AMERICA'S GOVERNMENTS

AMERICA'S

A Fact Book of Census Data
on the Organization, Finances, and Employment
of Federal, State, and Local Governments

1979 EDITION
Based on 1977 Census of Governments Data
and Annual Census Data on Finances and
Employment for the Same Year

GOVERNMENTS

Compiled by

RICHARD P. NATHAN
and
MARY M. NATHAN

**A WILEY—INTERSCIENCE
PUBLICATION**

JOHN WILEY & SONS

New York Chichester
Brisbane Toronto

Library of Congress Cataloging in Publication Data:

Nathan, Richard P
    America's governments.

    "Based on 1977 Census of Governments data and annual
census data on finances and employment for the same year."
    "A Wiley-Interscience publication."
    Bibliography: p.

    1.   United States—Politics and government—1977—
2.   Finances, Public—United States—Statistics.
3.   United States—Officials and employees—Statistics.
4.   Political statistics.   I.   Nathan, Mary M., joint
author.   II.   United States. Bureau of the Census.
III.   Title.

JK464 1979.N37   350′.000973   79-18575
ISBN 0-471-05671-5

Printed in the United States of America

10 9 8 7 6 5 4 3 2 1

PREFACE

The idea for this volume grew out of work done by the Brookings Institution beginning in 1972 to monitor the effects of Federal grants-in-aid on State and local governments. Noting the lack of a summary volume on the governmental data produced by the U.S. Bureau of the Census, a suggestion was made to the Bureau in 1975 that such a volume be prepared for the quinquennial Census of Governments in 1977. At first the Bureau seemed inclined to proceed, but unfortunately never did. This compilation was developed as a result. We hope it will enable a large number of persons to come to understand and use Census data on the number, nature and finances of America's governments. Several people aided us on this project. Allen D. Manvel, for twenty years Director of the Governments Division of the Census Bureau, made many important suggestions. Maurice Criz, Senior Advisor in the Division, provided valuable assistance throughout the project. Appreciation is also expressed to Robert Lawless of John Wiley and Sons for his understanding and cooperation.

RICHARD P. NATHAN
MARY M. NATHAN

Princeton, New Jersey
May 1979

CONTENTS

viii

x

xiii

HOW TO USE THIS VOLUME

Describes the contents of the volume, and indicates important points and data qualifications for users; contains charts that summarize significant characteristics of contemporary American federalism.

THERE ARE NEARLY 80,000 GOVERNMENTS IN THE UNITED STATES. THIS includes the Federal Government, the 50 States, 3042 counties, 18,862 municipalities, and 16,822 townships. The nation also had what the U.S. Bureau of the Census classified in 1977 as 25,962 special-district governments (water supply, fire protection, housing, cemeteries, etc.) and 15,174 independent school districts.

This volume contains data compiled from U.S. Bureau of the Census documents that describe the form, functions, and finances of America's governments. This material is organized for easy reference on a basis that pulls together the latest and most useful summary information and data from a variety of Census Bureau sources. The reader in a metropolitan area, for example, can use this volume to study: the way that governments are organized in the area, the finances and employment of all cities of 50,000 persons or more and counties of 100,000 or more, the ways these governments compare to others in their spending and employment patterns, comparative property tax rates, and the trends in State and local finances and employment over the past 25 years.

The charts in this introductory section show important characteristics of all governments. In 1977 Illinois had the largest number of local governments and Hawaii the smallest (Chart 1). Some States have very few (or no) separate governments for schools. In other States independent school districts accounted for a high proportion of all local governments in 1977.

For the three types of general-purpose local governments—counties, municipalities, and townships—small governments abound, although most people live in large ones (Charts 2, 3, 4). More than half of all municipal governments had a population of under 1000 in 1977, yet over 40% of the residents of cities lived in the 163 cities with 100,000 people or more. The same general pattern applies to school districts, although here the pattern has been shifting (Chart 5). In fact, the most dramatic change in American governmental structure in the past 25 years has been the consolidation of local school districts (Chart 7).

Both the big picture and facts about individual large local governments are featured in the Census data compiled for this volume. The volume is divided into four parts: (1) Organization, (2) Finances, (3) Employment, and (4) Historical Statistics. An annotated table of contents is provided for ready reference to text sections and to the 45 tables presented.* The volume also contains notes in italics by the compilers that describe the material presented and indicate certain caution signals regarding the use of the data for comparative purposes.

Although it may be a surprise to many readers, the narrative sections of the reports by the Census Bureau on governmental statistics are extremely readable. We suggest that users for whom this is a new subject begin by studying the text

---

*Throughout this volume letters are used for text tables and numbers for the full-page tables following the text.

sections interspersed throughout this volume. All text except the italicized sections is condensed from Census Bureau documents.

Understanding American federalism requires an immersion in the kind of facts and figures presented in this volume. Fortunately, the Census Bureau provides a wealth of data on American government. Since 1957 the Bureau has conducted a Census of Governments every 5 years ending in "2" and "7." The end product is a detailed set of volumes (often as many as twenty). The Bureau also issues 12 reports every year on various aspects of State and local finances and employment. Few students, even scholars and government officials, have access to all of this material from the quinquennial Census of Governments and the annual reports on government finances and employment.

In compiling this information from the Census of Governments conducted for 1977 and the annually published Census reports on the finances of State and local government for the same year, materials were selected that we believe will be useful to a wide audience—governmental officials, libraries, organization officials, experts in public policy, and students of government, public finance, and policy analysis. We particularly chose tables that show comparative data for individual large governmental units, so that the user can compare the major governments within a given State, or all large cities and counties in the nation. Although this is important and interesting to do, it requires considerable care. Comparative studies must take into account the wide differences that exist in the way State and local governments are organized and financed. In some States welfare is a State function. In others, it is administered by counties, with the State providing grants-in-aid for this purpose. In some cases fire protection, water supply, or sewerage is a municipal function, in others that of a special district. It is the dynamics of these different functional arrangements and fiscal flows that make our subject matter so complex and at the same time so interesting.

In short, contemporary American federalism is characterized by a multiplicity of governments; great diversity in their form, functions, and finances; and frequently a layering of these units (as discussed below) in the nation's most populated areas. There were over 1000 special districts in 1977 for each of the following functions— fire protection, water supply, soil conservation, housing, drainage, cemeteries, sewerage, and school buildings in 1977 (Chart 6). Some States (namely Alaska, Hawaii, Maryland, North Carolina, and Virginia) had no independent school districts in 1977. Nebraska had the largest number of independent school districts (1195); four States had more than 1000 (Chart 8).

Much of the data provided in this volume is organized by standard metropolitan statistical area (SMSA), of which there were 276 in 1977. As mentioned earlier, the interesting aspect of American federalism shown by the data on governments in SMSAs is the layering of local governments. Some metropolitan areas have many layers of government—a county, township, city, and several special districts. The Chicago area is a classic illustration of fragmentation and layering. The Chicago SMSA had 1214 local governments in 1977—1166 of which had property-taxing power.

For users interested in what governments in their area do and how they compare to other places, we recommend beginning with Table 6 in Part I, which shows the number and nature of all governments by county for all SMSAs. Although this is by far the longest table in the volume, it contains important basic information on the organization of local governments in 594 individual county areas that are part of an SMSA. The nation's SMSAs are shown on the map included in the chart section (Chart 11). (See also Charts 12–15.)

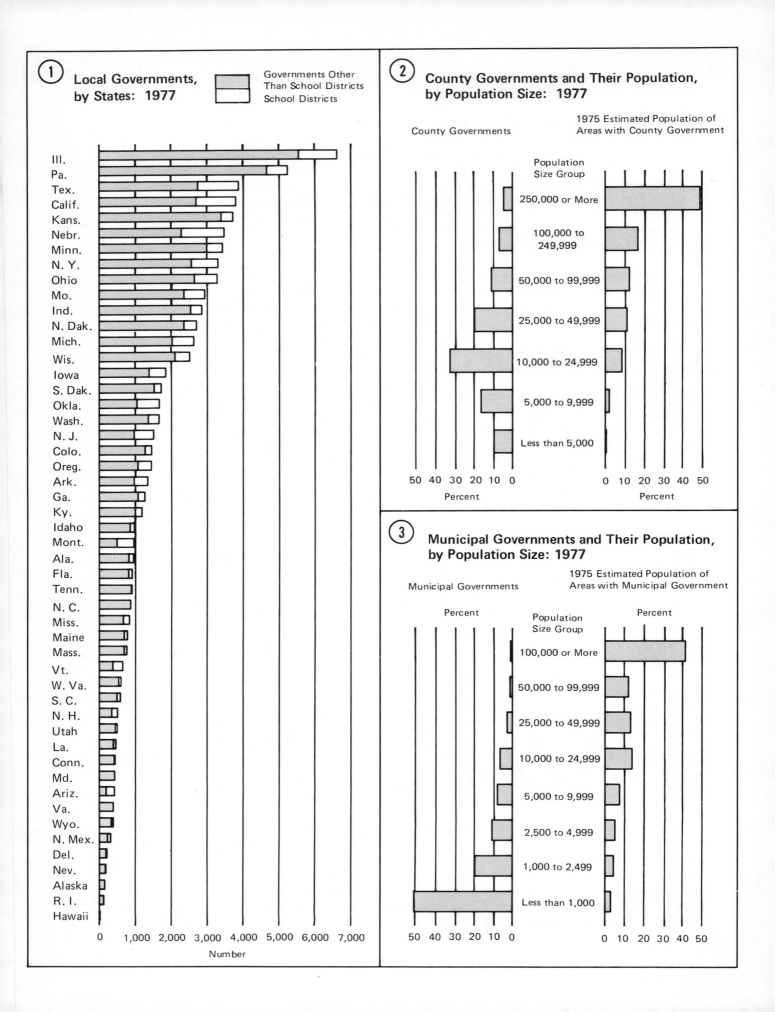

① Local Governments, by States: 1977

Governments Other Than School Districts
School Districts

Ill.
Pa.
Tex.
Calif.
Kans.
Nebr.
Minn.
N. Y.
Ohio
Mo.
Ind.
N. Dak.
Mich.
Wis.
Iowa
S. Dak.
Okla.
Wash.
N. J.
Colo.
Oreg.
Ark.
Ga.
Ky.
Idaho
Mont.
Ala.
Fla.
Tenn.
N. C.
Miss.
Maine
Mass.
Vt.
W. Va.
S. C.
N. H.
Utah
La.
Conn.
Md.
Ariz.
Va.
Wyo.
N. Mex.
Del.
Nev.
Alaska
R. I.
Hawaii

0   1,000   2,000   3,000   4,000   5,000   6,000   7,000
Number

② County Governments and Their Population, by Population Size: 1977

County Governments

1975 Estimated Population of Areas with County Government

Population Size Group

250,000 or More
100,000 to 249,999
50,000 to 99,999
25,000 to 49,999
10,000 to 24,999
5,000 to 9,999
Less than 5,000

50 40 30 20 10 0   0 10 20 30 40 50
Percent   Percent

③ Municipal Governments and Their Population, by Population Size: 1977

Municipal Governments

1975 Estimated Population of Areas with Municipal Government

Percent   Population Size Group   Percent

100,000 or More
50,000 to 99,999
25,000 to 49,999
10,000 to 24,999
5,000 to 9,999
2,500 to 4,999
1,000 to 2,499
Less than 1,000

50 40 30 20 10 0   0 10 20 30 40 50

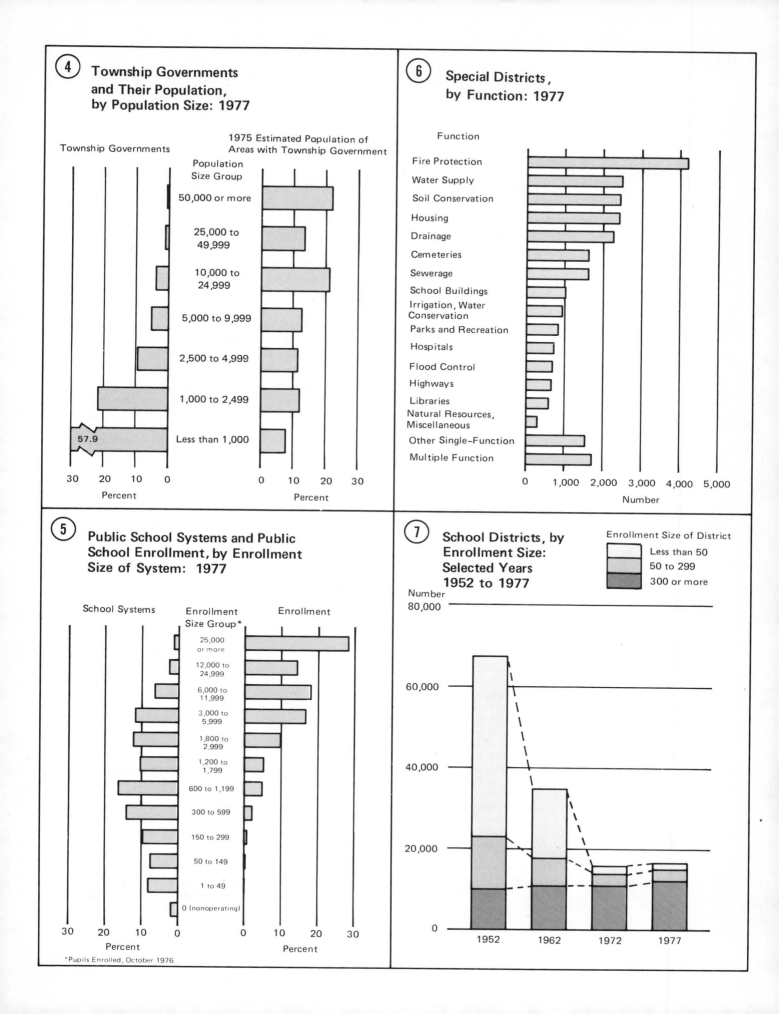

4 Township Governments and Their Population, by Population Size: 1977

Township Governments

1975 Estimated Population of Areas with Township Government

Population Size Group

50,000 or more

25,000 to 49,999

10,000 to 24,999

5,000 to 9,999

2,500 to 4,999

1,000 to 2,499

Less than 1,000

57.9

Percent: 30 20 10 0 | 0 10 20 30

Percent

6 Special Districts, by Function: 1977

Function

Fire Protection
Water Supply
Soil Conservation
Housing
Drainage
Cemeteries
Sewerage
School Buildings
Irrigation, Water Conservation
Parks and Recreation
Hospitals
Flood Control
Highways
Libraries
Natural Resources, Miscellaneous
Other Single-Function
Multiple Function

Number: 0 1,000 2,000 3,000 4,000 5,000

5 Public School Systems and Public School Enrollment, by Enrollment Size of System: 1977

School Systems

Enrollment Size Group*

Enrollment

25,000 or more
12,000 to 24,999
6,000 to 11,999
3,000 to 5,999
1,800 to 2,999
1,200 to 1,799
600 to 1,199
300 to 599
150 to 299
50 to 149
1 to 49
0 (nonoperating)

Percent: 30 20 10 0 | 0 10 20 30

Percent

*Pupils Enrolled, October 1976

7 School Districts, by Enrollment Size: Selected Years 1952 to 1977

Enrollment Size of District
Less than 50
50 to 299
300 or more

Number
80,000

60,000

40,000

20,000

0

1952   1962   1972   1977

Governmental Finances

Part II of this volume discusses governmental finances; it is divided into five sections. The first section presents summary data on Federal, State, and local finances. The next three sections deal separately with the finances of States, counties, and cities.

The fifth section of Part II focuses on property taxation, an especially controversial subject in the current period. The Census Bureau periodically collects comparative data on this complicated source of predominantly local revenue. As part of the quinquennial Census of Governments, the Bureau conducts a special survey that compares "effective property tax rates" for some 500 local areas. (Effective property tax rates show property taxes as a percentage of the sales value of taxable real estate.) The data presented in this volume indicate a wide range of effective property tax rates in 1976 from 0.13% to 6.77% for residential property (the latter rate for East Orange, New Jersey).

The financial data in Part II are presented for many individual governmental units. They include all States (State and local governments combined), all individual State governments, all counties with 100,000 persons or more (of which there were 332 in 1975), and 403 cities and selected townships of 50,000 persons or more as of 1975. Comparative data are presented in per capita terms and, where possible, in relation to personal income (i.e., per $1000 of personal income). The latter provides a basis for considering revenue and expenditure effort.

As stressed throughout this volume, the use of all of these data for comparative purposes (except in the case of the State-local totals) is made difficult by virtue of the diversity of functions and finances and the layering of local governments in American federalism. Local jurisdictions also have different accounting systems and fiscal years. Although the Census Bureau seeks to present uniform data on State and local finances, differences can occur for these reasons.

To provide a quick overview of governmental revenue and expenditures in 1977, two pie charts are presented in the chart section of this introductory statement (Charts 16 and 17). Several points are highlighted:

- The importance of insurance trust revenue (i.e., Social Security taxes) to the Federal government.

- The relative importance of Federal grants and property tax revenue (they account for equal shares of State-local revenue).

- The dominance of education in State-local spending (it is nearly three times as large as spending for public welfare).

- The relatively small share of State and local expenditure devoted to public welfare.

Government Employment

The third section of this volume is on government employment. Part III is divided into three sections. The first section summarizes the data for all governments as of October 1977. The other two sections of Part III present employment data for

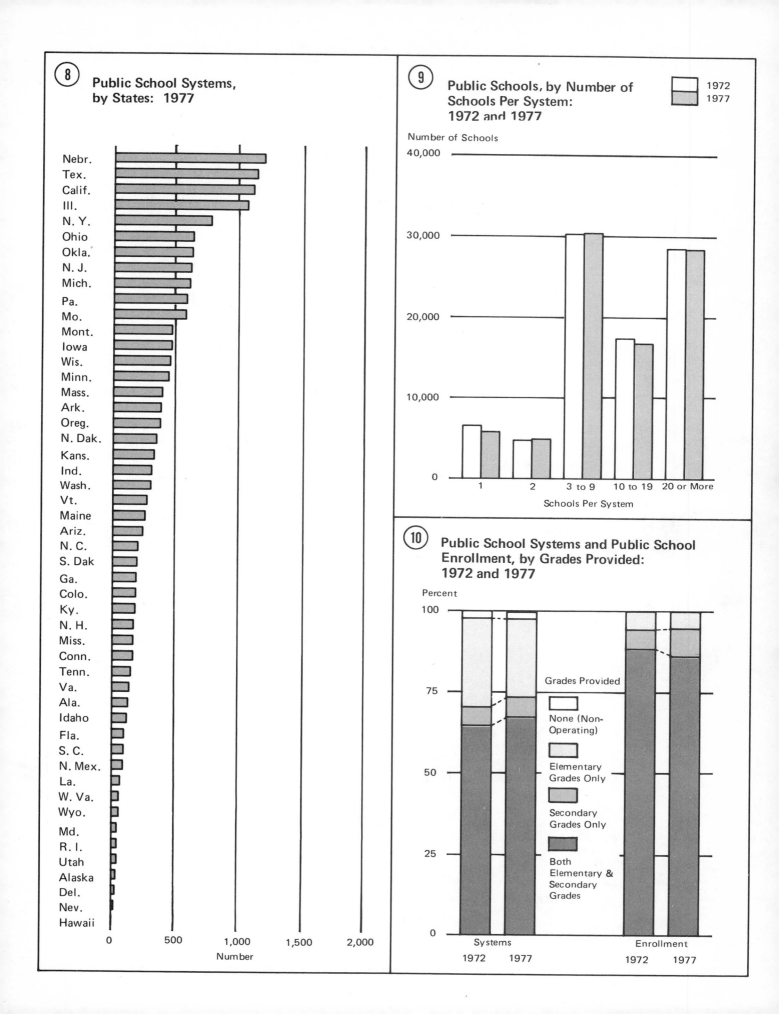

8 Public School Systems, by States: 1977

Nebr.
Tex.
Calif.
Ill.
N. Y.
Ohio
Okla.
N. J.
Mich.
Pa.
Mo.
Mont.
Iowa
Wis.
Minn.
Mass.
Ark.
Oreg.
N. Dak.
Kans.
Ind.
Wash.
Vt.
Maine
Ariz.
N. C.
S. Dak
Ga.
Colo.
Ky.
N. H.
Miss.
Conn.
Tenn.
Va.
Ala.
Idaho
Fla.
S. C.
N. Mex.
La.
W. Va.
Wyo.
Md.
R. I.
Utah
Alaska
Del.
Nev.
Hawaii

0   500   1,000   1,500   2,000
Number

9 Public Schools, by Number of Schools Per System: 1972 and 1977

1972
1977

Number of Schools

40,000

30,000

20,000

10,000

0

1   2   3 to 9   10 to 19   20 or More
Schools Per System

10 Public School Systems and Public School Enrollment, by Grades Provided: 1972 and 1977

Percent

100

75

50

25

0

Grades Provided

None (Non-Operating)

Elementary Grades Only

Secondary Grades Only

Both Elementary & Secondary Grades

Systems
1972   1977

Enrollment
1972   1977

STANDARD METROPOLITAN STATISTICAL AREAS

AREAS DEFINED BY OFFICE OF MANAGEMENT AND BUDGET, OCTOBER 1975

xx

(11)

U.S. DEPARTMENT OF COMMERCE
BUREAU OF THE CENSUS

BOUNDARIES

International
Extent of SMSA

ALBERS EQUAL AREA PROJECTION - STANDARD PARALLELS 29½° and 45½°

0 100 200 300 400 500 MILES

HONOLULU

0 100 200 MILES

ANCHORAGE

0 100 200 300 400 500 MILES

SAN JUAN

MAYAGUEZ   PONCE   CAGUAS

0 100 MILES

0 100 MILES

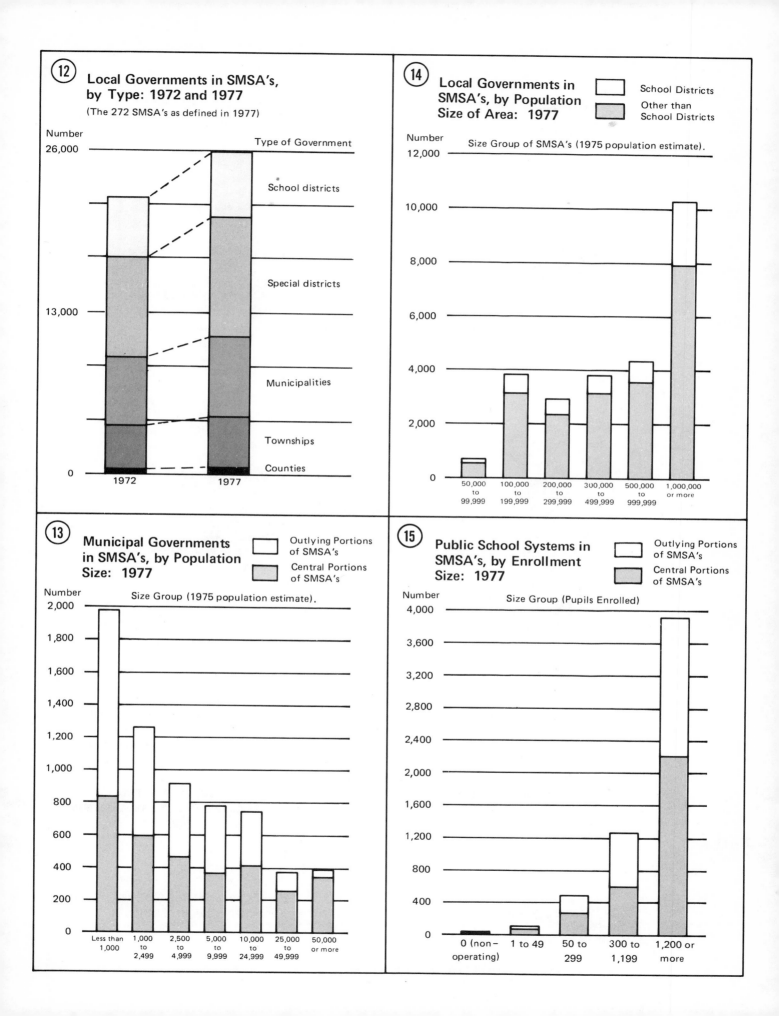

12 **Local Governments in SMSA's, by Type: 1972 and 1977**

(The 272 SMSA's as defined in 1977)

Number

Type of Government

School districts

Special districts

Municipalities

Townships

Counties

1972   1977

14 **Local Governments in SMSA's, by Population Size of Area: 1977**

☐ School Districts
▩ Other than School Districts

Number

Size Group of SMSA's (1975 population estimate).

50,000 to 99,999 | 100,000 to 199,999 | 200,000 to 299,999 | 300,000 to 499,999 | 500,000 to 999,999 | 1,000,000 or more

13 **Municipal Governments in SMSA's, by Population Size: 1977**

☐ Outlying Portions of SMSA's
▩ Central Portions of SMSA's

Number

Size Group (1975 population estimate).

Less than 1,000 | 1,000 to 2,499 | 2,500 to 4,999 | 5,000 to 9,999 | 10,000 to 24,999 | 25,000 to 49,999 | 50,000 or more

15 **Public School Systems in SMSA's, by Enrollment Size: 1977**

☐ Outlying Portions of SMSA's
▩ Central Portions of SMSA's

Number

Size Group (Pupils Enrolled)

0 (non-operating) | 1 to 49 | 50 to 299 | 300 to 1,199 | 1,200 or more

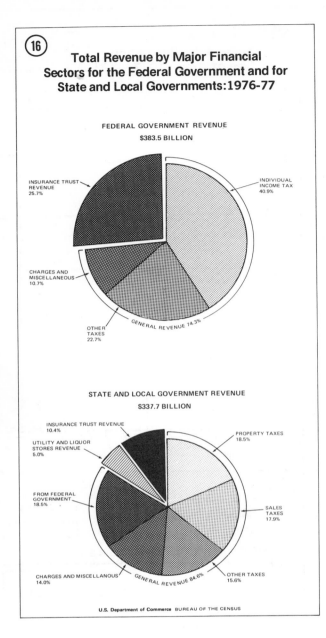

16 **Total Revenue by Major Financial Sectors for the Federal Government and for State and Local Governments:1976-77**

FEDERAL GOVERNMENT REVENUE
$383.5 BILLION

INSURANCE TRUST REVENUE 25.7%

INDIVIDUAL INCOME TAX 40.9%

CHARGES AND MISCELLANEOUS 10.7%

OTHER TAXES 22.7%

GENERAL REVENUE 74.3%

STATE AND LOCAL GOVERNMENT REVENUE
$337.7 BILLION

INSURANCE TRUST REVENUE 10.4%

UTILITY AND LIQUOR STORES REVENUE 5.0%

PROPERTY TAXES 18.5%

FROM FEDERAL GOVERNMENT 18.5%

SALES TAXES 17.9%

CHARGES AND MISCELLANOUS 14.0%

GENERAL REVENUE 84.6%

OTHER TAXES 15.6%

U.S. Department of Commerce BUREAU OF THE CENSUS

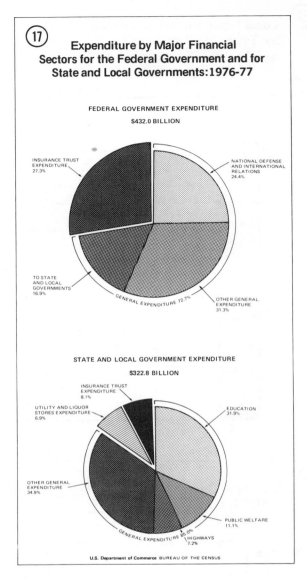

17 **Expenditure by Major Financial Sectors for the Federal Government and for State and Local Governments:1976-77**

FEDERAL GOVERNMENT EXPENDITURE
$432.0 BILLION

INSURANCE TRUST EXPENDITURE 27.3%

NATIONAL DEFENSE AND INTERNATIONAL RELATIONS 24.4%

TO STATE AND LOCAL GOVERNMENTS 16.9%

OTHER GENERAL EXPENDITURE 31.3%

GENERAL EXPENDITURE 72.7%

STATE AND LOCAL GOVERNMENT EXPENDITURE
$322.8 BILLION

INSURANCE TRUST EXPENDITURE 8.1%

UTILITY AND LIQUOR STORES EXPENDITURE 6.9%

EDUCATION 31.9%

OTHER GENERAL EXPENDITURE 34.9%

PUBLIC WELFARE 11.1%

HIGHWAYS 7.2%

GENERAL EXPENDITURE 85.0%

U.S. Department of Commerce BUREAU OF THE CENSUS

county and city governments. Data are presented showing total employment and payrolls in October 1977 by State for all State and local governments combined. Similar data are provided for all individual State governments, all counties of 100,000 persons or more, and all cities of 50,000 persons or more. For comparative purposes (though again the user should be cautious), tables are also presented in Part III showing levels of State and local employment per 10,000 persons. State and local employment and payrolls are much higher than for the Federal Government and have been rising at a faster rate over the past decade (Chart 18).

Historical Statistics

The final section of this volume is the shortest and contains three tables of historical statistics. (The Census Bureau publishes a summary volume of historical statis-

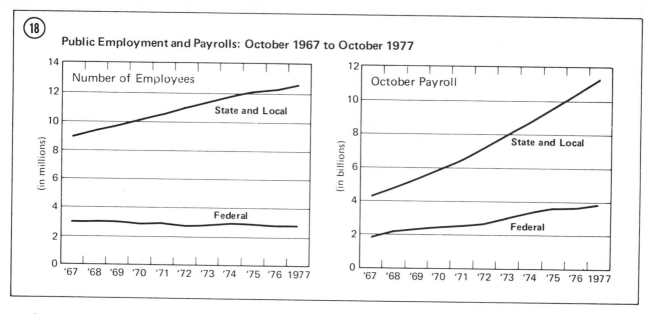

(18) Public Employment and Payrolls: October 1967 to October 1977

Number of Employees (in millions)

State and Local

Federal

'67 '68 '69 '70 '71 '72 '73 '74 '75 '76 1977

October Payroll (in billions)

State and Local

Federal

'67 '68 '69 '70 '71 '72 '73 '74 '75 '76 1977

tics as part of the quinquennial Census of Governments.) Part IV of this compilation contains three tables from the 1972 Census of Governments that show historical data, in one case going back to 1902. These tables enable the user of this volume to compare State and local finances by State in relation to personal income from 1953 to 1977. The tables in this section also present data from 1957 to 1972 on State and local employment by State, showing total employment, functional area data, and State and local employees per 10,000 people.

Guidance for Users

To give some guidance to users who want to find out about specific units of government in their area, several tables in this volume can be used to put together an effective composite picture. If it is a county in which one is interested, Table 6 in Part I shows the organization of all of the governments in the county, how many there are, what they do, how big they are, and how many students are enrolled in public schools in the county. Table 2 in Part IIC shows the county government's per capita revenue and expenditures if it is larger than 100,000 persons. Its per capita expenditures for particular functions can be compared to other counties in the same State and throughout the nation. Table 3 in Part IIE can be used to compare the property tax rates for major local governments in the county. Table 4 in Part IIIB can be used to study the level of employment and payroll of the county government with detail for major functional areas. Similar data can be found in Table 4 of Part IIIC for cities within the county with 50,000 persons or more. Users can profile and compare State governments and all large counties and cities on this basis.

The Appendix to this volume shows all of the publications for the 1977 Census of Governments. It also contains a list of the annual publications of the U.S. Bureau of the Census on governmental finances and employment.

RICHARD P. NATHAN
MARY M. NATHAN

xxiii

PART I

GOVERNMENTAL ORGANIZATION

Every 5 years since 1952, the U.S. Bureau of the Census has conducted a Census of Governments. The first volume on this census describes the organization of America's governments. It begins with an introductory statement that is condensed here to highlight in text and summary tables the principal characteristics of American State and local governments in 1977. Even though condensed, this is the longest introductory text section in this volume; it provides a valuable framework for all of the data used in this compilation. Table 6 in this section contains data on the governments in all county areas that are part of a standard metropolitan statistical area (SMSA). The central portion of the SMSA is shown by an asterisk at the top of the appropriate column. Throughout this volume letters are used for text tables and numbers for the full-page tables following the text.

There were 79,913 governmental units in the United States at the beginning of 1977. The 15,174 local school districts and 25,962 special districts accounted for a little over one-half of this total. The remainder includes the Federal Government, the 50 State governments, 3,042 counties, 18,862 municipalities, and 16,822 townships. The average number of governmental units per State is 1,598, but Illinois has 6,620 while Hawaii has only 19.

More than 3,000 governments are found in each of nine States, as follows:

California 3,806
Illinois 6,620
Kansas 3,725
Minnesota 3,437
Nebraska 3,485
New York 3,309
Ohio 3,285
Pennsylvania 5,246
Texas 3,883

Together, these nine States account for nearly one-half (46 percent) of all governmental units in the Nation.

The total number of governmental units in 1977 is 1,644 more than that reported for the 1972 Census of Governments. Following is a summary comparison of national totals by types of governments for 1977 with related numbers for 1972 and 1967. (A)

As this tabulation shows, there has been a reduction in the rate of decline in school district numbers during recent years. This decrease has been partly offset by an increase in number of municipalities and special districts. County governments have remained virtually unchanged in number while town-

Type of government	1977	1972	1967
Total	79,913	78,269	81,299
U.S. Government	1	1	1
State governments	50	50	50
Local governments	79,862	78,218	81,248
Counties	3,042	3,044	3,049
Municipalities	18,862	18,517	18,048
Townships	16,822	16,991	17,105
School districts	15,174	15,781	21,782
Special districts	25,962	23,885	21,264

ships have reflected small decreases over the past 10 years.

Types of Local Governments

The Bureau of the Census classifies local governments by five major types—counties, municipalities, townships, school districts, and special districts.

Counties

Organized county governments are found throughout the Nation except for Connecticut, Rhode Island, the District of Columbia, and limited portions of other States. Especially because these exceptional areas include New York City, Philadelphia, and several others of the most populous cities in the Nation (where the municipality operates, in effect, as a composite city-county unit), nearly 11 percent of the total U.S. population is not served by any separately organized county government.

In Louisiana, the counties are officially designated as "parishes," and the "boroughs" in Alaska resemble county governments in other States.

There are 137 county governments, located in 36 States, which serve populations of at least 250,000. These 137 county governments account for about 49 percent of the population served by all 3,042 county governments in the Nation. The overwhelming majority of county governments (78 percent) each serve fewer than 50,000 persons. (Table B)

The number of county governments per State ranges widely from the Texas total of 254 down to fewer than 20 in several States.

County governments   Number of States

100 or more 7

80 to 99 9

60 to 79 9

40 to 59 7

20 to 39 7

3 to 19 9

None 2

The average population served by a county government is 62,357, but Loving County, Tex., had only 114 inhabitants in 1975, while Los Angeles County, Calif., had almost 7 million.

Municipalities

For purposes of census classification, a municipality is a political subdivision within which a municipal corporation has been established to provide general local government for a specific population concentration in a defined area. A municipality may be legally termed a city, village, borough (except in Alaska), or town (except in the New England States, Minnesota, New York, and Wisconsin). In Alaska, the term "borough" corresponds to units classed as county governments and in New England, Minnesota, New York, and Wisconsin, the term "town" relates to an area subdivision which (although it may be legally termed a municipal corporation and have a similar governmental organization) has no necessary relationship to a concentration of population and thus corresponds to townships in other States. Similarly, although townships in New Jersey and Pennsylvania are legally termed municipal corporations, they have no necessary relation to a concentration of population and are thus treated for census purposes as a separate type of government.

A total of 18,862 municipalities are reported in existence as of early 1977. This is an increase of 345 over the number reported in the 1972 Census of Governments. Illinois, with 1,274 such governments at the beginning of 1977, has more municipalities than any other State. Texas has 1,066 municipalities, Pennsylvania has 1,015, Iowa 955, and Ohio 935. At the other extreme are seven States with fewer than 50 municipalities each— Connecticut, Hawaii, Maine, Massachusetts, Nevada, New Hampshire, and Rhode Island. It may be noted that five of these seven are New England States, where a town government often provides urban services ordinarily provided by municipalities in other States. (See Table C.)

More than 136 million of the inhabitants of the

Population-size group	County governments		Population served by county governments, 1975 (estimated)	
	Number	Percent	Number (1,000)	Percent
B United States	3,042	100.0	189,691	100.0
250,000 or more	137	4.5	92,392	48.7
100,000 to 249,999	206	6.8	32,085	16.9
50,000 to 99,999	336	11.1	23,503	12.4
25,000 to 49,999	596	19.6	20,976	11.1
10,000 to 24,999	980	32.2	16,079	8.5
5,000 to 9,999	496	16.3	3,758	2.0
Less than 5,000	291	9.6	897	0.5

Note: Because of rounding, population detail may not add to total.

Population-size group	Municipalities		Population served by municipalities 1975 (estimated)	
	Number	Percent	Number (1,000)	Percent
C United States	18,862	100.0	136,761	100.0
100,000 or more	163	0.9	56,534	41.3
50,000 to 99,999	230	1.2	16,091	11.8
25,000 to 49,999	514	2.7	17,939	13.1
10,000 to 24,999	1,212	6.4	19,002	13.9
5,000 to 9,999	1,461	7.8	10,299	7.5
2,500 to 4,999	2,004	10.6	7,040	5.2
1,000 to 2,499	3,664	19.4	5,872	4.3
Less than 1,000	9,614	51.0	3,985	2.9

Note: Because of rounding, population detail may not add to total.

United States live in areas with municipal government, and more than 56 million of these municipal residents live in the 163 cities of at least 100,000 population. The majority of municipalities (51 percent) have fewer than 1,000 inhabitants. However, these 9,614 small municipalities account for only 3 percent of the total municipally served population.

Townships

The term "townships" is applied to 16,822 organized governments, located in 20 States. This category includes governmental units officially designated as towns in the six New England States, New York, and Wisconsin and some "plantations" in Maine and "locations" in New Hampshire, as well as governments called townships in other areas. In Minnesota, the terms "town" and "township" are used interchangeably with reference to township governments. As distinguished from municipalities, which are created to serve specific population concentrations, townships exist to serve inhabitants of areas defined without regard to population concentrations. (See Table D.)

Townships range widely in scope of governmental powers and operations. Most of them, particularly in the North Central States, perform only a very limited range of services for predominantly rural areas. However, by general law in New England, New Jersey, and Pennsylvania, and to some degree in Michigan, New York, and Wisconsin, townships (or "towns") are vested with relatively broad powers

Area	Number of township governments	Estimated 1975 population (1,000)
D Total	16,822	48,344
6 New England States	1,425	6,700
3 Middle Atlantic States (New Jersey, New York, Pennsylvania	2,711	16,044
11 Other States	12,686	25,600

Note: Because of rounding, population detail may not add to total.

Population-size group	Township governments		Population served by townships, 1975 (estimated)	
	Number	Percent	Number (1,000)	Percent
United States	16,822	100.0	48,344	100.0
50,000 or more	103	0.6	10,539	21.8
25,000 to 49,999	190	1.1	6,479	13.4
10,000 to 24,999	660	3.9	10,185	21.1
5,000 to 9,999	870	5.2	6,081	12.6
2,500 to 4,999	1,595	9.5	5,505	11.4
1,000 to 2,499	3,657	21.7	5,808	12.0
Less than 1,000	9,747	57.9	3,747	7.8

Note: Because of rounding, population detail may not add to total.

and, where they include closely settled territory, perform functions commonly associated with municipal governments. In certain of the New England States, the towns are commonly responsible for local schools, as well as other governmental functions.

Township organization is generally restricted to the Northeastern and North Central States.

Since 1972, the number of township governments has shown a small decrease—from 16,991 in 1972 to 16,822 in 1977.

Only one State, Indiana, has township governments for all its area and population. In six States (Massachusetts, New Hampshire, New Jersey, Pennsylvania, Rhode Island, and Wisconsin), operating townships comprise all territory other than that served by municipalities. The same is true for Maine, except for "unorganized territory" which lacks any local government. Of the remaining 12 township States, there are eight where this kind of government appears only in certain counties as of early 1977: Illinois, in 85 of the 102 county areas; Kansas, in 103 of 105; Minnesota, in 85 of 87; Missouri, in 23 of 115; Nebraska, in 28 of 93; North Dakota, in 48 of 53; South Dakota, in 54 of 67; and Wisconsin, in 71 of 72 counties.

All municipal governments in Indiana, and some but not all municipalities in 10 other township States (Connecticut, Illinois, Kansas, Michigan, Minnesota, Missouri, Nebraska, New York, Ohio, and Vermont), operate within territory that is served also by township governments. In the remaining nine of the 20 township States, on the other hand, there is no geographic overlapping of these two kinds of units.

Of the nearly 17,000 township governments in the United States, only 953 had as many as 10,000 inhabitants in 1975 and nearly three-fifths of all townships have fewer than 1,000 inhabitants. (Table E)

School Districts

Of the 16,548 school systems in the United States in early 1977, only the 15,174 that are independent school districts enter into the count of separate units of government as shown in the various tables of this report. The other 1,374 "dependent" school systems are regarded as agencies of other governments—county, municipality, township, or State—and are excluded from the count of governmental units.

Because of the variety of State legislative provisions for the administration and operation of public schools, marked diversity is found in school organization throughout the United States. In 32 States, responsibility for public schools rests solely with school districts which are independent governmental units. In another two States—California and Ohio—all school systems that provide education through grade 12 are independent governments. However, each of these States has an institution of higher education operated by a city or county government. A "mixed" situation is found in 11 States, with the public schools that provide elementary and secondary education operated in some areas by independent school districts and elsewhere by some other type of government. In the District of Columbia and in five States (Alaska, Hawaii, Maryland, North Carolina, and Virginia) there are no independent school districts, and all public schools are administered by systems that are agencies of county or city governments, or of the State.

The 15,174 school districts reported for 1977 reflect a reduction in the rate of decline that has taken place in the number of school districts over the past 35 years, primarily as a result of school district consolidation and reorganization. As can be noted from

4

School year	Number of school districts
F	
1976-77	15,174
1971-72	15,781
1966-67	21,782
1961-62	34,678
1956-57	50,454
1951-52	67,355
1941-42	108,579

State	Number of school districts		Decrease	
	1977	1972	Number	Percent
G				
Illinois	1,063	1,177	114	9.7
Missouri	574	636	62	9.8
Montana	465	552	87	15.8
Nebraska	1,195	1,374	179	13.0

Table F, the present number of school districts is 96 percent of the 1972 total, less than 70 percent of the total 10 years ago, and only 14 percent of the 1942 total.

State	Number of school districts
H	
California	1,109
Illinois	1,063
Nebraska	1,195
Texas	1,138

Table G shows the four States that had the largest numerical decreases in school districts between 1972 and 1977.

Together these four States account for nearly 60 percent of the total decrease in number of school districts since 1972. Although there has been some decline in the number of school districts, the following four States each had more than 1,000 school districts in the 1976–77 school year.

These four States account for nearly 30 percent of all school districts in the Nation. The number of States having at least 1,000 school districts has decreased from 25 in 1942, 20 in 1952, 15 in 1962, 6 in 1967, to 4 in 1972 and in 1977. (Table H)

Special Districts

Special districts make up the most varied area of local government. With the exception of Alaska, these units are found in every State and in the District of Columbia. A majority of special districts are established to perform a single function, but some have been given authority by their enabling legislation to provide several kinds of services.

The 25,962 special districts counted in 1977 reflect an increase of 2,077 (8.7 percent) since 1972 when 23,885 such units were reported.

The following 11 States, each having at least 800 special districts, account for nearly 61 percent of all such local governments:

Illinois	.2,745
California	.2,227
Pennsylvania	.2,035
Texas	.1,425
Kansas	.1,219
Nebraska	.1,192
Washington	.1,060
Missouri	.1,007
New York	.964
Colorado	.950
Indiana	.885

An additional 17 States have at least 300 special districts—Alabama (336), Arkansas (424), Florida (361), Georgia (387), Idaho (612), Iowa (334), Kentucky (478), Massachusetts (328). Mississippi (304), Montana (311), New Jersey (380), North Carolina (302), North Dakota (587), Ohio (312), Oklahoma (406), Oregon (797), and Tennessee (471). There are six States with 200 to 299 such units, ten States with 100 to 199, and six States (as well as the District of Columbia) that have fewer than 100.

A number of interstate agencies are classified as special district governments and those which were in operation are included in these data. Each such

5

Function	Number	Percent
Total	25,962	100.0
Natural resources	6,595	25.4
Soil conservation	2,431	9.4
Drainage	2,255	8.7
Irrigation, water conservation	934	3.6
Flood control	681	2.6
Other natural resources activity	294	1.1
Fire protection	4,187	16.1
Urban water supply	2,480	9.6
Housing and urban renewal	2,408	9.2
Cemeteries	1,615	6.2
Sewerage	1,610	6.2
School building authorities	1,020	3.9
Parks and recreation	829	3.2
Highways	652	2.5
Hospitals	715	2.8
Libraries	586	2.3
Other single-function districts	1,545	6.0
Multiple function districts	1,720	6.6

Function	Number		Increase 1972 to 1977	
	1977	1972	Number	Percent
Fire protection	4,187	3,872	315	8.1
Housing and community redevelopment	2,408	2,271	137	6.0
Sewerage	1,610	1,411	199	14.1
Urban water supply	2,480	2,333	147	6.3

Item	Percent of special districts
Number of full-time employees, 1976:	
More than 20	6.2
6 to 20	6.0
1 to 5	20.2
None	67.6
Amount of debt, 1976:	
$5,000,000 or more	3.6
$1,000,000 to $4,999,999	8.1
$100,000 to $999,999	13.8
$1 to $99,999	11.3
None	63.1

entity is counted only once, being assigned geographically to the State where its headquarters is located.

Most special districts are established to perform a single function but some are authorized by their enabling legislation to provide several kinds of services. Table I summarizes the functional classification of special districts.

Table J is a tabulation of the functional classes of special districts that experienced the largest numerical increase in the 5-year period between 1972 and 1977.

That the major portion of all special districts conducts relatively small scale operations is evident from the statistics concerning number of full-time employees and the amount of indebtedness of special districts in 1976. (Table K)

One-fourth of all special districts serve an area with the same boundaries as those of some other local government—county, city, or township government. Although the vast majority of special districts are located wholly in a single county some 2,630 have territory extending into two or more counties, and 2,449 special districts have territory that includes part or all of a city of 25,000 inhabitants or more.

Public School Systems

The term "public school systems" includes two types of governmental entities with responsibility for providing public schools: (1) Those which are administratively and fiscally independent of any other government and are classified for Census Bureau reporting of governmental data as independent school district governments; and (2) those which lack sufficient autonomy to be classified as independent governmental units and each of which is treated as a dependent agency of some other government—a county, municipality, town or township, or State government.

6

Type of public school system	Public school systems	Public schools	Public school enrollment[1] (1,000)
	Number		
All public school systems	16,548	86,174	47,582
Independent school districts.	15,174	71,883	38,726
Other school systems.	1,374	14,291	8,856
State	3	381	184
County.	503	5,876	3,549
Municipal	284	5,598	3,992
Township (and "town")	584	2,436	1,132
	Percent		
All public school systems	100.0	100.0	100.0
Independent school districts.	91.7	83.4	81.4
Other school systems.	8.3	16.6	18.6
State	(Z)	0.4	0.4
County.	3.0	6.8	7.5
Municipal	1.7	6.5	8.4
Township (and "town")	3.5	2.8	2.4

Ⓛ

Z Less than 0.05 percent.

[1] Enrollment as of October 1976; includes 2,991,564 students enrolled in college-grade classes; see discussion of "College-grade coverage" below.

Table L summarizes, by type of system, the nationwide distribution of public school systems, schools, and enrollment in 1977.

In the foregoing summary, the three State-dependent systems are those of Alaska, Hawaii, and Maine. All public schools in Hawaii are administered directly as part of the State government, but in Alaska and Maine this arrangement applies only to certain sparsely populated areas.

The independent-district arrangement prevails in most parts of the country and is practically universal in the West. There are only five States in the entire Nation (Alaska, Hawaii, Maryland, North Carolina, and Virginia) plus the District of Columbia where all public school sytems are operated through school systems that are adjuncts of other governments, and such "dependent" systems account for a major share of public school enrollment in only five of the 13 States that have a composite arrangement, involving both independent school districts and other types of public school systems. These five exceptions are Connecticut, Maine, Massachusetts, Rhode Island, and Tennessee. In 40 of the 50 States, accordingly, all or a major fraction of all public school enrollment is accounted for by independent school districts.

School systems operating as adjuncts of counties appear mainly in the Southeast, but also in scattered instances elsewhere. Systems associated with township (or "town") governments are found only in New England and New Jersey. There are school systems operated by municipal governments in each of 14 States and the District of Columbia but in most of these States some other pattern predominates.

Public School Enrollment

Public school enrollment totaled 47.6 million in October 1976, with independent school districts accounting for 38.7 million, or 81 percent of the total number of pupils enrolled. In this report "number of pupils enrolled" covers not only pupils in elementary and high school classes (through grade 12) but also students enrolled at the college level in educational institutions operated by local governments.

Some 2 percent of all public school systems in the Nation in 1977—308 out of a total of 16,548—do not operate schools. Instead these "nonoperating" systems carry out their responsibilities by providing transportation and paying tuition or reinbursement to other school systems for any public school students who live in their respective areas.

The enrollment counted for each public school system is intended to cover not only pupils enrolled from within its own area but also any nonresident pupils transferred in from other areas. On this basis zero enrollment is reported for nonoperating school systems, since the pupils they send elsewhere are included in the figures for the school systems that do provide schools.

The 1,656 largest school systems—those having

7

Enrollment size (number of pupils)	Number of school systems		Percent change 1971-72 to 1976-77
	1976-77	1971-72	
United States	16,548	17,238	−4.0
25,000 or more	209	194	7.2
12,000 to 24,999	414	423	−2.1
6,000 to 11,999	1,033	990	4.3
3,000 to 5,999	1,892	1,913	−1.1
1,800 to 2,999	1,987	1,952	1.8
1,200 to 1,799	1,671	1,650	1.3
600 to 1,199	2,641	2,635	0.2
300 to 599	2,295	2,366	−3.0
150 to 299	1,561	1,645	−5.1
50 to 149	1,224	1,416	−13.6
15 to 49	659	905	−27.1
1 to 14	654	770	−15.1
0 (nonoperating)	308	378	−18.5

(M)

6,000 or more pupils—account for 60 percent of all public school enrollment in the Nation, and the 5,550 school systems with 1,200 to 5,999 pupils account for 32 percent. Thus, only 8 percent of all public school pupils are in systems with enrollments under 1,200.

The decrease in number of school systems during the past 5 years has been concentrated among those systems with small enrollments. Some decrease is reported in the number of systems in each size class below the 600-pupil level and some increase in the number in most size classes of systems above this enrollment size. (Table M)

Grade Coverage

School systems vary widely in the scope of their educational responsibilities.

Of the 16,240 school systems which operate schools, 3,983 provide elementary grades only. Although this represents 25 percent of all operating school systems, enrollment in these systems accounts for only 5 percent (2.3 million) of all public school enrollment.

The 1,018 school systems providing only secondary grades enrolled 4.2 million students in Oc-tober 1976. Typically, these are systems that maintain high schools for grades 9 through 12; however, this group also includes locally administered institutions of higher education and composite high school-junior college systems as well as those high school systemswhich provide grade 8, or grades 7 and 8, in addition to higher grades.

The remaining 11,239 school systems provide both elementary and secondary education. (Some of these also provide college-level education.) This group representing 69 percent of all systems maintaining schools, enrolled 40.9 million pupils in October 1976, or 86 percent of all public school enrollment.

The reduction in school systems in the past 5 years was accounted for mainly by systems providing only elementary grades and those which do not actually operate schools, as shown below. (N)

Number of Schools

Of the 86,174 public schools in operation in 1977, 45,106 or 52 percent, were under the jurisdiction of the 1,871 school systems which operated 10 or more schools each. At the other extreme, there were 5,779 school systems having a single school. Of the

Item	Number of public school systems		Change 1972 to 1977	
	1977	1972	Number	Percent
United States	16,548	17,238	−690	−4.0
Systems providing—				
Elementary grades only	3,983	4,716	−733	−15.5
Secondary grades only	1,018	985	33	3.4
Both elementary and secondary grades	11,239	11,159	80	0.7
Systems not operating schools	308	378	−70	−18.5

(N)

O

Number of local governments	Number of county areas	Percent of county areas
Total	3,121	100.0
200 or more	5	0.2
100 to 199	79	2.5
75 to 99	108	3.5
50 to 74	300	9.6
25 to 49	838	26.9
10 to 24	1,104	35.4
5 to 9	547	17.5
Less than 5	140	4.5

Average Number of Local Governments per County by State, 1977

"Low" average (less than 15)	"Middle" average (15 to 44)	"High" average (45 or more)
Alabama . . . 14	Arizona . . . 30	California . . . 66
Alaska . . . 12	Arkansas . . . 18	Connecticut . . . 54
Florida . . . 14	Colorado . . . 23	Delaware . . . 70
Georgia . . . 8	Idaho . . . 22	Illinois . . . 65
Hawaii . . . 5	Indiana . . . 31	Maine . . . 49
Kentucky . . . 10	Iowa . . . 19	Massachusetts . . . 55
Louisiana . . . 7	Kansas . . . 35	New Hampshire . . . 51
Mississippi . . . 10	Maryland . . . 18	New Jersey . . . 72
Nevada . . . 11	Michigan . . . 32	New York . . . 57
New Mexico . . . 10	Minnesota . . . 40	North Dakota . . . 51
North Carolina . . . 9	Missouri . . . 26	Pennsylvania . . . 78
South Carolina . . . 13	Montana . . . 17	Vermont . . . 46
Tennessee . . . 10	Nebraska . . . 37	
Virginia . . . 3	Ohio . . . 37	
West Virginia . . . 11	Oklahoma . . . 22	
	Oregon . . . 40	
	Rhode Island . . . 24	
	South Dakota . . . 26	
	Texas . . . 15	
	Utah . . . 17	
	Washington . . . 43	
	Wisconsin . . . 35	
	Wyoming . . . 17	

P

remaining school systems, 2,450 each operated two schools and 6,140 operated from three to nine schools.

Systems operating 10 schools or more, which comprise only 11 percent of all school systems, accounted for 58 percent (27.6 million) of all public school enrollment. On the other hand, the systems operating one of two schools, which represent 50 percent of all public school systems, reported only 11 percent (5.1 million) of the total enrollment.

There has been a decline in the number of public schools in the Nation since 1972, when 87,393 were reported. Most of this change resulted from consolidation or annexation of former one-school systems, which decreased in number from 6,545 to 5,779.

For the Nation as a whole, the number of local governments per county averages 26, as compared with 25 in 1972, 26 in 1967, 29 in 1962, 33 in 1957, 38 in 1952, and 50 in 1942. This average ranges from three local governments per county-type area in Virginia up to 78 per county area in Pennsylvania.

Only 3 percent (84) of the county-areas have as many as 100 local governments. On the other hand, 687 (22 percent) of all county areas have fewer than 10 units of government. (Table O)

There were five counties having 200 local governments or more in 1977, 1972, and 1967. This compares with 54 in 1942, 16 in 1952, and nine in 1957 and 1962. School district reorganization was mainly responsible for the decline in the number of these counties over the past 35 years. The five counties with 200 or more local governments in 1977 included two of the most populous counties in the Nation—Los Angeles County, Calif. (233 governments) and Cook County, Ill. (520 governments). The remaining three are Fresno County, Calif. (200 governments), Allegheny County, Pa. (325 governments), and Harris County, Tex. (308 governments). (Table P)

9

Type of government	United States	Inside SMSA's	Outside SMSA's	Percent in SMSA's
All local governments.	79,862	25,869	53,993	32.4
School districts	15,174	5,220	9,954	34.4
Other.	64,688	20,649	44,039	31.9
Counties	3,042	594	2,448	19.5
Municipalities	18,862	6,444	12,418	34.2
Townships	16,822	4,031	12,791	24.0
Special districts	25,962	9,580	16,382	36.9
Dependent school systems[1]	1,374	601	773	43.7

Ⓠ

[1] Not included in count of governments.

SMSA size group (Estimated 1975 population)	Number of SMSA's	Estimated population, 1975 (1,000)	Local governments, 1977
All SMSA's.	272	154,655	25,869
1,000,000 or more	35	85,991	10,266
500,000 to 999,999	37	25,764	4,349
300,000 to 499,999	43	16,049	3,805
200,000 to 299,999	48	11,997	2,924
100,000 to 199,999	84	12,648	3,826
50,000 to 99,999	25	2,206	699

Ⓡ

Note: Because of rounding, population detail may not add to total.

Type of local government	Local governments in the 272 SMSA's		Increase or decrease (—), 1972 to 1977	
	1977	1972	Number	Percent
Total	25,869	22,185	3,684	16.6
School districts	5,220	4,758	462	9.7
Other local governments	20,649	17,427	3,222	18.5
Counties	594	444	150	33.8
Municipalities	6,444	5,467	977	17.9
Townships	4,031	3,462	569	16.4
Special districts	9,580	8,054	1,526	19.0

Ⓢ

Type of special district	United States	Inside SMSA's	Outside SMSA's	Percent in SMSA's
Total	25,962	9,580	16,382	36.9
Natural resources	6,595	1,544	5,051	23.4
Other than natural resources.	19,367	8,036	11,331	41.5
Cemeteries.	1,615	212	1,403	13.1
Fire protection	4,187	1,738	2,449	41.5
Highways.	652	141	511	21.6
Hospitals.	715	186	529	26.0
Housing and community redevelopment	2,408	873	1,535	36.3
Libraries	586	224	362	38.2
Parks and recreation	829	427	402	51.5
School building authorities	1,020	613	407	60.1
Sewerage.	1,610	955	655	59.3
Urban water supply.	2,480	1,013	1,467	40.9
Other single-function districts	1,545	577	968	37.3
Multiple-function districts	1,720	1,077	643	62.6

Ⓣ

10

Most local governments in the United States operate entirely within a single county, but there are more than 7,500 units whose territory extends into two counties or more.

Local Governments in Metropolitan Areas

Statistics are summarized separately in various tables for local governments and public school systems in standard metropolitan statistical areas (SMSA's), as designated by the U.S. Office of Management and Budget with the advice of the Federal Committee on Standard Metropolitan Statistical Areas. This presentation applies to 272 SMSA's in the United States proper—i.e., excluding Puerto Rico, for which four SMSA's have also been defined. A number of new SMSA's have been recognized since the 1972 Census of Governments and territorial changes have also applied to some areas then designated.

Each standard metropolitan statistical area consists of a single county area or a group of contiguous counties, except that in New England such an area consists of a group of contiguous cities and towns. Each such area includes at least one "central city" of at least 50,000 inhabitants or—in some instances—contiguous twin cities which together meet this population minimum.

Slightly over 72 percent of the population of the United States reside within standard metropolitan statistical areas—155 million persons of the nationwide total of 213 million estimated for 1975. In 1977 these 272 areas encompassed 25,869 local governments, nearly one-third of all local governments in the Nation. Included in the 1977 total are 5,220 independent school districts, while an additional 601 school systems operated in metropolitan areas as adjuncts of other governments.

Metropolitan areas have experienced similar developments in local governments as has the Nation as a whole—namely, a net increase in local governments generally. However, because of changes in the composition of standard metropolitan statistical areas since 1972, there has been an increase in the number of school districts inside SMSA's, in contrast to the trend in the Nation as a whole.

A considerable fraction of all special districts is found in SMSA's, and this is particularly true of certain functions.

More than 34 percent of the municipal governments in the entire Nation and nearly four-fifths of all municipal residents were located in standard metropolitan statistical areas in 1977. These areas include all municipalities of 50,000 inhabitants or more, as well as a considerable proportion of all other sizable municipalities. However, within SMSA's as well as elsewhere, the majority of municipal governments are units of relatively small population as can be seen from Table U.

The number of local governments per area ranges from only a few each in a number of SMSA's, mainly in the South, up to a total of more than 250 in each of 23 SMSA's, as shown in Table V.

Criteria for Classifying Governmental Units

Governmental services in the United States are provided through a complex structure made up of numerous public bodies and agencies. In addition to the widely recognized pattern of Federal, State, county, municipal, and township governments, there exist many offshoots from the regular structure in the form of single-function and multiple-function districts, authorities, commissions, boards, and other entities that have varying degrees of autonomy. The basic pattern differs widely from State to State. Moreover, various classes of local units within a particular State also differ in their characteristics.

Before attempting to identify and count units of government, therefore, it is necessary to define what is to be counted and to establish standards for classifying the various types of governmental entities that are encountered. The discussion below sets forth the definitions and criteria that have been used by the Bureau of the Census in classifying and counting governmental units for this report. Following is a summary definition:

A government is an organized entity which, in addition to having governmental character, has sufficient discretion in the management of its own affairs to distinguish it as separate from the administrative structure of any other governmental unit.

To be counted as a government, any entity must possess all three of the attributes reflected in the foregoing definition: Existence as an organized entity, governmental character, and substantial autonomy. Following are some of the characteristics which are taken as evidence of these attributes.

Existence as an Organized Entity

Evidence on this score is provided by the presence of some form of organization and the possession of some corporate powers, such as perpetual

Population-size groups of municipalities	United States	Inside SMSA's	Outside SMSA's	Percent in SMSA's
	Number of municipalities			
Total	18,862	6,444	12,418	34.2
50,000 or more	393	391	¹2	99.5
25,000 to 49,999	514	374	140	72.8
10,000 to 24,999	1,212	744	468	61.4
5,000 to 9,999	1,461	779	682	53.3
2,500 to 4,999	2,004	915	1,089	45.7
1,000 to 2,499	3,664	1,262	2,402	34.4
Less than 1,000	9,614	1,979	7,635	20.6
	Estimated 1975 population (1,000)			
Total	136,761	109,271	27,491	79.9
50,000 or more	72,625	72,522	103	99.9
25,000 to 49,999	17,939	13,126	4,813	73.2
10,000 to 24,999	19,002	11,812	7,189	62.2
5,000 to 9,999	10,299	5,536	4,762	53.8
2,500 to 4,999	7,040	3,248	3,793	46.1
1,000 to 2,499	5,872	2,073	3,799	35.3
Less than 1,000	3,985	955	3,030	24.0

Note: Because of rounding, population detail may not add to total.

¹ Kokomo, Indiana and Lawrence, Kansas subsequently designated SMSA's.

Standard metropolitan statistical area	Local governments, 1977			Estimated population, 1975 (1,000)
	Total	Central portion	Outlying portion	
Chicago, Ill.	1,214	520	694	7,015
Philadelphia, Pa.-N.J.	864	11	853	4,807
Pittsburgh, Pa..	744	325	419	2,322
St. Louis, Mo.-Ill.	615	6	609	2,367
Houston, Tex..	488	308	180	2,286
Minneapolis-St. Paul, Minn.-Wis.	406	104	302	2,011
Nassau-Suffolk, N.Y.	370	—	370	2,657
Dallas-Fort Worth, Tex.	368	121	247	2,544
New York, N.Y.-N.J.	362	3	359	9,562
Detroit, Mich.	349	93	256	4,431
Denver-Boulder, Colo.	329	66	263	1,413
Indianapolis, Ind.	316	63	253	1,138
San Francisco-Oakland, Calif..	298	68	230	3,140
Kansas City, Mo.-Kans..	280	45	235	1,290
Allentown-Bethlehem-Easton, Pa.-N.J.. . . .	273	163	110	624
Newark, N.J.	268	49	219	1,999
Cincinnati, Ohio-Ky.-Ind.	265	79	186	1,381
Seattle-Everett, Wash.	262	262	—	1,407
Northeast Pennsylvania.	261	220	41	635
Peoria, Ill..	260	89	171	354
Omaha, Nebr.-Ia.	260	126	134	573
Albany-Schenectady-Troy, N.Y.	258	155	103	798
Portland, Ore.-Wash.	257	65	192	1,083

—Represents zero or rounds to zero.

12

succession, the right to sue and be sued, have a name, make contracts, acquire and dispose of property, and the like.

Designation of a class of units in law as "municipal corporations," "public corporations," "bodies corporate and politic," and the like indicates that such units are organized entities. On the other hand, some entities not so specifically stated by law to be corporations do have sufficient powers to be recognized as governmental units.

Obviously, the mere right to exist is not sufficient. Where a former governmental unit has ceased to operate—e.g., receives no revenue, conducts no activities, and has no officers currently—it is not counted as an existing government.

Governmental Character

This characteristic is indicated where officers of the entity are popularly elected or are appointed by public officials. A high degree of responsibility to the public, demonstrated by requirements for public reporting or for accessibility of records to public inspection, is also taken as critical evidence of governmental character.

Governmental character is attributed to any entities having power to levy property taxes, power to issue debt paying interest exempt from Federal taxation, or responsibility for performing a function commonly regarded as governmental in nature. However, a lack of these attributes or of evidence about them does not preclude a class of units being recognized as governmental in character, if it meets the indicated requirements as to officers or public accountability. Thus, some "special districts" exist which have no taxing powers and are empowered only to provide electric power or other public utility services also widely rendered privately, but are counted as local governments because of provisions as to their administration and public accountability.

Substantial Autonomy

This requirement is met where, subject to statutory limitations and any supervision of local governments by the State, an entity has considerable fiscal and administrative independence. Fiscal independence generally derives from power of the entity to determine its budget without review and detailed modification by other local officials or governments, to determine taxes to be levied for its support, to fix and collect charges for its services, or to issue debt without review by another local government.

Administrative independence is closely related to the basis for selection of the entity's governing body. Accordingly, a public agency is classified as an independent unit of government if it has independent fiscal powers and in addition (1) has a popularly elected governing body; (2) has a governing body representing two or more State or local governments; or (3) even in the event its governing body is appointed, performs functions that are essentially different from those of, and are not subject to specification by, its creating government.

13

Table 1. Total Number of Governmental Units: 1942 to 1977

State	All governmental units[1] 1977	1972	1967	1962	1957	1952	1942[2]	Change (– denotes decrease) 1972 to 1977 Number	Percent	1967 to 1977 Number	Percent
UNITED STATES	79 913	78 269	81 299	91 237	102 392	116 807	155 116	1 644	2.1	-1 386	-1.7
ALABAMA	950	876	797	733	617	548	511	74	8.4	153	19.2
ALASKA	151	121	62	57	42	49	(NA)	30	24.8	89	143.5
ARIZONA	421	407	395	379	367	367	499	14	3.4	26	6.6
ARKANSAS	1 347	1 284	1 253	1 209	1 127	1 089	3 705	63	4.9	94	7.5
CALIFORNIA	3 807	3 820	3 865	4 023	3 879	3 764	4 149	-13	-0.3	-58	-1.5
COLORADO	1 460	1 320	1 253	1 194	1 666	1 953	2 358	140	10.6	207	16.5
CONNECTICUT	435	429	414	398	384	363	349	6	1.4	21	5.1
DELAWARE	211	159	171	208	132	108	70	52	32.7	40	23.4
DISTRICT OF COLUMBIA	2	3	2	2	2	2	2	-1	-33.3	-	-
FLORIDA	912	866	828	765	672	617	503	46	5.3	84	10.1
GEORGIA	1 264	1 244	1 204	1 219	1 121	976	946	20	1.6	60	5.0
HAWAII	20	20	20	21	22	15	(NA)	-	-	-	-
IDAHO	973	902	872	835	843	938	1 666	71	7.9	101	11.6
ILLINOIS	6 621	6 386	6 454	6 453	6 510	7 723	15 854	235	3.7	167	2.6
INDIANA	2 855	2 793	2 670	3 092	2 989	3 050	3 043	62	2.2	185	6.9
IOWA	1 853	1 819	1 803	2 643	4 906	5 857	7 519	34	1.9	50	2.8
KANSAS	3 726	3 716	3 669	5 411	6 214	6 933	11 115	10	0.3	57	1.6
KENTUCKY	1 184	1 136	953	873	822	796	771	48	4.2	231	24.2
LOUISIANA	459	835	834	629	584	489	523	-376	-45.0	-375	-37.5
MAINE	780	715	699	659	645	664	584	65	9.1	81	11.6
MARYLAND	427	404	362	352	328	328	207	23	5.7	65	18.0
MASSACHUSETTS	767	683	655	587	573	584	409	84	12.3	112	17.1
MICHIGAN	2 634	2 650	2 904	3 819	5 160	6 766	8 106	-16	-0.6	-270	-9.3
MINNESOTA	3 438	3 396	4 185	5 213	6 298	9 026	10 398	42	1.2	-747	-17.8
MISSISSIPPI	836	797	784	773	672	693	1 792	39	4.9	52	6.6
MISSOURI	2 938	2 808	2 918	3 728	5 307	7 002	10 740	130	4.6	20	0.7
MONTANA	959	993	1 104	1 388	1 503	1 598	2 175	-34	-3.4	-145	-13.1
NEBRASKA	3 486	3 562	4 392	5 124	6 658	7 981	8 307	-76	-2.1	-906	-20.6
NEVADA	183	185	147	137	110	243	163	-2	-1.1	36	24.5
NEW HAMPSHIRE	507	500	516	551	545	551	546	7	1.4	-9	-1.7
NEW JERSEY	1 518	1 457	1 422	1 396	1 217	1 151	1 143	61	4.2	96	6.8
NEW MEXICO	314	310	308	306	317	289	225	4	1.3	6	1.9
NEW YORK	3 310	3 307	3 486	3 803	4 189	5 483	8 339	3	0.1	-176	-5.0
NORTH CAROLINA	875	803	753	675	624	608	603	72	9.0	122	16.2
NORTH DAKOTA	2 708	2 727	2 758	3 029	3 968	3 968	4 066	-19	-0.7	-50	-1.8
OHIO	3 286	3 260	3 284	3 360	3 667	3 936	4 021	26	0.8	2	0.1
OKLAHOMA	1 676	1 684	1 774	1 960	2 332	2 771	5 100	-8	-0.5	-98	-5.5
OREGON	1 448	1 447	1 457	1 470	1 526	1 723	2 332	1	0.1	-9	-0.6
PENNSYLVANIA	5 247	4 936	4 999	6 202	5 073	5 156	5 263	311	6.3	248	5.0
RHODE ISLAND	121	116	110	98	91	89	54	5	4.3	11	10.0
SOUTH CAROLINA	586	584	562	553	503	413	2 057	2	0.3	24	4.3
SOUTH DAKOTA	1 728	1 771	3 511	4 464	4 808	4 917	4 919	-43	-2.4	-1 783	-50.8
TENNESSEE	906	882	792	658	560	435	328	24	2.7	114	14.4
TEXAS	3 884	3 625	3 447	3 328	3 485	7 360	8 508	259	7.1	437	12.7
UTAH	493	460	446	424	398	385	303	33	7.2	47	10.5
VERMONT	648	659	657	425	409	414	398	-11	-1.7	-9	-1.4
VIRGINIA	390	394	374	381	367	366	323	-4	-1.0	16	4.3
WASHINGTON	1 667	1 683	1 653	1 647	1 577	1 539	1 906	-16	-1.0	14	0.8
WEST VIRGINIA	596	509	456	390	362	350	326	87	17.1	140	30.7
WISCONSIN	2 519	2 449	2 491	3 727	5 731	7 258	8 508	70	2.9	28	1.1
WYOMING	386	384	473	465	489	519	531	2	0.5	-87	-18.4

- Represents zero or rounds to zero.

NA Not available.

[1] Including the Federal Government, the 50 State governments, and all types of local governments—counties, municipalities, townships, school districts, and special districts.

[2] The figures shown for 1942, being based on less intensive and detailed survey efforts than data reported for subsequent years, are subject to limitations of comparability for some States.

Table 2. Local Governments and Public School Systems, by Type, and by State: 1977

State	Local governments								Public school systems	
	Total	With property-taxing power[1]	Without property-taxing power	Counties	Municipalities	Townships	School districts	Special districts	Total	Other than school districts[3]
UNITED STATES, TOTAL	79 862	67 780	12 082	3 042	18 862	16 822	15 174	25 962	16 548	1 374
ALABAMA	949	613	336	67	419	-	127	336	127	-
ALASKA	150	150	-	8	142	-	-	-	32	32
ARIZONA	420	418	2	14	70	-	230	106	237	7
ARKANSAS	1 346	923	423	75	467	-	380	424	380	1
CALIFORNIA	3 806	3 595	211	57	413	-	1 109	2 227	1 110	1
COLORADO	1 459	1 394	65	62	262	-	185	950	185	-
CONNECTICUT	434	359	75	-	33	149	16	236	165	149
DELAWARE	210	85	125	3	55	-	25	127	26	1
DISTRICT OF COLUMBIA	2	-	2	-	1	-	-	1	2	2
FLORIDA	911	686	225	66	389	-	95	361	95	-
GEORGIA	1 263	876	387	158	530	-	188	387	188	-
HAWAII	19	4	15	3	1	-	-	15	1	1
IDAHO	972	792	180	44	199	-	117	612	117	-
ILLINOIS	6 620	5 522	1 098	102	1 274	1 436	1 063	2 745	1 063	-
INDIANA	2 854	2 216	638	91	563	1 008	307	885	307	-
IOWA	1 852	1 738	114	99	955	-	464	334	464	-
KANSAS	3 725	3 365	360	105	625	1 449	327	1 219	327	-
KENTUCKY	1 183	975	208	119	405	-	181	478	181	-
LOUISIANA	458	456	2	62	300	-	66	30	66	-
MAINE	779	610	169	16	24	475	86	178	256	170
MARYLAND	426	194	232	23	151	-	-	252	40	40
MASSACHUSETTS	766	512	254	12	39	312	75	328	389	314
MICHIGAN	2 633	2 489	144	83	531	1 245	606	168	606	-
MINNESOTA	3 437	3 431	6	87	855	1 792	440	263	440	-
MISSISSIPPI	835	681	154	82	283	-	166	304	166	-
MISSOURI	2 937	2 317	620	114	916	326	574	1 007	574	-
MONTANA	958	818	140	56	126	-	465	311	465	-
NEBRASKA	3 485	3 248	237	93	534	471	1 195	1 192	1 195	-
NEVADA	182	117	65	16	17	-	17	132	17	-
NEW HAMPSHIRE	506	478	28	10	13	221	159	103	168	9
NEW JERSEY	1 517	1 254	263	21	335	232	549	380	615	66
NEW MEXICO	313	285	28	32	93	-	88	100	88	-
NEW YORK	3 309	3 296	13	57	618	930	740	964	773	33
NORTH CAROLINA	874	644	230	100	472	-	-	302	200	200
NORTH DAKOTA	2 707	2 608	99	53	361	1 360	346	587	346	-
OHIO	3 285	3 116	169	88	935	1 319	631	312	632	1
OKLAHOMA	1 675	1 284	391	77	567	-	625	406	625	-
OREGON	1 447	1 200	247	36	239	-	375	797	375	-
PENNSYLVANIA	5 246	3 282	1 964	66	1 015	1 549	581	2 035	581	-
RHODE ISLAND	120	90	30	-	8	31	3	78	40	37
SOUTH CAROLINA	585	507	78	46	264	-	93	182	93	-
SOUTH DAKOTA	1 727	1 632	95	64	311	1 010	194	148	194	-
TENNESSEE	905	447	458	94	326	-	14	471	147	133
TEXAS	3 883	3 248	635	254	1 066	-	1 138	1 425	1 138	-
UTAH	492	422	70	29	216	-	40	207	40	-
VERMONT	647	623	24	14	57	237	272	67	272	-
VIRGINIA	389	324	65	95	229	-	-	65	136	136
WASHINGTON	1 666	1 453	213	39	265	-	302	1 060	302	-
WEST VIRGINIA	595	338	257	55	227	-	55	258	55	-
WISCONSIN	2 518	2 379	139	72	576	1 270	410	190	452	42
WYOMING	385	285	100	23	90	-	55	217	55	-

- Represents zero or rounds to zero.

[1] See text, "Local Governments and Taxing Areas."

[2] Excludes areas corresponding to counties but having no organized county governments.

[3] School systems operated as part of a State, county, municipal, or township government. The count of "All types of local governments" does not include these numbers.

15

Table 3. Number of County Governments in 1977 and Their Estimated 1975 Populations, by Population Size, and by State

(Population amounts in thousands)

State	Total Number	Total Population	250,000 or more Number	250,000 or more Population	100,000 to 249,999 Number	100,000 to 249,999 Population	50,000 to 99,999 Number	50,000 to 99,999 Population
UNITED STATES, TOTAL	3 042	189 691	137	92 392	206	32 085	336	23 503
ALABAMA	67	3 616	2	980	4	593	11	762
ALASKA	8	83	-	-	-	-	-	-
ARIZONA	14	2 212	2	1 652	-	-	5	353
ARKANSAS	75	2 110	1	308	1	109	7	465
CALIFORNIA	57	20 533	16	17 690	11	1 820	7	545
COLORADO	62	2 056	2	595	6	946	1	62
CONNECTICUT	-	-	-	-	-	-	-	-
DELAWARE	3	579	1	399	-	-	2	180
DISTRICT OF COLUMBIA	-	-	-	-	-	-	-	-
FLORIDA	66	7 715	7	4 642	11	1 711	7	507
GEORGIA	158	4 771	2	1 031	6	966	9	607
HAWAII	3	163	-	-	-	-	2	130
IDAHO	44	814	-	-	1	135	3	186
ILLINOIS	102	11 197	6	7 161	11	1 793	10	672
INDIANA	91	4 532	2	836	8	1 136	13	936
IOWA	99	2 861	1	297	4	551	5	381
KANSAS	105	2 280	1	345	3	567	4	243
KENTUCKY	119	3 201	1	697	1	130	8	549
LOUISIANA	62	2 935	1	399	5	764	11	737
MAINE	16	1 058	-	-	4	558	2	190
MARYLAND	23	3 270	4	2 231	2	244	8	585
MASSACHUSETTS	12	5 086	7	4 604	3	411	1	64
MICHIGAN	83	9 111	6	5 281	11	1 810	12	803
MINNESOTA	87	3 921	2	1 372	5	781	2	139
MISSISSIPPI	82	2 341	-	-	3	475	7	425
MISSOURI	114	4 242	2	1 592	4	539	6	423
MONTANA	56	746	-	-	1	182	3	246
NEBRASKA	93	1 544	1	412	1	145	1	75
NEVADA	16	565	1	331	1	169	-	-
NEW HAMPSHIRE	10	812	-	-	2	403	4	282
NEW JERSEY	21	7 334	12	6 226	4	713	5	395
NEW MEXICO	32	1 144	1	362	1	135	5	309
NEW YORK	57	10 594	9	6 612	13	2 117	20	1 349
NORTH CAROLINA	100	5 441	3	935	7	1 110	28	1 986
NORTH DAKOTA	53	637	-	-	-	-	3	206
OHIO	88	10 735	9	5 902	13	1 882	23	1 661
OKLAHOMA	77	2 715	2	959	1	105	5	324
OREGON	36	2 284	1	530	5	915	5	339
PENNSYLVANIA	66	10 044	12	5 694	18	2 838	12	807
RHODE ISLAND	-	-	-	-	-	-	-	-
SOUTH CAROLINA	46	2 816	2	526	4	672	12	877
SOUTH DAKOTA	64	665	-	-	1	134	2	166
TENNESSEE	94	3 725	3	1 295	1	168	9	602
TEXAS	254	12 237	6	5 754	12	2 043	20	1 482
UTAH	29	1 203	1	512	3	414	-	-
VERMONT	14	472	-	-	1	106	1	55
VIRGINIA	95	2 968	1	513	4	550	6	343
WASHINGTON	39	3 559	4	2 135	3	427	6	446
WEST VIRGINIA	55	1 799	-	-	2	329	9	599
WISCONSIN	72	4 589	3	1 582	7	961	12	892
WYOMING	23	376	-	-	-	-	2	118

See footnotes at end of table.

Table 3. Number of County Governments in 1977 and Their Estimated 1975 Populations, by Population Size, and by State—Continued

(Population amounts in thousands)

| State | Population-size group—Continued | | | | | | | | Exhibit | |
| | 25,000 to 49,999 | | 10,000 to 24,999 | | 5,000 to 9,999 | | Less than 5,000 | | County-type areas without county government[1] | |
	Number	Population	Number	Population	Number	Population	Number	Population	Number	Population
UNITED STATES, TOTAL	596	20 976	980	16 079	496	3 758	291	897	80	23 345
ALABAMA	23	831	27	450	-	-	-	-	-	-
ALASKA	1	44	2	22	1	7	4	10	4	282
ARIZONA	4	158	3	49	1	7	-	-	-	-
ARKANSAS	16	530	37	592	13	105	-	-	-	-
CALIFORNIA	8	292	9	149	4	34	2	4	1	665
COLORADO	1	26	15	251	18	128	19	47	1	485
CONNECTICUT	-	-	-	-	-	-	-	-	8	3 100
DELAWARE	-	-	-	-	-	-	-	-	-	-
DISTRICT OF COLUMBIA	-	-	-	-	-	-	-	-	1	712
FLORIDA	14	540	16	243	8	61	3	12	1	562
GEORGIA	23	798	63	1 006	43	324	12	39	1	160
HAWAII	1	33	-	-	-	-	-	-	1	705
IDAHO	5	183	12	187	12	91	11	32	-	-
ILLINOIS	24	849	37	626	13	92	1	4	-	-
INDIANA	28	940	34	639	5	40	1	5	1	781
IOWA	14	507	60	998	15	127	-	-	-	-
KANSAS	12	397	23	375	30	230	32	123	-	-
KENTUCKY	21	712	59	904	26	198	3	11	1	186
LOUISIANA	16	564	24	425	5	46	-	-	2	871
MAINE	7	245	3	65	-	-	-	-	-	-
MARYLAND	4	108	5	102	-	-	-	-	1	852
MASSACHUSETTS	-	-	-	-	1	8	1	2	2	728
MICHIGAN	19	733	23	395	11	88	-	-	-	-
MINNESOTA	24	845	42	702	10	75	2	8	-	-
MISSISSIPPI	19	649	42	701	10	88	1	2	-	-
MISSOURI	19	632	55	851	24	189	4	17	1	525
MONTANA	4	162	13	179	16	112	20	48	1	(Z)
NEBRASKA	8	269	20	288	31	239	31	79	-	-
NEVADA	-	-	5	59	3	19	6	11	1	25
NEW HAMPSHIRE	3	104	1	22	-	-	-	-	-	-
NEW JERSEY	-	-	-	-	-	-	-	-	-	-
NEW MEXICO	6	250	2	39	5	40	6	21	-	-
NEW YORK	12	473	9	161	-	-	1	4	5	7 482
NORTH CAROLINA	25	865	25	453	11	87	-	-	-	-
NORTH DAKOTA	1	46	12	188	17	122	20	74	-	-
OHIO	30	1 042	13	247	-	-	-	-	-	-
OKLAHOMA	24	815	26	383	16	116	3	13	-	-
OREGON	8	308	6	152	5	33	3	6	-	-
PENNSYLVANIA	15	585	6	101	5	18	-	-	1	1 816
RHODE ISLAND	-	-	-	-	-	-	-	-	5	931
SOUTH CAROLINA	16	556	11	177	1	8	-	-	-	-
SOUTH DAKOTA	1	38	15	226	23	162	23	72	3	16
TENNESSEE	30	1 011	33	568	14	103	4	12	1	448
TEXAS	32	1 111	83	1 342	46	344	55	161	-	-
UTAH	2	77	9	140	5	34	9	26	-	-
VERMONT	6	220	4	81	1	6	1	4	-	-
VIRGINIA	23	783	37	606	22	167	2	6	41	2 013
WASHINGTON	9	347	9	160	4	28	4	16	-	-
WEST VIRGINIA	14	473	17	295	12	100	1	5	-	-
WISCONSIN	21	737	24	388	3	23	2	6	-	-
WYOMING	3	88	6	92	8	61	4	17	-	-

Note: Because of rounding, population detail may not add to totals.

- Represents zero or rounds to zero.
Z Less than 500.
[1] See "Relation to Other Classifications and Listings" in text.

17

Table 4. Number of Municipal Governments in 1977 and Their Estimated 1975 Populations, by Population Size, and by State

(Population amounts in thousands)

| State | Total | | Population-size group | | | | | | | | | |
| | | | 300,000 or more | | 200,000 to 299,999 | | 100,000 to 199,999 | | 50,000 to 99,999 | | 25,000 to 49,999 | |
	Number	Population	Number	Population	Number	Population	Number	Population	Number	Population	Number	Population
UNITED STATES, TOTAL	18 862	136 761	46	38 319	18	4 665	99	13 550	230	16 091	514	17 939
ALABAMA	419	2 153	-	-	1	276	3	486	2	120	9	298
ALASKA	142	291	-	-	-	-	1	161	-	-	1	30
ARIZONA	70	1 645	1	665	1	296	-	-	4	334	2	61
ARKANSAS	467	1 245	-	-	-	-	1	141	3	183	5	153
CALIFORNIA	413	15 990	6	5 388	1	261	14	1 897	51	3 613	73	2 533
COLORADO	262	1 931	1	485	-	-	4	523	3	209	8	261
CONNECTICUT	33	1 332	-	-	-	-	5	620	5	379	7	246
DELAWARE	55	194	-	-	-	-	-	-	1	76	1	27
DISTRICT OF COLUMBIA	1	712	1	712	-	-	-	-	-	-	-	-
FLORIDA	389	4 827	2	900	2	515	4	503	6	443	26	927
GEORGIA	530	2 420	1	436	-	-	3	391	2	127	6	222
HAWAII	1	705	1	705	-	-	-	-	-	-	-	-
IDAHO	199	531	-	-	-	-	-	-	1	100	3	105
ILLINOIS	1 274	9 405	1	3 099	-	-	2	271	15	1 025	47	1 628
INDIANA	563	3 543	1	715	-	-	5	709	4	264	13	493
IOWA	955	2 096	-	-	-	-	2	303	5	384	9	302
KANSAS	625	1 755	-	-	1	265	2	287	2	132	5	164
KENTUCKY	405	1 651	1	336	-	-	1	186	1	51	5	165
LOUISIANA	300	2 261	1	560	1	294	1	186	3	213	6	233
MAINE	24	358	-	-	-	-	-	-	1	66	2	73
MARYLAND	151	1 456	1	852	-	-	-	-	-	-	6	206
MASSACHUSETTS	39	2 872	1	637	-	-	5	645	12	880	17	630
MICHIGAN	531	5 948	1	1 335	-	-	6	880	16	1 199	25	896
MINNESOTA	855	3 000	1	378	1	280	-	-	3	229	17	583
MISSISSIPPI	283	1 151	-	-	-	-	1	167	-	-	8	303
MISSOURI	916	3 287	2	997	-	-	2	243	3	211	10	332
MONTANA	126	428	-	-	-	-	-	-	2	130	2	56
NEBRASKA	534	1 153	1	371	-	-	1	163	-	-	1	33
NEVADA	17	372	-	-	-	-	1	146	1	78	2	69
NEW HAMPSHIRE	13	331	-	-	-	-	-	-	2	144	1	29
NEW JERSEY	335	4 457	1	340	1	244	3	342	9	582	25	878
NEW MEXICO	93	745	-	-	1	279	-	-	-	-	6	210
NEW YORK	618	12 048	2	7 889	1	267	3	485	7	499	22	725
NORTH CAROLINA	472	2 408	-	-	1	281	4	532	4	241	8	273
NORTH DAKOTA	361	412	-	-	-	-	-	-	1	56	3	113
OHIO	935	7 444	4	1 955	2	458	2	234	12	799	28	938
OKLAHOMA	567	2 086	2	698	-	-	-	-	3	186	8	256
OREGON	239	1 303	1	357	-	-	-	-	2	171	3	105
PENNSYLVANIA	1 015	6 620	2	2 274	-	-	2	235	7	483	17	580
RHODE ISLAND	8	542	-	-	-	-	1	168	3	232	3	125
SOUTH CAROLINA	264	1 092	-	-	-	-	1	112	3	178	4	142
SOUTH DAKOTA	311	423	-	-	-	-	-	-	1	74	2	75
TENNESSEE	326	2 593	2	1 085	-	-	2	345	1	52	7	227
TEXAS	1 066	9 948	6	3 998	1	215	7	842	15	1 057	23	794
UTAH	216	836	-	-	-	-	1	170	2	125	2	66
VERMONT	57	160	-	-	-	-	-	-	-	-	1	37
VIRGINIA	229	2 351	-	-	3	733	6	683	1	63	5	209
WASHINGTON	265	1 984	1	487	-	-	2	325	1	65	9	337
WEST VIRGINIA	227	780	-	-	-	-	-	-	2	136	5	166
WISCONSIN	576	3 211	1	666	-	-	1	168	7	502	14	536
WYOMING	90	274	-	-	-	-	-	-	-	-	2	88

See footnotes at end of table.

18

Table 4. Number of Municipal Governments in 1977 and Their Estimated 1975 Populations, by Population Size, and by State—Continued

(Population amounts in thousands)

Population-size group—Continued / Exhibit

State	10,000 to 24,999: Number	10,000 to 24,999: Population	5,000 to 9,999: Number	5,000 to 9,999: Population	2,500 to 4,999: Number	2,500 to 4,999: Population	1,000 to 2,499: Number	1,000 to 2,499: Population	Less than 1,000: Number	Less than 1,000: Population	Population outside areas with municipal government	Percent of population in areas with municipal government
UNITED STATES, TOTAL	1 212	19 001	1 461	10 299	2 004	7 039	3 664	5 873	9 614	3 984	76 273	64.2
ALABAMA	24	340	35	243	52	177	75	124	218	88	1 462	59.6
ALASKA	1	17	2	14	4	16	10	19	122	35	74	79.7
ARIZONA	6	96	14	96	20	64	18	30	4	3	567	74.4
ARKANSAS	17	259	22	151	34	118	76	121	309	119	865	59.0
CALIFORNIA	90	1 552	59	427	68	249	30	57	21	13	5 208	75.4
COLORADO	10	150	14	95	22	79	43	64	157	66	610	76.0
CONNECTICUT	3	48	2	17	4	16	3	5	3	2	1 768	43.0
DELAWARE	1	22	3	20	4	14	15	24	30	10	385	33.5
DISTRICT OF COLUMBIA	-	-	-	-	-	-	-	-	-	-	-	100.0
FLORIDA	47	744	56	404	62	227	64	106	120	59	3 450	58.3
GEORGIA	29	459	36	250	71	252	99	161	283	121	2 511	49.1
HAWAII	-	-	-	-	-	-	-	-	-	-	163	81.2
IDAHO	6	106	6	42	23	80	33	52	127	48	282	65.3
ILLINOIS	103	1 600	91	651	129	463	246	381	640	286	1 792	84.0
INDIANA	37	578	36	248	50	182	134	216	283	140	1 770	66.7
IOWA	12	191	34	241	56	200	140	215	697	259	765	73.3
KANSAS	25	361	15	103	37	128	104	173	434	143	525	77.0
KENTUCKY	20	304	28	192	46	161	101	160	202	96	1 736	48.7
LOUISIANA	21	314	23	161	34	125	69	111	141	64	1 545	59.4
MAINE	9	154	7	54	2	7	2	3	1	1	700	33.8
MARYLAND	10	160	12	89	16	53	41	66	65	29	2 666	35.3
MASSACHUSETTS	4	80	-	-	-	-	-	-	-	-	2 942	49.4
MICHIGAN	43	691	52	359	71	252	148	243	169	93	3 163	65.3
MINNESOTA	37	585	38	278	70	247	133	216	555	203	921	76.5
MISSISSIPPI	17	261	20	141	35	116	63	102	139	61	1 190	49.2
MISSOURI	34	508	48	327	71	241	137	220	609	207	1 480	69.0
MONTANA	4	68	6	44	15	54	31	47	66	30	318	57.4
NEBRASKA	9	167	19	123	16	56	75	109	412	130	391	74.7
NEVADA	2	41	3	21	2	8	4	6	2	-	218	63.1
NEW HAMPSHIRE	7	131	3	26	-	-	-	-	-	-	481	40.8
NEW JERSEY	75	1 102	93	671	55	203	47	79	26	15	2 876	60.8
NEW MEXICO	7	110	9	67	9	29	18	31	43	19	399	65.1
NEW YORK	51	853	83	592	102	351	169	274	178	113	6 028	66.7
NORTH CAROLINA	26	397	32	215	54	182	105	174	238	113	3 033	44.3
NORTH DAKOTA	4	52	5	36	4	13	42	64	302	78	225	64.7
OHIO	97	1 562	88	623	105	375	190	306	407	195	3 291	69.3
OKLAHOMA	18	297	30	209	45	151	101	160	360	129	629	76.8
OREGON	19	296	19	127	30	108	55	86	112	54	981	57.0
PENNSYLVANIA	66	920	138	956	167	587	249	405	367	182	5 240	55.8
RHODE ISLAND	1	17	-	-	-	-	-	-	-	-	389	58.2
SOUTH CAROLINA	15	212	28	196	34	111	53	89	126	51	1 724	38.8
SOUTH DAKOTA	6	78	4	26	10	37	34	52	254	80	258	62.1
TENNESSEE	22	334	32	215	44	152	70	111	146	72	1 580	62.1
TEXAS	81	1 243	98	689	147	520	240	387	448	203	2 289	81.3
UTAH	13	193	14	100	19	68	44	71	121	44	367	69.5
VERMONT	2	30	5	40	3	11	19	31	27	12	312	33.9
VIRGINIA	17	299	24	168	20	66	49	77	104	52	630	47.2
WASHINGTON	24	388	15	93	38	135	65	99	110	54	1 575	55.7
WEST VIRGINIA	8	128	13	90	31	102	66	104	102	54	1 019	43.4
WISCONSIN	29	450	42	315	62	216	139	218	281	139	1 378	70.0
WYOMING	3	53	7	54	10	37	15	24	53	17	102	72.9

Note: Because of rounding, detail may not add to total.

- Represents zero or rounds to zero.

Table 5. Number of Township Governments in 1977 and Their Estimated 1975 Population, by Population Size, and by State

(Population amounts in thousands. Includes "towns" in the 6 New England States, New York, and Wisconsin)

State	Total (areas with township government) Number	Total (areas with township government) Population	100,000 or more Number	100,000 or more Population	50,000 to 99,999 Number	50,000 to 99,999 Population	25,000 to 49,999 Number	25,000 to 49,999 Population	10,000 to 24,999 Number	10,000 to 24,999 Population	5,000 to 9,999 Number	5,000 to 9,999 Population	2,500 to 4,999 Number	2,500 to 4,999 Population	1,000 to 2,499 Number	1,000 to 2,499 Population	Less than 1,000 Number	Less than 1,000 Population	Exhibit: Percent of 1975 population in areas with township government
UNITED STATES, TOTAL . .	16 822	48 344	31	5 041	72	4 798	190	6 477	660	10 185	870	6 080	1 595	5 504	3 657	5 807	9 747	3 747	22.7
NEW ENGLAND STATES, TOTAL. . .	1 425	6 700	-	-	10	565	34	1 064	157	2 492	152	1 084	200	713	329	528	543	254	55.0
CONNECTICUT.	149	1 820	-	-	7	390	9	306	43	710	37	272	25	97	25	43	3	3	58.7
MAINE.	475	701	-	-	-	-	-	-	4	57	23	165	49	172	126	196	273	112	66.3
MASSACHUSETTS . . .	312	2 944	-	-	3	175	22	679	85	1 343	66	458	49	187	47	79	40	22	50.6
NEW HAMPSHIRE . . .	221	481	-	-	-	-	-	-	5	75	15	110	43	143	68	107	90	46	59.2
RHODE ISLAND . . .	31	389	-	-	-	-	3	79	16	257	4	30	6	20	1	2	1	1	41.8
VERMONT.	237	366	-	-	-	-	-	-	4	50	7	49	28	94	62	101	136	71	77.5
MIDDLE ATLANTIC STATES, TOTAL.	2 711	16 044	11	2 826	24	1 601	62	2 138	233	3 576	312	2 163	534	1 872	888	1 473	647	394	43.0
NEW JERSEY	232	2 877	-	-	8	537	19	688	71	1 134	36	260	53	182	41	73	4	2	39.2
NEW YORK	930	7 925	11	2 826	10	668	27	885	83	1 274	136	924	206	735	299	510	158	102	43.8
PENNSYLVANIA . . .	1 549	5 242	-	-	6	396	16	565	79	1 167	140	979	275	955	548	890	485	290	44.2
OTHER STATES HAVING TOWNSHIP GOVERNMENTS, TOTAL. . .	12 686	25 600	20	2 915	38	2 632	94	3 275	270	4 118	406	2 833	861	2 919	2 440	3 808	8 557	3 099	46.7
ILLINOIS	1 436	5 772	13	1 759	21	1 557	39	1 373	75	1 155	74	495	137	468	377	577	700	388	69.4
INDIANA.	1 008	5 308	7	1 156	11	732	18	674	50	807	79	573	156	539	401	637	286	190	99.9
KANSAS	1 449	783	-	-	-	-	-	-	4	48	5	40	27	89	155	237	1 258	370	34.3
MICHIGAN	1 245	3 480	-	-	3	188	9	294	46	715	86	613	198	665	454	751	449	255	38.2
MINNESOTA.	1 792	911	-	-	-	-	-	-	1	12	3	17	17	56	156	222	1 615	604	23.2
MISSOURI	326	323	-	-	-	-	-	-	4	47	5	37	19	66	38	59	260	114	6.8
NEBRASKA	471	214	-	-	-	-	-	-	-	-	-	-	4	11	39	60	428	142	13.9
NORTH DAKOTA . . .	1 360	180	-	-	-	-	-	-	1	11	2	13	-	-	8	11	1 349	144	28.3
OHIO	1 319	5 089	-	-	3	155	28	934	83	1 238	136	938	237	806	479	771	353	246	47.4
SOUTH DAKOTA . . .	1 010	173	-	-	-	-	-	-	-	-	-	-	2	6	6	9	1 002	158	25.4
WISCONSIN.	1 270	1 367	-	-	-	-	-	-	6	85	16	107	64	213	327	474	857	488	29.8

Note: Because of rounding, detail may not add to total.

- Represents zero or rounds to zero.

Table 6. Local Governments and Public School Systems in Individual SMSA's: 1977

Item	Anniston	Birmingham					Florence			Gadsden
	Calhoun County (entire SMSA)	Total	Jefferson County*	St. Clair County	Shelby County	Walker County	Total	Colbert County	Lauderdale County*	Etowah County (entire SMSA)
NUMBER OF LOCAL GOVERNMENTS										
ALL TYPES, TOTAL	20	113	52	17	23	21	34	15	19	21
WITH PROPERTY-TAXING POWER	14	84	44	13	12	15	21	11	10	16
WITHOUT PROPERTY-TAXING POWER	6	29	8	4	11	6	13	4	9	5
COUNTY GOVERNMENTS	1	4	1	1	1	1	2	1	1	1
MUNICIPALITIES	8	66	34	11	10	11	13	6	7	12
WITH A POPULATION OF--										
50,000 OR MORE	-	1	1	-	-	-	-	-	-	1
25,000 TO 49,999	1	1	1	-	-	-	1	-	1	-
10,000 TO 24,999	-	7	6	-	-	1	1	1	-	-
5,000 TO 9,999	3	8	6	1	1	-	2	2	-	1
2,500 TO 4,999	1	11	7	-	2	2	-	-	-	3
1,000 TO 2,499	1	14	3	4	4	3	3	2	1	1
LESS THAN 1,000	2	24	10	6	3	5	6	1	5	6
TOWNSHIP GOVERNMENTS	-	-	-	-	-	-	-	-	-	-
SCHOOL DISTRICTS	5	14	9	1	1	3	6	4	2	3
SPECIAL DISTRICTS	6	29	8	4	11	6	13	4	9	5
WITH PROPERTY-TAXING POWER	-	-	-	-	-	-	-	-	-	-
SINGLE FUNCTION DISTRICTS	-	-	-	-	-	-	-	-	-	-
CEMETERIES	-	-	-	-	-	-	-	-	-	-
EDUCATION (SCHOOL BUILDING DISTRICTS)	-	-	-	-	-	-	-	-	-	-
FIRE PROTECTION	-	-	-	-	-	-	2	-	2	-
HIGHWAYS	-	-	-	-	-	-	-	-	-	-
HEALTH	-	-	-	-	-	-	-	-	-	-
HOSPITALS	-	3	1	1	1	-	1	1	-	1
HOUSING AND URBAN RENEWAL	4	16	6	2	3	5	3	2	1	3
LIBRARIES	-	-	-	-	-	-	-	-	-	-
NATURAL RESOURCES, TOTAL	1	4	1	1	1	1	2	1	1	1
DRAINAGE	-	-	-	-	-	-	-	-	-	-
FLOOD CONTROL	-	-	-	-	-	-	-	-	-	-
IRRIGATION, WATER CONSERVATION	-	-	-	-	-	-	-	-	-	-
SOIL CONSERVATION	1	4	1	1	1	1	2	1	1	1
OTHER AND COMPOSITE PURPOSES	-	-	-	-	-	-	-	-	-	-
PARKS AND RECREATION	-	-	-	-	-	-	-	-	-	-
SEWERAGE	-	1	-	-	1	-	-	-	-	-
UTILITIES, TOTAL	1	5	-	-	5	-	3	-	3	-
WATER SUPPLY	1	5	-	-	5	-	2	-	2	-
ELECTRIC POWER	-	-	-	-	-	-	-	-	-	-
GAS SUPPLY	-	-	-	-	-	-	1	-	1	-
TRANSIT	-	-	-	-	-	-	-	-	-	-
OTHER	-	-	-	-	-	-	-	-	-	-
MULTIPLE-FUNCTION DISTRICTS	-	-	-	-	-	-	2	-	2	-
SEWERAGE AND WATER SUPPLY	-	-	-	-	-	-	-	-	-	-
NATURAL RESOURCES AND WATER SUPPLY	-	-	-	-	-	-	-	-	-	-
OTHER	-	-	-	-	-	-	2	-	2	-
SCHOOL SYSTEMS										
TOTAL	5	14	9	1	1	3	6	4	2	3
DEPENDENT SCHOOL SYSTEMS	-	-	-	-	-	-	-	-	-	-
BY ENROLLMENT SIZE OCTOBER 1976										
100,000 OR MORE PUPILS	-	-	-	-	-	-	-	-	-	-
50,000 TO 99,999 PUPILS	-	2	2	-	-	-	-	-	-	-
25,000 TO 49,999 PUPILS	-	-	-	-	-	-	-	-	-	-
12,000 TO 24,999 PUPILS	-	-	-	-	-	-	-	-	-	-
6,000 TO 11,999 PUPILS	1	3	-	1	1	1	2	-	2	2
3,000 TO 5,999 PUPILS	1	2	2	-	-	-	1	1	-	-
1,200 TO 2,999 PUPILS	3	6	5	-	-	1	3	3	-	1
300 TO 1,199 PUPILS	-	1	-	-	-	1	-	-	-	-
50 TO 299 PUPILS	-	-	-	-	-	-	-	-	-	-
1 TO 49 PUPILS	-	-	-	-	-	-	-	-	-	-
POPULATION, 1975 (ESTIMATED)										
TOTAL	106 491	791 073	644 688	33 529	48 289	64 567	123 318	49 997	73 321	95 381
IN MUNICIPALLY GOVERNED AREAS	55 593	544 655	478 876	¹14 695	¹24 330	26 754	69 592	32 187	37 405	¹70 596
WITH A 1975 POPULATION OF--										
50,000 OR MORE	-	276 273	276 273	-	-	-	-	-	-	50 357
25,000 TO 49,999	30 622	31 531	31 531	-	-	-	34 402	-	34 402	-
10,000 TO 24,999	-	107 555	95 769	-	-	11 786	11 885	11 885	-	-
5,000 TO 9,999	20 132	54 613	41 007	6 066	7 540	-	16 491	16 491	-	7 212
2,500 TO 4,999	2 652	38 958	24 336	-	7 801	6 821	-	-	-	9 330
1,000 TO 2,499	1 222	23 276	5 356	5 303	6 876	5 741	4 007	2 921	1 086	1 214
LESS THAN 1,000	965	12 449	4 604	3 326	2 113	2 406	2 807	890	1 917	2 483
OUTSIDE MUNICIPALLY GOVERNED AREAS	50 898	246 418	165 812	18 834	23 959	37 813	53 726	17 810	35 916	24 785
IN TOWNSHIP-GOVERNED AREAS	-	-	-	-	-	-	-	-	-	-
ENROLLMENT OF PUBLIC SCHOOL SYSTEMS										
TOTAL	21 742	153 660	120 733	8 300	11 016	13 611	26 534	11 212	15 322	19 258
THROUGH GRADE 12	21 742	153 660	120 733	8 300	11 016	13 611	26 534	11 212	15 322	19 258
COLLEGE GRADES	-	-	-	-	-	-	-	-	-	-

Alabama (see also Georgia)

¹Excludes population of intercounty municipalities where majority of inhabitants live in another county.

Table 6. Local Governments and Public School Systems in Individual SMSA's: 1977—Continued

Alabama (see also Georgia)--Continued

Item	Huntsville Total	Limestone County	Madison County*	Marshall County	Mobile Total	Baldwin County	Mobile County*	Montgomery Total	Autauga County	Elmore County	Montgomery County*
NUMBER OF LOCAL GOVERNMENTS											
ALL TYPES, TOTAL	48	12	16	20	44	24	20	27	8	13	6
WITH PROPERTY-TAXING POWER	27	8	9	10	23	12	11	15	5	7	3
WITHOUT PROPERTY-TAXING POWER	21	4	7	10	21	12	9	12	3	6	3
COUNTY GOVERNMENTS	3	1	1	1	2	1	1	3	1	1	1
MUNICIPALITIES	17	5	6	6	19	10	9	8	3	4	1
WITH A POPULATION OF--											
50,000 OR MORE	1	-	1	-	1	-	1	1	-	-	1
25,000 TO 49,999	-	-	-	-	1	-	1	-	-	-	-
10,000 TO 24,999	2	1	-	1	-	-	-	1	1	-	-
5,000 TO 9,999	3	-	-	3	4	2	2	-	-	-	-
2,500 TO 4,999	1	-	1	-	4	2	2	2	-	2	-
1,000 TO 2,499	1	-	1	-	4	2	2	1	-	1	-
LESS THAN 1,000	9	4	3	2	5	4	1	3	2	1	-
TOWNSHIP GOVERNMENTS	-	-	-	-	-	-	-	-	-	-	-
SCHOOL DISTRICTS	7	2	2	3	2	1	1	4	1	2	1
SPECIAL DISTRICTS	21	4	7	10	21	12	9	12	3	6	3
WITH PROPERTY-TAXING POWER	-	-	-	-	-	-	-	-	-	-	-
SINGLE FUNCTION DISTRICTS	-	-	-	-	-	-	-	-	-	-	-
CEMETERIES	-	-	-	-	-	-	-	-	-	-	-
EDUCATION (SCHOOL BUILDING DISTRICTS)	-	-	-	-	-	-	-	-	-	-	-
FIRE PROTECTION	-	-	-	-	-	-	-	-	-	-	-
HIGHWAYS	-	-	-	-	-	-	-	-	-	-	-
HEALTH	-	-	-	-	-	-	-	-	-	-	-
HOSPITALS	2	1	-	1	1	1	-	1	-	1	-
HOUSING AND URBAN RENEWAL	7	1	2	4	5	2	3	3	1	1	1
LIBRARIES	-	-	-	-	-	-	-	-	-	-	-
NATURAL RESOURCES, TOTAL	3	1	1	1	3	2	1	3	1	1	1
DRAINAGE	-	-	-	-	-	-	-	-	-	-	-
FLOOD CONTROL	-	-	-	-	-	-	-	-	-	-	-
IRRIGATION, WATER CONSERVATION	-	-	-	-	-	-	-	-	-	-	-
SOIL CONSERVATION	3	1	1	1	3	2	1	3	1	1	1
OTHER AND COMPOSITE PURPOSES	-	-	-	-	-	-	-	-	-	-	-
PARKS AND RECREATION	-	-	-	-	-	-	-	-	-	-	-
SEWERAGE	-	-	-	-	-	-	-	-	-	-	-
UTILITIES, TOTAL	4	-	1	3	7	4	3	1	-	1	-
WATER SUPPLY	3	-	1	2	6	4	2	1	-	1	-
ELECTRIC POWER	-	-	-	-	-	-	-	-	-	-	-
GAS SUPPLY	1	-	-	1	1	-	1	-	-	-	-
TRANSIT	-	-	-	-	-	-	-	-	-	-	-
OTHER	1	-	1	-	-	-	-	1	-	-	1
MULTIPLE-FUNCTION DISTRICTS	4	1	2	1	5	3	2	3	1	2	-
SEWERAGE AND WATER SUPPLY	-	-	-	-	1	-	1	-	-	-	-
NATURAL RESOURCES AND WATER SUPPLY	-	-	-	-	-	-	-	-	-	-	-
OTHER	4	1	2	1	4	3	1	3	1	2	-
SCHOOL SYSTEMS											
TOTAL	7	2	2	3	2	1	1	4	1	2	1
DEPENDENT SCHOOL SYSTEMS	-	-	-	-	-	-	-	-	-	-	-
BY ENROLLMENT SIZE OCTOBER 1976											
100,000 OR MORE PUPILS	-	-	-	-	-	-	-	-	-	-	-
50,000 TO 99,999 PUPILS	1	-	1	-	1	-	1	-	-	-	-
25,000 TO 49,999 PUPILS	-	-	-	-	-	-	-	1	-	-	1
12,000 TO 24,999 PUPILS	-	-	-	-	1	1	-	-	-	-	-
6,000 TO 11,999 PUPILS	3	1	1	1	-	-	-	2	1	1	-
3,000 TO 5,999 PUPILS	-	-	-	-	-	-	-	-	-	-	-
1,200 TO 2,999 PUPILS	3	1	-	2	-	-	-	1	-	1	-
300 TO 1,199 PUPILS	-	-	-	-	-	-	-	-	-	-	-
50 TO 299 PUPILS	-	-	-	-	-	-	-	-	-	-	-
1 TO 49 PUPILS	-	-	-	-	-	-	-	-	-	-	-
POPULATION, 1975 (ESTIMATED)											
TOTAL	285 509	43 310	183 285	58 914	403 341	68 073	335 268	250 355	28 846	40 302	181 207
IN MUNICIPALLY GOVERNED AREAS	186 279	14 942	142 723	28 614	286 920	25 423	261 497	182 304	18 348	10 613	153 343
WITH A 1975 POPULATION OF--											
50,000 OR MORE	136 419	-	136 419	-	196 441	-	196 441	153 343	-	-	153 343
25,000 TO 49,999	-	-	-	-	39 319	-	39 319	-	-	-	-
10,000 TO 24,999	23 932	13 637	-	10 295	-	-	-	17 356	17 356	-	-
5,000 TO 9,999	17 771	-	-	17 771	30 364	13 345	17 019	-	-	-	-
2,500 TO 4,999	3 286	-	3 286	-	11 160	6 066	5 094	9 055	-	9 055	-
1,000 TO 2,499	1 395	-	1 395	-	6 636	3 443	3 193	1 280	-	1 280	-
LESS THAN 1,000	3 476	1 305	1 623	548	3 000	2 569	431	1 270	992	278	-
OUTSIDE MUNICIPALLY GOVERNED AREAS	99 230	28 368	40 562	30 300	116 421	42 650	73 771	68 051	10 498	29 689	27 864
IN TOWNSHIP-GOVERNED AREAS	-	-	-	-	-	-	-	-	-	-	-
ENROLLMENT OF PUBLIC SCHOOL SYSTEMS											
TOTAL	65 091	9 934	41 806	13 351	80 141	14 681	65 460	51 481	7 179	8 339	35 963
THROUGH GRADE 12	65 091	9 934	41 806	13 351	80 141	14 681	65 460	51 481	7 179	8 339	35 963
COLLEGE GRADES	-	-	-	-	-	-	-	-	-	-	-

Table 6. Local Governments and Public School Systems in Individual SMSA's: 1977—Continued

Item	Tuscaloosa — Tuscaloosa County (entire SMSA)	Anchorage — Anchorage Borough (entire SMSA)	Phoenix — Maricopa County (entire SMSA)	Tucson — Pima County (entire SMSA)	Fayetteville-Springdale — Total	Benton County	Washington County*
NUMBER OF LOCAL GOVERNMENTS							
ALL TYPES, TOTAL	10	1	115	24	69	41	28
WITH PROPERTY-TAXING POWER	6	1	115	23	47	25	22
WITHOUT PROPERTY-TAXING POWER	4	-	-	1	22	16	6
COUNTY GOVERNMENTS	1	-	1	1	2	1	1
MUNICIPALITIES	3	1	19	3	29	17	12
WITH A POPULATION OF--							
50,000 OR MORE	1	1	5	1	-	-	-
25,000 TO 49,999	-	-	-	-	1	-	1
10,000 TO 24,999	1	-	1	-	2	1	1
5,000 TO 9,999	-	-	3	1	2	2	1
2,500 TO 4,999	-	-	7	-	-	-	-
1,000 TO 2,499	-	-	3	1	7	3	4
LESS THAN 1,000	1	-	3	1	17	11	6
TOWNSHIP GOVERNMENTS	-	-	-	-	-	-	-
SCHOOL DISTRICTS	2	-	56	17	16	7	9
SPECIAL DISTRICTS	4	-	39	3	22	16	6
WITH PROPERTY-TAXING POWER	-	-	39	2	-	-	-
SINGLE FUNCTION DISTRICTS	-	-	-	-	-	-	-
CEMETERIES	-	-	-	-	-	-	-
EDUCATION (SCHOOL BUILDING DISTRICTS)	-	-	-	-	-	-	-
FIRE PROTECTION	-	-	-	-	-	-	-
HIGHWAYS	-	-	4	-	9	9	-
HEALTH	-	-	-	-	-	-	-
HOSPITALS	1	-	1	-	-	-	-
HOUSING AND URBAN RENEWAL	2	-	-	-	5	2	3
LIBRARIES	-	-	-	-	-	-	-
NATURAL RESOURCES, TOTAL	1	-	28	3	2	1	1
DRAINAGE	-	-	2	-	-	-	-
FLOOD CONTROL	-	-	-	-	-	-	-
IRRIGATION, WATER CONSERVATION	-	-	26	3	-	-	-
SOIL CONSERVATION	1	-	-	-	2	1	1
OTHER AND COMPOSITE PURPOSES	-	-	-	-	-	-	-
PARKS AND RECREATION	-	-	-	-	-	-	-
SEWERAGE	-	-	1	-	-	-	-
UTILITIES, TOTAL	-	-	4	-	4	2	2
WATER SUPPLY	-	-	-	-	4	2	2
ELECTRIC POWER	-	-	4	-	-	-	-
GAS SUPPLY	-	-	-	-	-	-	-
TRANSIT	-	-	-	-	-	-	-
OTHER	-	-	-	-	-	-	-
MULTIPLE-FUNCTION DISTRICTS	-	-	1	-	2	2	-
SEWERAGE AND WATER SUPPLY	-	-	-	-	1	1	-
NATURAL RESOURCES AND WATER SUPPLY	-	-	-	-	-	-	-
OTHER	-	-	1	-	1	1	-
SCHOOL SYSTEMS							
TOTAL	2	1	57	18	16	7	9
DEPENDENT SCHOOL SYSTEMS	-	1	1	1	-	-	-
BY ENROLLMENT SIZE OCTOBER 1976							
100,000 OR MORE PUPILS	-	-	-	-	-	-	-
50,000 TO 99,999 PUPILS	-	-	-	1	-	-	-
25,000 TO 49,999 PUPILS	-	1	4	-	-	-	-
12,000 TO 24,999 PUPILS	1	-	4	1	-	-	-
6,000 TO 11,999 PUPILS	1	-	8	2	1	-	1
3,000 TO 5,999 PUPILS	-	-	5	1	2	1	1
1,200 TO 2,999 PUPILS	-	-	12	3	2	2	-
300 TO 1,199 PUPILS	-	-	10	3	10	4	6
50 TO 299 PUPILS	-	-	11	3	1	-	1
1 TO 49 PUPILS	-	-	3	2	-	-	-
0 PUPILS (NONOPERATING)	-	-	-	2	-	-	-
POPULATION, 1975 (ESTIMATED)							
TOTAL	122 169	161 018	1 221 414	443 958	146 890	58 709	88 181
IN MUNICIPALLY GOVERNED AREAS	¹82 884	161 018	1 072 627	303 850	98 164	¹35 720	62 444
WITH A 1975 POPULATION OF--							
50,000 OR MORE	69 425	161 018	998 978	296 457	-	-	-
25,000 TO 49,999	-	-	-	-	33 405	-	33 405
10,000 TO 24,999	13 383	-	19 706	-	34 815	14 316	20 499
5,000 TO 9,999	-	-	23 125	6 218	13 124	13 124	-
2,500 TO 4,999	-	-	24 712	-	-	-	-
1,000 TO 2,499	-	-	6 106	1 175	9 115	3 903	5 212
LESS THAN 1,000	76	-	-	-	7 705	4 377	3 328
OUTSIDE MUNICIPALLY GOVERNED AREAS	39 285	-	148 787	140 108	48 726	22 989	25 737
IN TOWNSHIP-GOVERNED AREAS	-	-	-	-	-	-	-
ENROLLMENT OF PUBLIC SCHOOL SYSTEMS							
TOTAL	23 504	40 183	292 712	112 986	31 188	12 426	18 762
THROUGH GRADE 12	23 504	40 183	269 372	92 983	31 188	12 426	18 762
COLLEGE GRADES	-	-	23 340	20 003	-	-	-

Table 6. Local Governments and Public School Systems in Individual SMSA's: 1977—Continued

Item	Arkansas (see also Tennessee and Texas)--Continued — Fort Smith — Total	Crawford County	Sebastian County*	Le Flore County (Okla.)	Sequoyah County (Okla.)	Little Rock-North Little Rock — Total	Pulaski County*	Saline County	Pine Bluff — Jefferson County (entire SMSA)	California — Anaheim-Santa Ana-Garden Grove — Orange County (entire SMSA)	Bakersfield — Kern County (entire SMSA)
NUMBER OF LOCAL GOVERNMENTS											
ALL TYPES, TOTAL	112	19	20	46	27	79	58	21	39	108	146
WITH PROPERTY-TAXING POWER	88	14	18	33	23	22	10	12	18	108	140
WITHOUT PROPERTY-TAXING POWER	24	5	2	13	4	57	48	9	21	-	6
COUNTY GOVERNMENTS	4	1	1	1	1	2	1	1	1	1	1
MUNICIPALITIES	43	8	11	15	9	11	6	5	6	26	11
WITH A POPULATION OF--											
50,000 OR MORE	1	-	1	-	-	2	2	-	1	11	1
25,000 TO 49,999	-	-	-	-	-	-	-	-	-	6	-
10,000 TO 24,999	-	-	-	-	-	2	1	1	-	8	2
5,000 TO 9,999	3	1	-	1	1	1	1	1	-	1	3
2,500 TO 4,999	2	-	1	1	1	-	-	-	-	1	3
1,000 TO 2,499	13	2	2	6	3	2	1	1	1	-	1
LESS THAN 1,000	24	5	7	7	5	4	1	3	4	-	1
TOWNSHIP GOVERNMENTS	-	-	-	-	-	-	-	-	-	-	-
SCHOOL DISTRICTS	41	5	6	17	13	9	3	6	11	33	51
SPECIAL DISTRICTS	24	5	2	13	4	57	48	9	21	48	83
WITH PROPERTY-TAXING POWER	-	-	-	-	-	-	-	-	-	48	77
SINGLE FUNCTION DISTRICTS											
CEMETERIES	-	-	-	-	-	-	-	-	-	3	7
EDUCATION (SCHOOL BUILDING DISTRICTS)	-	-	-	-	-	-	-	-	-	-	-
FIRE PROTECTION	-	-	-	-	-	2	2	-	-	-	-
HIGHWAYS	-	-	-	-	-	1	1	-	-	-	1
HEALTH	-	-	-	-	-	-	-	-	-	1	4
HOSPITALS	-	-	-	-	-	-	-	-	-	-	4
HOUSING AND URBAN RENEWAL	7	2	1	4	-	2	2	-	-	-	2
LIBRARIES	-	-	-	-	-	-	-	-	-	3	-
NATURAL RESOURCES, TOTAL	10	3	1	4	2	5	4	1	13	6	25
DRAINAGE	-	-	-	-	-	2	2	-	9	1	-
FLOOD CONTROL	3	2	-	-	1	1	1	-	4	1	2
IRRIGATION, WATER CONSERVATION	2	-	-	2	-	-	-	-	-	3	17
SOIL CONSERVATION	5	1	1	2	1	2	1	1	-	1	5
OTHER AND COMPOSITE PURPOSES	-	-	-	-	-	-	-	-	-	1	1
PARKS AND RECREATION	-	-	-	-	-	-	-	-	-	3	8
SEWERAGE	-	-	-	-	-	16	14	2	8	11	1
UTILITIES, TOTAL	7	-	-	5	2	25	22	3	-	11	19
WATER SUPPLY	7	-	-	5	2	25	22	3	-	10	18
ELECTRIC POWER	-	-	-	-	-	-	-	-	-	-	-
GAS SUPPLY	-	-	-	-	-	-	-	-	-	-	-
TRANSIT	-	-	-	-	-	-	-	-	-	1	1
OTHER	-	-	-	-	-	-	-	-	-	2	1
MULTIPLE-FUNCTION DISTRICTS	-	-	-	-	-	6	3	3	-	8	11
SEWERAGE AND WATER SUPPLY	-	-	-	-	-	3	-	3	-	3	8
NATURAL RESOURCES AND WATER SUPPLY	-	-	-	-	-	-	-	-	-	1	1
OTHER	-	-	-	-	-	3	3	-	-	4	2
SPECIAL DISTRICTS BY AREA SERVED											
SCHOOL SYSTEMS											
TOTAL	41	5	6	17	13	9	3	6	11	33	51
DEPENDENT SCHOOL SYSTEMS	-	-	-	-	-	-	-	-	-	-	-
BY ENROLLMENT SIZE OCTOBER 1976											
100,000 OR MORE PUPILS	-	-	-	-	-	-	-	-	-	-	-
50,000 TO 99,999 PUPILS	-	-	-	-	-	-	-	-	-	-	-
25,000 TO 49,999 PUPILS	-	-	-	-	-	1	1	-	-	7	-
12,000 TO 24,999 PUPILS	1	-	1	-	-	1	1	-	-	11	3
6,000 TO 11,999 PUPILS	-	-	-	-	-	1	1	-	1	5	-
3,000 TO 5,999 PUPILS	1	1	-	-	-	2	-	2	1	7	3
1,200 TO 2,999 PUPILS	6	1	1	2	2	-	-	-	2	2	12
300 TO 1,199 PUPILS	23	3	4	11	5	2	-	2	3	1	15
50 TO 299 PUPILS	10	-	-	4	6	2	-	2	4	-	14
1 TO 49 PUPILS	-	-	-	-	-	-	-	-	-	-	4
TOTAL	201 804	30 137	109 094	35 904	26 669	348 471	308 294	40 177	83 750	1 699 666	349 874
IN MUNICIPALLY GOVERNED AREAS	125 135	15 281	76 630	21 314	11 910	255 448	235 208	[1]20 240	[1]58 459	1 488 359	142 084
WITH A 1975 POPULATION OF--											
50,000 OR MORE	66 663	-	66 663	-	-	202 911	202 911	-	54 631	1 133 815	77 264
25,000 TO 49,999	-	-	-	-	-	-	-	-	-	204 320	-
10,000 TO 24,999	-	-	-	-	-	40 969	24 249	16 720	-	143 759	28 523
5,000 TO 9,999	21 523	9 500	-	5 966	6 057	5 860	5 860	-	-	6 465	20 467
2,500 TO 4,999	5 394	-	2 809	2 585	-	-	-	-	-	-	13 019
1,000 TO 2,499	21 596	3 549	3 605	10 022	4 420	3 967	1 596	2 371	1 842	-	2 105
LESS THAN 1,000	9 959	2 232	3 553	2 741	1 433	1 741	592	1 149	1 986	-	706
OUTSIDE MUNICIPALLY GOVERNED AREAS	76 669	14 856	32 464	14 590	14 759	93 023	73 086	19 937	25 291	211 307	207 790
IN TOWNSHIP-GOVERNED AREAS	-	-	-	-	-	-	-	-	-	-	-
ENROLLMENT OF PUBLIC SCHOOL SYSTEMS											
TOTAL	41 365	7 063	17 696	8 917	7 689	72 098	62 984	9 114	20 083	513 967	104 125
THROUGH GRADE 12	41 365	7 063	17 696	8 917	7 689	72 098	62 984	9 114	20 083	420 992	83 115
COLLEGE GRADES	-	-	-	-	-	-	-	-	-	92 975	21 010

					California--Continued						
Item	Fresno	Los Angeles-Long Beach	Modesto	Oxnard-Simi Valley-Ventura	Riverside-San Bernardino-Ontario			Sacramento			
	Fresno County (entire SMSA)	Los Angeles County (entire SMSA)	Stanislaus County (entire SMSA)	Ventura County (entire SMSA)	Total	Riverside County*	San Bernardino County*	Total	Placer County	Sacramento County*	Yolo County
NUMBER OF LOCAL GOVERNMENTS											
ALL TYPES, TOTAL	200	232	107	73	230	114	116	212	66	99	47
WITH PROPERTY-TAXING POWER	191	228	98	69	219	108	111	186	64	86	36
WITHOUT PROPERTY-TAXING POWER	9	4	9	4	11	6	5	26	2	13	11
COUNTY GOVERNMENTS	1	1	1	1	2	1	1	3	1	1	1
MUNICIPALITIES	15	78	9	9	31	17	14	12	5	4	3
WITH A POPULATION OF--											
50,000 OR MORE	1	23	1	4	3	1	2	1	-	1	-
25,000 TO 49,999	-	24	-	1	6	2	4	2	-	-	2
10,000 TO 24,999	2	20	1	2	9	4	5	1	1	-	-
5,000 TO 9,999	3	4	2	2	7	6	1	2	1	1	-
2,500 TO 4,999	5	-	3	-	4	3	1	4	2	1	1
1,000 TO 2,499	4	3	2	-	2	1	1	-	-	-	-
LESS THAN 1,000	-	4	-	-	-	-	-	2	1	1	-
TOWNSHIP GOVERNMENTS	-	-	-	-	-	-	-	-	-	-	-
SCHOOL DISTRICTS	55	95	29	21	66	28	38	42	20	17	5
SPECIAL DISTRICTS	129	58	68	42	131	68	63	155	40	77	38
WITH PROPERTY-TAXING POWER	120	54	59	38	120	62	58	129	38	64	27
SINGLE FUNCTION DISTRICTS											
CEMETERIES	14	5	3	3	14	11	3	17	6	5	6
EDUCATION (SCHOOL BUILDING DISTRICTS)	-	-	-	-	-	-	-	-	-	-	-
FIRE PROTECTION	8	-	19	-	8	2	6	45	15	22	8
HIGHWAYS	-	-	1	-	-	-	-	-	-	-	-
HEALTH	4	4	2	1	2	2	-	2	1	1	-
HOSPITALS	3	2	4	1	7	4	3	2	1	1	-
HOUSING AND URBAN RENEWAL	2	2	2	3	4	1	3	2	-	1	1
LIBRARIES	1	2	-	-	2	2	-	-	-	-	-
NATURAL RESOURCES, TOTAL	46	3	27	12	15	9	6	44	2	25	17
DRAINAGE	3	-	1	3	1	1	-	10	-	6	4
FLOOD CONTROL	2	-	-	-	-	-	-	3	-	2	2
IRRIGATION, WATER CONSERVATION	28	-	15	7	3	1	2	6	1	3	2
SOIL CONSERVATION	7	3	4	2	9	6	3	6	1	3	2
OTHER AND COMPOSITE PURPOSES	6	-	7	-	2	1	1	19	-	11	8
PARKS AND RECREATION	4	5	1	4	8	6	2	11	2	9	-
SEWERAGE	4	-	4	6	8	6	2	4	2	1	1
UTILITIES, TOTAL	30	25	1	8	37	13	24	18	6	11	1
WATER SUPPLY	30	24	1	7	37	13	24	16	6	9	1
ELECTRIC POWER	-	-	-	-	-	-	-	1	-	1	-
GAS SUPPLY	-	-	-	-	-	-	-	-	-	-	-
TRANSIT	-	1	-	1	-	-	-	1	-	1	-
OTHER	3	-	-	2	2	1	1	1	-	1	-
MULTIPLE-FUNCTION DISTRICTS	10	8	4	2	24	11	13	11	6	1	4
SEWERAGE AND WATER SUPPLY	5	3	1	1	6	3	3	9	5	-	4
NATURAL RESOURCES AND WATER SUPPLY	2	4	-	1	3	2	1	1	-	1	-
OTHER	3	1	3	-	15	6	9	1	1	-	-
SCHOOL SYSTEMS											
TOTAL	55	96	29	21	66	28	38	42	20	17	5
DEPENDENT SCHOOL SYSTEMS	-	1	-	-	-	-	-	-	-	-	-
BY ENROLLMENT SIZE OCTOBER 1976											
100,000 OR MORE PUPILS	-	2	-	-	-	-	-	-	-	-	-
50,000 TO 99,999 PUPILS	1	1	-	-	-	-	-	-	-	-	-
25,000 TO 49,999 PUPILS	-	6	-	1	1	-	1	2	-	2	-
12,000 TO 24,999 PUPILS	1	19	1	3	6	2	4	3	-	2	1
6,000 TO 11,999 PUPILS	2	30	2	3	15	8	7	5	1	3	1
3,000 TO 5,999 PUPILS	2	21	3	5	7	2	5	4	2	1	1
1,200 TO 2,999 PUPILS	6	7	6	5	15	7	8	7	5	2	-
300 TO 1,199 PUPILS	28	5	9	3	10	5	5	10	4	4	2
50 TO 299 PUPILS	14	4	5	3	11	4	7	10	7	3	-
1 TO 49 PUPILS	1	1	3	1	1	-	1	1	1	-	-
POPULATION, 1975 (ESTIMATED)											
TOTAL	445 727	6 986 898	223 664	437 853	1 225 945	529 074	696 871	880 001	90 912	687 888	101 201
IN MUNICIPALLY GOVERNED AREAS	260 095	5 981 474	134 322	351 047	734 061	330 644	403 417	370 419	34 655	275 311	60 453
WITH A 1975 POPULATION OF--											
50,000 OR MORE	176 528	4 750 420	83 540	275 556	315 828	150 612	165 216	260 822	-	260 822	-
25,000 TO 49,999	-	867 581	-	25 350	192 509	60 503	132 006	57 920	-	-	57 920
10,000 TO 24,999	31 704	324 689	18 007	36 415	158 106	65 553	92 553	20 256	20 256	-	-
5,000 TO 9,999	23 812	31 013	16 983	13 726	48 963	41 267	7 696	15 905	6 663	9 242	-
2,500 TO 4,999	19 467	-	11 083	-	15 380	11 577	3 803	13 869	7 000	4 336	2 533
1,000 TO 2,499	8 584	5 326	4 709	-	3 275	1 132	2 143	-	-	-	-
LESS THAN 1,000	-	2 445	-	-	-	-	-	1 647	736	911	-
OUTSIDE MUNICIPALLY GOVERNED AREAS	185 632	1 005 424	89 342	86 806	491 884	198 430	293 454	509 582	56 257	412 577	40 748
IN TOWNSHIP-GOVERNED AREAS	-	-	-	-	-	-	-	-	-	-	-
ENROLLMENT OF PUBLIC SCHOOL SYSTEMS											
TOTAL	131 683	1 638 073	60 493	130 424	335 540	133 292	202 248	227 229	30 784	170 183	26 262
THROUGH GRADE 12	110 453	1 338 741	52 153	104 209	282 688	115 875	166 813	196 870	23 257	147 351	26 262
COLLEGE GRADES	21 230	299 332	8 340	26 215	52 852	17 417	35 435	30 359	7 527	22 832	-

Table 6. Local Governments and Public School Systems in Individual SMSA's: 1977—Continued

Item	Salinas-Seaside-Monterey — Monterey County (entire SMSA)	San Diego — San Diego County (entire SMSA)	San Francisco-Oakland — Total	Alameda County*	Contra Costa County	Marin County	San Francisco County*	San Mateo County	San Jose — Santa Clara County (entire SMSA)	Santa Barbara Santa Maria-Lompoc — Santa Barbara County (entire SMSA)
NUMBER OF LOCAL GOVERNMENTS										
ALL TYPES, TOTAL	87	149	298	61	83	70	7	77	74	72
WITH PROPERTY-TAXING POWER	84	148	271	53	69	70	5	74	72	71
WITHOUT PROPERTY-TAXING POWER	3	1	27	8	14	-	2	3	2	1
COUNTY GOVERNMENTS	1	1	4	1	1	1	-	1	1	1
MUNICIPALITIES	12	13	59	13	15	11	1	19	15	5
WITH A POPULATION OF--										
50,000 OR MORE	1	4	12	6	2	-	1	3	5	1
25,000 TO 49,999	2	4	15	4	3	2	-	6	4	1
10,000 TO 24,999	2	4	15	2	7	3	-	3	3	1
5,000 TO 9,999	-	-	9	-	-	4	-	5	2	1
2,500 TO 4,999	5	1	5	1	1	2	-	1	1	1
1,000 TO 2,499	1	-	1	-	1	-	-	-	-	-
LESS THAN 1,000	1	-	2	-	1	-	-	1	-	-
TOWNSHIP GOVERNMENTS	-	-	-	-	-	-	-	-	-	-
SCHOOL DISTRICTS	27	48	88	22	19	21	2	24	37	26
SPECIAL DISTRICTS	47	87	147	25	48	37	4	33	21	40
WITH PROPERTY-TAXING POWER	44	86	120	17	34	37	2	30	19	39
SINGLE FUNCTION DISTRICTS	-	-	-	-	-	-	-	-	-	-
CEMETERIES	8	6	2	-	2	-	-	-	1	7
EDUCATION (SCHOOL BUILDING DISTRICTS)	-	-	-	-	-	-	-	-	-	-
FIRE PROTECTION	12	20	21	3	4	9	-	5	2	6
HIGHWAYS	-	2	1	-	1	-	-	1	-	2
HEALTH	1	1	6	1	2	1	1	1	1	1
HOSPITALS	2	4	8	2	3	1	-	2	2	1
HOUSING AND URBAN RENEWAL	2	-	12	5	4	-	1	2	-	1
LIBRARIES	-	-	-	-	-	-	-	-	-	-
NATURAL RESOURCES, TOTAL	4	13	22	2	15	2	1	2	-	5
DRAINAGE	-	-	1	-	-	1	-	-	-	-
FLOOD CONTROL	-	-	2	1	1	-	-	-	-	-
IRRIGATION, WATER CONSERVATION	-	7	2	-	2	-	-	-	1	2
SOIL CONSERVATION	4	6	3	-	1	1	-	1	2	-
OTHER AND COMPOSITE PURPOSES	-	-	14	1	11	-	1	1	-	3
PARKS AND RECREATION	6	2	14	3	5	3	-	3	3	2
SEWERAGE	2	7	28	3	8	12	-	5	6	6
UTILITIES, TOTAL	5	17	19	2	3	6	-	8	3	4
WATER SUPPLY	5	17	15	-	3	5	-	7	3	3
ELECTRIC POWER	-	-	-	-	-	-	-	-	-	-
GAS SUPPLY	-	-	-	-	-	-	-	-	-	-
TRANSIT	-	-	4	2	-	1	-	1	-	1
OTHER	3	2	3	-	-	-	-	3	-	1
MULTIPLE-FUNCTION DISTRICTS	2	13	11	4	1	3	1	2	-	5
SEWERAGE AND WATER SUPPLY	2	4	3	1	-	1	-	1	-	2
NATURAL RESOURCES AND WATER SUPPLY	-	4	1	1	-	-	-	-	-	-
OTHER	-	5	7	2	1	2	1	1	-	3
SCHOOL SYSTEMS										
TOTAL	27	48	88	22	19	21	2	24	37	26
DEPENDENT SCHOOL SYSTEMS	-	-	-	-	-	-	-	-	-	-
BY ENROLLMENT SIZE OCTOBER 1976										
100,000 OR MORE PUPILS	-	1	-	-	-	-	-	-	-	-
50,000 TO 99,999 PUPILS	-	-	2	1	-	-	1	-	-	-
25,000 TO 49,999 PUPILS	-	1	6	2	2	-	1	1	2	-
12,000 TO 24,999 PUPILS	1	8	6	3	2	2	-	1	10	1
6,000 TO 11,999 PUPILS	4	6	20	8	3	2	-	7	8	3
3,000 TO 5,999 PUPILS	2	8	13	3	3	4	-	3	7	5
1,200 TO 2,999 PUPILS	3	6	17	2	5	4	-	6	5	1
300 TO 1,199 PUPILS	5	9	15	2	1	2	-	6	2	7
50 TO 299 PUPILS	5	8	3	1	1	1	-	-	1	7
1 TO 49 PUPILS	4	1	6	1	1	4	-	-	1	2
POPULATION, 1975 (ESTIMATED)										
TOTAL	267 828	1 584 583	3 140 306	1 090 353	584 047	220 424	664 520	580 962	1 174 171	279 693
IN MUNICIPALLY GOVERNED AREAS	198 888	1 204 874	2 703 957	961 059	410 660	154 476	664 520	513 242	1 042 169	142 277
WITH A 1975 POPULATION OF--										
50,000 OR MORE	70 438	966 393	1 824 876	790 750	164 827	-	664 520	204 779	848 411	72 125
25,000 TO 49,999	65 949	165 173	533 479	141 536	105 210	81 486	-	205 247	112 680	33 595
10,000 TO 24,999	40 138	68 535	265 041	24 756	135 011	38 692	-	66 582	61 908	24 296
5,000 TO 9,999	-	-	62 271	-	-	29 026	-	33 245	16 046	9 194
2,500 TO 4,999	20 208	4 773	15 857	4 017	3 709	5 272	-	2 859	3 124	3 067
1,000 TO 2,499	1 925	-	1 788	-	1 788	-	-	-	-	-
LESS THAN 1,000	230	-	645	-	115	-	-	530	-	-
OUTSIDE MUNICIPALLY GOVERNED AREAS	68 940	379 709	436 349	129 294	173 387	65 948	-	67 720	132 002	137 416
IN TOWNSHIP-GOVERNED AREAS	-	-	-	-	-	-	-	-	-	-
ENROLLMENT OF PUBLIC SCHOOL SYSTEMS										
TOTAL	68 172	403 776	689 343	256 991	155 051	50 453	95 750	131 098	351 677	71 782
THROUGH GRADE 12	53 125	323 700	554 373	208 088	134 340	39 776	69 250	102 919	274 702	58 353
COLLEGE GRADES	15 047	80 076	134 970	48 903	20 711	10 677	26 500	28 179	76 975	13 429

Table 6. Local Governments and Public School Systems in Individual SMSA's: 1977—Continued

Item	California—Continued Santa Cruz / Santa Cruz County (entire SMSA)	Santa Rosa / Sonoma County (entire SMSA)	Stockton / San Joaquin County (entire SMSA)	Vallejo-Fairfield-Napa Total	Napa County*	Solano County*	Colorado / Colorado Springs Total	El Paso County*	Teller County
NUMBER OF LOCAL GOVERNMENTS									
ALL TYPES, TOTAL	47	92	121	66	22	44	80	67	13
WITH PROPERTY-TAXING POWER	46	91	82	58	22	36	77	65	12
WITHOUT PROPERTY-TAXING POWER	1	1	39	8	-	8	3	2	1
COUNTY GOVERNMENTS	1	1	1	2	1	1	2	1	1
MUNICIPALITIES	4	8	6	11	4	7	11	8	3
WITH A POPULATION OF—									
50,000 OR MORE	-	1	1	2	-	2	1	1	-
25,000 TO 49,999	1	1	1	1	1	-	-	-	-
10,000 TO 24,999	1	1	2	1	-	1	-	-	-
5,000 TO 9,999	2	1	-	1	-	1	1	1	-
2,500 TO 4,999	-	4	2	-	-	-	1	1	-
1,000 TO 2,499	-	-	-	6	3	3	2	1	1
LESS THAN 1,000	-	-	-	-	-	-	6	4	2
TOWNSHIP GOVERNMENTS	-	-	-	-	-	-	-	-	-
SCHOOL DISTRICTS	12	42	19	13	6	7	17	15	2
SPECIAL DISTRICTS	30	41	95	40	11	29	50	43	7
WITH PROPERTY-TAXING POWER	29	40	56	32	11	21	47	41	6
SINGLE FUNCTION DISTRICTS									
CEMETERIES	-	-	-	-	-	-	-	-	-
EDUCATION (SCHOOL BUILDING DISTRICTS)	1	2	2	8	2	6	-	-	-
FIRE PROTECTION	-	-	-	-	-	-	-	-	-
HIGHWAYS	14	17	21	2	1	1	12	11	1
HEALTH	-	1	-	2	1	1	-	-	-
HOSPITALS	-	-	3	2	1	1	1	-	1
HOUSING AND URBAN RENEWAL	-	3	1	3	-	3	-	-	-
LIBRARIES	-	-	-	-	-	-	-	-	-
NATURAL RESOURCES, TOTAL	3	6	58	16	2	14	5	4	1
DRAINAGE	-	1	5	1	-	1	-	-	-
FLOOD CONTROL	-	-	4	2	1	1	-	-	-
IRRIGATION, WATER CONSERVATION	-	-	9	2	-	2	1	1	-
SOIL CONSERVATION	2	4	3	4	1	3	1	1	1
OTHER AND COMPOSITE PURPOSES	1	1	37	7	-	7	3	2	-
PARKS AND RECREATION	4	5	-	1	-	1	2	2	-
SEWERAGE	1	1	2	3	1	2	11	10	1
UTILITIES, TOTAL	5	4	5	1	1	-	10	8	2
WATER SUPPLY	4	4	4	1	1	-	10	8	2
ELECTRIC POWER	-	-	-	-	-	-	-	-	-
GAS SUPPLY	-	-	-	-	-	-	-	-	-
TRANSIT	1	-	1	-	-	-	-	-	-
OTHER	1	-	1	-	-	-	-	-	-
MULTIPLE-FUNCTION DISTRICTS									
SEWERAGE AND WATER SUPPLY	1	2	2	4	3	1	9	8	1
NATURAL RESOURCES AND WATER SUPPLY	1	2	1	3	3	-	9	8	1
OTHER	-	-	1	1	-	1	-	-	-
SCHOOL SYSTEMS									
TOTAL	12	42	19	13	6	7	17	15	2
DEPENDENT SCHOOL SYSTEMS	-	-	-	-	-	-	-	-	-
BY ENROLLMENT SIZE OCTOBER 1976									
100,000 OR MORE PUPILS	-	-	-	-	-	-	-	-	-
50,000 TO 99,999 PUPILS	-	-	-	-	-	-	-	-	-
25,000 TO 49,999 PUPILS	-	-	1	-	-	-	-	-	-
12,000 TO 24,999 PUPILS	1	1	2	-	-	-	1	1	-
6,000 TO 11,999 PUPILS	1	2	1	3	1	2	1	1	-
3,000 TO 5,999 PUPILS	2	3	2	2	1	1	2	2	-
1,200 TO 2,999 PUPILS	4	6	4	1	1	-	3	2	1
300 TO 1,199 PUPILS	-	15	-	4	1	3	3	2	-
50 TO 299 PUPILS	4	13	8	2	1	1	4	4	-
1 TO 49 PUPILS	-	2	1	1	1	-	3	2	1
POPULATION, 1975 (ESTIMATED)									
TOTAL	156 108	246 557	299 576	277 451	90 272	187 179	286 649	280 929	5 720
IN MUNICIPALLY GOVERNED AREAS	68 036	130 436	188 205	228 525	55 911	172 614	197 164	194 235	[1]2 929
WITH A 1975 POPULATION OF—									
50,000 OR MORE	-	65 087	117 600	120 945	-	120 945	179 584	179 584	-
25,000 TO 49,999	36 807	30 810	31 903	76 370	46 557	29 813	-	-	-
10,000 TO 24,999	18 243	12 667	33 304	10 629	-	10 629	-	-	-
5,000 TO 9,999	12 986	6 138	-	-	-	-	7 401	7 401	-
2,500 TO 4,999	-	15 734	5 398	20 581	9 354	11 227	4 206	4 206	-
1,000 TO 2,499	-	-	-	-	-	-	3 083	1 164	1 919
LESS THAN 1,000	-	-	-	-	-	-	2 890	1 880	1 010
OUTSIDE MUNICIPALLY GOVERNED AREAS	88 072	116 121	111 371	48 926	34 361	14 565	89 485	86 694	2 791
IN TOWNSHIP-GOVERNED AREAS	-	-	-	-	-	-	-	-	-
ENROLLMENT OF PUBLIC SCHOOL SYSTEMS									
TOTAL	39 285	66 090	86 665	74 182	22 714	51 468	64 665	63 068	1 597
THROUGH GRADE 12	30 297	53 459	69 681	59 717	17 081	42 636	64 665	63 068	1 597
COLLEGE GRADES	8 988	12 631	16 984	14 465	5 633	8 832	-	-	-

27

Table 6. Local Governments and Public School Systems in Individual SMSA's: 1977—Continued

Colorado--Continued

Item	Denver-Boulder — Total	Adams County	Arapahoe County	Boulder County*	Denver County*	Douglas County	Gilpin County	Jefferson County	Fort Collins — Larimer County (entire SMSA)	Greeley — Weld County (entire SMSA)	Pueblo — Pueblo County (entire SMSA)
NUMBER OF LOCAL GOVERNMENTS											
ALL TYPES, TOTAL	329	46	96	42	24	21	7	93	58	92	26
WITH PROPERTY-TAXING POWER	323	44	95	41	22	21	7	93	55	85	24
WITHOUT PROPERTY-TAXING POWER	6	2	1	1	2	-	-	-	3	7	2
COUNTY GOVERNMENTS	6	1	1	1	-	1	1	1	1	1	1
MUNICIPALITIES	39	7	10	10	1	1	2	8	6	28	3
WITH A POPULATION OF--											
50,000 OR MORE	5	-	1	1	1	-	-	2	1	-	1
25,000 TO 49,999	5	1	2	1	-	-	-	1	1	1	-
10,000 TO 24,999	6	4	-	1	-	-	-	1	-	-	-
5,000 TO 9,999	3	1	1	-	-	-	-	1	-	2	-
2,500 TO 4,999	5	-	2	2	-	1	-	-	1	9	-
1,000 TO 2,499	3	-	2	1	-	-	-	-	2	16	2
LESS THAN 1,000	12	1	2	4	-	-	2	3	1	-	-
TOWNSHIP GOVERNMENTS	-	-	-	-	-	-	-	-	-	-	-
SCHOOL DISTRICTS	20	7	7	2	1	1	1	1	3	13	2
SPECIAL DISTRICTS	264	31	78	29	22	18	3	83	48	50	20
WITH PROPERTY-TAXING POWER	258	29	77	28	20	18	3	83	45	43	18
SINGLE FUNCTION DISTRICTS											
CEMETERIES	1	-	-	-	-	1	-	-	-	-	-
EDUCATION (SCHOOL BUILDING DISTRICTS)	-	-	-	-	-	-	-	-	-	-	-
FIRE PROTECTION	51	9	11	9	2	4	2	14	7	18	4
HIGHWAYS	2	2	-	-	-	-	-	-	-	-	-
HEALTH	-	-	-	-	-	-	-	-	-	4	-
HOSPITALS	2	1	-	-	1	-	-	-	4	1	1
HOUSING AND URBAN RENEWAL	-	-	-	-	-	-	-	-	-	-	-
LIBRARIES	-	-	-	-	-	-	-	-	-	-	-
NATURAL RESOURCES, TOTAL	12	2	3	4	1	-	1	1	4	12	4
DRAINAGE	-	-	-	-	-	-	-	-	1	3	-
FLOOD CONTROL	1	-	-	-	1	-	-	-	1	6	1
IRRIGATION, WATER CONSERVATION	4	-	2	2	-	-	-	-	2	3	3
SOIL CONSERVATION	7	2	1	2	-	-	1	1	-	-	-
OTHER AND COMPOSITE PURPOSES	-	-	-	-	-	-	-	-	-	-	-
PARKS AND RECREATION	16	2	5	-	-	2	-	7	2	16	15
SEWERAGE	48	2	16	3	4	-	-	22	11	2	1
UTILITIES, TOTAL	61	7	21	5	7	2	-	19	19	10	2
WATER SUPPLY	60	7	21	5	6	2	-	19	19	10	2
ELECTRIC POWER	-	-	-	-	-	-	-	-	-	-	-
GAS SUPPLY	1	-	-	-	-	1	-	-	-	1	-
TRANSIT	1	-	-	-	1	-	-	-	-	-	-
OTHER	3	-	1	-	-	1	1	-	-	-	-
MULTIPLE-FUNCTION DISTRICTS	68	8	19	8	6	7	-	20	3	2	5
SEWERAGE AND WATER SUPPLY	65	8	18	8	6	6	-	19	-	1	3
NATURAL RESOURCES AND WATER SUPPLY	-	-	-	-	-	-	-	-	-	-	-
OTHER	3	-	1	-	-	1	-	1	-	-	2
SCHOOL SYSTEMS											
TOTAL	20	7	7	2	1	1	1	1	3	13	2
DEPENDENT SCHOOL SYSTEMS	-	-	-	-	-	-	-	-	-	-	-
BY ENROLLMENT SIZE OCTOBER 1976											
100,000 OR MORE PUPILS	-	-	-	-	-	-	-	-	-	-	-
50,000 TO 99,999 PUPILS	2	-	-	-	1	-	-	1	-	-	-
25,000 TO 49,999 PUPILS	-	-	-	-	-	-	-	-	-	-	1
12,000 TO 24,999 PUPILS	7	2	3	2	-	-	-	-	-	2	1
6,000 TO 11,999 PUPILS	2	2	1	1	-	1	-	-	1	1	-
3,000 TO 5,999 PUPILS	3	-	1	1	-	-	-	1	-	4	-
1,200 TO 2,999 PUPILS	1	2	1	-	-	1	-	-	1	3	-
300 TO 1,199 PUPILS	3	2	1	-	-	-	1	-	-	3	-
50 TO 299 PUPILS	2	-	-	-	-	-	-	-	-	-	-
1 TO 49 PUPILS	-	-	-	-	-	-	-	-	-	-	-
POPULATION, 1975 (ESTIMATED)											
TOTAL	1 413 318	215 460	216 744	165 071	484 531	15 693	1 855	313 964	117 738	107 365	125 665
IN MUNICIPALLY GOVERNED AREAS	1 185 698	[1]118 661	199 611	[1]135 867	484 531	[1]2 726	601	[1]243 701	87 505	73 962	106 008
WITH A 1975 POPULATION OF--											
50,000 OR MORE	875 755	-	118 060	78 560	484 531	-	-	194 604	55 984	-	105 312
25,000 TO 49,999	160 581	35 318	63 995	31 831	-	-	-	29 437	25 282	47 362	-
10,000 TO 24,999	104 186	76 155	-	15 167	-	-	-	12 864	-	-	-
5,000 TO 9,999	17 259	6 350	5 648	-	-	-	-	5 261	-	-	-
2,500 TO 4,999	19 168	-	8 622	7 820	-	2 726	-	-	2 653	6 496	-
1,000 TO 2,499	3 401	-	2 208	1 193	-	-	-	-	3 395	13 499	-
LESS THAN 1,000	5 348	838	1 078	1 296	-	-	601	1 535	191	6 605	696
OUTSIDE MUNICIPALLY GOVERNED AREAS	227 620	96 799	17 133	29 204	-	12 967	1 254	70 263	30 233	33 403	19 657
IN TOWNSHIP-GOVERNED AREAS	-	-	-	-	-	-	-	-	-	-	-
ENROLLMENT OF PUBLIC SCHOOL SYSTEMS											
TOTAL	311 757	51 900	63 143	37 957	72 775	4 902	111	80 969	21 156	24 960	27 748
THROUGH GRADE 12	311 757	51 900	63 143	37 957	72 775	4 902	111	80 969	21 156	21 460	27 748
COLLEGE GRADES	-	-	-	-	-	-	-	-	-	3 500	-

Item	Bridgeport	Bristol	Danbury	Hartford	Meriden	New Britain	New Haven–West Haven	New London–Groton–Norwich Total	Connecticut portion*	Rhode Island portion
NUMBER OF LOCAL GOVERNMENTS										
ALL TYPES, TOTAL	26	5	12	85	2	9	40	42	33	9
WITH PROPERTY-TAXING POWER	18	4	11	70	1	6	32	37	29	8
WITHOUT PROPERTY-TAXING POWER	8	1	1	15	1	3	8	5	4	1
COUNTY GOVERNMENTS	–	–	–	–	–	–	–	–	–	–
MUNICIPALITIES	4	1	1	1	1	1	3	2	2	–
WITH A POPULATION OF--										
50,000 OR MORE	1	1	1	1	1	1	2	–	–	–
25,000 TO 49,999	2	–	–	–	–	–	1	2	2	–
10,000 TO 24,999	1	–	–	–	–	–	–	–	–	–
5,000 TO 9,999	–	–	–	–	–	–	–	–	–	–
2,500 TO 4,999	–	–	–	–	–	–	–	–	–	–
1,000 TO 2,499	–	–	–	–	–	–	–	–	–	–
LESS THAN 1,000	–	–	–	–	–	–	–	–	–	–
TOWNSHIP GOVERNMENTS	5	2	6	36	–	3	12	15	13	2
SCHOOL DISTRICTS	–	1	–	1	–	–	1	1	1	–
SPECIAL DISTRICTS	17	1	5	47	1	5	24	24	17	7
WITH PROPERTY-TAXING POWER	9	–	4	32	–	2	16	19	13	6
SINGLE FUNCTION DISTRICTS										
CEMETERIES	–	–	–	–	–	–	–	–	–	–
EDUCATION (SCHOOL BUILDING DISTRICTS)	–	–	–	–	–	–	–	–	–	–
FIRE PROTECTION	3	–	3	10	–	–	3	11	5	6
HIGHWAYS	–	–	–	4	–	–	–	–	–	–
HEALTH	–	–	–	–	–	–	–	–	–	–
HOSPITALS	–	–	–	–	–	–	–	–	–	–
HOUSING AND URBAN RENEWAL	7	1	1	13	1	3	7	5	4	1
LIBRARIES	–	–	–	–	–	–	–	–	–	–
NATURAL RESOURCES, TOTAL	–	–	–	–	–	–	–	–	–	–
DRAINAGE	–	–	–	–	–	–	–	–	–	–
FLOOD CONTROL	–	–	–	–	–	–	–	–	–	–
IRRIGATION, WATER CONSERVATION	–	–	–	–	–	–	–	–	–	–
SOIL CONSERVATION	–	–	–	–	–	–	–	–	–	–
OTHER AND COMPOSITE PURPOSES	–	–	–	–	–	–	–	–	–	–
PARKS AND RECREATION	–	–	–	–	–	–	–	–	–	–
SEWERAGE	–	–	–	2	–	1	–	–	–	–
UTILITIES, TOTAL	1	–	–	1	–	–	–	–	–	–
WATER SUPPLY	–	–	–	1	–	–	–	–	–	–
ELECTRIC POWER	–	–	–	–	–	–	–	–	–	–
GAS SUPPLY	–	–	–	–	–	–	–	–	–	–
TRANSIT	1	–	–	–	–	–	–	–	–	–
OTHER	6	–	1	14	–	1	14	8	8	–
MULTIPLE-FUNCTION DISTRICTS	–	–	–	3	–	–	–	–	–	–
SEWERAGE AND WATER SUPPLY	–	–	–	1	–	–	–	–	–	–
NATURAL RESOURCES AND WATER SUPPLY	–	–	–	–	–	–	–	–	–	–
OTHER	–	–	–	2	–	–	–	–	–	–
SCHOOL SYSTEMS										
TOTAL	10	3	7	38	1	4	15	17	15	2
DEPENDENT SCHOOL SYSTEMS	10	2	7	37	1	4	14	16	14	2
BY ENROLLMENT SIZE OCTOBER 1976										
100,000 OR MORE PUPILS	–	–	–	–	–	–	–	–	–	–
50,000 TO 99,999 PUPILS	–	–	–	–	–	–	–	–	–	–
25,000 TO 49,999 PUPILS	–	–	–	1	–	–	–	–	–	–
12,000 TO 24,999 PUPILS	–	–	–	–	–	–	–	–	–	–
6,000 TO 11,999 PUPILS	1	–	1	–	–	–	1	–	–	–
3,000 TO 5,999 PUPILS	6	1	–	6	1	2	3	1	1	–
1,200 TO 2,999 PUPILS	1	–	4	8	–	2	7	8	7	1
300 TO 1,199 PUPILS	1	2	2	15	–	–	3	3	3	–
50 TO 299 PUPILS	1	–	–	7	–	–	1	5	4	1
1 TO 49 PUPILS	–	–	–	1	–	–	–	–	–	–
POPULATION, 1975 (ESTIMATED)										
TOTAL	395 045	73 950	129 481	731 742	57 697	145 093	414 471	251 609	228 083	23 526
IN MUNICIPALLY GOVERNED AREAS	233 961	58 560	54 512	138 152	57 697	78 556	179 847	71 516	71 516	–
WITH A 1975 POPULATION OF--										
50,000 OR MORE	142 960	58 560	54 512	138 152	57 697	78 556	179 847	–	–	–
25,000 TO 49,999	79 018	–	–	–	–	–	–	71 516	71 516	–
10,000 TO 24,999	11 983	–	–	–	–	–	–	–	–	–
5,000 TO 9,999	–	–	–	–	–	–	–	–	–	–
2,500 TO 4,999	–	–	–	–	–	–	–	–	–	–
1,000 TO 2,499	–	–	–	–	–	–	–	–	–	–
LESS THAN 1,000	–	–	–	–	–	–	–	–	–	–
OUTSIDE MUNICIPALLY GOVERNED AREAS	161 084	15 390	74 969	593 590	–	66 537	234 624	180 093	156 567	23 526
IN TOWNSHIP-GOVERNED AREAS	161 084	15 390	74 969	593 590	–	66 537	234 624	180 093	156 567	23 526
ENROLLMENT OF PUBLIC SCHOOL SYSTEMS										
TOTAL	86 461	15 934	30 233	154 129	10 274	25 713	80 772	50 033	44 946	5 087
THROUGH GRADE 12	86 461	15 934	30 233	154 129	10 274	25 713	80 772	50 033	44 946	5 087
COLLEGE GRADES	–	–	–	–	–	–	–	–	–	–

Connecticut (see also Massachusetts)

29

Table 6. Local Governments and Public School Systems in Individual SMSA's: 1977—Continued

Item	Connecticut (Continued)			Wilmington, Delaware				Washington, D.C.	
	Norwalk	Stamford	Waterbury	Total	New Castle County*	Salem County (N.J.)	Cecil County (Md.)	Total	District of Columbia*
NUMBER OF LOCAL GOVERNMENTS									
ALL TYPES, TOTAL	9	17	19	81	29	39	13	92	2
WITH PROPERTY-TAXING POWER	8	15	17	67	26	32	9	78	1
WITHOUT PROPERTY-TAXING POWER	1	2	2	14	3	7	4	14	1
COUNTY GOVERNMENTS	-	-	-	3	1	1	1	7	-
MUNICIPALITIES	1	1	2	24	12	4	8	63	1
WITH A POPULATION OF--									
50,000 OR MORE	1	1	1	1	1	-	-	2	1
25,000 TO 49,999	-	-	1	1	1	-	-	3	-
10,000 TO 24,999	-	-	-	-	-	-	-	9	-
5,000 TO 9,999	-	-	-	4	1	2	1	10	-
2,500 TO 4,999	-	-	-	3	2	1	-	9	-
1,000 TO 2,499	-	-	-	8	3	1	4	13	-
LESS THAN 1,000	-	-	-	7	4	-	3	17	-
TOWNSHIP GOVERNMENTS	3	3	9	11	-	11	-	-	-
SCHOOL DISTRICTS	-	-	3	24	12	12	-	-	-
SPECIAL DISTRICTS	5	13	5	19	4	11	4	22	1
WITH PROPERTY-TAXING POWER	4	11	3	5	1	4	-	8	-
SINGLE FUNCTION DISTRICTS	-	-	-	-	-	-	-	-	-
CEMETERIES	-	-	-	-	-	-	-	-	-
EDUCATION (SCHOOL BUILDING DISTRICTS)	-	-	-	2	-	2	-	-	-
FIRE PROTECTION	-	1	-	3	1	2	-	3	-
HIGHWAYS	-	-	-	-	-	-	-	-	-
HEALTH	-	-	-	-	-	-	-	-	-
HOSPITALS	-	-	-	-	-	-	-	-	-
HOUSING AND URBAN RENEWAL	1	3	2	5	2	2	1	5	-
LIBRARIES	-	-	-	-	-	-	-	-	-
NATURAL RESOURCES, TOTAL	-	-	-	3	-	1	2	7	-
DRAINAGE	-	-	-	-	-	-	-	1	-
FLOOD CONTROL	-	-	-	-	-	-	-	-	-
IRRIGATION, WATER CONSERVATION	-	-	-	-	-	-	-	-	-
SOIL CONSERVATION	-	-	-	3	-	1	2	6	-
OTHER AND COMPOSITE PURPOSES	-	-	-	-	-	-	-	-	-
PARKS AND RECREATION	-	2	-	1	1	-	-	-	-
SEWERAGE	-	-	-	5	-	4	1	-	-
UTILITIES, TOTAL	2	-	1	-	-	-	-	1	1
WATER SUPPLY	1	-	1	-	-	-	-	-	-
ELECTRIC POWER	1	-	-	-	-	-	-	-	-
GAS SUPPLY	-	-	-	-	-	-	-	1	1
TRANSIT	-	-	-	-	-	-	-	-	-
OTHER	-	7	1	-	-	-	-	3	-
MULTIPLE-FUNCTION DISTRICTS	2	-	1	-	-	-	-	3	-
SEWERAGE AND WATER SUPPLY	-	-	-	-	-	-	-	-	-
NATURAL RESOURCES AND WATER SUPPLY	-	-	-	-	-	-	-	-	-
OTHER	2	-	1	-	-	-	-	3	-
SCHOOL SYSTEMS									
TOTAL	4	4	9	29	13	14	2	15	2
DEPENDENT SCHOOL SYSTEMS	4	4	6	5	1	2	2	15	2
BY ENROLLMENT SIZE OCTOBER 1976									
100,000 OR MORE PUPILS	-	-	-	-	-	-	-	4	1
50,000 TO 99,999 PUPILS	-	-	-	-	-	-	-	1	-
25,000 TO 49,999 PUPILS	-	-	-	-	-	-	-	5	-
12,000 TO 24,999 PUPILS	1	1	1	3	2	-	1	2	1
6,000 TO 11,999 PUPILS	1	1	-	2	2	-	-	-	-
3,000 TO 5,999 PUPILS	1	2	4	6	6	-	-	2	-
1,200 TO 2,999 PUPILS	1	-	4	9	3	5	1	-	-
300 TO 1,199 PUPILS	-	-	-	5	-	5	-	-	-
50 TO 299 PUPILS	-	-	-	4	-	4	-	-	-
1 TO 49 PUPILS	-	-	-	-	-	-	-	-	-
0 PUPILS (NONOPERATING)	-	-	-	-	-	-	-	1	-
POPULATION, 1975 (ESTIMATED)									
TOTAL	127 563	202 848	226 135	517 848	399 354	62 489	56 005	3 021 801	711 518
IN MUNICIPALLY GOVERNED AREAS	76 688	105 151	132 890	158 453	[1]126 501	17 771	14 181	1 205 762	711 518
WITH A 1975 POPULATION--									
50,000 OR MORE	76 688	105 151	107 065	76 152	76 152	-	-	816 738	711 518
25,000 TO 49,999	-	-	25 825	26 645	26 645	-	-	109 331	-
10,000 TO 24,999	-	-	-	-	-	-	-	148 437	-
5,000 TO 9,999	-	-	-	27 710	8 809	13 024	5 877	74 212	-
2,500 TO 4,999	-	-	-	10 757	7 754	3 003	-	30 437	-
1,000 TO 2,499	-	-	-	12 986	5 054	1 744	6 188	20 112	-
LESS THAN 1,000	-	-	-	4 203	2 087	-	2 116	6 495	-
OUTSIDE MUNICIPALLY GOVERNED AREAS	50 875	97 697	93 245	359 395	272 853	44 718	41 824	1 816 039	-
IN TOWNSHIP-GOVERNED AREAS	50 875	97 697	93 245	44 719	-	44 719	-	-	-
ENROLLMENT OF PUBLIC SCHOOL SYSTEMS									
TOTAL	27 948	37 882	44 492	106 502	78 726	13 472	14 304	661 303	132 695
THROUGH GRADE 12	27 948	37 882	44 492	104 996	78 726	13 472	12 798	626 427	125 908
COLLEGE GRADES	-	-	-	1 506	-	-	1 506	34 876	6 787

Table 6. Local Governments and Public School Systems in Individual SMSA's: 1977—Continued

	District of Columbia--Continued Washington--Continued							
Item	Charles County (Md.)	Montgomery County (Md.)	Prince Georges County (Md.)	Alexandria city (Va.)	Arlington County (Va.)	Fairfax city (Va.)	Fairfax County (Va.)	Falls Church city (Va.)
NUMBER OF LOCAL GOVERNMENTS								
ALL TYPES, TOTAL	5	26	33	1	1	1	5	1
WITH PROPERTY-TAXING POWER	3	22	29	1	1	1	4	1
WITHOUT PROPERTY-TAXING POWER	2	4	4	-	-	-	1	1
COUNTY GOVERNMENTS	1	1	1	-	1	-	1	-
MUNICIPALITIES	2	14	27	1	-	1	3	1
WITH A POPULATION OF--								
50,000 OR MORE	-	-	-	1	-	-	-	-
25,000 TO 49,999	-	1	2	-	-	-	-	-
10,000 TO 24,999	-	2	3	-	-	1	1	1
5,000 TO 9,999	-	-	7	-	-	-	1	-
2,500 TO 4,999	-	2	6	-	-	-	1	-
1,000 TO 2,499	2	4	4	-	-	-	-	-
LESS THAN 1,000	-	5	5	-	-	-	1	-
TOWNSHIP GOVERNMENTS	-	-	-	-	-	-	-	-
SCHOOL DISTRICTS	-	-	-	-	-	-	-	-
SPECIAL DISTRICTS	2	11	5	-	-	-	1	-
WITH PROPERTY-TAXING POWER	-	7	1	-	-	-	-	-
SINGLE FUNCTION DISTRICTS								
CEMETERIES	-	-	-	-	-	-	-	-
EDUCATION (SCHOOL BUILDING DISTRICTS)	-	-	-	-	-	-	-	-
FIRE PROTECTION	-	-	-	-	-	-	-	-
HIGHWAYS	-	-	-	-	-	-	-	-
HEALTH	-	3	-	-	-	-	-	-
HOSPITALS	-	-	-	-	-	-	-	-
HOUSING AND URBAN RENEWAL	-	2	3	-	-	-	-	-
LIBRARIES	-	-	-	-	-	-	-	-
NATURAL RESOURCES, TOTAL	2	1	1	-	-	-	1	-
DRAINAGE	-	-	-	-	-	-	-	-
FLOOD CONTROL	1	-	-	-	-	-	-	-
IRRIGATION, WATER CONSERVATION	-	-	-	-	-	-	-	-
SOIL CONSERVATION	1	1	1	-	-	-	1	-
OTHER AND COMPOSITE PURPOSES	-	-	-	-	-	-	-	-
PARKS AND RECREATION	-	-	-	-	-	-	-	-
SEWERAGE	-	-	-	-	-	-	-	-
UTILITIES, TOTAL	-	-	-	-	-	-	-	-
WATER SUPPLY	-	-	-	-	-	-	-	-
ELECTRIC POWER	-	-	-	-	-	-	-	-
GAS SUPPLY	-	-	-	-	-	-	-	-
TRANSIT	-	-	-	-	-	-	-	-
OTHER	-	3	-	-	-	-	-	-
MULTIPLE-FUNCTION DISTRICTS	-	2	1	-	-	-	-	-
SEWERAGE AND WATER SUPPLY	-	-	-	-	-	-	-	-
NATURAL RESOURCES AND WATER SUPPLY	-	-	-	-	-	-	-	-
OTHER	-	2	1	-	-	-	-	-
SCHOOL SYSTEMS								
TOTAL	2	2	2	1	1	1	1	1
DEPENDENT SCHOOL SYSTEMS	2	2	2	1	1	1	1	1
BY ENROLLMENT SIZE OCTOBER 1976								
100,000 OR MORE PUPILS	-	1	1	-	-	-	1	-
50,000 TO 99,999 PUPILS	-	-	-	-	-	-	-	-
25,000 TO 49,999 PUPILS	-	-	-	-	-	-	-	-
12,000 TO 24,999 PUPILS	1	1	-	1	1	-	-	-
6,000 TO 11,999 PUPILS	-	-	1	-	-	-	-	-
3,000 TO 5,999 PUPILS	-	-	-	-	-	-	-	-
1,200 TO 2,999 PUPILS	1	-	-	-	-	-	-	1
300 TO 1,199 PUPILS	-	-	-	-	-	-	-	-
50 TO 299 PUPILS	-	-	-	-	-	-	-	-
1 TO 49 PUPILS	-	-	-	-	-	-	-	-
0 PUPILS (NONOPERATING)	-	-	-	-	-	2	-	-
POPULATION, 1975 (ESTIMATED)								
TOTAL	60 546	571 558	677 848	105 220	155 518	21 858	512 915	10 360
IN MUNICIPALLY GOVERNED AREAS	3 140	99 709	¹188 143	105 220	-	21 858	27 139	10 360
WITH A 1975 POPULATION--								
50,000 OR MORE	-	-	-	105 220	-	-	-	-
25,000 TO 49,999	-	44 299	65 032	-	-	-	-	-
10,000 TO 24,999	-	41 157	42 312	-	-	21 858	19 709	10 360
5,000 TO 9,999	-	-	50 700	-	-	-	7 222	-
2,500 TO 4,999	-	5 831	21 935	-	-	-	-	-
1,000 TO 2,499	3 140	6 795	6 023	-	-	-	-	-
LESS THAN 1,000	-	1 627	2 141	-	-	-	208	-
OUTSIDE MUNICIPALLY GOVERNED AREAS	57 406	471 849	489 705	-	155 518	-	485 776	-
IN TOWNSHIP-GOVERNED AREAS	-	-	-	-	-	-	-	-
ENROLLMENT OF PUBLIC SCHOOL SYSTEMS								
TOTAL	18 860	130 809	156 671	13 423	19 072	-	134 674	1 512
THROUGH GRADE 12	16 680	116 825	144 746	13 423	19 072	-	134 674	1 512
COLLEGE GRADES	2 180	13 984	11 925	-	-	-	-	-

Table 6. Local Governments and Public School Systems in Individual SMSA's: 1977—Continued

Item	District of Columbia--Continued — Washington--Continued — Loudoun County (Va.)	Manassas city (Va.)	Manassas Park city (Va.)	Prince William County (Va.)	Florida — Daytona Beach — Volusia County (entire SMSA)	Fort Lauderdale-Hollywood — Broward County (entire SMSA)	Fort Myers — Lee County (entire SMSA)	Gainesville — Alachua County (entire SMSA)
NUMBER OF LOCAL GOVERNMENTS								
ALL TYPES, TOTAL	9	1	1	6	27	52	27	16
WITH PROPERTY-TAXING POWER	8	1	1	5	23	41	20	13
WITHOUT PROPERTY-TAXING POWER	1	-	-	1	4	11	7	3
COUNTY GOVERNMENTS	1	-	-	1	1	1	1	1
MUNICIPALITIES	7	1	1	4	14	29	3	9
WITH A POPULATION OF--								
50,000 OR MORE	-	-	-	-	-	2	-	1
25,000 TO 49,999	-	-	-	-	1	7	1	-
10,000 TO 24,999	-	1	-	-	3	10	1	-
5,000 TO 9,999	1	-	1	-	3	1	-	2
2,500 TO 4,999	-	-	-	1	1	4	-	3
1,000 TO 2,499	1	-	-	2	3	1	1	3
LESS THAN 1,000	5	-	-	1	3	4	-	-
TOWNSHIP GOVERNMENTS	-	-	-	-	-	-	-	-
SCHOOL DISTRICTS	-	-	-	-	2	2	2	2
SPECIAL DISTRICTS	1	-	-	1	10	20	21	4
WITH PROPERTY-TAXING POWER	-	-	-	-	6	9	14	1
SINGLE FUNCTION DISTRICTS	-	-	-	-	-	-	-	-
CEMETERIES	-	-	-	-	-	-	-	-
EDUCATION (SCHOOL BUILDING DISTRICTS)	-	-	-	-	1	1	9	1
FIRE PROTECTION	-	-	-	-	-	-	3	-
HIGHWAYS	-	-	-	-	-	-	-	-
HEALTH	-	-	-	-	3	2	1	-
HOSPITALS	-	-	-	-	3	3	1	2
HOUSING AND URBAN RENEWAL	-	-	-	-	-	-	1	-
LIBRARIES	-	-	-	-	1	9	6	1
NATURAL RESOURCES, TOTAL	1	-	-	1	-	5	3	-
DRAINAGE	-	-	-	-	-	3	1	-
FLOOD CONTROL	-	-	-	-	-	1	-	-
IRRIGATION, WATER CONSERVATION	-	-	-	1	1	-	1	1
SOIL CONSERVATION	1	-	-	-	-	-	1	-
OTHER AND COMPOSITE PURPOSES	-	-	-	-	-	-	-	-
PARKS AND RECREATION	-	-	-	-	1	1	-	-
SEWERAGE	-	-	-	-	-	-	-	-
UTILITIES, TOTAL	-	-	-	-	-	-	-	-
WATER SUPPLY	-	-	-	-	-	-	-	-
ELECTRIC POWER	-	-	-	-	-	-	-	-
GAS SUPPLY	-	-	-	-	-	-	-	-
TRANSIT	-	-	-	-	-	-	-	-
OTHER	-	-	-	-	1	2	-	-
MULTIPLE-FUNCTION DISTRICTS	-	-	-	-	-	2	-	-
SEWERAGE AND WATER SUPPLY	-	-	-	-	-	-	-	-
NATURAL RESOURCES AND WATER SUPPLY	-	-	-	-	-	2	-	-
OTHER	-	-	-	-	-	-	-	-
SCHOOL SYSTEMS								
TOTAL	1	(1)	-	1	2	2	2	2
DEPENDENT SCHOOL SYSTEMS	1	-	-	1	-	-	-	-
BY ENROLLMENT SIZE OCTOBER 1976								
100,000 OR MORE PUPILS	-	-	-	-	-	1	-	-
50,000 TO 99,999 PUPILS	-	-	-	-	1	-	1	-
25,000 TO 49,999 PUPILS	-	-	-	1	-	-	-	1
12,000 TO 24,999 PUPILS	1	-	-	-	-	1	-	1
6,000 TO 11,999 PUPILS	-	-	-	-	1	-	1	-
3,000 TO 5,999 PUPILS	-	-	-	-	-	-	-	-
1,200 TO 2,999 PUPILS	-	-	-	-	-	-	-	-
300 TO 1,199 PUPILS	-	-	-	-	-	-	-	-
50 TO 299 PUPILS	-	-	-	-	-	-	-	-
1 TO 49 PUPILS	-	-	-	-	-	-	-	-
POPULATION, 1975 (ESTIMATED)								
TOTAL	48 828	13 041	9 215	123 376	207 206	848 190	154 161	121 945
IN MUNICIPALLY GOVERNED AREAS	10 813	13 041	9 215	5 606	128 951	702 439	58 281	83 932
WITH A 1975 POPULATION OF--								
50,000 OR MORE	-	-	-	-	-	271 961	-	72 236
25,000 TO 49,999	-	-	-	-	48 037	223 304	36 170	-
10,000 TO 24,999	-	13 041	-	-	44 263	179 835	19 763	-
5,000 TO 9,999	7 075	-	9 215	-	24 959	9 719	-	5 573
2,500 TO 4,999	-	-	-	2 671	4 102	14 967	-	4 008
1,000 TO 2,499	1 634	-	-	2 520	5 194	1 494	2 348	2 115
LESS THAN 1,000	2 104	-	-	415	2 396	1 159	-	-
OUTSIDE MUNICIPALLY GOVERNED AREAS	38 015	-	-	117 770	78 255	145 751	95 880	38 013
IN TOWNSHIP-GOVERNED AREAS	-	-	-	-	-	-		
ENROLLMENT OF PUBLIC SCHOOL SYSTEMS								
TOTAL	14 060	-	-	39 527	40 016	156 120	30 882	27 837
THROUGH GRADE 12	14 060	-	-	39 527	35 624	138 120	27 503	21 781
COLLEGE GRADES	-	-	-	-	4 392	18 000	3 379	6 056

Item	Florida--Continued								
	Jacksonville						Lakeland-Winter Haven	Melbourne-Titusville-Cocoa Beach	Miami
	Total	Baker County	Clay County	Duval County*	Nassau County	St. Johns County	Polk County (entire SMSA)	Brevard County (entire SMSA)	Dade County (entire SMSA)
NUMBER OF LOCAL GOVERNMENTS									
ALL TYPES, TOTAL	43	7	8	9	9	10	30	29	33
WITH PROPERTY-TAXING POWER	35	5	7	8	7	8	23	23	30
WITHOUT PROPERTY-TAXING POWER	8	2	1	1	2	2	7	6	3
COUNTY GOVERNMENTS	4	1	1	-	1	1	1	1	1
MUNICIPALITIES	17	2	4	5	3	3	17	15	27
WITH A POPULATION OF--									
50,000 OR MORE	1	-	-	1	-	-	-	-	3
25,000 TO 49,999	-	-	-	-	-	-	1	2	3
10,000 TO 24,999	2	-	-	1	-	1	3	3	4
5,000 TO 9,999	3	-	1	1	1	-	2	3	4
2,500 TO 4,999	3	1	1	1	-	-	4	4	5
1,000 TO 2,499	3	-	1	1	1	-	4	4	2
LESS THAN 1,000	5	1	1	1	-	1	3	3	6
TOWNSHIP GOVERNMENTS	-	-	--	-	-	-	-	-	-
SCHOOL DISTRICTS	6	1	1	2	1	1	2	2	2
SPECIAL DISTRICTS	16	3	2	2	4	5	10	11	3
WITH PROPERTY-TAXING POWER	8	1	1	1	2	3	3	5	-
SINGLE FUNCTION DISTRICTS	-	-	-	-	-	-	-	-	-
CEMETERIES	-	-	-	-	-	-	-	-	-
EDUCATION (SCHOOL BUILDING DISTRICTS)	-	-	-	-	-	-	-	-	-
FIRE PROTECTION	-	-	-	-	-	-	1	-	-
HIGHWAYS	-	-	-	-	-	-	-	-	-
HEALTH	2	-	-	-	1	1	-	-	-
HOSPITALS	4	1	1	1	1	-	-	2	-
HOUSING AND URBAN RENEWAL	2	1	-	-	-	1	4	4	3
LIBRARIES	-	-	-	-	-	-	-	2	-
NATURAL RESOURCES, TOTAL	6	1	1	1	1	2	5	2	-
DRAINAGE	1	-	-	-	-	1	3	2	-
FLOOD CONTROL	-	-	-	-	-	-	-	-	-
IRRIGATION, WATER CONSERVATION	-	-	-	-	-	-	1	-	-
SOIL CONSERVATION	5	1	1	1	1	1	1	-	-
OTHER AND COMPOSITE PURPOSES	-	-	-	-	-	-	-	-	-
PARKS AND RECREATION	-	-	-	-	-	-	-	-	-
SEWERAGE	-	-	-	-	-	-	-	-	-
UTILITIES, TOTAL	-	-	-	-	-	-	-	-	-
WATER SUPPLY	-	-	-	-	-	-	-	-	-
ELECTRIC POWER	-	-	-	-	-	-	-	-	-
GAS SUPPLY	-	-	-	-	-	-	-	-	-
TRANSIT	-	-	-	-	-	-	-	-	-
OTHER	2	-	-	-	-	2	-	1	-
MULTIPLE-FUNCTION DISTRICTS	-	-	-	-	-	-	-	-	-
SEWERAGE AND WATER SUPPLY	-	-	-	-	-	-	-	-	-
NATURAL RESOURCES AND WATER SUPPLY	-	-	-	-	-	-	-	-	-
OTHER	-	-	-	-	-	-	-	-	-
SCHOOL SYSTEMS									
TOTAL	6	1	1	2	1	1	2	2	2
DEPENDENT SCHOOL SYSTEMS	-	-	-	-	-	-	-	-	-
BY ENROLLMENT SIZE OCTOBER 1976									
100,000 OR MORE PUPILS	1	-	-	1	-	-	-	-	1
50,000 TO 99,999 PUPILS	-	-	-	-	-	-	-	-	-
25,000 TO 49,999 PUPILS	-	-	-	-	-	-	1	1	1
12,000 TO 24,999 PUPILS	2	-	1	1	-	-	-	-	-
6,000 TO 11,999 PUPILS	2	-	-	-	1	1	-	1	-
3,000 TO 5,999 PUPILS	1	1	-	-	-	-	1	-	-
1,200 TO 2,999 PUPILS	-	-	-	-	-	-	-	-	-
300 TO 1,199 PUPILS	-	-	-	-	-	-	-	-	-
50 TO 299 PUPILS	-	-	-	-	-	-	-	-	-
1 TO 49 PUPILS	-	-	-	-	-	-	-	-	-
POPULATION, 1975 (ESTIMATED)									
TOTAL	692 795	12 491	51 169	562 282	28 158	38 695	273 996	231 918	1 439 481
IN MUNICIPALLY GOVERNED AREAS	606 065	4 301	14 696	562 282	10 334	¹14 452	129 344	143 820	808 321
WITH A 1975 POPULATION OF--									
50,000 OR MORE	535 030	-	-	535 030	-	-	-	-	576 827
25,000 TO 49,999	-	-	-	-	-	-	49 705	69 322	123 210
10,000 TO 24,999	26 893	-	-	13 843	-	13 050	43 051	36 086	57 091
5,000 TO 9,999	23 138	-	8 149	7 288	7 701	-	15 358	22 528	26 460
2,500 TO 4,999	13 296	3 942	4 737	4 617	-	-	13 754	14 340	18 549
1,000 TO 2,499	4 455	-	1 224	1 504	1 727	-	6 817	-	3 835
LESS THAN 1,000	3 253	359	586	-	906	1 402	659	1 544	2 349
OUTSIDE MUNICIPALLY GOVERNED AREAS	86 730	8 190	36 473	-	17 824	24 243	144 652	88 098	631 160
IN TOWNSHIP-GOVERNED AREAS	-	-	-	-	-	-	-	-	-
ENROLLMENT OF PUBLIC SCHOOL SYSTEMS									
TOTAL	158 403	3 439	15 398	122 982	7 649	8 935	60 986	61 685	278 253
THROUGH GRADE 12	146 091	3 439	15 398	110 670	7 649	8 935	55 959	52 656	240 248
COLLEGE GRADES	12 312	-	-	12 312	-	-	5 027	9 029	38 005

	Florida--Continued										
	Orlando				Pensacola			Sarasota	Tallahassee		
Item	Total	Orange County*	Osceola County	Seminole County	Total	Escambia County*	Santa Rosa County	Sarasota County (entire SMSA)	Total	Leon County*	Wakulla County
NUMBER OF LOCAL GOVERNMENTS											
ALL TYPES, TOTAL	41	22	5	14	15	8	7	21	11	6	5
WITH PROPERTY-TAXING POWER	32	18	4	10	10	5	5	14	9	5	4
WITHOUT PROPERTY-TAXING POWER	9	4	1	4	5	3	2	7	2	1	1
COUNTY GOVERNMENTS	3	1	1	1	2	1	1	1	2	1	1
MUNICIPALITIES	22	13	2	7	5	2	3	3	3	1	2
WITH A POPULATION OF--											
50,000 OR MORE	1	1	-	-	1	1	-	-	1	1	-
25,000 TO 49,999	-	-	-	-	-	-	-	1	-	-	-
10,000 TO 24,999	5	1	1	3	-	-	-	1	-	-	-
5,000 TO 9,999	6	4	1	1	2	-	2	1	-	-	-
2,500 TO 4,999	4	1	-	3	-	-	-	-	-	-	-
1,000 TO 2,499	2	2	-	-	-	-	-	-	-	-	-
LESS THAN 1,000	4	4	-	-	2	1	1	-	2	-	2
TOWNSHIP GOVERNMENTS	-	-	-	-	-	-	-	-	-	-	-
SCHOOL DISTRICTS	5	2	1	2	3	2	1	1	3	2	1
SPECIAL DISTRICTS	11	6	1	4	5	3	2	16	3	2	1
WITH PROPERTY-TAXING POWER	2	2	-	-	-	-	-	9	1	1	-
SINGLE FUNCTION DISTRICTS	-	-	-	-	-	-	-	-	-	-	-
CEMETERIES	-	-	-	-	-	-	-	-	-	-	-
EDUCATION (SCHOOL BUILDING DISTRICTS)	-	-	-	-	-	-	-	-	-	-	-
FIRE PROTECTION	-	-	-	-	-	-	-	4	-	-	-
HIGHWAYS	-	-	-	-	-	-	-	6	-	-	-
HEALTH	-	-	-	-	-	-	-	-	-	-	-
HOSPITALS	1	1	-	-	-	-	-	1	-	-	-
HOUSING AND URBAN RENEWAL	4	2	-	2	2	1	1	2	-	-	-
LIBRARIES	-	-	-	-	-	-	-	-	-	-	-
NATURAL RESOURCES, TOTAL	5	2	1	2	2	1	1	1	3	2	1
DRAINAGE	1	1	-	-	-	-	-	-	-	-	-
FLOOD CONTROL	1	-	-	1	-	-	-	-	1	1	-
IRRIGATION, WATER CONSERVATION	-	-	-	-	-	-	-	-	-	-	-
SOIL CONSERVATION	3	1	1	1	2	1	1	1	2	1	1
OTHER AND COMPOSITE PURPOSES	-	-	-	-	-	-	-	-	-	-	-
PARKS AND RECREATION	-	-	-	-	1	1	-	-	-	-	-
SEWERAGE	-	-	-	-	-	-	-	-	-	-	-
UTILITIES, TOTAL	-	-	-	-	-	-	-	-	-	-	-
WATER SUPPLY	-	-	-	-	-	-	-	-	-	-	-
ELECTRIC POWER	-	-	-	-	-	-	-	-	-	-	-
GAS SUPPLY	-	-	-	-	-	-	-	-	-	-	-
TRANSIT	-	-	-	-	-	-	-	-	-	-	-
OTHER	1	1	-	-	-	-	-	1	-	-	-
MULTIPLE-FUNCTION DISTRICTS	-	-	-	-	-	-	-	1	-	-	-
SEWERAGE AND WATER SUPPLY	-	-	-	-	-	-	-	1	-	-	-
NATURAL RESOURCES AND WATER SUPPLY	-	-	-	-	-	-	-	-	-	-	-
OTHER	-	-	-	-	-	-	-	-	-	-	-
SCHOOL SYSTEMS											
TOTAL	5	2	1	2	3	2	1	1	3	2	1
DEPENDENT SCHOOL SYSTEMS	-	-	-	-	-	-	-	-	-	-	-
BY ENROLLMENT SIZE OCTOBER 1976											
100,000 OR MORE PUPILS	-	-	-	-	-	-	-	-	-	-	-
50,000 TO 99,999 PUPILS	1	1	-	-	-	-	-	-	-	-	-
25,000 TO 49,999 PUPILS	1	-	-	1	1	1	-	-	-	-	-
12,000 TO 24,999 PUPILS	-	-	-	-	1	-	1	1	1	1	-
6,000 TO 11,999 PUPILS	2	1	1	-	1	1	-	-	-	-	-
3,000 TO 5,999 PUPILS	1	-	-	1	-	-	-	-	-	-	-
1,200 TO 2,999 PUPILS	-	-	-	-	-	-	-	-	2	1	1
300 TO 1,199 PUPILS	-	-	-	-	-	-	-	-	-	-	-
50 TO 299 PUPILS	-	-	-	-	-	-	-	-	-	-	-
1 TO 49 PUPILS	-	-	-	-	-	-	-	-	-	-	-
POPULATION, 1975 (ESTIMATED)											
TOTAL	582 664	409 970	37 693	135 001	269 231	223 120	46 111	160 927	133 776	124 714	9 062
IN MUNICIPALLY GOVERNED AREAS	254 368	169 366	19 670	65 332	78 262	64 563	13 699	[1]62 806	84 508	83 725	783
WITH A 1975 POPULATION OF--											
50,000 OR MORE	113 179	113 179	-	-	64 168	64 168	-	-	83 725	83 725	-
25,000 TO 49,999	-	-	-	-	-	-	-	47 089	-	-	-
10,000 TO 24,999	85 269	22 932	12 793	49 544	-	-	-	11 283	-	-	-
5,000 TO 9,999	39 159	25 711	6 877	6 571	12 888	-	12 888	-	-	-	-
2,500 TO 4,999	12 185	2 968	-	9 217	-	-	-	4 434	-	-	-
1,000 TO 2,499	3 192	3 192	-	-	-	-	-	-	-	-	-
LESS THAN 1,000	1 384	1 384	-	-	1 206	395	811	-	783	-	783
OUTSIDE MUNICIPALLY GOVERNED AREAS	328 296	240 604	18 023	69 669	190 969	158 557	32 412	98 121	49 268	40 989	8 279
IN TOWNSHIP-GOVERNED AREAS	-	-	-	-	-	-	-	-	-	-	-
ENROLLMENT OF PUBLIC SCHOOL SYSTEMS											
TOTAL	135 243	91 447	7 723	36 073	67 249	55 064	12 185	23 799	26 715	24 499	2 216
THROUGH GRADE 12	123 954	83 717	7 723	32 514	59 363	47 178	12 185	23 799	23 829	21 613	2 216
COLLEGE GRADES	11 289	7 730	-	3 559	7 886	7 886	-	-	2 886	2 886	-

Table 6. Local Governments and Public School Systems in Individual SMSA's: 1977—Continued

	Florida--Continued					Georgia (see also Tennessee)		
	Tampa-St. Petersburg				West Palm Beach-Roca Raton	Albany		
Item	Total	Hillsborough County*	Pasco County	Pinellas County*	Palm Beach County (entire SMSA)	Total	Dougherty County*	Lee County
NUMBER OF LOCAL GOVERNMENTS								
ALL TYPES, TOTAL	57	10	11	36	72	11	6	5
WITH PROPERTY-TAXING POWER	46	7	10	29	51	7	3	4
WITHOUT PROPERTY-TAXING POWER	11	3	1	7	21	4	3	1
COUNTY GOVERNMENTS	3	1	1	1	1	2	1	1
MUNICIPALITIES	33	3	6	24	37	3	1	2
WITH A POPULATION OF--								
50,000 OR MORE	3	1	-	2	1	1	1	-
25,000 TO 49,999	2	-	-	2	4	-	-	-
10,000 TO 24,999	5	2	-	3	4	-	-	-
5,000 TO 9,999	3	-	1	2	6	-	-	-
2,500 TO 4,999	10	-	2	8	4	-	-	-
1,000 TO 2,499	6	-	1	5	8	1	-	1
LESS THAN 1,000	4	-	2	2	10	1	-	1
TOWNSHIP GOVERNMENTS	-	-	-	-	-	-	-	-
SCHOOL DISTRICTS	6	2	2	2	2	2	1	1
SPECIAL DISTRICTS	15	4	2	9	32	4	3	1
WITH PROPERTY-TAXING POWER	4	1	1	2	11	-	-	-
SINGLE FUNCTION DISTRICTS	-	-	-	-	-	-	-	-
CEMETERIES	-	-	-	-	-	-	-	-
EDUCATION (SCHOOL BUILDING DISTRICTS)	-	-	-	-	-	-	-	-
FIRE PROTECTION	2	-	-	2	-	-	-	-
HIGHWAYS	-	-	-	-	-	-	-	-
HEALTH	1	-	1	-	-	-	-	-
HOSPITALS	-	-	-	-	3	-	-	-
HOUSING AND URBAN RENEWAL	7	2	-	5	5	1	1	1
LIBRARIES	-	-	-	-	-	2	1	-
NATURAL RESOURCES, TOTAL	3	1	1	1	20	1	1	-
DRAINAGE	-	-	-	-	12	-	-	-
FLOOD CONTROL	-	-	-	-	5	-	-	-
IRRIGATION, WATER CONSERVATION	-	-	-	-	2	-	-	-
SOIL CONSERVATION	3	1	1	1	1	1	1	-
OTHER AND COMPOSITE PURPOSES	-	-	-	-	-	-	-	-
PARKS AND RECREATION	1	1	-	-	-	-	-	-
SEWERAGE	-	-	-	-	-	-	-	-
UTILITIES, TOTAL	1	-	-	1	-	-	-	-
WATER SUPPLY	-	-	-	-	-	-	-	-
ELECTRIC POWER	-	-	-	-	-	-	-	-
GAS SUPPLY	-	-	-	-	-	-	-	-
TRANSIT	1	-	-	1	-	-	-	-
OTHER	-	-	-	-	2	-	-	-
MULTIPLE-FUNCTION DISTRICTS	-	-	-	-	2	-	-	-
SEWERAGE AND WATER SUPPLY	-	-	-	-	1	-	-	-
NATURAL RESOURCES AND WATER SUPPLY	-	-	-	-	1	-	-	-
OTHER	-	-	-	-	1	-	-	-
SCHOOL SYSTEMS								
TOTAL	6	2	2	2	2	2	1	1
DEPENDENT SCHOOL SYSTEMS	-	-	-	-	-	-	-	-
BY ENROLLMENT SIZE OCTOBER 1976								
100,000 OR MORE PUPILS	1	1	-	-	-	-	-	-
50,000 TO 99,999 PUPILS	1	-	-	1	1	-	-	-
25,000 TO 49,999 PUPILS	-	-	-	-	-	-	-	-
12,000 TO 24,999 PUPILS	3	-	1	1	1	1	1	-
6,000 TO 11,999 PUPILS	-	-	-	-	-	-	-	-
3,000 TO 5,999 PUPILS	-	-	-	-	1	-	-	-
1,200 TO 2,999 PUPILS	1	-	-	1	-	1	-	1
300 TO 1,199 PUPILS	-	-	-	-	-	-	-	-
50 TO 299 PUPILS	-	-	-	-	-	-	-	-
1 TO 49 PUPILS	-	-	-	-	-	-	-	-
POPULATION, 1975 (ESTIMATED)								
TOTAL	1 347 677	577 497	126 640	643 540	455 451	100 138	90 752	9 386
IN MUNICIPALLY GOVERNED AREAS	797 400	308 095	20 496	468 809	328 410	75 385	73 373	2 012
WITH A 1975 POPULATION OF--								
50,000 OR MORE	581 798	280 340	-	301 458	61 471	73 373	73 373	-
25,000 TO 49,999	66 977	-	-	66 977	130 773	-	-	-
10,000 TO 24,999	72 788	27 755	-	45 033	62 848	-	-	-
5,000 TO 9,999	25 203	-	8 830	16 373	44 146	-	-	-
2,500 TO 4,999	37 633	-	8 687	28 946	13 439	-	-	-
1,000 TO 2,499	10 687	-	1 709	8 978	11 769	1 329	-	1 329
LESS THAN 1,000	2 314	-	1 270	1 044	3 964	683	-	683
OUTSIDE MUNICIPALLY GOVERNED AREAS	550 277	269 402	106 144	174 731	127 041	24 753	17 379	7 374
IN TOWNSHIP-GOVERNED AREAS	-	-	-	-	-	-	-	-
ENROLLMENT OF PUBLIC SCHOOL SYSTEMS								
TOTAL	254 594	126 435	23 717	104 442	77 468	23 559	21 062	2 497
THROUGH GRADE 12	227 596	114 097	22 075	91 424	69 656	23 559	21 062	2 497
COLLEGE GRADES	26 998	12 338	1 642	13 018	7 812	-	-	-

Item	Total	Butts County	Cherokee County	Clayton County	Cobb County	De Kalb County	Douglas County	Fayette County	Forsyth County	Fulton County*	Gwinnett County
						Georgia (see also Tennessee)--Continued					
						Atlanta					
NUMBER OF LOCAL GOVERNMENTS											
ALL TYPES, TOTAL	172	7	10	11	15	17	5	7	6	26	21
WITH PROPERTY-TAXING POWER	112	5	7	9	9	11	3	7	3	13	15
WITHOUT PROPERTY-TAXING POWER.	60	2	3	2	6	6	2	-	3	13	6
COUNTY GOVERNMENTS	15	1	1	1	1	1	1	1	1	1	1
MUNICIPALITIES	77	3	5	7	6	8	1	5	1	10	12
WITH A POPULATION OF--											
50,000 OR MORE	1	-	-	-	-	-	-	-	-	1	-
25,000 TO 49,999	2	-	-	-	1	-	-	-	-	1	-
10,000 TO 24,999	8	-	-	1	1	1	1	-	-	2	1
5,000 TO 9,999	13	-	-	3	2	3	-	-	-	1	2
2,500 TO 4,999	19	1	1	2	2	2	-	2	1	3	3
1,000 TO 2,499	11	-	1	-	-	1	-	-	-	1	2
LESS THAN 1,000.	23	2	3	1	-	1	-	3	-	1	4
TOWNSHIP GOVERNMENTS	-	-	-	-	-	-	-	-	-	-	-
SCHOOL DISTRICTS	20	1	1	1	2	2	1	1	1	2	2
SPECIAL DISTRICTS.	60	2	3	2	6	6	2	-	3	13	6
WITH PROPERTY-TAXING POWER	-	-	-			-	-	-	-	-	-
SINGLE FUNCTION DISTRICTS.	-	-	-	-	-	-	-	-	-	-	-
CEMETERIES	-	-	-	-	-	-	-	-	-	-	-
EDUCATION (SCHOOL BUILDING DISTRICTS). . . .	-	-	-	-	-	-	-	-	-	-	-
FIRE PROTECTION.	-	-	-	-	-	-	-	-	-	-	-
HIGHWAYS	-	-	-	-	-	-	-	-	-	-	-
HEALTH	-	-	-	-	-	-	-	-	-	-	-
HOSPITALS.	16	1	1	-	2	2	1	-	-	2	1
HOUSING AND URBAN RENEWAL.	30	1	1	1	2	4	1	-	1	8	3
LIBRARIES.	-	-	-	-	-	-	-	-	-	-	-
NATURAL RESOURCES, TOTAL	2	-	-	-	-	-	-	-	-	1	-
DRAINAGE	-	-	-	-	-	-	-	-	-	-	-
FLOOD CONTROL.	-	-	-	-	-	-	-	-	-	-	-
IRRIGATION, WATER CONSERVATION	-	-	-	-	-	-	-	-	-	-	-
SOIL CONSERVATION.	2	-	-	-	-	-	-	-	-	1	-
OTHER AND COMPOSITE PURPOSES	-	-	-	-	-	-	-	-	-	-	-
PARKS AND RECREATION	1	-	-	-	1	-	-	-	-	-	-
SEWERAGE	-	-	-	-	-	-	-	-	-	-	-
UTILITIES, TOTAL	7	-	1	1	1	-	-	-	-	2	-
WATER SUPPLY	5	-	1	1	1	-	-	-	-	1	-
ELECTRIC POWER	1	-	-	-	-	-	-	-	-	1	-
GAS SUPPLY	-	-	-	-	-	-	-	-	-	1	-
TRANSIT.	1	-	-	-	-	-	-	-	-	-	-
OTHER.	1	-	-	-	-	-	-	-	-	-	1
MULTIPLE-FUNCTION DISTRICTS.	3	-	-	-	-	-	-	-	1	-	1
SEWERAGE AND WATER SUPPLY.	3	-	-	-	-	-	-	-	1	-	1
NATURAL RESOURCES AND WATER SUPPLY	-	-	-	-	-	-	-	-	-	-	-
OTHER.	-	-	-	-	-	-	-	-	-	-	-
SCHOOL SYSTEMS											
TOTAL.	20	1	1	1	2	2	1	1	1	2	2
DEPENDENT SCHOOL SYSTEMS	-	-	-	-	-	-	-	-	-	-	-
BY ENROLLMENT SIZE OCTOBER 1976											
100,000 OR MORE PUPILS	-	-	-	-	1	1	-	-	-	1	-
50,000 TO 99,999 PUPILS.	3	-	-	-	-	-	-	-	-	1	1
25,000 TO 49,999 PUPILS.	3	-	-	1	-	-	-	-	-	1	1
12,000 TO 24,999 PUPILS.	-	-	-	-	-	-	-	-	-	-	-
6,000 TO 11,999 PUPILS	5	-	1	-	1	1	1	-	1	-	-
3,000 TO 5,999 PUPILS.	6	-	-	-	1	1	-	1	1	-	-
1,200 TO 2,999 PUPILS.	1	1	-	-	-	-	-	-	-	-	1
300 TO 1,199 PUPILS.	2	-	-	-	-	-	-	-	-	-	-
50 TO 299 PUPILS	-	-	-	-	-	-	-	-	-	-	-
1 TO 49 PUPILS	-	-	-	-	-	-	-	-	-	-	-
POPULATION, 1975 (ESTIMATED)											
TOTAL.	1 790 128	12 113	38 994	130 516	239 832	450 599	45 263	17 721	22 016	580 600	113 247
IN MUNICIPALLY GOVERNED AREAS.	838 272	4 858	¹7 337	¹44 851	70 626	¹51 874	¹11 868	8 078	2 682	536 647	¹50 053
WITH A 1975 POPULATION OF--											
50,000 OR MORE	436 057	-	-	-	-	-	-	-	-	436 057	-
25,000 TO 49,999	67 944	-	-	-	31 317	-	-	-	-	36 627	-
10,000 TO 24,999	140 271	-	-	20 414	18 960	20 241	11 868	-	-	42 330	15 207
5,000 TO 9,999	95 013	-	-	18 415	12 368	22 314	-	-	-	7 029	17 269
2,500 TO 4,999	66 986	3 971	3 715	5 731	7 981	7 049	-	6 765	2 682	11 953	11 567
1,000 TO 2,499	21 925	-	1 787	-	-	1 505	-	-	-	2 467	4 038
LESS THAN 1,000.	10 076	887	1 835	291	-	765	-	1 313	-	184	1 972
OUTSIDE MUNICIPALLY GOVERNED AREAS	951 856	7 255	31 657	85 665	169 206	398 725	33 395	9 643	19 334	43 953	63 194
IN TOWNSHIP-GOVERNED AREAS	-	-	-	-	-	-	-	-	-	-	-
ENROLLMENT OF PUBLIC SCHOOL SYSTEMS											
TOTAL.	405 041	2 750	9 312	32 344	55 554	102 027	11 249	5 090	5 432	117 989	29 995
THROUGH GRADE 12	390 953	2 750	9 312	32 344	55 554	87 939	11 249	5 090	5 432	117 989	29 995
COLLEGE GRADES	14 088	-	-	-	-	14 088	-	-	-	-	-

Table 6. Local Governments and Public School Systems in Individual SMSA's: 1977—Continued

Item	Atlanta--Continued					Augusta			
	Henry County	Newton County	Paulding County	Rockdale County	Walton County	Total	Columbia County	Richmond County*	Aiken County (S.C.)
NUMBER OF LOCAL GOVERNMENTS									
ALL TYPES, TOTAL	10	10	7	6	14	31	6	8	17
WITH PROPERTY-TAXING POWER	6	7	4	3	10	24	4	5	15
WITHOUT PROPERTY-TAXING POWER	4	3	3	3	4	7	2	3	2
COUNTY GOVERNMENTS	1	1	1	1	1	3	1	1	1
MUNICIPALITIES	4	5	2	1	7	13	2	3	8
WITH A POPULATION OF--									
50,000 OR MORE	-	-	-	-	-	1	-	1	-
25,000 TO 49,999	-	-	-	-	-	-	-	-	-
10,000 TO 24,999	-	1	-	-	-	2	-	-	2
5,000 TO 9,999	-	-	-	1	1	-	-	-	-
2,500 TO 4,999	1	-	1	-	-	1	1	-	-
1,000 TO 2,499	2	2	-	-	2	4	1	1	2
LESS THAN 1,000	1	2	1	-	4	5	-	1	4
TOWNSHIP GOVERNMENTS	-	-	-	-	-	-	-	-	-
SCHOOL DISTRICTS	1	1	1	1	2	3	1	1	1
SPECIAL DISTRICTS	4	3	3	3	4	12	2	3	7
WITH PROPERTY-TAXING POWER	-	-	-	-	-	5	-	-	5
SINGLE FUNCTION DISTRICTS	-	-	-	-	-	-	-	-	-
CEMETERIES	-	-	-	-	-	-	-	-	-
EDUCATION (SCHOOL BUILDING DISTRICTS)	-	-	-	-	-	-	-	-	-
FIRE PROTECTION	-	-	-	-	-	-	-	-	-
HIGHWAYS	-	-	-	-	-	-	-	-	-
HEALTH	-	-	-	-	-	-	-	-	-
HOSPITALS	1	1	1	1	1	1	-	1	-
HOUSING AND URBAN RENEWAL	2	1	1	1	3	3	1	1	1
LIBRARIES	-	-	-	-	-	-	-	-	-
NATURAL RESOURCES, TOTAL	-	-	-	1	-	3	1	1	1
DRAINAGE	-	-	-	-	-	-	-	-	-
FLOOD CONTROL	-	-	-	-	-	-	-	-	-
IRRIGATION, WATER CONSERVATION	-	-	-	-	-	-	-	-	-
SOIL CONSERVATION	-	-	-	1	-	3	1	1	1
OTHER AND COMPOSITE PURPOSES	-	-	-	-	-	-	-	-	-
PARKS AND RECREATION	-	-	-	-	-	-	-	-	-
SEWERAGE	-	-	-	-	-	-	-	-	-
UTILITIES, TOTAL	-	1	1	-	-	3	-	-	3
WATER SUPPLY	-	1	1	-	-	3	-	-	3
ELECTRIC POWER	-	-	-	-	-	-	-	-	-
GAS SUPPLY	-	-	-	-	-	-	-	-	-
TRANSIT	-	-	-	-	-	-	-	-	-
OTHER	-	-	-	-	-	-	-	-	-
MULTIPLE-FUNCTION DISTRICTS	1	-	-	-	-	2	-	-	2
SEWERAGE AND WATER SUPPLY	1	-	-	-	-	2	-	-	2
NATURAL RESOURCES AND WATER SUPPLY	-	-	-	-	-	-	-	-	-
OTHER	-	-	-	-	-	-	-	-	-
SCHOOL SYSTEMS									
TOTAL	1	1	1	1	2	3	1	1	1
DEPENDENT SCHOOL SYSTEMS	-	-	-	-	-	-	-	-	-
BY ENROLLMENT SIZE OCTOBER 1976									
100,000 OR MORE PUPILS	-	-	-	-	-	-	-	-	-
50,000 TO 99,999 PUPILS	-	-	-	-	-	-	-	-	-
25,000 TO 49,999 PUPILS	-	-	-	-	-	-	-	-	-
12,000 TO 24,999 PUPILS	-	-	-	-	-	1	-	1	1
6,000 TO 11,999 PUPILS	1	1	-	1	-	1	1	-	-
3,000 TO 5,999 PUPILS	-	-	1	-	1	1	-	-	-
1,200 TO 2,999 PUPILS	-	-	-	-	1	-	-	-	-
300 TO 1,199 PUPILS	-	-	-	-	1	-	-	-	-
50 TO 299 PUPILS	-	-	-	-	-	-	-	-	-
1 TO 49 PUPILS	-	-	-	-	-	-	-	-	-
POPULATION, 1975 (ESTIMATED)									
TOTAL	28 897	32 077	21 832	27 471	28 950	279 757	28 365	156 151	95 241
IN MUNICIPALLY GOVERNED AREAS	8 030	15 599	3 086	8 312	14 371	94 727	4 825	55 822	34 080
WITH A 1975 POPULATION OF--									
50,000 OR MORE	-	-	-	-	-	54 019	-	54 019	-
25,000 TO 49,999	-	-	-	-	-	-	-	-	-
10,000 TO 24,999	-	11 251	-	-	-	27 860	-	-	27 860
5,000 TO 9,999	-	-	-	8 312	9 306	-	-	-	-
2,500 TO 4,999	3 038	-	2 534	-	-	3 170	3 170	-	-
1,000 TO 2,499	4 141	3 593	-	-	4 394	7 352	1 655	1 351	4 346
LESS THAN 1,000	851	755	552	-	671	2 326	-	452	1 874
OUTSIDE MUNICIPALLY GOVERNED AREAS	20 867	16 478	18 746	19 159	14 579	185 030	23 540	100 329	61 161
IN TOWNSHIP-GOVERNED AREAS	-	-	-	-	-	-	-	-	-
ENROLLMENT OF PUBLIC SCHOOL SYSTEMS									
TOTAL	6 205	7 353	5 336	7 397	7 008	62 131	7 679	31 218	23 234
THROUGH GRADE 12	6 205	7 353	5 336	7 397	7 008	62 131	7 679	31 218	23 234
COLLEGE GRADES	-	-	-	-	-	-	-	-	-

Item	Columbus				Macon				
	Total	Chatta-hoochee County	Muscogee County*	Russell County (Ala.)	Total	Bibb County*	Houston County	Jones County	Twiggs County
NUMBER OF LOCAL GOVERNMENTS									
ALL TYPES, TOTAL	17	3	5	9	21	6	9	3	3
WITH PROPERTY-TAXING POWER	11	3	3	5	15	4	5	3	3
WITHOUT PROPERTY-TAXING POWER	6	-	2	4	6	2	4	-	-
COUNTY GOVERNMENTS	2	1	-	1	4	1	1	1	1
MUNICIPALITIES	5	1	2	2	7	2	3	1	1
WITH A POPULATION OF--									
50,000 OR MORE	1	-	1	-	1	1	-	-	-
25,000 TO 49,999	1	-	-	1	1	-	1	-	-
10,000 TO 24,999	-	-	-	-	-	-	-	-	-
5,000 TO 9,999	-	-	-	-	1	-	1	-	-
2,500 TO 4,999	-	-	-	-	-	-	-	-	-
1,000 TO 2,499	1	1	-	-	3	-	1	1	1
LESS THAN 1,000	2	-	1	1	1	1	-	-	-
TOWNSHIP GOVERNMENTS	-	-	-	-	-	-	-	-	-
SCHOOL DISTRICTS	4	1	1	2	4	1	1	1	1
SPECIAL DISTRICTS	6	-	2	4	6	2	4	-	-
WITH PROPERTY-TAXING POWER	-	-	-	-	-	-	-	-	-
SINGLE FUNCTION DISTRICTS	-	-	-	-	-	-	-	-	-
CEMETERIES	-	-	-	-	-	-	-	-	-
EDUCATION (SCHOOL BUILDING DISTRICTS)	-	-	-	-	-	-	-	-	-
FIRE PROTECTION	-	-	-	-	-	-	-	-	-
HIGHWAYS	-	-	-	-	-	-	-	-	-
HEALTH	-	-	-	-	-	-	-	-	-
HOSPITALS	-	-	-	-	2	1	1	-	-
HOUSING AND URBAN RENEWAL	2	-	1	1	2	1	1	-	-
LIBRARIES	-	-	-	-	-	-	-	-	-
NATURAL RESOURCES, TOTAL	2	-	1	1	1	-	1	-	-
DRAINAGE	-	-	-	-	-	-	-	-	-
FLOOD CONTROL	-	-	-	-	-	-	-	-	-
IRRIGATION, WATER CONSERVATION	-	-	-	-	-	-	-	-	-
SOIL CONSERVATION	2	-	1	1	1	-	1	-	-
OTHER AND COMPOSITE PURPOSES	-	-	-	-	-	-	-	-	-
PARKS AND RECREATION	-	-	-	-	-	-	-	-	-
SEWERAGE	-	-	-	-	-	-	-	-	-
UTILITIES, TOTAL	-	-	-	-	-	-	-	-	-
WATER SUPPLY	-	-	-	-	-	-	-	-	-
ELECTRIC POWER	-	-	-	-	-	-	-	-	-
GAS SUPPLY	-	-	-	-	-	-	-	-	-
TRANSIT	-	-	-	-	-	-	-	-	-
OTHER	1	-	-	1	1	-	1	-	-
MULTIPLE-FUNCTION DISTRICTS	1	-	-	1	-	-	-	-	-
SEWERAGE AND WATER SUPPLY	-	-	-	-	-	-	-	-	-
NATURAL RESOURCES AND WATER SUPPLY	-	-	-	-	-	-	-	-	-
OTHER	1	-	-	1	-	-	-	-	-
SCHOOL SYSTEMS									
TOTAL	4	1	1	2	4	1	1	1	1
DEPENDENT SCHOOL SYSTEMS	-	-	-	-	-	-	-	-	-
BY ENROLLMENT SIZE OCTOBER 1976									
100,000 OR MORE PUPILS	-	-	-	-	-	-	-	-	-
50,000 TO 99,999 PUPILS	-	-	-	-	-	-	-	-	-
25,000 TO 49,999 PUPILS	1	-	1	-	1	1	-	-	-
12,000 TO 24,999 PUPILS	-	-	-	-	1	-	1	-	-
6,000 TO 11,999 PUPILS	-	-	-	-	-	-	-	-	-
3,000 TO 5,999 PUPILS	2	-	-	2	1	-	-	1	-
1,200 TO 2,999 PUPILS	1	-	-	-	1	-	-	-	1
300 TO 1,199 PUPILS	1	1	-	-	-	-	-	-	-
50 TO 299 PUPILS	-	-	-	-	-	-	-	-	-
1 TO 49 PUPILS	-	-	-	-	-	-	-	-	-
POPULATION, 1975 (ESTIMATED)									
TOTAL	222 043	15 772	160 103	46 168	237 416	142 978	71 616	14 781	8 041
IN MUNICIPALLY GOVERNED AREAS	188 211	1 291	160 103	26 817	175 468	121 385	50 442	¹2 368	¹1 273
WITH A 1975 POPULATION OF--									
50,000 OR MORE	159 352	-	159 352	-	121 157	121 157	-	-	-
25,000 TO 49,999	26 048	-	-	26 048	39 696	-	39 696	-	-
10,000 TO 24,999	-	-	-	-	-	-	-	-	-
5,000 TO 9,999	-	-	-	-	8 259	-	8 259	-	-
2,500 TO 4,999	-	-	-	-	-	-	-	-	-
1,000 TO 2,499	1 291	1 291	-	-	6 128	-	2 487	2 368	1 273
LESS THAN 1,000	1 520	-	751	769	228	228	-	-	-
OUTSIDE MUNICIPALLY GOVERNED AREAS	33 832	14 481	-	19 351	61 948	21 593	21 174	12 413	6 768
IN TOWNSHIP-GOVERNED AREAS	-	-	-	-	-	-	-	-	-
ENROLLMENT OF PUBLIC SCHOOL SYSTEMS									
TOTAL	45 086	383	35 605	9 098	49 603	28 176	15 959	3 439	2 029
THROUGH GRADE 12	45 086	383	35 605	9 098	49 603	28 176	15 959	3 439	2 029
COLLEGE GRADES	-	-	-	-	-	-	-	-	-

Item	Georgia (see also Tennessee)--Continued Savannah — Total	Bryan County	Chatham County*	Effingham County	Hawaii Honolulu — Honolulu County (entire SMSA)	Idaho Boise City — Ada County (entire SMSA)	Illinois Bloomington-Normal — McLean County (entire SMSA)	Illinois Champaign-Urbana-Rantoul — Champaign County (entire SMSA)
NUMBER OF LOCAL GOVERNMENTS								
ALL TYPES, TOTAL	26	4	16	6	4	43	114	166
WITH PROPERTY-TAXING POWER	19	4	10	5	1	34	94	99
WITHOUT PROPERTY-TAXING POWER	7	-	6	1	3	9	20	67
COUNTY GOVERNMENTS	3	1	1	1	-	1	1	1
MUNICIPALITIES	13	2	8	3	1	5	21	23
WITH A POPULATION OF--								
50,000 OR MORE	1	-	1	-	1	1	-	1
25,000 TO 49,999	-	-	-	-	-	-	2	1
10,000 TO 24,999	-	-	-	-	-	-	-	1
5,000 TO 9,999	1	-	1	-	-	-	-	-
2,500 TO 4,999	2	-	2	-	-	2	1	-
1,000 TO 2,499	7	2	3	2	-	-	4	8
LESS THAN 1,000	2	-	1	1	-	2	14	12
TOWNSHIP GOVERNMENTS	-	-	-	-	-	-	31	30
SCHOOL DISTRICTS	3	1	1	1	-	3	13	18
SPECIAL DISTRICTS	7	-	6	1	3	34	48	94
WITH PROPERTY-TAXING POWER	-	-	-	-	-	25	28	27
SINGLE FUNCTION DISTRICTS								
CEMETERIES	-	-	-	-	-	-	-	-
EDUCATION (SCHOOL BUILDING DISTRICTS)	-	-	-	-	-	7	2	-
FIRE PROTECTION	-	-	-	-	-	-	-	-
HIGHWAYS	1	-	1	-	-	8	20	18
HEALTH	-	-	-	-	-	1	-	-
HOSPITALS	2	-	1	1	-	-	-	-
HOUSING AND URBAN RENEWAL	1	-	1	-	1	-	2	1
LIBRARIES	-	-	-	-	-	2	1	-
NATURAL RESOURCES, TOTAL	1	-	1	-	3	8	18	68
DRAINAGE	-	-	-	-	-	2	17	67
FLOOD CONTROL	-	-	-	-	-	-	-	-
IRRIGATION, WATER CONSERVATION	-	-	-	-	-	4	-	-
SOIL CONSERVATION	-	-	-	-	-	2	-	-
OTHER AND COMPOSITE PURPOSES	1	-	1	-	3	-	1	1
PARKS AND RECREATION	-	-	-	-	-	2	3	3
SEWERAGE	-	-	-	-	-	5	1	2
UTILITIES, TOTAL	1	-	1	-	-	-	-	1
WATER SUPPLY	-	-	-	-	-	-	-	-
ELECTRIC POWER	-	-	-	-	-	-	-	-
GAS SUPPLY	-	-	-	-	-	-	-	-
TRANSIT	1	-	1	-	-	-	-	1
OTHER	1	-	1	-	-	-	1	-
MULTIPLE-FUNCTION DISTRICTS	-	-	-	-	-	-	-	1
SEWERAGE AND WATER SUPPLY	-	-	-	-	-	-	-	1
NATURAL RESOURCES AND WATER SUPPLY	-	-	-	-	-	-	-	-
OTHER	-	-	-	-	-	-	-	-
SCHOOL SYSTEMS								
TOTAL	3	1	1	1	(¹)	3	13	18
DEPENDENT SCHOOL SYSTEMS	-	-	-	-	-	-	-	-
BY ENROLLMENT SIZE OCTOBER 1976								
100,000 OR MORE PUPILS	-	-	-	-	-	-	-	-
50,000 TO 99,999 PUPILS	-	-	-	-	-	-	-	-
25,000 TO 49,999 PUPILS	1	-	1	-	-	-	-	-
12,000 TO 24,999 PUPILS	-	-	-	-	-	1	-	-
6,000 TO 11,999 PUPILS	-	-	-	-	-	1	2	2
3,000 TO 5,999 PUPILS	1	-	-	1	-	-	-	2
1,200 TO 2,999 PUPILS	1	1	-	-	-	1	1	3
300 TO 1,199 PUPILS	-	-	-	-	-	-	8	5
50 TO 299 PUPILS	-	-	-	-	-	-	2	6
1 TO 49 PUPILS	-	-	-	-	-	-	-	-
POPULATION, 1975 (ESTIMATED)								
TOTAL	207 185	8 128	183 304	15 753	705 381	134 653	114 284	162 304
IN MUNICIPALLY GOVERNED AREAS	134 879	2 567	128 079	4 233	705 381	109 494	91 536	¹131 919
WITH A 1975 POPULATION OF--								
50,000 OR MORE	110 348	-	110 348	-	705 381	99 771		58 398
25,000 TO 49,999	-	-	-	-	-	-	74 845	34 418
10,000 TO 24,999	-	-	-	-	-	-	-	21 533
5,000 TO 9,999	5 999	-	5 999	-	-	-	-	-
2,500 TO 4,999	5 999	-	5 999	-	-	8 021	2 679	-
1,000 TO 2,499	11 557	2 567	5 600	3 390	-	-	5 990	11 987
LESS THAN 1,000	976	-	133	843	-	1 702	8 022	5 583
OUTSIDE MUNICIPALLY GOVERNED AREAS	72 306	5 561	55 225	11 520	-	25 159	22 748	30 385
IN TOWNSHIP-GOVERNED AREAS	-	-	-	-	-	-	114 285	162 314
ENROLLMENT OF PUBLIC SCHOOL SYSTEMS								
TOTAL	40 286	2 252	34 185	3 849	-	32 917	21 922	34 491
THROUGH GRADE 12	40 286	2 252	34 185	3 849	-	32 917	21 922	28 122
COLLEGE GRADES	-	-	-	-	-	-	-	6 369

Illinois (see also Iowa and Missouri)--Continued

Item	Chicago Total	Cook County*	Du Page County	Kane County	Lake County	McHenry County	Will County	Decatur Macon County (entire SMSA)	Kankakee Kankakee County (entire SMSA)
NUMBER OF LOCAL GOVERNMENTS									
ALL TYPES, TOTAL	1 214	520	170	85	185	100	154	86	101
WITH PROPERTY-TAXING POWER	1 166	507	170	82	173	96	138	63	73
WITHOUT PROPERTY-TAXING POWER	48	13	-	3	12	4	16	23	28
COUNTY GOVERNMENTS	6	1	1	1	1	1	1	1	1
MUNICIPALITIES	261	121	29	20	43	24	24	11	16
WITH A POPULATION OF--									
50,000 OR MORE	12	8	-	2	1	-	1	1	-
25,000 TO 49,999	32	22	6	1	2	-	1	-	1
10,000 TO 24,999	67	45	10	2	6	2	2	-	1
5,000 TO 9,999	42	23	7	3	3	2	4	1	2
2,500 TO 4,999	41	12	3	3	11	4	8	1	2
1,000 TO 2,499	33	6	2	5	13	2	5	7	2
LESS THAN 1,000	34	5	1	4	7	14	3	2	9
TOWNSHIP GOVERNMENTS	113	29	9	16	18	17	24	17	17
SCHOOL DISTRICTS	315	152	47	11	53	22	30	9	15
SPECIAL DISTRICTS	519	217	84	37	70	36	75	48	52
WITH PROPERTY-TAXING POWER	471	204	84	34	58	32	59	25	24
SINGLE FUNCTION DISTRICTS	-	-	-	-	-	2	1	5	1
CEMETERIES	5	2	-	-	-	2	1	5	1
EDUCATION (SCHOOL BUILDING DISTRICTS)	-	-	-	-	-	-	-	-	-
FIRE PROTECTION	146	41	28	19	16	17	25	11	5
HIGHWAYS	6	-	3	-	-	-	3	-	-
HEALTH	11	4	4	-	2	-	1	1	-
HOSPITALS	5	1	1	-	1	1	1	1	1
HOUSING AND URBAN RENEWAL	5	1	-	-	2	1	1	1	1
LIBRARIES	61	31	6	2	10	4	8	-	1
NATURAL RESOURCES, TOTAL	44	8	4	3	10	4	15	22	28
DRAINAGE	35	6	2	2	7	3	15	21	26
FLOOD CONTROL	4	-	2	-	2	-	-	-	1
IRRIGATION, WATER CONSERVATION	1	1	-	-	-	-	-	-	-
SOIL CONSERVATION	4	1	-	1	1	1	-	1	1
OTHER AND COMPOSITE PURPOSES	-	-	-	-	-	-	-	-	-
PARKS AND RECREATION	166	90	29	8	17	6	16	4	2
SEWERAGE	48	27	7	3	9	1	1	3	3
UTILITIES, TOTAL	10	6	1	-	2	-	1	-	-
WATER SUPPLY	6	4	1	-	1	-	-	-	-
ELECTRIC POWER	-	-	-	-	-	-	-	-	-
GAS SUPPLY	-	-	-	-	-	-	-	-	-
TRANSIT	4	2	-	-	1	-	1	-	-
OTHER	4	2	-	1	1	-	-	-	1
MULTIPLE-FUNCTION DISTRICTS	8	4	1	1	-	-	2	1	-
SEWERAGE AND WATER SUPPLY	8	4	1	1	-	-	2	-	-
NATURAL RESOURCES AND WATER SUPPLY	-	-	-	-	-	-	-	1	-
OTHER	-	-	-	-	-	-	-	-	-
SCHOOL SYSTEMS									
TOTAL	315	152	47	11	53	22	30	9	15
DEPENDENT SCHOOL SYSTEMS	-	-	-	-	-	-	-	-	-
BY ENROLLMENT SIZE OCTOBER 1976									
100,000 OR MORE PUPILS	1	1	-	-	-	-	-	-	-
50,000 TO 99,999 PUPILS	1	1	-	-	-	-	-	-	-
25,000 TO 49,999 PUPILS	1	-	-	1	-	-	-	-	-
12,000 TO 24,999 PUPILS	7	3	1	1	1	-	1	1	1
6,000 TO 11,999 PUPILS	33	19	6	3	2	-	3	-	-
3,000 TO 5,999 PUPILS	50	31	8	2	4	3	2	-	6
1,200 TO 2,999 PUPILS	110	59	14	2	21	6	8	4	6
300 TO 1,199 PUPILS	96	35	17	2	19	9	14	4	2
50 TO 299 PUPILS	15	3	-	-	6	4	2	-	-
1 TO 49 PUPILS	1	-	1	-	-	-	-	-	-
POPULATION, 1975 (ESTIMATED)									
TOTAL	7 015 251	5 369 328	553 670	262 675	407 373	125 981	296 224	126 439	96 228
IN MUNICIPALLY GOVERNED AREAS	6 482 809	¹5 222 848	¹436 969	¹228 605	¹321 712	¹73 562	¹199 113	103 343	¹59 278
WITH A 1975 POPULATION OF--									
50,000 OR MORE	3 831 354	3 555 111	-	136 709	65 133	-	74 401	89 604	-
25,000 TO 49,999	1 067 996	726 849	213 775	25 446	74 449	-	27 477	-	27 961
10,000 TO 24,999	1 047 718	715 568	153 448	26 848	95 656	28 265	27 933	-	10 276
5,000 TO 9,999	304 099	168 371	54 926	19 382	18 506	13 521	29 393	3 525	9 431
2,500 TO 4,999	156 025	43 669	10 325	10 041	45 727	17 741	28 522	8 579	5 705
1,000 TO 2,499	56 361	10 548	3 847	8 686	19 144	4 158	9 978	1 635	2 391
LESS THAN 1,000	19 256	2 732	648	1 493	3 097	9 877	1 409	1 635	3 514
OUTSIDE MUNICIPALLY GOVERNED AREAS	532 442	146 480	116 701	34 070	85 661	52 419	97 111	23 096	36 950
IN TOWNSHIP-GOVERNED AREAS	3 852 421	2 206 499	553 669	262 673	407 376	125 984	296 220	126 443	96 227
ENROLLMENT OF PUBLIC SCHOOL SYSTEMS									
TOTAL	1 498 819	1 055 943	154 471	78 364	104 172	31 053	74 816	29 859	23 425
THROUGH GRADE 12	1 351 798	951 315	138 325	72 205	95 175	28 536	66 242	27 144	21 317
COLLEGE GRADES	147 021	104 628	16 146	6 159	8 997	2 517	8 574	2 715	2 108

Item	Illinois (see also Iowa and Missouri)—Continued									
	Peoria				Rockford			Springfield		
	Total	Peoria County*	Tazewell County	Woodford County	Total	Boone County	Winnebago County*	Total	Menard County	Sangamon County*
NUMBER OF LOCAL GOVERNMENTS										
ALL TYPES, TOTAL	260	89	106	65	92	23	69	118	18	100
WITH PROPERTY-TAXING POWER	241	83	101	57	86	23	63	109	14	95
WITHOUT PROPERTY-TAXING POWER	19	6	5	8	6	-	6	9	4	5
COUNTY GOVERNMENTS	3	1	1	1	2	1	1	2	1	1
MUNICIPALITIES	45	14	16	15	13	3	10	30	5	25
WITH A POPULATION OF--										
50,000 OR MORE	1	1	-	-	1	-	1	1	-	1
25,000 TO 49,999	1	-	1	-	-	-	-	-	-	-
10,000 TO 24,999	2	-	2	-	2	1	1	-	-	-
5,000 TO 9,999	5	3	2	-	-	-	-	-	-	-
2,500 TO 4,999	2	-	1	1	1	-	1	4	1	3
1,000 TO 2,499	16	5	6	5	5	-	5	9	1	8
LESS THAN 1,000	18	5	4	9	4	2	2	16	3	13
TOWNSHIP GOVERNMENTS	56	20	19	17	23	9	14	27	-	27
SCHOOL DISTRICTS	49	19	21	9	14	2	12	16	3	13
SPECIAL DISTRICTS	107	35	49	23	40	8	32	43	9	34
WITH PROPERTY-TAXING POWER	88	29	44	15	34	8	26	34	5	29
SINGLE FUNCTION DISTRICTS										
CEMETERIES	-	-	-	-	-	-	-	-	-	-
EDUCATION (SCHOOL BUILDING DISTRICTS)	3	2	1	-	-	-	-	2	2	-
FIRE PROTECTION	-	-	-	-	-	-	-	-	-	-
HIGHWAYS	45	12	25	8	20	5	15	24	3	21
HEALTH	3	1	1	1	3	1	2	-	-	-
HOSPITALS	-	-	-	-	-	-	-	-	-	-
HOUSING AND URBAN RENEWAL	1	1	-	-	-	-	-	-	-	-
LIBRARIES	3	1	1	1	2	-	2	3	1	2
	6	3	2	1	2	-	2	-	-	-
NATURAL RESOURCES, TOTAL	15	2	7	6	2	-	2	5	3	2
DRAINAGE	10	1	4	5	1	-	1	3	2	1
FLOOD CONTROL	2	-	2	-	-	-	-	-	-	-
IRRIGATION, WATER CONSERVATION	-	-	-	-	-	-	-	-	-	-
SOIL CONSERVATION	3	1	1	1	1	-	1	2	1	1
OTHER AND COMPOSITE PURPOSES	-	-	-	-	-	-	-	-	-	-
PARKS AND RECREATION	15	4	8	3	4	2	2	2	-	2
SEWERAGE	8	4	3	1	4	-	4	1	-	1
UTILITIES, TOTAL	6	4	1	1	2	-	2	5	-	5
WATER SUPPLY	4	3	-	1	1	-	1	4	-	4
ELECTRIC POWER	-	-	-	-	-	-	-	-	-	-
GAS SUPPLY	-	-	-	-	-	-	-	-	-	-
TRANSIT	2	1	1	-	1	-	1	1	-	1
OTHER	1	1	-	-	1	-	1	1	-	1
MULTIPLE-FUNCTION DISTRICTS	1	-	-	1	-	-	-	-	-	-
SEWERAGE AND WATER SUPPLY	1	-	-	1	-	-	-	-	-	-
NATURAL RESOURCES AND WATER SUPPLY	-	-	-	-	-	-	-	-	-	-
OTHER	-	-	-	-	-	-	-	-	-	-
SCHOOL SYSTEMS										
TOTAL	49	19	21	9	14	2	12	16	3	13
DEPENDENT SCHOOL SYSTEMS	-	-	-	-	-	-	-	-	-	-
BY ENROLLMENT SIZE OCTOBER 1976										
100,000 OR MORE PUPILS	-	-	-	-	-	-	-	-	-	-
50,000 TO 99,999 PUPILS	-	-	-	-	-	-	-	-	-	-
25,000 TO 49,999 PUPILS	-	-	-	-	-	-	-	-	-	-
12,000 TO 24,999 PUPILS	-	-	-	-	1	-	1	-	-	-
6,000 TO 11,999 PUPILS	2	2	-	-	-	-	-	1	-	1
3,000 TO 5,999 PUPILS	3	-	3	-	2	-	2	1	-	1
1,200 TO 2,999 PUPILS	9	4	4	1	1	1	-	-	-	-
300 TO 1,199 PUPILS	28	10	10	8	2	-	2	4	1	3
50 TO 299 PUPILS	7	3	4	-	6	1	5	10	2	8
1 TO 49 PUPILS	-	-	-	-	2	-	2	-	-	-
POPULATION, 1975 (ESTIMATED)										
TOTAL	353 939	199 023	125 189	29 727	271 632	26 592	245 040	180 514	10 761	169 753
IN MUNICIPALLY GOVERNED AREAS	272 669	¹157 036	¹98 907	¹16 726	189 271	18 074	171 197	124 320	5 615	118 705
WITH A 1975 POPULATION OF--										
50,000 OR MORE	125 983	125 983	-	-	145 459	-	145 459	87 418	-	87 418
25,000 TO 49,999	32 254	-	32 254	-	-	-	-	-	-	-
10,000 TO 24,999	35 027	-	35 027	-	28 951	16 744	12 207	-	-	-
5,000 TO 9,999	37 003	20 511	16 492	-	-	-	-	-	-	-
2,500 TO 4,999	6 203	-	3 166	3 037	3 772	-	3 772	12 987	2 832	10 155
1,000 TO 2,499	27 391	7 678	9 251	10 462	8 035	-	8 035	15 302	1 142	14 160
LESS THAN 1,000	8 808	2 864	2 717	3 227	3 054	1 330	1 724	8 613	1 641	6 972
OUTSIDE MUNICIPALLY GOVERNED AREAS	81 270	41 987	26 282	13 001	82 361	8 518	73 843	56 194	5 146	51 048
IN TOWNSHIP-GOVERNED AREAS	353 936	199 023	125 187	29 726	271 632	26 593	245 039	169 749	-	169 749
ENROLLMENT OF PUBLIC SCHOOL SYSTEMS										
TOTAL	86 645	49 893	28 934	7 818	69 502	6 616	62 886	39 448	2 902	36 546
THROUGH GRADE 12	74 497	37 745	28 934	7 818	60 726	6 616	54 110	33 420	2 902	30 518
COLLEGE GRADES	12 148	12 148	-	-	8 776	-	8 776	6 028	-	6 028

	Anderson	Bloomington	Evansville					
Item	Madison County (entire SMSA)	Monroe County (entire SMSA)	Total	Gibson County	Posey County	Vanderburgh County*	Warrick County	Henderson County (Ky.)
NUMBER OF LOCAL GOVERNMENTS								
ALL TYPES, TOTAL	54	32	112	34	29	17	25	7
WITH PROPERTY-TAXING POWER	40	18	89	28	22	13	20	6
WITHOUT PROPERTY-TAXING POWER.	14	14	23	6	7	4	5	1
COUNTY GOVERNMENTS	1	1	5	1	1	1	1	1
MUNICIPALITIES	16	3	25	10	5	2	6	2
WITH A POPULATION OF--								
50,000 OR MORE	1	-	1	-	-	1	-	-
25,000 TO 49,999	-	1	-	-	-	-	-	1
10,000 TO 24,999	1	-	1	-	-	-	-	1
5,000 TO 9,999	1	-	3	1	1	-	1	-
2,500 TO 4,999	1	-	3	2	-	-	1	-
1,000 TO 2,499	5	1	3	1	1	1	1	-
LESS THAN 1,000	7	1	14	6	3	1	3	1
TOWNSHIP GOVERNMENTS	14	11	38	10	10	8	10	-
SCHOOL DISTRICTS	5	2	9	3	3	1	1	1
SPECIAL DISTRICTS.	18	15	35	10	10	5	7	3
WITH PROPERTY-TAXING POWER	4	1	12	4	3	1	2	2
SINGLE FUNCTION DISTRICTS.	-	-	-	-	-	-	-	-
CEMETERIES	-	-	-	-	-	-	-	-
EDUCATION (SCHOOL BUILDING DISTRICTS). . .	11	12	13	4	5	1	3	-
FIRE PROTECTION.	-	-	-	-	-	-	-	-
HIGHWAYS	-	-	-	-	-	-	-	-
HEALTH	-	-	-	-	-	-	-	-
HOSPITALS.	1	-	3	-	1	1	1	-
HOUSING AND URBAN RENEWAL.	1	1	-	-	-	-	-	1
LIBRARIES.	4	1	11	4	3	1	2	1
NATURAL RESOURCES, TOTAL	2	1	6	2	1	1	1	1
DRAINAGE	1	-	1	1	-	-	-	-
FLOOD CONTROL.	-	-	1	1	-	-	-	-
IRRIGATION, WATER CONSERVATION . . .	-	-	-	-	-	-	-	-
SOIL CONSERVATION.	1	1	5	1	1	1	1	1
OTHER AND COMPOSITE PURPOSES	-	-	-	-	-	-	-	-
PARKS AND RECREATION	-	-	-	-	-	-	-	-
SEWERAGE	-	-	-	-	-	-	-	-
UTILITIES, TOTAL	-	-	1	1	-	-	-	1
WATER SUPPLY	-	-	1	1	-	-	-	1
ELECTRIC POWER	-	-	-	-	-	-	-	-
GAS SUPPLY	-	-	-	-	-	-	-	-
TRANSIT.	-	-	-	-	-	-	-	-
OTHER.	-	-	1	-	-	-	1	-
MULTIPLE-FUNCTION DISTRICTS.	-	-	-	-	-	-	-	-
SEWERAGE AND WATER SUPPLY.	-	-	-	-	-	-	-	-
NATURAL RESOURCES AND WATER SUPPLY	-	-	-	-	-	-	-	-
OTHER.	-	-	-	-	-	-	-	-
SCHOOL SYSTEMS								
TOTAL.	5	2	9	3	3	1	1	1
DEPENDENT SCHOOL SYSTEMS	-	-	-	-	-	-	-	-
BY ENROLLMENT SIZE OCTOBER 1976								
100,000 OR MORE PUPILS	-	-	-	-	-	-	-	-
50,000 TO 99,999 PUPILS.	-	-	-	-	-	-	-	-
25,000 TO 49,999 PUPILS.	-	-	1	-	-	-	1	-
12,000 TO 24,999 PUPILS.	1	1	2	-	-	-	-	1
6,000 TO 11,999 PUPILS	-	-	1	-	1	-	1	1
3,000 TO 5,999 PUPILS.	3	-	1	-	1	-	-	-
1,200 TO 2,999 PUPILS.	1	1	4	3	1	-	-	-
300 TO 1,199 PUPILS.	-	-	1	-	1	-	-	-
50 TO 299 PUPILS	-	-	-	-	-	-	-	-
1 TO 49 PUPILS	-	-	-	-	-	-	-	-
POPULATION, 1975 (ESTIMATED)								
TOTAL.	138 548	88 925	287 720	31 358	22 849	162 848	34 049	36 616
IN MUNICIPALLY GOVERNED AREAS.	100 216	51 212	198 174	17 209	10 103	134 316	12 762	23 784
WITH A 1975 POPULATION OF--								
50,000 OR MORE	69 486	-	133 566	-	-	133 566	-	-
25,000 TO 49,999	-	48 955	-	-	-	-	-	22 832
10,000 TO 24,999	10 581	-	22 832	-	-	-	-	-
5,000 TO 9,999	5 730	-	20 056	7 445	7 136	-	5 475	-
2,500 TO 4,999	2 972	-	8 990	5 779	-	-	3 211	-
1,000 TO 2,499	9 334	1 963	4 361	1 013	1 096	-	2 252	-
LESS THAN 1,000.	2 113	294	8 369	2 972	1 871	750	1 824	952
OUTSIDE MUNICIPALLY GOVERNED AREAS	38 332	37 713	89 546	14 149	12 746	28 532	21 287	12 832
IN TOWNSHIP-GOVERNED AREAS	138 546	88 924	251 105	31 358	22 849	162 848	34 050	-
ENROLLMENT OF PUBLIC SCHOOL SYSTEMS								
TOTAL.	31 075	15 154	56 585	6 482	5 299	28 166	8 242	8 396
THROUGH GRADE 12	31 075	15 154	56 585	6 482	5 299	28 166	8 242	8 396
COLLEGE GRADES	-	-	-	-	-	-	-	-

Indiana (see also Kentucky and Ohio)

Item	Fort Wayne					Gary-Hammond-East Chicago		
	Total	Adams County	Allen County*	De Kalb County	Wells County	Total	Lake County*	Porter County
NUMBER OF LOCAL GOVERNMENTS								
ALL TYPES, TOTAL	126	27	40	36	23	140	92	48
WITH PROPERTY-TAXING POWER	104	23	32	30	19	91	54	37
WITHOUT PROPERTY-TAXING POWER	22	4	8	6	4	49	38	11
COUNTY GOVERNMENTS	4	1	1	1	1	2	1	1
MUNICIPALITIES	23	4	6	8	5	29	18	11
WITH A POPULATION OF--								
50,000 OR MORE	-	-	-	-	-	2	2	-
25,000 TO 49,999	1	-	1	-	-	2	2	-
10,000 TO 24,999	-	-	-	-	-	3	3	-
5,000 TO 9,999	4	1	1	1	1	7	5	2
2,500 TO 4,999	2	1	1	1	-	5	4	1
1,000 TO 2,499	5	1	1	1	1	3	2	1
LESS THAN 1,000	11	1	3	4	1	7	1	6
TOWNSHIP GOVERNMENTS	56	12	20	15	9	23	11	12
SCHOOL DISTRICTS	13	3	4	3	3	25	16	9
SPECIAL DISTRICTS	30	7	9	9	5	61	46	15
WITH PROPERTY-TAXING POWER	8	3	1	3	1	12	8	4
SINGLE FUNCTION DISTRICTS								
CEMETERIES	-	-	-	-	-	-	-	-
EDUCATION (SCHOOL BUILDING DISTRICTS)	-	-	-	-	-	-	-	-
FIRE PROTECTION	15	3	5	4	3	43	33	10
HIGHWAYS	-	-	-	-	-	-	-	-
HEALTH	-	-	-	-	-	-	-	-
HOSPITALS	1	-	1	-	-	-	-	-
HOUSING AND URBAN RENEWAL	1	-	1	-	-	3	3	-
LIBRARIES	9	3	1	4	1	11	7	4
NATURAL RESOURCES, TOTAL	4	1	1	1	1	2	1	1
DRAINAGE	-	-	-	-	-	-	-	-
FLOOD CONTROL	-	-	-	-	-	-	-	-
IRRIGATION, WATER CONSERVATION	-	-	-	-	-	-	-	-
SOIL CONSERVATION	-	-	-	-	-	-	-	-
OTHER AND COMPOSITE PURPOSES	4	1	1	1	1	2	1	1
PARKS AND RECREATION	-	-	-	-	-	-	-	-
SEWERAGE	-	-	-	-	-	2	2	-
UTILITIES, TOTAL	-	-	-	-	-	-	-	-
WATER SUPPLY	-	-	-	-	-	-	-	-
ELECTRIC POWER	-	-	-	-	-	-	-	-
GAS SUPPLY	-	-	-	-	-	-	-	-
TRANSIT	-	-	-	-	-	-	-	-
OTHER	-	-	-	-	-	-	-	-
MULTIPLE-FUNCTION DISTRICTS								
SEWERAGE AND WATER SUPPLY	-	-	-	-	-	-	-	-
NATURAL RESOURCES AND WATER SUPPLY	-	-	-	-	-	-	-	-
OTHER	-	-	-	-	-	-	-	-
SCHOOL SYSTEMS								
TOTAL	13	3	4	3	3	25	16	9
DEPENDENT SCHOOL SYSTEMS	-	-	-	-	-	-	-	-
BY ENROLLMENT SIZE OCTOBER 1976								
100,000 OR MORE PUPILS	-	-	-	-	-	-	-	-
50,000 TO 99,999 PUPILS	-	-	-	-	-	-	-	-
25,000 TO 49,999 PUPILS	1	-	1	-	-	1	1	-
12,000 TO 24,999 PUPILS	1	-	1	-	-	1	1	-
6,000 TO 11,999 PUPILS	-	-	-	-	-	4	3	1
3,000 TO 5,999 PUPILS	2	-	1	1	-	9	7	2
1,200 TO 2,999 PUPILS	8	3	1	2	2	4	3	1
300 TO 1,199 PUPILS	1	-	-	-	1	6	1	5
50 TO 299 PUPILS	-	-	-	-	-	-	-	-
1 TO 49 PUPILS	-	-	-	-	-	-	-	-
POPULATION, 1975 (ESTIMATED)								
TOTAL	373 164	27 434	288 796	32 057	24 877	643 084	546 757	96 327
IN MUNICIPALLY GOVERNED AREAS	238 226	12 757	195 573	¹18 730	¹11 166	563 117	500 430	62 687
WITH A 1975 POPULATION OF--								
50,000 OR MORE	185 299	-	185 299	-	-	272 438	272 438	-
25,000 TO 49,999	-	-	-	-	-	98 188	98 188	-
10,000 TO 24,999	-	-	-	-	-	134 590	90 960	43 630
5,000 TO 9,999	30 743	8 018	6 400	7 800	8 525	35 287	28 469	6 818
2,500 TO 4,999	7 919	3 107	-	4 812	-	10 454	7 523	2 931
1,000 TO 2,499	8 547	1 018	1 467	4 170	1 892	11 440	2 448	8 992
LESS THAN 1,000	5 718	614	2 407	1 948	749	720	404	316
OUTSIDE MUNICIPALLY GOVERNED AREAS	134 938	14 677	93 223	13 327	13 711	79 967	46 327	33 640
IN TOWNSHIP-GOVERNED AREAS	373 162	27 434	288 795	32 057	24 876	643 085	546 758	96 327
ENROLLMENT OF PUBLIC SCHOOL SYSTEMS								
TOTAL	77 846	5 784	58 401	7 766	5 895	141 552	116 649	24 903
THROUGH GRADE 12	77 846	5 784	58 401	7 766	5 895	141 552	116 649	24 903
COLLEGE GRADES	-	-	-	-	-	-	-	-

Indiana (see also Kentucky and Ohio)--Continued

Item	Total	Indianapolis — Boone County	Hamilton County	Hancock County	Hendricks County	Johnson County	Marion County*	Morgan County	Shelby County	Lafayette–West Lafayette — Tippecanoe County (entire SMSA)	Muncie — Delaware County (entire SMSA)
NUMBER OF LOCAL GOVERNMENTS											
ALL TYPES, TOTAL	316	34	40	29	46	40	63	36	28	38	40
WITH PROPERTY-TAXING POWER	232	25	29	23	35	28	41	28	23	24	27
WITHOUT PROPERTY-TAXING POWER.	84	9	11	6	11	12	22	8	5	14	13
COUNTY GOVERNMENTS	7	1	1	1	1	1	-	1	1	1	1
MUNICIPALITIES	67	7	8	7	10	8	18	7	2	5	6
WITH A POPULATION OF--											
50,000 OR MORE	1	-	-	-	-	-	1	-	-	-	1
25,000 TO 49,999	1	-	-	-	-	-	1	-	-	1	-
10,000 TO 24,999	10	1	2	1	-	2	2	1	1	1	-
5,000 TO 9,999	4	-	-	-	2	1	-	1	-	-	-
2,500 TO 4,999	2	-	-	-	-	1	1	-	-	-	-
1,000 TO 2,499	16	2	4	2	-	2	5	1	1	3	5
LESS THAN 1,000.	33	4	2	4	7	2	9	4	1	-	-
TOWNSHIP GOVERNMENTS	88	12	9	9	12	9	9	14	14	13	12
SCHOOL DISTRICTS	44	3	6	4	6	6	11	4	4	3	7
SPECIAL DISTRICTS.	110	11	16	8	17	16	25	10	7	16	14
WITH PROPERTY-TAXING POWER	26	2	5	2	6	4	3	2	2	2	1
SINGLE FUNCTION DISTRICTS.	-	-	-	-	-	-	-	-	-	-	-
CEMETERIES	-	-	-	-	-	-	-	-	-	-	-
EDUCATION (SCHOOL BUILDING DISTRICTS). . . .	71	8	10	5	9	10	18	7	4	12	9
FIRE PROTECTION.	-	-	-	-	-	-	-	-	-	-	-
HIGHWAYS	-	-	-	-	-	-	-	-	-	-	-
HEALTH	-	-	-	-	-	-	-	-	-	-	-
HOSPITALS.	-	-	-	-	-	-	-	-	-	-	2
HOUSING AND URBAN RENEWAL. . . .	1	-	-	-	-	-	1	-	-	-	-
LIBRARIES.	25	2	5	2	6	4	3	2	1	2	1
NATURAL RESOURCES, TOTAL	8	1	1	1	1	1	1	1	1	2	2
DRAINAGE	-	-	-	-	-	-	-	-	-	-	-
FLOOD CONTROL.	-	-	-	-	-	-	-	-	-	1	1
IRRIGATION, WATER CONSERVATION	-	-	-	-	-	-	-	-	-	-	-
SOIL CONSERVATION.	8	1	1	1	1	1	1	1	1	1	1
OTHER AND COMPOSITE PURPOSES	-	-	-	-	-	-	-	-	-	-	-
PARKS AND RECREATION	-	-	-	-	-	1	-	-	-	1	-
SEWERAGE	3	-	-	-	-	1	1	-	-	-	-
UTILITIES, TOTAL	1	-	-	-	-	-	1	-	-	-	-
WATER SUPPLY	-	-	-	-	-	-	-	-	-	-	-
ELECTRIC POWER	-	-	-	-	-	-	-	-	-	-	-
GAS SUPPLY	1	-	-	-	-	-	1	-	-	-	-
TRANSIT.	-	-	-	-	-	-	-	-	-	-	-
OTHER.	-	-	-	-	-	-	-	-	-	-	-
MULTIPLE-FUNCTION DISTRICTS.	1	-	-	-	-	1	-	-	-	-	-
SEWERAGE AND WATER SUPPLY.	-	-	-	-	-	-	-	-	-	-	-
NATURAL RESOURCES AND WATER SUPPLY	-	-	-	-	-	-	-	-	-	-	-
OTHER.	1	-	-	-	-	1	-	-	-	-	-
SCHOOL SYSTEMS											
TOTAL.	44	3	6	4	6	6	11	4	4	3	7
DEPENDENT SCHOOL SYSTEMS	-	-	-	-	-	-	-	-	-	-	-
BY ENROLLMENT SIZE OCTOBER 1976											
100,000 OR MORE PUPILS	-	-	-	-	-	-	-	-	-	-	-
50,000 TO 99,999 PUPILS.	1	-	-	-	-	-	1	-	-	-	-
25,000 TO 49,999 PUPILS.	-	-	-	-	-	-	-	-	-	-	-
12,000 TO 24,999 PUPILS.	3	-	-	-	-	-	3	-	-	-	1
6,000 TO 11,999 PUPILS	4	-	1	-	-	-	2	1	-	2	1
3,000 TO 5,999 PUPILS.	12	1	1	1	2	3	2	1	1	-	1
1,200 TO 2,999 PUPILS.	22	2	4	3	4	3	3	1	2	1	4
300 TO 1,199 PUPILS.	2	-	-	-	-	-	-	1	1	-	-
50 TO 299 PUPILS	-	-	-	-	-	-	-	-	-	-	-
1 TO 49 PUPILS	-	-	-	-	-	-	-	-	-	-	-
POPULATION, 1975 (ESTIMATED)											
TOTAL.	1 137 702	32 618	68 260	40 294	61 290	66 880	782 141	48 480	38 792	112 408	128 989
IN MUNICIPALLY GOVERNED AREAS.	949 567	15 428	33 092	18 306	25 873	41 552	781 088	19 000	¹15 228	¹71 540	86 314
WITH A 1975 POPULATION OF--											
50,000 OR MORE	714 790	-	-	-	-	-	714 790	-	-	-	78 329
25,000 TO 49,999	25 485	-	-	-	-	-	25 485	-	-	48 894	-
10,000 TO 24,999	127 598	10 038	24 023	11 531	-	27 693	29 389	10 551	14 373	20 297	-
5,000 TO 9,999	28 110	-	-	-	17 020	5 318	-	5 772	-	-	-
2,500 TO 4,999	9 503	-	-	-	4 973	4 530	-	-	-	-	7 985
1,000 TO 2,499	27 648	3 341	7 765	4 052	-	2 811	8 609	1 070	-	-	-
LESS THAN 1,000.	16 433	2 049	1 304	2 723	3 880	1 200	2 815	1 607	855	2 349	-
OUTSIDE MUNICIPALLY GOVERNED AREAS	188 135	17 190	35 168	21 988	35 417	25 328	1 053	29 480	23 564	40 868	42 675
IN TOWNSHIP-GOVERNED AREAS	1 138 760	32 617	68 261	40 297	61 293	66 880	782 141	48 479	38 792	112 409	128 986
ENROLLMENT OF PUBLIC SCHOOL SYSTEMS											
TOTAL.	247 228	7 670	17 840	10 201	15 112	18 092	156 914	12 236	9 163	19 593	27 117
THROUGH GRADE 12	247 228	7 670	17 840	10 201	15 112	18 092	156 914	12 236	9 163	19 593	27 117
COLLEGE GRADES	-	-	-	-	-	-	-	-	-	-	-

Table 6. Local Governments and Public School Systems in Individual SMSA's: 1977—Continued

Indiana (see also Kentucky and Ohio)--Continued

Item	South Bend Total	Marshall County	St. Joseph County*	Terre Haute Total	Clay County	Sullivan County	Vermillion County	Vigo County*
NUMBER OF LOCAL GOVERNMENTS								
ALL TYPES, TOTAL	81	36	45	97	25	24	21	27
WITH PROPERTY-TAXING POWER	59	27	32	76	20	20	17	19
WITHOUT PROPERTY-TAXING POWER	22	9	13	21	5	4	4	8
COUNTY GOVERNMENTS	2	1	1	4	1	1	1	1
MUNICIPALITIES	15	6	9	24	6	7	7	4
WITH A POPULATION OF--								
50,000 OR MORE	1	-	1	1	-	-	-	1
25,000 TO 49,999	1	-	1	-	-	-	-	-
10,000 TO 24,999	-	-	-	-	-	-	-	-
5,000 TO 9,999	1	1	-	2	1	-	1	-
2,500 TO 4,999	1	1	-	1	-	1	-	-
1,000 TO 2,499	7	3	4	6	-	2	2	2
LESS THAN 1,000	4	1	3	14	5	4	4	1
TOWNSHIP GOVERNMENTS	23	10	13	37	11	9	5	12
SCHOOL DISTRICTS	10	5	5	6	1	2	2	1
SPECIAL DISTRICTS	31	14	17	26	6	5	6	9
WITH PROPERTY-TAXING POWER	9	5	4	5	1	1	2	1
SINGLE FUNCTION DISTRICTS	-	-	-	-	-	-	-	-
CEMETERIES	-	-	-	-	-	-	-	-
EDUCATION (SCHOOL BUILDING DISTRICTS)	17	8	9	10	3	-	3	4
FIRE PROTECTION	-	-	-	-	-	-	-	-
HEALTH	-	-	-	-	-	-	-	-
HOSPITALS	-	-	-	-	-	-	-	-
HOUSING AND URBAN RENEWAL	2	-	2	3	1	1	-	1
LIBRARIES	9	5	4	5	1	1	2	1
NATURAL RESOURCES, TOTAL	2	1	1	7	1	3	1	2
DRAINAGE	-	-	-	-	-	-	-	-
FLOOD CONTROL	-	-	-	3	-	2	-	-
IRRIGATION, WATER CONSERVATION	-	-	-	-	-	-	-	1
SOIL CONSERVATION	2	1	1	4	1	1	1	1
OTHER AND COMPOSITE PURPOSES	-	-	-	-	-	-	-	-
PARKS AND RECREATION	-	-	-	-	-	-	-	-
SEWERAGE	-	-	-	-	-	-	-	-
UTILITIES, TOTAL	-	-	-	1	-	-	-	1
WATER SUPPLY	-	-	-	1	-	-	-	1
ELECTRIC POWER	-	-	-	-	-	-	-	-
GAS SUPPLY	-	-	-	-	-	-	-	-
TRANSIT	-	-	-	-	-	-	-	-
OTHER	-	-	-	-	-	-	-	-
MULTIPLE-FUNCTION DISTRICTS	1	-	1	-	-	-	-	-
SEWERAGE AND WATER SUPPLY	-	-	-	-	-	-	-	-
NATURAL RESOURCES AND WATER SUPPLY	-	-	-	-	-	-	-	-
OTHER	1	-	1	-	-	-	-	-
SCHOOL SYSTEMS								
TOTAL	10	5	5	6	1	2	2	1
DEPENDENT SCHOOL SYSTEMS	-	-	-	-	-	-	-	-
BY ENROLLMENT SIZE OCTOBER 1976								
100,000 OR MORE PUPILS	-	-	-	-	-	-	-	-
50,000 TO 99,999 PUPILS	-	-	-	-	-	-	-	-
25,000 TO 49,999 PUPILS	1	-	1	-	-	-	-	-
12,000 TO 24,999 PUPILS	-	-	-	-	-	-	-	1
6,000 TO 11,999 PUPILS	2	-	2	1	-	-	-	1
3,000 TO 5,999 PUPILS	-	-	-	1	1	-	-	-
1,200 TO 2,999 PUPILS	5	3	2	3	-	2	1	-
300 TO 1,199 PUPILS	2	2	-	1	-	-	1	-
50 TO 299 PUPILS	-	-	-	-	-	-	-	-
1 TO 49 PUPILS	-	-	-	-	-	-	-	-
POPULATION, 1975 (ESTIMATED)								
TOTAL	278 372	37 941	240 431	171 202	24 306	19 541	16 846	110 509
IN MUNICIPALLY GOVERNED AREAS	178 954	16 993	161 961	97 533	10 573	9 413	9 587	67 960
WITH A 1975 POPULATION OF--								
50,000 OR MORE	117 478	-	117 478	63 998	-	-	-	63 998
25,000 TO 49,999	36 523	-	36 523	-	-	-	-	-
10,000 TO 24,999	-	-	-	-	-	-	-	-
5,000 TO 9,999	7 919	7 919	-	12 750	7 562	-	5 188	-
2,500 TO 4,999	3 592	3 592	-	4 384	-	4 384	-	-
1,000 TO 2,499	11 122	4 846	6 276	7 974	-	2 160	2 099	3 715
LESS THAN 1,000	2 320	636	1 684	8 427	3 011	2 869	2 300	247
OUTSIDE MUNICIPALLY GOVERNED AREAS	99 418	20 948	78 470	73 669	13 733	10 128	7 259	42 549
IN TOWNSHIP-GOVERNED AREAS	278 369	37 940	240 429	171 204	24 305	19 542	16 848	110 509
ENROLLMENT OF PUBLIC SCHOOL SYSTEMS								
TOTAL	54 304	7 964	46 340	33 569	5 080	4 341	3 670	20 478
THROUGH GRADE 12	54 304	7 964	46 340	33 569	5 080	4 341	3 670	20 478
COLLEGE GRADES	-	-	-	-	-	-	-	-

Iowa (see also Nebraska)

Item	Cedar Rapids Linn County (entire SMSA)	Davenport-Rock Island-Moline Total	Scott County*	Henry County (Ill.)	Rock Island County (Ill.)*	Des Moines Total	Polk County*	Warren County	Dubuque Dubuque County (entire SMSA)
NUMBER OF LOCAL GOVERNMENTS									
ALL TYPES, TOTAL	39	197	30	89	78	90	65	25	26
WITH PROPERTY-TAXING POWER	39	176	29	77	70	87	62	25	26
WITHOUT PROPERTY-TAXING POWER	-	21	1	12	8	3	3	-	-
COUNTY GOVERNMENTS	1	3	1	1	1	2	1	1	1
MUNICIPALITIES	17	47	17	15	15	30	17	13	21
WITH A POPULATION OF--									
50,000 OR MORE	1	1	1	-	-	1	1	-	1
25,000 TO 49,999	-	2	-	-	2	-	-	-	-
10,000 TO 24,999	1	3	1	1	1	3	3	-	-
5,000 TO 9,999	-	3	-	1	2	2	1	1	-
2,500 TO 4,999	2	5	2	2	1	4	3	1	1
1,000 TO 2,499	4	11	3	4	4	5	4	1	3
LESS THAN 1,000	9	22	10	7	5	15	5	10	16
TOWNSHIP GOVERNMENTS	-	42	-	24	18	-	-	-	-
SCHOOL DISTRICTS	12	25	5	10	10	15	10	5	2
SPECIAL DISTRICTS	9	80	7	39	34	43	37	6	2
WITH PROPERTY-TAXING POWER	9	59	6	27	26	40	34	6	2
SINGLE FUNCTION DISTRICTS	-	-	-	-	-	-	-	-	-
CEMETERIES	-	2	-	-	2	-	-	-	-
EDUCATION (SCHOOL BUILDING DISTRICTS)	-	-	-	-	-	-	-	-	-
FIRE PROTECTION	6	31	4	12	15	4	-	4	-
HIGHWAYS	-	-	-	-	-	-	-	-	-
HEALTH	-	-	-	-	-	-	-	-	-
HOSPITALS	-	2	-	1	1	1	-	-	-
HOUSING AND URBAN RENEWAL	-	4	-	1	3	1	1	-	-
LIBRARIES	-	3	1	1	1	-	-	-	1
NATURAL RESOURCES, TOTAL	1	24	2	15	7	2	1	1	1
DRAINAGE	-	19	1	14	4	-	-	-	-
FLOOD CONTROL	-	1	-	-	1	-	-	-	-
IRRIGATION, WATER CONSERVATION	-	1	-	-	1	-	-	-	-
SOIL CONSERVATION	1	3	1	1	1	2	1	1	1
OTHER AND COMPOSITE PURPOSES	-	-	-	-	-	-	-	-	-
PARKS AND RECREATION	-	3	-	3	-	-	-	-	-
SEWERAGE	2	8	-	5	3	3	2	1	-
UTILITIES, TOTAL	-	1	-	-	1	33	33	-	-
WATER SUPPLY	-	-	-	-	-	32	32	-	-
ELECTRIC POWER	-	-	-	-	-	-	-	-	-
GAS SUPPLY	-	-	-	-	-	-	-	-	-
TRANSIT	-	1	-	-	1	1	1	-	-
OTHER	-	2	-	1	1	-	-	-	-
MULTIPLE-FUNCTION DISTRICTS	-	-	-	-	-	-	-	-	-
SEWERAGE AND WATER SUPPLY	-	-	-	-	-	-	-	-	-
NATURAL RESOURCES AND WATER SUPPLY	-	-	-	-	-	-	-	-	-
OTHER	-	-	-	-	-	-	-	-	-
SCHOOL SYSTEMS									
TOTAL	12	25	5	10	10	15	10	5	2
DEPENDENT SCHOOL SYSTEMS	-	-	-	-	-	-	-	-	-
BY ENROLLMENT SIZE OCTOBER 1976									
100,000 OR MORE PUPILS	-	-	-	-	-	-	-	-	-
50,000 TO 99,999 PUPILS	-	-	-	-	-	-	-	-	-
25,000 TO 49,999 PUPILS	-	-	-	-	-	1	1	-	-
12,000 TO 24,999 PUPILS	1	1	1	-	-	-	-	-	1
6,000 TO 11,999 PUPILS	-	3	-	-	3	1	1	-	-
3,000 TO 5,999 PUPILS	2	5	2	1	2	5	4	1	1
1,200 TO 2,999 PUPILS	2	6	2	2	2	4	2	2	-
300 TO 1,199 PUPILS	7	10	-	7	3	4	2	2	-
50 TO 299 PUPILS	-	-	-	-	-	-	-	-	-
1 TO 49 PUPILS	-	-	-	-	-	-	-	-	-
POPULATION, 1975 (ESTIMATED)									
TOTAL	164 145	370 197	149 082	55 802	165 313	328 391	296 881	31 510	93 191
IN MUNICIPALLY GOVERNED AREAS	¹143 356	314 107	¹136 860	39 052	138 195	289 498	¹271 155	¹18 343	73 360
WITH A 1975 POPULATION OF--									
50,000 OR MORE	108 998	99 941	99 941	-	93 599	194 168	194 168	-	61 754
25,000 TO 49,999	-	93 599	-	-	93 599	-	-	-	-
10,000 TO 24,999	18 214	59 764	24 379	15 587	19 798	50 093	50 093	-	-
5,000 TO 9,999	-	19 113	-	6 696	12 417	16 683	7 016	9 667	-
2,500 TO 4,999	6 941	14 864	5 287	6 162	3 415	14 113	11 245	2 868	3 595
1,000 TO 2,499	5 157	16 401	4 004	6 902	5 495	8 939	6 511	2 428	4 228
LESS THAN 1,000	4 046	10 425	3 249	3 705	3 471	5 502	2 122	3 380	3 783
OUTSIDE MUNICIPALLY GOVERNED AREAS	20 789	56 090	12 222	16 750	27 118	38 893	25 726	13 167	19 831
IN TOWNSHIP-GOVERNED AREAS	-	221 117	-	55 809	165 308	-	-	-	-
ENROLLMENT OF PUBLIC SCHOOL SYSTEMS									
TOTAL	41 451	89 724	36 633	13 243	39 848	73 939	66 395	7 544	17 263
THROUGH GRADE 12	37 249	80 424	33 802	13 243	33 379	68 870	61 326	7 544	17 263
COLLEGE GRADES	4 202	9 300	2 831	-	6 469	5 069	5 069	-	-

Table 6. Local Governments and Public School Systems in Individual SMSA's: 1977—Continued

Item	Iowa (see also Nebraska)--Continued				Kansas (see also Missouri)						
	Sioux City			Waterloo-Cedar Falls	Topeka				Wichita		
	Total	Woodbury County*	Dakota County (Nebr.)	Black Hawk County (entire SMSA)	Total	Jefferson County	Osage County	Shawnee County*	Total	Butler County	Sedgwick County*
NUMBER OF LOCAL GOVERNMENTS											
ALL TYPES, TOTAL	46	27	19	17	167	66	55	46	143	63	80
WITH PROPERTY-TAXING POWER	40	25	15	17	139	60	45	34	132	57	75
WITHOUT PROPERTY-TAXING POWER	6	2	4	-	28	6	10	12	11	6	5
COUNTY GOVERNMENTS	2	1	1	1	3	1	1	1	2	1	1
MUNICIPALITIES	20	15	5	9	22	8	9	5	30	13	17
WITH A POPULATION OF--											
50,000 OR MORE	1	1	-	1	1	-	-	1	1	-	1
25,000 TO 49,999	-	-	-	1	-	-	-	-	1	1	-
10,000 TO 24,999	-	-	-	-	-	-	-	-	1	1	-
5,000 TO 9,999	1	-	1	-	-	-	-	-	3	1	2
2,500 TO 4,999	-	-	-	1	-	-	-	-	2	-	2
1,000 TO 2,499	3	2	1	3	5	1	2	2	7	3	4
LESS THAN 1,000	15	12	3	3	16	7	7	2	16	8	8
TOWNSHIP GOVERNMENTS	-	-	-	-	40	12	16	12	56	29	27
SCHOOL DISTRICTS	11	7	4	6	17	6	5	6	20	10	10
SPECIAL DISTRICTS	13	4	9	1	85	39	24	22	35	10	25
WITH PROPERTY-TAXING POWER	7	2	5	1	57	33	14	10	24	4	20
SINGLE FUNCTION DISTRICTS	-	-	-	-	-	-	-	-	-	-	-
CEMETERIES	-	-	-	-	-	-	-	-	-	-	-
EDUCATION (SCHOOL BUILDING DISTRICTS)	-	-	-	-	35	21	13	1	6	-	6
FIRE PROTECTION	3	-	3	-	-	-	-	-	-	-	-
HIGHWAYS	-	-	-	-	-	-	-	-	-	-	-
HEALTH	-	-	-	-	-	-	-	-	-	-	-
HOSPITALS	-	-	-	-	-	-	-	-	-	-	-
HOUSING AND URBAN RENEWAL	1	-	1	-	4	1	2	1	2	1	1
LIBRARIES	1	1	-	-	1	-	-	1	-	-	-
NATURAL RESOURCES, TOTAL	6	3	3	1	20	11	2	7	14	5	9
DRAINAGE	4	2	2	-	14	8	-	6	4	-	4
FLOOD CONTROL	-	-	-	-	3	2	1	-	8	4	4
IRRIGATION, WATER CONSERVATION	-	-	-	-	-	-	-	-	-	-	-
SOIL CONSERVATION	1	1	-	1	3	1	1	1	2	1	1
OTHER AND COMPOSITE PURPOSES	1	-	1	-	-	-	-	-	-	-	-
PARKS AND RECREATION	-	-	-	-	-	-	-	-	-	-	-
SEWERAGE	-	-	-	-	1	-	-	1	-	-	-
UTILITIES, TOTAL	1	-	1	-	22	5	7	10	9	4	5
WATER SUPPLY	-	-	-	-	22	5	7	10	9	4	5
ELECTRIC POWER	1	-	1	-	-	-	-	-	-	-	-
GAS SUPPLY	-	-	-	-	-	-	-	-	-	-	-
TRANSIT	-	-	-	-	-	-	-	-	-	-	-
OTHER	-	-	-	-	-	-	-	-	-	-	-
MULTIPLE-FUNCTION DISTRICTS	1	-	1	-	2	1	-	1	4	-	4
SEWERAGE AND WATER SUPPLY	1	-	1	-	-	-	-	-	3	-	3
NATURAL RESOURCES AND WATER SUPPLY	-	-	-	-	-	-	-	-	-	-	-
OTHER	-	-	-	-	2	1	-	1	1	-	1
SCHOOL SYSTEMS											
TOTAL	11	7	4	6	17	6	5	6	20	10	10
DEPENDENT SCHOOL SYSTEMS	-	-	-	-	-	-	-	-	-	-	-
BY ENROLLMENT SIZE OCTOBER 1976											
100,000 OR MORE PUPILS	-	-	-	-	-	-	-	-	-	-	-
50,000 TO 99,999 PUPILS	-	-	-	-	-	-	-	-	-	-	-
25,000 TO 49,999 PUPILS	-	-	-	-	-	-	-	-	-	-	-
12,000 TO 24,999 PUPILS	1	1	-	1	1	-	-	1	1	-	1
6,000 TO 11,999 PUPILS	-	-	-	1	-	-	-	-	-	-	-
3,000 TO 5,999 PUPILS	-	-	-	-	2	-	-	2	2	-	2
1,200 TO 2,999 PUPILS	1	-	1	1	3	-	1	2	8	4	4
300 TO 1,199 PUPILS	7	6	1	3	11	6	4	1	8	5	3
50 TO 299 PUPILS	2	-	2	-	-	-	-	-	1	1	-
1 TO 49 PUPILS	-	-	-	-	-	-	-	-	-	-	-
POPULATION, 1975 (ESTIMATED)											
TOTAL	119 013	103 692	15 321	133 589	177 974	13 223	13 757	150 994	384 920	39 696	345 224
IN MUNICIPALLY GOVERNED AREAS	104 840	94 257	¹10 583	¹123 034	135 141	5 547	7 788	121 806	323 194	25 617	¹297 577
WITH A 1975 POPULATION OF--											
50,000 OR MORE	85 719	85 719	-	77 681	119 203	-	-	119 203	264 901	-	264 901
25,000 TO 49,999	-	-	-	33 184	-	-	-	-	-	-	-
10,000 TO 24,999	-	-	-	-	-	-	-	-	11 694	11 694	-
5,000 TO 9,999	8 421	-	8 421	-	-	-	-	-	22 701	6 254	16 447
2,500 TO 4,999	-	-	-	4 761	-	-	-	-	6 437	-	6 437
1,000 TO 2,499	4 478	3 269	1 209	5 519	6 798	1 070	3 594	2 134	9 995	4 582	5 413
LESS THAN 1,000	6 222	5 269	953	1 889	9 140	4 477	4 194	469	7 466	3 087	4 379
OUTSIDE MUNICIPALLY GOVERNED AREAS	14 173	9 435	4 738	10 555	42 833	7 676	5 969	29 188	61 726	14 079	47 647
IN TOWNSHIP-GOVERNED AREAS	-	-	-	-	56 329	13 223	11 315	31 791	102 073	21 747	80 326
ENROLLMENT OF PUBLIC SCHOOL SYSTEMS											
TOTAL	23 583	20 112	3 471	26 896	40 760	3 952	3 108	33 700	79 610	11 408	68 202
THROUGH GRADE 12	23 583	20 112	3 471	25 061	35 930	3 952	3 108	28 870	77 856	9 654	68 202
COLLEGE GRADES	-	-	-	1 835	4 830	-	-	4 830	1 754	1 754	-

Table 6. Local Governments and Public School Systems in Individual SMSA's: 1977—Continued

| | Kentucky (see also Indiana, Ohio, Tennessee, and West Virginia) | | | | | | |
| | Lexington-Fayette | | | | | | |
Item	Total	Bourbon County	Clark County	Lexington-Fayette Urban County*	Jessamine County	Scott County	Woodford County
NUMBER OF LOCAL GOVERNMENTS							
ALL TYPES, TOTAL	41	8	4	4	9	7	9
WITH PROPERTY-TAXING POWER	33	8	3	2	7	7	6
WITHOUT PROPERTY-TAXING POWER.	8	-	1	2	2	-	3
COUNTY GOVERNMENTS	5	1	1	-	1	1	1
MUNICIPALITIES	12	3	1	1	2	3	2
WITH A POPULATION OF--							
50,000 OR MORE	1	-	-	1	-	-	-
25,000 TO 49,999	-	-	-	-	-	-	-
10,000 TO 24,999	1	-	1	-	-	-	-
5,000 TO 9,999	4	1	-	-	1	1	1
2,500 TO 4,999	1	-	-	-	1	-	-
1,000 TO 2,499	1	-	-	-	-	-	1
LESS THAN 1,000.	4	2	-	-	-	2	-
TOWNSHIP GOVERNMENTS	-	-	-	-	-	-	-
SCHOOL DISTRICTS	7	2	1	1	1	1	1
SPECIAL DISTRICTS.	17	2	1	2	5	2	5
WITH PROPERTY-TAXING POWER	9	2	-	-	3	2	2
SINGLE FUNCTION DISTRICTS.							
CEMETERIES	-	-	-	-	-	-	-
EDUCATION (SCHOOL BUILDING DISTRICTS). . . .	-	-	-	-	-	-	-
FIRE PROTECTION.	2	-	-	-	1	-	1
HIGHWAYS	-	-	-	-	-	-	-
HEALTH	-	-	-	-	-	-	-
HOSPITALS.	-	-	-	-	-	-	-
HOUSING AND URBAN RENEWAL.	-	-	-	-	-	-	-
LIBRARIES.	3	1	-	-	1	1	-
NATURAL RESOURCES, TOTAL	5	1	-	1	1	1	1
DRAINAGE	-	-	-	-	-	-	-
FLOOD CONTROL.	-	-	-	-	-	-	-
IRRIGATION, WATER CONSERVATION	-	-	-	-	-	-	-
SOIL CONSERVATION.	5	1	-	1	1	1	1
OTHER AND COMPOSITE PURPOSES	-	-	-	-	-	-	-
PARKS AND RECREATION	-	-	-	-	-	-	-
SEWERAGE	-	-	-	-	-	-	-
UTILITIES, TOTAL	7	-	1	1	2	-	3
WATER SUPPLY	7	-	1	1	2	-	3
ELECTRIC POWER	-	-	-	-	-	-	-
GAS SUPPLY	-	-	-	-	-	-	-
TRANSIT.	-	-	-	-	-	-	-
OTHER.	-	-	-	-	-	-	-
MULTIPLE-FUNCTION DISTRICTS.	-	-	-	-	-	-	-
SEWERAGE AND WATER SUPPLY.	-	-	-	-	-	-	-
NATURAL RESOURCES AND WATER SUPPLY	-	-	-	-	-	-	-
OTHER.	-	-	-	-	-	-	-
SCHOOL SYSTEMS							
TOTAL.	7	2	1	1	1	1	1
DEPENDENT SCHOOL SYSTEMS	-	-	-	-	-	-	-
BY ENROLLMENT SIZE OCTOBER 1976							
100,000 OR MORE PUPILS	-	-	-	-	-	-	-
50,000 TO 99,999 PUPILS.	-	-	-	-	-	-	-
25,000 TO 49,999 PUPILS.	1	-	-	1	-	-	-
12,000 TO 24,999 PUPILS.	-	-	-	-	-	-	-
6,000 TO 11,999 PUPILS	-	-	-	-	-	-	-
3,000 TO 5,999 PUPILS.	4	-	1	-	1	1	1
1,200 TO 2,999 PUPILS.	2	2	-	-	-	-	-
300 TO 1,199 PUPILS.	-	-	-	-	-	-	-
50 TO 299 PUPILS	-	-	-	-	-	-	-
1 TO 49 PUPILS	-	-	-	-	-	-	-
POPULATION, 1975 (ESTIMATED)							
TOTAL.	287 392	18 815	26 133	186 048	21 375	18 654	16 367
IN MUNICIPALLY GOVERNED AREAS.	239 755	8 465	15 922	186 048	11 235	9 496	8 589
WITH A 1975 POPULATION OF--							
50,000 OR MORE	186 048	-	-	186 048	-	-	-
25,000 TO 49,999	-	-	-	-	-	-	-
10,000 TO 24,999	15 922	-	15 922	-	-	-	-
5,000 TO 9,999	30 795	7 298	-	-	7 565	8 892	7 040
2,500 TO 4,999	3 670	-	-	-	3 670	-	-
1,000 TO 2,499	1 549	-	-	-	-	-	1 549
LESS THAN 1,000.	1 771	1 167	-	-	-	604	-
OUTSIDE MUNICIPALLY GOVERNED AREAS	47 637	10 350	10 211	-	10 140	9 158	7 778
IN TOWNSHIP-GOVERNED AREAS	-	-	-	-	-	-	-
ENROLLMENT OF PUBLIC SCHOOL SYSTEMS							
TOTAL.	56 140	4 108	5 553	34 334	4 369	4 045	3 731
THROUGH GRADE 12	56 140	4 108	5 553	34 334	4 369	4 045	3 731
COLLEGE GRADES	-	-	-	-	-	-	-

Item	Kentucky (see also Indiana, Ohio, Tennessee, and West Virginia)--Continued							Louisiana		
	Louisville						Owensboro	Alexandria		
	Total	Bullitt County	Jefferson County*	Oldham County	Clark County (Ind.)	Floyd County (Ind.)	Daviess County (entire SMSA)	Total	Grant Parish	Rapides Parish*
NUMBER OF LOCAL GOVERNMENTS										
ALL TYPES, TOTAL	215	13	122	19	43	18	9	21	8	13
WITH PROPERTY-TAXING POWER	173	11	111	16	24	11	5	21	8	13
WITHOUT PROPERTY-TAXING POWER. . . .	42	2	11	3	19	7	4	-	-	-
COUNTY GOVERNMENTS	5	1	1	1	1	1	1	2	1	1
MUNICIPALITIES	92	5	76	3	5	3	2	15	5	10
WITH A POPULATION OF--										
50,000 OR MORE	1	-	1	-	-	-	1	1	-	1
25,000 TO 49,999	1	-	-	-	-	1	1	1	-	1
10,000 TO 24,999	5	-	3	-	2	-	-	1	-	1
5,000 TO 9,999	1	-	-	-	2	1	-	-	-	-
2,500 TO 4,999	4	1	2	-	1	-	-	-	-	-
1,000 TO 2,499	26	3	20	2	-	1	-	6	1	5
LESS THAN 1,000	54	1	50	1	1	1	1	7	4	3
TOWNSHIP GOVERNMENTS	17	-	-	-	12	5	-	-	-	-
SCHOOL DISTRICTS	8	1	2	1	3	1	2	2	1	1
SPECIAL DISTRICTS	93	6	43	14	22	8	4	2	1	1
WITH PROPERTY-TAXING POWER . . .	51	4	32	11	3	1	-	2	1	1
SINGLE FUNCTION DISTRICTS. . . .										
CEMETERIES	-	-	-	-	-	-	-	-	-	-
EDUCATION (SCHOOL BUILDING DISTRICTS). .	17	-	-	-	13	4	-	-	-	-
FIRE PROTECTION.	32	2	21	9	-	-	-	-	-	-
HIGHWAYS	4	-	4	-	-	-	-	-	-	-
HEALTH	-	-	-	-	-	-	-	-	-	-
HOSPITALS.	-	-	-	-	-	-	-	-	-	-
HOUSING AND URBAN RENEWAL. . . .	4	-	1	-	2	1	-	-	-	-
LIBRARIES.	5	1	-	1	2	1	-	-	-	-
NATURAL RESOURCES, TOTAL	8	1	1	1	3	2	1	2	1	1
DRAINAGE	2	-	-	-	1	1	-	-	-	-
FLOOD CONTROL.	2	-	-	-	1	1	-	2	1	1
IRRIGATION, WATER CONSERVATION . . .	-	-	-	-	-	-	-	-	-	-
SOIL CONSERVATION.	6	1	1	1	2	1	1	-	-	-
OTHER AND COMPOSITE PURPOSES . . .	-	-	-	-	-	-	-	-	-	-
PARKS AND RECREATION	-	-	-	-	-	-	-	-	-	-
SEWERAGE	14	-	14	-	-	-	1	-	-	-
UTILITIES, TOTAL	6	2	1	3	-	-	2	-	-	-
WATER SUPPLY	5	2	-	3	-	-	2	-	-	-
ELECTRIC POWER	-	-	-	-	-	-	-	-	-	-
GAS SUPPLY	-	-	-	-	-	-	-	-	-	-
TRANSIT.	1	-	1	-	-	-	-	-	-	-
OTHER.	1	-	-	-	1	-	-	-	-	-
MULTIPLE-FUNCTION DISTRICTS. . . .	2	-	1	-	1	-	-	-	-	-
SEWERAGE AND WATER SUPPLY. . . .	2	-	1	-	1	-	-	-	-	-
NATURAL RESOURCES AND WATER SUPPLY . .	-	-	-	-	-	-	-	-	-	-
OTHER.	-	-	-	-	-	-	-	-	-	-
SCHOOL SYSTEMS										
TOTAL.	8	1	2	1	3	1	2	2	1	1
DEPENDENT SCHOOL SYSTEMS	-	-	-	-	-	-	-	-	-	-
BY ENROLLMENT SIZE OCTOBER 1976										
100,000 OR MORE PUPILS	1	-	1	-	-	-	-	-	-	-
50,000 TO 99,999 PUPILS.	-	-	-	-	-	-	-	-	-	-
25,000 TO 49,999 PUPILS.	-	-	-	-	-	-	-	-	-	-
12,000 TO 24,999 PUPILS.	2	-	-	-	-	-	-	1	-	1
6,000 TO 11,999 PUPILS.	1	1	-	-	1	1	2	-	-	-
3,000 TO 5,999 PUPILS.	3	-	-	1	2	-	-	1	1	-
1,200 TO 2,999 PUPILS.	-	-	-	-	-	-	-	-	-	-
300 TO 1,199 PUPILS	1	-	1	-	-	-	-	-	-	-
50 TO 299 PUPILS	-	-	-	-	-	-	-	-	-	-
1 TO 49 PUPILS	-	-	-	-	-	-	-	-	-	-
POPULATION, 1975 (ESTIMATED)										
TOTAL.	887 882	33 476	696 832	17 752	83 040	56 782	80 730	135 418	14 330	121 088
IN MUNICIPALLY GOVERNED AREAS.	537 500	9 749	436 977	3 931	47 018	39 825	51 413	72 962	3 836	69 126
WITH A 1975 POPULATION OF--										
50,000 OR MORE	335 954	-	335 954	-	-	-	50 788	-	-	-
25,000 TO 49,999	37 492	-	-	-	-	37 492	-	49 481	-	49 481
10,000 TO 24,999	79 452	-	42 444	-	37 008	-	-	11 456	-	11 456
5,000 TO 9,999	5 949	-	-	-	5 949	-	-	-	-	-
2,500 TO 4,999	12 523	3 308	5 504	-	3 711	-	-	-	-	-
1,000 TO 2,499	40 121	6 000	29 070	3 405	-	1 646	-	9 065	1 916	7 149
LESS THAN 1,000	26 009	441	24 005	526	350	687	625	2 960	1 920	1 040
OUTSIDE MUNICIPALLY GOVERNED AREAS	350 382	23 727	259 855	13 821	36 022	16 957	29 317	62 456	10 494	51 962
IN TOWNSHIP-GOVERNED AREAS	139 822	-	-	-	83 039	56 783	-	-	-	-
ENROLLMENT OF PUBLIC SCHOOL SYSTEMS										
TOTAL.	165 016	10 385	117 629	4 679	19 762	12 561	15 618	30 632	3 670	26 962
THROUGH GRADE 12	165 016	10 385	117 629	4 679	19 762	12 561	15 618	30 632	3 670	26 962
COLLEGE GRADES	-	-	-	-	-	-	-	-	-	-

	Louisiana--Continued							
	Baton Rouge					Lafayette	Lake Charles	Monroe
Item	Total	Ascension Parish	East Baton Rouge Parish*	Livingston Parish	West Baton Rouge Parish	Lafayette Parish (entire SMSA)	Calcasieu Parish (entire SMSA)	Ouachita Parish (entire SMSA)
NUMBER OF LOCAL GOVERNMENTS								
ALL TYPES, TOTAL	26	6	4	10	6	8	11	7
WITH PROPERTY-TAXING POWER	26	6	4	10	6	8	11	7
WITHOUT PROPERTY-TAXING POWER.	-	-	-	-	-	-	-	-
COUNTY GOVERNMENTS	3	1	-	1	1	1	1	1
MUNICIPALITIES	17	3	3	8	3	6	6	4
WITH A POPULATION OF--								
50,000 OR MORE	1	-	1	-	-	1	1	1
25,000 TO 49,999	-	-	-	-	-	-	-	1
10,000 TO 24,999	1	-	1	-	-	-	1	1
5,000 TO 9,999	5	2	1	1	1	-	-	-
2,500 TO 4,999	-	-	-	-	-	1	3	2
1,000 TO 2,499	4	1	-	2	1	4	1	-
LESS THAN 1,000.	6	-	-	5	1	-	-	-
TOWNSHIP GOVERNMENTS	-	-	-	-	-	-	-	-
SCHOOL DISTRICTS	4	1	1	1	1	1	1	2
SPECIAL DISTRICTS.	2	1	-	-	1	-	3	-
WITH PROPERTY-TAXING POWER	2	1	-	-	1	-	3	-
SINGLE FUNCTION DISTRICTS.	-	-	-	-	-	-	-	-
CEMETERIES	-	-	-	-	-	-	-	-
EDUCATION (SCHOOL BUILDING DISTRICTS). .	-	-	-	-	-	-	-	-
FIRE PROTECTION.	-	-	-	-	-	-	-	-
HIGHWAYS	-	-	-	-	-	-	-	-
HEALTH	-	-	-	-	-	-	-	-
HOSPITALS.	-	-	-	-	-	-	-	-
HOUSING AND URBAN RENEWAL.	-	-	-	-	-	-	-	-
LIBRARIES.	-	-	-	-	-	-	-	-
NATURAL RESOURCES, TOTAL	2	1	-	-	1	-	-	-
DRAINAGE	-	-	-	-	-	-	-	-
FLOOD CONTROL.	2	1	-	-	1	-	-	-
IRRIGATION, WATER CONSERVATION	-	-	-	-	-	-	-	-
SOIL CONSERVATION.	-	-	-	-	-	-	-	-
OTHER AND COMPOSITE PURPOSES	-	-	-	-	-	-	-	-
PARKS AND RECREATION	-	-	-	-	-	-	-	-
SEWERAGE	-	-	-	-	-	-	-	-
UTILITIES, TOTAL	-	-	-	-	-	-	-	-
WATER SUPPLY	-	-	-	-	-	-	-	-
ELECTRIC POWER	-	-	-	-	-	-	-	-
GAS SUPPLY	-	-	-	-	-	-	-	-
TRANSIT.	-	-	-	-	-	-	-	-
OTHER.	-	-	-	-	-	-	3	-
MULTIPLE-FUNCTION DISTRICTS.	-	-	-	-	-	-	-	-
SEWERAGE AND WATER SUPPLY.	-	-	-	-	-	-	-	-
NATURAL RESOURCES AND WATER SUPPLY . . .	-	-	-	-	-	-	-	-
OTHER.	-	-	-	-	-	-	-	-
SCHOOL SYSTEMS								
TOTAL.	4	1	1	1	1	1	1	2
DEPENDENT SCHOOL SYSTEMS	-	-	-	-	-	-	-	-
BY ENROLLMENT SIZE OCTOBER 1976								
100,000 OR MORE PUPILS	-	-	-	-	-	-	-	-
50,000 TO 99,999 PUPILS.	1	-	1	-	-	-	-	-
25,000 TO 49,999 PUPILS.	-	-	-	-	-	1	1	-
12,000 TO 24,999 PUPILS.	1	-	-	1	-	-	-	1
6,000 TO 11,999 PUPILS	1	1	-	-	-	-	-	1
3,000 TO 5,999 PUPILS.	1	-	-	-	1	-	-	-
1,200 TO 2,999 PUPILS.	-	-	-	-	-	-	-	-
300 TO 1,199 PUPILS.	-	-	-	-	-	-	-	-
50 TO 299 PUPILS	-	-	-	-	-	-	-	-
1 TO 49 PUPILS	-	-	-	-	-	-	-	-
POPULATION, 1975 (ESTIMATED)								
TOTAL.	411 725	40 691	310 922	42 590	17 522	125 233	151 334	125 447
IN MUNICIPALLY GOVERNED AREAS.	346 520	14 036	310 922	13 651	7 911	84 388	106 921	79 367
WITH A 1975 POPULATION OF--								
50,000 OR MORE	294 394	-	294 394	-	-	75 430	76 087	61 016
25,000 TO 49,999	-	-	-	-	-	-	-	-
10,000 TO 24,999	10 693	-	10 693	-	-	-	17 527	15 678
5,000 TO 9,999	32 539	12 820	5 835	8 080	5 804	-	11 257	-
2,500 TO 4,999	-	-	-	-	-	2 668	-	-
1,000 TO 2,499	5 537	1 216	-	2 923	1 398	6 290	2 050	2 673
LESS THAN 1,000.	3 357	-	-	2 648	709	-	-	-
OUTSIDE MUNICIPALLY GOVERNED AREAS	65 205	26 655	-	28 939	9 611	40 845	44 413	46 080
IN TOWNSHIP-GOVERNED AREAS	-	-	-	-	-	-	-	-
ENROLLMENT OF PUBLIC SCHOOL SYSTEMS								
TOTAL.	95 590	10 522	68 451	12 606	4 011	28 047	34 065	29 612
THROUGH GRADE 12	95 590	10 522	68 451	12 606	4 011	28 047	34 065	29 612
COLLEGE GRADES	-	-	-	-	-	-	-	-

Table 6. Local Governments and Public School Systems in Individual SMSA's: 1977—Continued

Item	Louisiana--Continued								
	New Orleans					Shreveport			
	Total	Jefferson Parish	Orleans Parish*	St. Bernard Parish	St. Tammany Parish	Total	Bossier Parish	Caddo Parish*	Webster Parish
NUMBER OF LOCAL GOVERNMENTS									
ALL TYPES, TOTAL	25	8	3	4	10	35	7	15	13
WITH PROPERTY-TAXING POWER	25	8	3	4	10	35	7	15	13
WITHOUT PROPERTY-TAXING POWER	-	-	-	-	-	-	-	-	-
COUNTY GOVERNMENTS	3	1	-	1	1	3	1	1	1
MUNICIPALITIES	15	6	1	-	8	26	4	11	11
WITH A POPULATION OF--									
50,000 OR MORE	1	-	1	-	-	1	-	1	-
25,000 TO 49,999	2	2	-	-	-	1	-	1	-
10,000 TO 24,999	3	2	-	-	1	1	1	-	-
5,000 TO 9,999	1	-	-	-	1	1	-	-	1
2,500 TO 4,999	1	-	-	-	1	1	-	1	1
1,000 TO 2,499	2	1	-	-	1	4	2	-	2
LESS THAN 1,000	5	1	-	-	4	17	1	9	7
TOWNSHIP GOVERNMENTS	-	-	-	-	-	-	-	-	-
SCHOOL DISTRICTS	4	1	1	1	1	3	1	1	1
SPECIAL DISTRICTS	3	-	1	2	-	3	1	2	-
WITH PROPERTY-TAXING POWER	3	-	1	2	-	3	1	2	-
SINGLE FUNCTION DISTRICTS	-	-	-	-	-	-	-	-	-
CEMETERIES	-	-	-	-	-	-	-	-	-
EDUCATION (SCHOOL BUILDING DISTRICTS)	-	-	-	-	-	-	-	-	-
FIRE PROTECTION	-	-	-	-	-	-	-	-	-
HIGHWAYS	-	-	-	-	-	-	-	-	-
HEALTH	-	-	-	-	-	-	-	-	-
HOSPITALS	-	-	-	-	-	-	-	-	-
HOUSING AND URBAN RENEWAL	-	-	-	-	-	-	-	-	-
LIBRARIES	-	-	-	-	-	-	-	-	-
NATURAL RESOURCES, TOTAL	2	-	1	1	-	2	1	1	-
DRAINAGE	-	-	-	-	-	-	-	-	-
FLOOD CONTROL	2	-	1	1	-	2	1	1	-
IRRIGATION, WATER CONSERVATION	-	-	-	-	-	-	-	-	-
SOIL CONSERVATION	-	-	-	-	-	-	-	-	-
OTHER AND COMPOSITE PURPOSES	-	-	-	-	-	-	-	-	-
PARKS AND RECREATION	-	-	-	-	-	-	-	-	-
SEWERAGE	-	-	-	-	-	-	-	-	-
UTILITIES, TOTAL	-	-	-	-	-	1	-	1	-
WATER SUPPLY	-	-	-	-	-	1	-	1	-
ELECTRIC POWER	-	-	-	-	-	-	-	-	-
GAS SUPPLY	-	-	-	-	-	-	-	-	-
TRANSIT	-	-	-	-	-	-	-	-	-
OTHER	1	-	-	1	-	-	-	-	-
MULTIPLE-FUNCTION DISTRICTS	-	-	-	-	-	-	-	-	-
SEWERAGE AND WATER SUPPLY	-	-	-	-	-	-	-	-	-
NATURAL RESOURCES AND WATER SUPPLY	-	-	-	-	-	-	-	-	-
OTHER	-	-	-	-	-	-	-	-	-
SCHOOL SYSTEMS									
TOTAL	4	1	1	1	1	3	1	1	1
DEPENDENT SCHOOL SYSTEMS	-	-	-	-	-	-	-	-	-
BY ENROLLMENT SIZE OCTOBER 1976									
100,000 OR MORE PUPILS	-	-	-	-	-	-	-	-	-
50,000 TO 99,999 PUPILS	2	1	1	-	-	-	-	-	-
25,000 TO 49,999 PUPILS	-	-	-	-	-	1	-	1	-
12,000 TO 24,999 PUPILS	2	-	-	1	1	1	1	-	-
6,000 TO 11,999 PUPILS	-	-	-	-	-	1	-	-	1
3,000 TO 5,999 PUPILS	-	-	-	-	-	-	-	-	-
1,200 TO 2,999 PUPILS	-	-	-	-	-	-	-	-	-
300 TO 1,199 PUPILS	-	-	-	-	-	-	-	-	-
50 TO 299 PUPILS	-	-	-	-	-	-	-	-	-
1 TO 49 PUPILS	-	-	-	-	-	-	-	-	-
POPULATION, 1975 (ESTIMATED)									
TOTAL	1 094 423	399 016	559 770	58 188	77 449	348 936	69 870	239 078	39 988
IN MUNICIPALLY GOVERNED AREAS	700 874	104 434	559 770	-	36 670	271 138	¹50 281	194 166	26 691
WITH A 1975 POPULATION OF--									
50,000 OR MORE	559 770	-	559 770	-	-	185 711	-	185 711	-
25,000 TO 49,999	73 703	73 703	-	-	-	46 565	46 565	-	-
10,000 TO 24,999	49 155	28 141	-	-	21 014	13 813	-	-	13 813
5,000 TO 9,999	8 187	-	-	-	8 187	6 138	-	-	6 138
2,500 TO 4,999	3 608	-	-	-	3 608	4 114	-	4 114	-
1,000 TO 2,499	3 568	1 944	-	-	1 624	5 821	2 819	-	3 002
LESS THAN 1,000	2 883	646	-	-	2 237	8 976	897	4 341	3 738
OUTSIDE MUNICIPALLY GOVERNED AREAS	393 549	294 582	-	58 188	40 779	77 798	19 589	44 912	13 297
IN TOWNSHIP-GOVERNED AREAS	-	-	-	-	-	-	-	-	-
ENROLLMENT OF PUBLIC SCHOOL SYSTEMS									
TOTAL	197 412	70 426	93 364	15 170	18 452	76 318	19 834	47 096	9 388
THROUGH GRADE 12	196 852	70 426	93 364	14 610	18 452	74 576	18 092	47 096	9 388
COLLEGE GRADES	560	-	-	560	-	1 742	1 742	-	-

Table 6. Local Governments and Public School Systems in Individual SMSA's: 1977—Continued

| Item | Maine | | Maryland (see also Delaware and District of Columbia) | | | | | | |
| | Lewiston-Auburn | Portland | Baltimore | | | | | | |
			Total	Anne Arundel County	Baltimore City*	Baltimore County	Carroll County	Harford County	Howard County
NUMBER OF LOCAL GOVERNMENTS									
ALL TYPES, TOTAL	10	25	29	6	2	2	11	6	2
WITH PROPERTY-TAXING POWER	3	18	19	3	1	1	9	4	1
WITHOUT PROPERTY-TAXING POWER	7	7	10	3	1	1	2	2	1
COUNTY GOVERNMENTS	-	-	5	1	-	1	1	1	1
MUNICIPALITIES	2	4	14	2	1	-	8	3	-
WITH A POPULATION OF--									
50,000 OR MORE	-	1	1	-	1	-	-	-	-
25,000 TO 49,999	1	-	1	1	-	-	-	-	-
10,000 TO 24,999	1	3	2	-	-	-	1	2	-
5,000 TO 9,999	-	-	2	-	-	-	1	1	-
2,500 TO 4,999	-	-	1	-	-	-	1	-	-
1,000 TO 2,499	-	-	5	-	-	-	5	-	-
LESS THAN 1,000	-	-	2	1	-	-	1	-	-
TOWNSHIP GOVERNMENTS	1	9	-	-	-	-	-	-	-
SCHOOL DISTRICTS	-	2	-	-	-	-	-	-	-
SPECIAL DISTRICTS	7	10	10	3	1	1	2	2	1
WITH PROPERTY-TAXING POWER	-	3	-	-	-	-	-	-	-
SINGLE FUNCTION DISTRICTS	-	-	-	-	-	-	-	-	-
CEMETERIES	-	-	-	-	-	-	-	-	-
EDUCATION (SCHOOL BUILDING DISTRICTS)	-	-	-	-	-	-	-	-	-
FIRE PROTECTION	-	-	-	-	-	-	-	-	-
HIGHWAYS	-	-	-	-	-	-	-	-	-
HEALTH	-	-	-	-	-	-	-	-	-
HOSPITALS	-	-	-	-	-	-	-	1	-
HOUSING AND URBAN RENEWAL	2	3	4	2	1	-	-	-	-
LIBRARIES	-	-	-	-	-	-	-	-	-
NATURAL RESOURCES, TOTAL	1	1	5	1	-	1	1	1	1
DRAINAGE	-	-	-	-	-	-	-	-	-
FLOOD CONTROL	-	-	-	-	-	-	-	-	-
IRRIGATION, WATER CONSERVATION	-	-	-	-	-	-	-	-	-
SOIL CONSERVATION	1	1	5	1	-	1	1	1	1
OTHER AND COMPOSITE PURPOSES	-	-	-	-	-	-	-	-	-
PARKS AND RECREATION	-	-	-	-	-	-	-	-	-
SEWERAGE	2	2	-	-	-	-	-	-	-
UTILITIES, TOTAL	2	4	-	-	-	-	-	-	-
WATER SUPPLY	2	3	-	-	-	-	-	-	-
ELECTRIC POWER	-	-	-	-	-	-	-	-	-
GAS SUPPLY	-	-	-	-	-	-	-	-	-
TRANSIT	-	1	-	-	-	-	-	-	-
OTHER	-	-	-	-	-	-	-	-	-
MULTIPLE-FUNCTION DISTRICTS	-	-	1	-	-	-	1	-	-
SEWERAGE AND WATER SUPPLY	-	-	1	-	-	-	1	-	-
NATURAL RESOURCES AND WATER SUPPLY	-	-	-	-	-	-	-	-	-
OTHER	-	-	-	-	-	-	-	-	-
SCHOOL SYSTEMS									
TOTAL	3	14	14	2	2	5	1	2	2
DEPENDENT SCHOOL SYSTEMS	3	12	14	2	2	5	1	2	2
BY ENROLLMENT SIZE OCTOBER 1976									
100,000 OR MORE PUPILS	-	-	2	-	1	1	-	-	-
50,000 TO 99,999 PUPILS	-	-	1	1	-	-	-	-	-
25,000 TO 49,999 PUPILS	-	-	1	-	-	-	-	1	-
12,000 TO 24,999 PUPILS	-	1	2	-	-	1	-	-	1
6,000 TO 11,999 PUPILS	2	1	5	1	1	3	-	1	-
3,000 TO 5,999 PUPILS	-	2	1	1	-	-	-	-	1
1,200 TO 2,999 PUPILS	1	10	2	-	-	1	-	-	-
300 TO 1,199 PUPILS	-	1	-	-	-	-	-	-	-
50 TO 299 PUPILS	-	-	-	-	-	-	-	-	-
1 TO 49 PUPILS	-	-	-	-	-	-	-	-	-
POPULATION, 1975 (ESTIMATED)									
TOTAL	72 114	181 246	2 147 850	344 056	851 698	637 114	80 607	136 381	97 994
IN MUNICIPALLY GOVERNED AREAS	64 349	115 952	938 869	32 464	851 698	-	20 324	34 383	-
WITH A 1975 POPULATION OF--									
50,000 OR MORE	-	65 785	851 698	-	851 698	-	-	-	-
25,000 TO 49,999	41 045	-	32 458	32 458	-	-	-	-	-
10,000 TO 24,999	23 304	50 167	25 135	-	-	-	-	25 135	-
5,000 TO 9,999	-	-	17 873	-	-	-	8 625	9 248	-
2,500 TO 4,999	-	-	2 543	-	-	-	2 543	-	-
1,000 TO 2,499	-	-	8 176	-	-	-	8 176	-	-
LESS THAN 1,000	-	-	986	6	-	-	980	-	-
OUTSIDE MUNICIPALLY GOVERNED AREAS	7 765	65 294	1 208 981	311 592	-	637 114	60 283	101 998	97 994
IN TOWNSHIP-GOVERNED AREAS	7 765	65 294	-	-	-	-	-	-	-
ENROLLMENT OF PUBLIC SCHOOL SYSTEMS									
TOTAL	16 511	38 583	486 628	83 826	169 663	149 351	19 763	37 347	26 678
THROUGH GRADE 12	16 511	38 583	434 651	77 282	160 212	118 792	19 763	33 947	24 655
COLLEGE GRADES	-	-	51 977	6 544	9 451	30 559	-	3 400	2 023

52

Table 6. Local Governments and Public School Systems in Individual SMSA's: 1977—Continued

Item	Boston	Brockton	Fall River Total	Fall River Massachusetts portion*	Fall River Rhode Island portion*	Fitchburg-Leominster	Lawrence-Haverhill Total	Lawrence-Haverhill Massachusetts portion*	Lawrence-Haverhill New Hampshire portion*
NUMBER OF LOCAL GOVERNMENTS									
ALL TYPES, TOTAL	190	18	19	11	8	12	27	20	7
WITH PROPERTY-TAXING POWER	107	10	13	7	6	9	19	12	7
WITHOUT PROPERTY-TAXING POWER	83	8	6	4	2	3	8	8	-
COUNTY GOVERNMENTS	-	-	-	-	-	-	-	-	-
MUNICIPALITIES	17	1	1	1	-	2	2	2	-
WITH A POPULATION OF--									
50,000 OR MORE	9	1	1	1	-	-	1	1	-
25,000 TO 49,999	7	-	-	-	-	2	1	1	-
10,000 TO 24,999	1	-	-	-	-	-	-	-	-
5,000 TO 9,999	-	-	-	-	-	-	-	-	-
2,500 TO 4,999	-	-	-	-	-	-	-	-	-
1,000 TO 2,499	-	-	-	-	-	-	-	-	-
LESS THAN 1,000	-	-	-	-	-	-	-	-	-
TOWNSHIP GOVERNMENTS	75	7	7	4	3	4	16	9	7
SCHOOL DISTRICTS	9	2	-	-	-	2	-	-	-
SPECIAL DISTRICTS	89	8	11	6	5	4	9	9	-
WITH PROPERTY-TAXING POWER	6	-	5	2	3	1	1	1	-
SINGLE FUNCTION DISTRICTS	-	-	-	-	-	-	-	-	-
CEMETERIES	-	-	-	-	-	-	-	-	-
EDUCATION (SCHOOL BUILDING DISTRICTS)	1	-	-	-	-	-	-	-	-
FIRE PROTECTION	1	-	1	1	-	-	-	-	-
HIGHWAYS	-	-	-	-	-	-	-	-	-
HEALTH	-	-	-	-	-	-	-	-	-
HOSPITALS	-	-	-	-	-	-	-	-	-
HOUSING AND URBAN RENEWAL	77	7	6	4	2	3	8	8	-
LIBRARIES	-	-	-	-	-	-	-	-	-
NATURAL RESOURCES, TOTAL	1	1	-	-	-	-	-	-	-
DRAINAGE	-	-	-	-	-	-	-	-	-
FLOOD CONTROL	-	-	-	-	-	-	-	-	-
IRRIGATION, WATER CONSERVATION	-	-	-	-	-	-	-	-	-
SOIL CONSERVATION	1	1	-	-	-	-	-	-	-
OTHER AND COMPOSITE PURPOSES	-	-	-	-	-	-	-	-	-
PARKS AND RECREATION	-	-	-	-	-	-	-	-	-
SEWERAGE	3	-	-	-	-	-	-	-	-
UTILITIES, TOTAL	7	-	3	-	3	1	1	1	-
WATER SUPPLY	5	-	3	-	3	1	1	1	-
ELECTRIC POWER	-	-	-	-	-	-	-	-	-
GAS SUPPLY	-	-	-	-	-	-	-	-	-
TRANSIT	2	-	-	-	-	-	-	-	-
OTHER	-	-	-	-	-	-	-	-	-
MULTIPLE-FUNCTION DISTRICTS	-	-	1	1	-	-	-	-	-
SEWERAGE AND WATER SUPPLY	-	-	-	-	-	-	-	-	-
NATURAL RESOURCES AND WATER SUPPLY	-	-	-	-	-	-	-	-	-
OTHER	-	-	1	1	-	-	-	-	-
SCHOOL SYSTEMS									
TOTAL	99	9	10	8	2	7	14	11	3
DEPENDENT SCHOOL SYSTEMS	90	7	10	8	2	5	14	11	-
BY ENROLLMENT SIZE OCTOBER 1976									
100,000 OR MORE PUPILS	-	-	-	-	-	-	-	-	-
50,000 TO 99,999 PUPILS	1	-	-	-	-	-	-	-	-
25,000 TO 49,999 PUPILS	-	-	-	-	-	-	-	-	-
12,000 TO 24,999 PUPILS	5	1	1	1	-	-	-	-	-
6,000 TO 11,999 PUPILS	22	-	-	-	-	2	4	4	-
3,000 TO 5,999 PUPILS	37	-	5	4	1	1	2	1	1
1,200 TO 2,999 PUPILS	20	7	1	1	-	1	2	2	-
300 TO 1,199 PUPILS	13	1	3	2	1	3	6	4	2
50 TO 299 PUPILS	1	-	-	-	-	-	-	-	-
1 TO 49 PUPILS	-	-	-	-	-	-	-	-	-
POPULATION, 1975 (ESTIMATED)									
TOTAL	2 890 368	163 260	183 183	152 767	30 416	97 201	270 129	226 335	43 794
IN MUNICIPALLY GOVERNED AREAS	1 545 816	95 878	100 430	100 430	-	74 469	111 767	111 767	-
WITH A 1975 POPULATION OF--									
50,000 OR MORE	1 252 121	95 878	100 430	100 430	-	-	67 390	67 390	-
25,000 TO 49,999	268 979	-	-	-	-	74 469	44 377	44 377	-
10,000 TO 24,999	24 716	-	-	-	-	-	-	-	-
5,000 TO 9,999	-	-	-	-	-	-	-	-	-
2,500 TO 4,999	-	-	-	-	-	-	-	-	-
1,000 TO 2,499	-	-	-	-	-	-	-	-	-
LESS THAN 1,000	-	-	-	-	-	-	-	-	-
OUTSIDE MUNICIPALLY GOVERNED AREAS	1 344 552	67 382	82 753	52 337	30 416	22 732	158 362	114 568	43 794
IN TOWNSHIP-GOVERNED AREAS	1 344 552	67 382	82 753	52 337	30 416	22 732	158 362	114 568	43 794
ENROLLMENT OF PUBLIC SCHOOL SYSTEMS									
TOTAL	539 984	35 093	36 932	33 008	3 924	20 939	48 405	41 524	6 881
THROUGH GRADE 12	534 270	35 093	36 932	33 008	3 924	20 939	48 405	41 524	6 881
COLLEGE GRADES	5 714	-	-	-	-	-	-	-	-

53

Item	Lowell Total	Lowell Massachusetts portion*	Lowell New Hampshire portion	New Bedford	Pittsfield	Springfield-Chicopee-Holyoke Total	Springfield-Chicopee-Holyoke Massachusetts portion*	Springfield-Chicopee-Holyoke Connecticut portion	Worcester	Ann Arbor Washtenaw County (entire SMSA)
NUMBER OF LOCAL GOVERNMENTS										
ALL TYPES, TOTAL	16	14	2	16	19	54	53	1	59	45
WITH PROPERTY-TAXING POWER	10	8	2	10	14	29	28	1	39	41
WITHOUT PROPERTY-TAXING POWER	6	6	-	6	5	25	25	-	20	4
COUNTY GOVERNMENTS	-	-	-	-	-	-	-	-	-	1
MUNICIPALITIES	1	1	-	1	1	5	5	-	1	8
WITH A POPULATION OF--										
50,000 OR MORE	1	1	-	1	1	2	2	-	1	1
25,000 TO 49,999	-	-	-	-	-	2	2	-	-	1
10,000 TO 24,999	-	-	-	-	-	-	-	-	-	-
5,000 TO 9,999	-	-	-	-	-	1	1	-	-	1
2,500 TO 4,999	-	-	-	-	-	-	-	-	-	2
1,000 TO 2,499	-	-	-	-	-	-	-	-	-	2
LESS THAN 1,000	-	-	-	-	-	-	-	-	-	1
TOWNSHIP GOVERNMENTS	7	6	1	7	7	19	18	1	24	20
SCHOOL DISTRICTS	1	-	1	1	3	1	1	-	6	11
SPECIAL DISTRICTS	7	7	-	7	8	29	29	-	28	5
WITH PROPERTY-TAXING POWER	1	1	-	1	3	4	4	-	8	1
SINGLE FUNCTION DISTRICTS	-	-	-	-	-	-	-	-	-	-
CEMETERIES	-	-	-	-	-	-	-	-	-	-
EDUCATION (SCHOOL BUILDING DISTRICTS)	-	-	-	-	-	-	-	-	-	-
FIRE PROTECTION	-	-	-	1	2	3	3	-	-	-
HIGHWAYS	-	-	-	-	-	-	-	-	-	-
HEALTH	-	-	-	-	-	-	-	-	-	-
HOSPITALS	-	-	-	-	-	-	-	-	-	1
HOUSING AND URBAN RENEWAL	6	6	-	4	3	22	22	-	14	-
LIBRARIES	-	-	-	-	-	-	-	-	-	-
NATURAL RESOURCES, TOTAL	-	-	-	-	1	2	2	-	3	1
DRAINAGE	-	-	-	-	~	-	-	-	-	-
FLOOD CONTROL	-	-	-	-	-	-	-	-	-	-
IRRIGATION, WATER CONSERVATION	-	-	-	-	-	-	-	-	-	-
SOIL CONSERVATION	-	-	-	-	1	2	2	-	3	1
OTHER AND COMPOSITE PURPOSES	-	-	-	-	-	-	-	-	-	-
PARKS AND RECREATION	-	-	-	-	-	-	-	-	-	-
SEWERAGE	-	-	-	-	-	-	-	-	-	-
UTILITIES, TOTAL	1	1	-	1	2	2	2	-	10	-
WATER SUPPLY	1	1	-	-	2	1	1	-	10	-
ELECTRIC POWER	-	-	-	-	-	1	1	-	-	-
GAS SUPPLY	-	-	-	-	-	-	-	-	-	-
TRANSIT	-	-	-	1	-	-	-	-	-	-
OTHER	-	-	-	1	-	-	-	-	-	-
MULTIPLE-FUNCTION DISTRICTS	-	-	-	-	-	-	-	-	1	3
SEWERAGE AND WATER SUPPLY	-	-	-	-	-	-	-	-	1	3
NATURAL RESOURCES AND WATER SUPPLY	-	-	-	-	-	-	-	-	-	-
OTHER	-	-	-	-	-	-	-	-	-	-
SCHOOL SYSTEMS										
TOTAL	7	6	1	9	7	26	25	1	29	11
DEPENDENT SCHOOL SYSTEMS	6	6	-	8	4	25	24	1	23	-
BY ENROLLMENT SIZE OCTOBER 1976										
100,000 OR MORE PUPILS	-	-	-	-	-	-	-	-	-	-
50,000 TO 99,999 PUPILS	-	-	-	-	-	-	-	-	-	-
25,000 TO 49,999 PUPILS	-	-	-	-	-	1	1	-	1	-
12,000 TO 24,999 PUPILS	1	1	-	1	-	-	-	-	-	1
6,000 TO 11,999 PUPILS	3	3	-	-	1	3	3	-	-	2
3,000 TO 5,999 PUPILS	1	1	-	2	-	7	7	-	3	2
1,200 TO 2,999 PUPILS	2	1	1	1	4	9	8	1	15	5
300 TO 1,199 PUPILS	-	-	-	5	2	5	5	-	9	1
50 TO 299 PUPILS	-	-	-	-	-	1	1	-	1	-
1 TO 49 PUPILS	-	-	-	-	-	-	-	-	-	-
POPULATION, 1975 (ESTIMATED)										
TOTAL	229 446	222 167	7 279	166 841	94 288	549 211	541 917	7 294	378 193	244 724
IN MUNICIPALLY GOVERNED AREAS	91 493	91 493	-	100 133	54 893	339 341	339 341	-	171 566	148 978
WITH A 1975 POPULATION OF										
50,000 OR MORE	91 493	91 493	-	100 133	54 893	228 561	228 561	-	171 566	103 542
25,000 TO 49,999	-	-	-	-	-	110 780	110 780	-	-	26 745
10,000 TO 24,999	-	-	-	-	-	-	-	-	-	-
5,000 TO 9,999	-	-	-	-	-	-	-	-	-	6 313
2,500 TO 4,999	-	-	-	-	-	-	-	-	-	8 304
1,000 TO 2,499	-	-	-	-	-	-	-	-	-	3 630
LESS THAN 1,000	-	-	-	-	-	-	-	-	-	444
OUTSIDE MUNICIPALLY GOVERNED AREAS	137 953	130 674	7 279	66 708	39 395	209 870	202 576	7 294	206 627	95 746
IN TOWNSHIP-GOVERNED AREAS	137 953	130 674	7 279	66 708	39 395	209 870	202 576	7 294	206 627	103 599
ENROLLMENT OF PUBLIC SCHOOL SYSTEMS										
TOTAL	48 394	46 494	1 900	28 765	22 561	105 649	103 924	1 725	75 017	52 268
THROUGH GRADE 12	48 394	46 494	1 900	28 765	22 561	105 649	103 924	1 725	75 017	45 568
COLLEGE GRADES	-	-	-	-	-	-	-	-	-	6 700

Massachusetts (see also Rhode Island)--Continued

Michigan (see also Ohio)

Table 6. Local Governments and Public School Systems in Individual SMSA's: 1977—Continued

	Michigan (see also Ohio)--Continued										
	Battle Creek			Bay City	Detroit						
Item	Total	Barry County	Calhoun County*	Bay County (entire SMSA)	Total	Lapeer County	Livingston County	Macomb County	Oakland County	St. Clair County	Wayne County*
NUMBER OF LOCAL GOVERNMENTS											
ALL TYPES, TOTAL	70	26	44	29	349	36	30	54	94	42	93
WITH PROPERTY-TAXING POWER	68	25	43	25	327	34	26	50	90	41	86
WITHOUT PROPERTY-TAXING POWER.	2	1	1	4	22	2	4	4	4	1	7
COUNTY GOVERNMENTS	2	1	1	1	6	1	1	1	1	1	1
MUNICIPALITIES	13	5	8	4	107	9	4	15	37	8	34
WITH A POPULATION OF--											
50,000 OR MORE	-	-	-	-	15	-	-	4	5	-	6
25,000 TO 49,999	1	-	1	1	15	-	-	1	3	1	10
10,000 TO 24,999	1	-	1	-	20	-	-	2	7	-	11
5,000 TO 9,999	3	1	2	1	15	1	1	2	5	3	3
2,500 TO 4,999	-	-	-	-	19	-	1	3	10	1	4
1,000 TO 2,499	4	2	2	2	14	3	2	3	4	2	-
LESS THAN 1,000.	4	2	2	-	9	5	-	-	3	1	-
TOWNSHIP GOVERNMENTS	36	16	20	14	102	18	16	12	23	23	10
SCHOOL DISTRICTS	17	3	14	5	108	6	5	22	29	8	38
SPECIAL DISTRICTS.	2	1	1	5	26	2	4	4	4	2	10
WITH PROPERTY-TAXING POWER	-	-	-	1	4	-	-	-	-	1	3
SINGLE FUNCTION DISTRICTS.											
CEMETERIES	-	-	-	-	-	-	-	-	-	-	-
EDUCATION (SCHOOL BUILDING DISTRICTS). . .	-	-	-	-	-	-	-	-	-.	-	-
FIRE PROTECTION	-	-	-	-	-	-	-	-	-	-	-
HIGHWAYS	-	-	-	-	-	-	-	-	-	-	-
HEALTH	-	-	-	-	-	-	-	-	-	-	-
HOSPITALS.	-	-	-	-	5	-	-	-	1	1	3
HOUSING AND URBAN RENEWAL.	-	-	-	-	-	-	-	-	-	-	-
LIBRARIES.	-	-	-	-	-	-	-	-	-	-	-
NATURAL RESOURCES, TOTAL	2	1	1	1	8	1	3	1	1	1	1
DRAINAGE	-	-	-	-	-	-	-	-	-	-	-
FLOOD CONTROL.	-	-	-	-	-	-	-	-	-	-	-
IRRIGATION, WATER CONSERVATION	-	-	-	-	-	-	-	-	-	-	-
SOIL CONSERVATION.	2	1	1	1	8	1	3	1	1	1	1
OTHER AND COMPOSITE PURPOSES	-	-	-	-	-	-	-	-	-	-	-
PARKS AND RECREATION	-	-	-	-	1	-	-	-	-	-	1
SEWERAGE	-	-	-	-	3	-	1	1	-	-	1
UTILITIES, TOTAL	-	-	-	4	2	-	-	-	1	-	1
WATER SUPPLY	-	-	-	3	1	-	-	-	1	-	1
ELECTRIC POWER	-	-	-	-	-	-	-	-	-	-	-
GAS SUPPLY	-	-	-	-	-	-	-	-	-	-	-
TRANSIT.	-	-	-	1	1	-	-	-	-	-	1
OTHER.	-	-	-	-	5	-	-	2	1	-	2
MULTIPLE-FUNCTION DISTRICTS.											
SEWERAGE AND WATER SUPPLY.	-	-	-	-	2	1	-	-	-	-	1
NATURAL RESOURCES AND WATER SUPPLY . . .	-	-	-	-	2	1	-	-	-	-	1
OTHER.	-	-	-	-	-	-	-	-	-	-	-
SCHOOL SYSTEMS											
TOTAL.	17	3	14	5	108	6	5	22	29	8	38
DEPENDENT SCHOOL SYSTEMS	-	-	-	-	-	-	-	-	-	-	-
BY ENROLLMENT SIZE OCTOBER 1976											
100,000 OR MORE PUPILS	-	-	-	-	1	-	-	-	-	-	1
50,000 TO 99,999 PUPILS.	-	-	-	-	-	-	-	-	-	-	-
25,000 TO 49,999 PUPILS.	-	-	-	-	4	-	-	2	-	-	2
12,000 TO 24,999 PUPILS.	-	-	-	1	13	-	-	1	7	1	4
6,000 TO 11,999 PUPILS	2	-	2	1	30	1	1	7	10	-	11
3,000 TO 5,999 PUPILS.	5	1	4	1	37	-	2	9	10	2	14
1,200 TO 2,999 PUPILS.	5	2	3	1	21	3	2	3	2	5	6
300 TO 1,199 PUPILS.	3	-	3	-	1	1	-	-	-	-	-
50 TO 299 PUPILS	-	-	-	-	-	-	-	-	-	-	-
1 TO 49 PUPILS	2	-	2	1	1	1	-	-	-	-	-
POPULATION, 1975 (ESTIMATED)											
TOTAL.	184 928	41 430	143 498	120 099	4 431 014	61 985	77 714	669 813	972 916	130 749	2 517 837
IN MUNICIPALLY GOVERNED AREAS.	87 047	12 571	174 476	156 193	3 603 736	14 429	14 178	1517 063	1647 089	159 876	2 351 101
WITH A 1975 POPULATION OF--											
50,000 OR MORE	-	-	-	-	2 548 048	-	-	403 762	346 780	-	1 797 506
25,000 TO 49,999	43 338	-	43 338	47 215	527 464	-	-	42 693	98 604	35 739	350 428
10,000 TO 24,999	14 033	-	14 033	-	328 346	-	-	37 218	121 452	-	169 676
5,000 TO 9,999	19 669	7 055	12 614	5 395	99 092	5 761	7 330	15 946	34 285	16 493	19 277
2,500 TO 4,999	-	-	-	-	72 249	-	3 241	-	38 194	4 147	14 214
1,000 TO 2,499	7 497	4 258	3 239	3 583	23 019	5 132	3 607	4 991	6 164	3 125	-
LESS THAN 1,000.	2 510	1 258	1 252	-	5 518	3 536	-	-	1 610	372	-
OUTSIDE MUNICIPALLY GOVERNED AREAS	97 881	28 859	69 022	63 906	827 278	47 556	63 536	152 750	325 827	70 873	166 736
IN TOWNSHIP-GOVERNED AREAS	106 275	34 377	71 898	63 609	894 801	54 121	67 142	161 469	366 059	72 289	173 721
ENROLLMENT OF PUBLIC SCHOOL SYSTEMS											
TOTAL.	45 395	8 593	36 802	29 987	1 031 022	15 394	18 884	195 244	239 060	34 616	527 824
THROUGH GRADE 12	38 873	8 593	30 280	20 987	941 950	15 394	18 884	170 340	220 660	30 124	486 548
COLLEGE GRADES	6 522		6 522	9 000	89 072			24 904	18 400	4 492	41 276

55

Item	Michigan (see also Ohio)--Continued						
	Flint			Grand Rapids			Jackson
	Total	Genesee County*	Shiawassee County	Total	Kent County*	Ottawa County	Jackson County (entire SMSA)
NUMBER OF LOCAL GOVERNMENTS							
ALL TYPES, TOTAL	93	55	38	93	56	37	41
WITH PROPERTY-TAXING POWER	90	54	36	90	54	36	40
WITHOUT PROPERTY-TAXING POWER.	3	1	2	3	2	1	1
COUNTY GOVERNMENTS	2	1	1	2	1	1	1
MUNICIPALITIES	25	14	11	20	13	7	7
WITH A POPULATION OF--							
50,000 OR MORE	1	1	-	2	2	-	-
25,000 TO 49,999	1	1	-	2	1	1	1
10,000 TO 24,999	1	-	1	4	3	1	-
5,000 TO 9,999	5	5	-	1	-	1	-
2,500 TO 4,999	4	2	2	5	3	2	-
1,000 TO 2,499	6	3	3	3	1	2	4
LESS THAN 1,000.	7	2	5	3	3	-	2
TOWNSHIP GOVERNMENTS	33	17	16	38	21	17	19
SCHOOL DISTRICTS	30	22	8	28	19	9	13
SPECIAL DISTRICTS.	3	1	2	5	2	3	1
WITH PROPERTY-TAXING POWER	-	-	-	2	-	2	-
SINGLE FUNCTION DISTRICTS.	-	-	-	-	-	-	-
CEMETERIES	-	-	-	-	-	-	-
EDUCATION (SCHOOL BUILDING DISTRICTS). . .	-	-	-	-	-	-	-
FIRE PROTECTION.	-	-	-	-	-	-	-
HIGHWAYS	-	-	-	-	-	-	-
HEALTH	-	-	-	-	-	-	-
HOSPITALS.	-	-	-	1	-	1	-
HOUSING AND URBAN RENEWAL.	-	-	-	-	-	-	-
LIBRARIES.	-	-	-	-	-	-	-
NATURAL RESOURCES, TOTAL	2	1	1	3	2	1	1
DRAINAGE	-	-	-	-	-	-	-
FLOOD CONTROL.	-	-	-	-	-	-	-
IRRIGATION, WATER CONSERVATION	-	-	-	-	-	-	-
SOIL CONSERVATION.	2	1	1	3	2	1	1
OTHER AND COMPOSITE PURPOSES	-	-	-	-	-	-	-
PARKS AND RECREATION	-	-	-	-	-	-	-
SEWERAGE	-	-	-	1	-	1	-
UTILITIES, TOTAL	-	-	-	-	-	-	-
WATER SUPPLY	-	-	-	-	-	-	-
ELECTRIC POWER	-	-	-	-	-	-	-
GAS SUPPLY	-	-	-	-	-	-	-
TRANSIT.	-	-	-	-	-	-	-
OTHER.	1	-	1	-	-	-	-
MULTIPLE-FUNCTION DISTRICTS.	-	-	-	-	-	-	-
SEWERAGE AND WATER SUPPLY.	-	-	-	-	-	-	-
NATURAL RESOURCES AND WATER SUPPLY . . .	-	-	-	-	-	-	-
OTHER.	-	-	-	-	-	-	-
SCHOOL SYSTEMS							
TOTAL.	30	22	8	28	19	9	13
DEPENDENT SCHOOL SYSTEMS	-	-	-	-	-	-	-
BY ENROLLMENT SIZE OCTOBER 1976							
100,000 OR MORE PUPILS	-	-	-	-	-	-	-
50,000 TO 99,999 PUPILS.	-	-	-	-	-	-	-
25,000 TO 49,999 PUPILS.	1	1	-	1	1	-	-
12,000 TO 24,999 PUPILS.	-	-	-	-	-	-	-
6,000 TO 11,999 PUPILS	4	3	1	2	2	-	2
3,000 TO 5,999 PUPILS.	10	9	1	10	6	4	1
1,200 TO 2,999 PUPILS.	12	8	4	13	9	4	8
300 TO 1,199 PUPILS.	3	1	2	2	1	1	2
50 TO 299 PUPILS	-	-	-	-	-	-	-
1 TO 49 PUPILS	-	-	-	-	-	-	-
POPULATION, 1975 (ESTIMATED)							
TOTAL.	518 736	449 518	69 218	564 157	423 601	140 556	146 542
IN MUNICIPALLY GOVERNED AREAS.	291 752	[1]257 656	34 096	379 443	[1]322 489	56 954	[1]50 040
WITH A 1976 POPULATION OF--							
50,000 OR MORE	174 218	174 218	-	245 864	245 864	-	-
25,000 TO 49,999	33 762	33 762	-	53 317	25 113	28 204	43 994
10,000 TO 24,999	17 903	-	17 903	49 739	37 624	12 115	-
5,000 TO 9,999	36 199	36 199	-	5 293	-	5 293	-
2,500 TO 4,999	14 292	6 784	7 508	16 416	9 562	6 854	-
1,000 TO 2,499	10 104	5 313	4 791	6 725	2 237	4 488	4 582
LESS THAN 1,000.	5 274	1 380	3 894	2 089	2 089	-	1 464
OUTSIDE MUNICIPALLY GOVERNED AREAS	226 984	191 862	35 122	184 714	101 112	83 602	96 502
IN TOWNSHIP-GOVERNED AREAS	238 673	198 555	40 118	196 457	106 450	90 007	102 547
ENROLLMENT OF PUBLIC SCHOOL SYSTEMS							
TOTAL.	144 098	124 906	19 192	124 862	94 563	30 299	40 847
THROUGH GRADE 12	134 598	115 406	19 192	117 631	87 332	30 299	31 601
COLLEGE GRADES	9 500	9 500	-	7 231	7 231	-	9 246

Table 6. Local Governments and Public School Systems in Individual SMSA's: 1977—Continued

	Michigan (see also Ohio)--Continued							
	Kalamazoo-Portage			Lansing-East Lansing				
Item	Total	Kalamazoo County*	Van Buren County	Total	Clinton County	Eaton County	Ingham County*	Ionia County
NUMBER OF LOCAL GOVERNMENTS								
ALL TYPES, TOTAL	81	36	45	152	33	37	41	41
WITH PROPERTY-TAXING POWER	79	35	44	145	31	36	38	40
WITHOUT PROPERTY-TAXING POWER	2	1	1	7	2	1	3	1
COUNTY GOVERNMENTS	2	1	1	4	1	1	1	1
MUNICIPALITIES	20	9	11	36	8	10	8	10
WITH A POPULATION OF--								
50,000 OR MORE	1	1	-	2	-	-	2	-
25,000 TO 49,999	1	1	-	-	-	-	-	-
10,000 TO 24,999	-	-	-	-	-	-	-	-
5,000 TO 9,999	1	-	1	7	1	3	1	2
2,500 TO 4,999	2	-	2	2	-	-	1	1
1,000 TO 2,499	10	5	5	14	4	5	3	2
LESS THAN 1,000	5	2	3	11	3	2	1	5
TOWNSHIP GOVERNMENTS	33	15	18	64	16	16	16	16
SCHOOL DISTRICTS	22	10	12	41	6	9	13	13
SPECIAL DISTRICTS	4	1	3	7	2	1	3	1
WITH PROPERTY-TAXING POWER	2	-	2	-	-	-	-	-
SINGLE FUNCTION DISTRICTS								
CEMETERIES	-	-	-	-	-	-	-	-
EDUCATION (SCHOOL BUILDING DISTRICTS)	-	-	-	-	-	-	-	-
FIRE PROTECTION	-	-	-	-	-	-	-	-
HIGHWAYS	-	-	-	-	-	-	-	-
HEALTH	-	-	-	-	-	-	-	-
HOSPITALS	-	-	-	-	-	-	-	-
HOUSING AND URBAN RENEWAL	2	-	2	-	-	-	-	-
LIBRARIES	-	-	-	-	-	-	-	-
NATURAL RESOURCES, TOTAL	2	1	1	4	1	1	1	1
DRAINAGE	-	-	-	-	-	-	-	-
FLOOD CONTROL	-	-	-	-	-	-	-	-
IRRIGATION, WATER CONSERVATION	-	-	-	-	-	-	-	-
SOIL CONSERVATION	-	-	-	-	-	-	-	-
OTHER AND COMPOSITE PURPOSES	2	1	1	4	1	1	1	1
PARKS AND RECREATION	-	-	-	-	-	-	-	-
SEWERAGE	-	-	-	1	1	-	-	-
UTILITIES, TOTAL	-	-	-	-	-	-	-	-
WATER SUPPLY	-	-	-	-	-	-	-	-
ELECTRIC POWER	-	-	-	-	-	-	-	-
GAS SUPPLY	-	-	-	-	-	-	-	-
TRANSIT	-	-	-	-	-	-	-	-
OTHER	-	-	-	1	-	-	1	-
MULTIPLE-FUNCTION DISTRICTS								
SEWERAGE AND WATER SUPPLY	-	-	-	1	-	-	1	-
NATURAL RESOURCES AND WATER SUPPLY	-	-	-	1	-	-	1	-
OTHER	-	-	-	-	-	-	-	-
SCHOOL SYSTEMS								
TOTAL	22	10	12	41	6	9	13	13
DEPENDENT SCHOOL SYSTEMS	-	-	-	-	-	-	-	-
BY ENROLLMENT SIZE OCTOBER 1976								
100,000 OR MORE PUPILS	-	-	-	-	-	-	-	-
50,000 TO 99,999 PUPILS	-	-	-	-	-	-	-	-
25,000 TO 49,999 PUPILS	-	-	-	-	-	-	-	-
12,000 TO 24,999 PUPILS	1	1	-	1	-	-	1	-
6,000 TO 11,999 PUPILS	1	1	-	1	-	-	1	-
3,000 TO 5,999 PUPILS	4	3	1	10	1	3	5	1
1,200 TO 2,999 PUPILS	9	3	6	13	3	3	4	3
300 TO 1,199 PUPILS	6	2	4	6	2	1	2	1
50 TO 299 PUPILS	-	-	-	1	-	-	-	1
1 TO 49 PUPILS	1	-	1	9	-	2	-	7
POPULATION, 1975 (ESTIMATED)								
TOTAL	263 100	201 366	61 734	445 231	52 495	77 804	267 581	47 351
IN MUNICIPALLY GOVERNED AREAS	150 787	129 092	21 695	259 861	[1]15 651	[1]29 933	192 159	22 118
WITH A 1975 POPULATION OF--								
50,000 OR MORE	79 542	79 542	-	177 230	-	-	177 230	-
25,000 TO 49,999	38 641	38 641	-	-	-	-	-	-
10,000 TO 24,999	-	-	-	-	-	-	-	-
5,000 TO 9,999	6 108	-	6 108	47 236	7 756	21 511	6 050	11 919
2,500 TO 4,999	5 589	-	5 589	7 220	-	-	3 127	4 093
1,000 TO 2,499	17 669	9 185	8 484	22 110	6 170	7 288	5 220	3 432
LESS THAN 1,000	3 238	1 724	1 514	6 065	1 725	1 134	532	2 674
OUTSIDE MUNICIPALLY GOVERNED AREAS	112 313	72 274	40 039	185 370	36 844	47 871	75 422	25 233
IN TOWNSHIP-GOVERNED AREAS	129 321	79 137	50 184	205 483	42 396	51 574	80 175	31 338
ENROLLMENT OF PUBLIC SCHOOL SYSTEMS								
TOTAL	64 107	46 468	17 639	124 201	11 665	18 722	81 054	12 760
THROUGH GRADE 12	58 185	40 546	17 639	107 099	11 665	18 722	63 952	12 760
COLLEGE GRADES	5 922	5 922	-	17 102	-	-	17 102	-

57

Table 6. Local Governments and Public School Systems in Individual SMSA's: 1977—Continued

| Item | Michigan (see also Ohio)--Continued | | | | Minnesota (see also North Dakota) | | | |
| | Muskegon-Norton Shores-Muskegon Heights | | | Saginaw | Duluth-Superior | | | Minneapolis-St. Paul |
	Total	Muskegon County*	Oceana County	Saginaw County (entire SMSA)	Total	St. Louis County*	Douglas County* (Wis.)	Total
NUMBER OF LOCAL GOVERNMENTS								
ALL TYPES, TOTAL	75	45	30	54	151	124	27	406
WITH PROPERTY-TAXING POWER	71	42	29	50	150	124	26	403
WITHOUT PROPERTY-TAXING POWER	4	3	1	4	1	-	1	3
COUNTY GOVERNMENTS	2	1	1	1	2	1	1	10
MUNICIPALITIES	18	11	7	8	33	27	6	175
WITH A POPULATION OF--								
50,000 OR MORE	-	-	-	1	1	1	-	3
25,000 TO 49,999	1	1	-	-	1	-	1	13
10,000 TO 24,999	2	2	-	-	2	2	-	20
5,000 TO 9,999	-	-	-	-	2	2	-	20
2,500 TO 4,999	4	4	-	2	8	8	-	29
1,000 TO 2,499	6	2	4	4	2	2	-	33
LESS THAN 1,000	5	2	3	1	17	12	5	57
TOWNSHIP GOVERNMENTS	32	16	16	27	85	69	16	101
SCHOOL DISTRICTS	19	14	5	13	21	18	3	67
SPECIAL DISTRICTS	4	3	1	5	10	9	1	53
WITH PROPERTY-TAXING POWER	-	-	-	1	7	7		41
SINGLE FUNCTION DISTRICTS	-	-	-	-	-	-	-	-
CEMETERIES	-	-	-	-	-	-	-	-
EDUCATION (SCHOOL BUILDING DISTRICTS)	-	-	-	-	-	-	-	-
FIRE PROTECTION	-	-	-	-	-	-	-	-
HIGHWAYS	-	-	-	-	-	-	-	1
HEALTH	-	-	-	-	-	-	-	4
HOSPITALS	-	-	-	-	-	-	-	-
HOUSING AND URBAN RENEWAL	-	-	-	-	7	6	1	21
LIBRARIES	-	-	-	-	-	-	-	-
NATURAL RESOURCES, TOTAL	3	2	1	3	2	2	-	22
DRAINAGE	-	-	-	-	-	-	-	1
FLOOD CONTROL	-	-	-	-	-	-	-	10
IRRIGATION, WATER CONSERVATION	-	-	-	-	-	-	-	9
SOIL CONSERVATION	3	2	1	3	2	2	-	2
OTHER AND COMPOSITE PURPOSES	-	-	-	-	-	-	-	-
PARKS AND RECREATION	-	-	-	-	-	-	-	1
SEWERAGE	-	-	-	-	1	1	-	1
UTILITIES, TOTAL	-	-	-	1	-	-	-	1
WATER SUPPLY	-	-	-	1	-	-	-	-
ELECTRIC POWER	-	-	-	-	-	-	-	-
GAS SUPPLY	-	-	-	-	-	-	-	-
TRANSIT	-	-	-	-	-	-	-	1
OTHER	1	1	-	1	-	-	-	1
MULTIPLE-FUNCTION DISTRICTS	-	-	-	-	-	-	-	1
SEWERAGE AND WATER SUPPLY	-	-	-	-	-	-	-	-
NATURAL RESOURCES AND WATER SUPPLY	-	-	-	-	-	-	-	-
OTHER	-	-	-	-	-	-	-	1
SCHOOL SYSTEMS								
TOTAL	19	14	5	13	22	18	4	67
DEPENDENT SCHOOL SYSTEMS	-	-	-	-	1	1	1	-
BY ENROLLMENT SIZE OCTOBER 1976								
100,000 OR MORE PUPILS	-	-	-	-	-	-	-	-
50,000 TO 99,999 PUPILS	-	-	-	-	-	-	-	1
25,000 TO 49,999 PUPILS	-	-	-	-	-	-	-	2
12,000 TO 24,999 PUPILS	-	-	-	2	1	1	-	4
6,000 TO 11,999 PUPILS	1	1	-	1	1	1	1	15
3,000 TO 5,999 PUPILS	6	6	-	3	2	2	-	12
1,200 TO 2,999 PUPILS	6	4	2	7	10	8	2	23
300 TO 1,199 PUPILS	4	2	2	-	7	6	1	10
50 TO 299 PUPILS	2	1	1	-	1	1	-	-
1 TO 49 PUPILS	-	-	-	-	-	-	-	-
POPULATION, 1975 (ESTIMATED)								
TOTAL	178 309	157 646	20 663	226 682	260 599	216 220	44 379	2 010 880
IN MUNICIPALLY GOVERNED AREAS	106 418	98 831	7 587	99 623	202 010	169 221	32 789	1 884 634
WITH A 1975 POPULATION OF--								
50,000 OR MORE	-	-	-	86 202	93 971	93 971	-	736 857
25,000 TO 49,999	44 176	44 176	-	-	30 038	-	30 038	459 328
10,000 TO 24,999	37 039	37 039	-	-	27 711	27 711	-	350 364
5,000 TO 9,999	-	-	-	-	12 763	12 763	-	152 494
2,500 TO 4,999	14 067	14 067	-	6 616	28 023	28 023	-	106 169
1,000 TO 2,499	8 698	2 510	6 188	6 354	2 816	2 816	-	52 330
LESS THAN 1,000	2 438	1 039	1 399	451	6 688	3 937	2 751	27 092
OUTSIDE MUNICIPALLY GOVERNED AREAS	71 891	58 815	13 076	127 059	58 589	46 999	11 590	126 246
IN TOWNSHIP-GOVERNED AREAS	80 951	62 366	18 585	135 022	53 983	42 391	11 592	127 248
ENROLLMENT OF PUBLIC SCHOOL SYSTEMS								
TOTAL	46 805	42 287	4 518	65 169	60 051	48 647	11 404	434 980
THROUGH GRADE 12	42 155	37 637	4 518	65 169	57 731	48 647	9 084	434 980
COLLEGE GRADES	4 650	4 650	-	-	2 320	-	2 320	-

Table 6. Local Governments and Public School Systems in Individual SMSA's: 1977—Continued

Item	Minnesota (see also North Dakota)--Continued									
	Minneapolis-St. Paul									
	Anoka County	Carver County	Chisago County	Dakota County	Hennepin County*	Ramsey County*	Scott County	Washington County	Wright County	St. Croix County (Wis.)
NUMBER OF LOCAL GOVERNMENTS										
ALL TYPES, TOTAL	32	31	28	48	71	33	29	41	48	45
WITH PROPERTY-TAXING POWER	32	31	28	48	71	33	29	41	48	42
WITHOUT PROPERTY-TAXING POWER	-	-	-	-	-	-	-	-	-	3
COUNTY GOVERNMENTS	1	1	1	1	1	1	1	1	1	1
MUNICIPALITIES	17	12	11	20	42	15	8	23	15	12
WITH A POPULATION OF--										
50,000 OR MORE	-	-	-	-	2	1	-	-	-	-
25,000 TO 49,999	3	-	-	1	7	2	-	-	-	-
10,000 TO 24,999	2	-	-	6	5	5	-	2	-	-
5,000 TO 9,999	2	2	-	2	6	3	1	3	-	1
2,500 TO 4,999	5	-	-	2	8	1	3	7	2	1
1,000 TO 2,499	3	3	5	-	6	2	2	4	6	2
LESS THAN 1,000	2	7	6	9	8	1	2	7	7	8
TOWNSHIP GOVERNMENTS	4	11	10	13	1	1	11	9	20	21
SCHOOL DISTRICTS	6	4	4	9	16	5	5	4	8	6
SPECIAL DISTRICTS	4	3	2	5	11	11	4	4	4	5
WITH PROPERTY-TAXING POWER	3	2	1	4	10	10	3	3	3	2
SINGLE FUNCTION DISTRICTS										
CEMETERIES	-	-	-	-	-	-	-	-	-	-
EDUCATION (SCHOOL BUILDING DISTRICTS)	-	-	-	-	-	-	-	-	-	-
FIRE PROTECTION	-	-	-	-	-	-	-	-	-	-
HIGHWAYS	-	-	-	-	-	-	-	-	-	-
HEALTH	-	-	-	-	-	-	-	-	-	-
HOSPITALS	-	-	-	-	-	1	-	-	-	-
HOUSING AND URBAN RENEWAL	2	-	1	4	7	2	1	1	1	3
LIBRARIES	-	-	-	-	-	-	-	1	1	-
NATURAL RESOURCES, TOTAL	2	3	1	1	3	3	3	2	2	2
DRAINAGE	1	-	-	-	-	-	-	-	-	-
FLOOD CONTROL	-	2	-	-	-	-	-	-	-	-
IRRIGATION, WATER CONSERVATION	-	-	-	-	-	-	-	-	-	-
SOIL CONSERVATION	-	-	-	-	2	2	2	1	1	-
OTHER AND COMPOSITE PURPOSES	1	1	1	1	1	1	1	1	1	2
PARKS AND RECREATION	-	-	-	-	1	-	-	-	-	-
SEWERAGE	-	-	-	-	-	1	-	-	-	-
UTILITIES, TOTAL	-	-	-	-	-	1	-	-	-	-
WATER SUPPLY	-	-	-	-	-	1	-	-	-	-
ELECTRIC POWER	-	-	-	-	-	-	-	-	-	-
GAS SUPPLY	-	-	-	-	-	-	-	-	-	-
TRANSIT	-	-	-	-	-	1	-	-	-	-
OTHER	-	-	-	-	-	1	-	-	-	-
MULTIPLE-FUNCTION DISTRICTS										
SEWERAGE AND WATER SUPPLY	-	-	-	-	-	1	-	-	-	-
NATURAL RESOURCES AND WATER SUPPLY	-	-	-	-	-	-	-	-	-	-
OTHER	-	-	-	-	-	1	-	-	-	-
SCHOOL SYSTEMS										
TOTAL	6	4	4	9	16	5	5	4	8	6
DEPENDENT SCHOOL SYSTEMS	-	-	-	-	-	-	-	-	-	-
BY ENROLLMENT SIZE OCTOBER 1976										
100,000 OR MORE PUPILS	-	-	-	-	-	-	-	-	-	-
50,000 TO 99,999 PUPILS	-	-	-	-	-	-	-	-	-	-
25,000 TO 49,999 PUPILS	1	-	-	-	1	-	-	-	-	-
12,000 TO 24,999 PUPILS	-	-	-	-	-	1	-	-	-	-
6,000 TO 11,999 PUPILS	1	-	-	2	3	1	-	-	-	-
3,000 TO 5,999 PUPILS	4	1	-	5	6	3	-	3	-	-
1,200 TO 2,999 PUPILS	-	2	2	1	1	-	-	-	1	3
300 TO 1,199 PUPILS	-	1	2	1	5	-	4	1	5	3
50 TO 299 PUPILS	-	-	-	-	-	-	1	-	2	-
1 TO 49 PUPILS	-	-	-	-	-	-	-	-	-	-
POPULATION, 1975 (ESTIMATED)										
TOTAL	186 328	33 609	22 074	166 793	915 603	456 006	39 604	104 145	47 852	38 866
IN MUNICIPALLY GOVERNED AREAS	179 132	21 619	9 999	157 614	[1]915 603	[1]447 524	25 426	[1]90 604	[1]19 492	[1]17 621
WITH A 1975 POPULATION OF--										
50,000 OR MORE	-	-	-	-	457 322	279 535	-	-	-	-
25,000 TO 49,999	92 938	-	-	30 098	273 121	63 171	-	-	-	-
10,000 TO 24,999	45 633	-	-	99 256	94 244	78 730	-	32 501	-	-
5,000 TO 9,999	14 369	12 496	-	16 432	52 098	17 991	9 053	24 198	-	5 857
2,500 TO 4,999	20 636	-	-	9 175	25 516	3 788	11 098	25 316	6 811	3 829
1,000 TO 2,499	4 469	5 345	6 908	-	8 818	4 105	4 856	5 390	9 089	3 350
LESS THAN 1,000	1 087	3 778	3 091	2 653	4 484	204	419	3 199	3 592	4 585
OUTSIDE MUNICIPALLY GOVERNED AREAS	7 196	11 990	12 075	9 179	-	8 482	14 178	13 541	28 360	21 245
IN TOWNSHIP-GOVERNED AREAS	7 362	12 028	12 076	9 215	1 531	5 839	15 374	13 470	30 293	20 060
ENROLLMENT OF PUBLIC SCHOOL SYSTEMS										
TOTAL	58 669	7 046	5 793	47 152	170 037	86 564	10 152	27 393	13 156	9 018
THROUGH GRADE 12	58 669	7 046	5 793	47 152	170 037	86 564	10 152	27 393	13 156	9 018
COLLEGE GRADES	-	-	-	-	-	-	-	-	-	-

Item	Rochester — Olmsted County (entire SMSA)	St. Cloud — Total	Benton County	Sherburne County	Stearns County*	Biloxi-Gulfport — Total	Hancock County	Harrison County*	Stone County
NUMBER OF LOCAL GOVERNMENTS									
ALL TYPES, TOTAL	32	127	24	21	82	26	7	14	5
WITH PROPERTY-TAXING POWER	31	127	24	21	82	19	5	10	4
WITHOUT PROPERTY-TAXING POWER	1	-	-	-	-	7	2	4	1
COUNTY GOVERNMENTS	1	3	1	1	1	3	1	1	1
MUNICIPALITIES	6	39	5	5	29	7	2	4	1
WITH A POPULATION OF--									
50,000 OR MORE	1	-	-	-	-	-	-	-	-
25,000 TO 49,999	-	1	-	-	1	2	-	2	-
10,000 TO 24,999	-	-	-	-	-	2	1	1	-
5,000 TO 9,999	-	1	1	-	-	2	1	1	-
2,500 TO 4,999	1	5	-	1	4	3	1	1	1
1,000 TO 2,499	1	6	1	1	4	-	-	-	-
LESS THAN 1,000	3	26	3	3	20	-	-	-	-
TOWNSHIP GOVERNMENTS	18	60	12	11	37	-	-	-	-
SCHOOL DISTRICTS	5	16	2	3	11	9	2	5	2
SPECIAL DISTRICTS	2	9	4	1	4	7	2	4	1
WITH PROPERTY-TAXING POWER	-	6	3	-	3	-	-	-	-
SINGLE FUNCTION DISTRICTS	-	-	-	-	-	-	-	-	-
CEMETERIES	-	-	-	-	-	-	-	-	-
EDUCATION (SCHOOL BUILDING DISTRICTS)	-	-	-	-	-	-	-	-	-
FIRE PROTECTION	-	-	-	-	-	-	-	-	-
HIGHWAYS	-	-	-	-	-	-	-	-	-
HEALTH	-	-	-	-	-	-	-	-	-
HOSPITALS	-	5	2	-	3	3	1	2	-
HOUSING AND URBAN RENEWAL	-	-	-	-	-	-	-	-	-
LIBRARIES	-	-	-	-	-	-	-	-	-
NATURAL RESOURCES, TOTAL	1	3	1	1	1	3	1	1	1
DRAINAGE	-	-	-	-	-	-	-	-	-
FLOOD CONTROL	-	-	-	-	-	-	-	-	-
IRRIGATION, WATER CONSERVATION	-	-	-	-	-	-	-	-	-
SOIL CONSERVATION	1	3	1	1	1	3	1	1	1
OTHER AND COMPOSITE PURPOSES	-	-	-	-	-	-	-	-	-
PARKS AND RECREATION	1	-	-	-	-	-	-	-	-
SEWERAGE	-	-	-	-	-	-	-	-	-
UTILITIES, TOTAL	-	1	1	-	-	-	-	-	-
WATER SUPPLY	-	-	-	-	-	-	-	-	-
ELECTRIC POWER	-	-	-	-	-	-	-	-	-
GAS SUPPLY	-	-	-	-	-	-	-	-	-
TRANSIT	-	1	1	-	-	-	-	-	-
OTHER	-	-	-	-	-	1	-	1	-
MULTIPLE-FUNCTION DISTRICTS	-	-	-	-	-	-	-	-	-
SEWERAGE AND WATER SUPPLY	-	-	-	-	-	-	-	-	-
NATURAL RESOURCES AND WATER SUPPLY	-	-	-	-	-	-	-	-	-
OTHER	-	-	-	-	-	-	-	-	-
SCHOOL SYSTEMS									
TOTAL	5	16	2	3	11	9	2	5	2
DEPENDENT SCHOOL SYSTEMS	-	-	-	-	-	-	-	-	-
BY ENROLLMENT SIZE OCTOBER 1976									
100,000 OR MORE PUPILS	-	-	-	-	-	-	-	-	-
50,000 TO 99,999 PUPILS	-	-	-	-	-	-	-	-	-
25,000 TO 49,999 PUPILS	-	-	-	-	-	-	-	-	-
12,000 TO 24,999 PUPILS	1	1	-	-	1	-	-	-	-
6,000 TO 11,999 PUPILS	-	-	-	-	-	3	-	3	-
3,000 TO 5,999 PUPILS	-	1	-	1	-	2	-	1	1
1,200 TO 2,999 PUPILS	2	9	2	-	7	4	2	1	1
300 TO 1,199 PUPILS	2	5	-	2	3	-	-	-	-
50 TO 299 PUPILS	-	-	-	-	-	-	-	-	-
1 TO 49 PUPILS	-	-	-	-	-	-	-	-	-
POPULATION, 1975 (ESTIMATED)									
TOTAL	87 732	151 073	23 037	25 881	102 155	170 264	18 249	143 528	8 487
IN MUNICIPALLY GOVERNED AREAS	¹63 210	82 123	¹6 997	¹6 933	¹68 193	114 792	10 287	101 493	3 012
WITH A 1975 POPULATION OF--									
50,000 OR MORE	56 211	-	-	-	-	-	-	-	-
25,000 TO 49,999	-	40 621	-	-	40 621	89 533	-	89 533	-
10,000 TO 24,999	-	-	-	-	-	13 953	6 746	7 207	-
5,000 TO 9,999	-	5 219	5 219	-	-	-	-	-	-
2,500 TO 4,999	3 466	16 036	-	3 654	12 382	11 306	3 541	4 753	3 012
1,000 TO 2,499	1 867	10 578	1 148	1 584	7 846	-	-	-	-
LESS THAN 1,000	1 666	9 669	630	1 695	7 344	-	-	-	-
OUTSIDE MUNICIPALLY GOVERNED AREAS	24 522	68 950	16 040	18 948	33 962	55 472	7 962	42 035	5 475
IN TOWNSHIP-GOVERNED AREAS	23 825	72 900	11 827	15 139	45 934	-	-	-	-
ENROLLMENT OF PUBLIC SCHOOL SYSTEMS									
TOTAL	21 459	38 203	4 410	6 250	27 543	41 472	3 829	29 903	7 740
THROUGH GRADE 12	21 459	38 203	4 410	6 250	27 543	35 773	3 829	29 903	2 041
COLLEGE GRADES	-	-	-	-	-	5 699	-	-	5 699

Table 6. Local Governments and Public School Systems in Individual SMSA's: 1977—Continued

Item	Mississippi (see also Tennessee)--Continued			Pascagoula-Moss Point	Missouri				
	Jackson				Columbia	Kansas City			
	Total	Hinds County*	Rankin County	Jackson County	Boone County	Total	Cass County	Clay County	Jackson County*
NUMBER OF LOCAL GOVERNMENTS									
ALL TYPES, TOTAL	28	16	12	10	21	280	39	47	45
WITH PROPERTY-TAXING POWER	25	15	10	8	19	227	36	38	43
WITHOUT PROPERTY-TAXING POWER	3	1	2	2	2	53	3	9	2
COUNTY GOVERNMENTS	2	1	1	1	1	7	1	1	1
MUNICIPALITIES	15	8	7	3	8	107	17	21	18
WITH A POPULATION OF--									
50,000 OR MORE	1	1	-	-	1	4	-	-	2
25,000 TO 49,999	-	-	-	1	-	3	-	1	1
10,000 TO 24,999	2	1	1	2	-	12	1	2	3
5,000 TO 9,999	1	-	1	-	-	6	1	1	-
2,500 TO 4,999	1	-	1	-	1	7	1	-	2
1,000 TO 2,499	4	3	1	-	-	17	1	4	3
LESS THAN 1,000	6	3	3	-	6	58	13	13	7
TOWNSHIP GOVERNMENTS	-	-	-	-	-	11	-	-	-
SCHOOL DISTRICTS	6	5	1	4	8	53	12	7	13
SPECIAL DISTRICTS	5	2	3	2	4	102	9	18	13
WITH PROPERTY-TAXING POWER	2	1	1	-	2	49	6	9	11
SINGLE FUNCTION DISTRICTS	-	-	-	-	-	-	-	-	-
CEMETERIES	-	-	-	-	-	6	-	-	-
EDUCATION (SCHOOL BUILDING DISTRICTS)	-	-	-	-	-	-	-	-	-
FIRE PROTECTION	-	-	-	-	1	14	4	-	9
HIGHWAYS	-	-	-	-	1	19	1	5	-
HEALTH	-	-	-	-	-	1	-	-	-
HOSPITALS	-	-	-	-	-	1	-	1	-
HOUSING AND URBAN RENEWAL	-	-	-	1	1	4	-	2	-
LIBRARIES	-	-	-	-	1	3	1	1	-
NATURAL RESOURCES, TOTAL	4	1	3	1	-	21	1	2	-
DRAINAGE	1	-	1	-	-	12	1	1	-
FLOOD CONTROL	1	-	1	-	-	7	-	1	-
IRRIGATION, WATER CONSERVATION	-	-	-	-	-	-	-	-	-
SOIL CONSERVATION	2	1	1	1	-	2	-	-	-
OTHER AND COMPOSITE PURPOSES	-	-	-	-	-	-	-	-	-
PARKS AND RECREATION	-	-	-	-	-	2	-	-	1
SEWERAGE	-	-	-	-	-	-	-	-	-
UTILITIES, TOTAL	1	1	-	-	-	30	2	7	3
WATER SUPPLY	1	1	-	-	-	29	2	7	2
ELECTRIC POWER	-	-	-	-	-	-	-	-	-
GAS SUPPLY	-	-	-	-	-	-	-	-	-
TRANSIT	-	-	-	-	-	1	-	-	-
OTHER	-	-	-	-	-	-	-	-	-
MULTIPLE-FUNCTION DISTRICTS	-	-	-	-	-	1	-	-	-
SEWERAGE AND WATER SUPPLY	-	-	-	-	-	-	-	-	-
NATURAL RESOURCES AND WATER SUPPLY	-	-	-	-	-	-	-	-	-
OTHER	-	-	-	-	-	1	-	-	-
SCHOOL SYSTEMS									
TOTAL	6	5	1	4	8	53	12	7	13
DEPENDENT SCHOOL SYSTEMS	-	-	-	-	-	-	-	-	-
BY ENROLLMENT SIZE OCTOBER 1976									
100,000 OR MORE PUPILS	-	-	-	-	-	-	-	-	-
50,000 TO 99,999 PUPILS	-	-	-	-	-	1	-	-	1
25,000 TO 49,999 PUPILS	1	1	-	-	-	2	-	-	-
12,000 TO 24,999 PUPILS	-	-	-	-	1	5	-	1	4
6,000 TO 11,999 PUPILS	2	1	1	3	-	5	-	-	3
3,000 TO 5,999 PUPILS	2	2	-	1	-	8	1	2	2
1,200 TO 2,999 PUPILS	-	-	-	-	1	13	4	1	2
300 TO 1,199 PUPILS	1	1	-	-	5	13	4	1	1
50 TO 299 PUPILS	-	-	-	-	1	5	2	2	-
1 TO 49 PUPILS	-	-	-	-	-	1	1	-	-
POPULATION, 1975 (ESTIMATED)									
TOTAL	285 327	228 521	56 806	105 186	87 230	1 290 110	47 767	133 198	634 589
IN MUNICIPALLY GOVERNED AREAS	210 912	183 208	27 704	61 562	69 874	1 218 623	31 331	[1]70 540	[2]688 756
WITH A 1975 POPULATION OF--									
50,000 OR MORE	166 512	166 512	-	-	63 227	833 176	-	-	[2]584 010
25,000 TO 49,999	-	-	-	30 403	-	88 693	-	29 063	32 999
10,000 TO 24,999	27 189	11 434	15 755	31 159	-	187 169	14 454	25 969	56 106
5,000 TO 9,999	5 922	-	5 922	-	-	36 770	6 090	5 025	-
2,500 TO 4,999	3 321	-	3 321	-	3 568	23 199	3 475	-	7 478
1,000 TO 2,499	5 224	3 868	1 356	-	-	27 334	1 796	6 562	4 982
LESS THAN 1,000	2 744	1 394	1 350	-	3 079	22 282	5 516	3 921	3 181
OUTSIDE MUNICIPALLY GOVERNED AREAS	74 415	45 313	29 102	43 624	17 356	125 654	16 436	62 658	-
IN TOWNSHIP-GOVERNED AREAS	-	-	-	-	-	12 189	-	-	-
ENROLLMENT OF PUBLIC SCHOOL SYSTEMS									
TOTAL	54 959	47 962	6 997	26 471	17 100	293 475	14 484	30 666	137 499
THROUGH GRADE 12	51 021	44 024	6 997	26 471	17 100	268 678	13 171	30 666	122 170
COLLEGE GRADES	3 938	3 938	-	-	-	24 797	1 313	-	15 329

Table 6. Local Governments and Public School Systems in Individual SMSA's: 1977—Continued

Item	Missouri--Continued										
	Kansas City--Continued				St. Joseph			St. Louis			
	Platte County	Ray County	Johnson County (Kans.)	Wyandotte County (Kans.)	Total	Andrew County	Buchanan County*	Total	Franklin County	Jefferson County	St. Charles County
NUMBER OF LOCAL GOVERNMENTS											
ALL TYPES, TOTAL	41	36	54	18	39	19	20	615	38	46	30
WITH PROPERTY-TAXING POWER	32	20	45	13	34	18	16	558	32	43	25
WITHOUT PROPERTY-TAXING POWER	9	16	9	5	5	1	4	57	6	3	5
COUNTY GOVERNMENTS	1	1	1	1	2	1	1	8	1	1	1
MUNICIPALITIES	17	11	20	3	14	8	6	194	11	11	8
WITH A POPULATION OF--											
50,000 OR MORE	-	-	1	1	1	-	1	3	-	-	1
25,000 TO 49,999	-	-	1	-	-	-	-	8	-	1	-
10,000 TO 24,999	-	-	6	-	-	-	-	22	-	1	1
5,000 TO 9,999	-	1	2	1	-	-	-	31	3	2	1
2,500 TO 4,999	2	-	2	-	1	1	-	34	2	2	1
1,000 TO 2,499	3	1	4	1	1	1	-	34	1	-	2
LESS THAN 1,000	12	9	4	-	11	6	5	62	5	6	3
TOWNSHIP GOVERNMENTS	-	-	9	2	-	-	-	61	-	-	-
SCHOOL DISTRICTS	4	5	7	5	9	4	5	113	11	12	5
SPECIAL DISTRICTS	19	19	17	7	14	6	8	239	15	22	16
WITH PROPERTY-TAXING POWER	10	3	8	2	9	5	4	182	9	19	11
SINGLE FUNCTION DISTRICTS	-	-	-	-	-	-	-	-	-	-	-
CEMETERIES	-	-	6	-	-	-	-	1	-	-	-
EDUCATION (SCHOOL BUILDING DISTRICTS)	-	-	-	-	-	-	-	-	-	-	-
FIRE PROTECTION	1	-	-	-	2	2	-	114	5	11	6
HIGHWAYS	5	8	-	-	-	-	-	13	4	3	-
HEALTH	-	1	-	-	1	-	1	12	4	5	1
HOSPITALS	-	-	-	-	-	-	-	2	-	-	-
HOUSING AND URBAN RENEWAL	-	-	-	2	-	-	-	10	-	-	1
LIBRARIES	-	1	-	-	1	-	1	4	1	-	1
NATURAL RESOURCES, TOTAL	4	8	3	3	5	1	4	26	1	-	4
DRAINAGE	2	4	2	2	1	-	1	14	-	-	3
FLOOD CONTROL	2	4	-	-	4	1	3	10	1	-	1
IRRIGATION, WATER CONSERVATION	-	-	-	-	-	-	-	-	-	-	-
SOIL CONSERVATION	-	-	1	1	-	-	-	2	-	-	-
OTHER AND COMPOSITE PURPOSES	-	-	-	-	-	-	-	-	-	-	-
PARKS AND RECREATION	-	-	1	-	2	-	2	13	-	-	-
SEWERAGE	-	-	-	-	-	-	-	17	-	-	-
UTILITIES, TOTAL	9	1	7	1	3	3	-	14	-	3	3
WATER SUPPLY	9	1	7	1	3	3	-	14	-	3	3
ELECTRIC POWER	-	-	-	-	-	-	-	-	-	-	-
GAS SUPPLY	-	-	-	-	-	-	-	-	-	-	-
TRANSIT	-	-	-	-	-	-	-	-	-	-	-
OTHER	-	-	-	-	-	-	-	4	-	-	-
MULTIPLE-FUNCTION DISTRICTS	-	-	-	1	-	-	-	9	-	-	-
SEWERAGE AND WATER SUPPLY	-	-	-	-	-	-	-	2	-	-	-
NATURAL RESOURCES AND WATER SUPPLY	-	-	-	1	-	-	-	-	-	-	-
OTHER	-	-	-	1	-	-	-	7	-	-	-
SCHOOL SYSTEMS											
TOTAL	4	5	7	5	9	4	5	113	11	12	5
DEPENDENT SCHOOL SYSTEMS	-	-	-	-	-	-	-	-	-	-	-
BY ENROLLMENT SIZE OCTOBER 1976											
100,000 OR MORE PUPILS	-	-	-	-	-	-	-	-	-	-	-
50,000 TO 99,999 PUPILS	-	-	-	-	-	-	-	1	-	-	-
25,000 TO 49,999 PUPILS	-	-	1	1	-	-	-	1	-	-	-
12,000 TO 24,999 PUPILS	-	-	-	-	1	-	1	6	-	-	3
6,000 TO 11,999 PUPILS	1	-	1	-	-	-	-	18	-	2	3
3,000 TO 5,999 PUPILS	-	-	1	2	1	-	1	14	2	1	1
1,200 TO 2,999 PUPILS	2	1	3	1	1	1	-	28	3	5	1
300 TO 1,199 PUPILS	1	3	1	1	4	1	3	28	2	3	-
50 TO 299 PUPILS	-	1	-	-	2	2	-	17	4	1	-
1 TO 49 PUPILS	-	-	-	-	-	-	-	-	-	-	-
POPULATION, 1975 (ESTIMATED)											
TOTAL	39 333	19 327	238 326	177 570	99 682	13 361	86 321	2 366 542	64 199	121 769	115 994
IN MUNICIPALLY GOVERNED AREAS	¹14 864	¹9 485	227 057	¹176 590	85 219	6 478	¹78 741	1 679 728	30 416	44 165	53 839
WITH A 1975 POPULATION OF--											
50,000 OR MORE	-	-	81 013	168 153	77 679	-	77 679	653 358	-	-	-
25,000 TO 49,999	-	-	26 631	-	-	-	-	282 468	-	-	36 168
10,000 TO 24,999	-	-	90 640	-	-	-	-	331 756	-	21 226	-
5,000 TO 9,999	-	5 017	13 862	6 776	-	-	-	211 762	19 740	13 198	9 091
2,500 TO 4,999	5 414	-	6 832	-	4 052	4 052	-	114 904	7 262	6 396	3 311
1,000 TO 2,499	4 608	1 218	6 507	1 661	1 087	1 087	-	57 524	1 500	-	4 373
LESS THAN 1,000	4 842	3 250	1 572	-	2 401	1 339	1 062	27 956	1 914	3 345	896
OUTSIDE MUNICIPALLY GOVERNED AREAS	24 469	9 842	11 269	980	14 463	6 883	7 580	686 814	33 783	77 604	62 155
IN TOWNSHIP-GOVERNED AREAS	-	-	11 328	861	-	-	-	560 186	-	-	-
ENROLLMENT OF PUBLIC SCHOOL SYSTEMS											
TOTAL	10 235	4 173	56 443	39 975	24 171	2 951	21 220	501 932	14 917	33 877	26 285
THROUGH GRADE 12	10 235	4 173	51 488	36 775	20 457	2 951	17 506	455 776	14 917	31 983	26 285
COLLEGE GRADES	-	-	4 955	3 200	3 714	-	3 714	46 156	-	1 894	-

	Missouri--Continued						Springfield			Montana
	St. Louis--Continued									Billings
Item	St. Louis city*	St. Louis County	Clinton County (Ill.)	Madison County (Ill.)	Monroe County (Ill.)	St. Clair County (Ill.)	Total	Christian County	Greene County*	Yellowstone County
NUMBER OF LOCAL GOVERNMENTS										
ALL TYPES, TOTAL	6	150	65	130	24	126	50	30	20	42
WITH PROPERTY-TAXING POWER	3	145	58	113	18	121	35	16	19	24
WITHOUT PROPERTY-TAXING POWER	3	5	7	17	6	5	15	14	1	18
COUNTY GOVERNMENTS	-	1	1	1	1	1	2	1	1	1
MUNICIPALITIES	1	91	12	26	6	28	14	5	9	3
WITH A POPULATION OF--										
50,000 OR MORE	1	1	-	-	-	1	1	-	1	1
25,000 TO 49,999	-	4	-	2	-	1	-	-	-	-
10,000 TO 24,999	-	14	-	3	-	4	-	-	-	-
5,000 TO 9,999	-	18	-	4	-	3	-	-	-	-
2,500 TO 4,999	-	15	2	4	2	6	2	1	1	1
1,000 TO 2,499	-	15	4	6	-	6	2	1	1	-
LESS THAN 1,000	-	24	6	7	4	7	9	3	6	1
TOWNSHIP GOVERNMENTS	-	-	15	24	-	22	-	-	-	-
SCHOOL DISTRICTS	2	24	12	16	3	28	15	7	8	15
SPECIAL DISTRICTS	3	34	25	63	14	47	19	17	2	23
WITH PROPERTY-TAXING POWER	-	29	18	46	8	42	4	3	1	5
SINGLE FUNCTION DISTRICTS										
CEMETERIES	-	-	-	-	1	-	-	-	-	3
EDUCATION (SCHOOL BUILDING DISTRICTS)	-	-	-	-	-	-	-	-	-	-
FIRE PROTECTION	-	25	12	27	4	24	-	-	-	-
HIGHWAYS	-	3	-	2	1	-	14	14	-	-
HEALTH	-	-	-	-	-	2	-	-	-	-
HOSPITALS	-	-	-	1	-	1	1	-	1	-
HOUSING AND URBAN RENEWAL	1	2	1	3	-	2	1	-	1	-
LIBRARIES	-	1	-	1	-	-	2	1	1	-
NATURAL RESOURCES, TOTAL	-	1	5	7	6	2	-	-	-	19
DRAINAGE	-	-	4	6	1	-	-	-	-	14
FLOOD CONTROL	-	1	-	1	4	2	-	-	-	-
IRRIGATION, WATER CONSERVATION	-	-	-	-	-	-	-	-	-	4
SOIL CONSERVATION	-	-	1	-	1	-	-	-	-	1
OTHER AND COMPOSITE PURPOSES	-	-	-	-	-	-	-	-	-	-
PARKS AND RECREATION	-	1	1	5	1	5	-	-	-	-
SEWERAGE	1	1	4	7	1	3	-	-	-	-
UTILITIES, TOTAL	-	-	2	5	-	1	2	2	-	1
WATER SUPPLY	-	-	2	5	-	1	2	2	-	1
ELECTRIC POWER	-	-	-	-	-	-	-	-	-	-
GAS SUPPLY	-	-	-	-	-	-	-	-	-	-
TRANSIT	-	-	-	-	-	-	-	-	-	-
OTHER	-	-	-	3	-	1	-	-	-	-
MULTIPLE-FUNCTION DISTRICTS										
SEWERAGE AND WATER SUPPLY	1	-	-	2	-	6	-	-	-	-
NATURAL RESOURCES AND WATER SUPPLY	-	-	-	1	-	1	-	-	-	-
OTHER	1	-	-	1	-	5	-	-	-	-
SCHOOL SYSTEMS										
TOTAL	2	24	12	16	3	28	15	7	8	15
DEPENDENT SCHOOL SYSTEMS	-	-	-	-	-	-	-	-	-	-
BY ENROLLMENT SIZE OCTOBER 1976										
100,000 OR MORE PUPILS	-	-	-	-	-	-	-	-	-	-
50,000 TO 99,999 PUPILS	1	-	-	-	-	-	-	-	-	-
25,000 TO 49,999 PUPILS	1	-	-	-	-	-	-	-	-	-
12,000 TO 24,999 PUPILS	-	4	-	1	-	1	1	-	1	1
6,000 TO 11,999 PUPILS	-	9	-	2	-	2	-	-	-	-
3,000 TO 5,999 PUPILS	-	3	-	4	-	3	-	-	-	-
1,200 TO 2,999 PUPILS	-	7	2	5	2	3	4	1	3	1
300 TO 1,199 PUPILS	-	1	3	3	1	15	9	5	4	3
50 TO 299 PUPILS	-	-	7	1	-	4	1	1	-	7
1 TO 49 PUPILS	-	-	-	-	-	-	-	-	-	3
POPULATION, 1975 (ESTIMATED)										
TOTAL	524 964	960 451	29 557	249 685	18 977	280 946	187 532	19 576	167 956	97 220
IN MUNICIPALLY GOVERNED AREAS	524 964	[1]612 648	[1]15 985	[1]174 112	10 123	[1]213 476	146 435	7 557	138 878	73 975
WITH A 1975 POPULATION OF--										
50,000 OR MORE	524 964	70 465	-	-	-	57 929	131 557	-	131 557	68 987
25,000 TO 49,999	-	126 924	-	75 614	-	43 762	-	-	-	-
10,000 TO 24,999	-	206 661	-	44 746	-	59 123	-	-	-	-
5,000 TO 9,999	-	122 370	-	28 235	-	19 128	-	-	-	-
2,500 TO 4,999	-	50 187	6 503	12 848	8 575	19 822	6 602	3 737	2 865	4 894
1,000 TO 2,499	-	25 085	6 540	9 100	-	10 926	3 308	2 061	1 247	-
LESS THAN 1,000	-	10 956	2 942	3 569	1 548	2 786	4 968	1 759	3 209	94
OUTSIDE MUNICIPALLY GOVERNED AREAS	-	347 803	13 572	75 573	8 854	67 470	41 097	12 019	29 078	23 245
IN TOWNSHIP-GOVERNED AREAS	-	-	29 555	249 687	-	280 944	-	-	-	-
ENROLLMENT OF PUBLIC SCHOOL SYSTEMS										
TOTAL	106 043	184 004	6 066	57 422	3 853	69 465	38 151	4 523	33 628	22 467
THROUGH GRADE 12	75 171	184 004	6 066	54 032	3 853	59 465	38 151	4 523	33 628	22 467
COLLEGE GRADES	30 872	-	-	3 390	-	10 000	-	-	-	-

Item	Montana--Continued Great Falls — Cascade County (entire SMSA)	Nebraska (see also Iowa) Lincoln — Lancaster County (entire SMSA)	Omaha Total	Omaha Douglas County*	Omaha Sarpy County	Omaha Pottawattamie County (Iowa)	Nevada Las Vegas — Clark County (entire SMSA)	Nevada Reno — Washoe County (entire SMSA)	New Hampshire (see also Massachusetts) Manchester	Nashua
NUMBER OF LOCAL GOVERNMENTS										
ALL TYPES, TOTAL	25	53	260	126	103	31	19	19	25	16
WITH PROPERTY-TAXING POWER	22	51	247	122	98	27	14	11	24	13
WITHOUT PROPERTY-TAXING POWER	3	2	13	4	5	4	5	8	1	3
COUNTY GOVERNMENTS	1	1	3	1	1	1	1	1	-	-
MUNICIPALITIES	4	13	26	7	5	14	4	2	1	1
WITH A POPULATION OF--										
50,000 OR MORE	1	1	2	1	-	1	1	1	1	1
25,000 TO 49,999	-	-	-	-	-	-	1	1	-	-
10,000 TO 24,999	-	-	1	-	1	-	1	-	-	-
5,000 TO 9,999	-	-	3	1	2	-	1	-	-	-
2,500 TO 4,999	-	-	1	-	-	1	-	-	-	-
1,000 TO 2,499	-	1	5	2	1	2	-	-	-	-
LESS THAN 1,000	3	11	14	3	1	10	-	-	-	-
TOWNSHIP GOVERNMENTS	-	-	-	-	-	-	-	-	7	4
SCHOOL DISTRICTS	14	19	32	16	6	10	1	1	9	7
SPECIAL DISTRICTS	6	20	199	102	91	6	13	15	8	4
WITH PROPERTY-TAXING POWER	3	18	186	98	86	2	8	7	7	1
SINGLE FUNCTION DISTRICTS										
CEMETERIES	1	-	-	-	-	-	-	-	-	-
EDUCATION (SCHOOL BUILDING DISTRICTS)	-	-	-	-	-	-	-	-	-	-
FIRE PROTECTION	-	10	15	10	5	-	2	2	2	-
HIGHWAYS	-	-	1	-	1	-	-	-	-	-
HEALTH	-	-	-	-	-	-	-	-	-	-
HOSPITALS	-	-	1	-	1	-	-	-	-	-
HOUSING AND URBAN RENEWAL	1	1	1	1	-	-	3	1	1	1
LIBRARIES	-	-	-	-	-	-	3	-	-	-
NATURAL RESOURCES, TOTAL	2	1	11	1	4	6	1	5	-	1
DRAINAGE	-	-	7	-	3	4	-	-	-	-
FLOOD CONTROL	-	-	-	-	-	-	-	-	-	-
IRRIGATION, WATER CONSERVATION	1	-	-	-	-	-	1	1	-	1
SOIL CONSERVATION	1	-	2	-	-	2	-	4	-	-
OTHER AND COMPOSITE PURPOSES	-	1	2	1	1	-	-	-	-	-
PARKS AND RECREATION	-	-	-	-	-	-	1	-	-	-
SEWERAGE	1	3	21	12	9	-	-	1	-	-
UTILITIES, TOTAL	1	-	2	2	-	-	2	-	5	2
WATER SUPPLY	1	-	-	-	-	-	1	-	5	2
ELECTRIC POWER	-	-	1	1	-	-	1	-	-	-
GAS SUPPLY	-	-	-	-	-	-	-	-	-	-
TRANSIT	-	-	1	1	-	-	-	-	-	-
OTHER	-	1	1	1	-	-	1	1	-	-
MULTIPLE-FUNCTION DISTRICTS	-	4	146	75	71	-	-	5	-	-
SEWERAGE AND WATER SUPPLY	-	-	1	-	1	-	-	2	-	-
NATURAL RESOURCES AND WATER SUPPLY	-	1	1	1	-	-	-	-	-	-
OTHER	-	3	144	74	70	-	-	3	-	-
SCHOOL SYSTEMS										
TOTAL	14	19	32	16	6	10	1	1	10	8
DEPENDENT SCHOOL SYSTEMS	-	-	-	-	-	-	-	-	1	1
BY ENROLLMENT SIZE OCTOBER 1976										
100,000 OR MORE PUPILS	-	-	-	-	-	-	-	-	-	-
50,000 TO 99,999 PUPILS	-	-	1	1	-	-	1	-	-	-
25,000 TO 49,999 PUPILS	-	1	-	-	-	-	-	1	-	-
12,000 TO 24,999 PUPILS	1	-	1	-	-	1	-	-	1	1
6,000 TO 11,999 PUPILS	-	-	3	2	1	-	-	-	-	1
3,000 TO 5,999 PUPILS	-	-	3	1	1	1	-	-	-	1
1,200 TO 2,999 PUPILS	-	2	2	1	-	1	-	-	3	3
300 TO 1,199 PUPILS	3	2	12	3	2	7	-	-	4	2
50 TO 299 PUPILS	4	2	-	-	-	-	-	-	2	-
1 TO 49 PUPILS	4	11	9	7	2	-	-	-	-	-
0 PUPILS (NONOPERATING)	2	1	1	1	-	-	-	-	-	-
POPULATION, 1975 (ESTIMATED)										
TOTAL	83 832	181 659	573 294	411 878	75 121	86 295	330 714	144 750	139 948	101 459
IN MUNICIPALLY GOVERNED AREAS	62 304	168 018	491 889	382 973	38 621	[1]70 295	206 120	109 736	83 417	61 002
WITH A 1975 POPULATION OF--										
50,000 OR MORE	60 868	163 112	430 115	371 455	-	58 660	146 030	78 097	83 417	61 002
25,000 TO 49,999	-	-	-	-	-	-	37 476	31 639	-	-
10,000 TO 24,999	-	-	20 964	-	20 964	-	16 488	-	-	-
5,000 TO 9,999	-	-	20 975	5 764	15 211	-	6 126	-	-	-
2,500 TO 4,999	-	-	3 517	-	-	3 517	-	-	-	-
1,000 TO 2,499	-	1 636	8 358	3 634	1 689	3 035	-	-	-	-
LESS THAN 1,000	1 436	3 270	7 960	2 120	757	5 083	-	-	-	-
OUTSIDE MUNICIPALLY GOVERNED AREAS	21 528	13 641	81 405	28 905	36 500	16 000	124 594	35 014	56 531	40 457
IN TOWNSHIP-GOVERNED AREAS	-	-	-	-	-	-	-	-	56 531	40 457
ENROLLMENT OF PUBLIC SCHOOL SYSTEMS										
TOTAL	18 700	33 665	119 390	78 928	18 126	22 336	82 848	30 450	26 826	29 332
THROUGH GRADE 12	18 700	31 898	116 080	77 869	18 126	20 085	82 848	30 450	26 826	29 332
COLLEGE GRADES	-	1 767	3 310	1 059	-	2 251	-	-	-	-

Table 6. Local Governments and Public School Systems in Individual SMSA's: 1977—Continued

New Jersey (see also Delaware, New York, and Pennsylvania)

Item	Atlantic City — Atlantic County (entire SMSA)	Jersey City — Hudson County (entire SMSA)	Long Branch-Asbury Park — Monmouth County (entire SMSA)	New Brunswick-Perth Amboy-Sayreville — Middlesex County (entire SMSA)	Newark Total	Newark Essex County*	Newark Morris County	Newark Somerset County	Newark Union County	Paterson-Clifton-Passaic — Passaic County (entire SMSA)	Trenton — Mercer County (entire SMSA)
NUMBER OF LOCAL GOVERNMENTS											
ALL TYPES, TOTAL	56	39	139	76	268	49	114	57	48	42	43
WITH PROPERTY-TAXING POWER	44	20	114	60	225	40	100	46	39	35	32
WITHOUT PROPERTY-TAXING POWER	12	19	25	16	43	9	14	11	9	7	11
COUNTY GOVERNMENTS	1	1	1	1	4	1	1	1	1	1	1
MUNICIPALITIES WITH A POPULATION OF--	17	10	38	15	62	18	19	12	13	13	5
50,000 OR MORE	-	3	-	-	5	4	-	-	1	3	1
25,000 TO 49,999	1	3	1	3	9	5	-	-	4	-	-
10,000 TO 24,999	5	2	5	6	13	3	3	3	4	5	1
5,000 TO 9,999	4	1	14	5	21	4	10	4	3	5	1
2,500 TO 4,999	2	-	5	-	8	2	4	1	1	-	1
1,000 TO 2,499	2	1	10	-	3	-	2	1	-	-	1
LESS THAN 1,000	3	-	3	1	3	-	-	3	-	-	-
TOWNSHIP GOVERNMENTS	6	2	15	10	41	4	20	9	8	3	8
SCHOOL DISTRICTS	15	6	52	21	95	17	40	21	17	17	9
SPECIAL DISTRICTS	17	20	33	29	66	9	34	14	9	8	20
WITH PROPERTY-TAXING POWER	5	1	8	13	23	-	20	3	-	1	9
SINGLE FUNCTION DISTRICTS											
CEMETERIES	-	-	-	-	-	-	-	-	-	-	-
EDUCATION (SCHOOL BUILDING DISTRICTS)	-	-	-	-	-	-	-	-	-	-	-
FIRE PROTECTION	5	-	8	13	14	-	11	3	-	-	9
HIGHWAYS	-	-	-	-	8	-	8	-	-	-	-
HEALTH	-	1	-	-	-	-	-	-	-	-	-
HOSPITALS	-	-	-	-	-	-	-	-	-	-	-
HOUSING AND URBAN RENEWAL	-	-	-	-	-	-	-	-	-	-	-
LIBRARIES	2	8	7	7	12	4	3	1	4	2	3
NATURAL RESOURCES, TOTAL	1	-	1	-	2	-	1	1	-	-	1
DRAINAGE	-	-	-	-	-	-	-	-	-	-	-
FLOOD CONTROL	-	-	-	-	-	-	-	-	-	-	-
IRRIGATION, WATER CONSERVATION	-	-	-	-	-	-	-	-	-	-	-
SOIL CONSERVATION	1	-	1	-	2	-	1	1	-	-	1
OTHER AND COMPOSITE PURPOSES	-	-	-	-	-	-	-	-	-	-	-
PARKS AND RECREATION	-	-	-	-	-	-	-	-	-	-	-
SEWERAGE	5	2	13	3	16	1	7	6	2	1	3
UTILITIES, TOTAL	-	-	-	1	-	-	-	-	-	1	-
WATER SUPPLY	-	-	-	1	-	-	-	-	-	1	-
ELECTRIC POWER	-	-	-	-	-	-	-	-	-	-	-
GAS SUPPLY	-	-	-	-	-	-	-	-	-	-	-
TRANSIT	-	-	-	-	-	-	-	-	-	-	-
OTHER	3	7	1	4	10	3	2	2	3	2	1
MULTIPLE-FUNCTION DISTRICTS											
SEWERAGE AND WATER SUPPLY	1	1	3	1	4	1	2	1	-	2	3
NATURAL RESOURCES AND WATER SUPPLY	1	-	2	1	3	-	2	1	-	2	2
OTHER	-	1	1	-	1	1	-	-	-	-	1
SCHOOL SYSTEMS											
TOTAL	25	9	55	26	109	23	42	23	21	21	11
DEPENDENT SCHOOL SYSTEMS	10	3	3	5	14	6	2	2	4	4	2
BY ENROLLMENT SIZE OCTOBER 1976											
100,000 OR MORE PUPILS	-	-	-	-	-	-	-	-	-	-	-
50,000 TO 99,999 PUPILS	-	-	-	-	1	1	-	-	-	-	-
25,000 TO 49,999 PUPILS	-	1	-	-	-	-	-	-	-	-	-
12,000 TO 24,999 PUPILS	-	-	-	-	-	-	-	-	-	1	-
6,000 TO 11,999 PUPILS	1	-	1	3	2	1	-	-	1	1	2
3,000 TO 5,999 PUPILS	3	3	4	4	14	7	2	1	4	3	1
1,200 TO 2,999 PUPILS	6	-	8	7	28	5	12	4	7	-	5
300 TO 1,199 PUPILS	10	3	9	6	30	5	11	9	5	9	1
50 TO 299 PUPILS	5	1	22	4	25	3	15	4	3	7	2
1 TO 49 PUPILS	-	1	8	2	5	1	1	2	1	-	-
0 PUPILS (NONOPERATING)	-	-	3	-	4	-	1	3	-	-	-
POPULATION, 1975 (ESTIMATED)											
TOTAL	188 106	577 519	492 030	592 771	1 999 025	882 487	393 624	202 091	520 823	452 664	318 374
IN MUNICIPALLY GOVERNED AREAS	146 310	517 821	220 528	256 845	1 363 069	792 678	137 159	82 614	350 618	369 778	125 988
WITH A 1975 POPULATION OF--											
50,000 OR MORE	-	369 978	-	-	627 751	523 346	-	-	104 405	265 697	101 365
25,000 TO 49,999	43 969	115 347	31 007	116 712	330 435	185 506	-	-	144 929	-	-
10,000 TO 24,999	58 940	24 564	61 636	101 821	210 646	44 348	48 634	46 047	71 617	66 792	13 806
5,000 TO 9,999	30 519	5 931	87 996	37 391	156 858	32 222	72 147	27 743	24 746	37 289	5 911
2,500 TO 4,999	7 719	-	19 992	-	30 520	7 256	13 916	4 427	4 921	-	2 591
1,000 TO 2,499	3 507	2 001	17 715	-	4 442	-	2 462	1 980	-	-	2 315
LESS THAN 1,000	1 656	-	2 182	921	2 417	-	-	2 417	-	-	-
OUTSIDE MUNICIPALLY GOVERNED AREAS	41 796	59 698	271 502	335 926	635 956	89 809	256 465	119 477	170 205	82 886	192 386
IN TOWNSHIP-GOVERNED AREAS	41 796	59 698	271 501	335 929	635 954	89 808	256 462	119 479	170 205	82 887	192 384
ENROLLMENT OF PUBLIC SCHOOL SYSTEMS											
TOTAL	41 102	66 845	107 129	126 720	403 143	177 317	94 037	46 201	85 588	85 348	62 024
THROUGH GRADE 12	37 065	66 845	107 129	122 224	390 772	170 768	90 117	44 299	85 588	85 348	55 571
COLLEGE GRADES	4 037	-	-	4 496	12 371	6 549	3 920	1 902	-	-	6 453

65

Table 6. Local Governments and Public School Systems in Individual SMSA's: 1977—Continued

Item	New Jersey (see also Delaware, New York, and Pennsylvania)--Continued Vineland-Millville-Bridgeton Cumberland County (entire SMSA)	New Mexico Albuquerque Total	Bernalillo County*	Sandoval County	New York Albany-Schenectady-Troy Total	Albany County*	Montgomery County	Rensselaer County*	Saratoga County	Schenectady County*
NUMBER OF LOCAL GOVERNMENTS										
ALL TYPES, TOTAL	36	21	9	12	258	55	35	61	68	39
WITH PROPERTY-TAXING POWER	29	20	9	11	258	55	35	61	68	39
WITHOUT PROPERTY-TAXING POWER.	7	1	-	1	-	-	-	-	-	-
COUNTY GOVERNMENTS	1	2	1	1	5	1	1	1	1	1
MUNICIPALITIES	4	8	3	5	41	9	11	7	11	3
WITH A POPULATION OF--										
50,000 OR MORE	1	1	1	-	3	1	-	1	-	1
25,000 TO 49,999	1	-	-	-	-	-	-	-	-	-
10,000 TO 24,999	1	-	-	-	4	2	1	-	1	-
5,000 TO 9,999	-	-	-	-	5	1	-	1	2	1
2,500 TO 4,999	-	-	-	-	9	4	1	1	3	-
1,000 TO 2,499	-	3	1	2	9	1	4	2	2	1
LESS THAN 1,000.	1	4	1	3	11	-	5	2	3	-
TOWNSHIP GOVERNMENTS	10	-	-	-	58	10	10	14	19	5
SCHOOL DISTRICTS	12	4	1	3	51	13	5	14	12	7
SPECIAL DISTRICTS.	9	7	4	3	103	22	8	25	25	23
WITH PROPERTY-TAXING POWER	2	6	4	2	103	22	8	25	25	23
SINGLE FUNCTION DISTRICTS.	-	-	-	-	-	-	-	-	-	-
CEMETERIES	-	-	-	-	-	-	-	-	-	-
EDUCATION (SCHOOL BUILDING DISTRICTS). . .	-	-	-	-	91	21	2	25	21	22
FIRE PROTECTION.	-	-	-	-	-	-	-	-	-	-
HIGHWAYS	2	-	-	-	11	-	6	-	4	1
HEALTH	-	-	-	-	-	-	-	-	-	-
HOSPITALS.	-	-	-	-	-	-	-	-	-	-
HOUSING AND URBAN RENEWAL.	3	-	-	-	-	-	-	-	-	-
LIBRARIES.	-	-	-	-	-	-	-	-	-	-
NATURAL RESOURCES, TOTAL	2	5	3	2	-	-	-	-	-	-
DRAINAGE	-	1	1	-	-	-	-	-	-	-
FLOOD CONTROL.	-	1	1	-	-	-	-	-	-	-
IRRIGATION, WATER CONSERVATION .	-	1	1	-	-	-	-	-	-	-
SOIL CONSERVATION.	2	3	1	2	-	-	-	-	-	-
OTHER AND COMPOSITE PURPOSES	-	-	-	-	-	-	-	-	-	-
PARKS AND RECREATION	-	-	-	-	-	-	-	-	-	-
SEWERAGE	2	-	-	-	-	-	-	-	-	-
UTILITIES, TOTAL	-	-	-	-	-	-	-	-	-	-
WATER SUPPLY	-	-	-	-	-	-	-	-	-	-
ELECTRIC POWER	-	-	-	-	-	-	-	-	-	-
GAS SUPPLY	-	-	-	-	-	-	-	-	-	-
TRANSIT.	-	-	-	-	-	-	-	-	-	-
OTHER.	-	1	-	1	1	1	-	-	-	-
MULTIPLE-FUNCTION DISTRICTS.	-	1	1	-	-	-	-	-	-	-
SEWERAGE AND WATER SUPPLY.	-	1	1	-	-	-	-	-	-	-
NATURAL RESOURCES AND WATER SUPPLY	-	-	-	-	-	-	-	-	-	-
OTHER.	-	-	-	-	-	-	-	-	-	-
SCHOOL SYSTEMS										
TOTAL.	16	4	1	3	54	13	6	15	12	8
DEPENDENT SCHOOL SYSTEMS	4	-	-	-	3	-	1	1	-	1
BY ENROLLMENT SIZE OCTOBER 1976										
100,000 OR MORE PUPILS	-	-	-	-	-	-	-	-	-	-
50,000 TO 99,999 PUPILS.	-	1	1	-	-	-	-	-	-	-
25,000 TO 49,999 PUPILS.	-	-	-	-	-	-	-	-	-	-
12,000 TO 24,999 PUPILS.	-	-	-	-	-	-	-	-	-	-
6,000 TO 11,999 PUPILS	3	-	-	-	8	3	-	2	2	1
3,000 TO 5,999 PUPILS.	-	-	-	-	13	3	1	3	3	3
1,200 TO 2,999 PUPILS.	1	1	-	1	23	4	4	6	6	3
300 TO 1,199 PUPILS.	8	2	-	2	4	1	1	1	1	1
50 TO 299 PUPILS	4	-	-	-	4	2	-	1	-	-
1 TO 49 PUPILS	-	-	-	-	1	-	-	1	-	-
0 PUPILS (NONOPERATING).	-	-	-	-	1	-	-	1	-	-
POPULATION, 1975 (ESTIMATED)										
TOTAL.	132 938	384 663	362 087	22 576	798 014	287 580	55 729	153 377	143 980	157 348
IN MUNICIPALLY GOVERNED AREAS.	99 947	287 108	281 629	5 479	413 358	163 609	37 093	78 220	51 728	82 708
WITH A 1975 POPULATION OF--										
50,000 OR MORE	53 637	279 401	279 401	-	245 618	110 311	-	60 312	-	74 995
25,000 TO 49,999	25 119	-	-	-	-	-	-	-	-	-
10,000 TO 24,999	20 545	-	-	-	78 939	29 624	24 430	-	24 885	-
5,000 TO 9,999	-	-	-	-	37 525	8 942	-	9 391	11 986	7 206
2,500 TO 4,999	-	-	-	-	29 313	13 071	2 644	3 727	9 871	-
1,000 TO 2,499	-	6 361	2 045	4 316	14 939	1 661	7 052	3 141	3 085	-
LESS THAN 1,000.	646	1 346	183	1 163	7 024	-	2 967	1 649	1 901	507
OUTSIDE MUNICIPALLY GOVERNED AREAS	32 991	97 555	80 458	17 097	384 656	123 971	18 636	75 157	92 252	74 640
IN TOWNSHIP-GOVERNED AREAS	32 993	-	-	-	457 951	147 644	31 298	83 676	112 980	82 353
ENROLLMENT OF PUBLIC SCHOOL SYSTEMS										
TOTAL.	33 704	87 931	83 410	4 521	162 727	45 156	13 013	35 802	38 329	30 427
THROUGH GRADE 12	31 940	87 931	83 410	4 521	150 585	45 156	10 413	28 790	38 329	27 897
COLLEGE GRADES	1 764	-	-	-	12 142	-	2 600	7 012	-	2 530

66

Table 6. Local Governments and Public School Systems in Individual SMSA's: 1977—Continued

New York--Continued

Item	Binghamton Total	Broome County*	Tioga County	Susquehanna County (Pa.)	Buffalo Total	Erie County*	Niagara County	Elmira — Chemung County (entire SMSA)	Nassau-Suffolk[1] Total	Nassau County	Suffolk County
NUMBER OF LOCAL GOVERNMENTS											
ALL TYPES, TOTAL	135	47	33	55	143	109	34	32	370	166	204
WITH PROPERTY-TAXING POWER	128	47	33	48	142	109	33	32	370	166	204
WITHOUT PROPERTY-TAXING POWER	7	-	-	7	1	-	1	-	-	-	-
COUNTY GOVERNMENTS	3	1	1	1	2	1	1	1	2	1	1
MUNICIPALITIES											
WITH A POPULATION OF--	27	8	6	13	26	18	8	6	95	66	29
50,000 OR MORE	1	1	-	-	2	1	1	-	-	-	-
25,000 TO 49,999	-	-	-	-	4	2	2	1	8	7	1
10,000 TO 24,999	2	2	-	-	4	4	-	1	9	7	2
5,000 TO 9,999	-	-	-	-	3	3	-	1	18	13	5
2,500 TO 4,999	2	-	2	-	7	6	1	1	15	11	4
1,000 TO 2,499	10	4	1	5	4	1	3	-	25	18	7
LESS THAN 1,000	12	1	3	8	2	1	1	3	20	10	10
TOWNSHIP GOVERNMENTS	52	16	9	27	37	25	12	11	13	3	10
SCHOOL DISTRICTS	25	13	6	6	40	30	10	3	130	57	73
SPECIAL DISTRICTS	28	9	11	8	38	35	3	11	130	39	91
WITH PROPERTY-TAXING POWER	21	9	11	-	37	35	2	11	130	39	91
SINGLE FUNCTION DISTRICTS											
CEMETERIES	-	-	-	-	-	-	-	-	-	-	-
EDUCATION (SCHOOL BUILDING DISTRICTS)	1	-	-	1	-	-	-	-	-	-	-
FIRE PROTECTION	17	9	8	-	36	34	2	11	130	39	91
HIGHWAYS	-	-	-	-	1	-	1	-	-	-	-
HEALTH	3	-	3	-	1	1	-	-	-	-	-
HOSPITALS	-	-	-	-	-	-	-	-	-	-	-
HOUSING AND URBAN RENEWAL	1	-	-	1	-	-	-	-	-	-	-
LIBRARIES	-	-	-	-	-	-	-	-	-	-	-
NATURAL RESOURCES, TOTAL	-	-	-	-	-	-	-	-	-	-	-
DRAINAGE	-	-	-	-	-	-	-	-	-	-	-
FLOOD CONTROL	-	-	-	-	-	-	-	-	-	-	-
IRRIGATION, WATER CONSERVATION	-	-	-	-	-	-	-	-	-	-	-
SOIL CONSERVATION	-	-	-	-	-	-	-	-	-	-	-
OTHER AND COMPOSITE PURPOSES	-	-	-	-	-	-	-	-	-	-	-
PARKS AND RECREATION	-	-	-	-	-	-	-	-	-	-	-
SEWERAGE	3	-	-	3	-	-	-	-	-	-	-
UTILITIES, TOTAL	1	-	-	1	-	-	-	-	-	-	-
WATER SUPPLY	1	-	-	1	-	-	-	-	-	-	-
ELECTRIC POWER	-	-	-	-	-	-	-	-	-	-	-
GAS SUPPLY	-	-	-	-	-	-	-	-	-	-	-
TRANSIT	-	-	-	-	-	-	-	-	-	-	-
OTHER	1	-	-	1	-	-	-	-	-	-	-
MULTIPLE-FUNCTION DISTRICTS	1	-	-	1	-	-	-	-	-	-	-
SEWERAGE AND WATER SUPPLY	-	-	-	-	-	-	-	-	-	-	-
NATURAL RESOURCES AND WATER SUPPLY	-	-	-	-	-	-	-	-	-	-	-
OTHER	1	-	-	1	-	-	-	-	-	-	-
SCHOOL SYSTEMS											
TOTAL	26	14	6	6	43	32	11	3	132	58	74
DEPENDENT SCHOOL SYSTEMS	1	1	-	-	3	2	1	-	2	1	1
BY ENROLLMENT SIZE OCTOBER 1976											
100,000 OR MORE PUPILS	-	-	-	-	-	-	-	-	-	-	-
50,000 TO 99,999 PUPILS	-	-	-	-	1	1	-	-	-	-	-
25,000 TO 49,999 PUPILS	-	-	-	-	-	-	-	-	-	-	-
12,000 TO 24,999 PUPILS	-	-	-	-	4	3	1	-	10	3	7
6,000 TO 11,999 PUPILS	4	4	-	-	6	4	2	2	32	14	18
3,000 TO 5,999 PUPILS	5	4	1	-	17	14	3	-	32	22	10
1,200 TO 2,999 PUPILS	16	6	5	5	12	7	5	1	30	18	12
300 TO 1,199 PUPILS	1	-	-	1	2	2	-	-	10	-	10
50 TO 299 PUPILS	-	-	-	-	1	1	-	-	12	-	12
1 TO 49 PUPILS	-	-	-	-	-	-	-	-	5	1	4
0 PUPILS (NONOPERATING)	-	-	-	-	1	1	-	-	1	-	1
POPULATION, 1975 (ESTIMATED)											
TOTAL	304 157	219 376	47 937	36 844	1 326 848	1 089 327	237 521	100 377	2 656 839	1 403 289	1 253 550
IN MUNICIPALLY GOVERNED AREAS	127 156	100 828	13 435	12 893	728 065	²571 597	156 468	52 343	632 527	511 012	121 515
WITH A 1975 POPULATION OF--											
50,000 OR MORE	60 666	60 666	-	-	487 933	407 160	80 773	-	-	-	-
25,000 TO 49,999	-	-	-	-	117 199	51 082	66 117	37 320	260 407	230 698	29 709
10,000 TO 24,999	33 404	33 404	-	-	68 502	68 502	-	-	144 756	119 643	25 113
5,000 TO 9,999	-	-	-	-	20 517	20 517	-	8 388	131 886	95 136	36 750
2,500 TO 4,999	9 557	-	9 557	-	25 099	21 833	3 266	4 684	45 618	33 020	12 598
1,000 TO 2,499	16 815	6 417	1 281	9 117	7 624	1 899	5 725	-	38 202	26 179	12 023
LESS THAN 1,000	6 714	341	2 597	3 776	1 191	604	587	1 951	11 658	6 336	5 322
OUTSIDE MUNICIPALLY GOVERNED AREAS	177 001	118 548	34 502	23 951	598 783	517 730	81 053	48 034	2 024 312	892 277	1 132 035
IN TOWNSHIP-GOVERNED AREAS	230 599	158 711	47 937	23 951	723 572	634 130	89 442	63 055	2 597 877	1 344 510	1 253 367
ENROLLMENT OF PUBLIC SCHOOL SYSTEMS											
TOTAL	84 897	62 558	12 510	9 829	258 525	205 171	53 354	19 819	629 689	285 631	344 058
THROUGH GRADE 12	80 250	57 911	12 510	9 829	245 272	195 968	49 304	19 819	594 305	268 175	326 130
COLLEGE GRADES	4 647	4 647	-	-	13 253	9 203	4 050	-	35 384	17 456	17 928

	New York--Continued						Poughkeepsie	Rochester
	New York City							
Item	Total	New York City*	Putnam County	Rockland County	Westchester County	Bergen County (N.J.)	Dutchess County (entire SMSA)	Total
NUMBER OF LOCAL GOVERNMENTS								
ALL TYPES, TOTAL	362	3	21	48	133	157	71	244
WITH PROPERTY-TAXING POWER	346	1	21	48	133	143	71	243
WITHOUT PROPERTY-TAXING POWER.	16	2	-	-	-	14	-	1
COUNTY GOVERNMENTS	4	-	1	1	1	1	1	5
MUNICIPALITIES	106	1	3	13	28	61	10	44
WITH A POPULATION OF--								
50,000 OR MORE	4	1	-	-	3	-	-	1
25,000 TO 49,999	8	-	-	-	1	7	1	-
10,000 TO 24,999	32	-	-	1	8	23	1	4
5,000 TO 9,999	37	-	-	4	13	20	1	7
2,500 TO 4,999	13	-	-	3	2	8	1	8
1,000 TO 2,499	7	-	2	3	3	1	4	19
LESS THAN 1,000.	5	-	1	2	-	2	2	5
TOWNSHIP GOVERNMENTS	38	-	6	5	18	9	20	77
SCHOOL DISTRICTS	135	-	6	9	48	72	15	52
SPECIAL DISTRICTS.	79	2	5	20	38	14	25	66
WITH PROPERTY-TAXING POWER	63	-	5	20	38	-	25	65
SINGLE FUNCTION DISTRICTS.	-	-	-	-	-	-	-	-
CEMETERIES	-	-	-	-	-	-	-	-
EDUCATION (SCHOOL BUILDING DISTRICTS). . . .	-	-	-	-	-	-	-	-
FIRE PROTECTION.	63	-	5	20	38	-	25	60
HIGHWAYS	-	-	-	-	-	-	-	-
HEALTH	-	-	-	-	-	-	-	5
HOSPITALS.	-	-	-	-	-	-	-	-
HOUSING AND URBAN RENEWAL.	7	-	-	-	-	7	-	-
LIBRARIES.	-	-	-	-	-	-	-	-
NATURAL RESOURCES, TOTAL	1	-	-	-	-	1	-	1
DRAINAGE	-	-	-	-	-	-	-	-
FLOOD CONTROL.	-	-	-	-	-	-	-	-
IRRIGATION, WATER CONSERVATION	1	-	-	-	-	1	-	-
SOIL CONSERVATION.	-	-	-	-	-	-	-	1
OTHER AND COMPOSITE PURPOSES	-	-	-	-	-	-	-	-
PARKS AND RECREATION	-	-	-	-	-	-	-	-
SEWERAGE	5	-	-	-	-	5	-	-
UTILITIES, TOTAL	-	-	-	-	-	-	-	-
WATER SUPPLY	-	-	-	-	-	-	-	-
ELECTRIC POWER	-	-	-	-	-	-	-	-
GAS SUPPLY	-	-	-	-	-	-	-	-
TRANSIT.	-	-	-	-	-	-	-	-
OTHER.	2	1	-	-	-	1	-	-
MULTIPLE-FUNCTION DISTRICTS.	1	1	-	-	-	-	-	-
SEWERAGE AND WATER SUPPLY.	-	-	-	-	-	-	-	-
NATURAL RESOURCES AND WATER SUPPLY	-	-	-	-	-	-	-	-
OTHER.	1	1	-	-	-	-	-	-
SCHOOL SYSTEMS								
TOTAL.	144	2	6	10	50	76	16	55
DEPENDENT SCHOOL SYSTEMS	9	2	-	1	2	4	1	3
BY ENROLLMENT SIZE OCTOBER 1976								
100,000 OR MORE PUPILS	2	2	-	-	-	-	-	-
50,000 TO 99,999 PUPILS.	-	-	-	-	-	-	-	1
25,000 TO 49,999 PUPILS.	1	-	-	-	1	-	-	1
12,000 TO 24,999 PUPILS.	2	-	-	2	-	-	1	2
6,000 TO 11,999 PUPILS	12	-	-	3	5	4	1	5
3,000 TO 5,999 PUPILS.	29	-	2	3	12	12	3	15
1,200 TO 2,999 PUPILS.	54	-	2	1	20	31	8	23
300 TO 1,199 PUPILS.	33	-	2	-	6	25	1	6
50 TO 299 PUPILS	8	-	-	1	5	2	2	1
1 TO 49 PUPILS	1	-	-	-	1	-	-	-
0 PUPILS (NONOPERATING).	2	-	-	-	-	2	-	2
POPULATION, 1975 (ESTIMATED)								
TOTAL.	9 561 504	7 481 613	69 276	251 114	879 241	880 260	234 511	971 465
IN MUNICIPALLY GOVERNED AREAS.	8 940 192	7 481 613	4 063	71 612	638 799	744 105	61 767	426 354
WITH A 1975 POPULATION OF--								
50,000 OR MORE	7 813 650	7 481 613	-	-	332 037	-	-	267 173
25,000 TO 49,999	263 439	-	-	-	48 327	215 112	31 608	-
10,000 TO 24,999	514 557	-	-	20 288	151 357	342 912	12 553	51 131
5,000 TO 9,999	283 056	-	-	34 568	96 372	152 116	6 479	45 800
2,500 TO 4,999	50 265	-	-	9 635	8 396	32 234	2 512	26 234
1,000 TO 2,499	13 073	-	3 449	5 843	2 310	1 471	6 869	32 878
LESS THAN 1,000.	2 152	-	614	1 278	-	260	1 746	3 138
OUTSIDE MUNICIPALLY GOVERNED AREAS	621 312		-	65 213	179 502	240 442	136 155	172 744	545 111
IN TOWNSHIP-GOVERNED AREAS	918 925		-	69 276	251 113	462 383	136 153	190 352	675 594
ENROLLMENT OF PUBLIC SCHOOL SYSTEMS								
TOTAL.	1 672 841	1 262 191	16 880	65 976	164 988	162 806	54 125	223 443
THROUGH GRADE 12	1 462 437	1 077 191	16 880	58 095	157 132	153 139	51 350	212 509
COLLEGE GRADES	210 404	185 000	-	7 881	7 856	9 667	2 775	10 934

68

	New York--Continued										
	Rochester--Continued					Syracuse				Utica-Rome	
Item	Livingston County	Monroe County*	Ontario County	Orleans County	Wayne County	Total	Madison County	Onondaga County*	Oswego County	Total	Herkimer County
NUMBER OF LOCAL GOVERNMENTS											
ALL TYPES, TOTAL	41	78	44	24	57	179	54	78	47	139	51
WITH PROPERTY-TAXING POWER	41	77	44	24	57	178	54	77	47	139	51
WITHOUT PROPERTY-TAXING POWER	-	1	-	-	-	1	-	1	1	-	-
COUNTY GOVERNMENTS	1	1	1	1	1	3	1	1	1	2	1
MUNICIPALITIES	9	11	10	4	10	39	11	16	12	33	11
WITH A POPULATION OF--											
50,000 OR MORE	-	1	-	-	-	1	-	1	-	1	-
25,000 TO 49,999	-	1	-	-	-	1	-	1	-	1	-
10,000 TO 24,999	-	1	2	-	1	3	1	-	2	-	-
5,000 TO 9,999	2	3	-	2	-	5	1	4	-	3	3
2,500 TO 4,999	2	3	-	-	3	11	4	5	2	10	3
1,000 TO 2,499	4	3	6	2	4	6	-	4	2	6	1
LESS THAN 1,000	1	-	2	-	2	13	5	2	6	12	4
TOWNSHIP GOVERNMENTS	17	19	16	10	15	56	15	19	22	45	19
SCHOOL DISTRICTS	8	19	9	5	11	36	10	17	9	29	11
SPECIAL DISTRICTS	6	28	8	4	20	45	17	25	3	30	9
WITH PROPERTY-TAXING POWER	6	27	8	4	20	44	17	24	3	30	9
SINGLE FUNCTION DISTRICTS											
CEMETERIES	-	-	-	-	-	-	-	-	-	-	-
EDUCATION (SCHOOL BUILDING DISTRICTS)	-	-	-	-	-	-	-	-	-	-	-
FIRE PROTECTION	-	-	-	-	-	-	-	-	-	-	-
HIGHWAYS	5	27	7	4	17	38	11	24	3	25	6
HEALTH	-	-	-	-	-	-	-	-	-	-	-
HOSPITALS	1	-	1	-	3	6	6	-	-	5	3
HOUSING AND URBAN RENEWAL	-	-	-	-	-	-	-	-	-	-	-
LIBRARIES	-	-	-	-	-	-	-	-	-	-	-
NATURAL RESOURCES, TOTAL	-	1	-	-	-	1	-	1	-	-	-
DRAINAGE	-	-	-	-	-	-	-	-	-	-	-
FLOOD CONTROL	-	-	-	-	-	-	-	-	-	-	-
IRRIGATION, WATER CONSERVATION	-	-	-	-	-	-	-	-	-	-	-
SOIL CONSERVATION	-	-	-	-	-	-	-	-	-	-	-
OTHER AND COMPOSITE PURPOSES	-	1	-	-	-	1	-	1	-	-	-
PARKS AND RECREATION	-	-	-	-	-	-	-	-	-	-	-
SEWERAGE	-	-	-	-	-	-	-	-	-	-	-
UTILITIES, TOTAL	-	-	-	-	-	-	-	-	-	-	-
WATER SUPPLY	-	-	-	-	-	-	-	-	-	-	-
ELECTRIC POWER	-	-	-	-	-	-	-	-	-	-	-
GAS SUPPLY	-	-	-	-	-	-	-	-	-	-	-
TRANSIT	-	-	-	-	-	-	-	-	-	-	-
OTHER	-	-	-	-	-	-	-	-	-	-	-
MULTIPLE-FUNCTION DISTRICTS											
SEWERAGE AND WATER SUPPLY	-	-	-	-	-	-	-	-	-	-	-
NATURAL RESOURCES AND WATER SUPPLY	-	-	-	-	-	-	-	-	-	-	-
OTHER	-	-	-	-	-	-	-	-	-	-	-
SCHOOL SYSTEMS											
TOTAL	8	21	10	5	11	38	10	19	9	31	12
DEPENDENT SCHOOL SYSTEMS	-	2	1	-	-	2	-	2	-	2	1
BY ENROLLMENT SIZE OCTOBER 1976											
100,000 OR MORE PUPILS	-	-	-	-	-	-	-	-	-	-	-
50,000 TO 99,999 PUPILS	-	-	-	-	-	-	-	-	-	-	-
25,000 TO 49,999 PUPILS	-	1	-	-	-	-	-	-	-	-	-
12,000 TO 24,999 PUPILS	-	2	-	-	-	3	-	3	-	1	-
6,000 TO 11,999 PUPILS	-	5	-	-	-	3	-	3	-	1	-
3,000 TO 5,999 PUPILS	-	8	3	1	3	10	2	3	5	5	-
1,200 TO 2,999 PUPILS	6	3	4	3	7	15	2	9	4	14	7
300 TO 1,199 PUPILS	2	-	3	1	-	7	6	1	-	8	5
50 TO 299 PUPILS	-	-	-	-	1	-	-	-	-	2	-
1 TO 49 PUPILS	-	-	-	-	-	-	-	-	-	-	-
0 PUPILS (NONOPERATING)	-	2	-	-	-	-	-	-	-	-	-
POPULATION, 1975 (ESTIMATED)											
TOTAL	56 892	708 642	85 060	38 328	82 543	647 828	65 469	472 708	109 651	334 046	67 969
IN MUNICIPALLY GOVERNED AREAS	26 564	314 067	[1]41 568	15 463	28 692	319 263	33 347	237 629	48 287	205 453	38 126
WITH A 1975 POPULATION OF--											
50,000 OR MORE	-	267 173	-	-	-	182 543	-	182 543	-	82 443	-
25,000 TO 49,999	-	-	-	-	-	-	-	-	-	49 014	-
10,000 TO 24,999	-	11 755	28 694	-	10 682	46 715	11 118	-	35 597	-	-
5,000 TO 9,999	12 311	21 187	-	12 302	-	33 634	5 011	28 623	-	24 986	24 986
2,500 TO 4,999	6 803	8 775	-	-	10 656	38 309	14 096	18 838	5 375	32 109	9 356
1,000 TO 2,499	7 083	5 177	11 351	3 161	6 106	9 341	-	6 293	3 048	9 059	1 018
LESS THAN 1,000	367	-	1 523	-	1 248	8 721	3 122	1 332	4 267	7 842	2 766
OUTSIDE MUNICIPALLY GOVERNED AREAS	30 328	394 575	43 492	22 865	53 851	328 565	32 122	235 079	61 364	128 593	29 843
IN TOWNSHIP-GOVERNED AREAS	56 891	441 468	56 365	38 327	82 543	417 762	54 352	289 359	74 051	192 853	61 096
ENROLLMENT OF PUBLIC SCHOOL SYSTEMS											
TOTAL	11 711	157 951	21 726	9 889	22 166	146 461	16 252	102 306	27 903	76 248	16 434
THROUGH GRADE 12	11 711	148 212	20 531	9 889	22 166	140 250	16 252	96 095	27 903	69 299	15 065
COLLEGE GRADES	-	9 739	1 195	-	-	6 211	-	6 211	-	6 949	1 369

Item	New York—Continued / Utica-Rome—Continued: Oneida County*	Asheville: Total	Asheville: Buncombe County*	Asheville: Madison County	Burlington: Almance County (entire SMSA)	Charlotte-Gastonia: Total	Charlotte-Gastonia: Gaston County*	Charlotte-Gastonia: Mecklenburg County*	Charlotte-Gastonia: Union County	Fayetteville: Cumberland County (entire SMSA)	Greensboro—Winston-Salem—High Point: Total
NUMBER OF LOCAL GOVERNMENTS											
ALL TYPES, TOTAL	88	21	13	8	9	42	18	12	12	12	50
WITH PROPERTY-TAXING POWER	88	15	10	5	6	34	16	9	9	9	37
WITHOUT PROPERTY-TAXING POWER	-	6	3	3	3	8	2	3	3	3	13
COUNTY GOVERNMENTS	1	2	1	1	1	3	1	1	1	1	6
MUNICIPALITIES	22	9	6	3	5	27	14	7	6	8	25
WITH A POPULATION OF—											
50,000 OR MORE	1	1	1	-	-	1	-	1	-	1	3
25,000 TO 49,999	1	-	-	-	1	1	1	-	-	-	3
10,000 TO 24,999	-	-	-	-	1	1	-	-	1	1	2
5,000 TO 9,999	-	-	-	-	1	3	3	-	-	1	1
2,500 TO 4,999	7	2	2	-	2	6	4	2	-	1	9
1,000 TO 2,499	5	4	2	2	1	8	2	3	3	-	7
LESS THAN 1,000	8	2	1	1	-	7	4	1	2	5	
TOWNSHIP GOVERNMENTS	26	-	-	-	-	-	-	-	-	-	-
SCHOOL DISTRICTS	18	-	-	-	-	-	-	-	-	-	-
SPECIAL DISTRICTS	21	10	6	4	3	12	3	4	5	3	19
WITH PROPERTY-TAXING POWER	21	4	3	1	-	4	1	1	2	-	6
SINGLE FUNCTION DISTRICTS	-	-	-	-	-	-	-	-	-	-	-
CEMETERIES	-	-	-	-	-	-	-	-	-	-	-
EDUCATION (SCHOOL BUILDING DISTRICTS)	-	-	-	-	-	-	-	-	-	-	-
FIRE PROTECTION	19	-	-	-	-	-	-	-	-	-	-
HIGHWAYS	-	-	-	-	-	-	-	-	-	-	-
HEALTH	2	-	-	-	-	1	-	1	-	-	1
HOSPITALS	-	-	-	-	-	-	-	-	-	-	-
HOUSING AND URBAN RENEWAL	-	4	1	3	2	4	1	1	2	1	5
LIBRARIES	-	-	-	-	-	-	-	-	-	-	-
NATURAL RESOURCES, TOTAL	-	2	1	1	1	4	1	2	1	2	8
DRAINAGE	-	-	-	-	-	1	-	1	-	1	-
FLOOD CONTROL	-	-	-	-	-	-	-	-	-	-	2
IRRIGATION, WATER CONSERVATION	-	-	-	-	-	-	-	-	-	-	-
SOIL CONSERVATION	-	2	1	1	1	3	1	1	1	1	6
OTHER AND COMPOSITE PURPOSES	-	-	-	-	-	-	-	-	-	-	-
PARKS AND RECREATION	-	-	-	-	-	-	-	-	-	-	-
SEWERAGE	-	3	3	-	-	2	-	-	2	-	3
UTILITIES, TOTAL	-	-	-	-	-	1	1	-	-	-	1
WATER SUPPLY	-	-	-	-	-	1	1	-	-	-	1
ELECTRIC POWER	-	-	-	-	-	-	-	-	-	-	-
GAS SUPPLY	-	-	-	-	-	-	-	-	-	-	-
TRANSIT	-	-	-	-	-	-	-	-	-	-	-
OTHER	-	-	-	-	-	-	-	-	-	-	1
MULTIPLE-FUNCTION DISTRICTS	-	1	1	-	-	-	-	-	-	-	-
SEWERAGE AND WATER SUPPLY	-	1	1	-	-	-	-	-	-	-	-
NATURAL RESOURCES AND WATER SUPPLY	-	-	-	-	-	-	-	-	-	-	-
OTHER	-	-	-	-	-	-	-	-	-	-	-
SCHOOL SYSTEMS											
TOTAL	19	4	3	1	3	6	2	2	2	3	15
DEPENDENT SCHOOL SYSTEMS	1	4	3	1	3	6	2	2	2	3	15
BY ENROLLMENT SIZE OCTOBER 1976											
100,000 OR MORE PUPILS	-	-	-	-	-	-	-	-	-	-	-
50,000 TO 99,999 PUPILS	-	-	-	-	-	1	-	1	-	-	1
25,000 TO 49,999 PUPILS	-	-	-	-	-	1	1	-	-	1	3
12,000 TO 24,999 PUPILS	1	1	1	-	1	1	-	1	-	-	2
6,000 TO 11,999 PUPILS	1	1	1	-	1	1	-	-	1	1	2
3,000 TO 5,999 PUPILS	5	-	-	-	-	1	-	-	1	1	5
1,200 TO 2,999 PUPILS	7	2	1	1	1	1	1	-	-	-	2
300 TO 1,199 PUPILS	3	-	-	-	-	-	-	-	-	-	1
50 TO 299 PUPILS	2	-	-	-	-	-	-	-	-	-	-
1 TO 49 PUPILS	-	-	-	-	-	-	-	-	-	-	-
POPULATION, 1975 (ESTIMATED)											
TOTAL	266 077	167 759	150 952	16 807	98 954	592 706	156 529	373 925	62 252	226 146	764 178
IN MUNICIPALLY GOVERNED AREAS	167 327	72 777	69 133	3 644	¹53 793	399 154	¹86 882	293 811	18 461	76 120	439 607
WITH A 1975 POPULATION OF—											
50,000 OR MORE	82 443	59 591	59 591	-	-	281 417	-	281 417	-	65 915	358 196
25,000 TO 49,999	49 014	-	-	-	37 586	49 343	49 343	-	-	-	-
10,000 TO 24,999	-	-	-	-	-	11 740	-	-	11 740	-	48 962
5,000 TO 9,999	-	-	-	-	8 926	16 104	16 104	-	-	5 476	11 034
2,500 TO 4,999	22 753	6 376	6 376	-	5 130	22 163	15 553	6 610	-	2 970	2 508
1,000 TO 2,499	8 041	5 662	2 566	3 096	2 151	14 441	4 055	4 936	5 450	-	15 223
LESS THAN 1,000	5 076	1 148	600	548	-	3 946	1 827	848	1 271	1 759	3 684
OUTSIDE MUNICIPALLY GOVERNED AREAS	98 750	94 982	81 819	13 163	45 161	193 552	69 647	80 114	43 791	150 026	324 571
IN TOWNSHIP-GOVERNED AREAS	131 757	-	-	-	-	-	-	-	-	-	-
ENROLLMENT OF PUBLIC SCHOOL SYSTEMS											
TOTAL	59 814	30 285	27 523	2 762	24 106	157 324	37 625	104 507	15 192	51 105	172 644
THROUGH GRADE 12	54 234	28 500	25 738	2 762	22 595	130 731	35 032	80 507	15 192	47 254	164 182
COLLEGE GRADES	5 580	1 785	1 785	-	1 511	26 593	2 593	24 000	-	3 851	8 462

	North Carolina (see also Virginia)--Continued							
	Greensboro--Winston-Salem--High Point--Continued						Raleigh-Durham	
Item	Davidson County	Forsyth County*	Guilford County*	Randolph County	Stokes County	Yadkin County	Total	Durham County*
NUMBER OF LOCAL GOVERNMENTS								
ALL TYPES, TOTAL	7	8	10	12	6	7	31	5
WITH PROPERTY-TAXING POWER	5	5	6	10	5	6	20	2
WITHOUT PROPERTY-TAXING POWER.	2	3	4	2	1	1	11	3
COUNTY GOVERNMENTS	1	1	1	1	1	1	3	1
MUNICIPALITIES	3	3	4	8	2	5	16	1
WITH A POPULATION OF--								
50,000 OR MORE	-	-	-	-	-	-	-	-
25,000 TO 49,999	-	1	2	-	-	-	2	1
10,000 TO 24,999	-	-	-	-	-	-	1	-
5,000 TO 9,999	2	-	-	1	-	-	2	-
2,500 TO 4,999	-	1	-	1	-	-	1	-
1,000 TO 2,499	-	-	-	-	-	1	3	-
LESS THAN 1,000	1	1	2	3	1	1	3	-
				3	1	3	4	
TOWNSHIP GOVERNMENTS	-	-	-	-	-	-	-	-
SCHOOL DISTRICTS	-	-	-	-	-	-	-	-
SPECIAL DISTRICTS.	3	4	5	3	3	1	12	3
WITH PROPERTY-TAXING POWER	1	1	1	1	2	-	1	-
SINGLE FUNCTION DISTRICTS.								
CEMETERIES	-	-	-	-	-	-	-	-
EDUCATION (SCHOOL BUILDING DISTRICTS). .	-	-	-	-	-	-	-	-
FIRE PROTECTION.	-	-	-	-	-	-	-	-
HIGHWAYS	-	-	-	-	-	-	-	-
HEALTH	-	-	-	-	-	-	-	-
HOSPITALS.	-	1	-	-	-	-	-	-
HOUSING AND URBAN RENEWAL.	1	1	2	1	-	-	6	1
LIBRARIES.	-	-	-	-	-	-	-	-
NATURAL RESOURCES, TOTAL	1	1	1	1	3	1	4	2
DRAINAGE	-	-	-	-	-	-	-	-
FLOOD CONTROL.	-	-	-	-	2	-	1	-
IRRIGATION, WATER CONSERVATION	-	-	-	-	-	-	-	1
SOIL CONSERVATION.	1	1	1	1	1	1	3	1
OTHER AND COMPOSITE PURPOSES	-	-	-	-	-	-	-	-
PARKS AND RECREATION	-	-	-	-	-	-	-	-
SEWERAGE	1	-	1	1	-	-	-	-
UTILITIES, TOTAL	-	1	-	-	-	-	1	-
WATER SUPPLY	-	1	-	-	-	-	1	-
ELECTRIC POWER	-	-	-	-	-	-	-	-
GAS SUPPLY	-	-	-	-	-	-	-	-
TRANSIT.	-	-	-	-	-	-	-	-
OTHER.	-	-	1	-	-	-	1	-
MULTIPLE-FUNCTION DISTRICTS.	-	-	-	-	-	-	-	-
SEWERAGE AND WATER SUPPLY.	-	-	-	-	-	-	-	-
NATURAL RESOURCES AND WATER SUPPLY	-	-	-	-	-	-	-	-
OTHER.	-	-	-	-	-	-	-	-
SCHOOL SYSTEMS								
TOTAL.	4	2	4	3	1	1	7	3
DEPENDENT SCHOOL SYSTEMS	4	2	4	3	1	1	7	3
BY ENROLLMENT SIZE OCTOBER 1976								
100,000 OR MORE PUPILS	-	-	-	-	-	-	-	-
50,000 TO 99,999 PUPILS.	-	-	-	-	-	-	1	-
25,000 TO 49,999 PUPILS.	-	1	2	-	-	-	-	-
12,000 TO 24,999 PUPILS.	1	-	-	1	-	-	1	1
6,000 TO 11,999 PUPILS	-	-	1	-	1	-	1	1
3,000 TO 5,999 PUPILS.	2	-	1	1	-	1	2	-
1,200 TO 2,999 PUPILS.	1	1	-	-	-	-	2	1
300 TO 1,199 PUPILS.	-	-	-	1	-	-	-	-
50 TO 299 PUPILS	-	-	-	-	-	-	-	-
1 TO 49 PUPILS	-	-	-	-	-	-	-	-
POPULATION, 1975 (ESTIMATED)								
TOTAL.	100 814	226 332	299 484	82 555	28 369	26 624	468 512	139 320
IN MUNICIPALLY GOVERNED AREAS.	¹33 800	147 564	220 880	¹29 534	1 549	6 280	314 476	¹101 224
WITH A 1975 POPULATION OF--								
50,000 OR MORE	-	141 018	217 178	-	-	-	235 455	101 224
25,000 TO 49,999	-	-	-	-	-	-	30 520	-
10,000 TO 24,999	32 700	-	-	16 262	-	-	24 982	-
5,000 TO 9,999	-	5 192	-	5 842	-	-	5 519	-
2,500 TO 4,999	-	-	-	-	-	2 508	9 678	-
1,000 TO 2,499	1 100	1 354	3 702	6 009	1 370	1 688	5 740	-
LESS THAN 1,000.	-	-	-	1 421	179	2 084	2 582	-
OUTSIDE MUNICIPALLY GOVERNED AREAS	67 014	78 768	78 604	53 021	26 820	20 344	154 036	38 096
IN TOWNSHIP-GOVERNED AREAS	-	-	-	-	-	-	-	-
ENROLLMENT OF PUBLIC SCHOOL SYSTEMS								
TOTAL.	26 094	47 344	67 978	18 550	6 894	5 784	96 636	29 172
THROUGH GRADE 12	24 099	45 170	64 465	17 770	6 894	5 784	91 619	26 905
COLLEGE GRADES	1 995	2 174	3 513	780	-	-	5 017	2 267

Item	North Carolina (see also Virginia)--Continued					North Dakota			Ohio (see also West Virginia)		
	Raleigh-Durham--Continued		Wilmington			Fargo-Moorhead			Akron		
	Orange County	Wake County*	Total	Brunswick County	New Hanover County*	Total	Cass County*	Clay County* (Minn.)	Total	Portage County	Summit County*
NUMBER OF LOCAL GOVERNMENTS											
ALL TYPES, TOTAL	9	17	25	17	8	161	109	52	102	43	59
WITH PROPERTY-TAXING POWER	5	13	19	14	5	157	106	51	98	42	56
WITHOUT PROPERTY-TAXING POWER	4	4	6	3	3	4	3	1	4	1	3
COUNTY GOVERNMENTS	1	1	2	1	1	2	1	1	2	1	1
MUNICIPALITIES	3	12	16	12	4	31	20	11	30	10	20
WITH A POPULATION OF--											
50,000 OR MORE	-	1	1	-	1	1	1	-	1	-	1
25,000 TO 49,999	1	-	-	-	-	1	-	1	3	1	2
10,000 TO 24,999	-	2	-	-	-	-	-	-	4	1	3
5,000 TO 9,999	1	-	-	-	-	1	1	-	6	2	4
2,500 TO 4,999	-	3	1	1	-	-	-	-	7	1	6
1,000 TO 2,499	1	2	3	1	2	4	1	3	4	3	1
LESS THAN 1,000	-	4	11	10	1	24	17	7	5	2	3
TOWNSHIP GOVERNMENTS	-	-	-	-	-	80	50	30	31	18	13
SCHOOL DISTRICTS	-	-	-	-	-	19	13	6	28	11	17
SPECIAL DISTRICTS	5	4	7	4	3	29	25	4	11	3	8
WITH PROPERTY-TAXING POWER	1	-	1	1	-	24	22	2	7	2	5
SINGLE FUNCTION DISTRICTS											
CEMETERIES	-	-	-	-	-	-	-	-	-	-	-
EDUCATION (SCHOOL BUILDING DISTRICTS)	-	-	-	-	-	-	-	-	-	-	-
FIRE PROTECTION	-	-	-	-	-	8	8	-	-	-	-
HIGHWAYS	-	-	-	-	-	-	-	-	-	-	-
HEALTH	-	-	-	-	-	-	-	-	-	-	-
HOSPITALS	-	-	1	1	-	-	-	-	1	-	1
HOUSING AND URBAN RENEWAL	3	2	1	-	1	3	1	2	1	-	1
LIBRARIES	-	-	-	-	-	-	-	-	2	1	1
NATURAL RESOURCES, TOTAL	1	1	3	2	1	4	2	2	3	2	1
DRAINAGE	-	-	1	1	-	-	-	-	-	-	-
FLOOD CONTROL	-	-	-	-	-	1	-	1	-	-	-
IRRIGATION, WATER CONSERVATION	-	-	-	-	-	1	1	-	-	-	-
SOIL CONSERVATION	1	1	2	1	1	2	1	1	3	2	1
OTHER AND COMPOSITE PURPOSES	-	-	-	-	-	-	-	-	-	-	-
PARKS AND RECREATION	-	-	-	-	-	11	11	-	1	-	1
SEWERAGE	-	-	-	-	-	-	-	-	-	-	-
UTILITIES, TOTAL	1	-	-	-	-	-	-	-	2	-	2
WATER SUPPLY	1	-	-	-	-	-	-	-	1	-	1
ELECTRIC POWER	-	-	-	-	-	-	-	-	-	-	-
GAS SUPPLY	-	-	-	-	-	-	-	-	-	-	-
TRANSIT	-	-	-	-	-	-	-	-	1	-	1
OTHER	-	1	-	-	-	3	3	-	1	-	1
MULTIPLE-FUNCTION DISTRICTS	-	-	2	1	1	-	-	-	-	-	-
SEWERAGE AND WATER SUPPLY	-	-	2	1	1	-	-	-	-	-	-
NATURAL RESOURCES AND WATER SUPPLY	-	-	-	-	-	-	-	-	-	-	-
OTHER	-	-	-	-	-	-	-	-	-	-	-
SCHOOL SYSTEMS											
TOTAL	2	2	3	1	2	19	13	6	28	11	17
DEPENDENT SCHOOL SYSTEMS	2	2	3	1	2	-	-	-	-	-	-
BY ENROLLMENT SIZE OCTOBER 1976											
100,000 OR MORE PUPILS	-	-	-	-	-	-	-	-	-	-	-
50,000 TO 99,999 PUPILS	-	1	-	-	-	-	-	-	-	-	-
25,000 TO 49,999 PUPILS	-	-	-	-	-	-	-	-	1	-	1
12,000 TO 24,999 PUPILS	-	-	1	-	1	-	-	-	3	-	3
6,000 TO 11,999 PUPILS	-	-	1	1	-	2	1	1	3	-	3
3,000 TO 5,999 PUPILS	2	-	-	-	-	1	1	-	12	4	8
1,200 TO 2,999 PUPILS	-	1	-	-	-	-	-	-	11	7	4
300 TO 1,199 PUPILS	-	-	1	-	1	9	4	5	1	-	1
50 TO 299 PUPILS	-	-	-	-	-	5	5	-	-	-	-
1 TO 49 PUPILS	-	-	-	-	-	-	-	-	-	-	-
0 PUPILS (NONOPERATING)	-	-	-	-	-	2	2	-	-	-	-
POPULATION, 1975 (ESTIMATED)											
TOTAL	67 324	261 868	127 770	32 523	95 247	126 616	79 838	46 778	667 157	132 257	534 900
IN MUNICIPALLY GOVERNED AREAS	37 609	175 643	66 291	7 755	58 536	105 924	69 104	36 820	496 799	64 879	431 920
WITH A 1975 POPULATION OF--											
50,000 OR MORE	-	134 231	53 818	-	53 818	56 058	56 058	-	251 747	-	251 747
25,000 TO 49,999	30 520	-	-	-	-	28 755	-	28 755	102 129	26 768	75 361
10,000 TO 24,999	-	24 982	-	-	-	-	-	-	65 534	12 212	53 322
5,000 TO 9,999	5 519	-	-	-	-	7 586	7 586	-	42 204	16 619	25 585
2,500 TO 4,999	-	9 678	3 721	3 721	-	-	-	-	25 910	3 595	22 315
1,000 TO 2,499	1 570	4 170	5 872	1 512	4 360	7 316	1 547	5 769	6 676	5 205	1 471
LESS THAN 1,000	-	2 582	2 880	2 522	358	6 209	3 913	2 296	2 599	480	2 119
OUTSIDE MUNICIPALLY GOVERNED AREAS	29 715	86 225	61 479	24 768	36 711	20 692	10 734	9 958	170 358	67 378	102 980
IN TOWNSHIP-GOVERNED AREAS	-	-	-	-	-	20 463	10 501	9 962	231 430	111 471	119 959
ENROLLMENT OF PUBLIC SCHOOL SYSTEMS											
TOTAL	11 026	56 438	30 061	7 825	22 236	26 440	15 382	11 058	142 015	29 593	112 422
THROUGH GRADE 12	11 026	53 688	29 061	7 825	21 236	26 440	15 382	11 058	142 015	29 593	112 422
COLLEGE GRADES	-	2 750	1 000	-	1 000	-	-	-	-	-	-

Table 6. Local Governments and Public School Systems in Individual SMSA's: 1977—Continued

	Ohio (see also West Virginia)--Continued										
	Canton			Cincinnati							
Item	Total	Carroll County	Stark County*	Total	Clermont County	Hamilton County*	Warren County	Boone County	Campbell County	Kenton County	Dearborn County
NUMBER OF LOCAL GOVERNMENTS											
ALL TYPES, TOTAL	84	25	59	265	39	79	38	9	31	32	37
WITH PROPERTY-TAXING POWER	80	23	57	242	38	76	35	8	27	30	28
WITHOUT PROPERTY-TAXING POWER	4	2	2	23	1	3	3	1	4	2	9
COUNTY GOVERNMENTS	2	1	1	7	1	1	1	1	1	1	1
MUNICIPALITIES	24	5	19	108	12	36	13	3	15	22	7
WITH A POPULATION OF--											
50,000 OR MORE	1	-	1	1	-	1	-	-	-	-	-
25,000 TO 49,999	2	-	2	2	-	1	-	-	-	-	-
10,000 TO 24,999	1	-	1	11	-	6	1	1	2	1	-
5,000 TO 9,999	1	-	1	23	-	14	2	-	2	5	-
2,500 TO 4,999	3	1	2	22	2	6	3	-	3	5	3
1,000 TO 2,499	9	1	8	19	4	7	2	1	2	3	-
LESS THAN 1,000	7	3	4	30	6	1	5	1	6	7	4
TOWNSHIP GOVERNMENTS	31	14	17	51	14	12	11	-	-	-	14
SCHOOL DISTRICTS	19	2	17	57	9	23	8	2	7	5	3
SPECIAL DISTRICTS	8	3	5	42	3	7	5	3	8	4	12
WITH PROPERTY-TAXING POWER	4	1	3	19	2	4	2	2	4	2	3
SINGLE FUNCTION DISTRICTS	-	-	-	-	-	-	-	-	-	-	-
CEMETERIES	-	-	-	-	-	-	-	-	-	-	-
EDUCATION (SCHOOL BUILDING DISTRICTS)	-	-	-	7	-	-	-	-	-	-	7
FIRE PROTECTION	-	-	-	2	-	-	-	-	-	-	-
HIGHWAYS	-	-	-	-	-	-	-	-	2	-	-
HEALTH	-	-	-	-	-	-	-	-	-	-	-
HOSPITALS	-	-	-	-	-	-	-	-	-	-	-
HOUSING AND URBAN RENEWAL	1	-	1	2	-	1	1	-	-	-	-
LIBRARIES	2	1	1	5	1	-	-	1	-	1	2
NATURAL RESOURCES, TOTAL	2	1	1	11	1	2	2	1	1	1	3
DRAINAGE	-	-	-	-	-	-	-	-	-	-	-
FLOOD CONTROL	-	-	-	2	1	-	-	-	-	-	-
IRRIGATION, WATER CONSERVATION	-	-	-	2	-	1	-	-	-	-	1
SOIL CONSERVATION	-	-	-	2	-	-	1	-	-	-	1
OTHER AND COMPOSITE PURPOSES	2	1	1	7	1	1	1	1	1	1	1
PARKS AND RECREATION	1	-	1	5	1	3	1	-	-	-	-
SEWERAGE	-	-	-	2	-	-	-	-	1	1	-
UTILITIES, TOTAL	1	-	1	7	-	1	-	1	4	1	-
WATER SUPPLY	-	-	-	5	-	-	-	1	3	1	-
ELECTRIC POWER	-	-	-	-	-	-	-	-	-	-	-
GAS SUPPLY	-	-	-	-	-	-	-	-	-	-	-
TRANSIT	1	-	1	2	-	1	-	-	1	-	-
OTHER	-	-	-	1	-	-	1	-	-	-	-
MULTIPLE-FUNCTION DISTRICTS	1	1	-	-	-	-	-	-	-	-	-
SEWERAGE AND WATER SUPPLY	1	1	-	-	-	-	-	-	-	-	-
NATURAL RESOURCES AND WATER SUPPLY	-	-	-	-	-	-	-	-	-	-	-
OTHER	-	-	-	-	-	-	-	-	-	-	-
SCHOOL SYSTEMS											
TOTAL	19	2	17	58	9	24	8	2	7	5	3
DEPENDENT SCHOOL SYSTEMS	-	-	-	1	-	1	-	-	-	-	-
BY ENROLLMENT SIZE OCTOBER 1976											
100,000 OR MORE PUPILS	-	-	-	1	-	1	-	-	-	-	-
50,000 TO 99,999 PUPILS	-	-	-	1	-	1	-	-	-	-	-
25,000 TO 49,999 PUPILS	-	-	-	1	-	1	-	-	-	-	-
12,000 TO 24,999 PUPILS	1	-	1	1	-	1	-	-	-	-	-
6,000 TO 11,999 PUPILS	3	-	3	9	1	5	3	-	2	2	1
3,000 TO 5,999 PUPILS	9	1	8	13	2	5	3	1	2	-	1
1,200 TO 2,999 PUPILS	5	-	5	25	4	10	5	-	3	1	2
300 TO 1,199 PUPILS	1	1	-	7	2	1	-	1	1	2	-
50 TO 299 PUPILS	-	-	-	1	-	-	-	-	1	-	-
1 TO 49 PUPILS	-	-	-	-	-	-	-	-	-	-	-
POPULATION, 1975 (ESTIMATED)											
TOTAL	400 399	24 352	376 047	1 381 196	108 886	900 284	88 745	37 367	84 911	129 819	31 184
IN MUNICIPALLY GOVERNED AREAS	211 594	¹6 652	204 942	931 645	¹18 740	¹652 371	¹40 833	16 877	71 809	116 019	14 996
WITH A 1975 POPULATION OF--											
50,000 OR MORE	101 852	-	101 852	412 564	-	412 564	-	-	-	-	-
25,000 TO 49,999	59 933	-	59 933	70 961	-	26 494	-	-	-	44 467	-
10,000 TO 24,999	16 795	-	16 795	156 659	-	78 797	10 792	14 664	38 921	13 485	-
5,000 TO 9,999	6 641	-	6 641	158 860	-	96 827	15 177	-	15 910	30 946	-
2,500 TO 4,999	10 489	4 113	6 376	84 406	7 685	22 495	9 909	-	11 818	19 963	12 536
1,000 TO 2,499	13 895	1 683	12 212	35 198	8 162	14 517	3 361	1 969	2 629	4 560	-
LESS THAN 1,000	1 989	856	1 133	12 997	2 893	677	1 594	244	2 531	2 598	2 460
OUTSIDE MUNICIPALLY GOVERNED AREAS	188 805	17 700	171 105	449 551	90 146	247 913	47 912	20 490	13 102	13 800	16 188
IN TOWNSHIP-GOVERNED AREAS	231 973	24 353	207 620	503 977	108 885	283 769	80 140	-	-	-	31 183
ENROLLMENT OF PUBLIC SCHOOL SYSTEMS											
TOTAL	86 071	4 414	81 657	365 268	26 769	261 365	23 016	9 123	14 614	22 167	8 214
THROUGH GRADE 12	86 071	4 414	81 657	329 989	26 769	226 086	23 016	9 123	14 614	22 167	8 214
COLLEGE GRADES	-	-	-	35 279	-	35 279	-	-	-	-	-

	Ohio (see also West Virginia)--Continued										
	Cleveland					Columbus					
Item	Total	Cuyahoga County*	Geauga County	Lake County	Medina County	Total	Delaware County	Fairfield County	Franklin County*	Madison County	Pickaway County
NUMBER OF LOCAL GOVERNMENTS											
ALL TYPES, TOTAL	211	101	33	39	38	196	32	40	65	28	31
WITH PROPERTY-TAXING POWER	202	98	31	37	36	184	30	37	63	25	29
WITHOUT PROPERTY-TAXING POWER.	9	3	2	2	2	12	2	3	2	3	2
COUNTY GOVERNMENTS	4	1	1	1	1	5	1	1	1	1	1
MUNICIPALITIES	89	56	5	18	10	62	7	14	26	6	9
WITH A POPULATION OF--											
50,000 OR MORE	5	5	-	-	-	1	-	-	1	-	-
25,000 TO 49,999	9	8	-	1	-	3	-	1	2	-	-
10,000 TO 24,999	28	20	-	5	3	8	1	-	6	1	1
5,000 TO 9,999	8	5	-	3	-	3	-	-	2	1	-
2,500 TO 4,999	10	6	2	1	1	7	1	1	3	2	-
1,000 TO 2,499	13	7	2	3	1	7	1	1	3	1	1
LESS THAN 1,000.	16	5	1	5	5	33	4	11	9	2	7
TOWNSHIP GOVERNMENTS	42	4	16	5	17	77	18	13	17	14	15
SCHOOL DISTRICTS	57	33	7	10	7	37	4	8	17	4	4
SPECIAL DISTRICTS.	19	7	4	5	3	15	2	4	4	3	2
WITH PROPERTY-TAXING POWER	10	4	2	3	1	3	-	1	2	-	-
SINGLE FUNCTION DISTRICTS.	-	-	-	-	-	-	-	-	-	-	-
CEMETERIES	-	-	-	-	-	-	-	-	-	-	-
EDUCATION (SCHOOL BUILDING DISTRICTS). . .	-	-	-	-	-	1	-	-	-	1	-
FIRE PROTECTION.	-	-	-	-	-	-	-	-	-	-	-
HIGHWAYS	-	-	-	-	-	-	-	-	-	-	-
HEALTH	-	-	-	-	-	-	-	-	-	-	-
HOSPITALS.	-	-	-	-	-	-	-	-	-	-	-
HOUSING AND URBAN RENEWAL.	3	1	-	1	1	2	-	-	1	1	-
LIBRARIES.	3	1	1	1	-	3	1	1	-	-	1
NATURAL RESOURCES, TOTAL	4	1	1	1	1	7	1	3	1	1	1
DRAINAGE	-	-	-	-	-	-	-	-	-	-	-
FLOOD CONTROL.	-	-	-	-	-	2	-	2	-	-	-
IRRIGATION, WATER CONSERVATION . . .	-	-	-	-	-	-	-	-	-	-	-
SOIL CONSERVATION.	4	1	1	1	1	5	1	1	1	1	1
OTHER AND COMPOSITE PURPOSES . . .	-	-	-	-	-	-	-	-	-	-	-
PARKS AND RECREATION	5	1	2	1	1	1	-	-	1	-	-
SEWERAGE	1	1	-	-	-	-	-	-	-	-	-
UTILITIES, TOTAL	1	1	-	-	-	1	-	-	1	-	-
WATER SUPPLY	-	-	-	-	-	-	-	-	-	-	-
ELECTRIC POWER	-	-	-	-	-	-	-	-	-	-	-
GAS SUPPLY	-	-	-	-	-	-	-	-	-	-	-
TRANSIT.	1	1	-	-	-	1	-	-	1	-	-
OTHER.	2	1	-	1	-	-	-	-	-	-	-
MULTIPLE-FUNCTION DISTRICTS.	-	-	-	-	-	-	-	-	-	-	-
SEWERAGE AND WATER SUPPLY.	-	-	-	-	-	-	-	-	-	-	-
NATURAL RESOURCES AND WATER SUPPLY . . .	-	-	-	-	-	-	-	-	-	-	-
OTHER.	-	-	-	-	-	-	-	-	-	-	-
SCHOOL SYSTEMS											
TOTAL.	57	33	7	10	7	37	4	8	17	4	4
DEPENDENT SCHOOL SYSTEMS	-	-	-	-	-	-	-	-	-	-	-
BY ENROLLMENT SIZE OCTOBER 1976											
100,000 OR MORE PUPILS	1	1	-	-	-	-	-	-	-	-	-
50,000 TO 99,999 PUPILS.	-	-	-	-	-	1	-	-	1	-	-
25,000 TO 49,999 PUPILS.	1	1	-	-	-	-	-	-	-	-	-
12,000 TO 24,999 PUPILS.	4	2	-	2	-	1	-	-	1	-	-
6,000 TO 11,999 PUPILS	11	9	-	1	1	5	-	1	4	-	-
3,000 TO 5,999 PUPILS.	16	9	1	3	3	9	1	-	6	-	2
1,200 TO 2,999 PUPILS.	17	7	4	3	3	18	3	5	4	4	2
300 TO 1,199 PUPILS.	6	3	2	1	-	3	-	2	1	-	-
50 TO 299 PUPILS	1	1	-	-	-	-	-	-	-	-	-
1 TO 49 PUPILS	-	-	-	-	-	-	-	-	-	-	-
POPULATION, 1975 (ESTIMATED)											
TOTAL.	1 966 725	1 592 613	68 144	206 881	99 087	1 068 514	50 836	84 568	858 239	31 304	43 567
IN MUNICIPALLY GOVERNED AREAS.	1 820 657	1 582 587	¹10 911	166 941	¹60 218	838 701	¹24 997	¹49 608	728 409	17 402	¹18 285
WITH A 1975 POPULATION OF--											
50,000 OR MORE	917 519	917 519	-	-	-	535 610	-	-	535 610	-	-
25,000 TO 49,999	303 288	263 765	-	39 523	-	99 582	-	37 952	61 630	-	-
10,000 TO 24,999	479 918	329 980	-	97 087	52 851	125 778	19 546	-	93 642	-	12 590
5,000 TO 9,999	53 532	33 042	-	20 490	-	26 334	-	-	18 322	8 012	-
2,500 TO 4,999	37 172	23 824	7 294	3 287	2 767	21 794	2 538	2 968	9 198	7 090	-
1,000 TO 2,499	20 312	11 766	3 160	3 864	1 522	11 158	1 230	1 483	4 908	1 628	1 909
LESS THAN 1,000.	8 916	2 691	457	2 690	3 078	18 445	1 683	7 205	5 099	672	3 786
OUTSIDE MUNICIPALLY GOVERNED AREAS	146 068	10 026	57 233	39 940	38 869	229 813	25 839	34 960	129 830	13 902	25 282
IN TOWNSHIP-GOVERNED AREAS	186 485	10 156	68 145	47 478	60 706	383 426	47 067	46 617	222 884	23 292	43 566
ENROLLMENT OF PUBLIC SCHOOL SYSTEMS											
TOTAL.	415 235	320 878	14 789	52 144	27 424	228 090	10 802	19 877	179 224	7 263	10 924
THROUGH GRADE 12	380 793	292 778	14 789	45 802	27 424	223 730	10 802	19 877	174 864	7 263	10 924
COLLEGE GRADES	34 442	28 100	-	6 342	-	4 360	-	-	4 360	-	-

Item	Ohio (see also West Virginia)—Continued					Hamilton-Middletown	Lima
	Dayton						
	Total	Greene County	Miami County	Montgomery County*	Preble County	Butler County (entire SMSA)	Total
NUMBER OF LOCAL GOVERNMENTS							
ALL TYPES, TOTAL	162	35	39	56	32	38	141
WITH PROPERTY-TAXING POWER	153	32	37	53	31	36	135
WITHOUT PROPERTY-TAXING POWER.	9	3	2	3	1	2	6
COUNTY GOVERNMENTS	4	1	1	1	1	1	4
MUNICIPALITIES	50	9	12	18	11	11	43
WITH A POPULATION OF--							
50,000 OR MORE	2	-	-	2	-	1	1
25,000 TO 49,999	2	2	-	-	-	1	-
10,000 TO 24,999	7	-	-	5	-	2	1
5,000 TO 9,999	6	1	2	3	1	1	3
2,500 TO 4,999	7	1	1	4	-	2	3
1,000 TO 2,499	9	2	2	1	4	-	9
LESS THAN 1,000	17	3	5	3	6	4	26
TOWNSHIP GOVERNMENTS	49	12	12	13	12	13	53
SCHOOL DISTRICTS	38	7	9	17	5	9	28
SPECIAL DISTRICTS.	21	6	5	7	3	4	13
WITH PROPERTY-TAXING POWER	12	3	3	4	2	2	7
SINGLE FUNCTION DISTRICTS.	-	-	-	-	-	-	-
CEMETERIES	-	-	-	-	-	-	-
EDUCATION (SCHOOL BUILDING DISTRICTS). . . .	-	-	-	-	-	-	-
FIRE PROTECTION.	-	-	-	-	-	-	-
HIGHWAYS	-	-	-	-	-	-	-
HEALTH	-	-	-	-	-	-	-
HOSPITALS.	-	-	-	-	-	-	-
HOUSING AND URBAN RENEWAL.	2	1	-	1	-	1	2
LIBRARIES.	4	1	1	1	1	-	2
NATURAL RESOURCES, TOTAL	5	1	2	1	1	2	3
DRAINAGE	-	-	-	-	-	-	-
FLOOD CONTROL.	1	-	1	-	-	1	-
IRRIGATION, WATER CONSERVATION . . .	-	-	-	-	-	-	-
SOIL CONSERVATION.	4	1	1	1	1	1	3
OTHER AND COMPOSITE PURPOSES	-	-	-	-	-	-	-
PARKS AND RECREATION	7	2	1	3	1	1	4
SEWERAGE	1	-	1	-	-	-	-
UTILITIES, TOTAL	-	-	-	-	-	-	1
WATER SUPPLY	-	-	-	-	-	-	-
ELECTRIC POWER	-	-	-	-	-	-	-
GAS SUPPLY	-	-	-	-	-	-	-
TRANSIT.	-	-	-	-	-	-	1
OTHER.	1	1	-	-	-	-	-
MULTIPLE-FUNCTION DISTRICTS.	1	-	-	1	-	-	-
SEWERAGE AND WATER SUPPLY.	1	-	-	1	-	-	-
NATURAL RESOURCES AND WATER SUPPLY	-	-	-	-	-	-	-
OTHER.	1	-	-	1	-	-	-
SCHOOL SYSTEMS							
TOTAL.	38	7	9	17	5	9	28
DEPENDENT SCHOOL SYSTEMS	-	-	-	-	-	-	-
BY ENROLLMENT SIZE OCTOBER 1976							
100,000 OR MORE PUPILS	-	-	-	-	-	-	-
50,000 TO 99,999 PUPILS.	-	-	-	-	-	-	-
25,000 TO 49,999 PUPILS.	1	-	-	1	-	1	-
12,000 TO 24,999 PUPILS.	2	-	-	-	-	-	-
6,000 TO 11,999 PUPILS	7	3	-	2	-	1	1
3,000 TO 5,999 PUPILS.	7	-	-	4	-	3	3
1,200 TO 2,999 PUPILS.	15	2	2	5	-	2	7
300 TO 1,199 PUPILS.	6	2	4	5	4	3	17
50 TO 299 PUPILS	-	2	3	-	1	-	-
1 TO 49 PUPILS	-	-	-	-	-	-	-
POPULATION, 1975 (ESTIMATED)							
TOTAL.	835 708	124 779	87 276	587 507	36 146	244 562	211 543
IN MUNICIPALLY GOVERNED AREAS.	534 047	77 008	56 724	¹384 498	15 817	¹173 815	125 969
WITH A 1975 POPULATION OF--							
50,000 OR MORE	275 935	-	-	275 935	-	66 469	51 372
25,000 TO 49,999	61 418	61 418	-	-	-	48 004	-
10,000 TO 24,999	103 353	-	38 609	64 744	-	43 033	10 879
5,000 TO 9,999	39 374	5 586	5 886	21 823	6 079	6 341	23 752
2,500 TO 4,999	29 672	4 366	6 785	18 521	-	7 877	10 328
1,000 TO 2,499	15 644	4 435	3 412	1 005	6 792	-	17 197
LESS THAN 1,000.	8 651	1 203	2 032	2 470	2 946	2 091	12 441
OUTSIDE MUNICIPALLY GOVERNED AREAS	301 661	47 771	30 552	203 009	20 329	70 747	85 574
IN TOWNSHIP-GOVERNED AREAS	487 073	96 016	87 277	273 716	30 064	123 747	160 176
ENROLLMENT OF PUBLIC SCHOOL SYSTEMS							
TOTAL.	191 315	30 156	21 252	130 402	9 505	49 974	47 351
THROUGH GRADE 12	178 681	30 156	21 252	117 768	9 505	49 974	47 351
COLLEGE GRADES	12 634	-	-	12 634	-	-	-

Ohio (see also West Virginia)--Continued

Item	Lima--Continued				Lorain-Elyria	Mansfield	Springfield			Steubenville-Weirton	
	Allen County*	Auglaize County	Putnam County	Van Wert County	Lorain County (entire SMSA)	Richland County (entire SMSA)	Total	Champaign County	Clark County*	Total	Jefferson County*
NUMBER OF LOCAL GOVERNMENTS											
ALL TYPES, TOTAL	40	32	42	27	56	41	62	29	33	65	44
WITH PROPERTY-TAXING POWER	36	32	41	26	52	39	57	27	30	53	42
WITHOUT PROPERTY-TAXING POWER.	4	-	1	1	4	2	5	2	3	12	2
COUNTY GOVERNMENTS	1	1	1	1	1	1	2	1	1	3	1
MUNICIPALITIES	10	9	15	9	15	9	17	7	10	27	20
WITH A POPULATION OF--											
50,000 OR MORE	1	-	-	-	2	1	1	-	1	-	-
25,000 TO 49,999	-	-	-	-	-	-	-	-	-	2	1
10,000 TO 24,999	-	-	-	1	2	-	1	1	-	2	2
5,000 TO 9,999	1	2	-	-	4	1	1	-	1	2	2
2,500 TO 4,999	2	-	1	-	2	2	-	-	-	4	1
1,000 TO 2,499	2	3	3	1	3	3	4	2	2	8	6
LESS THAN 1,000.	4	4	11	7	2	2	10	4	6	11	10
TOWNSHIP GOVERNMENTS	12	14	15	12	18	18	22	12	10	14	14
SCHOOL DISTRICTS	9	6	9	4	16	10	13	5	8	8	6
SPECIAL DISTRICTS.	8	2	2	1	6	3	8	4	4	13	3
WITH PROPERTY-TAXING POWER	4	2	1	-	2	1	3	2	1	1	1
SINGLE FUNCTION DISTRICTS.	-	-	-	-	-	-	-	-	-	-	-
CEMETERIES	-	-	-	-	-	-	-	-	-	-	-
EDUCATION (SCHOOL BUILDING DISTRICTS). . .	-	-	-	-	-	-	-	-	-	-	-
FIRE PROTECTION.	-	-	-	-	-	-	-	-	-	-	-
HIGHWAYS	-	-	-	-	-	-	-	-	-	-	-
HEALTH	-	-	-	-	-	-	-	-	-	-	-
HOSPITALS.	1	1	-	-	-	-	-	-	-	2	1
HOUSING AND URBAN RENEWAL.	1	-	-	-	1	1	1	-	1	-	1
LIBRARIES.	-	1	1	-	-	-	2	1	1	-	-
NATURAL RESOURCES, TOTAL	1	-	1	1	1	1	4	2	2	1	1
DRAINAGE	-	-	-	-	-	-	-	-	-	-	-
FLOOD CONTROL.	-	-	-	-	-	-	1	-	1	-	-
IRRIGATION, WATER CONSERVATION	-	-	-	-	-	-	1	1	-	-	-
SOIL CONSERVATION.	1	-	1	1	1	1	2	1	1	1	1
OTHER AND COMPOSITE PURPOSES	-	-	-	-	-	-	-	-	-	-	-
PARKS AND RECREATION	4	-	-	-	1	1	1	1	-	1	1
SEWERAGE	-	-	-	-	-	-	-	-	-	2	-
UTILITIES, TOTAL	1	-	-	-	1	-	-	-	-	5	-
WATER SUPPLY	-	-	-	-	1	-	-	-	-	5	-
ELECTRIC POWER	-	-	-	-	-	-	-	-	-	-	-
GAS SUPPLY	-	-	-	-	-	-	-	-	-	-	-
TRANSIT.	1	-	-	-	-	-	-	-	-	-	-
OTHER.	-	-	-	-	2	-	-	-	-	-	-
MULTIPLE-FUNCTION DISTRICTS.	-	-	-	-	-	-	-	-	-	2	-
SEWERAGE AND WATER SUPPLY.	-	-	-	-	-	-	-	-	-	1	-
NATURAL RESOURCES AND WATER SUPPLY	-	-	-	-	-	-	-	-	-	-	-
OTHER.	-	-	-	-	-	-	-	-	-	1	-
SCHOOL SYSTEMS											
TOTAL.	9	6	9	4	16	10	13	5	8	8	6
DEPENDENT SCHOOL SYSTEMS	-	-	-	-	-	-	-	-	-	-	-
BY ENROLLMENT SIZE OCTOBER 1976											
100,000 OR MORE PUPILS	-	-	-	-	-	-	-	-	-	-	-
50,000 TO 99,999 PUPILS.	-	-	-	-	-	-	-	-	-	-	-
25,000 TO 49,999 PUPILS.	-	-	-	-	-	-	-	-	-	-	-
12,000 TO 24,999 PUPILS.	-	-	-	-	2	-	1	-	1	-	-
6,000 TO 11,999 PUPILS	1	-	-	-	-	1	-	-	-	2	-
3,000 TO 5,999 PUPILS.	2	1	-	-	5	3	3	-	3	4	4
1,200 TO 2,999 PUPILS.	4	1	1	1	8	5	5	2	3	2	2
300 TO 1,199 PUPILS.	2	4	8	3	1	1	4	3	1	-	-
50 TO 299 PUPILS	-	-	-	-	-	-	-	-	-	-	-
1 TO 49 PUPILS	-	-	-	-	-	-	-	-	-	-	-
POPULATION, 1975 (ESTIMATED)											
TOTAL.	108 734	41 464	31 757	29 588	268 579	130 915	187 424	32 540	154 884	165 781	94 606
IN MUNICIPALLY GOVERNED AREAS.	71 732	24 545	14 951	¹14 741	¹215 315	¹80 047	108 501	18 289	¹90 212	103 284	61 372
WITH A 1975 POPULATION OF--											
50,000 OR MORE	51 372	-	-	-	137 381	56 916	77 317	-	77 317	-	-
25,000 TO 49,999	-	-	-	-	-	-	-	-	-	54 215	28 280
10,000 TO 24,999	-	-	-	10 879	30 251	-	12 217	12 217	-	13 173	13 173
5,000 TO 9,999	7 408	16 344	-	-	35 636	9 306	6 623	-	6 623	16 953	4 933
2,500 TO 4,999	6 475	-	3 853	-	6 982	7 516	-	-	-	12 254	8 830
1,000 TO 2,499	4 422	6 055	5 641	1 079	4 497	4 734	7 627	4 043	3 584	6 689	6 156
LESS THAN 1,000.	2 055	2 146	5 457	2 783	568	1 575	4 717	2 029	2 688		
OUTSIDE MUNICIPALLY GOVERNED AREAS	37 002	16 919	16 806	14 847	53 264	50 868	78 923	14 251	64 672	62 497	33 234
IN TOWNSHIP-GOVERNED AREAS	57 364	41 464	31 762	29 586	82 907	74 000	110 107	32 541	77 566	66 324	66 324
ENROLLMENT OF PUBLIC SCHOOL SYSTEMS											
TOTAL.	24 298	9 485	8 664	4 904	65 712	30 769	44 884	8 541	36 343	35 008	20 339
THROUGH GRADE 12	24 298	9 485	8 664	4 904	60 414	29 426	42 874	8 541	34 333	33 558	18 889
COLLEGE GRADES	-	-	-	-	5 298	1 343	2 010	-	2 010	1 450	1 450

Table 6. Local Governments and Public School Systems in Individual SMSA's: 1977—Continued

Item	Steubenville-Weirton--Continued		Toledo						Youngstown-Warren		
	Brooke County (W. Va.)	Hancock County* (W. Va.)	Total	Fulton County	Lucas County*	Ottawa County	Wood County	Monroe County (Mich.)	Total	Mahoning County*	Trumbull County*
NUMBER OF LOCAL GOVERNMENTS											
ALL TYPES, TOTAL	10	11	198	29	42	30	59	38	106	45	61
WITH PROPERTY-TAXING POWER	6	5	186	28	37	29	57	35	101	43	58
WITHOUT PROPERTY-TAXING POWER.	4	6	12	1	5	1	2	3	5	2	3
COUNTY GOVERNMENTS	1	1	5	1	1	1	1	1	2	1	1
MUNICIPALITIES	4	3	58	7	10	8	25	8	20	10	10
WITH A POPULATION OF--											
50,000 OR MORE	-	-	1	-	1	-	-	-	2	1	1
25,000 TO 49,999	-	1	-	-	-	-	-	-	-	-	-
10,000 TO 24,999	-	-	5	-	3	-	1	-	4	2	2
5,000 TO 9,999	-	-	4	1	-	1	2	-	3	1	2
2,500 TO 4,999	2	1	10	3	2	1	3	1	4	2	2
1,000 TO 2,499	1	1	15	1	2	2	6	4	4	4	-
LESS THAN 1,000.	1	-	23	2	2	4	13	2	3	-	3
TOWNSHIP GOVERNMENTS	-	-	69	12	11	12	19	15	38	14	24
SCHOOL DISTRICTS	1	1	43	8	8	7	10	10	35	14	21
SPECIAL DISTRICTS.	4	6	23	1	12	2	4	4	11	6	5
WITH PROPERTY-TAXING POWER	-	-	11	-	7	1	2	1	6	4	2
SINGLE FUNCTION DISTRICTS.	-	-	-	-	-	-	-	-	-	-	-
CEMETERIES	-	-	-	-	-	-	-	-	-	-	-
EDUCATION (SCHOOL BUILDING DISTRICTS).	-	-	-	-	-	-	-	-	-	-	-
FIRE PROTECTION.	-	-	-	-	-	-	-	-	-	-	-
HIGHWAYS	-	-	-	-	-	-	-	-	-	-	-
HEALTH	-	-	1	-	1	-	-	-	-	-	-
HOSPITALS.	-	-	-	-	-	-	-	-	-	-	-
HOUSING AND URBAN RENEWAL.	-	1	1	-	1	-	-	-	-	-	-
LIBRARIES.	-	-	2	-	1	-	1	-	2	1	1
NATURAL RESOURCES, TOTAL	-	-	8	1	3	2	1	1	2	1	1
DRAINAGE	-	-	-	-	-	-	-	-	-	-	-
FLOOD CONTROL.	-	-	3	-	2	1	-	-	-	-	-
IRRIGATION, WATER CONSERVATION . . .	-	-	-	-	-	-	-	-	-	-	-
SOIL CONSERVATION.	-	-	5	1	1	1	1	1	2	1	1
OTHER AND COMPOSITE PURPOSES . . .	-	-	-	-	-	-	-	-	-	-	-
PARKS AND RECREATION	-	-	4	-	3	-	1	-	5	2	3
SEWERAGE	1	1	-	-	-	-	-	-	1	1	-
UTILITIES, TOTAL	2	3	2	-	1	-	-	1	1	1	-
WATER SUPPLY	2	3	1	-	-	-	-	1	1	1	-
ELECTRIC POWER	-	-	-	-	-	-	-	-	-	-	-
GAS SUPPLY	-	-	-	-	-	-	-	-	-	-	-
TRANSIT.	-	-	1	-	1	-	-	-	-	-	-
OTHER.	-	-	4	-	1	-	-	1	2	-	-
MULTIPLE-FUNCTION DISTRICTS.	1	1	1	-	1	-	-	-	-	-	-
SEWERAGE AND WATER SUPPLY.	1	-	-	-	-	-	-	-	-	-	-
NATURAL RESOURCES AND WATER SUPPLY . .	-	-	-	-	-	-	-	-	-	-	-
OTHER.	-	1	1	-	1	-	-	-	-	-	-
SCHOOL SYSTEMS											
TOTAL.	1	1	43	8	8	7	10	10	35	14	21
DEPENDENT SCHOOL SYSTEMS	-	-	-	-	-	-	-	-	-	-	-
BY ENROLLMENT SIZE OCTOBER 1976											
100,000 OR MORE PUPILS	-	-	-	-	-	-	-	-	-	-	-
50,000 TO 99,999 PUPILS.	-	-	1	-	1	-	-	-	-	-	-
25,000 TO 49,999 PUPILS.	-	-	-	-	-	-	-	-	-	-	-
12,000 TO 24,999 PUPILS.	-	-	-	-	-	-	-	-	-	-	-
6,000 TO 11,999 PUPILS	1	1	4	-	2	-	-	2	3	2	1
3,000 TO 5,999 PUPILS.	-	-	7	-	4	1	1	1	4	1	3
1,200 TO 2,999 PUPILS.	-	-	20	5	-	2	7	6	17	7	10
300 TO 1,199 PUPILS.	-	-	8	3	1	1	2	1	10	3	7
50 TO 299 PUPILS	-	-	1	-	-	1	-	-	-	-	-
1 TO 49 PUPILS	-	-	2	-	-	-	-	2	-	-	-
POPULATION, 1975 (ESTIMATED)											
TOTAL.	31 049	40 126	778 810	35 566	476 657	38 828	100 665	127 094	548 558	307 339	241 219
IN MUNICIPALLY GOVERNED AREAS.	[1]10 627	31 285	560 984	16 933	428 499	15 973	[1]65 200	[1]34 379	301 879	[1]181 601	[1]120 278
WITH A 1975 POPULATION OF--											
50,000 OR MORE	-	-	367 650	-	367 650	-	-	-	192 689	132 203	60 486
25,000 TO 49,999	-	25 935	-	-	-	-	-	-	-	-	-
10,000 TO 24,999	-	-	99 132	-	49 826	-	24 694	24 612	65 108	27 438	37 670
5,000 TO 9,999	-	-	27 124	5 398	-	7 503	14 223	-	21 017	6 891	14 126
2,500 TO 4,999	8 627	3 393	33 842	9 031	7 532	3 014	11 540	2 725	15 030	8 153	6 877
1,000 TO 2,499	1 467	1 957	22 014	1 299	2 947	3 696	8 008	6 064	6 916	6 916	-
LESS THAN 1,000.	533	-	11 222	1 205	544	1 760	6 735	978	1 119	-	1 119
OUTSIDE MUNICIPALLY GOVERNED AREAS	20 422	8 841	217 826	18 633	48 158	22 855	35 465	92 715	246 679	125 738	120 941
IN TOWNSHIP-GOVERNED AREAS	-	-	298 800	35 563	69 360	38 829	56 340	98 708	383 384	145 271	238 113
ENROLLMENT OF PUBLIC SCHOOL SYSTEMS											
TOTAL.	6 223	8 446	164 500	11 081	90 841	8 782	21 730	32 066	108 695	55 687	53 008
THROUGH GRADE 12	6 223	8 446	158 682	10 283	90 841	8 782	18 738	30 038	108 695	55 687	53 008
COLLEGE GRADES	-	-	5 818	798	-	-	2 992	2 028	-	-	-

77

Table 6. Local Governments and Public School Systems in Individual SMSA's: 1977—Continued

		Oklahoma (see also Arkansas)							
	Lawton	Oklahoma City						Tulsa	
Item	Comanche County (entire SMSA)	Total	Canadian County	Cleveland County	McClain County	Oklahoma County*	Pottawatomie County	Total	Creek County
NUMBER OF LOCAL GOVERNMENTS									
ALL TYPES, TOTAL	33	133	20	18	25	38	32	192	38
WITH PROPERTY-TAXING POWER	24	115	17	16	18	36	28	141	28
WITHOUT PROPERTY-TAXING POWER	9	18	3	2	7	2	4	51	10
COUNTY GOVERNMENTS	1	5	1	1	1	1	1	6	1
MUNICIPALITIES	10	53	6	7	10	19	11	64	11
WITH A POPULATION OF--									
50,000 OR MORE	1	3	-	1	-	2	-	1	-
25,000 TO 49,999	-	3	-	1	-	1	1	-	-
10,000 TO 24,999	-	6	2	-	-	4	-	3	1
5,000 TO 9,999	-	3	1	-	-	1	1	4	-
2,500 TO 4,999	-	8	-	1	2	4	1	7	1
1,000 TO 2,499	1	6	-	1	1	2	2	14	3
LESS THAN 1,000	8	24	3	3	7	5	6	35	6
TOWNSHIP GOVERNMENTS	-	-	-	-	-	-	-	-	-
SCHOOL DISTRICTS	13	55	10	8	7	15	15	71	16
SPECIAL DISTRICTS	9	20	3	2	7	3	5	51	10
WITH PROPERTY-TAXING POWER	-	2	-	-	-	1	1	-	-
SINGLE FUNCTION DISTRICTS	-	-	-	-	-	-	-	-	-
CEMETERIES	-	-	-	-	-	-	-	-	-
EDUCATION (SCHOOL BUILDING DISTRICTS)	-	-	-	-	-	-	-	-	-
FIRE PROTECTION	-	-	-	-	-	-	-	1	-
HIGHWAYS	-	-	-	-	-	-	-	-	-
HEALTH	-	-	-	-	-	-	-	-	-
HOSPITALS	-	1	-	-	-	-	1	-	-
HOUSING AND URBAN RENEWAL	4	1	-	-	-	1	-	6	3
LIBRARIES	-	-	-	-	-	-	-	-	-
NATURAL RESOURCES, TOTAL	2	9	2	2	1	1	3	9	2
DRAINAGE	-	-	-	-	-	-	-	-	-
FLOOD CONTROL	-	3	-	1	-	-	2	3	1
IRRIGATION, WATER CONSERVATION	1	-	-	-	-	-	-	-	-
SOIL CONSERVATION	1	6	2	1	1	1	1	6	1
OTHER AND COMPOSITE PURPOSES	-	-	-	-	-	-	-	-	-
PARKS AND RECREATION	-	-	-	-	-	-	-	-	-
SEWERAGE	-	1	-	-	-	-	1	1	-
UTILITIES, TOTAL	3	8	1	-	6	-	1	33	5
WATER SUPPLY	3	8	1	-	6	-	1	33	5
ELECTRIC POWER	-	-	-	-	-	-	-	-	-
GAS SUPPLY	-	-	-	-	-	-	-	-	-
TRANSIT	-	-	-	-	-	-	-	-	-
OTHER	-	-	-	-	-	-	-	1	-
MULTIPLE-FUNCTION DISTRICTS	-	-	-	-	-	-	-	-	-
SEWERAGE AND WATER SUPPLY	-	-	-	-	-	-	-	-	-
NATURAL RESOURCES AND WATER SUPPLY	-	-	-	-	-	-	-	-	-
OTHER	-	-	-	-	-	-	-	-	-
SCHOOL SYSTEMS									
TOTAL	13	55	10	8	7	15	15	71	16
DEPENDENT SCHOOL SYSTEMS	-	-	-	-	-	-	-	-	-
BY ENROLLMENT SIZE OCTOBER 1976									
100,000 OR MORE PUPILS	-	-	-	-	-	-	-	-	-
50,000 TO 99,999 PUPILS	-	-	-	-	-	-	-	1	-
25,000 TO 49,999 PUPILS	-	1	-	-	-	1	-	-	-
12,000 TO 24,999 PUPILS	1	3	-	1	-	2	-	-	-
6,000 TO 11,999 PUPILS	-	2	-	1	-	1	-	1	-
3,000 TO 5,999 PUPILS	-	4	1	-	-	2	1	5	1
1,200 TO 2,999 PUPILS	-	7	2	1	-	2	2	10	1
300 TO 1,199 PUPILS	5	20	1	3	6	6	4	32	10
50 TO 299 PUPILS	7	18	6	2	1	1	8	20	3
1 TO 49 PUPILS	-	-	-	-	-	-	-	2	1
POPULATION, 1975 (ESTIMATED)									
TOTAL	105 059	746 323	40 460	99 128	18 597	537 939	50 199	585 682	49 291
IN MUNICIPALLY GOVERNED AREAS	82 215	715 309	[1]34 217	[1]90 290	[1]11 355	[2]539 919	[1]39 528	465 416	28 063
WITH A 1975 POPULATION OF--									
50,000 OR MORE	76 421	475 969	-	59 948	-	[2]416 021	-	331 726	-
25,000 TO 49,999	-	81 440	-	25 115	-	29 607	26 718	-	-
10,000 TO 24,999	-	97 172	27 841	-	-	69 331	-	45 673	14 997
5,000 TO 9,999	-	16 699	5 240	-	-	6 029	5 430	30 055	-
2,500 TO 4,999	-	26 826	-	2 728	7 098	13 560	3 440	26 383	4 385
1,000 TO 2,499	1 237	9 325	-	1 781	1 974	3 075	2 495	20 208	4 877
LESS THAN 1,000	4 557	7 878	1 136	718	2 283	2 296	1 445	11 371	3 804
OUTSIDE MUNICIPALLY GOVERNED AREAS	22 844	32 994	6 243	8 838	7 242	-	10 671	120 266	21 228
IN TOWNSHIP-GOVERNED AREAS	-	-	-	-	-	-	-	-	-
ENROLLMENT OF PUBLIC SCHOOL SYSTEMS									
TOTAL	24 178	162 200	11 227	25 623	4 717	109 010	11 623	133 618	12 532
THROUGH GRADE 12	24 178	162 200	11 227	25 623	4 717	109 010	11 623	133 618	12 532
COLLEGE GRADES	-	-	-	-	-	-	-	-	-

78

Table 6. Local Governments and Public School Systems in Individual SMSA's: 1977—Continued

Item	Oklahoma (see also Arkansas)--Continued					Oregon		
	Tulsa--Continued					Eugene-Springfield	Portland	
	Mayes County	Osage County	Rogers County	Tulsa County*	Wagoner County	Lane County (entire SMSA)	Total	Clackamas County
NUMBER OF LOCAL GOVERNMENTS								
ALL TYPES, TOTAL	29	36	30	35	24	82	257	97
WITH PROPERTY-TAXING POWER	21	29	21	28	14	73	218	86
WITHOUT PROPERTY-TAXING POWER	8	7	9	7	10	9	39	11
COUNTY GOVERNMENTS	1	1	1	1	1	1	4	1
MUNICIPALITIES	12	13	9	11	8	11	39	14
WITH A POPULATION OF--								
50,000 OR MORE	-	-	-	-	-	-	1	-
25,000 TO 49,999	-	-	-	1	-	1	1	-
10,000 TO 24,999	-	-	-	-	-	1	1	-
5,000 TO 9,999	-	-	-	2	-	-	7	3
2,500 TO 4,999	1	-	1	1	1	1	5	3
1,000 TO 2,499	-	1	-	4	1	3	6	1
LESS THAN 1,000	3	3	3	2	-	2	10	4
	8	9	5	1	6	3	9	3
TOWNSHIP GOVERNMENTS	-	-	-	-	-	-	-	-
SCHOOL DISTRICTS	8	15	11	16	5	18	69	30
SPECIAL DISTRICTS	8	7	9	7	10	52	145	52
WITH PROPERTY-TAXING POWER	-	-	-	-	-	43	106	41
SINGLE FUNCTION DISTRICTS	-	-	-	-	-	-	-	-
CEMETERIES	-	-	-	-	-	-	-	-
EDUCATION (SCHOOL BUILDING DISTRICTS)	-	-	-	-	-	-	5	1
FIRE PROTECTION	-	-	-	-	-	-	-	-
HIGHWAYS	-	-	-	-	1	21	41	16
HEALTH	-	-	-	-	-	1	2	2
HOSPITALS	-	-	-	-	-	-	-	-
HOUSING AND URBAN RENEWAL	1	1	-	1	-	1	4	1
LIBRARIES	-	-	-	-	-	-	1	-
NATURAL RESOURCES, TOTAL	1	1	2	1	2	10	27	4
DRAINAGE	-	-	-	-	-	-	17	1
FLOOD CONTROL	-	-	1	-	1	2	2	1
IRRIGATION, WATER CONSERVATION	-	-	-	-	-	8	4	2
SOIL CONSERVATION	1	1	1	1	1	-	4	-
OTHER AND COMPOSITE PURPOSES	-	-	-	-	-	-	-	-
PARKS AND RECREATION	-	-	-	-	-	2	4	2
SEWERAGE	-	1	-	-	-	-	4	2
UTILITIES, TOTAL	6	4	7	4	7	14	47	19
WATER SUPPLY	6	4	7	4	7	11	46	19
ELECTRIC POWER	-	-	-	-	-	2	-	-
GAS SUPPLY	-	-	-	-	-	-	-	-
TRANSIT	-	-	-	-	-	1	1	-
OTHER	-	-	-	1	-	1	5	1
MULTIPLE-FUNCTION DISTRICTS	-	-	-	-	-	1	5	4
SEWERAGE AND WATER SUPPLY	-	-	-	-	-	-	1	1
NATURAL RESOURCES AND WATER SUPPLY	-	-	-	-	-	-	-	-
OTHER	-	-	-	-	-	1	4	3
SCHOOL SYSTEMS								
TOTAL	8	15	11	16	5	18	69	30
DEPENDENT SCHOOL SYSTEMS	-	-	-	-	-	-	-	-
BY ENROLLMENT SIZE OCTOBER 1976								
100,000 OR MORE PUPILS	-	-	-	-	-	-	-	-
50,000 TO 99,999 PUPILS	-	-	-	-	-	-	1	-
25,000 TO 49,999 PUPILS	-	-	-	1	-	-	1	-
12,000 TO 24,999 PUPILS	-	-	-	-	-	-	1	-
6,000 TO 11,999 PUPILS	-	-	-	1	-	1	4	2
3,000 TO 5,999 PUPILS	-	-	-	4	-	2	6	3
1,200 TO 2,999 PUPILS	2	-	2	3	2	2	11	1
300 TO 1,199 PUPILS	3	6	6	5	2	4	7	3
50 TO 299 PUPILS	3	9	2	2	1	7	21	11
1 TO 49 PUPILS	-	-	1	-	-	1	13	8
0 PUPILS (NONOPERATING)	-	-	-	-	-	-	2	1
						1	3	1
POPULATION, 1975 (ESTIMATED)								
TOTAL	27 213	31 390	33 671	416 892	27 225	237 937	1 082 757	206 014
IN MUNICIPALLY GOVERNED AREAS	13 486	¹12 353	¹14 824	¹385 888	¹10 802	147 887	605 812	¹84 005
WITH A 1975 POPULATION OF--								
50,000 OR MORE	-	-	-	331 726	-	92 451	356 732	-
25,000 TO 49,999	-	-	-	-	-	33 432	47 742	-
10,000 TO 24,999	-	-	-	30 676	-	-	124 967	50 785
5,000 TO 9,999	7 797	-	9 897	6 073	6 288	6 652	38 892	22 892
2,500 TO 4,999	-	3 877	-	15 245	2 876	9 483	17 788	2 926
1,000 TO 2,499	3 449	5 803	3 927	2 152	-	3 488	15 570	6 379
LESS THAN 1,000	2 240	2 673	1 000	16	1 638	2 381	4 121	1 023
OUTSIDE MUNICIPALLY GOVERNED AREAS	13 727	19 037	18 847	31 004	16 423	90 050	476 945	122 009
IN TOWNSHIP-GOVERNED AREAS	-	-	-	-	-	-	-	-
ENROLLMENT OF PUBLIC SCHOOL SYSTEMS								
TOTAL	6 184	4 968	9 708	95 284	4 942	55 235	275 927	66 522
THROUGH GRADE 12	6 184	4 968	9 708	95 284	4 942	48 273	232 627	59 022
COLLEGE GRADES	-	-	-	-	-	6 962	43 300	7 500

Table 6. Local Governments and Public School Systems in Individual SMSA's: 1977—Continued

Item	Oregon--Continued						Pennsylvania (see also New York)	
	Portland--Continued			Salem			Allentown-Bethlehem-Easton	
	Multnomah County*	Washington County	Clark County (Wash.)	Total	Marion County*	Polk County	Total	Carbon County
NUMBER OF LOCAL GOVERNMENTS								
ALL TYPES, TOTAL	65	53	42	118	96	22	273	56
WITH PROPERTY-TAXING POWER	52	46	34	100	81	19	168	32
WITHOUT PROPERTY-TAXING POWER	13	7	8	18	15	3	105	24
COUNTY GOVERNMENTS	1	1	1	2	1	1	4	1
MUNICIPALITIES	6	12	7	22	18	4	47	12
WITH A POPULATION OF--								
50,000 OR MORE	1	-	-	1	1	-	2	-
25,000 TO 49,999	-	-	1	-	-	-	1	-
10,000 TO 24,999	1	3	-	-	-	-	3	-
5,000 TO 9,999	-	1	1	3	1	2	11	3
2,500 TO 4,999	2	2	1	3	2	1	12	4
1,000 TO 2,499	2	2	2	5	5	-	8	1
LESS THAN 1,000	-	4	2	10	9	1	10	4
TOWNSHIP GOVERNMENTS	-	-	-	-	-	-	61	11
SCHOOL DISTRICTS	16	14	9	42	37	5	53	6
SPECIAL DISTRICTS	42	26	25	52	40	12	108	26
WITH PROPERTY-TAXING POWER	29	19	17	34	25	9	-	-
SINGLE FUNCTION DISTRICTS	-	-	-	-	-	-	-	-
CEMETERIES	-	-	4	5	-	5	-	-
EDUCATION (SCHOOL BUILDING DISTRICTS)	-	-	-	-	-	-	30	8
FIRE PROTECTION	9	8	8	20	18	2	-	-
HIGHWAYS	-	-	-	10	10	-	1	1
HEALTH	-	-	-	-	-	-	1	-
HOSPITALS	-	-	-	-	-	-	2	1
HOUSING AND URBAN RENEWAL	1	1	1	1	-	1	6	1
LIBRARIES	-	-	1	-	-	-	-	-
NATURAL RESOURCES, TOTAL	11	6	6	12	8	4	1	-
DRAINAGE	7	4	5	2	2	-	-	-
FLOOD CONTROL	-	-	1	5	3	2	-	-
IRRIGATION, WATER CONSERVATION	1	1	-	3	2	1	-	-
SOIL CONSERVATION	3	1	-	2	1	1	1	-
OTHER AND COMPOSITE PURPOSES	-	-	-	-	-	-	-	-
PARKS AND RECREATION	-	2	-	-	-	-	-	-
SEWERAGE	1	-	1	2	2	-	28	5
UTILITIES, TOTAL	19	9	-	2	2	-	12	4
WATER SUPPLY	18	9	-	2	2	-	11	4
ELECTRIC POWER	-	-	-	-	-	-	-	-
GAS SUPPLY	-	-	-	-	-	-	-	-
TRANSIT	1	-	-	-	-	-	1	-
OTHER	1	-	3	-	-	-	11	2
MULTIPLE-FUNCTION DISTRICTS	-	-	1	-	-	-	16	5
SEWERAGE AND WATER SUPPLY	-	-	-	-	-	-	10	2
NATURAL RESOURCES AND WATER SUPPLY	-	-	1	-	-	-	-	-
OTHER	-	-	1	-	-	-	6	3
SCHOOL SYSTEMS								
TOTAL	16	14	9	42	37	5	54	6
DEPENDENT SCHOOL SYSTEMS	-	-	-	-	-	-	1	-
BY ENROLLMENT SIZE OCTOBER 1976								
100,000 OR MORE PUPILS	-	-	-	-	-	-	-	-
50,000 TO 99,999 PUPILS	1	-	-	-	-	-	-	-
25,000 TO 49,999 PUPILS	1	-	-	-	-	-	-	-
12,000 TO 24,999 PUPILS	-	1	1	1	1	-	2	-
6,000 TO 11,999 PUPILS	2	-	1	-	-	-	4	1
3,000 TO 5,999 PUPILS	5	4	1	-	-	-	7	1
1,200 TO 2,999 PUPILS	-	1	3	5	4	1	15	2
300 TO 1,199 PUPILS	3	5	2	8	8	-	17	3
50 TO 299 PUPILS	3	2	-	23	20	3	7	-
1 TO 49 PUPILS	-	-	1	3	3	-	-	-
0 PUPILS (NONOPERATING)	1	1	-	2	1	1	2	-
POPULATION, 1975 (ESTIMATED)								
TOTAL	530 412	191 741	154 590	205 848	166 920	38 928	623 628	52 289
IN MUNICIPALLY GOVERNED AREAS	[1]387 644	[1]72 556	[1]61 607	123 290	[1]106 695	[1]16 595	383 105	35 035
WITH A 1975 POPULATION OF--								
50,000 OR MORE	356 732	-	-	78 168	78 168	-	180 451	-
25,000 TO 49,999	-	-	47 742	-	-	-	29 263	-
10,000 TO 24,999	23 249	50 933	-	-	-	-	41 095	-
5,000 TO 9,999	-	9 881	6 119	21 791	9 134	12 657	71 391	17 164
2,500 TO 4,999	5 176	6 109	3 577	11 316	8 146	3 170	41 076	14 526
1,000 TO 2,499	2 487	3 500	3 204	7 306	7 306	-	13 554	1 169
LESS THAN 1,000	-	2 133	965	4 709	3 941	768	6 275	2 176
OUTSIDE MUNICIPALLY GOVERNED AREAS	142 768	119 185	92 983	82 558	60 225	22 333	240 523	17 254
IN TOWNSHIP-GOVERNED AREAS	-	-	-	-	-	-	240 526	17 253
ENROLLMENT OF PUBLIC SCHOOL SYSTEMS								
TOTAL	127 173	42 755	39 477	41 703	38 643	3 060	130 145	9 930
THROUGH GRADE 12	91 373	42 755	39 477	38 810	35 750	3 060	123 574	9 930
COLLEGE GRADES	35 800	-	-	2 893	2 893	-	6 571	-

Pennsylvania (see also New York)--Continued

Item	Allentown-Bethlehem-Easton--Continued			Altoona	Erie	Harrisburg				Johnstown	
	Lehigh County*	Northampton County*	Warren County (N.J.)	Blair County (entire SMSA)	Erie County (entire SMSA)	Total	Cumberland County	Dauphin County*	Perry County	Total	Cambria County*
NUMBER OF LOCAL GOVERNMENTS											
ALL TYPES, TOTAL	71	92	54	66	95	223	83	90	50	224	129
WITH PROPERTY-TAXING POWER	36	51	49	37	56	136	47	54	35	143	80
WITHOUT PROPERTY-TAXING POWER	35	41	5	29	39	87	36	36	15	81	49
COUNTY GOVERNMENTS	1	1	1	1	1	3	1	1	1	2	1
MUNICIPALITIES	9	21	5	9	18	38	12	17	9	59	34
WITH A POPULATION OF--											
50,000 OR MORE	1	1	-	1	1	1	-	1	-	-	-
25,000 TO 49,999	-	1	-	-	-	1	-	-	-	1	1
10,000 TO 24,999	1	-	2	-	-	-	3	-	-	-	-
5,000 TO 9,999	2	5	1	2	2	3	3	3	-	3	1
2,500 TO 4,999	3	3	2	1	4	5	2	3	-	10	9
1,000 TO 2,499	2	5	-	4	4	14	4	6	4	16	11
LESS THAN 1,000	-	6	-	1	7	10	1	4	5	29	12
TOWNSHIP GOVERNMENTS	15	17	18	15	22	66	22	23	21	55	30
SCHOOL DISTRICTS	11	11	25	8	15	27	10	13	4	26	14
SPECIAL DISTRICTS	35	42	5	33	39	89	38	36	15	82	50
WITH PROPERTY-TAXING POWER	-	-	-	-	-	-	-	-	-	-	-
SINGLE FUNCTION DISTRICTS											
CEMETERIES	-	-	-	-	-	-	-	-	-	-	-
EDUCATION (SCHOOL BUILDING DISTRICTS)	11	11	-	7	10	21	11	9	1	16	8
FIRE PROTECTION	-	-	-	-	-	-	-	-	-	-	-
HIGHWAYS	1	-	-	-	-	-	-	-	-	-	-
HEALTH	-	-	-	-	-	-	-	-	-	-	-
HOSPITALS	1	1	-	-	1	2	1	1	-	1	1
HOUSING AND URBAN RENEWAL	2	2	1	2	2	2	-	2	-	2	1
LIBRARIES	-	-	-	-	-	-	-	-	-	-	-
NATURAL RESOURCES, TOTAL	-	-	1	-	-	-	-	-	-	-	-
DRAINAGE	-	-	-	-	-	-	-	-	-	-	-
FLOOD CONTROL	-	-	-	-	-	-	-	-	-	-	-
IRRIGATION, WATER CONSERVATION	-	-	-	-	-	-	-	-	-	-	-
SOIL CONSERVATION	-	-	1	-	-	-	-	-	-	-	-
OTHER AND COMPOSITE PURPOSES	-	-	-	-	-	-	-	-	-	-	-
PARKS AND RECREATION	-	-	-	1	3	-	-	-	-	5	4
SEWERAGE	9	14	-	10	9	30	11	10	9	19	10
UTILITIES, TOTAL	4	4	-	3	5	8	2	4	2	21	15
WATER SUPPLY	3	4	-	2	4	7	2	3	2	19	13
ELECTRIC POWER	-	-	-	-	-	-	-	-	-	-	-
GAS SUPPLY	-	-	-	-	-	-	-	-	-	-	-
TRANSIT	1	-	-	1	1	1	-	1	-	2	2
OTHER	3	4	2	4	4	10	5	4	1	6	4
MULTIPLE-FUNCTION DISTRICTS	4	6	1	6	5	16	8	6	2	12	7
SEWERAGE AND WATER SUPPLY	3	4	1	5	4	9	5	3	1	7	5
NATURAL RESOURCES AND WATER SUPPLY	-	-	-	-	-	-	-	-	-	-	-
OTHER	1	2	-	1	1	7	3	3	1	5	2
SCHOOL SYSTEMS											
TOTAL	11	11	26	8	15	27	10	13	4	26	14
DEPENDENT SCHOOL SYSTEMS	-	-	1	-	-	-	-	-	-	-	-
BY ENROLLMENT SIZE OCTOBER 1976											
100,000 OR MORE PUPILS	-	-	-	-	-	-	-	-	-	-	-
50,000 TO 99,999 PUPILS	-	-	-	-	-	-	-	-	-	-	-
25,000 TO 49,999 PUPILS	-	-	-	-	-	-	-	-	-	-	-
12,000 TO 24,999 PUPILS	-	-	-	-	-	-	-	-	-	-	-
6,000 TO 11,999 PUPILS	1	1	-	1	1	-	-	-	-	1	1
3,000 TO 5,999 PUPILS	2	2	-	1	1	5	3	2	-	3	1
1,200 TO 2,999 PUPILS	2	3	1	1	3	7	4	3	-	14	2
300 TO 1,199 PUPILS	6	5	2	4	8	11	2	6	3	14	9
50 TO 299 PUPILS	-	-	14	2	1	4	1	2	1	8	2
1 TO 49 PUPILS	-	-	7	-	1	-	-	-	-	-	-
0 PUPILS (NONOPERATING)	-	-	2	-	-	-	-	-	-	-	-
POPULATION, 1975 (ESTIMATED)											
TOTAL	263 566	224 883	82 890	134 661	273 396	426 609	171 294	223 343	31 972	266 597	187 851
IN MUNICIPALLY GOVERNED AREAS	[1]143 765	162 022	42 283	83 066	[1]167 592	183 461	73 180	101 312	8 969	131 489	102 500
WITH A 1975 POPULATION OF--											
50,000 OR MORE	106 624	73 827	-	59 692	127 895	58 274	-	58 274	-	-	-
25,000 TO 49,999	-	29 263	-	-	-	-	-	-	-	40 044	40 044
10,000 TO 24,999	11 248	-	29 847	-	-	42 178	42 178	-	-	-	-
5,000 TO 9,999	11 574	35 805	6 848	12 634	12 296	38 631	16 495	22 136	-	18 912	6 222
2,500 TO 4,999	11 160	9 802	5 588	2 668	15 370	15 864	7 393	8 471	-	32 570	29 953
1,000 TO 2,499	3 159	9 226	-	7 641	8 376	23 622	6 805	10 116	6 691	26 669	19 543
LESS THAN 1,000	-	4 099	-	431	3 655	4 892	309	2 305	2 278	13 294	6 738
OUTSIDE MUNICIPALLY GOVERNED AREAS	119 801	62 861	40 607	51 595	105 804	243 148	98 114	122 031	23 003	135 108	85 351
IN TOWNSHIP-GOVERNED AREAS	99 390	83 276	40 607	51 596	105 803	244 495	99 458	122 035	23 002	135 113	85 355
ENROLLMENT OF PUBLIC SCHOOL SYSTEMS											
TOTAL	51 173	51 281	17 761	32 193	52 943	94 143	41 950	44 308	7 885	51 635	34 967
THROUGH GRADE 12	48 762	47 121	17 761	32 193	52 943	89 540	41 950	39 705	7 885	51 635	34 967
COLLEGE GRADES	2 411	4 160	-	-	-	4 603	-	4 603	-	-	-

Table 6. Local Governments and Public School Systems in Individual SMSA's: 1977—Continued

Item	Johnstown--Continued Somerset County	Lancaster Lancaster County (entire SMSA)	Northeast Pennsylvania Total	Lackawanna County*	Luzerne County*	Monroe County	Philadelphia Total	Bucks County
NUMBER OF LOCAL GOVERNMENTS								
ALL TYPES, TOTAL	95	142	261	75	145	41	864	125
WITH PROPERTY-TAXING POWER	63	81	171	53	91	27	570	75
WITHOUT PROPERTY-TAXING POWER	32	61	90	22	54	14	294	50
COUNTY GOVERNMENTS	1	1	3	1	1	1	7	1
MUNICIPALITIES	25	19	62	19	39	4	140	22
WITH A POPULATION OF--								
50,000 OR MORE	-	1	2	1	1	-	2	-
25,000 TO 49,999	-	-	1	-	1	-	3	-
10,000 TO 24,999	-	2	5	2	3	-	20	3
5,000 TO 9,999	2	5	17	8	7	2	35	2
2,500 TO 4,999	1	4	13	3	10	-	38	6
1,000 TO 2,499	5	7	14	4	9	1	25	6
LESS THAN 1,000	17	-	10	1	8	1	17	5
TOWNSHIP GOVERNMENTS	25	41	73	21	36	16	199	31
SCHOOL DISTRICTS	12	17	32	12	15	5	189	17
SPECIAL DISTRICTS	32	64	91	22	54	15	329	54
WITH PROPERTY-TAXING POWER	-	-	-	-	-	-	-	-
SINGLE FUNCTION DISTRICTS	-	-	-	-	-	-	-	-
CEMETERIES	-	-	-	-	-	-	-	-
EDUCATION (SCHOOL BUILDING DISTRICTS)	8	16	20	4	12	4	91	19
FIRE PROTECTION	-	-	-	-	-	-	27	-
HIGHWAYS	-	1	-	-	-	-	3	1
HEALTH	-	-	-	-	-	-	1	-
HOSPITALS	-	1	3	1	1	1	7	1
HOUSING AND URBAN RENEWAL	1	2	9	3	5	1	13	1
LIBRARIES	-	-	-	-	-	-	-	-
NATURAL RESOURCES, TOTAL	-	-	-	-	-	-	3	-
DRAINAGE	-	-	-	-	-	-	-	-
FLOOD CONTROL	-	-	-	-	-	-	-	-
IRRIGATION, WATER CONSERVATION	-	-	-	-	-	-	-	-
SOIL CONSERVATION	-	-	-	-	-	-	3	-
OTHER AND COMPOSITE PURPOSES	-	-	-	-	-	-	-	-
PARKS AND RECREATION	1	-	4	-	4	-	2	2
SEWERAGE	9	17	31	10	19	2	104	14
UTILITIES, TOTAL	6	12	5	2	2	1	14	3
WATER SUPPLY	6	11	2	-	1	1	13	3
ELECTRIC POWER	-	-	-	-	-	-	-	-
GAS SUPPLY	-	-	-	-	-	-	-	-
TRANSIT	-	1	3	2	1	-	1	-
OTHER	2	6	12	2	7	3	26	2
MULTIPLE-FUNCTION DISTRICTS	5	9	7	-	4	3	38	11
SEWERAGE AND WATER SUPPLY	2	9	4	-	2	2	29	9
NATURAL RESOURCES AND WATER SUPPLY	-	-	-	-	-	-	-	-
OTHER	3	-	3	-	2	1	9	2
SCHOOL SYSTEMS								
TOTAL	12	17	32	12	15	5	197	17
DEPENDENT SCHOOL SYSTEMS	-	-	-	-	-	-	8	-
BY ENROLLMENT SIZE OCTOBER 1976								
100,000 OR MORE PUPILS	-	-	-	-	-	-	1	-
50,000 TO 99,999 PUPILS	-	-	-	-	-	-	-	-
25,000 TO 49,999 PUPILS	-	-	-	-	-	-	-	-
12,000 TO 24,999 PUPILS	-	-	1	1	-	-	8	4
6,000 TO 11,999 PUPILS	-	1	3	-	3	-	25	5
3,000 TO 5,999 PUPILS	1	10	11	3	6	2	43	1
1,200 TO 2,999 PUPILS	5	6	12	6	4	2	48	5
300 TO 1,199 PUPILS	6	-	5	2	2	1	52	2
50 TO 299 PUPILS	-	-	-	-	-	-	15	-
1 TO 49 PUPILS	-	-	-	-	-	-	1	-
0 PUPILS (NONOPERATING)	-	-	-	-	-	-	4	-
POPULATION, 1975 (ESTIMATED)								
TOTAL	78 746	342 797	634 635	234 771	345 645	54 219	4 807 301	460 978
IN MUNICIPALLY GOVERNED AREAS	28 989	140 268	445 033	200 688	228 274	16 071	2 736 358	¹78 814
WITH A 1975 POPULATION OF--								
50,000 OR MORE	-	56 669	152 924	95 884	57 040	-	1 905 022	-
25,000 TO 49,999	-	-	29 610	-	29 610	-	110 543	-
10,000 TO 24,999	-	23 381	71 038	29 899	41 139	-	276 789	32 596
5,000 TO 9,999	12 690	35 254	112 959	55 411	43 262	14 286	260 160	15 542
2,500 TO 4,999	2 617	14 093	50 548	11 467	39 081	-	130 206	18 098
1,000 TO 2,499	7 126	10 871	23 158	7 355	14 587	1 216	42 783	8 814
LESS THAN 1,000	6 556	-	4 796	672	3 555	569	10 855	3 764
OUTSIDE MUNICIPALLY GOVERNED AREAS	49 757	202 529	189 602	34 083	117 371	38 148	2 070 943	382 164
IN TOWNSHIP-GOVERNED AREAS	49 758	202 532	189 598	34 082	117 368	38 148	2 070 935	381 157
ENROLLMENT OF PUBLIC SCHOOL SYSTEMS								
TOTAL	16 668	67 144	112 271	38 827	61 213	12 231	932 719	107 260
THROUGH GRADE 12	16 668	67 144	109 271	38 827	58 213	12 231	890 129	99 651
COLLEGE GRADES	-	-	3 000	-	3 000	-	42 590	7 609

82

Item	Chester County	Delaware County	Montgomery County	Philadelphia County*	Burlington County (N.J.)	Camden County (N.J.)	Gloucester County (N.J.)	Total	Allegheny County*	Beaver County
				Pennsylvania (see also New York)--Continued						
			Philadelphia--Continued					Pittsburgh		
NUMBER OF LOCAL GOVERNMENTS										
ALL TYPES, TOTAL	143	120	175	11	108	110	72	744	325	123
WITH PROPERTY-TAXING POWER	92	69	89	6	89	92	58	433	188	71
WITHOUT PROPERTY-TAXING POWER	51	51	86	5	19	18	14	311	137	52
COUNTY GOVERNMENTS	1	1	1	–	1	1	1	4	1	1
MUNICIPALITIES	16	28	24	1	9	29	11	193	85	31
WITH A POPULATION OF--										
50,000 OR MORE	–	–	–	1	–	1	–	1	1	–
25,000 TO 49,999	–	1	2	–	–	–	–	6	6	–
10,000 TO 24,999	3	4	1	–	1	6	2	25	13	3
5,000 TO 9,999	2	11	4	–	2	10	4	35	22	5
2,500 TO 4,999	4	7	8	–	4	7	2	39	20	7
1,000 TO 2,499	4	2	6	–	1	3	3	36	14	2
LESS THAN 1,000	3	3	3	–	1	2	–	51	9	14
TOWNSHIP GOVERNMENTS	57	21	38	–	31	8	13	117	42	22
SCHOOL DISTRICTS	14	19	26	5	40	41	27	105	53	16
SPECIAL DISTRICTS	55	51	86	5	27	31	20	325	144	53
WITH PROPERTY-TAXING POWER	–	–	–	–	–	–	–	–	–	–
SINGLE FUNCTION DISTRICTS	–	–	–	–	–	–	–	–	–	–
CEMETERIES	–	–	–	–	–	–	–	–	–	–
EDUCATION (SCHOOL BUILDING DISTRICTS)	21	21	30	–	–	–	–	102	53	13
FIRE PROTECTION	–	–	–	–	8	13	6	–	–	–
HIGHWAYS	–	–	–	–	2	–	–	–	–	–
HEALTH	–	–	–	–	–	–	1	3	1	–
HOSPITALS	1	2	2	1	–	–	–	6	5	1
HOUSING AND URBAN RENEWAL	1	2	1	1	3	3	1	6	3	1
LIBRARIES	–	–	–	–	–	–	–	–	–	–
NATURAL RESOURCES, TOTAL	–	–	–	–	1	1	1	2	2	–
DRAINAGE	–	–	–	–	–	–	–	1	1	–
FLOOD CONTROL	–	–	–	–	–	–	–	1	1	–
IRRIGATION, WATER CONSERVATION	–	–	–	–	–	–	–	–	–	–
SOIL CONSERVATION	–	–	–	–	1	1	1	–	–	–
OTHER AND COMPOSITE PURPOSES	–	–	–	–	–	–	–	–	–	–
PARKS AND RECREATION	–	–	–	–	–	–	–	7	4	1
SEWERAGE	20	14	34	–	8	10	4	89	33	11
UTILITIES, TOTAL	3	1	5	1	–	1	–	41	16	11
WATER SUPPLY	3	1	5	–	–	1	–	40	15	11
ELECTRIC POWER	–	–	–	–	–	–	–	–	–	–
GAS SUPPLY	–	–	–	–	–	–	–	–	–	–
TRANSIT	–	–	–	1	–	–	–	1	1	–
OTHER	5	8	8	2	–	–	1	43	16	9
MULTIPLE-FUNCTION DISTRICTS	4	3	6	–	5	3	6	26	11	6
SEWERAGE AND WATER SUPPLY	3	1	3	–	5	2	6	16	6	5
NATURAL RESOURCES AND WATER SUPPLY	–	–	–	–	–	–	–	–	–	–
OTHER	1	2	3	–	–	1	–	10	5	1
SCHOOL SYSTEMS										
TOTAL	14	19	26	5	45	43	28	105	53	16
DEPENDENT SCHOOL SYSTEMS	–	–	–	–	5	2	1	–	–	–
BY ENROLLMENT SIZE OCTOBER 1976										
100,000 OR MORE PUPILS	–	–	–	1	–	–	–	–	–	–
50,000 TO 99,999 PUPILS	–	–	–	–	–	–	–	1	1	–
25,000 TO 49,999 PUPILS	–	–	–	–	–	–	–	1	1	–
12,000 TO 24,999 PUPILS	–	–	–	1	1	2	–	1	1	–
6,000 TO 11,999 PUPILS	4	6	5	3	1	1	–	12	8	–
3,000 TO 5,999 PUPILS	3	9	15	–	6	5	4	38	17	6
1,200 TO 2,999 PUPILS	5	1	3	–	12	12	10	41	21	9
300 TO 1,199 PUPILS	2	3	3	–	16	17	9	11	4	1
50 TO 299 PUPILS	–	–	–	–	8	·2	5	–	–	–
1 TO 49 PUPILS	–	–	–	–	1	–	–	–	–	–
0 PUPILS (NONOPERATING)	–	–	–	–	–	4	–	–	–	–
POPULATION, 1975 (ESTIMATED)										
TOTAL	293 074	591 671	634 001	1 815 808	345 696	476 511	189 562	2 322 224	1 517 996	209 328
IN MUNICIPALLY GOVERNED AREAS	82 605	205 951	163 215	1 815 808	42 680	277 745	69 540	1 449 980	¹1 060 033	¹115 457
WITH A 1975 POPULATION OF--										
50,000 OR MORE	–	–	–	1 815 808	–	89 214	–	458 651	458 651	–
25,000 TO 49,999	–	48 529	62 014	–	–	–	–	181 815	181 815	–
10,000 TO 24,999	47 861	49 387	20 437	–	11 886	86 380	28 242	350 723	169 617	45 264
5,000 TO 9,999	13 918	81 961	31 924	–	14 649	74 412	27 754	236 184	149 239	34 902
2,500 TO 4,999	12 779	20 677	33 798	–	14 008	23 661	7 185	136 353	71 647	25 156
1,000 TO 2,499	5 979	3 423	12 623	–	1 541	4 044	6 359	59 613	24 790	3 588
LESS THAN 1,000	2 068	1 974	2 419	–	596	34	–	26 641	4 274	6 547
OUTSIDE MUNICIPALLY GOVERNED AREAS	210 469	385 720	470 786	–	303 016	198 766	120 022	872 244	457 963	93 871
IN TOWNSHIP-GOVERNED AREAS	210 463	385 717	471 793	–	303 013	198 769	120 023	869 647	455 626	92 852
ENROLLMENT OF PUBLIC SCHOOL SYSTEMS										
TOTAL	60 285	94 995	117 307	324 668	81 148	103 069	43 987	486 066	315 616	44 484
THROUGH GRADE 12	60 285	91 530	113 183	311 699	76 025	96 269	41 487	438 066	269 616	42 484
COLLEGE GRADES	–	3 465	4 124	12 969	5 123	6 800	2 500	48 000	46 000	2 000

Table 6. Local Governments and Public School Systems in Individual SMSA's: 1977—Continued

Item	Pittsburgh--Continued		Reading	Williams-port	York			Providence-Warwick-Pawtucket			Charleston-North Charleston
								(Pennsylvania see also New York)--Continued	Rhode Island		South Carolina (see also Georgia)
	Washington County	Westmore-land County	Berks County (entire SMSA)	Lycoming County (entire SMSA)	Total	Adams County	York County*	Total	Rhode Island portion*	Massa-chusetts portion*	Total
NUMBER OF LOCAL GOVERNMENTS											
ALL TYPES, TOTAL	133	163	170	89	223	69	154	75	67	8	43
WITH PROPERTY-TAXING POWER	85	89	107	62	136	46	90	54	46	8	38
WITHOUT PROPERTY-TAXING POWER	48	74	63	27	87	23	64	21	21	-	5
COUNTY GOVERNMENTS	1	1	1	1	2	1	1	-	-	-	3
MUNICIPALITIES	34	43	31	10	50	13	37	8	7	1	22
WITH A POPULATION OF--											
50,000 OR MORE	-	-	1	-	-	-	-	4	4	-	2
25,000 TO 49,999	-	-	-	1	1	-	1	3	2	1	-
10,000 TO 24,999	2	7	-	-	1	-	1	1	1	-	1
5,000 TO 9,999	4	4	2	2	3	1	2	-	-	-	2
2,500 TO 4,999	4	8	10	2	6	2	4	-	-	-	2
1,000 TO 2,499	10	10	13	3	14	2	12	-	-	-	6
LESS THAN 1,000	14	14	5	2	25	8	17	-	-	-	9
TOWNSHIP GOVERNMENTS	32	21	44	42	56	21	35	24	17	7	-
SCHOOL DISTRICTS	16	20	21	9	22	6	16	-	-	-	5
SPECIAL DISTRICTS	50	78	73	27	93	28	65	43	43	-	13
WITH PROPERTY-TAXING POWER	-	-	-	-	-	-	-	22	22	-	8
SINGLE FUNCTION DISTRICTS	-	-	-	-	-	-	-	-	-	-	-
CEMETERIES	-	-	-	-	-	-	-	-	-	-	-
EDUCATION (SCHOOL BUILDING DISTRICTS)	13	23	23	7	32	6	26	-	-	-	-
FIRE PROTECTION	-	-	-	-	1	-	1	-	-	-	4
HIGHWAYS	-	-	-	-	-	-	-	21	21	-	-
HEALTH	-	2	-	-	-	-	-	-	-	-	-
HOSPITALS	-	-	1	1	1	-	1	-	-	-	-
HOUSING AND URBAN RENEWAL	1	1	2	2	1	-	1	18	18	-	1
LIBRARIES	-	-	-	-	-	-	-	-	-	-	-
NATURAL RESOURCES, TOTAL	-	-	-	-	-	-	-	1	1	-	3
DRAINAGE	-	-	-	-	-	-	-	-	-	-	-
FLOOD CONTROL	-	-	-	-	-	-	-	-	-	-	-
IRRIGATION, WATER CONSERVATION	-	-	-	-	-	-	-	-	-	-	-
SOIL CONSERVATION	-	-	-	-	-	-	-	1	1	-	3
OTHER AND COMPOSITE PURPOSES	-	-	-	-	-	-	-	-	-	-	-
PARKS AND RECREATION	-	2	-	1	-	-	-	-	-	-	-
SEWERAGE	23	22	26	7	31	9	22	1	1	-	1
UTILITIES, TOTAL	5	9	10	2	7	1	6	1	1	-	2
WATER SUPPLY	5	9	9	2	5	1	4	1	1	-	2
ELECTRIC POWER	-	-	-	-	-	-	-	-	-	-	-
GAS SUPPLY	-	-	-	-	-	-	-	-	-	-	-
TRANSIT	-	-	1	-	2	-	2	-	-	-	-
OTHER	6	12	4	3	6	2	4	-	-	-	-
MULTIPLE-FUNCTION DISTRICTS	2	7	7	4	14	10	4	1	1	-	2
SEWERAGE AND WATER SUPPLY	2	3	5	3	11	7	4	-	-	-	1
NATURAL RESOURCES AND WATER SUPPLY	-	-	-	-	-	-	-	-	-	-	-
OTHER	-	4	2	1	3	3	-	1	1	-	1
SCHOOL SYSTEMS											
TOTAL	16	20	21	9	22	6	16	34	26	8	5
DEPENDENT SCHOOL SYSTEMS	-	-	-	-	-	-	-	34	26	8	-
BY ENROLLMENT SIZE OCTOBER 1976											
100,000 OR MORE PUPILS	-	-	-	-	-	-	-	-	-	-	-
50,000 TO 99,999 PUPILS	-	-	-	-	-	-	-	-	-	-	-
25,000 TO 49,999 PUPILS	-	-	-	-	-	-	-	-	-	-	1
12,000 TO 24,999 PUPILS	-	-	1	-	-	-	-	3	3	-	1
6,000 TO 11,999 PUPILS	1	3	1	1	1	-	1	5	4	1	1
3,000 TO 5,999 PUPILS	3	12	4	1	12	1	11	12	10	2	-
1,200 TO 2,999 PUPILS	9	2	13	7	8	4	4	10	8	2	1
300 TO 1,199 PUPILS	3	3	2	-	1	1	-	3	1	2	1
50 TO 299 PUPILS	-	-	-	-	-	-	-	1	-	1	-
1 TO 49 PUPILS	-	-	-	-	-	-	-	-	-	-	-
POPULATION, 1975 (ESTIMATED)											
TOTAL	214 611	380 289	305 017	115 181	347 509	61 842	285 667	903 841	810 313	93 528	371 350
IN MUNICIPALLY GOVERNED AREAS	92 259	182 231	¹159 026	63 244	135 757	21 296	114 461	545 731	513 217	32 514	165 412
WITH A 1975 POPULATION OF--											
50,000 OR MORE	-	-	81 592	-	-	-	-	400 004	400 004	-	118 986
25,000 TO 49,999	-	-	-	35 915	48 587	-	48 587	129 038	96 524	32 514	-
10,000 TO 24,999	31 901	103 941	-	-	15 209	-	15 209	16 689	16 689	-	11 752
5,000 TO 9,999	26 138	25 905	14 872	13 017	18 257	7 461	10 796	-	-	-	14 110
2,500 TO 4,999	11 785	27 765	39 241	7 937	17 678	5 808	11 870	-	-	-	7 131
1,000 TO 2,499	14 865	16 370	21 141	5 479	21 942	2 845	19 097	-	-	-	9 732
LESS THAN 1,000	7 570	8 250	2 180	896	14 084	5 182	8 902	-	-	-	3 701
OUTSIDE MUNICIPALLY GOVERNED AREAS	122 352	198 058	145 991	51 937	211 752	40 546	171 206	358 110	297 096	61 014	205 938
IN TOWNSHIP-GOVERNED AREAS	123 019	198 150	145 983	51 653	211 752	40 547	171 205	358 110	297 096	61 014	-
ENROLLMENT OF PUBLIC SCHOOL SYSTEMS											
TOTAL	44 699	81 267	64 950	27 054	71 986	13 067	58 919	172 352	151 186	21 166	81 084
THROUGH GRADE 12	44 699	81 267	64 950	25 412	71 986	13 067	58 919	172 352	151 186	21 166	81 084
COLLEGE GRADES	-	-	-	1 642	-	-	-	-	-	-	-

Item	Charleston-North Charleston--Continued			Columbia			Greenville-Spartanburg			
	Berkeley County	Charleston County*	Dorchester County	Total	Lexington County	Richland County*	Total	Greenville County*	Pickens County	Spartanburg County*
NUMBER OF LOCAL GOVERNMENTS										
ALL TYPES, TOTAL	10	22	11	37	22	15	92	33	14	45
WITH PROPERTY-TAXING POWER	8	20	10	34	21	13	84	29	13	42
WITHOUT PROPERTY-TAXING POWER.	2	2	1	3	1	2	8	4	1	3
COUNTY GOVERNMENTS	1	1	1	2	1	1	3	1	1	1
MUNICIPALITIES	6	11	5	20	15	5	28	8	7	13
WITH A POPULATION OF--										
50,000 OR MORE	-	2	-	1	-	1	1	1	-	-
25,000 TO 49,999	-	-	-	-	-	-	1	-	-	1
10,000 TO 24,999	1	-	-	2	2	-	2	1	1	-
5,000 TO 9,999	-	1	1	1	-	1	3	2	1	-
2,500 TO 4,999	1	1	-	2	2	-	6	3	2	1
1,000 TO 2,499	2	3	1	4	4	-	10	-	1	9
LESS THAN 1,000	2	4	3	10	7	3	5	1	2	2
TOWNSHIP GOVERNMENTS	-	-	-	-	-	-	-	-	-	-
SCHOOL DISTRICTS	1	1	3	7	5	2	9	1	1	7
SPECIAL DISTRICTS.	2	9	2	8	1	7	52	23	5	24
WITH PROPERTY-TAXING POWER	-	7	1	5	-	5	44	19	4	21
SINGLE FUNCTION DISTRICTS.	-	-	-	-	-	-	-	-	-	-
CEMETERIES	-	-	-	-	-	-	-	-	-	-
EDUCATION (SCHOOL BUILDING DISTRICTS). . . .	-	-	-	-	-	-	-	-	-	-
FIRE PROTECTION.	-	4	-	1	-	1	18	6	-	12
HIGHWAYS	-	-	-	-	-	-	-	-	-	-
HEALTH	-	-	-	-	-	-	-	-	-	-
HOSPITALS.	-	-	-	-	-	-	-	-	-	-
HOUSING AND URBAN RENEWAL.	-	1	-	1	-	1	3	2	-	1
LIBRARIES.	-	-	-	-	-	-	-	-	-	-
NATURAL RESOURCES, TOTAL	1	1	1	2	1	1	3	1	1	1
DRAINAGE	-	-	-	-	-	-	-	-	-	-
FLOOD CONTROL.	-	-	-	-	-	-	-	-	-	-
IRRIGATION, WATER CONSERVATION	-	-	-	-	-	-	-	-	-	-
SOIL CONSERVATION.	1	1	1	2	1	1	3	1	1	1
OTHER AND COMPOSITE PURPOSES	-	-	-	-	-	-	-	-	-	-
PARKS AND RECREATION	-	-	-	2	-	2	2	1	-	1
SEWERAGE	-	1	-	1	-	1	3	2	-	1
UTILITIES, TOTAL	-	1	1	-	-	-	12	1	4	7
WATER SUPPLY	-	1	1	-	-	-	12	1	4	7
ELECTRIC POWER	-	-	-	-	-	-	-	-	-	-
GAS SUPPLY	-	-	-	-	-	-	-	-	-	-
TRANSIT.	-	-	-	-	-	-	-	-	-	-
OTHER.	-	-	-	1	-	1	2	2	-	-
MULTIPLE-FUNCTION DISTRICTS.	1	1	-	-	-	-	9	8	-	1
SEWERAGE AND WATER SUPPLY.	1	-	-	-	-	-	3	3	-	-
NATURAL RESOURCES AND WATER SUPPLY	-	-	-	-	-	-	-	-	-	-
OTHER.	-	1	-	-	-	-	6	5	-	1
SCHOOL SYSTEMS										
TOTAL.	1	1	3	7	5	2	9	1	1	7
DEPENDENT SCHOOL SYSTEMS	-	-	-	-	-	-	-	-	-	-
BY ENROLLMENT SIZE OCTOBER 1976										
100,000 OR MORE PUPILS	-	-	-	-	-	-	-	-	-	-
50,000 TO 99,999 PUPILS.	-	1	-	1	-	1	1	1	-	-
25,000 TO 49,999 PUPILS.	-	-	-	1	-	1	-	-	-	-
12,000 TO 24,999 PUPILS.	1	-	-	-	-	-	1	-	1	-
6,000 TO 11,999 PUPILS	-	-	1	4	3	1	3	-	-	3
3,000 TO 5,999 PUPILS.	-	-	-	-	-	-	3	-	-	3
1,200 TO 2,999 PUPILS.	-	-	1	2	2	-	1	-	-	1
300 TO 1,199 PUPILS.	-	-	1	-	-	-	-	-	-	-
50 TO 299 PUPILS	-	-	-	-	-	-	-	-	-	-
1 TO 49 PUPILS	-	-	-	-	-	-	-	-	-	-
POPULATION, 1975 (ESTIMATED)										
TOTAL.	65 628	260 426	45 296	365 156	117 603	247 553	525 430	265 573	68 270	191 587
IN MUNICIPALLY GOVERNED AREAS.	20 485	136 148	8 779	161 520	41 319	120 201	188 882	93 045	28 570	¹67 267
WITH A 1975 POPULATION OF--										
50,000 OR MORE	-	118 986	-	111 616	-	111 616	58 518	58 518	-	-
25,000 TO 49,999	-	-	-	-	-	-	46 929	-	-	46 929
10,000 TO 24,999	11 752	-	-	23 754	23 754	-	23 596	11 435	12 161	-
5,000 TO 9,999	-	8 680	5 430	6 897	-	6 897	20 506	13 355	7 151	-
2,500 TO 4,999	4 170	2 961	-	7 434	7 434	-	20 363	9 473	6 351	4 539
1,000 TO 2,499	3 974	3 925	1 833	6 692	6 692	-	16 345	-	1 640	14 705
LESS THAN 1,000	589	1 596	1 516	5 127	3 439	1 688	2 625	264	1 267	1 094
OUTSIDE MUNICIPALLY GOVERNED AREAS	45 143	124 278	36 517	203 636	76 284	127 352	336 548	172 528	39 700	124 320
IN TOWNSHIP-GOVERNED AREAS	-	-	-	-	-	-	-	-	-	-
ENROLLMENT OF PUBLIC SCHOOL SYSTEMS										
TOTAL.	20 058	49 602	11 424	74 815	31 836	42 979	109 408	55 254	13 916	40 238
THROUGH GRADE 12	20 058	49 602	11 424	74 815	31 836	42 979	109 408	55 254	13 916	40 238
COLLEGE GRADES	-	-	-	-	-	-	-	-	-	-

Table 6. Local Governments and Public School Systems in Individual SMSA's: 1977—Continued

| | South Dakota | Tennessee | | | | | | | Clarksville-Hopkinsville |
| | Sioux Falls | Chattanooga | | | | | | | |
Item	Minnehaha County (entire SMSA)	Total	Hamilton County*	Marion County	Sequatchie County	Catoosa County (Ga.)	Dade County (Ga.)	Walker County (Ga.)	Total
NUMBER OF LOCAL GOVERNMENTS									
ALL TYPES, TOTAL	50	60	22	13	3	7	4	11	17
WITH PROPERTY-TAXING POWER	48	38	11	10	2	4	3	8	10
WITHOUT PROPERTY-TAXING POWER	2	22	11	3	1	3	1	3	7
COUNTY GOVERNMENTS	1	6	1	1	1	1	1	1	2
MUNICIPALITIES	10	27	10	8	1	2	1	5	6
WITH A POPULATION OF--									
50,000 OR MORE	1	1	1	-	-	-	-	-	1
25,000 TO 49,999	-	-	-	-	-	-	-	-	1
10,000 TO 24,999	-	2	2	-	-	-	-	-	-
5,000 TO 9,999	-	4	2	-	-	1	-	1	-
2,500 TO 4,999	-	3	1	1	-	-	-	1	-
1,000 TO 2,499	2	9	2	2	1	1	1	2	1
LESS THAN 1,000	7	8	2	5	-	-	-	1	3
TOWNSHIP GOVERNMENTS	24	-	-	-	-	-	-	-	-
SCHOOL DISTRICTS	7	5	-	1	-	1	1	2	1
SPECIAL DISTRICTS	8	22	11	3	1	3	1	3	8
WITH PROPERTY-TAXING POWER	6	-	-	-	-	-	-	-	1
SINGLE FUNCTION DISTRICTS	-	-	-	-	-	-	-	-	-
CEMETERIES	-	-	-	-	-	-	-	-	-
EDUCATION (SCHOOL BUILDING DISTRICTS)	-	-	-	-	-	-	-	-	-
FIRE PROTECTION	-	-	-	-	-	-	-	-	-
HIGHWAYS	-	-	-	-	-	-	-	-	-
HEALTH	-	-	-	-	-	-	-	-	-
HOSPITALS	-	1	-	-	-	-	-	1	-
HOUSING AND URBAN RENEWAL	-	6	1	1	-	2	-	2	1
LIBRARIES	-	-	-	-	-	-	-	-	-
NATURAL RESOURCES, TOTAL	2	4	1	1	1	1	-	-	2
DRAINAGE	-	-	-	-	-	-	-	-	-
FLOOD CONTROL	1	-	-	-	-	-	-	-	-
IRRIGATION, WATER CONSERVATION	-	-	-	-	-	-	-	-	-
SOIL CONSERVATION	1	4	1	1	1	1	-	-	2
OTHER AND COMPOSITE PURPOSES	-	-	-	-	-	-	-	-	-
PARKS AND RECREATION	-	-	-	-	-	-	-	-	-
SEWERAGE	5	-	-	-	-	-	-	-	-
UTILITIES, TOTAL	-	11	9	1	-	-	1	-	4
WATER SUPPLY	-	11	9	1	-	-	1	-	4
ELECTRIC POWER	-	-	-	-	-	-	-	-	-
GAS SUPPLY	-	-	-	-	-	-	-	-	-
TRANSIT	-	-	-	-	-	-	-	-	-
OTHER	-	-	-	-	-	-	-	-	-
MULTIPLE-FUNCTION DISTRICTS	1	-	-	-	-	-	-	-	1
SEWERAGE AND WATER SUPPLY	1	-	-	-	-	-	-	-	-
NATURAL RESOURCES AND WATER SUPPLY	-	-	-	-	-	-	-	-	1
OTHER	-	-	-	-	-	-	-	-	1
SCHOOL SYSTEMS									
TOTAL	7	9	2	2	1	1	1	2	2
DEPENDENT SCHOOL SYSTEMS	-	4	2	1	1	-	-	-	1
BY ENROLLMENT SIZE OCTOBER 1976									
100,000 OR MORE PUPILS	-	-	-	-	-	-	-	-	-
50,000 TO 99,999 PUPILS	-	-	-	-	-	-	-	-	-
25,000 TO 49,999 PUPILS	-	1	1	-	-	-	-	-	-
12,000 TO 24,999 PUPILS	1	1	1	-	-	-	-	-	1
6,000 TO 11,999 PUPILS	-	2	-	-	-	1	-	1	1
3,000 TO 5,999 PUPILS	-	1	-	1	-	-	-	-	-
1,200 TO 2,999 PUPILS	1	2	-	-	1	-	1	-	-
300 TO 1,199 PUPILS	5	1	-	-	-	-	-	1	-
50 TO 299 PUPILS	-	1	-	1	-	-	-	-	-
1 TO 49 PUPILS	-	-	-	-	-	-	-	-	-
POPULATION, 1975 (ESTIMATED)									
TOTAL	99 739	392 011	264 909	21 848	7 157	32 158	11 741	54 198	138 912
IN MUNICIPALLY GOVERNED AREAS	82 034	257 148	221 733	10 181	1 762	7 045	1 813	14 614	81 890
WITH A 1975 POPULATION OF--									
50,000 OR MORE	73 925	161 978	161 978	-	-	-	-	-	51 910
25,000 TO 49,999	-	-	-	-	-	-	-	-	26 448
10,000 TO 24,999	-	38 029	38 029	-	-	-	-	-	-
5,000 TO 9,999	-	26 186	14 741	-	-	5 255	-	6 190	-
2,500 TO 4,999	-	10 971	3 600	3 380	-	-	-	3 991	-
1,000 TO 2,499	3 943	16 128	2 988	3 953	1 762	1 790	1 813	3 822	2 012
LESS THAN 1,000	4 166	3 856	397	2 848	-	-	-	611	1 520
OUTSIDE MUNICIPALLY GOVERNED AREAS	17 705	134 863	43 176	11 667	5 395	25 113	9 928	39 584	57 022
IN TOWNSHIP-GOVERNED AREAS	17 708	-	-	-	-	-	-	-	-
ENROLLMENT OF PUBLIC SCHOOL SYSTEMS									
TOTAL	21 750	79 869	50 388	5 508	1 915	7 405	2 401	12 252	26 024
THROUGH GRADE 12	21 750	79 869	50 388	5 508	1 915	7 405	2 401	12 252	26 024
COLLEGE GRADES	-	-	-	-	-	-	-	-	-

86

	Clarksville-Hopkinsville--Continued		Johnson City-Kingsport-Bristol								
Item	Christian County* (Ky.)	Montgomery County*	Total	Carter County	Hawkins County	Sullivan County*	Unicoi County	Washington County*	Scott County (Va.)	Washington County (Va.)	Bristol City (Va.)
NUMBER OF LOCAL GOVERNMENTS											
ALL TYPES, TOTAL	9	8	76	12	18	17	7	7	9	5	1
WITH PROPERTY-TAXING POWER	8	2	30	3	6	4	2	3	7	4	1
WITHOUT PROPERTY-TAXING POWER	1	6	46	9	12	13	5	4	2	1	-
COUNTY GOVERNMENTS	1	1	7	1	1	1	1	1	1	1	-
MUNICIPALITIES	5	1	23	2	5	3	1	2	6	3	1
WITH A POPULATION OF--											
50,000 OR MORE	-	1	-	-	-	-	-	-	-	-	-
25,000 TO 49,999	1	-	3	-	-	2	-	1	-	-	-
10,000 TO 24,999	-	-	2	1	-	-	-	-	-	-	1
5,000 TO 9,999	-	-	1	-	-	-	-	-	-	1	-
2,500 TO 4,999	-	-	4	-	3	-	1	-	-	-	-
1,000 TO 2,499	1	-	7	-	1	1	-	1	2	2	-
LESS THAN 1,000	3	-	6	1	1	-	-	-	4	-	-
TOWNSHIP GOVERNMENTS	-	-	-	-	-	-	-	-	-	-	-
SCHOOL DISTRICTS	1	-	-	-	-	-	-	-	-	-	-
SPECIAL DISTRICTS	2	6	46	9	12	13	5	4	2	1	-
WITH PROPERTY-TAXING POWER	1	-	-	-	-	-	-	-	-	-	-
SINGLE FUNCTION DISTRICTS											
CEMETERIES	-	-	-	-	-	-	-	-	-	-	-
EDUCATION (SCHOOL BUILDING DISTRICTS)	-	-	-	-	-	-	-	-	-	-	-
FIRE PROTECTION	-	-	-	-	-	-	-	-	-	-	-
HIGHWAYS	-	-	-	-	-	-	-	-	-	-	-
HEALTH	-	-	-	-	-	-	-	-	-	-	-
HOSPITALS	-	-	-	-	-	-	-	-	-	-	-
HOUSING AND URBAN RENEWAL	-	1	6	1	1	2	1	1	-	-	-
LIBRARIES	-	-	-	-	-	-	-	-	-	-	-
NATURAL RESOURCES, TOTAL	1	1	8	1	1	2	1	1	1	1	-
DRAINAGE	-	-	-	-	-	-	-	-	-	-	-
FLOOD CONTROL	-	-	1	-	-	1	-	-	-	-	-
IRRIGATION, WATER CONSERVATION	-	-	-	-	-	-	-	-	-	-	-
SOIL CONSERVATION	1	1	7	1	1	1	1	1	1	1	-
OTHER AND COMPOSITE PURPOSES	-	-	-	-	-	-	-	-	-	-	-
PARKS AND RECREATION	-	-	-	-	-	-	-	-	-	-	-
SEWERAGE	-	-	1	-	-	-	-	-	1	-	-
UTILITIES, TOTAL	1	3	26	6	9	7	3	1	-	-	-
WATER SUPPLY	1	3	24	6	8	7	2	1	-	-	-
ELECTRIC POWER	-	-	-	-	-	-	-	-	-	-	-
GAS SUPPLY	-	-	2	-	1	-	1	-	-	-	-
TRANSIT	-	-	-	-	-	-	-	-	-	-	-
OTHER	-	-	2	1	-	-	-	1	-	-	-
MULTIPLE-FUNCTION DISTRICTS	-	1	3	-	1	2	-	-	-	-	-
SEWERAGE AND WATER SUPPLY	-	-	-	-	-	-	-	-	-	-	-
NATURAL RESOURCES AND WATER SUPPLY	-	-	-	-	-	-	-	-	-	-	-
OTHER	-	1	3	-	1	2	-	-	-	-	-
SCHOOL SYSTEMS											
TOTAL	1	1	13	2	2	3	1	2	1	1	1
DEPENDENT SCHOOL SYSTEMS	-	1	13	2	2	3	1	2	1	1	1
BY ENROLLMENT SIZE OCTOBER 1976											
100,000 OR MORE PUPILS	-	-	-	-	-	-	-	-	-	-	-
50,000 TO 99,999 PUPILS	-	-	-	-	-	-	-	-	-	-	-
25,000 TO 49,999 PUPILS	-	-	-	-	-	-	-	-	-	-	-
12,000 TO 24,999 PUPILS	-	1	1	-	-	1	-	-	-	-	-
6,000 TO 11,999 PUPILS	1	-	6	1	1	1	-	2	-	1	-
3,000 TO 5,999 PUPILS	-	-	4	-	-	1	1	-	1	-	1
1,200 TO 2,999 PUPILS	-	-	1	1	-	-	-	-	-	-	-
300 TO 1,199 PUPILS	-	-	1	-	1	-	-	-	-	-	-
50 TO 299 PUPILS	-	-	-	-	-	-	-	-	-	-	-
1 TO 49 PUPILS	-	-	-	-	-	-	-	-	-	-	-
POPULATION, 1975 (ESTIMATED)											
TOTAL	65 594	73 318	400 623	46 164	37 284	134 447	15 702	79 752	25 204	39 354	22 716
IN MUNICIPALLY GOVERNED AREAS	29 980	51 910	167 982	[1]12 870	[1]12 427	61 145	4 666	41 186	4 635	[1]8 337	22 716
WITH A 1975 POPULATION OF--											
50,000 OR MORE	-	51 910	-	-	-	-	-	-	-	-	-
25,000 TO 49,999	26 448	-	99 365	-	-	60 040	-	39 325	-	-	-
10,000 TO 24,999	-	-	35 270	12 554	-	-	-	-	-	-	22 716
5,000 TO 9,999	-	-	5 106	-	-	-	-	-	-	5 106	-
2,500 TO 4,999	-	-	15 164	-	10 498	-	4 666	-	-	-	-
1,000 TO 2,499	2 012	-	11 143	-	1 306	1 105	-	1 861	3 640	3 231	-
LESS THAN 1,000	1 520	-	1 934	316	623	-	-	-	995	-	-
OUTSIDE MUNICIPALLY GOVERNED AREAS	35 614	21 408	232 641	33 294	24 857	73 302	11 036	38 566	20 569	31 017	-
IN TOWNSHIP-GOVERNED AREAS	-	-	-	-	-	-	-	-	-	-	-
ENROLLMENT OF PUBLIC SCHOOL SYSTEMS											
TOTAL	10 532	15 492	88 160	9 994	8 608	30 259	3 178	16 799	5 520	9 692	4 110
THROUGH GRADE 12	10 532	15 492	88 160	9 994	8 608	30 259	3 178	16 799	5 520	9 692	4 110
COLLEGE GRADES	-	-	-	-	-	-	-	-	-	-	-

Table 6. Local Governments and Public School Systems in Individual SMSA's: 1977—Continued

	Tennessee--Continued									
	Knoxville					Memphis				
Item	Total	Anderson County	Blount County	Knox County*	Union County	Total	Shelby County*	Tipton County	Crittenden County (Ark.)	De Soto County (Miss.)
NUMBER OF LOCAL GOVERNMENTS										
ALL TYPES, TOTAL	39	13	10	10	6	68	12	13	33	10
WITH PROPERTY-TAXING POWER	17	6	6	2	3	40	7	9	15	9
WITHOUT PROPERTY-TAXING POWER	22	7	4	8	3	28	5	4	18	1
COUNTY GOVERNMENTS	4	1	1	1	1	4	1	1	1	1
MUNICIPALITIES	12	4	5	1	2	26	6	8	9	3
WITH A POPULATION OF--										
50,000 OR MORE	1	-	-	1	-	1	1	-	-	-
25,000 TO 49,999	1	1	-	-	-	1	-	-	1	-
10,000 TO 24,999	1	-	1	-	-	1	1	-	-	-
5,000 TO 9,999	2	1	1	-	-	3	2	1	-	-
2,500 TO 4,999	-	-	-	-	-	4	1	-	1	2
1,000 TO 2,499	2	2	-	-	-	5	1	2	1	1
LESS THAN 1,000	5	-	3	-	2	11	-	5	6	-
TOWNSHIP GOVERNMENTS	-	-	-	-	-	-	-	-	-	-
SCHOOL DISTRICTS	-	-	-	-	-	6	-	-	5	1
SPECIAL DISTRICTS	23	8	4	8	3	32	5	4	18	5
WITH PROPERTY-TAXING POWER	1	1	-	-	-	4	-	-	-	4
SINGLE FUNCTION DISTRICTS	-	-	-	-	-	-	-	-	-	-
CEMETERIES	-	-	-	-	-	-	-	-	-	-
EDUCATION (SCHOOL BUILDING DISTRICTS)	-	-	-	-	-	-	-	-	-	-
FIRE PROTECTION	-	-	-	-	-	-	-	-	-	-
HIGHWAYS	-	-	-	-	-	5	-	-	5	-
HEALTH	-	-	-	-	-	-	-	-	-	-
HOSPITALS	-	-	-	-	-	-	-	-	-	-
HOUSING AND URBAN RENEWAL	3	1	1	1	-	6	3	1	2	-
LIBRARIES	-	-	-	-	-	-	-	-	-	-
NATURAL RESOURCES, TOTAL	4	1	1	1	1	18	1	1	11	5
DRAINAGE	-	-	-	-	-	12	-	-	8	4
FLOOD CONTROL	-	-	-	-	-	2	-	-	2	-
IRRIGATION, WATER CONSERVATION	-	-	-	-	-	-	-	-	-	-
SOIL CONSERVATION	4	1	1	1	1	4	1	1	1	1
OTHER AND COMPOSITE PURPOSES	-	-	-	-	-	-	-	-	-	-
PARKS AND RECREATION	-	-	-	-	-	-	-	-	-	-
SEWERAGE	-	-	-	-	-	-	-	-	-	-
UTILITIES, TOTAL	12	6	2	3	1	1	-	1	-	-
WATER SUPPLY	10	4	2	3	1	1	-	1	-	-
ELECTRIC POWER	-	-	-	-	-	-	-	-	-	-
GAS SUPPLY	2	2	-	-	-	-	-	-	-	-
TRANSIT	-	-	-	-	-	-	-	-	-	-
OTHER	-	-	-	-	-	1	1	-	-	-
MULTIPLE-FUNCTION DISTRICTS	4	-	-	3	1	1	-	1	-	-
SEWERAGE AND WATER SUPPLY	3	-	-	3	-	-	-	-	-	-
NATURAL RESOURCES AND WATER SUPPLY	-	-	-	-	-	-	-	-	-	-
OTHER	1	-	-	-	1	1	-	1	-	-
SCHOOL SYSTEMS										
TOTAL	9	3	3	2	1	10	2	2	5	1
DEPENDENT SCHOOL SYSTEMS	9	3	3	2	1	4	2	2	-	-
BY ENROLLMENT SIZE OCTOBER 1976										
100,000 OR MORE PUPILS	-	-	-	-	-	1	1	-	-	-
50,000 TO 99,999 PUPILS	-	-	-	-	-	-	-	-	-	-
25,000 TO 49,999 PUPILS	2	-	-	2	-	-	-	-	-	-
12,000 TO 24,999 PUPILS	-	-	-	-	-	2	1	-	-	1
6,000 TO 11,999 PUPILS	2	1	1	-	-	2	-	1	1	-
3,000 TO 5,999 PUPILS	1	1	-	-	-	-	-	-	-	-
1,200 TO 2,999 PUPILS	3	-	2	-	1	2	-	-	2	-
300 TO 1,199 PUPILS	1	1	-	-	-	3	-	1	2	-
50 TO 299 PUPILS	-	-	-	-	-	-	-	-	-	-
1 TO 49 PUPILS	-	-	-	-	-	-	-	-	-	-
POPULATION, 1975 (ESTIMATED)										
TOTAL	435 473	61 911	69 816	293 405	10 341	866 864	736 754	29 917	51 074	49 119
IN MUNICIPALLY GOVERNED AREAS	247 316	¹35 426	26 833	183 383	1 674	752 593	697 373	10 729	36 686	7 805
WITH A 1975 POPULATION OF--										
50,000 OR MORE	183 383	-	-	183 383	-	661 319	661 319	-	-	-
25,000 TO 49,999	26 949	26 949	-	-	-	27 586	-	-	27 586	-
10,000 TO 24,999	18 653	-	18 653	-	-	19 491	19 491	-	-	-
5,000 TO 9,999	12 111	5 210	6 901	-	-	17 595	11 562	6 033	-	-
2,500 TO 4,999	-	-	-	-	-	13 022	3 626	-	3 258	6 138
1,000 TO 2,499	3 267	3 267	-	-	-	8 037	1 375	2 662	2 333	1 667
LESS THAN 1,000	2 953	-	1 279	-	1 674	5 543	-	2 034	3 509	-
OUTSIDE MUNICIPALLY GOVERNED AREAS	188 157	26 485	42 983	110 022	8 667	114 271	39 381	19 188	14 388	41 314
IN TOWNSHIP-GOVERNED AREAS	-	-	-	-	-	-	-	-	-	-
ENROLLMENT OF PUBLIC SCHOOL SYSTEMS										
TOTAL	92 375	15 215	14 910	59 642	2 608	171 133	138 356	7 551	12 298	12 928
THROUGH GRADE 12	92 375	15 215	14 910	59 642	2 608	171 133	138 356	7 551	12 298	12 928
COLLEGE GRADES	-	-	-	-	-	-	-	-	-	-

88

| | Tennessee--Continued | | | | | | | | |
| | Nashville-Davidson | | | | | | | | |
Item	Total	Cheatham County	Davidson County*	Dickson County	Robertson County	Rutherford County	Sumner County	Williamson County	Wilson County
NUMBER OF LOCAL GOVERNMENTS									
ALL TYPES, TOTAL	94	8	13	15	11	11	13	11	12
WITH PROPERTY-TAXING POWER	49	4	7	7	8	5	7	5	6
WITHOUT PROPERTY-TAXING POWER	45	4	6	8	3	6	6	6	6
COUNTY GOVERNMENTS	7	1	-	1	1	1	1	1	1
MUNICIPALITIES	39	3	7	6	7	4	6	3	3
WITH A POPULATION OF--									
50,000 OR MORE	1	-	1	-	-	-	-	-	-
25,000 TO 49,999	1	-	-	-	-	1	-	-	-
10,000 TO 24,999	5	-	-	-	1	-	2	1	1
5,000 TO 9,999	4	-	1	1	-	1	-	1	-
2,500 TO 4,999	6	-	3	1	1	1	1	1	-
1,000 TO 2,499	9	1	2	1	-	1	1	-	2
LESS THAN 1,000	13	2	-	4	5	1	2	1	-
TOWNSHIP GOVERNMENTS	-	-	-	-	-	-	-	-	-
SCHOOL DISTRICTS	3	-	-	-	-	-	-	1	2
SPECIAL DISTRICTS	45	4	6	8	3	6	6	6	6
WITH PROPERTY-TAXING POWER	-	-	-	-	-	-	-	-	-
SINGLE FUNCTION DISTRICTS	-	-	-	-	-	-	-	-	-
CEMETERIES	-	-	-	-	-	-	-	-	-
EDUCATION (SCHOOL BUILDING DISTRICTS)	-	-	-	-	-	-	-	-	-
FIRE PROTECTION	-	-	-	-	-	-	-	-	-
HIGHWAYS	-	-	-	-	-	-	-	-	-
HEALTH	-	-	-	-	-	-	-	-	-
HOSPITALS	-	-	-	-	-	-	-	-	-
HOUSING AND URBAN RENEWAL	7	-	1	1	1	1	2	1	-
LIBRARIES	-	-	-	-	-	-	-	-	-
NATURAL RESOURCES, TOTAL	9	1	1	1	2	1	1	1	1
DRAINAGE	-	-	-	-	-	-	-	-	-
FLOOD CONTROL	1	-	-	-	1	-	-	-	-
IRRIGATION, WATER CONSERVATION	-	-	-	-	-	-	-	-	-
SOIL CONSERVATION	8	1	1	1	1	1	1	1	1
OTHER AND COMPOSITE PURPOSES	-	-	-	-	-	-	-	-	-
PARKS AND RECREATION	-	-	-	-	-	-	-	-	-
SEWERAGE	-	-	-	-	-	-	-	-	-
UTILITIES, TOTAL	21	3	1	6	-	3	2	3	3
WATER SUPPLY	20	3	1	5	-	3	2	3	3
ELECTRIC POWER	-	-	-	-	-	-	-	-	-
GAS SUPPLY	1	-	-	1	-	-	-	-	-
TRANSIT	-	-	-	-	-	-	-	-	-
OTHER	2	-	1	-	-	-	-	-	1
MULTIPLE-FUNCTION DISTRICTS	6	-	2	-	-	1	1	1	1
SEWERAGE AND WATER SUPPLY	4	-	1	-	-	1	1	-	1
NATURAL RESOURCES AND WATER SUPPLY	-	-	-	-	-	-	-	-	-
OTHER	2	-	1	-	-	-	-	1	-
SCHOOL SYSTEMS									
TOTAL	12	1	1	1	1	2	1	2	3
DEPENDENT SCHOOL SYSTEMS	9	1	1	1	1	2	1	1	1
BY ENROLLMENT SIZE OCTOBER 1976									
100,000 OR MORE PUPILS	-	-	-	-	-	-	-	-	-
50,000 TO 99,999 PUPILS	1	-	1	-	-	-	-	-	-
25,000 TO 49,999 PUPILS	-	-	-	-	-	-	-	-	-
12,000 TO 24,999 PUPILS	2	-	-	-	-	1	1	-	-
6,000 TO 11,999 PUPILS	4	-	-	1	1	-	-	1	1
3,000 TO 5,999 PUPILS	2	1	-	-	-	1	-	-	-
1,200 TO 2,999 PUPILS	2	-	-	-	-	-	-	1	1
300 TO 1,199 PUPILS	1	-	-	-	-	-	-	-	1
50 TO 299 PUPILS	-	-	-	-	-	-	-	-	-
1 TO 49 PUPILS	-	-	-	-	-	-	-	-	-
POPULATION, 1975 (ESTIMATED)									
TOTAL	749 417	16 428	447 865	26 283	32 015	67 091	70 457	44 672	44 606
IN MUNICIPALLY GOVERNED AREAS	600 367	3 614	[1]447 865	9 863	[1]15 508	41 715	[1]43 458	[1]21 967	16 377
WITH A 1975 POPULATION OF--									
50,000 OR MORE	423 426	-	423 426	-	-	-	-	-	-
25,000 TO 49,999	29 937	-	-	-	-	29 937	-	-	-
10,000 TO 24,999	72 667	-	-	-	10 468	-	37 521	11 518	13 160
5,000 TO 9,999	29 834	-	7 785	6 748	-	6 845	-	8 456	-
2,500 TO 4,999	22 772	-	12 495	-	2 620	4 451	3 206	-	-
1,000 TO 2,499	15 666	2 296	4 159	1 487	-	-	2 514	1 993	3 217
LESS THAN 1,000	6 065	1 318	-	1 628	2 420	482	217	-	-
OUTSIDE MUNICIPALLY GOVERNED AREAS	149 050	12 814	-	16 420	16 507	25 376	26 999	22 705	28 229
IN TOWNSHIP-GOVERNED AREAS	-	-	-	-	-	-	-	-	-
ENROLLMENT OF PUBLIC SCHOOL SYSTEMS									
TOTAL	152 172	4 880	77 998	6 416	7 700	16 115	17 827	10 247	10 989
THROUGH GRADE 12	152 172	4 880	77 998	6 416	7 700	16 115	17 827	10 247	10 989
COLLEGE GRADES	-	-	-	-	-	-	-	-	-

Table 6. Local Governments and Public School Systems in Individual SMSA's: 1977—Continued

Item	Texas — Abilene Total	Callahan County	Jones County	Taylor County*	Amarillo Total	Potter County*	Randall County	Austin Total	Hays County	Travis County*	Beaumont-Port Arthur-Orange Total
NUMBER OF LOCAL GOVERNMENTS											
ALL TYPES, TOTAL	49	12	17	20	14	8	6	39	10	29	76
WITH PROPERTY-TAXING POWER	42	10	14	18	11	7	4	34	8	26	67
WITHOUT PROPERTY-TAXING POWER	7	2	3	2	3	1	2	5	2	3	9
COUNTY GOVERNMENTS	3	1	1	1	2	1	1	2	1	1	3
MUNICIPALITIES	17	4	5	8	3	1	2	11	3	8	23
WITH A POPULATION OF--											
50,000 OR MORE	1	-	-	1	1	1	-	1	-	1	2
25,000 TO 49,999	-	-	-	-	-	-	-	1	1	-	1
10,000 TO 24,999	-	-	-	-	1	-	1	-	-	-	4
5,000 TO 9,999	-	-	-	-	-	-	-	-	-	-	2
2,500 TO 4,999	3	-	3	-	-	-	-	2	1	1	4
1,000 TO 2,499	5	3	-	2	-	-	-	7	1	6	5
LESS THAN 1,000	8	1	2	5	1	-	1	-	-	-	5
TOWNSHIP GOVERNMENTS	-	-	-	-	-	-	-	-	-	-	-
SCHOOL DISTRICTS	17	4	5	8	6	5	1	9	3	6	17
SPECIAL DISTRICTS	12	3	6	3	3	1	2	17	3	14	33
WITH PROPERTY-TAXING POWER	5	1	3	1	-	-	-	12	1	11	24
SINGLE FUNCTION DISTRICTS											
CEMETERIES	-	-	-	-	-	-	-	-	-	-	-
EDUCATION (SCHOOL BUILDING DISTRICTS)	-	-	-	-	-	-	-	1	-	1	3
FIRE PROTECTION	-	-	-	-	-	-	-	-	-	-	-
HIGHWAYS	-	-	-	-	-	-	-	-	-	-	-
HEALTH	-	-	-	-	-	-	-	-	-	-	-
HOSPITALS	2	-	2	-	1	-	1	3	1	2	4
HOUSING AND URBAN RENEWAL	6	2	3	1	-	-	-	-	-	-	-
LIBRARIES	-	-	-	-	-	-	-	-	-	-	-
NATURAL RESOURCES, TOTAL	2	-	1	1	2	1	1	1	1	-	7
DRAINAGE	-	-	-	-	-	-	-	1	1	-	4
FLOOD CONTROL	-	-	-	-	-	-	-	-	-	-	-
IRRIGATION, WATER CONSERVATION	-	-	-	-	-	-	-	-	-	-	3
SOIL CONSERVATION	2	-	1	1	2	1	1	-	-	-	-
OTHER AND COMPOSITE PURPOSES	-	-	-	-	-	-	-	-	-	-	-
PARKS AND RECREATION	-	-	-	-	-	-	-	-	-	-	-
SEWERAGE	-	-	-	-	-	-	-	-	-	-	2
UTILITIES, TOTAL	2	1	-	1	-	-	-	8	-	8	-
WATER SUPPLY	2	1	-	1	-	-	-	7	-	7	-
ELECTRIC POWER	-	-	-	-	-	-	-	1	-	1	-
GAS SUPPLY	-	-	-	-	-	-	-	-	-	-	-
TRANSIT	-	-	-	-	-	-	-	-	-	-	-
OTHER	-	-	-	-	-	-	-	-	-	-	8
MULTIPLE-FUNCTION DISTRICTS	-	-	-	-	-	-	-	4	1	3	9
SEWERAGE AND WATER SUPPLY	-	-	-	-	-	-	-	3	-	3	7
NATURAL RESOURCES AND WATER SUPPLY	-	-	-	-	-	-	-	1	1	-	1
OTHER	-	-	-	-	-	-	-	-	-	-	1
SCHOOL SYSTEMS											
TOTAL	17	4	5	8	6	5	1	9	3	6	17
DEPENDENT SCHOOL SYSTEMS	-	-	-	-	-	-	-	-	-	-	-
BY ENROLLMENT SIZE OCTOBER 1976											
100,000 OR MORE PUPILS	-	-	-	-	-	-	-	1	-	1	-
50,000 TO 99,999 PUPILS	-	-	-	-	-	-	-	-	-	-	-
25,000 TO 49,999 PUPILS	-	-	-	-	1	1	-	-	-	-	3
12,000 TO 24,999 PUPILS	1	-	-	1	-	-	-	-	-	-	1
6,000 TO 11,999 PUPILS	-	-	-	-	2	1	1	2	1	1	5
3,000 TO 5,999 PUPILS	-	-	-	-	-	-	-	3	1	2	6
1,200 TO 2,999 PUPILS	-	-	-	-	3	3	-	2	1	1	1
300 TO 1,199 PUPILS	11	4	4	3	3	3	-	1	-	1	1
50 TO 299 PUPILS	5	-	1	4	-	-	-	-	-	-	-
1 TO 49 PUPILS	-	-	-	-	-	-	-	-	-	-	-
POPULATION, 1975 (ESTIMATED)											
TOTAL	130 617	9 238	15 989	105 390	157 004	93 462	63 542	396 891	35 052	361 839	350 521
IN MUNICIPALLY GOVERNED AREAS	117 264	4 885	[1]10 882	101 497	147 125	[2]138 743	[1]8 382	332 269	25 862	306 407	292 677
WITH A 1975 POPULATION OF--											
50,000 OR MORE	96 459	-	-	96 459	138 743	[2]138 743	-	301 147	-	301 147	167 253
25,000 TO 49,999	-	-	-	-	-	-	-	23 288	23 288	-	25 782
10,000 TO 24,999	-	-	-	-	8 140	-	8 140	-	-	-	58 275
5,000 TO 9,999	-	-	-	-	-	-	-	-	-	-	15 146
2,500 TO 4,999	9 924	-	9 924	-	-	-	-	3 753	2 021	1 732	14 526
1,000 TO 2,499	8 158	4 779	-	3 379	-	-	-	4 081	553	3 528	8 570
LESS THAN 1,000	2 723	106	958	1 659	242	-	242	-	-	-	3 125
OUTSIDE MUNICIPALLY GOVERNED AREAS	13 353	4 353	5 107	3 893	55 160	-	55 160	64 622	9 190	55 432	57 844
IN TOWNSHIP-GOVERNED AREAS	-	-	-	-	-	-	-	-	-	-	-
ENROLLMENT OF PUBLIC SCHOOL SYSTEMS											
TOTAL	26 744	2 281	3 505	20 958	36 478	32 835	3 643	74 436	7 616	66 820	80 549
THROUGH GRADE 12	26 744	2 281	3 505	20 958	31 748	28 105	3 643	74 436	7 616	66 820	80 549
COLLEGE GRADES	-	-	-	-	4 730	4 730	-	-	-	-	-

Table 6. Local Governments and Public School Systems in Individual SMSA's: 1977—Continued

Texas--Continued

Item	Beaumont-Port Arthur-Orange--Continued			Brownsville-Harlingen-San Benito	Bryan-College Station	Corpus Christi			Dallas-Fort Worth
	Hardin County	Jefferson County*	Orange County*	Cameron County (entire SMSA)	Brazos County (entire SMSA)	Total	Nueces County*	San Patricio County	Total
NUMBER OF LOCAL GOVERNMENTS									
ALL TYPES, TOTAL	15	35	26	62	9	60	34	26	368
WITH PROPERTY-TAXING POWER	14	31	22	50	7	50	29	21	336
WITHOUT PROPERTY-TAXING POWER	1	4	4	12	2	10	5	5	32
COUNTY GOVERNMENTS	1	1	1	1	1	2	1	1	11
MUNICIPALITIES	5	11	7	14	2	15	6	9	171
WITH A POPULATION OF--									
50,000 OR MORE	-	2	-	1	-	1	1	-	8
25,000 TO 49,999	-	-	1	1	2	-	-	-	6
10,000 TO 24,999	-	3	1	1	-	1	1	-	17
5,000 TO 9,999	1	-	1	1	-	4	-	4	10
2,500 TO 4,999	-	2	2	2	-	3	1	2	22
1,000 TO 2,499	3	2	-	4	-	3	1	2	26
LESS THAN 1,000	1	2	2	5	-	3	2	1	82
TOWNSHIP GOVERNMENTS	-	-	-	-	-	-	-	-	-
SCHOOL DISTRICTS	5	7	5	12	2	21	14	7	110
SPECIAL DISTRICTS	4	16	13	35	4	22	14	9	76
WITH PROPERTY-TAXING POWER	3	12	9	23	2	12	8	4	44
SINGLE FUNCTION DISTRICTS									
CEMETERIES	-	-	-	-	-	-	-	-	-
EDUCATION (SCHOOL BUILDING DISTRICTS)	-	-	-	-	-	-	-	-	-
FIRE PROTECTION	-	-	-	-	-	-	-	-	-
HIGHWAYS	-	-	3	-	-	2	2	-	1
HEALTH	-	-	-	-	-	-	-	-	-
HOSPITALS	-	-	-	-	-	-	-	-	-
HOUSING AND URBAN RENEWAL	-	2	2	6	1	2	1	1	6
LIBRARIES	-	-	-	-	-	6	2	4	21
NATURAL RESOURCES, TOTAL	1	4	2	19	1	5	3	2	21
DRAINAGE	-	3	1	3	-	3	2	1	1
FLOOD CONTROL	-	-	-	-	-	-	-	-	-
IRRIGATION, WATER CONSERVATION	-	-	-	-	-	-	-	-	12
SOIL CONSERVATION	-	-	-	14	-	-	-	-	1
OTHER AND COMPOSITE PURPOSES	1	1	1	2	1	2	1	1	7
PARKS AND RECREATION	-	-	-	-	-	-	-	-	-
SEWERAGE	-	-	-	-	-	-	-	-	-
UTILITIES, TOTAL	-	2	-	2	-	3	3	-	5
WATER SUPPLY	-	2	-	2	-	3	3	-	5
ELECTRIC POWER	-	-	-	-	-	-	-	-	-
GAS SUPPLY	-	-	-	-	-	-	-	-	-
TRANSIT	-	-	-	-	-	-	-	-	-
OTHER	1	5	2	3	-	2	1	1	1
MULTIPLE-FUNCTION DISTRICTS	2	3	4	5	2	2	1	1	21
SEWERAGE AND WATER SUPPLY	2	2	3	5	2	2	1	1	21
NATURAL RESOURCES AND WATER SUPPLY	-	1	1	-	-	-	-	-	-
OTHER	-	-	-	-	-	-	-	-	-
SCHOOL SYSTEMS									
TOTAL	5	7	5	12	2	21	14	7	110
DEPENDENT SCHOOL SYSTEMS	-	-	-	-	-	-	-	-	-
BY ENROLLMENT SIZE OCTOBER 1976									
100,000 OR MORE PUPILS	-	-	-	-	-	-	-	-	1
50,000 TO 99,999 PUPILS	-	-	-	-	-	-	-	-	1
25,000 TO 49,999 PUPILS	-	-	-	-	-	-	-	-	4
12,000 TO 24,999 PUPILS	-	-	-	-	-	1	1	-	4
6,000 TO 11,999 PUPILS	-	3	-	1	-	1	1	-	8
3,000 TO 5,999 PUPILS	-	-	1	2	1	1	1	-	3
1,200 TO 2,999 PUPILS	1	2	2	2	1	3	2	1	15
300 TO 1,199 PUPILS	3	1	2	4	-	9	4	5	22
50 TO 299 PUPILS	1	-	-	2	-	3	2	1	36
1 TO 49 PUPILS	-	1	-	1	-	3	3	-	19
POPULATION, 1975 (ESTIMATED)									
TOTAL	34 085	241 246	75 190	176 931	71 251	298 800	248 422	50 378	2 543 735
IN MUNICIPALLY GOVERNED AREAS	14 242	226 819	51 616	144 901	63 737	270 805	[1]231 959	38 846	2 394 264
WITH A 1975 POPULATION OF--									
50,000 OR MORE	-	167 253	-	72 157	-	214 838	214 838	-	1 684 358
25,000 TO 49,999	-	-	25 782	40 423	63 737	-	-	-	195 381
10,000 TO 24,999	-	47 519	10 756	17 436	-	10 912	10 912	-	266 314
5,000 TO 9,999	8 587	-	6 559	-	-	26 591	-	26 591	79 900
2,500 TO 4,999	-	7 387	7 139	6 920	-	10 866	3 429	7 437	85 686
1,000 TO 2,499	5 167	3 403	-	5 965	-	6 208	1 474	4 734	46 161
LESS THAN 1,000	488	1 257	1 380	2 000	-	1 390	1 306	84	36 464
OUTSIDE MUNICIPALLY GOVERNED AREAS	19 843	14 427	23 574	32 030	7 514	27 995	16 463	11 532	149 471
IN TOWNSHIP-GOVERNED AREAS	-	-	-	-	-	-	-	-	-
ENROLLMENT OF PUBLIC SCHOOL SYSTEMS									
TOTAL	9 265	51 621	19 663	64 246	12 726	81 675	67 179	14 496	623 062
THROUGH GRADE 12	9 265	51 621	19 663	59 945	12 726	73 738	59 242	14 496	568 863
COLLEGE GRADES	-	-	-	4 301	-	7 937	7 937	-	54 199

Item	Collin County	Dallas County*	Denton County	Ellis County	Hood County	Johnson County	Kaufman County	Parker County	Rockwall County	Tarrant County*	Wise County
					Texas--Continued						
					Dallas-Fort Worth--Continued						
NUMBER OF LOCAL GOVERNMENTS											
ALL TYPES, TOTAL	50	59	46	33	9	27	25	21	10	62	26
WITH PROPERTY-TAXING POWER	44	56	44	29	8	26	23	20	8	56	22
WITHOUT PROPERTY-TAXING POWER	6	3	2	4	1	1	2	1	2	6	4
COUNTY GOVERNMENTS	1	1	1	1	1	1	1	1	1	1	1
MUNICIPALITIES	25	27	28	13	3	10	10	6	5	33	11
WITH A POPULATION OF--											
50,000 OR MORE	-	6	-	-	-	-	-	-	-	2	-
25,000 TO 49,999	1	2	1	-	-	-	-	-	-	2	-
10,000 TO 24,999	1	5	1	2	-	2	1	1	-	4	-
5,000 TO 9,999	-	1	-	-	-	-	-	-	-	9	2
2,500 TO 4,999	2	6	-	1	1	1	1	-	1	7	-
1,000 TO 2,499	4	3	5	2	-	2	3	1	1	5	-
LESS THAN 1,000	17	4	21	8	2	5	5	4	3	4	9
TOWNSHIP GOVERNMENTS	-	-	-	-	-	-	-	-	-	-	-
SCHOOL DISTRICTS	15	15	11	10	3	11	7	11	2	18	7
SPECIAL DISTRICTS	9	16	6	9	2	5	7	3	2	10	7
WITH PROPERTY-TAXING POWER	3	13	4	5	1	4	5	2	-	4	3
SINGLE FUNCTION DISTRICTS	-	-	-	-	-	-	-	-	-	-	-
CEMETERIES	-	-	-	-	-	-	-	-	-	-	-
EDUCATION (SCHOOL BUILDING DISTRICTS)	-	-	-	-	-	1	-	-	-	-	-
FIRE PROTECTION	-	-	-	-	-	-	-	-	-	-	-
HIGHWAYS	-	-	-	-	-	-	-	-	-	-	-
HEALTH	-	-	-	-	-	-	-	-	-	-	-
HOSPITALS	-	2	-	-	-	1	-	1	-	1	1
HOUSING AND URBAN RENEWAL	5	1	1	3	1	-	1	1	2	3	3
LIBRARIES	-	-	-	-	-	-	-	-	-	-	-
NATURAL RESOURCES, TOTAL	1	6	1	5	1	1	4	-	-	2	-
DRAINAGE	-	-	-	1	-	-	-	-	-	-	-
FLOOD CONTROL	-	6	-	3	-	-	3	-	-	1	-
IRRIGATION, WATER CONSERVATION	-	-	-	-	-	-	-	-	-	1	-
SOIL CONSERVATION	1	-	1	1	1	1	1	-	-	-	-
OTHER AND COMPOSITE PURPOSES	-	-	-	-	-	-	-	-	-	-	-
PARKS AND RECREATION	-	-	-	-	-	-	-	-	-	-	-
SEWERAGE	-	-	-	-	-	-	-	-	-	-	-
UTILITIES, TOTAL	1	2	-	-	-	-	-	-	-	-	2
WATER SUPPLY	1	2	-	-	-	-	-	-	-	-	2
ELECTRIC POWER	-	-	-	-	-	-	-	-	-	-	-
GAS SUPPLY	-	-	-	-	-	-	-	-	-	-	-
TRANSIT	-	-	-	-	-	-	-	-	-	1	-
OTHER	-	-	-	-	-	-	-	-	-	-	-
MULTIPLE-FUNCTION DISTRICTS	2	5	4	1	-	2	2	1	-	3	1
SEWERAGE AND WATER SUPPLY	2	5	4	1	-	2	2	1	-	3	1
NATURAL RESOURCES AND WATER SUPPLY	-	-	-	-	-	-	-	-	-	-	-
OTHER	-	-	-	-	-	-	-	-	-	-	-
SCHOOL SYSTEMS											
TOTAL	15	15	11	10	3	11	7	11	2	18	7
DEPENDENT SCHOOL SYSTEMS	-	-	-	-	-	-	-	-	-	-	-
BY ENROLLMENT SIZE OCTOBER 1976											
100,000 OR MORE PUPILS	-	1	-	-	-	-	-	-	-	1	-
50,000 TO 99,999 PUPILS	-	-	-	-	-	-	-	-	-	1	-
25,000 TO 49,999 PUPILS	-	3	-	-	-	-	-	-	-	3	-
12,000 TO 24,999 PUPILS	1	4	-	-	-	-	-	-	-	-	-
6,000 TO 11,999 PUPILS	-	1	2	-	-	-	-	-	-	5	-
3,000 TO 5,999 PUPILS	1	3	-	2	-	2	1	1	-	5	2
1,200 TO 2,999 PUPILS	2	2	1	2	1	2	2	2	1	5	4
300 TO 1,199 PUPILS	8	1	7	4	-	3	4	2	1	2	1
50 TO 299 PUPILS	3	-	1	2	2	4	-	5	-	1	-
1 TO 49 PUPILS	-	-	-	-	-	-	-	1	-	-	-
POPULATION, 1975 (ESTIMATED)											
TOTAL	94 613	1 405 126	97 410	51 872	10 308	55 564	36 209	33 629	9 150	728 951	20 903
IN MUNICIPALLY GOVERNED AREAS	[1]71 894	[1]1 398 363	[1]82 710	[1]36 351	5 571	[1]36 036	[1]24 291	[1]15 404	[1]7 213	[1]704 924	11 507
WITH A 1975 POPULATION OF--											
50,000 OR MORE	-	1 215 451	-	-	-	-	-	-	-	468 907	-
25,000 TO 49,999	37 486	59 041	43 499	-	-	-	-	-	-	55 355	-
10,000 TO 24,999	14 293	82 214	21 664	25 640	-	26 548	13 251	11 991	-	70 713	-
5,000 TO 9,999	-	9 316	-	-	-	-	-	-	-	70 584	-
2,500 TO 4,999	6 298	24 731	-	3 334	4 927	2 774	4 286	-	4 192	28 081	7 063
1,000 TO 2,499	7 106	5 557	8 865	3 315	-	3 851	5 352	1 488	1 737	8 890	-
LESS THAN 1,000	6 711	2 053	8 682	4 062	644	2 863	1 402	1 925	1 284	2 394	4 444
OUTSIDE MUNICIPALLY GOVERNED AREAS	22 719	6 763	14 700	15 521	4 737	19 528	11 918	18 225	1 937	24 027	9 396
IN TOWNSHIP-GOVERNED AREAS	-	-	-	-	-	-	-	-	-	-	-
ENROLLMENT OF PUBLIC SCHOOL SYSTEMS											
TOTAL	28 826	334 114	21 619	12 291	2 315	13 874	8 964	8 797	2 826	184 890	4 546
THROUGH GRADE 12	28 826	301 324	21 619	12 291	2 315	13 874	8 964	7 388	2 826	164 890	4 546
COLLEGE GRADES	-	32 790	-	-	-	-	-	1 409	-	20 000	-

Table 6. Local Governments and Public School Systems in Individual SMSA's: 1977—Continued

	El Paso	Galveston-Texas City	Houston							Killeen-Temple
Item	El Paso County (entire SMSA)	Galveston County (entire SMSA)	Total	Brazoria County	Fort Bend County	Harris County*	Liberty County	Montgomery County	Waller County	Total
NUMBER OF LOCAL GOVERNMENTS										
ALL TYPES, TOTAL	20	39	488	51	34	308	31	50	14	49
WITH PROPERTY-TAXING POWER	18	36	450	48	33	282	26	48	13	39
WITHOUT PROPERTY-TAXING POWER	2	3	38	3	1	26	5	2	1	10
COUNTY GOVERNMENTS	1	1	6	1	1	1	1	1	1	2
MUNICIPALITIES	3	10	86	20	9	29	10	13	5	13
WITH A POPULATION OF--										
50,000 OR MORE	1	1	2	-	-	2	-	-	-	2
25,000 TO 49,999	-	1	1	-	-	1	-	-	-	-
10,000 TO 24,999	-	3	11	4	1	5	-	1	-	2
5,000 TO 9,999	-	1	12	2	3	5	2	-	-	2
2,500 TO 4,999	-	-	13	2	1	8	1	-	1	1
1,000 TO 2,499	2	1	16	4	1	4	1	-	3	1
LESS THAN 1,000	-	3	31	8	3	4	5	10	1	5
TOWNSHIP GOVERNMENTS	-	-	-	-	-	-	-	-	-	-
SCHOOL DISTRICTS	9	11	53	10	4	23	7	6	3	16
SPECIAL DISTRICTS	7	17	343	20	20	255	13	30	5	18
WITH PROPERTY-TAXING POWER	5	14	305	17	19	229	8	28	4	8
SINGLE FUNCTION DISTRICTS										
CEMETERIES	-	-	-	-	-	-	-	-	-	-
EDUCATION (SCHOOL BUILDING DISTRICTS)	-	-	-	-	-	-	-	-	-	-
FIRE PROTECTION	-	-	-	-	-	-	-	-	-	-
HIGHWAYS	-	-	-	-	-	-	-	-	-	-
HEALTH	-	-	-	-	-	-	-	-	-	-
HOSPITALS	-	-	3	3	-	-	-	-	-	-
HOUSING AND URBAN RENEWAL	1	2	4	-	-	2	2	-	-	7
LIBRARIES	-	-	-	-	-	-	-	-	-	-
NATURAL RESOURCES, TOTAL	1	5	24	7	2	2	10	1	2	5
DRAINAGE	-	5	14	6	1	-	6	-	1	-
FLOOD CONTROL	-	-	2	-	-	-	2	-	-	3
IRRIGATION, WATER CONSERVATION	-	-	1	-	-	1	-	-	-	-
SOIL CONSERVATION	1	-	7	1	1	1	2	1	1	2
OTHER AND COMPOSITE PURPOSES	-	-	-	-	-	-	-	-	-	-
PARKS AND RECREATION	-	-	-	-	-	-	-	-	-	-
SEWERAGE	-	-	1	-	-	1	-	-	-	-
UTILITIES, TOTAL	1	3	15	3	-	10	1	-	1	-
WATER SUPPLY	1	3	15	3	-	10	1	-	1	-
ELECTRIC POWER	-	-	-	-	-	-	-	-	-	-
GAS SUPPLY	-	-	-	-	-	-	-	-	-	-
TRANSIT	-	-	-	-	-	-	-	-	-	-
OTHER	-	1	2	1	-	1	-	-	-	-
MULTIPLE-FUNCTION DISTRICTS	4	6	294	6	18	239	-	29	2	6
SEWERAGE AND WATER SUPPLY	4	6	287	6	18	234	-	27	2	6
NATURAL RESOURCES AND WATER SUPPLY	-	-	1	-	-	-	-	1	-	-
OTHER	-	-	6	-	-	5	-	1	-	-
SCHOOL SYSTEMS										
TOTAL	9	11	53	10	4	23	7	6	3	16
DEPENDENT SCHOOL SYSTEMS	-	-	-	-	-	-	-	-	-	-
BY ENROLLMENT SIZE OCTOBER 1976										
100,000 OR MORE PUPILS	-	-	1	-	-	1	-	-	-	-
50,000 TO 99,999 PUPILS	1	-	-	-	-	-	-	-	-	-
25,000 TO 49,999 PUPILS	1	-	3	-	-	3	-	-	-	-
12,000 TO 24,999 PUPILS	-	1	6	-	1	4	-	1	-	1
6,000 TO 11,999 PUPILS	-	2	9	2	1	6	-	-	-	1
3,000 TO 5,999 PUPILS	1	3	10	4	-	5	-	1	-	3
1,200 TO 2,999 PUPILS	2	4	14	2	1	4	3	3	1	2
300 TO 1,199 PUPILS	3	-	8	1	1	-	3	1	2	6
50 TO 299 PUPILS	1	1	2	1	-	-	1	-	-	3
1 TO 49 PUPILS	-	-	-	-	-	-	-	-	-	-
POPULATION, 1975 (ESTIMATED)										
TOTAL	424 479	183 244	2 286 247	124 380	76 245	1 944 431	38 441	87 213	15 537	201 371
IN MUNICIPALLY GOVERNED AREAS	389 110	149 901	1 841 024	85 160	¹44 320	¹1 649 215	21 758	¹30 869	¹9 702	137 654
WITH A 1975 POPULATION OF--										
50,000 OR MORE	385 691	60 125	1 454 955	-	-	1 454 955	-	-	-	-
25,000 TO 49,999	-	40 939	48 191	-	-	48 191	-	-	-	88 825
10,000 TO 24,999	-	39 609	160 410	51 474	14 995	70 263	-	23 678	-	30 814
5,000 TO 9,999	-	6 331	86 670	16 693	22 492	34 868	12 617	-	-	7 971
2,500 TO 4,999	-	-	50 131	6 355	3 706	31 323	4 702	-	4 045	4 577
1,000 TO 2,499	3 419	1 229	25 686	6 971	1 662	6 346	2 257	3 082	5 368	2 729
LESS THAN 1,000	-	1 668	14 981	3 667	1 465	3 269	2 182	4 109	289	2 738
OUTSIDE MUNICIPALLY GOVERNED AREAS	35 369	33 343	445 223	39 220	31 925	295 216	16 683	56 344	5 835	63 717
IN TOWNSHIP-GOVERNED AREAS	-	-	-	-	-	-	-	-	-	-
ENROLLMENT OF PUBLIC SCHOOL SYSTEMS										
TOTAL	113 011	55 405	566 721	39 663	23 222	464 703	10 294	25 125	3 714	45 609
THROUGH GRADE 12	113 011	51 522	541 526	34 150	23 222	445 021	10 294	25 125	3 714	38 999
COLLEGE GRADES	-	3 883	25 195	5 513	-	19 682	-	-	-	6 610

Texas--Continued

Item	Killeen-Temple--Continued — Bell County*	Killeen-Temple--Continued — Coryell County	Laredo — Webb County (entire SMSA)	Longview — Total	Longview — Gregg County*	Longview — Harrison County	Lubbock — Lubbock County (entire SMSA)	McAllen-Pharr-Edinburg — Hidalgo County (entire SMSA)	Midland — Midland County (entire SMSA)	Odessa — Ector County (entire SMSA)	San Angelo — Tom Green County (entire SMSA)
NUMBER OF LOCAL GOVERNMENTS											
ALL TYPES, TOTAL	37	12	10	35	21	14	21	59	5	6	12
WITH PROPERTY-TAXING POWER	29	10	8	31	18	13	18	45	4	5	10
WITHOUT PROPERTY-TAXING POWER	8	2	2	4	3	1	3	14	1	1	2
COUNTY GOVERNMENTS	1	1	1	2	1	1	1	1	1	1	1
MUNICIPALITIES	9	4	1	14	8	6	6	15	1	2	1
WITH A POPULATION OF--											
50,000 OR MORE	-	-	1	1	1	-	1	-	1	1	-
25,000 TO 49,999	2	-	-	-	-	-	-	1	-	-	-
10,000 TO 24,999	1	1	-	1	-	1	-	5	-	-	-
5,000 TO 9,999	1	-	-	2	2	-	1	4	-	-	-
2,500 TO 4,999	-	1	-	1	1	-	-	1	-	-	-
1,000 TO 2,499	2	-	-	2	-	2	3	3	-	-	-
LESS THAN 1,000	3	2	-	7	4	3	1	1	-	1	-
TOWNSHIP GOVERNMENTS	-	-	-	-	-	-	-	-	-	-	-
SCHOOL DISTRICTS	11	5	5	14	8	6	8	15	2	2	6
SPECIAL DISTRICTS	16	2	3	5	4	1	6	28	1	1	4
WITH PROPERTY-TAXING POWER	8	-	1	1	1	-	3	14	-	-	2
SINGLE FUNCTION DISTRICTS											
CEMETERIES	-	-	-	-	-	-	-	-	-	-	-
EDUCATION (SCHOOL BUILDING DISTRICTS)	-	-	-	-	-	-	-	-	-	-	-
FIRE PROTECTION	-	-	-	-	-	-	-	-	-	-	-
HIGHWAYS	-	-	-	-	-	-	-	-	-	-	-
HEALTH	-	-	-	-	-	-	-	-	-	-	-
HOSPITALS	-	-	-	-	-	-	-	-	-	-	-
HOUSING AND URBAN RENEWAL	5	2	1	2	1	1	2	9	-	-	-
LIBRARIES	-	-	-	-	-	-	-	-	-	-	-
NATURAL RESOURCES, TOTAL	5	-	1	1	1	-	2	17	1	1	2
DRAINAGE	-	-	-	-	-	-	-	1	-	-	1
FLOOD CONTROL	3	-	-	-	-	-	1	16	-	-	1
IRRIGATION, WATER CONSERVATION	2	-	1	1	1	-	1	-	1	1	-
SOIL CONSERVATION	-	-	-	-	-	-	-	-	-	-	-
OTHER AND COMPOSITE PURPOSES	-	-	-	-	-	-	-	-	-	-	-
PARKS AND RECREATION	-	-	-	-	-	-	1	1	-	-	-
SEWERAGE	-	-	-	-	-	-	1	-	-	-	-
UTILITIES, TOTAL	-	-	-	-	-	-	-	-	-	-	2
WATER SUPPLY	-	-	-	-	-	-	-	-	-	-	2
ELECTRIC POWER	-	-	-	-	-	-	-	-	-	-	-
GAS SUPPLY	-	-	-	-	-	-	-	-	-	-	-
TRANSIT	-	-	-	-	-	-	-	-	-	-	-
OTHER	-	-	-	-	-	-	-	-	-	-	-
MULTIPLE-FUNCTION DISTRICTS	6	-	1	2	2	-	-	1	-	-	-
SEWERAGE AND WATER SUPPLY	6	-	1	1	1	-	-	1	-	-	-
NATURAL RESOURCES AND WATER SUPPLY	-	-	-	1	1	-	-	-	-	-	-
OTHER	-	-	-	-	-	-	-	-	-	-	-
SCHOOL SYSTEMS											
TOTAL	11	5	5	14	8	6	8	15	2	2	6
DEPENDENT SCHOOL SYSTEMS	-	-	-	-	-	-	-	-	-	-	-
BY ENROLLMENT SIZE OCTOBER 1976											
100,000 OR MORE PUPILS	-	-	-	-	-	-	-	-	-	-	-
50,000 TO 99,999 PUPILS	-	-	-	-	-	-	-	-	-	-	-
25,000 TO 49,999 PUPILS	-	-	-	-	-	-	1	-	-	-	-
12,000 TO 24,999 PUPILS	1	-	1	-	-	-	-	1	1	1	1
6,000 TO 11,999 PUPILS	1	-	-	2	1	1	-	4	-	-	-
3,000 TO 5,999 PUPILS	2	1	2	3	3	-	-	3	-	-	-
1,200 TO 2,999 PUPILS	1	1	-	2	1	1	3	3	1	-	2
300 TO 1,199 PUPILS	6	-	-	7	3	4	4	4	-	1	3
50 TO 299 PUPILS	-	3	2	-	-	-	-	-	-	-	-
1 TO 49 PUPILS	-	-	-	-	-	-	-	-	-	-	-
POPULATION, 1975 (ESTIMATED)											
TOTAL	156 781	44 590	81 009	126 157	81 798	44 359	197 248	227 853	69 214	97 460	74 534
IN MUNICIPALLY GOVERNED AREAS	[1]112 357	25 297	76 998	96 409	71 773	24 636	[1]175 935	169 413	62 950	84 851	66 099
WITH A 1975 POPULATION OF--											
50,000 OR MORE	-	-	76 998	52 034	52 034	-	163 525	-	62 950	84 476	66 099
25,000 TO 49,999	88 825	-	-	-	-	-	-	48 563	-	-	-
10,000 TO 24,999	10 989	19 825	-	21 132	-	21 132	-	86 544	-	-	-
5,000 TO 9,999	7 971	-	-	15 423	15 423	-	6 756	26 507	-	-	-
2,500 TO 4,999	-	4 577	-	3 058	3 058	-	-	2 987	-	-	-
1,000 TO 2,499	2 729	-	-	2 763	-	2 763	5 117	4 592	-	-	-
LESS THAN 1,000	1 843	895	-	1 999	1 258	741	537	220	-	375	-
OUTSIDE MUNICIPALLY GOVERNED AREAS	44 424	19 293	4 011	29 748	10 025	19 723	21 313	58 440	6 264	12 609	8 435
IN TOWNSHIP-GOVERNED AREAS	-	-	-	-	-	-	-	-	-	-	-
ENROLLMENT OF PUBLIC SCHOOL SYSTEMS											
TOTAL	37 878	7 731	27 612	35 418	24 498	10 920	41 496	68 535	16 281	26 845	16 019
THROUGH GRADE 12	31 268	7 731	24 346	31 722	20 802	10 920	41 496	68 535	16 281	23 134	16 019
COLLEGE GRADES	6 610	-	3 266	3 696	3 696	-	-	-	-	3 711	-

Table 6. Local Governments and Public School Systems in Individual SMSA's: 1977—Continued

Item	Texas--Continued San Antonio Total	Bexar County*	Comal County	Guadalupe County	Sherman-Denison Grayson County (entire SMSA)	Texarkana Total	Bowie County*	Little River County (Ark.)	Miller County* (Ark.)
NUMBER OF LOCAL GOVERNMENTS									
ALL TYPES, TOTAL	80	55	9	16	45	66	31	15	20
WITH PROPERTY-TAXING POWER	72	51	7	14	31	43	25	9	9
WITHOUT PROPERTY-TAXING POWER	8	4	2	2	14	23	6	6	11
COUNTY GOVERNMENTS	3	1	1	1	1	3	1	1	1
MUNICIPALITIES WITH A POPULATION OF--	27	20	2	5	15	16	8	5	3
50,000 OR MORE	1	1	-	-	-	-	-	-	-
25,000 TO 49,999	-	-	-	-	1	-	-	-	-
10,000 TO 24,999	3	1	1	1	1	1	1	-	-
5,000 TO 9,999	5	4	-	1	1	1	-	-	1
2,500 TO 4,999	6	6	-	1	-	-	-	-	-
1,000 TO 2,499	3	3	-	-	1	4	3	1	-
LESS THAN 1,000	9	5	1	3	9	6	1	3	2
TOWNSHIP GOVERNMENTS	-	-	-	-	-	-	-	-	-
SCHOOL DISTRICTS	22	16	2	4	14	22	14	3	5
SPECIAL DISTRICTS	28	18	4	6	15	25	8	6	11
WITH PROPERTY-TAXING POWER	20	14	2	4	1	2	2	-	-
SINGLE FUNCTION DISTRICTS									
CEMETERIES	-	-	-	-	-	-	-	-	-
EDUCATION (SCHOOL BUILDING DISTRICTS)	-	-	-	-	-	-	-	-	-
FIRE PROTECTION	-	-	-	-	-	-	-	-	-
HIGHWAYS	-	-	-	-	-	-	-	-	-
HEALTH	-	-	-	-	-	-	-	-	-
HOSPITALS	-	-	-	-	1	-	-	-	-
HOUSING AND URBAN RENEWAL	4	2	1	1	12	6	4	1	1
LIBRARIES	-	-	-	-	-	-	-	-	-
NATURAL RESOURCES, TOTAL	3	2	-	1	2	16	2	5	9
DRAINAGE	-	-	-	-	-	9	-	3	6
FLOOD CONTROL	-	-	-	-	1	4	1	1	2
IRRIGATION, WATER CONSERVATION	1	1	-	-	-	-	-	-	-
SOIL CONSERVATION	2	1	-	1	1	3	1	1	1
OTHER AND COMPOSITE PURPOSES	-	-	-	-	-	-	-	-	-
PARKS AND RECREATION	1	-	1	-	-	-	-	-	-
SEWERAGE	1	-	-	1	-	-	-	-	-
UTILITIES, TOTAL	4	3	1	-	-	2	2	-	-
WATER SUPPLY	4	3	1	-	-	2	2	-	-
ELECTRIC POWER	-	-	-	-	-	-	-	-	-
GAS SUPPLY	-	-	-	-	-	-	-	-	-
TRANSIT	-	-	-	-	-	-	-	-	-
OTHER	-	-	-	-	-	1	-	-	1
MULTIPLE-FUNCTION DISTRICTS	15	11	1	3	-	-	-	-	-
SEWERAGE AND WATER SUPPLY	14	10	1	3	-	-	-	-	-
NATURAL RESOURCES AND WATER SUPPLY	1	1	-	-	-	-	-	-	-
OTHER	-	-	-	-	-	-	-	-	-
SCHOOL SYSTEMS									
TOTAL	22	16	2	4	14	22	14	3	5
DEPENDENT SCHOOL SYSTEMS	-	-	-	-	-	-	-	-	-
BY ENROLLMENT SIZE OCTOBER 1976									
100,000 OR MORE PUPILS	-	-	-	-	-	-	-	-	-
50,000 TO 99,999 PUPILS	1	1	-	-	-	-	-	-	-
25,000 TO 49,999 PUPILS	3	3	-	-	-	-	-	-	-
12,000 TO 24,999 PUPILS	2	2	-	-	-	-	-	-	-
6,000 TO 11,999 PUPILS	2	2	-	-	-	-	-	-	-
3,000 TO 5,999 PUPILS	7	3	2	2	1	2	1	-	1
1,200 TO 2,999 PUPILS	4	4	-	-	2	5	4	1	-
300 TO 1,199 PUPILS	3	1	-	2	9	8	5	1	2
50 TO 299 PUPILS	-	-	-	-	2	6	4	1	1
1 TO 49 PUPILS	-	-	-	-	-	1	-	-	1
POPULATION, 1975 (ESTIMATED)									
TOTAL	981 566	912 934	29 478	39 154	78 831	115 753	69 918	11 837	33 998
IN MUNICIPALLY GOVERNED AREAS	883 592	¹837 590	¹20 430	25 572	61 094	77 445	49 218	5 819	22 408
WITH A 1975 POPULATION OF--									
50,000 OR MORE	773 248	773 248	-	-	-	-	-	-	-
25,000 TO 49,999	-	-	-	-	26 049	33 813	33 813	-	-
10,000 TO 24,999	48 174	11 112	20 308	16 754	22 413	21 249	-	-	21 249
5,000 TO 9,999	31 434	23 973	-	7 461	-	-	-	-	-
2,500 TO 4,999	22 648	22 648	-	-	2 835	13 188	9 493	3 695	-
1,000 TO 2,499	4 568	4 568	-	-	5 094	6 699	5 546	1 153	-
LESS THAN 1,000	3 520	2 041	122	1 357	4 703	2 496	366	971	1 159
OUTSIDE MUNICIPALLY GOVERNED AREAS	97 974	75 344	9 048	13 582	17 737	38 308	20 700	6 018	11 590
IN TOWNSHIP-GOVERNED AREAS	-	-	-	-	-	-	-	-	-
ENROLLMENT OF PUBLIC SCHOOL SYSTEMS									
TOTAL	253 317	235 133	7 346	10 838	20 695	29 882	18 926	3 083	7 873
THROUGH GRADE 12	224 317	206 133	7 346	10 838	16 923	27 194	16 238	3 083	7 873
COLLEGE GRADES	29 000	29 000	-	-	3 772	2 688	2 688	-	-

Item	Texas--Continued					Utah			
	Tyler	Waco	Wichita Falls			Provo-Orem	Salt Lake City-Ogden		
	Smith County (entire SMSA)	McLennan County (entire SMSA)	Total	Clay County	Wichita County*	Utah County (entire SMSA)	Total	Davis County	Salt Lake County*
NUMBER OF LOCAL GOVERNMENTS									
ALL TYPES, TOTAL	21	49	30	13	17	35	126	37	40
WITH PROPERTY-TAXING POWER	19	43	23	10	13	28	112	32	38
WITHOUT PROPERTY-TAXING POWER	2	6	7	3	4	7	14	5	2
COUNTY GOVERNMENTS	1	1	2	1	1	1	4	1	1
MUNICIPALITIES	7	20	9	4	5	16	43	16	9
WITH A POPULATION OF--									
50,000 OR MORE	1	-	1	-	1	1	2	-	1
25,000 TO 49,999	-	-	-	-	-	1	1	1	-
10,000 TO 24,999	-	-	-	-	-	2	8	2	3
5,000 TO 9,999	-	2	2	-	2	4	7	3	2
2,500 TO 4,999	-	4	2	1	1	1	9	5	2
1,000 TO 2,499	3	4	-	-	-	4	7	4	1
LESS THAN 1,000	3	9	4	3	1	3	9	1	1
TOWNSHIP GOVERNMENTS	-	-	-	-	-	-	-	-	-
SCHOOL DISTRICTS	9	19	10	5	5	3	8	1	4
SPECIAL DISTRICTS	4	9	9	3	6	15	71	19	26
WITH PROPERTY-TAXING POWER	2	3	2	-	2	8	57	14	24
SINGLE FUNCTION DISTRICTS	-	-	-	-	-	1	11	2	2
CEMETERIES	-	-	-	-	-	-	-	-	-
EDUCATION (SCHOOL BUILDING DISTRICTS)	-	-	-	-	-	-	-	-	-
FIRE PROTECTION	-	-	-	-	-	-	-	-	-
HIGHWAYS	-	-	-	-	-	-	5	2	2
HEALTH	-	-	-	-	-	-	-	-	-
HOSPITALS	-	1	1	-	1	-	-	-	-
HOUSING AND URBAN RENEWAL	-	4	4	1	3	-	-	-	-
LIBRARIES	-	-	-	-	-	-	-	-	-
NATURAL RESOURCES, TOTAL	1	2	3	1	2	9	16	5	3
DRAINAGE	-	-	-	-	-	3	1	-	1
FLOOD CONTROL	-	1	-	-	-	-	-	-	-
IRRIGATION, WATER CONSERVATION	-	-	1	-	1	3	7	3	1
SOIL CONSERVATION	1	1	2	1	1	3	8	2	1
OTHER AND COMPOSITE PURPOSES	-	-	-	-	-	-	-	-	-
PARKS AND RECREATION	-	-	-	-	-	-	3	-	2
SEWERAGE	-	-	-	-	-	1	15	6	6
UTILITIES, TOTAL	-	-	-	-	-	3	12	3	5
WATER SUPPLY	-	-	-	-	-	3	10	3	3
ELECTRIC POWER	-	-	-	-	-	-	1	-	1
GAS SUPPLY	-	-	-	-	-	-	-	-	-
TRANSIT	-	-	-	-	-	-	1	-	1
OTHER	-	-	-	-	-	-	1	-	-
MULTIPLE-FUNCTION DISTRICTS	3	2	1	1	-	1	8	1	6
SEWERAGE AND WATER SUPPLY	3	2	-	-	-	1	6	-	6
NATURAL RESOURCES AND WATER SUPPLY	-	-	-	-	-	-	1	-	1
OTHER	-	-	1	1	-	-	1	1	-
SCHOOL SYSTEMS									
TOTAL	9	19	10	5	5	3	8	1	4
DEPENDENT SCHOOL SYSTEMS	-	-	-	-	-	-	-	-	-
BY ENROLLMENT SIZE OCTOBER 1976									
100,000 OR MORE PUPILS	-	-	-	-	-	-	-	-	-
50,000 TO 99,999 PUPILS	-	-	-	-	-	-	1	-	1
25,000 TO 49,999 PUPILS	-	-	-	-	-	-	3	1	2
12,000 TO 24,999 PUPILS	1	1	1	-	1	1	2	-	-
6,000 TO 11,999 PUPILS	-	-	-	-	-	2	1	-	-
3,000 TO 5,999 PUPILS	1	1	1	-	1	-	1	-	1
1,200 TO 2,999 PUPILS	3	4	1	-	1	-	-	-	-
300 TO 1,199 PUPILS	4	9	4	2	2	-	-	-	-
50 TO 299 PUPILS	-	-	4	3	3	-	-	-	-
1 TO 49 PUPILS	-	-	-	-	-	-	-	-	-
POPULATION, 1975 (ESTIMATED)									
TOTAL	107 597	154 267	127 878	8 363	119 515	165 745	782 845	114 652	512 130
IN MUNICIPALLY GOVERNED AREAS	¹68 744	¹140 564	119 407	¹4 535	¹114 872	149 819	491 822	103 912	247 971
WITH A 1975 POPULATION OF--									
50,000 OR MORE	61 434	100 862	95 008	-	95 008	55 593	238 895	-	169 917
25,000 TO 49,999	-	-	-	-	-	35 584	30 358	30 358	-
10,000 TO 24,999	-	-	-	-	-	20 668	123 725	30 927	52 937
5,000 TO 9,999	-	14 101	15 931	-	15 931	27 375	51 046	19 051	17 351
2,500 TO 4,999	-	14 136	6 583	2 986	3 597	2 727	32 207	16 303	7 540
1,000 TO 2,499	5 400	7 736	-	-	-	6 616	11 626	6 397	-
LESS THAN 1,000	1 910	3 729	1 885	1 549	336	1 256	3 965	876	226
OUTSIDE MUNICIPALLY GOVERNED AREAS	38 853	13 703	8 471	3 828	4 643	15 926	291 023	10 740	264 159
IN TOWNSHIP-GOVERNED AREAS	-	-	-	-	-	-	-	-	-
ENROLLMENT OF PUBLIC SCHOOL SYSTEMS									
TOTAL	28 974	33 320	24 940	1 803	23 137	41 417	200 201	35 933	125 228
THROUGH GRADE 12	23 948	29 712	24 940	1 803	23 137	41 417	200 201	35 933	125 228
COLLEGE GRADES	5 026	3 608	-	-	-	-	-	-	-

Table 6. Local Governments and Public School Systems in Individual SMSA's: 1977—Continued

Column groups — Utah—Continued: Salt Lake City-Ogden—Continued (Tooele County, Weber County*). Virginia (see also District of Columbia and Tennessee): Lynchburg (Total, Amherst County, Appomattox County, Campbell County, Lynchburg city*); Newport News-Hampton (Total, Gloucester County, Hampton city*, James City County).

Item	Tooele County	Weber County*	Total (Lynchburg)	Amherst County	Appomattox County	Campbell County	Lynchburg city*	Total (Newport News-Hampton)	Gloucester County	Hampton city*	James City County
NUMBER OF LOCAL GOVERNMENTS											
ALL TYPES, TOTAL	15	34	10	3	3	3	1	9	1	1	1
WITH PROPERTY-TAXING POWER	12	30	9	2	3	3	1	7	1	1	1
WITHOUT PROPERTY-TAXING POWER	3	4	1	1	-	-	-	2	-	-	-
COUNTY GOVERNMENTS	1	1	3	1	1	1	-	3	1	-	1
MUNICIPALITIES	7	11	6	1	2	2	1	4	-	1	-
WITH A POPULATION OF--											
50,000 OR MORE	-	1	1	-	-	-	1	2	-	1	-
25,000 TO 49,999	-	-	-	-	-	-	-	-	-	-	-
10,000 TO 24,999	1	2	-	-	-	-	-	1	-	-	-
5,000 TO 9,999	-	2	-	-	-	-	-	1	-	-	-
2,500 TO 4,999	1	1	1	-	-	1	-	-	-	-	-
1,000 TO 2,499	1	2	2	1	1	-	-	-	-	-	-
LESS THAN 1,000	4	3	2	-	1	1	-	-	-	-	-
TOWNSHIP GOVERNMENTS	-	-	-	-	-	-	-	-	-	-	-
SCHOOL DISTRICTS	1	2	-	-	-	-	-	-	-	-	-
SPECIAL DISTRICTS	6	20	1	1	-	-	-	2	-	-	-
WITH PROPERTY-TAXING POWER	3	16	-	-	-	-	-	-	-	-	-
SINGLE FUNCTION DISTRICTS											
CEMETERIES	-	-	-	-	-	-	-	-	-	-	-
EDUCATION (SCHOOL BUILDING DISTRICTS)	-	7	-	-	-	-	-	-	-	-	-
FIRE PROTECTION	-	-	-	-	-	-	-	-	-	-	-
HIGHWAYS	-	-	-	-	-	-	-	-	-	-	-
HEALTH	-	-	-	-	-	-	-	-	-	-	-
HOSPITALS	-	1	-	-	-	-	-	-	-	-	-
HOUSING AND URBAN RENEWAL	-	-	-	-	-	-	-	-	-	-	-
LIBRARIES	-	-	-	-	-	-	-	-	-	-	-
NATURAL RESOURCES, TOTAL	3	5	1	1	-	-	-	-	-	-	-
DRAINAGE	-	-	1	1	-	-	-	-	-	-	-
FLOOD CONTROL	-	-	-	-	-	-	-	-	-	-	-
IRRIGATION, WATER CONSERVATION	-	3	-	-	-	-	-	-	-	-	-
SOIL CONSERVATION	3	2	-	-	-	-	-	-	-	-	-
OTHER AND COMPOSITE PURPOSES	-	-	-	-	-	-	-	-	-	-	-
PARKS AND RECREATION	1	-	-	-	-	-	-	1	-	-	-
SEWERAGE	1	2	-	-	-	-	-	-	-	-	-
UTILITIES, TOTAL	-	4	-	-	-	-	-	-	-	-	-
WATER SUPPLY	-	4	-	-	-	-	-	-	-	-	-
ELECTRIC POWER	-	-	-	-	-	-	-	-	-	-	-
GAS SUPPLY	-	-	-	-	-	-	-	-	-	-	-
TRANSIT	-	-	-	-	-	-	-	-	-	-	-
OTHER	1	-	-	-	-	-	-	1	-	-	-
MULTIPLE-FUNCTION DISTRICTS	-	1	-	-	-	-	-	-	-	-	-
SEWERAGE AND WATER SUPPLY	-	-	-	-	-	-	-	-	-	-	-
NATURAL RESOURCES AND WATER SUPPLY	-	1	-	-	-	-	-	-	-	-	-
OTHER	-	-	-	-	-	-	-	-	-	-	-
SCHOOL SYSTEMS											
TOTAL	1	2	4	1	1	1	1	6	1	1	(²)
DEPENDENT SCHOOL SYSTEMS	-	-	4	1	1	1	1	6	1	1	
BY ENROLLMENT SIZE OCTOBER 1976											
100,000 OR MORE PUPILS	-	-	-	-	-	-	-	-	-	-	-
50,000 TO 99,999 PUPILS	-	-	-	-	-	-	-	-	-	-	-
25,000 TO 49,999 PUPILS	-	-	-	-	-	-	-	2	-	1	-
12,000 TO 24,999 PUPILS	-	2	-	-	-	-	-	-	-	-	-
6,000 TO 11,999 PUPILS	1	-	2	-	-	1	1	1	-	-	-
3,000 TO 5,999 PUPILS	-	-	1	1	-	-	-	2	1	-	-
1,200 TO 2,999 PUPILS	-	-	1	-	1	-	-	1	-	-	-
300 TO 1,199 PUPILS	-	-	-	-	-	-	-	-	-	-	-
50 TO 299 PUPILS	-	-	-	-	-	-	-	-	-	-	-
1 TO 49 PUPILS	-	-	-	-	-	-	-	-	-	-	-
POPULATION, 1975 (ESTIMATED)											
TOTAL	22 936	133 127	142 987	27 555	11 139	41 227	63 066	347 220	17 215	125 013	17 840
IN MUNICIPALLY GOVERNED AREAS	18 679	121 260	69 669	1 087	1 740	3 776	63 066	281 731	-	125 013	-
WITH A 1975 POPULATION OF--											
50,000 OR MORE	-	68 978	63 066	-	-	-	63 066	263 773	-	125 013	-
25,000 TO 49,999	-	-	-	-	-	-	-	-	-	-	-
10,000 TO 24,999	12 905	26 956	-	-	-	-	-	10 641	-	-	-
5,000 TO 9,999	-	14 644	-	-	-	-	-	7 317	-	-	-
2,500 TO 4,999	3 657	4 707	2 842	-	-	2 842	-	-	-	-	-
1,000 TO 2,499	1 001	4 228	2 414	1 087	1 327	-	-	-	-	-	-
LESS THAN 1,000	1 116	1 747	1 347	-	413	934	-	-	-	-	-
OUTSIDE MUNICIPALLY GOVERNED AREAS	4 257	11 867	73 318	26 468	9 399	37 451	-	65 489	17 215	-	17 840
IN TOWNSHIP-GOVERNED AREAS	-	-	-	-	-	-	-	-	-	-	-
ENROLLMENT OF PUBLIC SCHOOL SYSTEMS											
TOTAL	6 584	32 456	30 747	5 829	2 893	10 300	11 725	79 913	3 782	29 413	-
THROUGH GRADE 12	6 584	32 456	30 747	5 829	2 893	10 300	11 725	79 913	3 782	29 413	-
COLLEGE GRADES	-	-	-	-	-	-	-	-	-	-	-

Table 6. Local Governments and Public School Systems in Individual SMSA's: 1977—Continued

Item	Virginia (see also District of Columbia and Tennessee)--Continued							
	Newport News-Hampton--Continued				Norfolk-Virginia Beach-Portsmouth			
	Newport News city*	Poquoson city	Williamsburg city	York County	Total	Chesapeake city	Norfolk city*	Portsmouth city*
NUMBER OF LOCAL GOVERNMENTS								
ALL TYPES, TOTAL	3	1	1	1	9	4	1	1
WITH PROPERTY-TAXING POWER	1	1	1	1	6	1	1	1
WITHOUT PROPERTY-TAXING POWER	2	-	-	-	3	3	-	-
COUNTY GOVERNMENTS	-	-	-	1	1	-	-	-
MUNICIPALITIES	1	1	1	-	5	1	1	1
WITH A POPULATION OF--								
50,000 OR MORE	1	-	-	-	4	1	1	1
25,000 TO 49,999	-	-	-	-	1	-	-	-
10,000 TO 24,999	-	-	1	-	-	-	-	-
5,000 TO 9,999	-	1	-	-	-	-	-	-
2,500 TO 4,999	-	-	-	-	-	-	-	-
1,000 TO 2,499	-	-	-	-	-	-	-	-
LESS THAN 1,000	-	-	-	-	-	-	-	-
TOWNSHIP GOVERNMENTS	-	-	-	-	-	-	-	-
SCHOOL DISTRICTS	-	-	-	-	-	-	-	-
SPECIAL DISTRICTS	2	-	-	-	3	3	-	-
WITH PROPERTY-TAXING POWER	-	-	-	-	-	-	-	-
SINGLE FUNCTION DISTRICTS	-	-	-	-	-	-	-	-
CEMETERIES	-	-	-	-	-	-	-	-
EDUCATION (SCHOOL BUILDING DISTRICTS)	-	-	-	-	-	-	-	-
FIRE PROTECTION	-	-	-	-	-	-	-	-
HIGHWAYS	-	-	-	-	-	-	-	-
HEALTH	-	-	-	-	-	-	-	-
HOSPITALS	-	-	-	-	1	1	-	-
HOUSING AND URBAN RENEWAL	-	-	-	-	-	-	-	-
LIBRARIES	-	-	-	-	-	-	-	-
NATURAL RESOURCES, TOTAL	-	-	-	-	1	1	-	-
DRAINAGE	-	-	-	-	-	-	-	-
FLOOD CONTROL	-	-	-	-	-	-	-	-
IRRIGATION, WATER CONSERVATION	-	-	-	-	-	-	-	-
SOIL CONSERVATION	-	-	-	-	1	1	-	-
OTHER AND COMPOSITE PURPOSES	-	-	-	-	-	-	-	-
PARKS AND RECREATION	1	-	-	-	1	1	-	-
SEWERAGE	-	-	-	-	-	-	-	-
UTILITIES, TOTAL	-	-	-	-	-	-	-	-
WATER SUPPLY	-	-	-	-	-	-	-	-
ELECTRIC POWER	-	-	-	-	-	-	-	-
GAS SUPPLY	-	-	-	-	-	-	-	-
TRANSIT	-	-	-	-	-	-	-	-
OTHER	1	-	-	-	-	-	-	-
MULTIPLE-FUNCTION DISTRICTS	-	-	-	-	-	-	-	-
SEWERAGE AND WATER SUPPLY	-	-	-	-	-	-	-	-
NATURAL RESOURCES AND WATER SUPPLY	-	-	-	-	-	-	-	-
OTHER	-	-	-	-	-	-	-	-
SCHOOL SYSTEMS								
TOTAL	1	1	1	1	6	1	1	1
DEPENDENT SCHOOL SYSTEMS	1	1	1	1	6	1	1	1
BY ENROLLMENT SIZE OCTOBER 1976								
100,000 OR MORE PUPILS	-	-	-	-	-	-	-	-
50,000 TO 99,999 PUPILS	-	-	-	-	1	-	-	-
25,000 TO 49,999 PUPILS	1	-	-	-	2	1	1	-
12,000 TO 24,999 PUPILS	-	-	-	-	1	-	-	1
6,000 TO 11,999 PUPILS	-	-	-	1	1	-	-	-
3,000 TO 5,999 PUPILS	-	-	1	-	-	-	-	-
1,200 TO 2,999 PUPILS	-	1	-	-	1	-	-	-
300 TO 1,199 PUPILS	-	-	-	-	-	-	-	-
50 TO 299 PUPILS	-	-	-	-	-	-	-	-
1 TO 49 PUPILS	-	-	-	-	-	-	-	-
POPULATION, 1975 (ESTIMATED)								
TOTAL	138 760	7 317	10 641	30 434	772 932	104 459	286 694	108 674
IN MUNICIPALLY GOVERNED AREAS	138 760	7 317	10 641	-	762 991	104 459	286 694	108 674
WITH A 1975 POPULATION OF--								
50,000 OR MORE	138 760	-	-	-	713 781	104 459	286 694	108 674
25,000 TO 49,999	-	-	-	-	49 210	-	-	-
10,000 TO 24,999	-	-	10 641	-	-	-	-	-
5,000 TO 9,999	-	7 317	-	-	-	-	-	-
2,500 TO 4,999	-	-	-	-	-	-	-	-
1,000 TO 2,499	-	-	-	-	-	-	-	-
LESS THAN 1,000	-	-	-	-	-	-	-	-
OUTSIDE MUNICIPALLY GOVERNED AREAS	-	-	-	30 434	9 941	-	-	-
IN TOWNSHIP-GOVERNED AREAS	-	-	-	-	-	-	-	-
ENROLLMENT OF PUBLIC SCHOOL SYSTEMS								
TOTAL	29 905	2 061	5 128	9 624	165 928	27 298	46 956	21 957
THROUGH GRADE 12	29 905	2 061	5 128	9 624	165 928	27 298	46 956	21 957
COLLEGE GRADES	-	-	-	-	-	-	-	-

Table 6. Local Governments and Public School Systems in Individual SMSA's: 1977—Continued

Virginia (see also District of Columbia and Tennessee)—Continued

Item	Suffolk city	Virginia Beach city*	Currituck County (N.C.)	Total	Colonial Heights city*	Dinwiddie County	Hopewell city*	Petersburg city*	Prince George County	Total	Charles City County
NUMBER OF LOCAL GOVERNMENTS											
ALL TYPES, TOTAL	1	1	1	8	1	2	2	2	1	14	1
WITH PROPERTY-TAXING POWER	1	1	1	6	1	2	1	1	1	9	1
WITHOUT PROPERTY-TAXING POWER	-	-	-	2	-	-	1	1	-	5	-
COUNTY GOVERNMENTS	-	-	1	2	-	1	-	-	1	7	1
MUNICIPALITIES	1	1	-	4	1	1	1	1	-	2	-
WITH A POPULATION OF--											
50,000 OR MORE	-	1	-	-	-	-	-	-	-	1	-
25,000 TO 49,999	1	-	-	1	-	-	-	1	-	-	-
10,000 TO 24,999	-	-	-	2	1	-	1	-	-	-	-
5,000 TO 9,999	-	-	-	-	-	-	-	-	-	1	-
2,500 TO 4,999	-	-	-	-	-	-	-	-	-	-	-
1,000 TO 2,499	-	-	-	1	-	1	-	-	-	-	-
LESS THAN 1,000	-	-	-	-	-	-	-	-	-	-	-
TOWNSHIP GOVERNMENTS	-	-	-	-	-	-	-	-	-	-	-
SCHOOL DISTRICTS	-	-	-	-	-	-	-	-	-	-	-
SPECIAL DISTRICTS	-	-	-	2	-	-	1	1	-	5	-
WITH PROPERTY-TAXING POWER	-	-	-	-	-	-	-	-	-	-	-
SINGLE FUNCTION DISTRICTS											
CEMETERIES	-	-	-	-	-	-	-	-	-	-	-
EDUCATION (SCHOOL BUILDING DISTRICTS)	-	-	-	-	-	-	-	-	-	-	-
FIRE PROTECTION	-	-	-	-	-	-	-	-	-	-	-
HIGHWAYS	-	-	-	-	-	-	-	-	-	-	-
HEALTH	-	-	-	-	-	-	-	-	-	1	-
HOSPITALS	-	-	-	-	-	-	-	-	-	-	-
HOUSING AND URBAN RENEWAL	-	-	-	2	-	-	1	1	-	-	-
LIBRARIES	-	-	-	-	-	-	-	-	-	-	-
NATURAL RESOURCES, TOTAL	-	-	-	-	-	-	-	-	-	4	-
DRAINAGE	-	-	-	-	-	-	-	-	-	-	-
FLOOD CONTROL	-	-	-	-	-	-	-	-	-	-	-
IRRIGATION, WATER CONSERVATION	-	-	-	-	-	-	-	-	-	-	-
SOIL CONSERVATION	-	-	-	-	-	-	-	-	-	-	-
OTHER AND COMPOSITE PURPOSES	-	-	-	-	-	-	-	-	-	4	-
PARKS AND RECREATION	-	-	-	-	-	-	-	-	-	-	-
SEWERAGE	-	-	-	-	-	-	-	-	-	-	-
UTILITIES, TOTAL	-	-	-	-	-	-	-	-	-	-	-
WATER SUPPLY	-	-	-	-	-	-	-	-	-	-	-
ELECTRIC POWER	-	-	-	-	-	-	-	-	-	-	-
GAS SUPPLY	-	-	-	-	-	-	-	-	-	-	-
TRANSIT	-	-	-	-	-	-	-	-	-	-	-
OTHER	-	-	-	-	-	-	-	-	-	-	-
MULTIPLE-FUNCTION DISTRICTS											
SEWERAGE AND WATER SUPPLY	-	-	-	-	-	-	-	-	-	-	-
NATURAL RESOURCES AND WATER SUPPLY	-	-	-	-	-	-	-	-	-	-	-
OTHER	-	-	-	-	-	-	-	-	-	-	-
SCHOOL SYSTEMS											
TOTAL	1	1	1	5	1	1	1	1	1	8	1
DEPENDENT SCHOOL SYSTEMS	1	1	1	5	1	1	1	1	1	8	1
BY ENROLLMENT SIZE OCTOBER 1976											
100,000 OR MORE PUPILS	-	-	-	-	-	-	-	-	-	-	-
50,000 TO 99,999 PUPILS	-	1	-	-	-	-	-	-	-	-	-
25,000 TO 49,999 PUPILS	-	-	-	-	-	-	-	-	-	3	-
12,000 TO 24,999 PUPILS	-	-	-	-	-	-	-	-	-	-	-
6,000 TO 11,999 PUPILS	1	-	-	1	-	-	-	1	-	1	-
3,000 TO 5,999 PUPILS	-	-	-	4	1	1	1	-	1	4	1
1,200 TO 2,999 PUPILS	-	-	1	-	-	-	-	-	-	-	-
300 TO 1,199 PUPILS	-	-	-	-	-	-	-	-	-	-	-
50 TO 299 PUPILS	-	-	-	-	-	-	-	-	-	-	-
1 TO 49 PUPILS	-	-	-	-	-	-	-	-	-	-	-
POPULATION, 1975 (ESTIMATED)											
TOTAL	49 210	213 954	9 941	125 746	17 472	20 998	23 580	45 245	18 451	585 203	6 752
IN MUNICIPALLY GOVERNED AREAS	49 210	213 954	-	86 828	17 472	531	23 580	45 245	-	236 212	-
WITH A 1975 POPULATION OF--											
50,000 OR MORE	-	213 954	-	-	-	-	-	-	-	232 652	-
25,000 TO 49,999	49 210	-	-	45 245	-	-	-	45 245	-	-	-
10,000 TO 24,999	-	-	-	41 052	17 472	-	23 580	-	-	-	-
5,000 TO 9,999	-	-	-	-	-	-	-	-	-	-	-
2,500 TO 4,999	-	-	-	-	-	-	-	-	-	-	-
1,000 TO 2,499	-	-	-	-	-	-	-	-	-	3 560	-
LESS THAN 1,000	-	-	-	531	-	531	-	-	-	-	-
OUTSIDE MUNICIPALLY GOVERNED AREAS	-	-	9 941	38 918	-	20 467	-	-	18 451	348 991	6 752
IN TOWNSHIP-GOVERNED AREAS	-	-	-	-	-	-	-	-	-	-	-
ENROLLMENT OF PUBLIC SCHOOL SYSTEMS											
TOTAL	11 259	56 099	2 359	29 288	3 990	5 247	5 283	9 230	5 538	117 856	1 816
THROUGH GRADE 12	11 259	56 099	2 359	29 288	3 990	5 247	5 283	9 230	5 538	117 856	1 816
COLLEGE GRADES	-	-	-	-	-	-	-	-	-	-	-

99

Virginia (see also District of Columbia and Tennessee)--Continued

Item	Richmond--Continued							Roanoke			
	Chesterfield County	Goochland County	Hanover County	Henrico County	New Kent County	Powhatan County	Richmond city*	Total	Botetourt County	Craig County	Roanoke city*
NUMBER OF LOCAL GOVERNMENTS											
ALL TYPES, TOTAL	2	2	3	1	2	1	2	11	4	3	1
WITH PROPERTY-TAXING POWER	1	1	2	1	1	1	1	10	4	2	1
WITHOUT PROPERTY-TAXING POWER	1	1	1	-	1	-	1	1	-	1	-
COUNTY GOVERNMENTS	1	1	1	1	1	1	-	3	1	1	-
MUNICIPALITIES	-	-	1	-	-	-	1	7	3	1	1
WITH A POPULATION OF--											
50,000 OR MORE	-	-	-	-	-	-	1	1	-	-	1
25,000 TO 49,999	-	-	-	-	-	-	-	-	-	-	-
10,000 TO 24,999	-	-	-	-	-	-	-	1	-	-	-
5,000 TO 9,999	-	-	-	-	-	-	-	1	-	-	-
2,500 TO 4,999	-	-	1	-	-	-	-	-	-	-	-
1,000 TO 2,499	-	-	-	-	-	-	-	1	1	-	-
LESS THAN 1,000	-	-	-	-	-	-	-	3	2	1	-
TOWNSHIP GOVERNMENTS	-	-	-	-	-	-	-	-	-	-	-
SCHOOL DISTRICTS	-	-	-	-	-	-	-	-	-	-	-
SPECIAL DISTRICTS	1	1	1	-	1	-	1	1	-	1	-
WITH PROPERTY-TAXING POWER	-	-	-	-	-	-	-	-	-	-	-
SINGLE FUNCTION DISTRICTS	1	1	1	-	1	-	1	1	-	1	-
CEMETERIES	-	-	-	-	-	-	-	-	-	-	-
EDUCATION (SCHOOL BUILDING DISTRICTS)	-	-	-	-	-	-	-	-	-	-	-
FIRE PROTECTION	-	-	-	-	-	-	-	-	-	-	-
HIGHWAYS	-	-	-	-	-	-	1	-	-	-	-
HEALTH	-	-	-	-	-	-	-	-	-	-	-
HOSPITALS	-	-	-	-	-	-	-	-	-	-	-
HOUSING AND URBAN RENEWAL	-	-	-	-	-	-	-	-	-	-	-
LIBRARIES	-	-	-	-	-	-	-	-	-	-	-
NATURAL RESOURCES, TOTAL	1	1	1	-	1	-	-	1	-	1	-
DRAINAGE	-	-	-	-	-	-	-	-	-	-	-
FLOOD CONTROL	-	-	-	-	-	-	-	-	-	-	-
IRRIGATION, WATER CONSERVATION	-	-	-	-	-	-	-	-	-	-	-
SOIL CONSERVATION	1	1	1	-	1	-	-	1	-	1	-
OTHER AND COMPOSITE PURPOSES	-	-	-	-	-	-	-	-	-	-	-
PARKS AND RECREATION	-	-	-	-	-	-	-	-	-	-	-
SEWERAGE	-	-	-	-	-	-	-	-	-	-	-
UTILITIES, TOTAL	-	-	-	-	-	-	-	-	-	-	-
WATER SUPPLY	-	-	-	-	-	-	-	-	-	-	-
ELECTRIC POWER	-	-	-	-	-	-	-	-	-	-	-
GAS SUPPLY	-	-	-	-	-	-	-	-	-	-	-
TRANSIT	-	-	-	-	-	-	-	-	-	-	-
OTHER	-	-	-	-	-	-	-	-	-	-	-
MULTIPLE-FUNCTION DISTRICTS	-	-	-	-	-	-	-	-	-	-	-
SEWERAGE AND WATER SUPPLY	-	-	-	-	-	-	-	-	-	-	-
NATURAL RESOURCES AND WATER SUPPLY	-	-	-	-	-	-	-	-	-	-	-
OTHER	-	-	-	-	-	-	-	-	-	-	-
SCHOOL SYSTEMS											
TOTAL	1	1	1	1	1	1	1	5	1	1	1
DEPENDENT SCHOOL SYSTEMS	1	1	1	1	1	1	1	5	1	1	1
BY ENROLLMENT SIZE OCTOBER 1976											
100,000 OR MORE PUPILS	-	-	-	-	-	-	-	-	-	-	-
50,000 TO 99,999 PUPILS	-	-	-	-	-	-	-	-	-	-	-
25,000 TO 49,999 PUPILS	1	-	-	1	-	-	1	-	-	-	-
12,000 TO 24,999 PUPILS	-	-	-	-	-	-	-	2	-	-	1
6,000 TO 11,999 PUPILS	-	-	1	-	-	-	-	1	-	-	-
3,000 TO 5,999 PUPILS	-	-	-	-	-	-	-	1	1	-	-
1,200 TO 2,999 PUPILS	-	1	-	-	1	1	-	-	-	-	-
300 TO 1,199 PUPILS	-	-	-	-	-	-	-	1	-	1	-
50 TO 299 PUPILS	-	-	-	-	-	-	-	-	-	-	-
1 TO 49 PUPILS	-	-	-	-	-	-	-	-	-	-	-
0 PUPILS (NONOPERATING)	-	-	-	-	-	-	-	-	-	-	-
POPULATION, 1975 (ESTIMATED)											
TOTAL	103 240	11 050	47 397	167 728	7 351	9 033	232 652	212 021	20 605	3 822	100 585
IN MUNICIPALLY GOVERNED AREAS	-	-	3 560	-	-	-	232 652	134 847	2 239	225	100 585
WITH A 1975 POPULATION OF--											
50,000 OR MORE	-	-	-	-	-	-	232 652	100 585	-	-	100 585
25,000 TO 49,999	-	-	-	-	-	-	-	-	-	-	-
10,000 TO 24,999	-	-	-	-	-	-	-	24 042	-	-	-
5,000 TO 9,999	-	-	-	-	-	-	-	7 756	-	-	-
2,500 TO 4,999	-	-	3 560	-	-	-	-	-	-	-	-
1,000 TO 2,499	-	-	-	-	-	-	-	1 278	1 278	-	-
LESS THAN 1,000	-	-	-	-	-	-	-	1 186	961	225	-
OUTSIDE MUNICIPALLY GOVERNED AREAS	103 240	11 050	43 837	167 728	7 351	9 033	-	77 174	18 366	3 597	-
IN TOWNSHIP-GOVERNED AREAS	-	-	-	-	-	-	-	-	-	-	-
ENROLLMENT OF PUBLIC SCHOOL SYSTEMS											
TOTAL	26 483	2 415	11 445	35 052	1 718	2 405	36 522	45 209	4 897	825	15 973
THROUGH GRADE 12	26 483	2 415	11 445	35 052	1 718	2 405	36 522	45 209	4 897	825	15 973
COLLEGE GRADES	-	-	-	-	-	-	-	-	-	-	-

Item	Virginia (see also District of Columbia and Tennessee)--Continued		Washington (see also Oregon)						
	Roanoke--Continued		Richland-Kennewick			Seattle-Everett			Spokane
	Roanoke County	Salem city	Total	Benton County*	Franklin County	Total	King County*	Snohomish County*	Spokane County (entire SMSA)
NUMBER OF LOCAL GOVERNMENTS									
ALL TYPES, TOTAL	2	1	67	44	23	262	166	96	64
WITH PROPERTY-TAXING POWER	2	1	48	28	20	235	154	81	55
WITHOUT PROPERTY-TAXING POWER	-	-	19	16	3	27	12	15	9
COUNTY GOVERNMENTS	1	-	2	1	1	2	1	1	1
MUNICIPALITIES	1	1	9	5	4	46	28	18	11
WITH A POPULATION OF--									
50,000 OR MORE	-	-	-	-	-	2	2	-	1
25,000 TO 49,999	-	-	1	1	-	2	1	1	-
10,000 TO 24,999	-	1	2	1	1	8	5	3	-
5,000 TO 9,999	1	-	-	-	-	2	2	-	1
2,500 TO 4,999	-	-	1	1	-	11	7	4	1
1,000 TO 2,499	-	-	3	2	1	11	5	6	3
LESS THAN 1,000	-	-	2	-	2	10	6	4	5
TOWNSHIP GOVERNMENTS	-	-	-	-	-	-	-	-	-
SCHOOL DISTRICTS	-	-	10	6	4	34	20	14	14
SPECIAL DISTRICTS	-	-	46	32	14	180	117	63	38
WITH PROPERTY-TAXING POWER	-	-	27	16	11	153	105	48	29
SINGLE FUNCTION DISTRICTS.									
CEMETERIES	-	-	-	-	-	-	-	-	-
EDUCATION (SCHOOL BUILDING DISTRICTS)	-	-	2	-	2	-	-	-	5
FIRE PROTECTION	-	-	10	5	5	60	36	24	12
HIGHWAYS	-	-	-	-	-	-	-	-	-
HEALTH	-	-	2	2	-	1	1	-	1
HOSPITALS	-	-	3	2	1	6	3	3	1
HOUSING AND URBAN RENEWAL	-	-	2	1	1	4	3	1	1
LIBRARIES	-	-	1	1	-	2	1	1	1
NATURAL RESOURCES, TOTAL	-	-	17	15	2	23	7	16	6
DRAINAGE	-	-	7	7	-	17	7	10	-
FLOOD CONTROL	-	-	-	-	-	6	-	6	-
IRRIGATION, WATER CONSERVATION	-	-	10	8	2	-	-	-	-
SOIL CONSERVATION	-	-	-	-	-	-	-	-	6
OTHER AND COMPOSITE PURPOSES	-	-	-	-	-	-	-	-	-
PARKS AND RECREATION	-	-	-	-	-	2	1	1	-
SEWERAGE	-	-	-	-	-	22	16	6	2
UTILITIES, TOTAL	-	-	4	3	1	48	41	7	7
WATER SUPPLY	-	-	1	1	-	48	41	7	7
ELECTRIC POWER	-	-	3	2	1	-	-	-	-
GAS SUPPLY	-	-	-	-	-	-	-	-	-
TRANSIT	-	-	-	-	-	-	-	-	-
OTHER	-	-	4	2	2	3	1	2	-
MULTIPLE-FUNCTION DISTRICTS.									
SEWERAGE AND WATER SUPPLY	-	-	1	1	-	9	7	2	3
NATURAL RESOURCES AND WATER SUPPLY	-	-	-	-	-	4	4	-	2
OTHER	-	-	1	1	-	5	3	2	1
SCHOOL SYSTEMS									
TOTAL	1	1	10	6	4	34	20	14	14
DEPENDENT SCHOOL SYSTEMS	1	1	-	-	-	-	-	-	-
BY ENROLLMENT SIZE OCTOBER 1976									
100,000 OR MORE PUPILS	-	-	-	-	-	-	-	-	-
50,000 TO 99,999 PUPILS	-	-	-	-	-	-	-	-	-
25,000 TO 49,999 PUPILS	-	-	-	-	-	1	1	-	-
12,000 TO 24,999 PUPILS	-	-	-	-	-	1	1	-	-
6,000 TO 11,999 PUPILS	1	-	-	-	-	8	7	1	1
3,000 TO 5,999 PUPILS	-	-	2	2	-	3	2	1	1
1,200 TO 2,999 PUPILS	-	-	1	-	1	5	2	3	3
300 TO 1,199 PUPILS	-	-	2	1	1	8	4	4	4
50 TO 299 PUPILS	-	-	2	2	-	5	1	4	2
1 TO 49 PUPILS	-	-	1	-	1	1	1	-	1
0 PUPILS (NONOPERATING)	-	1	2	1	1	2	1	1	2
POPULATION, 1975 (ESTIMATED)									
TOTAL	62 967	24 042	105 022	77 373	27 649	1 406 746	1 142 544	264 202	306 338
IN MUNICIPALLY GOVERNED AREAS	7 756	24 042	71 340	54 509	16 831	852 368	[1]718 361	134 007	189 666
WITH A 1975 POPULATION OF--									
50,000 OR MORE	-	-	-	-	-	552 456	552 456	-	173 698
25,000 TO 49,999	-	-	29 543	29 543	-	75 156	26 785	48 371	-
10,000 TO 24,999	-	24 042	33 545	19 015	14 530	151 741	91 584	60 157	-
5,000 TO 9,999	7 756	-	-	-	-	11 427	11 427	-	6 573
2,500 TO 4,999	-	-	3 111	3 111	-	40 895	26 100	14 795	3 474
1,000 TO 2,499	-	-	4 542	2 840	1 702	15 148	6 784	8 364	4 578
LESS THAN 1,000	-	-	599	-	599	5 545	3 225	2 320	1 343
OUTSIDE MUNICIPALLY GOVERNED AREAS	55 211	-	33 682	22 864	10 818	554 378	424 183	130 195	116 672
IN TOWNSHIP-GOVERNED AREAS	-	-	-	-	-	-	-	-	-
ENROLLMENT OF PUBLIC SCHOOL SYSTEMS									
TOTAL	23 514	-	27 511	20 835	6 676	302 413	239 415	62 998	57 303
THROUGH GRADE 12	23 514	-	27 511	20 835	6 676	302 413	239 415	62 998	57 303
COLLEGE GRADES	-	-	-	-	-	-	-	-	-

Table 6. Local Governments and Public School Systems in Individual SMSA's: 1977—Continued

Item	Washington (see also Oregon)--Continued Tacoma — Pierce County (entire SMSA)	Yakima — Yakima County (entire SMSA)	West Virginia (see also Ohio) Charleston — Total	Kanawha County*	Putnam County	Huntington-Ashland — Total	Cabell County*	Wayne County	Boyd County* (Ky.)
NUMBER OF LOCAL GOVERNMENTS									
ALL TYPES, TOTAL	74	66	61	47	14	88	14	11	14
WITH PROPERTY-TAXING POWER	67	49	24	16	8	69	6	6	11
WITHOUT PROPERTY-TAXING POWER	7	17	37	31	6	19	8	5	3
COUNTY GOVERNMENTS	1	1	2	1	1	5	1	1	1
MUNICIPALITIES	18	14	20	14	6	24	3	4	2
WITH A POPULATION OF--									
50,000 OR MORE	1	-	1	1	-	1	1	-	-
25,000 TO 49,999	-	1	-	-	-	1	-	-	1
10,000 TO 24,999	1	-	2	2	-	1	-	-	-
5,000 TO 9,999	1	2	2	2	-	1	-	-	1
2,500 TO 4,999	5	3	2	1	1	5	-	1	1
1,000 TO 2,499	3	4	6	5	1	11	2	2	-
LESS THAN 1,000	7	4	7	3	4	4	-	1	-
TOWNSHIP GOVERNMENTS	-	-	-	-	-	14	-	-	-
SCHOOL DISTRICTS	15	15	2	1	1	15	1	1	3
SPECIAL DISTRICTS	40	36	37	31	6	30	9	5	8
WITH PROPERTY-TAXING POWER	33	19	-	-	-	11	1	-	5
SINGLE FUNCTION DISTRICTS	-	-	-	-	-	-	-	-	-
CEMETERIES	-	-	-	-	-	-	-	-	-
EDUCATION (SCHOOL BUILDING DISTRICTS)	-	-	-	-	-	-	-	-	-
FIRE PROTECTION	23	13	-	-	-	5	-	-	3
HIGHWAYS	-	-	1	1	-	-	-	-	-
HEALTH	-	1	-	-	-	-	-	-	-
HOSPITALS	-	-	-	-	-	-	-	-	-
HOUSING AND URBAN RENEWAL	1	1	4	4	-	2	1	-	-
LIBRARIES	1	1	-	-	-	1	-	-	-
NATURAL RESOURCES, TOTAL	7	16	1	1	-	5	1	-	2
DRAINAGE	7	-	-	-	-	-	-	-	-
FLOOD CONTROL	-	-	-	-	-	1	-	-	1
IRRIGATION, WATER CONSERVATION	-	16	-	-	-	-	-	-	-
SOIL CONSERVATION	-	-	1	1	-	4	1	-	1
OTHER AND COMPOSITE PURPOSES	-	-	-	-	-	-	-	-	-
PARKS AND RECREATION	2	-	-	-	-	2	1	-	2
SEWERAGE	2	2	14	12	2	5	2	1	-
UTILITIES, TOTAL	2	1	11	7	4	5	2	2	1
WATER SUPPLY	2	-	10	6	4	4	1	2	1
ELECTRIC POWER	-	1	-	-	-	-	-	-	-
GAS SUPPLY	-	-	-	-	-	-	-	-	-
TRANSIT	-	-	1	1	-	1	1	-	-
OTHER	1	1	1	1	-	1	1	-	-
MULTIPLE-FUNCTION DISTRICTS	1	-	5	5	-	4	1	2	-
SEWERAGE AND WATER SUPPLY	-	-	4	4	-	4	1	2	-
NATURAL RESOURCES AND WATER SUPPLY	-	-	-	-	-	-	-	-	-
OTHER	1	-	1	1	-	-	-	-	-
SCHOOL SYSTEMS									
TOTAL	15	15	2	1	1	15	1	1	3
DEPENDENT SCHOOL SYSTEMS	-	-	-	-	-	-	-	-	-
BY ENROLLMENT SIZE OCTOBER 1976									
100,000 OR MORE PUPILS	-	-	-	-	-	-	-	-	-
50,000 TO 99,999 PUPILS	-	-	-	-	-	-	-	-	-
25,000 TO 49,999 PUPILS	1	-	1	1	-	-	-	-	-
12,000 TO 24,999 PUPILS	1	-	-	-	-	1	1	-	-
6,000 TO 11,999 PUPILS	3	1	1	-	1	1	-	1	2
3,000 TO 5,999 PUPILS	2	2	-	-	-	4	-	-	2
1,200 TO 2,999 PUPILS	4	6	-	-	-	6	-	-	-
300 TO 1,199 PUPILS	3	6	-	-	-	3	-	-	1
50 TO 299 PUPILS	1	-	-	-	-	-	-	-	-
1 TO 49 PUPILS	-	-	-	-	-	-	-	-	-
POPULATION, 1975 (ESTIMATED)									
TOTAL	415 707	155 516	255 964	225 037	30 927	289 649	103 654	38 357	52 560
IN MUNICIPALLY GOVERNED AREAS	199 628	81 591	135 497	[1]126 935	[1]8 562	156 391	72 999	[1]8 718	31 232
WITH A 1975 POPULATION OF--									
50,000 OR MORE	151 267	-	67 348	67 348	-	68 811	68 811	-	-
25,000 TO 49,999	-	49 264	-	-	-	27 456	-	-	27 456
10,000 TO 24,999	16 205	-	30 460	30 460	-	13 959	-	-	-
5,000 TO 9,999	6 014	12 988	16 855	16 855	-	9 220	-	-	-
2,500 TO 4,999	17 782	10 701	7 250	2 537	4 713	17 482	-	4 792	3 776
1,000 TO 2,499	4 893	6 294	8 739	7 577	1 162	17 213	4 188	3 111	-
LESS THAN 1,000	3 467	2 344	4 845	2 158	2 687	2 250	-	815	-
OUTSIDE MUNICIPALLY GOVERNED AREAS	216 079	73 925	120 467	98 102	22 365	133 258	30 655	29 639	21 328
IN TOWNSHIP-GOVERNED AREAS	-	-	-	-	-	60 870	-	-	-
ENROLLMENT OF PUBLIC SCHOOL SYSTEMS									
TOTAL	89 406	37 148	53 539	45 365	8 174	64 400	19 818	10 511	10 939
THROUGH GRADE 12	89 406	37 148	53 539	45 365	8 174	64 400	19 818	10 511	10 939
COLLEGE GRADES	-	-	-	-	-	-	-	-	-

Table 6. Local Governments and Public School Systems in Individual SMSA's: 1977—Continued

West Virginia (see also Ohio)--Continued

Item	Huntington-Ashland--Continued		Parkersburg-Marietta				Wheeling			
	Greenup County	Lawrence County (Ohio)	Total	Wirt County	Wood County*	Washington County* (Ohio)	Total	Marshall County	Ohio County*	Belmont County
NUMBER OF LOCAL GOVERNMENTS										
ALL TYPES, TOTAL	17	32	53	3	12	38	69	18	9	42
WITH PROPERTY-TAXING POWER	16	30	45	3	5	37	51	7	7	37
WITHOUT PROPERTY-TAXING POWER.	1	2	8	-	7	1	18	11	2	5
COUNTY GOVERNMENTS	1	1	3	1	1	1	3	1	1	1
MUNICIPALITIES	8	7	11	1	3	7	23	5	5	13
WITH A POPULATION OF--										
50,000 OR MORE	-	-	-	-	-	-	-	-	-	-
25,000 TO 49,999	-	-	1	-	1	-	1	-	1	-
10,000 TO 24,999	-	1	2	-	1	1	2	1	-	1
5,000 TO 9,999	1	-	1	-	-	1	2	-	-	2
2,500 TO 4,999	1	2	1	-	1	-	6	3	-	3
1,000 TO 2,499	5	2	2	-	-	2	5	1	1	3
LESS THAN 1,000.	1	2	4	1	-	3	7	-	3	4
TOWNSHIP GOVERNMENTS	-	14	22	-	-	22	16	-	-	16
SCHOOL DISTRICTS	3	7	8	1	1	6	9	1	1	7
SPECIAL DISTRICTS.	5	3	9	-	7	2	18	11	2	5
WITH PROPERTY-TAXING POWER	4	1	1	-	-	1	-	-	-	-
SINGLE FUNCTION DISTRICTS.										
CEMETERIES	-	-	-	-	-	-	-	-	-	-
EDUCATION (SCHOOL BUILDING DISTRICTS). . .	-	-	-	-	-	-	-	-	-	-
FIRE PROTECTION.	2	-	-	-	-	-	-	-	-	-
HIGHWAYS	-	-	-	-	-	-	-	-	-	-
HEALTH	-	-	-	-	-	-	-	-	-	-
HOSPITALS.	-	-	-	-	-	-	-	-	-	-
HOUSING AND URBAN RENEWAL.	-	1	1	-	1	-	5	3	1	1
LIBRARIES.	1	-	1	-	-	1	-	-	-	-
NATURAL RESOURCES, TOTAL	1	1	2	-	1	1	2	-	-	1
DRAINAGE	-	-	-	-	-	-	-	-	-	-
FLOOD CONTROL.	-	-	-	-	-	-	-	-	-	-
IRRIGATION, WATER CONSERVATION	-	-	-	-	-	-	-	-	-	-
SOIL CONSERVATION.	1	1	2	-	1	1	2	1	-	1
OTHER AND COMPOSITE PURPOSES	-	-	-	-	-	-	-	-	-	-
PARKS AND RECREATION	-	1	-	-	-	-	-	-	-	-
SEWERAGE	-	-	-	-	-	-	2	1	-	1
UTILITIES, TOTAL	-	-	3	-	3	-	9	6	1	2
WATER SUPPLY	-	-	3	-	3	-	9	6	1	2
ELECTRIC POWER	-	-	-	-	-	-	-	-	-	-
GAS SUPPLY	-	-	-	-	-	-	-	-	-	-
TRANSIT.	-	-	-	-	-	-	-	-	-	-
OTHER.	-	-	-	-	-	-	-	-	-	-
MULTIPLE-FUNCTION DISTRICTS.	1	-	2	-	2	-	-	-	-	-
SEWERAGE AND WATER SUPPLY.	1	-	2	-	2	-	-	-	-	-
NATURAL RESOURCES AND WATER SUPPLY	-	-	-	-	-	-	-	-	-	-
OTHER.	-	-	-	-	-	-	-	-	-	-
SCHOOL SYSTEMS										
TOTAL.	3	7	8	1	1	6	9	1	1	7
DEPENDENT SCHOOL SYSTEMS	-	-	-	-	-	-	-	-	-	-
BY ENROLLMENT SIZE OCTOBER 1976										
100,000 OR MORE PUPILS	-	-	-	-	-	-	-	-	-	-
50,000 TO 99,999 PUPILS.	-	-	-	-	-	-	-	-	-	-
25,000 TO 49,999 PUPILS.	-	-	-	-	-	-	-	-	-	-
12,000 TO 24,999 PUPILS.	-	-	-	-	-	-	-	-	-	-
6,000 TO 11,999 PUPILS	-	-	1	-	1	-	-	-	-	-
3,000 TO 5,999 PUPILS.	2	-	1	-	-	1	2	1	1	-
1,200 TO 2,999 PUPILS.	-	6	5	-	-	4	7	-	-	7
300 TO 1,199 PUPILS.	1	1	1	1	-	1	-	-	-	-
50 TO 299 PUPILS	-	-	-	-	-	-	-	-	-	-
1 TO 49 PUPILS	-	-	-	-	-	-	-	-	-	-
POPULATION, 1975 (ESTIMATED)										
TOTAL.	34 209	60 869	151 660	4 523	87 449	59 688	181 491	38 841	60 283	82 367
IN MUNICIPALLY GOVERNED AREAS.	20 508	22 934	80 826	944	52 810	27 072	114 957	22 419	48 727	¹43 811
WITH A 1975 POPULATION OF--										
50,000 OR MORE	-	-	-	-	-	-	-	-	-	-
25,000 TO 49,999	-	-	38 882	-	38 882	-	44 369	-	44 369	-
10,000 TO 24,999	-	13 959	27 110	-	10 936	16 174	23 223	12 930	-	10 293
5,000 TO 9,999	9 220	-	7 158	-	-	7 158	14 241	-	-	14 241
2,500 TO 4,999	2 920	5 994	2 992	-	2 992	-	19 886	7 942	-	11 944
1,000 TO 2,499	7 538	2 376	2 523	-	-	2 523	8 665	1 547	2 370	4 748
LESS THAN 1,000.	830	605	2 161	944	-	1 217	4 573	-	1 988	2 585
OUTSIDE MUNICIPALLY GOVERNED AREAS	13 701	37 935	70 834	3 579	34 639	32 616	66 534	16 422	11 556	38 556
IN TOWNSHIP-GOVERNED AREAS	-	60 870	43 512	-	-	43 512	82 368	-	-	82 368
ENROLLMENT OF PUBLIC SCHOOL SYSTEMS										
TOTAL.	8 783	14 349	35 075	1 254	20 226	13 595	32 679	8 479	9 199	15 001
THROUGH GRADE 12	8 783	14 349	35 075	1 254	20 226	13 595	32 679	8 479	9 199	15 001
COLLEGE GRADES	-	-	-	-	-	-	-	-	-	-

103

Item	Wisconsin (see also Minnesota)									
	Appleton-Oshkosh				Eau Claire			Green Bay	Kenosha	La Crosse
	Total	Calumet County	Outagamie County*	Winnebago County*	Total	Chippewa County	Eau Claire County*	Brown County (entire SMSA)	Kenosha County (entire SMSA)	La Crosse County (entire SMSA)
NUMBER OF LOCAL GOVERNMENTS										
ALL TYPES, TOTAL	99	23	50	26	67	39	28	37	31	25
WITH PROPERTY-TAXING POWER	85	21	40	24	63	38	25	32	30	24
WITHOUT PROPERTY-TAXING POWER.	14	2	10	2	4	1	3	5	1	1
COUNTY GOVERNMENTS	3	1	1	1	2	1	1	1	1	1
MUNICIPALITIES	22	6	11	5	12	7	5	6	4	6
WITH A POPULATION OF--										
50,000 OR MORE	2	-	1	1	-	-	-	1	1	-
25,000 TO 49,999	-	-	-	-	1	-	1	1	-	1
10,000 TO 24,999	3	-	1	2	1	1	-	1	-	1
5,000 TO 9,999	2	-	2	-	-	-	-	1	-	1
2,500 TO 4,999	5	3	1	1	2	1	1	-	1	-
1,000 TO 2,499	4	-	3	1	4	3	1	3	2	2
LESS THAN 1,000	6	3	3	-	4	2	2	-	-	2
TOWNSHIP GOVERNMENTS	45	9	20	16	36	23	13	18	8	12
SCHOOL DISTRICTS	14	5	7	2	9	5	4	7	14	4
SPECIAL DISTRICTS.	15	2	11	2	8	3	5	5	4	2
WITH PROPERTY-TAXING POWER	1	-	1	-	4	2	2	-	3	1
SINGLE FUNCTION DISTRICTS.	-	-	-	-	-	-	-	-	-	-
CEMETERIES	-	-	-	-	-	-	-	-	-	-
EDUCATION (SCHOOL BUILDING DISTRICTS). . . .	-	-	-	-	-	-	-	-	-	-
FIRE PROTECTION.	-	-	-	-	-	-	-	-	-	-
HIGHWAYS	-	-	-	-	-	-	-	-	-	-
HEALTH	-	-	-	-	-	-	-	-	-	-
HOSPITALS.	-	-	-	-	-	-	-	-	-	-
HOUSING AND URBAN RENEWAL.	5	2	2	1	4	1	3	4	-	1
LIBRARIES.	-	-	-	-	-	-	-	-	-	-
NATURAL RESOURCES, TOTAL	9	-	8	1	4	2	2	-	4	1
DRAINAGE	9	-	8	1	-	-	-	-	1	-
FLOOD CONTROL.	-	-	-	-	-	-	-	-	-	-
IRRIGATION, WATER CONSERVATION	-	-	-	-	-	-	-	-	-	-
SOIL CONSERVATION.	-	-	-	-	-	-	-	-	-	-
OTHER AND COMPOSITE PURPOSES	-	-	-	-	4	2	2	-	3	1
PARKS AND RECREATION	-	-	-	-	-	-	-	-	-	-
SEWERAGE	1	-	1	-	-	-	-	1	-	-
UTILITIES, TOTAL	-	-	-	-	-	-	-	-	-	-
WATER SUPPLY	-	-	-	-	-	-	-	-	-	-
ELECTRIC POWER	-	-	-	-	-	-	-	-	-	-
GAS SUPPLY	-	-	-	-	-	-	-	-	-	-
TRANSIT.	-	-	-	-	-	-	-	-	-	-
OTHER.	-	-	-	-	-	-	-	-	-	-
MULTIPLE-FUNCTION DISTRICTS.	-	-	-	-	-	-	-	-	-	-
SEWERAGE AND WATER SUPPLY.	-	-	-	-	-	-	-	-	-	-
NATURAL RESOURCES AND WATER SUPPLY	-	-	-	-	-	-	-	-	-	-
OTHER.	-	-	-	-	-	-	-	-	-	-
SCHOOL SYSTEMS										
TOTAL.	19	5	9	5	12	7	5	9	14	6
DEPENDENT SCHOOL SYSTEMS	5	-	2	3	3	2	1	2	-	2
BY ENROLLMENT SIZE OCTOBER 1976										
100,000 OR MORE PUPILS	-	-	-	-	-	-	-	-	-	-
50,000 TO 99,999 PUPILS.	-	-	-	-	-	-	-	-	-	-
25,000 TO 49,999 PUPILS.	-	-	-	-	-	-	-	-	1	-
12,000 TO 24,999 PUPILS.	2	-	1	1	-	-	-	1	1	-
6,000 TO 11,999 PUPILS	2	-	1	1	1	-	1	-	1	1
3,000 TO 5,999 PUPILS.	2	-	1	1	1	1	-	2	-	1
1,200 TO 2,999 PUPILS.	8	2	4	2	3	2	1	5	-	2
300 TO 1,199 PUPILS.	4	2	2	-	7	4	3	1	9	2
50 TO 299 PUPILS	1	1	-	-	-	-	-	-	3	-
1 TO 49 PUPILS	-	-	-	-	-	-	-	-	-	-
POPULATION, 1975 (ESTIMATED)										
TOTAL.	283 700	29 038	124 414	130 248	122 094	49 603	72 491	169 467	122 621	85 855
IN MUNICIPALLY GOVERNED AREAS.	196 926	[1]10 889	[1]92 268	[1]93 769	76 752	[1]21 802	54 950	115 995	87 256	62 090
WITH A 1975 POPULATION OF--										
50,000 OR MORE	109 289	-	59 182	50 107	-	-	-	91 189	80 727	-
25,000 TO 49,999	-	-	-	-	47 852	-	47 852	-	-	49 082
10,000 TO 24,999	50 197	-	11 250	38 947	12 904	12 904	-	14 488	-	7 273
5,000 TO 9,999	12 028	-	12 028	-	-	-	-	5 921	-	-
2,500 TO 4,999	14 753	9 044	3 115	2 594	7 436	3 205	4 231	-	3 175	-
1,000 TO 2,499	7 118	-	4 997	2 121	6 061	4 648	1 413	4 397	3 354	4 467
LESS THAN 1,000	3 541	1 845	1 696	-	2 499	1 045	1 454	-	-	1 268
OUTSIDE MUNICIPALLY GOVERNED AREAS	86 774	18 149	32 146	36 479	45 342	27 801	17 541	53 472	35 365	23 765
IN TOWNSHIP-GOVERNED AREAS	84 895	13 646	34 769	36 480	45 342	26 434	18 908	53 475	35 365	23 766
ENROLLMENT OF PUBLIC SCHOOL SYSTEMS										
TOTAL.	67 567	5 056	35 139	27 372	27 187	10 641	16 546	41 635	33 018	18 284
THROUGH GRADE 12	59 462	5 056	27 034	27 372	24 437	10 641	13 796	37 895	26 044	14 496
COLLEGE GRADES	8 105	-	8 105	-	2 750	-	2 750	3 740	6 974	3 788

Item	Wisconsin (see also Minnesota)--Continued						
	Madison	Milwaukee					Racine
	Dane County (entire SMSA)	Total	Milwaukee County*	Ozaukee County	Washington County	Waukesha County	Racine County (entire SMSA)
NUMBER OF LOCAL GOVERNMENTS							
ALL TYPES, TOTAL	85	154	37	19	37	61	39
WITH PROPERTY-TAXING POWER	77	146	33	18	34	61	31
WITHOUT PROPERTY-TAXING POWER	8	8	4	1	3	-	8
COUNTY GOVERNMENTS	1	4	1	1	1	1	1
MUNICIPALITIES WITH A POPULATION OF--	24	58	19	8	7	24	9
50,000 OR MORE	1	3	3	-	-	-	1
25,000 TO 49,999	-	5	1	-	-	4	1
10,000 TO 24,999	3	13	10	1	1	1	-
5,000 TO 9,999	1	9	2	3	1	3	1
2,500 TO 4,999	5	8	2	1	2	3	2
1,000 TO 2,499	9	10	1	2	2	5	2
LESS THAN 1,000	5	10	-	1	1	8	3
TOWNSHIP GOVERNMENTS	[1]35	32	-	6	13	13	9
SCHOOL DISTRICTS	16	47	13	3	10	21	12
SPECIAL DISTRICTS	9	13	4	1	6	2	8
WITH PROPERTY-TAXING POWER	1	5	-	-	3	2	-
SINGLE FUNCTION DISTRICTS.							
CEMETERIES	-	-	-	-	-	-	-
EDUCATION (SCHOOL BUILDING DISTRICTS)	-	-	-	-	-	-	-
FIRE PROTECTION	-	-	-	-	-	-	-
HIGHWAYS	-	-	-	-	-	-	-
HEALTH	-	-	-	-	-	-	-
HOSPITALS	-	-	-	-	-	-	-
HOUSING AND URBAN RENEWAL	6	2	2	-	-	-	-
LIBRARIES	-	-	-	-	-	-	-
NATURAL RESOURCES, TOTAL	2	10	1	1	6	2	8
DRAINAGE	2	5	1	1	3	-	8
FLOOD CONTROL	-	-	-	-	-	-	-
IRRIGATION, WATER CONSERVATION	-	-	-	-	-	-	-
SOIL CONSERVATION	-	-	-	-	-	-	-
OTHER AND COMPOSITE PURPOSES	-	5	-	-	3	2	-
PARKS AND RECREATION	-	-	-	-	-	-	-
SEWERAGE	1	1	1	-	-	-	-
UTILITIES, TOTAL	-	-	-	-	-	-	-
WATER SUPPLY	-	-	-	-	-	-	-
ELECTRIC POWER	-	-	-	-	-	-	-
GAS SUPPLY	-	-	-	-	-	-	-
TRANSIT	-	-	-	-	-	-	-
OTHER	-	-	-	-	-	-	-
MULTIPLE-FUNCTION DISTRICTS.							
SEWERAGE AND WATER SUPPLY	-	-	-	-	-	-	-
NATURAL RESOURCES AND WATER SUPPLY	-	-	-	-	-	-	-
OTHER	-	-	-	-	-	-	-
SCHOOL SYSTEMS							
TOTAL	17	56	19	5	10	22	12
DEPENDENT SCHOOL SYSTEMS	1	9	6	2	-	1	-
BY ENROLLMENT SIZE OCTOBER 1976							
100,000 OR MORE PUPILS	-	1	1	-	-	-	-
50,000 TO 99,999 PUPILS	-	-	-	-	-	-	-
25,000 TO 49,999 PUPILS	1	1	1	-	-	-	-
12,000 TO 24,999 PUPILS	-	1	1	-	-	-	1
6,000 TO 11,999 PUPILS	1	7	2	-	-	1	-
3,000 TO 5,999 PUPILS	3	16	7	3	1	4	1
1,200 TO 2,999 PUPILS	8	13	6	1	4	5	1
300 TO 1,199 PUPILS	4	7	2	1	4	2	6
50 TO 299 PUPILS	-	10	-	-	3	7	4
1 TO 49 PUPILS	-	-	-	-	-	-	-
POPULATION, 1975 (ESTIMATED)							
TOTAL	301 668	1 409 363	1 012 335	64 519	76 730	255 779	175 781
IN MUNICIPALLY GOVERNED AREAS	[1]239 225	1 306 805	1 012 335	[1]50 250	[1]43 914	200 306	115 141
WITH A 1975 POPULATION OF--							
50,000 OR MORE	168 196	791 394	791 394	-	-	-	94 744
25,000 TO 49,999	-	171 823	31 647	-	-	140 176	-
10,000 TO 24,999	32 470	213 637	162 897	15 079	21 989	13 672	-
5,000 TO 9,999	7 020	76 198	16 620	26 794	15 475	17 309	8 548
2,500 TO 4,999	14 638	30 341	8 328	3 714	-	18 299	7 123
1,000 TO 2,499	14 489	16 903	1 449	3 812	5 831	5 811	3 520
LESS THAN 1,000	2 412	6 509	-	851	619	5 039	1 206
OUTSIDE MUNICIPALLY GOVERNED AREAS	62 443	102 558	-	14 269	32 816	55 473	60 640
IN TOWNSHIP-GOVERNED AREAS	62 331	102 433	-	14 085	32 874	55 474	60 637
ENROLLMENT OF PUBLIC SCHOOL SYSTEMS							
TOTAL	66 197	318 464	209 548	15 056	18 725	75 135	36 915
THROUGH GRADE 12	58 814	269 457	171 898	15 056	18 725	63 778	36 915
COLLEGE GRADES	7 383	49 007	37 650	-	-	11 357	-

PART II
GOVERNMENTAL FINANCES

Every year, the Census Bureau issues a series of reports on the finances of State and local governments. Part II of this volume contains four sections of these data—a general section and sections on State, county, and city finances. Comparative data have been provided on specific places. For example, in Part A, which summarizes State and local finances in 1977, per capita data are presented in Table 7 so that users can compare their State as a whole (State and local finances combined) with other States. Table 8 presents similar comparative data per $1000 of personal income, which gives an indication of differences in levels of revenue and expenditure effort. Users are reminded that, whereas comparisons of State and local finances on a combined basis are relatively straightforward, there are problems in disaggregating these data for State governments and for all or particular localities, because of the differences in the financial and functional responsibilities of State and local governments. Other caveats that should be entered involve the timing and accounting system for the finance data. As pointed out in the text, jurisdictions vary in terms of the fiscal year used. It is also important to note that different budget and accounting systems are used by State and local units in the U.S. Whereas the Census Bureau seeks to draw financial data together on a uniform basis, problems can occur due to differences in the way the books are kept among jurisdictions.

A — SUMMARY OF GOVERNMENTAL FINANCES IN 1977

Total Federal, State, and local governmental revenue from all sources amounted to $657.3 billion for fiscal 1976-77, up $86.1 billion from the prior year. Tax revenues collected by all governments in 1976-77 came to $419.7 billion, as compared to $358.2 billion for 1975-76.[1] (Table A)

Governmental expenditures in fiscal 1976-77 were $680.3 billion, up $55.3 billion from the prior year sum of $625.1 billion.

Indebtedness of all governments at the end of fiscal 1976-77 was $966.7 billion, including a Federal gross debt (as of September 30, 1977) of $709.1 billion. State and local government debt increased $17.0 billion during fiscal 1976-77 to a record total of $257.5 billion.

Governmental financial data are presented within broad activity sectors, including "general government," "utilities," "liquor stores," and "insurance trust activities."

Revenue by Source

The national totals of governmental revenue include a basic distinction between intergovernmental revenue and revenue from "own sources" of the several levels of government. Revenue from "own sources" was distributed among the several levels of government for fiscal year 1976-77 as shown in Table B.

The distribution of revenue in Table C in terms of final recipient level of government shows the effect of intergovernmental transfers. Total local revenue is increased from 18.2 percent to 29.5 percent of all revenue if allowance is made for intergovernmental revenue from Federal and State sources.

The Federal General Revenue Sharing program represented an important source of State and local revenue in fiscal 1976-77. Total funds distributed to States in this program amounted to $2.3 billion; an additional $4.5 billion was paid to local governments (cities, towns, townships, and counties) in fiscal 1976-77.

General Revenue

Taxes show marked differences of emphasis among the three levels of government. While individual and corporate income taxes provide the major Federal income sources, local governments rely primarily on property tax revenues. State governments rely on a combination of general and selective sales and gross receipts taxes for more than half of their tax revenue.

Of the total national tax yield, 58.1 percent was collected by the Federal Government, 24.1 percent by State governments, and 17.8 percent by local governments.

Charges and miscellaneous general revenue consist mainly of "current charges" received from performance of specific services and from sales of commodities (other than utility and liquor store proceeds) benefiting those persons charged. Amounts received are reported here on a gross basis without offset for costs of operations or purchases.

The major source of Federal current charges revenue was postal receipts, which provided 49.4 per-

---

[1]The financial statistics for 1976-77 relate to governmental fiscal years which ended June 30, 1977, or at some date within the 12 previous months. The following governments are exceptions, and are included as though they were part of the June 30 group: States of Alabama (including school districts) and Michigan, ending September 30; New York State, ending March 31; and State of Texas (including school districts), ending August 31.

Governmental Revenue: 1976-77

Item	Amount (millions of dollars)				Percent				Percent increase from prior fiscal year		
	All govern-ments	Federal	State	Local	All gov-ern-ments	Fed-eral	State	Local	All gov-ern-ments	Fed-eral	State and local
Revenue from all sources.............	657,321	383,524	204,475	196,321	100.0	100.0	100.0	100.0	15.1	18.1	11.4
Intergovernmental revenue............	(1)	1,375	48,676	76,948	(1)	0.4	23.8	39.2	(1)	3.3	12.6
Revenue from own sources............	657,321	382,149	155,799	119,373	100.0	99.6	76.2	60.8	15.1	18.1	11.1
General revenue from own sources.	506,862	283,641	121,191	102,031	77.1	74.0	59.3	52.0	15.6	19.3	11.3
Taxes...........	419,721	243,842	101,085	74,794	63.9	63.6	49.4	38.1	17.2	21.1	12.2
Charges and miscellaneous general revenue........	87,142	39,799	20,106	27,237	13.3	10.4	9.8	13.9	8.8	9.6	8.2
Current charges......	56,828	25,083	12,768	18,977	8.6	6.5	6.2	9.7	9.6	11.3	8.3
All other.....	30,313	14,716	7,338	8,259	4.6	3.8	3.6	4.2	7.4	6.9	7.9
Utility revenue...	14,191	–	–	14,191	2.2	–	–	7.2	12.9	–	12.9
Liquor stores revenue..........	2,612	–	2,244	368	0.4	–	1.1	0.2	2.3	–	2.3
Insurance trust revenue.........	133,656	98,508	32,365	2,783	20.3	25.7	15.8	1.4	13.5	14.8	9.9

Note: Because of rounding, detail may not add to totals.

– Represents zero or rounds to zero.

1Net of duplicative intergovernmental transactions.

109

Level of government	Amount (millions of dollars)	Percent
(B) Total own-source revenue.....	657,321	100.0
Federal......................	382,149	58.1
State........................	155,799	23.7
Local........................	119,373	18.2

Level of government	Amount (millions of dollars)	Percent
(C) Total final revenue.....	657,321	100.0
Federal......................	320,949	48.8
State........................	142,789	21.7
Local........................	193,584	29.5

cent of total Federal charges. Other significant components of Federal current charges include amounts received for equipment, services and supplies related to national defense and international relations (21.4 percent), and "natural resources" charges, mainly from agricultural product sales (17.9 percent of total Federal charges).

State and local government amounts from current charges are derived mainly from higher education institutional fees and charges (24.3 percent), hospital charges (25.5 percent), school lunch sales (5.1 percent), and sewerage charges (7.8 percent).

Governmental expenditure according to final spending level—i.e., in terms of direct expenditure, or for "own purposes" by each level of government is shown in Table D.

As shown below in Table E, a different distribution results if governmental spending is treated in terms of the financing rather than the final spending level of government, i.e., by treating amounts represented by intergovernmental transactions as expenditure of the originating rather than the recipient government.

Level of government	Amount (millions of dollars)	Percent
(D) Total final expenditure...	680,329	100.0
Federal......................	358,935	52.8
State........................	128,778	18.9
Local........................	192,616	28.3

Level of government	Amount (millions of dollars)	Percent
(E) Total financing expenditure..	680,329	100.0
Federal......................	430,594	63.3
State........................	137,683	20.2
Local........................	112,052	16.5

Tax Revenue: 1976-77

(F) Item	Amount (millions of dollars)				Percent				Percent increase from prior fiscal year		
	All governments	Federal	State	Local	All governments	Federal	State	Local	All governments	Federal	State and local
Total taxes...	419,721	243,842	101,085	74,794	100.0	100.0	100.0	100.0	17.2	21.1	12.2
Income............	250,036	211,617	34,667	3,752	59.6	86.8	34.3	5.0	22.1	22.3	20.6
Individual........	185,970	156,725	25,493	3,752	44.3	64.3	25.2	5.0	19.1	19.1	19.0
Corporation.......	64,066	54,892	9,174	(1)	15.3	22.5	9.1	(1)	31.6	32.6	26.1
Property...........	62,535	–	2,260	60,275	14.9	–	2.2	80.6	9.7	–	9.7
Sales, gross receipts, and customs	83,775	23,180	52,362	8,232	20.0	9.5	51.8	11.0	9.8	6.7	11.1
Customs duties....	5,394	5,394	–	–	1.3	2.2	–	–	20.0	20.0	–
General sales and gross receipts...	36,313	–	30,896	5,417	8.7	–	30.6	7.2	13.3	–	13.3
Selective sales and gross receipts...........	42,068	17,786	21,466	2,815	10.0	7.3	21.2	3.8	5.9	3.3	7.9
All other..........	23,375	9,045	11,796	2,534	5.6	3.7	11.7	3.4	16.4	35.3	6.8

Note: Because of rounding, detail may not add to totals.

- Represents zero or rounds to zero.
[1] Minor amounts included in individual income tax figures.

111

Expenditure by Sector and by Function

Governmental expenditures comprise four categories including general expenditure, utility expenditure, liquor stores expenditure, and insurance trust expenditure.

National defense and international relations is a most significant general expenditure functional category, amounting to 20.5 percent of all general expenditures. Federal payments in this area, accounting for 33.6 percent of Federal general expenditures, are mainly for military functions. Federal veterans benefits, interest on war debt, civil defense activities, and other defense-related operations closely related to defense efforts are classified in other functional categories. All defense-related activities of State and local governments, including National Guard, civil defense, and armory activities, have been classified in the residual "Other" functional class; hence, reported defense expenditures are entirely those of the Federal Government. The relative importance of defense and intergovernmental relations expenditure to total general expenditures for current and prior years is given in Table G.

Education ranks first in governmental expenditure, amounting to 21.5 percent of total general government payments. As indicated in Table H, a substantial portion of Federal and State spending for education is in the form of intergovernmental payments. The largest Federal education expenditure was for grants-in-aid to local schools. State intergovernmental payments, including Federal amounts channeled through the States, provided 48.8 percent of local government education direct expenditure. Higher education institutions receive a substantial amount of State education monies with minor amounts going for local school supervision, for provision of State schools for the handicapped, and for other special programs.

Institutions of higher education consist of publicly operated universities, colleges, junior colleges, and other schools beyond the high school level. Amounts for such auxiliary activities as dormitories, dining halls, and bookstores are included with higher education expenditure, but related payments for hospital services and for agricultural experiment and extension activities are reported under other functional categories.

Natural resources include expenditures for conservation and development of agricultural, forest, mineral, and for similar resources. Federal government payments, accounting for 79.0 percent of governmental natural resource payments, are mainly for gross amounts of commodity purchases in the form of price stabilization programs. No exclusion is made of commodities resold during the year or transferred to Federal aid programs. Other Federal natural resources programs are: Multi-purpose power and reclamation projects; activities in soil conservation and reclamation, forestry and parks, mineral resources, and agricultural research; and farm crop and mortgage insurance.

Highways comprise the provision and maintenance of highway facilities, including toll turnpikes, bridges, and tunnels and ferries, as well as regular roads, highways, and city streets. About 4.9 percent of all State government expenditure, but a considerably smaller proportion of Federal and local government spending, involve payments for highway facilities. State and local government capital outlays for highway facilities decreased 12.0 percent from the prior year amount of $14.2 billion to $12.5 billion for fiscal 1976-77, reflecting reduced Federal highway aid for State and local government highway construction.

Both Federal and State highway expenditure involve substantial amounts for intergovernmental payments, as can be seen in Table I (in millions of dollars).

Public welfare relates to assistance to needy

112

Fiscal year	Expenditure for national defense and international relations as a percent of total general expenditure of--	
(G)	The Federal Government	All governments
1976-77.........	33.6	20.5
1975-76.........	34.7	21.1
1974-75.........	37.9	22.1
1973-74.........	39.0	23.0
1972-73.........	39.8	23.8
1971-72.........	42.9	25.7

Item	Federal (millions of dollars)	State (millions of dollars)	Local (millions of dollars)
(H) Total educa-tion expend-iture.......	18,041	64,037	76,064
Intergovernmental expenditure.......	10,205	36,964	331
Direct expenditure.	7,836	27,073	75,733
Local schools....	-	651	70,692
Institutions of higher education	-	21,166	5,039
Other...........	7,836	5,257	2

- Represents zero or rounds to zero.

Item	Federal	State	Local
(I) Total highway expenditure.....	6,431	17,496	9,275
Intergovernmental expenditure..........	6,173	3,631	35
Direct expenditure.....	258	13,865	9,239
Capital outlay.......	68	9,370	3,035
Construction.......	65	8,573	2,502
Other capital outlay...........	3	798	533
Current operation....	190	4,495	6,204

Item	Federal	State	Local
(J) Total public wel-fare expenditure	34,424	32,779	12,499
Intergovernmental expenditure..........	19,520	10,133	581
Direct expenditure.....	14,904	22,646	11,918
Categorical cash assistance..........	6,151	5,308	4,784
Other cash assistance	1,000	511	764
Other public welfare.	7,753	16,827	6,370

persons as well as support to welfare institutions. Cash assistance payments under the "categorical" programs—old age assistance, aid to families with dependent children, aid to the blind, and aid to the disabled—account for a substantial share of all public welfare expenditure. State and local amounts include any applicable cash benefits in excess of, or supplementary to, those financed with Federal participation. Other cash assistance is mainly for gen-eral relief, which is wholly financed from State and local sources. Other public welfare spending comprises vendor payments under various public welfare programs, including the federally supported medical care program commonly known as Medicaid, as well as institutional care for the needy, and administration of welfare activities.

Individual States vary in the degree to which they directly undertake public welfare activities or dele-

113

Governmental Expenditure by Function: 1976-77

Item	Amount (millions of dollars)	Percent of total	Percent of general expenditure	Percent increase or decrease (-) from prior fiscal year		
				All governments	Federal	State and local[1]
Total expenditure......................	680,329	100.0	(X)	8.8	10.5	6.1
Direct general expenditure....................	514,001	75.6	100.0	8.0	11.5	6.8
National defense and international relations...................................	105,596	15.5	20.5	7.8	7.8	(X)
All other general expenditure..............	408,405	60.0	79.5	8.7	12.7	6.8
Education.................................	110,643	16.3	21.5	4.1	-13.3	5.8
Public welfare...........................	49,468	7.3	9.6	9.6	8.9	10.0
Interest on general debt.................	44,670	6.6	8.7	12.9	13.5	11.0
Health and hospitals.....................	30,050	4.4	5.8	9.0	9.0	9.0
Highways.................................	23,362	3.4	4.5	-3.5	-12.2	-3.4
Natural resources........................	23,798	3.5	4.6	22.8	27.8	7.3
Postal service...........................	14,641	2.2	2.8	6.5	6.5	(X)
Police protection........................	11,723	1.7	2.3	9.2	11.5	8.9
Veterans' services, n.e.c.................	10,219	1.5	2.0	9.3	9.4	-12.9
Sanitation...............................	8,873	1.3	1.7	7.7	(X)	7.7
Local fire protection....................	4,293	0.6	0.8	10.1	(X)	10.1
Other functions..........................	76,665	11.3	14.9	9.3	9.2	9.5
Utility expenditure...........................	20,108	3.0	(X)	15.2	(X)	15.2
Liquor stores expenditure.....................	2,143	0.3	(X)	2.5	(X)	2.5
Insurance trust expenditure..................	144,076	21.2	(X)	10.5	16.3	-9.8

X Not applicable.
[1]Excludes intergovernmental expenditure.

114

gate this responsibility to local governments. The amounts the States transfer to local governments for welfare programs (including money from Federal sources) provide a major portion of the total expenditure of local governments for public welfare.

Summary figures on intergovernmental and direct expenditures for public welfare in fiscal 1976-77 are shown in Table J (in millions of dollars).

Public welfare expenditure by all governments totaled $49.5 billion in fiscal 1976-77, an increase of $4.3 billion or 9.6 percent from the prior year. Since the 1974-75 fiscal year the Federal Government, in connection with the Supplemental Security Income program, has administered direct categorical cash assistance payments to blind, aged and disabled recipients, including for some States supplementation to Federal minimum direct categorical aid.

Health and hospitals involve operation and provision of hospital and public health facilities or programs. State and local governments account for about 75 percent of all governmental spending for public health and hospital services.

A major portion of total spending in this category is for construction, operation, and maintenance of public hospitals. The remainder includes payments to private hospitals for care of patients or for public support, as well as for public health services other than hospitals.

Postal service comprises Federal Government expenditure for the postal service on a gross basis in Federal expenditure totals for Census Bureau reports. This is in contrast to the usual practice of including only the net postal deficit in overall U.S. Budget data.

Item	Amount (millions of dollars)	Percent increase or decrease (-) from 1975-76
(L) Debt outstanding, total.......	257,532	7.1
Long-term....................	244,147	10.1
Full faith and credit.....	137,749	5.1
Nonguaranteed.............	106,398	17.3
Short-term.................	13,385	-28.7
Net long-term debt outstanding	212,333	8.5

Financial assets	Amount (millions of dollars)	Percent of total	Percent increase or decrease (-) from 1975-76
Total..........	272,028	100.0	11.8
Insurance trust systems.............	133,662	49.1	11.2
(M) Unemployment compensation.........	4,968	1.8	11.9
Employee retirement	123,481	45.4	10.9
Other.............	5,213	1.9	17.3
Other than insurance trust systems.......	138,366	50.9	12.4
Cash and deposits..	65,482	24.1	13.3
Federal securities.	35,041	12.9	22.9
State and local government securities........	6,347	2.3	-3.1
Nongovernmental securities........	31,496	11.6	4.2

Item	Per capita amount, 1976-77	
	Lowest State[1]	Highest State[1]
Total general revenue...........	931.80	3,730.70
From Federal Government.......	188.35	766.95
All general revenue from own sources.....................	660.46	2,963.75
Tax revenue.................	494.08	2,295.71
Property tax..............	59.66	1,317.75
Other taxes..............	235.97	977.96
Charges and miscellaneous general revenue...........	148.39	668.05
Total general expenditure.......	876.20	3,275.33
Education.....................	353.71	1,072.57
Local schools..............	221.33	826.80
Institutions of higher education..................	60.95	214.21
Highways.....................	62.42	468.53
Public welfare...............	55.31	384.17
Health and hospitals..........	45.38	171.57
Police protection.............	21.88	149.94
Local fire protection.........	8.00	49.07
Sewerage.....................	7.67	86.47
Total debt outstanding.........	344.63	5,651.12

(N)

[1] The District of Columbia is included as a "State" area in this presentation.

Police protection largely reflects local government payments for police protection and traffic safety activities. Federal expenditure under this heading relates primarily to the Federal Bureau of Investigation, Immigration and Naturalization Service, Bureau of Narcotics, and Secret Service. State expenditure so reported is mainly for highway police activities.

Sanitation activities are classified as a distinctive function only at the local level. A major portion of the local expenditure for this function is for the provision and operation of sewerage facilities; the balance is for refuse collection and disposal and street cleaning.

Government Indebtedness

As summarized in Table L, the major portion of all State and local government debt is long-term indebtedness. More than half of such long-term obligations is full faith and credit debt, for which the credit of the government is unconditionally pledged. Nonguaranteed obligations include debt issued for industrial aid and pollution control; governmental finance data does not reflect expenditure or fund balances derived from proceeds of these obligations when the funds are privately administered.

Cash and Security Holdings

Table M shows financial assets of State and local governments. About one-half of all holdings represents assets of employee-retirement or other insurance trust systems. Other major holdings by purpose include holdings of bond funds pending disbursement, and holdings of sinking funds and other debt offsets.

Data by States

Marked interstate variation is evident in the financial scale of State and local governments. This may be illustrated by the figures above in Table N, which indicate the highest and lowest of the per capita statewide averages for various financial items.

The Federal Government supplied 21.9 percent of total general revenue of State and local governments during fiscal 1976-77. This proportion varied considerably, however, with Federal payments generally ranging from about 17.9 percent of the aggregate up to 58.0 percent.

Table 1 Governmental Revenue by Source and Level of Government: 1977

Sources	Amount (millions of dollars)					Per capita		
	All governments	Federal Government	State and local governments			Total	Federal Government	State and local governments
			Total	State	Local			
TOTAL REVENUE.	[1]657 321	383 524	[1]337 747	204 475	196 321	[1]3 038.48	1 772.85	[1]1 561.24
TOTAL GENERAL REVENUE.	[1]506 862	285 016	[1]285 796	169 866	178 979	[1]2 342.98	1 317.49	[1]1 321.10
INTERGOVERNMENTAL REVENUES	([1])	1 375	62 575	48 676	76 948	([1])	6.36	289.26
FROM FEDERAL GOVERNMENT.	([1])	-	62 575	45 938	16 637	([1])	-	289.26
FROM STATE GOVERNMENTS	([1])	1 375	([1])	-	60 311	([1])	6.36	([1])
FROM LOCAL GOVERNMENTS	([1])	-	([1])	2 737	-	([1])	-	([1])
REVENUE FROM OWN SOURCES	657 321	382 149	275 172	155 799	119 373	3 038.48	1 766.49	1 271.89
GENERAL REVENUE FROM OWN SOURCES	506 862	283 641	223 221	121 191	102 031	2 342.98	1 311.14	1 031.85
TAXES.	419 721	243 842	175 879	101 085	74 794	1 940.17	1 127.17	813.00
PROPERTY.	62 535	-	62 535	2 260	60 275	289.07	-	289.07
INDIVIDUAL INCOME.	185 970	156 725	29 245	25 493	3 752	859.65	724.47	135.19
CORPORATION INCOME	64 066	54 892	9 174	9 174	([2])	296.15	253.74	42.41
SALES AND GROSS RECEIPTS	83 775	23 180	60 595	52 362	8 232	387.25	107.15	280.10
CUSTOMS DUTIES	5 394	5 394	-	-	-	24.93	24.93	-
GENERAL SALES AND GROSS RECEIPTS .	36 313	-	36 313	30 896	5 417	167.86	-	167.86
SELECTIVE SALES AND GROSS RECEIPTS	42 068	17 786	24 282	21 466	2 815	194.46	82.22	112.24
MOTOR FUEL	14 067	4 903	9 164	9 088	75	65.02	22.66	42.36
ALCOHOLIC BEVERAGES.	7 651	5 387	2 264	2 120	144	35.36	24.90	10.46
TOBACCO PRODUCTS	6 031	2 399	3 632	3 500	131	27.88	11.09	16.79
PUBLIC UTILITIES	6 941	2 780	4 161	2 363	1 798	32.09	12.85	19.24
OTHER.	7 379	2 317	5 062	4 395	667	34.11	10.71	23.40
MOTOR VEHICLE AND OPERATORS LICENSES	4 941	-	4 941	4 587	354	22.84	-	22.84
DEATH AND GIFT TAX	9 132	7 327	1 805	1 805	([3])	42.21	33.87	8.34
ALL OTHER.	9 302	1 718	7 584	5 404	2 180	43.00	7.94	35.06
CHARGES AND MISCELLANEOUS GENERAL REVENUE .	87 142	39 799	47 343	20 106	27 237	402.82	183.97	218.84
CURRENT CHARGES.	56 828	25 083	31 745	12 768	18 977	262.69	115.95	146.66
NATIONAL DEFENSE AND INTERNATIONAL RELATIONS	5 362	5 362	-	-	-	24.79	24.79	-
POSTAL SERVICE	12 396	12 396	-	-	-	57.30	57.30	-
EDUCATION.	10 384	74	10 310	6 818	3 492	48.00	0.34	47.66
SCHOOL LUNCH SALES	1 622	-	1 622	-	1 622	7.50	-	7.50
INSTITUTIONS OF HIGHER EDUCATION	7 795	74	7 721	6 678	1 043	36.03	0.34	35.69
OTHER.	968	-	968	140	828	4.47	-	4.47
HOSPITALS.	8 135	43	8 092	2 370	5 722	37.60	0.20	37.41
SEWERAGE	2 488	-	2 483	-	2 488	11.50	-	11.50
SANITATION OTHER THAN SEWERAGE . .	662	-	662	-	662	3.06	-	3.06
LOCAL PARKS AND RECREATION	626	-	626	-	626	2.89	-	2.89
NATURAL RESOURCES.	5 165	4 478	687	557	130	23.88	20.57	3.18
HOUSING AND URBAN RENEWAL.	1 529	568	961	44	916	7.07	2.63	4.44
AIR TRANSPORTATION	1 263	13	1 250	141	1 109	5.84	0.06	5.78
WATER TRANSPORT AND TERMINALS. . .	898	315	583	168	415	4.15	1.46	2.70
PARKING FACILITIES	287	-	287	-	287	1.33	-	1.33
OTHER.	7 633	1 834	5 799	2 669	3 130	35.28	8.48	26.81
MISCELLANEOUS GENERAL REVENUE. . . .	30 313	14 716	15 597	7 338	8 259	140.12	68.03	72.10
SPECIAL ASSESSMENTS.	884	-	884	22	862	4.09	-	4.09
SALE OF PROPERTY	891	569	322	106	215	4.12	2.63	1.49
INTEREST EARNINGS.	11 667	4 869	6 798	3 475	3 323	53.93	22.51	31.42
OTHER.	16 872	9 278	7 594	3 734	3 859	77.99	42.89	35.10
UTILITY REVENUE.	14 191	-	14 191	-	14 191	65.60	-	65.60
LIQUOR STORES REVENUE.	2 612	-	2 612	2 244	368	12.07	-	12.07
INSURANCE TRUST REVENUE.	133 656	98 508	35 148	32 365	2 783	617.83	455.36	162.47

Note: Because of rounding, detail may not add to totals. Local government amounts are estimates subject to sampling variation.

- Represents zero or rounds to zero.
[1]Duplicative transactions between levels of government are excluded; see text.
[2]Minor amount included in individual income tax figures.
[3]Minor amount included in "All other" taxes.

(Millions of dollars)

State and level of government	Total general revenue	Intergovernmental revenue		All general revenue from own sources	Taxes				Charges and miscella-neous general revenue
		From Federal Government	Other (local-State and State-local)		Total[1]	Property	General sales	Income	
UNITED STATES, TOTAL	285 796.5	62 575.2	([2])	223 221.3	175 878.7	62 534.9	36 312.9	38 418.7	47 342.6
STATE GOVERNMENTS.	169 866.1	45 938.3	2 737.2	121 190.6	101 084.6	2 259.8	30 895.9	34 666.3	20 105.9
LOCAL GOVERNMENTS.	178 979.0	16 636.9	60 311.4	102 030.7	74 794.0	60 275.1	5 417.0	3 752.4	27 236.6
ALABAMA.	3 787.6	1 082.7	([2])	2 704.9	1 870.7	220.1	593.3	358.1	834.2
STATE GOVERNMENT . . .	2 650.0	875.3	22.2	1 752.6	1 403.7	34.1	454.8	337.8	348.9
LOCAL GOVERNMENTS. . .	1 833.2	207.4	673.4	952.4	467.0	186.0	138.5	20.4	485.3
ALASKA	1 518.1	311.8	([2])	1 206.2	934.4	536.3	31.4	246.1	271.9
STATE GOVERNMENT . . .	1 220.3	273.8	0.3	946.2	773.5	409.8	-	246.1	172.7
LOCAL GOVERNMENTS. . .	499.6	38.1	201.5	260.0	160.9	126.6	31.4	-	99.2
ARIZONA.	2 896.6	523.7	([2])	2 372.9	1 897.8	727.9	606.3	242.4	475.1
STATE GOVERNMENT . . .	1 734.7	363.6	7.0	1 364.1	1 160.1	129.8	502.9	242.4	204.0
LOCAL GOVERNMENTS. . .	1 862.3	160.0	693.4	1 008.8	737.8	598.1	103.4	-	271.0
ARKANSAS	1 997.8	581.8	([2])	1 416.0	1 059.3	234.8	275.0	231.0	356.7
STATE GOVERNMENT . . .	1 395.1	461.3	4.3	929.5	802.9	1.7	274.3	231.0	126.5
LOCAL GOVERNMENTS. . .	1 012.4	120.4	405.4	486.6	256.4	233.1	0.7	-	230.2
CALIFORNIA	36 321.7	7 423.3	([2])	28 898.4	23 842.9	10 025.1	5 243.6	5 262.5	5 055.5
STATE GOVERNMENT . . .	20 737.3	5 768.2	625.9	14 343.2	12 589.1	439.4	4 314.0	5 262.5	1 754.1
LOCAL GOVERNMENTS. . .	25 029.4	1 655.1	8 819.1	14 555.2	11 253.8	9 585.7	929.6	-	3 301.4
COLORADO	3 631.2	767.4	([2])	2 863.7	2 157.6	822.8	563.9	419.5	706.2
STATE GOVERNMENT . . .	2 001.5	606.0	6.7	1 388.8	1 077.3	2.4	359.6	419.5	311.6
LOCAL GOVERNMENTS. . .	2 315.5	161.4	679.2	1 474.9	1 080.3	820.3	204.3	-	394.6
CONNECTICUT.	3 975.9	710.2	([2])	3 265.7	2 750.9	1 282.1	583.5	261.1	514.8
STATE GOVERNMENT . . .	2 327.0	541.3	2.9	1 782.8	1 457.1	-	583.5	261.1	325.6
LOCAL GOVERNMENTS. . .	2 050.0	168.8	398.3	1 482.9	1 293.8	1 282.1	-	-	189.2
DELAWARE	854.9	199.9	([2])	655.0	482.7	78.0	-	206.7	172.3
STATE GOVERNMENT . . .	638.3	136.4	1.6	500.2	390.9	-	-	197.0	109.3
LOCAL GOVERNMENTS. . .	380.0	63.5	161.7	154.8	91.8	78.0	-	9.6	63.0
DISTRICT OF COLUMBIA . .	2 023.8	1 174.0	([2])	849.8	738.7	165.8	141.1	256.6	111.1
FLORIDA.	9 066.1	1 779.7	([1])	7 286.4	5 309.2	1 783.6	1 398.6	194.2	1 977.2
STATE GOVERNMENT . . .	4 851.1	1 126.8	26.7	3 697.6	3 274.8	68.6	1 398.6	194.2	422.8
LOCAL GOVERNMENTS. . .	6 402.6	652.9	2 160.9	3 588.8	2 034.4	1 715.1	-	-	1 554.4
GEORGIA.	5 576.8	1 373.4	([2])	4 203.4	3 074.7	956.8	773.3	666.5	1 128.7
STATE GOVERNMENT . . .	3 180.6	980.0	7.8	2 192.8	1 906.5	9.9	687.4	666.5	286.3
LOCAL GOVERNMENTS. . .	3 268.7	393.5	864.7	2 010.6	1 168.2	946.9	85.9	-	842.4
HAWAII	1 573.3	458.8	([2])	1 114.5	872.1	149.2	341.0	230.6	242.4
STATE GOVERNMENT . . .	1 228.9	345.3	5.9	877.7	685.7	-	341.0	230.6	192.0
LOCAL GOVERNMENTS. . .	383.5	113.5	33.2	236.8	186.4	149.2	-	-	50.4
IDAHO.	982.1	270.4	([2])	711.7	547.9	175.4	103.9	143.5	163.8
STATE GOVERNMENT . . .	659.7	224.5	2.1	433.1	367.8	0.2	103.9	143.5	65.3
LOCAL GOVERNMENTS. . .	523.9	45.9	199.4	278.6	180.1	175.1	-	-	98.5
ILLINOIS	14 360.5	2 816.1	([2])	11 544.4	9 674.0	3 576.5	2 240.8	1 797.8	1 870.4
STATE GOVERNMENT . . .	8 166.5	2 076.2	55.9	6 034.3	5 319.5	4.8	1 842.3	1 797.8	714.8
LOCAL GOVERNMENTS. . .	8 840.9	739.8	2 591.0	5 510.1	4 354.4	3 571.7	398.5	-	1 155.6
INDIANA.	5 525.7	1 003.9	([2])	4 521.8	3 477.6	1 293.6	1 045.6	600.6	1 044.2
STATE GOVERNMENT . . .	3 437.1	761.2	9.0	2 666.9	2 162.9	23.6	1 045.6	565.5	504.0
LOCAL GOVERNMENTS. . .	3 404.2	242.7	1 306.6	1 854.8	1 314.7	1 270.1	-	35.1	540.2
IOWA	3 559.9	716.9	([2])	2 843.0	2 155.2	837.2	346.8	539.3	687.8
STATE GOVERNMENT . . .	2 154.5	558.6	37.2	1 558.7	1 292.5	0.1	346.8	539.3	266.1
LOCAL GOVERNMENTS. . .	2 302.3	158.3	859.7	1 284.3	862.7	837.1	-	-	421.6
KANSAS	2 775.2	546.2	([2])	2 229.0	1 692.3	696.0	339.3	331.9	536.7
STATE GOVERNMENT . . .	1 604.0	424.5	11.1	1 168.4	969.0	15.4	326.7	331.9	199.4
LOCAL GOVERNMENTS. . .	1 594.2	121.7	411.9	1 060.6	723.3	680.5	12.6	-	337.3
KENTUCKY	3 660.0	973.3	([2])	2 686.7	2 079.1	389.3	463.8	600.7	607.6
STATE GOVERNMENT . . .	2 650.5	767.5	5.8	1 877.2	1 560.4	43.4	463.8	469.4	316.8
LOCAL GOVERNMENTS. . .	1 582.9	205.8	567.6	809.5	518.8	345.9	-	131.3	290.8
LOUISIANA.	4 744.8	1 224.6	([2])	3 520.2	2 494.0	388.8	809.6	228.9	1 026.1
STATE GOVERNMENT . . .	3 216.1	966.7	13.8	2 235.6	1 718.7	0.1	481.7	228.9	517.0
LOCAL GOVERNMENTS. . .	2 498.6	257.9	956.2	1 284.6	775.4	388.6	327.9	-	509.2

See footnotes at end of table.

Table 2. General Revenue of State and Local Governments by Source and Level of Government, by State: 1977—Continued

(Millions of dollars)

State and level of government	Total general revenue	Intergovernmental revenue — From Federal Government	Intergovernmental revenue — Other (local-State and State-local)	All general revenue from own sources	Taxes — Total¹	Taxes — Property	Taxes — General sales	Taxes — Income	Charges and miscellaneous general revenue
MAINE.	1 274.2	399.2	(²)	875.1	714.1	258.1	169.7	110.4	161.0
STATE GOVERNMENT . . .	862.8	274.0	8.1	580.8	468.5	14.3	169.7	110.4	112.4
LOCAL GOVERNMENTS. . .	631.4	125.2	212.0	294.2	245.6	243.7	-		48.6
MARYLAND	5 960.2	1 228.8	(²)	4 731.4	3 691.8	1 098.8	465.8	1 300.4	1 039.6
STATE GOVERNMENT . . .	3 491.9	805.2	24.3	2 662.4	2 127.7	72.4	465.8	922.0	534.7
LOCAL GOVERNMENTS. . .	3 868.2	423.6	1 375.6	2 069.0	1 564.1	1 026.3	-	378.4	504.8
MASSACHUSETTS.	8 672.5	1 897.1	(²)	6 775.4	5 792.8	2 841.5	441.9	1 588.8	982.6
STATE GOVERNMENT . . .	4 968.6	1 323.9	167.4	3 477.3	2 934.3	0.6	441.9	1 588.8	543.1
LOCAL GOVERNMENTS. . .	5 013.4	573.2	1 142.2	3 298.1	2 858.5	2 840.9	-		439.6
MICHIGAN	13 184.9	2 841.2	(²)	10 343.9	8 016.8	3 029.8	1 407.0	2 442.5	2 327.0
STATE GOVERNMENT . . .	7 891.4	2 042.2	85.8	5 763.5	4 843.7	117.7	1 407.0	2 254.8	919.8
LOCAL GOVERNMENTS. . .	8 078.6	798.8	2 699.4	4 580.3	3 173.1	2 912.1	-	187.6	1 407.2
MINNESOTA.	5 951.6	1 236.3	(²)	4 715.3	3 601.7	1 077.3	469.6	1 215.0	1 113.6
STATE GOVERNMENT . . .	3 867.7	912.2	39.4	2 916.0	2 485.6	3.1	466.7	1 215.0	430.5
LOCAL GOVERNMENTS. . .	3 765.4	324.0	1 642.1	1 799.3	1 116.2	1 074.2	2.9		683.1
MISSISSIPPI.	2 474.5	700.8	(²)	1 773.7	1 260.1	277.6	475.5	177.5	513.6
STATE GOVERNMENT . . .	1 759.4	578.8	11.9	1 168.7	969.3	3.6	475.5	177.5	199.4
LOCAL GOVERNMENTS. . .	1 315.7	122.0	588.7	605.0	290.9	274.0	-		314.2
MISSOURI	4 870.3	1 166.7	(²)	3 703.5	2 923.5	927.1	728.2	581.4	780.1
STATE GOVERNMENT . . .	2 632.8	789.1	3.6	1 840.2	1 598.1	4.5	596.4	495.4	242.1
LOCAL GOVERNMENTS. . .	2 954.6	377.7	713.4	1 863.4	1 325.4	922.6	131.8	86.0	538.0
MONTANA.	1 076.2	310.4	(²)	765.8	582.7	275.4	-	136.8	183.2
STATE GOVERNMENT . . .	670.0	265.7	5.3	399.0	312.4	15.6	-	136.6	86.6
LOCAL GOVERNMENTS. . .	579.5	44.7	168.0	366.9	270.3	259.7	-	-	96.6
NEBRASKA	1 977.8	359.9	(²)	1 617.9	1 208.1	557.0	221.1	212.5	409.9
STATE GOVERNMENT . . .	1 044.1	273.4	22.2	748.5	612.9	2.9	198.7	212.5	135.6
LOCAL GOVERNMENTS. . .	1 204.7	86.5	248.8	869.4	595.1	554.0	22.4	-	274.2
NEVADA	946.5	175.0	(²)	771.5	564.8	180.8	134.4	-	206.7
STATE GOVERNMENT . . .	527.4	142.3	6.5	378.6	329.1	22.1	115.7	-	49.5
LOCAL GOVERNMENTS. . .	591.2	32.6	165.6	392.9	235.7	158.7	18.7	-	157.2
NEW HAMPSHIRE.	881.3	202.4	(²)	678.9	525.0	324.7		39.6	153.9
STATE GOVERNMENT . . .	461.5	158.6	10.2	292.7	200.2	6.2	-	39.6	92.5
LOCAL GOVERNMENTS. . .	506.7	43.8	76.7	386.1	324.8	318.5	-		61.4
NEW JERSEY	10 177.3	1 957.5	(²)	8 219.8	6 826.6	3 430.8	913.1	1 042.4	1 393.2
STATE GOVERNMENT . . .	5 370.3	1 430.3	75.0	3 865.0	3 103.7	80.5	913.1	1 042.4	761.3
LOCAL GOVERNMENTS. . .	6 568.9	527.3	1 686.9	4 354.8	3 722.9	3 350.3	-	-	631.9
NEW MEXICO	1 560.1	427.3	(²)	1 132.8	743.2	135.0	267.0	56.1	389.5
STATE GOVERNMENT . . .	1 215.3	326.0	11.8	877.6	597.6	16.1	257.2	56.1	280.0
LOCAL GOVERNMENTS. . .	759.6	101.4	403.0	255.2	145.6	118.9	9.7		109.6
NEW YORK	34 119.9	6 515.1	(²)	27 604.8	22 444.8	8 033.8	3 918.3	7 158.5	5 160.0
STATE GOVERNMENT . . .	18 805.6	4 843.1	1 034.8	12 927.7	10 743.2	24.2	2 218.2	5 822.0	2 184.4
LOCAL GOVERNMENTS. . .	27 164.0	1 672.0	10 814.9	14 677.1	11 701.5	8 009.6	1 700.2	1 336.5	2 975.6
NORTH CAROLINA	5 685.4	1 555.0	(²)	4 130.4	3 275.2	771.9	649.9	986.4	855.2
STATE GOVERNMENT . . .	4 026.3	1 213.3	18.2	2 794.8	2 384.8	38.0	511.5	986.4	410.0
LOCAL GOVERNMENTS. . .	3 237.3	341.8	1 560.0	1 335.6	890.4	733.8	138.4	-	445.2
NORTH DAKOTA	923.5	238.9	(²)	684.6	445.1	146.1	110.2	76.8	239.4
STATE GOVERNMENT . . .	677.9	214.2	11.9	451.7	296.3	2.6	110.2	76.8	155.4
LOCAL GOVERNMENTS. . .	401.4	24.7	143.9	232.9	148.8	143.5	-	-	84.1
OHIO	11 290.1	2 260.9	(²)	9 029.2	6 856.6	2 668.6	1 203.3	1 483.9	2 172.7
STATE GOVERNMENT . . .	6 061.5	1 656.4	45.7	4 359.4	3 570.8	108.3	1 135.5	930.4	788.6
LOCAL GOVERNMENTS. . .	7 889.1	604.5	2 614.7	4 669.8	3 285.8	2 560.3	67.8	553.5	1 384.0
OKLAHOMA	3 144.9	803.9	(²)	2 340.9	1 681.8	378.8	341.3	287.5	659.1
STATE GOVERNMENT . . .	2 110.1	584.5	21.8	1 503.8	1 139.0	-	205.1	287.5	364.8
LOCAL GOVERNMENTS. . .	1 620.2	219.4	563.7	837.1	542.8	378.8	136.2	-	294.3
OREGON	3 489.4	891.1	(²)	2 598.3	1 884.5	838.8	(Z)	653.0	713.9
STATE GOVERNMENT . . .	1 965.3	615.1	9.9	1 340.3	973.1	0.1	-	653.0	367.2
LOCAL GOVERNMENTS. . .	2 052.2	276.0	518.2	1 258.0	911.3	838.7	(Z)	-	346.7
PENNSYLVANIA	13 978.8	3 145.6	(²)	10 833.2	9 074.6	2 370.3	1 524.5	2 601.4	1 758.6
STATE GOVERNMENT . . .	8 588.4	2 239.3	72.7	6 276.4	5 590.8	62.5	1 524.5	1 844.1	685.6
LOCAL GOVERNMENTS. . .	7 927.8	906.3	2 464.7	4 556.8	3 483.7	2 307.8	-	757.3	1 073.0

See footnotes at end of table.

(Millions of dollars)

State and level of government	Total general revenue	Intergovernmental revenue		All general revenue from own sources	Taxes				Charges and miscellaneous general revenue
		From Federal Government	Other (local-State and State-local)		Total[1]	Property	General sales	Income	
RHODE ISLAND	1 264.0	345.4	(2)	918.6	741.3	305.4	141.8	144.6	177.3
STATE GOVERNMENT . . .	850.5	259.9	2.7	588.0	438.8	5.7	141.8	144.6	149.2
LOCAL GOVERNMENTS. . .	556.0	85.5	139.9	330.6	302.4	299.7	-	-	28.1
SOUTH CAROLINA	2 921.0	750.7	(2)	2 170.3	1 578.6	369.1	415.3	397.0	591.7
STATE GOVERNMENT . . .	2 135.4	610.9	23.0	1 501.5	1 187.6	4.8	415.3	397.0	313.9
LOCAL GOVERNMENTS. . .	1 326.4	139.8	517.8	668.9	391.1	364.3	-	-	277.8
SOUTH DAKOTA	820.4	218.9	(2)	601.5	433.6	211.4	111.4	2.5	167.9
STATE GOVERNMENT . . .	493.0	185.2	5.6	302.2	200.1	-	101.0	2.5	102.0
LOCAL GOVERNMENTS. . .	400.5	33.7	67.4	299.4	233.5	211.4	10.4	-	65.9
TENNESSEE.	4 295.2	1 098.4	(2)	3 196.9	2 425.0	607.8	929.2	178.4	771.8
STATE GOVERNMENT . . .	2 625.9	817.4	16.3	1 792.2	1 529.5	-	733.6	178.4	262.7
LOCAL GOVERNMENTS. . .	2 389.3	281.0	703.7	1 404.6	895.5	607.8	195.6	-	509.2
TEXAS.	13 671.2	2 726.3	(2)	10 944.8	8 178.3	2 984.9	1 997.1	-	2 766.5
STATE GOVERNMENT . . .	8 090.2	2 066.0	16.5	6 007.6	4 750.1	42.8	1 695.8	-	1 257.6
LOCAL GOVERNMENTS. . .	7 739.8	660.3	2 142.3	4 937.2	3 428.2	2 942.2	301.2	-	1 509.0
UTAH	1 511.1	415.8	(2)	1 095.3	827.0	241.7	266.9	183.1	268.4
STATE GOVERNMENT . . .	1 040.2	344.0	8.1	688.2	531.3	0.2	226.9	183.1	156.9
LOCAL GOVERNMENTS. . .	776.6	71.8	297.6	407.2	295.7	241.5	40.0	-	111.5
VERMONT.	689.2	202.9	(2)	486.3	391.3	159.7	32.5	87.2	95.0
STATE GOVERNMENT . . .	485.9	181.4	2.2	302.3	229.8	0.3	32.5	87.2	72.5
LOCAL GOVERNMENTS. . .	264.2	21.5	58.6	184.0	161.5	159.4	-	-	22.6
VIRGINIA	5 711.3	1 298.3	(2)	4 413.0	3 468.1	997.5	572.2	873.2	944.8
STATE GOVERNMENT . . .	3 576.4	927.3	37.4	2 611.8	2 053.8	22.1	426.8	873.2	557.9
LOCAL GOVERNMENTS. . .	3 191.1	371.1	1 018.9	1 801.2	1 414.3	975.4	145.4	-	386.9
WASHINGTON	5 376.1	1 273.9	(2)	4 102.2	3 004.0	934.5	1 284.9	-	1 098.2
STATE GOVERNMENT . . .	3 449.0	899.0	57.4	2 492.7	2 100.0	303.2	1 172.6	-	392.6
LOCAL GOVERNMENTS. . .	3 025.0	375.0	1 040.6	1 609.5	904.0	631.3	112.3	-	705.5
WEST VIRGINIA.	2 019.0	580.0	(2)	1 439.0	1 157.1	208.6	447.4	188.0	282.0
STATE GOVERNMENT . . .	1 552.2	502.8	1.0	1 048.4	903.4	0.9	447.4	188.0	145.0
LOCAL GOVERNMENTS. . .	890.3	77.2	422.5	390.6	253.6	207.7	-	-	137.0
WISCONSIN.	6 327.4	1 250.3	(2)	5 077.2	4 048.3	1 389.5	667.9	1 395.7	1 028.9
STATE GOVERNMENT . . .	4 227.3	1 017.6	31.2	3 178.5	2 733.3	91.9	667.9	1 395.7	445.2
LOCAL GOVERNMENTS. . .	4 137.5	232.7	2 006.1	1 898.7	1 315.0	1 297.6	(Z)	-	583.7
WYOMING.	753.9	197.8	(2)	556.1	401.3	163.3	104.7	-	154.8
STATE GOVERNMENT . . .	488.5	182.1	3.2	303.2	233.3	9.0	94.6	-	69.8
LOCAL GOVERNMENTS. . .	379.1	15.6	110.5	253.0	168.0	154.3	10.1	-	85.0

Note: Because of rounding, detail may not add to totals. Local government amounts are estimates subject to sampling variation; see text.

- Represents zero or rounds to zero.
Z Less than half the unit of measurement shown.
[1] Including amounts for categories not shown separately.
[2] Duplicative transactions between levels of government are excluded; see text.

Table 3. State and Local Government General Revenue by Origin and Allocation, and Level of Government: 1977

(Dollar amounts in millions)

State	Total general revenue	By originating level of government (before transfers among governments) Amount Federal	State	Local	Percent Federal	State	Local	By final recipient level of government (after intergovernmental transfers) Amount State	Local	Percent State	Local
UNITED STATES	285 796.5	62 575.2	121 190.6	102 030.7	21.9	42.4	35.7	[1]109 554.7	176 241.8	38.3	61.7
ALABAMA	3 787.6	1 082.7	1 752.6	952.4	28.6	46.3	25.1	1 976.6	1 811.0	52.2	47.8
ALASKA	1 518.1	311.8	946.2	260.0	20.5	62.3	17.1	1 018.8	499.3	67.1	32.9
ARIZONA	2 896.6	523.7	1 364.1	1 008.8	18.1	47.1	34.8	1 041.3	1 855.3	35.9	64.1
ARKANSAS	1 997.8	581.8	929.5	486.6	29.1	46.5	24.4	989.7	1 008.1	49.5	50.5
CALIFORNIA	36 321.7	7 423.3	14 343.2	14 555.2	20.4	39.5	40.1	11 918.2	24 403.5	32.8	67.2
COLORADO	3 631.2	767.4	1 388.8	1 474.9	21.1	38.2	40.6	1 322.4	2 308.8	36.4	63.6
CONNECTICUT	3 975.9	710.2	1 782.8	1 482.9	17.9	44.8	37.3	1 928.8	2 047.1	48.5	51.5
DELAWARE	854.9	199.9	500.2	154.8	23.4	58.5	18.1	476.6	378.3	55.7	44.3
DISTRICT OF COLUMBIA	2 023.8	1 174.0	(X)	849.8	58.0	(X)	42.0	(X)	2 023.8	(X)	100.0
FLORIDA	9 066.1	1 779.7	3 697.6	3 588.8	19.6	40.8	39.6	2 690.2	6 375.9	29.7	70.3
GEORGIA	5 576.8	1 373.4	2 192.8	2 010.6	24.6	39.3	36.1	2 315.9	3 260.9	41.5	58.5
HAWAII	1 573.3	458.8	877.7	236.8	29.2	55.8	15.1	1 195.7	377.6	76.0	24.0
IDAHO	982.1	270.4	433.1	278.6	27.5	44.1	28.4	460.3	521.8	46.8	53.2
ILLINOIS	14 360.5	2 816.1	6 034.3	5 510.1	19.6	42.0	38.4	5 575.4	8 785.0	38.8	61.2
INDIANA	5 525.7	1 003.9	2 666.9	1 854.8	18.2	48.3	33.6	2 130.4	3 395.2	38.6	61.4
IOWA	3 559.9	716.9	1 558.7	1 284.3	20.1	43.8	36.1	1 294.8	2 265.1	36.4	63.6
KANSAS	2 775.2	546.2	1 168.4	1 060.6	19.7	42.1	38.2	1 192.1	1 583.1	43.0	57.0
KENTUCKY	3 660.0	973.3	1 877.2	809.5	26.6	51.3	22.1	2 082.9	1 577.1	56.9	43.1
LOUISIANA	4 744.8	1 224.6	2 235.6	1 284.6	25.8	47.1	27.1	2 260.0	2 484.9	47.6	52.4
MAINE	1 274.2	399.2	580.8	294.2	31.3	45.6	23.1	650.9	623.4	51.1	48.9
MARYLAND	5 960.2	1 228.8	2 662.4	2 069.0	20.6	44.7	34.7	2 116.3	3 843.9	35.5	64.5
MASSACHUSETTS	8 672.5	1 897.1	3 477.3	3 298.1	21.9	40.1	38.0	3 826.4	4 846.0	44.1	55.9
MICHIGAN	13 184.9	2 841.1	5 763.5	4 580.3	21.5	43.7	34.7	5 192.1	7 992.8	39.4	60.6
MINNESOTA	5 951.6	1 236.3	2 916.0	1 799.3	20.8	49.0	30.2	2 225.6	3 726.0	37.4	62.6
MISSISSIPPI	2 474.5	700.8	1 168.7	605.0	28.3	47.2	24.5	1 170.7	1 303.8	47.3	52.7
MISSOURI	4 870.3	1 166.7	1 840.2	1 863.4	24.0	37.8	38.3	1 919.3	2 950.9	39.4	60.6
MONTANA	1 076.2	310.4	399.0	366.9	28.8	37.1	34.1	502.0	574.2	46.6	53.4
NEBRASKA	1 977.8	359.9	748.5	869.4	18.2	37.8	44.0	795.3	1 182.5	40.2	59.8
NEVADA	946.5	175.0	378.6	392.9	18.5	40.0	41.5	361.8	584.7	38.2	61.8
NEW HAMPSHIRE	881.3	202.4	292.7	386.1	23.0	33.2	43.8	384.9	496.4	43.7	56.3
NEW JERSEY	10 177.3	1 957.5	3 865.0	4 354.8	19.2	38.0	42.8	3 683.3	6 494.0	36.2	63.8
NEW MEXICO	1 560.1	427.3	877.6	255.2	27.4	56.3	16.4	812.3	747.8	52.1	47.9
NEW YORK	34 119.9	6 515.1	12 927.7	14 677.1	19.1	37.9	43.0	7 990.7	26 129.2	23.4	76.6
NORTH CAROLINA	5 685.4	1 555.0	2 794.8	1 335.6	27.4	49.2	23.5	2 466.3	3 219.1	43.4	56.6
NORTH DAKOTA	923.5	238.9	451.7	232.9	25.9	48.9	25.2	534.0	389.5	57.8	42.2
OHIO	11 290.1	2 260.9	4 359.4	4 669.8	20.0	38.6	41.4	3 446.8	7 843.3	30.5	69.5
OKLAHOMA	3 144.9	803.9	1 503.8	837.1	25.6	47.8	26.6	1 546.4	1 598.5	49.2	50.8
OREGON	3 489.4	891.1	1 340.3	1 258.0	25.5	38.4	36.1	1 447.2	2 042.3	41.5	58.5
PENNSYLVANIA	13 978.8	3 145.6	6 276.4	4 556.8	22.5	44.9	32.6	6 123.8	7 855.1	43.8	56.2
RHODE ISLAND	1 264.0	345.4	588.0	330.6	27.3	46.5	26.2	710.6	553.3	56.2	43.8
SOUTH CAROLINA	2 921.0	750.7	1 501.5	668.9	25.7	51.4	22.9	1 617.6	1 303.4	55.4	44.6
SOUTH DAKOTA	820.4	218.9	302.2	299.4	26.7	36.8	36.5	425.6	394.9	51.9	48.1
TENNESSEE	4 295.2	1 098.4	1 792.2	1 404.6	25.6	41.7	32.7	1 922.2	2 373.0	44.8	55.2
TEXAS	13 671.2	2 726.3	6 007.6	4 937.2	19.9	43.9	36.1	5 947.9	7 723.3	43.5	56.5
UTAH	1 511.1	415.8	688.2	407.2	27.5	45.5	26.9	742.6	768.5	49.1	50.9
VERMONT	689.2	202.9	302.3	184.0	29.4	43.9	26.7	427.3	262.0	62.0	38.0
VIRGINIA	5 711.3	1 298.3	2 611.8	1 801.2	22.7	45.7	31.5	2 557.5	3 153.8	44.8	55.2
WASHINGTON	5 376.1	1 273.9	2 492.7	1 609.5	23.7	46.4	29.9	2 408.4	2 967.7	44.8	55.2
WEST VIRGINIA	2 019.0	580.0	1 048.4	390.6	28.7	51.9	19.3	1 129.7	889.3	56.0	44.0
WISCONSIN	6 327.4	1 250.3	3 178.5	1 898.7	19.8	50.2	30.0	2 221.2	4 106.3	35.1	64.9
WYOMING	753.9	197.8	303.2	253.0	26.2	40.2	33.6	378.0	376.0	50.1	49.9

Note: Because of rounding, detail may not add to totals. Local government data are estimates subject to sampling variation; see text.

X Not applicable.

[1]Data not adjusted for Federal receipts of $1,375 million from State governments (mainly for Supplemental Security Income Program).

Table 4. State and Local Government Direct General Expenditure by Function and Level of Government, by State: 1977

(Millions of dollars)

State and level of government	Direct general expenditure for all functions Total	Other than capital outlay	Education Total	Other than capital outlay	Local schools Total	Other than capital outlay	Institutions of higher education	Other education	Highways Total	Other than capital outlay	Public welfare
UNITED STATES, TOTAL	273 001.8	234 222.8	102 805.2	93 570.6	71 342.7	65 361.2	26 205.1	5 257.4	23 104.5	10 607.5	34 564.0
STATE GOVERNMENT	103 535.1	86 656.2	27 072.7	24 158.9	650.8	441.3	21 165.8	5 256.1	13 865.3	4 403.1	22 646.0
LOCAL GOVERNMENTS	169 466.7	147 566.7	75 732.5	69 411.7	70 692.0	64 919.9	5 039.3	1.3	9 239.2	6 204.3	11 918.0
ALABAMA	3 696.3	3 020.1	1 454.9	1 287.4	816.7	733.8	491.7	146.5	435.4	169.2	375.9
STATE GOVERNMENT	1 862.1	1 472.8	671.2	562.0	33.1	8.4	491.7	146.5	293.0	60.7	367.0
LOCAL GOVERNMENTS	1 834.2	1 547.3	783.7	725.4	783.7	725.4	-	-	142.4	108.6	8.9
ALASKA	1 333.1	973.4	436.5	353.3	336.5	276.8	87.2	12.8	190.7	47.4	57.3
STATE GOVERNMENT	793.8	569.6	183.2	134.8	83.1	58.2	87.2	12.8	161.6	34.3	56.4
LOCAL GOVERNMENTS	539.2	403.8	253.4	218.5	253.4	218.5	-	-	29.1	13.2	0.9
ARIZONA	2 853.4	2 327.7	1 288.4	1 112.1	840.0	709.0	408.2	40.1	285.1	104.5	127.0
STATE GOVERNMENT	964.4	778.9	349.0	316.4	-	-	308.9	40.1	184.5	49.5	110.4
LOCAL GOVERNMENTS	1 889.0	1 548.8	939.4	795.7	840.0	709.0	99.4	-	100.6	55.0	16.6
ARKANSAS	1 878.6	1 549.5	758.4	675.6	488.7	444.4	209.5	60.1	262.1	116.9	237.2
STATE GOVERNMENT	947.5	747.1	264.1	226.0	-	-	203.9	60.1	192.5	62.4	235.1
LOCAL GOVERNMENTS	931.0	802.3	494.3	449.7	488.7	444.4	5.6	-	69.6	54.5	2.1
CALIFORNIA	32 532.1	29 368.2	12 217.8	11 252.8	8 186.9	7 626.2	3 683.5	347.5	1 504.6	848.8	5 178.6
STATE GOVERNMENT	9 942.0	9 100.2	2 774.8	2 518.1	31.8	31.8	2 395.4	347.5	683.4	280.9	2 634.0
LOCAL GOVERNMENTS	22 590.1	20 268.1	9 443.1	8 734.7	8 155.1	7 594.4	1 288.0	-	821.2	567.9	2 544.6
COLORADO	3 524.6	2 911.7	1 587.0	1 392.2	1 027.6	895.9	518.0	41.4	334.1	137.8	323.8
STATE GOVERNMENT	1 268.6	1 029.6	516.5	462.6	-	-	475.0	41.4	203.4	47.3	160.2
LOCAL GOVERNMENTS	2 256.0	1 882.1	1 070.5	929.6	1 027.6	895.9	43.0	-	130.6	90.6	163.6
CONNECTICUT	3 579.3	3 188.8	1 296.0	1 211.5	993.9	944.0	209.2	92.9	244.5	163.4	437.5
STATE GOVERNMENT	1 607.0	1 426.9	302.0	267.5	-	-	209.2	92.9	155.2	87.9	400.2
LOCAL GOVERNMENTS	1 972.3	1 761.8	994.0	944.0	993.9	944.0	-	(Z)	89.3	75.6	37.3
DELAWARE	848.7	710.2	345.9	316.6	204.7	194.1	113.2	28.0	67.7	34.0	74.0
STATE GOVERNMENT	474.4	393.0	141.2	122.5	-	-	113.2	28.0	55.5	23.4	73.3
LOCAL GOVERNMENTS	374.3	317.2	204.7	194.1	204.7	194.1	-	-	12.2	10.5	0.8
DISTRICT OF COLUMBIA	1 424.0	1 292.4	321.8	288.8	271.5	238.7	50.3	-	52.8	31.6	265.1
FLORIDA	9 287.5	7 515.2	3 438.2	3 016.7	2 476.6	2 196.6	861.1	100.5	726.0	270.5	488.3
STATE GOVERNMENT	2 886.0	2 231.1	618.5	534.3	10.4	10.4	507.6	100.5	471.9	89.1	442.1
LOCAL GOVERNMENTS	6 401.5	5 284.0	2 819.7	2 482.4	2 466.2	2 186.2	353.5	-	254.0	181.4	46.2
GEORGIA	5 060.9	4 330.5	1 860.5	1 687.6	1 300.8	1 177.3	456.3	103.4	476.7	196.5	516.1
STATE GOVERNMENT	2 121.3	1 757.2	567.7	499.7	19.3	(Z)	445.1	103.4	307.1	79.0	508.0
LOCAL GOVERNMENTS	2 939.6	2 573.4	1 292.8	1 187.9	1 281.5	1 177.3	11.2	0.1	169.6	117.5	8.0
HAWAII	1 714.1	1 365.2	478.2	408.4	292.7	254.5	174.3	11.2	133.4	60.1	189.5
STATE GOVERNMENT	1 313.5	1 073.1	477.6	407.7	292.1	253.9	174.3	11.2	93.8	36.0	188.8
LOCAL GOVERNMENTS	400.6	292.1	0.7	0.7	0.7	0.7	-	-	39.6	24.1	0.6
IDAHO	977.7	776.4	375.1	324.9	240.9	210.4	115.9	18.3	159.6	64.0	78.5
STATE GOVERNMENT	464.1	352.0	121.0	105.4	-	-	102.7	18.3	105.1	20.6	75.3
LOCAL GOVERNMENTS	513.6	424.4	254.1	219.5	240.9	210.4	13.2	-	54.5	43.5	3.2
ILLINOIS	14 237.0	12 068.9	5 357.1	4 914.7	3 815.5	3 522.8	1 302.4	239.2	1 403.6	547.5	2 082.2
STATE GOVERNMENT	5 703.8	4 729.7	1 127.2	1 011.9	7.5	-	880.5	239.2	884.7	219.6	2 007.7
LOCAL GOVERNMENTS	8 533.1	7 339.2	4 229.9	3 902.8	3 808.0	3 522.8	421.9	-	519.0	327.9	74.5
INDIANA	5 080.1	4 321.4	2 286.6	2 044.1	1 555.0	1 361.8	638.9	92.7	496.0	205.9	474.8
STATE GOVERNMENT	1 851.5	1 532.3	723.0	673.7	-	-	630.3	92.7	287.5	69.5	268.4
LOCAL GOVERNMENTS	3 228.6	2 789.1	1 563.6	1 370.4	1 555.0	1 361.8	8.6	-	208.5	136.4	206.3
IOWA	3 556.3	2 985.8	1 499.7	1 421.9	1 006.4	957.0	431.0	62.3	520.5	250.1	361.5
STATE GOVERNMENT	1 391.8	1 137.7	412.3	393.9	-	-	350.0	62.3	265.1	88.8	307.5
LOCAL GOVERNMENTS	2 164.4	1 848.1	1 087.4	1 028.1	1 006.4	957.0	81.0	-	255.4	161.3	53.9
KANSAS	2 775.5	2 270.2	1 102.0	1 006.7	725.1	665.0	348.9	28.0	339.9	147.1	296.5
STATE GOVERNMENT	1 143.1	931.8	319.1	290.8	-	-	291.1	28.0	197.1	58.2	291.6
LOCAL GOVERNMENTS	1 632.4	1 338.4	782.9	715.9	725.1	665.0	57.8	-	142.8	88.9	4.9
KENTUCKY	3 479.5	2 806.9	1 359.8	1 176.3	833.0	726.1	399.7	127.1	456.8	161.4	471.6
STATE GOVERNMENT	1 986.2	1 555.4	533.7	457.1	6.9	6.9	399.7	127.1	403.7	124.9	462.4
LOCAL GOVERNMENTS	1 493.2	1 251.5	826.1	719.2	826.1	719.2	(Z)	-	53.1	36.5	9.2
LOUISIANA	4 733.5	3 723.7	1 570.3	1 408.4	1 076.0	977.5	387.7	106.6	661.9	208.9	442.2
STATE GOVERNMENT	2 294.1	1 681.4	503.1	439.7	9.5	9.5	387.0	106.6	489.8	101.7	437.2
LOCAL GOVERNMENTS	2 439.4	2 042.3	1 067.2	968.7	1 066.6	968.1	0.6	-	172.0	107.2	5.0
MAINE	1 214.9	1 011.4	405.4	383.4	294.1	274.6	90.1	21.2	158.8	97.9	170.2
STATE GOVERNMENT	578.4	515.3	113.8	111.2	2.5	2.5	90.1	21.2	107.3	55.4	164.7
LOCAL GOVERNMENTS	636.6	496.1	291.6	272.1	291.6	272.1	-	-	51.5	42.5	5.5

See footnotes at end of table.

122

Table 4. State and Local Government Direct General Expenditure by Function and Level of Government, by State: 1977—Continued

(Millions of dollars)

State and level of government	Health and hospitals		Police protection	Fire protection	Sewerage		Sanitation other than sewerage	Local parks and recreation	Financial administration	General control	Interest on general debt	All other general expenditure
	Total	Other than capital outlay			Total	Other than capital outlay						
UNITED STATES, TOTAL	22 542.4	20 471.1	10 380.4	4 293.3	6 536.9	2 328.9	2 335.9	3 870.5	4 433.4	6 264.5	11 393.6	40 463.4
STATE GOVERNMENT	11 209.4	10 123.1	1 569.4	-	-	-	-	-	2 223.1	1 760.0	5 136.3	18 052.9
LOCAL GOVERNMENTS	11 333.0	10 348.0	8 811.0	4 293.3	6 536.9	2 328.9	2 335.9	3 870.5	2 210.2	4 504.5	6 257.3	22 410.5
ALABAMA	481.8	412.8	102.3	45.5	82.2	22.4	32.4	49.0	43.0	66.6	133.6	393.8
STATE GOVERNMENT	221.1	200.4	19.5	-	-	-	-	-	19.8	22.7	50.4	197.3
LOCAL GOVERNMENTS	260.7	212.5	82.8	45.5	82.2	22.4	32.4	49.0	23.2	43.8	83.1	196.6
ALASKA	45.3	41.6	35.0	16.1	34.0	8.5	11.8	12.3	36.1	55.5	66.8	335.6
STATE GOVERNMENT	29.9	29.3	15.5	-	-	-	-	-	19.7	38.0	49.2	240.5
LOCAL GOVERNMENTS	15.4	12.3	19.6	16.1	34.0	8.5	11.8	12.3	16.4	17.5	17.6	95.1
ARIZONA	203.5	191.0	148.1	42.3	57.6	15.0	38.7	57.1	61.9	86.2	71.0	386.5
STATE GOVERNMENT	90.6	86.8	31.4	-	-	-	-	-	30.0	15.7	4.4	148.4
LOCAL GOVERNMENTS	113.0	104.2	116.7	42.3	57.6	15.0	38.7	57.1	31.9	70.5	66.5	238.0
ARKANSAS	177.4	154.4	53.5	21.0	22.6	9.5	12.8	11.2	38.2	29.5	49.0	205.0
STATE GOVERNMENT	79.4	70.3	14.5	-	-	-	-	-	27.0	10.2	6.9	117.8
LOCAL GOVERNMENTS	98.0	84.0	39.1	21.0	22.6	9.5	12.8	11.2	11.1	19.2	42.1	87.9
CALIFORNIA	2 348.5	2 253.1	1 427.6	652.8	631.8	231.0	190.4	633.8	625.2	912.8	687.3	5 520.9
STATE GOVERNMENT	712.5	688.0	211.7	-	-	-	-	-	289.3	146.1	286.8	2 203.5
LOCAL GOVERNMENTS	1 636.1	1 565.1	1 215.9	652.8	631.8	231.0	190.4	633.8	335.9	766.7	400.5	3 317.4
COLORADO	267.8	251.9	127.3	64.9	85.3	35.9	16.0	80.2	72.7	103.0	78.3	384.2
STATE GOVERNMENT	134.1	131.4	19.9	-	-	-	-	-	32.3	42.1	7.7	152.4
LOCAL GOVERNMENTS	133.7	120.5	107.4	64.9	85.3	35.9	16.0	80.2	40.4	60.9	70.6	231.8
CONNECTICUT	221.9	192.5	140.4	83.1	109.8	38.9	27.5	40.5	57.0	78.4	234.4	608.2
STATE GOVERNMENT	186.5	158.2	25.1	-	-	-	-	-	27.2	45.7	160.9	304.1
LOCAL GOVERNMENTS	35.5	34.3	115.3	83.1	109.8	38.9	27.5	40.5	29.7	32.7	73.5	304.1
DELAWARE	43.2	39.5	28.1	6.1	40.0	13.2	5.9	11.5	15.8	24.1	48.9	137.5
STATE GOVERNMENT	43.0	39.3	10.5	-	-	-	-	-	10.5	15.6	33.4	91.4
LOCAL GOVERNMENTS	0.2	0.2	17.5	6.1	40.0	13.2	5.9	11.5	5.3	8.5	15.5	46.1
DISTRICT OF COLUMBIA	118.4	116.3	103.5	33.9	59.7	15.5	24.4	23.1	20.8	46.5	82.2	271.9
FLORIDA	1 026.1	952.9	477.6	164.3	435.6	109.9	139.9	194.0	169.2	278.4	325.0	1 424.9
STATE GOVERNMENT	417.6	403.7	64.3	-	-	-	-	-	54.6	100.0	99.5	617.5
LOCAL GOVERNMENTS	608.5	549.2	413.3	164.3	435.6	109.9	139.9	194.0	114.6	178.4	225.5	807.4
GEORGIA	763.8	722.3	178.3	68.8	84.9	38.1	56.8	53.2	87.7	115.4	162.1	636.6
STATE GOVERNMENT	265.7	259.1	26.6	-	-	-	-	-	36.6	31.5	64.4	313.6
LOCAL GOVERNMENTS	498.0	463.3	151.7	68.8	84.9	38.1	56.8	53.2	51.0	84.0	97.7	323.0
HAWAII	106.9	95.1	48.3	24.8	56.3	9.0	12.5	42.3	25.6	45.3	90.5	460.6
STATE GOVERNMENT	100.3	91.1	0.3	-	-	-	-	-	17.1	31.3	76.1	328.2
LOCAL GOVERNMENTS	6.5	4.1	48.0	24.8	56.3	9.0	12.5	42.3	8.5	13.9	14.5	132.4
IDAHO	71.1	66.0	32.7	9.3	14.1	5.3	6.8	8.8	21.3	21.8	10.9	167.7
STATE GOVERNMENT	35.9	32.7	6.0	-	-	-	-	-	10.3	8.9	2.5	99.1
LOCAL GOVERNMENTS	35.3	33.3	26.7	9.3	14.1	5.3	6.8	8.8	10.9	12.9	8.5	68.6
ILLINOIS	972.6	794.5	656.3	248.0	394.4	183.7	133.7	283.2	173.2	335.5	489.9	1 707.5
STATE GOVERNMENT	573.3	435.1	59.8	-	-	-	-	-	89.3	88.0	198.8	675.3
LOCAL GOVERNMENTS	399.3	359.4	596.5	248.0	394.4	183.7	133.7	283.2	83.9	247.5	291.1	1 032.2
INDIANA	525.7	487.6	168.6	78.6	126.7	65.4	24.1	52.8	80.5	104.0	123.6	538.2
STATE GOVERNMENT	215.4	204.2	35.4	-	-	-	-	-	40.5	24.8	28.1	228.5
LOCAL GOVERNMENTS	310.3	283.4	133.2	78.6	126.7	65.4	24.1	52.8	40.0	79.2	95.6	309.7
IOWA	294.8	268.3	93.6	32.4	94.9	26.6	19.3	43.0	65.6	79.3	54.3	397.2
STATE GOVERNMENT	150.1	128.8	18.8	-	-	-	-	-	29.2	17.7	5.8	185.3
LOCAL GOVERNMENTS	144.8	139.4	74.7	32.4	94.9	26.6	19.3	43.0	36.5	61.6	48.5	211.9
KANSAS	257.9	184.8	96.8	35.2	50.9	21.7	32.1	29.2	44.5	66.1	71.8	352.7
STATE GOVERNMENT	126.9	97.0	10.2	-	-	-	-	-	26.6	19.7	12.8	139.0
LOCAL GOVERNMENTS	130.9	87.8	86.5	35.2	50.9	21.7	32.1	29.2	17.9	46.4	59.0	213.7
KENTUCKY	204.6	189.4	109.5	37.2	55.4	26.9	23.3	24.2	38.8	59.7	172.5	466.0
STATE GOVERNMENT	119.7	114.3	35.3	-	-	-	-	-	26.1	25.1	95.4	284.7
LOCAL GOVERNMENTS	84.9	75.1	74.3	37.2	55.4	26.9	23.3	24.2	12.7	34.6	77.1	181.3
LOUISIANA	557.1	477.9	182.2	53.3	68.6	31.1	47.8	65.3	69.7	95.4	194.5	725.3
STATE GOVERNMENT	303.3	256.7	36.1	-	-	-	-	-	32.0	36.3	73.8	382.6
LOCAL GOVERNMENTS	253.8	221.2	146.2	53.3	68.6	31.1	47.8	65.3	37.8	59.1	120.7	342.7
MAINE	49.2	44.6	30.8	20.7	88.5	7.1	4.7	13.0	17.5	26.9	47.3	181.9
STATE GOVERNMENT	39.4	35.0	7.2	-	-	-	-	-	10.7	12.1	27.8	95.4
LOCAL GOVERNMENTS	9.8	9.6	23.6	20.7	88.5	7.1	4.7	13.0	6.8	14.9	19.5	86.5

See footnotes at end of table.

(Millions of dollars)

State and level of government	Direct general expenditure for all functions — Total	Other than capital outlay	Education — Total	Other than capital outlay	Local schools — Total	Other than capital outlay	Institutions of higher education	Other education	Highways — Total	Other than capital outlay	Public welfare
MARYLAND	6 013.0	4 891.3	2 353.8	2 084.0	1 705.4	1 485.8	529.6	118.8	466.2	141.0	586.3
STATE GOVERNMENT. .	2 112.8	1 775.5	515.1	484.1	-	-	396.4	118.8	210.4	49.9	320.5
LOCAL GOVERNMENTS .	3 900.2	3 115.8	1 838.7	1 599.9	1 705.4	1 485.8	133.2	-	255.8	91.1	265.9
MASSACHUSETTS	7 968.4	7 237.1	2 612.1	2 411.4	2 098.5	1 985.1	356.6	156.9	516.2	300.6	1 371.1
STATE GOVERNMENT. .	3 394.9	3 063.9	511.5	424.4	-	-	354.6	156.8	291.3	121.8	1 330.9
LOCAL GOVERNMENTS .	4 573.5	4 173.2	2 100.6	1 987.0	2 098.5	1 985.1	2.0	0.1	224.9	178.9	40.3
MICHIGAN	12 687.3	11 161.1	5 060.0	4 678.4	3 499.1	3 211.3	1 302.5	258.4	906.8	368.2	1 996.0
STATE GOVERNMENT. .	4 800.9	4 308.8	1 296.6	1 237.6	-	--	1 038.2	258.4	392.0	62.7	1 767.8
LOCAL GOVERNMENTS .	7 886.4	6 852.3	3 763.4	3 440.8	3 499.1	3 211.3	264.3	-	514.8	305.5	228.3
MINNESOTA	5 803.2	4 845.5	2 167.2	1 984.8	1 508.9	1 392.9	568.0	90.2	613.9	281.0	773.0
STATE GOVERNMENT. .	2 023.7	1 728.6	658.2	591.9	-	-	568.0	90.2	285.1	103.3	393.3
LOCAL GOVERNMENTS .	3 779.5	3 116.9	1 508.9	1 392.9	1 508.9	1 392.9	-	-	328.8	177.7	379.7
MISSISSIPPI	2 431.6	1 971.7	905.2	818.3	534.9	494.1	298.9	71.3	375.7	156.6	234.0
STATE GOVERNMENT. .	1 135.4	885.4	316.0	281.3	3.8	3.8	240.8	71.3	214.7	48.4	229.3
LOCAL GOVERNMENTS .	1 296.2	1 086.2	589.2	537.0	531.1	490.3	58.1	-	161.0	108.2	4.7
MISSOURI.	4 523.6	3 823.5	1 834.6	1 706.4	1 328.5	1 240.0	447.9	58.2	508.1	201.5	449.3
STATE GOVERNMENT. .	1 740.8	1 410.2	424.6	389.2	-	-	366.4	58.2	351.1	90.4	435.3
LOCAL GOVERNMENTS .	2 782.7	2 413.4	1 410.0	1 317.1	1 328.5	1 240.0	81.5	-	157.1	111.1	14.0
MONTANA	1 072.3	847.1	438.0	404.6	317.2	291.3	100.7	20.1	197.7	67.8	78.7
STATE GOVERNMENT. .	498.4	363.0	115.2	107.9	-	-	95.1	20.1	154.0	38.6	68.3
LOCAL GOVERNMENTS .	573.9	484.1	322.8	296.8	317.2	291.3	5.6	-	43.7	29.2	10.4
NEBRASKA.	1 799.1	1 482.2	763.9	698.4	541.7	498.1	197.1	25.1	260.2	108.6	141.6
STATE GOVERNMENT. .	680.1	534.3	212.4	191.6	-	-	187.2	25.1	135.1	29.3	117.9
LOCAL GOVERNMENTS .	1 119.0	947.9	551.5	506.8	541.7	498.1	9.9	-	125.1	79.3	23.8
NEVADA.	930.4	780.2	293.5	260.8	211.4	190.6	71.8	10.4	108.0	48.4	57.8
STATE GOVERNMENT. .	353.4	273.8	82.1	70.1	-	-	71.8	10.4	80.6	31.4	45.3
LOCAL GOVERNMENTS .	577.0	506.4	211.4	190.6	211.4	190.6	-	-	27.4	17.0	12.5
NEW HAMPSHIRE	947.9	749.1	337.9	302.1	225.7	211.5	97.3	15.0	148.4	73.6	113.2
STATE GOVERNMENT. .	454.9	335.7	112.2	90.5	-	-	97.3	15.0	105.2	43.3	81.0
LOCAL GOVERNMENTS .	493.0	413.4	225.7	211.5	225.7	211.5	-	-	43.2	30.3	32.2
NEW JERSEY.	9 722.8	8 666.1	3 475.8	3 312.2	2 577.9	2 459.1	590.1	307.8	562.2	354.7	1 239.3
STATE GOVERNMENT. .	3 423.8	2 922.2	744.6	707.5	-	-	436.8	307.8	272.9	141.1	648.2
LOCAL GOVERNMENTS .	6 299.0	5 743.9	2 731.1	2 604.7	2 577.9	2 459.1	153.3	-	289.2	213.6	591.2
NEW MEXICO.	1 400.3	1 185.6	642.9	570.9	430.5	379.8	186.5	25.9	149.7	76.5	109.0
STATE GOVERNMENT. .	663.6	561.5	216.4	195.1	4.0	4.0	186.5	25.9	115.3	53.2	106.8
LOCAL GOVERNMENTS .	736.7	624.3	426.5	375.8	426.5	375.8	-	-	34.4	23.2	2.1
NEW YORK.	32 177.9	28 838.1	9 643.5	9 081.1	7 265.4	7 016.1	1 714.2	663.9	1 472.4	907.1	5 321.1
STATE GOVERNMENT. .	8 175.2	6 540.2	1 653.7	1 383.9	-	-	989.8	663.9	563.6	196.0	114.8
LOCAL GOVERNMENTS .	24 002.7	22 297.8	7 989.8	7 697.2	7 265.4	7 016.1	724.4	-	908.8	711.1	5 206.3
NORTH CAROLINA. . . .	5 426.0	4 538.6	2 417.4	2 178.9	1 570.9	1 412.4	747.0	99.5	513.3	206.7	432.4
STATE GOVERNMENT. .	2 148.3	1 748.7	653.1	601.4	15.7	5.7	537.9	99.5	422.6	150.0	182.8
LOCAL GOVERNMENTS .	3 277.7	2 789.9	1 764.3	1 577.6	1 555.2	1 406.7	209.1	-	90.7	56.7	249.6
NORTH DAKOTA.	854.3	698.5	322.7	296.1	195.6	182.6	112.1	15.1	149.5	60.8	68.0
STATE GOVERNMENT. .	465.5	376.3	122.9	109.5	-	-	107.9	15.1	90.3	24.7	59.6
LOCAL GOVERNMENTS .	388.8	322.3	199.8	186.6	195.6	182.6	4.2	-	59.1	36.2	8.4
OHIO.	11 871.5	10 096.6	4 868.6	4 506.4	3 582.7	3 361.3	1 146.3	139.6	933.9	465.6	1 327.3
STATE GOVERNMENT. .	3 943.7	3 216.6	1 039.5	925.3	-	-	899.9	139.6	472.4	141.5	952.9
LOCAL GOVERNMENTS .	7 927.8	6 880.0	3 829.1	3 581.1	3 582.7	3 361.3	246.4	(Z)	461.5	324.1	374.5
OKLAHOMA.	2 937.0	2 444.8	1 172.3	1 037.9	735.1	641.3	376.5	60.7	311.2	159.6	360.5
STATE GOVERNMENT. .	1 400.4	1 204.0	428.5	389.8	5.4	5.4	362.3	60.7	180.9	64.5	357.4
LOCAL GOVERNMENTS .	1 536.5	1 240.9	743.8	648.1	729.6	635.8	14.2	-	130.3	95.1	3.1
OREGON.	3 359.7	2 858.8	1 386.7	1 222.7	912.3	808.7	420.8	53.6	262.6	140.3	351.0
STATE GOVERNMENT. .	1 396.8	1 228.2	358.2	310.8	-	-	304.6	53.6	138.8	46.7	340.2
LOCAL GOVERNMENTS .	1 962.9	1 630.6	1 028.5	912.0	912.3	808.7	116.2	-	123.8	93.6	10.8
PENNSYLVANIA.	13 746.5	12 132.5	4 898.8	4 490.0	3 678.7	3 334.1	718.3	501.8	1 161.0	606.2	2 367.2
STATE GOVERNMENT. .	6 180.7	5 516.2	1 135.7	1 053.4	28.7	-	605.3	501.8	824.4	362.2	2 091.3
LOCAL GOVERNMENTS .	7 565.8	6 616.3	3 763.1	3 436.6	3 650.1	3 334.1	113.0	-	336.7	244.0	275.9
RHODE ISLAND.	1 199.7	1 073.7	421.4	400.8	279.7	264.1	107.6	34.2	62.8	37.9	212.4
STATE GOVERNMENT. .	641.5	598.3	141.7	136.7	-	-	107.6	34.2	37.2	18.2	197.0
LOCAL GOVERNMENTS .	558.2	475.4	279.7	264.1	279.7	264.1	-	-	25.6	19.7	15.4
SOUTH CAROLINA. . . .	2 814.3	2 414.3	1 144.4	1 031.0	710.3	635.6	330.2	104.0	179.5	104.2	242.2
STATE GOVERNMENT. .	1 559.7	1 313.7	469.5	422.4	35.4	27.0	330.2	104.0	140.7	74.3	236.9
LOCAL GOVERNMENTS .	1 254.6	1 100.6	674.9	608.6	674.9	608.6	(Z)	-	38.8	29.9	5.3

See footnotes at end of table.

Table 4. State and Local Government Direct General Expenditure by Function and Level of Government, by State: 1977—Continued

(Millions of dollars)

State and level of government	Health and hospitals Total	Health and hospitals Other than capital outlay	Police protection	Fire protection	Sewerage Total	Sewerage Other than capital outlay	Sanitation other than sewerage	Local parks and recreation	Financial administration	General control	Interest on general debt	All other general expenditure
MARYLAND	418.4	374.2	226.5	98.4	175.1	61.0	64.4	143.2	113.1	127.0	269.4	971.2
STATE GOVERNMENT. .	265.4	235.8	41.5	-	-	-	-	-	73.1	52.4	142.8	491.6
LOCAL GOVERNMENTS .	153.0	138.4	185.0	98.4	175.1	61.0	64.4	143.2	40.0	74.6	126.6	479.6
MASSACHUSETTS	583.8	545.3	315.6	226.1	112.3	34.4	66.6	69.7	112.6	171.2	472.7	1 338.1
STATE GOVERNMENT. .	359.3	335.8	37.8	-	-	-	-	-	52.0	51.3	301.8	459.0
LOCAL GOVERNMENTS .	224.5	209.5	277.8	226.1	112.3	34.4	66.6	69.7	60.7	119.9	170.9	879.3
MICHIGAN	1 064.2	990.0	501.1	182.9	306.1	139.2	87.7	152.4	173.5	321.6	435.7	1 499.2
STATE GOVERNMENT. .	465.6	435.8	65.6	-	-	-	-	-	80.9	73.5	105.1	553.9
LOCAL GOVERNMENTS .	598.6	554.1	435.5	182.9	306.1	139.2	87.7	152.4	92.6	248.1	330.7	945.3
MINNESOTA	470.0	434.7	146.5	53.5	192.3	53.7	20.4	103.4	88.8	127.1	212.1	834.9
STATE GOVERNMENT. .	214.7	206.2	18.0	-	-	-	-	-	38.7	27.0	54.8	333.9
LOCAL GOVERNMENTS .	255.3	228.5	128.6	53.5	192.3	53.7	20.4	103.4	50.1	100.0	157.3	501.1
MISSISSIPPI	288.3	262.2	64.7	22.8	18.4	9.6	20.4	13.1	30.4	43.5	81.9	333.4
STATE GOVERNMENT. .	99.1	93.6	19.6	-	-	-	-	-	15.2	11.9	40.3	189.4
LOCAL GOVERNMENTS .	189.1	168.7	45.1	22.8	18.4	9.6	20.4	13.1	15.2	31.6	41.6	144.0
MISSOURI.	417.4	384.3	193.0	71.2	125.7	36.0	27.5	80.4	58.3	94.9	124.0	539.1
STATE GOVERNMENT. .	204.0	192.6	33.9	-	-	-	-	-	24.3	28.5	20.6	218.5
LOCAL GOVERNMENTS .	213.5	191.7	159.0	71.2	125.7	36.0	27.5	80.4	34.0	66.4	103.4	320.6
MONTANA	55.2	48.4	26.1	8.6	12.6	6.3	5.5	8.2	27.3	27.2	17.7	169.5
STATE GOVERNMENT. .	35.7	33.1	5.6	-	-	-	-	-	20.8	10.4	3.5	84.9
LOCAL GOVERNMENTS .	19.4	15.3	20.5	8.6	12.6	6.3	5.5	8.2	6.5	16.9	14.2	84.6
NEBRASKA.	153.4	139.3	50.1	19.6	38.6	11.6	9.7	22.2	32.3	42.1	40.0	225.3
STATE GOVERNMENT. .	76.0	68.6	10.3	-	-	-	-	-	13.6	12.2	2.8	99.9
LOCAL GOVERNMENTS .	77.4	70.7	39.8	19.6	38.6	11.6	9.7	22.2	18.7	29.9	37.3	125.4
NEVADA.	102.1	91.1	52.9	23.9	10.9	6.9	2.3	28.2	25.3	36.0	31.5	158.0
STATE GOVERNMENT. .	28.6	21.7	7.0	-	-	-	-	-	15.9	9.1	2.5	82.2
LOCAL GOVERNMENTS .	73.6	69.5	45.9	23.9	10.9	6.9	2.3	28.2	9.4	26.9	28.9	75.8
NEW HAMPSHIRE	64.0	42.4	30.0	17.7	31.2	7.3	4.5	5.5	13.1	18.5	35.3	128.6
STATE GOVERNMENT. .	53.9	34.6	5.4	-	-	-	-	-	8.1	6.9	16.4	65.7
LOCAL GOVERNMENTS .	10.1	7.8	24.5	17.7	31.2	7.3	4.5	5.5	5.0	11.6	18.9	62.9
NEW JERSEY.	551.8	492.8	431.1	165.2	281.2	90.6	81.0	151.4	146.7	257.5	467.3	1 912.5
STATE GOVERNMENT. .	342.8	290.1	58.1	-	-	-	-	-	75.0	68.1	235.8	978.3
LOCAL GOVERNMENTS .	209.0	202.6	372.9	165.2	281.2	90.6	81.0	151.4	71.7	189.4	231.5	934.2
NEW MEXICO.	107.9	95.5	59.3	19.0	18.0	6.0	13.3	17.5	36.6	38.6	29.5	159.1
STATE GOVERNMENT. .	76.1	71.0	12.6	-	-	-	-	-	22.6	23.1	6.5	84.2
LOCAL GOVERNMENTS .	31.8	24.5	46.7	19.0	18.0	6.0	13.3	17.5	13.9	15.5	23.0	74.9
NEW YORK.	2 788.8	2 596.2	1 296.5	478.4	690.7	173.9	406.7	367.9	409.3	599.5	2 841.1	5 862.2
STATE GOVERNMENT. .	1 272.7	1 187.1	93.1	-	-	-	-	-	212.7	150.3	1 603.7	2 510.7
LOCAL GOVERNMENTS .	1 516.1	1 409.1	1 203.4	478.4	690.7	173.9	406.7	367.9	196.6	449.2	1 237.4	3 351.5
NORTH CAROLINA. . . .	526.7	465.1	179.0	57.1	93.7	39.3	53.5	54.0	89.2	113.3	120.0	776.4
STATE GOVERNMENT. .	296.8	281.3	43.9	-	-	-	-	-	47.3	60.7	61.1	380.0
LOCAL GOVERNMENTS .	229.9	183.8	135.0	57.1	93.7	39.3	53.5	54.0	41.9	52.5	59.0	396.4
NORTH DAKOTA.	31.0	28.7	18.4	5.9	13.3	2.4	4.6	6.4	14.3	14.3	17.2	188.7
STATE GOVERNMENT. .	28.2	26.5	4.1	-	-	-	-	-	7.9	6.0	3.5	142.8
LOCAL GOVERNMENTS .	2.8	2.2	14.4	5.9	13.3	2.4	4.6	6.4	6.3	8.2	13.7	45.8
OHIO.	1 068.1	869.1	431.8	213.2	282.7	153.3	94.8	144.6	191.2	238.5	405.6	1 671.4
STATE GOVERNMENT. .	514.6	379.8	44.0	-	-	-	-	-	110.6	32.7	173.4	603.7
LOCAL GOVERNMENTS .	553.4	489.3	387.8	213.2	282.7	153.3	94.8	144.6	80.6	205.9	232.2	1 067.7
OKLAHOMA.	243.6	214.6	88.2	42.3	69.9	11.6	23.2	41.3	38.7	58.3	97.3	390.2
STATE GOVERNMENT. .	125.1	113.1	21.1	-	-	-	-	-	17.4	23.1	45.6	201.5
LOCAL GOVERNMENTS .	118.6	101.5	67.2	42.3	69.9	11.6	23.2	41.3	21.3	35.2	51.7	188.7
OREGON.	191.8	186.2	113.9	79.1	107.9	40.3	6.0	42.3	97.1	95.3	153.8	472.3
STATE GOVERNMENT. .	127.9	125.7	22.9	-	-	-	-	-	60.3	28.8	106.7	212.9
LOCAL GOVERNMENTS .	63.9	60.5	91.0	79.1	107.9	40.3	6.0	42.3	36.8	66.5	47.2	259.3
PENNSYLVANIA.	921.9	862.5	504.0	140.9	278.5	147.6	107.8	131.7	215.4	333.2	840.7	1 845.4
STATE GOVERNMENT. .	671.2	635.3	118.4	-	-	-	-	-	127.9	84.8	391.6	735.5
LOCAL GOVERNMENTS .	250.7	227.2	385.6	140.9	278.5	147.6	107.8	131.7	87.6	248.4	449.1	1 109.9
RHODE ISLAND.	96.0	84.1	38.6	28.9	58.2	15.9	7.8	9.2	21.1	26.5	46.5	170.1
STATE GOVERNMENT. .	94.5	82.6	7.0	-	-	-	-	-	13.8	18.5	24.7	106.9
LOCAL GOVERNMENTS .	1.5	1.5	31.6	28.9	58.2	15.9	7.8	9.2	7.3	8.0	21.8	63.1
SOUTH CAROLINA. . . .	358.1	335.0	79.9	23.0	38.0	16.2	26.2	16.3	40.0	49.0	90.2	527.4
STATE GOVERNMENT. .	206.5	193.9	21.4	-	-	-	-	-	22.0	14.2	49.0	399.5
LOCAL GOVERNMENTS .	151.6	141.1	58.5	23.0	38.0	16.2	26.2	16.3	18.0	34.8	41.2	127.8

See footnotes at end of table.

Table 4. State and Local Government Direct General Expenditure by Function and Level of Government, by State: 1977—Continued

(Millions of dollars)

State and level of government	Direct general expenditure for all functions Total	Direct general expenditure for all functions Other than capital outlay	Education Total	Education Other than capital outlay	Local schools Total	Local schools Other than capital outlay	Institutions of higher education	Other education	Highways Total	Highways Other than capital outlay	Public welfare
SOUTH DAKOTA	813.3	648.3	311.2	275.9	208.6	188.1	91.2	11.4	135.1	72.3	70.4
STATE GOVERNMENT. .	429.6	324.0	102.6	87.9	-	-	91.2	11.4	90.3	38.4	67.5
LOCAL GOVERNMENTS .	383.8	324.3	208.6	188.1	208.6	188.1	-	-	44.8	33.9	2.9
TENNESSEE	4 266.1	3 484.6	1 593.7	1 376.7	1 027.8	905.9	405.8	160.2	490.4	217.1	430.9
STATE GOVERNMENT. .	1 833.3	1 470.3	565.9	470.8	-	-	405.8	160.2	310.1	93.7	411.4
LOCAL GOVERNMENTS .	2 432.8	2 014.3	1 027.8	905.9	1 027.8	905.9	-	-	180.2	123.4	19.5
TEXAS	12 873.1	10 693.6	5 595.1	4 855.1	3 691.3	3 213.0	1 746.5	157.3	1 136.6	455.6	1 200.2
STATE GOVERNMENT. .	5 133.2	4 281.3	1 671.8	1 435.0	13.7	13.7	1 501.9	156.2	693.6	214.2	1 173.6
LOCAL GOVERNMENTS .	7 739.9	6 412.3	3 923.3	3 420.1	3 677.6	3 199.3	244.6	1.1	443.0	241.3	26.5
UTAH.	1 523.0	1 231.5	759.4	638.0	471.5	386.1	257.2	30.6	157.2	53.4	120.6
STATE GOVERNMENT. .	750.9	600.1	287.9	251.9	-	-	257.2	30.6	117.8	28.0	117.0
LOCAL GOVERNMENTS .	772.1	631.4	471.5	386.1	471.5	386.1	-	-	39.4	25.4	3.6
VERMONT	618.0	554.5	240.9	232.5	148.0	144.0	76.6	16.2	86.4	47.4	80.6
STATE GOVERNMENT. .	374.5	325.9	92.9	88.5	-	-	76.6	16.2	54.2	20.7	80.4
LOCAL GOVERNMENTS .	243.4	228.5	148.0	144.0	148.0	144.0	-	-	32.2	26.6	0.2
VIRGINIA.	5 671.8	4 616.0	2 182.9	2 000.6	1 519.4	1 365.8	539.9	123.5	742.0	261.9	515.0
STATE GOVERNMENT. .	2 456.3	1 941.6	663.5	634.8	-	-	539.9	123.5	614.5	193.8	272.6
LOCAL GOVERNMENTS .	3 215.5	2 674.5	1 519.4	1 365.8	1 519.4	1 365.8	-	-	127.5	68.1	242.3
WASHINGTON.	4 963.9	4 153.9	2 024.2	1 816.1	1 286.5	1 166.2	644.2	93.4	501.9	211.6	512.2
STATE GOVERNMENT. .	2 267.5	1 856.7	785.6	649.9	48.0	-	644.2	93.4	306.5	83.9	504.3
LOCAL GOVERNMENTS .	2 696.3	2 297.2	1 238.6	1 166.2	1 238.6	1 166.2	-	-	195.4	127.8	7.9
WEST VIRGINIA	2 013.6	1 633.2	742.9	664.6	553.4	486.5	147.0	42.5	361.0	157.0	187.8
STATE GOVERNMENT. .	1 129.2	891.3	189.6	178.1	-	-	147.0	42.5	341.7	140.8	187.0
LOCAL GOVERNMENTS .	884.4	741.9	553.4	486.5	553.4	486.5	-	-	19.4	16.2	0.8
WISCONSIN	6 147.0	5 473.2	2 496.2	2 331.1	1 572.3	1 482.9	822.3	101.6	612.1	365.2	940.5
STATE GOVERNMENT. .	2 088.7	1 851.4	718.4	662.0	-	-	616.8	101.6	223.1	87.9	538.7
LOCAL GOVERNMENTS .	4 058.3	3 621.8	1 777.8	1 669.1	1 572.3	1 482.9	205.5	-	389.0	277.3	401.8
WYOMING	638.3	479.8	258.6	219.3	170.8	140.6	77.5	10.4	112.2	35.6	26.7
STATE GOVERNMENT. .	283.7	193.5	68.0	60.5	-	-	57.6	10.4	92.7	21.2	25.7
LOCAL GOVERNMENTS .	354.7	286.4	190.7	158.7	170.8	140.6	19.9	-	19.5	14.4	1.0

Note: Because of rounding, detail may not add to totals. Local government amounts are subject to sampling variation; see text.

- Represents zero or rounds to zero.
Z Less than half the unit of measurement shown.

(Millions of dollars)

State and level of government	Health and hospitals		Police protection	Fire protection	Sewerage		Sanitation other than sewerage	Local parks and recreation	Financial administration	General control	Interest on general debt	All other general expenditure
	Total	Other than capital outlay			Total	Other than capital outlay						
SOUTH DAKOTA	54.3	31.0	19.3	5.6	5.3	2.7	2.9	9.3	19.7	20.3	15.9	144.1
STATE GOVERNMENT	46.1	23.0	5.7	-	-	-	-	-	9.7	11.1	10.5	86.1
LOCAL GOVERNMENTS	8.2	7.9	13.6	5.6	5.3	2.7	2.9	9.3	10.0	9.2	5.4	58.0
TENNESSEE	470.4	435.2	141.2	74.7	120.1	33.0	56.6	53.6	61.9	87.8	165.6	519.3
STATE GOVERNMENT	184.7	173.8	15.7	-	-	-	-	-	33.3	29.5	53.8	228.8
LOCAL GOVERNMENTS	285.7	261.4	125.5	74.7	120.1	33.0	56.6	53.6	28.6	58.3	111.8	290.5
TEXAS	1 271.3	1 150.3	449.0	197.5	360.3	115.1	114.4	162.1	215.7	245.2	498.6	1 426.9
STATE GOVERNMENT	687.0	605.1	79.9	-	-	-	-	-	79.0	54.8	113.3	580.1
LOCAL GOVERNMENTS	584.3	545.2	369.1	197.5	360.3	115.1	114.4	162.1	136.7	190.4	385.3	846.9
UTAH	85.6	79.6	41.9	16.1	22.2	7.2	8.2	17.5	28.0	31.4	25.7	209.3
STATE GOVERNMENT	62.1	56.6	8.8	-	-	-	-	-	16.4	9.9	7.1	124.0
LOCAL GOVERNMENTS	23.5	23.0	33.1	16.1	22.2	7.2	8.2	17.5	11.6	21.5	18.6	85.3
VERMONT	34.2	32.5	13.7	8.3	5.4	4.0	1.0	3.0	12.4	13.5	29.8	88.8
STATE GOVERNMENT	33.0	31.4	6.9	-	-	-	-	-	9.5	8.1	22.4	67.1
LOCAL GOVERNMENTS	1.2	1.2	6.8	8.3	5.4	4.0	1.0	3.0	2.9	5.4	7.4	21.7
VIRGINIA	473.3	428.6	197.7	82.8	192.1	58.0	57.4	68.8	116.7	117.5	184.8	740.7
STATE GOVERNMENT	365.0	340.0	52.2	-	-	-	-	-	55.5	38.7	45.1	349.2
LOCAL GOVERNMENTS	108.3	88.6	145.5	82.8	192.1	58.0	57.4	68.8	61.2	78.8	139.7	391.5
WASHINGTON	274.5	251.8	168.5	81.4	93.8	42.4	40.4	97.3	108.7	105.9	171.8	783.1
STATE GOVERNMENT	150.0	140.0	28.6	-	-	-	-	-	50.8	27.0	65.9	348.8
LOCAL GOVERNMENTS	124.5	111.8	139.9	81.4	93.8	42.4	40.4	97.3	58.0	78.9	105.9	434.3
WEST VIRGINIA	139.9	130.8	40.7	17.1	23.0	12.9	10.1	13.5	30.9	34.2	86.4	326.1
STATE GOVERNMENT	91.8	83.5	12.7	-	-	-	-	-	22.2	17.4	63.5	203.3
LOCAL GOVERNMENTS	48.1	47.3	27.9	17.1	23.0	12.9	10.1	13.5	8.7	16.8	22.9	122.8
WISCONSIN	441.5	403.1	203.1	89.2	159.4	73.5	46.2	103.7	87.5	129.9	169.6	667.9
STATE GOVERNMENT	168.0	146.4	14.7	-	-	-	-	-	48.2	31.5	74.0	272.1
LOCAL GOVERNMENTS	273.4	256.8	188.4	89.2	159.4	73.5	46.2	103.7	39.3	98.4	95.8	395.8
WYOMING	57.2	50.2	18.0	4.7	6.6	2.5	3.9	5.1	13.1	15.2	21.8	95.2
STATE GOVERNMENT	18.3	17.7	4.8	-	-	-	-	-	9.3	6.7	3.9	54.2
LOCAL GOVERNMENTS	38.9	32.5	13.1	4.7	6.6	2.5	3.9	5.1	3.8	8.4	17.9	41.0

Table 5. Governmental Expenditure for Capital Outlay, by Function and Level of Government: 1977

(Millions of dollars)

Function	Total capital outlay					Construction expenditure only				
	All governments	Federal Government	State and local governments			All governments	Federal Government	State and local governments		
			Total	State	Local			Total	State	Local
ALL FUNCTIONS.	74 893	29 997	44 896	16 885	28 011	43 497	7 429	36 068	13 712	22 355
NATIONAL DEFENSE AND INTERNATIONAL RELATIONS	21 541	21 541	-	-	-	2 291	2 291	-	-	-
OTHER, TOTAL	53 352	8 456	44 896	16 885	28 011	41 206	5 138	36 068	13 712	22 355
SPACE RESEARCH AND TECHNOLOGY. . . .	185	185	-	-	-	105	105	-	-	-
EDUCATION	9 237	2	9 235	2 914	6 321	6 460	-	6 460	1 974	4 486
LOCAL SCHOOLS.	5 982	-	5 982	209	5 772	4 291	-	4 291	186	4 105
INSTITUTIONS OF HIGHER EDUCATION .	2 861	-	2 861	2 313	548	1 837	-	1 837	1 458	379
OTHER.	394	2	392	391	1	332	-	332	331	1
HIGHWAYS	12 565	68	12 497	9 462	3 035	11 232	65	11 167	8 665	2 502
HEALTH AND HOSPITALS	2 667	596	2 071	1 086	985	2 042	374	1 668	891	777
SEWERAGE	4 208	-	4 208	-	4 208	4 009	-	4 009	-	4 009
LOCAL PARKS AND RECREATION	1 109	-	1 109	-	1 109	769	-	769	-	769
NATURAL RESOURCES.	6 529	5 276	1 253	953	301	4 611	3 817	794	545	249
HOUSING AND URBAN RENEWAL.	1 944	605	1 339	93	1 247	1 085	-	1 085	92	992
AIR TRANSPORTATION	905	318	587	106	481	713	200	513	95	418
WATER TRANSPORT AND TERMINALS. . . .	648	283	365	118	247	571	270	301	96	206
LOCAL UTILITIES.	6 107	-	6 107	-	6 107	5 286	-	5 286	-	5 286
WATER SUPPLY	2 302	-	2 302	-	2 302	2 029	-	2 029	-	2 029
ELECTRIC POWER	2 175	-	2 175	-	2 175	1 953	-	1 953	-	1 953
TRANSIT.	1 573	-	1 573	-	1 573	1 258	-	1 258	-	1 258
GAS SUPPLY	57	-	57	-	57	46	-	46	-	46
ALL OTHER.	7 246	1 122	6 124	2 154	3 970	4 324	307	4 017	1 355	2 662

Note: Because of rounding, detail may not add to totals. Local government amounts are estimates subject to sampling variation; see text.

- Represents zero or rounds to zero.

Table 6. Finances of State and Local Governmentally Administered Employee-Retirement Systems: 1977

(Millions of dollars)

Item	All systems	State-administered systems	Locally administered systems		
			Total	Municipal	Other
RECEIPTS, TOTAL	25 347	19 287	6 059	1 891	4 168
EMPLOYEE CONTRIBUTIONS.	5 233	4 223	1 011	674	337
GOVERNMENT CONTRIBUTIONS.	12 369	8 898	3 472	2 762	710
FROM STATE.	4 960	4 847	113	55	58
FROM LOCAL GOVERNMENTS.	7 410	4 051	3 359	2 707	652
EARNINGS ON INVESTMENTS	7 744	6 167	1 577	1 158	419
BENEFITS AND WITHDRAWAL PAYMENTS, TOTAL	9 559	6 930	2 629	2 091	538
BENEFITS.	8 455	6 048	2 407	1 935	472
WITHDRAWALS	1 104	882	222	156	66
CASH AND SECURITY HOLDINGS AT END OF FISCAL YEAR, TOTAL	123 481	94 913	28 569	21 414	7 291
CASH AND DEPOSITS	1 701	818	883	623	260
GOVERNMENTAL SECURITIES	15 816	10 096	5 720	4 791	930
FEDERAL	12 188	9 500	2 689	1 803	886
UNITED STATES TREASURY.	6 568	4 729	1 839	1 181	658
FEDERAL AGENCY.	5 620	4 770	850	622	228
STATE AND LOCAL	3 628	596	3 032	2 988	44
NONGOVERNMENTAL SECURITIES.	105 964	83 998	21 966	15 896	6 070
CORPORATE BONDS	56 847	45 364	11 482	8 051	3 431
CORPORATE STOCKS.	27 976	21 733	6 243	4 389	1 854
MORTGAGES	10 889	10 228	661	405	256
OTHER	10 251	6 673	3 578	3 051	527

Note: Because of rounding, detail may not add to totals.

Table 7. Per Capita Amounts of Financial Items for State and Local Governments, by State: 1977

State	General revenue							Direct general expenditure		
	Total	From Federal Government	All general revenue from own sources	Taxes			Charges and miscellaneous general revenue	Total	Capital outlay	Other than capital outlay
				Total	Property	Other				
UNITED STATES AVERAGE .	1 321.10	289.26	1 031.85	813.01	289.07	523.94	218.84	1 261.96	179.25	1 082.70
MEDIAN STATE.	1 261.57	293.34	982.44	748.60	249.38	466.14	221.22	1 201.13	192.80	1 013.81
ALABAMA	1 026.46	293.42	733.04	506.97	59.66	447.31	226.07	1 001.72	183.26	818.46
ALASKA.	3 730.00	766.10	2 963.75	2 295.71	1 317.75	977.96	668.05	3 275.33	883.76	2 391.57
ARIZONA	1 261.57	228.08	1 033.49	826.58	317.05	509.53	206.91	1 242.76	228.95	1 013.81
ARKANSAS.	931.80	271.34	660.46	494.08	109.53	384.55	166.38	876.20	153.50	722.70
CALIFORNIA.	1 658.83	339.02	1 319.80	1 088.92	457.85	631.07	230.89	1 485.76	144.50	1 341.26
COLORADO.	1 386.47	293.02	1 093.45	823.82	314.16	509.67	269.63	1 345.77	234.01	1 111.76
CONNECTICUT	1 279.24	228.50	1 050.74	885.10	412.53	472.57	165.63	1 151.64	125.66	1 025.98
DELAWARE.	1 468.93	343.45	1 125.48	829.36	134.09	695.27	296.12	1 458.25	238.16	1 220.27
DISTRICT OF COLUMBIA. . .	2 933.04	701.44	1 231.59	1 070.58	240.29	830.29	160.99	2 063.79	190.77	1 873.02
FLORIDA	1 072.66	210.56	862.09	628.16	211.03	417.13	233.93	1 098.85	209.70	889.16
GEORGIA	1 104.75	272.07	832.69	609.10	189.54	419.56	223.59	1 002.55	144.68	857.87
HAWAII.	1 757.85	512.64	1 245.22	974.39	166.72	807.67	270.83	1 915.24	389.86	1 525.38
IDAHO	1 145.97	315.52	830.44	639.36	204.63	434.73	191.08	1 140.80	234.83	905.98
ILLINOIS.	1 277.06	250.43	1 026.63	860.29	318.05	542.24	166.33	1 266.07	192.81	1 073.27
INDIANA	1 036.71	188.35	848.36	652.45	242.71	409.74	195.91	953.12	142.35	810.77
IOWA.	1 236.51	249.03	987.49	748.60	290.81	457.79	238.89	1 235.24	198.15	1 037.09
KANSAS.	1 193.13	234.82	958.31	727.56	299.22	428.34	230.75	1 193.25	217.24	976.01
KENTUCKY.	1 058.41	281.46	776.95	601.25	112.59	488.67	175.70	1 006.21	194.50	811.71
LOUISIANA	1 210.10	312.33	897.78	636.07	99.15	536.92	261.71	1 207.21	257.53	949.68
MAINE	1 174.40	367.89	806.51	658.12	237.85	420.27	148.39	1 119.76	187.58	932.18
MARYLAND.	1 440.01	296.89	1 143.13	891.97	265.46	626.50	251.16	1 452.77	271.02	1 181.75
MASSACHUSETTS	1 499.91	328.10	1 171.81	1 001.87	491.44	510.43	169.95	1 378.13	126.47	1 251.66
MICHIGAN.	1 444.29	311.21	1 133.08	878.17	331.89	546.29	254.90	1 389.78	167.18	1 222.60
MINNESOTA	1 497.26	311.02	1 186.24	906.10	271.02	635.08	280.14	1 459.92	240.92	1 219.00
MISSISSIPPI	1 035.79	293.34	742.44	527.46	116.22	411.24	214.98	1 017.84	192.52	825.32
MISSOURI.	1 014.43	243.02	771.41	608.93	193.10	415.83	162.48	942.21	145.81	796.40
MONTANA	1 414.19	407.85	1 006.34	765.66	361.83	403.83	240.68	1 409.03	295.91	1 113.13
NEBRASKA.	1 267.00	230.54	1 036.46	773.90	356.80	417.10	262.56	1 152.50	203.00	949.50
NEVADA.	1 495.22	276.40	1 218.82	892.24	285.59	606.65	326.58	1 469.80	237.20	1 232.60
NEW HAMPSHIRE	1 038.02	238.42	799.60	618.36	382.39	235.97	181.24	1 116.53	234.23	882.30
NEW JERSEY.	1 388.63	267.09	1 121.54	931.45	468.11	463.34	190.09	1 326.62	144.18	1 182.44
NEW MEXICO.	1 311.02	359.09	951.93	624.58	113.44	511.14	327.35	1 176.74	180.24	996.50
NEW YORK.	1 903.59	363.48	1 540.10	1 252.22	448.21	804.01	287.88	1 795.24	186.33	1 608.91
NORTH CAROLINA.	1 029.03	281.45	747.58	592.79	139.71	453.08	154.79	982.08	160.62	821.47
NORTH DAKOTA.	1 414.21	365.89	1 048.33	681.69	223.67	458.02	366.64	1 308.26	238.53	1 069.73
OHIO.	1 055.06	211.28	843.77	640.74	249.38	391.36	203.03	1 109.38	165.87	943.52
OKLAHOMA.	1 118.77	285.99	832.78	598.30	134.74	463.56	234.48	1 044.81	175.07	869.74
OREGON.	1 468.62	375.04	1 093.58	793.13	353.03	440.09	300.45	1 414.03	210.82	1 203.21
PENNSYLVANIA.	1 186.15	266.92	919.23	770.01	201.13	568.88	149.22	1 166.44	136.95	1 029.49
RHODE ISLAND.	1 351.84	369.39	982.44	792.82	326.68	466.14	189.62	1 283.06	134.74	1 148.33
SOUTH CAROLINA.	1 015.65	261.02	754.63	548.90	128.35	420.55	205.72	978.55	139.07	839.47
SOUTH DAKOTA.	1 190.78	317.71	873.07	629.35	306.87	322.48	243.72	1 180.45	239.46	940.99
TENNESSEE	999.12	255.49	743.63	564.09	141.38	422.71	179.54	992.34	181.77	810.56
TEXAS	1 065.56	212.50	853.07	637.44	232.65	404.78	215.63	1 003.36	169.88	833.48
UTAH.	1 191.74	327.92	863.83	652.18	190.58	461.60	211.65	1 201.14	229.92	971.22
VERMONT	1 426.95	420.06	1 006.88	810.10	330.66	479.44	196.78	1 279.41	131.47	1 147.93
VIRGINIA.	1 112.23	252.84	859.39	675.39	194.25	481.15	184.00	1 104.54	205.61	898.93
WASHINGTON.	1 469.68	348.26	1 121.42	821.22	255.45	565.76	300.21	1 356.99	221.42	1 135.58
WEST VIRGINIA	1 086.09	312.01	774.07	622.40	112.23	510.17	151.67	1 083.15	204.63	878.52
WISCONSIN	1 360.45	268.82	1 091.63	870.41	298.75	571.66	221.22	1 321.65	144.88	1 176.77
WYOMING	1 856.94	487.12	1 369.82	988.43	402.32	586.11	381.39	1 572.23	390.40	1 181.83

See footnotes at end of table.

Table 7. Per Capita Amounts of Financial Items for State and Local Governments, by State: 1977—Continued

	Direct general expenditure--Continued										
	Education								Highways		
				Local schools			Institutions of higher education	Other education			
State	Total	Capital outlay	Other than capital outlay	Total	Capital outlay	Other than capital outlay			Total	Capital outlay	Other than capital outlay
UNITED STATES AVERAGE .	475.22	42.69	432.53	329.79	27.65	302.14	121.13	24.30	106.80	57.77	49.03
MEDIAN STATE.	463.69	43.15	421.12	319.80	28.68	298.22	127.95	22.70	124.18	72.14	52.62
ALABAMA	394.28	45.38	348.90	221.33	22.46	198.87	133.25	39.70	118.00	72.14	45.86
ALASKA.	1 072.57	204.47	868.09	826.80	146.78	680.02	214.21	31.55	468.53	351.97	116.57
ARIZONA	561.14	76.79	484.35	365.87	57.08	308.79	177.80	17.48	124.19	78.65	45.53
ARKANSAS.	353.71	38.58	315.13	227.95	20.69	207.26	97.72	28.04	122.26	67.73	54.53
CALIFORNIA.	557.99	44.07	513.92	373.90	25.61	348.29	168.23	15.87	68.71	29.95	38.77
COLORADO.	605.96	74.38	531.58	392.35	50.29	342.06	197.79	15.83	127.56	74.93	52.63
CONNECTICUT	416.99	27.18	389.80	319.80	16.07	303.73	67.30	29.89	78.65	26.06	52.59
DELAWARE.	594.33	50.43	543.87	351.75	18.28	333.48	194.57	48.11	116.27	57.90	58.38
DISTRICT OF COLUMBIA. . .	466.40	47.82	418.58	393.53	47.66	345.88	72.87	-	76.53	30.75	45.78
FLORIDA	406.79	49.87	356.92	293.01	33.13	259.89	101.88	11.89	85.89	53.89	32.00
GEORGIA	368.56	34.24	334.32	257.68	24.45	233.22	90.39	20.49	94.44	55.51	38.92
HAWAII.	534.32	78.04	456.28	327.07	42.66	284.41	194.74	12.51	149.02	81.91	67.10
IDAHO	437.65	58.59	379.06	281.08	35.62	245.46	135.22	21.35	186.21	111.50	74.72
ILLINOIS.	476.40	39.34	437.06	339.31	26.03	313.28	115.82	21.27	124.82	76.13	48.69
INDIANA	429.01	45.50	383.51	291.74	36.25	255.49	119.88	17.39	93.05	54.43	38.62
IOWA.	520.91	27.01	493.90	349.57	17.16	332.40	149.70	21.65	180.80	93.92	86.88
KANSAS.	473.76	40.94	432.82	311.75	25.86	285.88	149.98	12.03	146.14	82.88	63.26
KENTUCKY.	393.23	53.06	340.17	240.89	30.91	209.98	115.60	36.75	132.09	85.43	46.66
LOUISIANA	400.48	41.29	359.19	274.43	25.12	249.31	98.87	27.18	168.80	115.52	53.28
MAINE	373.64	20.32	353.33	271.07	17.96	253.11	83.06	19.51	146.40	56.17	90.24
MARYLAND.	568.68	65.19	503.49	412.04	53.06	358.97	127.95	28.69	112.64	78.58	34.06
MASSACHUSETTS	451.76	34.71	417.05	362.94	19.62	343.32	61.68	27.14	89.28	37.28	52.00
MICHIGAN.	554.28	41.80	512.47	383.29	31.53	351.77	142.68	28.30	99.33	59.00	40.33
MINNESOTA	545.20	45.88	499.32	379.60	29.20	350.40	142.89	22.70	154.44	83.75	70.69
MISSISSIPPI	378.89	36.36	342.53	223.91	17.08	206.82	125.13	29.86	157.25	91.69	65.56
MISSOURI.	382.12	26.70	355.42	276.70	18.42	258.28	93.28	12.13	105.84	63.87	41.97
MONTANA	575.61	43.87	531.73	416.88	34.08	382.81	132.34	26.39	259.78	170.71	89.07
NEBRASKA.	489.37	41.96	447.41	347.01	27.95	319.06	126.26	16.09	166.71	97.16	69.55
NEVADA.	463.70	51.76	411.94	333.96	32.79	301.17	113.35	16.39	170.66	94.27	76.39
NEW HAMPSHIRE	398.05	42.26	355.79	265.84	16.69	249.15	114.55	17.65	174.80	88.11	86.69
NEW JERSEY.	474.25	22.32	451.93	351.74	16.21	335.53	80.51	42.00	76.70	28.31	48.39
NEW MEXICO.	540.21	60.46	479.75	361.73	42.56	319.18	156.74	21.74	125.81	61.56	64.25
NEW YORK.	538.02	31.38	506.65	405.35	13.91	391.44	95.64	37.04	82.14	31.53	50.61
NORTH CAROLINA.	437.54	43.16	394.38	284.32	28.68	255.64	135.21	18.01	92.91	55.49	37.41
NORTH DAKOTA.	494.22	40.75	453.46	299.56	19.98	279.58	171.60	23.06	228.88	135.72	93.17
OHIO.	454.97	33.85	421.12	334.80	20.70	314.11	107.12	13.05	87.27	43.76	43.51
OKLAHOMA.	417.04	47.82	369.21	261.50	33.38	228.12	133.93	21.60	110.70	53.90	56.79
OREGON.	583.62	69.01	514.62	383.97	43.61	340.35	177.10	22.56	110.50	51.46	59.05
PENNSYLVANIA.	415.68	34.69	380.99	312.15	29.24	282.91	60.95	42.58	98.52	47.08	51.44
RHODE ISLAND.	450.70	22.01	428.69	299.11	16.63	282.48	115.03	36.56	67.22	26.68	40.54
SOUTH CAROLINA.	397.92	39.42	358.50	246.97	25.97	220.99	114.80	36.15	62.42	26.19	36.23
SOUTH DAKOTA.	451.69	51.18	400.51	302.75	29.80	272.95	132.39	16.55	196.05	91.12	104.93
TENNESSEE	370.71	50.48	320.23	239.07	28.35	210.72	94.38	37.26	114.07	63.58	50.50
TEXAS	436.09	57.67	378.42	287.71	37.28	250.43	136.12	12.26	88.59	53.08	35.51
UTAH.	598.87	95.70	503.17	371.84	67.32	304.52	202.87	24.16	123.99	81.84	42.15
VERMONT	498.80	17.42	481.38	306.49	8.27	298.23	158.67	33.63	178.87	80.83	98.04
VIRGINIA.	425.10	35.51	389.59	295.90	29.93	265.97	105.15	24.06	144.49	93.50	50.99
WASHINGTON.	553.35	56.88	496.47	351.70	32.89	318.81	176.12	25.53	137.22	79.36	57.86
WEST VIRGINIA	399.64	42.16	357.48	297.66	35.97	261.69	79.10	22.87	194.21	109.74	84.47
WISCONSIN	536.70	35.49	501.21	338.06	19.22	318.84	176.80	21.85	131.61	53.10	78.51
WYOMING	637.03	96.96	540.07	420.69	74.31	346.39	190.83	25.50	276.44	188.73	87.71

See footnotes at end of table.

131

State	Public welfare	Health and hospitals			Police protection	Fire protection	Sewerage			Sanitation other than sewerage
		Total	Capital outlay	Other than capital outlay			Total	Capital outlay	Other than capital outlay	
UNITED STATES AVERAGE .	159.77	104.20	9.57	94.63	47.98	19.85	30.22	19.45	10.77	10.80
MEDIAN STATE.	124.03	98.24	8.71	84.17	40.34	15.96	25.64	18.27	8.96	8.86
ALABAMA	101.87	130.58	18.70	111.88	27.71	12.33	22.29	16.21	6.08	8.79
ALASKA.	140.77	111.18	8.88	102.30	86.09	39.51	83.64	62.64	21.00	28.97
ARIZONA	55.31	88.64	5.46	83.18	64.50	18.42	25.09	18.57	6.51	16.86
ARKANSAS.	110.64	82.76	10.77	72.00	24.97	9.78	10.55	6.14	4.41	5.99
CALIFORNIA.	236.51	107.26	4.36	102.90	65.20	29.81	28.85	18.31	10.55	8.70
COLORADO.	123.64	102.26	6.06	96.20	48.61	24.77	32.58	18.88	13.70	6.13
CONNECTICUT	140.78	71.41	9.48	61.93	45.17	26.75	35.34	22.83	12.51	8.86
DELAWARE.	127.20	74.25	6.38	67.87	48.23	10.50	68.65	45.97	22.67	10.14
DISTRICT OF COLUMBIA. . .	384.17	171.57	3.09	168.49	149.94	49.07	86.47	64.01	22.46	35.37
FLORIDA	57.77	121.40	8.67	112.74	56.50	19.44	51.54	38.54	13.00	16.56
GEORGIA	102.23	151.30	8.21	143.09	35.33	13.64	16.82	9.27	7.55	11.25
HAWAII.	211.70	119.41	13.13	106.27	53.98	27.76	62.86	52.77	10.09	13.96
IDAHO	91.60	83.00	6.01	77.00	38.12	10.86	16.46	10.24	6.22	7.89
ILLINOIS.	185.17	86.49	15.84	70.65	58.36	22.05	35.07	18.74	16.33	11.89
INDIANA	89.07	98.62	7.14	91.48	31.63	14.74	23.78	11.52	12.26	4.52
IOWA.	125.56	102.40	9.23	93.18	32.50	11.25	32.97	23.72	9.25	6.71
KANSAS.	127.48	110.86	31.40	79.46	41.60	15.11	21.90	12.56	9.34	13.81
KENTUCKY.	136.39	59.18	4.41	54.77	31.68	10.75	16.01	8.22	7.78	6.75
LOUISIANA	112.78	142.08	20.21	121.87	46.48	13.60	17.48	9.56	7.92	12.19
MAINE	156.85	45.38	4.27	41.11	28.38	19.08	81.55	75.02	6.53	4.31
MARYLAND.	141.66	101.10	10.69	90.41	54.72	23.77	42.30	27.56	14.74	15.55
MASSACHUSETTS	237.14	100.96	6.65	94.31	54.58	39.10	19.42	13.48	5.94	11.53
MICHIGAN.	218.65	116.57	8.13	108.44	54.89	20.04	33.53	18.28	15.25	9.60
MINNESOTA	194.47	118.24	8.89	109.35	36.87	13.45	48.38	34.87	13.51	5.14
MISSISSIPPI	97.94	120.66	10.90	109.76	27.08	9.53	7.71	3.68	4.03	8.52
MISSOURI.	93.58	86.95	6.90	80.05	40.19	14.84	26.19	18.70	7.49	5.73
MONTANA	103.35	72.50	8.89	63.60	34.31	11.28	16.52	8.28	8.24	7.25
NEBRASKA.	90.74	98.25	8.98	89.26	32.07	12.53	24.70	17.24	7.46	6.24
NEVADA.	91.34	161.37	17.37	144.00	83.57	37.69	17.19	6.32	10.88	3.58
NEW HAMPSHIRE	133.36	75.39	25.49	49.91	35.29	20.87	36.76	28.18	8.58	5.26
NEW JERSEY.	169.10	75.28	8.05	67.23	58.82	22.53	38.37	26.01	12.36	11.05
NEW MEXICO.	91.56	90.66	10.39	80.27	49.82	15.96	15.14	10.11	5.03	11.16
NEW YORK.	296.87	155.59	10.74	144.85	72.33	26.69	38.53	28.83	9.70	22.69
NORTH CAROLINA.	78.27	95.33	11.16	84.18	32.39	10.33	16.96	9.85	7.11	9.69
NORTH DAKOTA.	104.12	47.52	3.56	43.96	28.24	9.08	20.35	16.73	3.62	7.12
OHIO.	124.04	99.81	18.59	81.22	40.35	19.93	26.41	12.09	14.32	8.86
OKLAHOMA.	128.25	86.67	10.32	76.35	31.39	15.05	24.88	20.75	4.13	8.24
OREGON.	147.74	80.74	2.38	78.36	47.94	33.27	45.39	28.43	16.96	2.52
PENNSYLVANIA.	200.86	78.23	5.04	73.19	42.76	11.96	23.64	11.11	12.53	9.14
RHODE ISLAND.	227.15	102.70	12.81	89.90	41.26	30.91	62.27	45.27	17.00	8.39
SOUTH CAROLINA.	84.20	124.51	8.04	116.47	27.78	8.00	13.21	7.57	5.64	9.12
SOUTH DAKOTA.	102.14	78.82	33.88	44.94	27.98	8.15	7.67	3.73	3.94	4.15
TENNESSEE	100.23	109.42	8.18	101.24	32.84	17.37	27.93	20.26	7.67	13.16
TEXAS	93.54	99.09	9.43	89.66	35.00	15.40	28.08	19.12	8.97	8.92
UTAH.	95.11	67.48	4.74	62.75	33.02	12.67	17.50	11.83	5.67	6.49
VERMONT	166.80	70.77	3.39	67.38	28.42	17.15	11.23	2.92	8.31	1.97
VIRGINIA.	100.29	92.18	8.71	83.47	38.51	16.13	37.42	26.12	11.29	11.18
WASHINGTON.	140.02	75.05	6.22	68.83	46.05	22.26	25.64	14.04	11.60	11.06
WEST VIRGINIA	101.02	75.24	4.88	70.36	21.88	9.19	12.40	5.44	6.96	5.42
WISCONSIN	202.21	94.92	8.24	86.67	43.67	19.19	34.27	18.47	15.80	9.93
WYOMING	65.84	140.93	17.38	123.54	44.23	11.58	16.31	10.22	6.09	9.50

See footnotes at end of table.

State	Direct general expenditure--Continued					Debt outstanding at end of fiscal year		Cash and security holdings at end of fiscal year	
	Local parks and recreation	Financial adminis- tration	General control	Interest on general debt	All other general expendi- ture	Total	Long-term only	Insurance trust systems	Other than insurance trust systems
UNITED STATES AVERAGE .	17.89	20.49	28.96	52.67	187.11	1 190.46	1 128.59	617.86	639.60
MEDIAN STATE.	13.51	20.01	27.95	38.52	168.32	1 017.40	952.70	433.76	579.25
ALABAMA	13.28	11.65	18.04	36.16	106.73	848.66	820.82	384.93	402.84
ALASKA.	30.17	88.78	136.37	164.17	824.57	5 651.12	5 574.79	1 126.54	3 752.54
ARIZONA	24.87	26.95	37.55	30.91	168.33	1 241.63	1 233.75	706.79	692.15
ARKANSAS.	5.21	17.80	13.74	22.86	95.91	547.15	522.16	271.97	298.13
CALIFORNIA.	28.94	28.55	41.69	31.39	252.14	965.38	948.26	1 061.68	781.95
COLORADO.	30.62	27.75	39.31	29.89	146.63	838.11	811.45	710.46	644.95
CONNECTICUT	13.02	18.33	25.23	75.42	195.70	1 638.72	1 498.30	475.26	520.35
DELAWARE.	19.79	27.16	41.43	84.00	236.32	1 978.85	1 970.25	249.14	604.39
DISTRICT OF COLUMBIA. . .	33.51	30.09	67.41	119.15	394.10	3 672.99	3 440.96	118.12	678.04
FLORIDA	22.96	20.02	32.94	38.45	168.59	964.98	952.71	352.40	564.01
GEORGIA	10.54	17.36	22.87	32.11	126.11	825.80	803.20	411.53	429.33
HAWAII.	47.26	28.61	50.58	101.15	514.63	2 022.98	1 992.22	969.89	655.73
IDAHO	10.31	24.80	25.49	12.76	195.64	344.63	319.85	324.27	536.17
ILLINOIS.	25.18	15.40	29.84	43.57	151.84	1 042.95	940.27	543.33	515.38
INDIANA	9.91	15.10	19.51	23.19	100.98	520.00	504.90	201.48	496.83
IOWA.	14.94	22.80	27.56	18.86	137.97	501.73	494.31	364.26	506.73
KANSAS.	12.55	19.13	28.41	30.87	151.63	972.63	934.92	321.75	595.26
KENTUCKY.	7.00	11.23	17.26	49.89	134.76	1 226.28	1 210.89	356.10	626.27
LOUISIANA	16.65	17.78	24.32	49.60	184.97	1 275.79	1 263.52	518.87	579.26
MAINE	11.99	16.11	24.83	43.62	167.62	948.27	863.05	209.91	512.91
MARYLAND.	34.60	27.33	30.68	65.08	234.65	1 557.04	1 523.04	597.97	444.34
MASSACHUSETTS	12.06	19.48	29.60	81.75	231.47	1 573.00	1 375.87	315.67	492.83
MICHIGAN.	16.69	19.01	35.23	47.73	164.23	1 017.40	986.57	639.74	504.48
MINNESOTA	26.02	22.35	31.97	53.36	210.05	1 278.89	1 231.27	583.40	859.28
MISSISSIPPI	5.49	12.72	18.21	34.27	139.55	792.64	770.01	288.57	327.16
MISSOURI.	16.75	12.14	19.77	25.83	112.30	644.17	632.35	433.76	436.01
MONTANA	10.74	35.92	35.78	23.21	222.80	697.48	686.70	498.29	820.18
NEBRASKA.	14.25	20.66	26.98	25.64	144.36	2 020.67	1 938.49	186.61	915.25
NEVADA.	44.50	40.01	56.83	49.69	249.66	1 140.54	1 135.65	939.03	796.72
NEW HAMPSHIRE	6.49	15.45	21.79	41.58	151.44	853.56	803.22	323.44	243.50
NEW JERSEY.	20.66	20.02	35.14	63.76	260.95	1 218.52	1 122.46	631.38	578.75
NEW MEXICO.	14.75	30.74	32.46	24.75	133.72	744.67	739.43	452.94	1 383.24
NEW YORK.	20.52	22.83	33.45	158.51	327.05	2 573.38	2 344.56	1 375.62	1 027.66
NORTH CAROLINA.	9.77	16.15	20.50	21.72	140.52	487.80	454.98	554.30	403.29
NORTH DAKOTA.	9.73	21.88	21.85	26.34	288.94	640.34	637.20	232.77	1 026.83
OHIO.	13.51	17.86	22.29	37.90	156.19	833.19	723.51	727.52	391.86
OKLAHOMA.	14.68	13.78	20.73	34.60	139.81	799.32	785.54	217.50	637.12
OREGON.	17.79	40.87	40.12	64.75	198.76	1 715.45	1 684.02	637.67	1 577.30
PENNSYLVANIA.	11.17	18.28	28.27	71.34	156.59	1 419.58	1 350.30	550.58	424.43
RHODE ISLAND.	9.81	22.61	28.38	49.78	181.88	1 188.04	1 078.85	446.98	587.50
SOUTH CAROLINA.	5.68	13.91	17.05	31.38	183.37	806.41	785.45	471.66	407.28
SOUTH DAKOTA.	13.49	28.64	29.45	23.11	209.11	518.95	497.47	234.54	835.70
TENNESSEE	12.47	14.39	20.41	38.53	120.80	1 115.41	1 056.78	319.35	545.54
TEXAS	12.64	16.81	19.11	38.86	111.22	1 017.98	999.95	384.59	803.98
UTAH.	13.79	22.10	24.79	20.25	165.07	541.32	540.75	383.60	470.83
VERMONT	6.28	25.70	27.96	61.65	183.81	1 254.69	1 197.60	374.33	688.48
VIRGINIA.	13.39	22.74	22.89	35.99	144.24	838.69	780.10	306.15	506.53
WASHINGTON.	26.61	29.73	28.96	46.97	214.07	2 302.11	2 278.20	739.64	1 212.68
WEST VIRGINIA	7.24	16.61	18.40	46.50	175.41	1 042.14	1 021.85	423.24	668.13
WISCONSIN	22.30	18.81	27.93	36.51	143.60	846.30	831.01	790.45	543.05
WYOMING	12.58	32.23	37.40	53.74	234.42	1 147.84	1 147.83	567.73	1 562.51

Note: Because of rounding, detail may not add to totals. These amounts are subject to sampling variation; see text.

- Represents zero or rounds to zero.

Table 8. Relation of State and Local Government Financial Items to State Personal Income, by State: 1977

| State | General revenue per $1,000 of personal income | | | | | | Direct general expenditure per $1,000 of personal income | | | | | |
| | Total | From Federal Government | All State and local general revenue sources | Taxes | | Charges and miscellaneous general revenue | All general expenditure | Education | | Highways | Public welfare | Health and hospitals |
				Total	Property only			Total	Local schools only			
UNITED STATES AVERAGE .	208.08	45.56	162.52	128.05	45.53	34.47	198.76	74.85	51.94	16.82	25.16	16.41
MEDIAN STATE.	209.86	50.42	158.62	120.12	38.93	36.88	204.89	77.15	51.42	21.65	20.03	15.58
ALABAMA	202.40	57.86	144.54	99.96	11.76	44.58	197.52	77.74	43.64	23.27	20.09	25.75
ALASKA.	381.53	78.36	303.15	234.82	134.79	68.33	335.02	109.71	84.57	47.92	14.40	11.37
ARIZONA	220.00	39.77	180.23	144.15	55.29	36.08	216.72	97.86	63.80	21.66	9.64	15.46
ARKANSAS.	191.95	55.89	136.05	101.78	22.56	34.27	180.49	72.86	46.96	25.19	22.79	17.05
CALIFORNIA.	236.02	48.24	187.78	154.93	65.14	32.85	211.40	79.39	53.20	9.78	33.65	15.26
COLORADO.	218.31	46.14	172.17	129.72	49.47	42.45	211.90	95.41	61.78	20.09	19.47	16.10
CONNECTICUT	173.40	30.97	142.43	119.97	55.92	22.45	156.10	56.52	43.35	10.66	19.08	9.68
DELAWARE.	208.92	48.85	160.08	117.96	19.07	42.12	207.40	84.53	50.03	16.54	18.09	10.56
DISTRICT OF COLUMBIA. . .	357.44	207.35	150.09	130.47	29.28	19.62	251.50	56.84	47.96	9.33	46.82	20.91
FLORIDA	178.85	35.11	143.74	104.74	35.19	39.01	183.22	67.83	48.86	14.32	9.63	20.24
GEORGIA	202.23	49.80	152.43	111.50	34.70	40.93	183.52	67.47	47.17	17.29	18.71	27.70
HAWAII.	253.84	74.03	179.81	140.70	24.07	39.11	276.56	77.16	47.23	21.52	30.57	17.24
IDAHO	209.67	57.73	151.94	116.98	37.44	34.96	208.73	80.07	51.43	34.07	16.76	15.19
ILLINOIS.	174.06	34.13	139.93	117.26	43.35	22.67	172.56	64.93	46.25	17.01	25.24	11.79
INDIANA	167.50	30.43	137.06	105.41	39.21	31.65	153.99	69.31	47.14	15.03	14.39	15.93
IOWA.	198.62	40.00	158.62	120.25	46.71	38.37	198.42	83.67	56.15	29.04	20.17	16.45
KANSAS.	185.70	36.55	149.15	113.24	46.57	35.91	185.71	73.73	48.52	22.74	19.84	17.25
KENTUCKY.	198.49	52.78	145.71	112.76	21.11	32.95	188.70	73.75	45.18	24.77	25.58	11.10
LOUISIANA	228.53	58.98	169.55	120.13	18.72	49.42	227.99	75.63	51.83	31.88	21.30	26.83
MAINE	221.95	69.53	152.42	124.38	44.95	28.04	211.63	70.62	51.23	27.67	29.64	8.58
MARYLAND.	209.03	43.10	165.93	129.47	38.53	36.46	210.88	82.55	59.81	16.35	20.56	14.68
MASSACHUSETTS	226.60	49.57	177.03	151.36	74.25	25.67	208.20	68.25	54.83	13.49	35.83	15.25
MICHIGAN.	214.44	46.21	168.23	130.39	49.28	37.85	206.35	82.30	56.91	14.75	32.46	17.31
MINNESOTA	242.77	50.43	192.34	146.92	43.94	45.42	236.72	88.40	61.55	25.04	31.53	19.17
MISSISSIPPI	232.06	65.72	166.34	118.18	26.04	48.17	228.04	84.89	50.17	35.23	21.94	27.03
MISSOURI.	170.92	40.95	129.98	102.60	32.54	27.38	158.75	64.38	46.62	17.83	15.77	14.65
MONTANA	251.27	72.47	178.81	136.04	64.29	42.76	250.36	102.27	74.07	46.16	18.36	12.88
NEBRASKA.	209.29	38.08	171.21	127.84	58.94	43.37	190.38	80.84	57.32	27.54	14.99	16.23
NEVADA.	216.68	40.05	176.63	129.30	41.39	47.33	213.00	67.20	48.40	24.73	13.24	23.39
NEW HAMPSHIRE	178.32	40.96	137.37	106.23	65.69	31.14	191.81	68.38	45.67	30.03	22.91	12.95
NEW JERSEY.	187.94	36.15	151.79	126.06	63.36	25.73	179.55	64.19	47.60	10.38	22.89	10.19
NEW MEXICO.	250.94	68.73	182.21	119.55	21.71	62.66	225.24	103.40	69.24	24.08	17.53	17.35
NEW YORK.	268.82	51.33	217.49	176.83	63.30	40.65	253.52	75.98	57.24	11.60	41.92	21.97
NORTH CAROLINA.	190.65	52.14	138.51	109.83	25.88	28.68	181.95	81.06	52.68	17.21	14.50	17.66
NORTH DAKOTA.	245.54	63.53	182.01	118.36	38.83	63.66	227.15	85.81	52.01	39.74	18.08	8.25
OHIO.	164.72	32.99	131.73	100.04	38.93	31.70	173.20	71.03	52.27	13.63	19.37	15.58
OKLAHOMA.	199.19	50.92	148.27	106.53	23.99	41.75	186.03	74.25	46.56	19.71	22.83	15.43
OREGON.	239.33	61.12	178.21	129.25	57.53	48.96	230.43	95.11	62.57	18.01	24.08	13.16
PENNSYLVANIA.	183.00	41.18	141.82	118.80	31.03	23.02	179.96	64.13	48.16	15.20	30.99	12.07
RHODE ISLAND.	215.47	58.88	156.59	126.37	52.07	30.22	204.51	71.84	47.68	10.71	36.21	16.37
SOUTH CAROLINA.	199.22	51.20	148.02	107.67	25.18	40.35	191.95	78.05	48.44	12.24	16.52	24.42
SOUTH DAKOTA.	233.61	62.33	171.28	123.47	60.20	47.81	231.59	88.61	59.40	38.46	20.04	15.46
TENNESSEE	190.00	48.59	141.42	107.27	26.89	34.14	188.71	70.50	45.46	21.69	19.06	20.81
TEXAS	176.55	35.21	141.34	105.61	38.55	35.73	166.24	72.25	47.67	14.68	15.50	16.42
UTAH.	230.00	63.29	166.72	125.87	36.78	40.85	231.82	115.58	71.76	23.93	18.36	13.02
VERMONT	267.45	78.73	188.72	151.84	61.97	36.88	239.80	93.49	57.45	33.52	31.26	13.26
VIRGINIA.	178.99	40.69	138.30	108.69	31.26	29.61	177.76	68.41	47.62	23.25	16.14	14.83
WASHINGTON.	218.82	51.85	166.97	122.27	38.03	44.70	202.04	82.39	52.36	20.43	20.85	11.17
WEST VIRGINIA	203.10	58.35	144.75	116.39	20.99	28.36	202.55	74.73	55.66	36.32	18.89	14.07
WISCONSIN	224.46	44.35	180.11	143.61	49.29	36.50	218.06	88.55	55.78	21.71	33.36	15.66
WYOMING	290.75	76.27	214.48	154.76	62.99	59.72	246.17	99.74	65.87	43.28	10.31	22.07

Note: Because of rounding, detail may not add to totals. These data are estimates subject to sampling variation; see text.

134

Table 9. Population and Personal Income, by State: 1977

State	Total population, excluding Armed Forces overseas (thousands)		Personal income calendar year 1976[2]		State	Total population, excluding Armed Forces overseas (thousands)		Personal income calendar year 1976[2]	
	July 1, 1977 (provisional estimates)[1]	July 1, 1976 (provisional estimates)[1]	Amount (millions of dollars)	Per capita		July 1, 1977 (provisional estimates)[1]	July 1, 1976 (provisional estimates)[1]	Amount (millions of dollars)	Per capita
ALL STATES.	216 332	214 659	1 373 511	6 399	MISSOURI . . .	4 801	4 778	28 494	5 963
					MONTANA. . . .	761	753	4 283	5 688
ALABAMA	3 690	3 665	18 714	5 106	NEBRASKA . . .	1 561	1 553	9 450	6 085
ALASKA.	407	382	3 979	10 416	NEVADA	633	610	4 368	7 161
ARIZONA	2 296	2 270	13 166	5 800	NEW HAMPSHIRE.	849	822	4 942	6 012
ARKANSAS.	2 144	2 190	10 408	4 753					
CALIFORNIA. . . .	21 896	21 520	153 892	7 151					
					NEW JERSEY . .	7 329	7 336	54 152	7 382
COLORADO.	2 619	2 583	16 633	6 439	NEW MEXICO . .	1 190	1 168	6 217	5 323
CONNECTICUT . . .	3 108	3 117	22 929	7 356	NEW YORK . . .	17 924	18 084	126 925	7 019
DELAWARE.	582	582	4 092	7 031	NORTH CAROLINA	5 525	5 469	29 821	5 453
DISTRICT OF COLUMBIA.	690	702	5 662	8 067	NORTH DAKOTA .	653	643	3 761	5 849
FLORIDA	8 452	8 421	50 690	6 019					
					OHIO	10 701	10 690	68 541	6 412
					OKLAHOMA . . .	2 811	2 766	15 788	5 708
GEORGIA	5 048	4 970	27 576	5 548	OREGON	2 376	2 329	14 580	6 260
HAWAII.	895	887	6 198	6 988	PENNSYLVANIA .	11 785	11 862	76 385	6 439
IDAHO	857	831	4 684	5 637	RHODE ISLAND .	935	927	5 866	6 328
ILLINOIS.	11 245	11 229	82 503	7 347					
INDIANA	5 330	5 302	32 990	6 222					
					SOUTH CAROLINA	2 876	2 848	14 662	5 148
IOWA.	2 879	2 870	17 923	6 245	SOUTH DAKOTA .	689	686	3 512	5 119
KANSAS.	2 326	2 310	14 945	6 470	TENNESSEE. . .	4 299	4 214	22 606	5 364
KENTUCKY.	3 458	3 428	18 439	5 379	TEXAS.	12 830	12 487	77 436	6 201
LOUISIANA	3 921	3 841	20 762	5 405	UTAH	1 268	1 228	6 570	5 350
MAINE	1 085	1 070	5 741	5 365					
					VERMONT. . . .	483	476	2 577	5 414
MARYLAND.	4 139	4 144	28 514	6 881	VIRGINIA . . .	5 135	5 032	31 908	6 341
MASSACHUSETTS . .	5 782	5 809	38 272	6 588	WASHINGTON . .	3 658	3 612	24 569	6 802
MICHIGAN.	9 129	9 104	61 485	6 754	WEST VIRGINIA.	1 859	1 821	9 941	5 459
MINNESOTA	3 975	3 965	24 515	6 183	WISCONSIN. . .	4 651	4 609	28 190	6 116
MISSISSIPPI . . .	2 389	2 354	10 663	4 530	WYOMING. . . .	406	390	2 593	6 649

[1]Bureau of the Census, Current Population Reports, series P-25, No. 727, January 1978.
[2]U.S. Department of Commerce, Survey of Current Business, August 1977.

B — STATE GOVERNMENT FINANCES

Three tables are presented on State government finances following the introduction to this section. Table 1 shows summary data. Table 2 shows per-capita data for comparative purposes, and, as in the previous section, Table 3 shows key aspects of State government finances per $1000 of personal income. This gives a basis for comparing effort levels, although the user needs to be reminded again that comparisons are made difficult for State finances because local governmental finances and functions vary so widely from State to State.

Revenue of State governments from all sources totaled $204.5 billion in fiscal 1977.[1] State government expenditure amounted, to $191.2 billion.

Total revenue includes gross sales of liquor stores operated by 17 States, and contributions and investment earnings received by employee-retirement, unemployment compensation, and other insurance trust systems of State governments. Correspondingly, total expenditure includes gross amounts of purchases and other expenditures by State liquor stores, and payments of benefits and withdrawals by the State insurance trust systems.

State borrowing amounted to $11.1 billion during fiscal 1977 and debt redemption totaled $6.9 billion. State debt rose to a new high of $90.2 billion at the end of the fiscal year. Short-term debt decreased from $6.0 billion to $3.0 billion or 49.8 percent.

The data on cash and security holdings indicate an increase of $18.5 billion in assets from the prior year. Holdings of employee-retirement systems rose $9.1 billion. Unemployment compensation funds amounted to $5.0 billion.

136   General Revenue

State general revenue totaled $169.9 billion in fiscal 1977. Taxes provided $101.1 billion, or 59.5 percent of the 1977 total of State general revenue.

Intergovernmental revenue totaled $48.7 billion.

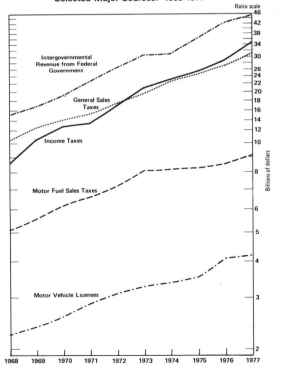

Figure 1. **Trends in State General Revenue From Selected Major Sources: 1968-1977**

[1]Fiscal 1977 data herein are for the State fiscal years ended on June 30, 1977, except for 4 States with other closing dates: Alabama and Michigan, September 30; New York, March 31; and Texas, August 31.

The 1977 figures include $2.3 billion in State receipts from the Federal General Revenue Sharing program.

State tax revenue was up 13.3 percent in 1977 from the 1976 total. General sales and gross receipts taxes provided $30.9 billion. The next ranking sales tax was the tax on motor fuel, which produced $9.1 billion. Tobacco sales tax collections were $3.5 billion in fiscal 1977. Sales taxes on public utilities totaled $2.4 billion. Altogether, general and selective sales and gross receipts taxes were up $5.0 billion to $52.4 billion, or more than one-half of the total collected from all State tax sources.

Motor vehicle license taxes produced $4.2 billion in 1977. This category includes truck mileage and weight taxes, and other motor carrier taxes except those measured by gross receipts, net income, or assessed valuation.

The yield from individual income taxes (imposed by 44 States) totaled $25.5 billion, up 18.9 percent from the 1976 figure. Corporation net income taxes amounted to $9.2 billion in 1977, or 26.1 percent more than in the previous year.

There were 13 State lotteries in operation during fiscal year 1977 providing $1,191.6 million gross revenue as indicated in Table O (in millions of dollars).

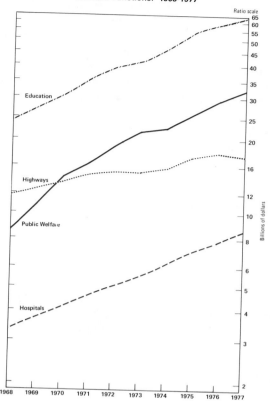

Figure 2. **Trends in State General Expenditure for Selected Functions: 1968-1977**

General Expenditure

State general expenditure amounted to $166.0 billion in fiscal 1977, or 8.0 percent more than in 1976.

Of the 1977 total, education accounted for a larger fraction of State spending than any other function. In 1977, the States spent $64.0 billion for education, or 7.4 percent more than in 1976.

State fiscal aid to local governments for support of

State Lotteries	Gross revenue	Disposition of funds		
		Prizes	Administration and other	Proceeds available for other purposes
Connecticut..	46.5	17.2	2.5	26.8
Delaware.....	6.3	3.1	2.2	1.1
Illinois.....	110.6	49.7	8.6	52.2
Maine........	6.4	2.9	2.0	1.6
Maryland.....	166.0	84.7	13.3	68.0
Massachusetts	148.5	67.8	14.1	66.6
Michigan.....	255.5	117.8	27.5	110.3
New Hampshire	7.6	3.2	1.9	2.5
New Jersey...	187.1	95.9	13.3	77.9
New York[1]....	31.8	28.6	8.6	-
Ohio........	105.8	29.0	11.2	60.9
Pennsylvania.	100.7	31.4	15.3	54.0
Rhode Island.	18.8	8.4	2.0	8.3

[1]Includes operations from August 1976.

137

public schools amounted to $37.0 billion in 1977, as compared with $34.1 billion in 1976. Expenditure for State institutions of higher education totaled $21.2 billion in 1977. This amount includes $2.5 billion for operation of auxiliary enterprises, such as dormitories and dining halls. State revenue from charges of these activities amounted to $2.8 billion. Amounts for education do not include expenditure for university-operated hospitals serving the public (classified under hospitals) or for agricultural experiment stations and extension services (classified under natural resources).

Expenditure for public welfare totaled $32.8 billion, an increase of $3.1 billion from 1976. This was largely accounted for by a 14.3 percent increase of medical vendor payments, from $11.0 billion in fiscal 1976 to $12.6 billion in 1977.

Some States supplement the Federal minimum grants with intergovernmental payments to the Federal Government or give supplemental checks directly to persons qualifying for these aid programs. State transfers to local governments for welfare services total $8.8 billion. However, wide variation exists among the States as to which unit of government provides particular welfare services.

State expenditure for highways in 1977 amount to $17.5 billion, or 3.3 percent less than in the previous year. About $3.6 billion was paid to local governments for highway purposes. Of the other $13.9 billion, $13.2 billion was for regular State highway facilities and the remainder was for toll roads and bridges (generally administered by semiautonomous agencies of the State governments).

Most direct expenditure by the States for highways consists of capital outlay-mainly construction but also involving the purchase of land and equipment. Capital expenditure for regular highway facilities decreased $1.5 billion from the previous year to $9.1 billion in fiscal 1977. Capital outlay for State toll highway facilities amounted to $291 million. Current spending for the operation of State toll facilities amounted to $392 million in 1977. Revenue from toll charges produced $1.0 billion.

Spending for hospitals, the fourth major State function, rose 11.8 percent to total $8.7 billion in 1977.

Expenditure by Character and Object

Total State spending for personal services was $35.8 billion, or 18.7 percent of all State expenditure in 1977. Personal service costs are mainly for "current operation," but include also some amounts for force-account construction.

Table P presents a summary of State expenditure by character and object.

Liquor Store Finances

Sales revenue of liquor stores which are operated by 17 State governments totaled $2.2 billion in 1977,

(P)

Item	1976-77 amount (millions of dollars)	Percent of total	Percent increase or decrease (-) from 1975-76
Total.........	191,238	100.0	5.1
Intergovernmental expenditure........	62,470	32.7	8.0
Direct expenditure...	128,768	67.3	4.6
Current operation..	75,857	39.7	11.3
Capital outlay.....	16,793	8.8	-6.7
Construction.....	13,620	7.1	-10.9
Purchase of land and existing structures......	1,696	0.9	33.1
Equipment........	1,477	0.8	1.9
Assistance and subsidies.........	7,556	4.0	3.6
Interest on debt...	5,136	2.7	24.1
Insurance benefits and repayments....	23,426	12.2	-8.0

138

and liquor stores expenditure amounted to $1.8 billion.

Insurance Trust Finances

Every State operates a system of unemployment insurance and one or more public-employee retirement systems. Most of the States also administer workmen's compensation systems, and a few have other social insurance systems involving the payment of cash benefits from accumulated fund reserves. Transactions of these various systems exclusive of administrative cost (treated as general expenditure) and of State contributions (classified as intragovernmental transactions)—are reported as insurance trust revenue and insurance trust expenditure.

Revenue of the State unemployment compensation systems totaled $15.2 billion in fiscal 1977, of which $6.5 billion was contributed by the Federal Government and the remaining $8.8 billion was largely derived from the State unemployment compensation payroll tax. Unemployment benefits paid in fiscal 1977 totaled $14.6 billion, of which $8.6 billion was regular compensation and $6.0 billion was for extended or special compensation. Fund balances of the State unemployment compensation systems amounted to $5.0 billion at the end of the 1977 fiscal year.

State-administered employee-retirement systems had revenue from contributions and investment earnings that totaled $14.4 billion in fiscal 1977, and made payments for benefits and withdrawals amounting to $6.9 billion.

Indebtedness, Borrowing and Debt Redemption

Of the $90.2 billion of State debt outstanding at the end of fiscal 1977, all except $3.0 billion was of long-term nature. In addition to $42.9 billion of long-term obligations backed by the States' full faith and credit, $44.3 billion of nonguaranteed debt was outstanding.

Net long-term State debt-allowing for debt offsets of $19.6 billion-amounted to $67.6 billion at the end of the 1977 fiscal year.

Table 1. Summary of State Government Finances: 1975 to 1977

Item	Amount (millions of dollars)			Percent increase or decrease (-)		Percent distribution, 1977	Per capita, 1977[1]
	1977	1976	1975	1976 to 1977	1975 to 1976		
REVENUE							
TOTAL	204 475	r183 821	r157 033	11.2	17.1	(X)	948.21
GENERAL REVENUE.	169 866	152 118	134 611	11.7	13.0	100.0	787.72
INTERGOVERNMENTAL REVENUE.	48 676	44 717	37 827	8.9	18.2	28.7	225.72
FROM FEDERAL GOVERNMENT.	45 938	42 013	36 148	9.3	16.2	27.0	213.03
PUBLIC WELFARE	18 723	16 867	14 247	11.0	18.4	11.0	86.82
EDUCATION.	9 035	8 661	7 879	4.3	9.9	5.3	41.90
HIGHWAYS	6 363	6 262	5 260	1.6	19.0	3.7	29.51
GENERAL REVENUE SHARING.	6 363	6 262	5 260	1.6	19.0	3.7	29.51
EMPLOYMENT SECURITY ADMINISTRATION . . .	2 266	2 102	2 066	7.8	1.8	1.3	10.51
HEALTH AND HOSPITALS	1 833	1 658	1 521	10.5	9.0	1.1	8.50
NATURAL RESOURCES.	1 532	1 235	1 102	24.0	12.1	0.9	7.11
AIRPORTS	637	642	599	-0.7	7.1	0.4	2.96
OTHER.	70	96	121	-27.4	-21.0	(Z)	0.32
	5 480	4 489	3 352	22.1	33.9	3.2	25.41
	2 737	2 704	1 680	1.2	61.0	1.6	12.69
FROM LOCAL GOVERNMENTS							
TAXES.	101 085	89 256	80 155	13.3	11.4	59.5	468.76
SALES AND GROSS RECEIPTS	52 362	47 391	43 346	10.5	9.3	30.8	242.82
GENERAL.	30 896	27 333	24 780	13.0	10.3	18.2	143.27
SELECTIVE.	21 466	20 058	18 566	7.0	8.0	12.6	99.55
MOTOR FUEL	9 088	8 660	8 255	4.9	4.9	5.4	42.15
TOBACCO PRODUCTS	3 500	3 462	3 286	1.1	5.4	2.1	16.23
ALCOHOLIC BEVERAGES.	2 120	2 057	1 963	3.0	4.8	1.2	9.83
INSURANCE.	2 336	1 960	1 751	19.2	12.0	1.4	10.83
PUBLIC UTILITIES	2 363	2 060	1 740	14.7	18.4	1.4	10.96
PARIMUTUELS.	721	719	676	0.3	6.3	0.4	3.34
OTHER.	1 338	1 139	894	17.5	27.4	0.8	6.20
LICENSE TAXES.	7 149	6 899	6 289	3.6	9.7	4.2	33.15
MOTOR VEHICLES	4 243	4 046	3 655	4.9	10.7	2.5	19.68
CORPORATIONS IN GENERAL.	1 041	1 135	1 041	-8.3	8.9	0.6	4.83
MOTOR VEHICLE OPERATORS.	344	310	286	10.8	8.7	0.2	1.60
HUNTING AND FISHING.	335	322	296	4.0	8.7	0.2	1.55
ALCOHOLIC BEVERAGES.	177	154	147	14.8	4.5	0.1	0.82
OTHER.	1 010	933	863	8.3	8.1	0.6	4.68
INDIVIDUAL INCOME.	25 493	21 448	18 819	18.9	14.0	15.0	118.22
CORPORATION NET INCOME	9 174	7 273	6 642	26.1	9.5	5.4	42.54
DEATH AND GIFT	1 805	1 513	1 418	19.2	6.7	1.1	8.37
PROPERTY	2 260	2 118	1 451	6.7	45.9	1.3	10.48
SEVERANCE.	2 168	2 029	1 741	6.9	16.5	1.3	10.05
DOCUMENTARY AND STOCK TRANSFER	630	545	415	15.6	31.3	0.4	2.92
OTHER.	44	40	33	9.3	19.8	(Z)	0.20
CHARGES AND MISCELLANEOUS GENERAL REVENUE. . .	20 106	18 145	16 629	10.8	9.1	11.8	93.24
CURRENT CHARGES.	12 768	11 652	10 437	9.6	11.7	7.5	59.21
EDUCATION.	6 818	6 347	5 751	7.4	10.4	4.0	31.62
STATE INSTITUTIONS OF HIGHER EDUCATION	6 678	6 212	5 625	7.5	10.4.	3.9	30.97
AUXILIARY ENTERPRISES.	2 830	2 628	2 326	7.7	13.0	1.7	13.12
OTHER.	3 848	3 584	3 299	7.4	8.7	2.3	17.85
OTHER EDUCATION.	140	136	126	3.1	7.3	0.1	0.65
HOSPITALS.	2 370	2 116	1 750	12.0	20.9	1.4	10.99
HIGHWAYS	1 106	1 054	991	5.0	6.3	0.7	5.13
TOLL FACILITIES.	1 016	960	907	5.8	5.9	0.6	4.71
OTHER.	90	93	84	-3.1	10.9	0.1	0.42
MISCELLANEOUS COMMERCIAL ACTIVITIES. . .	811	654	632	23.9	3.5	0.5	3.76
NATURAL RESOURCES.	557	359	318	55.3	12.9	0.3	2.58
OTHER.	1 106	1 123	994	-1.5	12.9	0.7	5.13
MISCELLANEOUS GENERAL REVENUE.	7 338	6 493	6 193	13.0	4.8	4.3	34.03
INTEREST EARNINGS.	3 475	3 387	3 731	2.6	-9.2	2.0	16.12
RENTS AND ROYALTIES.	957	958	711	-0.2	34.7	0.6	4.44
DONATIONS.	835	766	665	8.9	15.2	0.5	3.87
FINES AND FORFEITS	245	212	192	15.8	10.4	0.1	1.14
SALE OF PROPERTY	106	73	68	45.9	7.6	0.1	0.49
OTHER.	1 720	1 096	826	56.8	32.8	1.0	7.97
INSURANCE TRUST REVENUE.	32 365	r29 508	r20 293	9.7	45.4	100.0	150.09
EMPLOYEE RETIREMENT.	14 441	12 171	10 182	18.6	19.5	44.6	66.97
UNEMPLOYMENT COMPENSATION.	15 213	r15 068	r8 113	1.0	85.7	47.0	70.55
WORKMEN'S COMPENSATION	2 039	1 668	1 406	22.3	18.6	6.3	9.46
OTHER.	671	601	592	11.7	1.6	2.1	3.11
LIQUOR STORES REVENUE.	2 244	2 196	2 129	2.2	3.1	(X)	10.41

See footnotes at end of table.

Table 1. Summary of State Government Finances: 1975 to 1977—Continued

Item	Amount (millions of dollars)			Percent increase or decrease (-)		Percent distribution, 1977	Per capita, 1977[1]
	1977	1976	1975	1976 to 1977	1975 to 1976		
EXPENDITURE, BY CHARACTER AND OBJECT							
TOTAL	191 238	r180 926	r158 882	5.7	13.9	100.0	886.71
INTERGOVERNMENTAL EXPENDITURE	62 470	57 858	51 978	8.0	11.3	32.7	289.69
DIRECT EXPENDITURE	128 768	r123 069	r106 905	4.6	15.1	67.3	597.14
CURRENT OPERATION	75 857	68 175	60 793	11.3	12.1	39.7	351.77
CAPITAL OUTLAY	16 793	18 009	17 307	-6.7	4.1	8.8	77.88
CONSTRUCTION	13 620	15 285	14 443	-10.9	5.8	7.1	63.16
LAND AND EXISTING STRUCTURES	1 696	1 274	1 475	33.1	-13.6	0.9	7.86
EQUIPMENT	1 477	1 450	1 389	1.9	4.3	0.8	6.85
INSURANCE BENEFITS AND REPAYMENTS	23 426	r25 455	r18 860	-8.0	35.0	12.2	108.63
ASSISTANCE AND SUBSIDIES	7 556	7 290	6 673	3.6	9.2	4.0	35.04
INTEREST ON DEBT	5 136	4 140	3 272	24.1	26.5	2.7	23.82
EXHIBIT: TOTAL PERSONAL SERVICES	35 780	32 856	30 296	8.9	8.4	18.7	165.92
EXPENDITURE, BY FUNCTION							
TOTAL	191 238	r180 926	r158 882	5.7	13.9	–	884.00
GENERAL EXPENDITURE	165 995	153 690	138 303	8.0	11.1	100.0	769.77
INTERGOVERNMENTAL EXPENDITURE	62 470	57 858	51 978	8.0	11.3	37.6	289.69
STATE PAYMENTS TO FEDERAL GOVERNMENT	1 386	1 180	975	17.5	21.0	0.8	6.43
DIRECT EXPENDITURE	103 525	95 832	86 326	8.0	11.0	62.4	480.08
EDUCATION	64 037	59 630	54 012	7.4	10.4	38.6	296.96
INTERGOVERNMENTAL EXPENDITURE	36 975	34 084	31 110	8.5	9.6	22.3	171.46
DIRECT EXPENDITURE	27 062	25 546	22 902	5.9	11.5	16.3	125.50
STATE INSTITUTIONS OF HIGHER EDUCATION	21 166	19 707	17 696	7.4	11.4	12.8	98.15
CURRENT OPERATION	18 853	17 290	15 463	9.0	11.8	11.4	87.43
AUXILIARY ENTERPRISES	2 498	2 294	2 048	8.9	12.0	1.5	11.58
OTHER	16 355	14 996	13 415	9.1	11.8	9.9	75.84
CAPITAL OUTLAY	2 313	2 417	2 233	-4.3	8.2	1.4	10.73
LOCAL SCHOOLS	5 246	5 239	4 670	0.1	12.2	3.2	24.33
OTHER	651	600	536	8.5	11.9	0.4	3.02
PUBLIC WELFARE	32 779	29 633	25 559	10.6	15.9	19.8	152.01
INTERGOVERNMENTAL EXPENDITURE	10 133	9 476	8 102	6.9	17.0	6.1	46.99
SUPPLEMENTAL SECURITY INCOME PROGRAMS	1 377	1 169	965	17.8	21.1	0.8	6.38
DIRECT EXPENDITURE	22 646	20 157	17 457	12.3	15.5	13.6	105.02
VENDOR PAYMENTS FOR MEDICAL CARE	12 616	11 035	9 420	14.3	17.1	7.6	58.50
CASH ASSISTANCE PAYMENTS	5 819	5 556	4 986	4.7	11.4	3.5	26.98
CATEGORICAL PROGRAMS	5 308	5 203	4 661	2.0	11.6	3.2	24.61
OTHER	511	353	325	44.8	8.6	0.3	2.37
OTHER	4 212	3 566	3 052	18.1	16.8	2.5	19.53
HIGHWAYS	17 496	18 100	17 483	-3.3	3.5	10.5	81.14
INTERGOVERNMENTAL EXPENDITURE	3 631	3 241	3 225	12.0	0.5	2.2	16.84
DIRECT EXPENDITURE	13 865	14 860	14 258	-6.7	4.2	8.4	64.30
REGULAR HIGHWAY FACILITIES	13 183	14 223	13 583	-7.3	4.7	7.9	61.13
CURRENT OPERATION	4 103	3 615	3 386	13.5	6.8	2.5	18.97
CAPITAL OUTLAY	9 080	10 608	10 197	-14.4	4.0	5.5	41.97
TOLL HIGHWAY FACILITIES	683	636	675	7.4	-5.8	0.4	3.16
HOSPITALS	8 743	7 821	7 095	11.8	10.2	5.3	40.54
INTERGOVERNMENTAL EXPENDITURE	120	96	78	25.0	23.1	0.1	0.56
DIRECT EXPENDITURE	8 622	7 726	7 016	11.6	10.1	5.2	39.98
STATE HOSPITALS	8 364	7 572	6 891	10.5	9.9	5.0	38.79
CURRENT OPERATION	7 563	6 918	6 227	9.3	11.1	4.6	35.07
CAPITAL OUTLAY	801	655	663	22.3	-1.2	0.5	3.72
OTHER HOSPITALS (NONGOVERNMENTAL)	258	153	126	68.6	21.4	0.2	1.20
NATURAL RESOURCES	4 369	3 863	3 554	13.1	8.7	2.6	20.26
AGRICULTURE	1 548	1 516	1 373	2.1	10.4	0.9	7.18
FISH AND GAME	543	475	445	14.3	6.7	0.3	2.52
FORESTRY AND PARKS	1 602	1 243	1 164	28.9	6.8	1.0	7.43
OTHER	677	629	572	7.6	10.0	0.4	3.14
HEALTH	3 865	3 290	3 063	17.5	7.4	2.3	17.92
CORRECTION	2 882	2 480	2 203	16.2	12.6	1.7	13.37
FINANCIAL ADMINISTRATION	2 241	1 955	1 792	14.6	9.1	1.4	10.39
EMPLOYMENT SECURITY ADMINISTRATION	1 698	1 570	1 509	8.2	4.0	1.0	7.88
POLICE PROTECTION	1 690	1 569	1 423	7.7	10.3	1.0	7.84
GENERAL CONTROL	1 858	1 688	1 496	10.1	12.8	1.1	8.62
PROTECTIVE INSPECTION AND REGULATION, N.E.C.	1 189	1 090	999	9.1	9.1	0.7	5.51
MISCELLANEOUS COMMERCIAL ACTIVITIES	1 563	1 124	1 045	39.1	7.6	0.9	7.25
GENERAL PUBLIC BUILDINGS	557	566	568	-1.6	-0.4	0.3	2.58
AIRPORTS	235	369	366	-36.3	0.8	0.1	1.09
WATER TRANSPORT AND TERMINALS	276	243	221	13.6	10.0	0.2	1.28
LIBRARIES	236	229	215	3.1	6.5	0.1	1.09
HOUSING AND URBAN RENEWAL	353	465	632	-24.1	-26.4	0.2	1.64
VETERANS' SERVICES	54	64	363	-15.6	-82.3	(Z)	0.25
INTEREST ON DEBT	5 136	4 140	3 272	24.1	26.5	3.1	23.82
INTERGOVERNMENTAL EXPENDITURE, N.E.C.	9 323	8 760	7 414	6.4	18.2	5.6	43.09
GENERAL LOCAL GOVERNMENT SUPPORT	6 373	5 674	5 129	12.3	10.6	3.8	29.46
OTHER	2 950	3 086	2 285	-4.4	35.1	1.8	13.68
ALL OTHER	5 415	5 041	4 020	7.4	25.4	3.3	25.11

See footnotes at end of table.

141

Table 1. Summary of State Government Finances: 1975 to 1977—Continued

Item	Amount (millions of dollars) 1977	1976	1975	Percent increase or decrease (-) 1976 to 1977	1975 to 1976	Percent distribution, 1977	Per capita, 1977[1]
EXPENDITURE, BY FUNCTION--CONTINUED							
INSURANCE TRUST EXPENDITURE.	23 426	r25 455	r18 860	-8.0	35.0	100.0	108.63
UNEMPLOYMENT COMPENSATION.	14 611	r17 780	r12 245	-17.8	45.2	62.4	67.76
EMPLOYEE RETIREMENT.	6 930	6 045	5 160	14.6	17.2	29.6	32.14
WORKMEN'S COMPENSATION	1 326	1 070	910	23.9	17.6	5.7	6.15
OTHER.	559	559	545	(Z)	2.5	2.4	2.59
LIQUOR STORES EXPENDITURE.	1 817	1 781	1 719	2.0	3.6	-	8.43
INDEBTEDNESS AND DEBT TRANSACTIONS							
DEBT AT END FISCAL YEAR.	90 200	r84 825	72 127	6.3	17.6	100.0	418.29
LONG-TERM.	87 184	r78 814	67 548	10.6	16.7	96.7	404.30
NONGUARANTEED.	44 271	r39 972	33 812	10.8	18.2	49.1	205.30
FULL FAITH AND CREDIT.	42 913	r38 842	33 736	10.5	15.1	47.6	199.00
SHORT-TERM	3 016	6 011	4 579	-49.8	31.3	3.3	13.99
NET LONG-TERM DEBT AT END OF FISCAL YEAR	67 560	r62 934	58 388	7.4	7.8	-	313.30
FULL FAITH AND CREDIT ONLY	37 347	r34 129	29 503	9.4	15.7	-	173.19
LONG-TERM DEBT AT END OF FISCAL YEAR, BY FUNCTION:							
TOTAL.	87 184	r78 814	67 548	10.6	17.6	100.0	404.30
OTHER HIGHWAY FACILITIES	10 460	10 640	9 722	-1.7	9.5	12.0	48.51
STATE INSTITUTIONS OF HIGHER EDUCATION . . .	12 041	11 117	10 535	8.3	5.5	13.8	55.84
TOLL HIGHWAY FACILITIES.	6 203	6 409	6 610	-3.2	-3.0	7.1	28.77
LOCAL SCHOOLS.	4 048	4 034	3 895	0.4	3.6	4.6	18.77
OTHER EDUCATION.	3 259	2 908	2 591	12.1	12.2	3.7	15.11
HOSPITALS.	3 269	2 688	2 331	21.6	15.3	3.7	15.16
WATER TRANSPORT AND TERMINALS.	566	577	546	-2.0	5.7	0.6	2.62
VETERANS' BONUSES.	604	582	561	3.9	3.7	0.7	2.80
OTHER AND UNALLOCABLE.	46 734	r39 859	30 757	17.2	29.6	53.6	216.72
LONG-TERM DEBT ISSUED.	12 377	13 865	8 392	-10.7	65.2	100.0	57.39
FULL FAITH AND CREDIT.	5 842	6 365	4 335	-8.2	46.8	47.2	27.09
NONGUARANTEED.	6 534	7 500	4 057	-12.9	84.9	52.8	30.30
ORIGINAL ISSUES.	10 873	13 749	8 392	-20.9	63.8	87.9	50.42
REFUNDING ISSUES	1 504	117	-	(2)	(2)	12.1	6.97
LONG-TERM DEBT RETIRED	4 016	2 968	2 920	35.3	1.6	100.0	18.62
REDEEMED	3 678	2 915	2 908	26.2	0.2	91.6	17.06
REFUNDED	338	53	12	536.5	346.4	8.4	1.57
BORROWING.	11 101	15 805	9 663	-29.8	63.6	-	51.48
DEBT REDEMPTION.	6 875	3 585	2 922	91.8	22.7	-	31.88
CASH AND SECURITY HOLDINGS							
TOTAL	175 713	r157 210	140 748	11.8	11.7	100.0	814.84
CASH AND DEPOSITS, UNEMPLOYMENT COMPENSATION SYSTEMS	4 956	4 425	6 839	12.0	-35.3	2.8	22.98
OTHER CASH AND DEPOSITS.	21 647	18 477	18 744	17.2	-1.4	12.3	100.38
SECURITIES	149 110	r134 308	115 166	11.0	16.6	84.9	691.47
FEDERAL SECURITIES	29 108	22 787	19 415	27.7	17.4	16.6	134.98
UNITED STATES TREASURY	22 304	16 538	14 390	34.9	14.9	12.7	103.43
FEDERAL AGENCY	6 804	6 249	5 025	8.9	24.4	3.9	31.55
STATE AND LOCAL GOVERNMENT SECURITIES. . . .	6 732	7 142	1 637	-5.8	336.4	3.8	31.22
OTHER SECURITIES	113 271	r104 378	94 113	8.5	10.9	64.5	525.27
CASH AND SECURITY HOLDINGS OF INSURANCE TRUST SYSTEMS	105 082	r94 679	85 688	11.0	10.5	59.8	487.30
EMPLOYEE RETIREMENT.	94 913	85 811	74 642	10.6	15.0	54.0	440.14
UNEMPLOYMENT COMPENSATION.	4 956	4 425	6 839	12.0	-35.3	2.8	22.98
WORKMEN'S COMPENSATION	4 842	r4 151	3 897	16.7	6.5	2.8	22.45
OTHER INSURANCE TRUST SYSTEMS.	371	r292	309	27.1	-5.5	0.2	1.72
CASH AND SECURITY HOLDINGS, OTHER THAN INSURANCE TRUST SYSTEMS	70 631	62 531	55 061	13.0	13.6	40.2	327.54
BY PURPOSE OF HOLDING:							
OFFSETS TO LONG-TERM DEBT.	19 600	15 880	9 160	23.4	73.4	11.2	90.89
BOND FUNDS	7 923	7 447	8 103	6.4	-8.1	4.5	36.74
OTHER.	43 108	39 204	37 798	10.0	3.7	24.5	199.90
BY TYPE OF ASSET:							
CASH AND DEPOSITS.	20 572	17 527	17 751	17.4	-1.3	11.7	95.40
SECURITIES	50 059	45 004	37 310	11.2	20.6	28.5	232.14
FEDERAL GOVERNMENT SECURITIES.	18 540	14 516	13 286	27.7	9.3	10.5	85.98
STATE AND LOCAL GOVERNMENT SECURITIES . .	5 541	5 469	1 284	1.3	325.9	3.2	25.70
OTHER SECURITIES	25 978	25 019	22 740	3.8	10.0	14.8	120.47

Note: Because of rounding, detail may not add to totals. Per capita and percent figures are computed on the basis of amounts rounded to the nearest thousand.

- Represents zero or rounds to zero. r Revised. X Not applicable. Z Less than half the unit of measurement shown. [1] Based on provisional population as of July 1, 1977. [2] Excessive percentage increase due to lack of refunding bonds issued in prior years.

142

Table 2. Per Capita Amounts of Financial Items for State Governments: 1977

(Dollar amounts)

State	Total general revenue	Intergovernmental revenue from Federal Government Total[1]	Public welfare	Education	Highways	General revenue sharing	Employment security administration	Intergovernmental revenue from local governments	All taxes[1]	Sales and gross receipts taxes Total[1]	General[2]	Motor fuels
50-STATE AVERAGE .	787.72	213.03	86.82	41.90	29.51	10.51	8.50	12.69	468.76	242.82	143.27	42.15
MEDIAN STATE . . .	765.36	224.27	69.11	45.82	37.08	10.00	8.51	5.93	435.04	238.50	140.46	46.93
ALABAMA.	718.16	237.20	71.96	59.14	48.21	9.68	8.68	6.00	380.40	246.22	123.24	44.84
ALASKA	2 998.19	672.71	66.48	130.13	275.86	10.89	30.15	0.67	1 900.43	162.02	-	50.63
ARIZONA.	755.55	158.38	19.94	47.01	38.03	11.27	12.24	3.05	505.26	309.47	219.04	48.57
ARKANSAS	650.69	215.17	78.49	46.50	22.93	10.85	8.01	2.01	374.49	228.86	127.94	55.60
CALIFORNIA	947.08	263.44	127.76	43.35	24.73	10.62	7.34	28.59	574.95	274.24	197.02	37.06
COLORADO	764.23	231.38	65.68	53.42	49.06	9.23	7.24	2.55	411.33	210.06	137.29	39.09
CONNECTICUT.	748.72	174.18	73.57	28.31	14.83	9.09	9.39	0.94	468.83	338.78	187.73	51.21
DELAWARE	1 096.67	234.38	57.61	52.65	39.65	11.96	9.42	2.80	671.62	118.51	-	51.21
FLORIDA.	573.96	133.32	35.35	35.93	21.10	7.94	6.75	3.16	387.46	285.77	165.47	45.47
GEORGIA.	630.07	194.13	73.13	42.78	23.93	9.16	7.84	1.55	377.68	224.84	136.18	48.59
HAWAII	1 373.04	385.80	92.22	88.67	59.29	11.26	11.53	6.60	766.15	497.09	381.02	36.67
IDAHO.	769.78	261.95	59.90	39.47	66.53	9.55	11.17	2.47	429.20	205.29	121.19	52.42
ILLINOIS	726.23	184.64	85.78	32.12	30.06	9.96	8.34	4.97	473.06	268.11	163.83	36.08
INDIANA.	644.86	142.81	49.74	33.50	20.27	8.63	6.06	1.68	405.80	268.76	196.17	49.27
IOWA	748.35	194.03	60.65	47.00	34.05	9.49	7.12	12.93	448.94	198.72	120.45	46.23
KANSAS	689.60	182.49	69.61	45.02	32.64	8.49	7.95	4.77	416.60	223.84	140.46	51.16
KENTUCKY	766.48	221.95	76.25	48.12	37.90	10.82	3.66	1.69	451.24	242.37	134.14	53.32
LOUISIANA.	820.24	246.55	76.32	51.02	50.39	11.97	6.30	3.52	438.32	217.17	122.85	44.16
MAINE.	795.25	252.50	105.42	53.86	32.95	12.54	11.87	7.43	431.76	272.74	156.37	50.96
MARYLAND	843.65	194.53	66.45	35.31	39.22	11.83	5.71	5.86	514.06	239.00	112.55	45.60
MASSACHUSETTS. . . .	859.32	228.97	109.17	33.00	25.69	11.78	8.88	28.95	507.48	203.25	76.42	37.04
MICHIGAN	864.45	223.71	109.17	42.50	22.57	10.01	10.53	9.40	530.59	237.15	154.12	47.14
MINNESOTA.	973.00	229.49	103.56	50.60	33.32	11.86	6.92	9.91	625.30	247.39	117.40	49.59
MISSISSIPPI.	736.45	242.29	64.76	70.11	37.91	14.02	12.98	4.97	405.71	293.44	199.02	57.98
MISSOURI	548.38	164.35	52.63	31.62	30.65	8.65	7.97	0.74	332.87	193.59	124.23	42.61
MONTANA.	880.38	349.12	72.56	41.01	135.22	10.65	11.29	7.01	410.51	109.04	-	57.76
NEBRASKA	668.86	175.13	47.03	32.06	39.57	8.96	7.89	14.21	392.64	219.78	127.31	56.33
NEVADA	833.23	224.83	44.89	29.03	73.09	8.44	24.73	10.31	519.86	406.52	182.85	46.72
NEW HAMPSHIRE. . . .	543.62	186.78	61.77	32.81	38.29	8.54	7.44	12.06	235.84	134.26	-	47.44
NEW JERSEY	732.74	195.15	87.99	35.96	26.71	9.38	10.25	10.23	423.49	215.12	124.59	39.97
NEW MEXICO	1 021.28	273.92	71.97	74.13	47.44	12.09	8.18	9.89	502.19	316.03	216.17	54.46
NEW YORK	1 049.19	270.20	159.64	37.26	10.58	16.39	11.38	57.73	599.38	221.11	123.75	28.56
NORTH CAROLINA . . .	728.74	219.59	63.77	55.58	46.30	10.92	6.51	3.30	431.63	204.30	92.58	52.43
NORTH DAKOTA	1 038.07	328.07	62.02	53.91	81.22	9.39	2.89	18.29	453.80	252.60	168.80	45.60
OHIO	566.44	154.79	61.99	28.46	16.39	8.28	7.38	4.27	333.69	199.29	106.11	36.75
OKLAHOMA	750.67	207.95	90.89	45.71	26.66	8.58	8.83	7.75	405.19	175.55	72.96	44.05
OREGON	827.16	258.89	92.45	48.46	32.71	10.00	6.52	4.17	409.57	67.06	-	38.43
PENNSYLVANIA	728.76	190.01	95.83	29.41	24.95	9.81	9.94	6.17	474.40	238.01	129.36	42.35
RHODE ISLAND	909.68	277.93	120.71	50.79	15.90	13.13	12.77	2.84	469.35	272.49	151.63	43.57
SOUTH CAROLINA . . .	742.49	212.42	55.34	57.62	19.52	11.82	8.95	8.01	412.93	247.12	144.39	48.85
SOUTH DAKOTA	715.48	268.78	68.38	49.06	67.09	10.79	12.46	8.14	290.44	252.44	146.62	52.53
TENNESSEE.	610.82	190.13	65.36	41.25	36.26	9.48	7.84	3.80	355.79	262.76	170.65	44.85
TEXAS.	630.57	161.03	61.54	44.52	20.67	8.62	6.66	1.29	370.23	247.94	132.18	34.62
UTAH	820.36	271.28	68.61	73.85	55.60	9.81	14.14	6.35	418.99	242.47	178.98	43.12
VERMONT.	1 006.02	375.50	129.16	63.77	51.24	12.87	12.51	4.65	475.78	233.67	67.28	48.05
VIRGINIA	696.47	180.58	57.04	40.22	40.67	8.63	6.68	7.28	399.97	190.60	83.13	51.64
WASHINGTON	942.87	245.76	75.05	63.32	40.21	11.23	11.54	15.68	574.09	434.54	320.55	49.30
WEST VIRGINIA. . . .	834.96	270.49	64.98	45.14	90.78	12.54	8.84	0.52	485.97	348.64	240.69	43.23
WISCONSIN.	908.90	218.78	110.55	45.94	20.02	11.55	7.30	6.71	587.68	226.48	143.61	36.73
WYOMING.	1 203.11	448.58	33.62	63.77	120.31	8.70	16.15	7.82	574.72	326.51	232.96	67.67

- Represents zero or rounds to zero.

[1] Including amounts or categories not shown separately.

[2] Medians are based on those States having the specified items.

143

(Dollar amounts)

State	General revenue--Continued											
	Taxes--Continued							Total charges and miscellaneous general revenue[2]	Current charges			
	Sales and gross receipts taxes--Continued		Individual income[1]	Corporation net income[1]	Motor vehicle licenses	Death and gift[1]	Property[1]		Total[2]	State institutions of higher education	Hospitals	Toll highways[1]
	Tobacco products	Alcoholic beverages										
50-STATE AVERAGE	16.23	9.83	118.22	42.54	19.68	8.37	10.48	93.24	59.21	30.97	10.99	4.71
MEDIAN STATE	15.11	8.49	105.13	33.62	19.72	5.84	4.86	102.16	64.90	37.48	11.18	7.18
ALABAMA	13.43	19.31	70.97	20.56	9.25	1.14	9.24	94.55	81.82	42.09	21.84	-
ALASKA	11.92	19.60	516.80	87.89	27.03	0.47	1 006.80	424.38	146.49	24.38	0.51	-
ARIZONA	15.46	7.74	83.01	22.56	21.03	2.06	56.55	88.86	60.15	41.88	8.84	-
ARKANSAS	21.49	8.60	76.39	31.35	18.82	1.13	0.79	80.11	49.40	23.48	13.10	2.15
CALIFORNIA	12.40	5.82	165.37	74.97	15.72	16.73	20.07	118.96	87.18	67.45	14.08	-
COLORADO	12.69	7.61	129.41	30.77	15.94	10.12	0.93	104.77	57.84	21.05	11.62	13.05
CONNECTICUT	24.16	7.82	19.09	64.91	19.84	15.77	-	187.87	127.15	85.64	4.85	13.55
DELAWARE	21.04	7.51	288.66	49.89	33.93	13.16	-	50.02	33.72	16.41	3.96	8.28
FLORIDA	22.05	22.13	-	22.98	32.26	5.84	8.11	56.71	42.70	24.60	7.49	-
GEORGIA	14.78	15.12	98.19	33.85	8.66	3.03	1.96	214.49	151.83	30.93	25.81	-
HAWAII	11.52	18.13	226.84	30.84	0.13	4.59	-	76.16	37.12	26.74	2.17	-
IDAHO	9.33	7.72	131.24	36.21	28.56	4.15	0.27	63.57	38.05	23.46	4.83	7.22
ILLINOIS	15.76	6.79	125.69	34.18	29.03	7.43	0.42	94.57	75.21	51.58	12.48	4.81
INDIANA	9.67	5.31	89.92	16.17	17.07	4.95	4.42	92.44	73.82	48.77	16.56	-
IOWA	16.07	5.12	155.40	31.92	40.30	11.49	0.04					
KANSAS	13.80	7.44	89.93	52.76	25.00	7.55	6.64	85.74	64.87	36.70	13.29	8.40
KENTUCKY	6.44	4.32	97.79	37.96	12.49	5.56	12.55	91.61	60.63	32.67	11.33	5.09
LOUISIANA	14.53	11.56	34.08	24.29	9.69	5.10	0.04	131.84	59.03	34.61	9.12	0.30
MAINE	22.39	22.44	69.27	32.44	19.69	7.41	13.20	103.56	66.35	39.43	7.59	13.81
MARYLAND	13.13	6.81	194.91	27.86	18.25	4.79	17.50	129.19	86.32	36.71	15.98	12.87
MASSACHUSETTS	24.69	13.33	206.08	68.70	9.35	12.44	0.11	93.92	53.01	18.38	2.87	9.77
MICHIGAN	15.37	8.77	160.53	86.47	19.75	5.55	12.89	100.76	64.93	46.18	12.00	0.77
MINNESOTA	21.08	12.70	240.74	64.93	26.11	10.87	0.78	108.29	67.80	41.87	18.84	-
MISSISSIPPI	13.01	11.77	55.08	19.20	8.50	1.80	1.51	83.47	64.40	40.30	13.12	-
MISSOURI	12.38	4.85	81.15	22.03	20.04	4.11	0.94	50.42	38.94	27.79	6.55	-
MONTANA	15.15	12.00	146.99	32.80	16.70	8.52	20.55	113.75	54.64	43.96	2.31	-
NEBRASKA	14.48	6.62	109.29	26.87	22.35	1.19	1.87	86.87	64.44	40.33	14.80	-
NEVADA	17.58	16.64	-	-	27.31	-	34.92	78.23	57.05	26.89	1.08	-
NEW HAMPSHIRE	31.96	4.81	8.32	38.35	22.22	8.65	7.26	108.94	80.31	60.60	3.20	10.74
NEW JERSEY	23.03	7.34	96.83	45.41	25.65	11.87	10.98	103.87	69.74	19.63	9.27	22.35
NEW MEXICO	11.50	5.54	22.39	24.78	24.69	3.77	13.53	235.29	73.88	46.23	19.25	-
NEW YORK	18.64	8.38	252.56	72.25	15.93	11.12	1.35	121.87	66.89	13.99	7.63	8.54
NORTH CAROLINA	3.68	15.70	141.56	36.98	18.87	6.71	6.89	74.21	55.08	34.19	12.13	0.07
NORTH DAKOTA	13.12	9.56	84.28	33.38	35.94	5.59	3.99	237.90	184.92	64.94	12.47	4.41
OHIO	18.40	6.73	57.46	29.48	17.01	2.31	10.12	73.70	51.32	33.01	12.03	-
OKLAHOMA	18.48	12.08	77.14	25.13	34.49	9.77	-	129.78	101.45	59.82	11.02	9.37
OREGON	13.39	2.51	236.49	38.34	33.23	11.97	0.03	154.53	78.00	39.39	14.96	0.51
PENNSYLVANIA	21.04	9.03	99.96	56.51	22.72	12.43	5.31	58.17	39.73	21.61	7.29	6.82
RHODE ISLAND	26.09	7.68	111.00	43.68	18.26	9.59	6.14	159.56	108.44	38.24	50.11	4.16
SOUTH CAROLINA	8.20	25.76	100.97	37.07	10.16	3.75	1.68	109.13	90.33	27.38	12.36	-
SOUTH DAKOTA	13.10	10.11	-	3.63	15.69	8.17	-	148.11	97.76	51.94	0.98	-
TENNESSEE	15.78	9.89	5.21	36.30	20.71	9.68	-	61.10	46.22	30.88	9.40	-
TEXAS	22.41	11.80	-	-	19.14	5.19	3.33	98.02	40.61	29.29	7.11	1.00
UTAH	6.06	4.24	124.82	19.61	12.05	4.39	0.16	123.74	87.59	51.71	26.82	-
VERMONT	19.88	25.28	145.62	34.99	34.04	5.37	0.70	150.09	99.67	85.67	2.06	-
VIRGINIA	3.48	12.46	139.06	30.99	16.63	4.67	4.30	108.66	89.29	40.49	37.02	5.72
WASHINGTON	16.27	18.60	-	-	18.62	13.07	82.88	107.34	55.72	40.01	1.04	8.86
WEST VIRGINIA	15.08	3.14	88.58	12.55	20.89	4.89	0.48	77.98	51.04	25.72	11.66	7.14
WISCONSIN	18.14	8.31	245.98	54.11	19.53	11.45	19.76	95.73	71.37	44.15	22.68	-
WYOMING	11.51	3.15	-	-	74.51	8.85	22.29	171.99	58.52	40.20	2.34	-

- Represents zero or rounds to zero.
[1] Medians are based on those States having the specified items.
[2] Including amounts for categories not shown separately.

Table 2. Per Capita Amounts of Financial Items for State Governments: 1977—Continued

(Dollar amounts)

State	General expenditure												
	General expenditure for all functions[1]					Education				Public welfare		
	Total	Intergovernmental expenditure	Direct expenditure			Total	Intergovernmental expenditure[2]	All direct expenditure for education	State institutions of higher education only	Total	Intergovernmental expenditure[2]	Direct expenditure
			Total	Other than capital outlay	Capital outlay							
50-STATE AVERAGE .	769.77	239.69	480.08	402.23	77.45	296.96	171.46	125.50	98.15	152.01	46.99	105.02
MEDIAN STATE . . .	758.81	237.22	513.75	428.57	87.45	307.09	167.47	136.61	115.31	111.04	7.76	98.42
ALABAMA.	702.98	198.35	504.63	399.13	105.50	333.67	151.77	181.91	133.25	99.47	-	99.47
ALASKA	2 528.02	577.55	1 950.48	1 399.44	551.04	845.39	395.33	450.06	214.21	138.53	-	138.53
ARIZONA.	739.07	319.04	420.03	339.23	80.80	371.00	218.99	152.00	134.52	48.84	0.76	48.08
ARKANSAS	646.71	204.77	441.95	348.48	93.47	263.77	140.60	123.17	95.13	110.32	0.64	109.68
CALIFORNIA	868.37	414.31	454.05	415.61	38.45	318.57	191.84	126.72	109.40	248.91	128.61	120.30
COLORADO	748.10	263.73	484.37	393.12	91.25	370.97	173.77	197.20	181.38	111.77	50.58	61.18
CONNECTICUT.	688.36	171.31	517.05	459.11	57.94	209.12	111.94	97.18	67.30	135.00	6.24	128.76
DELAWARE	1 066.34	251.15	815.19	675.24	139.95	460.90	218.25	242.66	194.57	127.08	1.18	125.90
FLORIDA.	580.40	238.94	341.45	263.97	77.48	260.95	187.77	73.18	60.06	52.31	-	52.31
GEORGIA.	617.27	197.05	420.22	348.09	72.12	269.55	157.09	112.46	88.17	102.41	1.77	100.64
HAWAII	1 511.36	43.72	1 467.64	1 198.99	268.65	533.59	-	533.59	194.74	215.64	4.66	210.98
IDAHO.	798.38	256.89	541.49	410.71	130.78	313.74	172.54	141.20	119.85	87.84	-	87.84
ILLINOIS	758.35	251.12	507.23	420.61	86.63	276.05	175.81	100.24	78.30	187.89	9.35	178.54
INDIANA.	597.85	250.48	347.37	287.48	59.89	263.94	128.29	135.65	118.26	73.30	22.94	50.36
IOWA	796.54	313.09	483.45	395.18	88.27	348.68	205.46	143.22	121.57	114.69	7.87	106.82
KANSAS	684.00	192.57	491.43	400.61	90.82	290.74	153.56	137.18	125.15	125.54	0.17	125.37
KENTUCKY	745.44	171.05	574.39	449.80	124.59	294.93	140.58	154.35	115.59	133.72	-	133.72
LOUISIANA.	836.08	250.99	585.09	428.83	156.26	305.93	177.63	128.30	98.71	111.85	0.35	111.50
MAINE.	740.75	207.70	533.06	474.91	58.15	269.58	164.71	104.87	83.06	158.05	6.28	151.76
MARYLAND	858.65	348.19	510.46	428.97	81.49	304.84	180.39	124.45	95.76	137.78	60.36	77.43
MASSACHUSETTS.	822.64	235.50	587.14	529.90	57.25	233.46	145.00	88.46	61.34	251.98	21.80	230.17
MICHIGAN	837.91	312.01	525.90	471.99	53.91	316.08	174.05	142.03	113.72	217.94	24.29	193.65
MINNESOTA.	961.34	452.22	509.12	434.88	74.24	439.72	274.13	165.59	142.89	156.48	57.54	98.93
MISSISSIPPI.	727.65	252.37	475.28	370.63	104.65	312.99	180.72	132.27	100.80	95.99	-	95.99
MISSOURI	513.82	151.22	362.60	293.72	68.87	213.80	125.36	88.44	76.31	91.41	0.74	90.67
MONTANA.	877.66	222.74	654.92	477.01	177.91	326.29	174.93	151.36	124.98	91.68	1.95	89.73
NEBRASKA	639.69	204.03	435.66	342.28	93.38	212.12	76.08	136.04	119.95	84.96	9.47	75.50
NEVADA	805.32	247.02	558.30	432.53	125.76	324.09	194.35	129.74	113.35	74.61	2.98	71.63
NEW HAMPSHIRE.	647.77	111.97	535.80	395.40	140.40	179.64	47.43	132.21	114.55	95.45	-	95.45
NEW JERSEY	743.94	276.78	467.16	398.72	68.44	253.04	151.44	101.60	59.60	155.91	67.47	88.44
NEW MEXICO	892.44	334.78	557.65	471.89	85.76	441.18	259.35	181.83	156.74	89.79	-	89.79
NEW YORK	1 027.01	570.90	456.10	364.89	91.22	308.25	215.98	92.26	55.22	247.20	240.80	6.40
NORTH CAROLINA	718.22	329.39	388.83	356.10	32.73	345.40	227.20	118.21	97.37	81.03	47.95	33.08
NORTH DAKOTA	960.92	248.12	712.81	576.19	136.62	357.44	169.22	188.22	165.16	98.91	7.68	91.23
OHIO	599.00	230.47	368.53	300.59	67.95	238.12	140.98	97.14	84.10	102.19	13.14	89.05
OKLAHOMA	699.36	201.16	498.20	428.31	69.90	305.03	152.61	152.43	128.89	128.28	1.15	127.13
OREGON	800.23	212.35	587.87	516.91	70.96	289.10	138.33	150.77	128.21	144.19	0.99	143.20
PENNSYLVANIA	759.26	234.80	524.45	468.07	56.38	261.79	165.42	96.37	51.36	194.96	17.51	177.45
RHODE ISLAND	859.50	173.42	686.08	639.86	46.22	269.41	117.81	151.59	115.03	230.88	20.18	210.69
SOUTH CAROLINA	745.45	203.13	542.32	456.78	85.54	309.75	146.50	163.25	114.80	82.36	(Z)	82.36
SOUTH DAKOTA	732.81	109.35	623.46	470.31	153.14	224.96	76.02	148.93	132.39	98.25	0.34	97.90
TENNESSEE.	593.72	167.28	426.44	342.00	84.43	245.63	113.99	131.64	94.38	96.29	0.59	95.70
TEXAS.	572.81	172.71	400.09	333.69	66.40	297.78	167.47	130.30	117.06	91.48	-	91.48
UTAH	831.84	239.65	592.19	473.26	118.94	432.08	205.05	227.03	202.87	92.28	-	92.28
VERMONT.	954.32	178.91	775.41	674.81	100.61	309.04	116.74	192.30	158.67	174.24	7.76	166.48
VIRGINIA	685.18	206.83	478.35	378.10	100.25	269.81	140.60	129.20	105.15	96.52	43.42	53.09
WASHINGTON	914.70	294.81	619.89	507.58	112.31	427.14	212.38	214.76	176.12	144.85	6.98	137.86
WEST VIRGINIA.	838.81	231.37	607.44	479.44	128.00	317.23	215.25	101.98	79.10	100.61	-	100.61
WISCONSIN.	878.88	429.79	449.09	398.06	51.04	309.17	154.72	154.46	132.61	187.79	71.96	115.82
WYOMING.	991.31	292.64	698.67	476.49	222.18	336.29	168.87	167.42	141.92	63.32	-	63.32

- Represents zero or rounds to zero.
[1]Including amounts for categories not shown separately.
[2]Medians are based on those States having the specified items.

(Dollar amounts)

State	General expenditure--Continued												Total personal services expenditure
	Highways			Hospitals	Natural resources	Interest	Health	Correction	Financial adminis-tration	Employment security adminis-tration	General control		
	Total	Inter-govern-mental expendi-ture[1]	Direct expendi-ture										
50-STATE AVERAGE .	81.14	16.84	64.30	40.54	20.26	23.82	17.92	13.37	10.39	7.88	8.62		165.92
MEDIAN STATE . . .	101.37	14.28	79.88	39.47	23.33	14.50	17.94	12.26	10.65	7.95	9.09		177.92
ALABAMA.	101.14	21.73	79.41	46.15	17.94	13.66	16.28	7.95	5.37	7.45	6.16		172.48
ALASKA	396.96	-	396.96	33.57	170.86	120.81	64.54	53.93	48.42	35.12	93.36		770.02
ARIZONA.	104.86	24.51	80.35	30.58	16.02	1.93	10.71	12.71	13.06	10.20	6.85		178.37
ARKANSAS	115.83	26.04	89.78	31.53	22.47	3.21	11.45	7.95	12.61	7.61	4.94		144.82
CALIFORNIA	49.19	17.98	31.21	26.25	25.73	13.10	19.64	15.04	13.21	6.71	7.02		182.67
COLORADO	94.53	16.85	77.68	39.77	20.03	2.92	15.46	13.45	12.64	6.80	16.11		209.99
CONNECTICUT.	55.17	5.23	49.94	49.22	7.10	51.78	11.10	14.45	8.77	8.81	14.69		160.86
DELAWARE	98.75	3.44	95.31	45.66	35.90	57.43	28.19	29.93	18.06	9.25	28.52		300.32
FLORIDA.	69.16	13.32	55.83	26.43	31.86	11.77	23.48	20.62	6.49	6.15	11.83		128.92
GEORGIA.	69.94	9.11	60.83	35.52	22.20	12.76	24.70	13.35	7.26	6.03	6.23		155.50
HAWAII	104.77	-	104.77	83.56	79.57	84.99	28.87	17.04	19.14	12.12	35.00		561.81
IDAHO.	157.49	34.85	122.64	15.94	45.98	2.88	25.98	12.21	12.07	11.17	10.42		189.52
ILLINOIS	100.71	22.04	78.67	41.44	10.87	17.68	12.43	9.77	8.02	6.50	8.01		131.74
INDIANA.	83.05	29.11	53.93	30.88	14.77	5.26	10.26	8.70	7.59	6.37	4.73		141.46
IOWA	141.31	49.22	92.09	47.91	24.19	2.01	6.45	10.35	10.13	7.98	6.29		176.35
KANSAS	101.60	16.85	84.75	49.34	20.70	5.50	7.59	10.82	11.42	7.92	8.47		181.39
KENTUCKY	120.49	3.75	116.73	21.64	33.53	27.60	17.68	10.58	9.39	2.93	9.15		193.28
LOUISIANA.	135.37	10.44	124.93	63.73	26.32	18.83	15.33	30.01	8.97	6.92	9.36		184.97
MAINE.	102.81	3.90	98.92	23.26	31.14	25.66	14.99	9.31	9.88	10.44	11.31		160.12
MARYLAND	97.07	46.22	50.85	52.73	16.66	34.49	23.54	24.30	17.67	5.33	12.68		177.47
MASSACHUSETTS.	60.54	10.16	50.39	41.18	9.51	52.19	24.87	12.32	8.99	8.52	9.02		150.28
MICHIGAN	81.04	38.10	42.94	38.18	14.86	11.51	21.41	13.12	8.86	10.86	8.32		167.29
MINNESOTA.	96.28	24.55	71.73	42.56	29.38	13.79	14.04	10.26	9.74	6.43	7.53		191.97
MISSISSIPPI.	119.38	29.52	89.86	31.92	36.64	16.86	13.64	6.89	6.36	13.27	4.99		134.22
MISSOURI	82.82	9.70	73.12	34.36	12.06	4.30	9.08	7.88	5.51	7.48	5.94		133.45
MONTANA.	212.08	9.78	202.31	36.12	45.94	4.59	12.87	14.43	27.40	10.58	13.65		265.55
NEBRASKA	125.10	38.54	86.56	41.73	30.65	1.77	15.29	10.65	8.69	7.50	8.01		173.06
NEVADA	137.19	9.88	127.31	17.09	29.04	4.03	30.78	30.03	25.75	23.51	14.43		230.74
NEW HAMPSHIRE.	129.90	5.97	123.93	51.64	19.04	19.27	15.99	9.69	9.55	7.33	8.16		169.64
NEW JERSEY	41.10	3.86	37.24	40.30	30.51	32.17	12.27	9.64	10.46	7.04	9.52		126.20
NEW MEXICO	105.49	8.62	96.87	43.64	33.63	5.42	20.32	10.20	19.03	8.41	19.40		237.63
NEW YORK	38.46	7.02	31.44	61.60	12.07	89.47	24.80	17.17	11.88	9.15	10.56		163.30
NORTH CAROLINA	82.05	5.57	76.49	50.84	19.44	11.05	19.45	18.90	8.57	7.86	10.99		167.48
NORTH DAKOTA	170.12	31.77	138.35	34.92	45.41	5.41	11.30	6.46	12.16	3.03	9.24		243.52
OHIO	73.69	29.54	44.14	32.22	8.65	16.20	19.66	11.19	10.33	7.10	3.36		119.66
OKLAHOMA	94.50	30.16	64.34	39.17	20.13	16.22	6.06	15.15	6.20	8.97	8.22		184.90
OREGON	99.74	41.32	58.42	40.87	34.69	44.90	17.44	16.41	25.36	5.72	12.57		213.98
PENNSYLVANIA	80.32	10.37	69.95	50.14	13.74	33.23	18.20	9.28	10.85	9.60	9.23		146.81
RHODE ISLAND	40.21	0.42	39.79	67.81	13.42	26.46	33.27	16.68	14.77	13.33	19.83		241.09
SOUTH CAROLINA	63.20	14.28	48.92	45.31	21.26	17.04	28.12	14.32	7.65	9.64	4.94		198.61
SOUTH DAKOTA	137.80	6.73	131.07	57.75	33.52	15.22	14.01	8.74	14.06	14.50	16.13		221.79
TENNESSEE.	103.49	31.35	72.14	30.57	16.19	12.52	14.44	11.98	7.89	7.76	6.85		147.02
TEXAS.	54.63	0.57	54.06	45.66	13.00	8.83	7.90	7.18	6.16	6.97	4.40		144.04
UTAH	102.22	9.29	92.93	35.06	33.64	5.58	18.37	12.13	12.93	12.72	8.13		231.50
VERMONT.	124.22	11.98	112.24	31.10	45.17	46.33	37.23	17.04	19.66	13.11	16.83		234.25
VIRGINIA	126.90	7.24	119.66	49.66	13.02	8.79	22.40	17.79	11.13	5.03	7.57		180.42
WASHINGTON	102.70	18.90	83.80	27.55	43.96	18.01	22.62	17.50	13.88	10.30	7.52		231.71
WEST VIRGINIA.	183.79	-	183.79	31.76	27.51	34.16	19.31	6.93	11.99	8.00	9.39		169.29
WISCONSIN.	69.56	21.59	47.97	30.17	16.68	15.92	23.38	13.01	10.36	7.16	6.97		150.34
WYOMING.	255.66	27.33	228.33	29.77	54.13	9.73	18.72	11.68	22.83	22.12	16.59		280.75

- Represents zero or rounds to zero.
[1]Medians are based on those States having the specified items.

Table 2. Per Capita Amounts of Financial Items for State Governments: 1977—Continued

(Dollar amounts)

State	Gross debt at end of fiscal year					Net long-term debt at end of year		Cash and security holdings at end of fiscal year				
	Total debt	Long-term			Short-term[1]	Total	Full faith and credit[1]	Total	Insurance trust systems			Other than insurance trust systems
		Total	Full faith and credit[1]	Nonguar-anteed[1]					Total[2]	Employee retire-ment systems	Unemploy-ment compen-sation systems	
50-STATE AVERAGE .	418.29	404.30	199.00	205.30	13.99	313.30	173.19	814.84	487.30	440.14	22.98	327.54
MEDIAN STATE . . .	309.52	303.74	187.75	139.35	4.40	249.42	164.64	733.96	375.64	341.11	19.21	290.46
ALABAMA.	270.23	270.23	30.32	239.91	-	258.84	29.56	529.61	346.56	334.37	12.01	183.04
ALASKA	2 252.05	2 182.51	1 302.23	880.28	69.54	1 812.00	1 301.54	4 033.11	1092.52	903.60	188.11	2 940.59
ARIZONA	44.95	44.02	-	44.02	0.93	37.71	-	836.48	656.98	551.07	20.33	179.50
ARKANSAS	65.53	65.50	-	65.50	0.03	59.78	-	423.16	263.67	256.37	6.16	159.49
CALIFORNIA	307.94	306.49	260.50	45.99	1.44	239.18	197.09	1 084.60	765.59	692.37	37.07	319.02
COLORADO	75.32	75.32	-	75.32	-	44.08	-	811.00	587.82	532.61	16.45	223.18
CONNECTICUT.	1 021.05	1 020.45	774.64	245.82	0.60	893.61	733.64	724.68	375.95	356.65	19.06	348.73
DELAWARE	1 276.13	1 274.22	702.28	571.94	1.91	1 204.44	676.68	649.78	232.08	216.42	15.66	417.69
FLORIDA.	237.03	237.03	51.31	185.72	-	177.54	19.79	500.49	297.24	286.80	9.44	203.25
GEORGIA.	251.28	251.28	73.05	178.23	-	240.00	72.14	556.50	370.50	326.52	43.98	186.00
HAWAII	1 660.64	1 640.44	1 302.19	338.25	20.21	1 625.49	1 298.98	1 493.49	969.89	950.84	17.19	523.60
IDAHO.	60.98	59.36	1.27	58.09	1.61	36.15	1.16	682.77	322.72	235.72	59.07	360.06
ILLINOIS	360.50	345.43	145.13	200.30	15.07	274.73	140.66	516.82	337.18	325.00	12.16	179.64
INDIANA.	110.21	108.36	-	108.36	1.84	87.39	-	454.26	200.51	157.33	43.11	253.74
IOWA	43.05	43.05	-	43.05	-	40.37	-	493.17	307.12	292.41	14.71	186.04
KANSAS	173.18	173.17	-	173.17	0.01	156.87	-	575.44	296.70	234.52	62.19	278.74
KENTUCKY	590.11	590.11	95.80	494.31	-	428.03	95.80	795.78	331.73	292.80	36.76	464.06
LOUISIANA.	451.22	449.93	331.08	118.85	1.29	402.82	294.36	781.05	478.85	441.94	36.91	302.19
MAINE.	519.88	519.87	253.32	266.55	0.01	391.95	253.32	601.89	209.91	206.68	3.14	391.98
MARYLAND	737.15	737.15	499.32	237.83	-	696.10	488.89	666.49	449.92	424.83	12.90	216.56
MASSACHUSETTS.	893.75	786.68	554.03	232.64	107.07	634.03	552.00	504.72	192.29	174.16	17.96	312.43
MICHIGAN	213.71	207.05	81.01	126.05	6.66	139.61	78.61	632.18	415.23	365.81	37.31	216.95
MINNESOTA.	311.11	300.99	187.75	113.24	10.12	289.85	185.89	920.22	474.62	459.03	13.84	445.60
MISSISSIPPI.	339.93	338.90	303.70	35.20	1.03	324.87	301.28	455.48	286.30	241.63	44.65	169.18
MISSOURI	91.73	91.73	16.47	75.27	-	68.47	14.64	500.15	328.56	307.92	20.53	171.59
MONTANA.	133.24	133.24	9.72	123.51	-	110.25	8.76	934.16	493.29	417.49	7.05	440.87
NEBRASKA	37.99	37.99	-	37.99	-	24.01	-	272.56	97.23	67.53	28.87	175.33
NEVADA	86.26	86.26	57.34	28.92	-	67.98	43.66	1 210.85	939.03	690.01	22.40	271.83
NEW HAMPSHIRE.	427.77	403.04	263.72	139.32	24.73	390.70	253.87	407.59	322.56	282.52	40.04	85.03
NEW JERSEY	552.84	539.73	229.35	310.38	13.11	451.05	226.13	937.37	627.97	604.81	12.66	309.40
NEW MEXICO	178.21	178.08	21.00	157.09	0.13	139.92	17.19	1 542.36	452.29	425.76	26.53	1 090.07
NEW YORK	1 116.49	1 042.99	207.30	835.69	73.50	651.69	164.64	1 527.79	822.28	774.83	5.39	705.51
NORTH CAROLINA	146.15	146.06	114.57	31.49	0.09	140.49	112.08	774.06	548.97	505.01	43.21	225.09
NORTH DAKOTA	103.10	103.10	23.10	80.00	-	62.26	7.21	915.17	211.02	136.79	21.57	704.16
OHIO	299.53	286.91	186.07	100.85	12.62	263.00	185.70	864.41	708.95	555.60	18.50	155.46
OKLAHOMA	333.42	333.34	61.98	271.36	0.08	305.05	57.44	537.08	176.24	158.99	10.54	360.85
OREGON	1 023.25	1 023.25	1 015.23	8.02	-	96.27	96.27	1 837.79	618.73	425.02	27.86	1 219.06
PENNSYLVANIA	541.70	528.20	326.53	201.67	13.50	494.35	314.62	639.72	480.63	462.77	8.56	159.09
RHODE ISLAND	684.84	682.70	292.93	389.78	2.14	535.67	291.12	847.43	375.32	342.18	10.84	472.10
SOUTH CAROLINA	455.98	446.41	174.80	271.61	9.57	321.06	157.09	715.88	467.54	438.09	27.94	248.34
SOUTH DAKOTA	336.04	317.04	-	317.04	19.00	144.66	-	743.22	221.84	204.25	17.52	521.37
TENNESSEE.	279.87	255.05	160.93	94.12	24.82	188.23	160.00	505.35	265.01	228.61	36.39	240.34
TEXAS	165.63	165.63	69.05	96.58	-	138.05	53.95	787.89	336.29	316.94	19.35	451.59
UTAH	114.78	114.78	67.03	47.74	-	79.55	36.07	629.01	383.60	340.03	15.99	245.41
VERMONT.	941.09	940.58	523.68	416.90	0.51	785.29	523.68	933.50	359.19	347.92	11.21	574.30
VIRGINIA	169.92	147.37	7.98	139.39	22.55	56.57	7.98	517.21	246.79	231.03	15.76	270.42
WASHINGTON	385.94	385.94	305.97	79.98	-	322.78	305.97	981.16	675.91	527.79	13.45	305.25
WEST VIRGINIA.	718.03	707.49	461.75	245.74	10.54	622.98	461.75	940.07	416.03	234.99	33.30	524.04
WISCONSIN.	362.22	360.07	260.32	99.76	2.15	340.91	260.32	922.38	684.69	645.65	35.91	237.69
WYOMING.	180.49	180.49	-	180.49	-	79.06	-	1 769.27	566.26	388.12	94.75	1 203.01

Note: Per capita amounts are based on provisional population figures as of July 1, 1977, and are computed on the basis of amounts rounded to the nearest thousand.

- Represents zero or rounds to zero.
[1] Medians are based on those States having the specified items.
[2] Including amounts for categories not shown separately.

Table 3. Relation of State Government Finances to State Personal Income: 1977

State	General revenue per $1,000 of personal income						General expenditure per $1,000 of personal income					
			Taxes					Education				
	Total	Revenue from Federal Government	Total[1]	General sales or gross receipts[2]	Individual income[2]	Charges and miscellaneous	Total	Total[1]	Intergovernmental[2]	State institutions of higher education	Public welfare	Highways
50-STATE AVERAGE .	124.18	33.58	73.90	22.59	18.64	14.70	121.35	46.82	27.03	15.47	23.96	12.79
MEDIAN STATE . . .	134.77	36.81	76.00	24.17	18.01	16.71	131.74	50.98	27.36	19.56	18.78	16.03
ALABAMA.	141.60	46.77	75.01	24.30	13.99	18.64	138.61	65.79	29.93	26.27	19.61	19.94
ALASKA	306.68	68.81	194.39	-	52.86	43.41	258.58	86.47	40.44	21.91	14.17	40.60
ARIZONA.	131.76	27.62	88.11	38.20	14.48	15.50	128.89	64.70	38.19	23.46	8.52	18.29
ARKANSAS	134.04	44.32	77.14	26.35	15.74	12.16	133.22	54.34	28.96	19.60	22.73	23.86
CALIFORNIA	134.75	37.48	81.80	28.03	23.53	11.40	123.55	45.33	27.30	15.57	35.41	7.00
COLORADO	120.33	36.43	64.77	21.62	20.38	18.73	117.79	58.41	27.36	28.56	17.60	14.89
CONNECTICUT.	101.49	23.61	63.55	25.45	2.59	14.20	93.31	28.35	15.17	9.12	18.30	7.48
DELAWARE	155.98	33.34	95.52	-	41.06	26.72	151.66	65.55	32.22	27.67	18.07	14.04
FLORIDA.	95.70	22.23	64.60	27.59	-	8.34	96.77	43.51	31.31	10.01	8.72	11.53
GEORGIA.	115.34	35.54	69.14	24.93	17.97	10.38	113.00	49.34	28.76	16.14	18.75	12.80
HAWAII	198.27	55.71	110.63	55.02	32.76	30.97	218.24	77.05	-	28.12	31.14	15.13
IDAHO.	140.84	47.93	78.53	22.17	24.01	13.93	146.07	57.40	31.57	21.93	16.07	28.81
ILLINOIS	98.98	25.17	64.48	22.33	17.13	8.66	103.36	37.62	23.96	10.67	25.61	13.73
INDIANA.	104.19	23.07	65.56	31.69	14.53	15.28	96.59	42.64	20.73	19.11	11.84	13.42
IOWA	120.21	31.17	72.11	19.35	24.96	14.85	127.95	56.01	33.00	19.53	18.42	22.70
KANSAS	107.33	28.40	64.84	21.86	14.00	13.34	106.46	45.25	23.90	19.48	19.54	15.81
KENTUCKY	143.74	41.62	84.62	25.16	18.34	17.18	139.80	55.31	26.36	21.68	25.08	22.60
LOUISIANA.	154.91	46.56	82.78	23.20	6.44	24.90	157.90	57.78	33.55	18.64	21.12	25.56
MAINE.	150.30	47.72	81.60	29.55	13.09	19.57	140.00	50.95	31.13	15.70	29.87	19.43
MARYLAND	122.46	28.24	74.62	16.34	28.29	18.75	124.64	44.25	26.18	13.90	20.00	14.09
MASSACHUSETTS.	129.82	34.59	76.67	11.55	31.13	14.19	124.28	35.27	21.91	9.27	38.07	9.15
MICHIGAN	128.35	33.22	78.78	22.88	23.83	14.96	124.41	46.93	25.84	16.89	32.36	12.03
MINNESOTA.	157.77	37.21	101.39	19.04	39.03	17.56	155.88	71.30	44.45	23.17	25.37	15.61
MISSISSIPPI.	165.00	54.28	90.90	44.59	12.34	18.70	163.03	70.12	40.49	22.58	21.51	26.75
MISSOURI	92.40	27.69	56.09	20.93	13.67	8.50	86.57	36.02	21.12	12.86	15.40	13.95
MONTANA.	156.43	62.03	72.94	-	26.12	20.21	155.94	57.98	31.08	22.21	16.29	37.68
NEBRASKA	110.49	28.93	64.86	21.03	18.05	14.35	105.67	35.04	12.57	19.81	14.03	20.66
NEVADA	120.75	32.58	75.34	26.50	-	11.34	116.70	46.97	28.16	16.43	10.81	19.88
NEW HAMPSHIRE.	93.39	32.09	40.52	-	1.43	18.71	111.28	30.86	8.15	19.68	16.40	22.32
NEW JERSEY	99.17	26.41	57.32	16.86	13.10	14.06	100.69	34.25	20.50	8.07	21.10	5.56
NEW MEXICO	195.48	52.43	96.12	41.38	4.28	45.04	170.82	84.45	49.64	30.00	17.19	20.19
NEW YORK	148.16	38.16	84.64	17.48	35.67	17.21	145.03	43.53	30.50	7.80	34.91	5.43
NORTH CAROLINA	135.01	40.68	79.97	17.15	26.23	13.75	133.07	63.99	42.09	18.04	15.01	15.20
NORTH DAKOTA	180.23	56.96	78.79	29.31	14.63	41.31	166.84	62.06	29.38	28.68	17.17	29.54
OHIO	88.44	24.17	52.10	16.57	8.97	11.51	93.52	37.18	22.01	13.13	15.95	11.50
OKLAHOMA	133.65	37.02	72.14	12.99	13.73	23.11	124.52	54.31	27.17	22.95	22.84	16.83
OREGON	134.80	42.19	66.75	-	38.54	25.18	130.41	47.11	22.54	20.89	23.50	16.25
PENNSYLVANIA	112.44	29.32	73.19	19.96	15.42	8.98	117.14	40.39	25.52	7.92	30.08	12.39
RHODE ISLAND	145.00	44.30	74.81	24.17	17.69	25.43	137.00	42.94	18.78	18.33	36.80	6.41
SOUTH CAROLINA	145.64	41.67	81.00	28.32	19.81	21.41	146.22	60.76	28.74	22.52	16.16	12.40
SOUTH DAKOTA	140.37	52.73	56.98	28.77	-	29.06	143.77	44.13	14.91	25.97	19.27	27.04
TENNESSEE.	116.16	36.16	67.66	32.45	0.99	11.62	112.91	46.71	21.68	17.95	18.31	19.68
TEXAS.	104.48	26.68	61.34	21.90	-	16.24	94.91	49.34	27.75	19.40	15.16	9.05
UTAH	158.33	52.36	80.86	34.54	24.09	23.88	160.54	83.39	39.57	39.15	17.81	19.73
VERMONT.	188.55	70.38	89.17	12.61	27.29	28.13	178.87	57.92	21.88	29.74	32.66	23.28
VIRGINIA	112.08	29.06	64.37	13.38	22.38	17.49	110.27	43.42	22.63	16.92	15.53	20.42
WASHINGTON	140.38	36.59	85.47	47.73	-	15.98	136.19	63.60	31.62	26.22	21.57	15.29
WEST VIRGINIA.	156.14	50.58	90.88	45.01	16.56	14.58	156.86	59.32	40.25	14.79	18.81	34.37
WISCONSIN.	149.96	36.10	96.96	23.69	40.58	15.79	145.01	51.01	25.53	21.88	30.98	11.48
WYOMING.	188.38	70.24	89.99	36.48	-	26.93	155.21	52.66	26.44	22.22	9.91	40.03

Note: State financial amounts for fiscal year 1976-77 are related herein to personal income data as estimated for calendar 1976 (see table 21).

- Represents zero or rounds to zero.
[1] Includes amounts for categories not shown separately.
[2] Medians are based on those States having the specified items.

C — COUNTY GOVERNMENT FINANCES

This and the next section of Part II show county and city data; each contains a summary table and a table showing major financial items on a per capita basis. A very important recent change in the finances of local governments is the dramatic increase which has occurred in the amount of direct grant-in-aid funds received from the Federal Government. The size in these direct grants can be observed in these two sections; however, there were especially big increases in fiscal years 1978 and 1979 which do not show up in these tables, but are having a fundamental impact on fiscal federalism. These increases will show up in next year's data.

Revenue of all county governments during fiscal 1976–77 totaled $42.4 billion, an increase of $4.6 billion, or 12.3 percent, from the previous year's total.

General revenue of county governments, which excludes utility, liquor store, and employee-retirement amounts, was $41.4 billion in 1976–77 compared to $36.9 billion a year earlier.

County expenditure totaled $42.4 billion in 1976–77, up to 10.3 percent from the 1975-76 amount of $38.4 billion. General expenditure—i.e., spending other than for utility, liquor store, and employee-retirement purposes—totaled $41.3 billion in 1976-77, compared to $37.5 billion in 1975–76.

General Revenue

Intergovernmental revenue provided $18.8 billion or 45.3 percent of all county revenue in fiscal 1976-77, compared to 45.1 percent or $16.7 billion for fiscal 1975-76. Grants and shared tax amounts from the States, including certain Federal aid channeled through the States, provided $14.3 billion or 76.2 percent of all intergovernmental aid. Direct Federal aid to county governments amounted to $3.7 billion in fiscal 1976-77, of which $1.7 billion, or 8.9 percent

of county intergovernmental revenue, was in the form of General Revenue Sharing Grants. Percentages in this paragraph and in the one following, it should be noted, relate to general revenue whereas the percentage distributions in Table Q are based on total revenue from utilities, liquor stores and employee-retirement systems as well as general revenue sources.

County-imposed taxes yielded $15.9 billion in fiscal 1976-77 or about 38.3 percent of all general revenue of county governments. Property taxation continued as the predominant tax revenue source, supplying $12.9 billion or 31.1 percent of general revenue in fiscal 1976-77 and increasing 11.3 percent from the previous year's return of $11.6 billion.

Table Q illustrates the distribution of county government revenue in fiscal 1976-77.

General Expenditure

Public welfare, education, hospitals, and highways, in that order, were the leading county functions in terms of expenditure for general government purposes, and together accounted for 54.9 percent of the total.

As indicated by Table R public welfare received a larger share of county expenditure than any other

149

Item	Amount (millions of dollars)	Percent	Percent increase from 1975-76
Revenue from all sources................	42,426	100.0	12.3
Intergovernmental revenue............	18,787	44.3	12.7
Revenue from own sources.............	23,639	55.7	12.0
General revenue..................	22,654	53.4	11.8
Taxes........................	15,865	37.4	12.3
Charges and miscellaneous.......	6,789	16.0	10.7
Utility revenue..................	303	0.7	22.7
Liquor stores revenue............	156	0.4	2.0
Employee-retirement revenue......	526	1.2	18.7

Item	Amount (millions of dollars)	Percent	Percent increase or decrease (-) from 1975-76
Total expenditure..................	42,359	100.0	10.3
General expenditure...............	41,282	97.5	10.1
Public welfare..................	7,842	18.5	10.8
Education.......................	6,634	15.7	10.6
Hospitals.......................	4,346	10.3	12.6
Highways........................	3,849	9.1	3.1
General control.................	2,560	6.0	12.2
Health..........................	1,957	4.6	16.2
Police protection...............	1,916	4.5	11.3
Correction......................	1,244	2.9	12.1
Financial administration........	1,092	2.6	11.4
General public buildings........	933	2.2	-2.8
Interest on general debt........	992	2.3	10.7
All other.......................	7,917	18.7	10.3
Utility expenditure.............	579	1.4	16.3
Employee-retirement expenditure..	353	0.8	21.7
Liquor stores expenditure.......	138	0.3	5.3

function. County spending for public welfare tended to be concentrated in States where counties administer major assistance and general relief programs. Similarly, county spending for education was relatively high in those States where counties directly administer local public schools or directly support other education activities.

Expenditure by Character and Object

About $29.4 billion or 69.3 percent of all county expenditure in 1976-77 (including amounts for utility, insurance trust, and general government purposes) was for current operation. Expenditure for personal services—mainly for current operation, but also including any salary and wage payments for construction work performed on a force-account rather than contract basis—amounted to $16.3 billion in 1976-77 or 38.4 percent of all county expenditure.

Capital outlay—mostly for construction but also including spending for equipment and the purchase of land and existing structures—was $5.3 billion, or 12.5 percent of all county expenditure.

Indebtedness and Debt Transactions

As shown below, total county indebtedness at the end of fiscal 1976-77 was $22.6 billion. Of this amount, $21.4 billion, or 94.6 percent, represented long-term obligations. Short-term debt amounted to $1.2 billion. About $2.9 billion long-term debt was issued during fiscal 1976-77 while long-term debt retired amounted to $1.1 billion. The net difference resulted in an increase of $1.7 billion in county indebtedness during 1976-77.

Long-term full faith and credit debt, for which the credit of the county is unconditionally pledged, accounted for 71.1 percent of $15.2 billion of total long-term obligations. Nonguaranteed debt, obligations payable solely from pledged earnings of specific activities or facilities, from special assessments or from specific nonproperty taxes, was $6.2 billion or 28.9 percent of total long-term debt. Net long-term debt outstanding, representing gross long-term debt less amounts reserved for future debt retirement (debt offsets), amounted to $20.2 billion at the end of fiscal 1976—77.

Cash and Security Holdings

Cash and securities held by all county funds at the end of fiscal 1976-77 amounted to $17.7 billion, or 20.7 percent more than a year earlier. Of this total $5.6 billion was held by locally administered employee-retirement systems. $2.5 billion represented proceeds of bond issues pending disbursement, $1.2 billion was reserved as offsets to long-term debt, and the remaining $8.3 billion comprised holdings of all other county funds, including public trust and investment funds. The summary presented in Table T shows financial assets of county governments.

Employee-Retirement Systems

Employee contributions and earnings on retirement system investments of county-administered employee-retirement systems amounted to $526 million in fiscal 1976—77.

Benefits and withdrawals paid by county retire-

Item	Amount (millions of dollars)	Percent increase or decrease (−) from 1975-76
(S) Debt outstanding, total.......	22,590	10.9
Long-term...................	21,367	12.3
Full faith and credit.....	15,202	11.7
Nonguaranteed.............	6,165	13.8
Short-term.................	1,223	-8.9
Net long-term debt outstanding	20,195	11.5

151

Item	Amount (millions of dollars)	Percent	Percent increase or decrease (−) from 1975-76
Cash and security holdings at end of fiscal year...........................	17,653	100.0	20.7
Insurance trust:			
Employee retirement...........	5,595	31.7	37.8
Other than insurance trust....	12,058	68.3	14.1
By purpose:			
Bond funds.................	2,544	14.4	−1.0
Offsets to debt...........	1,172	6.6	28.5
Other and unallocable.....	8,342	47.3	13.3
By type:			
Cash and deposits.........	9,932	56.3	11.6
Securities................	2,126	12.0	27.0
Federal...............	1,551	8.8	17.6
State and local government...	94	0.5	571.4
Other (nongovernmental)......	481	2.7	41.1

ment systems in 1976-77 totaled $353 million, and their financial assets at the end of the fiscal year amounted to $5.6 billion.

County Utilities and Liquor Stores

In Census Bureau reporting on governmental finances, amounts relating to four types of enterprises operated by local governments are distinguished for reporting as pertaining to "utilities"—i.e., water supply, electric power, gas supply, and transit system. Of these four, only water supply involves any significant activity by county governments, and even this utility service is provided by only relatively few counties.

County-operated liquor stores are administered only by certain counties in Maryland and North Carolina.

Individual County Data

Financial amounts and per capita data for 332 counties of 100,000 inhabitants or more in 1973 are presented. The counties are arranged alphabetically by State. Any intercounty comparisons based upon these figures should be made with caution, and with due recognition of variations that exist among urban areas in the relevant role of the county government, as discussed below under "Coverage and Limitations of Data."

Organized county governments are found throughout the Nation except for Connecticut, Rhode Island, the District of Columbia, and limited portions of other States. Since these exceptional areas include New York City, Philadelphia, and several others of the most populous cities in the nation (where the municipality, in effect, operates as a composite city-county unit), nearly 12 percent of the total U.S. population is not served by any separately organized county government.

Coverage and Limitations of Data

Data in this report relate only to county governments and their dependent agencies, and do not include amounts for other local governments within or among county areas. Therefore, expenditure figures for "education" do not include spending by the separate school districts which administer public schools within many county areas. Variations in the assignment of governmental responsibility for public assistance, health, hospitals, public housing, and other functions to a lesser degree, also have an important effect upon reported amounts of county expenditure, revenue, and debt.

In addition, counties have reported financial data to the Census Bureau reflecting fiscal years of varying annual periods. Slightly more than one-half of all county governments in the Nation had a fiscal year corresponding directly with the calendar year in 1976, and over one-third of the counties ended their fiscal year on June 30. This report covers fiscal years that ended between July 1, 1976 and June 30, 1977.

For counties having 500,000 or greater population and for a limited number of smaller counties, the basic data were compiled by Census Bureau representatives from official reports and records, with the advice and assistance of local officials and employees. Information for other counties of over 100,000 inhabitants was supplied by local officials in response to a mail canvass that involved the use of detailed census questionnaires. The mail reports were examined intensively, and followup correspondence was used to supplement and verify questionable figures. Data in this report are subject to possible inaccuracies in classification, response and processing. Every effort is made to keep such errors to a minimum through care in examining, editing, and tabulating the data submitted.

The data presented for counties of less than 100,000 population are based on a sample which includes all counties with 1970 populations between 50,000 and 99,999 and a randomly selected sample of the smaller counties. The relative sampling error for the major financial categories has been calculated to be less than 5 percent at the 90 percent confidence level.

153

Table 1. Summary of County Government Finances: 1977 and Prior Periods

(Dollar amounts in millions)

Item	1976-77	1975-76	1974-75	1973-74	Percent increase or decrease (-) 1975-76 to 1976-77	Percent distribution 1976-77
REVENUE						
REVENUE, TOTAL	42 426	37 785	33 648	30 929	12.3	100.0
GENERAL REVENUE.	41 441	36 942	32 893	30 246	12.2	97.7
INTERGOVERNMENTAL REVENUE [1]	18 787	16 677	14 755	13 799	12.7	44.3
FROM FEDERAL GOVERNMENT.	3 741	2 911	2 385	2 320	28.5	8.8
GENERAL REVENUE SHARING.	1 671	1 612	1 595	1 722	3.7	3.9
FROM STATE GOVERNMENT.	14 315	13 156	11 842	11 023	8.8	33.7
GENERAL REVENUE FROM OWN SOURCES	22 654	20 265	18 138	16 466	11.8	53.4
TAXES.	15 865	14 130	12 660	11 662	12.3	37.4
PROPERTY	12 888	11 582	10 316	9 573	11.3	30.4
OTHER.	2 976	2 548	2 345	2 089	16.8	7.0
CHARGES AND MISCELLANEOUS.	6 789	6 135	5 478	4 784	10.7	16.0
CURRENT CHARGES.	4 966	4 346	3 704	3 393	14.3	11.7
INTEREST EARNINGS.	691	775	913	650	-10.8	1.6
SPECIAL ASSESSMENTS.	140	122	122	112	14.8	0.3
SALE OF PROPERTY	51	37	53	34	37.8	0.1
OTHER AND UNALLOCABLE.	941	856	685	595	9.9	2.2
UTILITY REVENUE.	303	247	201	178	22.7	0.7
LIQUOR STORES REVENUE.	156	153	146	133	2.0	0.4
EMPLOYEE-RETIREMENT REVENUE.	526	443	408	372	18.7	1.2
EXPENDITURE						
EXPENDITURE, TOTAL	42 359	38 397	33 510	29 505	10.3	100.0
BY CHARACTER AND OBJECT:						
INTERGOVERNMENTAL EXPENDITURE.	2 521	2 095	1 841	1 796	20.3	6.0
DIRECT EXPENDITURE	39 838	36 302	31 670	27 710	9.7	94.0
CURRENT OPERATION.	29 356	26 171	22 675	19 575	12.2	69.3
CAPITAL OUTLAY	5 308	5 456	5 012	3 982	-2.7	12.5
CONSTRUCTION.	4 226	4 484	3 979	3 131	-5.8	10.0
EQUIPMENT	206	708	687	570	-70.9	0.5
LAND AND EXISTING STRUCTURES.	876	273	346	281	220.9	2.0
ASSISTANCE PAYMENTS.	3 747	3 408	2 868	3 184	9.9	8.8
INTEREST ON DEBT	1 074	968	850	742	11.0	2.5
INSURANCE BENEFITS AND REPAYMENTS.	353	290	265	225	21.7	0.8
EXHIBIT: TOTAL PERSONAL SERVICES.	16 273	14 484	12 667	11 199	12.4	38.4
BY FUNCTION:						
GENERAL EXPENDITURE.	41 282	37 478	32 744	28 879	10.1	97.5
CAPITAL OUTLAY	5 063	5 236	4 850	3 862	-3.3	12.0
OTHER.	36 219	32 241	27 894	25 017	12.3	85.5
PUBLIC WELFARE	7 842	7 079	6 169	6 342	10.8	18.5
CASH ASSISTANCE PAYMENTS	3 747	3 408	2 868	3 184	9.9	8.8
MEDICAL VENDOR PAYMENTS.	922	1 000	936	927	-7.8	2.2
OTHER PUBLIC WELFARE	3 174	2 672	2 365	2 230	18.8	7.5
EDUCATION.	6 634	5 996	5 643	4 757	10.6	15.7
CAPITAL OUTLAY	669	699	734	532	-4.3	1.6
OTHER.	5 965	5 297	4 909	4 226	12.6	14.1
HIGHWAYS	3 849	3 733	3 458	3 118	3.1	9.1
CAPITAL OUTLAY	1 113	1 197	1 140	1 030	-7.0	2.6
OTHER.	2 736	2 536	2 318	2 088	7.9	6.5
HOSPITALS.	4 346	3 860	3 337	2 899	12.6	10.3
OWN HOSPITALS.	4 075	3 558	3 038	2 625	14.5	9.6
CAPITAL OUTLAY	416	366	309	201	13.7	1.0
OTHER.	3 659	3 191	2 729	2 425	14.7	8.6
OTHER HOSPITALS.	271	302	300	274	-10.3	0.6

See footnotes at end of table.

Table 1. **Summary of County Government Finances: 1977 and Prior Periods**—Continued

(Dollar amounts in millions)

Item	1976-77	1975-76	1974-75	1973-74	Percent increase or decrease (-) 1975-76 to 1976-77	Percent distribution 1976-77
EXPENDITURE--CONTINUED						
BY FUNCTION--CONTINUED						
GENERAL EXPENDITURE--CONTINUED						
GENERAL PUBLIC BUILDINGS	933	960	824	650	-2.8	2.2
CAPITAL OUTLAY	426	450	378	275	-5.3	1.0
OTHER	507	510	446	375	-0.6	1.2
GENERAL CONTROL	2 560	2 282	1 986	1 706	12.2	6.0
POLICE PROTECTION	1 916	1 721	1 450	1 210	11.3	4.5
FINANCIAL ADMINISTRATION	1 092	980	883	765	11.4	2.6
HEALTH	1 957	1 684	1 428	1 128	16.2	4.6
CORRECTION	1 244	1 110	980	818	12.1	2.9
NATURAL RESOURCES	558	664	510	429	-16.0	1.3
PARKS AND RECREATION	887	820	741	609	8.2	2.1
SEWERAGE	1 004	915	742	586	9.7	2.4
LIBRARIES	344	315	270	228	9.2	0.8
FIRE PROTECTION	342	303	252	200	12.9	0.8
INTEREST ON GENERAL DEBT	992	896	795	695	10.7	2.3
OTHER AND UNALLOCABLE	4 789	4 159	3 277	2 730	15.1	11.3
UTILITY EXPENDITURE	579	498	376	285	16.3	1.4
LIQUOR STORES EXPENDITURE	138	131	125	115	5.3	0.3
EMPLOYEE-RETIREMENT EXPENDITURE	353	290	265	225	21.7	0.8
DEBT						
DEBT OUTSTANDING AT END OF FISCAL YEAR	22 590	20 372	18 935	17 486	10.9	100.0
LONG-TERM	21 367	19 028	17 617	16 353	12.3	94.6
FULL-FAITH AND CREDIT	15 202	13 612	12 770	12 621	11.7	67.3
NONGUARANTEED	6 165	5 416	4 847	3 732	13.8	27.3
SHORT-TERM	1 223	1 343	1 318	1 133	-8.9	5.4
LONG-TERM DEBT BY PURPOSE:						
LOCAL SCHOOLS	2 219	2 165	2 299	2 157	2.5	9.8
OTHER	19 148	16 864	15 318	14 196	13.5	84.7
NET LONG-TERM DEBT OUTSTANDING	20 195	18 116	16 814	15 605	11.5	89.4
LONG-TERM DEBT ISSUED DURING YEAR	2 859	2 205	1 866	2 184	29.7	(X)
LONG-TERM DEBT RETIRED	1 143	949	922	841	20.4	(X)
INCREASE IN TOTAL DEBT DURING THE YEAR	1 694	1 285	1 126	1 387	31.8	(X)
CASH AND SECURITY HOLDINGS						
CASH AND SECURITY HOLDINGS AT END OF FISCAL YEAR	17 653	14 631	14 586	13 716	20.7	100.0
INSURANCE TRUST:						
EMPLOYEE RETIREMENT	5 595	4 059	3 848	3 427	37.8	31.7
OTHER THAN INSURANCE TRUST	12 058	10 572	10 738	10 289	14.1	68.3
BY PURPOSE:						
BOND FUNDS	2 544	2 569	2 574	2 638	-1.0	14.4
OFFSETS TO DEBT	1 172	912	803	749	28.5	6.6
OTHER AND UNALLOCABLE	8 342	7 366	361	6 903	13.3	47.3
BY TYPE:						
CASH AND DEPOSITS	9 932	8 899	9 112	8 548	11.6	56.3
SECURITIES	2 126	1 674	1 626	1 741	27.0	12.0
FEDERAL GOVERNMENT	1 551	1 319	1 224	1 302	17.6	8.8
FEDERAL AGENCY ONLY	99	100	(NA)	(NA)	-1.0	0.6
STATE AND LOCAL GOVERNMENT	94	14	17	24	571.4	0.5
OTHER (NONGOVERNMENTAL)	481	341	385	414	41.1	2.7

Note: Because of rounding, detail may not add to totals. Amounts for counties less than 50,000 population are estimates subject to sample variation; see text.

- Represents zero or rounds to zero.
NA Not available.
X Not applicable.
[1]Including amounts from categories not shown separately, From Local Governments.

155

Table 2. Per Capita Amounts of Selected Financial Items: 1977

Item	Alabama						Arizona	
	Calhoun	Jefferson	Madison	Mobile	Montgomery	Tuscaloosa	Maricopa	Pima
GENERAL REVENUE	48.36	169.95	64.28	83.95	59.47	125.98	174.77	244.07
INTERGOVERNMENTAL REVENUE	24.91	61.18	23.73	32.60	22.55	32.10	72.86	100.08
GENERAL REVENUE SHARING	3.82	9.88	4.22	7.09	3.17	6.31	6.32	10.67
TAX REVENUE	21.21	77.44	30.68	45.15	27.65	85.88	79.02	119.59
PROPERTY TAXES ONLY	17.58	23.44	16.87	32.58	13.91	16.09	75.06	114.78
CHARGES AND MISCELLANEOUS	2.23	31.32	9.86	6.20	9.27	8.00	22.89	24.40
GENERAL EXPENDITURE, ALL FUNCTIONS	46.08	185.16	62.95	82.11	52.70	126.06	158.30	313.44
CAPITAL OUTLAY	0.84	59.72	1.94	13.23	5.23	6.02	19.25	104.09
OTHER	45.24	125.45	61.00	68.89	47.47	120.04	139.05	209.35
PUBLIC WELFARE	0.55	9.16	0.76	1.24	2.03	-	2.07	6.17
EDUCATION	2.17	1.16	1.60	7.84	6.87	21.10	22.07	21.82
HIGHWAYS	17.14	22.17	18.57	21.68	11.47	25.37	12.06	23.65
HOSPITALS	-	22.38	-	5.34	-	-	39.40	59.09
GENERAL CONTROL	6.26	9.13	8.78	7.45	6.08	7.74	17.37	30.03
POLICE PROTECTION	2.62	7.24	4.41	6.04	4.26	6.08	7.83	25.84
FINANCIAL ADMINISTRATION	5.14	8.53	1.25	6.87	5.42	4.15	5.90	8.65
GENERAL PUBLIC BUILDINGS	0.92	3.82	0.65	1.04	2.08	2.28	3.06	23.16
HEALTH	2.41	15.80	2.51	9.24	4.40	6.15	11.66	11.11
CORRECTION	2.05	4.96	2.63	3.20	4.43	2.39	8.37	-
NATURAL RESOURCES	0.35	0.07	0.65	0.83	0.35	0.23	5.30	0.20
PARKS AND RECREATION	-	16.05	1.01	0.33	0.17	4.94	1.83	15.39
INTEREST ON GENERAL DEBT	0.41	4.66	1.85	4.60	0.18	0.83	4.23	8.39
OTHER AND UNALLOCABLE	6.06	60.04	18.26	6.41	4.96	44.79	17.14	79.92
TOTAL DEBT OUTSTANDING AT END OF FISCAL YEAR	8.04	67.74	56.18	94.66	5.00	27.99	100.56	177.98

Item	Arkansas	California						
	Pulaski	Alameda	Butte	Contra Costa	Fresno	Humboldt	Kern	Los Angeles
GENERAL REVENUE	34.36	346.27	368.42	443.16	514.16	440.57	533.51	449.90
INTERGOVERNMENTAL REVENUE	13.47	168.37	213.51	219.80	243.62	230.13	243.30	234.08
GENERAL REVENUE SHARING	3.24	12.98	15.34	11.04	18.54	16.15	24.66	13.76
TAX REVENUE	18.58	143.03	132.13	188.26	163.44	158.65	236.10	193.45
PROPERTY TAXES ONLY	18.38	136.18	103.18	173.12	143.24	145.04	211.14	186.91
CHARGES AND MISCELLANEOUS	2.31	34.87	22.78	35.10	107.10	51.80	54.11	22.37
GENERAL EXPENDITURE, ALL FUNCTIONS	33.84	341.35	354.36	412.47	486.45	403.40	528.13	419.61
CAPITAL OUTLAY	0.61	10.97	32.36	19.42	15.85	7.95	34.93	22.92
OTHER	33.23	330.38	322.00	393.04	470.60	395.45	493.20	396.69
PUBLIC WELFARE	1.62	149.42	106.46	144.81	159.01	118.95	144.24	174.84
EDUCATION	0.19	6.78	41.87	31.58	37.68	34.22	38.55	13.76
HIGHWAYS	8.69	8.41	44.46	17.59	31.02	51.29	29.36	10.56
HOSPITALS	-	29.88	0.02	47.49	81.74	6.85	57.62	46.59
GENERAL CONTROL	5.61	32.08	22.96	29.64	27.87	31.13	29.71	24.22
POLICE PROTECTION	4.98	9.74	23.76	13.60	30.12	31.20	30.08	18.84
FINANCIAL ADMINISTRATION	3.56	9.97	13.99	12.87	13.22	18.69	15.16	8.32
GENERAL PUBLIC BUILDINGS	1.46	0.34	6.43	4.19	4.07	6.94	16.49	2.79
HEALTH	0.42	33.54	20.73	12.20	39.49	23.68	22.99	21.64
CORRECTION	0.64	29.19	12.64	27.53	23.59	7.65	38.75	18.86
NATURAL RESOURCES	0.13	9.72	17.00	4.89	3.87	5.48	3.71	14.28
PARKS AND RECREATION	0.83	1.08	1.09	4.24	6.10	1.44	14.73	7.82
INTEREST ON GENERAL DEBT	-	1.01	-	1.91	0.23	0.25	-	4.15
OTHER AND UNALLOCABLE	5.71	20.21	42.92	59.91	28.45	65.64	86.73	52.93
TOTAL DEBT OUTSTANDING AT END OF FISCAL YEAR	-	23.44	-	29.60	9.10	6.80	-	85.16

See footnotes at end of table.

Table 2. Per Capita Amounts of Selected Financial Items: 1977—Continued

Item	California--Continued							
	Marin	Merced	Monterey	Orange	Riverside	Sacramento	San Bernardino	San Diego
GENERAL REVENUE.	339.62	595.66	357.89	243.51	440.02	537.85	436.74	285.44
INTERGOVERNMENTAL REVENUE.	150.26	324.61	159.32	104.89	244.47	282.41	228.97	151.78
GENERAL REVENUE SHARING.	6.43	16.27	12.82	7.01	19.21	13.55	16.99	9.98
TAX REVENUE.	155.24	160.54	136.69	110.88	150.63	168.05	151.75	107.58
PROPERTY TAXES ONLY.	145.53	145.57	124.96	101.36	132.34	134.46	133.70	96.61
CHARGES AND MISCELLANEOUS.	34.11	110.52	61.88	27.74	44.93	87.40	56.02	26.08
GENERAL EXPENDITURE, ALL FUNCTIONS .	299.46	537.72	369.64	233.68	427.31	525.49	402.73	271.82
CAPITAL OUTLAY	16.70	20.09	15.80	19.92	28.42	87.92	33.37	17.63
OTHER.	282.76	517.63	353.84	213.76	398.89	437.57	369.37	254.19
PUBLIC WELFARE	66.36	170.79	120.02	62.88	139.06	184.08	133.39	112.81
EDUCATION.	20.38	90.87	20.67	18.42	38.76	25.25	20.29	13.32
HIGHWAYS	14.35	34.19	26.03	13.79	20.83	14.50	12.46	11.42
HOSPITALS.	1.14	79.52	40.58	5.21	36.55	3.06	34.31	3.48
GENERAL CONTROL.	48.27	26.82	24.34	21.47	26.93	30.15	28.25	25.30
POLICE PROTECTION.	13.10	15.58	14.27	8.97	24.21	25.33	19.51	10.31
FINANCIAL ADMINISTRATION	13.94	14.46	10.17	7.33	14.70	15.18	10.06	12.05
GENERAL PUBLIC BUILDINGS	7.51	17.11	3.43	9.33	7.76	7.85	7.86	7.93
HEALTH	33.10	25.95	23.35	17.79	32.00	27.01	28.50	19.36
CORRECTION	22.99	16.51	14.73	15.66	24.65	22.91	21.17	19.76
NATURAL RESOURCES.	5.50	1.68	4.90	10.07	29.21	3.07	13.26	3.48
PARKS AND RECREATION	10.74	5.22	6.79	9.22	5.09	25.92	9.52	3.67
INTEREST ON GENERAL DEBT	4.36	-	1.71	1.49	2.45	3.07	4.41	1.50
OTHER AND UNALLOCABLE.	37.74	39.02	58.63	32.05	25.09	138.11	59.73	27.44
TOTAL DEBT OUTSTANDING AT END OF FISCAL YEAR	82.11	-	54.22	28.84	44.87	89.89	72.53	8.74

Item	California--Continued							
	San Joaquin	San Luis Obispo	San Mateo	Santa Barbara	Santa Clara	Santa Cruz	Solano	Sonoma
GENERAL REVENUE.	492.43	457.74	321.82	434.65	420.55	387.87	319.56	447.68
INTERGOVERNMENTAL REVENUE.	255.35	172.98	152.35	182.75	231.23	197.13	161.77	215.05
GENERAL REVENUE SHARING.	18.06	19.02	5.92	13.29	11.00	14.64	11.29	16.16
TAX REVENUE.	168.20	182.43	126.38	167.19	139.15	150.64	125.75	161.09
PROPERTY TAXES ONLY.	154.47	160.73	116.30	148.22	130.24	128.62	120.86	140.61
CHARGES AND MISCELLANEOUS.	68.89	102.33	43.10	84.70	50.17	40.09	32.04	71.54
GENERAL EXPENDITURE, ALL FUNCTIONS .	502.96	421.30	315.56	389.56	363.74	420.18	317.57	439.29
CAPITAL OUTLAY	19.41	12.77	10.32	25.94	18.75	11.92	10.28	23.61
OTHER.	483.55	408.53	305.25	363.61	344.99	408.26	307.29	415.68
PUBLIC WELFARE	200.10	109.24	100.19	88.36	130.28	150.50	114.23	142.79
EDUCATION.	21.21	31.35	35.88	34.51	35.15	23.61	26.57	41.15
HIGHWAYS	29.78	29.83	9.79	13.99	11.63	19.76	15.41	36.74
HOSPITALS.	67.41	49.03	20.07	30.04	41.74	-	-	58.91
GENERAL CONTROL.	35.55	34.28	21.75	34.61	22.68	37.65	28.41	29.18
POLICE PROTECTION.	24.62	24.67	12.58	20.31	20.63	18.70	20.62	23.17
FINANCIAL ADMINISTRATION	13.17	16.94	9.00	11.55	9.08	15.36	15.90	13.42
GENERAL PUBLIC BUILDINGS	9.08	19.88	2.25	10.29	9.65	8.49	12.53	15.44
HEALTH	32.25	15.97	27.80	26.89	25.40	22.41	19.65	26.88
CORRECTION	23.51	9.44	25.01	22.05	13.53	23.04	14.24	17.57
NATURAL RESOURCES.	4.39	6.45	3.98	27.06	2.34	2.15	9.70	5.01
PARKS AND RECREATION	6.61	11.07	5.56	8.87	7.09	2.95	0.89	2.91
INTEREST ON GENERAL DEBT	-	8.36	0.13	0.72	2.60	2.45	1.73	0.28
OTHER AND UNALLOCABLE.	35.30	54.79	41.58	60.31	31.94	93.12	37.70	25.84
TOTAL DEBT OUTSTANDING AT END OF FISCAL YEAR	-	181.30	0.26	23.11	63.28	94.67	35.53	125.18

See footnotes at end of table.

Table 2. Per Capita Amounts of Selected Financial Items: 1977—Continued

Item	California--Continued				Colorado			
	Stanislaus	Tulare	Ventura	Yolo	Adams	Arapahoe	Boulder	El Paso
GENERAL REVENUE.	506.99	489.97	405.71	433.42	190.75	94.91	147.25	124.97
INTERGOVERNMENTAL REVENUE.	300.48	294.28	180.67	197.16	95.26	32.31	60.72	57.87
GENERAL REVENUE SHARING.	13.48	24.67	9.12	13.48	5.82	3.16	6.14	8.15
TAX REVENUE.	140.70	150.67	173.54	185.42	61.04	50.31	75.16	55.43
PROPERTY TAXES ONLY.	124.02	132.60	163.11	158.80	59.58	47.83	71.67	53.94
CHARGES AND MISCELLANEOUS.	65.82	45.03	51.49	50.84	34.45	12.30	11.37	11.67
GENERAL EXPENDITURE, ALL FUNCTIONS .	489.33	471.59	397.42	415.39	193.92	83.36	137.99	105.60
CAPITAL OUTLAY	23.15	17.65	22.01	18.47	22.32	7.87	13.44	10.12
OTHER.	466.18	453.94	375.41	396.92	171.60	75.49	124.55	95.48
PUBLIC WELFARE	154.66	182.41	108.61	108.50	66.90	22.71	40.31	35.10
EDUCATION.	69.38	56.53	19.82	58.02	-	-	-	-
HIGHWAYS	19.53	29.79	14.55	38.32	22.66	9.09	18.17	19.59
HOSPITALS.	42.78	21.40	26.23	28.98	-	-	0.07	-
GENERAL CONTROL.	28.50	28.78	25.96	39.55	10.12	9.09	15.64	8.86
POLICE PROTECTION.	19.18	21.73	21.81	35.31	9.72	10.37	10.86	6.67
FINANCIAL ADMINISTRATION	14.75	8.87	11.76	16.69	5.34	5.30	8.22	3.26
GENERAL PUBLIC BUILDINGS	27.39	15.68	6.51	7.84	14.66	3.71	14.55	8.60
HEALTH	30.92	25.83	27.74	25.00	16.78	3.79	9.29	7.18
CORRECTION	19.21	10.62	19.78	12.95	0.73	3.08	5.37	3.93
NATURAL RESOURCES.	3.80	1.60	21.82	6.21	1.33	0.69	0.56	0.52
PARKS AND RECREATION	4.35	2.33	6.14	2.05	2.97	-	2.27	2.53
INTEREST ON GENERAL DEBT	0.21	0.01	1.50	0.11	15.46	0.47	-	(Z)
OTHER AND UNALLOCABLE.	54.68	66.00	85.20	35.87	27.24	15.06	12.68	9.34
TOTAL DEBT OUTSTANDING AT END OF FISCAL YEAR	5.81	0.39	56.05	-	240.99	5.83	-	-

Item	Colorado--Continued				Delaware	Florida		
	Jefferson	Larimer	Pueblo	Weld	New Castle	Alachua	Brevard	Broward
GENERAL REVENUE.	130.08	150.54	203.47	350.91	144.73	159.83	170.94	113.91
INTERGOVERNMENTAL REVENUE.	43.53	74.15	111.65	101.82	64.48	68.20	68.03	28.75
GENERAL REVENUE SHARING.	4.79	6.33	8.62	12.92	16.75	7.79	9.94	3.24
TAX REVENUE.	70.16	65.99	63.25	103.75	40.56	60.57	76.38	58.97
PROPERTY TAXES ONLY.	49.88	58.10	62.05	98.82	38.79	57.42	72.67	55.04
CHARGES AND MISCELLANEOUS.	16.39	10.40	28.57	145.34	39.69	31.06	26.53	26.19
GENERAL EXPENDITURE, ALL FUNCTIONS .	115.96	142.83	204.96	341.13	170.26	168.81	181.94	91.46
CAPITAL OUTLAY	19.60	15.87	15.82	45.20	45.16	32.57	32.80	9.80
OTHER.	96.36	126.95	189.14	295.93	125.10	136.23	149.14	81.66
PUBLIC WELFARE	27.82	43.49	105.99	70.33	0.92	5.89	5.98	4.19
EDUCATION.	-	-	-	-	-	-	-	-
HIGHWAYS	20.63	19.99	16.36	46.90	0.65	14.52	13.29	9.88
HOSPITALS.	-	-	-	120.16	-	13.91	-	-
GENERAL CONTROL.	8.48	19.85	6.76	20.52	9.98	23.01	17.55	7.52
POLICE PROTECTION.	6.23	9.04	6.52	7.32	18.87	19.67	18.34	15.07
FINANCIAL ADMINISTRATION	9.56	6.12	7.03	9.00	6.76	4.53	8.15	8.60
GENERAL PUBLIC BUILDINGS	2.39	3.26	13.58	29.88	10.31	-	5.20	1.48
HEALTH	6.47	10.03	12.49	26.70	-	4.93	5.70	6.10
CORRECTION	1.45	3.22	3.91	0.65	-	7.22	0.07	1.32
NATURAL RESOURCES.	1.12	0.76	0.64	2.07	4.54	1.58	2.60	0.87
PARKS AND RECREATION	13.39	1.70	1.97	0.07	19.19	8.43	12.20	2.80
INTEREST ON GENERAL DEBT	(Z)	0.10	20.69	0.30	9.76	13.55	9.58	0.29
OTHER AND UNALLOCABLE.	18.43	25.25	9.02	7.23	89.26	51.56	83.27	33.34
TOTAL DEBT OUTSTANDING AT END OF FISCAL YEAR	-	1.29	302.39	6.11	236.59	340.52	156.52	72.42

See footnotes at end of table.

Table 2. Per Capita Amounts of Selected Financial Items: 1977—Continued

Item	Florida--Continued							
	Dade	Escambia	Hills-borough	Lee	Leon	Manatee	Orange	Palm Beach
GENERAL REVENUE	438.96	181.66	237.29	190.74	116.56	238.62	175.97	182.81
INTERGOVERNMENTAL REVENUE	129.54	53.59	61.80	55.81	56.93	52.00	65.36	60.77
GENERAL REVENUE SHARING	11.48	7.75	9.57	10.51	7.10	8.70	8.63	4.88
TAX REVENUE	132.22	52.44	73.33	85.18	47.88	80.32	83.95	101.44
PROPERTY TAXES ONLY	106.96	50.45	67.61	77.16	44.15	73.56	79.91	96.97
CHARGES AND MISCELLANEOUS	177.21	75.64	102.16	49.75	11.75	106.31	26.67	20.60
GENERAL EXPENDITURE, ALL FUNCTIONS	393.09	178.44	245.58	182.50	119.77	411.95	212.71	168.16
CAPITAL OUTLAY	117.89	15.37	38.07	26.25	11.19	249.59	47.74	23.39
OTHER	275.19	163.07	207.51	156.26	108.58	162.36	164.97	144.77
PUBLIC WELFARE	6.06	6.35	4.33	8.54	2.25	4.26	14.73	13.62
EDUCATION	-	-	0.77	-	-	-	3.22	-
HIGHWAYS	14.88	15.93	17.98	25.47	8.16	32.28	17.25	23.89
HOSPITALS	76.57	38.15	62.24	-	-	-	-	-
GENERAL CONTROL	15.17	11.07	16.23	44.23	30.82	19.11	11.81	15.61
POLICE PROTECTION	29.07	20.74	15.69	25.34	20.62	19.47	30.41	25.34
FINANCIAL ADMINISTRATION	7.59	10.58	9.64	12.68	8.28	6.64	11.11	9.96
GENERAL PUBLIC BUILDINGS	4.64	1.96	1.84	3.29	1.53	1.81	6.36	5.82
HEALTH	11.96	6.40	5.21	3.87	8.10	4.14	3.57	6.66
CORRECTION	5.95	12.72	11.05	0.06	-	0.94	2.21	1.93
NATURAL RESOURCES	0.88	1.03	4.72	2.34	-	1.47	3.67	1.13
PARKS AND RECREATION	17.81	4.13	5.67	8.98	4.68	9.49	3.33	7.04
INTEREST ON GENERAL DEBT	24.10	12.67	23.61	2.19	3.48	34.95	5.84	2.56
OTHER AND UNALLOCABLE	178.39	36.71	66.59	45.53	31.82	277.38	99.19	54.58
TOTAL DEBT OUTSTANDING AT END OF FISCAL YEAR	418.55	304.70	441.10	91.90	-	884.96	128.50	45.65

Item	Florida--Continued						Georgia	
	Pasco	Pinellas	Polk	Sarasota	Seminole	Volusia	Bibb	Chatham
GENERAL REVENUE	194.69	132.13	173.06	134.83	126.46	143.42	93.94	178.72
INTERGOVERNMENTAL REVENUE	49.30	41.69	77.24	43.85	48.04	49.82	17.71	43.56
GENERAL REVENUE SHARING	9.69	4.90	10.63	7.37	7.41	7.95	6.96	13.34
TAX REVENUE	77.88	64.22	62.40	74.93	69.10	73.52	66.56	117.61
PROPERTY TAXES ONLY	70.17	60.41	57.23	70.52	64.05	68.95	62.48	82.22
CHARGES AND MISCELLANEOUS	67.51	26.22	33.43	16.05	9.33	20.08	9.67	17.55
GENERAL EXPENDITURE, ALL FUNCTIONS	178.84	120.49	174.71	135.89	119.71	146.97	89.08	124.39
CAPITAL OUTLAY	20.09	29.92	16.27	20.59	6.58	19.31	14.53	12.48
OTHER	158.75	90.56	158.45	115.29	113.13	127.67	74.55	111.91
PUBLIC WELFARE	4.37	6.02	5.18	4.93	1.61	2.17	9.67	2.77
EDUCATION	-	3.54	-	-	-	-	-	-
HIGHWAYS	29.29	10.43	23.25	8.47	15.85	27.03	9.88	17.09
HOSPITALS	45.30	(Z)	20.88	-	-	-	2.00	4.36
GENERAL CONTROL	15.52	10.11	23.67	18.91	16.12	6.58	14.23	8.39
POLICE PROTECTION	23.71	14.47	18.91	22.64	19.99	17.45	18.25	13.57
FINANCIAL ADMINISTRATION	9.86	6.51	10.58	11.84	7.44	9.56	7.52	6.72
GENERAL PUBLIC BUILDINGS	6.21	3.17	2.78	8.92	3.65	1.73	3.16	3.29
HEALTH	4.22	5.46	8.20	5.87	2.64	7.50	5.89	14.65
CORRECTION	0.27	2.41	1.82	4.41	1.19	7.20	3.56	5.32
NATURAL RESOURCES	1.21	2.80	3.53	3.36	1.25	3.39	0.42	0.07
PARKS AND RECREATION	2.07	10.53	1.21	6.30	2.37	4.66	2.46	2.46
INTEREST ON GENERAL DEBT	6.63	4.06	2.36	4.87	3.00	0.96	2.38	4.54
OTHER AND UNALLOCABLE	30.18	40.97	52.34	35.39	44.59	58.74	9.67	41.15
TOTAL DEBT OUTSTANDING AT END OF FISCAL YEAR	90.93	132.53	42.26	185.82	69.60	26.60	75.21	97.16

See footnotes at end of table.

Table 2. Per Capita Amounts of Selected Financial Items: 1977—Continued

Item	Georgia--Continued					Idaho	Illinois	
	Clayton	Cobb	De Kalb	Fulton	Richmond	Ada	Champaign	Cook
GENERAL REVENUE	177.29	146.03	259.98	225.33	150.32	86.55	74.31	115.45
INTERGOVERNMENTAL REVENUE	22.61	34.52	43.72	34.35	23.78	28.21	24.19	33.37
GENERAL REVENUE SHARING	12.01	8.23	11.33	15.81	12.85	4.49	3.39	3.67
TAX REVENUE	119.06	74.93	153.70	170.99	118.24	47.11	31.32	66.65
PROPERTY TAXES ONLY	113.56	64.40	97.13	104.01	76.22	45.85	24.64	59.53
CHARGES AND MISCELLANEOUS	35.62	36.58	62.57	20.00	8.29	11.23	18.80	15.43
GENERAL EXPENDITURE, ALL FUNCTIONS	161.08	152.48	266.81	227.23	117.19	122.08	67.76	90.30
CAPITAL OUTLAY	24.72	20.53	36.21	24.40	9.43	32.40	19.30	17.01
OTHER	136.36	131.95	230.60	202.83	107.76	89.67	48.46	73.29
PUBLIC WELFARE	0.97	0.89	1.14	6.27	0.65	5.35	11.56	0.02
EDUCATION	-	-	-	0.08	-	16.23	0.16	0.16
HIGHWAYS	18.83	10.58	17.29	9.25	10.72	-	19.17	9.14
HOSPITALS	2.34	4.15	12.82	34.95	14.62	-	-	28.61
GENERAL CONTROL	15.61	23.00	14.44	21.01	13.96	15.94	7.84	20.57
POLICE PROTECTION	21.67	19.70	20.29	4.72	14.76	36.75	6.38	2.41
FINANCIAL ADMINISTRATION	9.72	11.10	10.54	10.59	7.54	15.58	1.92	3.03
GENERAL PUBLIC BUILDINGS	3.82	0.85	5.04	5.97	1.74	5.01	1.10	1.91
HEALTH	6.87	7.41	11.58	18.04	7.99	6.16	3.70	1.12
CORRECTION	5.06	3.59	5.16	8.90	7.46	3.89	2.89	8.51
NATURAL RESOURCES	0.20	0.40	3.71	0.25	0.44	-	-	0.01
PARKS AND RECREATION	3.98	6.99	7.55	4.37	5.48	1.58	-	3.28
INTEREST ON GENERAL DEBT	1.41	3.95	8.39	6.30	1.78	1.97	0.43	1.65
OTHER AND UNALLOCABLE	70.60	59.87	148.87	96.52	30.07	13.61	12.61	9.87
TOTAL DEBT OUTSTANDING AT END OF FISCAL YEAR	163.96	357.58	295.72	112.46	84.92	31.45	10.47	40.67

Item	Illinois--Continued							
	Du Page	Kane	Lake	La Salle	McHenry	McLean	Macon	Madison
GENERAL REVENUE	97.52	57.15	109.19	86.32	73.99	88.87	70.48	61.83
INTERGOVERNMENTAL REVENUE	24.79	15.88	44.15	37.71	24.75	22.37	36.18	22.70
GENERAL REVENUE SHARING	3.79	3.21	3.50	5.15	3.55	4.23	2.83	3.42
TAX REVENUE	51.28	30.45	42.73	30.62	36.80	46.86	25.41	24.98
PROPERTY TAXES ONLY	43.71	26.02	36.72	24.33	26.81	42.26	22.71	19.30
CHARGES AND MISCELLANEOUS	21.45	10.82	22.31	17.99	12.44	19.64	8.89	14.15
GENERAL EXPENDITURE, ALL FUNCTIONS	99.55	58.87	102.89	96.22	82.22	72.61	69.03	54.34
CAPITAL OUTLAY	26.28	17.18	40.80	25.59	18.01	14.42	5.72	6.94
OTHER	73.27	41.69	62.09	70.63	64.21	58.19	63.31	47.40
PUBLIC WELFARE	5.65	0.56	9.06	4.95	6.43	3.86	3.61	4.44
EDUCATION	0.27	0.14	0.19	0.48	0.19	0.33	0.26	0.46
HIGHWAYS	17.97	18.76	14.92	38.61	23.26	21.94	14.60	11.05
HOSPITALS	0.34	0.51	0.45	2.94	0.38	-	-	7.47
GENERAL CONTROL	10.63	8.02	11.97	7.72	11.08	10.67	9.85	7.47
POLICE PROTECTION	6.74	5.20	7.02	5.14	11.65	7.13	6.71	4.53
FINANCIAL ADMINISTRATION	3.98	1.85	4.22	4.40	4.28	4.24	1.66	3.87
GENERAL PUBLIC BUILDINGS	5.12	1.26	1.04	6.05	5.58	3.44	1.78	1.29
HEALTH	9.27	0.58	7.91	4.52	6.09	4.63	3.35	6.27
CORRECTION	3.05	8.44	3.32	1.38	0.32	2.14	2.46	5.62
NATURAL RESOURCES	-	0.04	0.17	0.19	0.12	-	0.11	0.18
PARKS AND RECREATION	13.22	3.77	31.41	0.36	-	2.07	-	0.35
INTEREST ON GENERAL DEBT	6.11	0.65	3.40	-	0.72	4.69	-	1.10
OTHER AND UNALLOCABLE	17.21	9.09	7.80	19.50	12.12	7.48	24.63	7.71
TOTAL DEBT OUTSTANDING AT END OF FISCAL YEAR	113.85	18.91	117.03	-	11.79	72.89	-	15.86

See footnotes at end of table.

160

Table 2. Per Capita Amounts of Selected Financial Items: 1977—Continued

Item	Illinois--Continued							Indiana
	Peoria	Rock Island	St. Clair	Sangamon	Tazewell	Will	Winnebago	Allen
GENERAL REVENUE.	91.95	76.55	58.82	53.47	60.13	88.41	93.65	117.93
INTERGOVERNMENTAL REVENUE.	27.33	29.14	21.16	18.46	19.58	34.77	29.33	58.98
GENERAL REVENUE SHARING.	4.12	2.30	5.52	2.26	2.96	4.56	4.87	5.79
TAX REVENUE.	44.43	23.98	27.13	23.97	30.31	35.95	41.52	43.14
PROPERTY TAXES ONLY.	38.49	21.37	24.33	18.34	25.69	31.17	35.12	40.68
CHARGES AND MISCELLANEOUS.	20.19	23.42	10.54	11.05	10.23	17.69	22.80	15.82
GENERAL EXPENDITURE, ALL FUNCTIONS .	83.81	70.94	51.61	55.39	47.81	74.47	100.03	97.79
CAPITAL OUTLAY .	13.49	13.98	9.30	5.33	10.54	13.60	18.25	2.41
OTHER.	70.33	56.96	42.31	50.06	37.27	60.87	81.78	95.39
PUBLIC WELFARE .	10.54	12.37	2.24	1.04	3.12	6.01	9.80	38.64
EDUCATION.	0.38	0.10	0.18	0.22	0.27	0.25	0.55	0.54
HIGHWAYS .	24.00	20.94	9.29	15.70	15.81	15.78	32.35	12.46
HOSPITALS.	-	1.50	-	-	-	-	-	0.42
GENERAL CONTROL.	10.09	8.78	9.03	7.56	9.51	9.99	10.04	10.31
POLICE PROTECTION.	9.31	5.99	4.41	8.85	5.66	8.50	7.53	7.84
FINANCIAL ADMINISTRATION .	3.36	2.17	5.97	3.38	2.58	3.26	4.82	5.27
GENERAL PUBLIC BUILDINGS .	0.52	1.82	5.67	0.55	0.93	1.50	6.07	3.67
HEALTH .	10.10	4.37	3.45	0.94	4.90	5.89	6.29	3.09
CORRECTION .	3.10	1.23	4.25	2.63	2.01	1.44	6.82	0.56
NATURAL RESOURCES.	-	0.12	0.13	0.11	-	0.20	-	0.35
PARKS AND RECREATION .	-	1.36	0.02	-	0.30	-	3.61	3.53
INTEREST ON GENERAL DEBT .	0.35	0.01	2.24	-	-	1.03	1.56	0.95
OTHER AND UNALLOCABLE.	12.07	10.19	4.73	14.42	2.71	20.62	10.59	10.16
TOTAL DEBT OUTSTANDING AT END OF FISCAL YEAR .	7.91	0.48	39.14	-	0.78	17.97	30.35	18.65

Item	Indiana--Continued							
	Delaware	Elkhart	Lake	La Porte	Madison	St. Joseph	Tippecanoe	Vanderburgh
GENERAL REVENUE.	91.74	146.17	163.51	116.30	105.89	104.23	92.10	125.26
INTERGOVERNMENTAL REVENUE.	53.52	60.39	87.41	69.12	69.02	51.37	46.25	60.98
GENERAL REVENUE SHARING.	4.59	8.65	7.12	5.61	5.00	4.90	4.85	8.19
TAX REVENUE.	28.73	73.11	65.84	37.13	31.64	39.05	36.79	46.33
PROPERTY TAXES ONLY.	28.30	35.92	64.64	36.62	31.02	38.10	36.20	45.16
CHARGES AND MISCELLANEOUS.	9.50	12.67	10.27	10.05	5.24	13.81	9.06	17.94
GENERAL EXPENDITURE, ALL FUNCTIONS .	147.04	147.02	146.26	155.44	75.59	122.59	83.93	119.35
CAPITAL OUTLAY .	9.62	27.40	6.01	57.40	8.44	15.03	16.64	9.85
OTHER.	137.41	119.62	140.25	98.04	67.15	107.56	67.29	109.50
PUBLIC WELFARE .	43.48	34.37	79.19	32.61	29.61	43.33	20.70	53.37
EDUCATION.	0.29	5.86	3.16	1.33	0.10	-	1.68	0.31
HIGHWAYS .	23.44	42.56	4.95	21.21	13.84	19.61	23.56	14.55
HOSPITALS.	-	-	1.27	2.07	-	7.02	-	0.63
GENERAL CONTROL.	11.35	18.33	14.32	13.10	9.07	14.15	14.80	12.72
POLICE PROTECTION.	4.92	7.86	5.91	5.41	2.66	7.27	5.52	7.83
FINANCIAL ADMINISTRATION .	6.37	3.02	7.84	5.82	5.07	5.54	3.34	6.31
GENERAL PUBLIC BUILDINGS .	1.72	2.26	3.30	43.57	1.40	2.75	2.44	1.39
HEALTH .	8.14	3.32	4.52	3.93	1.21	4.99	2.36	2.39
CORRECTION .	3.16	2.82	6.93	1.14	4.53	0.68	0.49	1.47
NATURAL RESOURCES.	2.25	0.97	0.27	1.23	0.56	1.38	1.39	0.85
PARKS AND RECREATION .	-	1.53	3.28	-	-	1.50	1.20	1.95
INTEREST ON GENERAL DEBT .	1.12	0.99	2.06	2.30	0.92	0.76	0.22	0.33
OTHER AND UNALLOCABLE.	40.79	23.12	9.27	21.72	6.61	13.62	6.23	15.25
TOTAL DEBT OUTSTANDING AT END OF FISCAL YEAR .	26.05	16.40	20.35	51.01	21.65	18.70	22.24	8.38

See footnotes at end of table.

161

Table 2. Per Capita Amounts of Selected Financial Items: 1977—Continued

Item	Indiana--Continued Vigo	Iowa Black Hawk	Iowa Linn	Iowa Polk	Iowa Scott	Iowa Woodbury	Kansas Johnson	Kansas Sedgwick
GENERAL REVENUE.	107.78	102.37	118.02	149.10	81.33	136.11	145.44	93.28
INTERGOVERNMENTAL REVENUE.	51.02	38.12	41.85	38.36	21.92	55.93	35.95	18.81
GENERAL REVENUE SHARING.	8.98	6.60	7.69	7.27	5.65	7.85	3.55	5.83
TAX REVENUE.	47.45	51.26	64.85	81.58	43.65	50.31	91.58	55.38
PROPERTY TAXES ONLY.	47.00	49.30	62.30	79.78	41.55	48.48	66.72	51.50
CHARGES AND MISCELLANEOUS.	9.31	12.99	11.33	29.16	15.76	29.87	17.92	19.09
GENERAL EXPENDITURE, ALL FUNCTIONS .	96.01	107.09	112.16	157.42	92.33	134.76	157.57	88.85
CAPITAL OUTLAY	5.93	12.62	8.59	16.81	16.27	4.30	58.92	13.61
OTHER.	90.08	94.47	103.57	140.62	76.06	130.46	98.66	75.25
PUBLIC WELFARE	41.17	16.98	16.19	21.36	4.12	26.78	2.85	0.04
EDUCATION.	-	1.35	1.43	2.02	2.67	2.20	6.91	5.98
HIGHWAYS	10.34	12.74	17.84	11.81	11.12	20.64	19.91	16.28
HOSPITALS.	-	12.01	9.96	47.66	5.92	13.14	-	3.92
GENERAL CONTROL.	17.40	18.44	13.71	26.79	9.12	21.37	24.32	13.33
POLICE PROTECTION.	3.92	4.53	5.32	5.45	4.74	2.77	8.32	7.00
FINANCIAL ADMINISTRATION	5.33	9.86	7.95	10.87	8.33	7.86	3.64	5.38
GENERAL PUBLIC BUILDINGS	1.74	7.56	3.52	3.39	1.27	3.98	2.10	2.82
HEALTH	3.73	10.19	11.70	11.49	24.30	6.79	7.61	10.46
CORRECTION	1.06	2.39	8.66	3.77	3.08	1.15	2.38	6.42
NATURAL RESOURCES.	0.77	0.41	0.91	0.02	0.94	0.71	0.72	1.69
PARKS AND RECREATION	1.83	2.94	3.03	3.20	3.15	3.59	0.26	4.58
INTEREST ON GENERAL DEBT	-	1.12	0.69	0.63	0.26	-	5.95	0.97
OTHER AND UNALLOCABLE.	8.72	6.57	11.23	8.95	13.31	23.78	72.60	9.98
TOTAL DEBT OUTSTANDING AT END OF FISCAL YEAR	-	24.48	15.72	12.80	4.36	-	195.03	27.45

Item	Kansas--Continued Shawnee	Kansas--Continued Wyandotte	Kentucky Jefferson	Kentucky Kenton	Louisiana Caddo	Louisiana Calcasieu	Louisiana Jefferson	Louisiana Lafayette
GENERAL REVENUE.	100.22	85.14	157.08	150.09	74.07	287.60	376.24	114.40
INTERGOVERNMENTAL REVENUE.	18.21	22.79	50.70	45.42	35.80	92.57	77.57	67.59
GENERAL REVENUE SHARING.	5.06	5.67	11.83	6.46	4.67	10.76	18.08	7.19
TAX REVENUE.	57.17	56.33	63.34	32.38	24.87	69.45	153.76	38.00
PROPERTY TAXES ONLY.	52.99	38.44	31.12	29.82	24.26	67.56	74.93	24.08
CHARGES AND MISCELLANEOUS.	24.85	6.02	43.04	72.29	13.41	125.58	144.91	8.81
GENERAL EXPENDITURE, ALL FUNCTIONS .	96.06	75.32	154.39	133.45	67.78	275.50	397.11	117.96
CAPITAL OUTLAY	7.27	5.21	33.41	27.35	6.53	58.04	122.33	23.65
OTHER.	88.78	70.11	120.98	106.09	61.26	217.46	274.78	94.30
PUBLIC WELFARE	0.03	-	6.96	0.63	0.35	0.40	0.11	0.42
EDUCATION.	6.10	0.19	0.73	0.41	1.27	-	22.87	2.51
HIGHWAYS	11.36	12.74	10.18	9.09	15.28	34.06	67.93	24.74
HOSPITALS.	-	1.24	28.61	3.30	3.54	63.63	104.53	-
GENERAL CONTROL.	11.31	11.05	8.80	4.41	4.60	5.08	13.93	4.34
POLICE PROTECTION.	5.50	2.89	19.22	7.99	9.38	22.84	48.09	17.21
FINANCIAL ADMINISTRATION	4.81	7.07	2.46	0.41	4.16	7.42	6.71	6.23
GENERAL PUBLIC BUILDINGS	4.62	2.94	5.01	0.39	3.21	22.34	2.37	10.28
HEALTH	5.39	8.86	10.44	5.32	4.25	7.88	5.04	6.23
CORRECTION	11.46	5.12	8.30	1.14	6.40	3.13	1.28	2.36
NATURAL RESOURCES.	1.67	0.32	7.16	0.26	0.31	11.59	24.57	0.16
PARKS AND RECREATION	11.63	3.54	5.82	5.58	1.30	4.49	7.53	3.77
INTEREST ON GENERAL DEBT	1.81	0.38	9.20	21.63	1.99	50.74	25.22	6.39
OTHER AND UNALLOCABLE.	20.35	18.96	31.48	72.89	11.75	41.89	66.93	33.33
TOTAL DEBT OUTSTANDING AT END OF FISCAL YEAR	31.31	7.02	208.24	431.79	41.41	818.25	650.41	128.94

See footnotes at end of table.

162

Table 2. Per Capita Amounts of Selected Financial Items: 1977—Continued

Item	Louisiana--Continued		Maine			Maryland		
	Ouachita	Rapides	Cumberland	Penobscot	York	Anne Arundel	Baltimore	Harford
GENERAL REVENUE.	122.18	166.54	14.81	12.63	12.90	684.86	691.76	752.63
INTERGOVERNMENTAL REVENUE.	71.81	78.69	3.91	2.84	7.43	314.97	231.64	405.97
GENERAL REVENUE SHARING.	4.55	7.61	0.88	1.32	1.15	14.03	21.76	7.80
TAX REVENUE.	38.09	74.16	9.35	7.99	5.10	317.81	358.41	276.54
PROPERTY TAXES ONLY.	36.84	35.00	9.35	7.99	5.10	168.03	210.24	181.17
CHARGES AND MISCELLANEOUS.	12.28	13.69	1.55	1.80	0.37	52.08	101.70	70.12
GENERAL EXPENDITURE, ALL FUNCTIONS .	117.56	164.81	29.39	10.47	15.78	731.07	717.61	705.88
CAPITAL OUTLAY	23.58	26.38	16.53	0.42	0.06	128.03	84.54	136.87
OTHER.	93.98	138.43	12.86	10.05	15.72	603.04	633.07	569.00
PUBLIC WELFARE	0.26	0.55	-	0.07	0.42	37.35	21.85	46.22
EDUCATION.	1.33	18.33	-	-	-	422.22	427.98	529.73
HIGHWAYS	18.69	17.55	0.52	0.42	-	42.05	30.63	28.51
HOSPITALS.	7.33	-	-	-	-	0.96	-	-
GENERAL CONTROL.	8.11	8.80	3.60	4.46	3.27	18.70	9.68	11.59
POLICE PROTECTION.	12.85	14.82	2.04	0.83	1.06	30.30	39.16	11.35
FINANCIAL ADMINISTRATION	3.58	4.72	0.22	0.19	0.53	14.01	7.21	4.49
GENERAL PUBLIC BUILDINGS	4.85	6.28	0.80	1.20	0.33	18.14	6.65	3.84
HEALTH	7.25	6.25	0.05	0.01	0.08	14.97	14.36	5.89
CORRECTION	2.93	17.17	2.20	1.14	1.97	2.18	3.06	5.32
NATURAL RESOURCES.	1.72	2.84	0.24	0.24	0.30	6.13	0.14	0.55
PARKS AND RECREATION	0.81	1.59	16.87	0.18	0.01	13.43	13.28	11.85
INTEREST ON GENERAL DEBT	1.23	7.53	1.08	0.13	0.09	21.40	27.82	14.25
OTHER AND UNALLOCABLE.	46.63	58.37	1.78	1.59	7.73	89.21	115.77	32.28
TOTAL DEBT OUTSTANDING AT END OF FISCAL YEAR	59.21	160.78	16.89	1.91	2.10	783.19	663.86	515.75

Item	Maryland--Continued			Massachusetts				
	Montgomery	Prince Georges	Washington	Barnstable	Berkshire	Bristol	Essex	Hampden
GENERAL REVENUE.	858.28	783.15	545.68	56.29	26.37	19.36	29.03	28.45
INTERGOVERNMENTAL REVENUE.	215.31	293.02	283.25	7.65	2.38	2.39	3.79	2.90
GENERAL REVENUE SHARING.	14.11	18.82	18.36	3.94	1.58	1.49	1.32	1.94
TAX REVENUE.	555.32	379.92	223.88	33.49	20.97	14.39	21.18	22.92
PROPERTY TAXES ONLY.	356.08	252.50	144.47	33.08	20.59	14.18	20.97	22.74
CHARGES AND MISCELLANEOUS.	87.65	110.21	38.55	15.14	3.02	2.59	4.06	2.63
GENERAL EXPENDITURE, ALL FUNCTIONS .	952.53	783.57	546.25	53.18	23.67	18.93	26.86	43.76
CAPITAL OUTLAY	107.72	60.29	53.88	1.56	0.23	0.08	2.84	5.54
OTHER.	844.80	723.28	492.38	51.62	23.44	18.84	24.02	38.22
PUBLIC WELFARE	30.18	33.06	25.38	-	-	-	4.09	-
EDUCATION.	560.45	434.00	406.67	-	-	2.35	-	-
HIGHWAYS	24.61	14.48	29.06	0.71	1.11	1.27	0.49	0.25
HOSPITALS.	-	74.19	0.07	11.35	-	-	-	-
GENERAL CONTROL.	12.33	12.18	7.40	16.37	10.36	7.46	8.32	9.45
POLICE PROTECTION.	37.55	40.95	2.85	3.03	0.42	0.17	0.12	0.24
FINANCIAL ADMINISTRATION	5.68	9.79	2.68	0.48	0.40	0.30	0.58	0.27
GENERAL PUBLIC BUILDINGS	12.91	5.95	2.76	2.98	0.79	1.11	3.82	7.06
HEALTH	25.14	8.05	6.53	1.27	0.48	-	-	-
CORRECTION	8.66	5.73	2.42	6.60	4.36	2.06	5.43	21.55
NATURAL RESOURCES.	0.96	0.22	0.78	0.84	0.85	0.12	0.03	0.69
PARKS AND RECREATION	51.72	33.93	8.02	-	1.13	0.52	-	0.18
INTEREST ON GENERAL DEBT	20.88	24.23	17.54	0.85	0.10	0.09	1.24	1.70
OTHER AND UNALLOCABLE.	161.46	86.83	34.07	8.70	3.68	3.45	2.74	2.38
TOTAL DEBT OUTSTANDING AT END OF FISCAL YEAR	624.35	452.45	252.39	17.69	1.81	1.79	19.20	34.89

See footnotes at end of table.

Item	Massachusetts--Continued					Michigan		
	Hampshire	Middlesex	Norfolk	Plymouth	Worcester	Bay	Berrien	Calhoun
GENERAL REVENUE.	41.02	29.86	26.93	32.62	29.74	220.55	140.27	95.60
INTERGOVERNMENTAL REVENUE.	5.97	3.10	5.50	5.28	3.03	118.48	59.44	51.16
GENERAL REVENUE SHARING.	2.60	1.49	0.96	1.70	1.90	9.38	6.27	5.92
TAX REVENUE.	19.06	20.50	16.69	18.34	18.64	50.72	37.79	31.65
PROPERTY TAXES ONLY.	18.70	20.33	16.47	18.13	18.34	48.95	36.33	30.08
CHARGES AND MISCELLANEOUS.	15.99	6.26	4.75	9.01	8.07	51.36	43.04	12.79
GENERAL EXPENDITURE, ALL FUNCTIONS .	38.88	31.22	20.36	33.37	26.68	258.84	145.73	117.19
CAPITAL OUTLAY	2.63	2.91	1.46	4.22	1.24	75.72	22.54	13.21
OTHER.	36.25	28.31	18.90	29.15	25.44	183.12	123.18	103.99
PUBLIC WELFARE	-	-	-	-	-	32.50	6.92	18.35
EDUCATION.	-	-	1.88	-	-	-	-	-
HIGHWAYS	0.70	0.85	1.02	0.48	1.21	42.64	32.16	32.46
HOSPITALS.	11.02	4.35	4.39	6.05	4.70	1.31	29.15	1.38
GENERAL CONTROL.	7.90	9.57	2.66	9.09	8.50	19.76	19.84	26.31
POLICE PROTECTION.	0.31	-	0.16	0.99	0.09	8.28	6.31	9.55
FINANCIAL ADMINISTRATION	1.73	0.61	0.41	0.22	0.45	2.86	3.81	2.89
GENERAL PUBLIC BUILDINGS	1.66	5.67	1.80	5.35	2.49	2.02	2.68	-
HEALTH	-	(Z)	-	-	-	21.06	18.87	8.84
CORRECTION	7.90	5.34	3.85	6.12	5.77	13.67	4.00	0.88
NATURAL RESOURCES.	1.27	0.20	-	0.49	0.41	42.91	1.06	0.87
PARKS AND RECREATION	1.00	-	0.94	-	0.02	6.17	0.72	0.61
INTEREST ON GENERAL DEBT	1.63	1.20	0.37	0.53	0.70	13.44	8.57	1.41
OTHER AND UNALLOCABLE.	3.75	3.43	2.88	4.04	2.34	52.22	11.65	13.65
TOTAL DEBT OUTSTANDING AT END OF FISCAL YEAR	35.33	25.86	6.68	10.31	12.37	457.51	326.39	39.44

Item	Michigan--Continued							
	Genesee	Ingham	Jackson	Kalamazoo	Kent	Macomb	Monroe	Muskegon
GENERAL REVENUE.	153.74	173.81	243.10	105.55	147.16	122.22	206.48	215.90
INTERGOVERNMENTAL REVENUE.	76.88	52.06	176.84	61.57	72.92	76.06	100.61	124.52
GENERAL REVENUE SHARING.	6.47	5.89	5.62	5.47	4.45	4.04	5.52	8.03
TAX REVENUE.	38.89	38.84	33.73	33.68	30.98	33.74	45.15	33.31
PROPERTY TAXES ONLY.	37.74	37.39	32.20	31.94	28.31	32.53	43.51	32.96
CHARGES AND MISCELLANEOUS.	37.97	82.91	32.53	10.30	43.26	12.42	60.72	58.07
GENERAL EXPENDITURE, ALL FUNCTIONS .	182.52	182.41	265.94	102.81	125.91	111.04	179.32	242.34
CAPITAL OUTLAY	37.02	10.22	122.79	19.20	19.65	28.38	32.79	15.67
OTHER.	145.50	172.19	143.15	83.60	106.26	82.66	146.53	226.67
PUBLIC WELFARE	16.31	29.05	30.79	9.27	11.15	6.71	9.23	32.44
EDUCATION.	-	-	-	0.76	-	0.35	-	-
HIGHWAYS	26.21	17.11	28.84	28.47	21.64	14.98	41.04	26.36
HOSPITALS.	13.69	60.92	7.95	0.99	22.06	5.63	-	19.57
GENERAL CONTROL.	15.20	15.05	15.15	12.72	8.86	9.38	12.90	19.39
POLICE PROTECTION.	12.41	10.45	6.67	14.72	5.22	3.44	22.66	11.67
FINANCIAL ADMINISTRATION	3.86	3.47	3.60	3.56	1.72	3.00	3.90	2.81
GENERAL PUBLIC BUILDINGS	2.65	1.29	4.48	4.03	0.78	4.65	2.75	2.45
HEALTH	14.70	21.83	7.24	11.32	16.45	10.02	15.34	26.32
CORRECTION	4.06	0.67	1.98	4.50	8.62	8.83	1.29	0.02
NATURAL RESOURCES.	2.78	1.60	4.46	1.05	2.54	14.08	2.53	1.29
PARKS AND RECREATION	11.16	2.67	3.75	1.70	1.43	0.31	1.01	1.33
INTEREST ON GENERAL DEBT	20.14	2.80	14.64	2.87	2.89	8.32	39.73	10.72
OTHER AND UNALLOCABLE.	39.36	15.51	136.40	6.83	22.54	21.36	26.92	87.97
TOTAL DEBT OUTSTANDING AT END OF FISCAL YEAR	406.47	61.79	237.20	53.06	80.84	173.29	1 073.61	213.20

See footnotes at end of table.

164

Table 2. Per Capita Amounts of Selected Financial Items: 1977—Continued

Item	Michigan--Continued						Minnesota	
	Oakland	Ottawa	Saginaw	St. Clair	Washtenaw	Wayne	Anoka	Dakota
GENERAL REVENUE	172.42	103.42	189.20	221.19	141.49	211.30	156.35	154.31
INTERGOVERNMENTAL REVENUE	109.17	68.51	108.60	135.31	61.70	130.77	86.68	76.57
GENERAL REVENUE SHARING	3.42	4.64	6.07	8.57	5.40	5.29	7.58	7.74
TAX REVENUE	41.48	26.19	38.82	52.02	52.75	39.76	50.27	58.32
PROPERTY TAXES ONLY	39.37	25.70	37.57	49.89	50.94	38.94	48.71	58.16
CHARGES AND MISCELLANEOUS	21.77	8.72	41.78	33.86	27.04	40.77	19.41	19.42
GENERAL EXPENDITURE, ALL FUNCTIONS	173.31	93.73	202.43	295.92	148.47	206.35	163.16	145.20
CAPITAL OUTLAY	39.87	22.80	41.22	97.38	21.29	30.73	18.24	18.16
OTHER	133.44	70.93	161.21	198.54	127.18	175.62	144.93	127.04
PUBLIC WELFARE	8.69	7.09	19.08	22.66	12.21	52.42	69.37	61.53
EDUCATION	-	-	-	-	-	0.70	-	-
HIGHWAYS	23.03	32.12	26.94	37.43	25.22	19.99	19.41	27.30
HOSPITALS	6.41	-	29.44	0.89	0.74	20.89	-	-
GENERAL CONTROL	12.87	11.00	14.57	19.07	22.01	18.57	13.59	12.18
POLICE PROTECTION	5.74	7.23	7.05	7.35	16.02	3.11	11.69	6.28
FINANCIAL ADMINISTRATION	4.44	1.42	1.65	3.10	2.55	3.03	7.93	3.66
GENERAL PUBLIC BUILDINGS	4.50	1.42	2.20	3.96	3.52	2.04	6.15	1.21
HEALTH	11.03	19.11	25.59	21.06	28.50	15.39	4.08	5.74
CORRECTION	11.80	1.33	2.36	4.26	12.30	12.37	2.59	-
NATURAL RESOURCES	18.73	1.63	10.66	1.77	8.74	10.17	0.97	2.92
PARKS AND RECREATION	4.43	1.54	0.52	0.28	0.69	1.25	9.33	6.69
INTEREST ON GENERAL DEBT	17.29	3.25	7.17	16.55	3.55	7.28	0.17	0.02
OTHER AND UNALLOCABLE	44.35	6.59	55.21	157.53	12.41	39.16	17.88	17.67
TOTAL DEBT OUTSTANDING AT END OF FISCAL YEAR	352.81	101.31	120.23	497.92	120.86	132.79	3.54	0.48

Item	Minnesota--Continued			Mississippi			Missouri	
	Hennepin	Ramsey	St. Louis	Harrison	Hinds	Jackson	Clay	Greene
GENERAL REVENUE	292.80	338.76	306.57	222.00	120.48	333.49	53.18	36.39
INTERGOVERNMENTAL REVENUE	160.45	158.39	174.96	47.77	24.44	37.92	12.67	8.67
GENERAL REVENUE SHARING	9.93	9.41	17.16	17.09	7.79	17.41	4.32	4.30
TAX REVENUE	101.65	86.25	85.23	70.13	38.60	95.28	36.91	23.91
PROPERTY TAXES ONLY	100.94	85.75	83.99	46.23	38.56	74.67	36.52	23.10
CHARGES AND MISCELLANEOUS	30.69	94.11	46.38	104.10	57.44	200.28	3.60	3.82
GENERAL EXPENDITURE, ALL FUNCTIONS	283.73	346.29	316.57	224.23	114.80	348.04	41.92	36.12
CAPITAL OUTLAY	19.24	31.79	34.57	52.90	21.16	65.99	2.06	4.08
OTHER	264.50	314.50	282.00	171.33	93.64	282.05	39.87	32.04
PUBLIC WELFARE	124.41	147.22	168.06	3.00	0.69	2.14	0.50	1.54
EDUCATION	-	-	-	0.19	0.06	-	0.21	-
HIGHWAYS	11.73	15.04	63.59	32.45	22.20	40.20	6.75	11.76
HOSPITALS	52.95	87.31	-	68.31	50.96	148.17	-	0.54
GENERAL CONTROL	19.34	16.93	15.18	9.96	6.70	11.78	6.30	4.07
POLICE PROTECTION	6.49	4.25	10.81	7.70	4.12	5.42	8.10	3.89
FINANCIAL ADMINISTRATION	8.88	8.97	9.93	4.15	3.14	3.81	2.30	2.85
GENERAL PUBLIC BUILDINGS	2.57	0.13	6.42	15.33	1.26	3.80	2.20	1.34
HEALTH	15.93	11.00	10.92	6.21	2.56	5.57	3.29	1.67
CORRECTION	16.34	18.64	9.99	1.36	12.03	0.62	2.09	2.36
NATURAL RESOURCES	-	0.88	1.98	0.46	0.75	0.40	0.05	0.26
PARKS AND RECREATION	-	14.13	6.05	10.43	0.17	2.21	0.87	0.07
INTEREST ON GENERAL DEBT	3.91	4.07	0.07	27.09	2.54	28.77	-	-
OTHER AND UNALLOCABLE	21.19	17.71	13.56	37.59	7.62	95.16	9.27	5.79
TOTAL DEBT OUTSTANDING AT END OF FISCAL YEAR	76.64	112.86	2.06	462.01	59.15	655.97	-	-

See footnotes at end of table.

165

Table 2. Per Capita Amounts of Selected Financial Items: 1977—Continued

Item	Missouri—Continued				Nebraska		Nevada	
	Jackson	Jefferson	St. Charles	St. Louis	Douglas	Lancaster	Clark	Washoe
GENERAL REVENUE	102.40	52.62	49.55	138.25	170.97	120.03	441.07	557.12
INTERGOVERNMENTAL REVENUE	32.30	22.58	9.53	29.28	75.81	32.76	81.10	70.84
GENERAL REVENUE SHARING	5.41	4.37	4.53	8.27	5.22	4.72	12.94	9.98
TAX REVENUE	53.89	26.61	31.57	94.76	53.12	49.76	215.10	208.32
PROPERTY TAXES ONLY	48.47	25.60	29.53	55.86	50.27	46.35	100.18	120.50
CHARGES AND MISCELLANEOUS	16.21	3.43	8.45	14.21	42.05	37.50	144.87	277.96
GENERAL EXPENDITURE, ALL FUNCTIONS	100.89	35.94	41.42	132.30	164.76	111.69	409.75	496.70
CAPITAL OUTLAY	39.07	5.82	2.66	9.68	17.41	19.49	51.04	71.34
OTHER	61.82	30.11	38.77	122.62	147.35	92.21	358.71	425.37
PUBLIC WELFARE	1.37	1.26	0.94	0.62	39.43	19.53	34.59	20.11
EDUCATION	-	-	-	0.01	0.63	2.86	-	-
HIGHWAYS	5.12	10.01	14.94	17.76	8.42	26.14	13.25	41.53
HOSPITALS	22.49	-	-	11.80	28.21	1.64	65.46	236.28
GENERAL CONTROL	11.70	4.75	5.35	8.35	9.27	9.58	38.79	31.58
POLICE PROTECTION	1.80	5.26	8.85	14.06	4.62	6.75	37.54	25.80
FINANCIAL ADMINISTRATION	5.05	2.46	3.13	4.59	13.23	5.05	5.10	15.10
GENERAL PUBLIC BUILDINGS	1.58	2.53	1.09	2.69	4.32	3.97	3.54	40.48
HEALTH	0.43	2.60	0.76	7.67	21.81	18.41	12.08	10.98
CORRECTION	11.37	0.54	0.70	2.86	6.06	3.04	12.68	7.03
NATURAL RESOURCES	0.19	0.25	0.14	0.06	0.49	0.65	3.87	0.62
PARKS AND RECREATION	4.11	0.28	-	7.95	1.37	0.30	34.74	20.88
INTEREST ON GENERAL DEBT	8.90	0.44	0.41	4.45	3.54	5.06	19.60	10.79
OTHER AND UNALLOCABLE	26.77	5.56	5.14	49.42	23.36	8.71	128.49	35.52
TOTAL DEBT OUTSTANDING AT END OF FISCAL YEAR	352.56	8.77	-	100.69	66.19	102.37	653.06	266.63

Item	New Hampshire		New Jersey					
	Hillsborough	Rockingham	Atlantic	Bergen	Burlington	Camden	Cumberland	Essex
GENERAL REVENUE	44.94	45.05	293.29	151.74	166.78	268.49	254.66	340.45
INTERGOVERNMENTAL REVENUE	10.98	19.96	158.62	43.25	73.72	132.56	137.49	180.95
GENERAL REVENUE SHARING	1.22	2.18	6.67	2.96	4.91	7.41	9.95	9.21
TAX REVENUE	19.30	17.46	109.44	70.70	72.53	123.59	92.31	136.04
PROPERTY TAXES ONLY	19.30	17.46	108.86	69.63	72.50	122.60	91.91	134.87
CHARGES AND MISCELLANEOUS	14.66	7.62	25.23	37.79	20.53	12.34	24.86	23.45
GENERAL EXPENDITURE, ALL FUNCTIONS	51.66	42.31	294.29	155.81	166.92	280.96	250.61	348.03
CAPITAL OUTLAY	17.98	2.96	9.53	13.67	10.89	21.56	17.73	7.48
OTHER	33.68	39.35	284.76	142.14	156.02	259.40	232.88	340.55
PUBLIC WELFARE	39.31	24.63	121.79	16.40	38.46	99.57	103.35	156.56
EDUCATION	-	-	43.37	28.08	39.04	30.99	28.17	31.07
HIGHWAYS	-	-	13.76	10.69	18.35	11.65	10.85	9.03
HOSPITALS	-	-	7.98	32.53	8.59	26.13	12.75	49.39
GENERAL CONTROL	4.73	5.27	18.01	10.63	7.87	15.86	20.86	21.21
POLICE PROTECTION	1.24	2.54	2.66	4.28	0.19	4.22	3.41	4.25
FINANCIAL ADMINISTRATION	0.33	0.06	1.93	1.99	1.47	3.14	1.46	2.65
GENERAL PUBLIC BUILDINGS	0.77	5.19	11.05	3.63	2.54	13.85	3.71	5.75
HEALTH	-	-	7.45	2.76	4.63	13.15	10.43	1.37
CORRECTION	3.17	2.00	11.57	4.62	11.93	11.79	9.73	21.27
NATURAL RESOURCES	1.05	1.08	1.09	0.11	0.23	0.37	1.08	0.21
PARKS AND RECREATION	-	-	1.63	7.23	0.16	3.87	0.60	14.12
INTEREST ON GENERAL DEBT	1.03	1.29	3.18	4.35	2.13	4.30	4.77	4.66
OTHER AND UNALLOCABLE	0.03	0.27	48.82	28.51	31.33	42.07	39.44	26.50
TOTAL DEBT OUTSTANDING AT END OF FISCAL YEAR	32.74	14.37	52.03	98.87	93.44	92.78	104.25	86.31

See footnotes at end of table.

Item	New Jersey--Continued							
	Gloucester	Hudson	Mercer	Middlesex	Monmouth	Morris	Ocean	Passaic
GENERAL REVENUE.	158.80	249.77	234.19	219.65	192.50	164.91	185.09	209.86
INTERGOVERNMENTAL REVENUE.	69.93	140.34	95.48	94.86	84.49	52.45	81.40	103.22
GENERAL REVENUE SHARING.	5.72	9.13	7.32	5.95	5.48	4.46	6.92	6.39
TAX REVENUE.	74.04	91.02	119.36	99.42	89.46	90.71	89.34	82.98
PROPERTY TAXES ONLY.	74.03	90.63	118.31	98.69	88.42	89.45	87.28	82.98
CHARGES AND MISCELLANEOUS. . . .	14.83	18.41	19.36	25.37	18.55	21.75	14.35	23.66
GENERAL EXPENDITURE, ALL FUNCTIONS .	146.52	241.07	245.17	218.61	196.17	164.31	184.30	203.38
CAPITAL OUTLAY	1.65	6.91	27.96	18.80	4.26	10.04	15.71	8.86
OTHER.	144.87	234.16	217.21	199.81	191.91	154.27	168.59	194.52
PUBLIC WELFARE	44.54	106.99	87.61	55.82	76.16	30.15	47.77	85.17
EDUCATION.	30.47	10.89	43.06	38.90	31.52	30.35	32.29	23.65
HIGHWAYS	10.34	2.54	9.56	12.25	10.68	15.63	15.57	6.86
HOSPITALS.	4.91	49.36	16.17	21.79	8.28	7.56	4.30	22.63
GENERAL CONTROL.	9.65	18.42	13.26	13.95	7.81	13.05	14.69	16.06
POLICE PROTECTION.	5.23	6.99	4.79	1.86	1.28	5.83	3.76	1.18
FINANCIAL ADMINISTRATION	0.93	3.10	1.26	1.99	2.17	2.51	1.41	1.34
GENERAL PUBLIC BUILDINGS	3.78	4.03	3.03	7.18	3.23	6.14	4.00	2.78
HEALTH	4.16	1.97	5.86	5.20	5.25	7.11	6.81	2.57
CORRECTION	6.85	9.28	24.27	8.58	4.21	2.19	4.96	8.81
NATURAL RESOURCES.	0.37	0.19	0.68	1.17	0.84	1.35	1.42	0.19
PARKS AND RECREATION	0.28	3.38	5.80	11.66	4.44	7.89	2.40	2.60
INTEREST ON GENERAL DEBT	1.23	2.16	6.35	4.68	4.05	6.90	1.51	3.10
OTHER AND UNALLOCABLE.	23.74	21.77	23.47	33.57	36.26	27.65	43.42	26.45
TOTAL DEBT OUTSTANDING AT END OF FISCAL YEAR	19.91	47.80	113.33	105.85	75.68	117.62	35.71	59.15

Item	New Jersey--Continued		New Mexico	New York				
	Somerset	Union	Bernalillo	Albany	Broome	Chautauqua	Chemung	Dutchess
GENERAL REVENUE.	169.54	155.94	63.80	619.88	372.94	319.25	361.34	311.79
INTERGOVERNMENTAL REVENUE.	49.85	56.83	24.16	443.98	179.73	187.76	202.96	163.06
GENERAL REVENUE SHARING.	4.23	4.36	9.54	7.01	5.85	10.68	12.46	5.92
TAX REVENUE.	98.69	80.97	33.70	159.64	135.90	113.00	138.08	119.31
PROPERTY TAXES ONLY.	98.68	80.26	33.19	42.50	55.43	22.41	52.15	102.28
CHARGES AND MISCELLANEOUS. . . .	20.99	18.14	5.95	16.26	57.31	18.49	20.29	29.42
GENERAL EXPENDITURE, ALL FUNCTIONS .	181.44	157.96	63.24	917.20	375.25	342.30	346.74	291.76
CAPITAL OUTLAY	18.07	8.68	10.38	23.09	37.86	21.73	11.15	5.64
OTHER.	163.37	149.28	52.86	894.11	337.39	320.58	335.59	286.12
PUBLIC WELFARE	26.69	44.34	-	187.20	166.23	164.97	170.31	130.39
EDUCATION.	40.60	6.57	-	7.29	34.91	7.29	8.83	41.81
HIGHWAYS	19.38	5.32	3.19	15.25	22.36	35.47	20.73	14.61
HOSPITALS.	6.32	24.49	14.96	0.49	-	-	0.30	14.65
GENERAL CONTROL.	11.13	17.66	7.58	10.13	10.81	14.31	10.32	
POLICE PROTECTION.	2.94	1.06	7.47	5.00	4.75	8.00	6.29	6.43
FINANCIAL ADMINISTRATION	1.35	1.60	2.63	3.48	2.34	3.08	4.05	5.45
GENERAL PUBLIC BUILDINGS	3.64	4.98	1.26	2.16	5.29	3.62	7.96	3.94
HEALTH	6.37	2.49	2.20	14.13	20.47	17.57	13.19	22.12
CORRECTION	7.98	9.86	10.34	14.07	5.80	6.26	9.02	8.78
NATURAL RESOURCES.	2.13	0.66	0.08	1.92	1.82	6.31	2.98	1.36
PARKS AND RECREATION	9.23	13.45	2.99	5.72	8.12	2.46	7.94	3.07
INTEREST ON GENERAL DEBT	9.09	1.80	1.23	131.71	8.90	2.28	6.13	4.73
OTHER AND UNALLOCABLE.	34.59	23.70	9.30	518.66	83.44	70.68	78.70	34.43
TOTAL DEBT OUTSTANDING AT END OF FISCAL YEAR	188.65	53.96	39.34	2 794.70	220.61	37.78	146.34	101.00

See footnotes at end of table.

167

Table 2. Per Capita Amounts of Selected Financial Items: 1977—Continued

Item	New York--Continued							
	Erie	Monroe	Nassau	Niagara	Oneida	Onondaga	Orange	Oswego
GENERAL REVENUE.	427.64	469.28	511.65	448.50	298.24	543.64	362.80	341.93
INTERGOVERNMENTAL REVENUE.	210.84	253.28	162.92	285.56	196.85	276.87	218.05	197.25
GENERAL REVENUE SHARING.	11.10	7.88	11.72	9.78	7.93	11.41	9.95	11.91
TAX REVENUE.	180.61	133.17	299.38	124.48	62.39	214.93	119.85	129.79
PROPERTY TAXES ONLY.	80.61	58.93	187.00	59.33	61.02	96.34	118.00	128.38
CHARGES AND MISCELLANEOUS.	36.19	82.84	49.35	38.46	39.00	51.84	24.89	14.88
GENERAL EXPENDITURE, ALL FUNCTIONS .	496.59	493.54	577.91	456.66	294.21	473.05	373.07	344.42
CAPITAL OUTLAY	71.06	39.85	57.42	98.29	22.87	28.21	29.14	11.53
OTHER.	425.53	453.69	520.48	358.37	271.33	444.84	343.93	332.89
PUBLIC WELFARE	158.15	183.41	116.05	161.60	151.66	189.54	185.44	152.46
EDUCATION.	42.35	44.49	29.35	43.62	39.53	29.76	46.85	2.10
HIGHWAYS	19.13	13.77	35.46	12.33	11.93	25.48	13.15	38.38
HOSPITALS.	67.56	22.96	45.68	12.07	15.21	2.65	-	4.06
GENERAL CONTROL.	12.48	22.15	22.62	13.33	10.97	27.15	14.65	11.89
POLICE PROTECTION.	4.93	10.40	79.28	7.10	3.68	16.03	2.31	7.78
FINANCIAL ADMINISTRATION	7.58	8.53	5.13	2.02	5.92	5.51	4.88	9.75
GENERAL PUBLIC BUILDINGS	1.96	2.64	7.37	8.83	3.96	10.47	5.10	3.01
HEALTH	26.41	22.65	22.01	13.83	11.55	30.09	18.65	42.11
CORRECTION	10.93	13.12	13.55	6.25	3.79	9.85	7.90	7.76
NATURAL RESOURCES.	0.51	0.57	0.86	1.24	0.91	0.26	1.22	3.00
PARKS AND RECREATION	5.34	11.37	41.39	5.07	2.18	11.94	4.51	3.74
INTEREST ON GENERAL DEBT	11.95	17.11	27.22	5.24	6.11	18.09	6.16	1.68
OTHER AND UNALLOCABLE.	127.31	120.36	131.92	164.12	26.81	96.21	62.24	56.72
TOTAL DEBT OUTSTANDING AT END OF FISCAL YEAR	335.67	413.32	522.63	121.37	140.74	485.87	142.09	32.51

Item	New York--Continued							
	Rensselaer	Rockland	St. Lawrence	Saratoga	Schenectady	Steuben	Suffolk	Ulster
GENERAL REVENUE.	355.44	419.50	311.62	321.98	293.22	300.55	431.20	331.25
INTERGOVERNMENTAL REVENUE.	221.26	196.21	179.66	231.86	167.17	181.62	210.58	195.41
GENERAL REVENUE SHARING.	7.31	6.59	11.23	4.20	5.54	10.64	13.93	9.15
TAX REVENUE.	88.05	151.16	98.62	72.83	94.15	103.64	194.01	114.18
PROPERTY TAXES ONLY.	49.01	149.80	23.19	60.27	93.10	13.19	194.01	114.18
CHARGES AND MISCELLANEOUS.	46.13	72.13	33.35	17.29	31.90	15.29	93.55	81.46
							26.61	21.66
GENERAL EXPENDITURE, ALL FUNCTIONS .	356.67	449.18	304.22	351.03	302.22	275.78	495.99	349.38
CAPITAL OUTLAY	26.86	26.37	1.72	153.98	10.33	14.64	87.41	16.17
OTHER.	329.81	422.80	302.50	197.05	291.89	261.14	408.57	333.21
PUBLIC WELFARE	142.40	167.37	176.90	97.11	146.90	135.84	164.43	152.67
EDUCATION.	83.36	67.37	1.67	12.60	31.62	3.67	27.43	47.42
HIGHWAYS	17.83	15.36	21.65	20.62	16.77	58.32	12.26	35.82
HOSPITALS.	-	35.84	-	-	19.19	-	-	-
GENERAL CONTROL.	12.86	18.13	11.70	10.40	11.19	17.78	17.05	14.24
POLICE PROTECTION.	2.93	5.50	2.70	5.32	0.84	3.70	71.46	2.62
FINANCIAL ADMINISTRATION	4.18	4.06	2.20	3.10	2.83	3.61	-	6.61
GENERAL PUBLIC BUILDINGS	2.56	3.17	2.70	2.42	2.66	1.74	9.52	9.13
HEALTH	16.95	49.15	15.01	13.15	9.46	14.12	18.09	18.24
CORRECTION	7.90	5.92	4.94	4.51	7.70	8.18	9.64	9.18
NATURAL RESOURCES.	1.92	3.16	2.43	1.47	0.79	2.89	9.62	1.75
PARKS AND RECREATION	7.69	4.02	2.63	0.77	6.27	0.80	10.01	3.95
INTEREST ON GENERAL DEBT	5.99	16.37	11.92	1.41	1.14	0.23	19.88	2.15
OTHER AND UNALLOCABLE.	50.11	53.77	47.76	178.14	44.86	24.89	126.60	45.61
TOTAL DEBT OUTSTANDING AT END OF FISCAL YEAR	106.40	266.58	252.03	99.06	24.88	5.59	524.92	49.36

See footnotes at end of table.

168

Table 2. Per Capita Amounts of Selected Financial Items: 1977—Continued

Item	New York--Continued Westchester	North Carolina Buncombe	Cumberland	Durham	Forsyth	Gaston	Guilford	Mecklenburg
GENERAL REVENUE.	438.79	451.56	478.35	500.24	469.85	442.00	475.97	562.58
INTERGOVERNMENTAL REVENUE.	201.94	279.60	315.71	287.64	275.04	301.68	291.43	329.54
GENERAL REVENUE SHARING.	5.31	11.30	11.24	10.31	9.35	10.26	7.93	14.17
TAX REVENUE.	180.02	130.99	121.01	186.46	139.21	109.69	148.00	193.54
PROPERTY TAXES ONLY.	148.37	96.59	95.63	154.95	103.51	86.23	111.90	155.93
CHARGES AND MISCELLANEOUS.	56.83	40.97	41.63	26.13	55.60	30.63	36.53	39.50
GENERAL EXPENDITURE, ALL FUNCTIONS.	540.10	446.30	544.15	525.05	528.06	457.34	467.24	551.87
CAPITAL OUTLAY.	89.77	56.61	61.23	71.70	88.09	52.55	21.38	42.66
OTHER.	450.33	389.69	482.92	453.35	439.97	404.79	445.86	509.21
PUBLIC WELFARE.	252.50	37.41	59.77	86.02	63.83	46.69	62.50	68.33
EDUCATION.	17.78	294.13	413.36	304.72	321.34	301.31	308.81	367.34
HIGHWAYS.	2.92	-	-	-	-	-	-	-
HOSPITALS.	79.55	2.72	0.14	22.25	-	-	-	5.05
GENERAL CONTROL.	13.43	3.22	4.43	2.65	3.74	2.23	7.29	4.71
POLICE PROTECTION.	7.46	7.48	10.08	4.56	9.12	9.16	6.52	10.16
FINANCIAL ADMINISTRATION.	5.18	4.94	3.65	3.47	5.01	4.99	5.59	5.38
GENERAL PUBLIC BUILDINGS.	3.92	3.41	2.33	26.95	2.61	2.91	3.18	6.17
HEALTH.	23.73	15.42	13.36	24.58	50.63	19.13	27.67	29.43
CORRECTION.	11.94	2.83	1.76	1.87	2.63	0.91	5.06	4.44
NATURAL RESOURCES.	0.29	1.51	0.74	1.31	0.87	0.70	0.56	1.73
PARKS AND RECREATION.	12.28	3.52	1.06	0.47	26.56	0.77	-	1.79
INTEREST ON GENERAL DEBT.	6.03	0.79	7.21	10.29	9.17	10.36	7.97	10.02
OTHER AND UNALLOCABLE.	103.09	68.93	26.27	35.91	32.55	58.17	32.08	37.31
TOTAL DEBT OUTSTANDING AT END OF FISCAL YEAR.	114.06	13.49	227.07	225.63	260.33	180.70	207.67	270.13

Item	North Carolina--Continued Wake	Ohio Allen	Ashtabula	Butler	Clark	Clermont	Columbiana	Cuyahoga
GENERAL REVENUE.	469.19	170.30	119.06	135.49	151.07	159.23	95.56	185.00
INTERGOVERNMENTAL REVENUE.	279.07	97.37	61.35	84.53	82.99	72.46	49.89	90.38
GENERAL REVENUE SHARING.	8.03	6.11	4.39	3.70	6.01	4.79	4.51	6.30
TAX REVENUE.	158.11	37.48	27.83	29.14	42.99	22.54	22.64	58.63
PROPERTY TAXES ONLY.	120.19	17.94	26.15	21.85	30.64	20.61	20.07	37.65
CHARGES AND MISCELLANEOUS.	32.01	35.45	29.88	21.82	25.09	64.23	23.03	36.00
GENERAL EXPENDITURE, ALL FUNCTIONS.	446.06	164.24	121.96	124.18	144.36	154.83	90.33	198.18
CAPITAL OUTLAY.	59.96	45.78	0.87	20.46	18.59	42.08	15.06	34.69
OTHER.	386.10	118.45	121.09	103.72	125.77	112.75	75.27	163.49
PUBLIC WELFARE.	45.15	29.35	24.40	29.74	41.86	16.96	18.95	47.70
EDUCATION.	321.62	4.72	4.55	2.63	2.04	7.09	4.02	0.58
HIGHWAYS.	-	20.74	24.36	14.61	13.98	16.13	18.67	12.76
HOSPITALS.	6.93	0.13	0.13	-	-	0.16	-	53.18
GENERAL CONTROL.	3.39	10.89	7.23	8.50	6.08	9.21	9.37	12.16
POLICE PROTECTION.	5.72	6.80	8.48	3.83	4.62	4.61	4.91	1.97
FINANCIAL ADMINISTRATION.	2.03	3.37	2.76	4.22	3.68	3.93	3.34	4.92
GENERAL PUBLIC BUILDINGS.	4.86	18.70	2.06	10.84	2.40	5.86	3.21	26.06
HEALTH.	25.49	13.10	9.13	11.45	22.95	20.61	7.85	12.82
CORRECTION.	0.73	2.06	12.11	1.00	7.59	0.88	1.73	4.91
NATURAL RESOURCES.	1.97	3.43	0.22	0.34	0.52	0.83	0.51	0.07
PARKS AND RECREATION.	0.14	0.29	0.11	-	0.05	0.06	-	-
INTEREST ON GENERAL DEBT.	6.02	3.17	1.26	1.00	4.62	7.12	0.13	4.31
OTHER AND UNALLOCABLE.	22.01	47.50	25.19	36.03	33.98	61.39	17.64	16.74
TOTAL DEBT OUTSTANDING AT END OF FISCAL YEAR.	149.16	58.89	45.65	52.17	71.80	239.06	9.07	80.21

See footnotes at end of table.

Table 2. Per Capita Amounts of Selected Financial Items: 1977—Continued

Item	Ohio--Continued							
	Franklin	Greene	Hamilton	Lake	Licking	Lorain	Lucas	Mahoning
GENERAL REVENUE.	138.75	155.40	122.14	195.86	126.77	130.83	120.89	130.33
INTERGOVERNMENTAL REVENUE.	63.56	69.14	44.06	39.94	81.46	65.13	66.15	84.17
GENERAL REVENUE SHARING.	4.25	4.29	6.34	5.98	5.66	3.32	4.71	5.44
TAX REVENUE.	35.04	52.36	59.38	40.41	29.60	24.49	41.11	30.82
PROPERTY TAXES ONLY.	29.71	37.32	39.51	22.38	16.54	23.23	25.22	28.66
CHARGES AND MISCELLANEOUS.	40.15	33.90	18.69	115.51	15.71	41.21	13.63	15.33
GENERAL EXPENDITURE, ALL FUNCTIONS .	138.77	157.25	141.66	215.27	138.25	111.60	121.46	132.72
CAPITAL OUTLAY	33.28	17.04	12.43	42.29	18.81	24.07	17.35	16.10
OTHER.	105.49	140.22	129.23	172.98	119.44	87.53	104.12	116.63
PUBLIC WELFARE	53.66	22.98	40.69	17.12	19.91	22.43	48.76	52.84
EDUCATION.	1.20	4.41	3.40	-	3.42	3.73	1.75	2.30
HIGHWAYS	11.24	22.86	10.63	13.65	22.33	9.16	9.39	12.37
HOSPITALS.	1.51	2.22	20.70	72.13	-	-	0.63	-
GENERAL CONTROL.	10.85	11.21	9.96	8.87	10.86	6.99	10.97	9.16
POLICE PROTECTION.	5.46	6.33	7.41	4.22	5.06	2.37	4.80	2.30
FINANCIAL ADMINISTRATION	3.25	3.57	4.34	3.04	3.89	3.38	2.71	2.99
GENERAL PUBLIC BUILDINGS	5.45	0.49	8.60	3.12	10.60	4.75	1.78	3.82
HEALTH	15.89	27.97	10.18	20.28	10.82	14.48	13.29	13.26
CORRECTION	5.22	1.61	4.60	1.96	0.91	2.25	8.93	0.07
NATURAL RESOURCES.	0.18	1.34	0.09	0.87	1.16	0.23	0.41	0.10
PARKS AND RECREATION	3.73	3.76	0.10	-	-	-	1.49	-
INTEREST ON GENERAL DEBT	4.44	6.82	8.22	1.06	2.59	13.67	0.97	1.07
OTHER AND UNALLOCABLE.	16.69	41.69	12.77	68.95	46.70	28.17	15.57	32.43
TOTAL DEBT OUTSTANDING AT END OF FISCAL YEAR	139.74	173.35	136.50	48.22	52.98	261.09	29.83	30.05

Item	Ohio--Continued						Oklahoma	
	Montgomery	Portage	Richland	Stark	Summit	Trumbull	Comanche	Oklahoma
GENERAL REVENUE.	188.74	170.44	108.89	116.62	152.27	120.89	157.59	64.46
INTERGOVERNMENTAL REVENUE.	100.65	45.15	57.04	53.32	84.05	53.79	33.70	19.04
GENERAL REVENUE SHARING.	5.67	3.70	3.19	3.38	5.11	3.49	4.86	4.56
TAX REVENUE.	49.81	28.32	20.08	29.11	44.37	29.29	18.48	35.62
PROPERTY TAXES ONLY.	29.61	25.83	18.24	20.11	38.37	27.87	18.31	35.51
CHARGES AND MISCELLANEOUS.	38.28	96.97	31.76	34.18	23.85	37.81	105.41	9.80
GENERAL EXPENDITURE, ALL FUNCTIONS .	168.92	257.37	106.11	106.75	141.36	134.95	137.08	54.21
CAPITAL OUTLAY	11.14	86.55	22.60	24.57	20.90	18.05	5.42	5.39
OTHER.	157.79	170.82	83.50	82.18	120.46	116.90	131.66	48.82
PUBLIC WELFARE	45.58	16.00	21.02	21.05	38.21	28.36	0.40	2.10
EDUCATION.	3.60	2.32	4.59	0.82	1.86	5.02	4.12	7.74
HIGHWAYS	11.76	18.21	18.20	11.03	12.62	14.53	10.35	9.91
HOSPITALS.	-	154.35	-	5.62	5.09	27.00	98.16	-
GENERAL CONTROL.	14.59	11.02	10.49	7.40	7.34	8.20	4.36	5.98
POLICE PROTECTION.	9.27	8.51	6.19	5.81	3.40	4.03	4.20	1.60
FINANCIAL ADMINISTRATION	4.14	4.21	2.96	3.79	3.08	3.30	1.99	2.94
GENERAL PUBLIC BUILDINGS	10.32	1.63	2.35	4.17	4.59	2.10	2.38	3.93
HEALTH	33.38	12.97	12.44	11.34	21.31	10.05	3.90	3.75
CORRECTION	4.76	1.10	2.70	1.69	3.60	0.70	0.43	2.35
NATURAL RESOURCES.	0.14	1.11	0.64	0.69	0.02	0.41	0.85	0.19
PARKS AND RECREATION	1.22	-	-	-	0.01	0.02	-	-
INTEREST ON GENERAL DEBT	1.80	3.27	1.06	0.87	1.38	1.59	5.47	1.89
OTHER AND UNALLOCABLE.	28.37	22.67	23.46	32.46	38.84	29.65	0.47	11.82
TOTAL DEBT OUTSTANDING AT END OF FISCAL YEAR	145.45	186.28	25.70	41.97	36.03	50.00	107.09	42.09

See footnotes at end of table.

Table 2. Per Capita Amounts of Selected Financial Items: 1977—Continued

Item	Oklahoma--Continued Tulsa	Oregon Clackamas	Jackson	Lane	Marion	Multnomah	Washington	Penn-sylvania Allegheny
GENERAL REVENUE	77.97	139.26	231.54	243.69	110.60	165.33	204.05	144.73
INTERGOVERNMENTAL REVENUE	21.99	93.42	179.51	194.91	59.51	62.74	120.18	69.10
GENERAL REVENUE SHARING	5.72	3.68	1.58	3.61	7.05	12.41	5.22	8.40
TAX REVENUE	50.88	26.64	14.58	23.30	27.16	79.13	47.88	52.92
PROPERTY TAXES ONLY	50.51	19.29	11.11	18.25	22.56	68.61	32.91	51.59
CHARGES AND MISCELLANEOUS	5.10	19.20	37.46	25.47	23.94	23.45	35.99	22.72
GENERAL EXPENDITURE, ALL FUNCTIONS	66.15	132.32	183.28	248.63	99.23	145.46	217.15	143.72
CAPITAL OUTLAY	6.09	9.74	30.05	56.66	4.67	7.27	109.61	7.48
OTHER	60.06	122.57	153.22	191.97	94.57	138.20	107.54	136.24
PUBLIC WELFARE	2.37	0.14	6.04	8.86	0.22	7.79	0.04	12.65
EDUCATION	10.98	6.78	7.67	20.41	5.37	2.79	2.40	9.32
HIGHWAYS	6.13	28.97	37.88	36.65	20.78	15.33	18.29	7.26
HOSPITALS	-	-	-	-	-	2.68	-	12.12
GENERAL CONTROL	7.66	17.83	18.48	23.50	11.71	25.79	10.99	11.70
POLICE PROTECTION	3.55	14.30	16.10	14.45	12.51	17.44	12.04	3.47
FINANCIAL ADMINISTRATION	9.62	8.97	9.52	13.46	8.87	13.00	7.33	4.68
GENERAL PUBLIC BUILDINGS	3.90	0.91	10.35	30.59	5.96	0.99	2.80	4.52
HEALTH	7.90	7.01	16.71	14.10	11.87	21.81	8.01	21.00
CORRECTION	0.40	-	7.36	14.78	7.38	9.62	4.59	5.52
NATURAL RESOURCES	0.31	-	12.43	3.44	0.72	0.96	0.76	0.06
PARKS AND RECREATION	2.06	1.56	7.48	3.61	1.04	1.54	1.46	4.52
INTEREST ON GENERAL DEBT	1.12	4.44	0.17	0.57	-	0.37	6.56	12.17
OTHER AND UNALLOCABLE	10.17	41.40	33.08	64.23	12.80	25.35	141.89	34.73
TOTAL DEBT OUTSTANDING AT END OF FISCAL YEAR	29.67	59.51	3.80	45.98	-	1.56	135.20	270.37

Item	Pennsylvania--Continued Beaver	Berks	Blair	Bucks	Butler	Cambria	Centre	Chester
GENERAL REVENUE	83.20	91.86	71.36	84.19	108.84	102.10	79.08	93.28
INTERGOVERNMENTAL REVENUE	47.21	57.27	43.49	37.33	60.03	56.92	49.58	43.01
GENERAL REVENUE SHARING	7.35	4.23	5.47	5.85	6.01	7.90	5.68	5.02
TAX REVENUE	29.25	24.86	19.29	34.28	23.78	30.05	17.64	39.87
PROPERTY TAXES ONLY	29.25	24.86	19.29	33.99	21.01	30.04	17.64	39.38
CHARGES AND MISCELLANEOUS	6.74	9.73	8.58	12.58	25.04	15.14	11.85	10.40
GENERAL EXPENDITURE, ALL FUNCTIONS	78.73	94.62	73.59	107.84	97.82	104.28	81.04	101.80
CAPITAL OUTLAY	0.69	11.50	3.82	9.01	2.48	22.04	0.56	0.59
OTHER	78.04	83.13	69.77	98.82	95.34	82.24	80.48	101.21
PUBLIC WELFARE	12.72	31.77	24.10	16.71	13.64	29.23	35.83	21.86
EDUCATION	0.48	-	-	6.83	9.37	-	-	-
HIGHWAYS	1.75	3.44	4.84	2.34	2.01	0.29	1.66	1.68
HOSPITALS	7.81	4.89	-	-	-	-	0.45	-
GENERAL CONTROL	12.01	9.27	8.53	14.66	9.52	8.13	4.31	21.28
POLICE PROTECTION	0.44	1.14	0.17	0.89	0.14	0.19	0.14	4.46
FINANCIAL ADMINISTRATION	2.98	2.54	2.69	2.94	2.29	3.45	3.53	3.24
GENERAL PUBLIC BUILDINGS	1.70	5.24	1.97	2.20	0.58	22.32	0.84	1.23
HEALTH	1.10	10.26	12.65	14.76	10.51	8.38	9.15	11.88
CORRECTION	4.99	6.62	4.32	7.55	4.13	3.64	2.65	10.99
NATURAL RESOURCES	0.19	0.22	0.23	0.72	0.32	0.51	0.54	0.76
PARKS AND RECREATION	1.67	1.29	2.38	3.77	0.61	0.51	0.14	1.07
INTEREST ON GENERAL DEBT	1.68	0.49	1.65	1.37	6.91	3.41	1.01	0.71
OTHER AND UNALLOCABLE	29.20	17.47	10.07	33.10	37.79	24.22	20.79	22.63
TOTAL DEBT OUTSTANDING AT END OF FISCAL YEAR	37.55	9.32	24.06	36.72	127.97	51.82	17.03	17.91

See footnotes at end of table.

Table 2. Per Capita Amounts of Selected Financial Items: 1977—Continued

Item	Pennsylvania--Continued							
	Cumberland	Dauphin	Delaware	Erie	Fayette	Franklin	Lackawanna	Lancaster
GENERAL REVENUE.	72.15	105.15	118.77	116.06	44.09	74.95	74.60	76.74
INTERGOVERNMENTAL REVENUE.	22.24	63.63	62.04	52.15	23.44	27.85	34.13	42.96
GENERAL REVENUE SHARING.	3.52	6.10	6.02	6.80	6.98	6.61	7.48	3.56
TAX REVENUE.	36.77	32.57	53.39	32.51	15.02	26.84	27.17	22.58
PROPERTY TAXES ONLY.	34.11	29.73	53.39	32.37	14.32	26.57	27.17	22.58
CHARGES AND MISCELLANEOUS.	13.14	8.95	3.33	31.41	5.63	20.26	13.30	11.21
GENERAL EXPENDITURE, ALL FUNCTIONS .	76.31	117.66	124.05	94.57	42.55	61.22	73.64	65.33
CAPITAL OUTLAY	7.95	11.28	11.05	5.38	9.07	4.69	7.34	1.09
OTHER.	68.36	106.37	113.00	89.19	33.49	56.53	66.29	64.25
PUBLIC WELFARE	29.31	34.89	27.14	24.02	2.90	16.26	27.88	15.77
EDUCATION.	-	-	-	-	0.64	-	-	-
HIGHWAYS	6.05	2.68	1.82	2.33	5.08	1.15	2.99	1.71
HOSPITALS.	0.09	8.59	1.06	-	0.01	0.19	0.15	-
GENERAL CONTROL.	6.59	12.30	14.76	17.47	8.36	7.29	7.39	6.86
POLICE PROTECTION.	0.11	0.14	1.11	0.23	0.18	0.03	0.12	0.18
FINANCIAL ADMINISTRATION	3.43	4.69	3.46	2.92	3.14	3.22	4.75	2.75
GENERAL PUBLIC BUILDINGS	1.47	2.20	2.42	1.55	0.51	4.42	5.11	1.43
HEALTH	12.95	15.27	14.05	24.84	0.86	9.11	4.12	8.68
CORRECTION	4.80	9.95	9.57	11.44	2.51	6.97	3.37	6.50
NATURAL RESOURCES.	0.41	0.10	0.12	0.33	1.95	0.51	0.13	0.30
PARKS AND RECREATION	0.08	0.44	0.77	0.55	2.09	-	3.13	1.22
INTEREST ON GENERAL DEBT	1.72	1.97	3.78	1.95	0.34	0.10	2.69	3.24
OTHER AND UNALLOCABLE.	9.30	24.43	43.97	6.95	13.98	11.98	11.81	16.70
TOTAL DEBT OUTSTANDING AT END OF FISCAL YEAR	30.68	35.66	53.24	43.33	8.30	2.23	50.19	55.78

Item	Pennsylvania--Continued							
	Lawrence	Lebanon	Lehigh	Luzerne	Lycoming	Mercer	Montgomery	Northampton
GENERAL REVENUE.	69.66	72.18	117.59	53.57	84.37	68.74	94.39	98.60
INTERGOVERNMENTAL REVENUE.	41.45	30.28	48.26	21.82	35.27	25.14	38.12	41.51
GENERAL REVENUE SHARING.	5.82	5.86	6.52	6.21	7.93	6.92	3.16	6.64
TAX REVENUE.	20.22	27.24	52.42	22.46	35.01	25.79	42.33	42.45
PROPERTY TAXES ONLY.	20.22	27.24	52.42	22.46	33.21	23.34	42.00	42.44
CHARGES AND MISCELLANEOUS.	7.98	14.65	16.91	9.29	14.09	17.80	13.94	14.63
GENERAL EXPENDITURE, ALL FUNCTIONS .	74.40	68.18	119.40	56.87	78.09	72.55	101.56	113.32
CAPITAL OUTLAY	13.83	0.30	14.44	2.61	7.35	7.74	17.00	24.53
OTHER.	60.57	67.88	104.96	54.26	70.74	64.80	84.55	88.78
PUBLIC WELFARE	19.17	31.62	47.98	20.32	19.68	23.41	21.06	53.54
EDUCATION.	-	-	0.02	1.63	-	-	3.78	-
HIGHWAYS	2.42	1.43	1.18	4.58	2.11	2.34	3.01	2.46
HOSPITALS.	-	-	0.48	-	0.20	0.23	1.29	0.53
GENERAL CONTROL.	8.38	8.46	9.48	7.55	13.54	9.87	13.47	8.68
POLICE PROTECTION.	0.15	0.07	0.13	0.19	0.10	0.21	0.67	0.13
FINANCIAL ADMINISTRATION	2.74	2.57	3.74	4.86	5.19	3.23	4.31	2.87
GENERAL PUBLIC BUILDINGS	4.01	1.93	3.42	3.70	1.70	1.14	2.93	10.19
HEALTH	7.85	2.03	10.82	0.37	10.30	11.03	10.95	10.82
CORRECTION	3.86	4.45	8.02	4.02	7.58	11.46	11.94	7.35
NATURAL RESOURCES.	0.26	0.53	1.65	0.47	0.47	0.90	0.14	0.26
PARKS AND RECREATION	0.02	0.56	7.14	0.96	0.41	-	1.25	1.53
INTEREST ON GENERAL DEBT	0.08	1.46	5.27	0.69	1.45	0.65	1.70	3.01
OTHER AND UNALLOCABLE.	25.45	13.07	20.06	7.54	15.37	8.07	25.04	11.92
TOTAL DEBT OUTSTANDING AT END OF FISCAL YEAR	2.16	36.34	101.80	11.78	19.99	11.55	37.61	84.02

See footnotes at end of table.

Table 2. Per Capita Amounts of Selected Financial Items: 1977—Continued

Item	Pennsylvania--Continued				South Carolina			
	Schuylkill	Washington	West-moreland	York	Anderson	Charleston	Greenville	Lexington
GENERAL REVENUE.	93.17	69.22	84.92	65.01	54.83	132.13	105.80	185.57
INTERGOVERNMENTAL REVENUE.	45.09	35.21	47.00	30.93	35.78	38.80	44.77	41.19
GENERAL REVENUE SHARING.	9.14	6.22	5.17	3.68	5.93	17.39	12.38	15.65
TAX REVENUE.	27.30	27.45	22.48	22.33	11.21	47.47	46.57	55.55
PROPERTY TAXES ONLY.	25.72	27.45	22.39	22.06	11.13	45.84	44.24	51.33
CHARGES AND MISCELLANEOUS.	20.78	6.56	15.44	11.74	7.85	45.86	14.46	88.83
GENERAL EXPENDITURE, ALL FUNCTIONS .	93.47	70.25	86.73	67.94	51.24	112.96	105.40	207.20
CAPITAL OUTLAY	1.20	16.45	9.42	5.65	9.21	20.93	11.63	38.13
OTHER.	92.27	53.80	77.30	62.29	42.03	92.02	93.77	169.07
PUBLIC WELFARE	30.31	24.35	20.42	22.14	0.94	1.60	4.03	0.66
EDUCATION.	-	-	2.15	-	1.67	-	4.70	1.39
HIGHWAYS	3.16	1.99	2.53	2.96	14.21	6.59	11.37	9.42
HOSPITALS.	-	-	-	-	-	26.32	-	79.45
GENERAL CONTROL.	8.50	8.37	8.37	8.85	5.62	9.62	10.37	11.00
POLICE PROTECTION.	0.19	0.14	0.23	0.20	3.95	13.32	12.57	8.50
FINANCIAL ADMINISTRATION	5.21	3.29	3.85	2.52	2.79	4.76	7.29	5.67
GENERAL PUBLIC BUILDINGS	2.08	2.15	2.64	0.72	1.50	10.91	4.91	6.28
HEALTH	12.49	0.81	8.97	0.86	6.87	8.07	5.51	4.30
CORRECTION	7.10	3.69	3.75	6.34	4.78	3.12	3.28	2.25
NATURAL RESOURCES.	0.67	2.23	0.56	0.25	0.05	1.31	0.05	-
PARKS AND RECREATION	0.31	1.27	0.91	0.59	0.23	3.04	6.46	8.68
INTEREST ON GENERAL DEBT	0.20	1.53	1.67	0.71	0.50	6.70	6.53	15.25
OTHER AND UNALLOCABLE.	23.25	20.42	30.67	21.79	8.13	17.61	28.35	54.33
TOTAL DEBT OUTSTANDING AT END OF FISCAL YEAR	5.21	22.39	54.90	14.09	10.44	98.68	131.45	276.19

Item	South Carolina--Continued		Tennessee				Texas	
	Richland	Spartanburg	Hamilton	Knox	Shelby	Sullivan	Bell	Bexar
GENERAL REVENUE.	201.33	240.29	469.12	294.03	292.43	315.50	30.30	74.81
INTERGOVERNMENTAL REVENUE.	38.71	40.92	80.67	102.19	53.03	101.05	5.31	15.29
GENERAL REVENUE SHARING.	10.62	8.58	7.36	7.25	11.32	4.85	2.97	5.67
TAX REVENUE.	35.20	23.54	199.05	169.35	181.94	191.99	14.86	39.33
PROPERTY TAXES ONLY.	33.18	22.81	126.50	101.67	122.98	134.83	13.71	37.45
CHARGES AND MISCELLANEOUS.	127.43	175.83	189.40	22.50	57.46	22.46	10.13	20.19
GENERAL EXPENDITURE, ALL FUNCTIONS .	192.56	220.75	437.54	282.95	290.77	323.53	31.80	74.94
CAPITAL OUTLAY	6.69	12.63	31.47	49.09	27.22	35.35	1.54	8.34
OTHER.	185.88	208.12	406.08	233.86	263.56	288.17	30.26	66.60
PUBLIC WELFARE	0.90	1.52	23.17	12.09	0.99	2.10	0.85	1.42
EDUCATION.	1.30	0.45	156.42	166.18	107.38	215.60	-	-
HIGHWAYS	4.07	8.90	16.28	12.59	9.14	25.98	8.66	5.25
HOSPITALS.	119.56	122.15	145.18	-	74.22	-	-	42.23
GENERAL CONTROL.	12.22	19.89	6.72	11.13	13.87	5.85	7.95	6.88
POLICE PROTECTION.	8.71	6.07	6.36	4.68	5.42	6.85	2.48	3.96
FINANCIAL ADMINISTRATION	3.94	2.78	5.23	4.88	6.41	4.62	3.81	3.10
GENERAL PUBLIC BUILDINGS	5.20	0.68	3.69	1.25	1.78	0.55	1.26	1.01
HEALTH	3.03	13.16	9.57	7.16	11.00	5.05	1.12	0.63
CORRECTION	2.18	0.87	5.92	3.59	11.52	1.65	3.74	4.15
NATURAL RESOURCES.	0.04	0.50	0.18	0.17	0.82	0.22	0.22	1.65
PARKS AND RECREATION	1.70	0.13	0.96	2.03	4.06	0.57	-	0.90
INTEREST ON GENERAL DEBT	6.03	23.41	6.61	10.05	2.95	10.16	0.51	1.53
OTHER AND UNALLOCABLE.	23.69	20.23	51.24	47.15	41.22	44.33	1.21	2.24
TOTAL DEBT OUTSTANDING AT END OF FISCAL YEAR	102.54	470.74	135.02	208.77	87.13	168.56	16.33	29.39

See footnotes at end of table.

173

Table 2. Per Capita Amounts of Selected Financial Items: 1977—Continued

Item	Texas--Continued							
	Brazoria	Cameron	Dallas	El Paso	Galveston	Harris	Hidalgo	Jefferson
GENERAL REVENUE	105.74	57.86	90.21	83.78	142.42	107.21	46.99	57.67
INTERGOVERNMENTAL REVENUE	15.85	15.44	15.87	12.49	10.00	15.33	18.10	9.33
GENERAL REVENUE SHARING	8.20	7.19	4.13	4.84	5.59	5.70	12.25	4.86
TAX REVENUE	79.77	24.14	48.35	30.60	59.99	72.35	23.35	39.03
PROPERTY TAXES ONLY	76.74	22.92	46.17	29.53	58.46	69.48	22.40	36.12
CHARGES AND MISCELLANEOUS	10.12	18.28	26.00	40.69	72.43	19.53	5.54	9.31
GENERAL EXPENDITURE, ALL FUNCTIONS	92.02	50.98	87.09	67.69	127.18	115.54	42.29	50.40
CAPITAL OUTLAY	20.57	12.82	8.58	4.11	3.66	31.07	13.71	1.54
OTHER	71.45	38.16	78.51	63.58	123.52	84.47	28.58	48.85
PUBLIC WELFARE	1.42	1.84	3.10	1.48	3.39	2.68	2.04	1.80
EDUCATION	-	-	-	-	-	0.44	(Z)	-
HIGHWAYS	32.10	8.79	9.11	2.26	11.12	17.74	4.10	9.14
HOSPITALS	0.76	-	34.90	37.92	57.95	30.53	-	0.42
GENERAL CONTROL	8.96	6.60	11.21	5.12	10.89	12.84	4.74	11.53
POLICE PROTECTION	7.82	2.92	2.84	2.76	6.94	4.30	2.30	3.83
FINANCIAL ADMINISTRATION	6.66	4.98	4.77	3.36	8.11	6.64	5.58	4.24
GENERAL PUBLIC BUILDINGS	12.65	11.73	2.09	4.17	4.10	6.15	0.90	2.70
HEALTH	3.24	4.27	1.99	1.83	4.04	3.39	3.01	2.13
CORRECTION	3.76	4.34	5.75	2.68	1.28	7.41	13.49	3.82
NATURAL RESOURCES	0.91	0.32	0.10	0.14	1.85	10.54	0.29	0.27
PARKS AND RECREATION	0.47	1.52	(Z)	1.83	3.20	2.01	0.82	-
INTEREST ON GENERAL DEBT	2.21	1.36	4.12	0.37	7.83	5.75	1.83	0.47
OTHER AND UNALLOCABLE	11.05	2.31	7.10	3.77	6.46	5.12	3.19	10.06
TOTAL DEBT OUTSTANDING AT END OF FISCAL YEAR	49.73	26.41	88.73	9.61	168.70	124.02	41.58	13.35

Item	Texas--Continued							
	Lubbock	McLennan	Nueces	Smith	Tarrant	Taylor	Travis	Wichita
GENERAL REVENUE	54.82	74.55	201.16	43.24	77.48	30.99	51.52	36.15
INTERGOVERNMENTAL REVENUE	9.15	40.95	27.24	5.10	15.48	4.71	9.22	6.99
GENERAL REVENUE SHARING	5.10	3.71	9.99	3.28	4.35	3.39	3.73	3.65
TAX REVENUE	32.22	23.12	63.74	26.80	40.64	18.96	31.63	23.14
PROPERTY TAXES ONLY	28.96	20.08	62.78	23.43	38.20	15.17	29.55	19.89
CHARGES AND MISCELLANEOUS	13.46	10.48	110.17	11.33	21.36	7.33	10.67	6.02
GENERAL EXPENDITURE, ALL FUNCTIONS	69.43	67.98	190.95	37.40	69.29	29.49	50.31	33.46
CAPITAL OUTLAY	30.72	1.66	30.68	0.70	3.01	1.19	5.03	2.74
OTHER	38.71	66.32	160.27	36.70	66.28	28.30	45.28	30.72
PUBLIC WELFARE	0.74	1.02	4.21	0.61	2.35	1.33	3.39	2.91
EDUCATION	-	-	-	-	-	-	(Z)	-
HIGHWAYS	4.50	10.42	10.07	11.81	4.74	4.00	8.53	5.24
HOSPITALS	34.28	-	116.17	-	31.35	-	-	1.39
GENERAL CONTROL	5.72	5.24	11.02	6.29	8.59	7.57	9.04	6.58
POLICE PROTECTION	3.56	4.38	3.43	3.95	2.88	2.54	5.06	3.40
FINANCIAL ADMINISTRATION	3.41	3.55	5.39	3.83	4.53	4.57	4.23	2.84
GENERAL PUBLIC BUILDINGS	2.82	1.08	21.19	1.26	0.80	2.49	2.16	2.14
HEALTH	1.48	1.91	1.90	1.38	0.38	1.02	0.89	1.15
CORRECTION	1.81	3.17	3.49	1.89	3.60	2.93	11.00	2.37
NATURAL RESOURCES	0.20	0.23	0.45	0.48	0.15	0.35	0.30	0.48
PARKS AND RECREATION	1.95	-	2.17	-	1.21	0.08	0.29	-
INTEREST ON GENERAL DEBT	3.65	-	4.26	1.30	1.44	1.45	0.60	0.53
OTHER AND UNALLOCABLE	5.30	36.99	7.19	4.58	7.27	1.16	4.81	4.44
TOTAL DEBT OUTSTANDING AT END OF FISCAL YEAR	57.29	-	92.22	32.16	26.87	36.58	12.98	15.03

See footnotes at end of table.

174

Table 2. Per Capita Amounts of Selected Financial Items: 1977—Continued

Item	Utah				Vermont	Virginia		
	Davis	Salt Lake	Utah	Weber	Chittenden	Arlington	Fairfax	Henrico
GENERAL REVENUE.	52.44	135.63	43.59	101.98	2.59	844.09	851.23	555.40
INTERGOVERNMENTAL REVENUE.	19.65	45.49	14.93	37.43	0.32	221.60	250.17	179.17
GENERAL REVENUE SHARING.	4.97	12.30	7.55	6.66	0.25	10.52	9.81	7.92
TAX REVENUE.	20.65	76.81	23.08	39.71	2.13	545.22	502.17	300.09
PROPERTY TAXES ONLY.	18.58	60.63	19.77	36.29	2.13	410.19	395.33	195.32
CHARGES AND MISCELLANEOUS.	12.13	13.33	5.57	24.83	0.13	77.26	98.89	76.15
GENERAL EXPENDITURE, ALL FUNCTIONS .	49.64	137.35	44.84	98.38	1.94	756.40	841.36	586.53
CAPITAL OUTLAY	4.15	12.08	7.05	5.48	0.20	45.22	66.64	113.67
OTHER.	45.49	125.28	37.79	92.90	1.74	711.18	774.72	472.85
PUBLIC WELFARE	3.06	1.79	0.42	4.01	-	55.12	26.84	12.23
EDUCATION.	-	0.27	-	-	-	283.54	449.69	281.73
HIGHWAYS	2.62	10.93	5.50	7.00	-	34.65	0.93	39.69
HOSPITALS.	-	-	-	18.97	-	0.06	3.89	-
GENERAL CONTROL.	5.77	10.60	5.68	9.40	0.76	27.79	9.29	11.17
POLICE PROTECTION.	5.70	10.91	3.09	3.91	0.05	66.19	31.53	34.90
FINANCIAL ADMINISTRATION	2.54	6.89	3.76	4.81	0.04	18.75	14.35	13.77
GENERAL PUBLIC BUILDINGS	2.13	4.76	1.68	2.70	-	9.14	12.35	40.99
HEALTH	5.29	15.81	4.02	18.72	-	25.39	18.98	3.20
CORRECTION	0.85	4.88	6.49	3.51	0.21	10.94	3.02	8.59
NATURAL RESOURCES.	1.47	5.99	1.39	1.65	-	6.97	0.47	6.22
PARKS AND RECREATION	3.75	12.19	1.71	1.60	-	34.53	18.30	8.45
INTEREST ON GENERAL DEBT	1.98	1.66	0.01	0.12	0.48	34.66	29.91	16.04
OTHER AND UNALLOCABLE.	14.49	50.68	11.09	21.97	0.41	148.66	208.17	109.55
TOTAL DEBT OUTSTANDING AT END OF FISCAL YEAR	49.24	30.43	-	3.00	8.77	1 005.35	1 006.50	414.12

Item	Virginia--Continued	Washington						
	Prince William	Clark	King	Kitsap	Pierce	Snohomish	Spokane	Yakima
GENERAL REVENUE.	802.18	139.78	167.70	139.47	99.10	119.76	119.07	119.63
INTERGOVERNMENTAL REVENUE.	316.98	46.74	60.93	57.82	41.07	42.22	42.48	54.10
GENERAL REVENUE SHARING.	25.24	5.63	6.19	6.36	6.73	7.90	6.78	7.95
TAX REVENUE.	384.04	71.59	78.35	64.08	45.61	64.40	53.49	48.62
PROPERTY TAXES ONLY.	320.13	38.40	49.60	36.91	28.99	37.27	27.80	27.50
CHARGES AND MISCELLANEOUS.	101.16	21.45	28.42	17.56	12.41	13.14	23.10	16.91
GENERAL EXPENDITURE, ALL FUNCTIONS .	670.48	141.81	178.12	140.39	127.41	117.27	133.64	148.19
CAPITAL OUTLAY	50.81	12.91	18.93	22.11	18.76	11.86	31.68	13.18
OTHER.	619.67	128.90	159.19	118.28	108.65	105.42	101.96	135.02
PUBLIC WELFARE	31.64	0.09	0.15	12.31	4.46	0.37	0.01	1.49
EDUCATION.	451.42	16.21	20.09	15.48	11.78	19.11	12.51	11.16
HIGHWAYS	0.64	37.49	17.29	34.46	23.13	18.45	21.16	31.24
HOSPITALS.	-	0.77	24.18	-	-	-	1.14	1.38
GENERAL CONTROL.	15.39	11.43	14.04	14.77	10.25	11.81	10.51	13.47
POLICE PROTECTION.	30.98	15.34	10.79	9.99	14.21	13.55	9.84	8.55
FINANCIAL ADMINISTRATION	12.96	8.70	8.28	12.06	14.22	9.60	8.22	9.83
GENERAL PUBLIC BUILDINGS	5.24	2.89	1.56	3.14	4.13	2.82	3.40	2.83
HEALTH	13.09	9.57	16.32	10.83	11.47	7.23	23.37	10.60
CORRECTION	2.28	3.09	7.92	2.72	3.95	5.20	6.75	7.63
NATURAL RESOURCES.	0.64	2.34	1.79	1.83	1.77	2.26	1.64	0.60
PARKS AND RECREATION	11.52	7.44	22.05	8.01	5.87	4.25	2.61	2.03
INTEREST ON GENERAL DEBT	33.35	-	13.64	1.86	0.76	2.29	2.81	0.26
OTHER AND UNALLOCABLE.	61.32	26.45	20.01	12.90	21.42	20.33	29.67	47.13
TOTAL DEBT OUTSTANDING AT END OF FISCAL YEAR	720.88	4.85	259.30	48.62	20.72	48.04	56.18	4.47

See footnotes at end of table.

175

Table 2. Per Capita Amounts of Selected Financial Items: 1977—Continued

Item	West Virginia		Wisconsin			
	Cabell	Kanawha	Brown	Dane	Kenosha	Marathon
GENERAL REVENUE.	65.54	62.06	207.76	200.83	199.68	289.59
INTERGOVERNMENTAL REVENUE.	33.14	19.55	137.61	128.32	122.57	175.13
GENERAL REVENUE SHARING. . . .	7.93	10.10	10.50	6.75	9.39	10.88
TAX REVENUE.	24.31	32.85	42.51	40.70	34.73	37.87
PROPERTY TAXES ONLY.	24.15	32.74	42.24	40.29	34.72	37.79
CHARGES AND MISCELLANEOUS. . . .	8.09	9.66	27.63	31.81	42.37	76.59
GENERAL EXPENDITURE, ALL FUNCTIONS .	56.14	59.47	203.59	193.33	194.72	272.49
CAPITAL OUTLAY	1.00	7.94	37.52	16.47	6.72	18.66
OTHER.	55.14	51.53	166.07	176.85	188.00	253.83
PUBLIC WELFARE	-	0.88	58.18	62.36	97.00	28.33
EDUCATION.	-	-	4.06	6.09	0.40	8.44
HIGHWAYS	-	-	39.11	23.22	30.19	59.15
HOSPITALS.	-	-	31.43	16.31	2.02	75.53
GENERAL CONTROL.	5.22	8.13	8.05	17.06	10.41	11.74
POLICE PROTECTION.	3.94	3.06	15.31	17.79	14.54	10.85
FINANCIAL ADMINISTRATION	3.39	4.82	2.94	1.90	4.20	2.37
GENERAL PUBLIC BUILDINGS	2.30	6.71	2.81	3.04	1.47	1.72
HEALTH	14.59	5.29	0.60	12.72	16.29	11.85
CORRECTION	1.59	3.71	3.05	3.23	0.61	2.67
NATURAL RESOURCES.	0.30	0.14	1.86	1.79	0.73	2.40
PARKS AND RECREATION	2.48	4.75	4.23	7.32	9.46	5.76
INTEREST ON GENERAL DEBT	0.23	2.97	6.00	0.27	0.42	4.69
OTHER AND UNALLOCABLE.	22.12	19.01	25.96	20.24	6.97	46.99
TOTAL DEBT OUTSTANDING AT END OF FISCAL YEAR	9.99	64.88	124.74	4.90	12.31	102.31

Item	Wisconsin--Continued					
	Milwaukee	Outagamie	Racine	Rock	Waukesha	Winnebago
GENERAL REVENUE.	374.81	197.98	224.27	259.95	161.75	216.66
INTERGOVERNMENTAL REVENUE.	231.84	146.99	151.58	182.70	93.87	125.22
GENERAL REVENUE SHARING. . . .	13.90	9.32	9.84	8.63	5.41	10.13
TAX REVENUE.	62.53	32.63	36.10	30.89	38.24	35.36
PROPERTY TAXES ONLY.	61.93	32.57	35.97	30.82	38.22	35.16
CHARGES AND MISCELLANEOUS. . . .	80.44	18.37	36.60	46.35	29.63	56.08
GENERAL EXPENDITURE, ALL FUNCTIONS .	356.95	200.48	231.05	252.09	158.73	194.42
CAPITAL OUTLAY	25.72	11.31	19.01	9.43	5.78	9.34
OTHER.	331.22	189.17	212.05	242.66	152.94	185.08
PUBLIC WELFARE	137.91	64.37	92.67	100.39	43.82	60.96
EDUCATION.	0.88	3.97	7.21	2.81	24.80	-
HIGHWAYS	9.06	27.48	21.63	34.87	18.18	27.76
HOSPITALS.	96.78	33.84	36.98	34.59	22.33	0.39
GENERAL CONTROL.	17.97	10.54	14.61	12.59	9.26	9.17
POLICE PROTECTION.	4.38	9.81	12.52	13.63	10.57	9.62
FINANCIAL ADMINISTRATION	3.61	3.84	2.46	2.54	1.66	2.84
GENERAL PUBLIC BUILDINGS	2.17	5.43	4.18	2.05	2.86	1.77
HEALTH	5.20	17.20	15.29	17.33	9.59	66.46
CORRECTION	9.30	1.67	1.46	6.94	0.23	1.41
NATURAL RESOURCES.	0.17	1.55	1.37	0.99	1.18	1.93
PARKS AND RECREATION	34.50	1.44	9.23	0.58	5.61	1.61
INTEREST ON GENERAL DEBT	4.74	1.65	-	3.35	0.23	1.88
OTHER AND UNALLOCABLE.	30.28	17.70	11.43	19.42	8.40	8.61
TOTAL DEBT OUTSTANDING AT END OF FISCAL YEAR	139.39	36.89	-	52.99	3.24	42.51

Note: Because of rounding, detail may not add to totals.

- Represents zero or rounds to zero.

D — CITY GOVERNMENT FINANCES

Municipalities in the United States received $73.8 billion from all revenue sources and made expenditures totaling $70.6 billion in fiscal year 1976-77. Total revenue increased $6.9 billion or 10.4 percent and expenditure was $3.1 billion or 4.7 percent larger than the previous fiscal year.

General revenue of city governments, which excludes utility, liquor store, and employee-retirement amounts, was $60.9 billion in 1976–77 compared with $55.3 billion a year earlier.

General Revenue

City governments have been receiving an increasing proportion of their general revenue from Federal and State grants-in-aid and shared taxes. For example, during the past decade such intergovernmental revenue has increased from 26.7 percent to 38.0 percent of total city general revenue. Federal subventions increased during this period from 4.4 percent of general revenue to 14.6 percent, and State aid went from 22.2 to 23.4 percent, respectively. There has been a concomitant decline in the percentage from property taxes, which decreased from 36.5 to 25.7 percent during the same period. The proportion derived from nonproperty taxes remained steady at about 16-17 percent, while the proportion from charges and miscellaneous sources has decreased slightly (18.9 to 17.5 percent).

City-imposed taxes yielded $26.1 billion in fiscal 1976-77 or about 42.8 percent of all general revenue of city governments. Property taxation continued as the predominant tax revenue source supplying $15.7 billion. Other municipal tax amounts consisted of approximately $3.5 billion from general sales and gross receipts taxes, $2.3 billion from selective sales taxes, and $4.6 billion from licenses and miscellaneous other taxes.

Municipalities received about $14.2 billion from State governments in fiscal 1976-77. This, together with sums received directly from the Federal Government and from other local governments (mainly

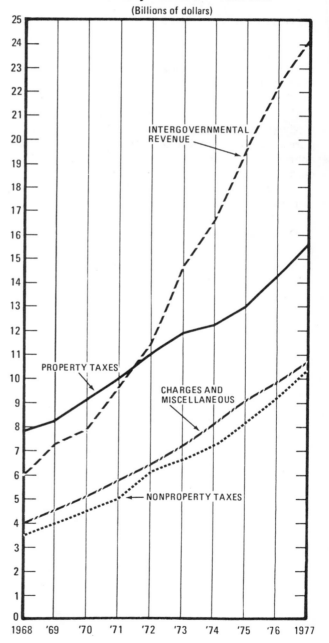

Trends in City General Revenue from Selected Major Sources: 1968-1977

(Billions of dollars)

177

counties), made the total of city intergovernmental revenue $24.2 billion, or about 39.7 percent of general revenue from all sources. Included in this total is $2.4 billion in general revenue sharing funds distributed by the Federal Government to municipalities under the State and Local Fiscal Assistance Act of 1972.

Sources other than taxes and intergovernmental revenue supplied $10.7 billion of municipal general revenue in fiscal 1976-77. This amount included $6.9 billion from current charges (other than for utility services, classed separately as utility revenue).

Table U below illustrates the distribution of municipal government revenue in fiscal 1976-77.

General Expenditure

As indicated below, education takes a larger share of city expenditure than any other function, even though most of this spending is by the small fraction of municipal governments (including New York City and some other very large units) that directly administer local public schools. In most cities, public schools are administered by independent school districts, for which financial data are not included in this report.

Table V is a summary functional distribution of municipal governments' general expenditure in fiscal 1976-77.

During the last 10 fiscal years, the percentage of general expenditure going for public welfare ranged from 7.9 to 8.8 percent. Comparable expenditure for education in this period has decreased slightly, from

15.8 to 13.6 percent; highways declined from 9.9 to 7.6 percent and fire protection from 6.5 to 6.2 percent.

Indebtedness and Debt Transactions

At the end of fiscal 1976-77, municipal indebtedness totaled $71.5 billion, or 3.9 percent more than a year earlier. The debt total included $38.6 billion of long-term indebtedness pledging the cities' full faith and credit, $28.3 billion of nonguaranteed long-term debt, and $4.6 billion of short-term debt.

During fiscal 1976-77, municipalities issued about $9.9 billion of long-term debt, including $2.7 billion for utility purposes. Their retirement of long-term debt during this fiscal year totaled $4.5 billion, including $949 million of utility indebtedness.

As shown in Table W, long-term debt is often nonguaranteed, i.e., obligations payable solely from pledged earnings of specific activities or facilities, from special assessments, or from specific nonproperty taxes. Net long-term debt represents gross long-term debt less amounts reserved for future debt retirement, which are commonly referred to as long-term debt offsets.

The changes in long and short-term debt outstanding at the end of fiscal 1976-77 from amounts reported for the previous fiscal year are accounted for partially by the indebtedness of New York City. Short-term indebtedness of New York City declined by $1.0 billion from fiscal 1975-76, long-term debt issued was $2.2 billion, and long-term debt retired was $1.3 billion.

178

Item	Amount (millions of dollars)	Percent	Percent increase from prior fiscal year
Revenue from all sources..	73,786	100.0	10.4
Intergovernmental revenue...........	24,176	32.7	8.7
Revenue from own sources...........	49,610	67.3	11.2
General revenue from own sources.	36,746	49.8	11.0
Taxes..........	26,067	35.3	11.7
Charges and miscellaneous general revenue	10,678	14.5	9.3
Utility revenue...	10,682	14.5	12.4
Liquor stores revenue.........	212	0.3	3.9
Insurance trust revenue.........	1,971	2.7	9.1

Function	Amount (millions of dollars)	Percent	Per capita amount (dollars)
Total general expenditure..	56,145	100.0	410.75
Education..........	7,633	13.6	55.84
Police protection...	6,445	11.5	47.15
Public welfare......	4,624	8.2	33.83
Highways...........	4,273	7.6	31.26
Sewerage...........	3,852	6.9	28.18
Fire protection.....	3,496	6.2	25.57
Interest on general debt..............	2,644	4.7	19.34
Parks and recreation	2,496	4.4	18.26
Hospitals...........	2,493	4.4	18.24
Sanitation other than sewerage......	1,901	3.4	13.91
General control.....	1,755	3.1	12.84
Housing and urban renewal...........	1,747	3.1	12.78
Financial adminis- tration...........	1,004	1.8	7.35
General public buildings..........	838	1.5	6.13
All other functions.	10,944	19.5	10.50

(V)

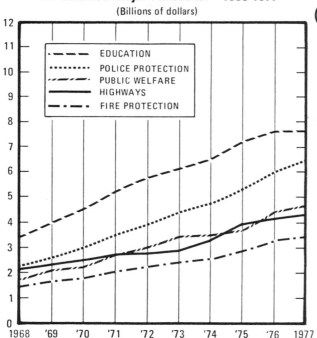

Trends in City General Expenditure for Selected Major Functions: 1968-1977
(Billions of dollars)

- — — — EDUCATION
- ········· POLICE PROTECTION
- ////// PUBLIC WELFARE
- ——— HIGHWAYS
- —·—·— FIRE PROTECTION

1968 '69 '70 '71 '72 '73 '74 '75 '76 1977

City Utilities and Liquor Stores

Municipal governments commonly operate water supply systems and some of them also operate other utilities—electric power, gas supply, and local transit systems.

(W)

Item	Amount (millions of dollars)	Percent increase or decrease (-) from 1975-76
Debt outstanding, total.......	71,497	3.9
Long-term..................	66,929	7.7
Full faith and credit.....	38,646	4.9
Nonguaranteed.............	28,283	11.9
Short-term.................	4,568	-31.6
Net long-term debt outstanding	61,046	6.5

City utility revenue in fiscal 1976–77 totaled $10.7 billion, including $3.8 billion for water supply systems and $5.3 billion for electric power systems. Utility expenditure amounted to $12.1 billion, of which $8.5 billion was for current operation. $2.7 billion was capital outlay, and the remainder was interest on utility debt.

Municipal long-term indebtedness for utilities at the end of the fiscal year amounted to $18.7 billion.

Finances of Municipal Employee-Retirement Systems

Municipal revenue in 1976-77 included employee-retirement revenue of $1.9 billion, consisting of employee contributions, earnings on retirement system investments, and State payments for employees covered by municipal systems.

179

Benefits and withdrawals paid by municipal retirement systems in 1976-77 totaled $2.1 billion, and
their financial assets at the end of the fiscal year
amounted to $21.2 billion.

Coverage and Limitations of Data

Data in this report relate only to municipal corporations and their dependent agencies, and do not
include amounts for other local governments overlying city areas. Therefore, expenditure figures for
"education" do not include spending by the separate
school districts which administer public schools
within most municipal areas. Variations in the assignment of governmental responsibility for public
assistance, health, hospitals, public housing, and
other functions to a lesser degree, also have an important effect upon reported amounts of city expenditure, revenue, and debt.

The 1976-77 fiscal years reported are those
which closed between July 1, 1976 and June 30,
1977. A majority of municipalities end their fiscal
years on December 31; the next most common financial period is the 12 months ending June 30.

The financial statistics reported here are based
mainly on a mail canvass that covered substantially
all cities with a 1970 population of 25,000 or more.
Estimates for minor revenue items, expenditure,
debt, and cash and security holdings were developed from data received from a scientifically de-
signed sample of city governments below that population size. As a result, the data covering the total of
all cities are subject to some sampling variations.
Calculations of the relative standard error of these
estimates indicate that for major items it is less than
one percent (at the two-thirds confidence level).

For the 46 cities with 300,000 inhabitants or more
and for a limited number of smaller cities, the basic
data were compiled by Census Bureau representatives from official reports and records, with the advice and assistance of local officers and employees.
Information for other cities was supplied by local officials in response to a mail canvass that involved
the use of detailed census questionnaires. The mail
reports were examined intensively, and followup
correspondence was used to supplement and verify
questionable figures.

180

Table 1. Summary of City Government Finances: 1973 to 1977

(Dollar amounts in millions)

Item	1976-77	1975-76	1974-75	1973-74	1972-73	Percent increase or decrease (-) 1975-76 to 1976-77	Percent distribution, 1976-77
REVENUE	73 786	66 856	59 744	52 822	48 461	10.4	(x)
GENERAL REVENUE	60 921	55 341	49 853	44 158	40 378	10.1	100.0
INTERGOVERNMENTAL REVENUE	24 176	22 234	19 648	16 624	14 697	8.7	39.7
FROM STATE GOVERNMENTS.	14 236	13 772	13 053	10 464	9 694	3.4	23.4
FROM FEDERAL GOVERNMENT	8 917	7 442	5 844	5 458	4 370	19.8	14.6
GENERAL REVENUE SHARING	2 380	2 185	2 208	2 349	1 606	8.9	2.0
FROM LOCAL GOVERNMENTS.	1 022	1 021	751	702	633	0.1	1.7
GENERAL REVENUE FROM OWN SOURCES.	36 746	33 107	30 205	27 534	25 681	11.0	60.3
TAXES	26 067	23 336	21 135	19 434	18 477	11.7	42.8
PROPERTY.	15 657	14 165	13 046	12 244	11 879	10.5	25.7
SALES AND GROSS RECEIPTS.	5 805	5 109	4 555	3 931	3 567	13.6	9.5
GENERAL	3 511	3 083	2 769	2 381	2 126	13.9	5.8
SELECTIVE	2 294	2 026	1 786	1 550	1 441	13.2	3.8
OTHER	4 604	4 063	3 534	3 259	3 031	13.3	7.6
CHARGES AND MISCELLANEOUS	10 678	9 771	9 071	8 100	7 204	9.3	17.5
CURRENT CHARGES	6 872	6 161	5 443	4 927	4 533	11.5	11.3
INTEREST EARNINGS	1 334	1 443	1 640	1 290	809	-7.6	2.2
SPECIAL ASSESSMENTS . :	525	527	502	489	507	-0.4	0.9
SALE OF PROPERTY.	128	171	167	213	245	-25.1	0.2
OTHER AND UNALLOCABLE	1 819	1 469	1 319	1 181	1 111	23.8	3.0
UTILITY REVENUE	10 682	9 504	8 217	7 067	6 619	12.4	100.0
WATER SUPPLY.	3 833	3 454	3 266	2 911	2 813	10.7	35.8
ELECTRIC POWER.	5 288	4 598	3 682	2 947	2 654	14.9	49.5
TRANSIT	944	929	821	807	764	1.6	8.8
GAS SUPPLY.	628	522	448	401	388	20.3	5.9
LIQUOR STORES REVENUE	212	204	192	173	164	3.9	2.0
INSURANCE TRUST REVENUE	1 971	1 807	1 482	1 424	1 300	9.1	(x)
EMPLOYEE RETIREMENT	1 889	1 692	1 460	1 405	1 283	11.6	(x)
UNEMPLOYMENT COMPENSATION (WASHINGTON, D.C.)	82	115	22	19	17	-28.7	(x)
EXPENDITURE	70 599	67 460	60 703	52 535	48 151	4.7	100.0
EXPENDITURE BY CHARACTER AND OBJECT:							
INTERGOVERNMENTAL EXPENDITURE	1 569	1 570	714	604	596	-0.1	2.2
DIRECT EXPENDITURE.	69 030	65 890	59 989	51 931	47 555	4.8	97.8
CURRENT OPERATION	50 287	46 705	41 451	36 192	32 665	7.7	71.2
CAPITAL OUTLAY.	11 273	11 923	12 054	9 904	9 182	-5.5	16.0
CONSTRUCTION.	9 115	9 729	9 780	7 841	7 153	-6.3	12.9
EQUIPMENT	1 575	1 475	1 436	1 138	953	6.8	2.2
LAND AND EXISTING STRUCTURES.	583	718	838	925	1 077	-18.8	0.8
ASSISTANCE PAYMENTS	1 794	1 787	1 594	1 575	1 799	0.4	2.5
INTEREST ON DEBT.	3 500	3 475	3 018	2 586	2 350	0.7	5.0
INSURANCE BENEFITS AND REPAYMENTS	2 177	2 000	1 872	1 674	1 559	8.9	3.1
EXHIBIT: TOTAL PERSONAL SERVICES	27 599	26 367	24 635	22 947	20 595	4.7	39.1
EXPENDITURE BY FUNCTION:							
GENERAL EXPENDITURE	56 145	54 425	48 935	42 786	39 134	3.2	100.0
CAPITAL OUTLAY.	8 570	9 312	9 577	7 863	7 201	-8.0	15.3
OTHER	47 575	45 113	39 358	34 923	31 803	5.5	84.7
EDUCATION	7 633	7 610	7 164	6 472	6 050	0.3	13.6
CAPITAL OUTLAY.	532	670	856	766	744	-20.6	0.9
OTHER	7 101	6 941	6 308	5 706	5 306	2.3	12.6
HIGHWAYS.	4 273	4 245	3 861	3 327	2 925	0.7	7.6
CAPITAL OUTLAY.	1 636	1 801	1 670	1 402	1 177	-9.2	2.9
OTHER	2 637	2 444	2 191	1 925	1 748	7.9	4.7
PUBLIC WELFARE.	4 624	4 544	3 846	3 490	3 413	1.8	8.2
CASH ASSISTANCE PAYMENTS.	1 794	1 787	1 594	1 575	1 799	0.4	3.2
OTHER PUBLIC WELFARE.	2 830	2 757	2 252	1 915	1 615	2.6	5.0
HOSPITALS	2 493	2 475	2 735	2 427	2 156	0.7	4.4
OWN HOSPITALS	2 220	2 179	1 986	1 820	1 653	1.9	4.0
CAPITAL OUTLAY.	170	171	176	153	143	-0.6	0.3
OTHER	2 050	2 008	1 810	1 667	1 510	2.1	3.7
OTHER HOSPITALS	273	296	749	607	502	-7.8	0.5
HEALTH.	797	987	906	793	678	-19.3	1.4
POLICE PROTECTION	6 445	6 015	5 420	4 797	4 434	7.1	11.5
FIRE PROTECTION	3 496	3 257	2 968	2 643	2 407	7.3	6.2
SEWERAGE.	3 852	3 664	3 415	2 575	2 360	5.1	6.9
CAPITAL OUTLAY.	2 282	2 296	2 255	1 576	1 518	-0.6	4.1
OTHER	1 571	1 368	1 160	999	841	14.8	2.8
SANITATION OTHER THAN SEWERAGE.	1 901	1 893	1 814	1 643	1 466	0.4	3.4
PARKS AND RECREATION.	2 496	2 558	2 274	1 998	1 723	-2.4	4.4
CAPITAL OUTLAY.	641	828	776	697	548	-22.6	1.1
OTHER	1 855	1 730	1 498	1 301	1 175	7.2	3.3
HOUSING AND URBAN RENEWAL	1 747	1 525	1 752	1 734	1 676	14.6	3.1
CAPITAL OUTLAY.	715	633	906	992	1 013	13.0	1.3
OTHER	1 032	892	846	742	664	15.7	1.8
AIRPORTS.	589	671	615	498	539	-12.2	1.0
WATER TRANSPORT AND TERMINALS	159	195	182	167	120	-18.5	0.3
PARKING FACILITIES.	263	264	249	188	185	-0.4	0.5
LIBRARIES	668	684	632	556	500	-2.3	1.2
FINANCIAL ADMINISTRATION.	1 004	912	819	719	636	10.1	1.8

See footnotes at end of table.

Table 1. Summary of City Government Finances: 1973 to 1977—Continued

(Dollar amounts in millions)

Item	1976-77	1975-76	1974-75	1973-74	1972-73	Percent increase or decrease (-) 1975-76 to 1976-77	Percent distribution, 1976-77
EXPENDITURE BY FUNCTION--CONTINUED							
GENERAL EXPENDITURE--CONTINUED							
GENERAL CONTROL	1 755	1 611	1 140	1 275	1 096	8.9	3.1
GENERAL PUBLIC BUILDINGS.	838	934	845	680	608	-10.3	1.5
CAPITAL OUTLAY.	270	375	358	269	252	-28.0	0.5
OTHER	568	560	487	411	357	1.4	1.0
INTEREST ON GENERAL DEBT.	2 644	2 683	2 294	1 918	1 736	-1.5	4.7
OTHER AND UNALLOCABLE	8 466	7 698	5 704	4 886	4 426	10.0	15.1
UTILITY EXPENDITURE	12 090	10 857	9 727	7 923	7 318	11.4	100.0
WATER SUPPLY.	4 467	3 958	3 776	3 188	2 987	12.9	36.9
ELECTRIC POWER.	5 275	4 560	3 779	2 981	2 709	15.7	43.6
TRANSIT	1 806	1 875	1 765	1 497	1 273	-3.7	14.9
GAS SUPPLY.	541	463	407	357	349	16.8	4.5
LIQUOR STORES EXPENDITURE	188	179	169	150	139	5.0	(x)
INSURANCE TRUST EXPENDITURE	2 177	2 000	1 872	1 674	1 559	8.9	(x)
EMPLOYEE RETIREMENT	2 091	1 878	1 828	1 644	1 534	11.3	(x)
UNEMPLOYMENT COMPENSATION (WASHINGTON, D.C.)	86	122	44	30	25	-29.5	(x)
GROSS DEBT OUTSTANDING.	71 497	68 797	65 239	61 187	56 041	3.9	100.0
LONG-TERM	66 929	62 119	55 789	53 390	49 286	7.7	93.6
FULL FAITH AND CREDIT	38 646	36 839	31 886	30 733	28 912	4.9	54.1
UTILITY DEBT ONLY	5 518	5 313	5 360	5 231	5 340	3.9	7.7
NONGUARANTEED	28 283	25 280	23 903	22 658	20 375	11.9	39.6
UTILITY DEBT ONLY	13 187	11 842	11 397	10 808	9 659	11.4	18.4
SHORT-TERM.	4 568	6 677	9 450	7 796	6 755	-31.6	6.4
NET LONG-TERM DEBT OUTSTANDING.	61 046	57 322	51 437	49 394	45 517	6.5	85.4
LONG-TERM DEBT ISSUED	9 874	9 684	5 754	6 827	6 140	2.0	100.0
GENERAL	7 149	8 274	4 435	5 267	4 620	-13.6	72.4
UTILITY	2 726	1 410	1 319	1 560	1 520	93.3	27.6
LONG-TERM DEBT RETIRED.	4 477	3 868	3 656	3 258	3 079	15.7	100.0
GENERAL	3 528	2 932	2 882	2 532	2 379	20.3	78.8
UTILITY	949	936	774	726	700	1.4	21.2
CASH AND SECURITY HOLDINGS AT END OF FISCAL YEAR	49 276	43 555	42 366	39 571	36 301	13.1	100.0
INSURANCE TRUST	21 185	19 052	17 496	16 030	15 529	11.2	43.0
EMPLOYEE RETIREMENT	21 174	19 037	17 475	15 985	15 473	11.2	43.0
UNEMPLOYMENT COMPENSATION (WASHINGTON, D.C.)	11	15	21	45	56	-26.7	-
OTHER THAN INSURANCE TRUST.	28 091	24 503	24 870	23 541	20 772	14.6	57.0
BY PURPOSE:							
OFFSETS TO DEBT	5 883	4 797	4 352	3 996	3 769	22.6	11.9
BOND FUNDS.	5 844	5 238	5 706	5 868	5 208	11.6	11.9
OTHER AND UNALLOCABLE	16 363	14 467	14 812	13 676	11 795	13.1	33.2
BY TYPE:							
CASH AND DEPOSITS	17 472	14 352	14 151	13 347	11 785	21.7	35.5
SECURITIES.	10 618	10 151	10 718	10 193	8 986	4.6	21.5
FEDERAL	6 938	6 103	6 788	6 813	6 260	13.7	14.1
STATE AND LOCAL GOVERNMENTS	377	961	916	721	727	-60.8	0.8
OTHER (NONGOVERNMENTAL)	3 303	3 087	3 015	2 659	1 999	7.0	6.7

Note: Because of rounding, detail may not add to totals. These data are estimates, subject to sampling variation. In particular, estimates here for components which do not appear in tables 3, 4, and 5 are based upon only a limited sample and may be subject to relatively sizable sampling variation.

- Represents zero or rounds to zero.
X Not applicable.

Table 2. Per Capita Amounts of Financial Items for Individual City and Selected Urban Town and Township Governments Having 50,000 Population or More: 1977

Item	Alabama						Alaska
	Birmingham	Gadsden	Huntsville	Mobile	Montgomery	Tuscaloosa	Anchorage
REVENUE							
GENERAL REVENUE	414.72	251.98	458.99	332.56	274.82	573.60	1 358.85
TAXES	192.07	143.61	131.92	132.08	133.71	55.18	406.14
PROPERTY	39.96	13.31	29.72	12.25	21.64	15.74	394.53
OTHER	152.11	130.31	102.20	119.83	112.07	39.44	11.61
INTERGOVERNMENTAL REVENUE	133.26	67.10	89.53	84.76	96.59	127.39	606.48
MISCELLANEOUS GENERAL REVENUE	89.39	41.27	237.55	115.71	44.51	391.03	346.23
EXPENDITURE							
GENERAL EXPENDITURE, ALL FUNCTIONS	336.12	227.20	425.34	366.08	238.44	587.32	1 399.71
TOTAL, EXCLUDING CAPITAL OUTLAY	298.59	210.97	344.50	206.64	187.89	433.32	1 152.78
GENERAL EXPENDITURE, SELECTED ITEMS:							
EDUCATION	2.38	2.42	19.06	-	0.30	0.35	624.01
HIGHWAYS	40.44	19.84	29.89	21.16	20.53	24.50	96.50
EXCLUDING CAPITAL OUTLAY	26.02	18.25	24.87	11.37	20.01	12.82	33.65
PUBLIC WELFARE	-	1.01	-	-	7.40	-	-
HEALTH AND HOSPITALS	1.37	3.36	158.30	3.35	0.91	420.80	22.85
POLICE PROTECTION	46.70	28.14	26.45	37.49	30.12	38.20	56.55
FIRE PROTECTION	35.25	30.48	22.07	33.70	30.64	28.64	57.15
SEWERAGE	29.85	9.04	8.69	120.93	7.23	11.45	68.86
EXCLUDING CAPITAL OUTLAY	20.88	8.02	8.05	11.41	6.68	8.87	37.64
SANITATION OTHER THAN SEWERAGE	7.91	17.77	10.64	13.78	20.68	20.54	27.06
PARKS AND RECREATION	33.25	13.07	14.04	27.92	23.33	4.08	45.59
HOUSING AND URBAN RENEWAL	(Z)	-	-	12.89	0.05	-	-
TOTAL DEBT	1 083.74	449.17	873.54	1 110.16	478.91	523.56	2 285.27
LONG-TERM, FULL FAITH AND CREDIT	823.26	109.94	438.43	424.05	218.99	149.12	1 323.57

Item	Arizona						Arkansas
	Glendale	Mesa	Phoenix	Scottsdale	Tempe	Tucson	Fort Smith
REVENUE							
GENERAL REVENUE	233.16	270.27	343.77	325.77	274.92	340.62	179.75
TAXES	93.41	75.92	128.46	136.05	99.20	150.24	39.90
PROPERTY	29.47	6.12	49.38	43.66	37.15	31.61	21.63
OTHER	63.94	69.80	79.08	92.39	62.05	118.63	18.27
INTERGOVERNMENTAL REVENUE	96.37	94.31	152.24	117.84	112.88	126.82	76.03
MISCELLANEOUS GENERAL REVENUE	43.38	100.04	63.06	71.88	62.84	63.55	63.81
EXPENDITURE							
GENERAL EXPENDITURE, ALL FUNCTIONS	202.56	273.35	360.47	332.20	223.86	368.16	153.44
TOTAL, EXCLUDING CAPITAL OUTLAY	155.90	178.53	264.99	271.96	171.45	293.91	133.98
GENERAL EXPENDITURE, SELECTED ITEMS:							
EDUCATION	-	-	1.61	-	-	-	-
HIGHWAYS	25.37	40.75	45.07	15.94	23.03	42.44	23.90
EXCLUDING CAPITAL OUTLAY	16.75	14.92	12.58	15.74	11.63	23.94	14.57
PUBLIC WELFARE	-	-	0.38	-	-	-	-
HEALTH AND HOSPITALS	-	-	0.29	-	-	-	0.97
POLICE PROTECTION	31.69	39.15	67.05	45.60	33.94	47.51	23.51
FIRE PROTECTION	19.03	26.57	28.52	10.60	17.52	28.74	20.38
SEWERAGE	10.92	6.40	25.75	3.44	10.78	21.62	-
EXCLUDING CAPITAL OUTLAY	4.64	5.37	6.29	3.44	9.69	8.87	-
SANITATION OTHER THAN SEWERAGE	17.69	18.18	26.18	24.21	16.12	22.31	15.25
PARKS AND RECREATION	24.94	22.92	27.27	33.07	38.88	40.98	9.07
HOUSING AND URBAN RENEWAL	6.56	-	13.06	15.90	9.00	12.48	-
TOTAL DEBT	123.08	694.30	597.58	361.66	357.96	555.37	219.58
LONG-TERM, FULL FAITH AND CREDIT	10.95	54.33	279.12	206.36	254.47	157.40	4.23

See footnotes at end of table.

183

Table 2. Per Capita Amounts of Financial Items for Individual City and Selected Urban Town and Township Governments Having 50,000 Population or More: 1977—Continued

Item	Arkansas--Continued			California			
	Little Rock	North Little Rock	Pine Bluff	Alameda	Alhambra	Anaheim	Bakersfield
REVENUE							
GENERAL REVENUE.	316.28	212.44	185.30	177.15	307.37	314.00	344.55
TAXES.	87.62	38.30	40.93	105.59	127.09	158.44	196.13
PROPERTY	41.43	25.50	19.16	66.91	77.64	68.47	75.61
OTHER.	46.19	12.81	21.76	38.67	49.44	89.97	120.52
INTERGOVERNMENTAL REVENUE.	141.31	114.98	94.25	47.11	91.76	73.79	109.92
MISCELLANEOUS GENERAL REVENUE.	87.35	59.16	50.12	24.45	88.53	81.79	38.49
EXPENDITURE							
GENERAL EXPENDITURE, ALL FUNCTIONS	237.96	289.55	204.55	165.11	376.69	316.20	331.42
TOTAL, EXCLUDING CAPITAL OUTLAY.	195.09	152.28	116.07	143.60	340.16	246.42	238.05
GENERAL EXPENDITURE, SELECTED ITEMS:							
EDUCATION.	0.51	-	-	-	-	-	-
HIGHWAYS	18.17	41.11	16.47	15.57	146.17	43.04	19.13
EXCLUDING CAPITAL OUTLAY	15.62	16.46	15.72	15.57	145.61	28.27	19.12
PUBLIC WELFARE	-	0.92	-	0.53	-	-	-
HEALTH AND HOSPITALS	1.99	62.48	2.65	-	17.08	-	-
POLICE PROTECTION.	30.58	34.55	24.45	33.06	44.55	56.01	66.32
FIRE PROTECTION.	36.35	26.37	14.44	31.70	39.53	31.52	47.59
SEWERAGE	21.90	13.60	16.38	0.01	1.30	-	61.06
EXCLUDING CAPITAL OUTLAY	12.69	13.60	5.25	-	1.28	-	7.80
SANITATION OTHER THAN SEWERAGE	13.77	14.10	10.58	0.01	12.02	12.55	20.26
PARKS AND RECREATION	14.30	18.21	56.09	26.13	14.35	57.00	6.51
HOUSING AND URBAN RENEWAL.	-	47.78	30.29	-	49.74	44.14	-
TOTAL DEBT	239.25	567.38	145.61	3.40	286.35	394.46	251.22
LONG-TERM, FULL FAITH AND CREDIT	29.00	189.52	74.59	3.19	285.68	49.07	50.61

Item	California--Continued						
	Bellflower	Berkeley	Buena Park	Burbank	Carson	Chula Vista	Compton
REVENUE							
GENERAL REVENUE.	108.46	400.80	210.07	373.75	342.43	226.13	265.81
TAXES.	42.90	171.89	118.56	194.46	173.47	124.27	123.11
PROPERTY	-	122.89	40.64	103.44	101.68	57.05	79.90
OTHER.	42.90	49.00	77.93	91.02	71.79	67.22	43.21
INTERGOVERNMENTAL REVENUE.	45.97	167.48	75.95	84.32	84.64	74.15	122.98
MISCELLANEOUS GENERAL REVENUE.	19.59	61.42	15.56	94.96	84.31	27.70	19.72
EXPENDITURE							
GENERAL EXPENDITURE, ALL FUNCTIONS	99.56	384.56	163.55	344.82	455.26	186.79	241.02
TOTAL, EXCLUDING CAPITAL OUTLAY.	76.33	358.82	145.08	324.52	361.34	170.13	229.54
GENERAL EXPENDITURE, SELECTED ITEMS:							
EDUCATION.	-	-	-	-	-	-	-
HIGHWAYS	29.02	27.63	26.91	26.84	30.68	35.60	34.87
EXCLUDING CAPITAL OUTLAY	14.98	14.25	19.73	26.20	18.60	24.08	34.17
PUBLIC WELFARE	-	-	-	-	-	-	-
HEALTH AND HOSPITALS	-	25.13	3.10	-	-	-	-
POLICE PROTECTION.	27.16	45.19	41.64	72.52	47.84	35.42	49.77
FIRE PROTECTION.	-	30.34	29.16	48.89	62.03	21.22	9.90
SEWERAGE	-	6.27	1.41	9.80	-	11.60	-
EXCLUDING CAPITAL OUTLAY	-	4.53	1.00	9.74	-	11.25	-
SANITATION OTHER THAN SEWERAGE	-	13.84	7.00	14.10	2.73	7.14	2.93
PARKS AND RECREATION	14.33	39.25	13.84	37.45	34.69	17.01	9.89
HOUSING AND URBAN RENEWAL.	0.37	3.14	-	5.42	156.07	3.81	17.01
TOTAL DEBT	6.75	45.05	43.82	121.53	845.48	71.96	218.85
LONG-TERM, FULL FAITH AND CREDIT	-	45.05	-	82.38	-	70.73	116.78

See footnotes at end of table.

184

Table 2. Per Capita Amounts of Financial Items for Individual City and Selected Urban Town and Township Governments Having 50,000 Population or More: 1977—Continued

Item	California--Continued						
	Concord	Costa Mesa	Daly City	Downey	El Cajon	El Monte	Fremont
REVENUE							
GENERAL REVENUE	240.58	264.18	163.28	188.67	218.96	183.61	190.92
TAXES	104.58	174.31	94.77	107.21	130.55	95.23	105.91
PROPERTY	42.42	63.65	50.29	23.37	39.52	36.31	49.11
OTHER	62.16	110.67	44.49	83.85	91.04	58.92	56.80
INTERGOVERNMENTAL REVENUE	65.85	58.74	54.81	61.40	57.35	77.08	58.73
MISCELLANEOUS GENERAL REVENUE	70.16	31.12	13.69	20.06	31.06	11.30	26.28
EXPENDITURE							
GENERAL EXPENDITURE, ALL FUNCTIONS	193.86	208.04	163.53	169.94	170.17	153.80	171.71
TOTAL, EXCLUDING CAPITAL OUTLAY	171.37	170.17	141.05	149.37	167.29	127.80	149.66
GENERAL EXPENDITURE, SELECTED ITEMS:							
EDUCATION	-	-	-	-	-	-	-
HIGHWAYS	28.36	38.04	16.33	21.34	14.37	24.33	28.73
EXCLUDING CAPITAL OUTLAY	27.40	23.50	13.72	16.33	14.24	12.84	18.08
PUBLIC WELFARE	-	-	-	-	-	-	-
HEALTH AND HOSPITALS	-	-	0.22	-	-	0.04	-
POLICE PROTECTION	49.58	50.13	36.02	44.12	36.06	47.34	31.29
FIRE PROTECTION	-	27.03	25.16	28.62	22.63	23.84	21.92
SEWERAGE	8.19	-	-	0.66	12.09	0.71	-
EXCLUDING CAPITAL OUTLAY	4.63	-	-	0.58	11.41	0.69	-
SANITATION OTHER THAN SEWERAGE	0.84	1.31	2.63	1.50	1.56	1.03	0.89
PARKS AND RECREATION	56.89	37.46	21.02	22.36	11.52	14.61	19.00
HOUSING AND URBAN RENEWAL	-	2.97	-	-	-	0.83	-
TOTAL DEBT	179.38	49.74	2.09	4.28	56.16	0.30	158.25
LONG-TERM, FULL FAITH AND CREDIT	146.77	49.17	2.03	3.06	6.70	0.30	47.64

Item	California--Continued						
	Fresno	Fullerton	Garden Grove	Glendale	Hawthorne	Hayward	Huntington Beach
REVENUE							
GENERAL REVENUE	401.69	269.98	209.62	274.37	201.42	314.22	260.52
TAXES	185.23	149.87	102.39	129.71	92.78	156.31	156.53
PROPERTY	81.70	78.88	55.39	53.79	36.40	61.12	70.47
OTHER	103.54	71.00	47.01	75.91	56.38	95.19	86.06
INTERGOVERNMENTAL REVENUE	123.75	79.45	81.74	69.36	46.61	89.01	66.26
MISCELLANEOUS GENERAL REVENUE	92.70	40.65	25.49	75.31	62.02	68.90	37.73
EXPENDITURE							
GENERAL EXPENDITURE, ALL FUNCTIONS	368.85	247.88	171.59	303.88	215.21	249.37	224.51
TOTAL, EXCLUDING CAPITAL OUTLAY	264.85	182.57	140.42	253.30	208.83	232.42	199.03
GENERAL EXPENDITURE, SELECTED ITEMS:							
EDUCATION	-	-	-	-	-	-	-
HIGHWAYS	57.89	51.18	32.61	30.86	20.63	22.97	23.90
EXCLUDING CAPITAL OUTLAY	29.14	21.72	16.69	29.68	20.54	18.65	13.03
PUBLIC WELFARE	-	-	-	-	-	-	-
HEALTH AND HOSPITALS	-	-	-	-	-	-	-
POLICE PROTECTION	57.76	41.94	37.01	36.73	42.11	53.63	43.58
FIRE PROTECTION	38.61	22.79	26.72	34.27	33.10	44.41	25.89
SEWERAGE	50.13	1.16	-	4.37	1.26	22.41	3.94
EXCLUDING CAPITAL OUTLAY	12.86	1.16	-	2.08	1.26	21.98	1.08
SANITATION OTHER THAN SEWERAGE	26.72	8.06	-	13.68	30.29	0.03	7.26
PARKS AND RECREATION	35.25	31.44	29.22	13.72	18.78	7.04	22.18
HOUSING AND URBAN RENEWAL	5.72	22.93	-	10.03	-	-	-
TOTAL DEBT	187.74	37.28	30.81	710.52	467.68	179.95	66.50
LONG-TERM, FULL FAITH AND CREDIT	120.86	28.52	-	6.04	-	78.93	34.87

See footnotes at end of table.

Table 2. Per Capita Amounts of Financial Items for Individual City and Selected Urban Town and Township Governments Having 50,000 Population or More: 1977—Continued

Item	California--Continued						
	Inglewood	Lakewood	Long Beach	Los Angeles	Modesto	Mountain View	Newport Beach
REVENUE							
GENERAL REVENUE.	341.13	157.16	478.93	424.65	280.79	384.06	339.48
TAXES.	167.82	84.84	175.65	216.17	134.69	186.86	234.33
PROPERTY	55.67	45.61	89.61	109.73	35.70	74.59	118.56
OTHER.	112.15	39.23	86.04	106.44	98.99	112.27	115.77
INTERGOVERNMENTAL REVENUE.	83.21	52.66	114.08	115.15	77.42	71.85	50.68
MISCELLANEOUS GENERAL REVENUE.	90.09	19.66	189.21	93.33	68.67	125.35	54.47
EXPENDITURE							
GENERAL EXPENDITURE, ALL FUNCTIONS	452.12	125.09	537.94	334.90	240.30	296.34	331.98
TOTAL, EXCLUDING CAPITAL OUTLAY.	427.26	115.47	428.65	292.34	193.15	238.47	278.19
GENERAL EXPENDITURE, SELECTED ITEMS:							
EDUCATION.	-	-	1.11	5.34	-	-	-
HIGHWAYS	35.93	16.25	18.58	28.79	30.42	33.49	54.08
EXCLUDING CAPITAL OUTLAY	35.35	11.86	14.34	17.46	14.66	18.91	26.89
PUBLIC WELFARE	-	-	-	-	-	-	-
HEALTH AND HOSPITALS	0.37	-	10.85	0.91	0.04	-	-
POLICE PROTECTION.	102.55	23.92	84.07	83.43	38.15	50.12	71.07
FIRE PROTECTION.	48.76	-	54.23	35.06	29.00	34.27	36.28
SEWERAGE	2.51	-	6.52	8.79	15.45	21.67	5.53
EXCLUDING CAPITAL OUTLAY	2.51	-	5.59	5.29	11.07	13.49	3.82
SANITATION OTHER THAN SEWERAGE	29.13	9.23	18.52	14.38	8.32	16.47	17.19
PARKS AND RECREATION	25.11	28.69	79.73	19.79	32.25	48.67	37.54
HOUSING AND URBAN RENEWAL.	35.79	-	17.25	9.16	1.94	0.74	0.68
TOTAL DEBT	759.29	44.99	382.72	975.05	14.75	520.10	7.87
LONG-TERM, FULL FAITH AND CREDIT	20.03	-	26.82	49.79	8.53	486.28	-

Item	California--Continued						
	Norwalk	Oakland	Ontario	Orange	Oxnard	Palo Alto	Pasadena
REVENUE							
GENERAL REVENUE.	121.25	570.89	284.64	244.08	267.36	402.17	417.16
TAXES.	53.77	205.59	115.28	137.65	117.28	159.80	217.14
PROPERTY	18.39	116.62	50.49	50.45	55.98	68.98	102.34
OTHER.	35.38	88.96	64.79	87.20	61.29	90.82	114.80
INTERGOVERNMENTAL REVENUE.	58.40	240.95	113.11	69.81	81.12	79.56	111.73
MISCELLANEOUS GENERAL REVENUE.	9.08	124.36	56.24	36.62	68.97	162.81	88.31
EXPENDITURE							
GENERAL EXPENDITURE, ALL FUNCTIONS	103.30	481.45	201.44	223.74	248.64	459.49	511.85
TOTAL, EXCLUDING CAPITAL OUTLAY.	88.43	391.49	173.33	194.80	205.43	416.67	384.21
GENERAL EXPENDITURE, SELECTED ITEMS:							
EDUCATION.	-	1.63	-	-	-	-	43.83
HIGHWAYS	22.00	36.71	14.33	39.01	27.00	23.68	26.37
EXCLUDING CAPITAL OUTLAY	13.87	25.95	10.03	18.59	14.22	18.61	-
PUBLIC WELFARE	-	-	-	0.11	-	-	10.37
HEALTH AND HOSPITALS	0.28	-	-	-	0.07	-	69.66
POLICE PROTECTION.	23.75	66.02	42.05	43.21	42.11	67.10	40.10
FIRE PROTECTION.	16.49	48.93	30.73	33.51	26.22	68.27	2.73
SEWERAGE	0.74	6.29	6.60	3.53	22.88	28.46	2.47
EXCLUDING CAPITAL OUTLAY	0.63	3.17	6.57	3.53	22.84	22.55	15.06
SANITATION OTHER THAN SEWERAGE	4.16	5.56	13.41	6.21	18.50	35.43	42.26
PARKS AND RECREATION	0.21	35.46	11.51	14.89	27.04	54.98	121.40
HOUSING AND URBAN RENEWAL.	3.06	16.34	-	-	0.03	3.88	-
TOTAL DEBT	-	508.05	120.27	81.70	167.41	173.40	522.78
LONG-TERM, FULL FAITH AND CREDIT	-	21.28	75.23	5.60	51.15	79.88	337.60

See footnotes at end of table.

186

Table 2. Per Capita Amounts of Financial Items for Individual City and Selected Urban Town and Township Governments Having 50,000 Population or More: 1977—Continued

Item	California--Continued						
	Pico Rivera	Pomona	Redondo Beach	Redwood City	Richmond	Riverside	Sacramento
REVENUE							
GENERAL REVENUE	150.05	283.65	320.11	289.18	675.70	255.45	373.79
TAXES	67.56	146.50	142.20	166.40	296.66	116.54	166.82
PROPERTY	27.94	59.20	74.18	99.32	205.69	31.02	85.79
OTHER	39.62	87.29	68.01	67.08	90.97	85.52	81.03
INTERGOVERNMENTAL REVENUE	63.85	106.13	89.68	61.12	300.70	80.88	98.66
MISCELLANEOUS GENERAL REVENUE	18.64	31.02	88.24	61.67	78.34	58.04	108.30
EXPENDITURE							
GENERAL EXPENDITURE, ALL FUNCTIONS	145.94	247.75	288.88	283.70	613.14	296.48	390.00
TOTAL, EXCLUDING CAPITAL OUTLAY	114.42	239.40	262.74	234.97	498.04	244.40	341.34
GENERAL EXPENDITURE, SELECTED ITEMS:							
EDUCATION	-	-	-	-	-	-	-
HIGHWAYS	19.87	26.61	18.03	19.39	83.74	39.01	10.76
EXCLUDING CAPITAL OUTLAY	14.12	21.89	15.00	15.84	21.56	28.08	10.75
PUBLIC WELFARE	-	-	-	-	-	-	-
HEALTH AND HOSPITALS	0.19	0.63	-	-	-	-	1.11
POLICE PROTECTION	31.44	49.24	53.17	73.45	73.27	51.01	66.59
FIRE PROTECTION	-	39.00	25.10	40.10	48.81	33.16	43.72
SEWERAGE	0.02	1.35	0.59	12.61	15.72	13.87	18.58
EXCLUDING CAPITAL OUTLAY	-	1.35	0.59	10.45	14.70	8.67	17.26
SANITATION OTHER THAN SEWERAGE	1.55	11.28	5.58	2.49	-	19.75	27.37
PARKS AND RECREATION	40.68	24.75	33.32	32.33	39.16	31.75	42.96
HOUSING AND URBAN RENEWAL	4.78	1.49	-	-	42.23	23.93	26.47
TOTAL DEBT	0.50	60.77	287.44	444.26	485.71	511.28	389.28
LONG-TERM, FULL FAITH AND CREDIT	-	37.37	-	2.68	144.52	32.57	217.64

Item	California--Continued						
	Salinas	San Bernardino	San Buenaventura	San Diego	San Francisco	San Jose	San Leandro
REVENUE							
GENERAL REVENUE	245.80	366.15	333.89	303.95	1 201.48	357.79	283.50
TAXES	139.36	177.30	154.43	128.02	537.32	143.69	163.38
PROPERTY	47.20	64.31	62.72	61.35	364.24	59.42	50.78
OTHER	92.15	112.99	91.71	66.67	173.08	84.27	112.60
INTERGOVERNMENTAL REVENUE	78.44	125.27	102.41	115.17	471.53	138.38	77.44
MISCELLANEOUS GENERAL REVENUE	28.01	63.58	77.05	60.76	192.63	75.72	42.67
EXPENDITURE							
GENERAL EXPENDITURE, ALL FUNCTIONS	241.03	350.88	354.49	252.37	1 045.36	328.48	285.96
TOTAL, EXCLUDING CAPITAL OUTLAY	199.65	304.27	259.66	214.71	884.76	198.63	237.32
GENERAL EXPENDITURE, SELECTED ITEMS:							
EDUCATION	-	-	-	7.02	4.33	-	-
HIGHWAYS	35.34	33.24	96.81	20.05	24.61	29.78	29.59
EXCLUDING CAPITAL OUTLAY	13.53	26.70	33.20	10.81	11.31	12.10	11.35
PUBLIC WELFARE	-	-	-	0.02	216.88	-	-
HEALTH AND HOSPITALS	-	-	-	0.63	143.76	-	0.03
POLICE PROTECTION	50.63	60.96	45.87	39.12	75.99	43.56	39.97
FIRE PROTECTION	32.75	41.09	41.80	23.58	56.74	25.57	31.08
SEWERAGE	6.93	21.35	38.16	22.14	69.15	95.01	19.73
EXCLUDING CAPITAL OUTLAY	6.74	20.85	31.49	10.54	8.42	12.74	13.08
SANITATION OTHER THAN SEWERAGE	-	19.25	-	11.86	9.25	3.65	10.25
PARKS AND RECREATION	29.13	20.30	49.97	38.18	43.66	34.20	27.51
HOUSING AND URBAN RENEWAL	6.15	-	3.69	4.15	35.38	1.74	11.43
TOTAL DEBT	108.45	449.65	200.94	168.81	939.37	248.35	74.95
LONG-TERM, FULL FAITH AND CREDIT	80.71	419.20	137.21	50.46	821.07	150.79	28.53

See footnotes at end of table.

Table 2. Per Capita Amounts of Financial Items for Individual City and Selected Urban Town and Township Governments Having 50,000 Population or More: 1977—Continued

Item	California--Continued						
	San Mateo	Santa Ana	Santa Barbara	Santa Clara	Santa Monica	Santa Rosa	Simi Valley
REVENUE							
GENERAL REVENUE.	290.40	260.87	432.55	411.76	390.61	573.69	134.58
TAXES.	142.08	139.47	151.04	159.31	154.96	161.66	55.65
PROPERTY	68.32	59.06	58.05	65.49	56.15	62.96	21.93
OTHER.	73.76	80.40	92.99	93.82	98.81	98.70	33.72
INTERGOVERNMENTAL REVENUE.	104.19	93.12	183.72	87.07	139.67	328.70	53.78
MISCELLANEOUS GENERAL REVENUE.	44.13	28.29	97.79	165.39	95.98	83.33	25.15
EXPENDITURE							
GENERAL EXPENDITURE, ALL FUNCTIONS	248.36	239.46	470.70	450.70	278.13	522.52	95.04
TOTAL, EXCLUDING CAPITAL OUTLAY.	230.71	202.53	281.10	316.32	252.74	219.31	87.82
GENERAL EXPENDITURE, SELECTED ITEMS:							
EDUCATION.	-	-	-	-	-	-	-
HIGHWAYS	19.45	24.85	42.23	116.84	21.04	62.67	16.04
EXCLUDING CAPITAL OUTLAY	12.57	15.79	23.07	12.92	11.28	24.67	9.25
PUBLIC WELFARE	-	-	-	-	-	-	-
HEALTH AND HOSPITALS	-	-	0.15	-	-	-	-
POLICE PROTECTION.	51.14	60.57	49.15	41.99	54.87	35.14	29.39
FIRE PROTECTION.	34.59	30.46	28.34	33.61	27.07	24.89	-
SEWERAGE	11.60	1.33	143.31	23.18	5.43	261.63	9.90
EXCLUDING CAPITAL OUTLAY	11.60	0.46	24.86	16.01	4.96	18.67	9.90
SANITATION OTHER THAN SEWERAGE	1.40	6.07	0.75	19.44	15.72	1.95	-
PARKS AND RECREATION	25.68	21.57	26.72	26.89	27.44	32.33	-
HOUSING AND URBAN RENEWAL.	2.00	5.92	-	-	2.64	13.69	-
TOTAL DEBT	202.52	31.38	392.83	796.09	83.60	600.10	100.60
LONG-TERM, FULL FAITH AND CREDIT	95.53	0.20	203.05	98.31	15.36	440.83	-

Item	California--Continued						
	South Gate	Stockton	Sunnyvale	Torrance	Vallejo	West Covina	Westminister
REVENUE							
GENERAL REVENUE.	218.79	501.06	278.06	276.08	240.67	218.06	191.60
TAXES.	123.00	177.44	125.21	170.57	121.46	126.06	87.93
PROPERTY	67.19	65.31	57.88	54.58	51.95	70.40	28.42
OTHER.	55.82	112.13	67.33	115.99	69.51	55.66	59.51
INTERGOVERNMENTAL REVENUE.	64.71	219.94	68.82	72.50	86.53	61.15	80.29
MISCELLANEOUS GENERAL REVENUE.	31.08	103.68	84.04	33.01	32.68	30.85	23.38
EXPENDITURE							
GENERAL EXPENDITURE, ALL FUNCTIONS	184.79	536.38	313.54	197.35	228.65	185.58	150.18
TOTAL, EXCLUDING CAPITAL OUTLAY.	182.89	367.48	216.04	178.06	200.01	169.89	122.10
GENERAL EXPENDITURE, SELECTED ITEMS:							
EDUCATION.	-	-	0.24	-	-	-	-
HIGHWAYS	17.06	42.70	27.94	36.97	23.39	28.09	33.03
EXCLUDING CAPITAL OUTLAY	17.06	16.81	20.79	27.19	17.47	23.26	13.96
PUBLIC WELFARE	-	-	-	-	-	-	-
HEALTH AND HOSPITALS	-	-	-	1.41	-	1.11	-
POLICE PROTECTION.	53.31	69.82	46.90	13.61	39.36	39.51	46.03
FIRE PROTECTION.	30.60	51.94	35.89	39.24	30.62	25.55	24.75
SEWERAGE	0.39	133.42	77.10	1.48	-	0.74	-
EXCLUDING CAPITAL OUTLAY	0.39	22.97	8.34	1.45	-	0.67	-
SANITATION OTHER THAN SEWERAGE	9.32	10.59	23.21	7.09	-	0.40	1.80
PARKS AND RECREATION	18.03	35.18	39.85	26.55	3.06	20.15	10.46
HOUSING AND URBAN RENEWAL.	0.02	14.01	-	0.19	7.64	7.44	-
TOTAL DEBT	0.99	355.50	248.40	46.99	249.11	277.70	31.61
LONG-TERM, FULL FAITH AND CREDIT	-	355.50	197.70	17.76	116.10	125.36	-

See footnotes at end of table.

Table 2. Per Capita Amounts of Financial Items for Individual City and Selected Urban Town and Township Governments Having 50,000 Population or More: 1977—Continued

Item	California--Continued Whittier	Colorado Arvada	Aurora	Boulder	Colorado Springs	Denver	Fort Collins
REVENUE							
GENERAL REVENUE	173.73	146.11	232.28	248.71	324.18	740.40	310.34
TAXES	99.97	92.41	153.27	139.31	115.05	285.78	111.28
PROPERTY	24.87	21.06	40.13	33.80	34.40	114.79	20.88
OTHER	75.11	71.35	113.14	105.51	80.65	170.99	90.40
INTERGOVERNMENTAL REVENUE	43.42	25.17	27.10	46.77	71.34	246.10	102.96
MISCELLANEOUS GENERAL REVENUE	30.34	28.52	51.91	62.64	137.79	208.52	96.10
EXPENDITURE							
GENERAL EXPENDITURE, ALL FUNCTIONS	168.47	167.99	258.85	239.89	356.05	735.54	255.02
TOTAL, EXCLUDING CAPITAL OUTLAY	153.87	100.91	211.46	167.68	241.75	611.26	155.17
GENERAL EXPENDITURE, SELECTED ITEMS:							
EDUCATION	-	-	-	-	0.45	(Z)	-
HIGHWAYS	22.27	23.20	31.70	44.23	35.63	24.74	36.06
EXCLUDING CAPITAL OUTLAY	18.32	14.50	30.97	22.17	23.41	18.00	16.18
PUBLIC WELFARE	-	1.80	-	-	23.68	116.16	-
HEALTH AND HOSPITALS	-	-	-	6.17	87.91	101.34	0.71
POLICE PROTECTION	42.47	30.05	37.66	33.07	34.81	75.83	26.08
FIRE PROTECTION	30.54	-	24.02	15.92	22.12	43.42	18.90
SEWERAGE	0.74	14.75	16.97	22.84	20.65	41.90	67.81
EXCLUDING CAPITAL OUTLAY	0.60	14.48	16.20	14.47	15.55	32.83	10.57
SANITATION OTHER THAN SEWERAGE	17.68	0.34	2.48	2.60	1.99	18.12	0.14
PARKS AND RECREATION	22.43	62.07	29.98	29.33	28.91	67.77	34.78
HOUSING AND URBAN RENEWAL	-	-	2.98	2.04	11.17	15.21	6.93
TOTAL DEBT	14.71	207.50	635.63	221.09	883.74	817.91	175.68
LONG-TERM, FULL FAITH AND CREDIT	6.31	200.16	480.73	152.91	216.73	584.50	63.61

Item	Colorado--Continued Lakewood	Pueblo	Connecticut Bridgeport	Bristol	Danbury	East Hartford Town	Fairfield Town
REVENUE							
GENERAL REVENUE	146.17	248.96	671.74	620.13	645.34	572.73	523.67
TAXES	104.46	121.74	412.79	347.76	426.14	414.08	420.91
PROPERTY	12.27	31.13	410.18	344.95	423.10	410.72	418.76
OTHER	92.19	90.62	2.62	2.82	3.05	3.36	2.15
INTERGOVERNMENTAL REVENUE	33.03	75.65	180.14	229.39	175.43	140.49	45.97
MISCELLANEOUS GENERAL REVENUE	8.67	51.56	78.81	42.98	43.77	18.16	56.80
EXPENDITURE							
GENERAL EXPENDITURE, ALL FUNCTIONS	130.00	195.95	650.04	533.91	571.20	578.75	625.92
TOTAL, EXCLUDING CAPITAL OUTLAY	112.57	152.03	647.54	516.50	553.82	569.03	558.91
GENERAL EXPENDITURE, SELECTED ITEMS:							
EDUCATION	-	-	249.04	256.08	350.36	346.15	392.41
HIGHWAYS	32.17	27.80	12.79	21.19	33.28	17.09	19.64
EXCLUDING CAPITAL OUTLAY	20.79	18.69	12.79	17.38	31.06	16.48	19.64
PUBLIC WELFARE	-	-	31.31	5.12	3.36	4.53	1.82
HEALTH AND HOSPITALS	0.72	2.53	38.05	14.48	5.43	2.90	10.78
POLICE PROTECTION	32.36	37.76	54.69	27.58	38.30	33.82	36.14
FIRE PROTECTION	-	24.57	61.18	25.70	32.64	40.48	37.14
SEWERAGE	-	8.81	13.61	6.39	0.55	-	5.25
EXCLUDING CAPITAL OUTLAY	-	4.97	13.61	6.39	-	-	5.25
SANITATION OTHER THAN SEWERAGE	2.39	5.07	15.21	6.01	-	18.45	2.20
PARKS AND RECREATION	13.26	23.04	14.02	6.83	7.45	13.93	15.29
HOUSING AND URBAN RENEWAL	0.71	7.67	-	15.06	11.65	-	-
TOTAL DEBT	38.89	586.41	397.59	410.55	386.25	245.14	558.02
LONG-TERM, FULL FAITH AND CREDIT	38.89	68.04	347.93	266.91	340.38	245.14	521.78

See footnotes at end of table.

Table 2. Per Capita Amounts of Financial Items for Individual City and Selected Urban Town and Township Governments Having 50,000 Population or More: 1977—Continued

Item	Connecticut--Continued						
	Greenwich Town	Hartford	Meriden	New Britain	New Haven	Norwalk	Stamford
REVENUE							
GENERAL REVENUE.	949.80	1 278.71	620.99	613.51	636.22	616.88	862.72
TAXES.	658.58	573.56	343.54	407.63	440.32	469.45	605.45
PROPERTY	648.79	569.81	340.92	405.81	436.60	461.48	600.15
OTHER.	9.79	3.74	2.62	1.82	3.73	7.97	5.31
INTERGOVERNMENTAL REVENUE.	191.74	560.47	147.77	168.82	161.26	118.21	205.69
MISCELLANEOUS GENERAL REVENUE.	99.49	144.69	129.68	37.06	34.63	29.22	51.58
EXPENDITURE							
GENERAL EXPENDITURE, ALL FUNCTIONS	851.88	1 270.82	640.17	480.32	652.67	712.82	842.66
TOTAL, EXCLUDING CAPITAL OUTLAY.	810.80	1 114.60	593.20	468.26	538.59	580.47	796.28
GENERAL EXPENDITURE, SELECTED ITEMS:							
EDUCATION.	389.75	478.14	258.11	213.38	284.32	334.29	360.50
HIGHWAYS	30.77	24.13	21.16	16.27	21.35	28.67	43.12
EXCLUDING CAPITAL OUTLAY	19.47	23.44	15.56	16.23	16.20	22.83	43.12
PUBLIC WELFARE	54.90	105.72	5.72	6.03	32.10	7.72	17.75
HEALTH AND HOSPITALS	33.66	43.26	99.61	3.12	8.59	7.17	16.36
POLICE PROTECTION.	55.84	63.89	31.99	40.39	56.64	40.98	52.84
FIRE PROTECTION.	26.49	58.25	30.31	35.86	59.71	36.46	44.69
SEWERAGE	10.43	-	39.31	13.62	100.41	107.36	25.42
EXCLUDING CAPITAL OUTLAY	10.11	-	5.16	13.62	7.52	14.47	25.42
SANITATION OTHER THAN SEWERAGE . . .	13.06	12.70	3.40	11.84	4.41	15.53	33.26
PARKS AND RECREATION	47.43	45.20	8.53	9.90	13.13	13.44	24.75
HOUSING AND URBAN RENEWAL.	-	124.83	-	4.72	-	15.09	47.17
TOTAL DEBT	135.56	1 013.30	566.13	569.10	736.41	1 308.25	967.89
LONG-TERM, FULL FAITH AND CREDIT	135.56	834.65	310.00	364.39	640.43	823.64	913.67

Item	Connecticut--Continued			Delaware	District of Columbia	Florida	
	Waterbury	West Hartford Town	West Haven	Wilmington	Washington	Clearwater	Fort Lauderdale
REVENUE							
GENERAL REVENUE.	763.69	695.55	462.74	1 073.60	2 188.59	435.27	405.16
TAXES.	384.96	527.18	324.31	348.49	1 038.26	144.02	175.08
PROPERTY	380.81	523.59	323.31	186.78	233.06	67.65	104.51
OTHER.	4.16	3.59	1.00	161.70	805.20	76.37	70.57
INTERGOVERNMENTAL REVENUE.	347.98	122.32	116.51	540.31	1 023.17	135.89	114.07
MISCELLANEOUS GENERAL REVENUE.	30.76	46.05	21.92	184.80	127.16	155.36	116.01
EXPENDITURE							
GENERAL EXPENDITURE, ALL FUNCTIONS	589.05	696.84	522.73	1 084.74	2 146.26	509.01	392.19
TOTAL, EXCLUDING CAPITAL OUTLAY.	563.55	618.08	480.62	831.17	1 964.91	380.83	303.67
GENERAL EXPENDITURE, SELECTED ITEMS:							
EDUCATION.	244.87	412.33	259.61	408.25	481.67	-	-
HIGHWAYS	15.05	38.41	17.28	38.94	74.22	22.96	14.86
EXCLUDING CAPITAL OUTLAY	12.93	24.40	16.87	29.41	44.40	3.18	12.74
PUBLIC WELFARE	18.28	3.38	4.09	-	372.56	-	-
HEALTH AND HOSPITALS	6.86	4.08	3.11	-	166.38	-	-
POLICE PROTECTION.	42.09	39.52	38.75	71.37	201.93	72.52	76.72
FIRE PROTECTION.	44.97	31.53	-	67.40	70.85	38.77	38.96
SEWERAGE	17.76	20.69	36.87	161.81	83.85	110.30	84.50
EXCLUDING CAPITAL OUTLAY	11.53	13.26	14.21	44.31	21.78	24.56	22.01
SANITATION OTHER THAN SEWERAGE . . .	13.87	26.17	8.92	26.50	34.30	35.68	25.97
PARKS AND RECREATION	14.18	18.87	13.04	40.16	32.50	49.40	23.11
HOUSING AND URBAN RENEWAL.	34.63	2.25	16.87	-	52.61	2.19	2.85
TOTAL DEBT	739.46	379.16	440.36	1 030.48	2 123.44	667.60	586.27
LONG-TERM, FULL FAITH AND CREDIT	436.93	344.63	339.35	1 018.90	1 595.02	142.27	119.71

See footnotes at end of table.

190

Table 2. Per Capita Amounts of Financial Items for Individual City and Selected Urban Town and Township Governments Having 50,000 Population or More: 1977—Continued

Item	Florida—Continued						
	Gainesville	Hialeah	Hollywood	Jacksonville	Miami	Miami Beach	Orlando
REVENUE							
GENERAL REVENUE	338.85	197.76	368.25	411.69	288.50	474.29	486.57
TAXES	92.83	89.98	126.19	118.38	166.35	307.23	174.23
PROPERTY	54.29	42.57	70.21	77.25	104.18	200.45	98.43
OTHER	38.54	47.41	55.98	41.13	62.18	106.78	75.80
INTERGOVERNMENTAL REVENUE	154.83	67.54	169.90	159.24	87.04	75.80	137.42
MISCELLANEOUS GENERAL REVENUE	91.19	40.24	72.15	134.06	35.11	91.26	174.92
EXPENDITURE							
GENERAL EXPENDITURE, ALL FUNCTIONS	425.12	195.02	332.33	411.52	320.09	710.75	458.76
TOTAL, EXCLUDING CAPITAL OUTLAY	242.69	180.95	230.20	300.83	253.49	345.87	398.45
GENERAL EXPENDITURE, SELECTED ITEMS:							
EDUCATION	-	-	-	0.03	0.07	-	-
HIGHWAYS	16.72	5.68	21.53	20.37	25.51	9.55	31.83
EXCLUDING CAPITAL OUTLAY	16.63	5.40	15.91	17.52	20.65	7.63	27.49
PUBLIC WELFARE	0.84	0.27	-	7.59	-	2.91	-
HEALTH AND HOSPITALS	0.36	-	0.66	56.61	0.86	0.99	3.01
POLICE PROTECTION	41.64	48.74	59.63	42.17	72.48	72.21	82.44
FIRE PROTECTION	35.41	28.76	23.90	24.12	44.29	35.18	55.35
SEWERAGE	182.71	8.80	81.37	74.17	18.83	211.26	28.70
EXCLUDING CAPITAL OUTLAY	27.67	8.74	13.96	15.50	-	7.49	24.46
SANITATION OTHER THAN SEWERAGE	18.37	18.43	13.96	12.65	31.52	23.70	33.09
PARKS AND RECREATION	10.99	17.61	21.12	13.36	52.34	148.95	40.88
HOUSING AND URBAN RENEWAL	2.66	-	25.94	22.40	-	-	-
TOTAL DEBT	2 067.97	90.88	409.92	984.19	321.89	817.09	1 572.06
LONG-TERM, FULL FAITH AND CREDIT	74.34	2.34	48.19	106.95	285.36	678.48	154.22

Item	Florida—Continued					Georgia	
	Pensacola	St. Petersburg	Tallahassee	Tampa	West Palm Beach	Albany	Atlanta
REVENUE							
GENERAL REVENUE	348.35	307.80	529.07	478.90	415.72	180.94	491.70
TAXES	77.09	103.14	67.35	136.35	159.12	67.37	205.98
PROPERTY	24.78	53.85	29.72	61.21	98.00	41.87	132.43
OTHER	52.32	49.29	37.64	75.14	61.12	25.50	73.55
INTERGOVERNMENTAL REVENUE	158.66	114.58	84.40	222.16	159.44	56.57	128.31
MISCELLANEOUS GENERAL REVENUE	112.60	90.08	377.32	120.39	97.17	57.00	157.42
EXPENDITURE							
GENERAL EXPENDITURE, ALL FUNCTIONS	451.99	304.71	664.66	583.27	412.60	224.95	484.46
TOTAL, EXCLUDING CAPITAL OUTLAY	306.69	224.11	502.93	310.92	252.18	186.06	368.49
GENERAL EXPENDITURE, SELECTED ITEMS:							
EDUCATION	-	-	-	-	-	-	12.36
HIGHWAYS	25.43	31.19	29.68	32.65	21.91	23.65	30.58
EXCLUDING CAPITAL OUTLAY	14.40	15.47	17.06	21.97	16.38	12.42	20.75
PUBLIC WELFARE	-	-	-	0.27	-	-	0.70
HEALTH AND HOSPITALS	-	0.28	317.74	-	0.47	1.08	0.11
POLICE PROTECTION	48.17	56.32	35.99	59.63	65.36	44.14	65.72
FIRE PROTECTION	35.89	29.84	21.38	50.27	36.02	29.02	32.24
SEWERAGE	144.29	48.11	49.02	156.64	157.10	19.82	32.95
EXCLUDING CAPITAL OUTLAY	30.70	12.88	26.13	20.49	17.20	15.20	18.72
SANITATION OTHER THAN SEWERAGE	19.57	26.61	26.30	49.21	27.49	16.35	21.97
PARKS AND RECREATION	20.87	33.43	45.86	24.25	37.04	18.40	37.57
HOUSING AND URBAN RENEWAL	3.82	4.66	10.42	3.50	-	13.98	0.48
TOTAL DEBT	780.84	443.37	2 028.02	552.50	393.81	101.93	1 348.25
LONG-TERM, FULL FAITH AND CREDIT	-	93.08	332.47	87.88	114.30	77.88	429.28

See footnotes at end of table.

Item	Georgia--Continued				Hawaii	Idaho	Illinois
	Augusta	Columbus	Macon	Savannah	Honolulu	Boise City	Arlington Heights
REVENUE							
GENERAL REVENUE	330.83	270.20	261.15	325.41	405.97	265.05	227.80
TAXES	132.53	181.88	146.20	123.64	202.20	88.20	129.38
PROPERTY	85.60	73.97	84.07	84.01	162.08	79.93	56.00
OTHER	46.93	107.91	62.13	39.63	40.12	8.27	73.38
INTERGOVERNMENTAL REVENUE	97.84	49.56	69.08	148.48	150.92	128.89	38.72
MISCELLANEOUS GENERAL REVENUE	100.46	38.76	45.87	53.30	52.85	47.96	59.70
EXPENDITURE							
GENERAL EXPENDITURE, ALL FUNCTIONS	342.97	220.86	177.18	300.35	441.01	291.17	207.23
TOTAL, EXCLUDING CAPITAL OUTLAY	258.17	214.27	150.80	214.95	329.20	182.58	179.59
GENERAL EXPENDITURE, SELECTED ITEMS:							
EDUCATION	-	1.00	-	-	-	-	0.63
HIGHWAYS	29.05	20.25	21.24	33.71	38.56	-	33.49
EXCLUDING CAPITAL OUTLAY	21.38	20.02	14.15	18.80	23.24	-	25.49
PUBLIC WELFARE	-	0.53	0.50	-	-	-	1.10
HEALTH AND HOSPITALS	-	22.20	2.31	-	8.37	-	1.76
POLICE PROTECTION	42.30	33.96	33.80	38.35	50.50	29.09	29.61
FIRE PROTECTION	25.62	22.62	28.38	24.63	25.22	29.45	26.98
SEWERAGE	41.15	12.16	4.41	27.78	59.44	60.29	-
EXCLUDING CAPITAL OUTLAY	10.92	11.88	4.41	16.98	10.31	9.62	-
SANITATION OTHER THAN SEWERAGE	10.46	18.79	23.43	32.95	16.67	-	-
PARKS AND RECREATION	5.52	8.80	10.25	27.83	42.01	28.19	0.41
HOUSING AND URBAN RENEWAL	17.86	-	2.53	0.34	9.35	20.29	-
TOTAL DEBT	428.16	299.12	223.92	348.40	342.89	148.23	1 020.75
LONG-TERM, FULL FAITH AND CREDIT	156.85	161.28	99.21	97.00	292.64	9.97	5.71

Item	Illinois--Continued						
	Aurora	Champaign	Chicago	Cicero	Decatur	Des Plaines	East St. Louis
REVENUE							
GENERAL REVENUE	249.46	405.46	396.43	154.36	197.57	215.00	370.42
TAXES	172.10	107.62	211.29	100.64	112.16	151.04	96.51
PROPERTY	120.54	36.85	103.12	56.90	44.47	71.24	51.41
OTHER	51.56	70.77	108.17	43.74	67.69	79.80	45.11
INTERGOVERNMENTAL REVENUE	52.15	53.65	136.71	39.34	55.56	36.70	238.52
MISCELLANEOUS GENERAL REVENUE	25.21	244.19	48.43	14.37	29.85	27.26	35.39
EXPENDITURE							
GENERAL EXPENDITURE, ALL FUNCTIONS	258.66	408.49	377.81	151.03	167.38	261.73	335.05
TOTAL, EXCLUDING CAPITAL OUTLAY	184.17	361.48	329.04	128.90	121.78	196.60	300.32
GENERAL EXPENDITURE, SELECTED ITEMS:							
EDUCATION	-	-	5.63	-	-	-	-
HIGHWAYS	61.10	18.63	26.85	23.56	35.00	39.28	25.34
EXCLUDING CAPITAL OUTLAY	29.55	11.27	16.35	12.47	13.70	38.60	22.46
PUBLIC WELFARE	-	-	7.66	-	-	-	-
HEALTH AND HOSPITALS	3.14	216.96	17.87	1.67	-	1.92	2.93
POLICE PROTECTION	56.71	36.63	101.68	42.29	25.09	44.57	47.63
FIRE PROTECTION	33.85	26.78	34.87	22.59	22.09	33.33	28.52
SEWERAGE	3.34	3.32	10.67	2.46	16.65	4.19	9.60
EXCLUDING CAPITAL OUTLAY	-	3.32	5.81	2.29	2.10	4.19	9.60
SANITATION OTHER THAN SEWERAGE	11.81	-	28.33	21.69	1.47	12.04	4.18
PARKS AND RECREATION	10.10	29.18	4.48	-	0.30	-	17.30
HOUSING AND URBAN RENEWAL	-	4.01	5.62	-	2.25	-	54.20
TOTAL DEBT	327.27	223.57	436.07	51.07	306.45	282.28	228.56
LONG-TERM, FULL FAITH AND CREDIT	250.86	185.19	99.20	5.67	142.79	153.88	23.56

See footnotes at end of table.

192

Table 2. Per Capita Amounts of Financial Items for Individual City and Selected Urban Town and Township Governments Having 50,000 Population or More: 1977—Continued

Item	Illinois--Continued						
	Elgin	Evanston	Joliet	Oak Lawn	Oak Park	Peoria	Rockford
REVENUE							
GENERAL REVENUE	239.28	299.45	257.98	225.40	282.65	248.98	209.75
TAXES	130.35	204.73	173.96	117.22	194.59	161.04	129.81
PROPERTY	72.41	111.65	111.44	56.04	117.75	94.20	72.48
OTHER	57.94	93.08	62.53	61.19	76.84	66.83	57.33
INTERGOVERNMENTAL REVENUE	57.75	63.80	56.28	35.29	45.99	60.27	60.40
MISCELLANEOUS GENERAL REVENUE	51.18	30.91	27.74	72.89	42.08	27.67	19.54
EXPENDITURE							
GENERAL EXPENDITURE, ALL FUNCTIONS	234.56	295.38	219.57	191.02	258.85	315.34	181.91
TOTAL, EXCLUDING CAPITAL OUTLAY	156.04	255.31	197.99	143.67	219.58	207.79	150.10
GENERAL EXPENDITURE, SELECTED ITEMS:							
EDUCATION	-	-	-	-	-	-	-
HIGHWAYS	47.51	42.76	57.82	53.07	19.07	50.34	36.70
EXCLUDING CAPITAL OUTLAY	8.12	16.71	47.32	14.91	8.05	12.57	22.18
PUBLIC WELFARE	-	2.96	-	2.04	-	-	-
HEALTH AND HOSPITALS	1.44	11.86	-	0.29	3.73	-	1.68
POLICE PROTECTION	36.97	47.22	51.79	34.95	56.30	49.32	47.86
FIRE PROTECTION	36.13	26.41	33.17	28.18	30.73	33.08	29.27
SEWERAGE	1.57	2.19	-	9.80	8.47	1.60	1.84
EXCLUDING CAPITAL OUTLAY	1.47	2.18	-	5.70	2.56	1.60	1.84
SANITATION OTHER THAN SEWERAGE	7.06	13.15	10.85	11.46	15.53	15.17	8.26
PARKS AND RECREATION	31.53	35.19	-	-	18.14	1.01	0.10
HOUSING AND URBAN RENEWAL	0.05	3.35	-	-	-	37.35	4.69
TOTAL DEBT	188.66	216.66	406.28	382.21	421.23	173.93	164.55
LONG-TERM, FULL FAITH AND CREDIT	158.48	93.02	40.32	28.32	247.77	15.95	45.15

Item	Illinois--Continued			Indiana			
	Skokie	Springfield	Waukegan	Anderson	Evansville	Fort Wayne	Gary
REVENUE							
GENERAL REVENUE	227.81	322.04	260.53	234.16	247.91	309.47	206.61
TAXES	173.74	152.81	127.54	113.16	83.08	79.05	112.80
PROPERTY	101.01	77.51	66.62	112.61	82.19	78.47	111.69
OTHER	72.73	75.29	60.92	0.55	0.89	0.58	1.11
INTERGOVERNMENTAL REVENUE	37.78	116.84	59.69	79.48	107.80	170.76	86.57
MISCELLANEOUS GENERAL REVENUE	16.28	52.39	73.30	41.52	57.03	59.66	7.24
EXPENDITURE							
GENERAL EXPENDITURE, ALL FUNCTIONS	191.39	285.46	223.97	172.73	256.47	320.67	174.71
TOTAL, EXCLUDING CAPITAL OUTLAY	176.29	207.62	174.14	159.49	233.64	214.91	140.19
GENERAL EXPENDITURE, SELECTED ITEMS:							
EDUCATION	-	-	-	-	-	-	-
HIGHWAYS	20.30	57.19	67.09	28.01	24.83	20.18	12.92
EXCLUDING CAPITAL OUTLAY	11.36	29.01	26.04	26.08	24.83	10.24	10.59
PUBLIC WELFARE	0.34	-	-	-	-	-	-
HEALTH AND HOSPITALS	3.10	8.98	1.60	0.55	5.46	2.76	4.45
POLICE PROTECTION	45.81	39.85	53.44	28.02	17.95	28.15	30.45
FIRE PROTECTION	32.95	33.75	38.14	28.24	27.56	20.62	20.41
SEWERAGE	-	14.52	4.64	17.80	36.23	94.98	21.27
EXCLUDING CAPITAL OUTLAY	-	4.79	4.39	17.62	35.23	20.74	8.31
SANITATION OTHER THAN SEWERAGE	10.31	2.91	9.76	7.93	-	-	-
PARKS AND RECREATION	0.24	17.16	0.41	10.71	18.69	20.93	10.16
HOUSING AND URBAN RENEWAL	1.89	32.73	-	11.08	44.05	15.71	26.93
TOTAL DEBT	41.05	1 553.94	107.78	314.14	203.32	165.96	197.71
LONG-TERM, FULL FAITH AND CREDIT	32.76	8.47	7.68	47.78	58.61	50.63	143.15

See footnotes at end of table.

Table 2. Per Capita Amounts of Financial Items for Individual City and Selected Urban Town and Township Governments Having 50,000 Population or More: 1977—Continued

Item	Indiana--Continued					Iowa	
	Hammond	Indianapolis	Muncie	South Bend	Terre Haute	Cedar Rapids	Council Bluffs
REVENUE							
GENERAL REVENUE	207.85	425.59	215.79	251.65	225.73	424.54	241.85
TAXES	117.92	141.09	66.28	110.05	88.55	136.75	83.99
PROPERTY	116.87	137.14	65.79	109.12	87.46	132.07	79.95
OTHER	1.05	3.95	0.50	0.93	1.09	4.68	4.04
INTERGOVERNMENTAL REVENUE	80.29	203.38	110.55	93.41	89.75	180.27	80.12
MISCELLANEOUS GENERAL REVENUE	9.64	81.12	38.96	48.19	47.42	107.52	77.74
EXPENDITURE							
GENERAL EXPENDITURE, ALL FUNCTIONS	183.05	418.69	219.17	223.82	218.15	407.00	276.99
TOTAL, EXCLUDING CAPITAL OUTLAY	169.05	335.84	129.24	190.69	182.26	236.16	193.76
GENERAL EXPENDITURE, SELECTED ITEMS:							
EDUCATION	-	1.59	-	-	-	-	-
HIGHWAYS	16.55	37.88	19.43	29.98	21.75	71.07	43.52
EXCLUDING CAPITAL OUTLAY	16.55	23.99	18.18	17.30	12.56	31.62	24.92
PUBLIC WELFARE	-	55.45	-	-	-	15.14	-
HEALTH AND HOSPITALS	2.62	79.29	-	-	0.66	0.72	4.07
POLICE PROTECTION	31.05	52.58	23.48	34.47	23.92	26.62	37.21
FIRE PROTECTION	24.97	25.82	21.41	31.50	23.94	21.91	22.79
SEWERAGE	19.86	39.67	59.39	33.37	61.69	127.25	19.23
EXCLUDING CAPITAL OUTLAY	19.86	12.38	16.65	26.42	55.03	32.30	13.02
SANITATION OTHER THAN SEWERAGE	10.32	5.22	27.22	3.33	6.86	16.84	12.12
PARKS AND RECREATION	8.74	19.76	5.52	23.22	17.44	34.84	13.55
HOUSING AND URBAN RENEWAL	17.25	9.08	-	11.81	5.33	6.79	29.76
TOTAL DEBT	261.82	396.60	184.16	258.18	385.72	503.03	724.92
LONG-TERM, FULL FAITH AND CREDIT	261.82	390.34	155.50	54.01	221.10	348.54	261.47

Item	Iowa--Continued					Kansas	
	Davenport	Des Moines	Dubuque	Sioux City	Waterloo	Kansas City	Overland Park
REVENUE							
GENERAL REVENUE	352.84	342.44	332.14	379.45	321.53	356.98	133.95
TAXES	99.00	134.05	89.03	120.74	114.15	131.36	63.13
PROPERTY	92.34	121.80	85.10	109.08	109.59	122.79	45.24
OTHER	6.65	12.25	3.93	11.67	4.56	8.57	17.89
INTERGOVERNMENTAL REVENUE	199.95	117.64	164.23	168.33	136.03	157.45	36.53
MISCELLANEOUS GENERAL REVENUE	53.89	90.75	78.88	90.38	71.36	68.17	34.30
EXPENDITURE							
GENERAL EXPENDITURE, ALL FUNCTIONS	335.99	364.97	268.58	408.70	276.71	334.67	119.26
TOTAL, EXCLUDING CAPITAL OUTLAY	154.70	281.42	175.21	215.68	193.30	199.72	79.32
GENERAL EXPENDITURE, SELECTED ITEMS:							
EDUCATION	-	-	-	-	-	-	-
HIGHWAYS	47.20	85.59	21.33	75.18	31.67	34.61	42.07
EXCLUDING CAPITAL OUTLAY	28.68	34.40	14.14	22.08	17.79	15.52	16.89
PUBLIC WELFARE	-	-	-	-	1.29	-	-
HEALTH AND HOSPITALS	1.49	6.55	3.58	6.36	2.54	12.25	0.88
POLICE PROTECTION	22.17	51.99	24.29	32.86	31.54	41.85	29.07
FIRE PROTECTION	21.24	33.03	26.20	23.47	25.97	29.96	-
SEWERAGE	141.90	25.06	82.73	77.74	12.41	18.03	-
EXCLUDING CAPITAL OUTLAY	9.07	14.78	16.24	9.99	10.04	13.77	-
SANITATION OTHER THAN SEWERAGE	10.64	15.45	13.51	8.53	7.71	2.87	-
PARKS AND RECREATION	12.61	26.05	26.85	26.59	24.47	11.65	15.84
HOUSING AND URBAN RENEWAL	6.74	22.31	7.69	39.42	57.95	19.32	-
TOTAL DEBT	265.61	563.91	364.25	506.59	381.08	622.14	261.03
LONG-TERM, FULL FAITH AND CREDIT	244.99	231.12	139.75	350.60	344.78	141.69	144.01

Item	Kansas--Continued		Kentucky			Louisiana	
	Topeka	Wichita	Lexington	Louisville	Ownesboro	Baton Rouge	Lafayette
REVENUE							
GENERAL REVENUE	311.44	319.81	291.63	506.59	516.01	390.31	245.58
TAXES	121.51	116.94	191.50	165.65	90.34	189.31	108.86
PROPERTY	83.66	96.08	63.01	52.25	41.35	57.14	24.57
OTHER	37.85	20.86	128.49	113.40	48.99	132.17	84.29
INTERGOVERNMENTAL REVENUE	97.41	111.87	60.54	231.13	108.55	124.55	51.52
MISCELLANEOUS GENERAL REVENUE	92.52	91.00	39.59	109.81	317.12	76.45	85.20
EXPENDITURE							
GENERAL EXPENDITURE, ALL FUNCTIONS	501.20	401.43	264.14	481.18	518.19	380.68	324.02
TOTAL, EXCLUDING CAPITAL OUTLAY	233.65	261.46	245.68	365.01	426.87	284.79	215.15
GENERAL EXPENDITURE, SELECTED ITEMS:							
EDUCATION	0.01	-	-	0.09	-	0.56	-
HIGHWAYS	35.59	57.82	7.68	12.05	27.80	37.92	83.71
EXCLUDING CAPITAL OUTLAY	22.87	19.35	7.68	5.21	22.47	21.67	15.06
PUBLIC WELFARE	-	-	9.86	-	3.23	0.04	1.96
HEALTH AND HOSPITALS	227.86	14.31	16.84	18.03	296.31	15.44	-
POLICE PROTECTION	37.21	27.60	40.37	59.93	36.29	45.60	23.52
FIRE PROTECTION	36.89	22.55	37.24	30.86	28.88	23.37	18.30
SEWERAGE	23.65	23.73	16.18	61.68	17.50	20.66	22.21
EXCLUDING CAPITAL OUTLAY	10.75	7.88	15.97	29.61	13.82	5.53	18.28
SANITATION OTHER THAN SEWERAGE	14.74	8.44	28.46	24.17	30.48	15.93	21.30
PARKS AND RECREATION	17.55	17.11	20.82	28.24	15.24	45.63	34.77
HOUSING AND URBAN RENEWAL	0.21	5.98	12.31	80.51	7.15	-	5.95
TOTAL DEBT	628.47	1 177.30	451.57	1 034.44	2 924.96	899.28	1 530.68
LONG-TERM, FULL FAITH AND CREDIT	216.93	305.75	91.73	133.86	2 673.03	291.28	182.16

Item	Louisiana--Continued				Maine	Maryland	Massachusetts
	Lake Charles	Monroe	New Orleans	Shreveport	Portland	Baltimore	Boston
REVENUE							
GENERAL REVENUE	271.08	266.03	449.05	294.95	737.89	1 270.64	1 265.62
TAXES	118.52	138.44	170.65	132.54	358.76	339.52	686.87
PROPERTY	48.94	56.33	55.75	63.81	353.68	234.27	680.59
OTHER	69.58	82.11	114.90	68.73	5.08	105.25	6.28
INTERGOVERNMENTAL REVENUE	126.87	63.98	179.08	107.66	303.92	825.85	447.15
MISCELLANEOUS GENERAL REVENUE	25.69	63.61	99.31	54.75	75.21	105.27	131.58
EXPENDITURE							
GENERAL EXPENDITURE, ALL FUNCTIONS	292.76	271.19	413.76	243.74	847.09	1 293.94	1 224.18
TOTAL, EXCLUDING CAPITAL OUTLAY	157.53	228.27	348.46	186.83	757.56	990.23	1 108.28
GENERAL EXPENDITURE, SELECTED ITEMS:							
EDUCATION	-	-	2.15	-	351.81	355.98	420.29
HIGHWAYS	29.73	24.93	28.99	35.80	38.94	154.13	28.20
EXCLUDING CAPITAL OUTLAY	17.55	7.38	12.28	18.87	27.37	19.72	16.56
PUBLIC WELFARE	-	0.87	5.56	-	10.93	187.63	6.43
HEALTH AND HOSPITALS	-	5.46	19.24	0.23	41.47	77.95	123.08
POLICE PROTECTION	21.48	30.70	57.36	43.94	44.34	86.60	104.55
FIRE PROTECTION	22.24	29.19	28.48	31.73	46.51	46.62	63.04
SEWERAGE	100.45	12.98	27.97	25.18	10.54	47.63	12.09
EXCLUDING CAPITAL OUTLAY	11.33	4.18	18.14	11.18	2.91	14.17	8.04
SANITATION OTHER THAN SEWERAGE	12.93	24.09	15.76	22.97	9.69	27.21	22.69
PARKS AND RECREATION	23.68	34.20	30.09	17.93	36.30	36.61	27.42
HOUSING AND URBAN RENEWAL	32.15	20.90	1.14	3.38	68.43	51.43	49.54
TOTAL DEBT	345.25	889.54	462.97	335.11	674.11	585.27	872.12
LONG-TERM, FULL FAITH AND CREDIT	245.96	405.39	340.74	215.79	674.11	581.10	760.62

See footnotes at end of table.

195

Table 2. Per Capita Amounts of Financial Items for Individual City and Selected Urban Town and Township Governments Having 50,000 Population or More: 1977—Continued

Item	Massachusetts--Continued						
	Brockton	Brookline Town	Cambridge	Chicopee	Fall River	Framingham Town	Lawrence
REVENUE							
GENERAL REVENUE.	825.49	927.50	955.30	615.60	660.63	744.90	631.21
TAXES.	469.92	751.87	583.89	358.26	338.24	508.80	318.70
PROPERTY	468.15	749.95	579.13	356.27	336.43	507.11	316.77
OTHER.	1.77	1.92	4.75	1.99	1.80	1.69	1.93
INTERGOVERNMENTAL REVENUE.	323.16	137.02	188.39	226.79	305.63	197.73	291.33
MISCELLANEOUS GENERAL REVENUE.	32.41	38.60	183.02	30.55	16.77	38.37	21.18
EXPENDITURE							
GENERAL EXPENDITURE, ALL FUNCTIONS	830.44	819.21	1 034.73	567.27	730.92	752.72	635.03
TOTAL, EXCLUDING CAPITAL OUTLAY.	798.16	806.39	944.83	550.52	686.05	743.99	614.51
GENERAL EXPENDITURE, SELECTED ITEMS:							
EDUCATION.	388.39	357.24	301.75	298.44	323.00	464.31	296.93
HIGHWAYS	35.60	53.64	28.65	12.27	13.99	43.77	27.90
EXCLUDING CAPITAL OUTLAY	29.49	48.68	28.65	10.13	13.99	37.93	22.17
PUBLIC WELFARE	7.39	4.68	6.43	22.42	8.10	5.28	5.49
HEALTH AND HOSPITALS	2.85	13.69	165.59	3.36	4.69	4.81	9.91
POLICE PROTECTION.	51.26	64.42	59.91	37.18	41.31	35.20	40.53
FIRE PROTECTION.	48.38	79.43	74.19	43.81	45.15	46.83	55.97
SEWERAGE	15.77	19.98	12.47	7.65	7.68	14.69	15.14
EXCLUDING CAPITAL OUTLAY	13.42	19.98	12.47	2.61	4.01	14.69	13.99
SANITATION OTHER THAN SEWERAGE . . .	19.68	7.24	20.46	9.52	18.87	16.35	19.60
PARKS AND RECREATION	13.83	48.77	22.87	13.54	9.95	12.63	9.59
HOUSING AND URBAN RENEWAL.	10.00	-	88.31	4.29	1.68	6.45	10.68
TOTAL DEBT	525.04	313.03	678.43	637.03	450.01	351.92	165.62
LONG-TERM, FULL FAITH AND CREDIT	518.47	305.25	407.98	404.36	409.64	351.92	143.36

Item	Massachusetts--Continued						
	Lowell	Lynn	Malden	Medford	New Bedford	Newton	Pittsfield
REVENUE							
GENERAL REVENUE.	727.23	757.57	732.03	723.16	819.12	907.55	706.28
TAXES.	329.51	519.32	453.21	432.14	371.84	695.55	451.44
PROPERTY	327.10	516.46	451.45	431.04	370.15	693.83	448.38
OTHER.	2.42	2.86	1.76	1.10	1.69	1.72	3.06
INTERGOVERNMENTAL REVENUE.	383.37	216.14	251.69	272.64	423.68	182.42	222.94
MISCELLANEOUS GENERAL REVENUE.	14.34	22.11	27.13	18.38	23.61	29.58	31.90
EXPENDITURE							
GENERAL EXPENDITURE, ALL FUNCTIONS	775.25	835.13	818.37	802.78	873.28	915.04	823.93
TOTAL, EXCLUDING CAPITAL OUTLAY.	575.24	832.18	709.96	793.02	717.49	897.96	669.87
GENERAL EXPENDITURE, SELECTED ITEMS:							
EDUCATION.	328.57	336.43	287.50	337.90	421.57	419.32	442.55
HIGHWAYS	15.94	25.20	30.37	28.80	24.56	71.50	19.91
EXCLUDING CAPITAL OUTLAY	15.94	23.31	24.38	24.62	23.27	68.94	16.36
PUBLIC WELFARE	11.31	21.28	16.85	6.98	3.50	1.51	2.70
HEALTH AND HOSPITALS	6.96	18.05	6.15	5.00	7.37	7.36	7.76
POLICE PROTECTION.	38.65	60.60	40.82	48.40	43.20	58.85	34.83
FIRE PROTECTION.	42.99	70.28	55.17	51.16	42.87	54.00	45.85
SEWERAGE	201.23	8.55	1.17	28.04	18.69	13.90	63.07
EXCLUDING CAPITAL OUTLAY	2.86	8.55	0.91	28.04	18.32	13.60	8.09
SANITATION OTHER THAN SEWERAGE . . .	7.64	11.62	13.45	12.37	13.42	30.83	10.73
PARKS AND RECREATION	9.99	18.61	6.06	16.44	13.73	28.08	16.98
HOUSING AND URBAN RENEWAL.	-	1.01	53.78	-	19.85	8.02	23.17
TOTAL DEBT	295.32	342.19	502.80	150.16	1 085.84	218.48	530.32
LONG-TERM, FULL FAITH AND CREDIT	247.23	276.70	471.15	150.16	609.14	218.48	434.66

See footnotes at end of table.

Item	Massachusetts--Continued						Michigan
	Quincy	Somerville	Springfield	Waltham	Weymouth Town	Worcester	Ann Arbor
REVENUE							
GENERAL REVENUE.	1 012.68	534.69	666.56	726.99	690.10	857.17	385.67
TAXES.	545.93	324.83	327.98	557.64	473.85	429.51	129.55
PROPERTY	543.78	322.38	325.87	555.60	472.62	426.48	126.25
OTHER.	2.14	2.45	2.11	2.04	1.23	3.03	3.30
INTERGOVERNMENTAL REVENUE.	214.18	196.14	274.88	135.78	180.23	286.05	164.43
MISCELLANEOUS GENERAL REVENUE.	252.57	13.71	63.70	33.56	36.01	141.61	91.69
EXPENDITURE							
GENERAL EXPENDITURE, ALL FUNCTIONS	948.70	555.61	757.84	800.22	638.48	902.99	286.67
TOTAL, EXCLUDING CAPITAL OUTLAY.	916.01	547.86	616.13	743.83	608.98	853.74	264.94
GENERAL EXPENDITURE, SELECTED ITEMS:							
EDUCATION.	371.62	274.77	345.24	423.05	387.68	354.91	-
HIGHWAYS	47.85	23.78	54.76	27.00	25.59	41.55	27.82
EXCLUDING CAPITAL OUTLAY	36.48	19.69	21.66	26.33	18.15	38.50	23.13
PUBLIC WELFARE	3.72	3.63	4.41	4.50	4.08	13.16	-
HEALTH AND HOSPITALS	199.26	4.67	39.00	3.24	1.94	112.83	2.21
POLICE PROTECTION.	59.74	32.18	34.39	51.45	43.54	40.84	39.77
FIRE PROTECTION.	56.54	52.60	30.24	53.72	46.73	41.67	39.80
SEWERAGE	13.48	10.53	36.71	12.07	23.07	6.41	31.27
EXCLUDING CAPITAL OUTLAY	10.44	10.53	9.49	11.95	9.96	6.41	21.06
SANITATION OTHER THAN SEWERAGE	10.86	16.54	9.87	12.84	8.68	10.80	17.08
PARKS AND RECREATION	16.69	11.58	17.33	18.95	13.87	9.54	25.10
HOUSING AND URBAN RENEWAL.	16.51	7.09	4.57	0.53	-	12.87	8.19
TOTAL DEBT	258.60	380.02	367.80	361.77	416.88	364.91	351.54
LONG-TERM, FULL FAITH AND CREDIT	258.60	379.40	300.11	359.10	409.84	328.99	164.13

Item	Michigan--Continued						
	Dearborn	Dearborn Heights	Detroit	Farmington Hills	Flint	Grand Rapids	Kalamazoo
REVENUE							
GENERAL REVENUE.	430.17	162.38	671.88	187.85	812.11	432.99	312.89
TAXES.	217.05	71.52	246.75	67.83	153.57	99.07	99.65
PROPERTY	213.47	69.20	125.49	60.93	55.87	44.45	98.44
OTHER.	3.58	2.32	121.26	6.89	97.71	54.62	1.21
INTERGOVERNMENTAL REVENUE.	122.04	69.47	330.33	62.50	294.53	252.93	117.64
MISCELLANEOUS GENERAL REVENUE.	91.08	21.39	94.80	57.52	364.00	80.99	95.61
EXPENDITURE							
GENERAL EXPENDITURE, ALL FUNCTIONS	433.65	181.91	517.25	200.10	733.48	374.20	283.72
TOTAL, EXCLUDING CAPITAL OUTLAY.	361.14	169.35	427.46	150.64	578.88	272.18	262.13
GENERAL EXPENDITURE, SELECTED ITEMS:							
EDUCATION.	-	-	12.47	-	-	-	-
HIGHWAYS	42.64	43.45	31.29	54.54	27.02	31.34	40.32
EXCLUDING CAPITAL OUTLAY	30.01	41.56	11.72	24.11	19.96	24.92	31.83
PUBLIC WELFARE	-	1.82	0.49	-	-	-	1.40
HEALTH AND HOSPITALS	2.97	2.59	65.05	-	302.79	2.97	-
POLICE PROTECTION.	48.99	32.35	89.97	37.32	74.37	41.09	47.60
FIRE PROTECTION.	24.50	17.62	31.80	8.17	45.31	30.73	35.64
SEWERAGE	25.63	11.91	50.34	-	70.93	102.01	36.21
EXCLUDING CAPITAL OUTLAY	17.18	11.91	18.05	-	18.58	17.55	34.08
SANITATION OTHER THAN SEWERAGE	16.61	12.09	25.73	0.30	10.62	5.70	2.82
PARKS AND RECREATION	51.34	7.26	34.19	1.31	24.59	26.79	15.12
HOUSING AND URBAN RENEWAL.	44.99	4.71	31.81	-	32.92	22.22	2.46
TOTAL DEBT	243.33	32.18	512.13	164.66	440.74	198.15	231.45
LONG-TERM, FULL FAITH AND CREDIT	80.58	32.18	219.10	63.37	216.64	46.62	86.12

See footnotes at end of table.

197

Table 2. Per Capita Amounts of Financial Items for Individual City and Selected Urban Town and Township Governments Having 50,000 Population or More: 1977—Continued

Item	Michigan--Continued						
	Lansing	Livonia	Pontiac	Roseville	Royal Oak	Saginaw	St. Clair Shores
REVENUE							
GENERAL REVENUE.	484.10	257.97	1 158.75	215.29	220.42	418.44	188.13
TAXES.	153.91	102.45	247.95	93.31	106.92	142.90	87.01
PROPERTY	74.98	99.22	140.66	90.49	104.92	70.88	85.78
OTHER.	78.92	3.23	107.29	2.82	2.00	72.02	1.23
INTERGOVERNMENTAL REVENUE.	174.54	87.19	404.99	85.46	74.44	186.21	77.66
MISCELLANEOUS GENERAL REVENUE.	155.65	68.33	505.81	36.51	39.06	89.33	23.46
EXPENDITURE							
GENERAL EXPENDITURE, ALL FUNCTIONS	443.92	235.62	1 157.68	203.75	190.07	417.70	171.98
TOTAL, EXCLUDING CAPITAL OUTLAY.	362.59	212.43	1 026.56	198.90	188.11	352.24	164.61
GENERAL EXPENDITURE, SELECTED ITEMS:							
EDUCATION.	-	-	-	-	-	-	-
HIGHWAYS	36.27	32.68	37.96	22.14	20.90	41.16	19.51
EXCLUDING CAPITAL OUTLAY	11.91	28.46	28.74	19.33	20.90	26.15	18.22
PUBLIC WELFARE	-	-	-	-	0.15	-	-
HEALTH AND HOSPITALS	0.49	0.15	363.74	-	-	2.81	-
POLICE PROTECTION.	53.04	40.68	100.25	47.20	32.39	61.07	31.98
FIRE PROTECTION.	41.49	28.59	42.70	23.68	22.09	48.34	18.84
SEWERAGE	46.30	14.43	77.95	9.03	15.22	36.26	14.20
EXCLUDING CAPITAL OUTLAY	20.63	8.64	27.82	9.03	14.33	21.24	14.20
SANITATION OTHER THAN SEWERAGE	6.27	14.70	17.24	10.89	16.44	12.08	9.62
PARKS AND RECREATION	37.32	14.22	71.54	7.19	7.72	38.42	16.83
HOUSING AND URBAN RENEWAL.	44.60	0.60	18.94	-	-	48.87	-
TOTAL DEBT	474.56	526.83	986.68	37.41	57.85	538.05	102.11
LONG-TERM, FULL FAITH AND CREDIT	199.68	491.64	300.04	9.63	27.63	280.60	56.09

Item	Michigan--Continued						Minnesota
	Southfield	Sterling Heights	Taylor	Warren	Westland	Wyoming	Bloomington
REVENUE							
GENERAL REVENUE.	350.46	528.63	255.59	298.34	170.81	277.34	244.45
TAXES.	190.41	115.37	133.84	114.64	70.53	66.35	88.21
PROPERTY	185.42	109.30	131.23	112.20	68.95	64.30	65.57
OTHER.	4.99	6.06	2.61	2.44	1.58	2.05	22.64
INTERGOVERNMENTAL REVENUE.	78.36	341.12	86.26	131.02	66.91	111.80	63.84
MISCELLANEOUS GENERAL REVENUE.	81.68	72.15	35.48	52.68	33.37	99.19	92.40
EXPENDITURE							
GENERAL EXPENDITURE, ALL FUNCTIONS	313.81	292.37	252.88	268.59	174.83	222.90	200.34
TOTAL, EXCLUDING CAPITAL OUTLAY.	292.98	200.40	236.45	218.60	166.60	188.39	177.60
GENERAL EXPENDITURE, SELECTED ITEMS:							
EDUCATION.	-	-	-	-	-	-	-
HIGHWAYS	30.29	27.49	20.84	22.31	39.30	20.60	16.56
EXCLUDING CAPITAL OUTLAY	25.51	13.64	13.83	15.78	36.11	19.49	16.01
PUBLIC WELFARE	-	-	-	-	-	-	-
HEALTH AND HOSPITALS	0.01	-	2.54	-	1.64	0.09	5.79
POLICE PROTECTION.	67.22	79.49	43.68	71.77	32.94	37.78	28.75
FIRE PROTECTION.	36.08	23.94	20.31	29.77	19.30	11.05	11.59
SEWERAGE	11.90	25.88	15.36	19.25	9.28	35.67	28.99
EXCLUDING CAPITAL OUTLAY	11.87	25.62	15.36	14.98	9.28	25.83	16.20
SANITATION OTHER THAN SEWERAGE	7.99	10.17	-	8.61	11.45	0.85	1.68
PARKS AND RECREATION	27.17	14.59	16.98	10.68	13.31	15.61	33.24
HOUSING AND URBAN RENEWAL.	-	-	1.34	0.96	-	-	6.79
TOTAL DEBT	238.73	38.42	255.33	194.54	286.79	688.56	592.83
LONG-TERM, FULL FAITH AND CREDIT	182.82	25.54	86.00	108.07	28.10	597.91	525.60

See footnotes at end of table.

Table 2. Per Capita Amounts of Financial Items for Individual City and Selected Urban Town and Township Governments Having 50,000 Population or More: 1977—Continued

Item	Minnesota--Continued				Mississippi	Missouri	
	Duluth	Minneapolis	Rochester	St. Paul	Jackson	Columbia	Florissant
REVENUE							
GENERAL REVENUE.	496.72	471.15	270.21	467.84	393.00	256.98	67.69
TAXES.	107.82	179.49	93.83	134.43	112.93	104.40	34.9d
PROPERTY	66.18	154.28	78.47	95.99	102.61	21.68	16.48
OTHER.	41.64	25.21	15.35	38.44	10.33	82.72	18.51
INTERGOVERNMENTAL REVENUE.	229.80	212.89	95.80	229.43	181.42	82.18	24.72
MISCELLANEOUS GENERAL REVENUE.	159.09	78.78	80.59	103.98	98.65	70.40	7.99
EXPENDITURE							
GENERAL EXPENDITURE, ALL FUNCTIONS	482.55	494.47	229.72	488.19	390.90	249.10	73.65
TOTAL, EXCLUDING CAPITAL OUTLAY.	369.56	383.49	190.27	389.02	284.06	153.25	56.72
GENERAL EXPENDITURE, SELECTED ITEMS:							
EDUCATION.	-	0.02	-	0.19	-	-	-
HIGHWAYS	83.56	71.15	55.01	51.77	53.79	35.48	15.20
EXCLUDING CAPITAL OUTLAY	27.84	31.50	33.13	25.11	22.71	12.97	11.25
PUBLIC WELFARE	0.21	-	-	0.39	5.41	-	0.10
HEALTH AND HOSPITALS	0.46	16.11	-	12.19	1.98	6.45	1.11
POLICE PROTECTION.	38.32	50.73	31.67	45.82	40.54	32.19	25.46
FIRE PROTECTION.	38.11	32.47	28.23	37.24	31.69	32.41	-
SEWERAGE	20.29	38.55	14.52	44.38	34.21	54.53	2.46
EXCLUDING CAPITAL OUTLAY	15.55	29.87	9.16	33.18	9.19	10.94	-
SANITATION OTHER THAN SEWERAGE	2.58	21.42	3.95	9.30	22.38	15.88	0.03
PARKS AND RECREATION	50.42	58.95	35.14	39.43	25.57	20.75	18.39
HOUSING AND URBAN RENEWAL.	0.97	27.06	-	73.45	1.71	-	0.71
TOTAL DEBT	787.72	542.70	122.48	1 131.46	657.99	680.50	47.97
LONG-TERM, FULL FAITH AND CREDIT	337.23	433.45	107.19	607.29	392.18	26.73	42.72

Item	Missouri--Continued					Montana	
	Independence	Kansas City	St. Joseph	St. Louis	Springfield	Billings	Great Falls
REVENUE							
GENERAL REVENUE.	252.36	538.51	307.73	561.03	368.42	308.29	293.24
TAXES.	97.23	272.48	91.80	309.62	82.10	97.97	79.75
PROPERTY	28.60	52.06	45.04	66.04	48.11	86.68	71.96
OTHER.	68.63	220.42	46.76	243.59	33.99	11.29	7.79
INTERGOVERNMENTAL REVENUE.	43.00	153.75	164.74	162.30	222.79	78.42	97.05
MISCELLANEOUS GENERAL REVENUE.	112.13	112.28	51.19	89.10	63.53	131.89	116.45
EXPENDITURE							
GENERAL EXPENDITURE, ALL FUNCTIONS	253.02	497.13	304.16	511.87	361.48	252.84	308.93
TOTAL, EXCLUDING CAPITAL OUTLAY.	165.48	405.10	139.78	448.73	145.43	169.96	183.00
GENERAL EXPENDITURE, SELECTED ITEMS:							
EDUCATION.	-	27.29	-	1.01	-	0.03	-
HIGHWAYS	18.97	46.15	17.06	19.35	65.39	54.00	35.39
EXCLUDING CAPITAL OUTLAY	18.86	25.74	16.93	12.57	13.07	18.83	12.58
PUBLIC WELFARE	-	1.44	0.90	6.74	1.13	1.32	-
HEALTH AND HOSPITALS	5.21	33.01	6.58	105.61	14.25	2.00	3.22
POLICE PROTECTION.	26.85	70.88	22.77	82.17	23.88	27.08	29.10
FIRE PROTECTION.	23.37	35.20	24.27	25.90	20.99	26.02	22.23
SEWERAGE	87.94	37.30	126.88	0.71	133.14	11.61	101.33
EXCLUDING CAPITAL OUTLAY	14.68	10.02	11.65	0.31	12.22	11.61	18.04
SANITATION OTHER THAN SEWERAGE	0.78	12.97	2.43	12.44	4.36	16.00	24.45
PARKS AND RECREATION	10.24	45.09	11.42	45.87	12.24	7.86	25.02
HOUSING AND URBAN RENEWAL.	7.20	13.96	16.52	15.96	27.59	3.84	3.34
TOTAL DEBT	486.76	673.98	180.36	310.50	1 070.24	592.58	392.88
LONG-TERM, FULL FAITH AND CREDIT	205.33	195.70	95.91	192.25	162.58	42.41	36.52

. See footnotes at end of table.

199

Table 2. Per Capita Amounts of Financial Items for Individual City and Selected Urban Town and Township Governments Having 50,000 Population or More: 1977—Continued

Item	Nebraska		Nevada		New Hampshire		New Jersey
	Lincoln	Omaha	Las Vegas	Reno	Manchester	Nashua	Bayonne
REVENUE							
GENERAL REVENUE.	360.40	316.92	284.90	439.42	725.10	564.65	295.28
TAXES.	137.05	136.12	112.52	148.98	413.51	408.30	211.43
PROPERTY	83.34	79.01	59.19	70.67	405.01	402.07	187.16
OTHER.	53.71	57.11	53.32	78.31	8.50	6.23	24.27
INTERGOVERNMENTAL REVENUE.	87.63	137.24	132.04	153.32	234.62	122.88	70.09
MISCELLANEOUS GENERAL REVENUE.	135.72	43.56	40.34	137.11	76.97	33.47	13.75
EXPENDITURE							
GENERAL EXPENDITURE, ALL FUNCTIONS	370.15	299.61	241.61	396.97	752.53	569.69	250.63
TOTAL, EXCLUDING CAPITAL OUTLAY.	252.75	203.20	237.16	321.18	580.79	520.44	245.79
GENERAL EXPENDITURE, SELECTED ITEMS:							
EDUCATION.	3.24	0.10	-	-	282.58	299.40	-
HIGHWAYS	75.65	38.77	17.91	43.64	148.30	33.08	9.16
EXCLUDING CAPITAL OUTLAY	17.41	17.72	16.94	29.94	51.26	29.43	8.82
PUBLIC WELFARE	-	0.25	-	0.13	14.77	4.13	2.46
HEALTH AND HOSPITALS	74.03	4.50	0.68	-	4.72	3.21	8.35
POLICE PROTECTION.	33.15	32.22	83.94	98.43	50.51	37.83	48.70
FIRE PROTECTION.	19.99	24.75	44.89	52.84	36.24	35.75	42.73
SEWERAGE	39.48	64.38	9.33	45.92	2.01	22.10	0.31
EXCLUDING CAPITAL OUTLAY	11.75	12.99	7.68	20.78	2.01	10.02	0.31
SANITATION OTHER THAN SEWERAGE	3.86	16.80	4.40	-	10.03	10.18	14.49
PARKS AND RECREATION	35.09	18.00	21.89	35.21	11.51	9.46	13.10
HOUSING AND URBAN RENEWAL.	7.17	8.21	1.95	-	4.65	-	-
TOTAL DEBT	942.26	315.11	128.18	289.86	566.59	596.13	163.67
LONG-TERM, FULL FAITH AND CREDIT	98.43	255.48	121.50	277.62	566.59	596.13	66.38

Item	New Jersey—Continued						
	Bloomfield	Camden	Cherry Hill Township	Clifton	Dover Township	East Orange	Edison Township
REVENUE							
GENERAL REVENUE.	249.80	373.70	276.67	463.48	182.88	713.16	657.91
TAXES.	200.20	166.06	209.55	354.91	131.51	481.98	546.91
PROPERTY	176.34	125.73	171.50	315.69	97.40	455.80	435.71
OTHER.	23.87	40.33	38.06	39.22	34.11	26.18	111.20
INTERGOVERNMENTAL REVENUE.	34.01	158.42	28.39	90.99	29.47	191.11	95.42
MISCELLANEOUS GENERAL REVENUE.	15.59	49.22	38.72	17.57	21.90	40.07	15.57
EXPENDITURE							
GENERAL EXPENDITURE, ALL FUNCTIONS	195.16	347.80	258.26	377.57	222.38	680.75	621.68
TOTAL, EXCLUDING CAPITAL OUTLAY.	193.88	347.80	227.93	371.68	161.26	666.94	607.33
GENERAL EXPENDITURE, SELECTED ITEMS:							
EDUCATION.	-	-	-	201.38	-	329.84	419.00
HIGHWAYS	7.52	11.87	13.97	7.88	24.38	15.08	14.70
EXCLUDING CAPITAL OUTLAY	7.46	11.87	13.88	7.70	22.28	14.17	12.54
PUBLIC WELFARE	2.20	20.29	0.28	0.24	0.74	26.98	1.30
HEALTH AND HOSPITALS	4.95	7.59	2.60	3.83	2.62	9.32	4.00
POLICE PROTECTION.	44.50	73.31	29.39	33.15	51.06	53.26	45.64
FIRE PROTECTION.	36.75	62.41	0.06	36.28	1.05	43.57	24.78
SEWERAGE	1.17	15.78	21.59	11.78	0.24	8.64	16.54
EXCLUDING CAPITAL OUTLAY	1.17	15.78	20.44	10.58	-	5.30	10.67
SANITATION OTHER THAN SEWERAGE	9.78	22.10	7.89	14.66	12.99	15.89	2.43
PARKS AND RECREATION	6.92	4.11	25.66	4.23	22.58	11.48	4.35
HOUSING AND URBAN RENEWAL.	0.96	-	-	-	0.03	0.34	-
TOTAL DEBT	152.39	206.18	283.44	172.24	138.49	388.64	503.46
LONG-TERM, FULL FAITH AND CREDIT	122.43	206.18	85.41	111.83	100.55	384.55	406.55

See footnotes at end of table.

Table 2. Per Capita Amounts of Financial Items for Individual City and Selected Urban Town and Township Governments Having 50,000 Population or More: 1977—Continued

Item	New Jersey--Continued						
	Elizabeth	Hamilton Township (Mercer County)	Irvington	Jersey City	Middletown Township	Newark	Parsippany-Troy Hills Township
REVENUE							
GENERAL REVENUE	535.49	192.54	355.02	635.09	162.88	1 086.47	168.83
TAXES	387.51	132.31	171.18	352.82	138.02	395.92	122.11
PROPERTY	340.92	42.35	151.61	273.57	107.44	293.80	101.13
OTHER	46.59	89.96	19.57	79.25	30.58	102.12	20.96
INTERGOVERNMENTAL REVENUE	127.35	27.42	45.95	263.19	15.19	655.25	19.12
MISCELLANEOUS GENERAL REVENUE	20.63	32.82	137.90	19.08	9.67	35.30	27.60
EXPENDITURE							
GENERAL EXPENDITURE, ALL FUNCTIONS	632.89	185.35	367.93	680.82	122.52	981.29	177.47
TOTAL, EXCLUDING CAPITAL OUTLAY	592.64	170.85	367.48	645.71	122.52	934.01	163.42
GENERAL EXPENDITURE, SELECTED ITEMS:							
EDUCATION	306.90	-	-	267.19	-	443.30	-
HIGHWAYS	18.77	32.22	10.65	12.57	22.19	11.84	28.26
EXCLUDING CAPITAL OUTLAY	18.56	29.06	10.65	8.61	22.19	8.89	21.36
PUBLIC WELFARE	10.56	1.17	7.05	7.70	0.39	83.87	1.12
HEALTH AND HOSPITALS	10.28	4.67	129.10	31.15	2.61	13.23	4.19
POLICE PROTECTION	61.77	35.07	44.56	89.98	32.17	96.47	40.12
FIRE PROTECTION	52.78	9.84	42.86	58.80	6.06	64.65	7.62
SEWERAGE	15.83	23.47	12.08	4.92	-	11.80	17.74
EXCLUDING CAPITAL OUTLAY	4.11	12.73	12.08	2.43	-	11.80	17.74
SANITATION OTHER THAN SEWERAGE	15.55	10.30	6.00	20.38	1.55	16.83	12.25
PARKS AND RECREATION	7.10	4.20	4.23	7.85	5.74	17.05	7.96
HOUSING AND URBAN RENEWAL	1.79	-	-	12.94	-	3.77	-
TOTAL DEBT	388.60	109.47	171.13	515.61	189.34	483.87	415.52
LONG-TERM, FULL FAITH AND CREDIT	369.42	109.47	128.00	476.38	189.34	460.92	181.15

Item	New Jersey--Continued						New Mexico
	Paterson	Trenton	Union City	Union township (Union County)	Vineland	Woodbridge Township	Albuquerque
REVENUE							
GENERAL REVENUE	538.91	397.25	285.40	242.11	494.12	222.92	378.85
TAXES	246.99	222.24	193.87	186.04	260.57	162.43	101.55
PROPERTY	217.36	191.69	175.87	146.73	239.83	67.78	63.92
OTHER	29.63	30.54	18.01	39.31	20.73	94.65	37.63
INTERGOVERNMENTAL REVENUE	277.47	154.01	84.85	39.64	195.74	50.86	197.19
MISCELLANEOUS GENERAL REVENUE	14.45	21.00	6.69	16.43	37.81	9.63	80.13
EXPENDITURE							
GENERAL EXPENDITURE, ALL FUNCTIONS	682.19	302.31	295.07	247.24	556.35	202.32	352.36
TOTAL, EXCLUDING CAPITAL OUTLAY	597.50	274.30	288.14	217.21	537.04	180.18	291.32
GENERAL EXPENDITURE, SELECTED ITEMS:							
EDUCATION	348.80	-	-	-	366.95	-	-
HIGHWAYS	15.11	10.31	10.96	18.00	15.42	24.40	30.09
EXCLUDING CAPITAL OUTLAY	9.41	7.64	8.11	13.05	15.42	17.99	12.91
PUBLIC WELFARE	9.77	8.38	4.41	2.45	2.09	0.68	-
HEALTH AND HOSPITALS	18.99	12.11	6.70	3.11	9.08	3.54	3.88
POLICE PROTECTION	66.40	67.85	40.51	57.58	32.70	33.24	52.23
FIRE PROTECTION	45.79	52.19	40.97	55.05	7.10	-	36.09
SEWERAGE	15.19	8.68	6.42	17.28	-	26.44	26.00
EXCLUDING CAPITAL OUTLAY	13.30	3.24	6.42	2.29	-	12.65	8.08
SANITATION OTHER THAN SEWERAGE	13.12	11.61	22.28	19.74	4.05	14.25	24.40
PARKS AND RECREATION	7.25	8.18	5.74	6.32	6.79	8.09	29.42
HOUSING AND URBAN RENEWAL	-	5.79	-	-	0.09	-	8.39
TOTAL DEBT	333.41	248.33	165.67	109.21	693.25	349.57	502.83
LONG-TERM, FULL FAITH AND CREDIT	231.02	105.16	140.46	34.12	535.25	290.35	293.24

See footnotes at end of table.

Table 2. Per Capita Amounts of Financial Items for Individual City and Selected Urban Town and Township Governments Having 50,000 Population or More: 1977—Continued

Item	New York						
	Albany	Binghampton	Buffalo	Mount Vernon	New Rochelle	New York City	Niagara Falls
REVENUE							
GENERAL REVENUE	394.83	765.59	996.65	352.76	384.43	1 915.36	782.71
TAXES	187.82	230.56	244.30	209.55	241.55	806.40	206.44
PROPERTY	180.92	171.25	234.37	153.52	221.28	437.14	145.01
OTHER	6.91	59.31	9.93	56.04	20.27	370.21	61.43
INTERGOVERNMENTAL REVENUE	168.06	229.98	673.93	114.04	86.23	907.51	517.95
MISCELLANEOUS GENERAL REVENUE	38.94	305.05	78.42	29.16	56.65	261.45	58.32
EXPENDITURE							
GENERAL EXPENDITURE, ALL FUNCTIONS	439.30	684.40	905.15	359.46	359.27	1 628.77	672.19
TOTAL, EXCLUDING CAPITAL OUTLAY	351.68	643.14	702.58	324.08	333.64	1 574.35	327.55
GENERAL EXPENDITURE, SELECTED ITEMS:							
EDUCATION	-	-	302.23	2.75	-	351.38	-
HIGHWAYS	31.47	34.01	29.49	28.09	22.17	21.26	11.64
EXCLUDING CAPITAL OUTLAY	22.85	20.92	22.49	27.63	21.39	17.71	9.84
PUBLIC WELFARE	-	14.06	0.14	0.77	0.97	471.81	-
HEALTH AND HOSPITALS	1.14	252.68	2.98	0.87	0.42	143.16	-
POLICE PROTECTION	60.98	41.41	60.20	51.49	52.59	95.03	47.09
FIRE PROTECTION	39.14	44.11	43.89	35.80	45.88	39.92	34.43
SEWERAGE	53.71	15.69	131.46	1.77	5.30	23.19	195.28
EXCLUDING CAPITAL OUTLAY	16.08	14.90	15.79	1.77	3.33	6.29	6.25
SANITATION OTHER THAN SEWERAGE	15.38	7.81	17.63	18.20	19.46	35.22	17.80
PARKS AND RECREATION	24.71	22.43	19.71	16.24	21.00	16.80	29.59
HOUSING AND URBAN RENEWAL	26.47	24.35	77.32	6.21	12.26	65.14	166.76
TOTAL DEBT	834.68	758.27	662.77	216.91	436.27	1 989.01	866.58
LONG-TERM, FULL FAITH AND CREDIT	270.15	253.01	352.96	91.10	314.03	1 556.51	369.89

Item	New York--Continued						North Carolina
	Rochester	Schenectady	Syracuse	Troy	Utica	Yonkers	Asheville
REVENUE							
GENERAL REVENUE	884.42	244.34	718.87	517.79	294.54	744.91	296.99
TAXES	322.08	119.59	186.02	110.03	103.88	478.54	115.82
PROPERTY	312.24	102.19	178.66	72.66	97.73	333.73	107.35
OTHER	9.84	17.40	7.36	37.37	6.15	144.81	8.47
INTERGOVERNMENTAL REVENUE	508.05	92.29	466.53	367.97	140.46	220.59	138.56
MISCELLANEOUS GENERAL REVENUE	54.28	32.46	66.32	39.79	50.20	45.78	42.61
EXPENDITURE							
GENERAL EXPENDITURE, ALL FUNCTIONS	827.68	275.02	640.16	409.49	281.05	691.64	253.85
TOTAL, EXCLUDING CAPITAL OUTLAY	813.47	274.63	571.86	239.39	235.29	656.21	228.44
GENERAL EXPENDITURE, SELECTED ITEMS:							
EDUCATION	386.02	-	318.93	-	-	318.97	-
HIGHWAYS	38.58	11.96	18.70	21.57	14.06	9.83	24.87
EXCLUDING CAPITAL OUTLAY	38.58	11.96	11.21	11.97	8.83	9.21	18.36
PUBLIC WELFARE	-	-	-	-	-	0.08	-
HEALTH AND HOSPITALS	-	4.60	-	2.02	0.17	-	1.18
POLICE PROTECTION	52.87	40.47	48.55	50.29	34.31	49.52	34.43
FIRE PROTECTION	46.69	41.58	42.37	63.50	47.44	43.54	32.44
SEWERAGE	1.86	13.07	4.95	5.44	16.10	1.89	5.50
EXCLUDING CAPITAL OUTLAY	1.86	13.00	3.83	4.99	16.10	1.40	5.44
SANITATION OTHER THAN SEWERAGE	29.54	14.60	13.18	7.91	15.06	18.52	25.27
PARKS AND RECREATION	20.25	11.31	17.16	11.11	11.80	10.49	23.90
HOUSING AND URBAN RENEWAL	9.77	44.08	45.16	155.43	53.44	26.14	-
TOTAL DEBT	1 099.30	231.88	537.68	386.89	531.82	783.78	347.20
LONG-TERM, FULL FAITH AND CREDIT	906.04	159.68	236.88	224.48	395.42	643.14	153.97

See footnotes at end of table.

Table 2. Per Capita Amounts of Financial Items for Individual City and Selected Urban Town and Township Governments Having 50,000 Population or More: 1977—Continued

Item	North Carolina--Continued						
	Charlotte	Durham	Fayetteville	Greensboro	High Point	Raleigh	Wilmington
REVENUE							
GENERAL REVENUE	370.12	338.20	211.83	330.03	383.83	345.17	283.27
TAXES	148.07	109.09	67.13	128.74	132.38	141.32	109.26
PROPERTY	143.03	105.44	63.75	123.62	128.31	134.42	104.83
OTHER	5.04	3.66	3.38	5.12	4.08	6.89	4.44
INTERGOVERNMENTAL REVENUE	163.88	136.56	90.19	133.05	163.10	146.70	115.44
MISCELLANEOUS GENERAL REVENUE	58.17	92.55	54.51	68.24	88.34	57.16	58.55
EXPENDITURE							
GENERAL EXPENDITURE, ALL FUNCTIONS	335.22	357.35	184.48	355.83	356.92	405.09	244.70
TOTAL, EXCLUDING CAPITAL OUTLAY	240.73	234.91	139.36	301.02	292.30	251.93	198.60
GENERAL EXPENDITURE, SELECTED ITEMS:							
EDUCATION	-	-	-	-	-	-	-
HIGHWAYS	61.83	42.35	21.28	44.67	57.49	42.14	40.75
EXCLUDING CAPITAL OUTLAY	32.85	23.10	12.44	33.09	29.02	19.50	23.21
PUBLIC WELFARE	-	-	-	-	-	2.14	-
HEALTH AND HOSPITALS	0.12	-	-	0.99	0.08	1.47	-
POLICE PROTECTION	39.15	44.19	34.89	50.00	43.53	41.53	34.82
FIRE PROTECTION	28.58	34.33	23.89	27.06	40.60	30.62	34.15
SEWERAGE	30.20	81.89	31.28	19.87	15.08	22.24	21.57
EXCLUDING CAPITAL OUTLAY	15.92	20.98	18.08	15.94	11.97	8.97	17.11
SANITATION OTHER THAN SEWERAGE	29.43	20.39	17.90	15.25	34.68	23.99	21.74
PARKS AND RECREATION	14.36	20.11	11.03	59.83	37.26	25.01	28.95
HOUSING AND URBAN RENEWAL	12.50	11.42	7.89	17.36	21.82	6.00	17.06
TOTAL DEBT	586.87	536.73	484.44	288.37	721.51	505.63	204.97
LONG-TERM, FULL FAITH AND CREDIT	551.03	401.63	482.62	274.47	685.73	505.63	177.39

Item	North Carolina-- Continued	North Dakota	Ohio				
	Winston-- Salem	Fargo	Akron	Canton	Cincinnati	Cleveland	Cleveland Heights
REVENUE							
GENERAL REVENUE	407.62	289.86	347.68	297.47	1 160.29	449.19	221.41
TAXES	122.10	72.10	139.83	131.77	239.69	150.64	113.04
PROPERTY	115.84	55.01	36.32	14.78	67.31	51.87	50.68
OTHER	6.25	17.09	103.52	116.99	172.38	88.77	62.36
INTERGOVERNMENTAL REVENUE	214.37	78.76	123.87	86.24	495.87	193.63	45.72
MISCELLANEOUS GENERAL REVENUE	71.15	139.00	83.97	79.46	424.73	104.92	62.65
EXPENDITURE							
GENERAL EXPENDITURE, ALL FUNCTIONS	360.70	382.21	411.21	346.80	1 101.23	500.18	231.75
TOTAL, EXCLUDING CAPITAL OUTLAY	305.62	215.65	281.58	236.80	920.89	390.89	187.50
GENERAL EXPENDITURE, SELECTED ITEMS:							
EDUCATION	-	-	-	-	359.67	1.01	-
HIGHWAYS	46.58	81.36	77.65	100.60	43.93	38.95	58.35
EXCLUDING CAPITAL OUTLAY	30.44	13.56	33.67	29.22	22.10	23.18	15.02
PUBLIC WELFARE	-	0.62	-	-	-	2.81	-
HEALTH AND HOSPITALS	1.01	15.36	13.49	16.26	173.24	13.77	1.58
POLICE PROTECTION	62.11	42.46	41.34	47.21	77.45	94.41	34.53
FIRE PROTECTION	24.82	29.85	27.01	37.32	50.44	42.00	22.78
SEWERAGE	29.66	62.77	37.27	29.80	97.05	37.07	26.36
EXCLUDING CAPITAL OUTLAY	18.52	5.24	21.95	18.43	39.53	34.89	26.34
SANITATION OTHER THAN SEWERAGE	27.28	20.30	33.64	1.46	22.02	22.15	16.27
PARKS AND RECREATION	22.56	0.57	15.09	15.25	43.50	20.16	9.87
HOUSING AND URBAN RENEWAL	32.63	11.72	28.19	41.14	27.87	21.73	1.29
TOTAL DEBT	475.75	725.25	565.95	519.59	589.89	679.57	162.00
LONG-TERM, FULL FAITH AND CREDIT	382.36	14.00	270.34	7.12	429.50	341.59	158.87

See footnotes at end of table.

Table 2. Per Capita Amounts of Financial Items for Individual City and Selected Urban Town and Township Governments Having 50,000 Population or More: 1977—Continued

Item	Ohio--Continued						
	Columbus	Dayton	Elyria	Euclid	Hamilton	Kettering	Lakewood
REVENUE							
GENERAL REVENUE	298.54	443.08	210.28	291.34	289.41	146.14	486.02
TAXES	127.81	218.65	103.98	176.63	102.89	94.34	100.07
PROPERTY	15.87	47.47	31.16	99.37	19.45	31.41	48.78
OTHER	111.94	171.17	72.82	77.26	83.44	62.93	51.29
INTERGOVERNMENTAL REVENUE	91.73	141.00	55.65	62.38	135.67	38.03	51.26
MISCELLANEOUS GENERAL REVENUE	78.99	83.43	50.65	52.33	50.85	13.77	334.69
EXPENDITURE							
GENERAL EXPENDITURE, ALL FUNCTIONS	309.10	454.51	255.97	267.28	222.83	138.52	421.94
TOTAL, EXCLUDING CAPITAL OUTLAY	269.95	393.35	238.00	221.63	182.67	117.76	395.47
GENERAL EXPENDITURE, SELECTED ITEMS:							
EDUCATION	-	-	-	-	-	0.03	-
HIGHWAYS	26.07	23.97	71.88	44.04	18.17	31.72	15.17
EXCLUDING CAPITAL OUTLAY	18.48	16.60	63.21	38.37	9.16	19.23	14.33
PUBLIC WELFARE	-	6.7	-	-	0.08	1.97	-
HEALTH AND HOSPITALS	10.12	13.4.	14.85	0.49	5.90	1.89	249.62
POLICE PROTECTION	55.76	60.46	25.99	38.49	36.41	23.42	21.45
FIRE PROTECTION	34.90	.45	26.26	27.50	29.26	9.31	16.94
SEWERAGE	38.91	16.95	15.11	40.49	28.89	0.01	15.49
EXCLUDING CAPITAL OUTLAY	22.84	13.82	13.11	18.51	15.77	-	15.49
SANITATION OTHER THAN SEWERAGE	15.82	16.75	17.13	26.65	10.32	-	18.17
PARKS AND RECREATION	24.04	29.90	16.64	22.29	10.47	11.48	14.44
HOUSING AND URBAN RENEWAL	0.87	61.79	2.97	5.53	14.86	-	5.03
TOTAL DEBT	593.34	394.24	367.02	375.55	313.27	26.06	354.16
LONG-TERM, FULL FAITH AND CREDIT	457.74	286.34	251.11	349.72	109.72	26.05	97.64

Item	Ohio--Continued						
	Lima	Lorain	Mansfield	Parma	Springfield	Toledo	Warren
REVENUE							
GENERAL REVENUE	289.73	215.01	222.36	121.42	222.50	331.70	191.47
TAXES	77.01	81.74	98.65	68.26	120.08	118.78	88.19
PROPERTY	12.01	24.51	25.44	23.55	11.39	17.33	15.81
OTHER	65.00	57.23	73.21	44.71	108.68	101.44	72.38
INTERGOVERNMENTAL REVENUE	124.00	79.30	65.46	34.97	57.98	129.61	57.65
MISCELLANEOUS GENERAL REVENUE	88.73	53.98	58.24	18.18	44.44	83.31	45.63
EXPENDITURE							
GENERAL EXPENDITURE, ALL FUNCTIONS	464.36	237.98	254.55	109.93	220.16	376.04	164.50
TOTAL, EXCLUDING CAPITAL OUTLAY	221.27	192.91	127.54	105.95	173.62	299.78	144.00
GENERAL EXPENDITURE, SELECTED ITEMS:							
EDUCATION	-	-	-	-	-	-	-
HIGHWAYS	24.25	27.76	23.28	12.94	14.47	34.63	20.20
EXCLUDING CAPITAL OUTLAY	20.81	17.42	8.21	12.86	10.71	24.83	12.93
PUBLIC WELFARE	0.02	-	-	-	0.13	-	-
HEALTH AND HOSPITALS	163.57	5.98	3.95	1.23	5.38	16.09	3.04
POLICE PROTECTION	29.92	18.76	28.99	18.65	37.20	47.46	32.24
FIRE PROTECTION	32.10	21.93	23.98	16.92	32.62	37.77	28.60
SEWERAGE	77.16	19.56	28.29	3.43	12.30	44.12	12.83
EXCLUDING CAPITAL OUTLAY	15.98	15.75	8.70	2.92	9.75	25.49	11.75
SANITATION OTHER THAN SEWERAGE	9.89	10.28	4.09	9.00	8.70	17.06	13.64
PARKS AND RECREATION	10.22	10.85	4.36	11.46	15.66	18.75	10.18
HOUSING AND URBAN RENEWAL	5.65	53.28	16.34	-	35.32	29.29	7.74
TOTAL DEBT	963.44	373.61	348.64	105.39	137.74	381.30	215.07
LONG-TERM, FULL FAITH AND CREDIT	144.61	38.96	157.95	18.04	32.71	99.57	68.41

See footnotes at end of table.

Table 2. Per Capita Amounts of Financial Items for Individual City and Selected Urban Town and Township Governments Having 50,000 Population or More: 1977—Continued

Item	Ohio Continued — Youngstown	Oklahoma — Lawton	Oklahoma — Midwest City	Oklahoma — Norman	Oklahoma — Oklahoma City	Oklahoma — Tulsa	Oregon — Eugene
REVENUE							
GENERAL REVENUE	250.52	234.43	293.04	317.91	440.97	369.72	370.11
TAXES	123.69	81.17	73.37	66.67	172.31	149.68	137.03
PROPERTY	25.35	12.40	16.78	9.04	60.99	34.90	120.05
OTHER	98.34	68.76	56.58	57.63	111.32	114.78	16.98
INTERGOVERNMENTAL REVENUE	85.67	100.48	28.06	30.36	180.79	130.78	131.79
MISCELLANEOUS GENERAL REVENUE	41.16	52.77	191.62	220.87	87.87	89.26	101.29
EXPENDITURE							
GENERAL EXPENDITURE, ALL FUNCTIONS	272.99	211.04	261.07	287.42	410.26	376.78	418.88
TOTAL, EXCLUDING CAPITAL OUTLAY	228.81	121.68	261.07	277.47	261.34	231.73	328.18
GENERAL EXPENDITURE, SELECTED ITEMS:							
EDUCATION	-	-	-	-	-	-	-
HIGHWAYS	30.04	35.10	7.24	13.95	40.01	20.97	32.86
EXCLUDING CAPITAL OUTLAY	18.85	11.83	7.24	11.66	17.83	13.82	31.65
PUBLIC WELFARE	1.00	-	-	-	-	-	-
HEALTH AND HOSPITALS	4.43	1.03	147.99	158.39	-	10.94	-
POLICE PROTECTION	40.04	30.00	24.49	25.67	33.58	35.48	43.37
FIRE PROTECTION	32.67	19.33	18.82	16.56	33.61	29.61	37.01
SEWERAGE	25.60	34.07	4.85	6.67	93.52	33.64	16.55
EXCLUDING CAPITAL OUTLAY	9.67	3.40	4.85	6.34	7.53	6.55	16.53
SANITATION OTHER THAN SEWERAGE	8.59	10.10	11.46	15.75	10.13	11.91	7.02
PARKS AND RECREATION	9.96	7.65	6.83	15.91	31.15	49.12	44.23
HOUSING AND URBAN RENEWAL	7.79	23.40	-	-	17.37	18.70	27.65
TOTAL DEBT	320.53	317.05	112.42	170.05	1 052.19	731.15	2 279.47
LONG-TERM, FULL FAITH AND CREDIT	136.28	317.05	79.71	73.91	598.26	370.47	

Item	Oregon—Continued — Portland	Oregon—Continued — Salem	Pennsylvania — Abington township (Montgomery County)	Pennsylvania — Allentown	Pennsylvania — Altoona	Pennsylvania — Bethlehem	Pennsylvania — Bristol township
REVENUE							
GENERAL REVENUE	393.40	398.28	130.05	214.60	155.67	264.73	94.54
TAXES	171.70	143.20	88.30	117.33	71.99	110.77	48.22
PROPERTY	128.35	120.54	73.33	68.48	44.91	70.68	43.83
OTHER	43.35	22.67	14.98	48.84	27.07	40.09	4.46
INTERGOVERNMENTAL REVENUE	137.00	152.72	20.21	53.24	57.19	109.07	30.31
MISCELLANEOUS GENERAL REVENUE	84.70	102.36	21.54	44.02	26.49	44.89	15.94
EXPENDITURE							
GENERAL EXPENDITURE, ALL FUNCTIONS	361.75	410.13	146.69	228.34	170.78	297.34	95.67
TOTAL, EXCLUDING CAPITAL OUTLAY	298.73	326.86	106.29	189.40	133.10	194.33	88.37
GENERAL EXPENDITURE, SELECTED ITEMS:							
EDUCATION	1.55	-	-	-	-	-	-
HIGHWAYS	29.39	78.09	27.10	18.53	19.72	29.53	17.15
EXCLUDING CAPITAL OUTLAY	22.61	35.04	14.46	17.25	13.99	19.99	12.59
PUBLIC WELFARE	-	-	-	-	-	-	-
HEALTH AND HOSPITALS	1.58	-	1.23	3.25	1.29	4.08	0.09
POLICE PROTECTION	65.79	44.80	31.18	36.01	31.18	32.49	32.39
FIRE PROTECTION	45.22	43.38	5.68	22.45	23.12	23.28	3.73
SEWERAGE	59.05	53.46	27.44	30.51	10.60	59.94	-
EXCLUDING CAPITAL OUTLAY	25.48	38.75	16.44	13.32	10.05	7.31	-
SANITATION OTHER THAN SEWERAGE	5.97	2.49	13.54	12.86	0.70	3.98	12.92
PARKS AND RECREATION	38.86	28.50	11.18	14.04	5.55	16.36	2.86
HOUSING AND URBAN RENEWAL	10.38	52.63	-	19.85	-	42.76	-
TOTAL DEBT	152.00	472.94	73.99	145.65	28.16	264.50	9.97
LONG-TERM, FULL FAITH AND CREDIT	73.71	354.56	73.99	143.71	28.16	237.41	9.97

See footnotes at end of table.

Table 2. Per Capita Amounts of Financial Items for Individual City and Selected Urban Town and Township Governments Having 50,000 Population or More: 1977—Continued

Item	Pennsylvania--Continued						
	Erie	Harrisburg	Haverford township	Lancaster	Lower Merion Township	Penn-Hills township	Philadelphia
REVENUE							
GENERAL REVENUE	275.92	296.15	118.84	238.31	199.00	97.85	667.86
TAXES	100.05	93.18	64.40	87.86	147.97	56.15	359.69
PROPERTY	70.30	57.13	57.20	58.94	131.08	32.92	96.06
OTHER	29.75	36.05	7.20	28.92	16.89	23.22	263.63
INTERGOVERNMENTAL REVENUE	128.57	95.31	24.77	100.00	17.20	31.37	217.82
MISCELLANEOUS GENERAL REVENUE	47.30	107.66	29.67	50.45	33.83	10.33	90.36
EXPENDITURE							
GENERAL EXPENDITURE, ALL FUNCTIONS	264.15	263.45	112.68	258.59	197.17	105.87	603.96
TOTAL, EXCLUDING CAPITAL OUTLAY	199.39	253.53	107.97	222.71	187.67	94.37	527.15
GENERAL EXPENDITURE, SELECTED ITEMS:							
EDUCATION	-	-	-	-	-	-	5.52
HIGHWAYS	21.34	22.50	25.10	28.55	28.62	15.70	21.22
EXCLUDING CAPITAL OUTLAY	17.24	20.42	23.20	16.92	27.70	14.15	17.76
PUBLIC WELFARE	-	-	-	0.72	-	-	27.42
HEALTH AND HOSPITALS	-	0.79	2.00	3.53	2.18	-	55.70
POLICE PROTECTION	25.89	47.62	28.94	34.92	49.80	28.37	94.01
FIRE PROTECTION	24.25	26.82	3.79	34.55	7.97	1.66	30.30
SEWERAGE	26.50	15.00	10.07	23.52	15.27	17.86	37.50
EXCLUDING CAPITAL OUTLAY	26.35	15.00	8.27	23.52	13.51	14.06	11.83
SANITATION OTHER THAN SEWERAGE	5.73	31.68	8.74	1.38	22.96	12.75	27.33
PARKS AND RECREATION	10.83	7.36	7.85	0.16	12.11	3.07	28.12
HOUSING AND URBAN RENEWAL	13.55	40.52	-	27.62	-	-	24.79
TOTAL DEBT	226.94	179.62	74.48	76.14	152.45	68.68	861.89
LONG-TERM, FULL FAITH AND CREDIT	168.38	139.98	74.48	47.38	152.45	68.68	621.90

Item	Pennsylvania--Continued					Rhode Island	
	Pittsburgh	Reading	Scranton	Upper Darby township	Wilkes-Barre	Cranston	Pawtucket
REVENUE							
GENERAL REVENUE	329.42	249.63	217.34	119.50	615.83	531.87	596.47
TAXES	162.77	95.10	94.59	66.30	85.36	343.04	317.09
PROPERTY	90.76	58.87	35.47	57.39	48.65	339.51	314.65
OTHER	72.01	36.23	59.12	8.92	36.71	3.54	2.44
INTERGOVERNMENTAL REVENUE	137.06	109.18	76.48	28.30	489.36	157.06	261.82
MISCELLANEOUS GENERAL REVENUE	29.59	45.36	46.26	24.90	41.11	31.77	17.56
EXPENDITURE							
GENERAL EXPENDITURE, ALL FUNCTIONS	336.65	235.91	908.72	123.99	624.72	526.44	552.18
TOTAL, EXCLUDING CAPITAL OUTLAY	289.87	180.34	905.65	117.70	254.80	491.24	486.59
GENERAL EXPENDITURE, SELECTED ITEMS:							
EDUCATION	-	-	-	-	-	280.31	252.78
HIGHWAYS	35.49	32.90	5.41	11.68	11.96	24.62	43.72
EXCLUDING CAPITAL OUTLAY	11.69	20.88	5.41	11.68	8.80	21.27	15.68
PUBLIC WELFARE	0.07	-	0.01	-	1.35	16.79	19.13
HEALTH AND HOSPITALS	0.58	5.49	0.53	1.38	4.31	3.54	0.47
POLICE PROTECTION	54.17	35.92	25.03	35.94	28.91	29.27	33.79
FIRE PROTECTION	39.79	23.12	29.74	5.29	49.60	34.08	31.36
SEWERAGE	2.57	13.00	17.63	4.87	11.34	22.68	13.27
EXCLUDING CAPITAL OUTLAY	2.52	5.37	17.63	4.87	2.77	10.76	13.20
SANITATION OTHER THAN SEWERAGE	20.90	2.43	8.21	6.18	3.65	8.38	9.23
PARKS AND RECREATION	18.89	19.12	1.88	6.71	42.58	10.18	13.02
HOUSING AND URBAN RENEWAL	28.44	45.07	11.91	-	342.74	1.63	60.09
TOTAL DEBT	300.39	201.92	128.10	33.87	93.34	422.61	345.54
LONG-TERM, FULL FAITH AND CREDIT	259.68	153.75	47.63	33.87	32.33	422.61	329.57

See footnotes at end of table.

Item	Rhode Island--Continued		South Carolina				South Dakota
	Providence	Warwick	Charleston	Columbia	Greenville	North Charleston	Sioux Falls
REVENUE							
GENERAL REVENUE.	624.45	548.65	291.60	258.47	260.83	79.67	304.01
TAXES.	347.07	376.33	120.76	78.97	150.55	38.84	158.81
PROPERTY	344.00	373.69	96.35	61.44	112.29	27.79	95.15
OTHER.	3.07	2.63	24.41	17.52	38.26	11.05	63.66
INTERGOVERNMENTAL REVENUE.	257.07	159.05	59.77	115.13	75.16	34.49	73.68
MISCELLANEOUS GENERAL REVENUE.	20.31	13.28	111.07	64.37	35.12	6.34	71.52
EXPENDITURE							
GENERAL EXPENDITURE, ALL FUNCTIONS	520.83	622.61	282.83	224.95	221.81	70.87	257.54
TOTAL, EXCLUDING CAPITAL OUTLAY.	490.91	579.89	209.26	168.13	179.74	65.22	187.08
GENERAL EXPENDITURE, SELECTED ITEMS:							
EDUCATION.	219.49	371.97	0.35	-	-	-	-
HIGHWAYS	33.24	24.71	22.67	18.01	20.68	4.46	26.73
EXCLUDING CAPITAL OUTLAY	21.92	12.61	15.57	11.64	16.39	4.46	18.16
PUBLIC WELFARE	37.59	8.49	4.40	-	-	-	-
HEALTH AND HOSPITALS	1.07	1.08	0.40	7.50	-	-	4.84
POLICE PROTECTION.	44.75	44.55	50.46	30.98	37.36	18.94	28.69
FIRE PROTECTION.	45.62	40.63	62.64	28.59	32.50	11.21	25.50
SEWERAGE .	15.39	20.34	22.06	50.93	4.89	-	20.76
EXCLUDING CAPITAL OUTLAY	15.38	3.67	20.92	9.77	4.55	-	14.12
SANITATION OTHER THAN SEWERAGE	15.34	7.29	18.18	17.52	35.20	9.39	3.00
PARKS AND RECREATION	15.63	7.32	44.08	14.94	17.84	3.30	34.98
HOUSING AND URBAN RENEWAL.	19.85	-	1.98	0.64	20.44	-	31.38
TOTAL DEBT .	237.94	455.93	310.41	337.32	351.11	0.26	160.66
LONG-TERM, FULL FAITH AND CREDIT	237.94	299.31	71.34	1.52	65.48	0.26	62.02

Item	Tennessee				Texas		
	Chattanooga	Knoxville	Memphis	Nashville-Davidson	Abilene	Amarillo	Arlington
REVENUE							
GENERAL REVENUE.	710.89	508.26	528.32	684.59	156.55	381.83	203.22
TAXES.	159.60	129.64	130.00	335.77	89.60	149.33	112.88
PROPERTY	130.64	102.60	100.75	215.31	48.30	99.23	61.25
OTHER.	28.96	27.04	29.25	120.46	41.30	50.09	51.63
INTERGOVERNMENTAL REVENUE.	462.58	297.61	329.99	224.21	22.05	33.33	21.07
MISCELLANEOUS GENERAL REVENUE.	88.72	81.01	68.33	124.61	44.90	199.17	69.27
EXPENDITURE							
GENERAL EXPENDITURE, ALL FUNCTIONS	703.84	541.46	540.94	740.29	127.00	355.72	203.27
TOTAL, EXCLUDING CAPITAL OUTLAY.	530.23	491.59	466.84	550.22	110.03	296.25	179.04
GENERAL EXPENDITURE, SELECTED ITEMS:							
EDUCATION.	248.04	224.76	233.18	289.71	-	-	-
HIGHWAYS	28.28	12.06	30.83	45.93	11.98	51.19	27.95
EXCLUDING CAPITAL OUTLAY	19.90	11.78	12.12	20.02	10.54	18.00	7.74
PUBLIC WELFARE	9.77	1.94	1.10	8.15	-	-	2.04
HEALTH AND HOSPITALS	5.38	0.74	0.64	57.06	3.51	128.97	2.35
POLICE PROTECTION.	50.88	60.23	48.26	47.01	18.82	29.01	23.49
FIRE PROTECTION.	40.31	41.22	41.96	25.12	15.29	19.16	16.41
SEWERAGE .	130.17	31.96	35.42	95.15	5.61	25.99	10.03
EXCLUDING CAPITAL OUTLAY	16.08	19.82	9.87	12.92	5.01	8.14	10.03
SANITATION OTHER THAN SEWERAGE	23.06	28.75	30.58	16.54	12.46	22.52	3.93
PARKS AND RECREATION	22.98	25.50	33.93	16.45	12.80	10.99	32.21
HOUSING AND URBAN RENEWAL.	9.32	-	-	0.12	-	-	-
TOTAL DEBT .	395.92	956.34	1 128.37	971.16	238.70	225.59	871.20
LONG-TERM, FULL FAITH AND CREDIT	367.60	673.90	631.69	484.05	144.10	193.16	669.47

See footnotes at end of table.

207

Table 2. Per Capita Amounts of Financial Items for Individual City and Selected Urban Town and Township Governments Having 50,000 Population or More: 1977—Continued

Item	Texas--Continued						
	Austin	Beaumont	Brownsville	Corpus Christi	Dallas	El Paso	Fort Worth
REVENUE							
GENERAL REVENUE.	334.51	239.03	159.90	228.17	335.10	201.41	315.15
TAXES.	125.29	121.60	71.86	112.88	210.16	90.60	135.95
PROPERTY	84.38	72.38	35.59	75.41	139.04	55.73	87.97
OTHER.	40.91	49.23	36.27	37.46	71.11	34.87	47.97
INTERGOVERNMENTAL REVENUE.	77.48	43.57	41.84	69.74	52.92	48.90	100.93
MISCELLANEOUS GENERAL REVENUE.	131.74	73.85	46.20	45.56	72.02	61.91	78.28
EXPENDITURE							
GENERAL EXPENDITURE, ALL FUNCTIONS	434.50	267.41	155.80	188.23	305.53	181.17	318.16
TOTAL, EXCLUDING CAPITAL OUTLAY. . . .	303.69	178.19	140.15	157.43	238.41	140.78	198.94
GENERAL EXPENDITURE, SELECTED ITEMS:							
EDUCATION.	0.35	-	-	-	-	-	0.41
HIGHWAYS	27.37	81.90	15.54	26.04	28.44	11.20	29.92
EXCLUDING CAPITAL OUTLAY	9.05	22.33	8.32	13.65	10.41	6.63	10.35
PUBLIC WELFARE	1.53	-	-	0.64	-	0.01	-
HEALTH AND HOSPITALS	105.02	5.35	3.06	5.19	5.52	4.56	5.15
POLICE PROTECTION.	36.54	30.99	23.49	28.12	50.44	26.10	40.84
FIRE PROTECTION.	21.32	28.64	15.05	18.76	29.67	16.36	26.09
SEWERAGE	71.74	9.39	19.73	12.30	30.71	31.77	91.07
EXCLUDING CAPITAL OUTLAY	10.88	8.14	14.11	9.48	7.32	6.00	9.05
SANITATION OTHER THAN SEWERAGE	10.33	11.09	10.35	12.40	11.93	8.12	13.96
PARKS AND RECREATION	30.49	12.57	10.39	23.48	26.40	12.67	16.91
HOUSING AND URBAN RENEWAL.	8.35	0.08	-	-	-	-	(Z)
TOTAL DEBT	1 406.03	457.69	564.33	307.88	572.53	161.88	513.61
LONG-TERM, FULL FAITH AND CREDIT	266.87	412.96	207.77	270.16	361.62	97.18	370.09

Item	Texas--Continued						
	Galveston	Garland	Grand Prarie	Houston	Irving	Laredo	Lubbock
REVENUE							
GENERAL REVENUE.	443.96	208.42	213.61	309.76	186.49	231.86	253.91
TAXES.	139.98	89.38	101.77	183.04	125.61	79.74	117.08
PROPERTY	90.73	59.33	69.47	113.83	85.81	30.17	72.72
OTHER.	49.25	30.05	32.30	69.21	39.80	49.57	44.35
INTERGOVERNMENTAL REVENUE.	48.93	56.61	33.62	47.26	10.41	105.90	79.79
MISCELLANEOUS GENERAL REVENUE.	255.05	62.43	78.22	79.46	50.47	46.22	57.04
EXPENDITURE							
GENERAL EXPENDITURE, ALL FUNCTIONS	476.71	240.86	253.00	294.22	199.08	249.77	250.21
TOTAL, EXCLUDING CAPITAL OUTLAY. . . .	426.18	154.01	176.59	227.18	150.79	174.43	176.44
GENERAL EXPENDITURE, SELECTED ITEMS:							
EDUCATION.	-	-	-	0.24	-	-	-
HIGHWAYS	18.66	65.86	61.82	23.07	18.38	80.57	22.15
EXCLUDING CAPITAL OUTLAY	18.46	16.12	22.03	6.52	8.98	39.81	11.30
PUBLIC WELFARE	0.27	0.61	-	-	-	5.62	0.40
HEALTH AND HOSPITALS	8.68	2.04	2.64	12.16	1.81	14.91	4.16
POLICE PROTECTION.	37.90	25.61	28.94	51.83	19.06	15.78	27.59
FIRE PROTECTION.	22.82	18.76	18.01	35.38	16.49	24.05	41.63
SEWERAGE	25.56	26.53	7.14	43.87	8.16	14.66	11.64
EXCLUDING CAPITAL OUTLAY	25.36	6.68	6.60	17.62	5.00	5.88	4.59
SANITATION OTHER THAN SEWERAGE	19.58	15.23	11.77	11.89	8.85	9.43	21.95
PARKS AND RECREATION	15.00	13.56	34.85	15.50	23.32	9.35	15.07
HOUSING AND URBAN RENEWAL.	2.15	-	0.14	-	-	-	7.49
TOTAL DEBT	512.50	959.43	590.48	594.50	661.50	167.55	459.76
LONG-TERM, FULL FAITH AND CREDIT	331.64	299.78	408.47	327.91	201.04	38.77	297.72

See footnotes at end of table.

Table 2. Per Capita Amounts of Financial Items for Individual City and Selected Urban Town and Township Governments Having 50,000 Population or More: 1977—Continued

Item	Texas--Continued						
	Mesquite	Midland	Odessa	Pasadena	Port Arthur	Richardson	San Angelo
REVENUE							
GENERAL REVENUE	157.69	198.24	151.85	165.51	224.43	194.46	195.63
TAXES	106.07	113.06	99.20	105.46	104.64	130.48	93.77
PROPERTY	64.94	66.72	47.78	64.02	67.65	91.42	57.25
OTHER	41.13	46.34	51.42	41.44	36.99	39.06	36.52
INTERGOVERNMENTAL REVENUE	15.78	7.99	10.54	15.17	73.04	8.08	71.24
MISCELLANEOUS GENERAL REVENUE	35.85	77.19	42.12	44.88	46.75	55.90	30.62
EXPENDITURE							
GENERAL EXPENDITURE, ALL FUNCTIONS	149.27	166.64	120.46	156.16	229.42	198.01	177.72
TOTAL, EXCLUDING CAPITAL OUTLAY	146.80	154.19	112.80	127.68	191.12	157.39	121.29
GENERAL EXPENDITURE, SELECTED ITEMS:							
EDUCATION	-	-	-	-	-	-	-
HIGHWAYS	13.71	24.21	16.08	20.90	42.78	40.72	26.13
EXCLUDING CAPITAL OUTLAY	11.96	18.46	15.58	9.80	20.84	11.32	11.80
PUBLIC WELFARE	-	-	-	0.17	0.17	-	2.38
HEALTH AND HOSPITALS	2.13	3.07	0.72	2.94	6.26	1.47	5.46
POLICE PROTECTION	26.53	28.53	29.76	33.89	27.93	23.06	26.19
FIRE PROTECTION	24.38	21.08	20.37	3.57	22.22	21.71	20.20
SEWERAGE	7.31	6.26	6.18	15.27	19.72	14.04	46.35
EXCLUDING CAPITAL OUTLAY	6.75	6.18	5.30	12.09	14.21	7.81	4.30
SANITATION OTHER THAN SEWERAGE	14.43	10.10	16.16	15.39	16.90	19.23	2.18
PARKS AND RECREATION	15.36	16.90	1.27	20.91	8.83	15.12	7.55
HOUSING AND URBAN RENEWAL	-	-	-	-	-	0.22	-
TOTAL DEBT	331.28	265.02	114.27	409.24	271.00	462.85	164.62
LONG-TERM, FULL FAITH AND CREDIT	221.74	121.84	56.50	303.03	231.12	337.52	93.72

Item	Texas--Continued				Utah			Virginia
	San Antonio	Tyler	Waco	Witchita Falls	Ogden	Provo	Salt Lake City	Alexandria
REVENUE								
GENERAL REVENUE	208.54	186.10	282.24	185.77	199.11	280.02	284.60	1 069.27
TAXES	78.39	103.23	113.99	104.00	94.33	69.27	151.66	554.92
PROPERTY	49.23	52.10	68.12	62.53	43.70	29.19	59.24	398.35
OTHER	29.15	51.13	45.87	41.47	50.64	40.08	92.42	156.59
INTERGOVERNMENTAL REVENUE	77.77	30.75	115.61	36.90	62.22	140.50	36.44	438.29
MISCELLANEOUS GENERAL REVENUE	52.38	52.07	52.65	44.87	42.55	70.24	96.51	75.27
EXPENDITURE								
GENERAL EXPENDITURE, ALL FUNCTIONS	241.95	188.63	250.69	144.95	173.42	329.29	282.22	1 030.01
TOTAL, EXCLUDING CAPITAL OUTLAY	183.89	140.74	225.94	121.91	151.50	128.49	222.01	745.77
GENERAL EXPENDITURE, SELECTED ITEMS:								
EDUCATION	0.85	-	-	-	-	-	-	292.12
HIGHWAYS	19.63	29.45	30.32	29.33	13.82	22.75	39.18	32.20
EXCLUDING CAPITAL OUTLAY	10.59	14.93	16.04	14.10	13.18	10.36	15.64	17.39
PUBLIC WELFARE	1.22	0.42	-	-	-	-	-	72.89
HEALTH AND HOSPITALS	10.55	2.90	13.20	5.68	0.16	0.23	-	22.01
POLICE PROTECTION	34.29	29.23	44.75	22.36	25.98	21.84	54.19	56.13
FIRE PROTECTION	21.48	21.71	25.98	16.19	24.94	15.47	37.29	43.16
SEWERAGE	27.65	23.60	18.64	10.77	10.71	163.31	6.79	233.29
EXCLUDING CAPITAL OUTLAY	5.75	5.75	15.94	8.35	8.76	7.21	6.55	7.74
SANITATION OTHER THAN SEWERAGE	11.78	17.42	11.92	13.34	9.08	10.04	8.20	18.24
PARKS AND RECREATION	31.31	7.76	15.68	10.40	18.67	18.98	15.66	25.77
HOUSING AND URBAN RENEWAL	4.16	-	15.23	-	-	-	-	19.73
TOTAL DEBT	737.63	346.89	317.03	263.91	63.43	109.91	190.19	1 235.44
LONG-TERM, FULL FAITH AND CREDIT	148.06	190.12	271.86	163.82	15.95	70.17	173.00	1 155.69

See footnotes at end of table.

Item	Virginia--Continued							
	Chesapeake	Hampton	Lynchburg	Newport News	Norfolk	Portsmouth	Richmond	Roanoke
REVENUE								
GENERAL REVENUE	649.97	656.73	630.83	701.52	759.73	723.30	942.24	822.85
TAXES	266.63	274.75	324.37	318.64	268.60	255.49	459.17	392.71
PROPERTY	185.34	183.95	183.05	227.33	133.21	146.02	272.82	209.63
OTHER	81.30	90.80	141.33	91.31	135.39	109.47	186.35	183.08
INTERGOVERNMENTAL REVENUE	338.32	327.24	244.00	324.84	419.24	379.49	366.09	330.23
MISCELLANEOUS GENERAL REVENUE	45.01	54.75	62.46	58.04	71.90	88.32	116.99	99.91
EXPENDITURE								
GENERAL EXPENDITURE, ALL FUNCTIONS	589.82	637.05	733.83	632.49	730.47	781.80	967.10	726.78
TOTAL, EXCLUDING CAPITAL OUTLAY	517.68	588.93	542.56	582.34	579.33	655.44	837.99	615.04
GENERAL EXPENDITURE, SELECTED ITEMS:								
EDUCATION	289.54	276.95	368.49	310.64	219.53	247.75	268.50	266.59
HIGHWAYS	46.10	15.10	30.16	13.46	23.53	62.38	64.74	18.59
EXCLUDING CAPITAL OUTLAY	31.74	11.09	20.57	13.20	18.25	28.64	26.28	14.52
PUBLIC WELFARE	49.00	78.30	53.93	58.77	91.26	102.75	164.94	79.39
HEALTH AND HOSPITALS	15.07	3.93	25.67	14.82	36.34	21.63	21.96	5.33
POLICE PROTECTION	27.70	54.09	37.58	26.83	38.56	39.64	47.21	27.18
FIRE PROTECTION	20.29	17.10	29.03	19.41	23.55	27.21	37.27	29.75
SEWERAGE	17.96	5.55	19.93	6.41	5.47	9.69	59.80	33.75
EXCLUDING CAPITAL OUTLAY	4.71	3.30	7.04	5.41	3.77	9.69	35.99	11.20
SANITATION OTHER THAN SEWERAGE	12.00	11.26	6.98	19.34	13.64	16.93	23.28	16.30
PARKS AND RECREATION	13.27	26.22	18.19	13.29	32.86	23.21	31.44	11.06
HOUSING AND URBAN RENEWAL	8.09	9.78	12.61	25.04	112.61	72.89	61.76	45.44
TOTAL DEBT	566.79	661.92	621.27	697.19	812.41	728.90	1 519.72	748.21
LONG-TERM, FULL FAITH AND CREDIT	539.79	631.74	510.27	643.04	646.89	669.73	1 360.41	748.21

Item	Virginia--Continued	Washington				West Virginia		Wisconsin
	Virginia Beach	Bellevue	Seattle	Spokane	Tacoma	Charleston	Huntington	Appleton
REVENUE								
GENERAL REVENUE	601.93	327.51	525.00	396.79	427.30	441.60	346.75	639.10
TAXES	274.15	129.58	196.37	120.82	167.24	185.86	126.59	253.49
PROPERTY	158.38	59.94	81.15	50.80	48.21	61.69	42.17	251.80
OTHER	115.77	69.64	115.21	70.03	119.03	124.16	84.42	1.69
INTERGOVERNMENTAL REVENUE	276.49	96.66	185.75	199.79	153.25	124.96	174.41	284.44
MISCELLANEOUS GENERAL REVENUE	51.29	101.28	142.88	76.18	106.81	130.78	45.75	101.16
EXPENDITURE								
GENERAL EXPENDITURE, ALL FUNCTIONS	601.99	300.21	476.92	340.31	478.11	311.52	232.10	658.49
TOTAL, EXCLUDING CAPITAL OUTLAY	499.34	247.10	385.46	207.51	369.68	268.75	206.89	574.72
GENERAL EXPENDITURE, SELECTED ITEMS:								
EDUCATION	276.48	-	2.56	0.03	-	-	0.80	307.05
HIGHWAYS	51.31	68.92	40.27	20.92	85.37	38.80	21.55	55.32
EXCLUDING CAPITAL OUTLAY	30.03	34.84	13.29	18.27	35.13	29.90	19.44	25.43
PUBLIC WELFARE	28.71	0.02	-	3.36	-	0.06	-	4.12
HEALTH AND HOSPITALS	12.38	0.64	18.67	0.18	25.68	4.68	3.01	4.73
POLICE PROTECTION	34.36	37.39	67.94	40.79	49.44	39.56	40.28	46.01
FIRE PROTECTION	14.33	26.86	47.38	35.84	49.26	31.66	34.79	33.78
SEWERAGE	17.23	37.28	42.11	129.20	18.54	23.31	17.03	69.19
EXCLUDING CAPITAL OUTLAY	3.74	27.98	35.20	12.50	14.99	23.31	16.45	28.72
SANITATION OTHER THAN SEWERAGE	16.73	0.84	23.27	23.45	22.67	17.82	18.44	12.33
PARKS AND RECREATION	21.45	23.65	74.70	28.67	14.83	21.32	9.58	27.96
HOUSING AND URBAN RENEWAL	-	-	22.81	-	7.96	19.96	26.19	
TOTAL DEBT	518.35	352.13	1 009.26	95.09	1 528.38	443.01	104.63	631.73
LONG-TERM, FULL FAITH AND CREDIT	485.31	176.96	296.04	66.83	65.22	103.02	13.01	430.91

See footnotes at end of table.

210

Table 2. Per Capita Amounts of Financial Items for Individual City and Selected Urban Town and Township Governments Having 50,000 Population or More: 1977—Continued

Item	Wisconsin--Continued							
	Green Bay	Kenosha	Madison	Milwaukee	Oshkosh	Racine	Wautosa	West Allis
REVENUE								
GENERAL REVENUE.	720.19	243.80	691.05	379.95	608.92	342.27	593.87	615.12
TAXES.	237.07	83.32	334.12	124.80	227.23	130.17	321.94	307.93
PROPERTY	234.89	80.85	326.30	119.82	224.22	127.44	315.64	303.60
OTHER.	2.18	2.47	7.82	4.99	3.01	2.73	6.30	4.33
INTERGOVERNMENTAL REVENUE.	382.00	127.86	262.15	191.25	305.85	167.59	211.98	265.59
MISCELLANEOUS GENERAL REVENUE.	101.12	32.62	94.78	63.99	75.84	44.51	59.95	41.60
EXPENDITURE								
GENERAL EXPENDITURE, ALL FUNCTIONS	793.12	204.54	711.69	348.84	632.91	375.69	589.52	592.83
TOTAL, EXCLUDING CAPITAL OUTLAY.	670.72	199.33	656.39	291.49	578.82	260.14	521.89	553.69
GENERAL EXPENDITURE, SELECTED ITEMS:								
EDUCATION.	378.02	-	332.59	0.04	333.33	-	312.19	325.46
HIGHWAYS	69.65	11.30	55.01	40.48	56.06	34.67	61.47	34.90
EXCLUDING CAPITAL OUTLAY	38.96	11.07	34.07	20.02	34.37	17.49	17.98	23.68
PUBLIC WELFARE	2.35	-	6.32	-	4.65	-	-	-
HEALTH AND HOSPITALS	5.40	4.74	7.69	12.48	4.35	7.05	4.14	7.19
POLICE PROTECTION.	43.99	34.83	53.96	70.54	38.40	47.34	36.22	39.13
FIRE PROTECTION.	42.20	30.15	45.16	30.82	37.64	31.83	37.50	34.86
SEWERAGE	72.51	13.11	27.34	21.53	51.63	92.68	9.89	16.52
EXCLUDING CAPITAL OUTLAY	55.53	13.01	23.19	13.60	35.28	10.91	8.55	7.31
SANITATION OTHER THAN SEWERAGE	19.30	14.57	17.66	25.56	14.89	11.94	20.15	13.30
PARKS AND RECREATION	25.41	12.29	32.70	18.08	17.48	28.41	8.60	2.82
HOUSING AND URBAN RENEWAL.	26.56	-	31.48	25.76	0.52	9.37	-	1.90
TOTAL DEBT	745.82	351.64	527.65	384.51	547.97	362.71	514.49	451.86
LONG-TERM, FULL FAITH AND CREDIT	612.01	276.95	366.42	220.81	547.97	339.28	433.89	303.49

Note: Per capita data is based on city population estimated for July 1, 1975, as given in table 5.

- Represents zero or rounds to zero.

211

E – PROPERTY TAXATION

In conjunction with the quinquennial Census of Governments, the Census Bureau conducts what really should be described as a special research project on property taxes. The data for the latest survey are for 1976.

The Bureau selected a sample of over 100,000 sales of real property as the basis for estimating the ratio of sales prices to assessed value. Among the calculations made from this information, the Bureau produced comparative data on "effective property tax rates" for nearly 500 places, including most cities of 50,000 persons or more. This is the best way to compare property taxes, because it eliminates the great variation that occurs in assessment practices by directly comparing the taxes levied to the sales price. Effective tax rates are shown in Table 3 in this section. All property taxes are included whether paid to local governments, school or other special districts, or State governments. Essex County, New Jersey stands out with effective rates in 1976 equal to between 3% and 7% of sales value. Rates in Los Angeles County, California range from 3% in Compton to 1.5% in Downey, though this was pre-California Proposition 13.

Table 1 in this section shows 1976 local property taxes by State and gives per capita comparisons and comparisons per $1000 of personal income. On the latter basis, Alaska and New Jersey rank highest, with $120.45 and $66.60 respectively.

Table 2 provides an insight into the methodology used for this special survey by showing the standard error for the assessment-sales ratios by State and type of property.

In the 20-year period, 1956 to 1976, property values assessed for local general property taxation have increased from $280.3 billion to $1,229.1 billion. In just five years, 1971 to 1976, assessed values have increased by $511.3 billion.

In 10 years the average sales price of a previously occupied single family house (each based on sampling for the survey involved) has increased by 118 percent, from $15,878 to $34,557. During the same period median area tax bills for the sampled properties have increased by $328.29 or 112 percent, from $293.74 in 1966 to $662.03 in 1976. It should be noted that although the tax bills have increased dramatically, effective tax rates have actually declined from 1.85 percent to 1.80 percent.

In fiscal 1966, property tax revenue, mostly of local governments but including State collections as well, amounted to an average, nationwide, of $46.36 per $1,000 of personal income. The figure for the median State (Michigan) was $45.20. Ten years later the nationwide average had decreased to $45.33 per $1,000 of personal income and the figure for the median State (Texas) was $38.63.

Taxable property in the United States amounted to more than $1,229.1 billion in assessed value in 1976, an increase of $511.3 billion, or 71 percent, over the corresponding aggregate for 1971. The 1976 total includes $992.5 billion in real property, $151.8 billion in personalty, and $84.8 billion of State-assessed property not classified within real and personal components.

For this ratio study of assessed values and sales prices, the Bureau obtained 110,000 in-scope transfers of real property in 1,939 assessing jurisdictions, and after survey processing, calculated an overall aggregate assessment-sales price ratio of 31.3 percent for all types of realty taken as a single class. An inherent limitation of any such ratio study immediately becomes apparent. A sample of sales is a sample of a subset, since the *sales universe* constitutes only a small percentage of all realty in the country. Within that essential qualification, if the unadjusted aggregate ratio is applied to the nationwide total of $992.5 billion in real property assessed value, a sales-generated market value estimate for all real property in 1976 approximates $3,171 billion. The calculation is conceptually improved a bit if the size-weighted ratio of 31.0 percent is used, in which case the imputed market value becomes $3,202 billion.

The "taxable property values" which the Census Bureau surveys are assessed values. As such they constitute official determinations by more than 13,500 local assessors of the value, officially set in 1976 for tax purposes, of about 100 million real property parcels and additional millions of personal property accounts.

Tax Rates

The rates which are applied to assessed values to produce expected revenue are nominal rates. They are one of the two major types of rates receiving attention in this survey. In the census definition, the nominal tax rate, whether one levy from one governmental unit, or a composite of levies from all units taxing the assessed value, is the quotient of the total annual tax bill divided by the assessed value of the property. It can vary within a single assessing jurisdiction depending on the extent to which the taxing units involved overlap. It can be relatively high or low depending on the de facto assessment level, the levying unit's functional responsibilities and need for funds, legal tax rates limits, and other factors.

The second rate dealt with in this survey is the effective tax rate. This is not a levy at all, except in equivalent terms when assessed values and market values and sales prices in fact equal each other. The Bureau defines the effective tax rate as the quotient of total annual tax bill divided by the sales per price of the property.

For this survey effective rates have been calculated for cities of 50,000 population or more, together with their surrounding counties, in those circumstances where the sales sample available is sufficient to support the statistical computations necessary. Three use categories are covered, namely, single-family (non-farm) houses, vacant platted lots, and all types of realty considered as a single group.

Demonstration of Nominal and Effective Rates

The following example illustrates nominal rates and effective rates in operation.

Example - Demonstration of rates

Item	Alpha City		Omega City	
	Property 1	Property 2	Property 3	Property 4
Sales price (SP)	$50,000	$50,000	$50,000	$50,000
Gross assessed value (GAV) . .	15,000	15,000	30,000	40,000
Assessment-sales price ratio, percent (R)	30	30	60	80
Applicable partial exemption for homestead (H).	6,000	—	—	—
Net assessed value (NAV, GAV minus H)	9,000	15,000	30,000	40,000
Total tax bill (B)	720	1,200	1,200	1,600
Nominal tax rate, percent (NTR) (B divided by NAV) .	8.0	8.0	4.0	4.0
Effective tax rate, percent (B) divided by SP).	1.4	2.4	2.4	3.2

— Represents zero or rounds to zero.

213

Consider properties 1 and 2 in Alpha City, and properties 3 and 4 in Omega City. Despite the fact that each property sold for $50,000, there are significant variations in nominal and effective rates. Properties 1 and 2 in Alpha City have identical assessments to start with, but property 1 received the benefit of a $6,000 homestead exemption, with the result that its effective rate is only 1.4 percent instead of 2.4 percent. In Omega City, properties 3 and 4 sold for identical amounts but have assessed values differing by $10,000. Here the effect is an effective rate for property 3 that is 25 percent less than the one for property 4. The example exhibits a common occurrence in today's increasingly complicated assessment environment—properties identical in value subject to signnificant differences in effective rates, and therefore in tax bills. In this example, the range extends from 1.4 percent to 3.2 percent.

The great merit of the effective tax rate is its analytical effectiveness. Since its basis is sales price and not assessed value, this rate avoids the built-in variety of assessment levels and makes possible intra-jurisdictional and cross-jurisdictional comparisons of property tax burdens.

Moreover, the effective rate concept gets down to the net tax bill, what the taxpayer actually pays as property tax, after any exemption, for example, of part of an assessed value for homestead. The effective rate usually is not, however, net of circuit-breaker tax credits or rebates, since the latter are commonly associated with administration of the State income tax.

Effective Rates, All Types of Realty

More than three out of every five "all types" rates fell below 2 percent in 1976. Five years ago two out of five were in a corresponding position. There are, however, more instances in 1976 of relatively high rates, those about 4 percent, in cities of less than 100,000 population.

Effective Tax Rates
Single-Family (Nonfarm) Houses

Survey findings show that almost two-thirds of cities with populations of 100,000 or more (92 out of 144) have median effective rates of less than 2 percent. The proportion is substantially higher than the corresponding relationship for 1971.

It is evident at the same time that the number of cities with higher rates is declining. Ten years ago 13 out of 122 cities had effective rates of 3 percent or more for single-family houses. Only two of such rates reached 4 percent. In 1971 the group at 3 percent or more comprised 22 cities out of 146. Half of them penetrated the 4 percent level and beyond. The shift apparent in 1976 results is noteworthy. Only 17 out of 144 rates equal or exceed 3 percent, and only three (Camden, Jersey City, and Trenton) stand at 4 percent or above.

Data for smaller cities (those with populations between 50,000 and 100,000) exhibit somewhat similar patterns, except that the 1976 proportion below 2 percent is somewhat less than that for the larger cities.

Effective Tax Rates. Selected Use Categories and Selected Local Areas: 1971 and 1976

(Rates in percent)

Area	All types of realty		Single-family (nonfarm) houses		Vacant platted lots	
	1971	1976	1971	1976	1971	1976
Cities with population 50,000 or more:						
Number of cities	349	358	349	353	113	109
Median effective rate	2.1	1.8	2.1	1.8	1.6	1.3
Number of "balance of county" areas	(NA)	134	(NA)	128	(NA)	103
Median effective rate	(NA)	1.2	(NA)	1.2	(NA)	0.9
Cities with population 50,000 to 99,999:						
Number of cities	203	214	203	209	43	43
Median effective rate	2.2	1.9	2.2	1.9	1.3	1.3
Cities with population 100,000 or more:						
Number of cities	146	144	146	144	70	65
Median effective rate	2.0	1.6	2.0	1.6	1.8	1.2

NA Not available.

Effective rate positions, single-family houses, selected cities: 1971 and 1976

State	Effective rate less than 1 percent		State	Effective rate 4 percent or more	
	1971	1976		1971	1976
Alabama	Birmingham Gadsden Huntsville Mobile Montgomery Tuscaloosa	Birmingham Gadsden Huntsville Mobile Montgomery Tuscaloosa	Connecticut		New Britain
Arkansas		Fort Smith Pine Bluff	Massachusetts	Arlington Boston Brockton Fall River Lynn Medford Somerville Springfield Worcester	Arlington Brockton Brookline Fall River Somerville
Florida		Hollywood West Palm Beach			
Hawaii	Honolulu	Honolulu	Michigan	Livonia	
Kentucky	Owensboro		New Jersey	Camden Jersey City Newark Paterson Trenton	Camden Cherry Hill East Orange Irvington Jersey City Trenton
Louisiana	Baton Rouge Lafayette Lake Charles New Orleans	Baton Rouge Lafayette Lake Charles Monroe City New Orleans Shreveport (part)	New York	Binghamton Buffalo Utica	New Rochelle Troy
Missouri		Independence (part)			
North Carolina		Winston-Salem	Wisconsin	Milwaukee	
Ohio		Elyria Lima			
Oklahoma		Lawton Norman Tulsa (part)			
Pennsylvania	Penn Hills Twp.				
South Carolina		Charleston Greenville			
Tennessee		Nashville			
Utah		Provo Salt Lake City			
Virginia	Virginia Beach	Virginia Beach			
Washington		Seattle			
West Virginia	Charleston Huntington (part)	Charleston Huntington (part)			

215

Median Effective Tax Rates, Selected Use Categories and Selected Cities: 1971 and 1976

Property use category and median effective tax rate	Cities having a population of 100,000 or more		Cities having a population of 50,000 to 99,999	
	1971[1]	1976[2]	1971[1]	1976[2]
All types of property—				
Total.	146	144	203	214
Less than 1 percent	11	14	7	17
1.0 to 1.4 percent	24	49	30	49
1.5 to 1.9 percent	35	28	31	52
2.0 to 2.4 percent	29	25	70	46
2.5 to 2.9 percent	22	9	36	20
3.0 to 3.4 percent	11	8	11	7
3.5 to 3.9 percent	3	6	11	11
4.0 to 4.9 percent	8	5	5	8
5.0 percent or more	3	—	2	4
Single-family (nonfarm) houses—				
Total.	146	144	203	209
Less than 1 percent	11	16	7	17
1.0 to 1.4 percent	22	45	27	47
1.5 to 1.9 percent	39	31	35	56
2.0 to 2.4 percent	31	26	68	43
2.5 to 2.9 percent	21	9	37	21
3.0 to 3.4 percent	7	9	13	7
3.5 to 3.9 percent	4	5	9	7
4.0 to 4.9 percent	9	3	7	9
5.0 percent or more	2	—	—	2
Vacant platted lots—				
Total.	70	65	43	43
Less than 1 percent	14	23	10	11
1.0 to 1.4 percent	13	17	16	14
1.5 to 1.9 percent	14	10	8	9
2.0 to 2.4 percent	10	10	2	4
2.5 to 2.9 percent	9	2	3	4
3.0 to 3.4 percent	3	2	2	—
3.5 to 3.9 percent	2	1	2	—
4.0 to 4.9 percent	5	—	—	1
5.0 percent or more	—	—	—	—

— Represents zero or rounds to zero.
[1] City population based on 1970 Census.
[2] City population based on 1973 estimates.

216

Table 1. Property Tax Revenue of State and Local Governments, by State: 1976

Area	Amount (millions of dollars)						Total amount per $1,000 of personal income (dollars)	Per capita amounts		As a percent of total tax revenue			As a percent of all general revenue		
	Total	State¹	Local government--selected types					Total (dollars)	Local governments (dollars)	State and local governments	States	Local governments	State and local governments	States	Local governments
			Total local²	Counties	Munici-palities	School districts									
UNITED STATES.	57 001.5	2 177.9	54 883.6	11 582.0	14 165.2	24 399.0	45.33	265.54	255.68	36.4	2.4	81.2	22.3	1.4	33.7
ALABAMA	210.3	31.4	178.9	63.0	39.1	75.8	12.53	57.37	48.81	12.6	2.5	42.1	6.3	1.3	10.7
ALASKA	400.4	306.4	94.0	22.8	71.2	-	120.45	1 048.12	246.07	55.3	51.2	75.0	31.3	29.4	21.8
ARIZONA	640.6	114.7	525.9	177.8	55.7	289.3	53.79	282.18	231.67	38.6	11.3	81.8	24.7	7.4	15.1
ARKANSAS	213.5	1.8	211.7	38.1	19.8	152.5	21.83	101.20	100.38	22.3	0.2	91.3	11.4	0.1	22.9
CALIFORNIA	8 935.7	374.7	8 561.0	2 761.6	1 170.2	4 148.9	64.13	415.23	397.82	43.1	3.5	85.7	28.1	2.1	37.4
COLORADO	700.8	1.7	699.1	111.9	89.3	469.9	46.20	271.29	270.65	37.3	0.2	76.3	21.4	0.1	34.2
CONNECTICUT	1 150.1	(X)	1 150.1	(X)	474.1	4.6	53.28	368.93	368.98	47.4	(X)	99.1	32.9	(X)	60.4
DELAWARE	75.7	-	75.7	18.0	19.3	38.4	19.38	130.12	130.07	16.9	(z)	85.4	9.5	(z)	21.2
DISTRICT OF COLUMBIA	147.1	(X)	147.1	(X)	147.1	(X)	26.53	209.50	209.50	22.7	-	-	9.2	-	-
FLORIDA	1 611.4	58.2	1 553.2	460.7	298.4	742.5	34.25	191.36	184.44	33.8	2.0	84.9	19.8	1.3	27.5
GEORGIA	884.3	6.6	877.7	290.1	155.6	431.5	35.30	177.94	176.60	32.4	0.4	83.5	17.6	0.2	30.7
HAWAII	153.9	(X)	153.9	36.7	117.2	(X)	27.13	173.52	173.51	18.6	(X)	81.0	10.8	(X)	43.2
IDAHO	158.0	0.3	157.7	38.9	27.0	79.4	37.31	190.12	189.77	32.2	0.1	97.5	17.7	0.1	33.6
ILLINOIS	3 188.5	4.5	3 184.0	320.8	624.1	1 878.8	42.14	283.95	283.55	36.9	0.1	82.6	24.5	0.1	40.8
INDIANA	1 197.6	25.0	1 172.6	151.5	274.4	677.3	39.89	225.88	221.16	38.4	1.3	97.5	23.9	0.8	38.2
IOWA	796.7	0.1	796.6	191.3	163.2	441.1	45.68	277.60	277.56	39.6	(z)	98.2	24.0	(z)	37.7
KANSAS	633.1	13.9	619.2	143.6	117.0	344.6	46.36	274.06	268.05	42.1	1.6	95.2	25.5	1.0	44.0
KENTUCKY	359.0	37.3	321.7	68.3	57.5	188.1	21.71	104.74	93.84	19.1	2.7	67.4	10.7	1.5	22.0
LOUISIANA	346.6	0.2	346.4	99.4	90.1	134.5	18.65	90.26	90.18	14.8	(z)	50.4	7.9	(z)	15.5
MAINE	317.8	131.5	186.3	10.3	82.6	8.3	62.67	297.01	174.11	44.2	24.8	99.1	27.1	14.8	15.5
MARYLAND	991.9	59.8	932.1	683.6	221.8	(X)	37.38	239.36	224.93	29.4	3.1	65.9	18.5	1.9	35.6
MASSACHUSETTS	2 500.9	0.5	2 500.4	80.1	1 188.6	4.3	70.31	430.52	430.44	47.7	(z)	99.4	32.0	(z)	54.6
MICHIGAN	2 951.7	121.0	2 830.7	317.1	589.0	1 842.9	52.22	324.22	310.93	43.3	3.2	92.8	25.5	1.8	38.7
MINNESOTA	1 007.9	2.2	1 005.7	273.0	199.2	494.9	44.22	254.20	253.64	30.9	0.1	96.4	18.7	0.1	29.6
MISSISSIPPI	258.0	3.3	254.7	86.7	52.4	114.2	27.14	109.59	108.20	22.5	0.4	94.2	11.4	0.2	21.1
MISSOURI	931.1	4.4	926.7	147.0	120.6	616.9	35.48	194.87	193.95	34.2	0.3	72.4	20.9	0.2	34.2
MONTANA	263.7	16.8	246.9	136.0	28.2	82.4	65.06	350.25	327.89	49.4	6.0	96.4	27.1	2.8	45.5
NEBRASKA	495.0	0.1	494.9	99.8	68.1	317.1	52.76	318.78	318.67	48.5	(z)	93.0	28.5	(z)	47.2
NEVADA	166.0	20.0	146.0	56.2	20.3	67.5	42.17	272.02	239.34	33.2	6.8	70.7	19.3	4.1	27.2
NEW HAMPSHIRE	286.0	5.6	280.4	14.5	88.8	132.8	65.80	347.91	341.12	60.9	3.0	98.1	36.6	1.3	61.6
NEW JERSEY	3 275.3	71.2	3 204.1	633.6	847.7	1 438.0	66.60	446.48	436.76	56.3	3.1	90.9	38.0	1.7	32.7
NEW MEXICO	119.7	13.8	105.9	25.3	22.4	55.3	21.86	102.51	90.67	17.1	2.4	35.7	8.4	1.2	15.6
NEW YORK	7 446.8	25.9	7 420.9	912.7	3 643.7	2 291.9	62.60	411.79	410.36	36.1	0.3	68.5	23.8	0.2	28.8
NORTH CAROLINA	712.0	32.7	679.3	462.8	215.7	(X)	26.38	130.19	124.21	24.7	1.6	82.5	14.6	1.0	22.9
NORTH DAKOTA	136.5	1.7	134.8	43.9	16.7	63.4	37.38	212.28	209.64	31.8	0.6	95.3	16.4	0.3	35.7
OHIO	2 390.7	98.1	2 292.6	298.1	239.8	1 632.7	38.24	223.65	214.46	38.2	3.0	77.7	23.1	1.7	33.2
OKLAHOMA	342.6	(X)	342.6	81.5	43.7	217.3	24.06	123.84	123.86	23.4	(X)	73.7	12.5	(X)	25.0
OREGON	775.5	0.1	775.4	73.6	104.6	553.2	58.74	332.95	332.93	47.3	(z)	95.4	25.3	(z)	44.3
PENNSYLVANIA	2 083.2	60.1	2 023.1	297.2	302.1	1 312.7	29.63	175.62	170.55	25.7	1.2	67.8	16.4	0.7	28.2
RHODE ISLAND	272.7	5.3	267.4	(X)	157.6	103.4	50.37	294.14	288.46	41.4	1.4	99.1	24.3	0.7	53.1
SOUTH CAROLINA	329.7	3.9	325.8	73.4	55.1	188.5	25.33	115.76	114.40	23.7	0.4	92.9	12.5	0.2	25.8
SOUTH DAKOTA	197.6	(X)	197.6	40.7	25.4	127.6	58.73	288.08	288.05	48.3	(X)	91.1	25.9	(X)	53.0
TENNESSEE	545.7	(X)	545.7	310.0	234.4	1.0	26.62	129.49	129.50	26.3	(X)	67.8	14.3	(X)	24.8
TEXAS	2 662.0	36.7	2 625.3	470.9	613.7	1 480.7	38.63	213.18	210.24	36.7	0.9	86.2	21.5	0.5	36.5
UTAH	210.8	0.2	210.6	45.4	26.7	129.5	35.50	171.65	171.50	29.0	(z)	83.2	15.5	(z)	31.0
VERMONT	150.7	4.6	146.1	0.7	15.2	97.4	62.74	307.88	306.93	41.5	0.2	98.8	23.3	0.1	59.2
VIRGINIA	868.6	20.0	848.6	485.0	363.7	(X)	30.23	172.63	168.64	28.3	1.1	68.3	17.1	0.6	29.3
WASHINGTON	852.1	271.5	580.6	148.6	92.7	295.4	38.46	235.91	160.74	32.4	14.7	74.3	18.8	9.2	21.9
WEST VIRGINIA	192.9	0.4	192.5	39.6	20.6	132.0	21.76	105.96	105.71	18.1	(z)	82.0	10.1	(z)	23.8
WISCONSIN	1 330.2	126.7	1 203.5	183.5	449.7	537.2	50.95	288.60	261.12	36.5	3.3	98.4	22.9	3.3	31.6
WYOMING	137.1	7.0	130.1	56.6	4.3	66.8	59.78	351.61	333.59	41.5	3.6	94.9	20.9	1.6	39.2

Note: Financial data are derived from data assembled for the annual Bureau of the Census report, Governmental Finances in 1975-76, except that the per capita figures here, being based on revised population estimates, as of July 1, 1976, differ in some instances from per capita figures appearing in that earlier report. Local government amounts are estimates subject to sampling variation. Because of rounding, detail may not add to totals.

- Represents zero or rounds to zero.
X Not applicable.
Z Less than 0.05 percent.
¹Data compiled from the annual Bureau of the Census report, State Tax Collections.
²Amounts shown are mainly from local general property taxes, but also include collections of local special property taxes in some States. Such collections (for which separate estimates are not available) are believed to make up a very minor percentage of all local property tax revenue.

Table 2. Measurable Sales of Ordinary Real Estate During A 6-Month Period, by Type of Property, by State: 1976

State	Ordinary real estate involved in measurable sales during a 6-month period					Percentage ratio of assessed value to sales price of sold properties			Approximate market value of all assessed ordinary real estate as indicated by measurable sales[2]		Exhibit: Assessed value of all ordinary real estate 1976[3]
	Number of properties[1]	Assessed value (thousand dollars)	Aggregate sales price (thousand dollars)	Percent of assessment roll totals — Number of properties[1]	Percent of assessment roll totals — Assessed value	Statewide size-weighted average	Aggregate assessment-sales price ratio — Statewide	Aggregate assessment-sales price ratio — SMSA portion of State	Total (thousand dollars)	Average value per parcel (dollars)	(thousand dollars)
UNITED STATES											
ALL TYPES OF PROPERTY	1 855 782	18 391 923	58 724 673	2.1	2.4	31.0	31.3 ±0.3	31.4 ±0.3	2 511 761 504	28 932	778 437 199
RESIDENTIAL (NONFARM), TOTAL .	1 288 601	14 958 898	46 201 796	2.5	2.8	30.8	32.4 ±0.2	31.9 ±0.2	1 744 965 968	33 605	538 273 454
SINGLE-FAMILY	1 196 863	13 477 008	41 406 506	2.5	2.8	30.7	32.5 ±0.2	32.1 ±0.2	1 573 104 640	32 271	482 168 565
MULTIFAMILY	91 738	1 481 890	4 795 290	2.9	2.6	32.2	30.9 ±0.7	30.0 ±0.7	174 020 158	54 722	56 104 889
ACREAGE	171 397	1 104 591	5 304 825	1.2	1.0	22.3	20.8 ±1.2	21.1 ±1.2	486 721 600	35 070	108 596 611
VACANT PLATTED LOTS	338 320	821 982	2 867 716	1.9	2.5	27.0	28.7 ±0.9	28.1 ±0.9	122 260 292	6 992	33 061 951
COMMERCIAL AND INDUSTRIAL . .	57 464	1 506 452	4 350 336	1.6	1.5	35.7	34.6 ±1.8	35.7 ±2.2	275 548 400	78 201	98 505 183
ALABAMA											
ALL TYPES OF PROPERTY	30 412	71 511	665 780	2.7	3.0	10.8	10.7 ±0.8	10.9 ±0.9	22 300 150	19 665	2 403 147
RESIDENTIAL (NONFARM), TOTAL .	19 782	57 588	504 119	2.5	3.2	10.7	11.4 ±0.4	11.3 ±0.4	16 697 475	20 971	1 782 092
SINGLE-FAMILY	19 155	55 955	489 460	2.4	3.3	10.6	11.4 ±0.5	11.4 ±0.4	16 217 101	20 557	1 716 965
MULTIFAMILY	627	1 633	14 659	8.5	2.5	12.2	11.1 ±2.1	10.9 ±2.2	534 415	72 759	65 127
ACREAGE	3 780	4 251	84 952	2.6	2.1	5.3	5.0 ±1.7	4.8 ±2.8	3 938 265	26 989	206 763
VACANT PLATTED LOTS	6 047	5 475	49 035	3.9	11.5	7.1	11.2 ±2.3	10.2 ±2.3	666 572	4 349	47 436
COMMERCIAL AND INDUSTRIAL . .	803	4 197	27 674	2.1	1.1	16.7	15.2 ±5.4	15.7 ±6.9	2 202 994	57 093	366 856
ALASKA											
ALL TYPES OF PROPERTY	5 250	201 478	289 581	2.8	4.2	67.2	69.6 ±2.9	68.8 ±3.1	7 208 282	38 070	4 843 813
RESIDENTIAL (NONFARM), TOTAL .	3 125	144 504	198 987	4.1	4.9	69.3	72.6 ±2.3	71.5 ±0.3	4 224 160	55 585	2 928 634
SINGLE-FAMILY	2 677	117 041	158 728	3.8	4.5	71.9	73.7 ±2.2	72.7 ±2.5	3 612 450	50 880	2 596 877
MULTIFAMILY	448	27 463	40 259	9.0	8.3	68.6	68.2 ±6.4	(4) (4)	483 425	96 801	331 757
ACREAGE	191	3 504	6 036	4.5	1.3	57.8	58.1±12.7	(4) (4)	460 943	108 304	266 402
VACANT PLATTED LOTS	1 756	25 704	36 750	1.7	2.9	66.0	69.9±15.1	(4) (4)	1 332 832	13 080	879 785
COMMERCIAL AND INDUSTRIAL . .	(4)	(4)	(4)	(4)	(4)	(4)	(4) (4)	(4) (4)	(4)	(4)	(4)
ARIZONA											
ALL TYPES OF PROPERTY	17 481	46 253	410 602	1.2	1.5	11.7	11.3 ±0.6	11.5 ±0.5	26 287 713	17 723	3 086 107
RESIDENTIAL (NONFARM), TOTAL .	10 344	38 844	324 508	1.9	1.9	12.0	12.0 ±0.5	12.2 ±0.3	16 836 057	31 274	2 028 368
SINGLE-FAMILY	9 939	35 962	305 299	2.0	2.0	11.7	11.8 ±0.4	12.0 −	15 619 539	30 842	1 823 457
MULTIFAMILY	405	2 882	19 209	1.3	1.4	14.3	15.0 ±2.3	15.4 ±2.9	1 434 377	44 952	204 911
ACREAGE	(4)	(4)	(4)	(4)	(4)	(4)	(4) (4)	(4) (4)	(4)	(4)	(4)
VACANT PLATTED LOTS	5 319	3 382	41 857	0.8	1.1	8.2	8.1 ±0.1	6.3 ±1.5	3 700 992	5 258	304 230
COMMERCIAL AND INDUSTRIAL . .	(4)	(4)	(4)	(4)	(4)	(4)	(4) (4)	(4) (4)	(4)	(4)	(4)
ARKANSAS											
ALL TYPES OF PROPERTY	26 183	41 037	448 568	1.8	2.3	8.6	9.1 ±0.7	11.5 ±0.4	21 106 894	14 771	1 811 892
RESIDENTIAL (NONFARM), TOTAL .	12 483	31 470	288 969	2.3	3.0	10.2	10.9 ±0.4	12.6 ±0.4	10 337 371	19 179	1 049 333
SINGLE-FAMILY	12 039	29 249	271 771	2.3	2.9	10.1	10.8 ±0.4	12.5 ±0.4	9 976 853	18 835	1 002 770
MULTIFAMILY	444	2 221	17 198	4.8	4.8	13.1	12.9 ±2.1	13.5 ±2.1	354 234	38 012	46 563
ACREAGE	5 379	3 089	80 986	1.0	0.6	4.1	3.8 ±0.8	5.7 ±1.2	11 719 725	20 990	481 667
VACANT PLATTED LOTS	7 334	2 704	38 625	2.5	4.6	6.2	7.0 ±0.9	8.5 ±1.2	951 945	3 270	59 069
COMMERCIAL AND INDUSTRIAL . .	987	3 774	39 988	2.4	1.7	9.4	9.4 ±2.0	(4) (4)	2 369 695	58 566	221 823
CALIFORNIA											
ALL TYPES OF PROPERTY	254 397	2 166 561	12 506 520	3.6	3.7	17.2	17.3 ±0.3	17.4 ±0.3	337 266 128	47 589	58 165 360
RESIDENTIAL (NONFARM), TOTAL .	200 830	1 811 221	10 225 064	4.0	4.0	17.7	17.7 ±0.1	17.7 ±0.1	253 400 524	49 942	44 748 200
SINGLE-FAMILY	178 346	1 480 863	8 369 668	3.9	3.9	17.7	17.7 ±0.1	17.7 ±0.1	217 395 630	47 519	38 437 635
MULTIFAMILY	22 484	330 358	1 855 396	4.5	5.2	17.6	17.8 ±0.5	17.7 ±0.6	35 773 253	71 696	6 310 565
ACREAGE	16 928	128 658	933 867	3.8	3.0	13.1	13.8 ±1.6	13.5 ±2.1	32 468 113	73 615	4 248 185
VACANT PLATTED LOTS	29 171	76 680	460 157	2.3	3.1	16.4	16.7 ±1.1	17.1 ±1.1	15 196 598	12 220	2 498 522
COMMERCIAL AND INDUSTRIAL . .	7 468	150 002	887 432	2.3	2.2	17.1	16.9 ±2.3	17.1 ±2.4	39 105 971	119 047	6 670 453
COLORADO											
ALL TYPES OF PROPERTY	40 779	238 939	1 376 696	3.5	4.1	16.8	17.4 ±0.8	18.2 ±0.6	34 927 247	30 096	5 864 740
RESIDENTIAL (NONFARM), TOTAL .	29 997	201 627	1 100 739	4.4	5.0	18.0	18.3 ±0.6	18.5 ±0.6	22 586 027	32 896	4 062 429
SINGLE-FAMILY	28 349	181 297	983 567	4.3	4.7	18.1	18.4 ±0.4	18.7 ±0.3	21 170 804	31 968	3 831 146
MULTIFAMILY	1 648	20 330	117 172	6.8	8.8	15.9	17.4 ±3.7	17.1 ±4.1	1 450 234	59 595	231 283
ACREAGE	2 877	14 129	143 083	1.6	2.2	9.3	9.9 ±2.6	11.9 ±3.1	7 009 052	38 172	655 098
VACANT PLATTED LOTS	7 156	10 352	65 820	3.1	4.0	14.7	15.7 ±1.3	16.5 ±1.7	1 779 901	7 734	260 981
COMMERCIAL AND INDUSTRIAL . .	749	12 831	67 054	1.2	1.4	19.3	19.1 ±2.9	18.8 ±2.9	4 583 522	76 170	886 232
CONNECTICUT											
ALL TYPES OF PROPERTY	15 050	304 084	711 459	1.6	1.8	42.1	42.7 ±2.0	43.6 ±2.2	40 902 289	43 977	17 205 698
RESIDENTIAL (NONFARM), TOTAL .	12 467	273 493	622 101	1.7	1.9	42.4	44.0 ±2.0	44.3 ±2.2	34 237 600	46 289	14 521 483
SINGLE-FAMILY	11 298	251 141	569 388	1.7	1.9	42.2	44.1 ±2.2	44.5 ±2.4	30 893 297	46 303	13 038 820
MULTIFAMILY	1 169	22 352	52 713	1.6	1.5	42.9	42.4 ±3.2	42.3 ±3.4	3 453 301	47 660	1 482 663
ACREAGE	814	7 385	30 565	2.8	2.9	24.8	24.2 ±8.1	25.6±14.1	1 033 058	35 758	256 579
VACANT PLATTED LOTS	1 446	10 666	27 209	1.2	2.2	31.0	39.2 ±5.9	40.0 ±6.3	1 550 268	12 517	480 023
COMMERCIAL AND INDUSTRIAL . .	323	12 540	31 584	0.9	0.6	40.1	39.7 ±6.6	44.9 ±5.7	4 856 974	128 894	1 947 613
DELAWARE											
ALL TYPES OF PROPERTY	1 812	19 226	58 710	0.8	0.8	31.9	32.7 ±2.6	36.5 ±4.3	7 542 755	34 046	2 405 244
RESIDENTIAL (NONFARM), TOTAL .	1 094	14 358	41 626	0.7	0.8	32.9	34.5 ±2.7	36.6 ±4.5	5 428 801	35 077	1 784 635
SINGLE-FAMILY	1 052	13 999	40 218	0.7	0.8	33.0	34.8 ±2.8	36.5 ±4.5	5 390 004	34 846	1 776 584
MULTIFAMILY	(4)	(4)	(4)	(4)	(4)	(4)	(4) (4)	(4) (4)	(4)	(4)	(4)
ACREAGE	194	1 123	5 013	0.8	0.5	23.1	22.4 ±5.4	(4) (4)	991 310	38 472	228 757
VACANT PLATTED LOTS	448	863	4 824	1.3	0.9	22.5	17.9 ±7.3	(4) (4)	427 489	12 825	96 295
COMMERCIAL AND INDUSTRIAL . .	(4)	(4)	(4)	(4)	(4)	(4)	(4) (4)	(4) (4)	(4)	(4)	(4)

See footnotes at end of table.

218

Table 2. Measurable Sales of Ordinary Real Estate During A 6-Month Period, by Type of Property, by State: 1976—Continued

Item	Number of properties[1]	Assessed value (thousand dollars)	Aggregate sales price (thousand dollars)	Percent of assessment roll totals — Number of properties[1]	Percent of assessment roll totals — Assessed value	Statewide size-weighted average	Aggregate assessment-sales price ratio — Statewide	Aggregate assessment-sales price ratio — SMSA portion of State	Total (thousand dollars)	Average value per parcel (dollars)	Exhibit: Assessed value of all ordinary real estate 1976[3] (thousand dollars)
STATES--CONTINUED											
DISTRICT OF COLUMBIA											
ALL TYPES OF PROPERTY	3 630	136 409	201 913	2.6	2.7	68.0	67.6 ±3.7	67.6 ±3.7	7 407 482	52 125	5 035 159
RESIDENTIAL (NONFARM), TOTAL	3 240	119 086	179 133	2.8	2.8	66.9	66.5 ±2.8	66.5 ±2.8	6 287 606	54 664	4 205 048
SINGLE-FAMILY	2 715	102 535	155 435	2.6	2.9	65.0	66.0 ±3.1	66.0 ±3.1	5 515 873	52 591	3 584 669
MULTIFAMILY	525	16 551	23 698	5.2	2.7	65.5	69.8 ±6.8	69.8 ±6.8	947 319	93 433	620 379
ACREAGE	-	-	-	-	-	-	-	-	-	-	-
VACANT PLATTED LOTS	240	1 899	2 142	1.2	0.7	(4)	(4) (4)	(4) (4)	(4)	(4)	290 832
COMMERCIAL AND INDUSTRIAL	150	15 424	20 638	2.1	2.9	(4)	(4) (4)	(4) (4)	(4)	(4)	539 279
FLORIDA[5]											
ALL TYPES OF PROPERTY	163 432	3 271 695	5 537 926	3.6	4.1	59.4	59.1 ±1.6	59.5 ±1.7	133 293 064	29 607	79 119 108
RESIDENTIAL (NONFARM), TOTAL	107 647	2 509 379	4 059 500	4.3	4.6	61.4	61.8 ±1.2	61.9 ±1.2	88 212 143	34 956	54 127 880
SINGLE-FAMILY	100 934	2 322 671	3 762 639	4.3	4.9	60.6	61.7 ±1.2	61.8 ±1.3	78 887 217	33 631	47 840 636
MULTIFAMILY	6 713	186 708	296 861	3.8	3.0	65.3	62.9 ±4.9	64.4 ±5.2	9 625 755	54 111	6 287 244
ACREAGE	8 680	163 265	341 421	2.8	1.8	52.6	47.8 ±7.9	48.4 ±9.5	17 555 342	55 706	9 226 041
VACANT PLATTED LOTS	41 007	221 020	452 226	2.7	3.4	48.9	48.9 ±3.8	47.3 ±4.0	13 445 433	8 985	6 572 088
COMMERCIAL AND INDUSTRIAL	6 098	378 031	684 779	3.7	4.1	57.9	55.2 ±9.5	55.7 ±9.9	15 869 235	95 097	9 193 099
GEORGIA											
ALL TYPES OF PROPERTY	33 976	287 453	944 204	1.8	1.9	30.8	30.4 ±1.6	30.9 ±1.6	50 198 606	27 053	15 444 075
RESIDENTIAL (NONFARM), TOTAL	22 186	220 612	675 466	1.9	2.4	31.6	32.7 ±1.1	32.6 ±0.7	29 519 017	25 205	9 316 632
SINGLE-FAMILY	21 173	210 802	643 422	1.8	2.4	31.4	32.8 ±1.0	32.6 ±0.8	28 418 427	24 567	8 928 339
MULTIFAMILY	1 013	9 810	32 044	7.0	2.5	34.8	30.6 ±4.9	30.9 ±2.5	1 114 306	77 286	388 293
ACREAGE	3 783	25 232	130 768	1.3	0.7	19.5	19.3 ±4.9	16.8 ±7.5	18 007 331	60 772	3 512 765
VACANT PLATTED LOTS	7 103	17 154	62 319	2.3	2.7	28.7	27.5 ±3.3	26.3 ±3.7	2 206 864	7 051	633 076
COMMERCIAL AND INDUSTRIAL	904	24 455	75 651	1.2	1.2	32.3	32.3 ±4.5	34.6 ±2.4	6 134 761	81 722	1 981 602
HAWAII[6]											
ALL TYPES OF PROPERTY	2 800	79 242	187 879	1.1	1.2	43.0	42.2 ±7.9	50.4 ±2.7	15 983 593	63 229	6 878 164
RESIDENTIAL (NONFARM), TOTAL	1 630	64 309	129 240	1.2	1.2	49.5	49.8 ±2.4	50.9 ±2.9	10 866 465	76 706	5 382 957
SINGLE-FAMILY	1 520	59 641	119 182	1.8	1.6	50.2	50.0 ±2.6	51.4 ±3.2	7 208 971	84 121	3 621 662
MULTIFAMILY	(4)	(4)	(4)	(4)	(4)	(4)	(4) (4)	(4) (4)	(4)	(4)	(4)
ACREAGE	340	3 430	33 877	3.8	1.3	8.1	(4) (4)	(4) (4)	3 199 689	355 916	260 092
VACANT PLATTED LOTS	800	10 103	20 779	0.8	1.5	47.9	(4) (4)	(4) (4)	1 378 133	14 262	660 614
COMMERCIAL AND INDUSTRIAL	(4)	(4)	(4)	(4)	(4)	(4)	(4) (4)	(4) (4)	(4)	(4)	(4)
IDAHO											
ALL TYPES OF PROPERTY	11 407	26 171	305 311	2.8	2.5	9.1	8.6 ±0.6	8.7 ±0.3	11 593 519	28 201	1 054 650
RESIDENTIAL (NONFARM), TOTAL	7 507	20 723	217 739	3.9	4.0	9.5	9.5 ±4.5	8.9 ±0.2	5 379 034	28 101	512 805
SINGLE-FAMILY	7 211	19 371	205 793	3.8	3.9	9.4	9.4 ±0.4	8.9 ±0.2	5 319 189	27 986	501 164
MULTIFAMILY	296	1 352	11 946	22.0	11.6	12.8	11.3 ±2.4	(4) (4)	91 054	67 598	11 641
ACREAGE	1 412	2 659	44 836	1.1	0.7	6.3	5.9 ±2.2	(4) (4)	6 071 947	48 185	385 410
VACANT PLATTED LOTS	2 111	1 061	20 452	2.7	2.7	5.2	5.2 ±0.1	5.7 ±0.9	749 557	9 617	39 318
COMMERCIAL AND INDUSTRIAL	377	1 728	22 284	2.4	1.5	8.9	7.8 ±2.3	(4) (4)	1 310 697	83 330	117 117
ILLINOIS											
ALL TYPES OF PROPERTY	55 468	483 517	1 862 552	1.4	1.3	26.0	26.0 ±0.9	26.3 ±0.8	145 682 542	36 479	37 851 617
RESIDENTIAL (NONFARM), TOTAL	42 620	412 782	1 536 272	1.6	1.7	26.7	26.9 ±0.6	26.7 ±0.5	91 328 214	34 640	24 366 532
SINGLE-FAMILY	39 540	373 402	1 400 368	1.7	1.9	26.3	26.7 ±0.6	26.4 ±0.5	76 635 927	33 127	20 164 541
MULTIFAMILY	3 080	39 380	135 904	1.0	0.9	29.0	29.0 ±2.1	28.9 ±2.2	14 491 928	44 855	4 201 991
ACREAGE	2 789	25 940	165 756	0.5	0.4	15.2	15.6 ±2.5	14.7 ±5.1	47 869 027	94 017	7 274 466
VACANT PLATTED LOTS	8 663	14 870	57 778	1.3	1.3	29.0	25.7 ±2.2	25.8 ±2.1	4 049 545	6 105	1 175 807
COMMERCIAL AND INDUSTRIAL	1 396	29 925	102 746	0.8	0.6	29.6	29.1 ±6.1	32.3 ±5.2	17 029 853	92 192	5 034 812
INDIANA											
ALL TYPES OF PROPERTY	49 944	177 803	1 193 206	2.3	2.3	14.8	14.9 ±0.5	15.8 ±0.5	52 223 375	24 144	7 746 899
RESIDENTIAL (NONFARM), TOTAL	35 245	144 788	884 064	2.8	2.9	16.2	16.4 ±0.4	16.7 ±0.3	30 735 911	24 557	4 990 133
SINGLE-FAMILY	33 540	138 145	849 028	2.7	2.9	16.1	16.3 ±0.4	16.5 ±0.3	29 967 905	24 259	4 813 926
MULTIFAMILY	1 705	6 643	35 036	10.5	3.8	17.5	19.0 ±1.1	19.3 ±2.3	1 006 685	61 798	176 207
ACREAGE	4 661	13 147	187 095	1.2	0.7	7.6	7.0 ±1.4	8.2 ±3.5	23 191 260	62 168	1 768 762
VACANT PLATTED LOTS	8 602	4 635	40 524	1.8	2.4	10.5	11.4 ±2.0	11.7 ±2.2	1 864 530	3 991	195 449
COMMERCIAL AND INDUSTRIAL	1 436	15 233	81 523	2.0	1.9	18.5	18.7 ±2.7	16.0 ±3.0	4 277 526	60 101	792 555
IOWA											
ALL TYPES OF PROPERTY	20 877	408 281	573 884	1.0	1.2	70.0	71.1 ±1.9	74.9 ±2.7	49 818 563	24 848	34 860 654
RESIDENTIAL (NONFARM), TOTAL	16 062	359 550	485 332	2.2	2.6	71.8	74.1 ±1.3	76.9 ±1.5	19 053 820	25 946	13 687 373
SINGLE-FAMILY	15 424	338 235	457 079	2.1	2.5	71.8	74.0 ±1.3	76.6 ±1.3	18 486 968	25 535	13 268 018
MULTIFAMILY	638	21 315	28 253	6.1	5.1	77.5	75.4 ±7.1	80.9 ±11.9	540 832	52 038	419 355
ACREAGE	1 110	19 817	41 610	0.1	0.1	46.5	47.6 ±8.2	(4) (4)	38 274 611	38 347	17 785 805
VACANT PLATTED LOTS	3 063	7 175	20 366	1.7	2.7	26.4	35.2 ±5.7	33.5 ±8.1	989 097	5 371	260 987
COMMERCIAL AND INDUSTRIAL	642	21 739	26 576	0.7	0.7	82.4	81.8 ±16.3	(4) (4)	3 792 496	42 945	3 126 489
KANSAS											
ALL TYPES OF PROPERTY	28 431	79 739	649 383	2.0	2.1	12.3	12.3 ±0.5	12.9 ±0.5	31 408 946	21 966	3 849 770
RESIDENTIAL (NONFARM), TOTAL	19 526	64 554	497 630	2.9	3.5	12.8	13.0 ±0.4	13.4 ±0.5	14 425 260	21 097	1 850 517
SINGLE-FAMILY	18 786	61 687	478 513	3.1	3.5	12.7	12.9 ±0.4	13.4 ±0.5	13 983 791	22 763	1 770 567
MULTIFAMILY	740	2 867	19 117	1.1	3.6	13.7	15.0 ±1.1	14.6 ±1.3	581 502	8 376	79 950
ACREAGE	2 057	6 134	80 003	0.4	0.4	7.6	7.7 ±1.7	6.1 ±1.9	20 877 234	42 048	1 594 352
VACANT PLATTED LOTS	6 072	4 061	36 547	2.9	8.1	8.1	11.1 ±3.4	10.2 ±3.7	615 575	2 984	50 000
COMMERCIAL AND INDUSTRIAL	776	4 990	35 203	1.8	1.4	13.3	14.2 ±2.6	13.4 ±2.2	2 669 347	61 651	354 901

See footnotes at end of table.

Table 2. Measurable Sales of Ordinary Real Estate During A 6-Month Period, by Type of Property, by State: 1976—Continued

State	Ordinary real estate involved in measurable sales during a 6-month period					Percentage ratio of assessed value to sales price of sold properties			Approximate market value of all assessed ordinary real estate as indicated by measurable sales[2]		Exhibit: Assessed value of all ordinary real estate 1976[3]
	Number of properties[1]	Assessed value (thousand dollars)	Aggregate sales price (thousand dollars)	Percent of assessment roll totals — Number of properties[1]	Percent of assessment roll totals — Assessed value	Statewide size-weighted average	Aggregate assessment-sales price ratio — Statewide	Aggregate assessment-sales price ratio — SMSA portion of State	Total (thousand dollars)	Average value per parcel (dollars)	(thousand dollars)
STATES--CONTINUED											
KENTUCKY											
ALL TYPES OF PROPERTY.	21 879	425 749	585 179	2.1	2.0	72.0	72.8 ±1.8	76.6 ±2.3	29 778 205	28 423	21 437 458
RESIDENTIAL (NONFARM), TOTAL .	15 974	339 141	444 991	2.3	2.7	74.0	76.2 ±1.4	78.0 ±2.2	17 103 613	24 253	12 657 983
SINGLE-FAMILY.	15 357	318 785	417 581	2.2	2.6	74.0	76.3 ±1.3	78.3 ±1.9	16 569 256	23 828	12 258 690
MULTIFAMILY.	617	20 356	27 410	6.3	5.1	73.1	74.3 ±9.9	74.7±11.9	545 966	55 389	399 293
ACREAGE.	2 940	53 094	91 526	1.3	0.9	60.7	58.0 ±5.8	55.7±10.8	10 088 657	44 552	6 121 054
VACANT PLATTED LOTS.	2 343	11 769	17 104	3.2	3.2	66.3	68.8 ±9.6	83.3±13.9	552 680	7 486	366 328
COMMERCIAL AND INDUSTRIAL. . .	622	21 745	31 558	1.5	0.9	72.1	68.9 ±9.7	79.4 ±8.0	3 178 388	75 317	2 292 093
LOUISIANA											
ALL TYPES OF PROPERTY.	22 346	51 629	529 075	1.7	1.8	9.6	9.8 ±0.5	10.5 ±0.4	29 637 689	22 485	2 834 145
RESIDENTIAL (NONFARM), TOTAL .	14 294	42 784	416 629	1.6	2.0	9.4	10.3 ±0.5	10.8 ±0.4	22 971 366	26 035	2 152 556
SINGLE-FAMILY.	12 960	36 876	368 184	1.5	1.9	9.0	10.0 ±0.5	10.5 ±0.4	21 269 486	25 425	1 918 801
MULTIFAMILY.	1 334	5 908	48 445	2.9	2.5	12.3	12.2 ±1.5	12.2 ±1.5	1 895 994	41 427	233 755
ACREAGE.	2 400	2 164	47 688	1.5	0.9	4.7	4.5 ±1.1	5.9 ±2.4	5 343 209	34 004	248 751
VACANT PLATTED LOTS.	5 073	3 508	44 047	2.0	3.2	7.0	8.0 ±2.0	7.3 ±0.1	1 599 564	6 433	111 292
COMMERCIAL AND INDUSTRIAL. . .	579	3 173	20 711	1.9	1.0	19.8	15.3 ±4.2	16.0 ±4.9	1 625 791	54 182	321 546
MAINE											
ALL TYPES OF PROPERTY.	9 877	139 551	251 694	1.7	2.0	53.5	55.4 ±3.6	57.6 ±4.2	12 921 922	22 101	6 916 881
RESIDENTIAL (NONFARM), TOTAL .	6 888	110 696	190 807	1.9	2.1	55.8	58.0 ±3.9	59.3 ±3.9	9 275 393	24 977	5 177 983
SINGLE-FAMILY.	6 170	95 722	165 666	1.8	2.1	55.5	57.8 ±4.6	59.6 ±4.6	8 366 694	23 995	4 647 356
MULTIFAMILY.	718	14 974	25 141	3.2	2.8	60.3	59.6 ±4.9	57.9 ±7.1	880 634	38 837	530 627
ACREAGE.	1 449	8 293	23 950	1.4	1.7	31.5	34.6 ±4.9	28.8 ±9.6	1 536 913	14 550	484 815
VACANT PLATTED LOTS.	1 057	3 673	8 050	1.3	2.0	39.9	45.6 ±9.8	35.2 ±8.5	452 496	5 452	180 625
COMMERCIAL AND INDUSTRIAL. . .	483	16 889	28 887	2.0	1.6	64.3	58.5 ±8.9	66.0±14.4	1 670 176	67 635	1 073 458
MARYLAND[6]											
ALL TYPES OF PROPERTY.	27 473	419 600	1 126 985	2.0	2.2	36.6	37.2 ±1.3	37.2 ±1.5	52 611 270	38 367	19 246 441
RESIDENTIAL (NONFARM), TOTAL .	21 664	367 130	931 902	2.2	2.4	39.1	39.4 ±0.9	39.0 ±0.5	39 785 486	40 387	15 553 204
SINGLE-FAMILY.	20 624	352 136	894 764	2.1	2.4	39.1	39.4 ±0.9	38.9 ±0.5	38 271 511	39 848	14 955 930
MULTIFAMILY.	1 040	14 994	37 138	4.2	2.5	40.8	40.4 ±3.3	41.0 ±3.5	1 465 443	59 378	597 274
ACREAGE.	2 251	19 538	100 905	2.6	1.7	19.0	19.4 ±7.8	14.7 ±7.4	5 936 509	69 749	1 127 507
VACANT PLATTED LOTS.	3 037	13 187	38 374	1.2	1.6	29.5	34.4 ±2.9	33.0 ±3.6	2 751 924	10 638	812 679
COMMERCIAL AND INDUSTRIAL. . .	(4)	(4)	(4)	(4)	(4)	(4)	(4) (4)	(4) (4)	(4)	(4)	(4)
MASSACHUSETTS											
ALL TYPES OF PROPERTY.	29 017	502 576	1 116 027	1.6	1.9	42.3	45.0 ±3.3	43.8 ±3.4	61 120 246	33 164	25 880 659
RESIDENTIAL (NONFARM), TOTAL .	24 890	447 968	1 007 558	1.9	2.1	41.3	44.5 ±3.4	44.9 ±3.3	51 633 345	38 528	21 343 182
SINGLE-FAMILY.	21 030	395 999	859 748	1.9	2.2	42.3	46.1 ±3.4	44.9 ±3.3	43 316 930	38 475	18 335 147
MULTIFAMILY.	3 860	51 969	147 810	1.8	1.7	30.8	35.2 ±4.4	33.9 ±4.4	9 764 177	45 566	3 008 035
ACREAGE.	1 016	6 807	16 555	1.7	2.9	29.9	41.1±13.6	40.4±14.5	773 867	12 975	231 380
VACANT PLATTED LOTS.	1 977	8 669	18 645	0.5	1.0	35.3	46.5±11.1	36.4 ±5.0	2 344 556	6 510	826 872
COMMERCIAL AND INDUSTRIAL. . .	1 134	39 132	73 269	1.4	1.1	59.8	53.4 ±6.6	53.7 ±7.2	5 814 139	70 036	3 479 225
MICHIGAN											
ALL TYPES OF PROPERTY.	50 923	559 492	1 377 884	1.4	1.5	40.6	40.6 ±0.8	41.7 ±0.7	92 285 396	25 149	37 510 262
RESIDENTIAL (NONFARM), TOTAL .	38 885	481 853	1 169 466	1.6	1.8	40.5	41.2 ±0.7	41.7 ±0.7	67 522 471	27 164	27 338 473
SINGLE-FAMILY.	37 786	468 386	1 138 025	1.6	1.8	40.5	41.2 ±0.7	41.7 ±0.7	63 912 058	26 846	25 864 356
MULTIFAMILY.	1 099	13 467	31 441	1.0	0.9	44.6	42.8 ±7.5	42.6 ±9.8	3 308 566	31 500	1 474 117
ACREAGE.	4 120	29 631	89 258	1.0	0.7	32.8	33.2 ±3.1	35.9 ±3.9	12 839 418	30 183	4 213 141
VACANT PLATTED LOTS.	6 699	18 913	44 880	1.1	1.7	40.5	42.1 ±2.9	43.3 ±3.5	2 702 561	4 517	1 095 223
COMMERCIAL AND INDUSTRIAL. . .	1 219	29 095	74 280	0.8	0.6	41.5	39.2 ±8.7	44.8 ±8.9	11 730 789	73 232	4 863 425
MINNESOTA											
ALL TYPES OF PROPERTY.	36 986	205 691	956 633	1.9	1.8	21.5	21.5 ±0.6	22.7 ±0.5	52 270 602	27 291	11 259 072
RESIDENTIAL (NONFARM), TOTAL .	23 350	177 845	787 328	2.4	2.5	22.4	22.6 ±0.5	23.5 ±0.4	31 820 015	32 509	7 121 837
SINGLE-FAMILY.	22 530	168 965	751 735	2.4	2.5	22.3	22.5 ±0.5	23.4 ±0.4	30 265 894	31 706	6 738 583
MULTIFAMILY.	820	8 880	35 593	3.4	2.3	24.9	24.9 ±3.6	24.3 ±3.3	1 541 313	63 617	383 254
ACREAGE.	5 594	12 784	95 705	1.0	0.5	14.1	13.4 ±2.5	12.5 ±2.5	18 349 656	33 571	2 583 845
VACANT PLATTED LOTS.	7 340	6 730	40 874	2.4	3.5	15.4	16.5 ±2.2	15.7 ±2.6	1 246 408	4 145	191 934
COMMERCIAL AND INDUSTRIAL. . .	702	8 332	32 726	0.8	0.6	27.8	25.5 ±4.7	(4) (4)	4 902 599	54 921	1 361 456
MISSISSIPPI											
ALL TYPES OF PROPERTY.	13 655	30 811	292 904	1.2	1.7	9.6	10.5 ±1.2	10.5 ±0.5	18 544 272	16 246	1 774 064
RESIDENTIAL (NONFARM), TOTAL .	8 486	23 879	206 810	1.6	2.3	10.6	11.5 ±0.6	10.8 ±0.5	9 955 924	18 700	1 052 357
SINGLE-FAMILY.	8 225	22 765	197 164	1.6	2.2	10.5	11.5 ±0.6	10.9 ±0.5	9 652 447	18 329	1 017 575
MULTIFAMILY.	261	1 114	9 646	4.5	3.2	11.0	11.5 ±2.9	(4) (4)	314 987	54 374	34 782
ACREAGE.	1 810	2 494	50 434	0.7	0.6	5.0	4.9 ±1.8	3.4 ±1.4	8 814 892	31 909	439 235
VACANT PLATTED LOTS.	2 935	1 495	16 101	1.0	2.0	7.1	9.3 ±2.8	7.1 ±1.4	1 037 278	3 435	73 365
COMMERCIAL AND INDUSTRIAL. . .	424	2 943	19 559	1.4	1.4	13.9	15.0 ±2.9	(4) (4)	1 502 284	48 747	209 107
MISSOURI											
ALL TYPES OF PROPERTY.	39 069	152 279	959 536	1.8	1.9	15.7	15.9 ±1.7	18.7 ±0.9	51 444 189	23 439	8 060 236
RESIDENTIAL (NONFARM), TOTAL .	24 390	111 347	634 643	2.1	2.2	17.5	17.5 ±1.8	19.2 ±0.7	29 507 642	25 730	5 167 348
SINGLE-FAMILY.	23 200	102 514	596 348	2.1	2.1	17.2	17.2 ±1.8	18.9 ±0.8	27 884 740	25 303	4 781 168
MULTIFAMILY.	1 190	8 833	38 295	2.5	2.3	23.8	23.1 ±2.6	23.2 ±2.8	1 623 213	34 151	386 180
ACREAGE.	6 377	17 378	182 219	1.3	1.1	9.8	9.5 ±1.2	8.1 ±2.5	15 610 945	31 012	1 529 698
VACANT PLATTED LOTS.	6 603	5 871	44 653	1.4	1.7	12.3	13.1 ±4.6	13.2 ±4.8	2 752 197	5 808	337 814
COMMERCIAL AND INDUSTRIAL. . .	1 699	17 683	98 021	2.4	1.7	20.8	18.0 ±7.2	25.6 ±5.7	4 934 632	69 751	1 025 376

See footnotes at end of table

220

Item	Number of properties[1]	Assessed value (thousand dollars)	Aggregate sales price (thousand dollars)	Percent of assessment roll totals — Number of properties[1]	Percent of assessment roll totals — Assessed value	Statewide size-weighted average	Aggregate assessment-sales price ratio — Statewide	Aggregate assessment-sales price ratio — SMSA portion of State	Approximate market value — Total (thousand dollars)	Approximate market value — Average value per parcel (dollars)	Exhibit: Assessed value of all ordinary real estate 1976[3] (thousand dollars)
STATES--CONTINUED											
MONTANA[6]											
ALL TYPES OF PROPERTY	11 838	17 002	325 655	2.7	3.2	5.3	5.2 ±0.7	6.1 ±0.6	10 084 574	22 974	536 764
RESIDENTIAL (NONFARM), TOTAL	6 919	11 687	193 057	3.6	4.3	5.7	6.1 ±0.9	6.0 ±0.5	4 773 958	24 957	271 521
SINGLE-FAMILY	6 333	10 314	173 572	3.4	4.0	5.6	5.9 ±0.9	5.6 ±0.4	4 571 126	24 473	258 128
MULTIFAMILY	586	1 373	19 485	13.0	10.3	7.2	7.0 ±2.4	(⁴) (⁴)	186 077	41 277	13 393
ACREAGE	2 357	2 791	88 681	1.5	1.6	3.6	3.1 ±2.5	(⁴) (⁴)	4 859 480	29 989	177 241
VACANT PLATTED LOTS	2 254	1 337	26 298	3.2	8.6	4.2	5.1 ±2.2	4.4 1.0	370 969	5 329	15 489
COMMERCIAL AND INDUSTRIAL	(⁴)	(⁴)	(⁴)	(⁴)	(⁴)	(⁴)	(⁴) (⁴)	(⁴) (⁴)	(⁴)	(⁴)	(⁴)
NEBRASKA											
ALL TYPES OF PROPERTY	18 778	98 175	547 209	2.5	2.2	18.6	17.9 ±1.4	19.2 ±1.3	24 146 955	32 128	4 499 761
RESIDENTIAL (NONFARM), TOTAL	14 467	86 111	444 027	4.1	5.3	18.4	19.4 ±1.0	20.1 ±0.7	8 783 581	24 952	1 612 553
SINGLE-FAMILY	13 607	76 923	402 907	4.0	5.0	18.2	19.1 ±0.9	20.0 ±0.6	8 374 520	24 371	1 527 156
MULTIFAMILY	860	9 188	41 120	10.2	10.8	21.3	22.3 ±4.5	21.1 ±3.7	400 769	47 694	85 397
ACREAGE	1 038	5 377	55 538	0.4	0.2	9.8	9.7 ±2.5	(⁴) (⁴)	24 356 183	88 285	2 382 504
VACANT PLATTED LOTS	2 724	3 051	24 237	3.1	4.9	10.3	12.6 ±2.9	11.8 ±3.9	600 845	6 903	61 967
COMMERCIAL AND INDUSTRIAL	549	3 636	23 407	1.5	0.8	25.5	15.5 ±14.1	(⁴) (⁴)	1 735 982	47 370	442 737
NEVADA											
ALL TYPES OF PROPERTY	7 598	53 790	235 377	2.9	2.9	20.8	22.9 ±2.1	23.4 ±2.4	8 989 780	33 761	1 870 423
RESIDENTIAL (NONFARM), TOTAL	5 493	46 806	200 189	3.8	3.7	22.6	23.4 ±2.5	23.8 ±2.7	5 532 231	37 942	1 250 303
SINGLE-FAMILY	5 195	42 367	170 475	3.7	3.6	24.2	24.9 ±0.8	25.4 ±0.8	4 883 849	34 387	1 180 357
MULTIFAMILY	298	4 439	29 714	7.9	6.3	15.4	14.9 ±8.8	15.0 ±9.1	453 117	119 746	69 946
ACREAGE	417	1 176	9 781	1.0	0.5	12.4	12.0 ±2.8	13.1 ±3.1	1 992 636	49 745	247 212
VACANT PLATTED LOTS	1 561	2 889	14 037	2.1	2.8	19.4	20.6 ±2.4	19.2 ±2.9	538 947	7 391	104 601
COMMERCIAL AND INDUSTRIAL	(⁴)	(⁴)	(⁴)	(⁴)	(⁴)	(⁴)	(⁴) (⁴)	(⁴) (⁴)	(⁴)	(⁴)	(⁴)
NEW HAMPSHIRE											
ALL TYPES OF PROPERTY	6 709	126 953	211 082	1.8	2.0	58.9	60.1 ±3.9	52.9 ±3.0	10 895 585	28 835	6 416 293
RESIDENTIAL (NONFARM), TOTAL	4 762	99 023	157 839	1.8	2.0	61.4	62.7 ±3.7	54.8 ±2.8	8 078 092	30 940	4 959 371
SINGLE-FAMILY	4 175	82 450	133 109	1.7	1.8	61.1	61.9 ±3.3	55.2 ±3.1	7 294 830	30 196	4 459 891
MULTIFAMILY	587	16 573	24 730	3.0	3.3	65.4	67.0 ±6.6	52.6 ±4.3	763 177	39 135	499 480
ACREAGE	970	10 109	20 144	1.5	2.5	42.4	50.2 ±10.1	39.6 ±0.4	939 569	14 646	398 400
VACANT PLATTED LOTS	611	3 029	6 242	1.8	3.2	42.0	48.5 ±19.8	34.6 ±8.3	223 888	6 558	94 062
COMMERCIAL AND INDUSTRIAL	366	14 792	26 857	2.0	1.5	58.2	55.1 ±7.7	(⁴) (⁴)	1 656 850	89 652	964 460
NEW JERSEY											
ALL TYPES OF PROPERTY	27 729	867 687	1 268 810	1.3	1.4	67.6	68.4 ±1.5	68.8 ±1.6	88 586 120	40 806	59 920 613
RESIDENTIAL (NONFARM), TOTAL	23 283	734 688	1 070 395	1.4	1.5	68.2	68.6 ±1.3	68.5 ±1.3	71 061 182	43 459	48 436 402
SINGLE-FAMILY	20 751	639 673	936 948	1.4	1.5	67.3	68.3 ±1.4	68.1 ±1.3	64 131 073	41 766	43 190 084
MULTIFAMILY	2 532	95 015	133 447	2.5	1.8	78.4	71.2 ±4.5	71.1 ±4.7	6 695 769	67 182	5 246 318
ACREAGE	1 000	18 645	39 681	1.5	1.5	48.3	47.0 ±12.2	50.9 ±16.1	2 632 138	38 808	1 271 877
VACANT PLATTED LOTS	2 092	15 538	27 127	0.6	0.6	56.9	57.3 ±9.8	55.2 ±11.9	4 564 590	12 864	2 595 431
COMMERCIAL AND INDUSTRIAL	1 354	98 816	131 607	1.2	1.3	73.0	75.1 ±8.5	77.3 ±8.8	10 431 979	92 215	7 616 903
NEW MEXICO											
ALL TYPES OF PROPERTY	9 738	28 602	167 788	1.3	1.4	17.1	17.0 ±1.5	20.7 ±1.4	11 642 234	15 897	1 989 564
RESIDENTIAL (NONFARM), TOTAL	4 244	20 786	112 087	1.6	1.7	18.3	18.5 ±1.1	20.5 ±0.9	6 609 499	25 291	1 212 772
SINGLE-FAMILY	4 023	18 605	103 094	1.6	1.6	17.9	18.0 ±0.8	20.5 ±1.0	6 325 365	24 447	1 131 614
MULTIFAMILY	(⁴)	(⁴)	(⁴)	(⁴)	(⁴)	(⁴)	(⁴) (⁴)	(⁴) (⁴)	(⁴)	(⁴)	(⁴)
ACREAGE	929	1 856	20 681	0.8	1.0	9.5	9.0 ±3.9	(⁴) (⁴)	2 009 767	17 565	191 399
VACANT PLATTED LOTS	4 156	2 466	14 504	1.2	1.1	17.8	17.0 ±2.5	18.4 ±3.7	1 279 453	3 768	227 198
COMMERCIAL AND INDUSTRIAL	409	3 494	20 516	2.4	1.0	18.2	17.0 ±4.2	(⁴) (⁴)	1 967 754	115 662	358 195
NEW YORK											
ALL TYPES OF PROPERTY	72 629	738 268	2 722 547	1.7	1.7	27.2	27.1 ±1.1	24.9 ±1.0	159 214 086	36 450	43 286 510
RESIDENTIAL (NONFARM), TOTAL	58 625	614 270	2 312 407	1.8	1.9	25.7	26.6 ±1.1	24.1 ±1.0	127 018 350	38 605	32 631 780
SINGLE-FAMILY	50 301	474 824	1 908 450	1.9	2.1	23.7	24.9 ±0.9	21.9 ±0.8	97 548 186	36 580	23 073 820
MULTIFAMILY	8 324	139 446	403 957	1.3	1.5	32.3	34.5 ±4.2	34.1 ±4.5	29 610 548	47 490	9 557 960
ACREAGE	5 346	26 215	97 459	1.8	1.6	29.9	26.9 ±7.9	25.9 ±7.9	5 333 757	18 016	1 595 020
VACANT PLATTED LOTS	5 649	9 731	52 861	1.0	0.7	27.4	18.4 ±4.0	15.6 ±3.9	5 048 343	9 267	1 382 309
COMMERCIAL AND INDUSTRIAL	3 009	88 052	259 820	1.3	1.1	35.2	33.9 ±5.3	33.5 ±5.4	21 825 994	92 134	7 677 401
NORTH CAROLINA											
ALL TYPES OF PROPERTY	59 902	792 648	1 272 995	2.5	2.4	63.6	62.3 ±6.3	66.4 ±1.7	51 719 213	21 957	32 907 745
RESIDENTIAL (NONFARM), TOTAL	30 541	590 112	919 989	2.5	2.8	61.6	64.1 ±5.3	67.8 ±1.5	33 803 306	27 167	20 818 582
SINGLE-FAMILY	29 749	573 181	891 997	2.4	2.9	61.2	64.3 ±5.4	68.0 ±1.6	32 750 734	26 742	20 047 357
MULTIFAMILY	792	16 931	27 992	4.1	2.2	66.3	60.5 ±5.8	63.1 ±5.3	1 162 965	59 508	771 225
ACREAGE	11 949	99 961	171 107	2.5	1.6	65.5	58.4 ±22.2	48.8 ±8.8	9 547 363	20 284	6 258 176
VACANT PLATTED LOTS	15 942	56 993	105 884	2.9	3.0	53.7	53.8 ±6.3	62.2 ±6.6	3 577 029	6 406	1 920 950
COMMERCIAL AND INDUSTRIAL	1 470	45 582	76 015	1.8	1.2	66.4	60.0 ±9.1	65.3 ±15.2	5 891 076	71 748	3 910 037
NORTH DAKOTA											
ALL TYPES OF PROPERTY	7 350	18 539	253 848	1.5	2.9	6.5	7.3 ±0.9	5.5 ±0.1	9 706 797	20 357	631 163
RESIDENTIAL (NONFARM), TOTAL	6 215	16 159	215 503	5.5	8.3	6.8	7.5 ±0.9	5.5 ±0.1	2 850 318	25 288	194 773
SINGLE-FAMILY	5 716	14 537	196 579	5.2	8.3	6.5	7.4 ±0.9	5.5 ±0.1	2 686 404	24 380	175 306
MULTIFAMILY	499	1 622	18 924	19.8	8.3	13.0	8.6 ±2.4	(⁴) (⁴)	150 241	59 501	19 467
ACREAGE	359	1 275	24 584	0.1	0.4	5.0	5.2 ±1.3	(⁴) (⁴)	7 215 788	26 611	362 348
VACANT PLATTED LOTS	568	241	4 383	0.8	4.4	5.7	5.5 ±1.8	(⁴) (⁴)	97 408	1 308	5 518
COMMERCIAL AND INDUSTRIAL	208	864	9 378	1.1	1.3	8.5	9.2 ±3.3	(⁴) (⁴)	810 894	43 894	68 524

See footnotes at end of table.

Table 2. Measurable Sales of Ordinary Real Estate During A 6-Month Period, by Type of Property, by State: 1976—Continued

State	Ordinary real estate involved in measurable sales during a 6-month period					Percentage ratio of assessed value to sales price of sold properties			Approximate market value of all assessed ordinary real estate as indicated by measurable sales[2]		Exhibit: Assessed value of all ordinary real estate 1976[3]
				Percent of assessment roll totals		Statewide size-weighted average	Aggregate assessment-sales price ratio				
	Number of properties[1]	Assessed value (thousand dollars)	Aggregate sales price (thousand dollars)	Number of properties[1]	Assessed value		Statewide	SMSA portion of State	Total (thousand dollars)	Average value per parcel (dollars)	(thousand dollars)
STATES--CONTINUED											
OHIO											
ALL TYPES OF PROPERTY	91 331	767 259	2 810 762	2.0	2.2	27.3	27.3 ±0.8	28.3 ±0.7	126 083 598	27 945	34 423 436
RESIDENTIAL (NONFARM), TOTAL	67 953	624 824	2 211 639	2.5	2.6	28.1	28.3 ±0.5	28.7 ±0.5	86 703 864	31 567	24 364 228
SINGLE-FAMILY	63 262	571 342	2 024 548	2.4	2.5	28.0	28.2 ±0.5	28.7 ±0.4	80 475 434	31 022	22 556 640
MULTIFAMILY	4 691	53 482	187 091	3.1	3.0	29.1	28.6 ±2.6	28.7 ±2.8	6 205 079	40 671	1 807 588
ACREAGE	7 371	56 210	289 381	1.4	1.2	18.6	19.4 ±2.8	21.6 ±3.7	24 195 661	47 265	4 506 995
VACANT PLATTED LOTS	12 916	22 844	88 955	1.3	1.8	23.6	25.7 ±2.0	25.7 ±2.3	5 390 276	5 279	1 272 480
COMMERCIAL AND INDUSTRIAL	3 091	63 381	220 787	1.3	1.5	31.1	28.7 ±5.2,	32.0 ±4.9	13 740 236	59 205	4 279 733
OKLAHOMA											
ALL TYPES OF PROPERTY	47 297	92 432	928 792	2.7	3.0	9.9	10.0 ±0.9	11.6 ±1.5	31 384 280	18 181	3 117 594
RESIDENTIAL (NONFARM), TOTAL	25 513	71 876	574 861	3.3	3.7	12.4	12.5 ±0.8	13.9 ±0.4	15 724 572	20 287	1 950 535
SINGLE-FAMILY	24 487	67 866	542 672	3.2	3.6	12.4	12.5 ±0.7	13.8 ±0.4	15 263 396	19 899	1 885 955
MULTIFAMILY	1 026	4 010	32 189	12.7	6.2	15.2	12.5 ±2.3	14.7 ±2.4	425 152	52 729	64 580
ACREAGE	6 000	7 898	180 507	1.7	1.1	4.7	4.4 ±1.3	5.9 ±1.6	15 271 526	43 281	718 581
VACANT PLATTED LOTS	13 730	4 607	71 707	2.5	5.5	5.6	6.4 ±1.5	5.7 ±1.8	1 489 147	2 765	83 117
COMMERCIAL AND INDUSTRIAL	2 054	8 051	101 717	3.4	2.2	8.7	7.9 ±5.2	7.2 ±5.3	4 219 325	70 783	365 361
OREGON											
ALL TYPES OF PROPERTY	50 735	1 029 571	1 424 836	4.5	4.3	71.5	72.3 ±2.2	76.7 ±2.3	33 383 725	29 638	23 861 693
RESIDENTIAL (NONFARM), TOTAL	32 831	820 179	1 084 561	5.4	5.6	74.9	75.6 ±2.2	78.3 ±2.2	19 454 531	32 118	14 568 547
SINGLE-FAMILY	31 145	753 565	999 391	5.3	5.6	74.8	75.4 ±2.1	78.3 ±1.9	18 121 980	30 659	13 556 307
MULTIFAMILY	1 686	66 614	85 170	11.5	6.6	83.5	78.2±11.1	77.6±16.1	1 212 272	82 777	1 012 240
ACREAGE	6 659	99 857	180 213	3.4	2.2	57.5	55.4 ±6.8	64.5±11.3	8 058 707	41 634	4 631 809
VACANT PLATTED LOTS	10 126	50 721	86 188	3.8	4.5	53.2	58.8 ±8.5	69.9 ±6.3	2 115 925	8 034	1 125 912
COMMERCIAL AND INDUSTRIAL	1 119	58 814	73 874	1.8	1.7	82.6	79.6±15.0	(4) (4)	4 282 421	67 207	3 535 425
PENNSYLVANIA											
ALL TYPES OF PROPERTY	63 245	323 029	1 781 689	1.5	1.6	17.9	18.1 ±0.7	18.6 ±0.8	114 346 987	27 003	20 425 841
RESIDENTIAL (NONFARM), TOTAL	47 509	258 792	1 450 577	1.5	1.6	17.2	17.8 ±0.6	18.2 ±0.7	93 993 512	29 198	16 199 184
SINGLE-FAMILY	43 261	224 315	1 302 920	1.4	1.5	16.8	17.2 ±0.5	17.5 ±5.3	90 208 452	29 098	15 172 142
MULTIFAMILY	4 248	34 477	147 657	3.6	3.4	23.4	23.3 ±3.4	24.2 ±3.8	4 380 161	36 816	1 027 042
ACREAGE	5 834	15 308	133 000	2.1	1.6	12.2	11.5 ±1.9	11.3 ±2.5	7 814 950	28 271	956 598
VACANT PLATTED LOTS	7 391	8 682	51 488	1.3	2.0	15.1	16.9 ±2.2	16.5 ±2.5	2 941 180	5 231	442 991
COMMERCIAL AND INDUSTRIAL	2 511	40 247	146 624	1.4	1.4	27.8	27.4 ±5.4	29.3 ±6.6	10 151 737	57 450	2 827 068
RHODE ISLAND											
ALL TYPES OF PROPERTY	5 194	77 434	169 101	1.5	1.9	43.7	45.8 ±5.8	48.0 ±7.4	9 556 386	27 084	4 178 814
RESIDENTIAL (NONFARM), TOTAL	3 772	64 492	138 557	1.6	2.0	43.0	46.5 ±5.7	48.5 ±7.3	7 683 774	33 015	3 304 437
SINGLE-FAMILY	3 071	53 544	117 637	1.5	1.9	41.1	45.5 ±6.8	47.6 ±8.7	6 742 340	33 824	2 773 514
MULTIFAMILY	701	10 948	20 920	2.1	2.1	51.9	52.3 ±4.3	53.0 ±3.6	1 023 850	30 651	530 923
ACREAGE	164	1 033	6 442	4.2	1.7	15.3	16.0 ±7.8	(4) (4)	385 931	98 779	59 133
VACANT PLATTED LOTS	1 025	3 071	8 475	1.0	1.5	32.3	36.2 ±8.1	37.4±11.2	650 492	6 528	209 988
COMMERCIAL AND INDUSTRIAL	233	8 838	15 627	1.4	1.5	58.5	56.6±23.4	64.5±29.8	1 033 935	62 470	605 256
SOUTH CAROLINA[6]											
ALL TYPES OF PROPERTY	21 986	16 144	503 769	1.7	2.0	3.3	3.2 ±0.4	3.3 ±0.2	24 761 546	19 555	811 871
RESIDENTIAL (NONFARM), TOTAL	13 904	12 475	380 772	1.9	2.3	3.2	3.3 ±0.2	3.4 ±0.1	16 434 746	22 127	531 934
SINGLE-FAMILY	13 492	11 942	366 277	1.8	2.4	3.2	3.3 ±0.2	3.4 ±0.1	15 925 466	21 776	505 616
MULTIFAMILY	412	533	14 495	3.6	2.0	4.5	3.7 ±1.0	3.1 ±0.9	590 201	51 799	26 318
ACREAGE	2 104	1 055	56 072	1.0	0.7	1.9	1.9 ±0.5	2.0 ±0.9	7 683 138	35 921	146 540
VACANT PLATTED LOTS	5 324	1 153	34 712	1.9	2.5	3.4	3.3 ±0.4	2.9 ±0.8	1 353 609	4 778	45 686
COMMERCIAL AND INDUSTRIAL	654	1 461	32 213	2.5	1.7	4.8	4.5 ±1.7	3.9 ±1.9	1 839 324	69 740	87 711
SOUTH DAKOTA											
ALL TYPES OF PROPERTY	5 477	35 012	134 241	1.1	1.3	25.6	26.1 ±2.2	31.3 ±1.1	10 740 677	20 691	2 748 463
RESIDENTIAL (NONFARM), TOTAL	3 647	25 866	91 202	2.5	2.9	28.8	28.4 ±1.2	31.4 ±1.1	3 130 940	21 839	902 129
SINGLE-FAMILY	3 486	24 367	86 746	2.5	2.9	28.0	28.1 ±1.3	31.7 ±1.1	3 042 430	21 489	851 717
MULTIFAMILY	161	1 499	4 456	9.0	3.0	38.9	33.6 ±6.2	(4) (4)	129 675	72 525	50 412
ACREAGE	618	3 910	24 541	0.2	0.3	15.1	15.9 ±4.2	(4) (4)	10 249 549	34 319	1 551 722
VACANT PLATTED LOTS	916	1 032	4 877	1.6	2.4	21.5	21.2 ±3.2	(4) (4)	195 754	3 498	42 129
COMMERCIAL AND INDUSTRIAL	296	4 204	13 621	1.4	1.7	29.8	30.9 ±4.9	(4) (4)	846 661	40 090	252 483
TENNESSEE[7]											
ALL TYPES OF PROPERTY	44 131	175 710	1 111 176	2.5	2.7	16.2	15.8 ±0.5	16.8 ±0.6	40 133 166	23 032	6 520 304
RESIDENTIAL (NONFARM), TOTAL	29 574	134 699	841 091	2.6	3.3	15.3	16.0 ±0.3	16.6 ±0.3	26 315 806	23 525	4 027 601
SINGLE-FAMILY	28 447	125 923	805 059	2.6	3.3	15.0	15.6 ±0.3	16.2 ±0.3	25 810 637	23 549	3 862 341
MULTIFAMILY	1 127	8 776	36 032	5.0	5.3	25.9	24.4 ±3.1	25.2 ±3.4	637 606	28 196	165 260
ACREAGE	5 061	13 660	143 352	2.1	1.3	9.8	9.5 ±1.4	9.5 ±3.2	10 557 536	44 411	1 035 038
VACANT PLATTED LOTS	8 193	9 516	58 334	2.7	4.1	15.5	16.3 ±1.4	18.0 ±2.1	1 488 208	4 827	230 939
COMMERCIAL AND INDUSTRIAL	1 303	17 835	68 399	1.7	1.5	27.6	26.1 ±3.6	27.9 ±4.9	4 445 794	57 154	1 226 726
TEXAS											
ALL TYPES OF PROPERTY	119 370	379 927	2 734 533	2.1	2.2	13.8	13.9 ±0.5	14.2 ±0.4	123 762 651	21 383	17 126 227
RESIDENTIAL (NONFARM), TOTAL	71 322	302 948	2 059 653	2.4	2.8	14.3	14.7 ±0.5	14.7 ±0.4	75 145 596	25 332	10 732 236
SINGLE-FAMILY	68 344	279 190	1 912 815	2.3	2.7	14.2	14.6 ±0.4	14.6 ±0.3	72 817 488	24 895	10 342 578
MULTIFAMILY	2 978	23 758	146 838	7.2	6.1	16.3	16.2 ±3.7	15.6 ±3.7	2 392 374	57 829	389 658
ACREAGE	9 014	23 063	282 148	0.7	0.7	8.7	8.2 ±1.4	9.7 ±1.8	39 754 777	32 747	3 445 565
VACANT PLATTED LOTS	36 017	26 938	219 669	2.5	3.5	11.5	12.3 ±1.0	12.3 ±1.0	6 782 083	4 697	777 075
COMMERCIAL AND INDUSTRIAL	3 017	26 978	173 063	1.8	1.2	17.1	15.6 ±3.8	15.1 ±4.1	12 676 560	77 465	2 171 351

See footnotes at end of table.

Table 2. Measurable Sales of Ordinary Real Estate During A 6-Month Period, by Type of Property, by State: 1976—Continued

State	Ordinary real estate involved in measurable sales during a 6-month period					Percentage ratio of assessed value to sales price of sold properties			Approximate market value of all assessed ordinary real estate as indicated by measurable sales[2]		Exhibit: Assessed value of all ordinary real estate 1976[3]
	Number of properties[1]	Assessed value (thousand dollars)	Aggregate sales price (thousand dollars)	Percent of assessment roll totals		Statewide size-weighted average	Aggregate assessment-sales price ratio		Total (thousand dollars)	Average value per parcel (dollars)	(thousand dollars)
				Number of properties[1]	Assessed value		Statewide	SMSA portion of State			
STATES--CONTINUED											
UTAH											
ALL TYPES OF PROPERTY	9 809	35 608	274 391	1.8	2.1	13.1	13.0 ±1.2	13.4 ±0.5	13 276 665	25 013	1 734 426
RESIDENTIAL (NONFARM), TOTAL	6 605	29 024	223 005	2.2	2.4	12.8	13.0 ±1.1	13.5 ±0.4	9 552 825	32 082	1 225 364
SINGLE-FAMILY	6 005	26 196	198 516	2.1	2.2	13.1	13.2 ±0.8	13.5 ±0.4	9 000 002	30 984	1 178 942
MULTIFAMILY	600	2 828	24 489	8.2	6.1	13.1	11.5 ±3.7	14.0 ±1.7	355 570	48 822	46 422
ACREAGE	935	2 177	21 155	1.0	1.0	11.2	10.3 ±3.8	13.1 ±6.8	1 930 395	19 660	216 971
VACANT PLATTED LOTS	1 975	2 773	17 173	1.6	2.8	15.2	16.1 ±2.6	13.8 ±1.7	646 723	5 388	98 354
COMMERCIAL AND INDUSTRIAL	(4)	(4)	(4)	(4)	(4)	(4)	(4) (4)	(4) (4)	(4)	(4)	(4)
VERMONT											
ALL TYPES OF PROPERTY	4 532	47 312	143 588	2.0	2.4	31.8	32.9 ±3.3	(8) -	6 213 959	27 344	1 973 880
RESIDENTIAL (NONFARM), TOTAL	3 364	36 374	109 498	2.2	2.6	31.9	33.2 ±2.7	(8) -	4 379 780	28 074	1 396 355
SINGLE-FAMILY	2 984	32 319	95 935	2.0	2.4	32.2	33.7 ±2.9	(8) -	4 173 899	27 585	1 343 043
MULTIFAMILY	380	4 055	13 563	8.1	7.6	29.2	29.9 ±3.1	(8) -	182 534	38 870	53 312
ACREAGE	676	4 198	13 111	1.2	1.3	30.6	32.0 ±6.4	(8) -	1 051 850	18 283	322 313
VACANT PLATTED LOTS	234	480	2 039	10.8	24.4	25.3	23.5 ±6.9	(8) -	7 765	3 572	1 967
COMMERCIAL AND INDUSTRIAL	258	6 260	18 940	2.2	2.5	31.3	33.1 ±10.5	(8) -	810 005	70 209	253 245
VIRGINIA											
ALL TYPES OF PROPERTY	43 618	542 854	1 555 862	2.2	2.8	32.8	34.9 ±3.3	40.6 ±2.3	59 567 105	29 839	19 537 365
RESIDENTIAL (NONFARM), TOTAL	30 300	467 298	1 256 272	2.6	3.3	33.6	37.2 ±2.7	41.6 ±2.1	42 397 471	36 361	14 251 062
SINGLE-FAMILY	29 075	450 561	1 206 436	2.6	3.5	32.9	37.3 ±2.8	41.7 ±2.1	39 176 659	35 556	12 891 101
MULTIFAMILY	1 225	16 737	49 836	1.9	1.2	34.6	33.6 ±5.3	38.9 ±5.9	3 925 294	61 163	1 359 961
ACREAGE	3 474	24 124	134 791	1.1	1.2	17.4	17.9 ±3.7	26.2 ±6.3	11 223 484	36 881	1 956 545
VACANT PLATTED LOTS	8 620	26 072	77 139	1.9	3.1	28.4	33.8 ±5.3	39.5 ±5.3	2 959 282	6 400	841 531
COMMERCIAL AND INDUSTRIAL	1 224	25 360	87 660	1.9	1.0	33.1	28.9 ±7.3	37.3 ±9.4	7 512 028	118 166	2 488 227
WASHINGTON											
ALL TYPES OF PROPERTY	54 065	906 563	1 422 856	2.8	2.7	64.2	63.7 ±3.9	61.5 ±2.1	51 573 475	26 864	33 116 112
RESIDENTIAL (NONFARM), TOTAL	34 850	726 527	1 121 395	3.6	3.5	64.5	64.8 ±2.2	64.3 ±1.4	31 873 163	32 862	20 553 141
SINGLE-FAMILY	33 186	679 745	1 054 992	3.5	3.6	64.0	64.4 ±2.2	63.8 ±1.4	29 467 391	31 416	18 855 787
MULTIFAMILY	1 664	46 782	66 403	5.2	2.8	74.2	70.5 ±6.3	71.8 ±4.4	2 286 489	71 616	1 697 354
ACREAGE	6 239	78 065	149 015	1.5	1.2	52.9	52.4 ±20.0	41.7 ±1.1	11 832 406	28 518	6 257 649
VACANT PLATTED LOTS	11 743	53 286	82 886	2.5	2.8	56.8	64.3 ±12.4	53.3 ±11.5	3 348 472	7 247	1 902 131
COMMERCIAL AND INDUSTRIAL	1 233	48 685	69 560	1.7	1.1	77.5	70.0 ±21.2	(4) (4)	5 680 509	77 885	4 403 191
WEST VIRGINIA											
ALL TYPES OF PROPERTY	14 430	61 934	242 656	1.6	1.8	25.4	25.5 ±1.8	26.9 ±1.5	13 547 969	15 066	3 442 045
RESIDENTIAL (NONFARM), TOTAL	7 012	44 247	165 584	1.4	1.8	25.4	26.7 ±1.3	27.4 ±1.1	9 710 572	19 445	2 461 978
SINGLE-FAMILY	6 539	40 251	153 272	1.3	1.7	24.9	26.3 ±1.4	26.9 ±1.1	9 564 135	19 462	2 377 576
MULTIFAMILY	473	3 996	12 312	5.9	4.7	33.5	32.5 ±3.4	32.7 ±4.9	251 845	31 583	84 402
ACREAGE	3 257	6 152	39 823	1.6	1.5	15.7	15.4 ±2.3	17.1 ±8.8	2 609 430	12 677	410 647
VACANT PLATTED LOTS	3 568	4 155	16 786	2.1	3.8	21.9	24.8 ±3.0	23.5 ±4.4	498 083	2 966	108 897
COMMERCIAL AND INDUSTRIAL	593	7 380	20 463	2.3	1.6	39.3	36.1 ±17.0	(4) (4)	1 172 152	44 927	460 523
WISCONSIN											
ALL TYPES OF PROPERTY	40 638	617 891	1 201 968	1.7	2.0	49.3	51.4 ±3.7	51.1 ±5.1	61 367 902	25 407	30 251 567
RESIDENTIAL (NONFARM), TOTAL	28 000	516 435	990 956	2.3	2.4	50.4	52.1 ±4.2	51.2 ±5.6	42 095 521	34 254	21 198 572
SINGLE-FAMILY	25 495	437 819	863 834	2.2	2.3	49.5	50.7 ±4.2	48.6 ±5.5	39 281 002	33 196	19 441 261
MULTIFAMILY	2 505	78 616	127 122	5.5	4.5	62.1	61.8 ±10.0	65.4 ±11.9	2 831 144	62 085	1 757 311
ACREAGE	4 603	23 547	64 064	0.7	0.6	41.3	36.8 ±8.1	35.1 ±12.8	9 622 240	14 645	3 977 559
VACANT PLATTED LOTS	6 523	18 986	51 520	1.5	2.0	33.4	36.9 ±9.7	39.8 ±15.1	2 882 173	6 623	961 437
COMMERCIAL AND INDUSTRIAL	1 512	58 923	95 428	1.6	1.4	64.1	61.7 ±8.1	62.9 ±12.6	6 416 851	68 071	4 113 999
WYOMING											
ALL TYPES OF PROPERTY	5 099	14 802	159 051	3.5	2.6	10.1	9.3 ±1.1	(8) -	5 557 746	38 477	563 410
RESIDENTIAL (NONFARM), TOTAL	3 290	11 669	116 057	4.0	3.8	10.0	10.1 ±0.5	(8) -	3 068 699	37 276	308 120
SINGLE-FAMILY	3 154	11 045	109 552	3.9	3.7	10.1	10.1 ±0.5	(8) -	2 932 324	36 204	294 950
MULTIFAMILY	(4)	(4)	(4)	(4)	(4)	(4)	(4) (4)	(8) -	(4)	(4)	(4)
ACREAGE	505	1 215	21 067	1.4	0.8	6.0	5.8 ±3.8	(8) -	2 691 932	74 751	160 902
VACANT PLATTED LOTS	1 060	772	10 057	5.6	8.4	5.2	7.7 ±2.8	(8) -	177 170	9 363	9 148
COMMERCIAL AND INDUSTRIAL	244	1 146	11 870	3.4	1.3	13.3	9.7 ±3.7	(8) -	640 742	89 165	85 240

Note: These data are estimates subject to sampling variation. Absolute sampling errors shown for aggregate assessment-sales price ratios are computed at the two standard error, 95 percent confidence level; see text. Because of rounding, detail may not add to totals.

- Represents zero or rounds to zero.

[1] These do not constitute estimates of gross turnover of realty because certain transfers were either nonrespondent to our mail canvass questionnaire or deemed not usable for ratio calculation and were necessarily excluded.

[2] For each type, the quotient of estimated assessed value divided by respective size-weighted average ratio.

[3] For each type, estimated on basis of respective aggregate assessed value sample expanded to reflect statewide totals.

[4] Ratios and/or market values not computed because of insufficient sales representation.

[5] Total values of real property include "highest and best use" assessments rather than "classified use" assessments for eligible properties in Baker, Clay, Collier, Glades, Jackson, Manatee, Nassau, Orange, Pasco, Putnam, St. Johns, and St. Lucie Counties.

[6] All properties in Hawaii, Maryland, and Montana, as well as "manufacturing" property in South Carolina, are assessed by a State agency. However, the values of such property are shown here as "locally assessed" for comparability with data for other States; see text.

[7] For Tennessee the estimate shown for multifamily residential is exclusive of any such property that may, because of differences in State and Bureau coding, be included in estimates for single-family houses or commercial property.

[8] There are no SMSA's in Vermont and Wyoming.

Table 3. Median Property Tax Rates and Assessment Ratios for Real Property Involved in Measurable Sales During a 6-Month Period, for Selected Local Areas: 1976

Area	Types of real property				Area	Types of real property			
	All types	Residential (nonfarm)		Vacant platted lots		All types	Residential (nonfarm)		Vacant platted lots
		Total	Single-family				Total	Single-family	
ALABAMA					**ARIZONA**				
ETOWAH COUNTY:					MARICOPA COUNTY:				
NOMINAL	2.95	3.16	3.16	2.60	NOMINAL	11.19	11.17	11.17	11.90
EFFECTIVE	0.27	0.32	0.32	0.15	EFFECTIVE	1.31	1.36	1.35	0.78
RATIO	8.9	9.7	9.7	5.2	RATIO	11.9	12.2	12.2	6.3
BALANCE OF COUNTY:					BALANCE OF COUNTY:				
NOMINAL	2.60	2.60	2.60	2.60	NOMINAL	10.17	9.83	9.83	10.74
EFFECTIVE	0.16	0.32	0.32	0.13	EFFECTIVE	0.98	1.06	1.06	0.40
RATIO	6.3	12.3	12.3	4.6	RATIO	11.1	12.1	12.1	4.2
GADSDEN:					GLENDALE:				
NOMINAL	3.60	3.25	3.25	3.60	NOMINAL	8.59	8.59	8.59	(1)
EFFECTIVE	0.33	0.32	0.32	0.37	EFFECTIVE	1.19	1.22	1.22	(1)
RATIO	9.9	9.4	9.4	10.2	RATIO	12.5	12.6	12.6	(1)
JEFFERSON COUNTY:					MESA:				
NOMINAL	4.45	4.45	4.45	3.77	NOMINAL	9.82	9.82	9.82	(1)
EFFECTIVE	0.48	0.48	0.48	0.42	EFFECTIVE	1.19	1.20	1.20	(1)
RATIO	11.9	11.9	11.9	11.7	RATIO	12.1	12.1	12.1	(1)
BALANCE OF COUNTY:					PHOENIX:				
NOMINAL	3.14	3.14	3.14	3.14	NOMINAL	11.82	11.81	11.81	14.07
EFFECTIVE	0.43	0.44	0.44	0.39	EFFECTIVE	1.46	1.47	1.46	1.27
RATIO	11.6	11.7	11.7	11.7	RATIO	12.1	12.2	12.2	8.0
BIRMINGHAM:					SCOTTSDALE:				
NOMINAL	4.50	4.45	4.45	4.94	NOMINAL	10.39	10.38	10.38	(1)
EFFECTIVE	0.55	0.55	0.55	0.53	EFFECTIVE	1.18	1.18	1.18	(1)
RATIO	12.2	12.1	12.1	12.0	RATIO	11.3	11.4	11.3	(1)
MADISON COUNTY:					TEMPE:				
NOMINAL	5.38	5.38	5.37	5.70	NOMINAL	11.49	11.49	11.49	(1)
EFFECTIVE	0.61	0.62	0.62	0.55	EFFECTIVE	1.41	1.41	1.41	(1)
RATIO	11.7	11.9	11.9	10.0	RATIO	12.3	12.4	12.4	(1)
BALANCE OF COUNTY:					PIMA COUNTY:				
NOMINAL	3.25	3.25	3.25	3.25	NOMINAL	11.45	11.44	11.44	12.44
EFFECTIVE	0.32	0.32	0.32	0.30	EFFECTIVE	1.31	1.32	1.32	0.90
RATIO	10.0	10.0	10.0	9.2	RATIO	11.4	11.5	11.5	8.4
HUNTSVILLE:					BALANCE OF COUNTY:				
NOMINAL	5.47	5.43	5.42	5.70	NOMINAL	11.58	11.52	11.52	12.44
EFFECTIVE	0.64	0.64	0.65	0.61	EFFECTIVE	1.23	1.23	1.23	1.11
RATIO	11.9	12.0	12.0	11.7	RATIO	11.1	11.2	11.2	8.3
MOBILE COUNTY:					TUCSON:				
NOMINAL	4.45	4.45	4.45	3.75	NOMINAL	11.44	11.44	11.44	12.75
EFFECTIVE	0.37	0.37	0.37	0.37	EFFECTIVE	1.34	1.34	1.34	0.89
RATIO	8.7	8.7	8.7	9.3	RATIO	11.6	11.7	11.7	8.4
BALANCE OF COUNTY:					**ARKANSAS**				
NOMINAL	3.75	3.75	3.75	3.75	JEFFERSON COUNTY:				
EFFECTIVE	0.32	0.33	0.33	0.31	NOMINAL	7.71	7.75	7.75	6.70
RATIO	8.2	8.3	8.3	7.7	EFFECTIVE	0.95	1.01	1.01	0.55
MOBILE:					RATIO	12.5	13.1	13.1	7.3
NOMINAL	4.45	4.45	4.45	4.45	BALANCE OF COUNTY:				
EFFECTIVE	0.41	0.39	0.39	0.64	NOMINAL	6.60	6.60	6.60	6.60
RATIO	9.1	8.8	8.8	14.3	EFFECTIVE	0.73	1.02	1.03	0.48
MONTGOMERY COUNTY:					RATIO	12.5	14.4	15.0	7.3
NOMINAL	3.35	3.35	3.35	2.10	PINE BLUFF:				
EFFECTIVE	0.24	0.25	0.25	0.09	NOMINAL	7.76	7.76	7.76	(1)
RATIO	12.4	13.0	13.0	3.6	EFFECTIVE	0.99	1.00	0.99	(1)
BALANCE OF COUNTY:					RATIO	12.7	12.9	12.8	(1)
NOMINAL	2.10	2.10	2.10	2.10	PULASKI COUNTY:				
EFFECTIVE	0.12	0.14	0.14	0.06	NOMINAL	7.60	7.78	7.78	7.09
RATIO	13.1	14.2	14.1	2.9	EFFECTIVE	1.04	1.04	1.04	1.03
MONTGOMERY:					RATIO	13.7	13.7	13.5	14.8
NOMINAL	3.35	3.35	3.35	(1)	BALANCE OF COUNTY:				
EFFECTIVE	0.28	0.28	0.28	(1)	NOMINAL	6.70	6.70	6.70	6.70
RATIO	12.1	12.2	12.2	(1)	EFFECTIVE	0.96	1.04	1.04	0.87
TUSCALOOSA COUNTY:					RATIO	13.9	15.3	15.3	12.3
NOMINAL	3.30	3.60	3.60	2.11	LITTLE ROCK:				
EFFECTIVE	0.35	0.38	0.37	0.16	NOMINAL	7.79	7.79	7.79	7.78
RATIO	11.8	11.9	12.0	6.4	EFFECTIVE	1.08	1.07	1.04	1.64
BALANCE OF COUNTY:					RATIO	13.7	13.4	13.3	21.0
NOMINAL	2.10	2.10	2.10	2.10	NORTH LITTLE ROCK:				
EFFECTIVE	0.20	0.21	0.21	0.13	NOMINAL	7.60	7.60	7.60	(1)
RATIO	9.5	11.4	11.4	5.9	EFFECTIVE	1.03	0.99	1.00	(1)
TUSCALOOSA:					RATIO	13.5	13.0	13.2	(1)
NOMINAL	3.60	3.60	3.60	3.60	SEBASTIAN COUNTY:				
EFFECTIVE	0.43	0.43	0.43	0.30	NOMINAL	7.22	7.23	7.23	7.23
RATIO	12.0	12.0	12.1	8.2	EFFECTIVE	0.80	0.84	0.84	0.70
ALASKA					RATIO	11.2	11.7	11.6	10.5
GREATER ANCHORAGE BOROUGH:					BALANCE OF COUNTY:				
NOMINAL	1.59	1.81	1.59	1.42	NOMINAL	6.95	7.17	7.17	6.83
EFFECTIVE	1.23	1.26	1.27	1.12	EFFECTIVE	0.67	0.76	0.76	0.70
RATIO	72.3	72.7	72.8	77.8	RATIO	10.0	10.6	10.6	10.3

See footnotes at end of table.

Table 3. Median Property Tax Rates and Assessment Ratios for Real Property Involved in Measurable Sales During a 6-Month Period, for Selected Local Areas: 1976—Continued

Area	All types	Residential (nonfarm) Total	Single-family	Vacant platted lots
ARKANSAS--CONTINUED				
SEBASTIAN COUNTY--CONTINUED:				
FORT SMITH:				
NOMINAL	7.23	7.23	7.23	7.22
EFFECTIVE	0.86	0.86	0.84	0.83
RATIO	11.9	11.9	11.7	11.6
CALIFORNIA				
ALAMEDA COUNTY:				
NOMINAL	12.85	12.85	12.85	13.18
EFFECTIVE	2.15	2.10	2.08	2.37
RATIO	19.1	19.1	19.1	18.4
BALANCE OF COUNTY:				
NOMINAL	12.83	12.83	12.83	(1)
EFFECTIVE	2.09	2.08	2.08	(1)
RATIO	19.0	19.0	19.0	(1)
ALAMEDA:				
NOMINAL	13.52	13.52	13.52	(1)
EFFECTIVE	2.38	2.31	2.41	(1)
RATIO	18.8	19.0	19.5	(1)
BERKELEY:				
NOMINAL	15.78	15.78	15.78	(1)
EFFECTIVE	2.64	2.53	2.45	(1)
RATIO	18.9	18.7	18.3	(1)
FREMONT:				
NOMINAL	12.51	12.51	12.51	(1)
EFFECTIVE	1.94	1.93	1.93	(1)
RATIO	19.1	19.1	19.1	(1)
HAYWARD:				
NOMINAL	12.85	12.85	12.85	(1)
EFFECTIVE	2.02	1.99	1.98	(1)
RATIO	19.4	19.1	19.1	(1)
OAKLAND:				
NOMINAL	14.45	14.45	14.45	(1)
EFFECTIVE	2.48	2.42	2.38	(1)
RATIO	19.3	19.2	19.2	(1)
SAN LEANDRO:				
NOMINAL	9.10	9.10	9.10	(1)
EFFECTIVE	1.61	1.57	1.53	(1)
RATIO	19.0	18.9	18.6	(1)
CONTRA COSTA COUNTY:				
NOMINAL	11.97	11.97	11.97	11.83
EFFECTIVE	1.85	1.80	1.79	2.25
RATIO	18.4	18.2	18.0	19.5
BALANCE OF COUNTY:				
NOMINAL	12.00	12.09	12.08	11.26
EFFECTIVE	1.83	1.78	1.76	2.25
RATIO	18.5	18.3	18.0	19.0
CONCORD:				
NOMINAL	11.90	11.90	11.90	(1)
EFFECTIVE	1.88	1.85	1.86	(1)
RATIO	18.2	18.2	18.2	(1)
RICHMOND:				
NOMINAL	13.65	13.65	13.65	(1)
EFFECTIVE	1.83	1.83	1.81	(1)
RATIO	18.3	18.0	18.0	(1)
FRESNO COUNTY:				
NOMINAL	11.09	12.24	12.24	10.03
EFFECTIVE	1.77	1.83	1.82	1.82
RATIO	18.3	19.2	19.2	20.4
BALANCE OF COUNTY:				
NOMINAL	10.55	10.57	10.57	10.03
EFFECTIVE	1.67	1.83	1.83	1.82
RATIO	18.2	19.6	19.6	20.6
FRESNO:				
NOMINAL	12.28	12.28	12.28	(1)
EFFECTIVE	1.85	1.85	1.81	(1)
RATIO	18.2	18.2	18.3	(1)
KERN COUNTY:				
NOMINAL	12.63	12.61	12.67	12.63
EFFECTIVE	1.50	1.18	1.17	1.75
RATIO	14.1	14.0	13.7	13.7
BALANCE OF COUNTY:				
NOMINAL	12.56	12.30	12.27	12.63
EFFECTIVE	1.50	1.23	1.23	1.75
RATIO	14.1	14.1	14.1	13.7
CALIFORNIA--CONTINUED				
KERN COUNTY--CONTINUED				
BAKERSFIELD:				
NOMINAL	13.57	13.57	13.58	(1)
EFFECTIVE	1.16	1.16	1.12	(1)
RATIO	13.1	13.1	12.1	(1)
LOS ANGELES COUNTY:				
NOMINAL	13.79	13.79	13.79	12.93
EFFECTIVE	2.12	2.12	2.11	1.90
RATIO	17.4	17.4	17.4	17.9
BALANCE OF COUNTY:				
NOMINAL	13.09	13.12	13.12	13.06
EFFECTIVE	1.99	1.97	1.94	2.41
RATIO	17.7	17.6	17.5	21.0
ALHAMBRA:				
NOMINAL	13.13	13.13	13.13	(1)
EFFECTIVE	2.10	2.11	1.62	(1)
RATIO	16.1	16.0	13.2	(1)
BELLFLOWER:				
NOMINAL	12.04	12.04	12.04	(1)
EFFECTIVE	1.99	1.98	2.16	(1)
RATIO	18.9	19.1	19.7	(1)
BURBANK:				
NOMINAL	11.42	11.42	11.42	(1)
EFFECTIVE	1.91	1.87	1.66	(1)
RATIO	17.7	17.3	17.2	(1)
CARSON:				
NOMINAL	12.74	12.74	12.74	(1)
EFFECTIVE	1.95	1.95	1.95	(1)
RATIO	18.5	18.5	18.7	(1)
COMPTON:				
NOMINAL	14.46	16.87	16.87	(1)
EFFECTIVE	2.90	2.90	2.90	(1)
RATIO	20.5	20.3	20.3	(1)
DOWNEY:				
NOMINAL	11.63	11.68	11.73	(1)
EFFECTIVE	1.47	1.47	1.46	(1)
RATIO	15.4	15.3	15.2	(1)
EL MONTE:				
NOMINAL	13.68	13.68	13.68	(1)
EFFECTIVE	2.18	2.15	2.14	(1)
RATIO	17.9	17.8	17.8	(1)
GLENDALE:				
NOMINAL	11.20	11.20	11.20	(1)
EFFECTIVE	1.89	1.89	1.81	(1)
RATIO	17.5	17.5	17.5	(1)
HAWTHORNE:				
NOMINAL	13.26	13.26	14.22	(1)
EFFECTIVE	2.39	2.39	2.26	(1)
RATIO	18.9	18.9	18.2	(1)
INGLEWOOD:				
NOMINAL	13.43	13.43	16.39	(1)
EFFECTIVE	2.69	2.70	2.65	(1)
RATIO	20.0	20.1	19.7	(1)
LAKEWOOD:				
NOMINAL	15.04	15.04	15.04	(1)
EFFECTIVE	2.32	2.32	2.32	(1)
RATIO	19.0	19.0	19.0	(1)
LONG BEACH:				
NOMINAL	12.86	13.00	14.84	(1)
EFFECTIVE	2.25	2.25	2.22	(1)
RATIO	17.7	17.7	17.5	(1)
LOS ANGELES:				
NOMINAL	13.79	13.88	15.18	7.29
EFFECTIVE	2.22	2.24	2.27	1.90
RATIO	16.9	16.9	16.9	17.9
NORWALK:				
NOMINAL	17.77	17.77	17.77	(1)
EFFECTIVE	2.24	2.24	2.24	(1)
RATIO	17.3	17.3	17.3	(1)
PASADENA:				
NOMINAL	14.03	14.10	14.45	14.03
EFFECTIVE	2.09	2.27	2.12	1.71
RATIO	14.9	16.2	15.1	12.2
PICO RIVERA:				
NOMINAL	18.58	18.62	18.62	(1)
EFFECTIVE	2.16	2.18	2.18	(1)
RATIO	17.0	17.1	17.1	(1)

See footnotes at end of table.

Table 3. Median Property Tax Rates and Assessment Ratios for Real Property Involved in Measurable Sales During a 6-Month Period, for Selected Local Areas: 1976—Continued

Area	All types	Residential (nonfarm) Total	Residential (nonfarm) Single-family	Vacant platted lots
CALIFORNIA--CONTINUED				
LOS ANGELES COUNTY--CONTINUED				
POMONA:				
NOMINAL	19.31	20.17	20.26	(1)
EFFECTIVE	2.56	2.55	2.56	(1)
RATIO	18.4	18.4	18.4	(1)
REDONDO BEACH:				
NOMINAL	12.42	12.42	15.62	(1)
EFFECTIVE	1.76	1.76	1.79	(1)
RATIO	14.4	14.4	14.6	(1)
SANTA MONICA:				
NOMINAL	10.81	10.81	10.81	(1)
EFFECTIVE	1.64	1.40	1.52	(1)
RATIO	15.1	13.0	14.1	(1)
SOUTH GATE:				
NOMINAL	12.66	12.74	12.66	(1)
EFFECTIVE	2.30	2.32	2.33	(1)
RATIO	18.2	19.0	19.8	(1)
TORRANCE:				
NOMINAL	13.06	13.25	13.40	(1)
EFFECTIVE	2.10	2.08	2.08	(1)
RATIO	19.4	18.9	18.9	(1)
WEST COVINA:				
NOMINAL	17.94	17.94	17.94	(1)
EFFECTIVE	2.30	2.28	2.28	(1)
RATIO	16.9	16.8	16.8	(1)
WHITTIER:				
NOMINAL	13.73	15.46	16.59	(1)
EFFECTIVE	2.13	2.29	2.29	(1)
RATIO	17.1	18.5	18.5	(1)
MONTEREY COUNTY:				
NOMINAL	10.49	10.50	10.50	(1)
EFFECTIVE	1.57	1.57	1.55	(1)
RATIO	18.6	18.6	18.4	(1)
BALANCE OF COUNTY:				
NOMINAL	10.16	10.16	9.78	(1)
EFFECTIVE	1.57	1.57	1.42	(1)
RATIO	18.4	18.6	18.4	(1)
SALINAS:				
NOMINAL	11.48	11.47	11.48	(1)
EFFECTIVE	1.60	1.59	1.56	(1)
RATIO	18.8	18.7	18.2	(1)
RIVERSIDE COUNTY:				
NOMINAL	11.53	11.40	11.40	12.49
EFFECTIVE	1.84	1.64	1.62	2.29
RATIO	17.2	17.4	17.3	17.4
BALANCE OF COUNTY:				
NOMINAL	11.85	11.51	11.51	12.49
EFFECTIVE	1.85	1.62	1.60	2.30
RATIO	16.9	16.9	16.7	17.5
RIVERSIDE:				
NOMINAL	11.25	11.25	11.25	(1)
EFFECTIVE	1.79	1.79	1.81	(1)
RATIO	18.8	19.3	19.7	(1)
SACRAMENTO COUNTY:				
NOMINAL	13.57	13.58	13.57	13.62
EFFECTIVE	1.82	1.79	1.75	3.06
RATIO	17.3	17.2	17.1	22.5
BALANCE OF COUNTY:				
NOMINAL	13.22	13.23	13.24	(1)
EFFECTIVE	1.83	1.80	1.79	(1)
RATIO	17.3	17.3	17.2	(1)
SACRAMENTO:				
NOMINAL	13.74	13.75	13.76	(1)
EFFECTIVE	1.82	1.74	1.65	(1)
RATIO	17.5	17.1	16.9	(1)
SAN BERNARDINO COUNTY:				
NOMINAL	12.95	12.96	12.96	12.95
EFFECTIVE	2.11	1.99	1.97	2.63
RATIO	18.8	18.8	18.8	20.4
BALANCE OF COUNTY:				
NOMINAL	12.89	12.90	12.90	12.93
EFFECTIVE	2.11	1.98	1.96	2.54
RATIO	18.8	18.8	18.8	20.3
ONTARIO:				
NOMINAL	13.21	13.21	13.21	(1)
EFFECTIVE	2.17	2.17	2.11	(1)
RATIO	19.1	19.1	19.0	(1)

Area	All types	Residential (nonfarm) Total	Residential (nonfarm) Single-family	Vacant platted lots
CALIFORNIA--CONTINUED				
SAN BERNARDINO COUNTY--CONTINUED				
SAN BERNARDINO:				
NOMINAL	13.37	13.37	13.36	(1)
EFFECTIVE	2.29	1.96	1.96	(1)
RATIO	19.2	18.8	19.1	(1)
SAN DIEGO COUNTY:				
NOMINAL	10.02	10.62	10.65	10.38
EFFECTIVE	1.65	1.64	1.64	1.76
RATIO	18.6	18.8	18.9	16.6
BALANCE OF COUNTY:				
NOMINAL	10.46	9.87	9.90	10.38
EFFECTIVE	1.69	1.69	1.66	1.79
RATIO	18.2	18.5	18.5	16.8
CHULA VISTA:				
NOMINAL	10.31	10.31	10.31	(1)
EFFECTIVE	1.73	1.73	1.68	(1)
RATIO	20.1	20.1	19.9	(1)
EL CAJON:				
NOMINAL	10.77	10.76	10.76	(1)
EFFECTIVE	1.80	1.69	1.69	(1)
RATIO	18.1	17.7	17.7	(1)
SAN DIEGO:				
NOMINAL	9.36	9.36	9.36	(1)
EFFECTIVE	1.57	1.57	1.57	(1)
RATIO	18.9	18.9	19.6	(1)
SAN JOAQUIN COUNTY:				
NOMINAL	12.03	12.03	12.03	(1)
EFFECTIVE	1.72	1.72	1.70	(1)
RATIO	18.3	18.3	16.1	(1)
BALANCE OF COUNTY:				
NOMINAL	11.25	11.25	11.25	(1)
EFFECTIVE	1.57	1.53	1.53	(1)
RATIO	17.8	16.1	15.9	(1)
STOCKTON:				
NOMINAL	12.06	12.06	12.06	(1)
EFFECTIVE	1.91	1.92	1.77	(1)
RATIO	18.6	18.7	18.9	(1)
SAN MATEO COUNTY:				
NOMINAL	9.91	9.91	9.91	11.73
EFFECTIVE	1.42	1.41	1.39	1.42
RATIO	15.7	15.8	15.8	13.3
BALANCE OF COUNTY:				
NOMINAL	10.27	10.22	10.22	(1)
EFFECTIVE	1.46	1.45	1.44	(1)
RATIO	16.3	16.3	16.3	(1)
DALY CITY:				
NOMINAL	11.76	11.76	11.76	(1)
EFFECTIVE	1.32	1.29	1.25	(1)
RATIO	13.7	13.6	13.6	(1)
REDWOOD CITY:				
NOMINAL	9.64	9.64	9.64	(1)
EFFECTIVE	1.43	1.43	1.43	(1)
RATIO	15.9	15.9	16.0	(1)
SAN MATEO:				
NOMINAL	9.61	9.61	9.61	(1)
EFFECTIVE	1.24	1.24	1.24	(1)
RATIO	15.1	15.2	15.4	(1)
SANTA BARBARA COUNTY:				
NOMINAL	11.56	11.62	11.62	10.99
EFFECTIVE	1.45	1.39	1.39	2.30
RATIO	14.7	14.1	14.2	21.8
BALANCE OF COUNTY:				
NOMINAL	11.62	11.69	11.69	11.23
EFFECTIVE	1.39	1.30	1.31	2.22
RATIO	14.2	13.2	13.3	19.8
SANTA BARBARA:				
NOMINAL	10.57	10.57	10.59	(1)
EFFECTIVE	1.94	1.68	1.70	(1)
RATIO	18.5	16.0	17.3	(1)
SANTA CLARA COUNTY:				
NOMINAL	12.12	12.12	12.12	12.49
EFFECTIVE	1.86	1.85	1.85	2.41
RATIO	18.6	18.6	18.6	16.6
BALANCE OF COUNTY:				
NOMINAL	12.16	12.17	12.16	(1)
EFFECTIVE	1.84	1.81	1.81	(1)
RATIO	18.5	18.5	18.6	(1)

See footnotes at end of table.

226

Area	Types of real property				Area	Types of real property			
	All types	Residential (nonfarm)		Vacant platted lots		All types	Residential (nonfarm)		Vacant platted lots
		Total	Single-family				Total	Single-family	
CALIFORNIA--CONTINUED					**CALIFORNIA--CONTINUED**				
SANTA CLARA COUNTY--CONTINUED					SAN FRANCISCO:[3]				
MOUNTAIN VIEW:					NOMINAL	11.50	11.50	11.50	(1)
NOMINAL	9.81	9.81	9.81	(1)	EFFECTIVE	1.45	1.35	1.31	(1)
EFFECTIVE	1.74	1.74	1.74	(1)	RATIO	13.9	13.7	14.0	(1)
RATIO	19.0	19.0	19.0	(1)	**COLORADO**				
PALO ALTO:					ADAMS COUNTY:				
NOMINAL	10.08	10.08	10.08	(1)	NOMINAL	9.37	9.37	9.37	8.77
EFFECTIVE	1.58	1.57	1.57	(1)	EFFECTIVE	1.57	1.58	1.56	1.11
RATIO	17.3	17.4	17.4	(1)	RATIO	17.4	17.6	17.2	12.7
SAN JOSE:					BALANCE OF COUNTY:				
NOMINAL	12.50	12.50	12.48	(1)	NOMINAL	8.98	8.98	8.98	8.77
EFFECTIVE	2.02	2.01	2.01	(1)	EFFECTIVE	1.53	1.55	1.54	1.11
RATIO	19.1	19.1	19.1	(1)	RATIO	17.1	17.4	17.3	12.7
SANTA CLARA:					AURORA (PART):				
NOMINAL	10.04	10.04	10.04	(1)	NOMINAL	9.67	9.67	9.67	(1)
EFFECTIVE	1.35	1.35	1.34	(1)	EFFECTIVE	1.77	1.77	1.64	(1)
RATIO	16.3	16.3	16.4	(1)	RATIO	18.4	18.4	16.7	(1)
SUNNYVALE:					ARAPAHOE COUNTY:				
NOMINAL	10.77	10.77	10.79	(1)	NOMINAL	8.70	8.70	8.70	9.20
EFFECTIVE	1.67	1.66	1.55	(1)	EFFECTIVE	1.59	1.61	1.60	1.48
RATIO	17.1	17.4	16.7	(1)	RATIO	18.8	18.8	18.8	17.9
SOLANO COUNTY:					BALANCE OF COUNTY:				
NOMINAL	11.28	11.28	11.28	13.34	NOMINAL	7.70	7.70	7.70	9.20
EFFECTIVE	1.64	1.63	1.61	1.79	EFFECTIVE	1.47	1.47	1.48	1.48
RATIO	17.6	18.8	18.0	14.8	RATIO	17.8	18.0	18.0	17.9
BALANCE OF COUNTY:					AURORA (PART):				
NOMINAL	11.05	11.28	11.28	39.27	NOMINAL	8.70	8.70	8.70	(1)
EFFECTIVE	1.59	1.57	1.57	1.60	EFFECTIVE	1.69	1.69	1.69	(1)
RATIO	17.5	18.8	18.8	14.8	RATIO	19.2	19.2	19.1	(1)
VALLEJO:					BOULDER COUNTY:				
NOMINAL	12.40	12.39	12.40	(1)	NOMINAL	9.50	9.70	9.51	9.60
EFFECTIVE	1.78	1.74	1.69	(1)	EFFECTIVE	1.47	1.54	1.54	1.08
RATIO	17.6	17.9	17.6	(1)	RATIO	15.1	15.6	15.6	11.1
SONOMA COUNTY:					BALANCE OF COUNTY:				
NOMINAL	10.65	10.84	10.80	9.14	NOMINAL	9.50	9.50	9.50	9.50
EFFECTIVE	1.62	1.70	1.65	1.57	EFFECTIVE	1.52	1.56	1.56	0.99
RATIO	19.1	19.4	19.4	17.49	RATIO	16.1	16.4	16.4	10.0
BALANCE OF COUNTY:					BOULDER:				
NOMINAL	9.59	10.08	9.63	8.47	NOMINAL	10.12	10.12	10.12	(1)
EFFECTIVE	1.46	1.54	1.53	1.34	EFFECTIVE	1.41	1.41	1.41	(1)
RATIO	18.6	19.0	19.1	16.2	RATIO	14.2	14.2	14.2	(1)
SANTA ROSA:					EL PASO COUNTY:				
NOMINAL	10.84	10.84	10.84	(1)	NOMINAL	7.88	7.88	7.88	7.88
EFFECTIVE	1.83	1.83	1.75	(1)	EFFECTIVE	1.71	1.70	1.72	1.87
RATIO	20.0	20.0	19.4	(1)	RATIO	22.1	22.0	22.1	26.0
STANISLAUS COUNTY:					BALANCE OF COUNTY:				
NOMINAL	10.64	10.66	10.68	10.95	NOMINAL	8.24	8.24	8.24	7.58
EFFECTIVE	1.65	1.64	1.65	1.76	EFFECTIVE	1.85	1.87	1.87	1.85
RATIO	19.1	19.4	19.7	17.1	RATIO	23.8	23.8	23.8	25.0
BALANCE OF COUNTY:					COLORADO SPRINGS:				
NOMINAL	10.09	10.17	10.08	(1)	NOMINAL	7.88	7.88	7.88	7.88
EFFECTIVE	1.71	1.50	1.50	(1)	EFFECTIVE	1.67	1.66	1.67	2.13
RATIO	17.4	18.3	18.3	(1)	RATIO	21.5	21.3	21.5	27.1
MODESTO:					JEFFERSON COUNTY:				
NOMINAL	10.68	10.68	10.68	(1)	NOMINAL	8.36	8.36	8.36	8.54
EFFECTIVE	1.64	1.64	1.65	(1)	EFFECTIVE	1.83	1.80	1.78	2.08
RATIO	19.9	19.8	19.8	(1)	RATIO	21.6	21.3	21.3	24.4
VENTURA COUNTY:					BALANCE OF COUNTY:				
NOMINAL	10.27	10.46	10.48	2.74	NOMINAL	8.54	8.24	8.24	8.54
EFFECTIVE	1.43	1.65	1.63	0.42	EFFECTIVE	1.89	1.73	1.73	2.08
RATIO	19.6	20.2	20.1	13.0	RATIO	22.4	20.4	20.4	24.4
BALANCE OF COUNTY:					ARVADA:				
NOMINAL	(2)	(2)	(2)	(2)	NOMINAL	8.36	8.36	8.36	8.36
EFFECTIVE	(2)	(2)	(2)	(2)	EFFECTIVE	1.78	1.80	1.78	1.20
RATIO	(2)	(2)	(2)	(2)	RATIO	21.3	21.4	21.3	14.4
OXNARD:					LAKEWOOD:				
NOMINAL	10.70	10.72	10.70	(1)	NOMINAL	8.53	8.53	8.53	8.60
EFFECTIVE	1.98	2.01	1.87	(1)	EFFECTIVE	1.83	1.84	1.83	0.94
RATIO	20.1	20.2	20.1	(1)	RATIO	21.6	21.7	21.6	11.3
SAN BUENAVENTURA:					LARIMER COUNTY:				
NOMINAL	10.32	10.32	10.31	(1)	NOMINAL	8.48	8.87	8.82	8.19
EFFECTIVE	1.66	1.66	1.65	(1)	EFFECTIVE	1.39	1.44	1.36	1.35
RATIO	19.0	19.0	19.0	(1)	RATIO	17.1	17.0	16.8	17.2
SIMI VALLEY:					BALANCE OF COUNTY:				
NOMINAL	12.11	12.11	12.11	(1)	NOMINAL	8.19	8.19	8.19	8.19
EFFECTIVE	1.99	1.99	1.99	(1)	EFFECTIVE	1.39	1.44	1.36	1.35
RATIO	20.0	20.0	20.0	(1)	RATIO	17.5	16.6	15.9	18.2

See footnotes at end of table.

Area	All types	Residential (nonfarm)		Vacant platted lots	Area	All types	Residential (nonfarm)		Vacant platted lots
		Total	Single-family				Total	Single-family	
COLORADO--CONTINUED					**DISTRICT OF COLUMBIA**				
LARIMER COUNTY--CONTINUED					WASHINGTON:				
FORT COLLINS:					NOMINAL	1.83	1.83	1.83	1.84
NOMINAL	9.06	9.06	9.06	(¹)	EFFECTIVE	1.25	1.24	1.23	1.55
EFFECTIVE	1.43	1.61	1.53	(¹)	RATIO.	68.4	67.9	67.2	79.8
RATIO	17.0	17.1	17.1	(¹)					
					FLORIDA				
PUEBLO COUNTY:									
NOMINAL	9.18	9.18	9.18	8.91	ALACHUA COUNTY:				
EFFECTIVE	1.37	1.54	1.53	0.97	NOMINAL.	2.12	2.46	2.26	(¹)
RATIO	15.0	16.8	16.7	11.4	EFFECTIVE.	1.25	1.27	1.25	(¹)
					RATIO.	63.5	65.2	63.5	(¹)
BALANCE OF COUNTY:									
NOMINAL	8.46	(¹)	(¹)	8.46	BALANCE OF COUNTY:				
EFFECTIVE	1.05	(¹)	(¹)	1.05	NOMINAL.	1.97	1.97	1.97	(¹)
RATIO	12.1	(¹)	(¹)	12.1	EFFECTIVE.	1.16	1.19	1.19	(¹)
					RATIO.	63.5	66.8	66.8	(¹)
PUEBLO:									
NOMINAL	9.18	9.18	9.18	9.18	GAINESVILLE:				
EFFECTIVE	1.49	1.53	1.52	0.76	NOMINAL.	2.65	2.65	2.65	(¹)
RATIO	16.2	16.7	16.5	8.4	EFFECTIVE.	1.56	1.56	1.51	(¹)
					RATIO.	63.5	63.5	63.0	(¹)
DENVER:									
NOMINAL	8.03	8.03	8.03	(¹)	BROWARD COUNTY:				
EFFECTIVE	1.35	1.34	1.33	(¹)	NOMINAL.	1.81	1.89	1.89	1.62
RATIO	16.8	16.7	16.5	(¹)	EFFECTIVE.	0.93	1.00	1.00	0.79
					RATIO.	60.2	64.3	63.9	49.0
CONNECTICUT									
					BALANCE OF COUNTY:				
FAIRFIELD COUNTY:					NOMINAL.	1.64	1.81	1.81	1.62
BRIDGEPORT:					EFFECTIVE.	0.88	0.97	0.97	0.79
NOMINAL	6.89	6.89	6.89	(¹)		59.8	65.7	56.9	49.0
EFFECTIVE	2.94	2.95	2.80	(¹)					
RATIO	43.5	44.2	40.6	(¹)	FORT LAUDERDALE:				
					NOMINAL.	2.06	2.06	2.06	2.06
DANBURY:					EFFECTIVE.	1.15	1.11	1.10	1.97
NOMINAL	7.03	7.03	7.03	(¹)	RATIO.	64.3	61.8	60.5	95.7
EFFECTIVE	1.78	1.77	1.87	(¹)					
RATIO	26.6	26.0	27.3	(¹)	HOLLYWOOD:				
					NOMINAL.	1.95	1.95	1.95	(¹)
NORWALK:					EFFECTIVE.	0.96	1.03	0.97	(¹)
NOMINAL	4.37	4.37	4.37	(¹)	RATIO.	56.9	58.7	57.9	(¹)
EFFECTIVE	2.01	1.98	1.96	(¹)					
RATIO	46.3	45.5	44.7	(¹)	DADE COUNTY:				
					NOMINAL.	1.72	1.72	1.72	1.72
STAMFORD:					EFFECTIVE.	1.16	1.15	1.12	1.10
NOMINAL	4.94	4.94	4.94	4.36	RATIO.	68.3	69.1	68.9	62.8
EFFECTIVE	2.08	2.14	2.07	2.06					
RATIO	45.0	45.0	44.8	48.3	BALANCE OF COUNTY:				
					NOMINAL.	1.72	1.72	1.72	1.72
HARTFORD COUNTY:					EFFECTIVE.	1.07	1.06	1.05	1.10
BRISTOL:					RATIO.	68.4	69.1	68.7	62.8
NOMINAL	7.57	7.57	7.57	7.57					
EFFECTIVE	2.27	2.31	2.23	2.07	HIALEAH:				
RATIO	30.0	30.5	29.5	27.4	NOMINAL.	2.17	2.17	2.17	(¹)
					EFFECTIVE.	1.31	1.31	1.32	(¹)
HARTFORD:					RATIO.	67.6	67.9	68.0	(¹)
NOMINAL	8.20	8.20	8.20	(¹)					
EFFECTIVE	3.29	3.20	3.09	(¹)	MIAMI:				
RATIO	40.9	39.9	37.7	(¹)	NOMINAL.	2.79	2.79	2.79	(¹)
					EFFECTIVE.	1.75	1.75	1.76	(¹)
NEW BRITAIN:					RATIO.	70.8	70.8	70.9	(¹)
NOMINAL	6.08	6.08	6.08	(¹)					
EFFECTIVE	4.00	4.00	4.17	(¹)	MIAMI BEACH:				
RATIO	65.7	65.7	68.6	(¹)	NOMINAL.	2.94	2.94	2.94	(¹)
					EFFECTIVE.	1.68	1.71	1.68	(¹)
NEW HAVEN COUNTY:					RATIO.	62.0	66.3	68.0	(¹)
MERIDEN:									
NOMINAL	7.27	7.27	7.27	(¹)	ESCAMBIA COUNTY:				
EFFECTIVE	2.39	2.27	2.27	(¹)	NOMINAL.	1.83	1.83	1.83	1.83
RATIO	32.1	31.5	31.5	(¹)	EFFECTIVE.	0.96	0.84	0.84	1.24
					RATIO.	60.0	61.1	61.1	67.7
NEW HAVEN:									
NOMINAL	8.66	8.66	8.66	(¹)	BALANCE OF COUNTY:				
EFFECTIVE	3.05	2.99	2.54	(¹)	NOMINAL.	1.83	1.83	1.83	1.83
RATIO	37.0	36.9	32.9	(¹)	EFFECTIVE.	0.83	0.80	0.80	0.98
					RATIO.	59.0	61.4	61.4	53.5
WATERBURY:									
NOMINAL	8.70	8.70	8.70	(¹)	PENSACOLA:				
EFFECTIVE	2.83	2.85	2.74	(¹)	NOMINAL.	2.23	2.23	2.23	1.83
RATIO	36.1	36.2	36.1	(¹)	EFFECTIVE.	1.47	1.08	1.08	1.54
					RATIO.	68.8	60.7	60.7	84.0
WEST HAVEN:									
NOMINAL	5.22	5.22	5.22	(¹)	HILLSBOROUGH COUNTY:				
EFFECTIVE	2.35	2.34	2.34	(¹)	NOMINAL.	1.89	1.89	1.89	1.89
RATIO	46.3	46.2	45.9	(¹)	EFFECTIVE.	1.05	1.04	1.03	1.17
					RATIO.	65.5	66.0	65.8	59.6
DELAWARE									
					BALANCE OF COUNTY:				
NEW CASTLE COUNTY:					NOMINAL.	1.88	1.88	1.88	1.88
WILMINGTON:					EFFECTIVE.	1.05	1.05	1.05	1.30
NOMINAL	3.95	3.95	3.95	(¹)	RATIO.	71.1	71.3	71.5	96.6
EFFECTIVE	1.59	1.78	1.78	(¹)					
RATIO	40.3	45.2	45.2	(¹)	TAMPA:				
					NOMINAL.	2.74	2.74	2.74	(¹)
					EFFECTIVE.	1.12	1.01	1.00	(¹)
					RATIO.	57.4	58.6	56.8	(¹)

See footnotes at end of table.

Table 3. Median Property Tax Rates and Assessment Ratios for Real Property Involved in Measurable Sales During a 6-Month Period, for Selected Local Areas: 1976—Continued

Area	All types	Residential (nonfarm) Total	Single-family	Vacant platted lots	Area	All types	Residential (nonfarm) Total	Single-family	Vacant platted lots
FLORIDA--CONTINUED					GEORGIA--CONTINUED				
LEON COUNTY:					DE KALB COUNTY:				
NOMINAL	1.64	1.64	1.64	1.29	BALANCE OF COUNTY:				
EFFECTIVE	0.95	0.92	0.90	1.03	NOMINAL	4.30	4.30	4.30	4.15
RATIO	76.4	76.5	75.5	76.4	EFFECTIVE	1.31	1.31	1.31	1.62
BALANCE OF COUNTY:					RATIO	35.4	35.3	35.3	40.0
NOMINAL	1.29	1.29	1.29	1.29	ATLANTA (PART):				
EFFECTIVE	0.85	0.84	0.83	0.99	NOMINAL	(2)	(2)	(2)	(2)
RATIO	81.0	81.9	81.6	76.4	EFFECTIVE	(2)	(2)	(2)	(2)
TALLAHASSEE:					RATIO	(2)	(2)	(2)	(2)
NOMINAL	1.64	1.64	1.64	(1)	DOUGHERTY COUNTY:				
EFFECTIVE	1.06	1.02	1.02	(1)	NOMINAL	3.67	3.67	3.81	3.22
RATIO	73.8	73.1	73.1	(1)	EFFECTIVE	1.11	1.11	1.05	1.14
ORANGE COUNTY:					RATIO	34.5	34.7	34.7	33.8
NOMINAL	1.89	1.92	1.92	1.77	BALANCE OF COUNTY:				
EFFECTIVE	1.27	1.27	1.26	1.25	NOMINAL	3.06	3.09	3.09	3.06
RATIO	79.5	80.7	80.7	65.1	EFFECTIVE	0.99	0.95	0.95	1.14
BALANCE OF COUNTY:					RATIO	35.1	34.7	34.7	37.1
NOMINAL	1.83	1.88	1.85	1.75	ALBANY:				
EFFECTIVE	1.25	1.23	1.23	1.29	NOMINAL	3.81	3.94	3.96	3.67
RATIO	80.9	81.6	81.6	74.9	EFFECTIVE	1.21	1.23	1.19	1.13
ORLANDO:					RATIO	34.5	35.1	35.1	33.2
NOMINAL	2.28	2.28	2.28	(1)					
EFFECTIVE	1.41	1.41	1.41	(1)	FULTON COUNTY:				
RATIO	78.5	79.3	79.3	(1)	NOMINAL	4.38	4.75	4.72	3.37
PALM BEACH COUNTY:					EFFECTIVE	1.23	1.22	1.20	1.14
NOMINAL	2.39	2.48	2.48	2.22	RATIO	32.7	32.7	32.9	31.7
EFFECTIVE	1.00	1.05	1.04	0.85	BALANCE OF COUNTY:				
RATIO	50.1	53.6	52.9	39.3	NOMINAL	3.42	3.43	3.44	3.35
BALANCE OF COUNTY:					EFFECTIVE	1.05	1.01	1.02	1.07
NOMINAL	2.48	2.48	2.48	2.51	RATIO	32.7	32.6	32.7	32.0
EFFECTIVE	1.07	1.08	1.08	0.96	ATLANTA (PART):				
RATIO	51.7	53.6	53.1	44.5	NOMINAL	5.93	5.77	5.69	5.93
WEST PALM BEACH:					EFFECTIVE	1.55	1.54	1.53	1.64
NOMINAL	2.21	2.16	2.16	2.21	RATIO	32.7	32.8	33.4	27.6
EFFECTIVE	0.85	0.86	0.84	0.82					
RATIO	43.8	55.2	51.9	37.5					
PINELLAS COUNTY:					RICHMOND COUNTY:				
NOMINAL	2.01	2.01	2.01	1.87	NOMINAL	5.87	5.87	5.87	3.82
EFFECTIVE	1.00	1.05	1.01	0.80	EFFECTIVE	1.55	1.43	1.39	2.06
RATIO	65.4	66.4	66.4	51.2	RATIO	34.7	33.6	33.2	54.0
BALANCE OF COUNTY:					BALANCE OF COUNTY:				
NOMINAL	1.86	1.86	1.87	1.85	NOMINAL	3.82	3.82	3.82	3.82
EFFECTIVE	0.94	0.96	0.96	0.78	EFFECTIVE	1.39	1.18	1.18	2.06
RATIO	66.1	67.5	67.9	49.6	RATIO	41.1	36.2	36.2	54.0
CLEARWATER:					AUGUSTA:				
NOMINAL	2.01	2.01	2.01	(1)	NOMINAL	5.87	5.87	5.87	5.87
EFFECTIVE	1.15	1.14	1.14	(1)	EFFECTIVE	1.68	1.63	1.60	2.74
RATIO	68.1	68.1	68.1	(1)	RATIO	33.1	32.2	31.3	45.5
ST. PETERSBURG:					COLUMBUS-MUSCOGEE:				
NOMINAL	2.13	2.14	2.14	2.12	NOMINAL	4.56	4.56	4.56	4.67
EFFECTIVE	1.11	1.11	1.11	0.80	EFFECTIVE	1.32	1.35	1.32	1.31
RATIO	64.1	64.2	64.4	51.3	RATIO	33.0	33.8	33.5	28.0
DUVAL COUNTY:									
JACKSONVILLE:					HAWAII				
NOMINAL	1.78	1.78	1.78	1.78	HONOLULU:				
EFFECTIVE	1.03	1.02	1.01	1.02	NOMINAL	1.54	1.54	1.54	1.54
RATIO	72.0	72.5	71.9	55.5	EFFECTIVE	0.66	0.65	0.65	0.82
					RATIO	53.0	53.1	54.3	53.2
GEORGIA									
BIBB COUNTY:					IDAHO				
NOMINAL	5.28	5.30	5.32	5.27	ADA COUNTY:				
EFFECTIVE	1.27	1.29	1.28	0.91	NOMINAL	16.07	16.07	16.07	11.84
RATIO	26.4	27.8	26.5	23.5	EFFECTIVE	1.23	1.37	1.35	0.59
BALANCE OF COUNTY:					RATIO	8.6	8.9	8.9	5.0
NOMINAL	3.87	(1)	(1)	(1)	BALANCE OF COUNTY:				
EFFECTIVE	0.66	(1)	(1)	(1)	NOMINAL	11.42	11.42	11.43	11.42
RATIO	22.9	(1)	(1)	(1)	EFFECTIVE	0.97	1.05	1.05	0.64
MACON (PART):					RATIO	8.2	9.0	8.9	6.1
NOMINAL	5.28	5.31	5.32	5.28	BOISE:				
EFFECTIVE	1.29	1.30	1.29	0.97	NOMINAL	16.25	16.25	16.25	16.25
RATIO	27.2	27.8	26.7	22.5	EFFECTIVE	1.47	1.51	1.52	0.53
CHATHAM COUNTY:					RATIO	8.8	8.8	8.9	3.3
SAVANNAH:									
NOMINAL	6.62	6.80	6.81	(1)					
EFFECTIVE	1.61	1.61	1.61	(1)					
RATIO	28.5	28.9	28.9	(1)					

See footnotes at end of table.

Table 3. Median Property Tax Rates and Assessment Ratios for Real Property Involved in Measurable Sales During a 6-Month Period, for Selected Local Areas: 1976—Continued

Area	All types	Residential (nonfarm) Total	Single-family	Vacant platted lots
ILLINOIS				
CHAMPAIGN COUNTY:				
NOMINAL	6.46	6.46	6.46	4.71
EFFECTIVE	1.70	1.77	1.77	1.29
RATIO	29.7	30.9	30.9	23.4
BALANCE OF COUNTY:				
NOMINAL	4.98	5.06	5.04	4.57
EFFECTIVE	1.55	1.64	1.64	1.20
RATIO	29.1	31.1	31.1	26.9
CHAMPAIGN:				
NOMINAL	6.46	6.46	6.46	(1)
EFFECTIVE	1.93	1.96	1.98	(1)
RATIO	30.6	30.9	30.9	(1)
COOK COUNTY:				
NOMINAL	8.82	8.82	8.82	(1)
EFFECTIVE	1.61	1.60	1.56	(1)
RATIO	19.1	18.9	18.2	(1)
BALANCE OF COUNTY:				
NOMINAL	8.09	8.05	8.17	(1)
EFFECTIVE	1.46	1.46	1.46	(1)
RATIO	18.2	18.1	18.0	(1)
ARLINGTON HEIGHTS (PART):				
NOMINAL	8.21	8.21	8.21	(1)
EFFECTIVE	1.45	1.45	1.45	(1)
RATIO	17.2	17.2	17.2	(1)
BERWYN:				
NOMINAL	5.90	5.90	5.74	(1)
EFFECTIVE	1.11	1.11	1.07	(1)
RATIO	18.4	18.4	18.4	(1)
CHICAGO (PART):				
NOMINAL	8.82	8.82	8.82	(1)
EFFECTIVE	1.71	1.71	1.66	(1)
RATIO	19.9	19.9	19.2	(1)
CICERO:				
NOMINAL	7.08	7.08	7.08	(1)
EFFECTIVE	1.14	1.14	1.14	(1)
RATIO	16.1	16.1	16.1	(1)
DES PLAINES:				
NOMINAL	7.79	7.79	7.79	(1)
EFFECTIVE	1.40	1.40	1.40	(1)
RATIO	17.8	17.8	17.8	(1)
OAK PARK:				
NOMINAL	10.90	10.90	10.90	(1)
EFFECTIVE	1.90	1.90	1.92	(1)
RATIO	16.8	16.8	17.2	(1)
SKOKIE:				
NOMINAL	8.68	8.68	(1)	(1)
EFFECTIVE	1.82	1.82	(1)	(1)
RATIO	15.2	15.2	(1)	(1)
DU PAGE COUNTY:				
NOMINAL	7.35	7.35	7.35	6.15
EFFECTIVE	1.93	1.93	1.92	1.47
RATIO	26.2	26.3	26.2	23.9
BALANCE OF COUNTY:				
NOMINAL	7.35	7.35	7.35	6.15
EFFECTIVE	1.93	1.93	1.92	1.47
RATIO	26.2	26.3	26.2	23.9
KANE COUNTY:				
NOMINAL	(NA)	(NA)	(NA)	(NA)
EFFECTIVE	(NA)	(NA)	(NA)	(NA)
RATIO	(NA)	(NA)	(NA)	(NA)
BALANCE OF COUNTY:				
NOMINAL	5.92	1.54	1.54	(1)
EFFECTIVE	1.68	1.66	1.66	(1)
RATIO	29.1	29.0	29.0	(1)
AURORA:				
NOMINAL	7.53	7.53	7.53	(1)
EFFECTIVE	2.28	2.27	2.28	(1)
RATIO	30.9	30.3	30.9	(1)
ELGIN (PART):				
NOMINAL	6.05	6.05	6.05	(1)
EFFECTIVE	1.61	1.80	1.56	(1)
RATIO	27.6	29.7	27.4	(1)
ILLINOIS—CONTINUED				
LAKE COUNTY:				
NOMINAL	7.47	7.44	7.43	8.31
EFFECTIVE	1.95	1.87	1.87	2.58
RATIO	25.8	25.0	24.5	28.5
BALANCE OF COUNTY:				
NOMINAL	7.44	7.43	7.43	8.85
EFFECTIVE	1.95	1.87	1.87	2.58
RATIO	25.9	25.1	24.9	28.5
WAUKEGAN:				
NOMINAL	8.23	8.50	8.37	(1)
EFFECTIVE	1.91	1.91	1.83	(1)
RATIO	21.5	21.5	20.9	(1)
MACON COUNTY:				
NOMINAL	5.38	5.38	5.38	5.30
EFFECTIVE	1.58	1.66	1.66	0.97
RATIO	31.5	32.9	32.9	23.7
BALANCE OF COUNTY:				
NOMINAL	4.98	4.98	4.98	(1)
EFFECTIVE	1.64	1.66	1.66	(1)
RATIO	33.8	35.7	35.7	(1)
DECATUR:				
NOMINAL	5.38	5.38	5.38	5.38
EFFECTIVE	1.47	1.62	1.62	0.92
RATIO	29.6	31.5	31.5	18.1
PEORIA COUNTY:				
NOMINAL	6.75	6.75	6.75	(1)
EFFECTIVE	1.83	1.83	1.83	(1)
RATIO	29.1	29.0	28.9	(1)
BALANCE OF COUNTY:				
NOMINAL	5.18	5.20	5.22	(1)
EFFECTIVE	1.04	0.93	0.90	(1)
RATIO	21.2	18.7	17.0	(1)
PEORIA:				
NOMINAL	6.75	6.75	6.75	(1)
EFFECTIVE	1.98	1.98	1.98	(1)
RATIO	29.4	30.0	29.7	(1)
ST. CLAIR COUNTY:				
NOMINAL	(2)	(2)	(2)	(2)
EFFECTIVE	(2)	(2)	(2)	(2)
RATIO	(2)	(2)	(2)	(2)
EAST ST. LOUIS:				
NOMINAL	3.63	3.63	3.63	(1)
EFFECTIVE	1.37	1.37	1.36	(1)
RATIO	32.0	32.0	32.0	(1)
SANGAMON COUNTY:				
NOMINAL	5.72	6.12	5.96	4.67
EFFECTIVE	1.43	1.53	1.54	1.32
RATIO	27.3	28.0	27.6	29.3
BALANCE OF COUNTY:				
NOMINAL	4.34	4.42	4.43	4.24
EFFECTIVE	1.09	1.12	1.12	0.93
RATIO	24.5	25.4	25.4	22.8
SPRINGFIELD:				
NOMINAL	6.12	6.12	6.12	6.11
EFFECTIVE	1.79	1.78	1.77	2.21
RATIO	29.8	29.5	29.3	40.0
WILL COUNTY:				
NOMINAL	8.04	8.07	8.07	6.82
EFFECTIVE	2.09	2.21	2.21	1.33
RATIO	29.5	30.3	31.0	20.5
BALANCE OF COUNTY:				
NOMINAL	6.81	7.77	8.04	(1)
EFFECTIVE	2.26	2.32	2.45	(1)
RATIO	32.0	33.7	34.1	(1)
JOLIET:				
NOMINAL	8.31	8.31	8.31	(1)
EFFECTIVE	1.88	1.83	1.81	(1)
RATIO	27.4	27.4	25.3	(1)
WINNEBAGO COUNTY:				
NOMINAL	5.78	5.78	5.78	4.57
EFFECTIVE	1.84	1.97	1.84	1.53
RATIO	35.2	35.3	35.2	30.6
BALANCE OF COUNTY:				
NOMINAL	4.80	5.14	5.14	(1)
EFFECTIVE	1.62	1.64	1.64	(1)
RATIO	32.7	35.0	35.0	(1)

See footnotes at end of table.

Table 3. Median Property Tax Rates and Assessment Ratios for Real Property Involved in Measurable Sales During a 6-Month Period, for Selected Local Areas: 1976—Continued

Area	Types of real property				Area	Types of real property			
	All types	Residential (nonfarm)		Vacant platted lots		All types	Residential (nonfarm)		Vacant platted lots
		Total	Single-family				Total	Single-family	
ILLINOIS--CONTINUED					**INDIANA--CONTINUED**				
WINNEBAGO COUNTY--CONTINUED:					VANDERBURGH COUNTY:				
ROCKFORD:					NOMINAL	8.96	9.01	9.01	6.04
NOMINAL	5.78	5.78	5.78	(¹)	EFFECTIVE	0.99	1.08	1.04	0.32
EFFECTIVE	2.05	2.04	1.98	(¹)	RATIO	15.1	15.5	15.3	6.3
RATIO	36.1	35.4	35.4	(¹)					
					BALANCE OF COUNTY:				
INDIANA					NOMINAL	6.03	6.03	6.03	5.99
					EFFECTIVE	0.59	0.77	0.77	0.25
ALLEN COUNTY:					RATIO	12.5	14.5	14.5	6.3
NOMINAL	8.47	8.48	8.48	5.90	EVANSVILLE:				
EFFECTIVE	1.19	1.30	1.30	0.56	NOMINAL	9.01	9.01	9.01	9.00
RATIO	19.7	19.9	19.9	10.7	EFFECTIVE	1.15	1.19	1.50	0.18
					RATIO	15.7	15.7	15.6	8.1
BALANCE OF COUNTY:					VIGO COUNTY:				
NOMINAL	5.82	5.48	5.48	5.90	NOMINAL	11.32	11.32	11.32	11.32
EFFECTIVE	0.92	0.99	0.99	0.56	EFFECTIVE	1.14	1.09	1.06	1.60
RATIO	19.1	19.8	19.8	10.7	RATIO	14.2	14.6	14.6	14.9
FORT WAYNE:									
NOMINAL	8.48	8.48	8.48	(¹)	BALANCE OF COUNTY:				
EFFECTIVE	1.59	1.57	1.57	(¹)	NOMINAL	7.61	7.61	7.61	7.27
RATIO	20.2	20.1	20.1	(¹)	EFFECTIVE	0.71	0.98	0.87	0.37
DELAWARE COUNTY:					RATIO	11.9	13.5	12.8	5.1
NOMINAL	8.46	8.46	8.46	(¹)	TERRE HAUTE:				
EFFECTIVE	1.27	1.27	1.26	(¹)	NOMINAL	11.32	11.32	11.32	11.32
RATIO	17.4	17.4	17.4	(¹)	EFFECTIVE	1.56	1.23	1.22	1.77
					RATIO	15.1	15.2	15.3	15.3
BALANCE OF COUNTY:									
NOMINAL	8.10	8.10	8.10	(¹)	**IOWA**				
EFFECTIVE	1.14	1.16	1.16	(¹)					
RATIO	17.4	17.5	17.5	(¹)	BLACK HAWK COUNTY:				
MUNCIE:					NOMINAL	3.30	3.30	3.30	2.74
NOMINAL	9.68	9.68	9.68	(¹)	EFFECTIVE	2.23	2.26	2.26	1.15
EFFECTIVE	1.44	1.46	1.44	(¹)	RATIO	70.1	71.0	71.0	44.6
RATIO	18.3	17.2	16.9	(¹)					
LAKE COUNTY:					BALANCE OF COUNTY:				
NOMINAL	14.71	15.15	15.11	13.03	NOMINAL	2.74	2.74	2.74	2.74
EFFECTIVE	1.71	1.81	1.81	1.17	EFFECTIVE	1.94	2.11	2.10	0.62
RATIO	11.6	12.0	11.9	7.6	RATIO	70.7	77.1	76.6	35.5
BALANCE OF COUNTY:					WATERLOO:				
NOMINAL	13.93	13.93	13.93	12.66	NOMINAL	3.30	3.30	3.30	3.30
EFFECTIVE	1.50	1.59	1.59	1.12	EFFECTIVE	2.31	2.33	2.32	1.48
RATIO	10.9	11.5	11.3	7.5	RATIO	70.1	70.4	70.2	44.7
GARY:					DUBUQUE COUNTY:				
NOMINAL	17.44	17.44	17.44	(¹)	NOMINAL	2.50	2.50	2.50	2.50
EFFECTIVE	2.42	2.41	2.41	(¹)	EFFECTIVE	1.95	2.14	2.11	0.33
RATIO	14.1	13.9	13.9	(¹)	RATIO	71.4	74.1	74.7	12.6
HAMMOND:					BALANCE OF COUNTY:				
NOMINAL	18.02	18.02	18.02	(¹)	NOMINAL	2.50	2.50	2.50	2.50
EFFECTIVE	1.80	1.77	1.80	(¹)	EFFECTIVE	1.75	1.85	1.85	0.51
RATIO	10.0	9.8	10.0	(¹)	RATIO	70.7	75.3	75.3	20.3
MADISON COUNTY:					DUBUQUE:				
NOMINAL	10.63	10.63	10.63	(¹)	NOMINAL	3.28	3.28	3.28	(¹)
EFFECTIVE	1.56	1.56	1.37	(¹)	EFFECTIVE	2.38	2.42	2.43	(¹)
RATIO	19.3	19.3	19.0	(¹)	RATIO	72.4	73.7	74.1	(¹)
BALANCE OF COUNTY:					LINN COUNTY:				
NOMINAL	7.53	7.53	7.53	(¹)	BALANCE OF COUNTY:				
EFFECTIVE	1.11	1.12	1.12	(¹)	NOMINAL	(²)	(²)	(²)	(²)
RATIO	17.4	17.4	17.4	(¹)	EFFECTIVE	(²)	(²)	(²)	(²)
ANDERSON:					RATIO	(²)	(²)	(²)	(²)
NOMINAL	10.63	10.63	10.63	(¹)					
EFFECTIVE	1.95	1.88	1.76	(¹)	CEDAR RAPIDS:				
RATIO	20.3	20.3	19.9	(¹)	NOMINAL	2.70	2.70	2.70	2.70
MARION COUNTY:					EFFECTIVE	2.15	2.18	2.17	1.46
NOMINAL	12.14	12.14	12.14	8.07	RATIO	79.8	80.8	80.3	54.1
EFFECTIVE	1.64	1.68	1.62	0.61	POLK COUNTY:				
RATIO	19.5	19.8	19.4	8.6	NOMINAL	3.53	3.53	3.53	3.11
BALANCE OF COUNTY:					EFFECTIVE	2.06	2.12	2.10	(²)
NOMINAL	8.01	8.01	8.01	8.04	RATIO	74.0	76.1	76.0	(²)
EFFECTIVE	1.25	1.29	1.26	0.56					
RATIO	18.6	19.1	19.1	7.4	BALANCE OF COUNTY:				
INDIANAPOLIS:					NOMINAL	3.10	3.10	3.10	3.10
NOMINAL	12.14	12.14	12.14	(¹)	EFFECTIVE	1.80	2.07	2.06	(²)
EFFECTIVE	2.16	2.16	2.10	(¹)	RATIO	69.9	75.7	75.3	(²)
RATIO	21.0	21.0	20.2	(¹)	DES MOINES:				
ST. JOSEPH COUNTY:					NOMINAL	3.53	3.53	3.53	3.53
SOUTH BEND:					EFFECTIVE	2.13	2.17	2.14	1.68
NOMINAL	10.17	10.17	10.17	(¹)	RATIO	75.7	76.3	76.1	42.1
EFFECTIVE	2.04	2.04	2.04	(¹)					
RATIO	20.3	20.3	20.3	(¹)					

See footnotes at end of table.

Area	All types	Residential (nonfarm) Total	Single-family	Vacant platted lots
IOWA--CONTINUED				
POTTAWATTAMIE COUNTY:				
NOMINAL	2.70	2.90	2.90	2.56
EFFECTIVE	2.22	2.43	2.43	0.15
RATIO	77.2	82.3	82.3	5.7
BALANCE OF COUNTY:				
NOMINAL	2.39	2.47	2.47	2.56
EFFECTIVE	1.02	2.31	2.31	0.15
RATIO	50.1	93.0	93.0	5.7
COUNCIL BLUFFS:				
NOMINAL	3.53	3.53	3.53	(1)
EFFECTIVE	2.60	2.60	2.60	(1)
RATIO	77.4	77.4	77.4	(1)
WOODBURY COUNTY:				
BALANCE OF COUNTY:				
NOMINAL	2.23	(1)	(1)	(1)
EFFECTIVE	1.51	(1)	(1)	(1)
RATIO	67.7	(1)	(1)	(1)
SIOUX CITY:				
NOMINAL	3.52	3.52	3.52	3.52
EFFECTIVE	2.35	2.39	2.41	1.29
RATIO	65.8	68.9	68.6	48.2
KANSAS				
JOHNSON COUNTY:				
NOMINAL	11.00	11.11	11.11	10.85
EFFECTIVE	1.28	1.32	1.32	0.63
RATIO	11.7	12.1	12.0	6.8
BALANCE OF COUNTY:				
NOMINAL	10.88	10.89	10.89	10.25
EFFECTIVE	1.20	1.29	1.28	0.63
RATIO	11.2	11.8	11.8	6.6
OVERLAND PARK:				
NOMINAL	11.34	11.34	11.34	11.28
EFFECTIVE	1.38	1.40	1.39	1.14
RATIO	12.3	12.3	12.3	9.6
SEDGWICK COUNTY:				
NOMINAL	10.48	10.48	10.48	10.48
EFFECTIVE	1.30	1.52	1.51	0.83
RATIO	12.9	14.8	14.7	8.0
BALANCE OF COUNTY:				
NOMINAL	10.48	10.48	10.48	10.48
EFFECTIVE	1.29	1.36	1.34	0.17
RATIO	12.9	14.1	13.9	2.0
WICHITA:				
NOMINAL	10.48	10.48	10.48	10.32
EFFECTIVE	1.35	1.56	1.55	0.83
RATIO	12.9	14.9	14.8	8.0
SHAWNEE COUNTY:				
NOMINAL	11.26	11.26	11.26	11.22
EFFECTIVE	1.29	1.31	1.31	0.27
RATIO	11.7	11.9	11.7	3.2
BALANCE OF COUNTY:				
NOMINAL	7.56	7.62	7.61	7.30
EFFECTIVE	0.64	0.95	0.93	0.11
RATIO	10.8	12.3	12.0	2.7
TOPEKA:				
NOMINAL	11.26	11.26	11.26	11.26
EFFECTIVE	1.33	1.33	1.32	0.56
RATIO	11.7	11.9	11.7	5.0
WYANDOTTE COUNTY:				
NOMINAL	18.46	18.47	18.48	18.26
EFFECTIVE	2.10	2.09	2.09	1.64
RATIO	11.3	11.2	11.2	8.9
BALANCE OF COUNTY:				
NOMINAL	15.22	16.43	16.43	14.00
EFFECTIVE	1.25	1.47	1.47	0.62
RATIO	8.1	10.2	10.2	5.0
KANSAS CITY:				
NOMINAL	18.48	18.48	18.48	18.42
EFFECTIVE	2.12	2.10	2.09	2.17
RATIO	11.4	11.3	11.2	11.3

Area	All types	Residential (nonfarm) Total	Single-family	Vacant platted lots
KENTUCKY				
DAVIESS COUNTY:				
NOMINAL	1.51	1.51	1.51	(1)
EFFECTIVE	1.03	1.05	1.05	(1)
RATIO	73.3	75.0	74.8	(1)
BALANCE OF COUNTY:				
NOMINAL	0.75	0.75	0.75	(1)
EFFECTIVE	0.44	0.44	0.44	(1)
RATIO	68.1	68.9	68.9	(1)
OWENSBORO:				
NOMINAL	1.51	1.51	1.51	(1)
EFFECTIVE	1.08	1.12	1.10	(1)
RATIO	74.6	75.4	75.0	(1)
JEFFERSON COUNTY:				
LOUISVILLE:				
NOMINAL	1.64	1.64	1.64	1.64
EFFECTIVE	1.33	1.35	1.31	1.04
RATIO	81.8	83.3	81.0	63.9
LEXINGTON-FAYETTE:				
NOMINAL	1.43	1.43	1.43	1.42
EFFECTIVE	1.14	1.12	1.09	1.33
RATIO	87.1	85.9	86.5	96.7
LOUISIANA				
CADDO PARISH:				
NOMINAL	(4)	(4)	(4)	(4)
EFFECTIVE	0.61	0.62	0.62	0.59
RATIO	18.0	18.1	18.0	12.5
BALANCE OF PARISH:				
NOMINAL	(4)	(4)	(4)	(4)
EFFECTIVE	0.23	0.24	0.24	(1)
RATIO	14.6	15.4	15.4	(1)
SHREVEPORT (PART):				
NOMINAL	(4)	(4)	(4)	(4)
EFFECTIVE	0.64	0.63	0.63	0.69
RATIO	18.2	18.2	18.1	13.9
CALCASIEU PARISH:				
LAKE CHARLES:				
NOMINAL	(4)	(4)	(4)	(1)
EFFECTIVE	0.31	0.36	0.36	(1)
RATIO	9.7	9.8	9.8	(1)
LAFAYETTE PARISH:				
LAFAYETTE:				
NOMINAL	(4)	(4)	(1)	(1)
EFFECTIVE	0.13	0.14	0.13	(1)
RATIO	3.9	4.0	4.2	(1)
QUACHITA PARISH:				
MONROE:				
NOMINAL	(4)	(4)	(4)	(1)
EFFECTIVE	0.35	0.35	0.35	(1)
RATIO	9.5	10.3	10.3	(1)
EAST BATON ROUGE PARISH:				
NOMINAL	4.97	4.97	4.97	4.97
EFFECTIVE	0.60	0.63	0.62	0.41
RATIO	11.7	12.5	12.1	8.2
NEW ORLEANS:				
NOMINAL	4.37	4.37	4.37	4.37
EFFECTIVE	0.54	0.52	0.46	0.55
RATIO	15.1	15.3	15.2	12.5
MAINE				
CUMBERLAND COUNTY:				
PORTLAND:				
NOMINAL	3.37	3.37	3.37	3.37
EFFECTIVE	2.53	2.56	2.56	2.50
RATIO	75.2	76.1	76.1	73.8
MARYLAND				
BALTIMORE COUNTY:				
NOMINAL	3.34	3.34	3.34	(1)
EFFECTIVE	1.31	1.32	1.31	(1)
RATIO	39.1	39.4	39.4	(1)

See footnotes at end of table.

Table 3. Median Property Tax Rates and Assessment Ratios for Real Property Involved in Measurable Sales During a 6-Month Period, for Selected Local Areas: 1976—Continued

Area	All types	Residential (nonfarm) Total	Single-family	Vacant platted lots
MARYLAND--CONTINUED				
MONTGOMERY COUNTY:				
NOMINAL	3.84	3.84	3.84	3.80
EFFECTIVE	1.58	1.60	1.60	1.53
RATIO	40.7	40.8	40.8	40.3
PRINCE GEORGES COUNTY:				
NOMINAL	4.15	4.15	4.15	(1)
EFFECTIVE	1.73	1.73	1.73	(1)
RATIO	41.8	41.8	41.9	(1)
BALTIMORE CITY:				
NOMINAL	6.11	6.11	6.11	(1)
EFFECTIVE	2.64	2.62	2.54	(1)
RATIO	42.2	41.8	40.9	(1)
MASSACHUSETTS				
BERKSHIRE COUNTY:				
PITTSFIELD:				
NOMINAL	6.72	6.72	6.72	(1)
EFFECTIVE	2.93	2.97	2.93	(1)
RATIO	44.2	44.2	43.4	(1)
BRISTOL COUNTY:				
FALL RIVER:				
NOMINAL	19.10	19.10	19.10	10.43
EFFECTIVE	4.81	6.59	4.36	1.51
RATIO	35.3	36.8	37.4	30.0
NEW BEDFORD:				
NOMINAL	13.66	13.66	13.66	17.05
EFFECTIVE	2.84	3.15	3.06	2.27
RATIO	20.5	22.6	21.9	13.3
HAMPDEN COUNTY:				
SPRINGFIELD:				
NOMINAL	8.55	8.55	8.55	(1)
EFFECTIVE	3.76	3.72	3.46	(1)
RATIO	43.9	43.8	40.5	(1)
MIDDLESEX COUNTY:				
ARLINGTON TOWN:				
NOMINAL	7.48	7.48	7.48	(1)
EFFECTIVE	4.33	4.32	4.24	(1)
RATIO	57.9	57.7	57.8	(1)
CAMBRIDGE:				
NOMINAL	17.95	17.95	17.95	(1)
EFFECTIVE	3.51	3.47	3.46	(1)
RATIO	19.9	19.6	19.3	(1)
FRAMINGHAM TOWN:				
NOMINAL	5.83	5.83	5.83	(1)
EFFECTIVE	3.39	3.34	3.32	(1)
RATIO	58.2	57.3	57.6	(1)
MEDFORD:				
NOMINAL	18.10	18.10	18.10	(1)
EFFECTIVE	3.57	3.57	3.55	(1)
RATIO	19.7	19.7	19.6	(1)
NEWTON:				
NOMINAL	16.44	16.44	16.43	(1)
EFFECTIVE	3.57	3.56	3.55	(1)
RATIO	21.9	22.1	21.9	(1)
SOMERVILLE:				
NOMINAL	23.75	23.75	23.75	(1)
EFFECTIVE	5.03	4.97	4.62	(1)
RATIO	21.2	20.9	19.5	(1)
WALTHAM:				
NOMINAL	5.86	5.86	5.86	(1)
EFFECTIVE	3.61	3.58	3.55	(1)
RATIO	61.6	61.1	60.6	(1)
NORFOLK COUNTY:				
BROOKLINE TOWN:				
NOMINAL	8.40	8.40	8.40	(1)
EFFECTIVE	4.24	4.18	4.22	(1)
RATIO	51.1	49.8	50.2	(1)
QUINCY:				
NOMINAL	19.48	19.48	19.48	(1)
EFFECTIVE	3.51	3.43	3.51	(1)
RATIO	19.4	19.3	18.9	(1)
WEYMOUTH TOWN:				
NOMINAL	6.44	6.44	6.44	(1)
EFFECTIVE	3.62	3.62	3.62	(1)
RATIO	56.9	56.9	56.9	(1)
MASSACHUSETTS--CONTINUED				
PLYMOUTH COUNTY:				
BROCKTON:				
NOMINAL	5.42	5.42	5.42	(1)
EFFECTIVE	4.35	4.35	4.25	(1)
RATIO	80.3	80.3	78.4	(1)
SUFFOLK COUNTY:				
BOSTON:				
NOMINAL	19.67	19.67	19.67	(1)
EFFECTIVE	4.94	4.68	3.81	(1)
RATIO	25.1	23.8	19.4	(1)
WORCESTER COUNTY:				
WORCESTER:				
NOMINAL	15.80	15.80	15.80	15.80
EFFECTIVE	3.92	4.39	3.34	3.16
RATIO	25.6	27.7	23.2	20.0
MICHIGAN				
GENESSEE COUNTY:				
FLINT:				
NOMINAL	5.31	5.31	5.31	5.32
EFFECTIVE	2.58	2.58	2.58	2.36
RATIO	48.7	48.5	48.5	44.5
INGHAM COUNTY:				
LANSING (PART):				
NOMINAL	5.77	5.57	5.77	(1)
EFFECTIVE	2.36	2.36	2.35	(1)
RATIO	41.0	40.8	40.7	(1)
KALAMAZOO COUNTY:				
KALAMAZOO:				
NOMINAL	6.59	6.59	6.59	(1)
EFFECTIVE	2.69	2.69	2.69	(1)
RATIO	40.6	40.6	40.6	(1)
KENT COUNTY:				
GRAND RAPIDS:				
NOMINAL	4.64	4.64	4.64	(1)
EFFECTIVE	1.97	1.95	1.95	(1)
RATIO	44.3	43.2	43.8	(1)
WYOMING:				
NOMINAL	5.04	5.04	5.04	5.00
EFFECTIVE	2.19	2.22	2.19	1.66
RATIO	44.2	45.0	44.2	36.7
MACOMB COUNTY:				
ST. CLAIR SHORES:				
NOMINAL	6.64	6.64	6.64	(1)
EFFECTIVE	2.94	2.94	2.92	(1)
RATIO	44.4	44.4	44.4	(1)
WARREN:				
NOMINAL	5.62	5.62	5.62	(1)
EFFECTIVE	2.40	2.43	2.43	(1)
RATIO	41.4	41.7	41.7	(1)
STERLING HEIGHTS:				
NOMINAL	5.38	5.38	5.38	(1)
EFFECTIVE	2.39	2.38	2.38	(1)
RATIO	44.9	44.8	44.8	(1)
CLINTON TOWNSHIP:				
NOMINAL	5.14	5.14	5.18	(1)
EFFECTIVE	2.16	2.16	2.16	(1)
RATIO	42.1	42.1	42.3	(1)
OAKLAND COUNTY:				
PONTIAC:				
NOMINAL	6.45	6.45	6.45	(1)
EFFECTIVE	2.73	2.73	2.72	(1)
RATIO	42.8	42.8	42.6	(1)
ROYAL OAK:				
NOMINAL	6.96	6.96	6.96	(1)
EFFECTIVE	2.91	2.91	2.91	(1)
RATIO	41.8	41.7	41.8	(1)
SOUTHFIELD:				
NOMINAL	5.95	5.95	5.95	(1)
EFFECTIVE	2.39	2.37	2.37	(1)
RATIO	40.1	39.8	39.8	(1)
FARMINGTON HILL:				
NOMINAL	5.54	5.54	5.54	(1)
EFFECTIVE	2.27	2.27	2.27	(1)
RATIO	40.9	41.0	41.0	(1)

See footnotes at end of table.

Area	All types	Residential (nonfarm) Total	Single-family	Vacant platted lots
MICHIGAN--CONTINUED				
OAKLAND COUNTY--CONTINUED				
WATERFORD TOWNSHIP:				
NOMINAL	5.27	5.27	5.27	(¹)
EFFECTIVE	2.03	2.03	2.03	(¹)
RATIO	39.2	38.6	39.9	(¹)
SAGINAW COUNTY:				
SAGINAW:				
NOMINAL	5.32	5.32	5.32	(¹)
EFFECTIVE	2.52	2.56	2.52	(¹)
RATIO	47.3	48.0	47.3	(¹)
WASHTENAW COUNTY:				
ANN ARBOR:				
NOMINAL	6.82	6.82	6.82	(¹)
EFFECTIVE	2.81	2.81	2.81	(¹)
RATIO	41.1	41.2	41.2	(¹)
WAYNE COUNTY:				
DEARBORN:				
NOMINAL	6.04	6.04	6.04	(¹)
EFFECTIVE	1.64	1.63	1.63	(¹)
RATIO	27.2	26.9	26.9	(¹)
DETROIT:				
NOMINAL	7.12	7.12	7.12	7.13
EFFECTIVE	3.46	3.47	3.47	3.37
RATIO	48.6	48.7	48.7	46.7
LIVONIA:				
NOMINAL	6.50	6.50	6.50	6.42
EFFECTIVE	2.60	2.60	2.60	2.48
RATIO	39.9	40.0	40.0	38.5
REDFORD TOWNSHIP:				
NOMINAL	5.73	5.73	5.73	(¹)
EFFECTIVE	2.16	2.14	2.14	(¹)
RATIO	41.6	41.6	41.6	(¹)
DEARBORN HEIGHTS:				
NOMINAL	4.63	4.62	4.62	(¹)
EFFECTIVE	2.58	2.60	2.60	(¹)
RATIO	54.3	54.4	54.4	(¹)
WESTLAND:				
NOMINAL	6.14	6.14	6.14	(¹)
EFFECTIVE	2.61	2.61	2.63	(¹)
RATIO	43.4	43.4	43.1	(¹)
TAYLOR:				
NOMINAL	6.85	6.85	6.85	6.85
EFFECTIVE	3.02	3.10	3.10	1.93
RATIO	44.3	45.3	45.3	28.1
MINNESOTA⁵				
HENNEPIN COUNTY:				
NOMINAL	8.07	7.87	7.87	10.26
EFFECTIVE	2.06	2.00	1.98	2.72
RATIO	25.4	25.4	25.4	26.5
BALANCE OF COUNTY:				
NOMINAL	7.69	7.56	7.54	10.56
EFFECTIVE	2.05	1.97	1.95	3.02
RATIO	26.4	26.3	26.2	30.5
BLOOMINGTON:				
NOMINAL	7.70	7.69	7.69	(¹)
EFFECTIVE	2.06	2.06	2.06	(¹)
RATIO	26.4	26.5	26.5	(¹)
MINNEAPOLIS:				
NOMINAL	9.07	9.00	8.86	(¹)
EFFECTIVE	2.06	2.06	2.04	(¹)
RATIO	23.0	23.0	23.0	(¹)
OLMSTED COUNTY:				
NOMINAL	7.47	6.82	6.81	8.91
EFFECTIVE	1.29	1.35	1.33	1.11
RATIO	18.6	19.3	19.3	14.9
BALANCE OF COUNTY:				
NOMINAL	7.73	6.33	6.33	8.91
EFFECTIVE	0.84	0.94	0.94	1.11
RATIO	15.3	16.7	16.7	14.9
ROCHESTER:				
NOMINAL	7.35	7.35	7.19	(¹)
EFFECTIVE	1.48	1.48	1.47	(¹)
RATIO	19.9	19.9	19.9	(¹)
MINNESOTA--CONTINUED				
RAMSEY COUNTY:				
NOMINAL	13.39	13.39	13.39	11.92
EFFECTIVE	2.68	2.68	2.64	4.15
RATIO	21.2	21.1	20.8	34.7
BALANCE OF COUNTY:				
NOMINAL	11.96	11.96	11.96	11.87
EFFECTIVE	2.47	2.47	2.47	3.18
RATIO	20.8	20.8	20.8	26.8
ST. PAUL:				
NOMINAL	13.39	13.39	13.39	(¹)
EFFECTIVE	2.90	2.87	2.78	(¹)
RATIO	21.7	21.5	20.8	(¹)
ST. LOUIS COUNTY:				
NOMINAL	9.26	7.63	7.63	12.06
EFFECTIVE	1.15	1.12	0.98	2.32
RATIO	16.3	16.3	16.2	30.3
BALANCE OF COUNTY:				
NOMINAL	7.86	4.51	4.51	10.13
EFFECTIVE	0.65	0.54	0.53	1.68
RATIO	11.9	14.2	14.2	17.1
DULUTH:				
NOMINAL	9.79	9.17	9.07	13.82
EFFECTIVE	2.08	1.88	1.87	4.92
RATIO	23.5	20.6	20.4	34.9
MISSISSIPPI				
HARRISON COUNTY:				
BILOXI:				
NOMINAL	16.54	16.33	16.33	(¹)
EFFECTIVE	1.23	1.25	1.25	(¹)
RATIO	7.2	7.4	7.4	(¹)
MISSOURI				
BOONE COUNTY:				
COLUMBIA:				
NOMINAL	6.94	6.94	6.94	(¹)
EFFECTIVE	1.07	1.09	1.26	(¹)
RATIO	15.3	15.7	18.1	(¹)
BUCHANAN COUNTY:				
ST. JOSEPH:				
NOMINAL	7.88	7.88	7.88	(¹)
EFFECTIVE	1.00	1.10	1.03	(¹)
RATIO	12.7	14.0	13.0	(¹)
CLAY COUNTY:				
KANSAS CITY (PART):				
NOMINAL	7.16	7.16	7.16	(¹)
EFFECTIVE	1.16	1.16	1.16	(¹)
RATIO	16.5	16.5	16.5	(¹)
GREENE COUNTY:				
SPRINGFIELD:				
NOMINAL	6.56	6.56	6.56	6.56
EFFECTIVE	1.03	1.11	1.12	0.20
RATIO	15.7	16.9	17.0	3.0
JACKSON COUNTY:				
INDEPENDENCE (PART):				
NOMINAL	6.40	6.40	6.40	6.40
EFFECTIVE	0.88	0.88	0.88	1.05
RATIO	14.0	13.8	13.8	16.4
KANSAS CITY (PART):				
NOMINAL	6.03	6.03	6.03	(¹)
EFFECTIVE	1.19	1.19	1.18	(¹)
RATIO	18.1	18.1	17.6	(¹)
PLATTE COUNTY:				
KANSAS CITY (PART):				
NOMINAL	7.97	7.97	7.97	(¹)
EFFECTIVE	1.60	1.53	1.53	(¹)
RATIO	20.6	20.2	20.2	(¹)
ST. LOUIS COUNTY:				
FLORISSANT:				
NOMINAL	9.20	9.20	9.20	(¹)
EFFECTIVE	1.88	1.87	1.87	(¹)
RATIO	20.4	20.3	20.3	(¹)
ST. LOUIS CITY:				
NOMINAL	6.48	6.48	6.48	(¹)
EFFECTIVE	1.96	1.92	1.64	(¹)
RATIO	30.2	29.6	25.4	(¹)

See footnotes at end of table.

Table 3. Median Property Tax Rates and Assessment Ratios for Real Property Involved in Measurable Sales During a 6-Month Period, for Selected Local Areas: 1976—Continued

Area	All types	Residential (nonfarm) Total	Single-family	Vacant platted lots	Area	All types	Residential (nonfarm) Total	Single-family	Vacant platted lots
MONTANA					**NEW HAMPSHIRE--CONTINUED**				
CASCADE COUNTY:					NASHUA:				
NOMINAL	28.57	28.57	28.57	28.57	NOMINAL	4.88	4.88	4.88	4.88
EFFECTIVE	1.57	1.57	1.56	1.05	EFFECTIVE	2.49	2.50	2.55	1.10
RATIO	5.6	5.6	5.5	4.0	RATIO	50.9	51.5	52.3	22.6
BALANCE OF COUNTY:									
NOMINAL	22.89	(1)	(1)	22.75	**NEW JERSEY[6]**				
EFFECTIVE	0.95	(1)	(1)	0.73	CAMDEN COUNTY:				
RATIO	4.6	(1)	(1)	3.0	CAMDEN:				
GREAT FALLS:					NOMINAL	7.31	7.31	7.31	(1)
NOMINAL	28.57	28.57	28.57	28.57	EFFECTIVE	4.11	4.11	4.54	(1)
EFFECTIVE	1.57	1.58	1.57	1.27	RATIO	56.2	56.2	62.0	(1)
RATIO	5.6	5.7	5.5	4.4	CHERRY HILL TOWNSHIP:				
YELLOWSTONE COUNTY:					NOMINAL	6.06	6.06	6.06	(1)
BILLINGS:					EFFECTIVE	4.03	4.03	4.03	(1)
NOMINAL	24.98	24.98	24.98	24.97	RATIO	66.3	66.3	66.3	(1)
EFFECTIVE	1.34	1.35	1.34	0.85	CUMBERLAND COUNTY:				
RATIO	5.32	5.36	5.34	3.20	VINELAND:				
NEBRASKA					NOMINAL	4.05	4.05	4.05	(1)
					EFFECTIVE	2.88	2.88	2.88	(1)
DOUGLAS COUNTY:					RATIO	73.3	73.0	73.0	(1)
NOMINAL	11.23	11.25	11.24	10.98	ESSEX COUNTY:				
EFFECTIVE	2.13	2.17	2.16	1.23	BLOOMFIELD TOWN:				
RATIO	19.4	19.8	19.7	13.1	NOMINAL	6.15	6.15	6.15	(1)
BALANCE OF COUNTY:					EFFECTIVE	3.77	3.77	3.64	(1)
NOMINAL	10.93	11.04	11.04	10.73	RATIO	61.3	61.3	59.2	(1)
EFFECTIVE	2.26	2.65	2.65	0.69	EAST ORANGE:				
RATIO	22.3	24.5	24.5	9.4	NOMINAL	11.54	11.54	11.54	(1)
OMAHA:					EFFECTIVE	6.54	7.12	6.77	(1)
NOMINAL	11.25	11.25	11.25	11.22	RATIO	56.6	61.6	58.6	(1)
EFFECTIVE	2.09	2.08	2.08	2.10	IRVINGTON TOWN:				
RATIO	18.9	18.8	18.7	18.7	NOMINAL	6.91	6.91	6.91	(1)
LANCASTER COUNTY:					EFFECTIVE	5.41	5.15	5.70	(1)
NOMINAL	10.35	10.35	10.35	10.35	RATIO	78.2	74.5	82.0	(1)
EFFECTIVE	1.62	1.66	1.65	0.82	NEWARK:				
RATIO	16.3	16.5	16.5	8.7	NOMINAL	9.36	9.36	9.36	(1)
BALANCE OF COUNTY:					EFFECTIVE	4.69	4.30	3.77	(1)
NOMINAL	7.55	7.63	7.63	7.39	RATIO	50.1	46.0	40.3	(1)
EFFECTIVE	0.90	1.18	1.18	0.74	HUDSON COUNTY:				
RATIO	12.1	15.9	15.9	9.8	BAYONNE:				
LINCOLN:					NOMINAL	6.30	6.30	(1)	(1)
NOMINAL	10.35	10.35	10.35	10.35	EFFECTIVE	3.13	3.13	(1)	(1)
EFFECTIVE	1.65	1.67	1.67	0.90	RATIO	49.7	49.7	(1)	(1)
RATIO	16.5	16.6	16.5	8.7	JERSEY CITY:				
NEVADA					NOMINAL	8.60	8.60	8.60	(1)
					EFFECTIVE	4.94	4.94	4.36	(1)
CLARK COUNTY:					RATIO	57.5	57.4	50.6	(1)
NOMINAL	4.99	5.00	5.00	4.95	UNION CITY:				
EFFECTIVE	1.21	1.25	1.26	0.55	NOMINAL	7.74	7.74	(1)	(1)
RATIO	24.5	25.2	25.3	14.6	EFFECTIVE	5.61	5.49	(1)	(1)
BALANCE OF COUNTY:					RATIO	72.5	71.0	(1)	(1)
NOMINAL	4.99	5.00	5.00	4.94	MERCER COUNTY:				
EFFECTIVE	1.17	1.23	1.24	0.59	HAMILTON TOWNSHIP:				
RATIO	23.7	24.9	25.1	14.7	NOMINAL	4.82	4.82	4.82	(1)
LAS VEGAS:					EFFECTIVE	2.64	2.69	2.70	(1)
NOMINAL	5.00	5.00	5.00	(1)	RATIO	54.5	55.8	56.1	(1)
EFFECTIVE	1.27	1.29	1.31	(1)	TRENTON:				
RATIO	25.7	25.8	26.1	(1)	NOMINAL	9.39	9.39	9.39	(1)
WASHOE COUNTY:					EFFECTIVE	4.62	4.89	4.89	(1)
NOMINAL	5.00	5.00	5.00	4.82	RATIO	49.2	52.1	52.1	(1)
EFFECTIVE	1.35	1.42	1.44	1.03	MIDDLESEX COUNTY:				
RATIO	27.3	28.3	28.5	21.9	EDISON TOWNSHIP:				
BALANCE OF COUNTY:					NOMINAL	3.81	3.81	3.81	(1)
NOMINAL	5.00	5.00	5.00	4.52	EFFECTIVE	2.72	2.65	2.72	(1)
EFFECTIVE	1.44	1.72	1.81	0.89	RATIO	71.3	69.5	71.3	(1)
RATIO	28.1	35.2	37.0	19.7	WOODBRIDGE TOWNSHIP:				
RENO:					NOMINAL	3.72	3.72	3.72	(1)
NOMINAL	5.15	5.17	5.17	5.00	EFFECTIVE	2.56	2.59	2.56	(1)
EFFECTIVE	1.32	1.28	1.23	1.47	RATIO	69.9	70.0	69.9	(1)
RATIO	25.9	25.4	24.5	29.3	MONMOUTH COUNTY:				
NEW HAMPSHIRE					MIDDLETOWN TOWNSHIP:				
					NOMINAL	4.45	4.45	4.45	(1)
HILLSBOROUGH COUNTY:					EFFECTIVE	2.83	2.83	2.83	(1)
MANCHESTER:					RATIO	63.2	63.2	63.2	(1)
NOMINAL	5.44	5.44	5.44	(1)	MORRIS COUNTY:				
EFFECTIVE	3.10	3.13	3.11	(1)	PARSIPPANY-TROY HILLS TOWNSHIP:				
RATIO	58.4	58.5	58.4	(1)	NOMINAL	5.06	5.08	5.09	(1)
					EFFECTIVE	2.96	2.94	2.91	(1)
					RATIO	60.0	59.5	59.0	(1)

See footnotes at end of table.

Table 3. Median Property Tax Rates and Assessment Ratios for Real Property Involved in Measurable Sales During a 6-Month Period, for Selected Local Areas: 1976—Continued

Area	All types	Residential (nonfarm) Total	Residential (nonfarm) Single-family	Vacant platted lots
NEW JERSEY--CONTINUED				
OCEAN COUNTY:				
DOVER TOWNSHIP:				
NOMINAL	2.26	2.26	2.26	(1)
EFFECTIVE	2.13	2.17	2.18	(1)
RATIO	94.0	96.0	96.1	(1)
PASSAIC COUNTY:				
CLIFTON:				
NOMINAL	3.16	3.16	3.16	(1)
EFFECTIVE	1.70	1.70	1.70	(1)
RATIO	53.8	53.8	53.7	(1)
PASSAIC:				
NOMINAL	5.59	5.59	(1)	(1)
EFFECTIVE	3.88	3.88	(1)	(1)
RATIO	67.2	67.2	(1)	(1)
PATERSON:				
NOMINAL	5.61	5.61	5.61	(1)
EFFECTIVE	3.70	3.70	3.55	(1)
RATIO	65.9	65.9	63.4	(1)
UNION COUNTY:				
ELIZABETH CITY:				
NOMINAL	2.85	2.85	2.85	(1)
EFFECTIVE	3.75	3.72	3.72	(1)
RATIO	131.2	130.2	130.2	(1)
UNION TOWNSHIP:				
NOMINAL	2.88	2.88	2.88	(1)
EFFECTIVE	2.23	2.29	2.34	(1)
RATIO	77.4	79.4	81.4	(1)
NEW MEXICO				
BERNALILLO COUNTY:				
NOMINAL	6.99	6.99	6.99	4.15
EFFECTIVE	1.30	1.31	1.31	0.68
RATIO	19.4	19.4	19.9	16.7
BALANCE OF COUNTY:				
NOMINAL	4.14	(1)	(1)	4.14
EFFECTIVE	0.69	(1)	(1)	0.22
RATIO	17.7	(1)	(1)	16.7
ALBUQUERQUE:				
NOMINAL	6.99	6.99	6.99	(1)
EFFECTIVE	1.32	1.32	1.33	(1)
RATIO	19.4	19.4	19.4	(1)
NEW YORK				
ALBANY COUNTY:				
ALBANY:				
NOMINAL	22.11	22.11	22.11	(1)
EFFECTIVE	3.90	3.68	3.46	(1)
RATIO	17.6	17.1	15.7	(1)
BROOME COUNTY:				
BINGHAMTON:				
NOMINAL	20.43	20.43	20.43	(1)
EFFECTIVE	3.72	2.82	2.75	(1)
RATIO	18.2	13.9	13.6	(1)
ERIE COUNTY:				
BUFFALO:				
NOMINAL	18.94	18.94	18.94	(1)
EFFECTIVE	3.90	3.85	3.72	(1)
RATIO	22.6	20.5	19.7	(1)
MONROE COUNTY:				
ROCHESTER:				
NOMINAL	16.68	16.68	16.68	(1)
EFFECTIVE	3.44	3.37	3.21	(1)
RATIO	21.2	20.8	19.7	(1)
NIAGARA COUNTY:				
NIAGARA FALLS:				
NOMINAL	12.33	12.33	12.33	(1)
EFFECTIVE	3.97	4.04	3.88	(1)
RATIO	32.2	32.8	31.5	(1)
ONEIDA COUNTY:				
ROME	(2)	(2)	(2)	(2)
UTICA:				
NOMINAL	9.57	9.57	9.57	(1)
EFFECTIVE	2.31	2.29	2.18	(1)
RATIO	24.5	24.4	23.2	(1)

Area	All types	Residential (nonfarm) Total	Residential (nonfarm) Single-family	Vacant platted lots
NEW YORK--CONTINUED				
ONONDAGA COUNTY:				
SYRACUSE:				
NOMINAL	13.93	13.92	13.92	(1)
EFFECTIVE	3.12	2.92	2.63	(1)
RATIO	23.0	22.1	18.8	(1)
RENSSELAER COUNTY:				
TROY:				
NOMINAL	17.18	17.18	17.18	(1)
EFFECTIVE	4.23	4.23	4.20	(1)
RATIO	26.2	26.2	25.0	(1)
SCHENECTADY COUNTY:				
SCHENECTADY:				
NOMINAL	19.53	19.53	19.54	(1)
EFFECTIVE	3.05	3.05	2.70	(1)
RATIO	16.9	16.9	15.6	(1)
WESTCHESTER COUNTY:				
MOUNT VERNON:				
NOMINAL	11.98	11.98	11.98	(1)
EFFECTIVE	3.51	3.00	3.21	(1)
RATIO	26.9	25.0	25.6	(1)
NEW ROCHELLE:				
NOMINAL	14.10	14.10	14.10	(1)
EFFECTIVE	4.15	4.17	4.19	(1)
RATIO	29.7	29.8	29.8	(1)
YONKERS:				
NOMINAL	11.56	11.52	11.56	(1)
EFFECTIVE	3.45	3.28	3.10	(1)
RATIO	31.4	29.9	27.6	(1)
NEW YORK CITY:				
NOMINAL	8.79	8.79	8.79	8.79
EFFECTIVE	2.30	2.21	1.91	2.44
RATIO	26.7	26.0	22.7	27.8
NORTH CAROLINA				
BUNCOMBE COUNTY:				
ASHEVILLE:				
NOMINAL	1.82	1.82	1.82	1.82
EFFECTIVE	1.25	1.26	1.26	1.22
RATIO	69.2	69.2	69.2	68.9
CUMBERLAND COUNTY:				
FAYETTEVILLE:				
NOMINAL	1.93	1.93	1.93	(1)
EFFECTIVE	1.17	1.22	1.22	(1)
RATIO	60.8	63.3	63.3	(1)
DURHAM COUNTY:				
NOMINAL	1.30	2.35	2.35	1.30
EFFECTIVE	0.97	1.16	1.13	0.60
RATIO	55.4	57.0	56.2	43.0
BALANCE OF COUNTY:				
NOMINAL	1.30	1.30	1.30	1.30
EFFECTIVE	0.69	0.71	0.71	0.55
RATIO	53.3	54.6	54.6	42.7
DURHAM:				
NOMINAL	2.35	2.35	2.35	2.35
EFFECTIVE	1.41	1.41	1.40	1.46
RATIO	59.3	59.3	59.2	62.0
FORSYTH COUNTY:				
NOMINAL	0.87	1.76	1.72	0.87
EFFECTIVE	0.50	0.60	0.53	0.27
RATIO	48.4	50.5	50.8	29.8
BALANCE OF COUNTY:				
NOMINAL	0.87	0.87	0.87	0.87
EFFECTIVE	0.40	0.44	0.44	0.26
RATIO	46.3	51.4	51.4	29.8
WINSTON SALEM:				
NOMINAL	1.77	1.77	1.77	1.76
EFFECTIVE	0.83	0.84	0.83	0.68
RATIO	48.8	48.8	48.7	38.8
GUILFORD COUNTY:				
GREENSBORO:				
NOMINAL	1.69	1.69	1.69	(1)
EFFECTIVE	1.04	1.04	1.04	(1)
RATIO	61.4	61.5	61.6	(1)
HIGH POINT (PART):				
NOMINAL	1.67	1.67	1.67	1.67
EFFECTIVE	1.04	1.12	1.14	0.79
RATIO	62.7	68.5	68.7	47.8

See footnotes at end of table.

Table 3. Median Property Tax Rates and Assessment Ratios for Real Property Involved in Measurable Sales During a 6-Month Period, for Selected Local Areas: 1976—Continued

Area	All types	Residential (nonfarm) Total	Single-family	Vacant platted lots
NORTH CAROLINA--CONTINUED				
MECKLENBURG COUNTY:				
NOMINAL	1.68	1.68	1.68	0.80
EFFECTIVE	1.28	1.32	1.33	0.59
RATIO	80.9	81.2	81.4	73.5
BALANCE OF COUNTY:				
NOMINAL	0.80	0.80	0.80	0.80
EFFECTIVE	0.62	0.63	0.63	0.59
RATIO	76.9	78.4	77.8	73.5
CHARLOTTE:				
NOMINAL	1.68	1.68	1.68	(1)
EFFECTIVE	1.38	1.38	1.38	(1)
RATIO	82.0	81.8	82.0	(1)
NEW HANOVER COUNTY:				
NOMINAL	0.83	0.85	0.82	0.69
EFFECTIVE	0.89	0.87	0.83	0.91
RATIO	88.3	90.8	92.8	85.0
BALANCE OF COUNTY:				
NOMINAL	0.73	0.79	0.77	0.69
EFFECTIVE	0.71	0.73	0.71	0.56
RATIO	89.6	91.9	93.0	81.5
WILMINGTON:				
NOMINAL	1.68	1.69	1.69	1.68
EFFECTIVE	1.54	1.58	1.60	1.40
RATIO	88.2	87.9	87.9	88.3
WAKE COUNTY:				
RALEIGH:				
NOMINAL	1.61	1.61	1.61	(1)
EFFECTIVE	1.27	1.29	1.30	(1)
RATIO	80.0	80.6	82.0	(1)
NORTH DAKOTA				
CASS COUNTY:				
NOMINAL	28.21	28.21	28.21	23.96
EFFECTIVE	1.51	1.51	1.51	2.16
RATIO	5.4	5.4	5.4	7.7
BALANCE OF COUNTY:				
NOMINAL	22.25	22.25	22.25	(1)
EFFECTIVE	1.34	1.28	1.28	(1)
RATIO	5.7	5.7	5.7	(1)
FARGO:				
NOMINAL	28.21	28.21	28.21	(1)
EFFECTIVE	1.51	1.51	1.51	(1)
RATIO	5.4	5.4	5.4	(1)
OHIO				
ALLEN COUNTY:				
NOMINAL	3.40	3.16	3.16	(1)
EFFECTIVE	0.87	0.85	0.87	(1)
RATIO	27.1	26.9	27.2	(1)
BALANCE OF COUNTY:				
NOMINAL	2.87	2.92	2.92	(1)
EFFECTIVE	0.78	0.82	0.82	(1)
RATIO	25.5	26.9	26.9	(1)
LIMA:				
NOMINAL	3.61	3.61	3.61	(1)
EFFECTIVE	1.01	0.91	0.92	(1)
RATIO	28.3	29.9	27.5	(1)
BUTLER COUNTY:				
NOMINAL	3.26	3.36	3.36	3.18
EFFECTIVE	0.80	0.87	0.87	0.59
RATIO	24.8	28.5	28.5	18.4
BALANCE OF COUNTY:				
NOMINAL	3.26	3.07	3.07	3.18
EFFECTIVE	0.80	0.88	0.88	0.59
RATIO	25.6	28.5	28.5	18.4
HAMILTON	(1)	(1)	(1)	(1)
CLARK COUNTY:				
NOMINAL	5.15	5.15	5.15	(1)
EFFECTIVE	1.10	1.10	1.10	(1)
RATIO	23.9	23.1	22.3	(1)
BALANCE OF COUNTY:				
NOMINAL	4.25	4.25	4.04	(1)
EFFECTIVE	1.05	1.05	0.98	(1)
RATIO	24.7	24.7	24.3	(1)
SPRINGFIELD:				
NOMINAL	5.15	5.15	5.15	(1)
EFFECTIVE	1.10	1.10	1.10	(1)
RATIO	22.2	22.1	22.0	(1)
OHIO--CONTINUED				
CUYAHOGA COUNTY:				
NOMINAL	6.79	6.97	6.84	6.71
EFFECTIVE	1.51	1.54	1.52	1.12
RATIO	30.2	30.5	30.5	26.3
BALANCE OF COUNTY:				
NOMINAL	6.53	6.49	6.49	6.71
EFFECTIVE	1.39	1.43	1.43	0.71
RATIO	29.2	29.7	29.7	12.2
CLEVELAND:				
NOMINAL	6.97	6.97	6.97	6.97
EFFECTIVE	1.81	1.80	1.79	2.20
RATIO	32.0	31.9	31.8	38.2
CLEVELAND HEIGHTS:				
NOMINAL	9.01	9.01	9.01	(1)
EFFECTIVE	2.20	2.20	2.20	(1)
RATIO	31.2	31.2	31.1	(1)
EUCLID:				
NOMINAL	6.23	6.23	6.23	(1)
EFFECTIVE	1.35	1.38	1.38	(1)
RATIO	30.4	30.4	30.4	(1)
LAKEWOOD:				
NOMINAL	7.79	7.79	7.79	(1)
EFFECTIVE	1.57	1.53	1.52	(1)
RATIO	28.5	28.5	28.5	(1)
PARMA:				
NOMINAL	5.52	5.52	5.52	(1)
EFFECTIVE	1.17	1.16	1.17	(1)
RATIO	30.2	29.9	29.8	(1)
FRANKLIN COUNTY:				
NOMINAL	4.04	4.04	4.04	3.86
EFFECTIVE	1.18	1.18	1.18	1.13
RATIO	29.4	29.4	29.4	30.1
BALANCE OF COUNTY:				
NOMINAL	4.04	4.28	4.28	3.85
EFFECTIVE	1.18	1.20	1.20	1.09
RATIO	29.3	29.1	29.1	28.6
COLUMBUS:				
NOMINAL	4.04	4.04	4.04	4.04
EFFECTIVE	1.18	1.18	1.18	1.41
RATIO	29.6	29.5	29.6	35.0
HAMILTON COUNTY:				
NOMINAL	4.54	4.54	4.54	4.16
EFFECTIVE	1.25	1.29	1.29	1.05
RATIO	29.0	29.2	29.5	22.6
BALANCE OF COUNTY:				
NOMINAL	4.38	4.42	4.42	4.03
EFFECTIVE	1.29	1.31	1.31	1.05
RATIO	30.0	30.3	30.3	22.6
CINCINNATI:				
NOMINAL	4.54	4.54	4.54	(1)
EFFECTIVE	1.23	1.22	1.20	(1)
RATIO	27.5	27.4	26.9	(1)
LORAIN COUNTY:				
NOMINAL	4.96	4.96	4.96	4.96
EFFECTIVE	1.11	1.13	1.12	0.77
RATIO	30.0	30.1	30.0	26.5
BALANCE OF COUNTY:				
NOMINAL	5.20	5.20	5.20	5.19
EFFECTIVE	1.16	1.17	1.17	1.14
RATIO	30.3	30.2	30.2	30.7
ELYRIA:				
NOMINAL	4.96	4.96	4.96	4.96
EFFECTIVE	0.67	0.99	0.99	0.39
RATIO	27.2	30.0	30.0	15.4
LORAIN:				
NOMINAL	4.83	4.83	4.83	4.83
EFFECTIVE	1.16	1.16	1.16	1.03
RATIO	31.2	31.4	31.2	26.5
LUCAS COUNTY:				
NOMINAL	4.87	4.65	4.65	6.26
EFFECTIVE	1.30	1.26	1.17	1.52
RATIO	36.0	36.6	36.1	35.0
BALANCE OF COUNTY:				
NOMINAL	5.12	4.18	4.18	6.22
EFFECTIVE	0.90	0.84	0.84	0.98
RATIO	27.6	27.8	27.8	20.3
TOLEDO:				
NOMINAL	4.84	4.65	4.66	6.26
EFFECTIVE	1.33	1.28	1.26	2.27
RATIO	37.4	37.7	37.4	43.8

See footnotes at end of table.

Table 3. Median Property Tax Rates and Assessment Ratios for Real Property Involved in Measurable Sales During a 6-Month Period, for Selected Local Areas: 1976—Continued

Area	All types	Residential (nonfarm) Total	Single-family	Vacant platted lots
OHIO--CONTINUED				
MAHONING COUNTY:				
NOMINAL	4.66	4.81	4.81	4.29
EFFECTIVE	1.26	1.32	1.31	0.72
RATIO	26.9	28.7	28.7	20.0
BALANCE OF COUNTY:				
NOMINAL	4.39	4.54	4.54	4.29
EFFECTIVE	1.21	1.31	1.31	0.71
RATIO	26.7	28.7	28.7	20.0
YOUNGSTOWN:				
NOMINAL	4.81	4.81	4.81	(¹)
EFFECTIVE	1.34	1.34	1.33	(¹)
RATIO	27.9	27.9	27.7	(¹)
MONTGOMERY COUNTY:				
NOMINAL	4.46	4.45	4.44	(¹)
EFFECTIVE	1.23	1.23	1.23	(¹)
RATIO	28.5	28.8	28.6	(¹)
BALANCE OF COUNTY:				
NOMINAL	4.36	4.28	4.32	(¹)
EFFECTIVE	1.17	1.20	1.20	(¹)
RATIO	27.5	28.0	27.9	(¹)
DAYTON:				
NOMINAL	4.65	4.65	4.65	(¹)
EFFECTIVE	1.55	1.43	1.43	(¹)
RATIO	30.6	30.4	30.5	(¹)
KETTERING:				
NOMINAL	4.11	4.11	4.11	(¹)
EFFECTIVE	1.20	1.20	1.20	(¹)
RATIO	29.1	29.1	29.1	(¹)
RICHLAND COUNTY:				
NOMINAL	3.69	3.69	3.69	3.84
EFFECTIVE	1.23	1.28	1.28	1.22
RATIO	31.6	33.9	34.8	30.5
BALANCE OF COUNTY:				
NOMINAL	3.96	3.69	3.80	4.01
EFFECTIVE	1.23	1.28	1.33	1.23
RATIO	30.8	31.6	33.4	30.8
MANSFIELD:				
NOMINAL	3.69	3.69	3.69	(¹)
EFFECTIVE	1.22	1.28	1.28	(¹)
RATIO	33.0	34.8	34.8	(¹)
STARK COUNTY:				
NOMINAL	3.08	3.08	3.08	2.82
EFFECTIVE	0.95	0.97	0.96	0.77
RATIO	32.5	32.8	32.6	25.6
BALANCE OF COUNTY:				
NOMINAL	2.97	2.97	2.97	2.82
EFFECTIVE	0.93	0.95	0.93	0.77
RATIO	31.7	32.4	31.8	25.6
CANTON:				
NOMINAL	3.33	3.33	3.33	(¹)
EFFECTIVE	1.03	1.03	1.00	(¹)
RATIO	35.7	35.4	35.0	(¹)
SUMMIT COUNTY:				
NOMINAL	4.49	4.49	4.49	(¹)
EFFECTIVE	1.35	1.34	1.34	(¹)
RATIO	30.2	30.2	30.2	(¹)
BALANCE OF COUNTY:				
NOMINAL	4.47	4.41	4.41	(¹)
EFFECTIVE	1.24	1.21	1.21	(¹)
RATIO	27.2	27.0	27.2	(¹)
AKRON:				
NOMINAL	4.49	4.49	4.49	(¹)
EFFECTIVE	1.42	1.43	1.41	(¹)
RATIO	32.3	32.4	32.3	(¹)
OHIO--CONTINUED				
TRUMBULL COUNTY:				
NOMINAL	4.07	4.07	4.07	3.81
EFFECTIVE	1.11	1.13	1.13	1.09
RATIO	28.3	28.1	28.2	29.3
BALANCE OF COUNTY:				
NOMINAL	3.87	3.87	3.80	3.81
EFFECTIVE	1.09	1.09	1.09	1.09
RATIO	28.5	27.5	28.7	29.3
WARREN:				
NOMINAL	4.07	4.07	4.07	(¹)
EFFECTIVE	1.15	1.15	1.14	(¹)
RATIO	28.2	28.2	28.1	(¹)
OKLAHOMA				
CANADIAN COUNTY:				
NOMINAL	9.25	9.25	9.25	9.48
EFFECTIVE	0.74	0.84	0.87	0.46
RATIO	10.9	12.9	12.9	4.9
BALANCE OF COUNTY:				
NOMINAL	9.25	9.25	9.25	9.25
EFFECTIVE	0.73	0.81	0.84	0.46
RATIO	11.1	12.8	12.9	5.0
OKLAHOMA CITY (PART):				
NOMINAL	10.86	(¹)	(¹)	10.42
EFFECTIVE	1.09	(¹)	(¹)	0.46
RATIO	10.0	(¹)	(¹)	4.4
CLEVELAND COUNTY:				
NOMINAL	8.13	8.13	8.13	10.16
EFFECTIVE	0.86	0.97	0.98	0.33
RATIO	11.2	13.9	14.4	3.0
BALANCE OF COUNTY:				
NOMINAL	9.79	10.16	10.16	(¹)
EFFECTIVE	0.77	1.04	1.04	(¹)
RATIO	13.3	13.9	13.9	(¹)
NORMAN:				
NOMINAL	8.13	8.13	8.13	(¹)
EFFECTIVE	0.88	0.93	0.95	(¹)
RATIO	11.2	13.5	14.4	(¹)
OKLAHOMA CITY (PART):				
NOMINAL	12.27	(¹)	(¹)	12.27
EFFECTIVE	0.39	(¹)	(¹)	0.33
RATIO	3.2	(¹)	(¹)	2.7
COMANCHE COUNTY:				
BALANCE OF COUNTY:				
NOMINAL	7.36	(¹)	(¹)	7.39
EFFECTIVE	0.27	(¹)	(¹)	0.27
RATIO	3.9	(¹)	(¹)	3.9
LAWTON:				
NOMINAL	8.22	8.22	8.22	8.22
EFFECTIVE	0.84	0.91	0.91	0.49
RATIO	12.9	13.1	13.1	6.0
MCCLAIN COUNTY:				
NOMINAL	7.88	7.53	7.53	(¹)
EFFECTIVE	0.67	0.66	0.66	(¹)
RATIO	8.7	9.1	9.1	(¹)
BALANCE OF COUNTY:				
NOMINAL	7.88	7.53	7.53	(¹)
EFFECTIVE	0.67	0.66	0.66	(¹)
RATIO	8.7	9.1	9.1	(¹)
OKLAHOMA CITY (PART) ...	(¹)	(¹)	(¹)	(¹)
OKLAHOMA COUNTY:				
NOMINAL	9.51	9.51	9.51	9.24
EFFECTIVE	0.98	1.01	1.00	0.48
RATIO	13.8	14.2	14.2	5.3
BALANCE OF COUNTY:				
NOMINAL	9.10	9.10	9.10	9.10
EFFECTIVE	0.87	0.91	0.91	0.27
RATIO	13.7	13.9	14.0	3.6
MIDWEST:				
NOMINAL	10.17	10.10	10.17	10.32
EFFECTIVE	1.04	1.06	1.06	0.72
RATIO	13.9	14.4	14.3	7.8

See footnotes at end of table.

Table 3. Median Property Tax Rates and Assessment Ratios for Real Property Involved in Measurable Sales During a 6-Month Period, for Selected Local Areas: 1976—Continued

Area	All types	Residential (nonfarm)		Vacant platted lots
		Total	Single-family	
OKLAHOMA--CONTINUED				
OKLAHOMA COUNTY--CONTINUED				
OKLAHOMA CITY (PART):				
NOMINAL	9.84	9.84	9.84	(1)
EFFECTIVE	1.06	1.11	1.09	(1)
RATIO	15.4	15.4	15.3	(1)
POTTAWATOMIE COUNTY:				
NOMINAL	7.71	7.81	7.81	7.29
EFFECTIVE	0.70	0.79	0.79	1.58
RATIO	13.6	15.0	15.0	22.9
BALANCE OF COUNTY:				
NOMINAL	7.71	7.81	7.81	7.29
EFFECTIVE	0.70	0.79	0.79	1.58
RATIO	13.6	15.0	15.0	22.9
OKLAHOMA CITY (PART)....	(1)	(1)	(1)	(1)
TULSA COUNTY:				
NOMINAL	8.32	8.32	8.32	9.34
EFFECTIVE	0.91	1.00	0.98	0.75
RATIO	14.2	15.1	15.0	7.7
BALANCE OF COUNTY:				
NOMINAL	9.49	8.58	8.68	9.54
EFFECTIVE	0.76	1.05	1.04	0.76
RATIO	11.0	14.9	14.9	7.7
TULSA (PART):				
NOMINAL	8.32	8.32	8.32	8.33
EFFECTIVE	0.97	0.99	0.97	0.69
RATIO	14.9	15.1	15.0	7.7
OREGON				
CLACKAMAS COUNTY:				
NOMINAL	2.69	2.70	2.72	2.76
EFFECTIVE	2.19	2.20	2.19	1.84
RATIO	79.7	81.5	81.1	70.2
BALANCE OF COUNTY:				
NOMINAL	2.69	2.70	2.72	2.76
EFFECTIVE	2.19	2.20	2.19	1.84
RATIO	79.7	81.5	81.1	70.2
PORTLAND (PART)	(1)	(1)	(1)	(1)
LANE COUNTY:				
BALANCE OF COUNTY:				
NOMINAL	2.54	2.58	2.55	2.60
EFFECTIVE	2.07	2.04	2.03	2.28
RATIO	83.7	83.7	83.2	84.4
EUGENE:				
NOMINAL	2.98	2.98	2.98	2.98
EFFECTIVE	2.14	2.32	2.31	1.96
RATIO	74.7	76.6	75.8	67.3
MARION COUNTY:				
NOMINAL	2.79	2.82	2.84	2.91
EFFECTIVE	2.01	2.09	2.06	1.26
RATIO	74.4	75.8	75.5	49.8
BALANCE OF COUNTY:				
NOMINAL	2.45	2.46	2.45	2.36
EFFECTIVE	1.78	1.82	1.82	1.07
RATIO	74.0	74.7	74.5	43.8
SALEM (PART):				
NOMINAL	3.15	3.15	3.15	3.15
EFFECTIVE	2.45	2.45	2.45	2.59
RATIO	77.8	77.8	77.8	82.3
MULTNOMAH COUNTY:				
NOMINAL	2.88	2.88	2.88	2.88
EFFECTIVE	2.40	2.37	2.36	2.69
RATIO	82.5	81.0	79.9	87.3
BALANCE OF COUNTY:				
NOMINAL	3.02	3.02	3.02	3.20
EFFECTIVE	2.43	2.40	2.38	2.65
RATIO	78.4	78.4	78.4	82.9
PORTLAND (PART):				
NOMINAL	2.88	2.88	2.88	2.88
EFFECTIVE	2.39	2.36	2.34	2.72
RATIO	83.0	81.7	81.1	92.6
POLK COUNTY:				
NOMINAL	2.59	2.59	2.59	(1)
EFFECTIVE	1.99	2.07	2.07	(1)
RATIO	75.0	81.9	81.9	(1)
BALANCE OF COUNTY:				
NOMINAL	2.52	2.59	2.59	(1)
EFFECTIVE	1.86	1.94	1.93	(1)
RATIO	72.5	75.9	76.7	(1)

Area	All types	Residential (nonfarm)		Vacant platted lots
		Total	Single-family	
OREGON--CONTINUED				
POLK COUNTY--CONTINUED				
SALEM (PART):				
NOMINAL	3.15	3.15	(1)	(1)
EFFECTIVE	2.58	2.75	(1)	(1)
RATIO	82.7	87.5	(1)	(1)
WASHINGTON COUNTY:				
NOMINAL	2.74	2.82	2.82	2.74
EFFECTIVE	2.23	2.38	2.37	1.98
RATIO	82.1	84.9	84.8	72.2
BALANCE OF COUNTY:				
NOMINAL	2.74	2.82	2.82	2.74
EFFECTIVE	2.23	2.38	2.37	1.98
RATIO	82.0	84.8	84.3	72.2
PORTLAND (PART)	(1)	(1)	(1)	(1)
PENNSYLVANIA				
ALLEGHENY COUNTY:				
PENN HILLS TOWNSHIP:				
NOMINAL	7.70	7.70	7.70	(1)
EFFECTIVE	1.95	1.96	1.95	(1)
RATIO	25.3	25.4	25.3	(1)
PITTSBURGH:[7]				
NOMINAL	7.95	7.90	7.87	8.60
EFFECTIVE	2.84	2.82	2.44	2.60
RATIO	35.9	36.0	31.0	30.0
BERKS COUNTY:				
READING:				
NOMINAL	14.46	14.46	14.46	(1)
EFFECTIVE	2.31	2.29	2.16	(1)
RATIO	16.6	15.9	15.0	(1)
BLAIR COUNTY:				
ALTOONA:				
NOMINAL	8.96	8.96	8.96	(1)
EFFECTIVE	1.84	1.82	1.81	(1)
RATIO	20.6	20.3	20.2	(1)
BUCKS COUNTY:				
BRISTOL TOWNSHIP:				
NOMINAL	20.01	20.01	20.01	(1)
EFFECTIVE	2.58	2.58	2.58	(1)
RATIO	12.9	12.9	12.9	(1)
DAUPHIN COUNTY:				
HARRISBURG:				
NOMINAL	11.45	11.44	11.44	(1)
EFFECTIVE	3.29	2.32	2.17	(1)
RATIO	26.8	20.2	19.0	(1)
DELAWARE COUNTY:				
CHESTER:				
NOMINAL	15.53	15.16	15.16	(1)
EFFECTIVE	1.39	1.31	1.31	(1)
RATIO	9.0	8.2	8.2	(1)
HAVERFORD TOWNSHIP:				
NOMINAL	23.76	23.76	23.76	(1)
EFFECTIVE	1.90	1.90	1.90	(1)
RATIO	8.0	8.0	8.0	(1)
UPPER DARBY TOWNSHIP:				
NOMINAL	23.67	23.67	23.67	(1)
EFFECTIVE	1.80	1.80	1.80	(1)
RATIO	7.6	7.6	7.6	(1)
ERIE COUNTY:				
ERIE:				
NOMINAL	12.28	12.33	12.40	(1)
EFFECTIVE	2.21	2.18	2.15	(1)
RATIO	17.9	17.4	17.4	(1)
LACKAWANNA COUNTY:				
SCRANTON:				
NOMINAL	14.60	14.60	14.60	(1)
EFFECTIVE	3.05	3.05	3.34	(1)
RATIO	19.3	19.3	23.3	(1)
LANCASTER COUNTY:				
LANCASTER:				
NOMINAL	15.78	15.78	15.78	(1)
EFFECTIVE	1.88	1.89	1.96	(1)
RATIO	11.9	12.0	12.4	(1)
LEHIGH COUNTY:				
ALLENTOWN:				
NOMINAL	6.54	6.54	6.54	(1)
EFFECTIVE	2.26	2.23	2.26	(1)
RATIO	34.6	34.0	34.6	(1)
BETHLEHEM (PART)	(1)	(1)	(1)	(1)

See footnotes at end of table.

Table 3. Median Property Tax Rates and Assessment Ratios for Real Property Involved in Measurable Sales During a 6-Month Period, for Selected Local Areas: 1976—Continued

Area	All types	Residential (nonfarm) Total	Single-family	Vacant platted lots
PENNSYLVANIA--CONTINUED				
LUZERNE COUNTY:				
WILKES BARRE:				
NOMINAL	11.00	11.00	(1)	(1)
EFFECTIVE	1.74	1.74	(1)	(1)
RATIO	14.7	14.7	(1)	(1)
MONTGOMERY COUNTY:				
ABINGTON TOWNSHIP:				
NOMINAL	17.25	17.25	17.25	(1)
EFFECTIVE	2.38	2.38	2.39	(1)
RATIO	13.8	13.8	13.9	(1)
LOWER MERION TOWNSHIP:				
NOMINAL	11.93	11.93	11.93	(1)
EFFECTIVE	1.66	1.66	1.66	(1)
RATIO	14.7	14.3	14.7	(1)
NORTHAMPTON COUNTY:				
BETHLEHEM (PART):				
NOMINAL	7.70	7.70	7.70	(1)
EFFECTIVE	2.00	2.00	2.00	(1)
RATIO	25.9	25.9	25.9	(1)
PHILADELPHIA:				
NOMINAL	6.17	6.17	6.17	(1)
EFFECTIVE	2.15	2.12	2.11	(1)
RATIO	34.8	34.3	34.1	(1)
RHODE ISLAND				
KENT COUNTY:				
WARWICK:				
NOMINAL	5.84	5.84	5.84	5.84
EFFECTIVE	2.12	2.13	2.12	2.08
RATIO	37.6	38.1	37.9	33.7
PROVIDENCE COUNTY:				
CRANSTON:				
NOMINAL	6.35	6.35	6.35	6.35
EFFECTIVE	1.98	2.00	1.91	1.52
RATIO	34.0	33.9	33.8	28.8
PAWTUCKET:				
NOMINAL	6.76	6.76	6.76	6.76
EFFECTIVE	1.97	1.92	1.92	1.70
RATIO	30.6	30.2	30.5	25.2
PROVIDENCE:				
NOMINAL	4.75	4.75	4.75	4.75
EFFECTIVE	3.37	3.43	3.10	2.19
RATIO	71.5	72.4	65.2	46.4
SOUTH CAROLINA				
CHARLESTON COUNTY:				
CHARLESTON:				
NOMINAL	29.75	29.75	29.75	(1)
EFFECTIVE	0.93	0.93	0.92	(1)
RATIO	3.2	3.2	3.2	(1)
GREENVILLE COUNTY:				
GREENVILLE:				
NOMINAL	31.93	31.93	31.93	(1)
EFFECTIVE	0.88	0.88	0.88	(1)
RATIO	2.9	2.9	2.8	(1)
RICHLAND COUNTY:				
COLUMBIA:				
NOMINAL	24.75	24.75	24.75	(1)
EFFECTIVE	1.10	1.10	1.15	(1)
RATIO	4.6	4.6	4.7	(1)
SOUTH DAKOTA				
MINNEHAHA COUNTY:				
NOMINAL	6.57	6.57	6.57	6.57
EFFECTIVE	1.98	1.99	2.03	1.86
RATIO	30.3	30.5	31.0	28.3
BALANCE OF COUNTY:				
NOMINAL	6.78	7.20	7.20	(1)
EFFECTIVE	1.74	1.87	1.87	(1)
RATIO	26.6	29.7	29.7	(1)
SIOUX FALLS (PART):				
NOMINAL	6.57	6.57	6.57	6.57
EFFECTIVE	2.03	2.01	2.04	2.84
RATIO	30.9	30.5	31.0	43.1
TENNESSEE				
HAMILTON COUNTY:				
NOMINAL	7.21	7.21	7.21	4.00
EFFECTIVE	1.03	1.03	0.99	1.08
RATIO	17.4	17.1	16.7	20.6
BALANCE OF COUNTY:				
NOMINAL	4.00	4.00	4.00	4.00
EFFECTIVE	0.73	0.72	0.71	0.80
RATIO	17.1	16.7	16.6	20.0
CHATTANOOGA:				
NOMINAL	7.21	7.21	7.21	7.21
EFFECTIVE	1.26	1.25	1.22	1.70
RATIO	17.6	17.4	16.9	23.5
KNOX COUNTY:				
NOMINAL	3.89	3.89	3.89	3.89
EFFECTIVE	0.75	0.81	0.80	0.60
RATIO	16.4	16.5	16.5	14.6
BALANCE OF COUNTY:				
NOMINAL	3.89	3.89	3.89	3.89
EFFECTIVE	0.64	0.65	0.65	0.56
RATIO	16.4	16.7	16.7	14.2
KNOXVILLE:				
NOMINAL	7.78	7.78	7.78	7.78
EFFECTIVE	1.29	1.26	1.26	1.54
RATIO	16.5	16.2	16.2	19.7
SHELBY COUNTY:				
MEMPHIS:				
NOMINAL	7.74	7.74	7.74	7.74
EFFECTIVE	1.14	1.12	1.09	1.82
RATIO	14.8	14.5	14.1	23.4
DAVIDSON COUNTY:				
NASHVILLE:				
NOMINAL	6.00	6.00	6.00	6.00
EFFECTIVE	1.02	1.00	0.99	1.03
RATIO	16.9	16.7	16.5	17.1
TEXAS				
HARRIS COUNTY:				
HOUSTON (PART): [8]				
NOMINAL	9.09	9.09	9.09	9.09
EFFECTIVE	1.10	1.04	1.04	1.42
RATIO	12.3	11.6	11.6	15.7
PASADENA	(2)	(2)	(2)	(2)
POTTER COUNTY:				
AMARILLO (PART):				
NOMINAL	8.10	8.10	8.10	8.10
EFFECTIVE	1.56	1.42	1.39	1.37
RATIO	19.2	17.5	17.2	16.9
UTAH				
SALT LAKE COUNTY:				
NOMINAL	9.24	9.14	9.19	10.06
EFFECTIVE	0.92	0.91	0.91	1.24
RATIO	10.0	9.9	9.9	11.9
BALANCE OF COUNTY:				
NOMINAL	9.24	9.14	9.19	9.44
EFFECTIVE	0.91	0.89	0.89	1.34
RATIO	10.3	9.8	9.8	13.0
SALT LAKE CITY:				
NOMINAL	9.24	9.24	9.19	10.16
EFFECTIVE	0.92	0.91	0.91	1.20
RATIO	10.0	10.0	9.9	11.9
UTAH COUNTY:				
NOMINAL	5.88	5.88	5.88	5.88
EFFECTIVE	0.93	0.95	0.95	0.70
RATIO	15.8	16.2	15.9	15.6
BALANCE OF COUNTY:				
NOMINAL	5.88	5.88	5.88	5.88
EFFECTIVE	0.95	0.94	0.94	0.99
RATIO	16.2	16.2	16.2	16.3
PROVO:				
NOMINAL	6.00	6.40	6.18	5.88
EFFECTIVE	0.91	0.99	0.97	0.51
RATIO	15.1	16.0	15.8	8.8

See footnotes at end of table.

Table 3. Median Property Tax Rates and Assessment Ratios for Real Property Involved in Measurable Sales During a 6-Month Period, for Selected Local Areas: 1976—Continued

Area	All types	Residential (nonfarm) Total	Single-family	Vacant platted lots
UTAH--CONTINUED				
WEBER COUNTY:				
NOMINAL	8.07	8.94	8.87	7.79
EFFECTIVE	1.09	1.10	1.07	1.06
RATIO	13.0	13.0	12.5	12.9
BALANCE OF COUNTY:				
NOMINAL	7.79	7.79	7.79	7.79
EFFECTIVE	1.01	1.00	0.99	1.06
RATIO	12.7	12.5	12.5	13.0
OGDEN:				
NOMINAL	9.02	9.02	9.02	(1)
EFFECTIVE	1.18	1.19	1.16	(1)
RATIO	13.1	13.2	12.9	(1)
VIRGINIA				
ARLINGTON COUNTY:				
NOMINAL	3.78	3.78	3.78	(1)
EFFECTIVE	1.36	1.37	1.37	(1)
RATIO	35.9	36.2	36.2	(1)
FAIRFAX COUNTY:				
NOMINAL	4.35	4.35	4.35	4.35
EFFECTIVE	1.43	1.43	1.43	1.37
RATIO	33.0	33.1	33.1	31.5
ALEXANDRIA:				
NOMINAL	3.50	3.50	3.50	(1)
EFFECTIVE	1.35	1.38	1.38	(1)
RATIO	39.2	39.5	39.6	(1)
CHESAPEAKE CITY:				
NOMINAL	3.22	3.22	3.22	3.22
EFFECTIVE	1.29	1.29	1.29	1.56
RATIO	39.9	39.9	39.9	50.0
HAMPTON:				
NOMINAL	3.75	3.75	3.75	(1)
EFFECTIVE	1.47	1.47	1.48	(1)
RATIO	39.1	39.1	39.4	(1)
LYNCHBURG:				
NOMINAL	2.80	2.80	2.80	2.80
EFFECTIVE	1.14	1.12	1.11	1.31
RATIO	40.6	40.0	39.8	46.7
NEWPORT NEWS:				
NOMINAL	3.00	3.00	3.00	(1)
EFFECTIVE	1.29	1.28	1.28	(1)
RATIO	43.0	42.8	42.7	(1)
NORFOLK:				
NOMINAL	2.70	2.70	2.70	2.70
EFFECTIVE	1.02	1.02	1.03	0.67
RATIO	37.8	37.8	37.9	24.7
PORTSMOUTH:				
NOMINAL	2.60	2.60	2.60	2.60
EFFECTIVE	1.24	1.29	1.28	1.24
RATIO	47.4	49.6	49.1	46.7
RICHMOND:				
NOMINAL	1.83	1.83	1.83	1.83
EFFECTIVE	1.56	1.57	1.58	0.83
RATIO	85.3	85.8	86.5	44.9
ROANOKE:				
NOMINAL	3.45	3.45	3.45	3.45
EFFECTIVE	1.04	1.04	1.06	1.03
RATIO	30.2	30.9	31.1	30.0
VIRGINIA BEACH:				
NOMINAL	1.45	1.45	1.45	1.45
EFFECTIVE	0.76	0.75	0.75	0.90
RATIO	52.1	51.8	51.8	58.2
WASHINGTON				
KING COUNTY:				
NOMINAL	1.34	1.34	1.34	1.34
EFFECTIVE	0.95	0.93	0.93	1.17
RATIO	69.8	69.2	69.2	70.9
BALANCE OF COUNTY:				
NOMINAL	1.30	1.30	1.29	1.44
EFFECTIVE	1.00	0.96	0.96	1.18
RATIO	72.5	72.2	72.2	77.2
BELLEVUE:				
NOMINAL	2.15	2.15	2.15	(1)
EFFECTIVE	1.54	1.54	1.55	(1)
RATIO	71.8	72.3	71.8	(1)
SEATTLE:				
NOMINAL	1.34	1.34	1.34	1.34
EFFECTIVE	0.88	0.88	0.88	1.10
RATIO	66.2	65.6	65.6	66.7

Area	All types	Residential (nonfarm) Total	Single-family	Vacant platted lots
WASHINGTON--CONTINUED				
PIERCE COUNTY:				
NOMINAL	2.16	2.41	2.41	1.77
EFFECTIVE	1.25	1.31	1.30	0.96
RATIO	62.2	62.3	62.1	59.2
BALANCE OF COUNTY:				
NOMINAL	1.72	2.10	2.10	1.38
EFFECTIVE	1.05	1.14	1.14	0.91
RATIO	59.9	60.7	59.5	63.8
TACOMA:				
NOMINAL	2.41	2.41	2.41	2.41
EFFECTIVE	1.50	1.51	1.50	1.40
RATIO	62.6	63.0	62.3	58.1
SPOKANE COUNTY:				
NOMINAL	1.99	1.99	1.99	1.99
EFFECTIVE	0.92	1.12	1.11	0.73
RATIO	48.2	57.3	56.3	37.0
BALANCE OF COUNTY:				
NOMINAL	1.96	1.99	1.99	1.99
EFFECTIVE	0.45	0.73	0.73	0.52
RATIO	28.0	49.3	49.3	30.8
SPOKANE:				
NOMINAL	1.99	1.99	1.99	1.99
EFFECTIVE	1.03	1.15	1.14	0.74
RATIO	55.0	58.5	57.3	37.0
WEST VIRGINIA				
CABELL COUNTY:				
NOMINAL	1.46	1.46	1.46	2.42
EFFECTIVE	0.35	0.34	0.32	0.37
RATIO	26.1	26.0	25.5	12.6
BALANCE OF COUNTY:				
NOMINAL	1.21	1.21	1.21	2.42
EFFECTIVE	0.30	0.27	0.27	0.36
RATIO	24.3	23.7	24.3	9.4
HUNTINGTON (PART):				
NOMINAL	2.18	1.82	1.46	(1)
EFFECTIVE	0.63	0.60	0.39	(1)
RATIO	28.1	28.1	26.7	(1)
KANAWHA COUNTY:				
NOMINAL	1.80	1.80	1.80	3.35
EFFECTIVE	0.46	0.43	0.41	0.87
RATIO	26.0	26.1	26.0	27.5
BALANCE OF COUNTY:				
NOMINAL	1.80	1.80	1.80	2.85
EFFECTIVE	0.42	0.40	0.39	0.80
RATIO	25.3	25.6	25.6	22.2
CHARLESTON (PART):				
NOMINAL	2.70	1.80	1.80	3.60
EFFECTIVE	0.66	0.63	0.61	1.03
RATIO	29.4	29.3	26.3	35.6
WISCONSIN				
BROWN COUNTY: GREEN BAY:				
NOMINAL	4.14	4.14	4.14	(1)
EFFECTIVE	1.79	1.85	1.85	(1)
RATIO	43.2	44.6	44.7	(1)
CALUMET COUNTY: APPLETON (PART):				
NOMINAL	2.94	2.94	2.94	(1)
EFFECTIVE	2.10	2.10	2.10	(1)
RATIO	71.2	71.2	71.2	(1)
DANE COUNTY: MADISON:				
NOMINAL	2.73	2.73	2.73	(1)
EFFECTIVE	2.40	2.40	2.41	(1)
RATIO	87.9	88.0	88.4	(1)
KENOSHA COUNTY: KENOSHA:				
NOMINAL	4.84	4.84	4.84	4.84
EFFECTIVE	2.09	2.11	2.10	1.11
RATIO	43.3	43.6	43.4	22.8
MILWAUKEE COUNTY: MILWAUKEE (PART):				
NOMINAL	4.29	4.29	4.29	4.29
EFFECTIVE	3.14	3.13	3.13	3.72
RATIO	73.2	72.9	72.9	86.7
WAUWATOSA:				
NOMINAL	5.29	5.29	5.29	(1)
EFFECTIVE	2.21	2.21	2.21	(1)
RATIO	41.8	41.8	41.8	(1)

See footnotes at end of table.

Table 3. Median Property Tax Rates and Assessment Ratios for Real Property Involved in Measurable Sales During a 6-Month Period, for Selected Local Areas: 1976—Continued

Area	Types of real property				Area	Types of real property			
	All types	Residential (nonfarm)		Vacant platted lots		All types	Residential (nonfarm)		Vacant platted lots
		Total	Single-family				Total	Single-family	
WISCONSIN--CONTINUED					**WISCONSIN--CONTINUED**				
MILWAUKEE COUNTY--CONTINUED					RACINE COUNTY:				
WEST ALLIS:					RACINE:				
NOMINAL	7.07	7.07	7.07	([1])	NOMINAL.	4.52	4.52	4.52	([1])
EFFECTIVE	2.25	2.17	2.17	([1])	EFFECTIVE.	2.02	2.01	1.98	([1])
RATIO	31.9	30.7	30.7	([1])	RATIO.	50.0	44.6	43.9	([1])
OUTAGAMIE COUNTY:					WINNEBAGO COUNTY:				
APPLETON (PART):					OSHKOSH:				
NOMINAL	2.94	2.94	2.94	([1])	NOMINAL.	6.62	6.62	6.62	([1])
EFFECTIVE	2.14	2.14	2.14	([1])	EFFECTIVE.	1.91	1.90	1.90	([1])
RATIO	72.6	72.2	70.3	([1])	RATIO.	28.9	28.7	28.7	([1])

Note: Nominal rate is total annual tax billing expressed as a percentage of taxable assessed value. Effective rate is total annual tax billing expressed as a percentage of the sales price. All rates and ratios are medians based on samples of measurable sales for the particular jurisdictions. See text for further discussion. All rates and ratios are percentages.

NA Not available.

[1]Data not presented where sample representation was insufficient or where cost limitations prevented collection of tax billing data.

[2]Data not presented where, on the basis of final review procedures, it was concluded that significant enumeration or processing error occurred.

[3]All assessed values and property tax bills used to compute ratios and tax rates are as of March 1, 1975.

[4]Nominal rates not shown because assessed values are frequently exempted from parish taxes, yet remain fully taxable for city purposes.

[5]Property tax bills used to compute tax rates for Minnesota jurisdictions exclude the State homestead tax credit, which amounts to $325, or 45 percent of the gross bill ("non-debt plus school debt taxes" on owner-occupied property), whichever is less.

[6]In New Jersey, tax bills are derived by applying the local tax rates to local, unequalized assessed values. However, the nominal rates shown in this table are the total annual tax bills expressed as percentages of the county equalized assessed values; see text.

[7]Pittsburgh tax rates are based on city, county and school district tax bills available for the 1976 or 1977 tax years.

[8]Tax rates for Houston were computed under the assumption that all properties sampled in the city of Houston were also in the Houston Independent School District. However, it is possible that a small minority of these properties could actually be in an adjacent school district which uses slightly different tax rates.

PART III

GOVERNMENT EMPLOYMENT

As in the case of the finance data, the material presented in this section on governmental employment is based on annual reports issued by the Census Bureau. The data are presented in three sections—a summary section and two additional sections on county and city employment. Individual State data are presented in the summary section. Table 4 in this summary section shows total State and local employment by State per 10,000 persons; these data provide a good basis for comparing the scope and labor intensity of governmental services by State. Comparative data for 342 counties over 100,000 persons are shown in the section on county employment data. Likewise, comparative data for 393 cities with over 50,000 persons are shown for the city data.

A – SUMMARY OF PUBLIC EMPLOYMENT IN 1977

Total civilian government employment in the United States was slightly more than 15.4 million as of October 1977. During the 12-month period of October 1976 to October 1977, State and local government employment increased by 389,000 workers, or 3.2 percent, to a total of 12,558,000 and Federal civilian employment increased by nearly 5,000 workers, or 0.2 percent, to 2,848,000.

Payrolls for all civilian government employees in October 1977 totaled $15.2 billion, an increase of 9.2 percent or nearly $1.3 billion over the amount for the month of October 1976. State and local government payrolls for the month of October 1977 were

$11.3 billion and Federal civilian payrolls for the same period were $3.9 billion.

Twenty-two percent of all persons counted as paid employees of State and local governments in October 1977 were employed on a part-time basis. When the number of these employees is discounted by applying average full-time earning rates it is found that the full-time equivalent of all State and local government employment was 10,498,000 in October 1977. Of this total, local governments accounted for approximately 72 percent, or 7,596,000 of the full-time equivalent employment.

Nearly one-half of the full-time equivalent number

of State and local government employees were in the education function in October 1977, a total of 5,106,000.

Trends in Public Employment

Total governmental employment in the United States has risen each year since 1953, with State and local governments accounting for most of the changes in this 24-year period. Civilian Federal employment reached a peak of approximately 3.4 million persons during World War II, was cut back to 2.0 million in 1947, and subsequently rose to 2.5 million in 1951. After several years of only minor changes, Federal civilian employment moved up to nearly 3.0 million in 1967 and has since receded to its present level of 2.8 million. Total employment of State and local governments dropped somewhat during World War II, from 3.4 million in 1941 to 3.2 million in 1945 but has since shown a significant increase nearly every year.

The 1976–77 increase in the full-time equivalent number of persons employed by State and local governments was 292,000 as compared with a rise of 108,000 during the previous year. Approximately two-thirds of the 1976–77 rise was accounted for by increased employment at the local government level. Recent annual rates of change in full-time equivalent employment and in October payrolls of State and local governments are indicated in Table A.[1]

The next summary, Table B, provides a summary of growth rates in full-time equivalent employment of State and local governments, by type of government.

Average October Earnings

Full-time employees of State and local governments were paid an average of $1,078 for the month of October 1977—$57 a month more than for October 1976.

There is a marked range in the average October earnings of full-time employees engaged in different functions as shown in Table C. In part, this results from differences in the proportion of highly trained personnel engaged in various fields. However, other factors may also be noted. For example, in the education function the relatively higher average October earnings are influenced in part by the fact that some employees are paid on a 9- or 10-month basis rather than uniformly throughout the calendar year. Also in the hospital function relatively low average monthly salaries are partly affected by the exclusion of any

payments for housing, meals or other "in kind" compensation supplementary to cash payments. Such perquisites are more commonly provided to hospital personnel than to public employees in other functions.

Generally higher pay rates in metropolitan and urban areas help to account for the higher average earnings for functions that are concentrated heavily in urban areas such as police and fire protection, water supply, and other local utilities.

Data by Type of Government

Table D shows the distribution of State and local government employment by type of Government in October 1977.

Data for State Areas

The number of Federal civilian employees working in various States ranges widely—from nearly 292,000 in California to fewer than 10,000 in each of seven States. This distribution is strongly influenced by the location of large-scale Federal establishments, including regional offices and field headquarters.

A wide interstate range appears also in employment of State and local governments—from more than 1 million in California and New York to fewer than 30,000 in Wyoming. Ranking the States by thier magnitude of State and local government employment generally resembles, but does not directly coincide with, their ranking in terms of total population.

Because of the differing proportions of part-time employment among areas, the relationship between public employment and population can best be considered in terms of full-time equivalent numbers. On this basis, State and local government employment in October 1977 ranged from approximately 402 per 10,000 population in Pennsylvania to 760 per 10,000 in the District of Columbia. Following is a distribution of the 50 States and the District of Columbia in terms of the full-time equivalent number of State and local government employees per 10,000 population:

Total 51

Less than 425 3
425–449 6
450–474 3

[1]Local Government data other than for 1957, 1962, 1967, and 1972 involve estimates based on a sample of governmental units.

244

Changes in State and Local Government Employment and Payrolls

Item	Year-to-year increase (percent)		
	All functions	Education	Other functions
Full-time equivalent employment:			
1976 to 1977..........	2.9	2.1	3.6
1975 to 1976..........	1.1	1.0	1.2
1974 to 1975..........	2.5	1.0	4.0
1973 to 1974..........	3.2	3.8	2.5
1972 to 1973..........	3.7	3.6	3.8
1971 to 1972..........	4.2	4.2	4.2
1970 to 1971..........	3.3	3.4	3.1
1969 to 1970..........	4.5	4.8	4.2
1968 to 1969..........	3.6	4.2	2.9
1967 to 1968..........	5.7	6.6	4.9
Average, 1972 to 1977..	2.6	2.2	3.0
Average, 1967 to 1977..	3.5	3.4	3.6
Average, 1957 to 1977..	4.0	4.6	3.5
October payrolls:			
1976 to 1977..........	8.9	8.3	9.5
1975 to 1976..........	7.6	7.2	7.9
1974 to 1975..........	9.7	8.3	11.6
1973 to 1974..........	10.2	10.4	10.0
1972 to 1973..........	10.7	9.7	11.8
1971 to 1972..........	9.9	9.0	10.9
1970 to 1971..........	8.1	6.7	9.6
1969 to 1970..........	12.5	12.0	13.0
1968 to 1969..........	10.5	11.2	9.7
1967 to 1968..........	12.8	13.4	12.1
Average, 1972 to 1977..	9.3	8.6	10.0
Average, 1967 to 1977..	10.3	9.9	10.9
Average, 1957 to 1977..	10.2	10.7	9.8

(A)

Changes in Employment for States and Types of Local Governments

Type of government	Year-to-year change in full-time equivalent employment (percent)	
	1976 to 1977	Average, 1977 to 1977
Total.................	2.9	3.5
State....................	3.7	4.1
Local...................	2.5	3.3
Counties................	6.5	4.7
Municipalities..........	1.6	2.2
Townships...............	2.0	3.6
School districts........	1.6	3.1
Special districts.......	0.8	5.6

(B)

245

State and Local Government Employment by Function

Function	Full-time equivalent employment	
	Number (thousands)	Percent
Total...................	10,498	100.0
Education...................	5,106	48.6
Local schools..............	3,929	37.4
Institutions of higher education.................	1,089	10.4
Other education............	88	.8
Hospitals...................	986	9.4
Police protection...........	561	5.4
Highways....................	557	5.3
Public welfare..............	356	3.4
General control.............	355	3.4
Financial administration.....	273	2.6
Local fire protection........	220	2.1
Correction..................	218	2.1
Health......................	197	1.9
Local utilities other than water supply[1]...............	190	1.8
Natural resources............	179	1.7
Local parks and recreation...	158	1.5
Sanitation other than sewerage....................	127	1.2
Water supply.................	121	1.2
Employment security adminis-tration.....................	108	1.0
Housing.....................	86	0.8
All other...................	701	6.7

Ⓒ

[1]Electric power, transit and gas supply systems.

State and Local Government Employment by Type of Government

Type of government	Employees (full-time and part-time)	
	Number (thousands)	Percent
Total...................	12,558	100.0
State.......................	3,467	27.6
Local.......................	9,091	72.4
County.....................	1,696	13.5
Municipal..................	2,487	19.8
Township..................	415	3.3
School district............	4 094	32.6
Special district...........	399	3.2

Ⓓ

246

475-499 15
500-524 10
525-549 6
500 or more 8

Local government employment, on a full-time equivalent basis, averaged 351 per 10,000 population, or two and two-thirds times the related average ratio for State government employment—134 per 10,000. The marked interstate differences in the relative magnitude of the State and local government components arise in part from differences in the allocation of responsibility for administration of various functions.

Comparison of the Number of State and Local Government Employees in Relation to Population

Function	State and local government full-time equivalent employment per 10,000 population		
	United States average	Highest State[1]	Lowest State[1]
Education[2].................	236.0	319.0	183.5
Local schools..........	181.6	223.7	156.7
Instructional staff..	127.1	164.2	110.3
Other................	54.6	70.5	37.1
Institutions of higher education............	50.4	104.9	26.4
All functions other than education[2]..............	249.2	389.9	201.1
Selected functions:			
Hospitals..............	45.6	88.5	16.4
Highways..............	25.8	49.6	15.9
Police protection......	25.9	40.5	15.8
Public welfare.........	16.4	32.0	9.3
General control.......	16.4	38.4	11.4
Financial administration.................	12.6	29.5	6.2
Local fire protection..	10.2	22.9	4.0

Ⓔ

[1]Excludes the District of Columbia because of its uniquely urban nature.
[2]Includes categories not shown separately.

247

Table 1. Public Employment and Payrolls, by Level of Government and by Function: October 1977 and 1976

Function	October 1977			October 1976			Percent increase or decrease (-), 1976 to 1977		
	All governments	Federal Government (civilian)[1]	State and local governments	All governments	Federal Government (civilian)[1]	State and local governments	All governments	Federal Government (civilian)[1]	State and local governments
EMPLOYEES (THOUSANDS)									
FULL-TIME AND PART-TIME	15 406	2 848	12 558	15 012	2 843	12 169	2.6	0.2	3.2
NATIONAL DEFENSE AND INTERNATIONAL RELATIONS	989	989	-	1 014	1 014	-	-2.5	-2.5	-
POSTAL SERVICE	652	652	-	661	661	-	-1.4	-1.4	-
SPACE RESEARCH AND TECHNOLOGY	24	24	-	25	25	-	-4.0	-4.0	-
EDUCATION	6 515	22	6 493	6 330	22	6 308	2.9	0.0	2.9
HIGHWAYS	592	5	587	587	5	582	0.9	-	0.9
HEALTH AND HOSPITALS	1 509	254	1 255	1 466	246	1 219	2.9	3.3	3.0
POLICE PROTECTION	684	56	628	670	57	613	2.1	-1.8	2.5
NATURAL RESOURCES	483	273	210	467	263	204	3.4	3.8	3.0
FINANCIAL ADMINISTRATION	415	108	307	399	106	293	4.0	1.9	4.8
GENERAL CONTROL	536	45	491	521	44	477	2.9	2.3	2.9
ALL OTHER	3 006	419	2 587	2 873	401	2 472	4.6	4.3	4.7
OCTOBER PAYROLLS (MILLIONS OF DOLLARS)									
TOTAL	15 197.8	3 918.4	11 279.4	r13 923.7	3 564.6	r10 359.1	9.2	9.9	8.9
NATIONAL DEFENSE AND INTERNATIONAL RELATIONS	1 326.9	1 326.9	-	1 244.0	1 244.0	-	6.7	6.7	-
POSTAL SERVICE	890.3	890.3	-	820.2	820.2	-	8.6	8.6	-
SPACE RESEARCH AND TECHNOLOGY	54.5	54.5	-	53.1	53.1	-	2.6	2.6	-
EDUCATION	5 781.8	28.8	5 753.0	r5 338.4	27.9	r5 310.4	8.3	3.1	8.3
HIGHWAYS	550.0	9.0	541.0	513.1	8.2	505.0	7.2	9.8	7.1
HEALTH AND HOSPITALS	1 390.8	318.5	1 072.4	1 258.6	277.1	981.4	10.5	14.9	9.3
POLICE PROTECTION	785.0	89.3	695.7	712.1	84.0	628.1	10.2	6.3	10.8
NATURAL RESOURCES	557.1	372.4	184.7	509.7	334.7	175.0	9.3	11.3	5.6
FINANCIAL ADMINISTRATION	409.0	140.4	268.5	370.7	129.2	241.4	10.3	8.7	11.2
GENERAL CONTROL	442.5	67.6	2 374.9	407.6	59.3	348.3	8.6	14.0	7.6
ALL OTHER	3 009.9	620.6	2 389.3	2 696.1	526.7	2 169.4	11.6	17.8	10.1

Note: Statistics for local governments are subject to sampling variation; see text for statement of reliability. Because of rounding, detail may not add to totals.

- Represents zero or rounds to zero.
r Revised.
[1] Comprises all Federal civilian employees, including those outside the United States. On a full-time equivalent basis, Federal employment totaled 2,720,024 in October 1977, or about 0.2 percent more than the 2,713,815 figure for October 1976. Federal figures on this basis are not available by function or by State.

Table 2. Employment and Payrolls of State and Local Governments, by Type of Government: 1953 to 1977

Item	State and local governments			State govern- ments	Local governments					
	Total	Education	Other functions		Total	Counties	Munici- palities	Townships	School districts	Special districts
EMPLOYEES (THOUSANDS)										
ALL EMPLOYEES (OCTO-BER 1977).	12 558	6 493	6 065	3 467	9 091	1 696	2 487	415	4 094	399
FULL-TIME	9 775	4 614	5 161	2 679	7 095	1 458	2 047	221	3 050	320
PART-TIME	2 783	1 879	904	788	1 995	238	440	194	1 044	79
FULL-TIME EQUIVA-LENT	10 504	5 106	5 395	2 902	7 602	1 543	2 141	249	3 325	344
FULL-TIME EQUIVALENT:										
1976 (OCTOBER). . .	10 206	5 003	5 204	2 799	7 409	1 448	2 107	245	3 272	335
1975 (OCTOBER). . .	10 098	4 952	5 146	2 744	7 354	1 408	2 142	237	3 243	324
1974 (OCTOBER). . .	9 852	4 901	4 950	2 653	7 199	1 343	2 127	233	3 183	312
1973 (OCTOBER). . .	9 578	4 751	4 827	2 547	7 031	1 318	2 109	232	3 074	298
1972 (OCTOBER). . .	9 237	4 585	4 651	2 487	6 750	1 242	2 029	215	2 981	283
1971 (OCTOBER). . .	8 806	4 403	4 403	2 384	6 422	1 153	1 960	200	2 865	244
1970 (OCTOBER). . .	8 528	4 258	4 271	2 302	6 226	1 098	1 922	192	2 786	228
1969 (OCTOBER). . .	8 160	4 063	4 097	2 179	5 981	1 053	1 858	191	2 656	221
1968 (OCTOBER). . .	7 879	3 898	3 982	2 085	5 795	1 034	1 813	185	2 555	207
1967 (OCTOBER). . .	7 455	3 658	3 797	1 946	5 509	973	1 715	175	2 449	196
1966 (OCTOBER). . .	7 263	3 543	3 720	1 864	5 399	948	1 701	181	2 369	200
1965 (OCTOBER). . .	6 937	3 337	3 600	1 751	5 186	893	1 638	177	2 287	191
1964 (OCTOBER). . .	6 586	3 132	3 454	1 639	4 947	859	1 584	165	2 164	176
1963 (OCTOBER). . .	6 282	2 948	3 334	1 558	4 724	804	1 549	154	2 056	161
1962 (OCTOBER). . .	5 958	2 730	3 228	1 478	4 480	784	1 486	145	1 901	165
1961 (OCTOBER). . .	5 845	2 652	3 193	1 435	4 410	760	1 491	149	1 836	152
1960 (OCTOBER). . .	5 570	2 525	3 045	1 353	4 217	738	1 447	(NA)	1 729	(NA)
1959 (OCTOBER)....	5 342	2 396	2 946	1 302	4 039	703	1 406	(NA)	1 635	(NA)
1958 (OCTOBER). . .	5 171	2 270	2 901	1 259	3 912	678	1 372	(NA)	1 572	(NA)
1957 (APRIL). . . .	4 793	2 093	2 700	1 154	3 638	647	1 297	122	1 452	120
1956 (OCTOBER). . .	4 687	2 032	2 655	1 136	3 551	632	1 292	110	1 415	103
1955 (OCTOBER). . .	4 487	1 935	2 552	1 081	3 406	604	1 252	109	1 341	100
1954 (OCTOBER). . .	4 309	1 826	2 483	1 024	3 284	587	1 234	102	1 264	97
1953 (OCTOBER). . .	4 126	1 737	2 389	966	3 160	561	1 200	105	1 197	98
MONTHLY PAYROLL (MILLIONS OF DOLLARS)										
1977 (OCTOBER), TOTAL	11 279.4	5 753.0	5 526.4	3 200.5	8 078.9	1 440.7	2 385.7	254.7	3 636.7	361.0
FOR FULL-TIME EMPLOYEES.	10 541.6	5 238.0	5 303.6	2 941.7	7 599.8	1 368.8	2 285.4	230.2	3 369.6	345.8
FOR PART-TIME EMPLOYEES.	737.8	515.0	222.7	258.7	479.1	71.9	100.3	24.5	267.1	15.2
TOTAL PAYROLL:										
1976 (OCTOBER). . .	ʳ10 359.1	ʳ5 310.4	5 048.6	2 893.7	ʳ7 465.1	1 295.2	2 235.4	237.0	ʳ3 371.3	326.5
1975 (OCTOBER). . .	9 640.1	4 960.3	4 679.7	2 652.7	6 987.4	1 183.4	2 129.3	214.7	3 160.3	299.6
1974 (OCTOBER). . .	8 791.5	4 579.5	4 212.0	2 409.5	6 382.0	1 057.2	1 985.3	199.8	2 881.7	258.0
1973 (OCTOBER). . .	8 014.9	4 184.8	3 830.1	2 158.2	5 856.8	951.7	1 855.3	192.4	2 622.9	234.4
1972 (OCTOBER). . .	7 240.0	3 814.3	3 425.8	1 936.6	5 303.4	857.4	1 654.0	166.4	2 427.9	197.8
1971 (OCTOBER). . .	6 382.2	3 382.4	2 999.7	1 741.7	4 640.5	722.4	1 481.8	137.8	2 146.1	152.3
1970 (OCTOBER). . .	5 906.4	3 169.7	2 736.7	1 612.2	4 294.2	639.5	1 360.7	122.3	2 031.7	140.0
1969 (OCTOBER). . .	5 252.3	2 830.6	2 421.7	1 430.5	3 821.7	571.6	1 195.6	114.4	1 816.3	123.9
1968 (OCTOBER). . .	4 751.9	2 544.8	2 207.1	1 256.6	3 495.2	531.8	1 097.1	107.2	1 644.0	115.2
1967 (OCTOBER). . .	4 213.2	2 244.0	1 969.2	1 105.5	3 107.7	465.4	971.5	96.2	1 475.0	99.6
1966 (OCTOBER). . .	3 798.2	2 020.3	1 777.9	975.2	3 823.0	414.4	891.7	87.1	1 332.9	96.9
1965 (OCTOBER). . .	3 400.3	1 777.7	1 622.5	849.2	2 551.1	377.3	818.2	80.5	1 188.6	86.5
1964 (OCTOBER). . .	3 097.2	1 607.9	1 489.3	761.1	2 336.1	345.5	760.5	71.7	1 079.9	78.6
1963 (OCTOBER). . .	2 840.3	1 463.8	1 376.6	696.4	2 143.9	311.2	707.9	64.9	992.3	67.6
1962 (OCTOBER). . .	2 619.3	1 325.1	1 294.2	634.6	1 984.7	295.4	662.3	59.8	899.3	67.8
1961 (OCTOBER). . .	2 419.9	1 204.6	1 215.3	586.2	1 833.7	272.2	630.4	59.9	811.6	60.2
1960 (OCTOBER). . .	2 215.0	1 095.0	1 120.0	524.1	1 690.6	254.2	583.4	(NA)	735.4	(NA)
1959 (OCTOBER). . .	2 041.7	999.3	1 042.4	485.4	1 556.3	229.1	547.9	(NA)	669.5	(NA)
1958 (OCTOBER). . .	1 885.8	905.7	980.1	446.5	1 439.3	212.8	511.2	(NA)	618.2	(NA)
1957 (APRIL). . . .	1 614.5	757.8	856.8	372.5	1 242.0	184.3	461.0	36.7	520.1	39.9
1956 (OCTOBER). . .	1 565.7	734.3	831.4	366.5	1 199.2	176.4	450.0	33.5	503.7	35.5
1955 (OCTOBER). . .	1 418.8	661.7	757.1	325.9	1 092.9	161.8	413.8	30.8	453.3	33.2
1954 (OCTOBER). . .	1 318.3	600.0	718.2	300.7	1 017.5	151.7	396.2	28.5	409.9	31.2
1953 (OCTOBER). . .	1 220.5	552.0	668.5	278.5	941.9	140.6	367.6	26.3	376.0	31.4

Note: Statistics for local governments except for 1972, 1967, 1962, and 1957, are subject to sampling variation; see text for statement of reliability. Because of rounding, detail may not add to totals.

NA not available.
ʳRevised.

Table 3 Employment and Payrolls of Local Governments, by Type of Government and by Function: October 1977

Function	All local governments	Counties	Munici- palities	Townships	School districts	Special districts
EMPLOYEES (FULL-TIME AND PART-TIME)						
ALL FUNCTIONS.	9 090 729	1 695 633	2 487 021	414 779	4 094 395	398 901
EDUCATION.	5 010 006	368 975	420 821	126 593	4 093 617	-
LOCAL SCHOOLS.	4 660 653	327 536	392 643	126 593	3 813 881	-
INSTRUCTIONAL PERSONNEL.	3 022 671	211 657	279 116	87 450	2 444 448	-
OTHER.	1 637 982	115 879	113 527	39 143	1 369 433	-
INSTITUTIONS OF HIGHER EDUCATION	349 353	41 439	28 178	-	279 736	-
INSTRUCTIONAL PERSONNEL.	175 481	22 168	15 015	-	138 298	-
OTHER.	173 872	19 271	13 163	-	141 438	-
FUNCTIONS OTHER THAN EDUCATION	4 080 723	1 326 658	2 066 200	288 186	778	398 901
HIGHWAYS	326 616	132 061	135 104	52 646	-	6 805
PUBLIC WELFARE	200 447	156 528	42 189	1 730	-	-
HOSPITALS.	497 635	244 927	129 206	2 136	-	121 366
HEALTH	118 446	75 942	37 429	2 024	-	3 051
POLICE PROTECTION.	558 157	118 254	400 494	39 409	-	-
LOCAL FIRE PROTECTION.	301 188	17 679	226 371	30 723	-	26 415
SEWERAGE	89 907	8 463	59 662	3 532	-	18 250
SANITATION OTHER THAN SEWERAGE	132 782	11 003	114 230	6 587	-	962
LOCAL PARKS AND RECREATION	220 659	40 353	149 142	12 238	-	18 926
NATURAL RESOURCES.	33 955	15 078	2 321	496	-	16 060
HOUSING AND URBAN RENEWAL.	90 111	3 188	40 709	182	-	46 032
AIRPORTS	18 944	3 883	10 365	88	-	4 608
WATER TRANSPORT AND TERMINALS.	8 831	405	3 182	12	-	5 232
CORRECTION	87 812	69 841	17 963	8	-	-
LOCAL LIBRARIES.	92 566	24 191	48 888	6 668	[1]778	12 041
FINANCIAL ADMINISTRATION	188 640	84 975	75 318	28 347	-	-
GENERAL CONTROL.	403 709	171 064	173 137	59 508	-	-
LOCAL UTILITIES.	323 370	8 632	202 544	5 348	-	106 846
WATER SUPPLY	130 943	6 088	99 753	4 293	-	20 809
ELECTRIC POWER	59 879	117	43 243	955	-	15 564
TRANSIT.	122 996	2 393	52 718	29	-	67 856
GAS SUPPLY	9 552	34	6 830	71	-	2 617
OTHER AND UNALLOCABLE.	386 948	140 191	197 946	36 504	-	12 307
OCTOBER PAYROLL (THOUSANDS OF DOLLARS)						
ALL FUNCTIONS.	8 078 898	1 440 688	2 385 727	254 707	3 636 746	361 030
EDUCATION.	4 515 525	320 704	441 924	116 741	3 636 156	-
LOCAL SCHOOLS.	4 260 213	286 586	415 012	116 741	3 441 873	-
INSTRUCTIONAL PERSONNEL.	3 349 357	228 839	342 048	96 114	2 682 356	-
OTHER.	910 855	57 747	72 963	20 628	759 517	-
INSTITUTIONS OF HIGHER EDUCATION	255 312	34 118	26 912	-	194 282	-
INSTRUCTIONAL PERSONNEL.	162 550	22 210	20 154	-	120 186	-
OTHER.	92 362	11 909	6 757	-	74 096	-
FUNCTIONS OTHER THAN EDUCATION	3 563 372	1 119 984	1 943 803	137 966	590	361 030
HIGHWAYS	266 461	106 297	122 023	31 345	-	6 795
PUBLIC WELFARE	169 091	127 118	40 898	1 074	-	-
HOSPITALS.	389 259	189 879	112 497	1 534	-	85 349
HEALTH	109 301	68 949	37 131	1 244	-	1 977
POLICE PROTECTION.	607 305	122 228	453 480	31 597	-	-
LOCAL FIRE PROTECTION.	291 608	20 814	249 123	12 343	-	9 328
SEWERAGE	87 212	8 553	54 811	3 151	-	20 697
SANITATION OTHER THAN SEWERAGE	111 731	9 215	96 484	5 222	-	810
LOCAL PARKS AND RECREATION	142 349	28 368	97 313	4 571	-	12 097
NATURAL RESOURCES.	25 729	13 180	1 950	333	-	10 266
HOUSING AND URBAN RENEWAL.	85 925	2 982	43 232	148	-	39 563
AIRPORTS	20 331	3 997	10 392	64	-	5 879
WATER TRANSPORT AND TERMINALS.	11 157	359	3 967	5	-	6 825
CORRECTION	90 837	68 677	22 156	4	-	-
LOCAL LIBRARIES.	55 157	14 072	32 513	3 099	[1]590	4 884
FINANCIAL ADMINISTRATION	145 614	71 277	64 104	10 233	-	-
GENERAL CONTROL.	273 976	152 165	107 731	14 079	-	-
LOCAL UTILITIES.	379 640	8 992	220 411	4 725	-	145 512
WATER SUPPLY	121 836	5 703	92 940	3 682	-	19 511
ELECTRIC POWER	74 760	128	51 086	990	-	22 556
TRANSIT.	173 529	3 132	70 018	19	-	100 360
GAS SUPPLY	9 515	29	6 367	34	-	3 086
OTHER AND UNALLOCABLE.	300 689	102 862	173 585	13 194	-	11 047

Note: Statistics are subject to sampling variation; see text for statement of reliability. Because of rounding, detail may not add to totals.

- Represents zero.

[1]Employees of Cleveland Public Library, a part of Cleveland City School District, are shown at libraries instead of education as is the case for other school library employees

Table 4. Number of Public Employees, by Level of Government and by State: October 1977

State	All employees (full-time and part-time)					Full-time equivalent employment of State and local governments					
	All governments	Federal (civilian)[1]	State and local governments			Number			Number per 10,000 population[2]		
			Total	State	Local	Total	State	Local	Total	State	Local
UNITED STATES, TOTAL ..	15 274 746	2 716 781	12 557 965	3 467 236	9 090 729	10 498 184	2 902 191	7 595 993	485	134	351
ALABAMA............	261 565	59 222	202 343	68 978	133 365	177 199	58 955	118 244	480	160	320
ALASKA	46 020	15 844	30 176	15 920	14 256	27 586	15 204	12 382	678	374	304
ARIZONA...........	185 389	34 539	150 850	40 859	109 991	126 673	33 590	93 083	552	146	405
ARKANSAS..........	132 242	18 295	113 947	37 742	76 205	95 806	31 946	63 860	447	149	298
CALIFORNIA........	1 669 540	291 603	1 377 937	289 076	1 088 861	1 087 861	231 957	855 645	497	106	391
COLORADO..........	225 197	48 633	176 564	56 104	120 460	141 701	41 738	99 963	541	159	382
CONNECTICUT.......	177 613	20 765	156 848	50 570	106 278	132 354	42 951	89 403	426	138	288
DELAWARE..........	40 738	5 170	35 568	16 816	18 752	30 865	14 439	16 426	530	248	282
DISTRICT OF COLUMBIA ...	259 543	204 729	54 814	-	54 814	52 459	-	52 459	760	-	760
FLORIDA...........	561 322	78 293	483 029	109 966	373 063	429 709	97 371	332 338	508	115	393
GEORGIA...........	384 023	75 707	308 316	89 060	219 256	273 904	77 469	196 435	543	153	389
HAWAII	82 137	24 917	57 220	42 864	14 356	47 397	34 036	13 361	530	380	149
IDAHO	66 170	10 320	55 850	19 969	35 881	43 935	15 081	28 854	513	176	337
ILLINOIS..........	724 993	102 967	622 026	141 853	480 173	494 004	116 104	377 900	439	103	336
INDIANA...........	328 022	39 139	288 883	82 985	205 898	235 938	61 115	174 823	443	115	328
IOWA	200 613	19 145	181 468	50 448	131 020	143 700	41 511	102 189	499	144	355
KANSAS............	181 370	22 944	158 426	49 698	108 728	123 629	38 026	85 603	532	163	368
KENTUCKY..........	207 745	35 403	172 342	63 989	108 353	145 945	55 450	90 495	422	160	262
LOUISIANA.........	252 674	31 199	221 475	79 648	141 827	199 240	68 021	131 219	508	173	335
MAINE.............	70 778	9 257	61 521	20 592	40 929	49 413	17 266	32 147	455	159	296
MARYLAND	376 664	133 085	243 579	76 681	166 898	216 907	72 184	144 723	524	174	350
MASSACHUSETTS.....	390 046	57 632	332 414	80 184	252 230	290 267	70 380	209 887	484	122	363
MICHIGAN..........	606 654	53 877	552 777	144 859	407 918	427 527	117 021	310 506	468	128	340
MINNESOTA.........	273 349	29 621	243 728	67 784	175 944	194 011	51 776	142 235	488	130	358
MISSISSIPPI.......	161 644	24 543	137 101	41 678	95 423	118 029	36 063	81 966	494	151	343
MISSOURI	320 434	66 084	254 350	75 052	179 298	213 206	61 486	151 720	444	128	316
MONTANA...........	65 689	12 309	53 380	19 735	33 645	42 525	15 191	27 334	559	200	359
NEBRASKA..........	124 978	15 703	109 275	31 097	78 178	88 766	26 657	62 109	569	171	398
NEVADA............	51 484	9 068	42 416	13 037	29 379	36 515	10 592	25 923	577	167	410
NEW HAMPSHIRE.....	63 801	13 348	50 453	17 235	33 218	37 906	13 518	24 388	446	159	287
NEW JERSEY	480 007	69 234	410 773	87 845	322 928	349 473	75 263	274 210	477	103	374
NEW MEXICO	105 760	27 197	78 563	32 740	45 823	68 475	27 855	40 590	575	234	341
NEW YORK	1 219 957	166 520	1 053 437	209 561	843 876	918 498	194 283	724 215	512	108	404
NORTH CAROLINA ...	353 900	41 627	312 273	99 472	212 801	278 808	86 899	191 609	504	157	347
NORTH DAKOTA	60 239	8 917	51 322	16 209	35 113	31 220	11 498	19 722	478	176	302
OHIO	653 825	92 351	561 474	136 273	425 201	454 257	109 355	344 902	424	102	322
OKLAHOMA	211 970	47 463	164 507	59 870	104 637	140 038	49 619	90 419	498	177	322
OREGON	186 572	25 904	160 668	52 954	107 714	197 487	41 219	86 268	537	173	363
PENNSYLVANIA	679 700	127 843	551 857	149 403	402 454	473 981	132 584	341 397	402	113	290
RHODE ISLAND	61 264	9 658	51 606	23 127	28 479	44 275	19 060	25 215	474	204	270
SOUTH CAROLINA ...	202 678	31 071	171 607	63 021	108 586	145 587	55 653	89 934	506	194	313
SOUTH DAKOTA	60 059	10 804	49 255	16 485	32 770	33 405	12 109	21 296	485	176	309
TENNESSEE.........	293 417	57 491	235 926	74 046	161 880	212 476	64 317	148 159	494	150	345
TEXAS.............	868 923	149 883	719 040	193 231	525 809	630 592	162 987	467 605	491	127	364
UTAH	116 507	35 078	81 429	33 178	48 251	63 541	26 364	37 177	501	208	293
VERMONT...........	35 867	4 333	31 534	12 955	18 579	23 745	10 750	12 995	492	223	269
VIRGINIA	441 286	142 226	299 060	105 219	193 841	261 799	89 292	172 507	510	174	336
WASHINGTON	287 090	57 688	229 402	84 890	144 512	188 934	65 843	123 091	516	180	336
WEST VIRGINIA.....	118 162	15 531	102 631	43 561	59 070	90 917	37 357	53 560	489	201	288
WISCONSIN.........	309 765	26 300	283 465	69 035	214 430	222 464	54 549	167 915	478	117	361
WYOMING...........	35 361	6 301	29 060	9 682	19 378	23 794	8 207	15 587	586	202	384

Note: Statistics for local governments are subject to sampling variation; see text for statement of reliability. Because of rounding, detail may not add to totals.

- Represents zero.

[1] Provisional Federal civilian employee data, by State, for December 1977 were not available at the time of publication; data are final figures for December 1976. Total accordingly differs from Federal data reported in table 1, which pertain to October 1977 and include employees working outside the United States.

[2] See table 11 for estimated populations as of July 1, 1977.

Table 5. State and Local Government Payrolls and Average Earnings of Full-Time State and Local Government Employees, by State: October 1977

State	Amount of payroll (thousands of dollars)			Percent of October payroll		Average earnings of full-time State and local government employees				
							Education employees			
	Total	State government	Local governments	State government	Local governments	All employees	All	Instructional personnel, local schools	Instructional personnel, institutions of higher education	Other than education employees
UNITED STATES, TOTAL . .	11 279 379	3 200 481	8 078 898	28.4	71.6	1 078	1 135	1 221	1 749	1 027
ALABAMA	155 601	60 704	94 897	39.0	61.0	883	951	967	1 554	826
ALASKA	47 538	25 601	21 937	53.9	46.1	1 721	1 830	1 908	2 603	1 645
ARIZONA	139 773	36 377	103 396	26.0	74.0	1 107	1 130	1 250	2 035	1 083
ARKANSAS	75 008	29 326	45 683	39.1	60.9	790	846	866	1 603	731
CALIFORNIA	1 476 339	324 760	1 151 579	22.0	78.0	1 360	1 425	1 581	2 041	1 310
COLORADO	152 961	49 396	103 565	32.3	67.7	1 087	1 091	1 159	1 465	1 082
CONNECTICUT	143 337	43 948	99 390	30.7	69.3	1 086	1 165	1 245	1 487	1 004
DELAWARE	33 036	15 431	17 604	46.7	53.3	1 068	1 168	1 189	1 952	970
DISTRICT OF COLUMBIA . . .	75 821	-	75 821	-	100.0	1 449	1 311	1 435	2 025	1 499
FLORIDA	421 207	103 313	317 894	24.5	75.5	983	1 037	1 095	1 928	942
GEORGIA	228 305	73 862	154 443	32.4	67.6	838	880	930	1 521	804
HAWAII	57 465	41 728	15 737	72.6	27.4	1 211	1 357	1 419	1 852	1 117
IDAHO	40 764	16 253	24 511	39.9	60.1	931	944	952	1 377	918
ILLINOIS	593 866	134 172	459 694	22.6	77.4	1 205	1 291	1 381	1 863	1 125
INDIANA	228 485	72 039	156 447	31.5	68.5	967	1 094	1 152	1 912	826
IOWA	151 133	52 471	98 662	34.7	65.3	1 054	1 098	1 071	1 858	998
KANSAS	113 580	39 409	74 171	34.7	65.3	923	987	990	1 572	856
KENTUCKY	128 608	53 899	74 709	41.9	58.1	890	947	963	1 678	833
LOUISIANA	171 401	61 897	109 504	36.1	63.9	863	948	1 029	1 628	779
MAINE	43 164	16 058	27 106	37.2	62.8	881	907	965	1 460	851
MARYLAND	243 740	75 836	167 904	31.1	68.9	1 127	1 233	1 441	1 469	1 028
MASSACHUSETTS	310 476	74 239	236 236	23.9	76.1	1 114	1 206	1 286	1 601	1 041
MICHIGAN	537 026	152 842	384 184	28.5	71.5	1 258	1 306	1 459	1 953	1 203
MINNESOTA	222 331	66 342	155 989	29.8	70.2	1 152	1 168	1 194	1 861	1 135
MISSISSIPPI	89 588	30 540	59 048	34.1	65.9	766	855	854	1 603	682
MISSOURI	199 810	59 383	140 428	29.7	70.3	941	995	1 058	1 586	892
MONTANA	43 785	17 036	26 749	38.9	61.1	1 032	1 129	1 135	1 600	937
NEBRASKA	81 102	24 414	56 688	30.1	69.9	916	922	975	1 607	910
NEVADA	40 314	13 380	26 934	33.2	66.8	1 114	1 043	1 136	1 681	1 164
NEW HAMPSHIRE	35 044	13 881	21 363	39.0	61.0	927	931	976	1 304	924
NEW JERSEY	402 894	87 546	315 348	21.7	78.3	1 157	1 310	1 458	1 925	1 023
NEW MEXICO	63 172	27 099	36 073	42.9	57.1	926	947	988	1 514	901
NEW YORK	1 148 525	218 487	930 038	19.0	81.0	1 255	1 411	1 615	1 766	1 163
NORTH CAROLINA	250 725	84 869	165 856	33.8	66.2	908	950	1 083	1 548	861
NORTH DAKOTA	31 941	12 439	19 502	38.9	61.1	1 037	1 136	1 200	1 756	920
OHIO	471 510	120 338	351 172	25.5	74.5	1 041	1 104	1 151	1 937	984
OKLAHOMA	118 566	45 662	72 904	38.5	61.5	848	927	953	1 610	776
OREGON	144 813	50 104	94 709	34.6	65.4	1 140	1 147	1 188	1 749	1 132
PENNSYLVANIA	501 843	153 536	348 307	30.6	69.4	1 065	1 067	1 149	1 900	1 062
RHODE ISLAND	47 789	19 959	27 830	41.8	58.2	1 081	1 239	1 387	1 639	950
SOUTH CAROLINA	121 858	52 026	69 832	42.7	57.3	835	888	901	2 046	784
SOUTH DAKOTA	29 277	11 913	17 364	40.7	59.3	879	900	885	1 500	854
TENNESSEE	178 028	55 987	122 041	31.4	68.6	846	918	1 011	1 535	793
TEXAS	588 036	164 387	423 648	28.0	72.0	937	980	1 030	1 630	887
UTAH	62 940	26 588	36 352	42.2	57.8	1 002	997	1 095	1 134	1 010
VERMONT	22 017	10 644	11 373	48.3	51.7	933	925	947	1 098	942
VIRGINIA	243 353	88 326	155 027	36.3	63.7	937	993	1 021	1 796	877
WASHINGTON	226 952	81 351	145 601	35.8	64.2	1 206	1 247	1 424	1 811	1 168
WEST VIRGINIA	81 341	34 174	47 168	42.1	58.0	892	988	1 038	2 034	780
WISCONSIN	240 209	67 798	172 410	28.2	71.8	1 087	1 125	1 143	1 480	1 044
WYOMING	22 971	8 905	14 067	38.8	61.2	972	1 037	1 035	1 608	917

Note: Statistics for local governments are subject to sampling variation; see text for statement of reliability. Because of rounding, detail may not add to totals.

- Represents zero.

252

Table 6. Employment and Payrolls of State and Local Governments, by Type of Government and by State: October 1977

State and type of government	Number of employees			October payroll, total (thousands of dollars)	Average earnings of full-time employees	
	Total	Full-time only	Full-time equivalent		All	Other than education employees
UNITED STATES, TOTAL.	12 557 965	9 774 669	10 498 184	11 279 379	1 078	1 027
STATES.	3 467 236	2 679 219	2 092 191	3 200 481	1 098	1 033
LOCAL, TOTAL.	9 090 729	7 095 450	7 595 993	8 078 898	1 071	1 025
COUNTIES.	1 695 633	1 457 734	1 542 919	1 440 688	938	919
MUNICIPALITIES.	2 487 021	2 046 673	2 141 056	2 385 727	1 116	1 090
TOWNSHIPS	414 779	221 226	249 493	254 707	1 040	961
SCHOOL DISTRICTS.	4 094 395	3 050 227	3 324 554	3 636 744	1 104	938
SPECIAL DISTRICTS	398 901	319 590	337 971	361 030	1 082	1 082
ALABAMA, TOTAL.	202 343	165 727	177 200	155 601	883	826
STATE	68 978	55 101	58 955	60 704	1 022	952
LOCAL, TOTAL.	133 365	110 626	118 244	94 897	813	752
COUNTIES.	17 211	15 655	16 211	11 295	694	694
MUNICIPALITIES.	36 424	31 656	32 656	26 107	799	799
SCHOOL DISTRICTS.	68 105	53 776	58 936	50 329	879	-
SPECIAL DISTRICTS	11 625	9 539	10 441	7 165	688	688
ALASKA, TOTAL	30 176	26 379	27 587	47 538	1 721	1 645
STATE	15 920	14 447	15 205	25 601	1 672	1 568
LOCAL, TOTAL.	14 256	11 932	12 382	21 937	1 781	1 811
BOROUGHS.	3 414	2 891	3 054	5 307	1 756	1 756
MUNICIPALITIES.	10 842	9 041	9 328	16 630	1 789	1 830
ARIZONA, TOTAL.	150 850	116 869	126 673	139 773	1 107	1 083
STATE	40 859	30 244	33 590	36 377	1 092	1 059
LOCAL, TOTAL.	109 991	86 625	93 083	103 396	1 113	1 093
COUNTIES.	16 284	15 297	15 618	15 135	967	970
MUNICIPALITIES.	23 776	19 553	20 817	23 042	1 110	1 110
SCHOOL DISTRICTS.	65 746	47 737	52 564	59 243	1 131	-
SPECIAL DISTRICTS	4 185	4 033	4 084	5 975	1 468	1 468
ARKANSAS, TOTAL	113 947	88 633	95 806	75 009	790	731
STATE	37 742	30 031	31 946	29 326	914	856
LOCAL, TOTAL.	76 205	58 602	63 860	45 683	727	627
COUNTIES.	13 411	11 333	12 264	6 752	552	552
MUNICIPALITIES.	17 651	11 516	12 276	8 597	699	699
SCHOOL DISTRICTS.	43 959	35 052	38 552	29 826	794	-
SPECIAL DISTRICTS	1 184	701	768	508	657	657
CALIFORNIA, TOTAL	1 377 937	997 486	1 087 602	1 476 340	1 360	1 310
STATE	289 076	207 152	231 957	324 761	1 401	1 350
LOCAL, TOTAL.	1 088 861	790 334	855 645	1 151 579	1 349	1 298
COUNTIES.	232 917	207 168	215 957	270 715	1 255	1 255
MUNICIPALITIES.	197 032	170 386	175 904	240 629	1 373	1,373
SCHOOL DISTRICTS.	592 574	357 318	406 265	570 092	1 411	-
SPECIAL DISTRICTS	66 338	55 462	57 519	70 143	1 225	1 225
COLORADO, TOTAL	176 564	129 892	141 701	152 961	1 087	1 082
STATE	56 104	38 329	41 738	49 396	1 185	1 192
LOCAL, TOTAL.	120 460	91 563	99 963	103 565	1 046	1 031
COUNTIES.	16 002	13 554	14 380	12 113	844	844
MUNICIPALITIES.	29 307	24 830	26 209	29 283	1 120	1 120
SCHOOL DISTRICTS.	69 343	49 519	55 083	57 527	1 059	-
SPECIAL DISTRICTS	5 808	3 660	4 291	4 641	1 115	1 115
CONNECTICUT, TOTAL.	156 848	125 596	132 354	143 338	1 086	1 052
STATE	50 570	40 963	42 951	43 948	1 019	954
LOCAL, TOTAL.	106 278	84 633	89 403	99 390	1 119	1 004
MUNICIPALITIES.	43 512	37 090	38 646	42 376	1 101	1 080
TOWNSHIPS	57 038	43 906	46 880	52 781	1 135	1 003
SCHOOL DISTRICTS.	2 017	1 585	1 665	1 813	1 093	-
SPECIAL DISTRICTS	3 711	2 052	2 212	2 420	1 115	1 115
DELAWARE, TOTAL	35 568	28 181	30 865	33 035	1 069	971
STATE	16 816	12 675	14 439	15 431	1 060	959
LOCAL, TOTAL.	18 752	15 506	16 426	17 604	1 075	992
COUNTIES.	2 575	2 172	2 285	2 049	891	891
MUNICIPALITIES.	4 835	3 890	4 142	4 582	1 106	1 068
SCHOOL DISTRICTS.	10 952	9 077	9 625	10 562	1 105	-
SPECIAL DISTRICTS	390	367	374	412	1 099	1 099

See footnotes at end of table.

253

Table 6. Employment and Payrolls of State and Local Governments, by Type of Government and by State: October 1977—Continued

State and type of government	Number of employees			October payroll, total (thousands of dollars)	Average earnings of full-time employees	
	Total	Full-time only	Full-time equivalent		All	Other than education employees
DISTRICT OF COLUMBIA, TOTAL	54 814	50 890	52 460	75 821	1 450	1 499
LOCAL, TOTAL.	54 814	50 890	52 460	75 821	1 450	1 499
MUNICIPALITIES.	47 717	43 793	45 363	65 068	1 416	1 462
SPECIAL DISTRICTS	7 097	7 097	7 097	11 753	1 656	1 656
FLORIDA, TOTAL.	483 029	404 401	429 709	421 207	983	942
STATE	109 966	92 138	97 371	103 313	1 057	965
LOCAL, TOTAL.	373 063	312 263	332 338	317 894	961	932
COUNTIES.	74 364	66 682	70 084	65 129	934	934
MUNICIPALITIES.	80 704	71 466	73 776	71 437	970	970
SCHOOL DISTRICTS.	192 778	152 020	164 850	162 248	991	-
SPECIAL DISTRICTS	25 217	22 095	23 628	19 080	808	808
GEORGIA, TOTAL.	308 316	258 955	273 905	228 305	838	805
STATE	89 060	73 587	77 469	73 862	950	885
LOCAL, TOTAL.	219 256	185 368	196 436	154 443	793	761
COUNTIES.	27 531	24 510	25 322	19 628	775	775
MUNICIPALITIES.	42 521	35 787	36 978	28 356	765	765
SCHOOL DISTRICTS.	110 359	91 395	97 825	79 439	826	-
SPECIAL DISTRICTS	38 845	33 676	36 311	27 020	747	747
HAWAII, TOTAL	57 220	44 279	47 397	57 465	1 211	1 211
STATE	42 864	31 188	34 036	41 728	1 222	1 055
LOCAL, TOTAL.	14 356	13 091	13 361	15 737	1 183	1 183
COUNTIES.	3 515	2 982	3 116	3 616	1 171	1 172
MUNICIPALITIES.	10 841	10 109	10 245	12 122	1 186	1 186
IDAHO, TOTAL.	55 850	39 831	43 935	40 764	931	918
STATE	19 969	13 352	15 081	16 253	1 075	1 063
LOCAL, TOTAL.	35 881	26 479	28 854	24 511	858	794
COUNTIES.	6 196	4 760	5 276	3 756	714	714
MUNICIPALITIES.	6 462	4 217	4 560	3 950	871	871
SCHOOL DISTRICTS.	20 823	15 901	17 184	15 295	901	-
SPECIAL DISTRICTS..	2 400	1 601	1 834	1 510	832	832
ILLINOIS, TOTAL	622 026	456 223	494 004	593 866	1 206	1 126
STATE	141 853	104 237	116 104	134 172	1 144	1 054
LOCAL, TOTAL.	480 173	351 986	377 900	459 694	1 224	1 156
COUNTIES.	46 298	40 859	42 506	39 561	933	933
MUNICIPALITIES.	114 139	85 541	89 851	113 129	1 264	1 264
TOWNSHIPS	16 388	4 685	5 968	4 007	668	668
SCHOOL DISTRICTS.	256 240	187 505	204 618	260 828	1 283	-
SPECIAL DISTRICTS	47 108	33 396	34 957	42 168	1 221	1 221
INDIANA, TOTAL.	288 883	216 242	235 939	228 485	967	827
STATE	82 985	53 885	61 116	72 039	1 154	996
LOCAL, TOTAL.	205 898	162 357	174 823	156 447	905	760
COUNTIES.	37 982	31 968	34 535	23 401	677	677
MUNICIPALITIES.	44 938	37 429	38 721	31 355	810	810
TOWNSHIPS	4 544	692	1 093	736	697	697
SCHOOL DISTRICTS.	112 190	88 668	96 230	96 952	1 025	-
SPECIAL DISTRICTS	6 244	3 600	4 244	4 004	979	979
IOWA, TOTAL	181 468	129 065	143 700	151 133	1 054	998
STATE	50 448	36 315	41 511	52 471	1 256	1 135
LOCAL, TOTAL.	131 020	92 750	102 189	98 662	974	903
COUNTIES.	20 418	16 460	18 233	14 800	819	819
MUNICIPALITIES.	27 669	16 664	18 121	17 804	988	988
SCHOOL DISTRICTS.	82 025	58 964	65 123	65 465	1 016	-
SPECIAL DISTRICTS	908	662	712	594	843	843
KANSAS, TOTAL	158 426	113 566	123 629	113 581	923	856
STATE	49 698	34 905	38 026	39 410	1 034	931
LOCAL, TOTAL.	108 728	78 661	85 603	74 171	875	808
COUNTIES.	16 961	13 519	14 443	9 577	663	663
MUNICIPALITIES.	25 896	17 056	18 357	16 059	877	877
TOWNSHIPS	2 363	594	800	542	681	681
SCHOOL DISTRICTS.	59 531	44 886	49 066	44 771	924	-
SPECIAL DISTRICTS	3 977	2 606	2 937	3 222	1 142	1 142
KENTUCKY, TOTAL	172 342	135 721	145 945	128 608	891	833
STATE	63 989	52 690	55 450	53 899	974	916
LOCAL, TOTAL.	108 353	83 031	90 495	74 709	837	744
COUNTIES.	13 888	11 872	12 520	7 854	627	627
MUNICIPALITIES.	23 562	19 186	20 174	16 054	797	797
SCHOOL DISTRICTS.	68 128	50 543	56 114	49 200	897	-
SPECIAL DISTRICTS	2 775	1 430	1 687	1 601	1 003	1 003

See footnotes at end of table.

State and type of government	Number of employees			October payroll, total (thousands of dollars)	Average earnings of full-time employees	
	Total	Full-time only	Full-time equivalent		All	Other than education employees
LOUISIANA, TOTAL	221 475	190 107	199 244	171 401	863	780
STATE	79 698	64 698	68 025	61 897	910	849
LOCAL, TOTAL	141 827	125 409	131 219	109 504	839	713
PARISHES	21 032	17 843	18 727	13 457	717	717
MUNICIPALITIES	34 439	30 588	31 649	22 374	708	708
SCHOOL DISTRICTS	85 867	76 503	80 367	73 242	920	-
SPECIAL DISTRICTS	489	475	476	431	904	904
MAINE, TOTAL	61 521	45 352	49 413	43 164	881	851
STATE	20 592	15 986	17 266	16 058	933	908
LOCAL, TOTAL	40 929	29 366	32 147	27 106	852	781
COUNTIES	1 393	877	1 002	660	656	656
MUNICIPALITIES	12 060	9 775	10 371	9 527	925	860
TOWNSHIPS	15 540	9 351	10 509	8 303	797	696
SCHOOL DISTRICTS	11 004	8 774	9 594	8 031	849	-
SPECIAL DISTRICTS	932	589	671	585	873	873
MARYLAND, TOTAL	243 579	205 356	216 907	243 740	1 127	1 028
STATE	76 681	67 866	72 184	75 836	1 058	1 046
LOCAL, TOTAL	166 898	137 490	144 723	167 904	1 160	1 014
COUNTIES	117 930	94 453	100 899	121 535	1 211	1 078
MUNICIPALITIES	45 354	39 528	40 287	42 162	1 036	913
SPECIAL DISTRICTS	3 614	3 509	3 537	4 207	1 188	1 188
MASSACHUSETTS, TOTAL	332 444	265 150	280 269	310 476	1 114	1 041
STATE	80 214	66 770	70 382	74 240	1 048	989
LOCAL, TOTAL	252 230	198 380	209 887	236 236	1 135	1 069
COUNTIES	7 494	6 677	7 109	6 920	973	973
MUNICIPALITIES	111 601	95 459	99 495	113 329	1 146	1 043
TOWNSHIPS	112 231	78 734	85 019	92 308	1 098	999
SCHOOL DISTRICTS	11 693	9 005	9 664	10 590	1 102	-
SPECIAL DISTRICTS	9 211	8 505	8 600	13 089	1 530	1 530
MICHIGAN, TOTAL	552 777	390 161	427 527	537 026	1 258	1 203
STATE	144 859	102 910	117 021	152 842	1 295	1 239
LOCAL, TOTAL	407 918	287 251	310 506	384 184	1 244	1 182
COUNTIES	46 473	41 502	43 146	44 419	1 031	1 031
MUNICIPALITIES	84 652	66 340	69 378	89 653	1 293	1 293
TOWNSHIPS	23 696	4 034	5 938	6 720	1 182	1 182
SCHOOL DISTRICTS	246 980	170 465	186 315	237 936	1 287	-
SPECIAL DISTRICTS	6 117	4 910	5 729	5 455	961	961
MINNESOTA, TOTAL	243 739	177 297	194 022	222 331	1 152	1 135
STATE	67 784	45 079	51 776	66 342	1 286	1 187
LOCAL, TOTAL	175 955	132 218	142 246	155 989	1 107	1 111
COUNTIES	32 269	26 028	28 503	29 361	1 032	1 032
MUNICIPALITIES	42 071	26 390	28 798	33 764	1 180	1 180
TOWNSHIPS	10 089	458	1 474	752	553	553
SCHOOL DISTRICTS	85 803	74 388	78 275	85 869	1 103	-
SPECIAL DISTRICTS	5 723	4 954	5 196	6 242	1 216	1 216
MISSISSIPPI, TOTAL	137 101	108 642	118 029	89 588	766	682
STATE	41 678	33 481	36 063	30 540	842	743
LOCAL, TOTAL	95 423	75 161	81 966	59 048	731	642
COUNTIES	20 687	17 769	18 952	11 535	609	609
MUNICIPALITIES	20 628	15 703	16 620	11 366	679	679
SCHOOL DISTRICTS	53 337	41 138	45 794	35 748	805	-
SPECIAL DISTRICTS	771	551	600	399	668	668
MISSOURI, TOTAL	254 350	198 632	213 206	199 811	941	892
STATE	75 052	57 119	61 486	59 383	954	887
LOCAL, TOTAL	179 298	141 513	151 720	140 428	936	894
COUNTIES	18 138	15 703	16 578	12 622	761	761
MUNICIPALITIES	48 165	38 666	40 526	39 086	966	966
TOWNSHIPS	2 134	306	512	294	563	563
SCHOOL DISTRICTS	102 989	80 608	87 432	83 183	967	-
SPECIAL DISTRICTS	7 872	6 230	6 672	5 242	800	800
MONTANA, TOTAL	53 380	39 958	42 525	43 785	1 032	937
STATE	19 735	14 299	15 191	17 036	1 116	1 023
LOCAL, TOTAL	33 645	25 659	27 334	26 749	986	838
COUNTIES	6 651	5 239	5 654	4 304	767	767
MUNICIPALITIES	5 575	3 798	4 097	3 879	949	949
SCHOOL DISTRICTS	20 909	16 320	17 234	18 334	1 070	-
SPECIAL DISTRICTS	510	302	349	232	667	667

See footnotes at end of table.

State and type of government	Number of employees			October payroll, total (thousands of dollars)	Average earnings of full-time employees	
	Total	Full-time only	Full-time equivalent		All	Other than education employees
NEBRASKA, TOTAL	109 275	80 206	88 766	81 102	916	910
STATE	31 097	23 847	26 657	24 414	903	864
LOCAL, TOTAL	78 178	56 359	62 109	56 688	922	937
COUNTIES	13 220	10 125	11 046	8 197	736	736
MUNICIPALITIES	16 314	10 878	11 832	11 198	945	945
TOWNSHIPS	607	85	156	88	593	593
SCHOOL DISTRICTS	40 181	29 352	32 898	29 456	908	-
SPECIAL DISTRICTS	7 856	5 919	6 177	7 750	1 270	1 270
NEVADA, TOTAL	42 416	34 564	36 515	40 314	1 114	1 164
STATE	13 037	10 070	10 592	13 380	1 263	1 257
LOCAL, TOTAL	29 379	24 494	25 923	26 934	1 053	1 114
COUNTIES	9 696	8 521	8 880	9 586	1 081	1 081
MUNICIPALITIES	4 531	4 142	4 244	5 102	1 205	1 205
SCHOOL DISTRICTS	14 020	11 069	11 825	11 405	980	-
SPECIAL DISTRICTS	1 132	762	974	841	994	994
NEW HAMPSHIRE, TOTAL	50 453	34 102	38 034	35 045	928	924
STATE	17 235	11 984	13 646	13 682	1 002	1 013
LOCAL, TOTAL	33 218	22 118	24 388	21 363	887	782
COUNTIES	2 529	2 074	2 288	1 527	668	668
MUNICIPALITIES	9 961	8 119	8 696	8 242	957	948
TOWNSHIPS	7 232	2 368	2 940	2 353	796	796
SCHOOL DISTRICTS	11 576	9 294	10 052	8 937	900	-
SPECIAL DISTRICTS	1 920	263	412	305	810	810
NEW JERSEY, TOTAL	410 773	331 802	349 473	402 894	1 157	1 023
STATE	87 845	71 227	75 263	87 546	1 160	1 088
LOCAL, TOTAL	322 928	260 575	274 210	315 348	1 156	994
COUNTIES	61 496	53 397	56 063	54 112	960	915
MUNICIPALITIES	96 923	79 597	83 354	90 585	1 090	1 037
TOWNSHIPS	25 997	18 707	20 073	20 540	1 025	1 043
SCHOOL DISTRICTS	130 208	101 551	107 181	142 176	1 342	-
SPECIAL DISTRICTS	8 304	7 323	7 539	7 935	1 055	1 055
NEW MEXICO, TOTAL	78 563	64 087	68 512	63 173	926	902
STATE	32 740	25 308	27 922	27 100	974	935
LOCAL, TOTAL	45 823	38 779	40 590	36 073	894	862
COUNTIES	3 979	3 364	3 589	2 979	835	835
MUNICIPALITIES	11 170	9 868	10 200	8 897	874	874
SCHOOL DISTRICTS	30 319	25 228	26 478	23 950	912	-
SPECIAL DISTRICTS	355	319	323	246	761	761
NEW YORK, TOTAL	1 053 437	868 320	918 499	1 148 526	1 255	1 163
STATE	209 561	188 254	194 283	218 487	1 123	1 099
LOCAL, TOTAL	843 876	680 066	724 216	930 039	1 292	1 190
COUNTIES	116 409	102 305	106 120	104 580	982	954
MUNICIPALITIES	428 927	356 808	378 854	507 605	1 344	1 286
TOWNSHIPS	50 323	28 994	32 381	31 757	983	983
SCHOOL DISTRICTS	238 428	183 188	197 929	271 829	1 397	-
SPECIAL DISTRICTS	9 789	8 771	8 932	14 268	1 603	1 603
NORTH CAROLINA, TOTAL	312 273	261 133	278 513	250 726	908	861
STATE	99 472	79 047	86 904	84 870	990	962
LOCAL, TOTAL	212 801	182 086	191 609	165 856	872	785
COUNTIES	168 313	142 454	150 966	132 596	888	744
MUNICIPALITIES	37 257	33 148	33 870	28 198	830	830
SPECIAL DISTRICTS	7 231	6 484	6 773	5 062	747	747
NORTH DAKOTA, TOTAL	51 322	27 873	31 220	31 941	1 037	920
STATE	16 209	10 595	11 498	12 439	1 078	966
LOCAL, TOTAL	35 113	17 278	19 722	19 502	1 012	867
COUNTIES	3 930	3 139	3 357	2 602	776	776
MUNICIPALITIES	6 270	2 635	2 954	2 924	991	991
TOWNSHIPS	8 453	90	455	225	503	503
SCHOOL DISTRICTS	15 425	11 345	12 738	13 616	1 089	-
SPECIAL DISTRICTS	1 035	69	218	136	691	691
OHIO, TOTAL	561 474	418 963	454 257	471 510	1 041	984
STATE	136 273	99 779	109 355	120 338	1 092	1 010
LOCAL, TOTAL	425 201	319 184	344 902	351 172	1 025	973
COUNTIES	71 544	65 222	67 920	54 395	801	801
MUNICIPALITIES	98 740	74 917	78 795	87 894	1 117	1 117
TOWNSHIPS	16 131	3 763	5 396	5 253	1 020	1 020
SCHOOL DISTRICTS	225 409	164 764	181 926	192 905	1 075	938
SPECIAL DISTRICTS[1]	13 377	10 518	10 865	10 725	998	998

See footnotes at end of table.

256

Table 6. Employment and Payrolls of State and Local Governments, by Type of Government and by State: October 1977—Continued

State and type of government	Number of employees			October payroll, total (thousands of dollars)	Average earnings of full-time employees	
	Total	Full-time only	Full-time equivalent		All	Other than education employees
OKLAHOMA, TOTAL	164 507	128 434	140 041	118 566	848	776
STATE	59 870	43 727	49 622	45 662	914	818
LOCAL, TOTAL	104 637	84 707	90 419	72 904	814	743
COUNTIES	14 783	13 346	13 893	8 308	598	598
MUNICIPALITIES	29 259	23 733	24 969	20 590	825	825
SCHOOL DISTRICTS	59 471	46 932	50 756	43 418	872	-
SPECIAL DISTRICTS	1 124	696	801	588	735	735
OREGON, TOTAL	160 668	115 662	127 487	144 813	1 140	1 132
STATE	52 954	36 499	41 219	50 104	1 213	1 136
LOCAL, TOTAL	107 714	79 163	86 278	94 709	1 106	1 129
COUNTIES	15 328	13 526	14 087	14 659	1 043	1 043
MUNICIPALITIES	15 738	12 778	13 273	15 829	1 196	1 196
SCHOOL DISTRICTS	68 279	46 478	52 210	56 445	1 090	-
SPECIAL DISTRICTS	8 369	6 381	6 698	7 776	1 178	1 178
PENNSYLVANIA, TOTAL	551 857	446 808	473 981	501 843	1 065	1 062
STATE	149 403	127 277	132 584	153 536	1 157	1 116
LOCAL, TOTAL	402 454	319 531	341 397	348 307	1 028	1 022
COUNTIES	47 394	42 705	44 797	33 971	758	758
MUNICIPALITIES	80 279	66 202	68 822	79 573	1 153	1 153
TOWNSHIPS	25 576	12 153	14 446	13 408	930	930
SCHOOL DISTRICTS	227 101	178 447	192 813	196 646	1 032	-
SPECIAL DISTRICTS	22 104	20 024	20 519	24 709	1 208	1 208
RHODE ISLAND, TOTAL	51 606	41 937	44 275	47 789	1 081	950
STATE	23 127	17 503	19 060	19 959	1 045	992
LOCAL, TOTAL	28 479	24 434	25 215	27 830	1 108	895
MUNICIPALITIES	16 081	14 379	14 711	16 578	1 129	925
TOWNSHIPS	11 053	8 980	9 396	10 289	1 102	877
SCHOOL DISTRICTS	358	321	331	417	1 255	-
SPECIAL DISTRICTS	987	754	777	546	702	702
SOUTH CAROLINA, TOTAL	171 607	139 930	145 587	121 858	835	784
STATE	63 021	52 463	55 653	52 026	933	852
LOCAL, TOTAL	108 586	87 467	89 934	69 832	777	716
COUNTIES	21 200	18 887	19 895	14 329	719	719
MUNICIPALITIES	16 299	12 879	13 332	9 484	709	709
SCHOOL DISTRICTS	67 132	52 145	53 014	43 341	818	-
SPECIAL DISTRICTS	3 955	3 556	3 693	2 678	727	727
SOUTH DAKOTA, TOTAL	49 255	31 095	33 405	29 277	879	854
STATE	16 485	11 270	12 109	11 913	985	937
LOCAL, TOTAL	32 770	19 825	21 296	17 364	819	760
COUNTIES	4 267	3 127	3 475	2 220	642	642
MUNICIPALITIES	6 984	3 528	4 086	3 524	869	869
TOWNSHIPS	3 249	-	198	139	-	-
SCHOOL DISTRICTS	17 989	13 099	13 436	11 429	849	-
SPECIAL DISTRICTS	281	71	101	53	520	520
TENNESSEE, TOTAL	235 926	199 776	212 476	178 028	847	793
STATE	74 046	60 925	64 317	55 987	868	812
LOCAL, TOTAL	161 880	138 851	148 159	122 041	837	783
COUNTIES	75 246	62 870	69 220	50 767	755	669
MUNICIPALITIES	81 156	71 664	74 256	67 671	912	848
SCHOOL DISTRICTS	1 142	967	1 035	707	703	-
SPECIAL DISTRICTS	4 336	3 350	3 648	2 897	800	800
TEXAS, TOTAL	719 040	593 489	630 592	588 035	937	887
STATE	193 231	151 980	162 987	164 387	1 007	944
LOCAL, TOTAL	525 809	441 509	467 605	423 648	913	858
COUNTIES	60 236	55 179	56 954	40 734	715	715
MUNICIPALITIES	125 907	113 486	116 236	106 737	919	919
SCHOOL DISTRICTS	325 147	260 020	281 216	263 915	952	-
SPECIAL DISTRICTS	14 519	12 824	13 199	12 262	930	930
UTAH, TOTAL	81 429	57 054	63 541	62 940	1 002	1 010
STATE	33 178	23 713	26 364	26 588	1 018	1 080
LOCAL, TOTAL	48 251	33 341	37 177	36 352	991	947
COUNTIES	7 478	6 088	6 548	6 047	931	931
MUNICIPALITIES	8 400	5 926	6 429	6 297	984	984
SCHOOL DISTRICTS	31 302	20 549	23 376	23 353	1 019	-
SPECIAL DISTRICTS	1 071	778	824	655	794	794

See footnotes at end of table.

257

Table 6. Employment and Payrolls of State and Local Governments, by Type of Government and by State: October 1977—Continued

State and type of government	Number of employees			October payroll, total (thousands of dollars)	Average earnings of full-time employees	
	Total	Full-time only	Full-time equivalent		All	Other than education employees
VERMONT, TOTAL.	31 534	21 369	23 747	22 017	933	942
STATE	12 955	9 989	10 752	10 644	984	979
LOCAL, TOTAL.	18 579	11 380	12 995	11 373	888	853
COUNTIES.	52	24	30	19	648	648
MUNICIPALITIES.	1 779	1 380	1 448	1 321	910	910
TOWNSHIPS	4 229	1 407	1 908	1 574	808	808
SCHOOL DISTRICTS.	11 659	8 470	9 408	8 335	900	-
SPECIAL DISTRICTS	860	99	201	125	753	753
VIRGINIA, TOTAL	299 060	241 222	261 799	243 353	937	877
STATE	105 219	82 709	89 292	88 326	984	877
LOCAL, TOTAL.	193 841	158 513	172 507	155 027	912	876
COUNTIES.	103 787	81 187	91 578	83 828	936	932
MUNICIPALITIES.	87 130	74 774	78 222	68 867	887	848
SPECIAL DISTRICTS	2 924	2 552	2 707	2 332	861	861
WASHINGTON, TOTAL	229 402	175 527	188 934	226 952	1 206	1 169
STATE	84 890	59 797	65 843	81 351	1 226	1 133
LOCAL, TOTAL.	144 512	115 730	123 091	145 601	1 195	1 193
COUNTIES.	20 637	17 313	18 093	18 805	1 041	1 041
MUNICIPALITIES.	30 215	23 193	24 460	30 809	1 264	1 264
SCHOOL DISTRICTS.	72 195	61 253	65 134	76 882	1 197	-
SPECIAL DISTRICTS	21 465	13 971	15 404	19 105	1 264	1 264
WEST VIRGINIA, TOTAL.	102 631	87 206	90 917	81 342	892	780
STATE	43 561	35 007	37 357	34 174	907	789
LOCAL, TOTAL.	59 070	52 199	53 560	47 168	881	764
COUNTIES.	6 321	5 433	5 731	3 778	659	659
MUNICIPALITIES.	10 953	8 284	8 872	7 343	830	830
SCHOOL DISTRICTS.	40 637	37 578	37 998	35 293	927	-
SPECIAL DISTRICTS	1 159	904	959	753	790	790
WISCONSIN, TOTAL.	283 465	203 519	222 464	240 208	1 087	1 044
STATE	69 035	49 222	54 549	67 798	1 245	1 176
LOCAL, TOTAL.	214 430	154 297	167 915	172 410	1 037	997
COUNTIES.	42 546	36 089	38 216	34 339	899	899
MUNICIPALITIES.	71 124	56 469	59 227	67 417	1 141	1 129
TOWNSHIPS	17 906	1 919	3 951	2 639	693	693
SCHOOL DISTRICTS.	81 898	59 081	65 736	67 273	1 034	-
SPECIAL DISTRICTS	956	739	785	742	939	939
WYOMING, TOTAL.	29 060	22 041	23 794	22 972	972	917
STATE	9 682	7 610	8 207	8 905	1 095	1 044
LOCAL, TOTAL.	19 378	14 431	15 587	14 067	907	810
COUNTIES.	4 219	3 597	3 810	2 808	738	738
MUNICIPALITIES.	3 251	2 429	2 571	2 323	907	907
SCHOOL DISTRICTS.	11 167	7 949	8 689	8 494	985	-
SPECIAL DISTRICTS	741	456	517	442	857	857

Note: Statistics for local governments are subject to sampling variation; see text for statement of reliability. Because of rounding, detail may not add to totals.

- Represents zero.

[1]Employees of the Cleveland Public Library, a part of the Cleveland City School District, are not considered as education employees as is the case for other school library employees.

Table 7. Full-Time Equivalent Employment of State and Local Governments, by Function and by State: October 1977

State	All functions		Education							
			Total		Local schools					
					State and local governments			State government only		
	State and local governments	State government only	State and local governments	State government only	Total	Instructional staff	Other	Total	Instructional staff	Other
UNITED STATES, TOTAL ..	10 498 184	2 902 191	5 106 275	1 004 626	3 929 218	2 748 770	1 180 448	15 809	11 523	4 286
ALABAMA.	177 199	58 955	83 450	24 514	58 936	42 542	16 394	-	-	-
ALASKA	27 586	15 204	11 719	4 468	8 988	6 198	2 790	1 737	1 310	427
ARIZONA.	126 673	33 590	68 559	15 665	48 445	32 626	15 819	-	-	-
ARKANSAS	95 806	31 946	50 455	11 903	38 151	26 930	11 221	-	-	-
CALIFORNIA	1 087 602	231 957	490 769	84 471	361 241	242 337	118 904	-	-	-
COLORADO	141 701	41 738	76 431	21 348	53 762	36 809	16 953	-	-	-
CONNECTICUT.	132 354	42 951	68 462	11 692	56 770	43 618	13 152	-	-	-
DELAWARE	30 865	14 439	16 025	4 745	11 280	7 997	3 283	-	-	-
DISTRICT OF COLUMBIA . . .	52 459	-	14 262		12 435	8 436	3 999	-	-	-
FLORIDA.	429 709	97 371	188 957	24 107	150 779	99 126	51 653	-	-	-
GEORGIA.	273 904	77 469	124 787	26 962	97 099	67 178	29 921	-	-	-
HAWAII	47 397	34 036	19 620	19 620	14 027	10 184	3 843	14 027	10 184	3 843
IDAHO.	43 935	15 081	22 334	5 150	16 647	12 525	4 122	-	-	-
ILLINOIS	494 004	116 104	246 268	41 650	190 234	133 276	56 958	-	-	-
INDIANA.	235 938	61 115	127 174	30 944	96 230	64 601	31 629	-	-	-
IOWA	143 700	41 511	81 134	16 011	61 921	43 353	18 568	-	-	-
KANSAS	123 629	38 026	65 233	16 167	46 244	32 690	13 554	-	-	-
KENTUCKY	145 945	55 450	76 265	20 151	56 114	40 248	15 866	-	-	-
LOUISIANA.	199 240	68 021	100 768	20 401	80 317	52 680	27 637	-	-	-
MAINE.	49 413	17 266	26 867	5 379	21 533	15 516	6 017	45	29	16
MARYLAND	216 907	72 184	107 930	24 225	78 560	53 938	24 622	-	-	-
MASSACHUSETTS.	280 267	70 380	127 224	16 799	110 378	82 050	28 328	-	-	-
MICHIGAN	427 527	117 021	234 102	47 787	177 852	118 227	59 625	-	-	-
MINNESOTA.	194 011	51 776	101 393	23 107	78 275	56 018	22 257	-	-	-
MISSISSIPPI.	118 029	36 063	58 830	13 036	42 909	30 715	12 194	-	-	-
MISSOURI	213 206	61 486	104 570	17 138	84 166	58 998	25 168	-	-	-
MONTANA.	42 525	15 191	21 231	3 997	17 024	12 495	4 529	-	-	-
NEBRASKA	88 766	26 657	43 114	10 216	31 795	23 453	8 342	-	-	-
NEVADA	36 515	10 592	15 202	3 377	11 825	8 252	3 573	-	-	-
NEW HAMPSHIRE.	37 906	13 518	18 572	4 233	14 339	11 190	3 149	-	-	-
NEW JERSEY	349 473	75 263	164 980	19 338	139 611	100 148	39 463	-	-	-
NEW MEXICO	68 475	27 885	37 964	11 486	26 478	19 234	7 244	-	-	-
NEW YORK	918 498	194 283	353 062	32 559	293 639	208 232	85 407	-	-	-
NORTH CAROLINA	278 508	86 899	149 374	31 274	110 656	76 935	33 721	-	-	-
NORTH DAKOTA	31 220	11 498	17 121	4 356	12 486	9 075	3 411	-	-	-
OHIO	454 257	109 355	225 127	43 830	177 089	126 388	50 701	-	-	-
OKLAHOMA	140 038	49 619	70 379	19 623	50 756	36 211	14 545	-	-	-
OREGON	127 487	41 219	65 011	12 801	46 126	31 968	14 158	-	-	-
PENNSYLVANIA	473 981	132 584	216 218	23 405	187 505	129 938	57 567	-	-	-
RHODE ISLAND	44 275	19 060	20 912	5 951	14 961	11 449	3 512	-	-	-
SOUTH CAROLINA	145 587	55 653	72 311	19 297	53 014	41 342	11 672	-	-	-
SOUTH DAKOTA	33 405	12 109	17 560	4 124	13 436	10 739	2 697	-	-	-
TENNESSEE.	212 476	64 317	93 675	22 803	70 872	48 630	22 242	-	-	-
TEXAS.	630 592	162 987	348 183	66 967	267 945	191 093	76 852	-	-	-
UTAH	63 541	26 364	37 435	14 059	23 376	16 994	6 382	-	-	-
VERMONT.	23 745	10 750	12 937	3 529	9 408	7 257	2 151	-	-	-
VIRGINIA	261 799	89 292	140 181	31 515	108 666	75 091	33 575	-	-	-
WASHINGTON	188 934	65 843	91 953	26 819	65 134	41 230	23 904	-	-	-
WEST VIRGINIA.	90 917	37 357	48 849	10 851	37 998	26 039	11 959	-	-	-
WISCONSIN.	222 464	54 549	120 040	28 158	83 700	60 774	22 926	-	-	-
WYOMING.	23 794	8 207	11 307	2 618	8 086	5 797	2 289	-	-	-

See footnotes at end of table.

259

Table 7. Full-Time Equivalent Employment of State and Local Governments, by Function and by State: October 1977—Continued

State	Education--Continued — Institutions of higher education						Other education (State)	All functions other than education	
	State and local governments			State government only				State and local governments	State government only
	Total	Instructional staff	Other	Total	Instructional staff	Other			
UNITED STATES, TOTAL . .	1 089 429	418 997	670 432	901 189	325 015	576 174	87 628	5 391 909	1 897 565
ALABAMA	20 915	7 697	13 218	20 915	7 697	13 218	3 599	93 749	34 441
ALASKA	2 303	1 096	1 207	2 303	1 096	1 207	428	15 867	10 736
ARIZONA	17 843	6 020	11 823	13 394	3 950	9 444	2 271	58 114	17 925
ARKANSAS	9 890	3 779	6 111	9 489	3 551	5 938	2 414	45 351	20 043
CALIFORNIA	124 563	48 756	75 807	79 506	27 050	52 456	4 965	596 833	147 486
COLORADO	22 119	7 091	15 028	20 798	6 487	14 311	550	65 270	20 390
CONNECTICUT	9 441	3 760	5 681	9 441	3 760	5 681	2 251	63 892	31 259
DELAWARE	4 497	1 302	3 195	4 497	1 302	3 195	248	14 840	9 694
DISTRICT OF COLUMBIA . . .	1 827	789	1 038	-	-	-	-	38 197	-
FLORIDA	36 034	13 065	22 969	21 963	7 281	14 682	2 144	240 752	73 264
GEORGIA	25 234	7 809	17 425	24 508	7 370	17 138	2 454	149 117	50 507
HAWAII	5 425	2 106	3 319	5 425	2 106	3 319	168	27 777	14 416
IDAHO	5 155	1 997	3 158	4 618	1 802	2 816	532	21 601	9 931
ILLINOIS	53 430	21 207	32 223	39 046	14 175	24 871	2 604	247 736	74 454
INDIANA	28 221	10 291	17 930	28 221	10 291	17 930	2 723	108 764	30 171
IOWA	17 732	6 566	11 166	14 530	4 943	9 587	1 481	62 566	25 500
KANSAS	18 231	8 040	10 191	15 409	6 677	8 732	758	58 396	21 859
KENTUCKY	16 557	5 465	11 092	16 557	5 465	11 092	3 594	69 680	35 299
LOUISIANA	17 918	6 916	11 002	17 868	6 868	11 000	2 533	93 472	47 620
MAINE	4 395	1 463	2 932	4 395	1 463	2 932	939	22 546	11 887
MARYLAND	27 306	12 210	15 096	22 161	10 036	12 125	2 064	108 977	47 959
MASSACHUSETTS	15 284	6 438	8 846	15 237	6 408	8 829	1 562	153 043	53 581
MICHIGAN	53 796	19 475	34 321	45 333	15 492	29 841	2 454	193 425	69 234
MINNESOTA	22 145	9 692	12 453	22 145	9 692	12 453	962	92 629	28 669
MISSISSIPPI	14 599	5 085	9 514	11 714	3 389	8 325	1 322	59 199	23 027
MISSOURI	18 605	9 903	8 702	15 339	8 345	6 994	1 799	108 636	44 348
MONTANA	3 735	1 646	2 089	3 525	1 531	1 994	472	21 294	11 194
NEBRASKA	10 560	3 874	6 686	9 457	3 420	6 037	759	45 652	16 441
NEVADA	3 124	1 090	2 034	3 124	1 090	2 034	253	21 313	7 215
NEW HAMPSHIRE	3 892	1 312	2 580	3 892	1 312	2 580	341	19 334	9 285
NEW JERSEY	23 038	9 126	13 912	17 007	6 664	10 343	2 331	184 493	55 925
NEW MEXICO	10 601	2 692	7 909	10 601	2 692	7 909	885	30 511	16 399
NEW YORK	55 742	25 632	30 110	28 878	10 732	18 146	3 681	565 436	161 724
NORTH CAROLINA	35 790	13 392	22 398	28 346	8 356	19 990	2 928	129 130	55 625
NORTH DAKOTA	4 218	1 810	2 408	3 939	1 655	2 284	417	14 099	7 142
OHIO	45 873	16 853	29 020	41 665	14 733	26 932	2 165	229 130	65 525
OKLAHOMA	17 874	6 250	11 624	17 874	6 250	11 624	1 749	69 659	29 996
OREGON	17 855	8 273	9 582	11 771	5 388	6 383	1 030	62 476	28 418
PENNSYLVANIA	26 066	10 264	15 802	20 758	7 479	13 279	2 647	257 763	109 179
RHODE ISLAND	4 890	1 565	3 325	4 890	1 565	3 325	1 061	23 363	13 109
SOUTH CAROLINA	14 088	3 992	10 096	14 088	3 992	10 096	5 209	73 276	36 356
SOUTH DAKOTA	3 800	1 379	2 421	3 800	1 379	2 421	324	15 845	7 985
TENNESSEE	19 822	6 502	13 320	19 822	6 502	13 320	2 981	118 801	41 514
TEXAS	76 606	25 964	50 642	63 335	19 366	43 969	3 632	282 409	96 020
UTAH	13 299	5 558	7 741	13 299	5 558	7 741	760	26 106	12 305
VERMONT	3 308	1 467	1 841	3 308	1 467	1 841	221	10 808	7 221
VIRGINIA	28 713	11 589	17 124	28 713	11 589	17 124	2 802	121 618	57 777
WASHINGTON	25 707	10 147	15 560	25 707	10 147	15 560	1 112	96 981	39 024
WEST VIRGINIA	9 369	3 248	6 121	9 369	3 248	6 121	1 482	42 068	26 506
WISCONSIN	34 957	16 265	18 692	26 775	11 412	15 363	1 383	102 424	26 391
WYOMING	3 037	1 089	1 948	2 434	792	1 642	184	12 487	5 589

See footnotes at end of table.

State	Highways		Public welfare		Hospitals		Health		Police protection	
	State and local governments	State government only	State and local governments	State government only	State and local governments	State government only	State and local governments	State government only	State and local governments	State government only
UNITED STATES, TOTAL	556 970	257 997	355 659	165 057	985 974	525 007	197 377	99 904	560 721	69 736
ALABAMA	14 305	5 567	4 200	3 650	25 067	10 103	3 071	1 420	7 592	866
ALASKA	1 843	1 590	669	613	668	422	529	425	931	304
ARIZONA	6 565	3 752	2 272	1 971	6 269	2 623	1 701	444	7 205	1 401
ARKANSAS	7 704	3 806	1 994	1 815	9 990	4 058	2 086	1 790	3 777	657
CALIFORNIA	34 788	13 744	37 264	2 072	87 905	29 653	26 491	6 592	64 555	9 448
COLORADO	7 725	3 167	3 928	978	9 260	4 809	2 986	676	6 974	824
CONNECTICUT	7 224	2 906	3 132	2 242	10 273	9 695	1 936	859	7 801	1 257
DELAWARE	1 573	1 258	1 108	1 108	1 667	1 667	849	849	1 544	582
DISTRICT OF COLUMBIA	1 057	-	2 637	-	2 951	-	3 241	-	4 905	-
FLORIDA	20 063	8 172	9 545	5 939	49 428	17 003	8 658	6 059	26 024	2 189
GEORGIA	14 324	6 817	5 131	4 910	44 682	12 815	9 005	6 358	11 975	1 749
HAWAII	1 898	937	910	832	3 026	3 026	1 620	1 494	2 442	-
IDAHO	3 115	1 537	1 303	1 154	2 784	940	1 056	1 031	2 022	218
ILLINOIS	21 329	7 360	15 814	11 585	39 246	21 286	6 646	1 974	33 033	1 935
INDIANA	11 983	5 129	6 854	1 196	24 900	10 372	2 545	917	11 209	1 564
IOWA	9 383	3 780	5 096	2 888	14 324	7 852	1 273	497	5 262	843
KANSAS	9 634	3 909	3 042	2 541	11 002	5 924	1 582	519	5 295	655
KENTUCKY	8 767	6 415	5 450	4 773	10 877	6 027	2 411	1 045	6 848	1 801
LOUISIANA	12 022	6 820	5 584	5 068	21 570	16 489	1 820	732	9 350	1 273
MAINE	4 982	3 028	1 138	1 098	2 169	1 724	576	354	2 199	463
MARYLAND	9 907	4 965	5 709	3 017	17 042	13 135	6 578	3 737	12 498	2 071
MASSACHUSETTS	12 971	5 202	7 749	6 700	29 399	18 445	3 051	1 435	16 567	1 566
MICHIGAN	16 582	4 680	15 287	13 371	37 835	19 339	6 670	1 813	23 105	2 931
MINNESOTA	12 424	4 957	7 934	1 223	17 747	8 478	2 597	1 034	7 753	815
MISSISSIPPI	8 965	2 885	3 204	3 086	16 484	5 690	2 231	1 751	4 760	777
MISSOURI	12 596	6 597	6 684	5 934	25 362	14 884	4 099	1 672	12 500	1 703
MONTANA	3 597	2 069	1 425	952	2 455	1 488	671	366	1 931	344
NEBRASKA	5 689	2 501	3 035	1 058	8 445	5 574	1 352	363	3 189	514
NEVADA	1 955	1 349	791	645	3 463	615	691	346	2 562	299
NEW HAMPSHIRE	3 580	2 150	2 716	936	2 440	2 021	488	393	1 803	275
NEW JERSEY	19 548	7 909	12 845	4 360	24 791	13 868	5 183	2 408	26 046	3 807
NEW MEXICO	3 991	2 748	1 545	1 530	4 818	3 714	751	644	3 223	549
NEW YORK	47 013	16 239	48 680	2 468	126 294	69 674	19 539	6 471	58 364	4 706
NORTH CAROLINA	15 013	11 910	8 213	1 301	24 695	15 161	6 268	1 464	12 709	2 796
NORTH DAKOTA	2 523	1 186	1 009	361	1 852	1 852	386	243	1 135	143
OHIO	23 129	8 670	17 212	1 352	36 011	22 528	8 821	2 405	23 371	1 930
OKLAHOMA	9 039	3 383	5 464	5 334	14 896	7 316	1 782	912	6 062	1 084
OREGON	6 925	3 132	4 765	3 878	7 701	5 711	2 194	706	5 571	1 173
PENNSYLVANIA	30 691	18 288	30 556	13 138	32 790	30 382	5 600	2 400	29 433	4 593
RHODE ISLAND	1 984	919	1 637	1 596	3 724	3 724	975	824	2 508	230
SOUTH CAROLINA	7 173	4 689	4 773	4 342	19 193	9 814	5 133	4 144	6 140	1 229
SOUTH DAKOTA	2 941	1 410	962	914	2 020	1 458	443	319	1 464	343
TENNESSEE	13 347	6 360	6 505	4 994	24 286	10 119	4 693	3 147	9 571	959
TEXAS	30 202	14 018	14 474	13 361	57 474	31 655	11 231	7 013	29 849	1 434
UTAH	3 294	1 922	1 989	1 296	3 643	2 963	911	543	2 741	438
VERMONT	2 147	1 043	638	636	1 149	1 149	396	383	950	383
VIRGINIA	15 973	11 701	6 245	721	20 043	17 647	6 132	5 078	11 037	1 656
WASHINGTON	10 742	5 126	5 469	5 072	11 814	7 563	2 630	671	7 919	1 266
WEST VIRGINIA	8 091	7 230	3 620	3 564	8 580	5 094	1 480	966	2 944	742
WISCONSIN	12 639	1 752	6 979	1 027	18 591	6 677	4 095	977	10 893	770
WYOMING	2 015	1 313	474	457	2 879	781	324	241	1 180	181

See footnotes at end of table.

Table 7. Full-Time Equivalent Employment of State and Local Governments, by Function and by State: October 1977—Continued

State	Fire protection (local)	Sewerage (local)	Sanitation other than sewerage (local)	Parks and recreation (local)	Natural resources State and local governments	Natural resources State government only	Correction State and local governments	Correction State government only	Libraries (local)
UNITED STATES, TOTAL	220 365	85 382	126 720	159 287	179 489	151 999	217 699	134 471	64 581
ALABAMA	3 405	860	4 239	1 813	3 159	3 060	2 300	1 536	521
ALASKA	425	129	166	217	1 549	1 538	591	575	93
ARIZONA	2 164	750	1 518	1 957	2 744	1 779	1 888	1 299	793
ARKANSAS	1 455	673	1 081	572	2 684	2 581	1 291	1 038	317
CALIFORNIA	26 180	6 860	7 248	25 887	19 496	12 150	31 466	12 135	10 566
COLORADO	2 391	1 295	774	2 788	2 275	1 866	2 422	1 633	1 088
CONNECTICUT	4 001	1 259	1 242	1 926	932	888	3 499	3 499	1 081
DELAWARE	232	275	271	471	702	702	848	848	66
DISTRICT OF COLUMBIA	1 488	611	2 011	1 235	-	-	2 258	-	477
FLORIDA	9 852	4 376	6 978	10 727	8 475	6 559	11 234	8 816	2 244
GEORGIA	5 404	2 006	5 363	3 118	4 893	4 664	5 565	3 915	980
HAWAII	1 326	560	571	1 646	1 521	1 504	573	572	-
IDAHO	773	271	137	436	2 547	1 863	560	423	213
ILLINOIS	11 384	6 149	4 483	10 457	4 806	4 261	7 599	4 424	3 720
INDIANA	5 058	2 432	1 947	3 039	3 165	2 603	3 296	1 887	2 249
IOWA	1 709	968	769	1 297	2 770	2 272	2 106	1 478	815
KANSAS	2 172	738	1 057	1 192	2 523	2 262	1 943	1 401	307
KENTUCKY	2 928	1 231	1 871	1 147	4 730	4 591	2 559	1 888	579
LOUISIANA	3 750	1 475	4 326	2 507	5 653	4 691	4 217	3 242	1 046
MAINE	1 109	339	233	375	1 408	1 357	801	609	196
MARYLAND	5 004	2 539	2 402	4 152	2 990	2 820	6 006	4 818	2 022
MASSACHUSETTS	13 284	1 571	2 399	2 990	2 891	2 384	4 765	2 919	3 602
MICHIGAN	7 666	2 615	4 338	5 287	6 136	5 486	8 105	4 948	1 911
MINNESOTA	2 082	1 653	798	2 863	3 734	3 252	2 933	1 471	1 409
MISSISSIPPI	1 775	913	2 142	758	3 866	3 611	1 262	981	298
MISSOURI	4 563	1 731	1 182	3 132	3 846	3 518	3 840	2 558	1 535
MONTANA	437	185	282	277	2 181	1 969	760	567	250
NEBRASKA	1 211	453	285	883	2 524	1 993	1 239	944	448
NEVADA	1 172	177	46	1 005	779	674	1 039	622	225
NEW HAMPSHIRE	1 136	234	296	247	716	674	524	359	272
NEW JERSEY	8 120	2 642	4 191	5 098	2 558	2 182	8 846	4 006	3 279
NEW MEXICO	1 066	474	681	942	1 718	1 379	855	669	316
NEW YORK	19 349	6 065	16 006	14 154	7 533	7 287	22 317	11 780	2 268
NORTH CAROLINA	4 081	2 278	4 870	2 605	5 664	4 770	6 703	5 881	1 088
NORTH DAKOTA	288	87	283	135	1 275	1 042	314	243	64
OHIO	10 233	5 828	5 075	6 179	5 470	4 489	9 266	6 536	3 163
OKLAHOMA	3 301	806	2 086	1 669	2 395	2 139	2 912	2 577	541
OREGON	3 110	1 178	255	1 408	3 914	3 394	2 855	1 713	606
PENNSYLVANIA	7 174	4 746	7 034	5 689	6 969	6 827	9 359	3 772	1 772
RHODE ISLAND	1 895	346	369	417	509	507	794	794	234
SOUTH CAROLINA	2 150	1 007	3 331	1 054	2 499	2 409	3 081	2 562	576
SOUTH DAKOTA	336	153	182	274	1 176	999	305	236	182
TENNESSEE	5 224	1 676	4 066	3 188	4 510	4 247	4 239	3 242	988
TEXAS	12 732	5 275	9 019	8 331	9 108	6 514	9 063	4 954	4 137
UTAH	1 018	310	414	750	1 220	1 059	882	726	461
VERMONT	330	113	55	193	1 003	882	488	488	47
VIRGINIA	4 774	2 749	3 801	4 464	4 005	3 599	8 265	5 935	1 684
WASHINGTON	4 339	1 502	926	2 875	6 420	5 508	4 878	3 262	1 863
WEST VIRGINIA	942	550	976	395	2 506	2 451	881	743	201
WISCONSIN	4 110	2 164	2 377	3 865	2 450	1 954	3 615	2 736	1 745
WYOMING	257	105	269	201	892	779	292	211	143

See footnotes at end of table.

Table 7. Full-Time Equivalent Employment of State and Local Governments, by Function and by State: October 1977—Continued

State	Employment security administration (State)	Financial administration — State and local governments	Financial administration — State government only	General control — State and local governments	General control — State government only	Local utilities — Water supply	Local utilities — Other	State liquor stores	Other and unallocable — State and local governments	Other and unallocable — State government only
UNITED STATES, TOTAL	107 692	272 997	115 263	355 212	81 014	120 556	189 569	14 203	622 468	186 546
ALABAMA.	1 614	3 712	1 574	4 450	1 983	2 265	1 826	990	8 360	2 078
ALASKA	557	1 200	800	1 561	1 189	298	260	–	4 181	2 723
ARIZONA.	1 378	3 883	1 240	4 778	607	1 356	3 154	–	7 739	1 431
ARKANSAS	1 374	2 314	1 032	2 773	595	1 123	413	–	3 730	1 297
CALIFORNIA	12 101	36 532	16 795	39 709	3 312	15 554	27 642	–	86 589	29 484
COLORADO	1 607	4 141	1 729	4 567	1 649	2 339	2 576	–	6 134	1 452
CONNECTICUT.	1 749	3 310	1 390	4 374	2 435	849	366	–	8 938	4 339
DELAWARE	276	974	574	1 400	890	152	149	–	2 283	940
DISTRICT OF COLUMBIA . . .	[1]304	562	–	2 270	–	562	7 097	–	4 531	–
FLORIDA.	2 866	11 962	3 431	14 845	5 022	5 600	5 631	–	32 244	7 208
GEORGIA.	1 487	5 014	1 383	7 703	2 342	3 788	3 738	–	15 041	4 067
HAWAII	483	1 219	896	2 285	1 380	842	30	–	6 825	3 292
IDAHO.	752	1 636	615	1 552	405	257	75	250	1 862	743
ILLINOIS	4 318	10 172	3 850	19 296	4 069	5 988	14 408	–	28 888	9 392
INDIANA.	1 813	5 400	1 738	8 011	867	1 886	2 612	–	10 365	2 085
IOWA	1 102	3 779	1 362	4 068	815	1 288	1 197	777	4 583	1 834
KANSAS	841	3 470	1 266	4 616	692	1 706	1 652	–	5 624	1 849
KENTUCKY	456	2 149	1 264	5 708	1 266	1 876	1 455	–	8 638	5 773
LOUISIANA.	2 081	5 592	2 425	5 309	1 395	2 784	801	–	8 585	3 404
MAINE.	615	1 583	720	1 578	647	422	80	262	2 481	1 010
MARYLAND	1 614	5 589	3 280	6 794	2 298	1 654	310	–	16 167	6 204
MASSACHUSETTS.	3 278	8 187	3 664	9 290	2 180	3 106	7 753	–	20 190	5 808
MICHIGAN	4 772	9 337	3 511	16 419	2 728	4 599	5 327	599	16 835	5 056
MINNESOTA.	1 788	5 236	1 678	7 241	1 296	1 663	3 618	–	9 156	2 677
MISSISSIPPI.	1 322	2 628	861	2 812	514	1 450	470	138	3 721	1 411
MISSOURI	2 355	4 575	1 909	7 350	1 593	2 406	2 437	–	8 443	1 625
MONTANA.	643	1 942	1 269	1 554	361	293	36	371	2 004	795
NEBRASKA	627	2 195	616	3 066	756	787	5 942	–	4 282	1 495
NEVADA	675	1 589	863	1 998	465	336	37	–	2 773	662
NEW HAMPSHIRE.	405	846	430	969	351	377	103	482	1 700	809
NEW JERSEY	4 043	8 821	3 757	15 380	3 258	2 520	856	–	29 726	6 327
NEW MEXICO	919	2 507	1 232	2 207	1 313	634	402	–	3 462	1 702
NEW YORK	10 979	21 837	11 745	28 979	7 452	7 127	39 693	–	69 239	12 923
NORTH CAROLINA	2 330	5 168	1 605	6 723	3 837	2 885	1 150	–	16 691	4 570
NORTH DAKOTA	504	1 102	414	1 283	236	275	51	–	1 533	918
OHIO	4 279	9 776	4 131	19 413	2 183	6 911	6 209	1 884	26 900	5 138
OKLAHOMA	1 223	3 314	1 257	4 227	1 333	1 979	575	–	7 388	3 438
OREGON	1 762	4 100	1 801	4 640	1 132	1 666	2 135	232	7 459	3 784
PENNSYLVANIA	7 023	14 666	6 935	19 077	3 547	4 288	10 578	4 404	25 914	7 870
RHODE ISLAND	800	1 361	793	1 437	821	495	–	–	3 979	2 101
SOUTH CAROLINA	1 308	3 691	1 713	3 849	1 138	1 491	403	–	6 424	3 008
SOUTH DAKOTA	427	1 383	355	1 444	606	330	160	–	1 663	918
TENNESSEE.	2 046	4 912	2 328	5 007	1 405	3 554	7 381	–	13 608	2 667
TEXAS.	5 003	15 873	4 601	16 646	1 669	10 536	7 924	–	25 532	5 798
UTAH	779	1 871	974	1 924	465	745	660	190	2 304	950
VERMONT.	415	657	471	655	465	178	186	167	1 041	739
VIRGINIA	1 663	6 465	2 376	6 444	2 270	2 567	1 185	1 587	12 535	3 544
WASHINGTON	3 316	5 944	2 205	5 774	938	2 020	7 425	1 014	10 111	3 083
WEST VIRGINIA.	898	2 390	1 265	2 576	1 044	707	173	822	3 336	1 687
WISCONSIN.	2 435	5 417	2 512	8 236	1 574	1 756	1 195	–	9 862	3 977
WYOMING.	277	1 014	628	945	226	286	31	34	869	461

Note: Statistics for local governments are subject to sampling variation; see text for statement of reliability.

– Represents zero.

[1]The category of Employment Security, normally a State function, is applied to the District of Columbia because of its unique governmental status. This amount, however, is included in local government totals as are all other data for the District of Columbia.

Table 8. Full-Time Equivalent Employment of State and Local Governments Per 10,000 Population, by Function and by State: October 1977

State	All functions	Education							
		Total	Local schools			Institutions of higher education			Other education
			Total	Instructional staff	Other	Total	Instructional staff	Other	
UNITED STATES, TOTAL	485.3	236.0	181.6	127.1	54.6	50.4	19.4	31.0	4.1
ALABAMA.	480.2	226.2	159.7	115.3	44.4	56.7	20.9	35.8	9.8
ALASKA	677.8	287.9	220.8	152.3	68.6	56.6	26.9	29.7	10.5
ARIZONA.	551.7	298.6	211.0	142.1	68.9	77.7	26.2	51.5	9.9
ARKANSAS	446.9	235.3	177.9	125.6	52.3	46.1	17.6	28.5	11.3
CALIFORNIA	496.7	224.1	165.0	110.7	54.3	56.9	22.3	34.6	2.3
COLORADO	541.1	291.8	205.3	140.5	64.7	84.5	27.1	57.4	2.1
CONNECTICUT.	425.9	220.3	182.7	140.3	42.3	30.4	12.1	18.3	7.2
DELAWARE	530.3	275.3	193.8	137.4	56.4	77.3	22.4	54.9	4.3
DISTRICT OF COLUMBIA . . .	760.3	206.7	180.2	122.3	58.0	26.5	11.4	15.0	-
FLORIDA.	508.4	223.6	178.4	117.3	61.1	42.6	15.5	27.2	2.5
GEORGIA.	542.6	247.2	192.4	133.1	59.3	50.0	15.5	34.5	4.9
HAWAII	529.6	219.2	156.7	113.8	42.9	60.6	23.5	37.1	1.9
IDAHO.	512.7	260.6	194.2	146.1	48.1	60.2	23.3	36.8	6.2
ILLINOIS	439.3	219.0	169.2	118.5	50.7	47.5	18.9	28.7	2.3
INDIANA.	442.7	238.6	180.5	121.2	59.3	53.0	19.3	33.6	5.1
IOWA	499.1	281.8	215.1	150.6	64.5	61.6	22.8	38.8	5.1
KANSAS	531.5	280.5	198.8	140.5	58.3	78.4	34.6	43.8	3.3
KENTUCKY	422.1	220.5	162.3	116.4	45.9	47.9	15.8	32.1	10.4
LOUISIANA.	508.1	257.0	204.8	134.4	70.5	45.7	17.6	28.1	6.5
MAINE.	455.4	247.6	198.5	143.0	55.5	40.5	13.5	27.0	8.7
MARYLAND	524.1	260.8	189.8	130.3	59.5	66.0	29.5	36.5	5.0
MASSACHUSETTS.	484.1	219.8	190.7	141.7	48.9	26.4	11.1	15.3	2.7
MICHIGAN	468.3	256.4	194.8	129.5	65.3	58.9	21.3	37.6	2.7
MINNESOTA.	488.1	255.1	196.9	140.9	56.0	55.7	24.4	31.3	2.4
MISSISSIPPI.	494.1	246.3	179.6	128.6	51.0	61.1	21.3	39.8	5.5
MISSOURI	444.1	217.8	175.3	122.9	52.4	38.8	20.6	18.1	3.7
MONTANA.	558.8	279.0	223.7	164.2	59.5	49.1	21.6	27.5	6.2
NEBRASKA	568.7	276.2	203.7	150.2	53.4	67.7	24.8	42.8	4.9
NEVADA	576.9	240.2	186.8	130.4	56.4	49.4	17.2	32.1	4.0
NEW HAMPSHIRE.	446.5	218.8	168.9	131.8	37.1	45.8	15.5	30.4	4.0
NEW JERSEY	476.8	225.1	190.5	136.6	53.8	31.4	12.5	19.0	3.2
NEW MEXICO	575.4	319.0	222.5	161.6	60.9	89.1	22.6	66.5	7.4
NEW YORK	512.4	197.0	163.8	116.2	47.6	31.1	14.3	16.8	2.1
NORTH CAROLINA	504.1	270.4	200.3	139.2	61.0	64.8	24.2	40.5	5.3
NORTH DAKOTA	478.1	262.2	191.2	139.0	52.2	64.6	27.7	36.9	6.4
OHIO	424.5	210.4	165.5	118.1	47.4	42.9	15.7	27.1	2.0
OKLAHOMA	498.2	250.4	180.6	128.8	51.7	63.6	22.2	41.4	6.2
OREGON	536.6	273.6	194.1	134.5	59.6	75.1	34.8	40.3	4.3
PENNSYLVANIA	402.1	183.5	159.1	110.3	48.8	22.1	8.7	13.4	2.2
RHODE ISLAND	473.5	223.7	160.0	122.4	37.6	52.3	16.7	35.6	11.3
SOUTH CAROLINA	506.2	251.4	184.3	143.7	40.6	49.0	13.9	35.1	18.1
SOUTH DAKOTA	484.8	254.9	195.0	155.9	39.1	55.2	20.0	35.1	4.7
TENNESSEE.	494.3	217.9	164.9	113.1	51.7	46.1	15.1	31.0	6.9
TEXAS.	491.5	271.4	208.8	148.9	59.9	59.7	20.2	39.5	2.8
UTAH	501.1	295.2	184.4	134.0	50.3	104.9	43.8	61.0	6.0
VERMONT.	491.6	267.9	194.8	150.2	44.5	68.5	30.4	38.1	4.6
VIRGINIA	509.8	273.0	211.6	146.2	65.4	55.9	22.6	33.3	5.5
WASHINGTON	516.5	251.4	178.1	112.7	65.3	70.3	27.7	42.5	3.0
WEST VIRGINIA.	489.1	262.8	204.4	140.1	64.3	50.4	17.5	32.9	8.0
WISCONSIN.	478.3	258.1	180.0	130.7	49.3	75.2	35.0	40.2	3.0
WYOMING.	586.1	278.5	199.2	142.8	56.4	74.8	26.8	48.0	4.5

See footnotes at end of table.

264

State	Functions other than education										
	Total	High-ways	Public welfare	Hospi-tals	Health	Police protec-tion	Fire protec-tion (local)	Sewerage (local)	Sanita-tion other than sewer-age (local)	Parks and recrea-tion (local)	Natural resources
UNITED STATES, TOTAL	249.2	25.8	16.4	45.6	9.1	25.9	10.2	3.9	5.9	7.3	8.3
ALABAMA	254.1	38.8	11.4	67.9	8.3	20.6	9.2	2.3	11.5	4.9	8.6
ALASKA	389.9	45.3	16.4	16.4	13.0	22.9	10.4	3.2	4.1	5.3	38.1
ARIZONA	253.1	28.6	9.9	27.3	7.4	31.4	9.4	3.3	6.6	8.5	12.0
ARKANSAS	211.5	35.9	9.3	46.6	9.7	17.6	6.8	3.1	5.0	2.7	12.5
CALIFORNIA	272.6	15.9	17.0	40.0	12.1	29.5	12.0	3.1	3.3	11.8	8.9
COLORADO	249.2	29.5	15.0	35.4	11.4	26.6	9.1	4.9	3.0	10.6	8.7
CONNECTIUCT	205.6	23.2	10.1	33.1	6.2	25.1	12.9	4.1	4.0	6.2	3.0
DELAWARE	255.0	27.0	19.0	28.6	14.6	26.5	4.0	4.7	4.7	8.1	12.1
DISTRICT OF COLUMBIA	553.6	15.3	38.2	42.8	47.0	71.1	21.6	8.9	29.1	17.9	-
FLORIDA	284.8	23.7	11.3	58.5	10.2	30.8	11.7	5.2	8.3	12.7	10.0
GEORGIA	295.4	28.4	10.2	88.5	17.8	23.7	10.7	4.0	10.6	6.2	9.7
HAWAII	310.4	21.2	10.2	33.8	18.1	27.3	14.8	·6.3	6.4	18.4	17.0
IDAHO	252.1	36.3	15.2	32.5	12.3	23.6	9.0	3.2	1.6	5.1	29.7
ILLINOIS	220.3	19.0	14.1	34.9	5.9	29.4	10.1	5.5	4.0	9.3	4.3
INDIANA	204.1	22.5	12.9	46.7	4.8	21.0	9.5	4.6	3.7	5.7	5.9
IOWA	217.3	32.6	·17.7	49.8	4.4	18.3	5.9	3.4	2.7	4.5	9.6
KANSAS	251.1	41.4	13.1	47.3	6.8	22.8	9.3	3.2	4.5	5.1	10.8
KENTUCKY	201.1	25.4	15.8	31.5	7.0	19.8	8.5	3.6	5.4	3.3	13.7
LOUISIANA	251.1	30.7	14.2	55.0	4.6	23.8	9.6	3.8	11.0	6.4	14.4
MAINE	207.8	45.9	10.5	20.0	5.3	20.3	10.2	3.1	2.1	3.5	13.0
MARYLAND	263.3	23.9	13.8	41.2	15.9	30.2	12.1	6.1	5.8	10.0	7.2
MASSACHUSETTS	264.4	22.4	13.4	50.8	5.3	28.6	22.9	2.7	4.1	5.2	5.0
MICHIGAN	211.9	18.2	16.7	41.4	7.3	25.3	8.4	2.9	4.8	5.8	6.7
MINNESOTA	233.0	31.3	20.0	44.6	6.5	19.5	5.2	4.2	2.0	7.2	9.4
MISSISSIPPI	247.8	37.5	13.4	69.0	9.3	19.9	7.4	3.8	9.0	3.2	16.2
MISSOURI	226.3	26.2	13.9	52.8	8.5	26.0	9.5	3.6	2.5	6.5	8.0
MONTANA	279.8	47.3	18.7	32.3	8.8	25.4	5.7	2.4	3.7	3.6	28.7
NEBRASKA	292.5	36.4	19.4	54.1	8.7	20.4	7.8	2.9	1.8	5.7	16.2.
NEVADA	·336.7	30.9	12.5	54.7	10.9	40.5	18.5	2.8	0.7	15.9	12.3
NEW HAMPSHIRE	227.7	42.2	32.0	28.7	5.7	21.2	13.4	2.8	3.5	2.9	8.4
NEW JERSEY	251.7	26.7	17.5	33.8	7.1	35.5	11.1	3.6	5.7	7.0	3.5
NEW MEXICO	256.4	33.5	13.0	40.5	6.3	27.1	9.0	4.0	5.7	7.9	14.4
NEW YORK	315.5	26.2	27.2	70.5	10.9	32.6	10.8	3.4	8.9	7.9	4.2
NORTH CAROLINA	233.7	27.2	14.9	44.7	11.3	23.0	7.4	4.1	8.8	4.7	10.3
NORTH DAKOTA	215.9	38.6	15.5	28.4	5.9	17.4	4.4	1.3	4.3	2.1	19.5
OHIO	214.1	21.6	16.1	33.7	8.2	21.8	9.6	5.4	4.7	5.8	5.1
OKLAHOMA	247.8	32.2	19.4	53.0	6.3	21.6	11.7	2.9	7.4	5.9	8.5
OREGON	263.0	29.1	20.1	32.4	9.2	23.5	13.1	5.0	1.1	5.9	16.5
PENNSYLVANIA	218.7	26.0	25.9	27.8	4.8	25.0	6.1	4.0	6.0	4.8	5.9
RHODE ISLAND	249.9	21.2	17.5	39.8	9.4	26.8	20.3	3.7	3.9	4.5	5.4
SOUTH CAROLINA	254.8	24.9	16.6	66.7	17.8	21.4	7.5	3.5	11.6	3.7	8.7
SOUTH DAKOTA	230.0	42.7	14.0	29.3	6.4	21.2	4.9	2.2	2.6	4.0	17.1
TENNESSEE	276.3	31.0	15.1	56.5	10.9	22.3	12.2	3.9	9.5	7.4	10.5
TEXAS	220.1	23.5	11.3	44.8	8.8	23.3	9.9	4.1	7.0	6.5	7.1
UTAH	205.9	26.0	15.7	28.7	7.2	21.6	8.0	2.4	3.3	5.9	9.6
VERMONT	223.8	44.5	13.2	23.8	8.2	19.7	6.8	2.3	1.1	4.0	20.8
VIRGINIA	236.8	31.1	12.2	39.0	11.9	21.5	9.3	5.4	7.4	8.7	7.8
WASHINGTON	265.1	29.4	15.0	32.3	7.2	21.7	11.9	4.1	2.5	7.9	17.6
WEST VIRGINIA	226.3	43.5	19.5	46.2	8.0	15.8	5.1	3.0	5.3	2.1	13.5
WISCONSIN	220.2	27.2	15.0	40.0	8.8	23.4	8.8	4.7	5.1	8.3	5.3
WYOMING	307.6	49.6	11.7	70.9	8.0	29.1	6.3	2.6	6.6	5.0	22.0

See footnotes at end of table.

265

Table 8. Full-Time Equivalent Employment of State and Local Governments Per 10,000 Population, by Function and by State: October 1977—Continued

| State | Functions other than education--Continued | | | | | | | | | Exhibit: Estimated State population July 1, 1976 (thousands) |
	Correction	Libraries (local)	Employment security administration (State)	Financial administration	General control	Local utilities — Water supply	Local utilities — Other	State liquor stores	Other and unallocable	
UNITED STATES, TOTAL	10.1	3.0	5.0	12.6	16.4	5.6	8.8	0.7	28.8	216 337
ALABAMA	6.2	1.4	4.4	10.1	12.1	6.1	4.9	2.7	22.7	3 690
ALASKA	14.5	2.3	13.7	29.5	38.4	7.3	6.4	-	102.7	407
ARIZONA	8.2	3.5	6.0	16.9	20.8	5.9	13.7	-	33.7	2 296
ARKANSAS	6.0	1.5	6.4	10.8	12.9	5.2	1.9	-	17.4	2 144
CALIFORNIA	14.4	4.8	5.5	16.7	18.1	7.1	12.6	-	39.5	21 896
COLORADO	9.2	4.2	6.1	15.8	17.4	8.9	9.8	-	23.4	2 619
CONNECTICUT	11.3	3.5	5.6	10.6	14.1	2.7	1.2	-	28.8	3 108
DELAWARE	14.6	1.1	4.7	16.7	24.1	2.6	2.6	-	39.2	582
DISTRICT OF COLUMBIA	32.7	6.9	¹4.4	8.1	32.9	8.1	102.9	-	65.7	690
FLORIDA	13.3	2.7	3.4	14.2	17.6	6.6	6.7	-	38.1	8 452
GEORGIA	11.0	1.7	2.9	9.9	15.3	7.5	7.4	-	29.8	5 048
HAWAII	6.4	-	5.4	13.6	25.5	9.4	0.3	-	76.3	895
IDAHO	6.5	2.5	8.8	19.1	18.1	3.0	0.9	2.9	21.7	857
ILLINOIS	6.8	3.3	3.8	9.0	17.2	5.3	12.8	-	25.7	11 245
INDIANA	6.2	4.2	3.4	10.1	15.0	3.5	4.9	-	19.4	5 330
IOWA	7.3	2.8	3.8	13.1	14.1	4.5	4.2	2.7	15.9	2 879
KANSAS	8.4	1.3	3.6	14.9	19.9	7.3	7.1	-	24.2	2 326
KENTUCKY	7.4	1.7	1.3	6.2	16.5	5.4	4.2	-	25.0	3 458
LOUISIANA	10.8	2.7	5.3	14.3	13.5	7.1	2.0	-	21.9	3 921
MAINE	7.4	1.8	5.7	14.6	14.5	3.9	0.7	2.4	22.9	1 085
MARYLAND	14.5	4.9	3.9	13.5	16.4	4.0	0.7	-	39.1	4 139
MASSACHUSETTS	8.2	6.2	5.7	14.2	16.0	5.4	13.4	-	34.9	5 789
MICHIGAN	8.9	2.1	5.2	10.2	18.0	5.0	5.8	0.7	18.4	9 129
MINNESOTA	7.4	3.5	4.5	13.2	18.2	4.2	9.1	-	23.0	3 975
MISSISSIPPI	5.3	1.2	5.5	11.0	11.8	6.1	2.0	0.6	15.6	2 389
MISSOURI	8.0	3.2	4.9	9.5	15.3	5.0	5.1	-	17.6	4 801
MONTANA	10.0	3.3	8.4	25.5	20.4	3.9	0.5	4.9	26.3	761
NEBRASKA	7.9	2.9	4.0	14.1	19.6	5.0	38.1	-	27.4	1 561
NEVADA	16.4	3.6	10.7	25.1	31.6	5.3	0.6	-	43.8	633
NEW HAMPSHIRE	6.2	3.2	4.8	10.0	11.4	4.4	1.2	5.7	20.0	849
NEW JERSEY	12.1	4.5	5.5	12.0	21.0	3.4	1.2	-	40.6	7 329
NEW MEXICO	7.2	2.7	7.7	21.1	18.5	5.3	3.4	-	29.1	1 190
NEW YORK	12.5	1.3	6.1	12.2	16.2	4.0	22.1	-	38.6	17 924
NORTH CAROLINA	12.1	2.0	4.2	9.4	12.2	5.2	2.1	-	30.2	5 525
NORTH DAKOTA	4.8	1.0	7.7	16.9	19.6	4.2	0.8	-	23.5	653
OHIO	8.7	3.0	4.0	9.1	18.1	6.5	5.8	1.8	25.1	10 701
OKLAHOMA	10.4	1.9	4.4	11.8	15.0	7.0	2.0	-	26.3	2 811
OREGON	12.0	2.6	7.4	17.3	19.5	7.0	9.0	1.0	31.4	2 376
PENNSYLVANIA	7.9	1.5	6.0	12.4	16.2	3.6	9.0	3.7	22.0	11 785
RHODE ISLAND	8.5	2.5	8.6	14.6	15.4	5.3	-	-	42.6	935
SOUTH CAROLINA	10.7	2.0	4.5	12.8	13.4	5.2	1.4	-	22.3	2 876
SOUTH DAKOTA	4.4	2.6	6.2	20.1	21.0	4.8	2.3	-	24.1	689
TENNESSEE	9.9	2.3	4.8	11.4	11.6	8.3	17.2	-	31.7	4 299
TEXAS	7.1	3.2	3.9	12.4	13.0	8.2	6.2	-	19.9	12 830
UTAH	7.0	3.6	6.1	14.8	15.2	5.9	5.2	1.5	18.2	1 268
VERMONT	10.1	1.0	8.6	13.6	13.6	3.7	3.9	3.5	21.6	483
VIRGINIA	16.1	3.3	3.2	12.6	12.5	5.0	2.3	3.1	24.4	5 135
WASHINGTON	13.3	5.1	9.1	16.2	15.8	5.5	20.3	2.8	27.6	3 658
WEST VIRGINIA	4.7	1.1	4.8	12.9	13.9	3.8	0.9	4.4	17.9	1 859
WISCONSIN	7.8	3.8	5.2	11.6	17.7	3.8	2.6	-	21.2	4 651
WYOMING	7.2	3.5	6.8	25.0	23.3	7.0	0.8	0.8	21.4	406

Note: Statistics for local governments are subject ot sampling variation; see text for statement of reliability. Because of rounding, detail may not add to totals.

- Represents zero.

¹The category of Employment Security, normally a State function, is applied to the District of Columbia because of its unique governmental status. However, this amount is included in local government totals as are all other data for the District of Columbia.

B — COUNTY GOVERNMENT EMPLOYMENT

County governments in 1977 continued a pattern of growth in employment and payrolls that has generally paralleled the continuous rise in the employment and payrolls of State and local governments since the mid-1940's. In the past year, from October 1976 to October 1977, the total number of county employees has risen at a higher rate (up 6.0 percent) than State governments (up 3.7 percent) and other types of local governments (cities up 1.8 percent, townships up 3.5 percent, school districts up 2.7 percent and special districts up 0.3 percent).

County governments made salary and wage payments for October 1977 amounting to $1.441 billion, representing payrolls for 1,696,000 employees. The 1,458,000 full-time county government employees accounted for 86 percent of all employees, and 95 percent of the total October payrolls ($1.369 billion).

Trends in County Employment

The county employment and payroll figures for October 1977 showed increases over the previous October as follows: Total employees up 6.0 percent (96,000), full-time equivalent employment up 6.5 percent (95,000), total October payroll up 11.2 percent ($145 million) and average October earnings of full-time employees up 4.3 percent ($39). Table F demonstrates that this rise marks a continuance of the upward trends in county employment and payrolls that have been underway since 1946.

During the 5-year period from 1972 to 1977, full-time equivalent employment in counties rose at an average annual rate of 4.4 percent and the payrolls increased at an average annual rate of 10.9 percent. Average October earnings of full-time county employees rose at an annual rate of 6.3 percent during this 5-year interval. Recent rates of increase in full-time equivalent employment, October payrolls and average monthly earnings in county government are shown in Table G.

For October 1977 the full-time equivalent employment per 10,000 population was 81.3 compared with 69.1 in 1972. If the education function is excluded, the full-time equivalent employment per 10,000 population was 64.4 in October 1977 and 54.6 in 1972.

Functions of County Governments

Individual county governments differ widely in the range of their responsibilities and services. One factor in this diversity is that counties were established to provide general local government to specific geographic locations that may have only vague resemblances to population concentrations. In addition, State law or local options establish widely differing parameters for the functioning of county governments.

The governmental functions most commonly conducted by counties include highways, public welfare, health, police protection, correction, financial administration and general control. However, other services provided by some counties, such as schools or hospitals, comprise a considerable portion of all county employment and payrolls.

In most parts of the United States, public schools are provided by school districts which operate as independent local governments. However, there are five States where public schools for elementary and secondary education are provided primarily by county governments (Alaska, Maryland, North Carolina, Tennessee, and Virginia), and in these States the education function represents about three-fifths to four-fifths of total county employment and payrolls.

In October 1977 the education and hospital functions accounted for more than one-third of all em-

267

Full-time equivalent employment	Year-to-year increase (percent)	October payrolls	Year-to-year increase (percent)	Average October earnings, full-time employees	Year-to-year increase (percent)
1976 to 1977.........	6.5	1976 to 1977.........	11.2	1976 to 1977.........	4.3
1975 to 1976.........	2.9	1975 to 1976.........	9.4	1975 to 1976.........	6.5
1974 to 1975.........	4.8	1974 to 1975.........	11.9	1974 to 1975.........	6.6
1973 to 1974.........	1.9	1973 to 1974.........	11.0	1973 to 1974.........	8.8
1972 to 1973.........	6.1	1972 to 1973.........	11.0	1972 to 1973.........	5.4
Average, 1972 to 1977	4.4	Average, 1972 to 1977	10.9	Average, 1972 to 1977	6.3

(F)

(G)

Function	Full-time equivalent employment (percent)	Total October payroll (percent)
Total................	100.0	100.0
Education.................	20.8	22.3
Hospitals.................	14.7	13.2
General control...........	10.2	10.6
public welfare............	9.6	8.8
Highways..................	8.3	7.4
Police protection.........	7.1	8.5
Financial administration...	5.2	4.9
Health....................	4.5	4.8
Correction................	4.2	4.8
Parks and recreation.......	2.1	2.0
Libraries.................	1.1	1.0
Fire protection...........	1.0	1.4
Natural resources.........	0.9	0.9
All other functions.......	10.2	9.5

ployment and payrolls of county governments. Table G shows percentage distributions of county government employment and payrolls, by function.

Data for Major Counties

There are 342 county governments which had an estimated population of 100,000 or more in 1975. Although the counties with 100,000 or more population comprise only about 10 percent of the total number of all county governments, they had approximately 61 percent of all county employment and 69 percent of all county payrolls in October 1977. It is also interesting to note that the full-time equivalent employment per 10,000 population is less in these large counties (79.7) than in all counties (81.3).

Excluded from Table 4 and the rest of this report are a number of consolidated city-county governments. These governments are classified for Census Bureau purposes as municipalities.

Table 1. Summary of Employment and Payrolls of County Governments by Function: October 1977 and Prior Years

Item	Amount						Year-to-year change (percent) 1976 to 1977	Average annual change (percent) 1972 to 1977
	1977	1976	1975	1974	1973	1972		
EMPLOYEES								
TOTAL	1 695 633	1 599 633	1 562 704	1 489 803	1 450 723	1 368 862	6.0	4.4
FULL-TIME	1 457 734	1 370 763	1 331 781	1 270 404	1 242 729	1 176 569	6.3	4.4
PART-TIME	237 899	228 870	230 923	219 399	207 994	192 293	4.0	4.3
FULL-TIME EQUIVALENT EMPLOYMENT .	1 542 919	1 448 314	1 408 135	1 343 219	1 318 332	1 242 166	6.5	4.4
BY FUNCTION:								
EDUCATION[1]	321 131	293 718	279 363	281 858	285 158	261 774	9.3	4.2
INSTRUCTIONAL STAFF	216 275	206 230	188 242	188 172	183 827	171 604	4.9	4.7
OTHER	104 856	87 488	91 121	93 686	101 331	90 170	19.9	3.1
HIGHWAYS.	127 972	127 464	129 476	125 462	125 613	123 601	0.4	0.7
PUBLIC WELFARE.	147 794	141 745	138 633	128 180	130 119	131 616	4.3	2.3
HOSPITALS	226 895	220 095	219 401	220 911	214 641	205 236	3.1	1.1
HEALTH.	69 946	62 051	61 527	55 682	51 325	47 037	12.7	8.3
POLICE PROTECTION	109 450	104 100	101 151	95 149	88 512	84 035	5.1	5.4
FIRE PROTECTION	15 150	14 178	13 077	11 442	10 667	9 810	6.9	9.1
PARKS AND RECREATION.	32 131	27 895	26 382	23 412	21 944	20 090	15.2	9.8
NATURAL RESOURCES	13 522	13 249	12 857	12 320	11 926	11 189	2.1	3.9
AIRPORTS.	3 694	3 404	3 598	3 491	3 460	3 015	8.5	4.1
CORRECTIONS	65 484	62 798	60 196	54 183	50 903	45 762	4.3	7.4
LIBRARIES	17 501	16 226	15 666	15 345	14 882	12 993	7.9	6.1
FINANCIAL ADMINISTRATION. . . .	80 773	72 720	69 806	67 372	66 403	62 286	11.1	5.3
GENERAL CONTROL	158 088	152 399	147 239	141 029	140 292	128 356	3.7	4.3
LOCAL UTILITIES	8 497	7 441	7 116	6 432	6 674	5 233	14.2	10.2
WATER SUPPLY.	6 005	5 258	5 173	4 691	5 300	3 916	14.2	8.9
ELECTRIC POWER.	117	220	162	186	149	173	-46.8	-7.5
TRANSIT	2 342	1 932	1 759	1 522	1 170	1 115	21.2	16.0
GAS SUPPLY.	33	31	22	33	55	29	6.5	2.6
ALL OTHER FUNCTIONS	144 891	128 831	122 647	100 951	95 813	90 128	12.5	10.0
FULL-TIME EQUIVALENT EMPLOYMENT PER 10,000 POPULATION.	81.3	76.3	74.2	72.0	73.4	69.1	6.6	3.3
OCTOBER PAYROLLS (THOUSANDS OF DOLLARS)								
TOTAL	1 440 688	1 295 190	1 183 427	1 057 218	951 692	857 398	11.2	10.9
FULL-TIME	1 368 774	1 232 595	1 125 909	1 006 386	905 808	818 386	11.0	10.8
PART-TIME	71 914	62 594	57 518	50 831	45 883	39 012	14.9	13.0
BY FUNCTION:								
EDUCATION[1]	320 705	284 776	251 746	241 281	232 787	205 206	12.6	9.3
INSTRUCTIONAL STAFF	251 049	227 305	195 266	185 589	181 463	161 021	10.5	9.3
OTHER	69 656	57 471	56 479	55 689	51 323	44 185	21.2	9.5
HIGHWAYS.	106 297	101 499	97 961	88 290	82 007	75 338	4.7	7.1
PUBLIC WELFARE.	127 118	114 065	106 169	91 528	84 617	82 586	11.4	8.9
HOSPITALS	189 879	174 617	161 958	152 911	135 475	123 668	8.7	9.0
HEALTH.	68 949	58 504	54 986	45 775	38 956	34 710	17.9	14.7
POLICE PROTECTION	122 228	110 095	100 408	88 660	70 412	65 553	11.0	13.3
FIRE PROTECTION	20 814	18 888	16 351	13 054	10 748	9 988	10.2	15.8
PARKS AND RECREATION.	28 368	24 212	22 095	17 978	14 902	13 997	17.2	15.2
NATURAL RESOURCES	13 180	12 364	11 027	9 819	8 091	7 777	6.6	11.1
AIRPORTS.	3 997	3 301	3 374	2 940	2 618	2 238	21.1	12.3
CORRECTION.	68 677	63 823	55 692	47 806	38 527	36 042	7.6	13.8
LIBRARIES	14 072	12 523	11 448	10 198	8 807	7 650	12.4	13.0
FINANCIAL ADMINISTRATION. . . .	71 277	61 459	55 646	49 858	44 531	40 024	16.0	12.2
GENERAL CONTROL	152 165	140 709	129 219	113 400	104 679	89 423	8.1	11.2
LOCAL UTILITIES	8 992	7 616	6 853	5 947	5 955	4 036	18.1	17.4
WATER SUPPLY.	5 703	4 917	4 498	4 042	4 542	2 840	16.0	15.0
ELECTRIC POWER.	128	210	165	111	119	104	-39.0	4.2
TRANSIT	3 132	2 462	2 176	1 769	1 259	1 073	27.2	23.9
GAS SUPPLY.	29	27	14	24	34	19	7.4	8.8
ALL OTHER FUNCTIONS	123 971	106 738	98 496	77 763	68 571	59 159	16.1	16.0
AVERAGE OCTOBER EARNINGS OF FULL-TIME EMPLOYEES (DOLLARS).	938	899	844	792	728	691	4.3	6.3
INSTRUCTIONAL STAFF	1 154	1 096	1 026	982	984	935	5.3	4.3
OTHER	902	865	815	760	686	656	4.3	6.6
EXHIBIT:								
POPULATION OF AREAS WITH COUNTY GOVERNMENTS (THOUSANDS)[2][3].	189 701	189 759	189 759	186 462	186 462	179 672	(X)	(X)
NUMBER OF COUNTY GOVERNMENTS[3]	3 040	3 042	3 042	3 044	3 044	3 044	(X)	(X)

Note: Statistics for 1972 are based on a complete census of all county governments. Data for other years are subject to sampling variation; see text for statement of reliability. Because of rounding, detail may not add to totals.

X Not applicable.
[1]Includes data for school systems and institutions of higher education operated by county governments.
[2]For 1972 data are based on 1970 populations; for 1973 and 1974 data are based on 1973 estimated populations, and for 1975, 1976 and 1977 data are based on 1975 estimated populations.
[3]Effective May 1977 the consolidated governments of Butte-Silver Bow County and Anaconda-Deer Lodge County, Montana were formed. These consolidated governments are treated for Census purposes as municipalities.

Table 2. Summary of Employment and Payrolls of County Governments by Function and by Population Size-Group: October 1977

Item	Total	300,000 or more	200,000 to 299,999	150,000 to 199,999	100,000 to 149,999	Less than 100,000
EMPLOYEES						
TOTAL.	1 695 633	706 038	151 848	67 648	106 623	663 476
FULL-TIME.	1 457 734	626 681	130 135	57 757	92 671	550 490
PART-TIME.	237 899	79 357	21 713	9 891	13 952	112 986
FULL-TIME EQUIVALENT EMPLOYMENT.	1 542 919	652 632	138 030	61 462	97 678	593 117
BY FUNCTION:						
EDUCATION.	321 131	81 071	26 658	13 309	19 824	180 269
INSTRUCTIONAL STAFF.	216 275	51 124	18 633	8 616	13 554	124 348
OTHER.	104 856	29 947	8 025	4 693	6 270	55 921
HIGHWAYS	127 972	29 107	8 350	4 793	8 698	77 024
PUBLIC WELFARE	147 794	71 543	19 507	8 234	10 927	37 583
HOSPITALS.	226 895	110 505	15 310	3 963	9 382	87 735
HEALTH	69 946	35 546	8 681	3 419	5 085	17 215
POLICE PROTECTION.	109 450	49 648	8 581	4 785	7 141	39 295
FIRE PROTECTION.	15 150	11 051	1 392	719	1 149	839
PARKS AND RECREATION	32 131	22 258	2 442	1 240	1 486	4 705
NATURAL RESOURCES.	13 522	6 081	1 197	411	687	5 146
AIRPORTS	3 694	2 570	256	78	264	526
CORRECTION	65 484	41 987	6 986	3 118	3 864	9 529
LIBRARIES.	17 501	8 728	1 874	958	1 665	4 276
FINANCIAL ADMINISTRATION	80 773	30 340	7 770	3 524	5 086	34 053
GENERAL CONTROL.	158 088	73 731	13 970	6 670	9 689	54 028
LOCAL UTILITIES.	8 497	6 047	209	288	630	1 323
WATER SUPPLY	6 005	4 038	129	244	470	1 124
ELECTRIC POWER	117	-	-	-	-	117
TRANSIT.	2 342	2 009	80	44	160	49
GAS SUPPLY	33	-	-	-	-	33
ALL OTHER FUNCTIONS[1]	144 891	72 419	14 847	5 953	12 101	39 571
FULL-TIME EQUIVALENT EMPLOYMENT PER 10,000 POPULATION	81.3	77.0	77.6	70.1	73.6	91.0
OCTOBER PAYROLLS (THOUSANDS OF DOLLARS)						
TOTAL.	1 440 688	732 857	126 803	55 894	83 719	441 415
FULL-TIME.	1 368 774	701 698	119 713	52 786	79 539	415 038
PART-TIME.	71 914	31 157	7 090	3 108	4 180	26 379
BY FUNCTION:						
EDUCATION.	320 705	108 888	27 246	14 054	19 166	151 351
INSTRUCTIONAL STAFF.	251 049	80 807	21 635	10 709	14 819	123 079
OTHER.	69 656	28 081	5 611	3 345	4 347	28 272
HIGHWAYS	106 297	31 480	7 999	4 264	7 419	55 135
PUBLIC WELFARE	127 118	70 101	15 396	6 190	8 110	27 321
HOSPITALS.	189 879	110 035	12 658	2 847	8 107	56 232
HEALTH	68 949	39 332	8 468	3 238	4 533	13 378
POLICE PROTECTION.	122 228	69 876	9 376	5 159	6 934	30 883
FIRE PROTECTION.	20 814	15 968	1 218	766	1 042	1 820
PARKS AND RECREATION	28 368	21 119	1 995	1 005	1 145	3 104
NATURAL RESOURCES.	13 180	7 923	1 091	313	530	3 323
AIRPORTS	3 997	3 074	224	73	204	422
CORRECTION	68 677	48 958	6 866	2 718	3 354	6 781
LIBRARIES.	14 072	7 970	1 481	744	1 208	2 669
FINANCIAL ADMINISTRATION	71 277	32 054	7 006	3 090	4 258	24 869
GENERAL CONTROL.	152 165	85 675	13 508	6 222	8 456	38 304
LOCAL UTILITIES.	8 992	6 860	208	252	522	1 150
WATER SUPPLY	5 703	3 986	129	217	418	953
ELECTRIC POWER	128	-	-	-	-	128
TRANSIT.	3 132	2 874	79	34	104	40
GAS SUPPLY	29	-	-	-	-	29
ALL OTHER FUNCTIONS[1]	123 971	73 543	12 063	4 959	8 731	24 675
AVERAGE OCTOBER EARNINGS OF FULL-TIME EMPLOYEES (DOLLARS)	938	1 121	919	909	858	753
INSTRUCTIONAL STAFF.	1 154	1 572	1 139	1 234	1 090	991
ALL OTHER.	902	1 083	884	855	820	679

Note: Statistics in the "Total" and "Less than 100,000" columns are subject to sampling variation; see text for statement of reliability. Because of rounding, detail may not add to totals.

- Represents zero or rounds to zero.
[1] Includes sewerage, sanitation other than sewerage, housing and urban renewal and water transport and terminals.

Table 3. Summary of Employment and Payrolls of All County Governments and County Governments With a Population of 100,000 or More: October 1977

EMPLOYEES

Item	All county governments	County governments with 100,000 or more population	
		Amount	Percent of all county governments total
TOTAL	1 695 633	1 032 157	60.9
FULL-TIME	1 457 734	907 244	62.2
PART-TIME	237 899	124 913	52.5
FULL-TIME EQUIVALENT EMPLOYMENT	1 542 919	949 802	61.6
BY FUNCTION:			
EDUCATION (COUNTY-OPERATED SCHOOLS AND COLLEGES)	321 131	140 862	43.9
INSTRUCTIONAL STAFF	216 275	91 927	42.5
OTHER	104 856	48 935	46.7
HIGHWAYS	127 972	50 948	39.8
PUBLIC WELFARE	147 794	110 211	74.6
HOSPITALS	226 895	139 160	61.3
HEALTH	69 946	52 731	75.4
POLICE PROTECTION	109 450	70 155	64.1
FIRE PROTECTION	15 150	14 311	94.5
PARKS AND RECREATION	32 131	27 426	85.4
NATURAL RESOURCES	13 522	8 376	61.9
AIRPORTS	3 694	3 168	85.8
CORRECTION	65 484	55 955	85.4
LIBRARIES	17 501	13 225	75.6
FINANCIAL ADMINISTRATION	80 773	46 720	57.8
GENERAL CONTROL	158 088	104 060	65.8
LOCAL UTILITIES	8 497	7 174	84.4
WATER SUPPLY	6 005	4 841	80.6
ELECTRIC POWER	117	-	-
TRANSIT	2 342	2 293	97.9
GAS SUPPLY	33	-	-
ALL OTHER FUNCTIONS[1]	144 891	105 320	72.7
FULL-TIME EQUIVALENT EMPLOYMENT PER 10,000 POPULATION	81.3	79.7	(X)

OCTOBER PAYROLLS (THOUSANDS OF DOLLARS)

Item	All county governments	County governments with 100,000 or more population	
		Amount	Percent of all county governments total
TOTAL	1 440 688	999 273	69.4
FULL-TIME	1 368 774	953 736	69.7
PART-TIME	71 914	45 535	63.3
BY FUNCTION:			
EDUCATION (COUNTY-OPERATED SCHOOLS AND COLLEGES)	320 705	169 354	52.8
INSTRUCTIONAL STAFF	251 049	127 970	51.0
OTHER	69 656	41 384	59.4
HIGHWAYS	106 297	51 162	48.1
PUBLIC WELFARE	127 118	99 797	78.5
HOSPITALS	189 879	133 647	70.4
HEALTH	68 949	55 571	80.6
POLICE PROTECTION	122 228	91 345	74.7
FIRE PROTECTION	20 814	18 994	91.3
PARKS AND RECREATION	28 368	25 264	89.1
NATURAL RESOURCES	13 180	9 857	74.8
AIRPORTS	3 997	3 575	89.4
CORRECTION	68 677	61 896	90.1
LIBRARIES	14 072	11 403	81.0
FINANCIAL ADMINISTRATION	71 277	46 408	65.1
GENERAL CONTROL	152 165	113 861	74.8
LOCAL UTILITIES	8 992	7 842	87.2
WATER SUPPLY	5 703	4 750	83.3
ELECTRIC POWER	128	-	-
TRANSIT	3 132	3 092	98.7
GAS SUPPLY	29	-	-
ALL OTHER FUNCTIONS[1]	123 971	99 296	80.1
AVERAGE OCTOBER EARNINGS OF:			
FULL-TIME EMPLOYEES (DOLLARS)	938	1 051	(X)
INSTRUCTIONAL STAFF	1 154	1 392	(X)
ALL OTHER	902	1 015	(X)

Note: Statistics in columns for "All county governments" are subject to sampling variation; see text for statement of reliability. Because of rounding, detail may not add to totals.

- Represents zero or rounds to zero.
X Not applicable.
[1] Includes sewerage, sanitation other than sewerage, housing and urban renewal, and water transport and terminals.

Table 4. Employees and Payrolls for Individual Counties Having 100,000 Population or More: October 1977

State and county	Population, 1975 (estimates)	All employees (full-time and part-time)	Full-time equivalent: Total	Education	Highways	Welfare	Hospitals	Health	Police	Correction	Financial administration and general control	Other	October payroll (thousands of dollars)	Average October earnings: Teachers	Other
ALABAMA															
CALHOUN	106 491	229	219	-	88	-	-	17	21	11	73	9	155	-	703
JEFFERSON	644 688	4 378	4 206	-	700	431	654	629	322	225	460	785	3 859	-	914
MADISON	183 285	652	622	-	139	-	-	35	55	18	118	257	443	-	711
MOBILE	335 268	1 197	1 154	-	234	-	-	229	139	71	413	68	998	-	866
MONTGOMERY[1]	181 207	570	555	-	156	2	-	62	-	61	184	90	402	-	726
TUSCALOOSA	122 169	588	538	-	203	1	-	41	81	20	116	76	413	-	760
ARIZONA															
MARICOPA	1 221 414	7 633	7 478	37	363	-	2 079	762	466	675	1 084	2 012	8 019	1 150	1 098
PIMA	443 958	4 081	3 901	5	366	160	779	236	377	301	978	699	3 945	666	1 002
ARKANSAS															
PULASKI	308 294	726	694	-	148	32	-	12	113	56	209	124	501	-	730
CALIFORNIA															
ALAMEDA	1 090 353	11 475	9 435	-	231	1 877	2 115	556	627	1 049	1 014	1 966	11 831	-	1 255
BUTTE	120 053	1 443	1 059	-	114	218	-	113	93	102	207	212	1 105	-	1 048
CONTRA COSTA	584 047	7 055	6 472	-	328	1 294	1 113	329	328	590	1 250	1 240	8 736	-	1 351
FRESNO	445 727	5 641	5 352	-	272	577	1 555	679	392	477	650	743	6 037	-	1 129
HUMBOLDT	105 912	1 578	1 439	-	154	182	55	167	172	71	280	358	1 593	-	1 110
KERN	349 874	5 640	5 532	-	232	749	1 032	306	408	434	816	555	6 496	-	1 174
LOS ANGELES[2]	6 986 898	82 563	78 384	31	1 561	12 157	19 500	5 228	5 712	5 946	12 870	15 979	107 705	2 111	1 375
MARIN	220 424	2 631	1 874	-	62	256	388	303	122	210	359	511	2 333	-	1 252
MERCED	118 290	1 908	1 712	-	118	279	459	140	201	73	303	289	1 757	-	1 023
MONTEREY	267 828	2 579	2 448	-	191	296	-	203	-	254	391	486	2 904	-	1 186
ORANGE	1 699 666	10 464	9 851	-	102	1 327	788	1 147	989	582	2 553	2 479	12 876	-	1 313
RIVERSIDE	529 074	6 151	5 805	-	331	867	161	640	829	752	764	1 004	6 873	-	1 185
SACRAMENTO	687 888	7 464	7 102	-	259	1 283	818	395	717	891	587	1 948	9 173	-	1 293
SAN BERNARDINO	696 871	9 451	9 154	-	424	953	977	701	670	1 279	1 523	2 174	10 153	-	1 102
SAN DIEGO	1 584 583	13 460	12 513	-	678	2 748	1 063	748	1 375	327	2 748	1 960	15 436	-	1 239
SAN JOAQUIN	299 576	5 396	4 907	-	249	752	320	529	319	102	842	826	5 007	-	1 023
SAN LUIS OBISPO	129 154	1 846	1 798	-	174	190	521	138	139	531	528	207	2 001	-	1 121
SAN MATEO	580 962	4 633	4 306	-	146	678	290	469	288	335	695	978	5 853	-	1 363
SANTA BARBARA	279 693	3 170	2 977	-	240	409	2 224	346	173	872	601	583	3 583	-	1 200
SANTA CLARA	1 174 171	12 095	11 399	-	299	1 966	-	1 479	890	124	1 971	1 698	14 241	-	1 254
SANTA CRUZ	156 108	1 539	1 514	-	115	309	-	258	130	148	400	178	1 689	-	1 113
SOLANO	187 179	1 649	1 560	-	85	257	560	212	163	226	483	212	1 873	-	1 201
SONOMA	246 557	4 204	3 388	-	217	345	416	269	203	209	693	875	3 867	-	1 144
STANISLAUS	223 664	2 782	2 594	-	74	390	201	254	273	178	429	549	2 620	-	1 014
TULARE	210 986	2 278	2 207	-	236	370	459	95	219	400	476	432	2 284	-	1 036
VENTURA	437 853	5 467	4 916	-	104	807	135	631	425	400	791	1 299	5 938	-	1 199
YOLO	101 201	1 443	1 263	-	103	150	-	113	126	100	260	276	1 413	-	1 125

See footnotes at end of table.

Table 4. Employees and Payrolls for Individual Counties Having 100,000 Population or More: October 1977—Continued

State and county	Population, 1975 (estimates)	All employees (full-time and part-time)	Full-time equivalent — Total	Education	Highways	Welfare	Hospitals	Health	Police	Correction	Financial administration and general control	Other	October payroll (thousands of dollars)	Avg. Oct. earnings — Teachers	Avg. Oct. earnings — Other
COLORADO															
ADAMS	215 460	1 247	1 181	-	122	227	-	230	111	28	284	179	1 110	-	940
ARAPAHOE	216 744	660	653	-	57	81	-	-	110	37	159	209	628	-	966
BOULDER	165 071	930	871	-	114	169	-	86	91	64	188	159	873	-	1 004
EL PASO	280 929	1 268	1 217	-	177	248	-	150	68	81	350	143	974	-	801
JEFFERSON	313 964	1 540	1 418	-	238	207	-	118	174	34	300	347	1 431	-	1 014
LARIMER [3]	117 738	582	563	-	105	140	-	62	57	11	143	45	430	-	761
PUEBLO	125 665	751	725	-	88	208	-	65	56	32	168	108	611	-	853
WELD	107 365	2 016	1 734	-	209	104	736	171	48	14	207	245	1 423	-	820
DELAWARE															
NEW CASTLE	399 354	1 955	1 733	-	-	-	-	-	332	-	383	1 018	1 677	-	964
FLORIDA															
ALACHUA [1]	121 945	1 167	986	-	109	89	-	53	176	59	222	278	718	-	734
BREVARD	231 918	2 152	1 925	-	218	24	-	16	202	33	457	975	1 376	-	721
BROWARD	848 190	4 630	4 570	-	262	60	-	168	430	180	726	2 740	4 354	-	951
DADE	1 439 481	25 023	22 631	-	812	575	5 346	964	3 010	529	2 357	9 038	25 746	-	1 144
ESCAMBIA	223 120	940	912	-	177	121	-	8	236	21	198	151	851	-	933
HILLSBOROUGH	577 497	6 742	6 382	-	324	748	2 091	59	500	314	872	1 474	5 820	-	912
LEE	154 161	1 589	1 516	-	147	237	-	14	228	2	184	704	1 276	-	843
LEON	124 714	598	582	-	92	5	-	24	151	29	84	197	455	-	782
MANATEE	121 471	506	493	-	202	5	-	26	112	39	142	84	381	-	772
ORANGE	409 970	3 721	3 682	-	366	585	-	133	442	227	518	967	3 103	-	842
PALM BEACH	455 451	3 629	3 541	-	342	337	167	22	435	192	877	411	3 358	-	948
PASCO	126 640	1 145	1 100	-	102	108	247	47	199	6	212	169	896	-	815
PINELLAS	643 540	3 058	3 030	-	231	101	-	22	379	135	898	329	2 958	-	975
POLK [1]	273 996	3 024	2 884	-	324	10	400	13	316	28	416	232	2 169	-	752
SARASOTA [1]	160 927	874	811	-	87	7	-	1	212	36	187	277	724	-	895
SEMINOLE [1]	135 001	1 160	1 157	-	140	10	380	7	118	32	194	210	929	-	803
VOLUSIA [1]	207 206	1 371	1 265	-	156	13	-	7	255	89	193	285	970	-	766
GEORGIA															
BIBB	142 978	625	597	-	87	12	-	75	88	28	188	119	460	-	767
CHATHAM	183 304	1 093	1 052	-	150	-	-	135	191	86	210	280	878	-	841
CLAYTON [3]	130 516	1 137	1 056	-	147	-	-	156	182	80	187	304	794	-	750
COBB	239 832	2 140	2 026	-	182	-	-	167	321	71	477	808	1 771	-	878
DE KALB [3]	450 599	4 319	4 243	-	351	8	-	383	569	99	747	2 086	3 569	-	840
FULTON	580 600	2 812	2 812	-	200	30	-	684	174	232	1 018	474	2 719	-	966
RICHMOND	156 151	1 097	985	-	72	-	-	77	170	97	207	362	684	-	693
IDAHO															
ADA	134 653	544	503	-	-	7	-	-	135	37	125	199	422	-	838

See footnotes at end of table.

273

Table 4. Employees and Payrolls for Individual Counties Having 100,000 Population or More: October 1977—Continued

State and county	Population, 1975 (estimates)	All employees (full-time and part-time)	Full-time equivalent — Total	Education	Highways	Welfare	Hospitals	Health	Police	Correction	Financial administration and general control	Other	October payroll (thousands of dollars)	Avg. Oct. earnings — Teachers	Avg. Oct. earnings — Other
ILLINOIS															
CHAMPAIGN	162 304	606	489	—	21	214	—	15	40	39	149	11	370	—	761
COOK[1]	5 369 328	20 747	20 089	—	945	34	8 746	160	761	1 987	6 022	1 434	21 707	—	1 079
DU PAGE	553 670	1 866	1 787	—	78	253	—	314	217	94	556	275	1 793	—	1 014
KANE	262 675	780	738	—	51	355	—	8	92	129	414	44	633	—	858
LAKE	407 373	1 755	1 624	—	105	67	—	264	172	122	405	201	1 472	—	915
LA SALLE	109 771	364	323	—	42	57	—	4	58	19	80	53	262	—	815
MCHENRY	125 981	384	363	—	26	124	—	34	80	22	128	16	332	—	918
MCLEAN	114 284	496	443	—	28	—	—	37	59	25	98	72	336	—	760
MACON	126 439	312	288	—	58	252	—	21	49	11	143	6	221	—	767
MADISON	249 685	1 823	1 628	—	181	186	—	25	146	75	271	678	1 653	—	756
PEORIA	199 023	815	748	—	52	249	—	136	133	16	187	38		—	878
ROCK ISLAND	165 313	833	691	—	28	—	—	41	86	17	126	144	508	—	738
ST. CLAIR	280 946	1 236	1 130	—	160	18	—	45	136	50	500	239	957	—	848
SANGAMON	169 753	440	421	—	53	190	—	2	97	60	185	24	381	—	905
TAZEWELL	125 189	347	311	—	11	—	—	50	38	25	163	6	254	—	818
WILL	296 224	937	887	—	70	260	—	133	154	14	267	59	751	—	850
WINNEBAGO	245 040	1 206	1 001	—	61	—	—	139	94	122	256	69	753	—	765
INDIANA															
ALLEN	288 796	1 829	1 634	—	127	715	—	55	125	129	304	179	1 298	—	802
DELAWARE	128 989	886	819	—	78	139	—	29	97	22	197	257	524	—	632
ELKHART	131 730	647	592	—	94	107	—	38	81	47	132	93	471	—	794
LAKE	546 757	3 247	3 125	—	90	107	—	46	245	214	1 034	389	2 601	—	834
LA PORTE	105 857	564	508	—	87	79	—	49	44	42	159	48	355	—	696
MADISON		549	534	—	64	112	133	16	41	43	194	64	358	—	670
ST. JOSEPH[3]	240 655	1 185	1 163	—	85	161	—	58	82	93	235	316	714	—	613
TIPPECANOE	112 408	549	538	—	47	91	—	6	46	3	108	237	319	—	590
VANDERBURGH	162 848	720	696	—	57	202	—	—	88	10	274	65	534	—	770
VIGO	110 509	866	865	—	73	126	—	44	37	16	198	371	525	—	606
IOWA															
BLACK HAWK[1]	133 589	616	563	—	36	76	—	124	38	65	184	40	431	—	754
LINN	164 145	890	800	—	100	173	—	91	45	126	201	64	788	—	987
POLK	296 881	1 799	1 693	—	91	117	599	6	65	143	544	128	1 347	—	809
SCOTT	149 082	477	477	—	44	52	—	36	44	32	174	95	370	—	775
WOODBURY[4]	103 692	422	401	—	64	38	—	14	21	12	131	121	318	—	796
KANSAS															
JOHNSON	238 326	1 018	994	—	47	51	101	50	108	62	330	346	755	—	759
SEDGWICK	345 224	1 509	1 470	—	218	—	—	102	98	105	574	272	1 348	—	916
SHAWNEE	150 994	696	644	—	67	—	—	—	72	84	210	211	507	—	787
WYANDOTTE	177 570	667	624	—	46	—	—	93	50	74	281	80	482	—	773

See footnotes at end of table.

Table 4. Employees and Payrolls for Individual Counties Having 100,000 Population or More: October 1977—Continued

State and county	Population, 1975 (estimates)	All employees (full-time and part-time)	Full-time equivalent — Total	Education	Highways	Welfare	Hospitals	Health	Police	Correction	Financial administration and general control	Other	October payroll (thousands of dollars)	Avg. Oct. earnings — Teachers	Avg. Oct. earnings — Other
KENTUCKY															
JEFFERSON[3]	696 832	4 310	4 131	–	161	471	1 055	354	569	303	954	264	3 437	–	832
KENTON[3]	129 819	373	345	–	37	2	33	31	49	–	28	165	233	–	678
LOUISIANA															
CADDO	239 078	906	858	–	151	–	–	62	56	105	323	161	646	–	752
CALCASIEU	151 334	1 395	1 310	–	229	61	377	63	46	27	181	326	1 047	–	805
JEFFERSON	399 016	6 050	5 658	–	494	111	1 761	133	280	57	1 225	1 597	4 284	–	758
LAFAYETTE	125 447	650	539	–	95	7	–	24	161	23	91	138	379	–	706
OUACHITA	125 447	1 087	1 012	–	118	20	100	58	120	23	153	420	663	–	660
RAPIDES	121 088	995	676	–	141	12	–	43	143	10	93	234	454	–	664
MAINE															
CUMBERLAND	208 111	160	146	–	–	–	–	–	35	54	43	14	122	–	826
PENOBSCOT	133 671	97	97	–	7	–	–	1	24	18	38	9	60	–	622
YORK	121 662	116	101	–	7	–	–	–	28	25	35	13	65	–	651
MARYLAND															
ANNE ARUNDEL[2]	344 056	10 820	9 728	6 522	471	265	–	75	545	37	426	1 387	11 110	1 358	934
BALTIMORE[2]	637 114	21 628	18 518	12 200	630	246	–	550	1 444	101	1 119	2 228	24 839	1 709	1 077
HARFORD[2]	136 381	4 231	4 231	3 183	321	119	–	93	93	36	149	328	4 214	1 141	822
MONTGOMERY[2]	571 558	25 317	18 853	12 255	302	372	–	510	1 079	155	792	388	29 158	1 900	1 287
PRINCE GEORGES[1][2]	677 848	25 811	22 986	15 090	686	369	1 946	63	1 237	216	1 209	2 170	28 137	1 742	926
WASHINGTON[1][2]	108 045	3 186	2 704	2 190	108	68	–	21	22	20	61	214	2 751	1 301	703
MASSACHUSETTS															
BARNSTABLE[3]	127 932	432	414	–	–	–	112	15	31	54	163	39	419	–	1 009
BERKSHIRE[3]	148 969	156	153	–	10	–	–	4	–	52	65	22	130	–	855
BRISTOL	463 813	481	465	57	–	–	–	–	–	88	290	30	458	–	966
ESSEX[2]	631 182	725	651	160	15	–	–	–	–	110	289	77	750	1 263	1 159
HAMPDEN	463 804	641	609	–	1	–	108	–	1	215	268	125	611	1 148	1 000
HAMPSHIRE	133 600	293	265	–	–	–	108	–	1	69	65	242	240	–	911
MIDDLESEX[3]	1 398 987	1 961	1 894	–	65	–	402	–	1	450	735	242	1 734	–	917
NORFOLK	619 994	879	840	57	19	–	248	–	1	189	289	37	789	1 237	930
PLYMOUTH	379 778	616	589	–	–	–	157	–	10	89	299	34	577	–	973
WORCESTER	648 095	1 005	973	–	33	–	223	–	–	99	294	324	991	1 015	
MICHIGAN															
BAY[1]	120 099	909	821	–	103	218	–	87	69	29	90	225	758	–	924
BERRIEN[1]	170 549	1 159	1 092	–	126	–	368	86	70	99	254	89	916	–	843
CALHOUN[1]	141 664	673	670	–	101	110	–	65	86	43	231	34	673	–	1 005
GENESEE	449 518	2 057	2 005	–	254	–	306	424	103	135	502	281	2 377	–	1 186
INGHAM	267 581	2 505	2 258	–	122	48	902	435	111	95	366	179	2 206	–	979
JACKSON	146 542	1 001	945	–	110	270	–	63	71	88	172	171	844	–	890

See footnotes at end of table.

Table 4. Employees and Payrolls for Individual Counties Having 100,000 Population or More: October 1977—Continued

State and county	Population, 1975 (estimates)	All employees (full-time and part-time)	Full-time equivalent — Total	Education	Highways	Welfare	Hospitals	Health	Police	Correction	Financial administration and general control	Other	October payroll (thousands of dollars)	Average October earnings — Teachers	Average October earnings — Other
MICHIGAN—CONTINUED															
KALAMAZOO	201 366	896	838	-	127	38	-	101	148	98	184	142	882	-	1 054
KENT	423 601	2 212	1 997	-	337	36	572	172	295	119	264	202	1 894	-	951
MACOMB	669 813	2 550	2 266	-	308	223	-	272	164	233	502	564	2 353	-	1 039
MONROE	127 094	885	838	-	121	13	-	125	127	58	180	214	839	-	1 004
MUSKEGON	157 646	1 202	1 120	-	107	204	69	95	100	18	235	292	1 024	-	915
OAKLAND	972 916	3 776	3 541	-	525	51	-	671	216	323	875	880	4 439	-	1 256
OTTAWA	140 556	526	541	-	151	20	-	105	63	31	111	26	541	-	1 066
SAGINAW	226 682	1 451	1 377	-	123	85	421	204	97	105	268	74	1 341	-	980
ST. CLAIR	130 749	794	692	-	181	53	-	111	35	66	170	76	829	-	1 207
WASHTENAW	244 724	1 510	1 291	-	127	8	-	263	139	117	332	305	1 760	-	1 364
WAYNE	2 517 837	8 470	8 336	-	585	1	2 311	490	483	944	2 203	1 319	12 689	-	1 523
MINNESOTA															
ANOKA	186 328	925	813	-	79	144	-	40	88	52	217	193	878	-	1 084
DAKOTA	166 793	639	570	-	60	151	-	-	55	15	200	89	630	-	1 111
HENNEPIN	915 603	7 741	6 912	-	398	1 531	2 118	296	276	622	1 047	624	8 345	-	1 215
RAMSEY	456 006	4 991	4 531	-	135	931	1 994	87	128	313	618	325	4 963	-	1 114
ST. LOUIS	216 220	2 582	2 442	-	343	1 154	-	112	99	182	308	244	2 579	-	1 060
MISSISSIPPI															
HARRISON	143 528	613	597	-	210	19	-	43	70	6	107	142	364	-	607
HINDS	228 521	1 550	1 457	-	243	17	836	16	75	60	152	58	1 029	-	708
JACKSON	105 186	1 514	1 403	-	99	10	942	-	62	33	68	189	1 069	-	760
MISSOURI															
CLAY	133 198	514	496	-	42	-	-	30	58	88	142	136	279	-	558
GREENE	167 956	436	431	-	139	-	-	11	55	31	136	59	269	-	625
JACKSON	634 589	1 726	1 726	-	120	-	-	-	81	451	882	192	1 424	-	825
JEFFERSON	121 769	321	301	-	79	-	-	34	49	10	91	38	220	-	732
ST. CHARLES	115 994	344	334	-	66	4	-	18	75	11	137	23	282	-	835
ST. LOUIS	960 451	4 775	4 658	-	496	150	780	358	762	247	754	1 111	4 588	-	984
NEBRASKA															
DOUGLAS	411 878	3 353	3 220	-	86	801	637	835	99	110	520	132	2 420	-	751
LANCASTER	181 659	1 109	1 050	-	101	626	-	-	64	47	153	59	895	-	852
NEVADA															
CLARK	330 714	5 004	4 777	-	90	104	902	188	1 114	286	754	1 339	5 396	-	1 140
WASHOE	144 750	2 834	2 669	-	116	29	1 424	134	200	61	419	286	2 831	-	1 060
NEW HAMPSHIRE															
HILLSBOROUGH	241 874	522	493	-	-	356	-	-	12	51	57	17	330	-	668
ROCKINGHAM	161 336	487	424	-	-	316	-	-	25	19	37	27	269	-	636

See footnotes at end of table.

Table 4. Employees and Payrolls for Individual Counties Having 100,000 Population or More: October 1977—Continued

State and county	Population, 1975 (estimates)	All employees (full-time and part-time)	Full-time equivalent — Total	Education	Highways	Welfare	Hospitals	Health	Police	Correction	Financial administration and general control	Other	October payroll (thousands of dollars)	Average October earnings — Teachers	Other
NEW JERSEY															
ATLANTIC [2,5]	188 106	2 195	2 087	845	132	401	-	43	40	165	228	233	1 967	1 496	888
BERGEN [2,6]	879 845	5 594	5 088	1 053	255	197	1 675	95	216	287	838	472	5 505	1 631	986
BURLINGTON [2,5]	345 696	2 569	2 189	751	243	135	141	72	146	153	147	401	2 255	1 635	811
CAMDEN [2,5,7]	476 511	5 571	4 881	921	235	750	860	116	88	406	535	970	4 713	1 254	927
CUMBERLAND [2,5]	132 938	1 146	1 096	168	96	150	162	32	26	149	79	234	892	1 678	731
ESSEX [2,6]	882 487	10 389	9 011	1 240	233	1 286	2 153	41	361	939	1 031	2 088	9 974	2 028	964
GLOUCESTER [2]	189 562	1 234	1 170	181	100	258	-	31	117	81	228	197	1 002	1 504	806
HUDSON [2]	577 519	4 534	4 447	140	96	479	1 571	8	216	425	915	574	3 588	1 274	800
MERCER [2]	318 374	2 708	2 315	586	168	281	263	33	42	270	317	355	2 396	1 602	956
MIDDLESEX [2,7]	592 771	5 755	5 292	847	317	531	673	190	88	371	827	448	5 118	1 609	908
MONMOUTH [2]	492 030	3 043	2 814	97	237	800	-	36	61	261	368	954	2 490	1 696	854
MORRIS [2]	393 624	3 250	2 608	523	201	739	-	24	83	163	421	454	2 649	2 003	924
OCEAN [2,7]	292 991	2 257	2 166	390	250	189	474	79	67	103	272	816	1 871	1 507	833
PASSAIC [2]	452 664	3 002	2 774	276	164	423	-	34	50	356	574	423	2 884	1 699	989
SOMERSET [2]	202 091	1 853	1 551	399	147	133	-	81	86	136	150	419	1 524	1 494	919
UNION [2]	520 823	2 924	2 690	228	109	257	605	22	60	302	492	615	3 010	1 296	1 110
NEW MEXICO															
BERNALILLO	362 087	872	824	-	65	-	-	14	207	31	214	293	774	-	950
NEW YORK															
ALBANY [2]	287 580	2 679	2 836	-	235	1 347	-	130	104	171	185	664	2 128	-	753
BROOME [2]	219 376	2 548	2 188	299	116	770	-	184	64	95	312	348	1 843	1 900	765
CHAUTAUQUA [2]	147 156	1 264	1 192	-	143	418	-	145	59	47	151	229	1 013	-	847
CHEMUNG [2]	100 377	1 183	1 037	-	60	267	-	67	40	58	60	485	846	-	811
DUTCHESS [2]	234 511	2 194	1 727	393	147	319	-	250	74	122	273	149	832	1 585	997
ERIE [1,2]	1 089 327	11 908	11 101	623	609	1 565	2 911	1 393	774	423	1 120	1 683	10 234	1 293	905
MONROE [2]	708 642	5 744	5 189	671	138	843	687	364	367	297	520	302	5 786	1 893	1 061
NASSAU [2]	1 403 289	22 925	21 030	1 138	929	2 510	3 242	753	4 375	1 013	2 295	4 775	24 642	2 092	1 150
NIAGARA [2]	237 521	2 072	1 824	355	80	420	213	146	164	41	261	144	1 890	1 647	966
ONEIDA [2]	266 077	1 561	1 512	-	169	355	199	87	62	94	147	399	1 246	-	822
ONONDAGA [2,9]	472 708	6 227	5 375	523	280	1 156	128	1 005	256	430	486	111	5 376	1 414	898
ORANGE [2]	241 811	2 557	2 052	388	171	931	-	83	35	80	189	175	2 103	1 939	927
OSWEGO [2]	109 651	1 139	1 068	-	129	347	-	50	56	62	157	267	854	-	803
RENSSELAER [2,5]	153 377	2 148	1 825	575	97	577	-	107	44	78	182	165	1 645	1 743	765
ROCKLAND [2]	251 114	2 474	2 419	-	99	738	200	409	100	112	344	417	2 221	-	920
ST. LAWRENCE [2]	117 048	1 270	1 243	-	137	216	-	95	35	54	65	641	812	-	654
SARATOGA	143 980	1 051	907	-	114	152	186	77	52	40	114	172	710	-	784
SCHENECTADY [2,5]	157 348	1 625	1 346	174	91	272	426	3	16	60	131	183	1 044	1 408	746
STEUBEN [2]	101 003	881	851	-	193	257	-	79	-	16	228	18	655	-	769
SUFFOLK [1,2]	1 253 550	12 785	11 860	1 038	385	1 511	-	923	3 083	567	1 850	2 503	13 367	1 740	1 092
ULSTER [2,8]	153 761	1 921	1 727	233	303	465	-	156	34	114	194	228	1 218	1 227	679
WESTCHESTER [2]	879 241	7 729	7 334	505	84	1 778	1 377	600	418	483	671	418	9 048	2 043	1 199

See footnotes at end of table.

Table 4. Employees and Payrolls for Individual Counties Having 100,000 Population or More: October 1977—Continued

State and county	Population, 1975 (estimates)	All employees (full-time and part-time)	Full-time equivalent										October payroll (thousands of dollars)	Average October earnings	
			Total	Education	Highways	Welfare	Hospitals	Health	Police	Correction	Financial administration and general control	Other		Teachers	Other
NORTH CAROLINA															
BUNCOMBE [2]	150 952	4 130	3 374	2 699	—	161	—	156	76	33	93	156	3 112	1 087	705
CUMBERLAND [2]	226 146	6 710	6 081	4 789	—	391	—	203	191	51	161	295	5 414	1 095	658
DURHAM [2]	139 320	4 414	3 686	2 929	—	317	—	194	26	24	55	141	3 409	1 048	755
FORSYTH [2]	226 332	6 903	5 907	4 495	—	401	—	265	130	41	256	319	5 741	1 138	804
GASTON [2]	156 529	4 299	3 774	3 130	—	147	—	173	61	28	68	167	3 596	1 124	707
GUILFORD [2]	299 484	8 751	7 814	6 137	—	441	—	531	140	86	183	296	8 091	1 151	801
MECKLENBURG [2]	373 925	11 466	9 545	7 465	—	548	—	545	181	102	191	513	9 845	1 155	875
WAKE [2]	261 868	7 154	6 092	5 065	—	274	—	200	83	27	105	338	6 059	1 088	834
OHIO															
ALLEN	108 734	771	756	—	74	191	—	31	59	30	132	239	603	—	798
ASHTABULA	101 940	699	666	—	74	257	—	77	86	18	125	29	484	—	727
BUTLER [1]	244 562	1 707	1 183	—	90	233	—	146	69	16	223	406	945	—	840
CLARK [1]	154 884	915	962	—	91	239	—	41	70	35	138	278	616	—	692
CLERMONT	108 886	775	760	—	63	92	—	39	32	211	166	157	597	—	787
COLUMBIANA [1]	113 182	561	518	—	65	84	2	86	27	25	130	99	412	—	790
CUYAHOGA [1]	1 592 613	12 305	12 101	—	477	2 519	3 992	531	315	283	1 367	2 617	10 606	—	871
FRANKLIN [3]	858 239	3 511	3 392	—	241	1 653	208	21	122	251	580	316	2 723	—	803
GREENE	124 779	736	688	—	70	221	—	57	65	11	172	92	597	—	867
HAMILTON	900 284	4 418	4 359	—	264	1 099	708	121	278	355	968	566	4 178	—	957
LAKE [1]	206 881	2 040	1 720	—	63	105	819	54	37	—	264	349	1 250	—	727
LICKING	113 316	474	450	—	96	54	—	82	52	53	128	53	342	—	764
LORAIN	268 579	1 091	1 040	—	111	324	—	51	52	177	272	177	800	—	769
LUCAS	476 657	2 568	2 418	—	110	1 164	—	37	128	158	584	237	2 227	—	922
MAHONING	307 339	1 831	1 815	—	264	604	—	55	76	78	286	452	1 258	—	692
MONTGOMERY	587 507	3 841	3 695	—	176	1 107	—	390	209	259	880	674	3 455	—	937
PORTAGE	132 257	2 139	1 988	—	81	142	835	41	62	20	147	660	1 719	—	860
RICHLAND	130 915	632	597	—	65	109	—	114	75	43	122	69	489	—	823
STARK [1]	376 047	2 151	2 009	—	161	436	164	223	140	99	324	462	1 572	—	781
SUMMIT [1]	534 900	3 146	3 101	—	209	506	234	—	215	116	545	1 276	2 363	—	761
TRUMBULL	241 219	1 475	1 415	—	113	305	231	135	84	16	267	264	1 259	—	889
OKLAHOMA															
COMANCHE	105 059	714	656	—	45	20	440	38	39	7	46	21	438	—	666
OKLAHOMA	537 939	1 134	1 085	—	117	41	—	105	65	85	352	320	853	—	786
TULSA	416 892	1 853	1 833	—	190	56	—	245	125	88	684	445	1 171	—	639
OREGON															
CLACKAMAS	206 014	982	855	—	152	41	—	46	124	63	281	148	1 033	—	1 207
JACKSON	112 235	931	859	—	182	—	—	86	94	69	224	204	840	—	978
LANE	237 937	1 987	1 922	—	212	417	—	202	184	167	481	259	1 997	—	1 042
MARION	166 920	814	752	—	112	—	—	126	81	109	248	76	747	—	993
MULTNOMAH	530 412	2 615	2 548	—	212	144	—	447	276	297	549	623	3 227	—	1 272
WASHINGTON	191 741	834	811	—	93	—	—	73	102	71	255	217	897	—	1 104

See footnotes at end of table.

Table 4. Employees and Payrolls for Individual Counties Having 100,000 Population or More: October 1977—Continued

State and county	Population, 1975 (estimates)	All employees (full-time and part-time)	Full-time equivalent Total	Education	Highways	Welfare	Hospitals	Health	Police	Correction	Financial administration and general control	Other	October payroll (thousands of dollars)	Average October earnings Teachers	Average October earnings Other
PENNSYLVANIA															
ALLEGHENY [1]	1 517 996	9 139	8 987	-	659	664	2 342	939	432	570	2 321	1 060	7 816	-	871
BEAVER [1]	209 328	637	580	-	9	62	-	1	80	59	229	140	513	-	864
BERKS	305 017	1 551	1 470	-	10	753	-	7	27	119	322	232	989	-	671
BLAIR	134 661	557	549	-	63	299	-	-	15	41	114	17	372	-	677
BUCKS	460 978	1 827	1 751	-	30	372	-	75	46	137	581	510	1 450	-	829
BUTLER	138 152	746	705	-	5	312	-	-	16	37	137	198	446	-	633
CAMBRIA	187 851	960	946	-	24	540	-	14	29	75	213	51	646	-	683
CENTRE	110 118	485	367	-	-	214	-	19	5	22	95	12	279	-	761
CHESTER	293 074	1 392	1 266	-	9	392	-	72	65	165	323	240	1 129	-	889
CUMBERLAND	171 294	877	754	-	1	412	-	15	13	64	99	150	551	-	731
DAUPHIN	223 343	1 328	1 132	-	3	561	-	9	35	95	290	139	1 011	-	890
DELAWARE	591 671	3 672	3 549	-	20	1 098	-	-	100	309	653	1 369	2 839	-	799
ERIE	273 396	712	688	-	21	99	-	60	24	139	245	121	635	-	925
FAYETTE	156 607	672	512	-	4	130	-	-	15	45	155	146	305	-	603
FRANKLIN	105 372	364	331	-	34	156	-	3	9	42	88	29	233	-	702
LACKAWANNA	234 771	889	889	-	87	476	-	-	13	59	242	65	606	-	681
LANCASTER [1]	342 797	2 154	2 082	-	-	534	-	14	36	172	332	907	1 307	-	627
LAWRENCE [1]	106 623	325	315	-	-	104	-	-	11	34	128	38	207	-	656
LEBANON	122 309	849	754	-	-	499	-	-	9	50	110	86	497	-	658
LEHIGH	263 566	1 605	1 554	-	20	809	-	58	-	157	419	91	1 168	-	735
LUZERNE	345 645	1 835	1 835	-	128	684	-	11	62	100	706	144	1 273	-	693
LYCOMING	114 897	534	503	-	9	180	-	-	8	18	79	209	438	-	873
MERCER [4]	127 741	327	321	-	-	214	-	-	-	33	59	14	161	-	499
MONTGOMERY [3]	634 001	1 891	1 731	-	32	465	-	-	101	187	651	270	1 390	-	801
NORTHAMPTON [3]	224 883	1 136	964	-	4	470	-	25	33	109	167	46	825	-	858
SCHUYLKILL	160 118	913	870	-	-	492	-	135	11	60	247	60	619	-	723
WASHINGTON	214 611	636	622	-	9	219	-	-	14	27	209	144	445	-	714
WESTMORELAND	380 289	1 637	1 538	-	24	716	-	-	65	89	352	292	1 300	-	849
YORK [3]	285 667	895	841	-	7	343	-	-	42	82	201	166	504	-	597
SOUTH CAROLINA															
ANDERSON	114 965	317	297	-	36	7	-	33	59	10	115	37	211	-	711
CHARLESTON	260 426	1 791	1 594	-	179	-	385	177	237	66	346	204	1 207	-	756
GREENVILLE	265 573	1 605	1 486	-	134	-	-	223	242	73	337	477	1 175	-	791
LEXINGTON	117 603	1 210	1 192	-	81	-	646	27	70	27	164	177	924	-	775
RICHLAND	247 553	2 982	2 899	-	107	-	1 960	39	192	50	351	200	2 413	-	827
SPARTANBURG	191 587	2 520	2 465	-	119	4	1 779	43	152	18	211	139	1 790	-	726
TENNESSEE															
HAMILTON	264 909	6 520	6 288	1 526	157	570	2 836	163	138	128	446	324	5 452	1 166	788
KNOX	293 405	3 678	3 468	2 422	64	61	-	50	179	65	159	468	2 997	1 006	726
SHELBY [5]	736 754	8 402	8 298	1 911	163	246	3 555	375	405	226	743	674	6 837	1 164	765
SULLIVAN [5]	134 447	2 277	2 042	1 541	168	10	-	56	75	-	125	67	1 828	1 100	631

See footnotes at end of table.

279

Table 4. Employees and Payrolls for Individual Counties Having 100,000 Population or More: October 1977—Continued

State and county	Population, 1975 (estimates)	All employees (full-time and part-time)	Full-time equivalent — Total	Education	Highways	Welfare	Hospitals	Health	Police	Correction	Financial administration and general control	Other	October payroll (thousands of dollars)	Avg. Oct. earnings — Teachers	Avg. Oct. earnings — Other
TEXAS															
BELL	156 781	331	321	–	66	–	–	1	37	53	149	15	237	–	739
BEXAR	912 934	4 535	4 355	–	164	–	2 607	–	245	365	777	197	3 155	–	724
BRAZORIA	124 380	535	489	–	137	2	–	10	64	25	161	90	417	–	854
CAMERON	176 931	493	487	–	76	–	–	58	50	71	174	52	328	–	672
DALLAS	1 405 126	5 955	5 821	–	188	188	2 974	55	343	711	1 197	165	5 347	–	918
EL PASO	424 479	1 763	1 702	–	74	12	758	–	101	204	364	189	1 138	–	670
GALVESTON	183 244	1 509	1 459	–	106	25	702	38	93	66	266	163	1 250	–	856
HARRIS	1 944 431	9 261	9 116	–	659	326	3 364	314	671	679	1 905	1 198	8 709	–	953
HIDALGO	227 853	710	696	–	51	19	–	91	66	101	275	93	436	–	626
JEFFERSON	241 246	705	700	–	101	21	–	25	74	89	269	121	653	–	932
LUBBOCK	197 248	421	403	–	29	–	–	43	81	70	120	52	273	–	678
MCLENNAN	154 267	602	477	–	82	6	–	60	52	72	157	48	364	–	767
NUECES	248 422	2 423	2 331	–	183	40	1 469	51	87	102	289	110	1 841	–	789
SMITH	107 597	262	258	–	67	5	–	8	35	22	100	21	190	–	735
TARRANT	728 951	2 864	2 637	–	152	36	1 154	22	195	239	701	138	2 186	–	831
TAYLOR	105 390	182	178	–	24	6	–	1	22	23	91	11	130	–	732
TRAVIS	361 839	1 111	1 004	–	129	26	–	16	110	281	358	84	965	–	963
WICHITA	119 515	251	251	–	31	33	–	2	28	29	107	21	209	–	801
UTAH															
DAVIS	114 652	358	278	–	13	34	–	54	43	6	46	82	259	–	948
SALT LAKE	512 130	3 790	3 431	–	269	482	–	178	479	65	743	1 215	3 566	–	1 043
UTAH	165 745	351	321	–	32	–	–	39	37	19	124	70	286	–	898
WEBER	133 127	947	873	–	32	126	244	40	42	40	95	254	672	–	793
VERMONT															
CHITTENDEN	105 559	8	6	–	–	–	–	–	–	–	6	–	5	–	718
VIRGINIA															
ARLINGTON [5]	155 518	5 291	4 395	2 092	180	118	–	81	402	48	371	1 103	5 922	1 752	1 184
FAIRFAX	512 915	21 473	20 001	14 121	53	200	–	301	883	125	667	3 651	24 476	1 390	1 098
HENRICO	167 728	5 578	5 199	3 380	182	52	–	–	396	65	195	929	4 869	1 093	950
PRINCE WILLIAM	123 376	4 489	4 264	3 262	14	78	–	–	165	35	159	551	4 520	1 150	982
WASHINGTON															
CLARK [1]	154 590	861	788	–	177	11	–	72	102	96	210	120	812	–	1 026
KING	1 142 544	5 172	4 044	–	432	4	–	251	503	601	1 130	1 123	5 245	–	1 301
KITSAP	116 710	801	699	–	105	–	–	80	73	27	167	247	709	–	1 017
PIERCE [1]	415 707	1 835	1 660	–	348	22	–	–	205	152	486	447	1 829	–	1 102
SNOHOMISH	264 202	1 383	1 451	–	207	–	–	80	123	119	294	628	1 306	–	900
SPOKANE	306 338	1 172	1 133	–	229	4	–	82	211	84	354	169	1 191	–	1 051
YAKIMA	155 516	803	797	–	124	90	–	95	83	88	222	95	711	–	891

See footnotes at end of table.

Table 4. Employees and Payrolls for Individual Counties Having 100,000 Population or More: October 1977—Continued

State and county	Population, 1975 (estimates)	All employees (full-time and part-time)	Full-time equivalent										October payroll (thousands of dollars)	Average October earnings	
			Total	Education	Highways	Welfare	Hospitals	Health	Police	Correction	Financial administration and general control	Other		Teachers	Other
WEST VIRGINIA															
CABELL	103 654	438	384	–	–	–	–	67	42	33	82	160	247	–	650
KANAWHA	225 037	619	565	–	–	16	–	76	77	19	230	147	443	–	785
WISCONSIN															
BROWN.	169 467	1 148	966	–	120	100	242	27	117	29	105	226	874	–	919
DANE	301 668	1 709	1 467	–	179	537	–	42	128	85	286	210	1 703	–	1 161
KENOSHA.	122 621	789	744	–	69	307	–	10	80	15	197	66	723	–	973
MARATHON	104 854	1 110	933	–	99	66	425	42	76	4	61	160	881	–	942
MILWAUKEE. . . .	1 012 335	10 323	10 323	–	358	1 077	4 047	255	204	398	1 331	2 653	10 924	–	1 058
OUTAGAMIE. . . .	124 414	872	724	–	97	94	231	11	61	9	187	34	685	–	947
RACINE	175 781	1 191	1 136	–	105	192	373	28	130	35	224	49	1 224	–	1 082
ROCK	133 993	979	927	–	102	106	356	54	98	25	118	68	805	–	872
WAUKESHA	255 779	1 381	1 292	–	98	154	345	90	131	55	171	248	1 232	–	952
WINNEBAGO. . . .	130 248	933	896	–	91	114	365	38	65	10	115	78	789	–	888

– Represents zero or rounds to zero.
[1] Data are for October 1976.
[2] Includes data for degree-granting institution(s) of higher education operated by the county government.
[3] Data are for October 1975.
[4] Data are for October 1974.
[5] Noneducation data are for October 1976.
[6] Secondary education data are for October 1975.
[7] Secondary education data are for October 1976.
[8] Noneducation data are for October 1975.
[9] Education data are for October 1976.

C — CITY GOVERNMENT EMPLOYMENT

Municipal government employment in October 1977 was 2,487,000, an increase of 44,000 employees, or 1.8 percent, from the number of employees in October 1976. Payrolls of municipal governments for October 1977 totaled $2.4 billion, an increase of 6.7 percent over the amount for October 1976.

Approximately 440,000 municipal employees were employed on a part-time basis in October 1977. When these part-time employees are counted in terms of average pay rates for full-time work in corresponding functions, they are found to be equivalent to only 94,000 full-time employees. Accordingly, the total of municipal government employment on a full-time equivalent basis in October 1977 is calculated at 2,141,000, an increase of 1.6 percent from the 2,107,000 full-time equivalent employment in October 1976 (Table H).

Table I provides a summary of municipal government employment and payrolls since 1946.

The average earnings of full-time noninstructional municipal employees in October 1977 was $1,077, an increase of $51, or 5.0 percent, from October 1976. Full-time instructional employees of school systems and higher education institutions operated by municipal governments had average earnings of $1,390 in October 1977, a 5.4 percent increase from the corresponding average pay for October 1976.

Since 1972, municipal employment (on a full-time equivalent basis) has risen 5.5 percent and the October payrolls of municipal governments have increased 44.2 percent. During this 5-year period, the average October earnings of full-time noninstructional municipal employees rose 37.7 percent; instructional employees' average October earnings increased 30.0 percent during this period.

There were 1,788,000 full-time equivalent municipal employees in October 1977 engaged in governmental functions other than education. This was equal to an average of 131 employees for each 10,000 municipal inhabitants.

Functions of City Governments

Individual city governments differ widely in the range of their responsibilities and services. Certain important services needed in urban areas may or may not be provided by the municipal government, depending on State law or local option.

Most municipal governments provide services in the following functions: Highways, police protection, fire protection, sewerage, sanitation other than sewerage, parks and recreation, financial administration and general control. However, other services provided by some municipalities, such as schools or hospitals, comprise a considerable portion of all city employment and payrolls.

In most parts of the United States, including a majority of urban areas, public schools are provided by schools districts which operate as independent local governments. While only 300 of 18,500 municipal governments operate schools, education is second only to police protection in percentage of municipal employment.

In October 1977, the education and police functions accounted for almost one-third of total municipal government employment. Table J shows percentage distributions of municipal employment, by function.

Data for Major Cities

The number of employees in the 393 cities which had an estimated population of 50,000 or more in 1975 increased 2.1 percent between October 1976 and October 1977 and the rate of increase in their October payroll amounts was 6.1.

These large cities engage a larger number of employees in relation to their population and have higher average salary payments for full-time employees than municipalities as a whole. They also differ in the functional distribution of their employ-

Item	Year-to-year change (percent)
Full-time equivalent employment:	
1976 to 1977...................	1.6
1975 to 1976...................	-1.7
1974 to 1975...................	0.6
1973 to 1974...................	0.8
1972 to 1973...................	4.0
Average, 1972 to 1977........	1.1
Average, 1967 to 1972........	3.3
Average, 1967 to 1977........	2.2
October payrolls:	
1976 to 1977...................	6.7
1975 to 1976...................	5.0
1974 to 1975...................	7.3
1973 to 1974...................	7.0
1972 to 1973...................	12.2
Average, 1972 to 1977........	7.6
Average, 1967 to 1972........	10.8
Average, 1967 to 1977........	9.4

(H)

Month and year	All employees (full-time and part-time) (thousands)	Monthly payroll (millions of dollars)	Month and year	All employees (full-time and part-time) (thousands)	Monthly payroll (millions of dollars)
October:			October:		
1977.................	2,487	2,386	1961...............	1,734	644
1976.................	2,443	2,235	1960...............	1,692	583
1975.................	2,506	2,129	1959...............	1,636	548
1974.................	2,491	1,985	1958...............	1,594	511
1973.................	2,471	1,855	April 1957..........	1,539	461
1972.................	2,376	1,654	October:		
1971.................	2,273	1,482	1956...............	1,485	450
1970.................	2,244	1,361	1955...............	1,436	414
1969.................	2,165	1,196	1954...............	1,420	396
1968.................	2,112	1,097	1953...............	1,382	367
			1952...............	1,341	345
1967.................	1,993	972	1951...............	1,297	315
1966.................	1,971	892	1950...............	1,311	290
1965.................	1,884	818	1949...............	1,281	270
1964.................	1,817	761	1948...............	1,249	266
1963.................	1,782	708	1947...............	1,202	236
1962.................	1,696	662	1946...............	1,155	206

(i)

ment. Table K shows percentage distributions of employment, by function, for the cities of 50,000 or more population.

In this report, statistics are shown for each of the 388 cities and 22 major urban towns and townships which had an estimated population of 50,000 or more in 1973. Intercity comparisons based on these figures should take account of the presence or absence of other overlying local governments, arrangements that apply for the operation of utilities, and the varying allocation of governmental responsibilities between the State and various types of local governments.

Within most cities, the county has a significant share of the responsibility for providing local government services. However, a number of cities either are completely or substantially consolidated with their county governments, operate outside the

283

Function	Percent of full-time equivalent employment October 1977
Total.....................	100.0
Police protection...............	16.6
Education........................	16.5
Fire protection..................	8.7
Highways.........................	6.0
Hospitals........................	5.7
Sanitation other than sewerage...	5.2
Parks and Recreation.............	5.1
Utilities other than water supply	4.7
General control..................	4.6
Water supply.....................	4.4
Financial administration.........	3.0
Sewerage.........................	2.7
Public welfare...................	1.9
Housing and urban renewal........	1.8
Libraries........................	1.7
Health...........................	1.6
Correction.......................	0.8
All other functions.............	9.0

(J)

Function for cities over 50,000	Percent of full-time equivalent employment October 1977
Total.....................	100.0
Education........................	19.4
Police protection...............	15.1
Fire protection..................	8.5
Hospitals........................	5.8
Parks and recreation.............	5.3
Utilities other than water supply	5.2
Sanitation other than sewerage...	4.5
Highways.........................	4.3
General control..................	4.0
Water supply.....................	3.5
Public welfare...................	2.6
Financial administration.........	2.4
Housing and urban renewal........	2.4
Health...........................	2.1
Sewerage.........................	2.0
Libraries........................	1.7
Correction.......................	1.1
All other functions.............	10.1

(K)

geographic limits of any county, or for other reasons have no county government operations within their boundaries.[2]

The major urban towns and townships for which data are provided are in four States (Connecticut, Massachusetts, New Jersey, and Pennsylvania) where such governments closely resemble municipalities in the span of their responsibilities.

[2]Anchorage, Baltimore, Baton Rouge, Boston, Columbus (Ga.), Denver, Honolulu, Indianapolis, Jacksonville, Lexington (Ky.), Nashville, New Orleans, New York City, Philadelphia, St. Louis, San Francisco, and Washington, D.C. as well as all of the cities in Connecticut, Rhode Island, and Virginia. Additionally, Washington, D.C. represents a unique case since it also performs some functions which commonly are handled by a State government.

Table 1. Summary of Employment and Payrolls of City Governments, by Function: October 1977 and Prior Years

Item	Amount						Year-to-year change 1976 to 1977 (percent)	Average annual change 1972 to 1977 (percent)
	1977	1976	1975	1974	1973	1972		
EMPLOYEES								
TOTAL	2 487 021	2 443 059	2 505 918	2 491 153	2 470 647	2 375 502	1.8	0.9
FULL-TIME	2 046 673	2 012 461	2 038 106	2 020 627	1 993 895	1 920 226	1.7	1.3
PART-TIME	440 348	430 598	467 812	470 526	476 752	455 276	2.3	-0.7
FULL-TIME EQUIVALENT EMPLOYMENT .	2 141 056	2 106 989	2 142 496	2 127 074	2 109 233	2 028 922	1.6	1.1
BY FUNCTION:								
EDUCATION (CITY-OPERATED SCHOOLS AND COLLEGES).	353 174	360 131	376 280	405 191	402 086	378 484	-1.9	-1.4
INSTRUCTIONAL STAFF	260 670	265 960	277 093	284 048	279 469	262 779	-2.0	-0.2
OTHERS.	92 504	94 171	99 187	121 143	122 617	115 705	-1.8	-4.4
HIGHWAYS.	128 234	124 095	128 584	121 897	122 287	118 744	3.3	1.5
PUBLIC WELFARE.	41 338	40 443	42 267	44 908	45 430	43 082	2.2	-0.8
HOSPITALS	122 051	123 243	127 613	130 877	132 997	129 364	-1.0	-1.2
HEALTH.	34 692	34 795	37 528	38 154	40 024	37 217	-0.3	-1.4
POLICE PROTECTION	354 637	346 774	349 387	344 002	337 280	319 004	2.3	2.1
FIRE PROTECTION	187 102	183 070	183 865	183 340	183 849	180 693	2.2	0.7
SEWERAGE.	57 241	55 329	54 535	52 234	50 035	45 591	3.5	4.7
SANITATION OTHER THAN SEWERAGE. . . .	110 267	106 614	107 616	111 917	111 306	108 715	3.4	0.3
PARKS AND RECREATION.	108 664	102 244	104 021	94 689	90 686	88 705	6.3	4.1
HOUSING AND URBAN RENEWAL	39 313	35 655	35 111	32 572	32 823	31 060	10.3	4.8
AIRPORTS.	9 895	9 774	9 617	9 377	8 887	8 111	1.3	4.1
WATER TRANSPORT AND TERMINALS	2 996	2 589	2 722	2 939	2 689	2 709	15.7	2.0
CORRECTION.	17 739	16 607	16 114	16 313	15 221	14 583	6.8	4.0
LIBRARIES	36 058	37 508	38 274	38 591	37 219	35 904	-3.9	0.1
FINANCIAL ADMINISTRATION.	64 500	61 983	61 439	58 947	58 745	54 824	4.1	3.3
GENERAL CONTROL	99 556	103 153	104 756	97 641	97 975	91 191	-3.5	1.8
LOCAL UTILITIES	194 757	197 195	200 410	201 649	195 784	189 258	-1.2	0.6
WATER SUPPLY.	93 699	91 924	92 292	92 208	88 296	83 660	1.9	2.3
ELECTRIC POWER.	42 310	44 535	45 736	46 858	45 855	44 257	-5.0	-0.9
TRANSIT	52 131	54 172	55 716	56 079	54 759	55 339	-3.8	-1.2
GAS SUPPLY.	6 617	6 564	6 666	6 504	6 874	5 996	0.8	2.0
ALL OTHER FUNCTIONS	178 842	165 787	162 357	141 836	143 910	151 689	7.8	3.3
FULL-TIME EQUIVALENT EMPLOYMENT PER 10,000 POPULATION[1]	156.6	154.1	156.7	160.8	159.5	153.4	1.6	0.4
OCTOBER PAYROLL (THOUSANDS OF DOLLARS)								
TOTAL	2 385 727	2 235 388	2 129 314	1 985 305	1 855 338	1 654 011	6.7	7.6
FULL-TIME	2 285 422	2 140 868	2 031 365	1 892 403	1 759 830	1 574 407	6.8	7.7
PART-TIME	100 305	94 520	97 948	92 902	95 508	79 604	6.1	4.7
BY FUNCTION:								
EDUCATION (CITY-OPERATED SCHOOLS AND COLLEGES).	441 924	431 314	424 568	425 354	414 534	352 068	2.5	4.7
INSTRUCTIONAL STAFF	362 202	352 385	346 173	337 987	327 385	283 152	2.8	5.0
OTHERS.	79 720	78 928	78 394	87 368	87 147	68 916	1.0	3.0
HIGHWAYS.	122 023	113 245	108 666	96 743	91 822	82 339	7.8	8.2
PUBLIC WELFARE.	40 898	38 588	35 610	37 395	33 748	30 117	6.0	6.3
HOSPITALS	112 497	109 101	108 230	99 584	94 829	84 786	3.1	5.8
HEALTH.	37 130	35 689	34 744	32 582	31 684	26 995	4.0	6.6
POLICE PROTECTION	453 479	407 226	384 234	349 232	323 164	297 884	11.4	8.8
FIRE PROTECTION	249 123	225 784	216 904	196 447	184 049	166 722	10.3	8.4
SEWERAGE.	54 811	50 544	46 407	42 153	38 094	32 526	8.4	11.0
SANITATION OTHER THAN SEWERAGE. . . .	96 484	92 368	88 285	86 964	81 776	73 328	4.5	5.6
PARKS AND RECREATION.	97 312	88 417	83 631	72 610	65 197	56 967	10.1	11.3
HOUSING AND URBAN RENEWAL	43 232	39 625	34 730	34 612	28 484	25 631	9.1	11.0
AIRPORTS.	10 391	9 782	9 150	8 108	7 365	6 083	6.2	11.3
WATER TRANSPORT AND TERMINALS	3 967	3 419	3 232	3 157	2 778	2 757	16.0	7.5
CORRECTION.	22 156	20 041	17 737	16 953	14 748	11 903	10.6	13.2
LIBRARIES	32 512	31 538	29 922	28 012	25 546	23 118	3.1	7.1
FINANCIAL ADMINISTRATION.	64 104	57 895	54 058	48 407	44 974	39 866	10.7	10.0
GENERAL CONTROL	107 731	110 034	100 676	89 153	83 846	72 522	-2.1	8.2
LOCAL UTILITIES	220 410	216 323	206 356	195 372	176 213	158 467	1.9	6.8
WATER SUPPLY.	92 939	86 676	80 839	75 787	68 277	60 274	7.2	9.1
ELECTRIC POWER.	51 085	51 236	48 461	45 991	42 531	37 960	-0.3	6.1
TRANSIT	70 104	72 358	71 336	68 319	60 577	56 157	3.2	4.5
GAS SUPPLY.	6 366	6 053	5 720	5 276	4 827	4 076	5.2	9.3
ALL OTHER FUNCTIONS:	175 535	154 455	142 173	122 466	112 478	107 932	13.6	10.2
AVERAGE OCTOBER EARNINGS OF FULL-TIME EMPLOYEES (DOLLARS).	1 116	1 063	997	936	882	820	5.0	6.4
INSTRUCTIONAL STAFF	1 390	1 319	1 239	1 182	1 163	1 073	5.4	5.3
ALL OTHER	1 077	1 026	960	898	839	782	5.0	6.6

Note: Because of rounding, detail may not add to totals. Data for 1972 are based on a complete census of all city governments. Data for other years on table are estimates subject to sampling variation; see text for statement of reliability.

[1]For 1972, 1973 and 1974 data are based on 1970 population of 132,244,000; for 1975, 1976 and 1977 data are based on 1975 estimated population of 136,685,000.

Table 2. Summary of Employment and Payrolls of City Governments, by Function and Population Size-Group: October 1977

Item	Total	Population size-groups (1970 population)						
		1,000,000 or more	500,000 to 999,999	300,000 to 499,999	200,000 to 299,999	100,000 to 199,999	50,000 to 99,999	Less than 50,000
EMPLOYEES								
TOTAL.	2 487 021	521 092	296 700	165 085	101 190	271 957	248 825	882 172
FULL-TIME.	2 046 673	458 472	272 888	153 656	91 647	237 096	214 432	618 482
PART-TIME.	440 348	62 620	23 812	11 429	9 543	34 861	34 393	263 690
FULL-TIME EQUIVALENT EMPLOYMENT. .	2 141 056	478 979	282 916	159 261	94 601	246 764	223 912	654 503
BY FUNCTION:								
EDUCATION (CITY OPERATED SCHOOLS AND COLLEGES).	353 174	96 725	48 949	21 226	22 176	59 224	40 220	64 654
TEACHERS	260 670	75 503	33 586	14 119	15 041	42 526	30 317	49 578
OTHER.	92 504	21 222	15 363	7 107	7 135	16 698	9 903	15 076
HIGHWAYS	128 234	14 528	10 686	7 851	4 611	12 137	13 493	64 928
PUBLIC WELFARE	41 338	27 242	5 856	1 362	1 557	2 434	897	1 990
HOSPITALS.	122 051	43 072	19 747	3 858	2 425	7 008	10 304	35 637
HEALTH	34 692	10 606	10 311	3 903	1 112	3 534	2 070	3 156
POLICE PROTECTION.	354 637	76 093	40 767	25 247	12 606	33 858	35 424	130 522
FIRE PROTECTION.	187 102	27 439	21 677	16 510	8 948	25 754	26 075	60 699
SEWERAGE	57 241	5 017	5 305	5 085	2 006	6 168	5 838	27 822
SANITATION OTHER THAN SEWERAGE	110 267	21 895	11 787	7 064	5 563	11 031	9 705	43 222
PARKS AND RECREATION	108 664	15 239	16 059	11 819	6 333	14 291	14 850	30 073
HOUSING AND URBAN RENEWAL.	39 313	18 119	5 672	2 250	2 508	4 069	2 812	3 883
AIRPORTS	9 895	2 687	2 116	1 167	597	1 294	816	1 218
WATER TRANSPORT AND TERMINALS.	2 996	864	321	915	16	67	467	346
CORRECTION	17 739	7 364	5 870	1 350	949	1 004	228	974
LIBRARIES.	36 058	4 747	5 176	3 573	1 948	4 781	5 556	10 277
FINANCIAL ADMINISTRATION	64 500	7 666	6 168	4 527	2 786	6 785	7 550	29 018
GENERAL CONTROL.	99 556	13 342	14 832	7 676	3 760	9 369	9 871	40 706
LOCAL UTILITIES.	194 757	58 614	22 343	11 705	5 455	17 316	14 120	65 204
WATER SUPPLY	93 699	12 278	9 996	7 665	4 075	9 114	8 882	41 689
ELECTRIC POWER	42 310	6 674	5 170	3 146	-	5 542	3 269	18 509
TRANSIT.	52 131	39 643	5 437	578	954	1 901	1 538	2 080
GAS SUPPLY	6 617	19	1 740	316	426	759	431	2 926
ALL OTHER FUNCTIONS.	178 842	27 720	29 274	22 173	9 245	26 640	23 616	40 174
FULL-TIME EQUIVALENT EMPLOYMENT PER 10,000 POPULATION	156.6	268.8	230.3	184.7	203.0	181.3	139.8	103.5
OCTOBER PAYROLL (THOUSANDS OF DOLLARS)								
TOTAL.	2 385 728	657 896	326 656	178 796	99 851	261 635	245 181	615 714
FULL-TIME.	2 285 423	631 736	317 640	174 981	97 198	252 740	235 840	575 288
PART-TIME.	100 305	26 160	9 015	3 815	2 653	8 895	9 341	40 427
BY FUNCTION:								
EDUCATION (CITY-OPERATED SCHOOLS AND COLLEGES).	441 925	143 149	66 127	27 874	24 127	65 655	48 313	66 681
TEACHERS	362 203	122 724	52 361	20 940	19 407	52 383	39 914	54 475
OTHER.	79 722	20 425	13 766	6 933	4 720	13 272	8 399	12 205
HIGHWAYS	122 023	17 542	11 140	8 494	4 467	11 498	13 448	55 435
PUBLIC WELFARE	40 898	27 395	6 621	1 189	1 344	2 042	797	1 510
HOSPITALS.	112 497	45 472	19 515	3 305	2 537	6 063	8 990	26 616
HEALTH	37 131	11 914	11 608	4 460	1 103	3 370	1 980	2 696
POLICE PROTECTION.	453 480	129 575	52 533	30 946	15 466	41 405	44 778	138 777
FIRE PROTECTION.	249 123	53 131	27 061	21 665	11 167	32 578	33 405	70 116
SEWERAGE	54 811	6 204	5 649	5 487	1 979	5 842	5 745	23 905
SANITATION OTHER THAN SEWERAGE	96 484	24 821	11 231	6 676	5 057	9 198	8 371	31 131
PARKS AND RECREATION	97 313	15 978	14 315	11 157	5 587	12 086	13 645	24 546
HOUSING AND URBAN RENEWAL.	43 232	21 304	6 417	2 291	2 598	4 115	2 783	3 725
AIRPORTS	10 392	3 206	2 331	1 289	600	1 166	730	1 068
WATER TRANSPORT AND TERMINALS.	3 967	1 259	397	1 330	26	75	530	352
CORRECTION	22 156	11 269	6 573	1 447	833	856	210	970
LIBRARIES.	32 513	4 721	4 814	3 217	1 706	4 241	5 224	8 590
FINANCIAL ADMINISTRATION	64 104	9 411	6 896	4 993	2 909	6 911	7 694	25 291
GENERAL CONTROL.	107 731	16 776	17 319	9 101	4 397	10 001	11 000	39 136
LOCAL UTILITIES.	220 411	80 982	26 368	13 415	5 489	19 482	14 692	59 982
WATER SUPPLY	92 940	15 420	10 759	8 248	4 081	9 047	8 863	36 521
ELECTRIC POWER	51 086	10 359	5 969	4 167	-	7 447	3 831	19 312
TRANSIT.	70 018	55 186	7 647	601	1 014	2 188	1 574	1 808
GAS SUPPLY	6 367	17	1 993	399	394	799	423	2 342
ALL OTHER FUNCTIONS.	175 536	33 787	29 743	20 460	8 461	25 051	22 846	35 189
AVERAGE OCTOBER EARNINGS OF FULL-TIME EMPLOYEES (DOLLARS)	1 116	1 377	1 163	1 138	1 060	1 068	1 099	929
TEACHERS	1 382	1 623	1 557	1 481	1 290	1 230	1 316	1 104
ALL OTHER.	1 079	1 334	1 111	1 104	1 016	1 033	1 065	914

Note: Because of rounding, detail may not add to totals. Data for cities of less than 50,000 population and totals for all cities are estimates subject to sampling variation; see text for statement of reliability.

Table 3. Summary of Employment and Payrolls of City Governments Having 50,000 Population or More, by Function: October 1977 and Prior Years

Item	Amount						Year-to-year change (percent) 1976 to 1977	Average annual rate of change (percent) 1972 to 1977
	1977	1976	1975	1974	1973	1972		
EMPLOYEES								
TOTAL	1 604 849	r1 572 187	1 629 602	1 651 019	1 629 488	1 608 161	2.1	(Z)
FULL-TIME	1 428 191	r1 407 033	1 449 489	1 448 819	1 429 860	1 395 149	1.5	0.5
PART-TIME	176 658	r165 154	180 113	202 200	199 628	213 012	7.0	-3.7
FULL-TIME EQUIVALENT EMPLOYMENT	1 486 553	r1 460 681	1 508 429	1 513 309	1 496 546	1 468 091	1.8	0.3
BY FUNCTION:								
EDUCATION (CITY-OPERATED SCHOOLS AND COLLEGES).	288 520	r289 787	312 122	334 981	336 123	314 227	-0.4	-1.7
HIGHWAYS.	63 306	60 681	64 885	60 925	61 772	60 366	4.3	1.0
POLICE PROTECTION	224 115	216 709	223 735	224 351	218 151	210 391	3.4	1.3
FIRE PROTECTION	126 403	123 706	126 066	126 670	124 994	123 811	2.2	0.4
SEWERAGE.	29 419	28 240	28 106	27 371	27 152	26 048	4.2	2.5
SANITATION OTHER THAN SEWERAGE.	67 045	64 109	66 247	69 479	70 933	71 550	4.6	-1.3
PARKS AND RECREATION.	78 591	72 667	72 711	68 062	66 002	65 568	8.2	3.7
LIBRARIES	25 781	27 255	28 436	28 801	28 608	27 270	-5.4	-1.1
FINANCIAL ADMINISTRATION.	35 482	33 721	33 877	33 100	32 896	32 208	5.2	1.9
GENERAL CONTROL	58 850	63 052	61 863	58 264	55 405	51 829	-6.7	2.6
WATER SUPPLY.	52 010	50 794	51 320	51 879	52 095	53 145	2.4	-0.4
ALL OTHER FUNCTIONS[1]	437 031	429 960	439 066	429 426	422 415	431 678	1.6	0.2
FULL-TIME EQUIVALENT EMPLOYMENT PER 10,000 POPULATION[2].	204.7	r201.1	207.7	208.8	206.4	202.5	1.8	0.2
OCTOBER PAYROLL (THOUSANDS OF DOLLARS)								
TOTAL	1 770 014	r1 668 368	1 611 673	1 516 144	1 396 463	1 269 707	6.1	6.9
FULL-TIME	1 710 135	r1 610 941	1 551 275	1 455 376	1 334 237	1 206 622	6.2	7.2
PART-TIME	59 878	r57 424	60 397	60 766	62 226	63 085	4.3	-1.0
BY FUNCTION:								
EDUCATION (CITY-OPERATED SCHOOLS AND COLLEGES).	375 245	r358 058	362 573	365 783	348 953	297 831	4.8	4.7
HIGHWAYS.	66 588	62 183	61 720	54 281	51 587	46 575	7.1	6.5
POLICE PROTECTION	314 703	282 330	271 530	248 677	227 865	215 953	11.5	7.8
FIRE PROTECTION	179 007	165 590	162 442	146 153	134 397	122 926	8.1	7.8
SEWERAGE.	30 906	28 620	26 661	24 474	22 301	19 584	8.0	9.6
SANITATION OTHER THAN SEWERAGE.	65 353	63 497	62 006	61 569	57 657	53 390	2.9	4.1
PARKS AND RECREATION.	72 767	64 697	60 731	53 828	48 364	44 621	12.5	10.3
LIBRARIES	23 923	23 725	22 786	21 373	19 554	17 289	0.8	6.7
FINANCIAL ADMINISTRATION.	38 813	34 762	32 448	29 628	27 216	24 757	11.7	9.4
GENERAL CONTROL	68 595	73 267	65 620	58 662	52 408	44 937	-6.4	8.8
WATER SUPPLY.	56 419	52 745	50 293	47 189	44 039	41 260	6.8	6.5
ALL OTHER FUNCTIONS[1]	477 695	454 525	432 864	404 527	362 121	340 584	5.1	7.0
AVERAGE OCTOBER EARNINGS OF FULL-TIME EMPLOYEES (DOLLARS).	1 197	1 141	1 070	1 006	933	873	4.9	6.5
TEACHERS.	1 450	1 377	1 300	1 244	(NA)	(NA)	5.3	(NA)
OTHER	1 156	1 092	1 027	964	(NA)	(NA)	5.9	(NA)

Note: Because of rounding, detail may not add to totals.

r Revised
NA Not available.   Z Less than one-half of one percent.
[1] Public welfare, hospitals, health, natural resources, housing and urban renewal, airports, water transport and terminals, correction, electric power, gas supply, transit utilities and "other and unallocable."
[2] Data for 1972, 1973 and 1974 are based on 1970 population of 72,670,000; and data for 1975, 1976 and 1977 are based on 1975 estimated population of 72,625,000 for all cities over 50,000 population.

Table 4. Employees and Payrolls for Individual Cities Having 50,000 Population or More: October 1977

City and State	Population, 1975 (estimates)	All employees (full-time and part-time)	Full-time equivalent Total	Education	Highways	Police	Fire	Sewerage	Sanitation	Parks	Financial administration and general control	Other	October payroll (thousands of dollars)	Teachers	Other
ALABAMA															
BIRMINGHAM	276 273	3 981	3 981	—	169	817	693	73	800	296	209	924	3 971	—	997
GADSDEN	50 357	881	877	—	112	95	119	17	102	72	49	311	684	—	782
HUNTSVILLE	136 419	3 267	3 121	—	231	321	267	74	164	138	75	1 851	2 492	—	804
MOBILE	196 441	2 631	2 550	—	226	499	429	82	212	294	174	634	2 385	—	935
MONTGOMERY	153 343	2 579	2 354	—	282	430	356	—	384	278	151	473	1 961	—	835
TUSCALOOSA	69 425	2 145	2 074	—	108	190	158	20	133	—	57	1 408	1 755	—	847
ALASKA															
ANCHORAGE[1][2]	161 018	6 306	5 644	3 213	92	211	239	73	46	95	215	1 460	10 445	1 995	1 778
ARIZONA															
GLENDALE	65 671	649	617	—	39	135	77	5	78	28	74	181	692	—	1 127
MESA	99 043	1 069	1 003	—	106	190	125	10	87	73	123	289	1 121	—	1 121
PHOENIX	664 721	9 486	8 650	—	272	1 977	792	190	600	607	776	3 436	10 098	—	1 177
SCOTTSDALE	77 529	845	760	—	28	158	—	6	49	105	145	269	945	—	1 254
TEMPE	84 072	779	670	—	60	151	87	10	47	87	68	160	772	—	1 154
TUCSON	296 457	4 496	4 281	—	296	694	428	95	307	365	504	1 592	4 595	—	1 088
ARKANSAS															
FORT SMITH	64 734	600	596	—	44	119	119	48	57	21	63	125	503	—	843
LITTLE ROCK	141 143	1 953	1 878	—	148	328	300	101	148	179	92	582	1 548	—	826
NORTH LITTLE ROCK	61 768	860	810	—	65	156	136	31	56	83	39	244	697	—	865
PINE BLUFF	54 631	573	565	—	52	118	76	18	4	26	42	229	364	—	645
CALIFORNIA															
ALAMEDA	72 017	693	585	—	62	121	110	—	—	74	54	164	865	—	1 492
ALHAMBRA	60 715	484	436	—	41	112	90	5	8	37	30	113	574	—	1 321
ANAHEIM	193 616	2 943	2 232	—	150	418	238	7	12	212	217	978	3 152	—	1 433
BAKERSFIELD	77 264	816	755	—	54	219	152	27	65	81	65	92	1 040	—	1 385
BELLFLOWER[3]	51 145	178	127	—	51	6	—	—	2	40	25	3	130	—	1 017
BERKELEY	110 465	1 847	1 498	—	91	277	156	38	166	127	166	477	2 132	—	1 443
BUENA PARK	61 840	492	415	—	32	145	75	3	14	23	53	70	588	—	1 429
BURBANK	86 001	1 433	1 320	—	108	191	114	18	47	115	132	595	1 872	—	1 429
CARSON[3]	78 671	402	300	—	37	—	—	—	6	68	68	121	387	—	1 296
CHULA VISTA	75 497	795	642	—	88	128	70	22	3	92	73	166	758	—	1 188
COMPTON	75 143	750	731	—	29	247	84	—	7	90	110	164	833	—	1 140
CONCORD	95 114	796	596	—	52	161	—	11	3	151	82	136	852	—	1 446
COSTA MESA	76 058	751	603	—	49	170	98	7	5	93	76	105	837	—	1 397
DALY CITY	72 741	627	535	—	26	128	75	—	7	42	48	209	694	—	1 307
DOWNEY	85 812	623	550	—	65	137	88	6	6	84	49	115	751	—	1 382

See footnotes at end of table.

Table 4. Employees and Payrolls for Individual Cities Having 50,000 Population or More: October 1977—Continued

City and State	Population, 1975 (estimates)	All employees (full-time and part-time)	Full-time equivalent Total	Education	Highways	Police	Fire	Sewerage	Sanitation	Parks	Financial administration and general control	Other	October payroll (thousands of dollars)	Avg. Oct. earnings Teachers	Avg. Oct. earnings Other
CALIFORNIA—CON.															
EL CAJON	60 404	523	479	—	45	148	88	12	3	56	62	65	594	—	1 244
EL MONTE	67 698	448	385	—	26	132	61	—	3	44	61	58	527	—	1 389
FREMONT	117 862	836	681	—	73	186	124	—	6	114	108	70	934	—	1 387
FRESNO	176 528	2 666	2 462	—	164	441	300	82	197	243	272	763	3 455	—	1 402
FULLERTON	93 692	917	753	—	102	182	102	—	3	54	93	217	978	—	1 307
GARDEN GROVE	118 454	859	792	—	32	170	93	—	—	81	50	366	1 236	—	1 575
GLENDALE	132 360	1 678	1 497	—	163	224	183	5	69	126	168	559	2 074	—	1 390
HAWTHORNE	53 953	415	326	—	27	94	58	2	—	29	73	43	533	—	1 649
HAYWARD	92 802	860	761	—	38	211	144	32	—	19	77	240	1 034	—	1 366
HUNTINGTON BEACH	149 706	1 415	1 105	—	138	298	165	12	12	125	145	210	1 707	—	1 564
INGLEWOOD	86 610	1 116	759	—	85	225	122	12	27	69	134	85	1 047	—	1 390
LAKEWOOD³	81 802	416	221	—	—	14	—	—	—	113	51	43	264	—	1 221
LONG BEACH	335 602	5 282	4 971	—	86	912	507	73	209	707	263	2 214	7 253	—	1 467
LOS ANGELES	2 727 399	45 707	45 460	—	1 966	10 502	3 337	514	1 237	4 996	3 508	19 400	66 086	—	1 464
MODESTO	83 540	867	788	—	81	174	110	36	42	143	90	112	1 024	—	1 300
MOUNTAIN VIEW	55 143	537	488	—	24	88	65	9	17	58	48	179	676	—	1 391
NEWPORT BEACH	61 853	796	714	—	65	190	110	11	45	73	57	163	1 012	—	1 424
NORWALK³	86 826	177	176	—	50	—	—	4	4	—	31	87	200	—	1 137
OAKLAND	330 651	5 233	4 879	—	334	937	570	49	50	566	316	2 057	7 389	—	1 522
ONTARIO	63 140	722	617	—	27	140	100	3	31	87	68	161	814	—	1 332
ORANGE	82 157	761	675	—	88	163	120	—	6	58	83	157	915	—	1 362
OXNARD	86 506	938	778	—	42	190	97	18	54	77	105	195	1 054	—	1 384
PALO ALTO	52 277	1 805	1 776	—	30	115	128	36	12	82	97	1 276	2 370	—	1 334
PASADENA	108 220	1 732	1 618	—	189	284	143	—	68	94	195	645	2 311	—	1 434
PICO RIVERA³	51 495	228	162	—	61	—	—	—	—	31	43	27	167	—	1 032
POMONA	82 275	1 069	846	—	54	183	144	4	53	95	102	211	1 234	—	1 486
REDONDO BEACH	62 400	605	474	—	28	108	68	1	16	54	46	153	704	—	1 515
REDWOOD CITY	54 160	652	530	—	55	90	80	8	6	52	59	180	674	—	1 277
RICHMOND	69 713	1 108	933	—	72	252	148	26	—	149	76	210	1 396	—	1 515
RIVERSIDE	150 612	1 894	1 648	—	113	309	183	40	140	194	132	537	2 176	—	1 334
SACRAMENTO	260 822	3 766	3 314	—	102	714	474	95	256	404	226	1 043	4 442	—	1 348
SALINAS	70 438	672	611	—	86	160	103	10	5	97	48	102	770	—	1 268
SAN BERNARDINO	102 076	1 661	1 427	—	97	265	167	33	84	108	72	601	1 925	—	1 357
SAN BUENAVENTURA	63 441	687	537	—	22	119	73	34	8	103	81	97	743	—	1 399
SAN DIEGO	773 996	7 570	7 118	—	461	1 395	773	179	326	745	752	2 487	9 807	—	1 387
SAN FRANCISCO	664 520	21 717	21 702	—	313	2 517	1 563	222	266	1 459	2 305	13 057	28 941	—	1 333
SAN JOSE	555 707	4 798	4 303	—	464	979	646	186	96	517	435	980	6 396	—	1 504
SAN LEANDRO	66 953	659	544	—	50	127	92	22	36	74	49	94	780	—	1 445
SAN MATEO	77 878	823	679	—	83	172	110	25	5	132	64	88	880	—	1 309
SANTA ANA	177 304	1 882	1 529	—	123	507	258	3	5	189	132	312	1 943	—	1 287
SANTA BARBARA	72 125	1 058	895	—	90	162	103	29	3	70	92	346	1 235	—	1 393
SANTA CLARA	82 822	992	890	—	75	162	140	8	36	100	108	261	1 315	—	1 490
SANTA MONICA	92 115	1 514	1 261	—	132	222	112	7	54	143	137	454	1 741	—	1 393

See footnotes at end of table.

Table 4. Employees and Payrolls for Individual Cities Having 50,000 Population or More: October 1977—Continued

City and State	Population, 1975 (estimates)	All employees (full-time and part-time)	Full-time equivalent Total	Education	Highways	Police	Fire	Sewerage	Sanitation	Parks	Financial administration and general control	Other	October payroll (thousands of dollars)	Average October earnings Teachers	Average October earnings Other
CALIFORNIA—CON.															
SANTA ROSA	65 087	660	583	-	81	113	79	35	4	49	83	139	743	-	1 283
SIMI VALLEY [2][3]	70 086	236	219	-	30	91	-	28	-	-	67	3	244	-	1 196
SOUTH GATE	56 560	440	381	-	40	124	-	2	2	85	26	102	474	-	1 262
STOCKTON	117 600	1 704	1 519	-	89	327	220	85	47	167	150	434	2 103	-	1 397
SUNNYVALE	102 462	1 170	544	-	61	107	91	14	9	119	45	98	890	-	1 638
TORRANCE	139 776	1 597	1 383	-	71	268	159	7	31	113	145	589	2 073	-	1 508
VALLEJO	70 681	506	491	-	42	140	91	3	5	23	65	130	695	-	1 420
WEST COVINA	75 783	754	490	-	51	124	74	3	5	82	39	112	605	-	1 254
WESTMINSTER	66 758	365	289	-	4	116	58	1	-	15	26	70	470	-	1 639
WHITTIER	72 059	487	371	-	28	128	-	2	33	48	22	110	522	-	1 420
COLORADO															
ARVADA	74 254	363	353	-	40	128	-	12	-	14	73	86	389	-	1 098
AURORA	118 060	1 264	1 124	-	127	252	182	32	6	153	103	269	1 331	-	1 196
BOULDER	78 560	1 127	1 079	-	46	138	66	41	4	457	110	217	1 073	-	1 070
COLORADO SPRINGS	179 584	3 406	3 063	-	142	394	244	129	11	203	100	1 840	3 363	-	1 111
DENVER	484 531	12 558	12 235	-	444	1 650	913	335	405	1 004	777	6 707	14 722	-	1 205
FORT COLLINS	55 984	722	593	-	20	92	66	32	-	70	74	239	625	-	1 073
LAKEWOOD	120 350	842	673	-	94	299	-	-	11	56	95	118	801	-	1 204
PUEBLO	105 312	1 110	935	-	103	235	154	36	11	89	60	247	939	-	1 002
CONNECTICUT															
BRIDGEPORT [4]	142 960	4 653	4 401	2 309	93	403	395	60	118	131	113	779	4 331	1 050	945
BRISTOL	58 560	1 902	1 588	912	42	102	97	26	32	58	59	260	1 938	1 209	1 258
DANBURY [5]	54 512	1 847	1 688	1 044	73	135	95	19	3	13	42	264	1 809	1 320	968
EAST HARTFORD TOWN	54 132	1 704	1 600	1 058	65	120	133	2	52	34	48	88	1 789	1 249	983
FAIRFIELD TOWN	58 084	2 027	1 605	1 022	46	122	94	16	5	54	66	180	2 047	1 506	1 119
GREENWICH TOWN	59 566	2 496	2 079	1 088	100	177	68	20	9	140	81	396	2 650	1 512	1 134
HARTFORD [5]	138 152	6 722	6 372	3 260	310	531	468	-	121	277	232	1 173	6 835	1 240	1 120
MERIDEN	57 697	2 128	1 662	1 013	43	119	108	14	15	67	57	492	2 005	1 141	993
NEW BRITAIN	78 556	1 994	1 662	808	85	167	147	-	-	43	91	321	1 939	1 352	1 037
NEW HAVEN [6]	126 845	4 164	3 890	2 097	77	468	470	55	106	95	147	375	4 100	1 158	1 014
NORWALK	76 688	2 557	2 352	1 509	95	211	151	35	35	73	123	120	2 776	1 394	1 002
STAMFORD [5]	105 151	3 359	3 264	1 998	97	239	199	69	113	51	122	376	3 808	1 325	999
WATERBURY [5]	107 065	3 516	3 152	1 505	71	331	280	69	120	160	189	427	3 292	1 446	838
WEST HARTFORD TOWN	66 605	2 539	1 840	1 156	35	157	110	11	54	74	59	184	2 618	1 766	1 179
WEST HAVEN	53 002	1 540	1 373	865	118	117	-	28	18	63	62	102	1 371	1 292	810
DELAWARE															
WILMINGTON	76 152	3 693	3 136	1 657	27	336	217	60	134	85	190	430	3 689	1 199	1 169

See footnotes at end of table.

Table 4. Employees and Payrolls for Individual Cities Having 50,000 Population or More: October 1977—Continued

City and State	Population, 1975 (estimates)	All employees (full-time and part-time)	Full-time equivalent										October payroll (thousands of dollars)	Average October earnings	
			Total	Education	Highways	Police	Fire	Sewerage	Sanitation	Parks	Financial administration and general control	Other		Teachers	Other
DISTRICT OF COLUMBIA															
WASHINGTON[7][8]	711 518	47 717	45 105	13 986	1 057	4 924	1 489	611	2 011	1 235	2 832	16 960	64 938	1 567	1 409
FLORIDA															
CLEARWATER	67 069	1 502	1 460	-	20	230	163	95	108	235	76	533	1 318	-	905
FORT LAUDERDALE	152 959	2 351	2 333	-	101	601	290	100	122	337	398	384	2 598	-	1 115
GAINESVILLE	72 236	1 346	1 318	-	105	211	168	74	36	111	186	427	1 357	-	1 032
HIALEAH	117 682	1 307	1 095	-	58	291	168	54	142	99	39	244	1 561	-	1 418
HOLLYWOOD	119 002	1 509	1 431	-	157	393	180	71	111	167	125	227	1 604	-	1 126
JACKSONVILLE[1]	535 030	11 660	10 936	-	468	1 599	869	438	249	315	863	6 135	10 765	-	986
MIAMI	365 082	4 439	4 423	-	315	1 148	732	-	581	586	463	598	5 144	-	1 164
MIAMI BEACH	94 063	1 516	1 481	-	34	330	135	40	96	371	162	231	1 786	-	1 208
ORLANDO	113 179	3 438	3 049	-	111	500	379	145	199	378	106	231	3 107	-	1 024
PENSACOLA	64 168	985	962	-	42	158	125	90	81	65	98	303	960	-	999
ST. PETERSBURG	234 389	3 865	3 668	-	221	665	309	-	306	580	406	1 181	3 300	-	903
TALLAHASSEE[2]	83 725	3 045	2 861	-	102	188	128	129	154	101	169	1 890	2 401	-	842
TAMPA	280 340	5 680	5 340	-	568	791	683	353	583	531	523	1 308	5 143	-	967
WEST PALM BEACH	61 471	1 242	1 189	-	35	213	133	104	140	214	80	270	1 086	-	915
GEORGIA															
ALBANY	73 373	1 098	1 032	-	66	219	162	67	80	66	67	305	874	-	845
ATLANTA	436 057	10 446	10 184	-	527	1 564	863	603	719	879	648	4 381	8 885	-	872
AUGUSTA[1]	54 019	1 046	1 014	-	31	195	141	115	73	51	70	338	700	-	689
COLUMBUS[1]	159 352	3 586	3 520	-	88	493	341	92	198	177	430	1 701	2 314	-	656
MACON	121 157	1 944	1 861	-	77	250	300	-	207	129	91	807	1 431	-	769
SAVANNAH	110 348	1 914	1 864	-	67	282	207	115	207	138	117	731	1 354	-	728
HAWAII															
HONOLULU	705 381	10 846	10 249	-	590	1 838	961	478	514	1 235	733	3 900	12 127	-	1 186
IDAHO															
BOISE CITY	99 771	906	894	-	-	177	179	67	-	164	102	205	867	-	971
ILLINOIS															
ARLINGTON HEIGHTS	70 019	468	397	-	47	105	87	11	-	-	24	123	581	-	1 488
AURORA[2]	76 955	714	632	-	44	187	125	16	39	23	48	150	883	-	1 414
BERWYN	49 618	333	283	-	8	77	59	28	28	8	34	41	302	-	1 101
CHAMPAIGN	58 398	1 275	1 066	-	24	122	80	11	-	40	26	763	1 168	-	1 113

See footnotes at end of table.

Table 4. Employees and Payrolls for Individual Cities Having 50,000 Population or More: October 1977—Continued

City and State	Population, 1975 (estimates)	All employees (full-time and part-time)	Full-time equivalent Total	Education	Highways	Police	Fire	Sewerage	Sanitation	Parks	Financial administration and general control	Other	October payroll (thousands of dollars)	Avg Oct earnings Teachers	Avg Oct earnings Other
ILLINOIS--CON.															
CHICAGO	3 099 391	47 261	45 441	-	3 682	16 204	4 874	870	3 117	489	2 073	14 132	62 895	-	1 390
CICERO[9]	63 444	511	420	-	35	113	82	-	40	-	45	105	364	-	862
DECATUR	89 604	646	620	-	37	139	119	8	12	4	44	257	675	-	1 086
DES PLAINES	55 828	514	417	-	42	115	87	10	24	3	28	108	592	-	1 442
EAST ST. LOUIS	57 929	946	903	-	77	176	112	32	14	72	163	257	888	-	982
ELGIN	59 754	535	454	-	51	118	77	8	18	33	46	103	601	-	1 327
EVANSTON	76 665	1 137	911	-	39	210	117	10	42	107	56	330	1 175	-	1 293
JOLIET	74 401	625	605	-	31	204	127	35	15	-	61	132	876	-	1 455
OAK LAWN	62 317	428	384	-	19	115	100	19	5	-	32	94	543	-	1 418
OAK PARK	59 773	812	627	-	19	191	88	5	57	44	52	171	802	-	1 299
PEORIA	125 983	1 026	973	-	91	322	198	10	50	-	75	227	1 362	-	1 413
ROCKFORD	145 459	1 304	1 252	-	51	286	263	17	2	-	104	529	1 456	-	1 168
SKOKIE[2]	67 674	596	531	-	24	138	125	10	46	-	50	138	662	-	1 262
SPRINGFIELD[2]	87 418	1 679	1 481	-	118	239	173	17	15	62	61	796	1 390	-	944
WAUKEGAN[2]	65 133	651	553	-	73	168	111	13	6	-	33	149	657	-	1 177
INDIANA															
ANDERSON	69 486	863	842	-	45	166	152	68	2	36	41	332	735	-	877
EVANSVILLE	133 566	913	853	-	136	316	284	87	-	202	62	766	1 521	-	821
FORT WAYNE	185 299	1 718	1 718	-	68	330	270	78	13	230	85	644	1 644	-	957
GARY	167 546	2 485	2 406	-	113	440	281	73	158	133	166	1 042	1 924	-	796
HAMMOND	104 892	1 448	1 282	-	91	243	185	81	81	60	60	481	1 064	-	836
INDIANAPOLIS[1]	714 878	11 636	11 464	-	412	1 503	845	355	311	708	1 468	5 862	9 155	-	799
MUNCIE	78 329	711	651	-	54	161	132	86	69	35	46	68	532	-	820
SOUTH BEND	117 478	1 602	1 488	-	102	329	278	99	25	138	48	469	1 351	-	935
TERRE HAUTE	63 998	664	630	-	60	181	145	73	-	42	31	98	466	-	754
IOWA															
CEDAR RAPIDS	108 998	1 228	1 117	-	89	197	143	68	101	89	70	360	1 153	-	1 037
COUNCIL BLUFFS	58 660	568	553	-	56	124	91	38	34	38	28	144	558	-	1 009
DAVENPORT	99 941	1 079	890	-	119	174	133	57	56	81	56	214	948	-	1 070
DES MOINES	194 168	2 505	2 323	-	203	404	301	147	131	153	213	771	2 705	-	1 167
DUBUQUE	61 754	662	585	-	38	89	100	46	37	61	40	174	712	-	1 217
SIOUX CITY	85 719	1 083	974	-	89	147	139	48	24	93	76	358	1 032	-	1 062
WATERLOO[2]	77 681	743	703	-	38	160	134	39	42	70	28	192	712	-	1 012

See footnotes at end of table.

Table 4. Employees and Payrolls for Individual Cities Having 50,000 Population or More: October 1977—Continued

City and State	Population, 1975 estimates	All employees (full-time and part-time)	Full-time equivalent										October payroll (thousands of dollars)	Average October earnings	
			Total	Education	Highways	Police	Fire	Sewerage	Sanitation	Parks	Financial administration and general control	Other		Teachers	Other
KANSAS															
KANSAS CITY[2]	168 153	2 016	1 976	—	184	494	419	118	34	162	207	358	1 294	—	814
OVERLAND PARK	81 013	342	325	—	62	125	—	—	1	50	59	28	345	—	1 065
TOPEKA	119 203	2 047	1 730	—	76	302	258	66	65	117	67	779	1 682	—	979
WICHITA	264 901	3 553	3 155	—	255	531	425	100	146	212	295	1 191	3 200	—	1 015
KENTUCKY															
LEXINGTON[1][2]	186 048	2 809	2 530	—	74	660	377	109	286	201	221	602	2 054	—	813
LOUISVILLE	335 954	6 636	6 095	—	47	1 055	754	578	382	599	736	1 944	5 325	—	878
OWENSBORO	50 788	1 835	1 741	—	51	115	96	42	109	47	51	1 230	1 491	—	856
LOUISIANA															
BATON ROUGE	294 394	3 772	3 656	—	288	717	525	104	242	241	536	1 003	3 321	—	907
LAFAYETTE	75 430	1 187	1 135	—	72	161	105	57	104	95	126	415	825	—	730
LAKE CHARLES	76 087	916	888	—	102	135	136	53	152	59	112	139	698	—	787
MONROE[2]	61 016	1 289	1 275	—	28	134	143	26	269	146	69	460	776	—	609
NEW ORLEANS	559 770	12 711	12 527	—	362	2 132	984	626	650	710	1 387	5 676	11 286	—	906
SHREVEPORT	185 711	2 996	2 837	—	63	495	366	204	446	367	159	737	2 040	—	720
MAINE															
PORTLAND[5]	59 857	2 914	2 882	1 193	86	219	277	14	46	196	116	735	2 711	1 434	826
MARYLAND															
BALTIMORE[7]	851 698	38 003	36 630	15 627	815	4 186	2 206	484	1 248	1 626	2 379	8 914	36 871	1 455	897
MASSACHUSETTS															
ARLINGTON TOWN	49 815	1 624	1 500	806	66	124	129	5	42	25	57	246	1 672	1 307	1 013
BOSTON[2]	636 725	27 617	24 937	8 424	556	2 871	2 083	93	114	732	1 936	8 128	33 608	2 081	1 090
BROCKTON	95 878	3 414	3 333	2 204	55	210	241	62	99	46	117	299	3 481	1 108	983
BROOKLINE TOWN[2]	52 590	1 904	1 764	762	86	168	228	7	102	120	60	231	2 650	2 040	1 291
CAMBRIDGE[5]	102 420	4 370	4 026	1 335	51	410	294	12	83	69	175	1 597	4 646	1 265	1 124
CHICOPEE[2]	57 771	2 171	1 745	901	50	131	165	14	44	34	84	453	1 705	1 121	932
FALL RIVER	100 430	3 528	3 201	1 451	170	291	314	36	88	77	146	628	1 178	1 132	903
FRAMINGHAM TOWN[5]	65 540	2 552	2 163	1 500	63	139	176	18	58	12	58	139	1 912	1 272	801
LAWRENCE	67 390	1 989	1 956	877	113	192	234	10	168	31	81	250	2 280	1 384	1 049
LOWELL	91 493	3 392	2 987	1 216	87	224	247	2	75	23	134	979	3 131	1 327	940

See footnotes at end of table.

Table 4. Employees and Payrolls for Individual Cities Having 50,000 Population or More: October 1977—Continued

City and State	Population, 1975 (estimates)	All employees (full-time and part-time)	Full-time equivalent — Total	Education	Highways	Police	Fire	Sewerage	Sanitation	Parks	Financial administration and general control	Other	October payroll (thousands of dollars)	Average October earnings — Teachers	Average October earnings — Other
MASSACHUSETTS—CON.															
LYNN6	79 327	3 195	2 774	1 426	63	198	295	32	76	35	78	571	3 492	1 361	1 188
MALDEN5	55 778	1 701	1 514	850	56	132	166	-	-	22	148	140	1 730	1 333	1 039
MEDFORD5	60 769	1 639	1 510	886	95	155	171	39	-	20	51	93	1 615	1 213	977
NEW BEDFORD	100 133	3 474	3 218	1 728	123	319	294	22	96	37	93	506	3 189	1 041	964
NEWTON2	88 559	3 693	3 017	1 681	192	241	269	37	134	62	109	292	3 501	1 417	1 017
PITTSFIELD6	54 893	1 968	1 837	1 136	80	108	156	24	38	26	56	213	2 054	1 141	1 096
QUINCY7	91 494	4 489	3 934	1 516	136	313	275	17	-	34	96	1 547	5 029	1 685	1 126
SOMERVILLE	80 798	2 542	2 275	989	55	162	203	11	82	22	76	675	2 742	1 414	1 079
SPRINGFIELD	170 790	7 061	6 233	2 731	173	529	514	195	193	294	338	1 266	6 742	1 047	989
WALTHAM2	56 251	1 944	1 783	1 004	59	151	181	11	69	32	82	194	1 992	1 178	1 074
WEYMOUTH TOWN5	56 815	1 849	1 827	1 097	43	144	154	22	36	22	38	271	1 985	1 330	1 063
WORCESTER	171 566	8 914	8 116	3 029	348	679	507	80	133	194	500	2 646	7 894	1 263	880
MICHIGAN															
ANN ARBOR2	103 542	1 463	1 267	-	54	186	119	50	57	87	146	568	1 481	-	1 179
DEARBORN5	98 986	1 694	1 389	-	92	314	130	16	67	201	144	425	1 868	-	1 360
DEARBORN HEIGHTS	79 239	446	385	-	38	111	70	30	-	13	48	75	487	-	1 274
DETROIT2	1 335 085	24 174	23 942	-	612	6 305	1 915	312	2 276	1 458	1 256	9 808	33 671	-	1 405
FARMINGTON HILLS	54 124	341	240	-	29	84	24	-	-	21	34	48	303	-	1 271
FLINT	174 218	4 365	3 974	-	147	497	296	85	90	156	287	2 416	4 677	-	1 181
GRAND RAPIDS	187 946	2 380	2 208	-	122	479	273	98	37	289	334	576	2 414	-	1 094
KALAMAZOO	79 542	1 142	1 076	-	120	211	153	62	-	74	148	308	1 208	-	1 127
LANSING	126 805	2 339	2 256	-	103	321	240	80	55	215	222	1 020	2 992	-	1 329
LINCOLN PARK	49 514	391	317	-	57	88	36	1	2	33	55	45	413	-	1 317
LIVONIA	114 881	982	787	-	115	223	108	18	-	75	101	147	1 120	-	1 439
PONTIAC	76 027	2 846	2 582	-	76	283	134	69	57	103	256	1 604	3 130	-	1 227
ROSEVILLE	58 141	337	313	-	28	97	47	13	16	12	49	64	468	-	1 500
ROYAL OAK	79 191	643	532	-	10	124	88	5	67	39	81	118	720	-	1 369
SAGINAW	86 202	1 360	1 264	-	58	225	134	86	19	173	97	472	1 351	-	1 084
ST. CLAIR SHORES	85 934	544	473	-	29	115	67	12	37	66	55	92	559	-	1 189
SOUTHFIELD	75 978	847	668	-	45	187	106	18	-	72	122	136	977	-	1 478
STERLING HEIGHTS	86 932	545	533	-	28	191	77	18	-	32	85	102	706	-	1 325
TAYLOR	76 626	480	427	-	65	119	58	13	36	41	56	39	565	-	1 321
WARREN	172 755	1 323	1 164	-	78	289	191	47	82	42	204	231	1 787	-	1 536
WESTLAND	92 689	440	398	-	41	107	65	11	3	29	72	70	549	-	1 382
WYOMING	57 918	525	394	-	32	114	33	26	-	28	63	98	482	-	1 219
MINNESOTA															
BLOOMINGTON	79 210	601	505	-	33	102	1	15	4	74	75	201	666	-	1 347
DULUTH	93 971	1 522	1 315	-	144	159	154	36	-	64	148	610	1 598	-	1 218
MINNEAPOLIS	378 112	6 080	5 337	-	628	908	533	140	188	660	541	1 739	7 531	-	1 414
ROCHESTER	56 211	751	611	-	64	111	92	23	12	65	35	209	721	-	1 187
ST. PAUL	279 535	3 766	3 483	-	298	712	511	55	169	520	295	923	4 831	-	1 391

See footnotes at end of table.

Table 4. Employees and Payrolls for Individual Cities Having 50,000 Population or More: October 1977—Continued

City and State	Population, 1975 (estimates)	All employees (full-time and part-time)	Full-time equivalent Total	Education	Highways	Police	Fire	Sewerage	Sanitation	Parks	Financial administration and general control	Other	October payroll (thousands of dollars)	Average October earnings Teachers	Average October earnings Other
MISSISSIPPI														
BILOXI.	46 407	530	503	—	46	105	86	29	51	42	46	98	325	—	648
JACKSON.	166 512	2 978	2 784	—	224	505	370	106	256	188	171	964	2 179	—	788
MISSOURI														
COLUMBIA	63 227	871	770	—	67	108	106	36	37	85	64	267	810	—	1 065
FLORISSANT . . .	70 465	316	236	—	20	99	—	—	1	44	29	43	216	—	946
INDEPENDENCE . .	111 481	1 192	1 106	—	58	188	165	69	7	71	112	436	1 162	—	1 055
KANSAS CITY. . .	472 529	7 047	6 950	—	518	1 755	1 016	305	101	629	594	2 032	7 951	—	1 146
ST. JOSEPH . . .	77 679	739	696	—	91	161	163	29	5	62	56	129	617	—	896
ST. LOUIS. . . .	524 964	14 995	14 478	—	579	2 848	995	—	475	931	1 179	7 471	14 178	—	983
SPRINGFIELD. . .	131 557	2 081	1 985	—	117	211	192	115	20	107	67	1 156	2 252	—	1 141
MONTANA														
BILLINGS	68 987	826	776	—	48	140	113	58	65	22	57	273	814	—	1 057
GREAT FALLS[2] . .	60 868	560	519	—	69	103	80	17	46	32	43	129	546	—	1 056
NEBRASKA														
LINCOLN.	163 112	3 244	2 933	—	191	295	244	78	70	227	186	1 642	2 882	—	990
OMAHA.	371 455	3 404	3 199	—	351	697	544	206	36	246	270	849	3 546	—	1 112
NEVADA														
LAS VEGAS. . . .	146 030	1 293	1 238	—	72	—	311	31	15	128	348	333	1 470	—	1 186
RENO	78 097	1 102	1 053	—	49	347	205	38	—	92	100	222	1 403	—	1 342
NEW HAMPSHIRE														
MANCHESTER . . .	83 417	2 900	2 648	1 341	154	200	217	33	86	58	74	485	2 645	1 102	938
NASHUA	61 002	1 860	1 633	992	38	154	117	34	60	26	73	139	1 611	1 075	936
NEW JERSEY														
BAYONNE[2]	73 574	2 066	1 882	852	56	240	199	37	74	68	76	280	2 382	1 450	1 182
BLOOMFIELD . . .	52 162	503	442	—	20	147	113	5	10	6	57	84	539	—	1 231
CAMDEN	89 214	1 882	1 811	—	72	441	327	14	58	24	104	771	1 655	—	917
CHERRY HILL TWP. .	68 794	517	430	—	49	131	1	31	35	6	77	100	500	—	1 184
CLIFTON[6]	79 467	1 770	1 470	844	60	166	153	11	13	30	68	125	1 923	1 613	1 107
DOVER TWP. . . .	63 653	558	489	—	55	192	—	—	49	—	64	129	549	—	1 136

See footnotes at end of table.

295

Table 4. Employees and Payrolls for Individual Cities Having 50,000 Population or More: October 1977—Continued

City and State	Population, 1975 (estimates)	All employees (full-time and part-time)	Full-time equivalent Total	Education	Highways	Police	Fire	Sewerage	Sanitation	Parks	Financial administration and general control	Other	October payroll (thousands of dollars)	Avg. Oct. earnings Teachers	Avg. Oct. earnings Other
NEW JERSEY--CON.															
EAST ORANGE	73 420	2 585	2 495	1 236	59	306	182	14	55	57	247	339	3 012	1 451	1 057
EDISON TWP	66 274	2 349	1 987	1 356	55	195	97	16	72	34	58	104	1 743	847	930
ELIZABETH	104 405	3 896	3 230	1 628	8	358	283	17	382	37	237	280	3 920	1 448	1 081
HAMILTON TWP (MERCER CO.)[2]	83 126	635	567	-	149	167	-	53	-	4	70	124	574	-	1 021
IRVINGTON[2]	58 196	752	688	-	30	186	152	4	37	35	60	184	750	-	1 088
JERSEY CITY	243 756	8 458	8 098	3 131	55	1 093	740	30	169	239	244	2 397	9 500	1 389	1 092
MIDDLETOWN TWP	58 535	430	332	-	128	98	-	-	-	-	57	48	304	-	909
NEWARK	339 568	17 847	17 521	8 102	237	1 672	965	46	440	223	701	5 135	18 366	1 377	908
PARSIPPANY-TROY HILLS TWP	50 104	448	410	-	69	91	1	48	-	18	51	132	408	-	1 001
PASSAIC	49 900	732	732	-	42	171	138	4	2	22	33	320	626	-	854
PATERSON[2]	136 098	4 453	4 110	2 172	150	499	422	46	61	61	164	535	4 382	1 211	971
TRENTON	101 365	2 164	2 079	-	99	471	288	54	65	97	123	882	2 305	-	1 116
UNION CITY	52 648	1 308	1 165	-	30	196	132	13	94	156	68	476	1 078	-	940
UNION TWP	51 113	474	375	-	24	153	133	2	1	1	30	32	478	-	1 286
VINELAND	53 637	2 048	1 701	1 132	43	124	19	-	18	17	90	258	1 900	1 335	968
WOODBRIDGE TWP	95 798	1 059	922	-	52	178	-	31	85	36	112	428	911	-	995
NEW MEXICO															
ALBUQUERQUE	279 401	4 262	4 045	-	101	732	499	127	226	483	413	1 464	4 237	-	1 054
NEW YORK															
ALBANY	110 311	2 845	2 727	-	108	461	334	10	72	383	172	1 187	1 791	-	651
BINGHAMTON	60 666	2 016	1 825	-	122	162	185	38	43	57	63	1 155	1 699	-	929
BUFFALO	407 160	13 653	12 588	5 609	221	1 395	1 071	300	506	249	266	2 971	16 895	1 881	1 105
MOUNT VERNON[2]	67 687	924	860	-	57	199	139	9	97	57	58	258	1 050	-	1 212
NEW ROCHELLE[2]	71 841	1 060	958	-	65	242	181	18	94	57	71	230	1 131	-	1 178
NEW YORK CITY[7]	7 481 613	349 306	310 606	96 725	6 015	29 405	11 861	1 925	10 213	4 964	8 100	141 398	429 051	1 623	1 314
NIAGARA FALLS	80 773	1 174	1 134	-	69	238	181	43	73	149	123	258	1 294	-	1 143
ROCHESTER[6]	267 173	9 762	8 544	4 763	162	791	688	-	412	290	355	1 083	11 475	1 833	1 080
ROME	49 014	1 113	951	-	46	75	99	6	17	16	51	641	837	-	884
SCHENECTADY	74 995	802	750	-	30	186	193	38	57	66	57	123	876	-	1 169
SYRACUSE	182 543	6 652	5 860	3 166	160	539	518	38	162	188	219	870	6 228	1 146	1 018
TROY	60 312	798	736	-	59	170	175	20	43	57	55	157	644	-	870
UTICA	82 443	1 439	1 380	-	6	211	233	11	49	397	113	360	1 373	-	999
YONKERS	192 509	5 618	4 625	2 401	8	516	425	28	236	138	128	745	6 620	1 701	1 270

See footnotes at end of table.

Table 4. Employees and Payrolls for Individual Cities Having 50,000 Population or More: October 1977—Continued

City and State	Population, 1975 (estimates)	All employees (full-time and part-time)	Full-time equivalent — Total	Education	Highways	Police	Fire	Sewerage	Sanitation	Parks	Financial administration and general control	Other	October payroll (thousands of dollars)	Avg. Oct. earnings — Teachers	Avg. Oct. earnings — Other
NORTH CAROLINA															
ASHEVILLE	59 591	1 199	1 111	-	64	158	144	25	100	145	68	407	771	...	697
CHARLOTTE	281 417	4 448	4 368	-	553	717	625	204	470	203	296	1 296	4 371	...	1 001
DURHAM	101 224	1 716	1 528	-	154	347	123	72	131	85	107	509	1 280	...	843
FAYETTEVILLE	65 915	1 178	1 144	-	86	209	138	61	129	67	71	383	883	...	773
GREENSBORO	155 848	2 521	2 036	-	119	439	286	113	161	166	110	642	2 006	...	986
HIGH POINT	61 330	1 268	1 152	-	78	189	179	39	111	106	104	346	983	...	856
RALEIGH	134 231	1 879	1 740	-	151	349	289	66	203	212	199	271	1 623	...	937
WILMINGTON	53 818	687	668	-	78	112	134	56	58	57	71	102	646	...	967
WINSTON-SALEM	141 018	2 193	2 078	-	107	457	187	64	240	270	149	604	1 721	...	831
NORTH DAKOTA															
FARGO	56 058	557	501	-	44	104	86	11	43	2	38	173	630	...	1 256
OHIO															
AKRON	251 747	3 390	3 165	-	430	523	341	214	169	204	420	864	3 902	...	1 231
CANTON	101 852	1 449	1 345	-	95	277	189	98	69	51	158	408	1 237	...	924
CINCINNATI	412 564	7 986	7 613	-	414	1 204	861	674	486	768	938	2 260	6 312	...	1 137
CLEVELAND	638 793	11 109	10 795	-	562	2 555	1 161	114	623	1 006	756	4 018	12 809	...	1 190
CLEVELAND HEIGHTS	51 141	553	460	-	21	92	76	11	32	15	63	150	343	...	751
COLUMBUS	535 610	7 321	7 179	-	419	1 352	904	352	587	596	740	2 229	8 242	...	1 150
DAYTON	205 986	2 935	2 915	-	78	730	435	96	166	107	399	904	3 671	...	1 260
ELYRIA	52 474	568	523	-	41	73	75	21	10	24	91	188	685	...	1 316
EUCLID[2]	63 307	764	710	-	70	128	97	45	78	19	84	283	776	...	1 091
HAMILTON	66 469	834	807	-	31	122	107	29	43	89	98	288	962	...	1 193
KETTERING	69 949	459	369	-	63	87	32	-	-	52	59	76	444	...	1 213
LAKEWOOD	65 395	1 638	1 477	-	51	98	76	23	89	52	37	1 051	1 463	...	996
LIMA	51 372	621	611	-	73	132	89	43	17	55	78	124	608	...	999
LORAIN[2]	84 907	845	788	-	47	111	107	47	77	35	66	298	742	...	946
MANSFIELD	56 916	805	624	-	44	112	102	35	20	22	75	214	570	...	932
PARMA	98 883	686	603	-	40	114	101	16	53	23	256	-	661	...	1 106
SPRINGFIELD	77 317	816	808	-	74	151	147	31	43	81	115	166	862	...	1 066
TOLEDO	367 650	3 959	3 818	-	264	858	572	269	408	209	451	787	5 069	...	1 331
WARREN	60 486	609	609	-	-	145	87	35	47	31	57	207	644	...	1 058
YOUNGSTOWN	132 203	1 850	1 751	-	135	297	233	69	74	52	194	697	1 770	...	1 010
OKLAHOMA															
LAWTON	76 421	767	743	-	74	137	107	40	83	58	105	139	657	...	887
MIDWEST CITY	50 105	994	892	-	21	95	80	-	53	20	51	572	721	...	813
NORMAN	59 948	1 221	1 192	-	57	124	106	30	63	74	74	669	966	...	816
OKLAHOMA CITY[2]	365 916	4 691	4 408	-	279	848	751	101	198	476	392	1 363	4 405	...	1 001
TULSA[2]	331 726	3 614	3 522	-	204	771	664	130	306	312	166	969	3 272	...	930

See footnotes at end of table.

Table 4. Employees and Payrolls for Individual Cities Having 50,000 Population or More: October 1977—Continued

City and State	Population, 1975 (estimates)	All employees (full-time and part-time)	Full-time equivalent										October payroll (thousands of dollars)	Average October earnings	
			Total	Education	Highways	Police	Fire	Sewerage	Sanitation	Parks	Financial administration and general control	Other		Teachers	Other
OREGON															
EUGENE	92 451	1 536	1 325	–	81	233	163	43	26	154	133	492	1 644	–	1 249
PORTLAND	356 732	4 534	4 338	–	483	952	669	306	76	516	554	782	6 344	–	1 467
SALEM	78 168	1 140	1 128	–	127	194	154	70	–	114	198	271	1 034	–	918
PENNSYLVANIA															
ABINGTON TWP	60 032	346	284	–	41	107	1	27	46	–	13	49	315	–	1 134
ALLENTOWN	106 624	962	927	–	81	203	179	68	35	71	107	183	1 063	–	1 152
ALTOONA	59 692	615	586	–	53	104	100	36	11	9	40	233	511	–	875
BETHLEHEM	73 827	842	778	–	46	178	116	33	8	87	82	228	796	–	1 028
BRISTOL TWP	66 184	265	240	–	73	115	–	–	2	6	13	31	237	–	1 018
CHESTER	48 529	715	649	–	30	172	54	–	51	32	45	265	644	–	996
ERIE[9]	127 895	1 410	1 222	–	89	252	214	84	75	50	134	324	973	–	809
HARRISBURG[2]	58 274	877	804	–	35	205	107	40	131	52	91	143	696	–	866
HAVERFORD TWP	55 385	321	281	–	49	101	–	9	28	–	33	61	280	–	1 009
LANCASTER	56 669	703	680	–	72	166	115	42	16	56	72	141	688	–	1 030
LOWER MERION TWP	60 099	467	421	–	43	150	5	15	65	–	26	117	512	–	1 226
PENN-HILLS TWP	62 605	338	252	–	58	98	1	47	–	–	22	26	254	–	995
PHILADELPHIA	1 815 808	38 593	37 768	–	1 208	9 949	3 108	670	4 046	2 182	5 023	11 582	49 187	–	1 303
PITTSBURGH	458 651	5 984	5 737	–	516	1 204	1 079	–	519	522	435	1 058	6 349	–	1 116
READING	81 592	934	847	–	54	204	108	37	15	92	88	249	854	–	1 017
SCRANTON	95 884	1 024	984	–	34	224	220	50	59	84	63	250	928	–	947
UPPER DARBY TWP[2]	91 521	596	481	–	30	195	5	28	69	48	44	62	490	–	1 017
WILKES-BARRE	57 040	624	616	–	37	120	110	15	31	28	69	206	590	–	959
RHODE ISLAND															
CRANSTON	74 381	2 340	2 148	1 316	78	206	170	35	5	12	98	228	2 499	1 491	913
PAWTUCKET	72 024	2 098	1 949	975	28	213	155	9	68	48	96	357	2 289	1 578	906
PROVIDENCE[6]	167 724	4 712	4 473	2 160	189	460	496	120	146	142	195	565	4 795	1 591	814
WARWICK	85 875	2 682	2 456	1 538	96	234	214	16	40	33	127	158	2 924	1 430	998
SOUTH CAROLINA															
CHARLESTON	57 470	1 355	1 317	–	83	280	214	–	143	198	95	304	1 043	–	791
COLUMBIA	111 616	1 585	1 544	–	103	247	255	86	208	151	146	348	1 288	–	835
GREENVILLE[2]	58 518	901	880	–	76	189	133	7	116	89	53	217	693	–	786
NORTH CHARLESTON	58 544	335	327	–	80	98	61	–	29	23	27	9	236	–	719
SOUTH DAKOTA															
SIOUX FALLS	73 925	875	773	–	85	136	121	45	5	76	47	258	867	–	1 123

See footnotes at end of table.

Table 4. Employees and Payrolls for Individual Cities Having 50,000 Population or More: October 1977—Continued

City and State	Population, 1975 (estimates)	All employees (full-time and part-time)	Full-time equivalent										October payroll (thousands of dollars)	Average October earnings	
			Total	Education	For selected functions									Teachers	Other
					Highways	Police	Fire	Sewerage	Sanitation	Parks	Financial administration and general control	Other			
TENNESSEE															
CHATTANOOGA	161 978	7 344	6 591	3 101	162	390	402	162	411	125	161	1 677	6 314	1 171	870
KNOXVILLE	183 383	5 675	5 484	2 748	113	405	456	131	139	133	79	1 280	5 061	918	918
MEMPHIS	661 319	26 315	24 657	10 912	469	1 615	1 650	350	1 585	1 686	138	6 252	24 531	1 237	878
NASHVILLE-DAVIDSON[1]	423 426	18 416	17 769	7 515	482	1 399	844	284	400	418	843	5 584	16 983	1 289	825
TEXAS															
ABILENE	96 459	1 068	1 025	--	70	144	141	26	112	113	67	352	873	--	854
AMARILLO	138 743	1 544	1 469	--	95	309	210	34	114	83	150	474	1 373	--	937
ARLINGTON	110 543	1 182	1 095	--	93	210	139	20	6	200	86	341	1 104	--	1 014
AUSTIN	301 147	6 711	6 325	--	180	763	519	222	195	463	648	3 335	6 461	--	1 024
BEAUMONT	113 696	1 336	1 320	--	182	239	215	63	122	101	130	268	1 385	--	1 051
BROWNSVILLE	72 157	948	927	--	135	123	84	43	91	95	76	280	623	--	672
CORPUS CHRISTI	214 838	2 969	2 861	--	164	399	320	128	217	297	240	1 096	2 691	--	942
DALLAS	812 797	13 596	13 391	--	592	2 694	1 514	430	710	901	1 701	4 849	14 546	--	1 088
EL PASO	385 691	4 192	4 109	--	268	902	480	112	467	237	340	1 303	14 466	--	1 087
FORT WORTH	358 364	4 973	4 786	--	322	854	605	288	311	683	594	1 129	4 450	--	933
GALVESTON	60 125	2 011	1 960	--	53	170	107	51	92	49	67	1 371	1 839	--	936
GARLAND	111 322	1 209	1 148	--	57	185	142	44	67	68	62	523	1 254	--	1 101
GRAND PRARIE	56 842	493	438	--	23	91	59	8	8	52	47	150	390	--	901
HOUSTON	1 326 809	16 051	15 762	--	1 045	3 728	2 344	726	1 006	1 150	1 048	4 715	16 606	--	1 057
IRVING	103 703	895	862	--	43	180	144	62	85	82	129	137	865	--	1 006
LAREDO[2]	76 998	988	974	--	147	83	109	30	127	53	42	383	613	--	632
LUBBOCK	163 525	1 852	1 771	--	90	282	262	54	132	164	211	576	1 453	--	824
MESQUITE	61 933	526	522	--	-	114	86	14	87	54	63	104	542	--	1 038
MIDLAND	62 950	711	695	--	83	145	108	18	38	51	67	185	644	--	926
ODESSA	84 476	622	593	--	33	154	124	24	49	-	101	108	599	--	1 010
PASADENA	94 670	824	777	--	105	203	6	36	111	66	89	161	754	--	976
PORT ARTHUR	53 557	714	702	--	67	125	89	38	65	22	76	220	727	--	1 040
RICHARDSON	59 190	639	574	--	48	105	101	18	62	67	53	120	584	--	1 024
SAN ANGELO	66 099	776	737	--	72	151	126	24	16	62	69	217	591	--	802
SAN ANTONIO	773 248	11 868	11 459	--	610	1 565	1 033	284	419	897	888	5 763	11 427	--	1 001
TYLER	61 434	680	646	--	38	118	97	23	101	32	48	189	547	--	850
WACO	97 607	1 471	1 418	--	157	240	166	33	109	142	138	433	1 130	--	800
WICHITA FALLS[2]	95 008	1 306	1 306	--	77	173	146	53	115	46	80	616	818	--	626
UTAH															
OGDEN	68 978	673	616	--	62	141	124	4	21	47	64	153	591	--	964
PROVO	55 593	581	462	--	19	76	51	13	32	34	55	182	521	--	1 137
SALT LAKE CITY	169 917	2 743	2 405	--	322	550	398	63	82	156	267	567	2 536	--	1 067

See footnotes at end of table.

Table 4. Employees and Payrolls for Individual Cities Having 50,000 Population or More: October 1977—Continued

City and State	Population, 1975 (estimates)	All employees (full-time and part-time)	Full-time equivalent Total	Education	Highways	Police	Fire	Sewerage	Sanitation	Parks	Financial administration and general control	Other	October payroll (thousands of dollars)	Teachers	Other
VIRGINIA															
ALEXANDRIA	105 220	4 009	3 342	1 661	71	283	198	67	80	75	239	668	4 007	1 337	1 146
CHESAPEAKE	104 459	4 452	4 384	2 720	253	298	159	41	87	141	153	532	3 941	1 012	822
HAMPTON	125 013	5 146	4 296	2 907	92	257	147	30	70	182	188	423	3 864	1 156	749
LYNCHBURG	63 066	2 402	2 186	1 136	82	174	164	19	67	79	104	361	2 041	1 090	844
NEWPORT NEWS	138 760	6 107	5 642	3 395	84	299	213	60	162	148	248	1 033	4 698	975	743
NORFOLK	286 694	12 116	10 944	4 636	281	749	493	98	284	661	405	3 337	9 625	1 036	825
PORTSMOUTH	108 674	4 700	4 163	2 138	71	252	219	68	156	122	168	969	3 567	953	825
RICHMOND	232 652	11 198	10 692	4 583	235	667	559	193	361	473	506	3 115	10 844	1 227	928
ROANOKE	100 585	3 963	3 583	1 763	184	266	244	53	285	47	118	623	6 436	1 147	853
VIRGINIA BEACH	213 954	8 773	8 095	5 063	355	564	200	41	280	227	274	1 091	6 733	1 027	699
WASHINGTON															
BELLEVUE	65 365	662	600	--	67	107	139	20	2	62	103	100	799	--	1 327
SEATTLE	487 091	9 550	8 456	--	731	1 395	992	64	81	867	1 267	3 059	11 679	--	1 390
SPOKANE	173 698	2 130	1 856	--	118	305	321	93	153	184	172	510	2 241	--	1 216
TACOMA	151 267	3 103	2 902	--	279	288	350	95	95	3	527	1 265	4 036	--	1 395
WEST VIRGINIA															
CHARLESTON	67 348	1 042	1 029	--	134	201	155	58	95	123	116	147	894	--	869
HUNTINGTON	68 811	935	901	--	99	177	156	80	164	4	95	126	785	--	871
WISCONSIN															
APPLETON	59 182	1 548	1 341	820	73	107	102	20	36	50	38	95	1 623	1 400	1 052
GREEN BAY	91 189	3 244	2 777	1 751	139	199	181	14	96	98	81	218	3 102	1 315	955
KENOSHA	80 727	881	808	--	89	189	136	19	40	79	53	203	887	--	1 100
MADISON	168 196	5 402	4 765	2 612	122	376	265	--	79	237	248	826	6 230	1 408	1 246
MILWAUKEE	665 796	9 765	9 319	--	1 275	2 315	1 125	311	862	89	676	2 666	12 098	--	1 296
OSHKOSH	50 107	1 503	1 465	882	69	103	98	32	27	34	57	163	1 367	949	925
RACINE	94 744	1 535	1 101	--	72	299	172	51	63	136	64	244	1 379	--	1 258
WAUWATOSA[5]	56 514	1 487	1 400	766	39	109	116	2	56	13	78	221	1 513	1 186	1 139
WEST ALLIS	69 084	1 876	1 673	952	16	161	140	6	90	25	122	161	2 298	1 581	1 223

[1] Data are for city and county (borough) consolidated government.

[2] Data are for October 1976.

[3] Employment and Payrolls are considerably limited due to contract arrangements with county governments for performance of certain municipal services.

[4] Education data are for October 1973.

[5] Education data are for October 1976.

[6] Noneducation data are for October 1976.

[7] Includes data for municipally operated institution(s) of higher education.

[8] Data for local schools are for October 1975.

[9] Data are for October 1974.

PART IV

HISTORICAL STATISTICS

The three tables in this section are from the 1972 Census of Governments. However, since 1977 data are provided in Parts I–III of this compilation, the user can combine them with the statistics in this section that run through 1972 to obtain an historical perspective. The first table in this section contains summary data on government finances back to 1902, although the figures are not adjusted for inflation. The second table shows selected State and local finance items by State per $1000 of personal income from 1957 to fiscal year 1972. The third table is on government employment and goes back to 1953. It shows State-by-State employment totals, percentages of employment by functional area, and employees per 10,000 persons.

Table 1. Finances of All Governments (Federal, State, and Local): 1902 to 1971-72

(Millions of dollars)

Item	1971-72	1970-71	1969-70	1968-69	1967-68	1966-67	1965-66	1964-65	1963-64
REVENUE									
TOTAL.	382 835	342 489	333 810	312 638	265 639	252 563	225 547	202 585	192 412
GENERAL REVENUE.	308 322	275 669	272 480	258 242	217 323	206 696	188 368	169 691	160 740
TAXES.	263 342	232 252	232 877	222 708	185 126	176 121	160 742	144 953	138 292
INDIVIDUAL INCOME.	109 964	98 130	101 224	96 157	76 034	67 352	60 206	52 882	52 488
CORPORATION INCOME	36 582	30 209	36 567	39 858	31 183	36 198	32 111	27 390	25 188
SALES, GROSS RECEIPTS, AND CUSTOMS	57 619	52 660	48 619	44 345	39 186	36 336	33 726	32 904	30 538
PROPERTY	42 877	37 852	34 054	30 673	27 747	26 047	24 670	22 583	21 241
OTHER.	16 301	13 402	12 413	11 675	10 976	10 188	10 029	9 194	8 838
CHARGES AND MISCELLANEOUS.	44 980	43 417	39 603	35 534	32 197	30 575	27 626	24 739	22 448
UTILITY AND LIQUOR STORES REVENUE.	9 829	9 359	8 614	7 840	7 502	6 911	6 619	6 355	5 975
INSURANCE TRUST REVENUE[1]	64 684	57 461	52 716	46 557	40 814	38 956	30 558	26 539	25 697
EMPLOYEE RETIREMENT.	10 524	9 366	8 206	7 133	6 240	5 492	4 870	4 494	4 078
UNEMPLOYMENT COMPENSATION.	3 713	3 215	3 224	3 174	3 103	3 421	3 476	3 387	3 404
OLD AGE, SURVIVORS, DISABILITY, AND HEALTH . . .	47 341	41 909	38 485	33 649	29 029	27 663	20 023	16 742	16 386
OTHER INSURANCE TRUST.	3 108	2 971	2 802	2 600	2 441	2 380	2 083	1 916	1 829
EXPENDITURE, BY CHARACTER AND OBJECT									
TOTAL.	399 098	369 423	332 985	308 344	282 645	257 800	224 813	205 682	196 431
CURRENT OPERATION.	226 953	214 713	197 020	181 547	165 515	153 458	130 488	122 614	111 496
CAPITAL OUTLAY	55 446	48 823	47 519	47 246	47 057	42 101	39 981	33 744	36 905
CONSTRUCTION	33 223	31 051	28 402	26 836	24 772	23 832	22 411	20 885	19 420
EQUIPMENT.	18 039	13 660	15 893	16 916	18 728	14 681	13 995	9 586	14 576
LAND AND EXISTING STRUCTURES	4 183	4 113	3 225	3 494	3 557	3 588	3 574	3 274	2 909
ASSISTANCE AND SUBSIDIES	28 005	25 357	20 764	18 288	16 450	14 694	13 363	12 493	12 750
INTEREST ON DEBT[1]	24 061	22 503	19 160	17 663	15 496	13 985	12 857	11 952	11 119
INSURANCE BENEFITS AND REPAYMENTS.	64 634	58 028	48 521	43 600	38 127	33 561	28 126	24 880	24 161
EXHIBIT: EXPENDITURE FOR PERSONAL SERVICES. . . .	133 764	120 107	110 499	99 068	89 375	81 270	72 963	65 724	61 361
EXPENDITURE, BY FUNCTION									
TOTAL.	399 098	369 423	332 985	308 344	282 645	257 800	224 813	205 682	196 431
GENERAL EXPENDITURE.	323 066	301 096	275 017	255 924	236 348	216 888	189 406	173 745	166 088
NATIONAL DEFENSE AND INTERNATIONAL RELATIONS . .	79 258	80 910	84 253	84 496	83 874	74 638	60 832	55 810	57 326
MILITARY FUNCTIONS ONLY.	71 995	73 639	76 550	77 179	76 747	66 782	53 770	48 385	49 341
POSTAL SERVICE	9 366	8 683	7 722	6 993	6 485	6 227	5 706	5 261	4 775
SPACE RESEARCH AND TECHNOLOGY.	3 369	3 334	3 691	4 189	4 645	5 359	5 869	5 058	4 140
EDUCATION.	70 918	64 042	55 771	50 377	43 614	40 214	34 837	29 613	27 342
INSTITUTIONS OF HIGHER EDUCATION	15 861	14 785	12 924	11 551	10 214	8 932	7 207	5 863	5 278
LOCAL SCHOOLS.	46 671	41 766	37 461	33 752	29 305	27 590	25 091	21 966	20 399
OTHER EDUCATION.	8 386	7 490	5 385	5 074	4 093	3 692	2 539	1 785	1 665
HIGHWAYS	19 453	18 396	16 746	15 738	14 654	14 033	12 895	12 348	11 828
PUBLIC WELFARE	23 604	20 446	17 517	14 730	11 245	9 592	6 965	6 420	5 880
CASH ASSISTANCE, CATEGORICAL PROGRAMS. . . .	9 847	8 662	6 917	5 737	4 849	4 388	3 829	3 697	3 491
CASH ASSISTANCE, OTHER	726	642	554	515	420	295	266	256	258
OTHER PUBLIC WELFARE	13 032	11 141	10 046	8 479	5 975	4 909	2 872	2 467	2 131
HOSPITALS.	12 796	11 141	9 693	8 593	7 801	6 951	6 297	5 867	5 461
HEALTH	4 392	3 694	3 895	3 337	2 778	2 506	2 065	1 805	1 618
POLICE PROTECTION.	6 559	5 706	4 903	4 242	3 700	3 331	3 033	2 792	2 586
LOCAL FIRE PROTECTION.	2 579	2 303	2 024	1 793	1 623	1 499	1 376	1 306	1 222
SANITATION	4 846	4 087	3 413	2 969	2 707	2 523	2 571	2 360	2 267
NATURAL RESOURCES.	14 228	13 740	11 469	10 024	9 200	10 145	10 301	11 121	10 042
STABILIZATION OF FARM PRICES AND INCOME. . . .	4 895	5 227	4 261	2 933	2 598	3 496	4 206	5 803	4 989
LOCAL PARKS AND RECREATION	2 318	2 109	1 888	1 645	1 412	1 291	1 187	1 104	1 022
HOUSING AND URBAN RENEWAL.	5 364	4 467	3 189	2 505	2 841	2 413	2 415	2 198	2 037
AIR TRANSPORTATION[2].	3 697	3 176	2 065	1 630	1 360	1 326	1 226	1 198	1 109
WATER TRANSPORT AND TERMINALS[3]	2 245	2 150	1 904	1 993	1 983	1 886	1 673	1 529	1 404
CORRECTION	2 223	1 979	1 709	1 457	1 335	1 199	1 077	1 033	939
SOCIAL INSURANCE ADMINISTRATION.	2 291	2 031	1 790	1 572	1 378	1 210	1 108	894	834
FINANCIAL ADMINISTRATION	4 068	3 612	3 284	2 885	2 566	2 387	2 178	2 074	1 957
GENERAL CONTROL.	4 097	3 567	3 086	2 678	2 400	2 150	1 927	1 768	1 626
INTEREST ON GENERAL DEBT[1].	23 143	21 688	18 411	16 992	14 873	13 405	12 278	11 430	10 649
OTHER AND UNALLOCABLE.	22 252	19 835	16 594	15 086	13 874	14 604	11 590	10 758	10 024
VETERANS' SERVICES NOT ELSEWHERE CLASSIFIED. .	6 882	6 411	5 388	5 046	4 740	4 448	4 531	4 210	4 208
UTILITY AND LIQUOR STORES EXPENDITURE.	11 398	10 300	9 447	8 820	8 170	7 350	7 282	7 058	6 184
INSURANCE TRUST EXPENDITURE.	64 634	58 028	48 521	43 600	38 127	33 561	28 126	24 880	24 161
EMPLOYEE RETIREMENT.	8 573	7 414	6 399	5 641	4 979	4 584	3 915	3 455	3 170
UNEMPLOYMENT COMPENSATION.	4 861	4 803	2 816	2 089	2 126	2 012	1 981	2 413	2 772
OLD AGE, SURVIVORS, DISABILITY, AND HEALTH . . .	46 949	41 959	35 828	32 474	27 951	23 919	19 793	16 618	15 830
OTHER INSURANCE TRUST.	4 252	3 851	3 478	3 396	3 071	3 046	2 437	2 393	2 388
INDEBTEDNESS									
DEBT OUTSTANDING AT END OF FISCAL YEAR	602 418	556 957	514 489	487 268	468 736	439 880	426 958	416 786	403 935
INCREASE OR DECREASE (-) IN DEBT DURING YEAR . . .	43 592	42 468	27 221	18 532	28 856	13 669	10 172	12 851	13 019

See footnotes at end of table.

Table 1. Finances of All Governments (Federal, State, and Local): 1902 to 1971-72—Continued

(Millions of dollars)

Item	1962–63	1962	1961	1960	1957	1954	1952	1950	1948
REVENUE									
TOTAL.	180 302	168 062	158 741	153 102	129 151	108 255	100 245	66 680	67 005
GENERAL REVENUE.	151 751	142 397	133 969	130 618	112 723	95 844	89 230	58 486	59 666
TAXES.	130 811	123 816	116 331	113 120	98 632	84 476	79 066	51 100	51 218
INDIVIDUAL INCOME.	50 855	48 608	43 951	43 178	37 374	30 669	28 919	16 533	19 848
CORPORATION INCOME	23 084	21 831	22 220	22 674	22 151	21 879	22 072	11 081	10 270
SALES, GROSS RECEIPTS, AND CUSTOMS	28 661	26 922	25 112	24 452	20 594	17 643	15 689	12 997	12 092
PROPERTY	19 833	19 054	18 002	16 405	12 864	9 967	8 652	7 349	6 126
OTHER.	8 378	7 402	7 047	6 411	5 650	4 317	3 735	3 140	2 881
CHARGES AND MISCELLANEOUS.	20 940	18 581	17 637	17 499	14 091	11 369	10 163	7 386	8 448
UTILITY AND LIQUOR STORES REVENUE.	5 532	5 308	5 116	4 877	4 127	3 496	3 108	2 712	2 511
INSURANCE TRUST REVENUE[1]	23 019	20 357	19 657	17 608	12 301	8 914	7 907	5 482	4 828
EMPLOYEE RETIREMENT.	3 729	3 438	3 190	2 868	2 130	1 502	1 253	965	672
UNEMPLOYMENT COMPENSATION.	3 331	2 967	2 669	2 476	1 799	1 488	1 612	1 190	1 337
OLD AGE, SURVIVORS, DISABILITY, AND HEALTH . . .	14 195	12 289	12 131	10 656	6 857	4 554	3 547	2 107	1 616
OTHER INSURANCE TRUST.	1 764	1 663	1 667	1 606	1 515	1 370	1 495	1 219	1 203
EXPENDITURE, BY CHARACTER AND OBJECT									
TOTAL.	184 996	176 240	164 875	151 288	125 463	111 332	99 847	70 334	55 081
CURRENT OPERATION.	103 471	98 146	91 723	81 654	68 966	62 494	56 112	51 584	43 226
CAPITAL OUTLAY	36 272	35 220	32 320	31 946	28 866	27 369	24 873	(NA)	(NA)
CONSTRUCTION	18 005	17 298	16 987	15 832	13 782	11 739	9 723	6 840	4 376
EQUIPMENT.	15 726	15 615	13 424	14 378	13 825	14 864	14 684		
LAND AND EXISTING STRUCTURES	2 543	2 307	1 909	1 736	1 259	767	³467	(⁴)	(⁴)
ASSISTANCE AND SUBSIDIES	11 716	11 660	10 931	10 402	9 488	8 271	8 387		
INTEREST ON DEBT[1]	10 277	9 586	9 710	9 690	6 873	5 713	4 986	5 017	4 866
INSURANCE BENEFITS AND REPAYMENTS.	23 259	21 628	20 191	17 596	11 269	7 984	5 489	6 894	2 614
EXHIBIT: EXPENDITURE FOR PERSONAL SERVICES. . . .	56 976	54 153	50 215	47 136	39 486	33 538	29 766	20 530	17 345
EXPENDITURE, BY FUNCTION									
TOTAL.	184 996	176 240	164 875	151 288	125 463	111 332	99 847	70 334	55 081
GENERAL EXPENDITURE.	156 002	149 159	139 161	128 600	109 765	100 365	91 291	60 701	50 088
NATIONAL DEFENSE AND INTERNATIONAL RELATIONS . . .	56 386	55 172	51 210	48 922	47 500	49 265	48 187	18 355	16 075
MILITARY FUNCTIONS ONLY.	47 973	46 950	43 068	41 340	39 073	40 519	38 962	12 118	10 642
POSTAL SERVICE	4 402	4 101	4 025	3 730	3 034	2 669	2 612	2 270	1 715
SPACE RESEARCH AND TECHNOLOGY.	2 529	1 242	735	395	-	-	-		-
EDUCATION.	24 480	22 814	21 214	19 404	15 098	11 196	9 598	9 647	7 721
INSTITUTIONS OF HIGHER EDUCATION	4 466	4 042	3 570	3 202	2 206	1 418	1 267	1 107	895
LOCAL SCHOOLS.	18 759	17 739	16 608	15 166	11 657	8 947	6 862	5 906	4 363
OTHER EDUCATION.	1 255	1 032	1 036	1 036	1 235	831	1 469	2 634	2 463
HIGHWAYS	11 315	10 508	9 995	9 565	7 931	5 586	4 714	3 872	3 071
PUBLIC WELFARE	5 538	5 147	4 779	4 462	3 534	3 103	2 830	2 964	2 144
CASH ASSISTANCE, CATEGORICAL PROGRAMS.	3 327	3 266	3 084	3 006	2 538	2 234	2 033	2 010	1 473
CASH ASSISTANCE, OTHER	250	259	335	310	195	308	303	538	357
OTHER PUBLIC WELFARE	1 961	1 623	1 362	1 145	801	561	493	416	314
HOSPITALS.	5 106	4 791	4 549	4 213	3 416	2 676	2 460	2 050	1 398
HEALTH	1 540	1 344	1 132	1 031	735	692	739	661	536
POLICE PROTECTION.	2 446	2 326	2 210	2 030	1 623	1 254	1 080	864	724
LOCAL FIRE PROTECTION.	1 161	1 124	1 087	995	810	653	586	488	406
SANITATION	1 996	1 958	1 774	1 727	1 443	1 058	992	834	670
NATURAL RESOURCES.	9 511	10 468	9 756	7 087	6 137	6 377	3 252	5 005	2 223
STABILIZATION OF FARM PRICES AND INCOME. . . .	4 993	5 963	5 508	3 404	3 283	3 863	638	2 712	592
LOCAL PARKS AND RECREATION	902	886	857	770	608	424	324	304	243
HOUSING AND URBAN RENEWAL.	1 688	1 701	1 320	1 142	624	742	875	573	245
AIR TRANSPORTATION[2].	1 097	1 082	1 065	842	508	372	352	214	136
WATER TRANSPORT AND TERMINALS[2]	1 384	1 388	1 273	1 142	862	765	718	410	414
CORRECTION	876	841	810	722	550	427	365	(⁴)	(⁴)
SOCIAL INSURANCE ADMINISTRATION.	740	727	636	539	424	316	238	(⁴)	(⁴)
FINANCIAL ADMINISTRATION	1 809	1 704	1 608	} 2 750	2 405	1 997	1 801	1 555	1 325
GENERAL CONTROL.	1 553	1 483	1 417						
INTEREST ON GENERAL DEBT[1]	9 846	9 173	9 309	9 332	6 603	5 515	4 814	4 862	4 722
OTHER AND UNALLOCABLE.	9 695	9 178	8 398	7 690	5 919	5 278	4 751	5 773	6 320
VETERANS' SERVICES NOT ELSEWHERE CLASSIFIED. .	3 961	4 224	4 049	3 801	3 224	2 913	2 570	3 258	3 926
UTILITY AND LIQUOR STORES EXPENDITURE.	5 736	5 453	5 523	5 088	4 429	3 482	3 067	2 739	2 379
INSURANCE TRUST EXPENDITURE.	23 260	21 628	20 191	17 596	11 269	7 484	5 489	6 894	2 614
EMPLOYEE RETIREMENT.	2 848	2 642	2 339	2 161	1 534	1 090	831	629	541
UNEMPLOYMENT COMPENSATION.	2 927	3 019	3 715	2 639	1 633	1 648	1 022	1 980	821
OLD AGE, SURVIVORS, DISABILITY, AND HEALTH . . .	15 015	13 669	11 889	10 798	6 515	3 276	1 983	726	512
OTHER INSURANCE TRUST.	2 470	2 298	2 248	1 997	1 589	1 471	1 653	3 559	740
INDEBTEDNESS									
DEBT OUTSTANDING AT END OF FISCAL YEAR	390 916	379 419	379 003	363 994	323 566	310 190	289 205	281 472	270 948
INCREASE OR DECREASE (−) IN DEBT DURING YEAR . . .	(NA)	14 756	7 708	7 470	1 947	10 338	5 867	7 703	−4 153

See footnotes at end of table.

303

Table 1. Finances of All Governments (Federal, State, and Local): 1902 to 1971-72—Continued

(Millions of dollars)

Item	1946	1944	1940	1936	1932	1927	1922	1913	1902
REVENUE									
TOTAL.	61 532	64 778	17 804	13 588	10 289	12 191	9 322	2 980	1 694
GENERAL REVENUE.	55 130	58 617	14 858	12 533	9 578	11 551	8 894	2 862	1 632
TAXES.	46 380	49 095	12 688	10 583	7 977	9 451	7 387	2 271	1 373
INDIVIDUAL INCOME.	16 579	20 043	1 183	819	479	949	2 040	—	—
CORPORATION INCOME	12 280	15 188	1 279	858	677	1 351		35	—
SALES, GROSS RECEIPTS, AND CUSTOMS	9 950	7 012	4 109	3 389	1 485	1 558	1 306	670	515
PROPERTY	4 986	4 604	4 430	4 093	4 487	4 730	3 321	1 332	706
OTHER.	2 586	2 249	1 687	1 424	849	862	721	234	152
CHARGES AND MISCELLANEOUS.	8 750	9 522	2 170	1 950	1 601	2 100	1 507	591	259
UTILITY AND LIQUOR STORES REVENUE.	2 033	1 633	998	747	463	403	266	116	62
INSURANCE TRUST REVENUE[1]	4 369	4 528	1 948	308	248	237	162	2	—
EMPLOYEE RETIREMENT.	571	498	214	158	126	92	59	2	—
UNEMPLOYMENT COMPENSATION.	1 282	1 518	931	23	—	—	—	—	—
OLD AGE, SURVIVORS, DISABILITY, AND HEALTH . . .	1 201	1 260	538	—	—	—	—	—	—
OTHER INSURANCE TRUST.	1 316	1 251	265	127	122	145	103	—	—
EXPENDITURE, BY CHARACTER AND OBJECT									
TOTAL.	79 707	109 947	20 417	16 758	12 437	11 220	9 297	3 215	1 660
CURRENT OPERATION.	70 356	101 201	14 624	12 551	8 968	7 560	6 398	2 451	1 350
CAPITAL OUTLAY	(NA)	(NA)	(NA)	(NA)	(NA)	(NA)	(NA)	(NA)	(NA)
CONSTRUCTION	2 536	5 117	3 139	2 427	1 876	2 095	1 397	561	202
EQUIPMENT.									
LAND AND EXISTING STRUCTURES . . . . . . }	(4)	(4)	(4)	(4)	(4)	(4)	(4)	(4)	(4)
ASSISTANCE AND SUBSIDIES									
INTEREST ON DEBT[1]	4 422	2 786	1 686	1 558	1 422	1 426	1 418	196	108
INSURANCE BENEFITS AND REPAYMENTS.	2 392	842	968	222	171	139	84	7	—
EXHIBIT: EXPENDITURE FOR PERSONAL SERVICES. . . .	28 413	26 760	7 649	6 353	4 729	4 255	3 303	1 427	970
EXPENDITURE, BY FUNCTION									
TOTAL.	79 707	109 947	20 417	16 758	12 437	11 220	9 297	3 215	1 660
GENERAL EXPENDITURE.	75 582	107 823	18 125	15 835	11 748	10 590	8 854	3 022	1 578
NATIONAL DEFENSE AND INTERNATIONAL RELATIONS . .	50 461	85 503	1 590	932	721	616	875	250	165
MILITARY FUNCTIONS ONLY.	42 677	74 670	1 567	916	702	599	864	245	162
POSTAL SERVICE	1 381	1 085	808	751	794	711	553	270	126
SPACE RESEARCH AND TECHNOLOGY.	—	—	—	—	—	—	—	—	—
EDUCATION.	3 711	2 805	2 827	2 365	2 325	2 243	1 713	582	258
INSTITUTIONS OF HIGHER EDUCATION	397	380	290	231	234	196	143	49	13
LOCAL SCHOOLS.	2 886	2 344	2 292	1 904	2 050	2 017	1 541	522	238
OTHER EDUCATION.	428	81	245	230	41	30	29	11	7
HIGHWAYS	1 680	1 215	2 177	1 945	1 766	1 819	1 296	419	175
PUBLIC WELFARE	1 435	1 150	1 314	997	445	161	128	57	41
CASH ASSISTANCE, CATEGORICAL PROGRAMS. . . .	1 014	842	611	731	366	79	57	17	11
CASH ASSISTANCE, OTHER	216	166	438						
OTHER PUBLIC WELFARE	205	142	265	266	79	82	71	40	30
HOSPITALS.	762	568	537	461	462	347	287	80	45
HEALTH	380	289	195	131	121	84	65	33	18
POLICE PROTECTION.	549	497	386	331	349	290	204	92	50
LOCAL FIRE PROTECTION.	294	251	235	205	210	203	158	76	40
SANITATION	370	245	207	204	223	312	189	97	51
NATURAL RESOURCES.	3 111	2 731	2 730	2 158	326	206	140	44	17
STABILIZATION OF FARM PRICES AND INCOME. . .	2 012	1 532	694	602	—	—	—	—	—
LOCAL PARKS AND RECREATION	179	123	162	104	147	153	85	57	29
HOUSING AND URBAN RENEWAL.	221	574	267	71	—	1	1	—	—
AIR TRANSPORTATION[2]	98	207	53	39	10	1	1	—	—
WATER TRANSPORT AND TERMINALS[3]	1 092	4 534	321	230	188	253	301	90	22
CORRECTION	(5)	(5)	(5)	(5)	(5)	(5)	(5)	(5)	(5)
SOCIAL INSURANCE ADMINISTRATION.	(5)	(5)	(5)	—	—	—	—	—	—
FINANCIAL ADMINISTRATION . . . . }	1 163	1 087	739	622	601	526	439	256	175
GENERAL CONTROL.									
INTEREST ON GENERAL DEBT[1]	4 286	2 650	1 522	1 455	1 323	1 348	1 370	170	97
OTHER AND UNALLOCABLE.	4 409	2 309	2 025	2 794	1 737	1 316	1 049	449	269
VETERANS' SERVICES NOT ELSEWHERE CLASSIFIED. .	2 588	530	501	1 699	928	579	505	177	141
UTILITY AND LIQUOR STORES EXPENDITURE.	1 733	1 281	1 324	701	518	491	359	186	82
INSURANCE TRUST EXPENDITURE.	2 392	842	968	222	171	139	84	7	—
EMPLOYEE RETIREMENT.	503	298	209	157	103	64	36	7	—
UNEMPLOYMENT COMPENSATION.	985	70	509	—	—	—	—	—	—
OLD AGE, SURVIVORS, DISABILITY, AND HEALTH . . .	321	185	16	—	—	—	—	—	—
OTHER INSURANCE TRUST.	584	289	234	65	68	75	48	—	—
INDEBTEDNESS									
DEBT OUTSTANDING AT END OF FISCAL YEAR	285 339	218 482	63 251	53 253	38 692	33 393	33 072	5 607	3 285
INCREASE OR DECREASE (−) IN DEBT DURING YEAR . . .	9 986	63 013	2 748	5 305	2 918	−57	432	(NA)	(NA)

Note: Duplicative transactions between levels of government are excluded in arriving at aggregates. For information on concepts, sources, data presentation, and historical changes in data classification, see introductory text.

NA Not available.
- Represents zero or rounds to zero.
[1]Excludes interest on Federal securities held by Federal agencies and funds (see text).
[2]Any State and local amounts prior to 1951 are included under "other and unallocable."
[3]Any Federal amounts are included in construction.
[4]Any amounts prior to 1951 are included in "current operation."
[5]Any amounts are included in "other and unallocable."

Table 2. Per Capita Amounts of Selected Items of Governmental Finances: 1902 to 1971-72

Item	1971-72			1970-71			1969-70			1968-69		
	All govern-ments	Federal Govern-ment	State and local govern-ments	All govern-ments	Federal Govern-ment	State and local govern-ments	All govern-ments	Federal Govern-ment	State and local govern-ments	All govern-ments	Federal Govern-ment	State and local govern-ments
GENERAL REVENUE	1 480.67	826.59	804.59	1 336.54	760.64	702.65	1 340.71	804.89	643.37	1 278.93	806.48	567.35
INTERGOVERNMENTAL REVENUE (FROM FEDERAL GOVERNMENT)	(¹)	-	150.52	(¹)	-	126.76	(¹)	-	107.54	(¹)	-	94.85
GENERAL REVENUE EXCLUDING INTERGOVERNMENTAL REVENUE	1 480.67	826.59	654.07	1 336.54	760.64	575.89	1 340.71	804.89	535.82	1 278.93	806.48	472.49
TAXES	1 264.66	738.28	526.38	1 126.04	665.57	460.47	1 145.85	718.78	427.06	1 102.95	723.04	379.94
INDIVIDUAL INCOME	528.08	454.96	73.13	475.77	418.07	57.69	498.06	444.86	53.20	476.21	432.09	44.11
CORPORATION INCOME	175.68	154.47	21.21	146.46	129.86	16.60	179.92	161.53	18.39	197.39	181.65	15.74
SALES, GROSS RECEIPTS, AND CUSTOMS	276.71	96.53	180.17	255.31	94.19	161.12	239.22	90.03	149.19	219.62	88.28	131.33
PROPERTY	205.91	-	205.91	183.51	-	183.51	167.56	-	167.56	151.92	-	151.92
OTHER TAXES, INCLUDING LICENSES	78.29	32.32	45.97	64.97	23.44	41.53	61.07	22.36	38.71	57.82	21.02	36.80
CHARGES AND MISCELLANEOUS	216.01	88.31	127.69	210.50	95.08	115.42	194.86	86.11	108.75	175.98	83.44	92.54
GENERAL EXPENDITURE	1 551.47	903.32	809.43	1 459.82	862.63	730.52	1 353.19	821.42	646.20	1 267.45	785.54	578.14
INTERGOVERNMENTAL EXPENDITURE	(¹)	161.28	(¹)	(¹)	133.33	(¹)	(¹)	114.43	(¹)	(¹)	96.18	(¹)
DIRECT GENERAL EXPENDITURE	1 551.47	742.04	809.43	1 459.82	729.30	730.52	1 353.19	706.99	646.20	1 267.45	689.36	578.14
NATIONAL DEFENSE AND INTERNATIONAL RELATIONS	380.62	380.62	-	392.28	392.28	-	414.56	414.56	-	418.46	418.46	-
MILITARY	345.74	345.74	-	357.03	357.03	-	376.66	376.66	-	382.22	382.22	-
POSTAL SERVICE	44.98	44.98	-	42.10	42.10	-	38.00	38.00	-	34.63	34.63	-
SPACE RESEARCH AND TECHNOLOGY	16.18	16.18	-	16.16	16.16	-	18.16	18.16	-	20.75	20.75	-
EDUCATION	340.57	24.51	316.06	310.50	22.44	288.05	274.42	15.02	259.39	249.49	15.55	233.94
INSTITUTIONS OF HIGHER EDUCATION	76.17	-	76.17	71.68	-	71.68	63.59	-	63.59	57.20	-	57.20
LOCAL SCHOOLS	224.13	-	224.13	202.50	-	202.49	184.32	-	184.32	167.15	-	167.15
OTHER EDUCATION	40.27	24.51	15.76	36.31	22.44	13.87	26.50	15.02	11.47	25.13	15.55	9.58
HIGHWAYS	93.42	2.07	91.35	89.19	1.46	87.73	82.40	1.57	80.83	77.94	1.59	76.35
PUBLIC WELFARE	113.35	11.95	101.41	99.13	10.76	88.36	86.19	13.96	72.23	72.95	12.98	59.97
HOSPITALS	61.45	11.29	50.17	54.02	9.96	44.05	47.69	9.00	38.69	42.56	7.83	34.72
HEALTH	21.09	8.72	12.37	17.91	7.64	10.27	19.16	10.28	8.88	16.53	9.05	7.47
POLICE PROTECTION	31.50	2.66	28.84	27.66	2.32	25.34	24.12	2.01	22.11	21.01	1.69	19.32
LOCAL FIRE PROTECTION	12.39	-	12.39	11.16	-	11.16	9.96	-	9.96	8.87	-	8.87
SANITATION	23.27	-	23.27	19.80	-	19.80	16.79	-	16.79	14.69	-	14.69
NATURAL RESOURCES	68.33	53.33	14.99	66.62	51.67	14.94	56.43	42.99	13.44	49.64	37.00	12.63
STABILIZATION OF FARM PRICES AND INCOME	23.51	23.51	-	25.34	25.34	-	20.97	20.97	-	14.53	14.53	-
LOCAL PARKS AND RECREATION	11.13	-	11.13	10.22	-	10.22	9.29	-	9.29	8.14	-	8.14
HOUSING AND URBAN RENEWAL	25.76	12.63	13.13	21.66	9.27	12.38	15.69	5.17	10.52	12.41	2.99	9.41
AIR TRANSPORTATION	17.75	11.62	6.14	15.40	10.25	5.14	10.16	5.39	4.77	8.07	4.49	3.57
WATER TRANSPORT AND TERMINALS	10.78	8.27	2.51	10.42	7.98	2.44	9.37	7.18	2.18	9.87	7.59	2.28
CORRECTION	10.68	0.53	10.14	9.59	0.46	9.13	8.41	0.41	8.00	7.22	0.33	6.88
SOCIAL SECURITY ADMINISTRATION	11.01	5.55	5.46	9.85	5.27	4.58	8.81	5.02	3.78	7.79	4.48	3.30
FINANCIAL ADMINISTRATION	19.54	7.53	12.01	17.51	6.50	11.01	16.16	6.17	9.99	14.29	5.34	8.94
GENERAL CONTROL	19.68	3.26	16.42	17.29	2.62	14.67	15.18	2.14	13.05	13.26	1.88	11.38
INTEREST ON GENERAL DEBT	111.14	82.19	28.95	105.15	80.48	24.67	90.59	69.07	21.52	84.15	65.67	18.48
OTHER AND UNALLOCABLE	106.86	54.16	52.70	96.16	49.68	46.49	81.64	40.88	40.76	74.69	37.06	37.62
VETERANS' SERVICES NOT ELSEWHERE CLASSIFIED	54.16	54.16	-	31.08	31.08	-	26.51	26.51	-	24.99	24.99	-
EXHIBIT: EXPENDITURE FOR PERSONAL SERVICES	636.77	258.93	377.84	582.32	240.22	342.10	543.70	233.72	339.97	490.63	214.80	275.82
DEBT OUTSTANDING AT END OF FISCAL YEAR	2 893.01	2 051.85	841.17	2 700.32	1 930.27	770.04	2 531.49	1 825.07	706.42	2 413.16	1 751.77	661.39

See footnotes at end of table.

Table 3. Selected Items of State and Local Government Finances, Per $1,000 of Personal Income, by States: 1957 to 1971-72

Item	1971-72	1966-67	1962	1957	1971-72	1966-67	1962	1957	1971-72	1966-67	1962	1957
	UNITED STATES AVERAGE				ALABAMA				ALASKA			
GENERAL REVENUE	195.47	157.11	132.47	109.44	201.26	171.32	114.62	121.56	347.41	320.04	206.82	¹(89.80)
FROM FEDERAL GOVERNMENT	36.57	26.48	17.90	11.02	56.00	42.13	34.77	24.20	115.17	165.75	69.90	(21.91)
FROM OWN SOURCES	158.90	130.63	114.57	98.42	145.27	129.18	109.85	97.37	232.24	154.29	136.92	(67.89)
TAXES	127.88	105.09	94.49	82.64	103.61	93.39	83.01	76.08	102.22	94.65	79.93	(55.57)
PROPERTY	50.02	44.87	43.33	36.89	15.31	16.57	16.84	15.37	25.00	23.30	18.29	(12.24)
OTHER	77.85	60.21	51.16	45.75	88.30	76.82	66.17	60.70	77.22	71.34	61.64	(43.33)
CHARGES AND MISCELLANEOUS	31.02	25.54	20.07	15.78	41.66	35.79	26.85	21.29	130.02	59.65	56.99	(12.33)
GENERAL EXPENDITURE	196.65	160.81	136.91	115.78	196.25	184.35	154.14	133.63	472.97	357.09	204.38	(90.53)
EDUCATION	76.79	65.32	50.52	40.53	74.59	77.18	56.42	42.32	159.57	92.74	64.28	(42.41)
HIGHWAYS	22.19	24.00	23.55	22.41	27.65	31.69	30.35	32.78	83.43	132.07	49.36	(7.82)
PUBLIC WELFARE	24.64	14.16	11.56	9.99	24.15	17.94	19.21	17.32	22.72	10.53	7.52	(7.86)
HEALTH AND HOSPITALS	15.19	11.44	9.87	8.95	20.57	12.87	11.47	8.02	14.34	9.48	14.86	(5.59)
ALL OTHER	57.84	45.89	41.41	33.90	49.29	44.67	36.70	33.19	192.91	112.27	68.36	(26.85)
TOTAL STATE-LOCAL DEBT	204.36	195.80	184.87	152.10	235.91	259.62	202.85	148.23	495.45	338.51	200.93	(82.30)

Item	1971-72	1966-67	1962	1957	1971-72	1966-67	1962	1957	1971-72	1966-67	1962	1957
	ARIZONA				ARKANSAS				CALIFORNIA			
GENERAL REVENUE	207.28	207.80	155.28	130.80	191.30	175.86	153.16	130.30	224.84	180.60	144.92	122.89
FROM FEDERAL GOVERNMENT	35.95	44.96	25.84	16.76	53.15	48.85	36.95	24.52	44.05	34.33	20.35	13.11
FROM OWN SOURCES	171.32	162.84	129.44	114.04	138.15	127.02	116.21	105.78	180.79	146.26	124.57	109.77
TAXES	137.54	128.42	103.67	91.09	103.58	99.86	92.94	86.69	149.87	119.77	104.56	93.06
PROPERTY	54.04	58.45	49.49	42.23	24.95	26.05	26.27	22.94	71.50	61.62	52.45	43.95
OTHER	83.50	69.97	54.19	48.86	78.63	73.81	66.67	63.75	78.37	58.15	52.12	49.11
CHARGES AND MISCELLANEOUS	33.78	34.42	25.77	22.96	35.57	27.16	23.27	19.09	30.92	26.50	20.01	16.72
GENERAL EXPENDITURE	211.72	212.94	167.02	146.34	172.03	177.38	148.09	127.91	213.21	189.24	151.21	125.70
EDUCATION	100.32	97.44	72.53	61.35	67.67	69.99	53.85	45.21	73.88	67.56	59.28	46.58
HIGHWAYS	25.75	40.74	31.33	26.94	27.22	33.74	34.42	29.54	16.57	20.57	18.95	18.39
PUBLIC WELFARE	10.78	9.71	9.74	9.55	23.71	21.16	18.27	16.56	40.92	25.02	13.39	11.70
HEALTH AND HOSPITALS	11.86	8.61	5.95	6.49	14.37	12.13	10.54	9.14	14.31	11.99	10.32	9.45
ALL OTHER	63.01	56.44	47.44	42.01	39.06	40.36	31.02	27.46	67.53	64.10	49.27	39.58
TOTAL STATE-LOCAL DEBT	171.42	194.62	177.15	151.23	161.09	159.94	137.18	140.64	191.84	202.68	177.76	128.72

Item	1971-72	1966-67	1962	1957	1971-72	1966-67	1962	1957	1971-72	1966-67	1962	1957
	COLORADO				CONNECTICUT				DELAWARE			
GENERAL REVENUE	209.11	187.50	156.21	134.07	171.12	125.43	110.93	86.06	198.32	156.71	107.35	73.83
FROM FEDERAL GOVERNMENT	43.78	34.99	25.29	19.76	24.23	16.99	11.82	4.68	35.74	21.04	10.53	6.71
FROM OWN SOURCES	165.33	152.51	130.92	114.31	146.89	108.44	99.11	81.38	162.59	135.67	96.83	67.12
TAXES	126.03	118.90	105.25	93.37	128.58	92.51	85.26	71.47	124.08	98.05	77.16	48.38
PROPERTY	51.47	54.50	50.21	47.40	63.52	48.13	45.68	35.75	21.42	19.46	15.81	11.59
OTHER	74.57	64.40	55.04	45.97	65.06	44.38	39.58	35.72	102.66	78.59	61.34	36.76
CHARGES AND MISCELLANEOUS	39.30	33.61	25.67	20.94	18.32	15.92	13.85	9.91	38.51	37.62	19.67	18.74
GENERAL EXPENDITURE	204.13	185.99	150.99	138.54	169.80	128.42	118.18	113.36	211.13	177.86	107.48	86.45
EDUCATION	91.67	87.00	64.10	50.59	65.59	47.98	40.60	32.64	98.90	69.42	45.15	34.72
HIGHWAYS	24.95	25.55	21.18	26.59	17.68	18.57	20.96	37.54	26.07	38.81	18.80	18.71
PUBLIC WELFARE	23.92	19.13	20.49	21.57	18.06	10.19	8.51	6.95	17.99	8.48	6.05	4.38
HEALTH AND HOSPITALS	14.22	12.39	10.23	8.33	10.44	7.52	6.92	7.25	9.41	8.23	6.52	6.20
ALL OTHER	49.37	41.92	34.99	31.46	58.03	44.12	41.18	28.98	68.17	52.92	30.96	22.44
TOTAL STATE-LOCAL DEBT	144.13	181.44	155.29	141.83	266.54	233.94	244.66	173.08	308.44	358.47	237.95	181.24

Item	1971-72	1966-67	1962	1957	1971-72	1966-67	1962	1957	1971-72	1966-67	1962	1957
	DISTRICT OF COLUMBIA				FLORIDA				GEORGIA			
GENERAL REVENUE	241.89	144.84	115.46	94.08	179.55	162.66	136.57	118.95	192.63	161.64	139.42	125.29
FROM FEDERAL GOVERNMENT	114.53	46.01	30.94	16.97	27.32	24.26	14.96	11.88	42.97	33.93	27.30	17.87
FROM OWN SOURCES	127.35	98.83	87.52	77.11	152.23	138.40	121.61	107.07	149.66	127.46	112.12	107.42
TAXES	103.63	86.40	72.48	69.21	115.67	105.33	95.12	85.89	108.84	96.89	86.98	86.52
PROPERTY	32.00	29.23	26.84	25.49	38.21	42.45	39.14	30.43	33.22	30.39	27.69	25.08
OTHER	71.62	57.17	45.64	43.72	77.46	62.88	55.97	55.46	75.62	66.50	59.30	61.44
CHARGES AND MISCELLANEOUS	23.72	12.43	12.04	7.90	36.55	33.07	26.50	21.18	40.81	30.57	25.14	20.90
GENERAL EXPENDITURE	241.87	150.70	131.10	89.45	180.49	164.01	138.74	127.19	189.64	161.61	145.06	129.95
EDUCATION	64.06	37.42	23.17	18.75	75.43	64.73	47.98	38.51	71.52	67.08	49.68	47.30
HIGHWAYS	15.98	16.23	23.32	7.65	21.26	24.13	21.45	26.32	20.85	24.75	28.69	22.36
PUBLIC WELFARE	32.90	12.52	10.22	5.63	12.32	9.44	8.59	9.18	23.74	13.10	13.81	14.40
HEALTH AND HOSPITALS	31.68	20.81	18.21	14.16	17.83	14.56	13.22	10.52	25.51	17.10	16.12	13.22
ALL OTHER	97.25	63.71	56.19	43.26	53.65	51.15	47.50	42.66	48.02	39.58	36.76	32.67
TOTAL STATE-LOCAL DEBT	185.59	111.63	91.12	41.13	166.96	208.78	181.20	164.75	172.52	189.59	184.32	161.01

Item	1971-72	1966-67	1962	1957	1971-72	1966-67	1962	1957	1971-72	1966-67	1962	1957
	HAWAII				IDAHO				ILLINOIS			
GENERAL REVENUE	226.47	213.15	170.19	¹(131.27)	210.04	190.96	160.30	137.13	177.04	117.40	110.73	87.93
FROM FEDERAL GOVERNMENT	51.64	49.44	32.93	(19.16)	49.99	35.81	34.23	21.75	34.66	15.89	12.46	6.11
FROM OWN SOURCES	174.84	163.71	137.26	(112.11)	160.05	155.15	126.08	115.38	142.38	101.51	98.28	81.82
TAXES	139.34	134.74	109.08	(91.96)	124.37	120.40	100.66	93.58	122.24	85.32	85.31	72.33
PROPERTY	26.60	27.33	17.45	(14.54)	43.95	44.25	48.88	46.97	50.88	41.70	45.59	37.41
OTHER	112.74	107.41	91.63	(77.42)	80.43	76.15	51.78	46.60	71.37	43.62	39.72	34.91
CHARGES AND MISCELLANEOUS	35.49	28.97	28.18	(20.15)	35.67	34.75	25.42	21.81	20.13	16.19	12.97	9.50
GENERAL EXPENDITURE	254.32	220.07	185.72	(156.07)	206.84	185.39	163.96	140.05	164.87	118.30	112.49	91.40
EDUCATION	83.19	80.10	57.60	(47.87)	82.25	72.97	55.90	49.11	64.46	48.37	41.13	31.61
HIGHWAYS	22.39	24.79	16.41	(24.47)	35.03	37.75	43.73	36.06	20.14	15.42	17.65	17.42
PUBLIC WELFARE	24.57	10.70	5.89	(7.84)	17.20	13.90	12.03	10.36	22.91	10.36	10.95	7.73
HEALTH AND HOSPITALS	16.68	14.32	14.09	(15.18)	15.97	11.45	10.52	9.72	10.68	8.90	6.69	5.97
ALL OTHER	107.49	90.16	91.73	(60.70)	56.39	49.32	41.78	34.80	46.68	35.25	36.08	28.67
TOTAL STATE-LOCAL DEBT	295.81	230.04	229.38	(199.99)	57.44	95.11	96.30	89.01	145.97	147.19	162.51	130.92

See footnotes at end of table.

Table 3. Selected Items of State and Local Government Finances, Per $1,000 of Personal Income, by States: 1957 to 1971-72—Continued

INDIANA / IOWA / KANSAS

Item	1971-72	1966-67	1962	1957	1971-72	1966-67	1962	1957	1971-72	1966-67	1962	1957
	INDIANA				IOWA				KANSAS			
GENERAL REVENUE	170.69	139.06	119.29	89.82	191.09	163.64	144.17	124.06	172.99	163.42	148.80	128.76
FROM FEDERAL GOVERNMENT	23.05	17.14	12.83	6.12	27.26	24.52	17.87	12.14	30.38	24.34	19.28	15.10
FROM OWN SOURCES	147.65	121.92	106.46	83.70	163.82	139.12	126.30	111.92	142.61	139.08	129.52	113.66
TAXES	115.27	96.61	85.93	69.31	129.51	111.27	105.02	95.82	110.99	110.14	106.77	96.05
PROPERTY	59.01	46.78	48.32	38.07	59.85	56.09	59.39	46.80	54.41	55.37	59.87	55.70
OTHER	56.25	49.53	37.61	31.24	69.66	55.17	45.63	49.02	56.57	54.77	46.90	40.35
CHARGES AND MISCELLANEOUS	32.38	25.31	20.53	14.39	34.31	27.86	21.28	16.10	31.62	28.94	22.75	17.61
GENERAL EXPENDITURE	168.93	134.79	124.67	100.89	194.80	163.80	146.43	127.64	165.35	156.62	148.84	148.18
EDUCATION	83.49	68.77	58.91	43.79	91.88	73.07	60.40	50.05	73.56	70.87	60.31	50.09
HIGHWAYS	19.52	19.75	20.67	18.23	36.47	36.69	34.29	35.61	27.39	28.64	32.70	44.49
PUBLIC WELFARE	12.67	5.78	5.98	5.78	16.11	11.05	12.30	11.43	11.84	10.95	11.88	12.03
HEALTH AND HOSPITALS	14.96	10.73	3.17	7.77	11.72	10.12	8.91	7.09	12.76	11.08	10.28	9.62
ALL OTHER	38.29	29.76	35.94	25.32	38.62	32.87	30.53	23.46	39.80	35.08	33.67	31.95
TOTAL STATE-LOCAL DEBT	118.63	111.47	121.28	86.95	99.59	85.76	85.03	63.04	139.16	155.70	178.03	169.67

KENTUCKY / LOUISIANA / MAINE

Item	1971-72	1966-67	1962	1957	1971-72	1966-67	1962	1957	1971-72	1966-67	1962	1957
	KENTUCKY				LOUISIANA				MAINE			
GENERAL REVENUE	186.72	171.22	137.92	109.15	229.28	200.15	189.49	162.77	223.47	154.23	139.55	114.78
FROM FEDERAL GOVERNMENT	45.40	46.24	27.97	15.85	47.69	42.42	37.34	24.03	50.97	29.65	21.87	13.84
FROM OWN SOURCES	141.32	124.97	109.94	93.30	181.59	157.73	152.15	138.74	172.50	124.57	117.67	100.94
TAXES	107.68	94.38	88.47	77.32	133.65	116.42	115.38	102.01	146.72	104.53	103.00	88.49
PROPERTY	22.57	25.51	26.80	28.07	26.91	23.86	26.08	22.22	66.06	50.69	54.40	44.24
OTHER	85.11	68.87	61.67	49.25	106.75	92.57	89.30	79.79	80.66	53.84	48.61	44.25
CHARGES AND MISCELLANEOUS	33.64	30.60	21.47	15.98	47.94	41.30	36.76	36.72	25.78	20.04	14.67	12.45
GENERAL EXPENDITURE	189.48	178.93	170.44	111.04	222.90	216.58	199.95	173.23	216.58	160.61	148.51	120.10
EDUCATION	72.38	70.56	56.01	40.36	82.92	82.70	63.92	54.28	77.31	63.10	53.99	35.95
HIGHWAYS	39.28	38.12	39.90	24.50	32.01	38.97	36.17	31.59	38.90	35.47	36.21	33.41
PUBLIC WELFARE	20.99	17.76	14.99	12.26	25.81	26.11	31.36	28.79	27.78	14.25	13.81	11.96
HEALTH AND HOSPITALS	11.18	10.35	8.13	7.22	18.98	14.74	12.38	10.11	9.13	7.88	7.92	6.89
ALL OTHER	45.65	42.14	51.40	26.70	63.18	54.06	56.13	48.46	63.46	39.91	36.57	31.89
TOTAL STATE-LOCAL DEBT	305.61	274.60	218.42	109.65	287.60	280.90	271.93	227.44	156.91	135.06	137.54	122.07

MARYLAND / MASSACHUSETTS / MICHIGAN

Item	1971-72	1966-67	1962	1957	1971-72	1966-67	1962	1957	1971-72	1966-67	1962	1957
	MARYLAND				MASSACHUSETTS				MICHIGAN			
GENERAL REVENUE	181.86	140.18	114.29	94.30	196.01	151.41	126.22	107.40	198.69	146.38	134.00	106.91
FROM FEDERAL GOVERNMENT	27.64	17.91	13.90	7.94	34.79	21.18	13.88	7.74	32.80	21.44	14.99	8.45
FROM OWN SOURCES	154.22	122.27	100.40	86.36	161.22	130.23	112.34	99.66	165.90	124.94	119.01	98.46
TAXES	125.24	101.31	83.37	72.28	142.10	113.39	99.56	89.71	131.67	98.08	98.22	82.51
PROPERTY	40.39	41.74	34.75	30.73	72.79	58.78	60.30	52.02	52.67	43.00	48.44	38.06
OTHER	84.84	59.59	48.62	41.55	69.32	54.61	39.26	37.69	79.01	55.08	49.78	44.45
CHARGES AND MISCELLANEOUS	28.99	20.97	17.03	14.08	19.12	16.84	12.78	9.95	34.23	26.86	20.79	15.95
GENERAL EXPENDITURE	194.36	146.02	121.12	110.44	196.28	143.56	124.75	123.95	197.34	156.16	143.89	119.48
EDUCATION	81.54	61.82	45.90	36.35	70.10	46.71	37.02	30.17	81.91	74.56	57.76	48.12
HIGHWAYS	18.48	17.94	19.38	25.88	14.52	15.40	17.37	25.67	17.46	18.62	25.19	21.55
PUBLIC WELFARE	19.16	10.67	5.69	4.25	36.27	16.93	14.11	13.38	27.35	11.81	9.87	7.45
HEALTH AND HOSPITALS	13.59	11.26	10.21	9.17	14.62	12.82	11.62	12.84	14.71	12.40	12.24	11.01
ALL OTHER	61.59	44.33	39.94	34.79	60.77	51.70	44.64	41.89	55.91	38.74	38.83	31.35
TOTAL STATE-LOCAL DEBT	217.99	215.87	226.24	226.71	207.26	206.88	204.19	190.21	165.99	150.13	158.50	108.87

MINNESOTA / MISSISSIPPI / MISSOURI

Item	1971-72	1966-67	1962	1957	1971-72	1966-67	1962	1957	1971-72	1966-67	1962	1957
	MINNESOTA				MISSISSIPPI				MISSOURI			
GENERAL REVENUE	225.46	184.48	157.41	131.42	232.53	199.93	177.03	163.63	167.36	141.10	113.36	92.47
FROM FEDERAL GOVERNMENT	37.82	30.26	19.28	12.84	63.88	50.88	36.59	27.87	33.27	26.08	20.28	15.26
FROM OWN SOURCES	187.63	154.22	138.13	118.57	168.65	149.05	140.44	135.77	134.09	115.02	93.08	77.21
TAXES	144.48	121.12	111.78	97.21	124.03	111.08	109.66	110.75	108.08	93.25	79.00	66.61
PROPERTY	57.78	60.10	61.35	50.32	28.08	30.74	32.74	30.45	40.06	38.12	33.67	29.57
OTHER	86.71	61.02	50.44	46.89	95.95	80.33	76.92	80.30	68.02	55.14	45.33	37.04
CHARGES AND MISCELLANEOUS	43.15	33.11	26.35	21.36	44.62	37.98	30.78	25.02	26.01	21.76	14.08	10.60
GENERAL EXPENDITURE	227.78	186.44	162.30	140.09	227.21	201.73	197.59	155.23	170.89	142.40	112.53	97.65
EDUCATION	101.95	82.13	64.93	54.17	83.14	79.74	69.88	52.07	69.77	60.42	40.77	33.56
HIGHWAYS	28.95	33.11	31.27	28.66	39.28	40.45	42.83	39.77	21.73	21.85	21.40	17.67
PUBLIC WELFARE	24.28	16.24	14.89	12.04	30.04	20.74	20.96	18.11	17.89	13.55	14.16	15.32
HEALTH AND HOSPITALS	14.81	11.78	11.12	12.25	21.82	15.43	15.95	11.10	13.41	10.49	8.43	6.97
ALL OTHER	57.79	43.18	40.08	32.97	52.93	45.37	47.97	34.18	48.09	36.09	27.78	24.13
TOTAL STATE-LOCAL DEBT	233.04	182.40	168.25	115.26	212.64	224.94	225.93	151.64	136.23	126.89	110.00	83.89

MONTANA / NEBRASKA / NEVADA

Item	1971-72	1966-67	1962	1957	1971-72	1966-67	1962	1957	1971-72	1966-67	1962	1957
	MONTANA				NEBRASKA				NEVADA			
GENERAL REVENUE	246.01	196.29	164.84	144.59	184.25	151.98	121.59	106.15	210.22	195.03	139.57	145.53
FROM FEDERAL GOVERNMENT	65.41	48.51	33.85	25.60	29.25	27.96	18.25	12.80	37.44	46.84	25.46	25.31
FROM OWN SOURCES	180.59	147.78	127.99	118.99	155.00	124.02	103.44	93.34	172.79	148.19	114.11	120.22
TAXES	145.22	115.54	103.57	98.43	115.90	93.18	80.34	76.29	128.95	110.28	86.69	93.28
PROPERTY	73.52	64.73	58.81	57.40	59.27	67.40	56.66	53.36	43.96	44.09	28.37	33.66
OTHER	71.70	50.80	44.76	41.03	56.63	25.78	23.67	22.94	84.99	66.19	58.33	59.62
CHARGES AND MISCELLANEOUS	35.37	32.24	24.42	20.56	39.09	30.85	23.11	17.05	43.84	37.91	27.42	26.94
GENERAL EXPENDITURE	230.47	193.95	156.76	147.94	176.39	155.09	124.01	110.11	219.34	205.58	152.86	148.87
EDUCATION	92.54	78.34	59.01	53.13	74.94	63.05	46.37	42.61	72.17	64.82	47.95	38.58
HIGHWAYS	54.30	51.82	42.68	41.52	29.67	33.68	32.36	27.79	30.32	42.98	31.35	36.11
PUBLIC WELFARE	17.42	10.72	9.93	10.92	14.92	9.21	7.60	7.52	12.70	8.79	6.36	6.19
HEALTH AND HOSPITALS	9.36	7.96	6.68	6.83	12.14	10.64	7.26	7.72	18.33	17.28	11.24	12.60
ALL OTHER	56.85	45.11	38.47	35.54	44.72	38.51	30.41	24.47	85.82	71.71	55.95	55.39
TOTAL STATE-LOCAL DEBT	104.27	126.47	120.20	113.38	259.71	207.74	192.52	189.56	199.60	211.82	117.99	101.95

See footnotes at end of table.

Item	1971-72	1966-67	1962	1957	1971-72	1966-67	1962	1957	1971-72	1966-67	1962	1957
	NEW HAMPSHIRE				NEW JERSEY				NEW MEXICO			
GENERAL REVENUE	177.77	136.85	129.50	104.87	166.09	125.80	107.61	85.38	260.14	236.18	185.20	172.02
FROM FEDERAL GOVERNMENT	30.20	23.18	23.16	9.76	25.80	14.10	9.32	3.95	77.16	71.09	41.32	38.70
FROM OWN SOURCES	147.57	113.67	106.34	95.11	140.29	111.71	98.29	81.43	182.98	165.09	143.88	133.32
TAXES	121.50	93.05	90.03	81.31	116.71	94.24	83.62	69.74	128.08	113.72	100.66	91.44
PROPERTY	73.38	58.99	57.27	51.05	66.67	53.67	54.11	44.65	26.38	25.61	25.34	21.38
OTHER	48.12	34.06	32.76	30.26	50.04	40.57	29.52	25.09	101.71	88.11	75.32	70.06
CHARGES AND MISCELLANEOUS	26.07	20.61	16.31	13.80	23.58	17.47	14.67	11.59	54.90	51.37	43.22	41.88
GENERAL EXPENDITURE	185.91	152.32	134.66	127.70	171.58	121.90	109.15	93.72	238.31	230.80	173.90	161.69
EDUCATION	72.53	64.32	43.53	38.37	67.13	47.89	40.11	31.44	109.44	115.10	81.08	63.52
HIGHWAYS	32.51	31.88	37.61	39.15	19.47	16.02	14.92	15.35	35.18	40.01	29.33	38.48
PUBLIC WELFARE	18.75	10.12	9.81	10.12	21.05	7.08	5.65	3.95	23.12	16.70	14.92	12.74
HEALTH AND HOSPITALS	11.43	8.68	8.55	9.05	9.91	8.41	7.43	7.29	14.31	11.63	8.34	9.03
ALL OTHER	50.69	37.32	35.10	31.01	54.02	42.50	41.04	35.69	56.26	47.36	40.24	37.92
TOTAL STATE-LOCAL DEBT	156.12	159.03	132.89	114.16	263.14	162.48	159.63	160.47	126.24	180.16	147.49	143.52
	NEW YORK				NORTH CAROLINA				NORTH DAKOTA			
GENERAL REVENUE	224.28	177.12	135.26	111.12	177.00	151.67	130.67	121.23	222.88	229.77	155.47	177.99
FROM FEDERAL GOVERNMENT	36.62	19.74	9.55	6.17	35.65	27.55	19.73	19.72	50.40	45.49	25.59	21.95
FROM OWN SOURCES	187.66	157.38	125.72	104.95	141.35	124.12	110.94	101.51	172.48	184.28	129.88	156.04
TAXES	157.75	132.30	106.93	90.40	112.52	99.75	90.15	84.20	120.74	116.34	92.48	114.80
PROPERTY	57.69	52.12	47.43	43.10	28.39	26.36	25.13	22.56	48.46	59.33	48.86	60.62
OTHER	100.06	80.18	59.50	47.29	84.12	73.39	65.02	61.65	72.29	57.01	43.62	54.18
CHARGES AND MISCELLANEOUS	29.92	25.07	18.79	14.56	28.83	24.37	20.79	17.31	51.74	67.94	37.40	41.24
GENERAL EXPENDITURE	250.68	176.89	138.21	116.99	174.25	152.65	132.22	120.98	216.74	234.74	163.52	177.10
EDUCATION	86.81	65.02	42.37	34.80	76.04	71.11	56.85	49.20	92.90	91.31	61.44	56.44
HIGHWAYS	16.05	17.16	18.29	15.85	23.17	24.53	22.76	25.25	41.89	51.73	39.57	50.14
PUBLIC WELFARE	36.26	17.06	10.56	8.71	17.02	10.57	10.54	8.86	17.02	15.39	11.13	13.78
HEALTH AND HOSPITALS	27.87	17.48	13.47	12.77	13.33	10.50	10.06	9.39	7.57	7.06	5.48	6.73
ALL OTHER	83.69	60.17	53.52	44.86	44.69	35.94	32.01	28.28	57.36	69.25	45.90	50.01
TOTAL STATE-LOCAL DEBT	345.86	290.26	273.81	237.17	113.26	131.16	120.64	136.18	113.50	137.90	111.93	90.26
	OHIO				OKLAHOMA				OREGON			
GENERAL REVENUE	153.67	123.68	115.93	88.41	199.09	187.16	161.42	140.97	212.78	180.46	151.99	142.25
FROM FEDERAL GOVERNMENT	22.83	17.86	14.74	7.06	49.14	46.66	34.73	24.65	49.42	34.81	28.61	19.83
FROM OWN SOURCES	130.84	105.83	101.19	81.35	149.94	140.51	126.70	116.32	163.36	145.65	123.38	122.42
TAXES	101.76	82.48	81.98	67.16	107.67	103.12	98.23	92.90	123.78	110.02	96.10	102.82
PROPERTY	44.44	42.66	42.38	32.23	29.27	33.90	30.64	28.21	61.56	52.23	45.57	43.61
OTHER	57.33	39.82	39.60	34.93	78.40	69.23	67.59	64.69	62.22	57.79	50.53	59.20
CHARGES AND MISCELLANEOUS	29.08	23.35	19.21	14.19	42.28	37.38	28.47	23.42	39.58	35.63	27.28	19.60
GENERAL EXPENDITURE	154.38	128.36	119.21	97.89	197.05	189.65	156.89	150.00	217.98	191.37	161.16	139.14
EDUCATION	66.69	54.58	44.59	35.62	74.49	75.59	56.66	53.54	93.13	88.25	64.65	54.02
HIGHWAYS	17.97	21.95	22.28	20.20	24.99	29.73	28.99	32.47	31.26	31.62	30.02	29.68
PUBLIC WELFARE	15.84	11.19	10.62	8.15	33.50	34.15	30.50	28.08	17.42	11.03	11.74	10.92
HEALTH AND HOSPITALS	11.67	7.38	7.35	6.52	13.22	9.90	8.35	7.07	10.24	9.24	8.54	6.77
ALL OTHER	42.21	33.26	34.27	27.40	50.85	40.28	32.39	28.84	65.93	51.23	46.22	37.75
TOTAL STATE-LOCAL DEBT	161.80	146.03	149.55	126.78	205.84	229.21	189.98	150.68	215.19	178.14	173.10	135.13
	PENNSYLVANIA				RHODE ISLAND				SOUTH CAROLINA			
GENERAL REVENUE	178.96	131.45	115.18	92.28	184.97	141.98	118.86	97.26	183.65	152.76	135.18	125.17
FROM FEDERAL GOVERNMENT	29.44	19.23	12.72	5.95	38.08	27.91	16.15	11.87	39.33	29.32	23.84	16.61
FROM OWN SOURCES	149.52	112.23	102.56	86.33	146.89	114.07	102.70	85.39	144.33	123.44	111.34	108.56
TAXES	126.16	94.15	86.87	75.53	126.66	97.78	91.97	76.82	110.38	96.19	87.86	87.19
PROPERTY	34.40	31.63	30.14	25.20	50.05	44.56	44.00	38.70	26.43	20.40	21.36	20.07
OTHER	91.76	62.51	56.73	50.33	76.61	53.22	47.97	38.12	83.95	75.79	66.49	67.12
CHARGES AND MISCELLANEOUS	23.36	18.08	15.59	10.80	20.23	16.29	10.73	8.56	33.95	27.25	23.48	21.37
GENERAL EXPENDITURE	180.00	134.97	118.49	92.00	178.87	161.24	124.10	106.04	180.66	149.83	131.21	128.69
EDUCATION	72.86	56.18	44.66	33.14	68.23	55.10	40.55	30.73	80.82	69.94	53.98	56.40
HIGHWAYS	20.49	21.03	18.94	15.81	12.66	28.65	18.44	18.49	20.79	23.76	24.73	21.18
PUBLIC WELFARE	23.30	10.64	10.03	6.89	31.93	17.37	12.80	11.83	11.90	7.47	8.98	10.57
HEALTH AND HOSPITALS	10.98	7.70	7.75	6.72	12.62	10.41	8.87	8.10	19.01	13.72	12.56	11.47
ALL OTHER	52.37	39.42	37.10	29.44	53.43	49.71	43.44	36.89	48.14	34.94	30.96	29.07
TOTAL STATE-LOCAL DEBT	217.89	198.91	184.08	149.37	209.04	207.95	172.19	161.15	159.42	124.51	136.95	151.07
	SOUTH DAKOTA				TENNESSEE				TEXAS			
GENERAL REVENUE	226.01	204.34	167.35	152.77	183.48	160.06	131.50	116.01	173.89	146.19	134.05	110.68
FROM FEDERAL GOVERNMENT	48.92	44.34	39.60	25.30	41.90	38.11	26.77	16.63	33.90	26.35	18.54	14.20
FROM OWN SOURCES	177.09	159.99	127.76	127.47	141.58	121.95	104.83	99.38	139.98	119.84	115.51	96.48
TAXES	132.48	124.44	102.22	103.39	108.80	95.30	85.42	83.12	106.71	90.56	90.90	76.03
PROPERTY	70.08	69.76	59.67	60.13	29.31	27.93	28.42	24.02	41.74	41.06	41.20	35.10
OTHER	62.40	54.68	42.55	43.26	79.49	67.38	57.00	59.10	64.97	49.39	49.70	40.94
CHARGES AND MISCELLANEOUS	44.61	35.55	25.54	24.08	32.77	26.65	19.42	16.26	33.28	29.38	24.61	20.45
GENERAL EXPENDITURE	214.23	204.95	161.04	155.25	187.19	176.75	142.95	113.76	175.12	152.38	132.93	113.53
EDUCATION	96.08	88.73	57.05	54.24	69.71	70.14	47.98	41.27	74.54	68.07	53.32	44.60
HIGHWAYS	44.70	54.50	54.92	49.95	25.59	32.88	34.71	24.30	24.94	28.82	28.01	24.47
PUBLIC WELFARE	17.61	13.07	10.61	10.35	18.27	12.22	10.85	10.37	17.42	10.64	10.20	9.46
HEALTH AND HOSPITALS	7.95	6.60	4.98	5.38	17.95	15.50	11.33	10.08	13.17	8.94	7.51	6.48
ALL OTHER	47.89	42.05	33.49	35.33	55.67	46.01	38.08	27.74	45.04	35.91	33.89	28.52
TOTAL STATE-LOCAL DEBT	57.67	64.00	46.44	41.97	234.15	233.04	226.09	199.10	207.17	211.64	205.22	178.01

See footnotes at end of table.

Item	1971-72	1966-67	1962	1957	1971-72	1966-67	1962	1957	1971-72	1966-67	1962	1957
	UTAH				VERMONT				VIRGINIA			
GENERAL REVENUE	224.10	205.22	153.61	131.51	267.71	198.07	187.35	133.36	168.70	139.85	112.09	104.01
FROM FEDERAL GOVERNMENT	59.65	53.15	30.58	19.14	61.96	49.47	53.99	17.50	31.75	25.88	18.09	9.72
FROM OWN SOURCES	164.45	152.07	123.02	112.37	205.74	148.60	133.36	115.86	136.94	113.97	94.01	94.29
TAXES	126.20	119.75	101.81	93.62	170.17	125.59	117.81	103.30	109.15	91.97	73.98	76.98
PROPERTY	43.00	49.52	44.93	41.01	73.02	50.38	53.21	46.45	31.11	27.63	26.57	23.91
OTHER	83.20	70.23	56.88	52.61	97.15	75.21	64.61	56.85	78.04	64.35	47.41	53.08
CHARGES AND MISCELLANEOUS	38.26	32.33	21.22	18.76	35.57	23.02	15.54	12.56	27.80	21.99	20.03	17.31
GENERAL EXPENDITURE	219.59	213.49	161.93	133.81	264.60	221.53	187.34	144.73	167.86	146.00	126.58	107.62
EDUCATION	108.71	113.62	79.18	60.40	107.38	84.95	63.54	49.13	73.06	62.58	47.45	38.08
HIGHWAYS	33.92	35.68	29.06	23.63	48.63	63.90	65.03	43.52	23.63	30.39	30.08	28.45
PUBLIC WELFARE	18.73	12.73	10.42	10.61	32.58	16.92	13.54	12.32	14.80	6.08	5.46	3.98
HEALTH AND HOSPITALS	9.86	9.26	6.90	7.20	11.37	7.90	9.02	8.99	10.08	9.73	8.13	8.27
ALL OTHER	48.37	42.20	36.37	31.97	64.64	47.86	36.21	30.77	46.29	37.22	35.46	28.84
TOTAL STATE-LOCAL DEBT	125.35	234.17	135.14	113.24	299.71	160.97	132.92	89.77	152.04	150.31	154.73	123.77

Item	1971-72	1966-67	1962	1957	1971-72	1966-67	1962	1957
	WASHINGTON				WEST VIRGINIA			
GENERAL REVENUE	212.94	177.43	153.38	124.13	208.21	174.73	140.88	96.08
FROM FEDERAL GOVERNMENT	39.40	29.96	21.74	13.90	60.44	47.19	27.05	12.21
FROM OWN SOURCES	173.54	147.47	131.63	110.23	147.77	127.55	113.84	83.87
TAXES	128.54	113.15	101.67	88.13	120.42	101.70	95.46	71.45
PROPERTY	46.86	34.84	31.37	26.09	24.76	27.11	25.98	18.13
OTHER	81.68	78.32	70.30	62.03	95.66	74.59	69.48	53.32
CHARGES AND MISCELLANEOUS	45.00	34.32	29.96	22.11	27.35	25.85	18.38	12.42
GENERAL EXPENDITURE	215.80	178.29	156.93	136.77	215.60	182.33	142.21	98.91
EDUCATION	86.07	76.31	63.75	50.69	77.95	73.54	53.92	40.30
HIGHWAYS	28.93	31.95	25.14	26.74	66.33	46.61	30.34	19.15
PUBLIC WELFARE	22.08	13.77	14.34	17.01	18.25	16.62	19.48	11.69
HEALTH AND HOSPITALS	10.68	8.83	8.23	7.71	11.82	9.52	7.37	5.59
ALL OTHER	68.04	47.43	45.47	34.62	41.25	36.04	31.10	22.18
TOTAL STATE-LOCAL DEBT	330.57	379.50	315.95	230.67	172.31	161.45	150.00	128.58

Item	1971-72	1966-67	1962	1957	1971-72	1966-67	1962	1957
	WISCONSIN				WYOMING			
GENERAL REVENUE	220.44	167.92	138.89	117.67	258.99	262.31	205.53	166.41
FROM FEDERAL GOVERNMENT	29.56	20.67	15.56	8.38	72.61	82.41	63.14	41.40
FROM OWN SOURCES	190.87	147.25	123.33	109.29	186.37	179.90	142.39	125.01
TAXES	160.60	122.49	104.33	94.68	125.85	126.22	103.75	93.30
PROPERTY	71.72	51.08	58.02	49.02	58.75	69.09	55.39	47.96
OTHER	88.87	71.41	46.32	45.67	67.10	57.13	48.36	45.34
CHARGES AND MISCELLANEOUS	30.28	24.76	19.00	14.61	60.53	53.69	38.64	31.71
GENERAL EXPENDITURE	216.99	179.25	151.73	123.25	260.97	266.84	206.31	160.06
EDUCATION	94.09	78.19	54.34	40.02	105.25	108.72	74.66	58.46
HIGHWAYS	28.82	30.20	32.71	27.99	59.24	78.78	63.88	45.14
PUBLIC WELFARE	21.72	13.80	10.99	9.23	11.06	9.45	8.58	8.45
HEALTH AND HOSPITALS	14.24	10.80	10.12	9.80	28.26	19.89	15.71	12.18
ALL OTHER	58.12	46.26	43.57	36.31	57.16	50.00	43.38	35.83
TOTAL STATE-LOCAL DEBT	162.59	146.05	123.25	79.19	150.85	194.79	148.57	102.08

Note: For information on concepts, sources, data presentation, and historical changes in data classification, see introductory text. Derived from data in table 18 and personal income estimates shown in table 21.

[1]Estimated. Data for years prior to statehood (shown in parentheses) not included in nationwide totals.

309

Table 4. Employment (Full-Time Equivalent) of State and Local Governments, by Level of Government and by Function, by States: 1972, 1967, 1962, 1957, and 1953

Item	October 1972	October 1967	October 1962	April 1957	October 1953	October 1972	October 1967	October 1962	April 1957	October 1953
	UNITED STATES					ALABAMA				
NUMBER OF EMPLOYEES										
TOTAL.	9 236 986	7 454 252	5 957 967	4 792 868	4 125 825	147 122	120 432	92 495	81 587	69 096
STATE GOVERNMENT	2 486 815	1 945 740	1 477 809	1 153 216	965 794	46 092	32 363	23 898	19 946	17 214
LOCAL GOVERNMENTS.	6 750 171	5 508 512	4 480 158	3 639 652	3 160 031	101 030	88 069	68 597	61 641	51 882
BY FUNCTION:										
EDUCATION.	4 585 476	3 658 498	2 729 653	2 092 541	1 737 224	70 517	60 256	43 160	41 262	35 589
HIGHWAYS	561 085	553 490	524 304	444 918	420 315	13 615	13 189	12 280	10 516	10 217
PUBLIC WELFARE	288 865	205 864	133 432	105 196	91 692	2 837	1 817	1 250	1 208	1 030
HEALTH AND HOSPITALS	1 052 994	844 878	694 480	559 431	447 846	22 959	15 640	11 072	7 571	4 612
POLICE PROTECTION.	487 300	380 778	318 083	268 925	229 558	6 303	4 923	3 855	3 441	2 982
LOCAL FIRE PROTECTION.	206 465	174 019	153 566	132 881	117 474	3 107	2 486	1 810	1 431	1 251
SANITATION	118 339	170 212	152 982	126 388	103 834	4 207	3 319	2 444	1 862	1 077
NATURAL RESOURCES.	160 987	139 883	121 640	106 296	98 922	2 674	2 415	2 501	2 401	2 041
LOCAL UTILITIES.	268 119	243 139	233 607	218 527	223 625	3 384	2 988	2 799	2 303	2 227
ALL OTHER.	1 507 356	1 083 491	896 221	737 765	655 335	17 519	13 399	11 325	9 592	8 070
PERCENT OF EMPLOYEES										
TOTAL.	100.0	100.0	100.0	100.0	100.0	100.0	100.0	100.0	100.0	100.0
STATE GOVERNMENT	26.9	26.1	24.8	24.1	23.4	31.3	26.9	25.8	24.4	24.9
LOCAL GOVERNMENTS.	73.1	73.9	75.2	75.9	76.6	68.7	73.1	74.2	75.6	75.1
BY FUNCTION:										
EDUCATION.	49.6	49.1	45.8	43.7	42.1	47.9	50.0	46.7	50.6	51.5
HIGHWAYS	6.1	7.4	8.8	9.3	10.2	9.3	11.0	13.3	12.9	14.8
PUBLIC WELFARE	3.1	2.8	2.2	2.2	2.2	1.9	1.5	1.4	1.5	1.5
HEALTH AND HOSPITALS	11.4	11.3	11.7	11.7	10.9	15.6	13.0	12.0	9.3	6.7
POLICE PROTECTION.	5.3	5.1	5.3	5.6	5.6	4.3	4.1	4.2	4.2	4.3
LOCAL FIRE PROTECTION.	2.2	2.3	2.6	2.6	2.8	2.1	2.1	2.0	1.8	1.8
SANITATION	1.3	2.3	2.6	2.6	2.5	2.9	2.7	2.6	2.3	1.6
NATURAL RESOURCES.	1.7	1.9	2.0	2.2	2.4	1.8	2.0	2.7	2.9	3.0
LOCAL UTILITIES.	2.9	3.3	3.9	4.6	5.4	2.3	2.5	3.0	2.8	3.2
ALL OTHER.	16.4	14.5	15.0	15.4	15.9	11.9	11.1	12.2	11.8	11.7
NUMBER OF STATE AND LOCAL GOVERNMENT EMPLOYEES PER 10,000 POPULATION										
TOTAL.	454.4	376.7	320.6	281.3	260.7	427.1	340.2	278.9	262.4	226.3
STATE GOVERNMENT	122.3	98.3	79.5	67.7	61.0	133.8	91.4	72.0	64.2	56.4
LOCAL GOVERNMENTS.	332.1	278.4	241.1	213.6	199.7	293.1	248.8	206.8	198.3	170.0
BY FUNCTION:										
EDUCATION.	225.6	184.9	146.9	122.8	109.8	204.7	170.2	130.1	132.7	116.6
HIGHWAYS	27.6	28.0	28.2	26.1	26.6	39.5	37.3	37.0	33.8	33.5
PUBLIC WELFARE	14.2	10.4	7.2	6.2	5.8	8.2	5.1	3.8	3.9	3.4
HEALTH AND HOSPITALS	51.8	42.7	37.3	32.8	28.3	66.7	44.2	33.4	24.4	15.1
POLICE PROTECTION.	24.0	19.2	17.1	15.8	14.5	18.3	13.9	11.6	11.1	9.8
LOCAL FIRE PROTECTION.	10.2	8.8	8.3	7.8	7.4	9.0	7.0	5.5	4.6	4.1
SANITATION	9.1	8.6	8.2	7.4	6.6	12.2	9.3	7.4	6.0	3.5
NATURAL RESOURCES.	7.8	7.1	6.6	6.2	6.3	7.8	6.8	7.5	7.7	6.7
LOCAL UTILITIES.	13.2	12.3	12.6	12.8	14.1	9.8	8.4	8.5	7.4	7.3
ALL OTHER.	70.9	54.7	48.2	43.3	41.4	50.9	38.0	34.1	30.9	26.4
	ALASKA					ARIZONA				
NUMBER OF EMPLOYEES										
TOTAL.	21 816	12 726	8 402	[1](4 244)	(NA)	93 741	66 654	50 151	32 119	24 091
STATE GOVERNMENT	11 751	6 804	4 613	(1 828)	(NA)	27 051	18 540	12 855	7 765	6 209
LOCAL GOVERNMENTS.	10 065	5 922	3 789	(2 416)	(NA)	66 690	48 114	37 297	24 354	17 882
BY FUNCTION:										
EDUCATION.	10 472	5 706	3 851	(2 208)	(NA)	52 305	35 924	26 601	15 462	11 065
HIGHWAYS	1 909	1 586	1 285	(155)	(NA)	5 842	6 327	5 118	3 401	2 948
PUBLIC WELFARE	421	243	104	(107)	(NA)	1 410	832	552	340	418
HEALTH AND HOSPITALS	895	711	391	(280)	(NA)	6 259	4 194	3 135	2 577	1 856
POLICE PROTECTION.	675	396	309	(222)	(NA)	5 107	3 290	2 408	1 445	1 076
LOCAL FIRE PROTECTION.	306	158	99	(69)	(NA)	1 392	1 087	899	533	426
SANITATION	197	95	77	(63)	(NA)	1 894	1 500	1 219	620	288
NATURAL RESOURCES.	835	591	352	(182)	(NA)	2 246	1 671	1 273	1 496	698
LOCAL UTILITIES.	219	248	191	(330)	(NA)	3 288	2 587	2 170	1 578	1 355
ALL OTHER.	5 887	2 992	1 742	(628)	(NA)	13 998	9 242	6 780	4 667	3 961
PERCENT OF EMPLOYEES										
TOTAL.	100.0	100.0	100.0	(100.0)	(NA)	100.0	100.0	100.0	100.0	100.0
STATE GOVERNMENT	53.9	53.5	54.9	(43.1)	(NA)	28.9	27.8	25.6	24.2	25.8
LOCAL GOVERNMENTS.	46.1	46.5	45.1	(56.9)	(NA)	71.1	72.2	74.4	75.8	74.2
BY FUNCTION:										
EDUCATION.	48.0	44.8	45.8	(52.0)	(NA)	55.8	53.9	53.0	48.1	45.9
HIGHWAYS	8.8	12.5	15.3	(3.7)	(NA)	6.2	9.5	10.2	10.6	12.2
PUBLIC WELFARE	1.9	1.9	1.2	(2.5)	(NA)	1.5	1.2	1.1	1.1	1.7
HEALTH AND HOSPITALS	4.1	5.6	4.7	(6.6)	(NA)	6.7	6.2	6.3	8.0	7.7

See footnotes at end of table.

Item	October 1972	October 1967	October 1962	April 1957	October 1953	October 1972	October 1967	October 1962	April 1957	October 1953
	ALASKA--CONTINUED					ARIZONA--CONTINUED				
PERCENT OF EMPLOYEES--CONTINUED										
BY FUNCTION--CONTINUED										
POLICE PROTECTION.	3.1	3.1	3.7	(5.2)	(NA)	5.4	4.9	4.8	4.5	4.5
LOCAL FIRE PROTECTION.	1.4	1.2	1.2	(1.6)	(NA)	1.5	1.6	1.8	1.7	1.8
SANITATION	0.9	0.8	0.9	(1.5)	(NA)	2.0	2.2	2.4	1.9	1.2
NATURAL RESOURCES.	3.8	4.6	4.2	(4.3)	(NA)	2.4	2.5	2.5	4.7	2.9
LOCAL UTILITIES.	1.0	1.9	2.3	(7.8)	(NA)	3.5	3.9	4.3	4.9	5.6
ALL OTHER.	27.0	23.6	20.7	(14.8)	(NA)	15.0	14.1	13.5	14.5	16.4
NUMBER OF STATE AND LOCAL GOVERNMENT EMPLOYEES PER 10,000 POPULATION										
TOTAL.	722.0	467.9	347.2	(183.7)	(NA)	528.8	407.9	337.5	285.5	269.5
STATE GOVERNMENT	388.9	250.1	190.6	(79.1)	(NA)	152.6	113.5	86.5	69.0	69.5
LOCAL GOVERNMENTS.	333.1	217.7	156.6	(104.6)	(NA)	376.2	294.5	251.0	216.5	200.0
BY FUNCTION:										
EDUCATION.	346.6	209.8	159.1	(95.6)	(NA)	295.1	219.9	179.0	137.4	123.8
HIGHWAYS	63.2	58.3	53.1	(6.7)	(NA)	33.0	38.7	34.4	30.2	33.0
PUBLIC WELFARE	13.9	8.9	4.3	(4.6)	(NA)	8.0	5.1	3.7	3.0	4.7
HEALTH AND HOSPITALS	29.6	26.2	16.2	(12.1)	(NA)	35.3	25.7	21.1	22.9	20.8
POLICE PROTECTION.	22.3	14.6	12.8	(9.6)	(NA)	28.8	20.1	16.2	12.8	12.0
LOCAL FIRE PROTECTION.	10.1	5.8	4.1	(3.0)	(NA)	7.8	6.7	6.1	4.7	4.8
SANITATION	6.5	3.5	3.2	(2.7)	(NA)	10.7	9.2	8.2	5.5	3.2
NATURAL RESOURCES.	27.6	21.7	14.5	(7.9)	(NA)	12.7	10.2	8.6	13.3	7.8
LOCAL UTILITIES.	7.2	9.1	7.9	(14.3)	(NA)	18.5	15.8	14.6	14.0	15.2
ALL OTHER.	195.0	110.0	72.0	(27.2)	(NA)	78.9	56.5	45.6	41.5	44.3
	ARKANSAS					CALIFORNIA				
NUMBER OF EMPLOYEES										
TOTAL.	76 213	66 549	49 911	43 909	36 852	953 235	780 502	624 439	454 598	379 261
STATE GOVERNMENT	25 840	21 166	15 927	12 714	10 560	199 914	173 957	143 397	98 211	77 349
LOCAL GOVERNMENTS.	50 373	45 383	33 984	31 195	26 292	753 321	606 545	481 041	356 387	301 912
BY FUNCTION:										
EDUCATION.	39 944	35 762	25 989	24 298	20 966	445 492	365 267	282 063	197 949	147 430
HIGHWAYS	6 566	6 528	5 862	5 032	4 592	38 571	39 770	36 077	30 185	23 946
PUBLIC WELFARE	1 802	1 142	870	652	644	38 835	25 374	13 761	9 372	8 391
HEALTH AND HOSPITALS	9 907	8 042	6 201	4 702	2 866	91 349	74 348	68 817	55 898	42 728
POLICE PROTECTION.	2 915	2 627	1 675	1 537	1 365	56 510	42 357	32 862	25 462	22 840
LOCAL FIRE PROTECTION.	1 335	1 456	854	711	670	23 448	20 943	18 218	14 953	10 549
SANITATION	1 264	1 471	860	629	572	11 583	10 044	9 301	6 767	6 792
NATURAL RESOURCES.	2 764	2 009	1 965	1 683	1 242	19 118	21 203	16 887	13 955	17 091
LOCAL UTILITIES.	1 385	1 134	967	1 081	650	37 917	34 683	31 389	23 498	21 621
ALL OTHER.	8 331	1 471	4 671	3 584	3 285	190 412	146 513	115 064	76 559	77 873
PERCENT OF EMPLOYEES										
TOTAL.	100.0	100.0	100.0	100.0	100.0	100.0	100.0	100.0	100.0	100.0
STATE GOVERNMENT	33.9	31.8	31.9	29.0	28.7	26.5	22.3	23.0	21.6	20.4
LOCAL GOVERNMENTS.	66.1	68.2	68.1	71.0	71.3	73.5	77.7	77.0	78.4	79.6
BY FUNCTION:										
EDUCATION.	52.4	53.7	52.1	55.3	56.9	46.7	46.8	45.2	43.5	38.9
HIGHWAYS	8.6	9.8	11.7	11.5	12.5	4.0	5.1	5.8	6.6	6.3
PUBLIC WELFARE	2.4	1.7	1.7	1.5	1.7	4.1	3.3	2.2	2.1	2.2
HEALTH AND HOSPITALS	13.0	12.1	12.4	10.7	7.8	9.6	9.5	11.0	12.3	11.3
POLICE PROTECTION.	3.8	3.9	3.4	3.5	3.7	5.9	5.4	5.3	5.6	6.0
LOCAL FIRE PROTECTION.	1.8	2.2	1.7	1.6	1.8	2.5	2.7	2.9	3.3	2.8
SANITATION	1.7	2.2	1.7	1.4	1.6	1.2	1.2	1.5	1.5	1.8
NATURAL RESOURCES.	3.6	3.0	3.9	3.8	3.4	2.0	2.7	2.7	3.1	4.5
LOCAL UTILITIES.	1.8	1.7	1.9	2.5	1.8	4.0	4.4	5.0	5.2	5.7
ALL OTHER.	10.9	9.7	9.4	8.2	8.9	19.9	18.9	18.4	16.8	20.5
NUMBER OF STATE AND LOCAL GOVERNMENT EMPLOYEES PER 10,000 POPULATION										
TOTAL.	396.3	338.2	271.0	253.4	207.0	477.5	407.5	366.7	318.7	309.6
STATE GOVERNMENT	134.4	107.6	86.5	73.4	59.3	100.1	90.8	84.2	68.9	63.1
LOCAL GOVERNMENTS.	261.9	230.6	184.5	180.0	147.7	377.3	316.7	282.5	249.9	246.4
BY FUNCTION:										
EDUCATION.	207.7	181.7	141.1	140.2	117.8	223.1	190.7	165.6	138.8	120.3
HIGHWAYS	34.1	33.2	31.8	29.0	25.8	19.3	20.8	21.2	21.2	19.5
PUBLIC WELFARE	9.4	5.8	4.7	3.8	3.6	19.5	13.2	8.1	6.6	6.8
HEALTH AND HOSPITALS	51.5	40.9	33.7	27.1	16.1	45.7	38.9	40.4	39.2	34.9
POLICE PROTECTION.	15.2	13.3	9.1	8.9	7.7	28.3	22.1	19.3	17.9	18.6
LOCAL FIRE PROTECTION.	6.9	7.4	4.6	4.1	3.8	11.7	10.9	10.7	10.5	8.6
SANITATION	6.6	7.5	4.7	3.6	3.2	5.8	5.2	5.5	4.7	5.5
NATURAL RESOURCES.	14.4	10.2	10.7	9.7	7.0	9.6	11.1	9.9	9.8	14.0
LOCAL UTILITIES.	7.2	5.8	5.2	6.2	3.7	19.0	18.1	18.4	16.5	17.6
ALL OTHER.	43.3	32.4	25.4	20.7	18.5	95.5	76.5	67.6	53.7	63.6

See footnotes at end of table.

Table 4. Employment (Full-Time Equivalent) of State and Local Governments, by Level of Government and by Function, by States: 1972, 1967, 1962, 1957, and 1953—Continued

Item	October 1972	October 1967	October 1962	April 1957	October 1953	October 1972	October 1967	October 1962	April 1957	October 1953
	COLORADO					CONNECTICUT				
NUMBER OF EMPLOYEES										
TOTAL	116 004	91 217	70 534	52 213	41 987	122 569	101 409	77 455	62 371	55 706
STATE GOVERNMENT	37 191	27 536	18 782	13 682	10 628	37 853	34 627	24 666	19 963	18 687
LOCAL GOVERNMENTS	78 813	63 681	51 752	38 531	31 359	84 716	66 782	52 789	42 408	37 019
BY FUNCTION:										
EDUCATION	65 527	49 872	36 831	25 308	18 651	64 485	52 089	34 941	25 689	21 945
HIGHWAYS	7 147	6 430	5 740	5 356	5 274	7 736	8 746	8 227	6 554	6 188
PUBLIC WELFARE	3 206	2 403	1 551	1 077	906	2 688	2 780	1 836	1 232	1 861
HEALTH AND HOSPITALS	10 400	9 834	7 688	5 321	4 246	10 457	9 623	8 232	7 859	7 106
POLICE PROTECTION	5 113	3 424	2 818	2 226	1 961	7 301	5 791	5 116	4 233	3 873
LOCAL FIRE PROTECTION	2 148	1 521	1 261	1 033	879	4 126	3 450	3 141	2 772	2 618
SANITATION	1 495	1 290	916	651	518	2 776	2 112	1 911	1 672	1 256
NATURAL RESOURCES	1 998	1 643	1 645	1 155	1 298	1 111	818	645	635	970
LOCAL UTILITIES	2 566	2 432	2 180	1 939	2 102	1 124	1 165	1 103	1 285	1 110
ALL OTHER	16 404	12 368	9 907	8 147	6 152	20 765	14 835	12 301	10 440	8 779
PERCENT OF EMPLOYEES										
TOTAL	100.0	100.0	100.0	100.0	100.0	100.0	100.0	100.0	100.0	100.0
STATE GOVERNMENT	32.1	30.2	26.6	26.2	25.3	30.9	34.1	31.8	32.0	33.5
LOCAL GOVERNMENTS	67.9	69.8	73.4	73.8	74.7	69.1	65.9	68.2	68.0	66.5
BY FUNCTION:										
EDUCATION	56.5	54.7	52.2	48.5	44.4	52.6	51.4	45.1	41.2	39.4
HIGHWAYS	6.2	7.0	8.1	10.3	12.6	6.3	8.6	10.6	10.5	11.1
PUBLIC WELFARE	2.8	2.6	2.2	2.1	2.2	2.2	2.7	2.4	2.0	3.3
HEALTH AND HOSPITALS	9.0	10.8	10.9	10.2	10.1	8.5	9.5	10.6	12.6	12.8
POLICE PROTECTION	4.4	3.8	4.0	4.3	4.7	6.0	5.7	6.6	6.8	7.0
LOCAL FIRE PROTECTION	1.9	1.7	1.8	2.0	2.1	3.4	3.4	4.1	4.4	4.7
SANITATION	1.3	1.4	1.3	1.2	1.2	2.3	2.1	2.5	2.7	2.3
NATURAL RESOURCES	1.7	1.8	2.3	2.2	3.1	0.9	0.8	0.8	1.0	1.7
LOCAL UTILITIES	2.2	2.7	3.1	3.7	5.0	0.9	1.1	1.4	2.1	2.0
ALL OTHER	14.0	13.5	14.0	15.6	14.7	16.9	14.7	15.9	16.7	15.8
NUMBER OF STATE AND LOCAL GOVERNMENT EMPLOYEES PER 10,000 POPULATION										
TOTAL	525.6	461.9	372.6	313.8	293.4	404.2	346.7	295.1	264.4	256.9
STATE GOVERNMENT	168.5	139.4	99.2	82.2	74.3	124.8	118.4	94.0	84.6	86.2
LOCAL GOVERNMENTS	357.1	322.4	273.4	231.6	219.1	279.4	228.3	201.1	179.8	170.8
BY FUNCTION:										
EDUCATION	296.9	252.5	194.6	152.1	130.3	212.7	178.1	133.1	108.9	101.2
HIGHWAYS	32.4	32.6	30.3	32.2	36.9	25.5	29.9	31.3	27.8	28.5
PUBLIC WELFARE	14.5	12.2	8.2	6.5	6.3	8.9	9.5	7.0	5.2	8.6
HEALTH AND HOSPITALS	47.1	49.8	40.6	32.0	29.7	34.5	32.9	31.4	33.3	32.8
POLICE PROTECTION	23.2	17.3	14.9	13.4	13.7	24.1	19.8	19.5	17.9	17.9
LOCAL FIRE PROTECTION	9.7	7.7	6.7	6.2	6.1	13.6	11.8	12.0	11.8	12.1
SANITATION	6.7	6.8	4.8	3.9	3.6	9.2	7.2	7.3	7.1	5.8
NATURAL RESOURCES	9.1	8.3	8.7	6.9	9.1	3.7	2.8	2.5	2.7	4.5
LOCAL UTILITIES	11.6	12.3	11.5	11.7	14.7	3.7	4.0	4.2	5.4	5.1
ALL OTHER	74.4	62.4	52.3	49.0	43.0	68.3	50.7	46.9	44.3	40.5
	DELAWARE					DISTRICT OF COLUMBIA				
NUMBER OF EMPLOYEES										
TOTAL	29 392	21 205	15 575	11 709	9 946	50 268	38 058	27 478	21 750	19 640
STATE GOVERNMENT	14 467	9 868	6 428	5 149	4 234	-	-	-	-	-
LOCAL GOVERNMENTS	14 925	11 337	9 147	6 560	5 712	50 268	38 058	27 478	21 750	19 640
BY FUNCTION:										
EDUCATION	16 053	10 999	7 718	5 156	4 215	14 770	12 509	7 570	6 080	5 311
HIGHWAYS	1 745	1 880	1 500	1 247	1 062	1 352	1 502	1 365	1 009	623
PUBLIC WELFARE	986	976	648	348	264	2 900	3 413	1 975	1 278	829
HEALTH AND HOSPITALS	2 385	1 899	1 488	1 246	1 023	8 197	5 217	3 539	2 815	2 925
POLICE PROTECTION	1 565	858	719	617	496	6 213	3 175	3 053	2 830	2 249
LOCAL FIRE PROTECTION	254	274	275	272	250	1 481	1 471	1 275	1 119	1 083
SANITATION	617	565	500	355	321	2 455	2 665	2 514	2 141	1 966
NATURAL RESOURCES	647	427	263	262	243	-	-	-	-	-
LOCAL UTILITIES	303	296	321	254	243	875	589	618	590	565
ALL OTHER	4 837	3 031	2 146	1 952	1 829	14 725	7 517	5 570	3 888	4 089
PERCENT OF EMPLOYEES										
TOTAL	100.0	100.0	100.0	100.0	100.0	100.0	100.0	100.0	100.0	100.0
STATE GOVERNMENT	49.2	46.5	41.3	44.0	42.6	-	-	-	-	-
LOCAL GOVERNMENTS	50.8	53.5	58.7	56.0	57.4	100.0	100.0	100.0	100.0	100.0
BY FUNCTION:										
EDUCATION	54.6	51.9	49.6	44.0	42.4	29.4	32.9	27.5	28.0	27.0
HIGHWAYS	5.9	8.9	9.6	10.6	10.7	2.7	3.9	5.0	4.6	3.2
PUBLIC WELFARE	3.4	4.6	4.2	3.0	2.7	5.8	9.0	7.2	5.9	4.2
HEALTH AND HOSPITALS	8.1	9.0	9.6	10.6	10.3	16.3	13.8	12.9	12.9	14.9

See footnotes at end of table.

312

Table 4. Employment (Full-Time Equivalent) of State and Local Governments, by Level of Government and by Function, by States: 1972, 1967, 1962, 1957, and 1953—Continued

Item	October 1972	October 1967	October 1962	April 1957	October 1953	October 1972	October 1967	October 1962	April 1957	October 1953
	DELAWARE--CONTINUED					DISTRICT OF COLUMBIA--CONTINUED				
PERCENT OF EMPLOYEES--CONTINUED										
BY FUNCTION--CONTINUED										
POLICE PROTECTION.	5.0	4.0	4.6	5.3	5.0	12.4	8.3	11.1	13.0	11.5
LOCAL FIRE PROTECTION.	0.9	1.3	1.8	2.3	2.5	2.9	3.9	4.6	5.1	5.5
SANITATION.	2.1	2.7	3.2	3.0	3.2	4.9	7.0	9.1	9.8	10.0
NATURAL RESOURCES.	2.2	2.0	1.7	2.2	2.4	-	-	-	-	-
LOCAL UTILITIES.	1.0	1.4	2.1	2.2	2.4	1.7	1.5	2.2	2.7	2.9
ALL OTHER.	16.8	14.2	13.8	16.7	18.4	23.9	19.7	20.3	17.9	20.8
NUMBER OF STATE AND LOCAL GOVERNMENT EMPLOYEES PER 10,000 POPULATION										
TOTAL.	536.3	405.4	333.5	274.9	283.4	664.5	470.4	348.3	285.1	242.5
STATE GOVERNMENT	264.0	188.7	137.6	120.9	120.6	-	-	-	-	-
LOCAL GOVERNMENTS.	272.3	216.8	195.9	154.0	162.8	664.5	470.4	348.3	285.1	242.5
BY FUNCTION:										
EDUCATION.	292.9	210.3	165.3	121.0	120.1	195.2	154.6	95.9	79.7	65.6
HIGHWAYS	31.8	35.9	32.1	29.3	30.3	17.9	18.6	17.3	13.2	7.7
PUBLIC WELFARE	18.0	18.7	13.9	8.2	7.5	38.3	42.2	25.0	16.7	10.2
HEALTH AND HOSPITALS	43.5	36.3	31.9	29.2	29.1	108.3	64.5	44.9	36.9	36.1
POLICE PROTECTION.	26.7	16.4	15.4	14.5	14.1	82.1	39.2	38.7	37.1	27.8
LOCAL FIRE PROTECTION.	4.6	5.2	5.9	6.4	7.1	19.6	18.2	16.2	14.7	13.4
SANITATION	11.1	10.8	10.7	8.3	9.1	32.5	32.9	31.9	28.1	24.3
NATURAL RESOURCES.	11.8	8.2	5.6	6.2	6.9	-	-	-	-	-
LOCAL UTILITIES.	5.5	5.7	6.9	6.0	6.9	11.6	7.3	7.8	7.7	7.0
ALL OTHER.	90.3	57.9	46.0	45.8	52.1	159.0	92.9	70.6	51.0	50.5
	FLORIDA					GEORGIA				
NUMBER OF EMPLOYEES										
TOTAL.	333 262	247 874	185 238	126 477	94 559	222 871	164 749	123 858	102 780	82 648
STATE GOVERNMENT	79 098	56 005	40 919	30 826	23 196	59 499	38 789	29 310	22 604	19 022
LOCAL GOVERNMENTS.	254 164	191 869	144 319	95 651	71 363	163 372	125 960	94 548	80 176	63 626
BY FUNCTION:										
EDUCATION.	155 517	115 709	80 649	51 049	37 153	102 863	81 969	58 453	49 956	41 024
HIGHWAYS	16 642	16 513	14 448	11 581	9 579	15 229	12 811	11 796	10 409	10 230
PUBLIC WELFARE	7 199	4 086	2 137	1 866	1 187	4 982	1 943	1 278	1 153	1 007
HEALTH AND HOSPITALS	43 137	34 307	26 472	16 768	13 245	44 997	28 255	19 354	14 012	7 520
POLICE PROTECTION.	18 711	13 215	10 493	7 001	4 945	9 387	6 596	5 307	4 693	3 856
LOCAL FIRE PROTECTION.	7 145	5 276	4 152	3 035	2 383	4 194	3 061	2 567	2 152	1 906
SANITATION	9 661	8 654	7 249	6 038	4 755	6 396	5 422	4 705	3 643	2 591
NATURAL RESOURCES.	7 766	5 752	4 846	5 132	2 884	4 561	3 796	3 584	3 287	2 500
LOCAL UTILITIES.	8 761	7 213	7 160	5 059	4 596	3 992	3 469	3 151	2 676	2 241
ALL OTHER.	58 723	37 149	27 634	18 948	13 832	26 290	17 427	13 655	10 799	9 773
PERCENT OF EMPLOYEES										
TOTAL.	100.0	100.0	100.0	100.0	100.0	100.0	100.0	100.0	100.0	100.0
STATE GOVERNMENT	23.7	22.6	22.1	24.4	24.5	26.7	23.5	23.7	22.0	23.0
LOCAL GOVERNMENTS.	76.3	77.4	77.9	75.6	75.5	73.3	76.5	76.3	78.0	77.0
BY FUNCTION:										
EDUCATION.	46.7	46.7	43.5	40.4	39.3	46.2	49.8	47.2	48.6	49.6
HIGHWAYS	5.0	6.7	7.8	9.2	10.1	6.8	7.8	9.5	10.1	12.4
PUBLIC WELFARE	2.2	1.6	1.2	1.5	1.3	2.2	1.2	1.0	1.1	1.2
HEALTH AND HOSPITALS	13.0	13.9	14.3	13.3	14.0	20.2	17.1	15.6	13.6	9.1
POLICE PROTECTION.	5.6	5.3	5.7	5.5	5.2	4.2	4.0	4.3	4.6	4.7
LOCAL FIRE PROTECTION.	2.1	2.1	2.2	2.4	2.5	1.9	1.9	2.1	2.1	2.3
SANITATION	2.9	3.5	3.9	4.8	5.0	2.9	3.3	3.8	3.5	3.1
NATURAL RESOURCES.	2.3	2.3	2.6	4.1	3.0	2.0	2.3	2.9	3.2	3.0
LOCAL UTILITIES.	2.6	2.9	3.9	4.0	4.9	1.8	2.1	2.5	2.6	2.7
ALL OTHER.	17.6	15.0	14.9	15.0	14.6	11.8	10.5	11.0	10.5	11.8
NUMBER OF STATE AND LOCAL GOVERNMENT EMPLOYEES PER 10,000 POPULATION										
TOTAL.	490.8	413.5	340.9	289.3	285.7	485.5	365.4	303.4	272.9	232.3
STATE GOVERNMENT	116.5	93.4	75.3	70.5	70.1	129.6	86.0	71.8	60.0	53.5
LOCAL GOVERNMENTS.	374.3	320.0	265.6	218.8	215.6	355.9	279.4	231.6	212.9	178.8
BY FUNCTION:										
EDUCATION.	229.0	193.0	148.4	116.8	112.2	224.1	181.8	143.2	132.7	115.3
HIGHWAYS	24.5	27.5	26.6	26.5	28.9	33.2	28.4	28.9	27.6	28.8
PUBLIC WELFARE	10.6	6.8	3.9	4.3	3.6	10.9	4.3	3.1	3.1	2.8
HEALTH AND HOSPITALS	63.5	57.2	48.7	38.4	40.0	98.1	62.7	47.4	37.2	21.1
POLICE PROTECTION.	27.6	22.0	19.3	16.0	14.9	20.5	14.6	13.0	12.5	10.8
LOCAL FIRE PROTECTION.	10.5	8.8	7.6	6.9	7.2	9.1	6.8	6.3	5.7	5.4
SANITATION	14.2	14.5	13.3	13.8	14.4	13.9	12.1	11.5	9.7	7.3
NATURAL RESOURCES.	11.4	9.6	8.9	11.7	8.7	9.9	8.4	8.8	8.7	7.0
LOCAL UTILITIES.	12.9	12.0	13.2	11.6	13.9	8.7	7.7	7.7	7.1	6.3
ALL OTHER.	86.6	62.1	50.9	43.3	41.8	57.2	38.6	33.4	28.7	27.5

See footnotes at end of table.

Item	October 1972	October 1967	October 1962	April 1957	October 1953	October 1972	October 1967	October 1962	April 1957	October 1953
	HAWAII					IDAHO				
NUMBER OF EMPLOYEES										
TOTAL.	40 303	31 932	22 525	[1](17 499)	(NA)	35 466	27 596	24 141	19 608	17 140
STATE GOVERNMENT	30 223	23 082	14 921	(10 758)	(NA)	11 843	8 253	7 310	5 816	5 441
LOCAL GOVERNMENTS.	10 080	8 850	7 604	(6 691)	(NA)	23 623	19 343	16 831	13 792	11 699
BY FUNCTION:										
EDUCATION.	20 077	15 911	9 000	(6 185)	(NA)	17 723	13 917	11 510	9 317	7 604
HIGHWAYS	1 994	1 900	2 160	(1 649)	(NA)	3 057	2 732	2 896	2 573	2 626
PUBLIC WELFARE	457	328	299	(274)	(NA)	549	382	223	190	209
HEALTH AND HOSPITALS	3 179	2 773	2 517	(2 352)	(NA)	3 624	2 846	2 462	1 607	1 255
POLICE PROTECTION.	2 282	1 416	1 118	(932)	(NA)	1 551	1 169	1 026	860	815
LOCAL FIRE PROTECTION.	1 211	906	667	(587)	(NA)	752	466	395	338	283
SANITATION	1 022	930	716	(597)	(NA)	256	232	229	154	133
NATURAL RESOURCES.	1 085	985	764	(512)	(NA)	2 043	1 559	1 662	1 419	1 316
LOCAL UTILITIES.	838	765	744	(656)	(NA)	293	308	385	316	299
ALL OTHER.	8 158	6 018	4 541	(3 705)	(NA)	5 618	3 985	3 351	2 834	2 600
PERCENT OF EMPLOYEES										
TOTAL.	100.0	100.0	100.0	(100.0)	(NA)	100.0	100.0	100.0	100.0	100.0
STATE GOVERNMENT	75.0	72.3	66.2	(61.7)	(NA)	33.4	29.9	30.3	29.7	31.7
LOCAL GOVERNMENTS.	25.0	27.7	33.8	(38.3)	(NA)	66.6	70.1	69.7	70.3	68.3
BY FUNCTION:										
EDUCATION.	49.8	49.8	40.0	(35.4)	(NA)	50.0	50.4	47.7	47.5	44.4
HIGHWAYS	4.9	6.0	9.6	(9.5)	(NA)	8.6	9.9	12.0	13.1	15.3
PUBLIC WELFARE	1.1	1.0	1.3	(1.6)	(NA)	1.5	1.4	0.9	1.0	1.2
HEALTH AND HOSPITALS	7.8	8.7	11.2	(13.5)	(NA)	10.2	10.3	10.2	8.2	7.3
POLICE PROTECTION.	5.7	4.4	5.0	(5.3)	(NA)	4.4	4.2	4.3	4.4	4.8
LOCAL FIRE PROTECTION.	3.0	2.8	3.0	(3.4)	(NA)	2.1	1.7	1.6	1.7	1.7
SANITATION	2.5	2.9	3.2	(3.4)	(NA)	0.7	0.8	0.9	0.8	0.8
NATURAL RESOURCES.	2.7	3.1	3.4	(2.9)	(NA)	5.8	5.6	6.9	7.2	7.7
LOCAL UTILITIES.	2.1	2.4	3.3	(3.8)	(NA)	0.8	1.1	1.6	1.6	1.7
ALL OTHER.	20.4	18.9	20.2	(21.2)	(NA)	15.9	14.6	13.9	14.5	15.2
NUMBER OF STATE AND LOCAL GOVERNMENT EMPLOYEES PER 10,000 POPULATION										
TOTAL.	523.5	432.1	325.0	(298.8)	(NA)	497.5	394.8	344.9	305.4	287.6
STATE GOVERNMENT	392.6	312.3	215.3	(184.2)	(NA)	166.1	118.1	104.4	90.6	91.3
LOCAL GOVERNMENTS.	130.9	119.8	109.7	(114.6)	(NA)	331.4	276.7	240.4	214.8	196.3
BY FUNCTION:										
EDUCATION.	260.8	215.3	129.9	(105.9)	(NA)	248.6	199.1	164.4	145.1	127.6
HIGHWAYS	25.9	25.7	31.2	(28.2)	(NA)	42.9	39.1	41.4	40.1	44.1
PUBLIC WELFARE	5.9	4.4	4.3	(4.7)	(NA)	7.7	5.5	3.2	3.0	3.5
HEALTH AND HOSPITALS	41.3	37.6	36.3	(40.3)	(NA)	50.9	40.7	35.2	25.0	21.1
POLICE PROTECTION.	29.6	19.2	16.1	(16.0)	(NA)	21.8	16.7	14.7	13.4	13.7
LOCAL FIRE PROTECTION.	15.7	12.3	9.6	(10.1)	(NA)	10.5	6.7	5.6	5.3	4.7
SANITATION	13.3	12.6	10.3	(10.2)	(NA)	3.6	3.3	3.3	2.4	2.2
NATURAL RESOURCES.	14.1	13.3	11.0	(8.8)	(NA)	28.7	22.3	23.8	22.1	22.1
LOCAL UTILITIES.	10.9	10.4	10.7	(11.2)	(NA)	4.1	4.4	5.5	4.9	5.0
ALL OTHER.	106.0	81.3	65.5	(63.4)	(NA)	78.7	57.0	47.9	44.1	43.6
	ILLINOIS					INDIANA				
NUMBER OF EMPLOYEES										
TOTAL.	460 485	383 063	303 118	243 687	211 674	212 183	180 881	147 008	118 965	100 933
STATE GOVERNMENT	108 414	91 675	60 676	48 752	38 682	54 953	48 850	37 190	28 908	23 486
LOCAL GOVERNMENTS.	352 071	291 388	242 442	194 935	172 992	157 230	132 031	109 818	90 057	77 447
BY FUNCTION:										
EDUCATION.	226 235	187 124	138 031	101 224	85 942	117 605	98 882	72 719	55 494	47 058
HIGHWAYS	19 364	22 517	22 433	14 619	13 747	11 430	12 167	11 831	9 341	8 818
PUBLIC WELFARE	15 162	12 143	8 288	6 835	4 485	4 913	3 621	2 834	2 247	2 141
HEALTH AND HOSPITALS	47 431	42 401	30 943	25 660	22 144	26 853	23 000	18 391	15 312	12 560
POLICE PROTECTION.	29 699	24 477	21 549	17 407	14 446	9 423	7 613	6 569	5 882	5 319
LOCAL FIRE PROTECTION.	10 784	8 712	8 026	7 084	5 455	5 178	4 511	4 074	3 503	3 162
SANITATION	9 929	8 143	6 440	8 022	6 552	3 818	3 521	3 035	2 244	1 653
NATURAL RESOURCES.	4 518	3 591	3 283	2 329	2 108	2 365	1 925	2 411	1 926	1 494
LOCAL UTILITIES.	18 883	18 874	18 893	19 628	23 209	4 806	4 664	4 533	4 715	4 268
ALL OTHER.	78 480	55 081	45 232	40 879	33 586	25 792	21 037	20 613	18 301	14 460
PERCENT OF EMPLOYEES										
TOTAL.	100.0	100.0	100.0	100.0	100.0	100.0	100.0	100.0	100.0	100.0
STATE GOVERNMENT	23.5	23.9	20.0	20.0	18.3	25.9	27.0	25.3	24.3	23.3
LOCAL GOVERNMENTS.	76.5	76.1	80.0	80.0	81.7	74.1	73.0	74.7	75.7	76.7
BY FUNCTION:										
EDUCATION.	49.1	48.8	45.5	41.5	40.6	55.4	54.6	49.5	46.6	46.6
HIGHWAYS	4.2	5.9	7.4	6.0	6.5	5.4	6.7	8.0	7.9	8.7
PUBLIC WELFARE	3.3	3.2	2.7	2.8	2.1	2.3	2.0	1.9	1.9	2.1
HEALTH AND HOSPITALS	10.3	11.0	10.2	10.5	10.5	12.5	12.7	12.5	12.9	12.4

See footnotes at end of table.

Table 4. Employment (Full-Time Equivalent) of State and Local Governments, by Level of Government and by Function, by States: 1972, 1967, 1962, 1957, and 1953—Continued

Item	October 1972	October 1967	October 1962	April 1957	October 1953	October 1972	October 1967	October 1962	April 1957	October 1953
	ILLINOIS--CONTINUED					INDIANA--CONTINUED				
PERCENT OF EMPLOYEES--CONTINUED										
BY FUNCTION--CONTINUED										
POLICE PROTECTION.	6.4	6.4	7.1	7.1	6.8	4.4	4.2	4.5	4.9	5.3
LOCAL FIRE PROTECTION.	2.3	2.3	2.6	2.9	2.6	2.4	2.5	2.8	2.9	3.1
SANITATION	2.2	2.1	2.1	3.3	3.1	1.8	2.0	2.1	1.9	1.6
NATURAL RESOURCES.	1.0	0.9	1.1	1.0	1.0	1.1	1.1	1.6	1.6	1.5
LOCAL UTILITIES.	4.1	4.9	6.2	8.1	11.0	2.3	2.6	3.1	4.0	4.2
ALL OTHER.	17.1	14.5	14.9	16.8	15.9	12.4	11.6	14.0	15.4	14.3
NUMBER OF STATE AND LOCAL GOVERNMENT EMPLOYEES PER 10,000 POPULATION										
TOTAL.	414.4	351.7	300.2	252.1	233.5	408.4	361.8	315.3	262.7	241.4
STATE GOVERNMENT	97.6	84.2	60.1	50.4	42.7	105.8	97.7	79.8	63.8	56.2
LOCAL GOVERNMENTS.	316.8	267.5	240.1	201.6	190.8	302.6	264.1	235.5	148.8	185.2
BY FUNCTION:										
EDUCATION.	203.6	171.8	136.7	104.7	94.8	226.4	197.6	155.9	122.5	112.5
HIGHWAYS	17.4	20.7	22.2	15.1	15.2	22.0	24.3	25.4	20.6	21.1
PUBLIC WELFARE	13.6	11.1	8.2	7.1	4.9	9.5	7.2	6.1	5.0	5.1
HEALTH AND HOSPITALS	42.7	38.9	30.6	26.5	24.4	51.7	46.0	39.4	33.8	30.0
POLICE PROTECTION.	26.7	22.5	21.3	18.0	15.9	18.1	15.2	14.1	13.0	12.7
LOCAL FIRE PROTECTION.	9.7	8.0	8.0	7.3	6.0	10.0	9.0	8.7	7.7	7.6
SANITATION.	9.0	7.5	6.4	8.3	7.2	7.3	7.0	6.5	5.0	4.0
NATURAL RESOURCES.	4.1	3.3	3.3	2.4	2.3	4.6	3.8	5.2	4.3	3.6
LOCAL UTILITIES.	17.0	17.3	18.7	20.3	25.6	9.3	9.3	9.7	10.4	10.2
ALL OTHER.	70.5	50.6	44.8	42.3	37.1	49.5	42.4	44.2	40.4	34.6
	IOWA					KANSAS				
NUMBER OF EMPLOYEES										
TOTAL.	123 948	108 163	92 868	81 872	75 157	107 400	95 448	79 574	68 464	57 574
STATE GOVERNMENT	33 367	29 897	24 542	20 913	19 434	31 599	27 891	21 164	17 662	15 194
LOCAL GOVERNMENTS.	90 581	78 266	68 326	60 959	55 723	75 801	67 557	58 410	50 802	42 380
BY FUNCTION:										
EDUCATION.	69 935	59 897	49 559	44 973	38 868	56 694	49 794	40 874	32 991	28 187
HIGHWAYS	10 350	9 604	9 600	8 490	9 076	9 201	9 287	9 427	8 961	8 619
PUBLIC WELFARE	3 867	3 252	2 605	2 128	1 684	2 397	2 129	1 672	1 401	1 234
HEALTH AND HOSPITALS	12 704	11 219	9 011	7 701	7 681	11 741	11 286	8 267	7 042	4 779
POLICE PROTECTION.	4 532	3 604	3 154	2 632	2 420	4 450	3 498	2 938	2 424	2 020
LOCAL FIRE PROTECTION.	1 998	1 635	1 604	1 148	1 112	2 440	1 794	1 491	1 326	1 038
SANITATION.	1 437	1 607	1 501	1 098	1 105	1 304	1 320	1 121	969	675
NATURAL RESOURCES.	2 164	2 240	2 575	1 393	1 422	2 299	2 282	1 754	1 132	1 009
LOCAL UTILITIES.	1 880	2 071	2 061	2 234	2 645	2 730	2 761	2 822	2 525	2 470
ALL OTHER.	15 081	13 034	11 201	10 075	9 144	14 104	11 297	9 210	9 693	7 543
PERCENT OF EMPLOYEES										
TOTAL.	100.0	100.0	100.0	100.0	100.0	100.0	100.0	100.0	100.0	100.0
STATE GOVERNMENT	26.9	27.6	26.4	25.5	25.9	29.4	29.2	26.6	25.8	26.4
LOCAL GOVERNMENTS.	73.1	72.4	73.6	74.5	74.1	70.6	70.8	73.4	74.2	73.6
BY FUNCTION:										
EDUCATION.	56.4	55.4	53.4	54.9	51.7	52.8	52.2	51.4	48.2	49.0
HIGHWAYS	8.4	8.9	10.3	10.4	12.1	8.6	9.7	11.8	13.1	15.0
PUBLIC WELFARE	3.1	3.0	2.8	2.6	2.2	2.2	2.2	2.1	2.0	2.1
HEALTH AND HOSPITALS	10.2	10.4	9.7	9.4	10.2	10.9	11.8	10.4	10.3	8.3
POLICE PROTECTION.	3.7	3.3	3.4	3.2	3.2	4.2	3.7	3.7	3.5	3.5
LOCAL FIRE PROTECTION.	1.6	1.5	1.7	1.4	1.5	2.3	1.9	1.9	1.9	1.8
SANITATION.	1.2	1.5	1.6	1.3	1.5	1.3	1.4	1.4	1.4	1.2
NATURAL RESOURCES.	1.7	2.1	2.8	1.7	1.9	2.1	2.4	2.2	1.7	1.8
LOCAL UTILITIES.	1.5	1.9	2.2	2.7	3.5	2.6	2.9	3.5	3.7	4.3
ALL OTHER.	12.2	12.0	12.1	12.3	12.2	13.0	11.8	11.6	14.2	13.1
NUMBER OF STATE AND LOCAL GOVERNMENT EMPLOYEES PER 10,000 POPULATION										
TOTAL.	438.7	392.9	334.8	301.4	285.9	477.5	419.6	359.3	321.7	288.7
STATE GOVERNMENT	118.1	108.6	88.5	77.0	73.9	140.5	122.6	95.5	83.0	76.2
LOCAL GOVERNMENTS.	320.6	284.3	246.3	224.4	212.0	337.0	297.0	263.7	238.7	212.5
BY FUNCTION:										
EDUCATION.	247.5	217.6	178.7	165.6	147.8	252.1	218.9	184.5	155.0	141.4
HIGHWAYS	36.6	34.9	34.6	31.3	34.5	40.9	40.8	42.6	42.1	43.2
PUBLIC WELFARE	13.7	11.8	9.4	7.8	6.4	10.7	9.4	7.6	6.6	6.2
HEALTH AND HOSPITALS	44.9	40.7	32.5	28.4	29.2	52.2	49.6	37.3	33.1	24.0
POLICE PROTECTION.	16.0	13.1	11.4	9.7	9.2	19.8	15.4	13.3	11.4	10.1
LOCAL FIRE PROTECTION.	7.1	5.9	5.8	4.2	4.2	11.0	7.9	6.7	6.2	5.2
SANITATION.	5.1	5.9	5.4	4.0	4.2	5.8	5.8	5.1	4.6	3.4
NATURAL RESOURCES.	7.7	8.1	9.3	5.1	5.4	10.2	10.0	7.9	5.3	5.1
LOCAL UTILITIES.	6.7	7.5	7.4	8.2	10.1	12.1	12.1	12.7	11.9	12.4
ALL OTHER.	53.4	47.4	40.4	37.1	34.8	62.7	49.7	41.6	45.5	37.8

See footnotes at end of table.

315

Item	October 1972	October 1967	October 1962	April 1957	October 1953	October 1972	October 1967	October 1962	April 1957	October 1953
	KENTUCKY					LOUISIANA				
NUMBER OF EMPLOYEES										
TOTAL.	125 280	106 130	81 862	69 795	57 338	176 455	147 362	119 827	98 154	78 886
STATE GOVERNMENT	45 259	36 707	24 449	21 903	16 336	59 096	51 399	40 590	35 128	28 891
LOCAL GOVERNMENTS.	80 021	69 423	57 413	47 892	41 002	117 359	95 963	79 237	63 026	49 995
BY FUNCTION:										
EDUCATION.	69 096	58 940	42 292	33 934	29 109	87 396	72 581	55 793	42 996	34 495
HIGHWAYS	10 700	10 687	9 652	9 039	7 991	12 568	13 940	11 722	10 311	8 801
PUBLIC WELFARE	3 649	2 631	1 353	593	1 172	4 535	3 101	2 490	2 722	2 205
HEALTH AND HOSPITALS	12 830	10 211	8 225	6 207	4 573	23 073	17 564	14 782	11 357	9 133
POLICE PROTECTION.	5 112	4 291	3 758	3 275	2 709	8 683	7 276	5 524	4 415	3 168
LOCAL FIRE PROTECTION.	2 202	1 885	1 563	1 360	1 199	3 243	2 761	2 487	2 182	2 082
SANITATION	2 165	2 139	1 635	1 274	805	4 704	3 751	3 389	2 683	2 003
NATURAL RESOURCES.	4 209	3 119	2 472	3 679	1 342	4 808	4 891	4 825	4 528	3 769
LOCAL UTILITIES.	2 154	2 009	2 116	1 703	1 485	3 612	3 890	3 609	3 561	2 857
ALL OTHER.	15 163	10 218	8 796	8 731	6 953	23 833	17 607	15 207	13 399	10 373
PERCENT OF EMPLOYEES										
TOTAL.	100.0	100.0	100.0	100.0	100.0	100.0	100.0	100.0	100.0	100.0
STATE GOVERNMENT	36.1	34.6	29.9	31.4	28.5	33.5	34.9	33.9	35.8	36.6
LOCAL GOVERNMENTS.	73.9	65.4	70.1	68.6	71.5	66.5	65.1	66.1	64.2	63.4
BY FUNCTION:										
EDUCATION.	55.2	55.5	51.7	48.6	50.8	49.5	49.3	46.6	43.8	43.7
HIGHWAYS	8.5	10.1	11.8	13.0	13.9	7.1	9.5	9.8	10.5	11.2
PUBLIC WELFARE	2.9	2.5	1.7	0.8	2.0	2.6	2.1	2.1	2.8	2.8
HEALTH AND HOSPITALS	10.2	9.6	10.0	8.9	8.0	13.1	11.9	12.3	11.6	11.6
POLICE PROTECTION.	4.1	4.0	4.6	4.7	4.7	4.9	4.9	4.6	4.5	4.0
LOCAL FIRE PROTECTION.	1.8	1.8	1.9	1.9	2.1	1.8	1.9	2.1	2.2	2.6
SANITATION	1.7	2.0	2.0	1.8	1.4	2.6	2.6	2.8	2.7	2.5
NATURAL RESOURCES.	3.4	2.9	3.0	5.3	2.3	2.7	3.3	4.0	4.6	4.8
LOCAL UTILITIES.	1.7	1.9	2.6	2.4	2.6	2.0	2.6	3.0	3.6	3.6
ALL OTHER.	10.4	9.7	10.7	12.5	12.1	13.7	11.9	12.7	13.7	13.1
NUMBER OF STATE AND LOCAL GOVERNMENT EMPLOYEES PER 10,000 POPULATION										
TOTAL.	389.2	332.8	265.4	238.4	197.5	484.4	402.4	355.5	315.1	275.2
STATE GOVERNMENT	140.6	115.1	79.3	74.8	56.3	162.2	140.4	120.4	112.8	100.8
LOCAL GOVERNMENTS.	248.6	217.7	186.2	163.6	141.2	322.2	262.1	235.1	202.3	174.4
BY FUNCTION:										
EDUCATION.	214.6	184.8	137.1	115.9	100.3	239.9	198.2	165.5	138.0	120.4
HIGHWAYS	33.2	33.5	31.3	30.9	27.5	34.5	38.1	34.8	33.1	30.7
PUBLIC WELFARE	11.3	8.3	4.4	2.0	4.0	12.4	8.5	7.4	8.7	7.7
HEALTH AND HOSPITALS	39.9	32.0	26.7	21.2	15.8	63.3	47.9	43.9	36.5	31.9
POLICE PROTECTION.	15.9	13.5	12.2	11.2	9.3	23.8	19.9	16.4	14.2	11.1
LOCAL FIRE PROTECTION.	6.8	5.9	5.1	4.6	4.1	8.9	7.5	7.4	7.0	7.2
SANITATION	6.7	6.7	5.3	4.4	2.8	12.9	10.3	10.1	8.6	6.9
NATURAL RESOURCES.	13.1	9.8	8.0	12.6	4.6	13.2	13.4	14.3	14.5	13.2
LOCAL UTILITIES.	6.7	6.3	6.9	5.8	5.1	9.9	10.6	10.7	11.4	10.0
ALL OTHER.	40.9	32.0	28.5	29.8	24.0	65.5	48.0	45.1	43.0	36.2
	MAINE					MARYLAND				
NUMBER OF EMPLOYEES										
TOTAL.	44 135	34 904	29 588	24 699	22 414	185 742	141 717	102 622	75 277	61 587
STATE GOVERNMENT	16 082	12 899	10 939	8 682	7 734	55 719	37 954	27 501	20 501	17 265
LOCAL GOVERNMENTS.	28 053	22 005	18 649	16 017	14 680	130 023	103 763	75 121	54 776	44 322
BY FUNCTION:										
EDUCATION.	23 807	18 276	13 759	11 077	10 046	96 443	73 638	48 709	32 416	24 756
HIGHWAYS	5 137	4 934	4 812	3 971	3 798	9 487	8 753	7 651	5 739	5 499
PUBLIC WELFARE	763	685	571	457	404	4 547	2 533	1 461	814	571
HEALTH AND HOSPITALS	2 817	2 407	2 399	1 909	1 816	20 214	16 511	12 898	9 988	8 694
POLICE PROTECTION.	1 810	1 355	1 192	966	883	11 468	8 799	7 138	5 767	4 184
LOCAL FIRE PROTECTION.	1 203	913	826	701	643	4 236	3 605	2 948	2 449	1 712
SANITATION	366	264	324	176	151	4 223	4 096	3 775	3 029	2 074
NATURAL RESOURCES.	1 412	1 227	1 199	809	1 060	1 892	1 365	1 089	990	958
LOCAL UTILITIES.	533	502	571	619	368	2 469	1 813	1 746	1 955	2 795
ALL OTHER.	6 287	4 341	3 937	4 014	3 245	30 763	20 604	15 208	12 130	10 344
PERCENT OF EMPLOYEES										
TOTAL.	100.0	100.0	100.0	100.0	100.0	100.0	100.0	100.0	100.0	100.0
STATE GOVERNMENT	36.4	37.0	37.0	35.2	34.5	30.0	26.8	26.8	27.2	28.0
LOCAL GOVERNMENTS.	63.6	63.0	63.0	64.8	65.5	70.0	73.2	73.2	72.8	72.0
BY FUNCTION:										
EDUCATION.	53.9	52.4	46.5	44.8	44.8	51.8	52.0	47.5	43.1	40.2
HIGHWAYS	11.4	14.1	16.3	16.1	16.9	5.1	6.2	7.5	7.6	8.9
PUBLIC WELFARE	1.7	2.0	1.9	1.9	1.8	2.5	1.8	1.4	1.1	0.9
HEALTH AND HOSPITALS	6.2	6.9	8.1	7.7	8.1	11.0	11.6	12.6	13.3	14.1

See footnotes at end of table.

Table 4. Employment (Full-Time Equivalent) of State and Local Governments, by Level of Government and by Function, by States: 1972, 1967, 1962, 1957, and 1953—Continued

Item	October 1972	October 1967	October 1962	April 1957	October 1953	October 1972	October 1967	October 1962	April 1957	October 1953
	MAINE--CONTINUED					MARYLAND--CONTINUED				
PERCENT OF EMPLOYEES--CONTINUED										
BY FUNCTION--CONTINUED										
POLICE PROTECTION.	4.0	3.9	4.0	3.9	3.9	6.2	6.2	7.0	7.7	6.8
LOCAL FIRE PROTECTION.	2.7	2.6	2.8	2.8	2.9	2.3	2.5	2.9	3.3	2.8
SANITATION	0.8	0.7	1.1	0.7	0.7	2.3	2.9	3.7	4.0	3.4
NATURAL RESOURCES.	3.1	3.5	4.1	3.3	4.7	1.0	1.0	1.1	1.3	1.6
LOCAL UTILITIES.	1.2	1.4	1.9	2.5	1.6	1.3	1.3	1.7	2.6	4.5
ALL OTHER.	15.0	12.5	13.3	16.3	14.5	15.7	14.5	14.8	16.1	16.8
NUMBER OF STATE AND LOCAL GOVERNMENT EMPLOYEES PER 10,000 POPULATION										
TOTAL.	444.2	358.7	302.5	261.9	245.5	473.3	384.9	317.4	262.0	239.9
STATE GOVERNMENT	161.8	132.6	111.9	92.1	84.7	142.0	103.1	85.1	71.4	67.3
LOCAL GOVERNMENTS.	282.4	226.2	190.7	169.9	160.8	331.3	281.8	232.4	190.7	172.7
BY FUNCTION:										
EDUCATION.	239.6	187.8	140.7	117.5	110.0	245.7	200.0	150.7	112.8	96.4
HIGHWAYS	51.7	50.7	49.2	42.1	41.6	24.2	23.8	23.7	20.0	21.4
PUBLIC WELFARE	7.7	7.0	5.8	4.8	4.4	11.6	6.9	4.5	2.8	2.2
HEALTH AND HOSPITALS	28.3	24.7	24.5	20.2	19.9	51.5	44.9	39.9	34.8	33.9
POLICE PROTECTION.	18.2	13.9	12.2	10.2	9.7	29.2	23.9	22.1	20.1	16.3
LOCAL FIRE PROTECTION.	12.1	9.4	8.4	7.4	7.0	10.8	9.8	9.1	8.5	6.7
SANITATION	3.7	2.7	3.3	1.9	1.7	10.8	11.1	11.7	10.5	8.1
NATURAL RESOURCES.	14.2	12.6	12.3	8.6	11.6	4.8	3.7	3.4	3.4	3.7
LOCAL UTILITIES.	5.4	5.2	5.8	6.6	4.0	6.3	4.9	5.4	6.8	10.9
ALL OTHER.	63.2	44.7	40.3	42.6	35.5	78.3	55.9	47.0	42.2	40.3
	MASSACHUSETTS					MICHIGAN				
NUMBER OF EMPLOYEES										
TOTAL.	254 888	204 164	175 893	153 548	147 958	380 479	322 308	257 888	217 863	179 096
STATE GOVERNMENT	66 246	48 712	41 542	33 940	31 691	96 481	80 218	58 830	52 805	34 204
LOCAL GOVERNMENTS.	188 642	155 452	134 351	119 608	116 267	283 998	242 090	199 058	165 058	144 892
BY FUNCTION:										
EDUCATION.	109 903	81 404	61 079	45 985	40 334	210 240	178 704	130 240	103 459	79 295
HIGHWAYS	14 399	14 542	15 590	13 937	14 141	18 422	18 848	17 516	15 910	17 183
PUBLIC WELFARE	6 754	5 826	4 914	4 214	4 811	9 790	5 284	4 241	4 209	3 112
HEALTH AND HOSPITALS	34 387	29 722	26 856	24 147	23 580	43 130	39 708	34 199	27 792	20 463
POLICE PROTECTION.	14 718	12 347	11 430	11 068	10 507	20 129	15 754	13 603	12 713	10 799
LOCAL FIRE PROTECTION.	12 886	11 242	10 455	10 414	9 858	8 057	7 077	6 346	5 421	4 944
SANITATION	4 201	4 106	3 049	3 330	3 298	6 611	5 788	6 911	5 849	4 833
NATURAL RESOURCES.	2 413	1 566	1 140	939	1 072	4 136	3 457	2 909	2 979	2 648
LOCAL UTILITIES.	11 033	9 683	10 181	10 128	11 168	8 543	7 991	7 520	9 165	11 665
ALL OTHER.	44 194	33 726	30 800	29 386	29 189	51 421	39 697	34 404	30 366	24 154
PERCENT OF EMPLOYEES										
TOTAL.	100.0	100.0	100.0	100.0	100.0	100.0	100.0	100.0	100.0	100.0
STATE GOVERNMENT	26.0	23.9	23.6	22.1	21.4	25.4	24.9	22.8	24.2	19.1
LOCAL GOVERNMENTS.	74.0	76.1	76.4	77.9	78.6	74.6	75.1	77.2	75.8	80.9
BY FUNCTION:										
EDUCATION.	43.1	39.9	34.7	29.9	27.3	55.3	55.4	50.5	47.5	44.3
HIGHWAYS	5.7	7.1	9.1	9.1	9.6	4.8	5.8	6.8	7.3	9.6
PUBLIC WELFARE	2.7	2.9	2.8	2.7	3.3	2.6	1.6	1.6	1.9	1.7
HEALTH AND HOSPITALS	13.5	14.5	15.3	15.7	15.9	11.4	12.4	13.3	12.8	11.4
POLICE PROTECTION.	5.8	6.0	6.5	7.2	7.1	5.3	4.9	5.3	5.8	6.0
LOCAL FIRE PROTECTION.	5.1	5.5	5.9	6.8	6.7	2.1	2.2	2.5	2.5	2.8
SANITATION	1.7	2.0	1.7	2.2	2.2	1.7	1.8	2.7	2.7	2.7
NATURAL RESOURCES.	0.9	0.8	0.6	0.6	0.7	1.1	1.1	1.1	1.4	1.5
LOCAL UTILITIES.	4.3	4.7	5.8	6.6	7.5	2.2	2.5	2.9	4.2	6.5
ALL OTHER.	17.2	16.6	17.5	19.1	19.7	13.5	12.3	13.3	13.9	13.5
NUMBER OF STATE AND LOCAL GOVERNMENT EMPLOYEES PER 10,000 POPULATION										
TOTAL.	448.0	376.6	339.0	311.5	307.9	428.4	375.5	321.2	287.8	262.5
STATE GOVERNMENT	116.4	89.9	80.1	68.9	65.9	108.6	93.5	73.3	69.8	50.1
LOCAL GOVERNMENTS.	331.6	286.8	259.0	242.7	241.9	319.8	282.0	247.9	218.1	212.4
BY FUNCTION:										
EDUCATION.	193.2	150.2	117.7	93.3	83.9	236.7	208.2	162.2	136.7	116.2
HIGHWAYS	25.3	26.8	30.8	28.3	29.4	20.7	22.0	21.8	21.0	25.2
PUBLIC WELFARE	11.9	10.7	9.5	8.5	10.0	11.0	6.2	5.3	5.6	4.6
HEALTH AND HOSPITALS	60.4	54.8	51.8	49.0	49.1	48.5	46.3	42.6	36.7	30.0
POLICE PROTECTION.	25.9	22.8	22.0	22.5	21.9	22.7	18.4	16.9	16.8	15.8
LOCAL FIRE PROTECTION.	22.6	20.7	20.2	21.1	20.5	9.1	8.2	7.9	7.2	7.2
SANITATION	7.4	7.6	5.9	6.8	6.9	7.4	6.8	8.6	7.7	7.1
NATURAL RESOURCES.	4.2	2.9	2.2	1.9	2.2	4.6	4.0	3.6	3.9	3.9
LOCAL UTILITIES.	19.4	17.9	19.6	20.5	23.2	9.6	9.3	9.4	12.1	17.1
ALL OTHER.	77.7	62.2	59.4	59.6	60.7	58.1	46.1	42.8	40.1	35.4

See footnotes at end of table.

Table 4. Employment (Full-Time Equivalent) of State and Local Governments, by Level of Government and by Function, by States: 1972, 1967, 1962, 1957, and 1953—Continued

Item	October 1972	October 1967	October 1962	April 1957	October 1953	October 1972	October 1967	October 1962	April 1957	October 1953
	MINNESOTA					MISSISSIPPI				
NUMBER OF EMPLOYEES										
TOTAL.	176 952	138 026	112 630	94 711	87 820	103 769	83 112	66 074	56 706	48 617
STATE GOVERNMENT	46 739	37 290	28 949	25 087	22 578	30 013	23 567	17 850	14 572	13 790
LOCAL GOVERNMENTS.	130 213	100 736	83 681	69 624	65 242	73 756	59 545	48 224	42 134	34 827
BY FUNCTION:										
EDUCATION.	97 075	73 225	57 601	45 556	41 032	53 465	42 272	32 635	29 275	25 022
HIGHWAYS	12 704	12 208	11 071	10 425	10 702	8 722	9 245	8 879	8 058	6 959
PUBLIC WELFARE	5 276	3 634	2 650	1 950	2 780	2 550	1 829	1 301	983	937
HEALTH AND HOSPITALS	19 082	16 232	11 704	11 258	9 336	16 353	11 861	8 482	5 937	3 700
POLICE PROTECTION.	6 499	4 801	4 060	3 459	3 084	3 926	3 127	2 333	1 929	1 661
LOCAL FIRE PROTECTION.	2 595	1 929	1 846	1 741	1 658	1 500	1 162	934	668	574
SANITATION	1 805	1 576	1 552	1 349	1 066	2 177	1 894	1 668	1 052	762
NATURAL RESOURCES.	2 947	2 660	2 689	2 067	2 508	3 376	2 739	2 553	2 682	3 528
LOCAL UTILITIES.	3 781	2 520	2 810	2 185	2 611	1 595	1 710	1 512	1 259	1 228
ALL OTHER.	25 188	19 241	16 645	14 721	13 043	10 105	7 273	5 778	4 863	4 246
PERCENT OF EMPLOYEES										
TOTAL.	100.0	100.0	100.0	100.0	100.0	100.0	100.0	100.0	100.0	100.0
STATE GOVERNMENT	26.4	27.0	25.7	26.5	25.7	28.9	28.4	27.0	25.7	28.4
LOCAL GOVERNMENTS.	73.6	73.0	74.3	73.5	74.3	71.1	71.6	73.0	74.3	71.6
BY FUNCTION:										
EDUCATION.	54.9	53.1	51.1	48.1	46.7	51.5	50.9	49.4	51.6	51.5
HIGHWAYS	7.2	8.8	9.8	11.0	12.2	8.4	11.1	13.4	14.2	14.3
PUBLIC WELFARE	3.0	2.6	2.4	2.1	3.2	2.5	2.2	2.0	1.7	1.9
HEALTH AND HOSPITALS	10.7	11.8	10.4	11.9	10.6	15.7	14.3	12.8	10.5	7.6
POLICE PROTECTION.	3.7	3.5	3.6	3.7	3.5	3.8	3.8	3.5	3.4	3.4
LOCAL FIRE PROTECTION.	1.5	1.4	1.6	1.8	1.9	1.4	1.4	1.4	1.2	1.2
SANITATION	1.0	1.1	1.4	1.4	1.2	2.1	2.3	2.5	1.9	1.6
NATURAL RESOURCES.	1.7	1.9	2.4	2.2	2.9	3.3	3.3	3.9	4.7	7.3
LOCAL UTILITIES.	2.1	1.8	2.5	2.3	3.0	1.5	2.1	2.3	2.2	2.5
ALL OTHER.	14.2	14.0	14.8	15.5	14.9	9.8	8.6	8.7	8.6	8.7
NUMBER OF STATE AND LOCAL GOVERNMENT EMPLOYEES PER 10,000 POPULATION										
TOTAL.	465.1	385.3	325.4	289.3	287.9	468.1	354.0	292.2	271.6	231.0
STATE GOVERNMENT	122.9	104.1	83.6	76.6	74.0	135.4	100.4	78.9	69.8	65.5
LOCAL GOVERNMENTS.	342.2	281.2	241.8	212.7	213.9	332.7	253.6	213.3	201.8	165.4
BY FUNCTION:										
EDUCATION.	255.2	204.4	166.4	139.1	134.5	241.2	180.0	144.3	140.2	118.9
HIGHWAYS	33.4	34.1	32.0	31.8	35.1	39.3	39.4	39.3	38.6	33.1
PUBLIC WELFARE	13.9	10.1	7.7	6.0	9.1	11.5	7.8	5.8	4.7	4.5
HEALTH AND HOSPITALS	50.1	45.3	33.8	34.4	30.6	73.8	50.5	37.5	28.4	17.6
POLICE PROTECTION.	17.1	13.4	11.7	10.6	10.1	17.7	13.3	10.3	9.2	7.9
LOCAL FIRE PROTECTION.	6.8	5.4	5.3	5.3	5.4	6.8	4.9	4.1	3.2	2.7
SANITATION	4.7	4.4	4.5	4.1	3.5	9.8	8.1	7.4	5.0	3.6
NATURAL RESOURCES.	7.7	7.4	7.8	6.3	8.2	15.2	11.7	11.3	12.8	16.8
LOCAL UTILITIES.	9.9	7.0	8.1	6.7	8.6	7.2	7.3	6.7	6.0	5.8
ALL OTHER.	66.1	53.8	48.1	45.0	42.8	45.6	31.0	25.6	23.3	20.2
	MISSOURI					MONTANA				
NUMBER OF EMPLOYEES										
TOTAL.	194 966	161 175	123 441	106 262	91 272	35 604	29 022	24 893	20 922	18 466
STATE GOVERNMENT	54 710	44 967	29 869	25 479	18 778	12 641	10 654	7 985	6 600	5 899
LOCAL GOVERNMENTS.	140 256	116 208	93 571	80 783	72 494	22 963	18 368	16 908	14 322	12 567
BY FUNCTION:										
EDUCATION.	99 043	82 002	57 411	46 952	41 648	18 653	14 572	12 403	9 920	8 127
HIGHWAYS	11 417	10 721	10 656	9 573	7 769	3 646	3 381	3 301	2 747	2 616
PUBLIC WELFARE	5 372	4 614	2 460	2 317	2 627	1 080	723	501	425	430
HEALTH AND HOSPITALS	28 382	20 248	15 852	14 160	9 925	2 651	2 411	1 835	1 299	905
POLICE PROTECTION.	11 353	9 151	7 721	6 278	5 847	1 537	1 157	1 062	889	762
LOCAL FIRE PROTECTION.	4 489	3 956	3 655	2 944	2 803	458	354	330	295	272
SANITATION	2 631	2 628	2 170	1 909	1 480	448	341	294	219	184
NATURAL RESOURCES.	3 580	3 198	2 147	2 573	1 650	1 174	1 243	1 138	1 191	1 292
LOCAL UTILITIES.	3 544	3 574	3 614	3 241	3 036	275	260	342	390	343
ALL OTHER.	25 155	21 083	17 756	16 315	14 487	5 682	4 580	4 039	3 547	3 535
PERCENT OF EMPLOYEES										
TOTAL.	100.0	100.0	100.0	100.0	100.0	100.0	100.0	100.0	100.0	100.0
STATE GOVERNMENT	28.1	27.9	24.2	24.0	20.6	35.5	36.7	32.1	31.5	31.9
LOCAL GOVERNMENTS.	71.9	72.1	75.8	76.0	79.4	64.5	63.3	67.9	68.5	68.1
BY FUNCTION:										
EDUCATION.	50.7	50.9	46.5	44.2	45.6	52.4	50.2	48.4	47.4	44.0
HIGHWAYS	5.8	6.7	8.6	9.0	8.5	10.2	11.6	13.3	13.1	14.2
PUBLIC WELFARE	2.7	2.9	2.0	2.2	2.9	3.0	2.5	2.0	2.0	2.3
HEALTH AND HOSPITALS	14.5	12.5	12.8	13.3	10.9	7.4	8.3	7.4	6.2	4.9

See footnotes at end of table.

Item	October 1972	October 1967	October 1962	April 1957	October 1953	October 1972	October 1967	October 1962	April 1957	October 1953
	MISSOURI--CONTINUED					MONTANA--CONTINUED				
PERCENT OF EMPLOYEES--CONTINUED										
BY FUNCTION--CONTINUED										
POLICE PROTECTION.	5.8	5.7	6.3	5.9	6.4	4.3	4.0	4.3	4.2	4.1
LOCAL FIRE PROTECTION.	2.3	2.5	3.0	2.8	3.1	1.3	1.2	1.3	1.4	1.5
SANITATION	1.3	1.7	1.8	1.8	1.6	1.3	1.1	1.2	1.0	1.0
NATURAL RESOURCES.	1.8	2.0	1.7	2.4	1.8	3.3	4.3	4.6	5.7	7.0
LOCAL UTILITIES.	1.8	2.2	2.9	3.1	3.3	0.8	0.9	1.4	1.9	1.9
ALL OTHER.	13.3	12.9	14.4	15.4	15.9	16.0	15.9	16.2	17.0	19.1
NUMBER OF STATE AND LOCAL GOVERNMENT EMPLOYEES PER 10,000 POPULATION										
TOTAL.	416.8	350.2	286.0	253.7	227.0	512.8	414.0	357.2	313.7	299.8
STATE GOVERNMENT	117.0	97.7	69.2	60.8	46.7	182.1	152.0	114.6	99.0	95.8
LOCAL GOVERNMENTS.	299.8	252.5	216.8	192.8	180.3	330.7	262.0	242.6	214.7	204.0
BY FUNCTION:										
EDUCATION.	211.7	178.1	133.0	112.1	103.6	268.6	207.9	172.8	148.7	131.9
HIGHWAYS	24.4	23.3	24.7	22.9	19.3	52.5	48.2	47.4	41.2	42.5
PUBLIC WELFARE	11.5	10.0	5.7	5.5	6.5	15.6	10.3	7.3	6.4	7.0
HEALTH AND HOSPITALS	60.6	44.0	36.7	33.8	24.7	38.1	34.4	26.3	19.5	14.7
POLICE PROTECTION.	24.3	19.9	17.9	15.0	14.5	22.1	16.5	15.2	13.3	12.4
LOCAL FIRE PROTECTION.	9.6	8.6	8.5	7.0	7.0	6.6	5.0	4.7	4.4	4.4
SANITATION	7.5	5.7	5.0	4.6	3.7	6.5	4.9	4.2	3.3	3.0
NATURAL RESOURCES.	7.7	6.9	5.0	6.1	4.1	16.9	17.7	16.3	17.9	21.0
LOCAL UTILITIES.	7.6	7.8	8.4	7.7	7.6	4.0	3.7	4.9	5.8	5.6
ALL OTHER.	53.7	45.9	41.1	38.9	36.0	81.9	65.4	57.9	53.2	57.4
	NEBRASKA					NEVADA				
NUMBER OF EMPLOYEES										
TOTAL.	78 045	60 784	52 202	45 614	41 500	29 196	20 772	13 368	9 103	6 824
STATE GOVERNMENT	23 254	16 785	13 817	11 232	9 895	7 920	5 657	3 529	2 240	1 939
LOCAL GOVERNMENTS.	54 791	43 999	38 385	34 382	31 605	21 276	15 115	9 840	6 863	4 885
BY FUNCTION:										
EDUCATION.	39 391	29 509	24 246	20 276	18 754	12 644	8 453	5 270	3 353	2 285
HIGHWAYS	5 663	4 929	5 322	4 284	4 638	2 172	2 118	1 610	1 308	1 044
PUBLIC WELFARE	2 017	1 087	698	558	445	503	309	161	101	82
HEALTH AND HOSPITALS	7 773	6 584	5 558	4 948	3 231	3 324	2 789	1 713	1 173	808
POLICE PROTECTION.	2 828	2 103	1 951	1 706	1 495	2 008	1 396	883	592	469
LOCAL FIRE PROTECTION.	1 136	920	779	690	605	939	700	397	268	158
SANITATION	693	840	546	382	254	197	187	126	113	90
NATURAL RESOURCES.	2 431	2 000	1 407	1 729	1 485	696	588	460	309	327
LOCAL UTILITIES.	5 761	5 114	5 258	5 267	5 068	305	229	191	135	75
ALL OTHER.	10 352	7 698	6 437	5 774	5 525	6 408	4 003	2 558	1 751	1 486
PERCENT OF EMPLOYEES										
TOTAL.	100.0	100.0	100.0	100.0	100.0	100.0	100.0	100.0	100.0	100.0
STATE GOVERNMENT	29.8	27.6	26.5	24.6	23.8	27.1	27.2	26.4	24.6	28.4
LOCAL GOVERNMENTS.	70.2	72.4	73.5	75.4	76.2	72.9	72.8	73.6	75.4	71.6
BY FUNCTION:										
EDUCATION.	50.5	48.5	46.4	44.5	45.2	43.3	40.7	39.4	36.8	33.5
HIGHWAYS	7.3	8.1	10.2	9.4	11.2	7.4	10.2	12.0	14.4	15.3
PUBLIC WELFARE	2.6	1.8	1.3	1.2	1.1	1.7	1.5	1.2	1.1	1.2
HEALTH AND HOSPITALS	10.0	10.8	10.6	10.8	7.8	11.4	13.4	12.8	12.9	11.8
POLICE PROTECTION.	3.6	3.5	3.7	3.7	3.6	6.9	6.7	6.6	6.5	6.9
LOCAL FIRE PROTECTION.	1.5	1.5	1.5	1.5	1.5	3.2	3.4	3.0	2.9	2.3
SANITATION	0.9	1.4	1.0	0.8	0.6	0.7	0.9	0.9	1.2	1.3
NATURAL RESOURCES.	3.1	3.3	2.7	3.8	3.6	2.4	2.8	3.4	3.4	4.8
LOCAL UTILITIES.	7.4	8.4	10.1	11.5	12.2	1.0	1.1	1.4	1.5	1.1
ALL OTHER.	13.1	12.7	12.3	12.7	13.3	22.0	19.3	19.1	19.2	21.8
NUMBER OF STATE AND LOCAL GOVERNMENT EMPLOYEES PER 10,000 POPULATION										
TOTAL.	525.5	423.6	361.0	327.2	314.9	597.4	467.8	382.0	350.1	349.9
STATE GOVERNMENT	156.6	117.0	95.6	80.6	75.1	162.1	127.4	100.8	86.2	99.4
LOCAL GOVERNMENTS.	368.9	306.6	265.5	246.6	239.8	435.3	340.4	281.1	264.0	250.5
BY FUNCTION:										
EDUCATION.	265.2	205.6	167.7	145.5	142.3	258.7	190.4	150.6	129.0	117.2
HIGHWAYS	38.1	34.3	36.8	30.7	35.2	44.4	47.7	46.0	50.3	53.5
PUBLIC WELFARE	13.6	7.6	4.8	4.0	3.4	10.3	7.0	4.6	3.9	4.2
HEALTH AND HOSPITALS	52.3	45.9	38.4	35.5	24.5	68.0	62.8	48.9	45.1	41.4
POLICE PROTECTION.	19.0	14.7	13.5	12.2	11.3	41.1	31.4	25.2	22.8	24.1
LOCAL FIRE PROTECTION.	7.6	6.4	5.4	4.9	4.6	19.2	15.8	11.3	10.3	8.1
SANITATION	4.6	5.8	3.8	2.7	1.9	4.1	4.2	3.6	4.3	4.6
NATURAL RESOURCES.	16.4	13.9	9.7	12.4	11.3	14.2	13.2	13.1	11.9	16.8
LOCAL UTILITIES.	38.8	35.6	36.4	37.8	38.5	6.2	5.2	5.5	5.2	3.8
ALL OTHER.	69.8	53.8	44.5	41.4	41.9	131.2	90.1	73.1	67.3	76.2

See footnotes at end of table.

Table 4. Employment (Full-Time Equivalent) of State and Local Governments, by Level of Government and by Function, by States: 1972, 1967, 1962, 1957, and 1953—Continued

Item	October 1972	October 1967	October 1962	April 1957	October 1953	October 1972	October 1967	October 1962	April 1957	October 1953
	NEW HAMPSHIRE					NEW JERSEY				
NUMBER OF EMPLOYEES										
TOTAL.	31 163	23 283	18 396	15 616	14 123	297 926	228 367	185 705	149 333	127 801
STATE GOVERNMENT	11 129	8 356	6 662	5 864	5 196	65 644	45 319	34 954	28 949	24 338
LOCAL GOVERNMENTS.	20 034	14 927	11 734	9 752	8 927	232 282	183 048	150 751	120 384	103 463
BY FUNCTION:										
EDUCATION.	15 910	10 972	7 635	5 776	5 000	147 824	109 032	81 850	58 726	49 082
HIGHWAYS	3 094	2 945	2 864	2 998	2 466	17 002	15 910	13 178	11 981	11 508
PUBLIC WELFARE	1 682	957	743	664	332	9 602	5 484	4 163	3 140	3 159
HEALTH AND HOSPITALS	2 507	2 248	2 018	1 704	1 839	26 596	23 980	21 625	20 154	15 439
POLICE PROTECTION.	1 478	1 038	792	659	616	23 105	17 167	14 899	13 143	11 013
LOCAL FIRE PROTECTION.	1 021	805	642	597	611	7 721	7 129	6 473	5 795	5 473
SANITATION	335	174	164	133	177	6 312	5 320	5 360	4 175	3 926
NATURAL RESOURCES.	663	672	598	514	615	2 389	2 159	2 140	1 693	1 450
LOCAL UTILITIES.	374	330	397	348	398	2 924	2 688	2 980	2 846	2 521
ALL OTHER.	4 099	3 142	2 544	2 223	2 069	54 451	39 498	33 037	27 680	24 230
PERCENT OF EMPLOYEES										
TOTAL.	100.0	100.0	100.0	100.0	100.0	100.0	100.0	100.0	100.0	100.0
STATE GOVERNMENT	35.7	35.9	36.2	37.6	36.8	22.0	19.8	18.8	19.4	19.0
LOCAL GOVERNMENTS.	64.3	64.1	63.8	62.4	63.2	78.0	80.2	81.2	80.6	81.0
BY FUNCTION:										
EDUCATION.	51.1	47.1	41.5	37.0	35.4	49.6	47.7	44.1	39.3	38.4
HIGHWAYS	9.9	12.6	15.6	19.2	17.5	5.7	7.0	7.1	8.0	9.0
PUBLIC WELFARE	5.4	4.1	4.0	4.3	2.4	3.2	2.4	2.2	2.1	2.5
HEALTH AND HOSPITALS	8.1	9.7	11.0	10.9	13.0	9.0	10.5	11.6	13.5	12.1
POLICE PROTECTION.	4.7	4.5	4.3	4.2	4.4	7.8	7.5	8.0	8.8	8.6
LOCAL FIRE PROTECTION.	3.3	3.5	3.5	3.8	4.3	2.6	3.1	3.5	3.9	4.3
SANITATION	1.1	0.7	0.9	0.9	1.3	2.2	2.4	2.9	2.8	3.1
NATURAL RESOURCES.	2.1	2.9	3.3	3.3	4.4	0.8	0.9	1.2	1.1	1.1
LOCAL UTILITIES.	1.2	1.4	2.2	2.2	2.8	1.0	1.2	1.6	1.9	2.0
ALL OTHER.	13.1	13.5	13.8	14.2	14.6	18.1	17.3	17.8	18.5	19.0
NUMBER OF STATE AND LOCAL GOVERNMENT EMPLOYEES PER 10,000 POPULATION										
TOTAL.	422.5	339.4	295.8	273.0	258.2	415.4	326.1	292.1	260.3	244.4
STATE GOVERNMENT	150.9	121.8	107.1	102.5	95.0	91.5	64.7	55.0	50.5	46.5
LOCAL GOVERNMENTS.	271.6	217.6	188.6	170.5	163.2	323.9	261.4	237.1	209.8	197.9
BY FUNCTION:										
EDUCATION.	215.7	159.9	122.7	101.0	91.4	206.1	155.7	128.8	102.4	93.9
HIGHWAYS	41.9	42.9	46.1	52.4	45.1	23.7	22.7	20.7	20.9	22.0
PUBLIC WELFARE	22.8	14.0	12.0	11.6	6.1	13.4	7.8	6.6	5.5	6.0
HEALTH AND HOSPITALS	33.9	32.7	32.4	29.8	33.6	37.1	34.2	34.0	35.1	29.5
POLICE PROTECTION.	20.0	15.1	12.7	11.5	11.3	32.2	24.5	23.4	22.9	21.1
LOCAL FIRE PROTECTION.	13.8	11.7	10.3	10.4	11.2	10.7	10.2	10.2	10.1	10.5
SANITATION	4.5	2.6	2.6	2.3	3.2	8.8	7.6	8.4	7.3	7.5
NATURAL RESOURCES.	9.0	9.8	9.6	9.0	11.2	3.3	3.1	3.4	3.0	2.8
LOCAL UTILITIES.	5.1	4.8	6.4	6.1	7.3	4.1	3.8	4.7	5.0	4.8
ALL OTHER.	55.7	45.9	40.9	38.9	37.8	·76.0	56.5	52.0	48.2	46.3
	NEW MEXICO					NEW YORK				
NUMBER OF EMPLOYEES										
TOTAL.	56 655	43 348	32 722	24 742	21 182	946 625	812 811	652 438	556 700	494 461
STATE GOVERNMENT	21 775	16 424	10 691	8 605	7 989	182 241	159 267	121 875	105 899	91 084
LOCAL GOVERNMENTS.	34 880	26 924	22 031	16 137	13 193	764 384	653 544	530 563	450 801	403 377
BY FUNCTION:										
EDUCATION.	31 409	23 709	17 973	12 905	11 111	375 217	315 147	221 347	167 488	136 704
HIGHWAYS	4 104	3 351	3 043	2 506	2 405	45 458	42 873	44 757	37 936	41 157
PUBLIC WELFARE	1 227	1 144	831	897	809	47 700	36 703	20 666	17 801	14 834
HEALTH AND HOSPITALS	5 308	4 025	2 383	1 644	1 099	141 097	116 149	104 624	93 354	80 407
POLICE PROTECTION.	2 559	1 754	1 344	970	704	60 256	54 085	45 132	40 992	34 373
LOCAL FIRE PROTECTION.	773	630	449	289	162	22 953	21 524	20 060	18 536	17 822
SANITATION	1 110	1 027	968	671	645	24 981	26 292	25 270	23 161	19 530
NATURAL RESOURCES.	1 462	1 150	993	941	1 082	9 353	8 009	5 573	5 112	5 200
LOCAL UTILITIES.	777	754	791	727	694	52 094	48 289	43 949	47 741	51 126
ALL OTHER.	7 926	5 804	3 950	3 192	2 471	167 516	143 740	121 062	104 579	93 308
PERCENT OF EMPLOYEES										
TOTAL.	100.0	100.0	100.0	100.0	100.0	100.0	100.0	100.0	100.0	100.0
STATE GOVERNMENT	38.4	37.9	32.7	34.8	37.7	19.3	19.6	18.7	19.0	18.4
LOCAL GOVERNMENTS.	61.6	62.1	67.3	65.2	62.3	80.7	80.4	81.3	81.0	81.6
BY FUNCTION:										
EDUCATION.	55.4	54.7	54.9	52.2	52.5	39.6	38.8	33.9	30.1	27.6
HIGHWAYS	7.2	7.7	9.3	10.1	11.4	4.8	5.3	6.9	6.8	8.3
PUBLIC WELFARE	2.2	2.6	2.5	3.6	3.8	5.0	4.5	3.2	3.2	3.0
HEALTH AND HOSPITALS	9.4	9.3	7.3	6.6	5.2	14.9	14.3	16.0	16.8	16.3

See footnotes at end of table.

Table 4. Employment (Full-Time Equivalent) of State and Local Governments, by Level of Government and by Function, by States: 1972, 1967, 1962, 1957, and 1953—Continued

Item	October 1972	October 1967	October 1962	April 1957	October 1953	October 1972	October 1967	October 1962	April 1957	October 1953
	NEW MEXICO--CONTINUED					NEW YORK--CONTINUED				
PERCENT OF EMPLOYEES--CONTINUED										
BY FUNCTION--CONTINUED										
POLICE PROTECTION.	4.5	4.0	4.1	3.9	3.3	6.4	6.7	6.9	7.4	7.0
LOCAL FIRE PROTECTION.	1.4	1.5	1.4	1.2	0.8	2.4	2.6	3.1	3.3	3.6
SANITATION	1.9	2.4	3.0	2.7	3.0	2.6	3.2	3.9	4.2	3.9
NATURAL RESOURCES.	2.6	2.7	3.0	3.8	5.1	1.0	1.0	0.9	0.9	1.1
LOCAL UTILITIES.	1.4	1.7	2.4	2.9	3.3	5.5	5.9	6.7	8.6	10.3
ALL OTHER.	14.0	13.4	12.1	12.9	11.7	17.8	17.7	18.6	18.8	18.9
NUMBER OF STATE AND LOCAL GOVERNMENT EMPLOYEES PER 10,000 POPULATION										
TOTAL.	557.6	432.2	328.2	292.1	280.2	518.9	443.3	372.9	340.0	318.5
STATE GOVERNMENT	214.3	163.7	107.2	101.6	105.7	99.9	86.9	69.7	64.7	58.7
LOCAL GOVERNMENTS.	343.3	268.4	221.0	190.5	174.5	419.0	356.4	303.2	275.3	259.8
BY FUNCTION:										
EDUCATION.	309.1	236.4	180.3	152.4	147.0	205.7	171.9	126.5	102.3	88.0
HIGHWAYS	40.4	33.4	30.5	29.6	31.8	24.9	23.4	25.6	23.2	26.5
PUBLIC WELFARE	12.1	11.4	8.3	10.6	10.7	26.2	20.0	11.8	10.9	9.6
HEALTH AND HOSPITALS	52.2	40.1	23.9	19.4	14.5	77.3	63.3	59.8	57.0	51.8
POLICE PROTECTION.	25.2	17.5	13.5	11.5	9.3	33.0	29.5	25.8	25.0	22.1
LOCAL FIRE PROTECTION.	7.6	6.3	4.5	3.4	2.1	12.6	11.7	11.5	11.3	11.5
SANITATION	10.9	10.3	9.7	7.9	8.5	13.6	14.3	14.4	14.1	12.6
NATURAL RESOURCES.	14.4	11.5	10.0	11.1	14.3	5.1	4.4	3.2	3.1	3.3
LOCAL UTILITIES.	7.6	7.5	7.9	8.6	9.2	28.6	26.3	25.1	29.2	32.9
ALL OTHER.	78.1	57.8	39.6	37.7	32.7	91.9	78.5	69.2	63.9	60.1
	NORTH CAROLINA					NORTH DAKOTA				
NUMBER OF EMPLOYEES										
TOTAL.	210 138	165 635	129 487	108 614	94 120	29 274	25 740	21 708	18 086	17 313
STATE GOVERNMENT	66 845	51 289	37 980	30 391	27 646	10 790	8 844	6 960	5 076	4 723
LOCAL GOVERNMENTS.	143 293	114 346	91 507	78 223	66 474	18 484	16 896	14 748	13 010	12 590
BY FUNCTION:										
EDUCATION.	113 904	91 793	67 102	57 388	50 021	17 081	14 517	11 761	10 096	9 177
HIGHWAYS	14 365	13 720	12 242	10 900	11 370	2 607	3 112	3 036	2 029	2 365
PUBLIC WELFARE	4 962	3 165	2 044	1 489	1 309	811	619	413	278	270
HEALTH AND HOSPITALS	23 095	16 397	13 173	10 810	7 905	1 851	1 653	1 434	1 046	1 028
POLICE PROTECTION.	9 450	6 415	5 438	4 473	3 929	977	773	697	618	565
LOCAL FIRE PROTECTION.	3 508	2 687	2 327	1 746	1 505	286	233	191	157	135
SANITATION	5 258	4 843	3 818	2 732	1 987	267	333	242	178	158
NATURAL RESOURCES.	4 097	4 464	4 049	3 255	2 931	1 027	950	612	691	614
LOCAL UTILITIES.	2 911	2 808	3 001	3 085	2 867	200	270	307	265	242
ALL OTHER.	28 588	19 343	16 294	12 736	10 296	4 167	3 280	3 015	2 728	2 759
PERCENT OF EMPLOYEES										
TOTAL.	100.0	100.0	100.0	100.0	100.0	100.0	100.0	100.0	100.0	100.0
STATE GOVERNMENT	31.8	31.0	29.3	28.0	29.4	36.9	34.4	32.1	28.1	27.3
LOCAL GOVERNMENTS.	68.2	69.0	70.7	72.0	70.6	63.1	65.6	67.9	71.9	72.7
BY FUNCTION:										
EDUCATION.	54.2	55.4	51.8	52.8	53.1	58.3	56.4	54.2	55.8	53.0
HIGHWAYS	6.8	8.3	9.5	10.0	12.1	8.9	12.1	14.0	11.2	13.7
PUBLIC WELFARE	2.4	1.9	1.6	1.4	1.4	2.8	2.4	1.9	1.5	1.6
HEALTH AND HOSPITALS	11.0	9.9	10.2	10.0	8.4	6.3	6.4	6.6	5.8	5.9
POLICE PROTECTION.	4.5	3.9	4.2	4.1	4.2	3.3	3.0	3.2	3.4	3.3
LOCAL FIRE PROTECTION.	1.7	1.6	1.8	1.6	1.6	1.0	0.9	0.9	0.9	0.8
SANITATION	2.5	2.9	2.9	2.5	2.0	0.9	1.3	1.1	1.0	0.9
NATURAL RESOURCES.	1.9	2.7	3.1	3.0	3.1	3.5	3.7	2.8	3.8	3.5
LOCAL UTILITIES.	1.4	1.7	2.3	2.8	3.0	0.7	1.0	1.4	1.5	1.4
ALL OTHER.	13.6	11.7	12.6	11.7	10.9	14.3	12.8	13.9	15.1	15.9
NUMBER OF STATE AND LOCAL GOVERNMENT EMPLOYEES PER 10,000 POPULATION										
TOTAL.	413.3	329.4	275.3	248.7	228.4	473.9	402.8	342.9	295.5	284.3
STATE GOVERNMENT	131.5	102.0	80.7	69.6	67.1	174.7	138.4	110.0	82.9	77.6
LOCAL GOVERNMENTS.	281.8	227.4	194.5	179.1	161.3	299.2	264.4	233.0	212.6	206.7
BY FUNCTION:										
EDUCATION.	224.0	182.5	142.6	131.4	121.4	276.5	227.2	185.8	165.0	150.7
HIGHWAYS	28.3	27.3	26.0	25.0	27.6	42.2	48.7	48.0	33.2	38.8
PUBLIC WELFARE	9.8	6.3	4.3	3.4	3.2	13.1	9.7	6.5	4.5	4.4
HEALTH AND HOSPITALS	45.5	32.6	28.0	24.7	19.2	29.9	25.9	22.7	17.1	16.9
POLICE PROTECTION.	18.6	12.8	11.6	10.2	9.5	15.8	12.1	11.0	10.1	9.3
LOCAL FIRE PROTECTION.	6.9	5.3	5.0	4.0	3.7	4.6	3.6	3.0	2.6	2.2
SANITATION	10.4	9.6	8.1	6.3	4.8	4.3	5.2	3.8	2.9	2.6
NATURAL RESOURCES.	8.1	8.9	8.6	7.5	7.1	16.6	14.9	9.7	11.3	10.1
LOCAL UTILITIES.	5.7	5.6	6.4	7.1	7.0	3.2	4.2	4.8	4.3	4.0
ALL OTHER.	56.0	38.5	34.6	29.2	25.0	67.6	51.3	47.6	44.6	45.3

See footnotes at end of table.

Table 4. Employment (Full-Time Equivalent) of State and Local Governments, by Level of Government and by Function, by States: 1972, 1967, 1962, 1957, and 1953—Continued

Item	October 1972	October 1967	October 1962	April 1957	October 1953	October 1972	October 1967	October 1962	April 1957	October 1953
	OHIO					OKLAHOMA				
NUMBER OF EMPLOYEES										
TOTAL.	426 010	346 721	295 979	238 962	205 635	119 234	99 683	78 495	68 468	63 996
STATE GOVERNMENT	100 660	71 055	62 690	49 307	37 853	41 215	33 628	24 264	19 967	18 841
LOCAL GOVERNMENTS.	325 350	275 666	233 289	189 655	167 782	78 019	66 055	54 231	48 501	45 155
BY FUNCTION:										
EDUCATION.	228 106	178 408	139 220	107 582	89 273	60 628	51 562	39 083	34 888	33 476
HIGHWAYS	23 585	25 137	24 467	21 108	19 509	9 894	8 635	8 374	7 572	6 426
PUBLIC WELFARE	14 459	12 191	9 215	6 599	5 042	3 832	3 224	2 044	1 436	1 222
HEALTH AND HOSPITALS . .	39 059	32 856	31 236	24 686	20 093	14 307	11 387	8 183	6 172	5 233
POLICE PROTECTION. . . .	20 676	16 545	13 995	12 798	10 816	4 932	3 824	3 085	2 791	2 754
LOCAL FIRE PROTECTION. .	10 151	8 786	8 093	7 118	7 054	2 784	2 225	1 683	1 424	1 293
SANITATION	10 194	9 606	8 648	7 312	5 871	2 493	2 168	1 928	1 553	1 271
NATURAL RESOURCES. . . .	5 056	3 530	3 191	3 196	2 182	2 540	2 899	2 620	2 143	2 145
LOCAL UTILITIES.	9 975	9 783	13 739	10 699	11 235	2 176	2 381	2 172	2 112	1 918
ALL OTHER.	64 749	49 879	44 175	37 864	34 560	16 648	11 378	9 323	8 377	8 258
PERCENT OF EMPLOYEES										
TOTAL.	100.0	100.0	100.0	100.0	100.0	100.0	100.0	100.0	100.0	100.0
STATE GOVERNMENT	23.6	20.5	21.2	20.6	18.4	34.6	33.7	30.9	29.2	29.4
LOCAL GOVERNMENTS.	76.4	79.5	78.8	79.4	81.6	65.4	66.3	69.1	70.8	70.6
BY FUNCTION:										
EDUCATION.	53.5	51.5	47.0	45.0	43.4	50.8	51.7	49.8	51.0	52.3
HIGHWAYS	5.5	7.2	8.3	8.8	9.5	7.5	8.7	10.7	11.1	10.0
PUBLIC WELFARE	3.4	3.5	3.1	2.8	2.5	3.2	3.2	2.6	2.1	1.9
HEALTH AND HOSPITALS . .	9.1	9.5	10.6	10.3	9.8	12.0	11.4	10.4	9.0	8.2
POLICE PROTECTION. . . .	4.9	4.8	4.7	5.4	5.3	4.1	3.8	3.9	4.1	4.3
LOCAL FIRE PROTECTION. .	2.4	2.5	2.7	3.0	3.4	2.3	2.2	2.1	2.1	2.0
SANITATION	2.4	2.8	2.9	3.1	2.9	2.1	2.2	2.5	2.3	2.0
NATURAL RESOURCES. . . .	1.2	1.0	1.1	1.3	1.1	2.1	2.9	3.3	3.1	3.4
LOCAL UTILITIES.	2.3	2.8	4.6	4.5	5.5	1.8	2.4	2.8	3.1	3.0
ALL OTHER.	15.3	14.4	14.9	15.8	16.8	14.1	11.5	11.9	12.2	12.9
NUMBER OF STATE AND LOCAL GOVERNMENT EMPLOYEES PER 10,000 POPULATION										
TOTAL.	399.8	331.5	294.9	253.9	239.4	465.8	399.5	320.7	300.0	293.3
STATE GOVERNMENT	94.5	67.9	62.5	52.4	44.1	161.0	134.8	99.1	87.5	86.3
LOCAL GOVERNMENTS.	305.3	263.6	232.4	201.5	195.3	304.8	264.7	221.5	212.5	206.9
BY FUNCTION:										
EDUCATION.	214.1	170.6	138.7	114.3	103.9	236.9	206.7	159.7	152.9	153.4
HIGHWAYS	22.1	24.0	24.4	22.4	22.7	34.7	34.6	34.2	33.2	29.5
PUBLIC WELFARE	13.6	11.7	9.2	7.0	5.9	15.0	12.9	8.4	6.3	5.6
HEALTH AND HOSPITALS . .	36.7	31.4	31.1	26.2	23.4	55.9	45.7	33.4	27.0	24.0
POLICE PROTECTION. . . .	19.4	15.8	13.9	13.6	12.6	19.3	15.3	12.6	12.2	12.6
LOCAL FIRE PROTECTION. .	9.5	8.4	8.1	7.6	8.2	10.9	8.9	6.9	6.2	5.9
SANITATION	9.5	9.2	8.6	7.8	6.8	9.8	8.7	7.9	6.8	5.8
NATURAL RESOURCES. . . .	4.7	3.4	3.2	3.4	2.5	9.9	11.6	10.7	9.4	9.8
LOCAL UTILITIES.	9.4	9.4	13.7	11.4	13.1	8.5	9.5	8.9	9.3	8.8
ALL OTHER.	60.8	47.6	44.0	40.2	40.2	65.0	45.6	38.1	36.7	37.8
	OREGON					PENNSYLVANIA				
NUMBER OF EMPLOYEES										
TOTAL.	105 080	84 492	70 743	56 776	47 345	448 209	366 848	307 881	251 112	218 481
STATE GOVERNMENT	34 275	28 389	23 036	18 618	15 224	131 004	106 835	88 462	70 311	60 293
LOCAL GOVERNMENTS.	70 805	56 103	47 437	38 158	32 121	317 205	260 013	219 420	180 801	158 188
BY FUNCTION:										
EDUCATION.	57 038	44 974	36 462	26 096	20 663	210 584	170 244	138 525	107 673	93 086
HIGHWAYS	7 311	7 243	6 928	6 323	5 856	31 689	32 742	31 796	27 970	24 358
PUBLIC WELFARE	3 295	2 075	1 464	1 097	946	23 062	16 168	10 651	7 114	5 308
HEALTH AND HOSPITALS . .	6 766	6 138	5 292	4 676	3 409	42 253	36 146	29 555	25 579	21 026
POLICE PROTECTION. . . .	4 684	3 607	2 964	2 456	2 335	27 530	23 334	20 079	17 394	14 879
LOCAL FIRE PROTECTION. .	2 457	1 858	1 607	1 376	1 277	6 648	6 449	6 483	6 534	6 337
SANITATION	989	744	641	423	412	9 465	8 846	8 445	6 303	5 355
NATURAL RESOURCES. . . .	2 832	2 950	2 395	2 289	2 149	5 893	3 877	3 481	3 042	2 284
LOCAL UTILITIES.	2 689	1 701	1 705	1 954	1 718	14 059	7 395	4 891	5 033	4 790
ALL OTHER.	17 019	13 202	11 015	10 086	8 580	77 026	61 647	53 975	44 470	41 058
PERCENT OF EMPLOYEES										
TOTAL.	100.0	100.0	100.0	100.0	100.0	100.0	100.0	100.0	100.0	100.0
STATE GOVERNMENT	32.6	33.6	32.7	32.8	32.2	29.2	29.1	28.7	28.0	27.6
LOCAL GOVERNMENTS.	67.4	66.4	67.3	67.2	67.8	70.8	70.9	71.3	72.0	72.4
BY FUNCTION:										
EDUCATION.	54.3	53.2	51.7	46.0	43.6	47.0	46.4	45.0	42.9	42.6
HIGHWAYS	7.0	8.6	9.8	11.1	12.4	7.1	8.9	10.3	11.1	11.1
PUBLIC WELFARE	3.1	2.5	2.1	1.9	2.0	5.1	4.4	3.6	2.8	2.4
HEALTH AND HOSPITALS . .	6.4	7.2	7.5	8.2	7.2	9.4	9.9	9.6	10.2	9.6

See footnotes at end of table.

Item	October 1972	October 1967	October 1962	April 1957	October 1953	October 1972	October 1967	October 1962	April 1957	October 1953
	OREGON--CONTINUED					PENNSYLVANIA--CONTINUED				
PERCENT OF EMPLOYEES--CONTINUED										
BY FUNCTION--CONTINUED										
POLICE PROTECTION	4.5	4.3	4.2	4.3	4.9	6.1	6.4	6.5	6.9	6.8
LOCAL FIRE PROTECTION	2.3	2.2	2.3	2.4	2.7	1.5	1.8	2.1	2.6	2.9
SANITATION	0.9	0.9	0.9	0.7	0.9	2.2	2.4	2.7	2.5	2.6
NATURAL RESOURCES	2.7	3.5	3.4	4.0	4.5	1.3	1.1	1.1	1.2	1.0
LOCAL UTILITIES	2.5	2.0	2.4	3.4	3.6	3.1	2.0	1.6	2.0	2.2
ALL OTHER	16.3	15.6	15.6	17.8	18.1	17.2	16.7	17.5	17.7	18.8
NUMBER OF STATE AND LOCAL GOVERNMENT EMPLOYEES PER 10,000 POPULATION										
TOTAL	502.4	422.7	390.0	331.6	295.7	380.0	315.5	270.5	229.2	204.9
STATE GOVERNMENT	163.9	142.0	127.5	108.8	95.1	111.1	91.9	77.7	64.2	56.5
LOCAL GOVERNMENTS	338.5	280.7	262.5	222.9	200.6	268.9	223.6	192.8	165.1	148.4
BY FUNCTION:										
EDUCATION	272.7	225.0	201.8	152.4	129.1	178.5	146.4	121.7	98.3	87.3
HIGHWAYS	35.0	36.2	38.3	36.9	36.6	26.9	28.2	27.9	25.5	22.8
PUBLIC WELFARE	15.8	10.4	8.1	6.4	5.9	19.5	13.9	9.4	6.5	5.0
HEALTH AND HOSPITALS	32.4	30.7	29.3	27.3	21.3	35.8	31.1	26.0	23.4	19.7
POLICE PROTECTION	22.4	18.0	16.4	14.3	14.6	23.3	20.1	17.6	15.9	14.0
LOCAL FIRE PROTECTION	11.7	9.3	8.9	8.0	8.0	5.6	5.7	5.7	6.0	5.9
SANITATION	4.8	3.8	3.5	2.5	2.6	8.1	7.6	7.4	5.8	5.0
NATURAL RESOURCES	13.5	14.8	13.3	13.4	13.4	5.0	3.3	3.1	2.8	2.1
LOCAL UTILITIES	12.9	8.5	9.4	11.4	10.7	11.9	6.4	4.3	4.6	4.5
ALL OTHER	81.2	66.0	61.0	58.9	53.6	65.3	53.0	47.4	40.6	38.5

Item	October 1972	October 1967	October 1962	April 1957	October 1953	October 1972	October 1967	October 1962	April 1957	October 1953
	RHODE ISLAND					SOUTH CAROLINA				
NUMBER OF EMPLOYEES										
TOTAL	40 101	31 449	25 853	22 147	19 838	116 777	84 077	66 354	60 527	51 213
STATE GOVERNMENT	16 655	12 474	9 293	7 737	7 048	39 633	25 924	19 759	16 944	14 248
LOCAL GOVERNMENTS	23 446	18 975	16 559	14 410	12 790	77 144	58 153	46 595	43 583	36 965
BY FUNCTION:										
EDUCATION	19 878	14 195	10 408	7 671	6 757	63 220	44 813	33 989	33 050	27 593
HIGHWAYS	1 970	2 351	2 258	1 980	1 990	7 260	6 527	6 351	6 226	5 755
PUBLIC WELFARE	1 491	1 191	887	890	901	2 323	1 205	838	736	704
HEALTH AND HOSPITALS	3 842	3 137	3 081	2 568	2 269	17 019	12 189	9 044	6 546	4 762
POLICE PROTECTION	2 255	1 886	1 807	1 707	1 580	4 534	3 201	2 872	2 699	2 478
LOCAL FIRE PROTECTION	1 740	1 449	1 345	1 297	1 193	1 414	1 088	914	716	632
SANITATION	691	678	618	722	545	2 618	2 448	1 916	1 584	1 390
NATURAL RESOURCES	492	495	370	425	350	2 592	2 518	2 431	2 217	1 755
LOCAL UTILITIES	488	522	516	500	493	1 783	1 500	1 343	1 046	944
ALL OTHER	7 254	5 545	4 564	4 387	3 760	14 014	8 588	6 656	5 707	5 200
PERCENT OF EMPLOYEES										
TOTAL	100.0	100.0	100.0	100.0	100.0	100.0	100.0	100.0	100.0	100.0
STATE GOVERNMENT	41.5	39.7	35.9	34.9	35.5	100.0	30.8	29.8	28.0	27.8
LOCAL GOVERNMENTS	58.5	60.3	64.1	65.1	64.5	33.9	69.2	70.2	72.0	72.2
BY FUNCTION:										
EDUCATION	49.6	45.1	40.3	34.6	34.1	54.1	53.3	51.2	54.6	53.9
HIGHWAYS	4.9	7.5	8.7	8.9	10.0	6.2	7.8	9.6	10.3	11.2
PUBLIC WELFARE	3.7	3.8	3.4	4.0	4.5	2.0	1.4	1.3	1.2	1.4
HEALTH AND HOSPITALS	9.6	10.0	11.9	11.6	11.4	14.6	14.5	13.6	10.8	9.3
POLICE PROTECTION	5.6	6.0	7.0	7.7	8.0	3.9	3.8	4.3	4.5	4.8
LOCAL FIRE PROTECTION	4.3	4.6	5.2	5.9	6.0	1.3	1.3	1.4	1.2	1.2
SANITATION	1.7	2.2	2.4	3.3	2.7	2.2	2.9	2.9	2.6	2.7
NATURAL RESOURCES	1.2	1.6	1.4	1.9	1.8	2.2	3.0	3.7	3.7	3.4
LOCAL UTILITIES	1.2	1.7	2.0	2.3	2.5	1.5	1.8	2.0	1.7	1.8
ALL OTHER	18.2	17.5	17.7	19.8	19.0	12.1	10.2	10.0	9.4	10.2
NUMBER OF STATE AND LOCAL GOVERNMENT EMPLOYEES PER 10,000 POPULATION										
TOTAL	422.3	349.4	294.5	260.2	243.4	450.6	323.5	271.1	266.2	234.8
STATE GOVERNMENT	175.4	138.6	105.8	90.9	86.5	111.2	99.7	80.7	74.5	65.3
LOCAL GOVERNMENTS	246.9	210.8	188.6	169.3	156.9	339.4	223.8	190.3	191.7	169.5
BY FUNCTION:										
EDUCATION	209.3	157.7	118.5	90.1	82.9	244.0	172.4	138.8	145.3	126.5
HIGHWAYS	20.7	26.1	25.7	23.3	24.4	28.0	25.1	25.9	27.4	26.4
PUBLIC WELFARE	15.7	13.2	10.1	10.5	11.1	9.0	4.6	3.4	3.2	3.2
HEALTH AND HOSPITALS	40.5	34.8	35.1	30.1	27.8	65.7	46.9	36.9	28.8	21.8
POLICE PROTECTION	23.7	21.0	20.6	20.1	19.4	17.5	12.3	11.7	11.9	11.4
LOCAL FIRE PROTECTION	18.3	16.1	15.3	15.2	14.6	5.5	4.2	3.7	3.1	2.9
SANITATION	7.2	7.6	7.0	8.5	6.7	10.1	9.4	7.8	7.0	6.4
NATURAL RESOURCES	5.2	5.5	4.2	5.0	4.3	10.0	9.7	9.9	9.7	8.0
LOCAL UTILITIES	5.1	5.8	5.9	5.9	6.0	6.9	5.8	5.5	4.6	4.3
ALL OTHER	76.5	61.6	52.0	51.6	46.1	54.0	33.1	27.2	25.1	23.8

See footnotes at end of table.

Table 4. Employment (Full-Time Equivalent) of State and Local Governments, by Level of Government and by Function, by States: 1972, 1967, 1962, 1957, and 1953—Continued

Item	October 1972	October 1967	October 1962	April 1957	October 1953	October 1972	October 1967	October 1962	April 1957	October 1953
	SOUTH DAKOTA					TENNESSEE				
NUMBER OF EMPLOYEES										
TOTAL.	31 630	28 791	23 757	20 772	18 664	182 625	145 726	111 353	91 416	76 850
STATE GOVERNMENT	10 678	9 424	6 975	5 473	4 789	53 071	38 794	28 132	20 815	15 761
LOCAL GOVERNMENTS.	20 952	19 367	16 781	15 299	13 875	129 554	106 932	83 221	70 601	61 089
BY FUNCTION:										
EDUCATION.	17 727	15 430	12 525	11 202	9 902	84 667	67 289	48 150	42 215	35 182
HIGHWAYS	3 442	3 686	3 446	2 643	2 741	12 891	13 197	12 600	10 574	9 594
PUBLIC WELFARE	734	505	417	273	257	4 322	2 671	1 734	1 288	1 297
HEALTH AND HOSPITALS	2 221	1 822	1 340	1 179	1 027	27 894	21 215	13 928	9 568	6 599
POLICE PROTECTION.	1 080	900	724	697	635	7 388	5 360	4 290	3 631	3 300
LOCAL FIRE PROTECTION.	294	275	211	197	160	4 384	3 157	2 351	1 885	1 608
SANITATION	224	279	260	176	150	4 434	3 893	3 509	2 930	2 133
NATURAL RESOURCES.	1 029	1 107	833	670	515	4 201	4 093	3 693	2 223	2 027
LOCAL UTILITIES.	362	452	467	584	452	9 873	9 424	9 264	7 731	7 171
ALL OTHER.	4 517	4 335	3 534	3 151	2 825	22 571	15 427	11 834	9 371	7 939
PERCENT OF EMPLOYEES										
TOTAL.	100.0	100.0	100.0	100.0	100.0	100.0	100.0	100.0	100.0	100.0
STATE GOVERNMENT	33.8	32.7	29.4	26.3	25.7	29.1	26.6	25.3	22.8	20.5
LOCAL GOVERNMENTS.	66.2	67.3	70.6	73.7	74.3	70.9	73.4	74.7	77.2	79.5
BY FUNCTION:										
EDUCATION.	56.0	53.6	52.7	53.9	53.1	46.4	46.2	43.2	46.2	45.8
HIGHWAYS	10.9	12.8	14.5	12.7	14.7	7.1	9.1	11.3	11.6	12.5
PUBLIC WELFARE	2.3	1.8	1.8	1.3	1.4	2.4	1.8	1.6	1.4	1.7
HEALTH AND HOSPITALS	7.0	6.3	5.6	5.7	5.5	15.3	14.5	12.5	10.5	8.6
POLICE PROTECTION.	3.4	3.1	3.0	3.4	3.4	4.0	3.7	3.9	4.0	4.3
LOCAL FIRE PROTECTION.	0.9	1.0	0.9	0.9	0.9	2.4	2.2	2.1	2.1	2.1
SANITATION	0.7	1.0	1.1	0.8	0.8	2.4	2.6	3.2	3.2	2.8
NATURAL RESOURCES.	3.3	3.8	3.5	3.2	2.8	2.3	2.8	3.3	2.4	2.6
LOCAL UTILITIES.	1.1	1.6	2.0	2.8	2.4	5.4	6.5	8.3	8.5	9.3
ALL OTHER.	14.4	15.0	14.9	15.2	15.1	12.3	10.6	10.6	10.3	10.3
NUMBER OF STATE AND LOCAL GOVERNMENT EMPLOYEES PER 10,000 POPULATION										
TOTAL.	474.8	427.2	329.5	311.9	288.0	465.3	374.4	304.9	266.2	231.5
STATE GOVERNMENT	160.3	139.8	96.7	82.2	73.9	135.2	99.7	77.0	60.6	47.5
LOCAL GOVERNMENTS.	314.5	287.3	232.7	229.7	214.1	330.1	274.7	227.9	205.6	184.1
BY FUNCTION:										
EDUCATION.	266.1	228.9	173.7	168.2	152.8	215.7	172.9	131.8	122.9	106.0
HIGHWAYS	51.7	54.7	47.8	39.7	42.3	32.8	33.9	34.5	30.8	28.9
PUBLIC WELFARE	11.0	7.5	5.8	4.1	4.0	11.0	6.9	4.8	3.8	3.9
HEALTH AND HOSPITALS	33.3	27.1	18.6	17.7	15.8	70.3	54.5	38.1	27.9	19.9
POLICE PROTECTION.	16.2	13.4	10.0	10.5	9.8	18.8	13.8	11.8	10.6	9.9
LOCAL FIRE PROTECTION.	4.4	4.1	2.9	3.0	2.5	11.2	8.1	6.4	5.5*	4.8
SANITATION	3.3	4.2	3.6	2.6	2.3	11.3	10.0	9.6	8.5	6.4
NATURAL RESOURCES.	15.4	16.4	11.6	10.1	7.9	10.7	10.5	10.1	6.5	6.1
LOCAL UTILITIES.	5.4	6.7	6.5	8.8	7.0	25.2	24.2	25.4	22.5	21.6
ALL OTHER.	67.9	64.2	49.0	47.3	43.6	58.3	39.6	32.4	27.3	23.9
	TEXAS					UTAH				
NUMBER OF EMPLOYEES										
TOTAL.	504 598	388 312	310 542	241 289	200 684	55 043	41 476	33 122	24 073	21 201
STATE GOVERNMENT	124 560	88 734	67 761	45 392	38 330	22 003	15 019	9 836	7 160	6 608
LOCAL GOVERNMENTS.	380 038	299 578	242 782	195 897	162 354	33 040	26 457	23 285	16 913	14 593
BY FUNCTION:										
EDUCATION.	273 687	209 641	159 854	121 629	100 018	33 655	25 238	19 012	12 988	11 394
HIGHWAYS	31 155	30 827	29 758	25 379	21 852	3 601	3 235	2 854	2 222	2 056
PUBLIC WELFARE	7 827	4 357	3 026	2 396	2 305	946	661	417	282	252
HEALTH AND HOSPITALS	57 683	39 035	28 778	19 468	13 855	4 015	2 675	2 480	2 005	1 426
POLICE PROTECTION.	21 760	16 374	13 845	10 699	8 450	2 212	1 569	1 303	1 077	863
LOCAL FIRE PROTECTION.	11 416	8 778	7 581	6 096	5 244	804	592	488	421	359
SANITATION	12 212	10 882	9 865	7 749	5 817	691	701	612	197	153
NATURAL RESOURCES.	9 321	6 445	5 932	4 701	4 841	1 311	959	865	637	755
LOCAL UTILITIES.	15 818	14 902	12 915	11 015	11 507	839	875	861	824	931
ALL OTHER.	63 719	47 071	38 989	32 157	26 795	6 969	4 971	4 228	3 420	3 012
PERCENT OF EMPLOYEES										
TOTAL.	100.0	100.0	100.0	100.0	100.0	100.0	100.0	100.0	100.0	100.0
STATE GOVERNMENT	24.7	22.9	21.8	18.8	19.1	40.0	36.2	29.7	29.7	31.2
LOCAL GOVERNMENTS.	75.3	77.1	78.2	81.2	80.9	60.0	63.8	70.3	70.3	68.8
BY FUNCTION:										
EDUCATION.	54.2	54.0	51.5	50.4	49.8	61.1	60.8	57.4	54.0	53.7
HIGHWAYS	6.2	7.9	9.6	10.5	10.9	6.5	7.8	8.6	9.2	9.7
PUBLIC WELFARE	1.6	1.1	1.0	1.0	1.1	1.7	1.6	1.3	1.2	1.2
HEALTH AND HOSPITALS	11.4	10.1	9.3	8.1	6.9	7.3	6.5	7.5	8.3	6.7

See footnotes at end of table.

Table 4. Employment (Full-Time Equivalent) of State and Local Governments, by Level of Government and by Function, by States: 1972, 1967, 1962, 1957, and 1953—Continued

Item	October 1972	October 1967	October 1962	April 1957	October 1953	October 1972	October 1967	October 1962	April 1957	October 1953
	TEXAS--CONTINUED					UTAH--CONTINUED				
PERCENT OF EMPLOYEES--CONTINUED										
BY FUNCTION--CONTINUED										
POLICE PROTECTION.	4.3	4.2	4.5	4.4	4.2	4.0	3.8	3.9	4.5	4.1
LOCAL FIRE PROTECTION.	2.3	2.3	2.4	2.5	2.6	1.5	1.4	1.5	1.7	1.7
SANITATION	2.4	2.8	3.2	3.2	2.9	1.3	1.7	1.8	0.8	0.7
NATURAL RESOURCES.	1.8	1.7	1.9	1.9	2.4	2.4	2.3	2.6	2.6	3.6
LOCAL UTILITIES.	3.1	3.8	4.2	4.6	5.7	1.5	2.1	2.6	3.4	4.4
ALL OTHER.	12.7	12.1	12.6	13.3	13.4	12.7	12.0	12.8	14.2	14.2
NUMBER OF STATE AND LOCAL GOVERNMENT EMPLOYEES PER 10,000 POPULATION										
TOTAL.	450.6	357.3	306.8	266.0	240.7	519.6	405.0	345.7	291.4	286.9
STATE GOVERNMENT	111.2	81.6	66.9	50.0	46.0	207.7	146.7	102.7	86.7	89.4
LOCAL GOVERNMENTS.	339.4	275.6	239.9	216.0	194.8	311.9	258.4	243.1	204.8	197.5
BY FUNCTION:										
EDUCATION.	244.4	192.9	157.9	134.1	120.0	317.7	246.5	198.5	157.2	154.2
HIGHWAYS	27.8	28.4	29.4	28.0	26.2	34.0	31.6	29.8	26.9	27.8
PUBLIC WELFARE	7.0	4.0	3.0	2.6	2.8	8.9	6.5	4.4	3.4	3.4
HEALTH AND HOSPITALS	51.5	35.9	28.4	21.5	16.6	37.9	26.1	25.9	24.3	19.3
POLICE PROTECTION.	19.4	15.1	13.7	11.8	10.1	20.9	15.3	13.6	13.0	11.7
LOCAL FIRE PROTECTION.	10.2	8.1	7.5	6.7	6.3	7.6	5.8	5.1	5.1	4.9
SANITATION	10.9	10.0	9.7	8.5	7.0	6.5	6.8	6.4	2.4	2.1
NATURAL RESOURCES.	8.3	5.9	5.9	5.2	5.8	12.4	9.4	9.0	7.7	10.2
LOCAL UTILITIES.	14.1	13.7	12.8	12.1	13.8	7.9	8.5	9.0	10.0	12.6
ALL OTHER.	57.1	43.3	38.5	35.5	32.1	65.8	48.5	44.1	41.4	40.8
	VERMONT					VIRGINIA				
NUMBER OF EMPLOYEES										
TOTAL.	22 227	15 252	12 431	10 057	9 595	207 522	157 615	118 306	96 798	84 823
STATE GOVERNMENT	9 995	6 956	5 416	4 038	3 848	70 627	51 411	38 753	31 916	29 661
LOCAL GOVERNMENTS.	12 232	8 296	7 015	6 019	5 747	136 895	106 204	79 553	64 882	55 162
BY FUNCTION:										
EDUCATION.	12 122	7 805	6 157	4 855	4 480	112 869	86 259	59 164	47 172	39 132
HIGHWAYS	2 333	2 143	2 236	1 807	1 987	15 269	13 387	12 174	12 174	12 818
PUBLIC WELFARE	373	328	255	159	157	4 408	2 371	1 408	1 370	1 265
HEALTH AND HOSPITALS	1 452	1 073	876	619	533	20 582	14 914	11 922	9 474	7 674
POLICE PROTECTION.	909	557	437	438	366	9 371	6 770	5 240	4 456	3 656
LOCAL FIRE PROTECTION.	385	219	191	188	213	3 628	2 700	2 247	1 806	1 484
SANITATION	147	135	49	52	27	4 828	4 371	3 791	3 118	2 386
NATURAL RESOURCES.	972	639	483	435	376	3 636	2 568	2 769	2 157	2 405
LOCAL UTILITIES.	220	234	245	323	304	2 824	2 524	2 150	1 828	1 931
ALL OTHER.	3 314	2 119	1 504	1 181	1 152	30 107	20 633	16 228	13 243	12 072
PERCENT OF EMPLOYEES										
TOTAL.	100.0	100.0	100.0	100.0	100.0	100.0	100.0	100.0	100.0	100.0
STATE GOVERNMENT	45.0	45.6	43.6	40.2	40.1	34.0	32.6	32.8	33.0	35.0
LOCAL GOVERNMENTS.	55.0	54.4	56.4	59.8	59.9	66.0	67.4	67.2	67.0	65.0
BY FUNCTION:										
EDUCATION.	54.5	51.2	49.5	48.3	46.7	54.4	54.7	50.0	48.7	46.1
HIGHWAYS	10.5	14.1	18.0	18.0	20.7	7.4	9.2	11.3	12.6	15.1
PUBLIC WELFARE	1.7	2.2	2.1	1.6	1.6	2.1	1.5	1.2	1.4	1.5
HEALTH AND HOSPITALS	6.5	7.0	7.0	6.2	5.6	9.9	9.4	10.1	9.8	9.0
POLICE PROTECTION.	4.1	3.7	3.5	4.4	3.8	4.5	4.3	4.4	4.6	4.3
LOCAL FIRE PROTECTION.	1.7	1.4	1.5	1.9	2.2	1.7	1.7	1.9	1.9	1.7
SANITATION	0.7	0.9	0.4	0.5	0.3	2.4	2.7	3.2	3.2	2.8
NATURAL RESOURCES.	4.4	4.2	3.9	4.3	3.9	1.7	1.6	2.3	2.2	2.8
LOCAL UTILITIES.	1.0	1.5	2.0	3.2	3.2	1.4	1.6	1.8	1.9	2.3
ALL OTHER.	14.9	13.8	12.1	11.7	12.0	14.5	13.3	13.7	13.7	14.2
NUMBER OF STATE AND LOCAL GOVERNMENT EMPLOYEES PER 10,000 POPULATION										
TOTAL.	499.7	365.8	321.2	267.5	253.2	446.1	347.5	278.5	251.8	238.5
STATE GOVERNMENT	224.7	166.8	139.9	107.4	101.5	151.8	113.3	91.2	83.0	83.4
LOCAL GOVERNMENTS.	275.0	198.9	181.3	160.1	151.6	294.3	234.1	187.3	168.8	155.1
BY FUNCTION:										
EDUCATION.	272.6	187.2	159.1	129.1	118.2	242.7	190.2	139.3	122.7	110.0
HIGHWAYS	52.5	51.4	57.8	48.1	52.4	32.8	32.0	31.5	31.7	36.0
PUBLIC WELFARE	8.4	7.9	6.6	4.2	4.1	9.5	5.2	3.3	3.6	3.6
HEALTH AND HOSPITALS	32.6	25.7	22.6	16.5	14.1	44.2	32.9	28.1	24.6	21.6
POLICE PROTECTION.	20.4	13.4	11.3	11.6	9.7	20.0	14.9	12.3	11.6	10.3
LOCAL FIRE PROTECTION.	8.7	5.3	4.9	5.0	5.6	7.8	6.0	5.3	4.7	4.2
SANITATION	3.3	3.2	1.3	1.4	0.7	10.3	9.6	8.9	8.1	6.7
NATURAL RESOURCES.	21.9	15.3	12.5	11.6	9.9	7.8	5.7	6.5	5.6	6.8
LOCAL UTILITIES.	4.9	5.6	6.3	8.6	8.0	6.1	5.6	5.1	4.8	5.4
ALL OTHER.	74.5	50.8	38.9	31.4	30.4	64.9	45.4	38.2	34.5	33.9

See footnotes at end of table.

Table 4. Employment (Full-Time Equivalent) of State and Local Governments, by Level of Government and by Function, by States: 1972, 1967, 1962, 1957, and 1953—Continued

Item	October 1972	October 1967	October 1962	April 1957	October 1953	October 1972	October 1967	October 1962	April 1957	October 1953
	WASHINGTON					WEST VIRGINIA				
NUMBER OF EMPLOYEES										
TOTAL.	170 511	135 074	110 006	88 311	75 911	82 081	66 901	54 650	44 795	44 611
STATE GOVERNMENT.	57 725	39 429	30 165	22 992	18 611	33 627	27 337	19 954	14 044	14 718
LOCAL GOVERNMENTS.	112 786	95 645	79 841	65 319	57 300	48 454	39 564	34 696	30 751	29 893
BY FUNCTION:										
EDUCATION.	84 493	69 938	54 632	38 532	31 447	43 841	36 376	28 892	25 664	25 640
HIGHWAYS	11 789	10 668	9 218	8 815	7 229	10 619	8 502	7 175	4 887	5 476
PUBLIC WELFARE	5 806	3 147	2 102	1 805	1 460	2 229	2 169	1 314	694	628
HEALTH AND HOSPITALS	12 462	10 425	9 319	7 777	7 028	9 064	6 349	5 035	3 352	2 820
POLICE PROTECTION.	6 905	4 869	4 243	3 655	3 280	2 433	2 028	1 822	1 790	1 611
LOCAL FIRE PROTECTION.	3 913	2 887	2 581	2 377	2 064	906	846	750	727	612
SANITATION	1 756	1 514	1 182	971	796	1 189	1 234	1 065	653	569
NATURAL RESOURCES.	4 774	3 862	3 421	3 173	2 867	1 689	1 334	1 197	1 206	1 210
LOCAL UTILITIES.	7 928	7 740	7 793	7 793	7 179	564	657	626	597	796
ALL OTHER.	30 685	20 024	15 517	13 413	12 561	9 547	7 406	6 776	5 225	5 249
PERCENT OF EMPLOYEES										
TOTAL.	100.0	100.0	100.0	100.0	100.0	100.0	100.0	100.0	100.0	100.0
STATE GOVERNMENT	33.9	29.2	27.4	26.0	24.5	41.0	40.9	36.5	31.4	33.0
LOCAL GOVERNMENTS.	66.1	70.8	72.6	74.0	75.5	59.0	59.1	63.5	68.6	67.0
BY FUNCTION:										
EDUCATION.	49.6	51.8	49.7	43.6	41.4	53.4	54.4	52.9	57.3	57.5
HIGHWAYS	6.9	7.9	8.4	10.0	9.5	12.9	12.7	13.1	10.9	12.3
PUBLIC WELFARE	3.4	2.3	1.9	2.0	1.9	2.7	3.2	2.4	1.5	1.4
HEALTH AND HOSPITALS	7.3	7.7	8.5	8.8	9.3	11.0	9.4	9.2	7.5	6.3
POLICE PROTECTION.	4.0	3.6	3.9	4.1	4.3	3.0	3.0	3.3	4.0	3.6
LOCAL FIRE PROTECTION.	2.3	2.1	2.3	2.7	2.7	1.1	1.3	1.4	1.6	1.4
SANITATION	1.1	1.2	1.1	1.1	1.0	1.5	0.9	1.9	1.5	1.3
NATURAL RESOURCES.	2.8	2.9	3.1	3.6	3.8	2.1	2.0	2.2	2.7	2.7
LOCAL UTILITIES.	4.6	5.7	7.1	8.8	9.5	0.7	1.0	1.1	1.3	1.8
ALL OTHER.	18.0	14.8	14.1	15.2	16.5	11.6	12.1	12.4	11.7	11.8
NUMBER OF STATE AND LOCAL GOVERNMENT EMPLOYEES PER 10,000 POPULATION										
TOTAL.	500.0	437.6	365.5	324.2	307.8	470.6	372.1	304.3	243.1	231.3
STATE GOVERNMENT	169.3	127.7	100.2	84.4	75.5	192.8	152.0	111.1	76.2	76.3
LOCAL GOVERNMENTS.	330.7	309.8	265.3	239.8	232.4	277.8	220.0	193.2	166.9	155.0
BY FUNCTION:										
EDUCATION.	247.7	226.6	181.5	141.5	127.5	251.3	202.3	160.9	139.3	132.9
HIGHWAYS	34.6	34.6	30.6	32.4	29.3	60.9	47.3	40.0	26.5	28.4
PUBLIC WELFARE	17.0	10.2	7.0	6.6	5.9	12.8	12.1	7.3	3.8	3.3
HEALTH AND HOSPITALS	36.6	33.8	31.0	28.5	28.5	52.0	35.3	28.0	18.2	14.6
POLICE PROTECTION.	20.2	15.8	14.1	13.4	13.3	13.9	11.3	10.2	9.7	8.4
LOCAL FIRE PROTECTION.	11.5	9.4	8.6	8.7	8.4	5.2	4.7	4.2	3.9	3.2
SANITATION	5.2	4.9	3.9	3.6	3.2	6.8	6.9	5.9	3.5	2.9
NATURAL RESOURCES.	14.0	12.5	11.4	11.6	11.6	9.7	7.4	6.7	6.5	6.3
LOCAL UTILITIES.	23.2	25.1	25.9	28.6	29.1	3.2	3.7	3.5	3.2	4.1
ALL OTHER.	90.0	64.7	51.6	49.2	50.9	54.8	41.1	37.7	28.4	27.2
	WISCONSIN					WYOMING				
NUMBER OF EMPLOYEES										
TOTAL.	199 060	156 866	127 675	97 879	90 014	22 522	17 851	14 816	11 632	9 922
STATE GOVERNMENT	52 171	38 711	27 322	19 313	17 694	7 184	6 009	4 422	3 325	2 955
LOCAL GOVERNMENTS.	146 889	118 155	100 353	78 566	72 320	15 338	11 842	10 394	8 307	6 967
BY FUNCTION:										
EDUCATION.	105 954	77 599	57 711	41 976	37 307	12 121	8 462	6 849	5 562	4 868
HIGHWAYS	13 909	12 296	12 293	10 949	11 367	1 946	2 090	1 819	1 363	1 344
PUBLIC WELFARE	5 970	5 890	3 736	3 862	3 196	393	519	376	256	173
HEALTH AND HOSPITALS	20 506	16 677	14 545	9 337	8 922	2 932	2 545	2 130	1 447	743
POLICE PROTECTION.	10 299	8 113	6 908	5 603	4 711	799	623	546	432	413
LOCAL FIRE PROTECTION.	4 780	3 793	3 284	2 917	2 548	216	198	246	139	115
SANITATION	3 971	3 968	4 226	3 191	3 163	283	256	231	174	119
NATURAL RESOURCES.	3 403	3 424	2 869	2 188	2 480	987	819	679	708	734
LOCAL UTILITIES.	2 127	2 168	2 290	1 937	1 941	265	201	249	250	167
ALL OTHER.	28 141	22 938	19 814	15 919	14 379	2 580	2 138	1 689	1 301	1 246
PERCENT OF EMPLOYEES										
TOTAL.	100.0	100.0	100.0	100.0	100.0	100.0	100.0	100.0	100.0	100.0
STATE GOVERNMENT	26.2	24.7	21.4	19.7	19.7	31.9	33.7	29.8	28.6	29.8
LOCAL GOVERNMENTS.	73.8	75.3	78.6	80.3	80.3	68.1	66.3	70.2	71.4	70.2
BY FUNCTION:										
EDUCATION.	53.2	49.5	45.2	42.9	41.4	53.8	47.4	46.2	47.8	49.1
HIGHWAYS	7.0	7.8	9.6	11.2	12.6	8.6	11.7	12.3	11.7	13.5
PUBLIC WELFARE	3.0	3.8	2.9	3.9	3.6	1.7	2.9	2.5	2.2	1.7
HEALTH AND HOSPITALS	10.3	10.6	11.4	9.5	9.9	13.0	14.3	14.4	12.4	7.5

See footnotes at end of table.

Item	October 1972	October 1967	October 1962	April 1957	October 1953	October 1972	October 1967	October 1962	April 1957	October 1953
	WISCONSIN--CONTINUED					WYOMING--CONTINUED				
PERCENT OF EMPLOYEES--CONTINUED										
BY FUNCTION--CONTINUED										
POLICE PROTECTION.	5.2	5.2	5.4	5.7	5.2	3.5	3.5	3.7	3.7	4.2
LOCAL FIRE PROTECTION.	2.4	2.4	2.6	3.0	2.8	1.0	1.1	1.7	1.2	1.2
SANITATION	1.9	2.5	3.3	3.3	3.5	1.2	1.4	1.6	1.5	1.2
NATURAL RESOURCES.	1.7	2.2	2.2	2.2	2.8	4.4	4.6	4.6	6.1	7.4
LOCAL UTILITIES.	1.1	1.4	1.8	2.0	2.2	1.2	1.1	1.7	2.1	1.7
ALL OTHER.	14.2	14.6	15.5	16.3	16.0	11.6	12.0	11.4	11.2	12.6
NUMBER OF STATE AND LOCAL GOVERNMENT EMPLOYEES PER 10,000 POPULATION										
TOTAL.	450.6	374.5	317.7	258.2	256.7	677.5	566.7	446.3	370.4	342.1
STATE GOVERNMENT	118.1	92.4	68.0	50.9	50.5	216.1	190.8	133.2	105.9	101.9
LOCAL GOVERNMENTS.	332.5	282.1	249.7	207.2	206.3	461.4	375.9	313.1	264.6	240.2
BY FUNCTION:										
EDUCATION.	239.8	185.2	143.6	110.7	106.4	364.6	268.6	206.3	177.1	167.9
HIGHWAYS	31.5	29.4	30.6	28.9	32.4	58.5	66.3	54.8	43.4	46.3
PUBLIC WELFARE	13.5	14.1	9.3	10.2	9.1	11.8	16.5	11.3	8.2	6.0
HEALTH AND HOSPITALS	46.4	39.9	36.2	24.6	25.4	88.2	80.8	64.2	46.1	25.6
POLICE PROTECTION.	23.3	19.4	17.2	14.8	13.4	24.0	19.8	16.5	13.8	14.2
LOCAL FIRE PROTECTION.	10.8	9.1	8.2	7.7	7.3	6.5	6.3	7.4	4.4	4.0
SANITATION	9.0	9.5	10.5	8.4	9.0	8.5	8.1	7.0	5.5	4.1
NATURAL RESOURCES.	7.7	8.2	7.1	5.8	7.1	29.7	26.0	20.5	22.5	25.3
LOCAL UTILITIES.	4.8	5.2	5.7	5.1	5.5	8.0	6.4	7.5	8.0	5.8
ALL OTHER.	63.8	54.5	49.3	42.0	41.0	77.7	67.9	50.9	41.4	43.0

Note: For information on concepts, sources, data presentation, and historical changes in data classification, see introductory text. Statistics here on public employees per 10,000 population are based on population figures

- Represents zero or rounds to zero.
NA Not available.
[1]Data for years prior to Statehood (shown in parentheses) not included in nationwide totals.

APPENDIX
PUBLICATIONS RELATED TO THIS VOLUME

This compilation is assembled from the quinquennial Census of Governments and the annual reports of the Governments Division of the U.S. Bureau of the Census on the finances and employment of America's governments. The titles of the recurrent reports and the volumes of the 1977 Census of Governments are shown below.

Recurrent Reports

Government Finances (Series GF)

(Published during the period of March–November each year)

No. 1. State Tax Collections in (year). National and State figures on tax collections of State governments, by type of tax. Includes detailed breakdowns of major tax categories. See also Quarterly Tax Report, below.

No. 2. Finances of Employee-Retirement Systems of State and local governments in (year). Figures for the Nation, by States, and for major individual systems, on the receipts, payments, and financial assets of employee-retirement systems administered by State and local governments.

No. 3. State Government Finances in (year). Detailed statistics, national and by States, with comparative totals for previous years. This report covers revenue by source, expenditure by function and by character and object, indebtedness and debt transactions, and cash and security holdings.

No. 4 City Government Finances in (year). National and size-group totals of municipal government finances, with comparative totals for previous years. Supplies financial statistics for each of the cities and selected townships having 50,000 inhabitants or more in 1970, and additional detail for each of the 48 largest cities.

No. 5. Governmental Finances in (year). National totals covering all governments—Federal, State, and local—with comparative summary data for previous years, and financial statistics for State and local governments, by States.

No. 6. Local Government Finances in Selected Metropolitan Areas and Large Counties: (year). Data on revenue, expenditure, and indebtedness of local governments for each of 74 populous standard metropolitan statistical areas.

No. 7. Chart Book of Governmental Data: (year). A graphic publication, providing charts and maps based mainly on data from recent annual and quarterly surveys, but including also presentations of historical trends.

No. 8. County Government Finances in (year). National and size-group totals of county government finances, with comparative totals for previous years. Presents financial statistics for individual counties having 100,000 inhabitants or more in 1972, and additional detail for the 62 largest counties.

Government Employment (Series GE)

(Published during the period of April–July each year)

No. 1. Public Employment in (year). National totals on employment of all governments (including the Federal Government), by function, and by type of government. Also shows State-by-State statistics on Federal civilian employees and, by function, on employment and payrolls of State and local governments.

No. 2. City Employment in (year). National totals on employment and payrolls of municipal governments, by function, with figures individually for the cities and 20 major towns and townships that had 50,000 population or more in 1970.

No. 3. Local Government Employment in Selected Metropolitan Areas and Large Counties: (year). Data for 74 standard metropolitan statistical areas, their county areas, and other county areas of 200,000 population or more.

No. 4. County Government Employment in (year). National and population size-group statistics by function for October employment and payrolls of county government, with comparative data for previous years. This report also presents employment and payroll data for individual county governments having 100,000 population or more.

Quarterly Tax (Series GT)

Quarterly Summary of State and Local Tax Revenue. These reports provide nationwide figures on tax revenue by level of government and type of tax; data on property tax collections for 200 major county areas; and data for individual State governments on collections of selected types of taxes.

Retirement Systems (Series GR)

Holdings of Selected Public Employee Retirement Systems (year). These quarterly reports supply summary nationwide figures on cash and securities held by 100 major State and local public employee-retirement systems.

1977 Census of Governments Reports

Every 5 years (in years ending in "2" and "7") the Census Bureau conducts a Census of Governments. Following are reports which will be issued for the 1977 census.

Volume 1. Part 1
Governmental Organization

This volume provides data nationally, by States, and for standard metropolitan statistical areas on county, municipal, and township governments by size classes; on school districts and other public school systems by size of enrollment, by kind of area served, by grades provided, and by number of schools operated; and on special districts by function performed. Also shown is the number of local governments, by type, in each county in the Nation. The volume also includes a summary description of governmental structure in each State.

Volume 1. Part 2
Popularly Elected Officials of State and Local Governments

This volume provides data nationally and by States on the number of popularly elected officials by type of government, by type of office, and by average number of elected officials by government. Also shown is the number of popularly elected officials in each county and in each standard metropolitan statistical area in the Nation. The volume also includes a summary description of legally authorized elective offices of State and local governments, by type of government, in each State.

Volume 2
Taxable Property Values and
Assessment-Sales Price Ratios

Preliminary-Assessed Valuation for Local General Property Taxation—Contains amounts of assessed value (gross and net) officially determined in 1976 for local general property taxation, for counties and for cities having a 1973 population of 50,000 or more with totals for States and their SMSA and non-SMSA components. Also contains tables which report the estimated distribution of locally assessed real property by property use class in each State. These tables show assessed valuation, numbers of taxable real properties, and percent distributions separately for the portion of each State located inside SMSA's, and State and National totals.

Final—Taxable Property Values—All data reported in the preliminary are reported here but in final form. In addition the final publication provides statistics, based on a sampling within more than 1,900 local assessing jurisdictions throughout the United

States, on real properties involved in measurable sales during a 6-month period of 1976. Statistics include effective tax rates, assessment-sales price ratios, and dispersion coefficients applicable to single-family (non-farm) houses and certain other realty, for States, local assessing jurisdictions classified by type, and selected local areas.

Volume 3
Public Employment

This volume consists of three separate paperbound reports on public employment.

No. 1. Employment of Major Local Governments—Statistics on October 1977 employment and payrolls of individual major local governments. Data are presented individually for all county governments, municipalities, and selected townships of 10,000 population or more, school districts and dependent school systems with 3,000 or more enrollment, and special districts with 100 or more full-time employees. Data reported include total, full-time, and full-time equivalent employment as well as payrolls and average monthly earnings. Full-time equivalent employment of counties and municipalities is shown for selected functions.

No. 2. Compendium of Public Employment—National data on October 1977 government employment and payrolls (including Federal Government), by function, and by type of government. State-by-State statistics are provided for all levels of government and, for State and local governments, are shown by governmental function. Additionally, statistics are presented by county areas for local governments; by population size groups for counties, municipalities, and townships; by enrollment size groups for school districts; and by employment size groups for special districts. Data are also presented by level of government on full-time employees covered by contributory retirement systems; health, hospital or disability insurance; and life insurance.

No. 3. Management-Labor Relations in State and Local Governments—National and State-by-State statistics on the number of full-time State and local employees who belong to an employee organization, type of labor relations policy practiced by State and local governments, number of written labor-management agreements, number and size of employee bargaining units, and number of work stoppages in State and local governments, by level of government and type of local government. Data on organized full-time employees and work stoppages are also shown for selected functions of State and local government. Statistics on work stoppages include number of employees involved, duration, days of idleness, major issues involved, and final methods of resolution.

Volume 4
Governmental Finances

This volume consists of five separate paperbound reports on government finances.

No. 1. Finances of School Districts—Statistics on revenue, expenditure, debt, and financial assets of school districts for fiscal year 1976—77. Figures are shown in detail for each State and, as to selected financial items, for enrollment-size groups of school districts and individual school districts enrolling 3,000 or more pupils.

No. 2. Finances of Special Districts—Data for fiscal year 1976—77 on finances of special districts, by State, and for selected large districts.

No. 3. Finances of County Governments—Statistics for the United States and for each State on revenue, expenditure, debt, and financial assets of County Governments for fiscal year 1976—77. Selected financial items are shown for groups of counties, classified by size of population, and for individual county governments.

No. 4. Finances of Municipalities and Township Governments—Data on revenue, expenditure, debt, and financial assets of municipalities and townships for their 1976—77 fiscal year. Detailed statistics are given for States. Selected financial items are reported for population-size groups of these governments, and for individual municipalities and townships having 10,000 or more inhabitants.

No. 5. Compendium of Government Finances—A comprehensive summary of the census findings on governmental finances for fiscal 1976—77 showing data for the Federal Government, individual States, and local governments by type of government, and data for State and local governments by State, including a breakdown by type of government. Figures are given separately for local governments within standard metropolitan statistical areas and for county areas. Also shown are per capita figures, percentage distributions, and State rankings.

No. 6. Finances of the Commonwealth of Puerto Rico—A summary of census findings on finances for the Commonwealth and municipio governments, including public utility and retirement systems.

Volume 5
Local Government in Metropolitan Areas

This volume presents the census findings for standard metropolitan statistical areas (SMSA's) in three major subject fields: Numbers of local governments by type and size, local government employment, and local government finances. Data are shown in terms of nationwide aggregates, for population-size groups of SMSA's and for the SMSA portion of each State, as well as for individual SMSA's and their component counties. Data are also shown for selected items of direct State expenditure in these areas.

Volume 6
Topical Studies

This volume consists of six separate paperbound reports on selected subjects.

No. 1. Employee-Retirement Systems of State and Local Governments—Membership, receipts, expenditures, number of beneficiaries and financial assets are presented for State and local government employee-retirement systems. Also shown are national and State totals by membership size and coverage class of systems, and individual-system data for those retirement systems with 200 or more members.

No. 2. Selected Personnel Expenditures of State and Local Governments—National expenditure data for employee payrolls, retirement, and insurance programs by State and local governments. Expenditures shown by State and type of government with reference to number of employees covered. Individual government data reported for counties over 100,000 population, cities over 50,000 and school districts with 25,000 or more pupils.

No. 3. State Payments to Local Governments—Programs for financial grants and reimbursements

to local governments in each State are described indicating the basis of allocation and amounts paid under each program during the fiscal year 1976–77. Statistics are also presented on State intergovernmental expenditure, by function and by type of recipient government, together with comparative historical data.

No. 4. Historical Statistics on Government Finances and Employment—Nationwide figures on governmental revenue, expenditure, and indebtedness, by Federal, State, and local levels of government, for selected years (1902 to 1966 and annually from 1967 to 1977). Nationwide figures on public employment are presented for the period since 1940. State-by-State data on the finances and employment of State and local governments appear for selected years since 1957.

No. 5. Graphic Summary—Charts and maps first issued in other reports of the census are assembled here with brief explanatory text and a reference guide to the subject matter reports where the underlying statistics appear.

No. 6. Regional Organizations—Presents baseline data on the organizational characteristics, expenditures, revenues, employment and source of Federal Grants for selected sub-State regional organizations. Data for each type of organization are presented by State. Explanatory text outlines survey methodology and criteria used in defining regional organizations.

Volume 7
Guide to 1977 Census of Governments

This report presents detailed samples of tables published in the 1977 Census of Government report series. It is a descriptive information source for users and potential users of data produced during the Census of Governments.

Volume 8
Procedural History

This volume summarizes the Census Bureau's procedures in collecting data on the financial transactions and employment of State and local governments. The historical presentation of these procedures begins with the Census Act of 1840 and continues to the 1977 Census of Governments.